Theories of Psychotherapy and Counseling
Concepts and Cases

5TH EDITION

Theories of Psychotherapy and Counseling
Concepts and Cases

Richard S. Sharf

University of Delaware

BROOKS/COLE

CENGAGE Learning

Australia • Brazil • Japan • Korea • Mexico • Singapore • Spain • United Kingdom • United States

BROOKS/COLE
CENGAGE Learning™

Theories of Psychotherapy and Counseling: Concepts and Cases, 5th Edition
Richard S. Sharf

Publisher: Linda Schreiber-Ganster

Acquisition Editor: Seth Dobrin

Associate Editor, Market Development: Arwen Renee Petty

Assistant Editor: Alicia McLaughlin

Editorial Assistant: Suzanna Kincaid

Media Editor: Elizabeth Momb

Marketing Manager: Trent Whatcott

Senior Marketing Communications Manager: Tami Strang

Content Project Management: PreMediaGlobal

Senior Art Director: Jennifer Wahi

Print Buyer: Judy Inouye

Compositor: PreMediaGlobal

Text Researcher: Sarah D'Stair

Photo Researcher: Carly Bergey

Rights Acquisition Specialist: Dean Dauphinais

Cover designer: Jeff Bane

Cover Illustration: Background image by CMB Design. Inset: *"The Water Lily Pond,"* pub. By Claude Monet (1899 Oil on Canvas)/The Art Resource.

For product information and technology assistance, contact us at **Cengage Learning Customer & Sales Support, 1-800-354-9706**

For permission to use material from this text or product, submit all requests online at **www.cengage.com/permissions.** Further permissions questions can be emailed to **permissionrequest@cengage.com.**

Library of Congress Control Number: 2010939588

ISBN-13: 978-0-8400-3366-6

ISBN-10: 0-8400-3366-4

Brooks/Cole
A Division of Cengage Learning, Inc
20 Davis Drive
Belmont, CA 94002
USA

Cengage Learning is a leading provider of customized learning solutions with office locations around the globe, including Singapore, the United Kingdom, Australia, Mexico, Brazil and Japan. Locate your local office at **international.cengage.com/region**.

Cengage Learning products are represented in Canada by Nelson Education, Ltd.

For your course and learning solutions, visit **www.cengage.com.**

Purchase any of our products at your local college store or at our preferred online store **www.cengagebrain.com.**

Instructors: Please visit **login.cengage.com** and log in to access instructor-specific resources.

Printed in the United States of America
1 2 3 4 5 6 7 14 13 12 11 10

For Jane, Jennie, and Alex

Brief Contents

Preface   xxii

CHAPTER 1   Introduction   1

CHAPTER 2   Psychoanalysis   28

CHAPTER 3   Jungian Analysis and Therapy   82

CHAPTER 4   Adlerian Therapy   123

CHAPTER 5   Existential Therapy   160

CHAPTER 6   Person-Centered Therapy   206

CHAPTER 7   Gestalt Therapy: An Experiential Therapy   240

CHAPTER 8   Behavior Therapy   280

CHAPTER 9   Rational Emotive Behavior Therapy   331

CHAPTER 10   Cognitive Therapy   369

CHAPTER 11   Reality Therapy   416

CHAPTER 12   Constructivist Approaches   452

CHAPTER 13   Feminist Therapy: A Multicultural Approach   484

CHAPTER 14   Family Therapy   533

CHAPTER 15   Other Psychotherapies   582

CHAPTER 16   Comparison and Critique   631

CHAPTER 17   Integrative Therapies   662

Glossary   691

Name Index   712

Subject Index   723

Contents

Preface   xxii

CHAPTER **1**   **Introduction   1**

Theory   2
Precision and Clarity   2
Comprehensiveness   3
Testability   3
Usefulness   3

Psychotherapy and Counseling   4

Theories of Psychotherapy and Counseling   5
Psychoanalysis   6
Jungian Analysis and Therapy   6
Adlerian Therapy   7
Existential Therapy   7
Person-Centered Therapy   7
Gestalt Therapy   7
Behavior Therapy   7
Rational Emotive Behavior Therapy   8
Cognitive Therapy   8
Reality Therapy   8
Constructivist Therapy   8
Feminist Therapy   9
Family Therapy   9
Other Psychotherapies   9
Integrative Therapy   9

Organization of the Chapters   10
History or Background   10
Personality Theories   11
Theories of Psychotherapy   11
Psychological Disorders   12
Brief Psychotherapy   16
Current Trends   17
Using a Theory with Other Theories   20
Research   20
Gender Issues   22
Multicultural Issues   22
Group Therapy   23

Ethics   23

My Theory of Psychotherapy and Counseling   24

Your Theory of Psychotherapy and Counseling   24

Suggested Readings   25

References   25

CHAPTER **2**   **Psychoanalysis   28**

History of Psychoanalysis   29

Freud's Drive Theory   33
  Drives and Instincts   33
  Levels of Consciousness   33
  Structure of Personality   34
  Defense Mechanisms   35
  Psychosexual Stages of Development   37

Ego Psychology   39
  Anna Freud   39
  Erik Erikson   40

Object Relations Psychology   41
  Donald Winnicott   42
  Otto Kernberg   43

Kohut's Self Psychology   43

Relational Psychoanalysis   45

Psychoanalytical Approaches to Treatment   47
  Therapeutic Goals   47
  Assessment   48
  Psychoanalysis, Psychotherapy, and Psychoanalytic Counseling   48
  Free Association   49
  Neutrality and Empathy   49
  Resistance   50
  Interpretation   51
  Interpretation of Dreams   51
  Interpretation and Analysis of Transference   52
  Countertransference   53
  Relational Responses   54

Psychological Disorders   54
  Treatment of Hysteria: Katharina   55
  Childhood Anxiety: Mary   56
  Borderline Disorders: Mr. R.   58
  Narcissistic Disorders: Mr. J.   59
  Depression: Sam   61

Brief Psychoanalytic Therapy   62

Current Trends   65

Using Psychoanalysis with Other Theories   66

Research   67

Gender Issues   70

Multicultural Issues   72

Group Therpy   73

Summary   74

Suggested Readings   75

References   76

CHAPTER 3   Jungian Analysis and Therapy   82

History of Jungian Analysis and Therapy   83

Theory of Personality   86
Levels of Consciousness   87
Archetypes   89
Personality Attitudes and Functions   91
Personality Development   94

Jungian Analysis and Therapy   96
Therapeutic Goals   96
Analysis, Therapy, and Counseling   96
Assessment   97
The Therapeutic Relationship   99
Stages of Therapy   99
Dreams and Analysis   100
Active Imagination   104
Other Techniques   104
Transference and Countertransference   105

Psychological Disorders   106
Depression: Young Woman   107
Anxiety Neurosis: Girl   108
Borderline Disorders: Ed   109
Psychotic Disorders: Patient   109

Brief Therapy   110

Current Trends   110

Using Jungian Concepts with Other Theories   111

Research   112

Gender Issues   113

Multicultural Issues   115

Group Therapy   116

Summary   117

Suggested Readings   118

References   118

CHAPTER 4   Adlerian Therapy   123

History of Adlerian Theory   124
Influences on Adlerian Psychology and Therapy   125

Adler's Theory of Personality   126
Style of Life   127
Social Interest   128
Inferiority and Superiority   129
Birth Order   130

Adlerian Theory of Therapy and Counseling   130
Goals of Therapy and Counseling   131
The Therapeutic Relationship   131
Assessment and Analysis   132
Insight and Interpretation   137
Reorientation   138

Psychological Disorders   **142**
Depression: Sheri   143
Generalized Anxiety: Robert   146
Eating Disorders: Judy   146
Borderline Disorders: Jane   147

Brief Therapy   **148**

Current Trends   **149**

Using Adlerian Therapy with Other Theories   **150**

Research   **151**

Gender Issues   **152**

Multicultural Issues   **153**

Group Counseling and Therapy   **154**

Summary   **155**

Suggested Readings   **155**

References   **156**

CHAPTER **5**   **Existential Therapy   160**

History of Existential Thought   **161**
Existential Philosophers   161
Originators of Existential Psychotherapy   164
Recent Contributors to Existential Psychotherapy   165

Existential Personality Theory   **166**
Being-in-the-World   166
Four Ways of Being   167
Time and Being   168
Anxiety   169
Living and Dying   170
Freedom, Responsibility, and Choice   171
Isolation and Loving   172
Meaning and Meaninglessness   173
Self-Transcendence   173
Striving for Authenticity   174
Development of Authenticity and Values   175

Existential Psychotherapy   **175**
Goals of Existential Psychotherapy   176
Existential Psychotherapy and Counseling   176
Assessment   177
The Therapeutic Relationship   178
Living and Dying   180
Freedom, Responsibility, and Choice   182
Isolation and Loving   184
Meaning and Meaninglessness   185

Psychological Disorders   **186**
Anxiety: Nathalie and Her Son   186
Depression: Catherine   189
Borderline Disorder: Anna   189
Obsessive-Compulsive Disorder: Female Patient   190
Alcoholism: Harry   190

Brief Therapy 191

Current Trends 193

Using Existential Therapy with Other Theories 194

Research 194

Gender Issues 196

Multicultural Issues 196

Group Counseling and Psychotherapy 198
Living and Dying 198
Freedom, Responsibility, and Choice 198
Isolation and Loving 199
Meaning and Meaninglessness 199

Summary 200

Suggested Readings 200

References 201

CHAPTER 6   **Person-Centered Therapy** 206

History of Person-Centered Therapy 207

Person-Centered Theory of Personality 211
Psychological Development 211
Development and Conditionality 212
Self-Regard and Relationships 212
The Fully Functioning Person 213

A Person-Centered Theory of Psychotherapy 213
Goals 213
Assessment 214
The Necessary and Sufficient Conditions for Client Change 214
The Client's Experience in Therapy 218
The Process of Person-Centered Psychotherapy 220

Psychological Disorders 221
Depression: Graduate Student 222
Grief and Loss: Justin 223
Borderline Disorder: Woman 225

Brief Therapy 226

Current Trends 226
Societal Implications 226
Theoretical Purity versus Eclecticism 227
Training Trends 227

Using Person-Centered Therapy with Other Theories 228

Research 229
Research on the Core Conditions 229
The Effectiveness of Person-Centered Therapy 230

Gender Issues 232

Multicultural Issues 232

Group Counseling 233

Summary   234

Suggested Readings   235

References   236

CHAPTER **7**   **Gestalt Therapy:
An Experiential Therapy   240**

History of Gestalt Therapy   241
Influences on the Development of Gestalt Therapy   243

Gestalt Theory of Personality   245
Gestalt Psychology and Gestalt Therapy   245
Contact   247
Contact Boundaries   248
Contact Boundary Disturbances   248
Awareness   250
The Present   251

Theory of Gestalt Psychotherapy   251
Goals of Therapy   252
The Therapeutic Relationship   253
Assessment in Gestalt Psychotherapy   253
Therapeutic Change   254
Enhancing Awareness   255
Integration and Creativity   263
Risks   264

Psychological Disorders   264
Depression: Woman   264
Anxiety: Man   265
Posttraumatic Stress Disorder: Holocaust Survivor   266
Substance Abuse: Mike   267

Brief Therapy   268

Current Trends   268

Using Gestalt Psychotherapy with Other Theories   269

Research   269

Gender Issues   271

Multicultural Issues   272

Group Therapy   273

Summary   275

Suggested Readings   275

References   276

CHAPTER **8**   **Behavior Therapy   280**

History of Behavior Therapy   281
Classical Conditioning   281
Operant Conditioning   282
Social Cognitive Theory   283
Current Status of Behavior Therapy   284

Behavior Theory of Personality   285
Positive Reinforcement   285
Negative Reinforcement   286
Extinction   286
Generalization   286
Discrimination   287
Shaping   287
Observational Learning   287

Theories of Behavior Therapy   289
Goals of Behavior Therapy   289
Behavioral Assessment   290
General Treatment Approach   291
Systematic Desensitization   292
Imaginal Flooding Therapies   294
In Vivo Therapies   295
Virtual Reality Therapy   296
Modeling Techniques   297
Self-Instructional Training: A Cognitive-Behavioral Approach   299
Stress Inoculation: A Cognitive-Behavioral Approach   299

Psychological Disorders   301
Generalized Anxiety Disorder: Claire   301
Depression: Jane   305
Obsessive-Compulsive Disorder: June   306
Phobic Disorder: Six-Year-Old Girl   308

Brief Therapy   309

Current Trends   309
Eye-Movement Desensitization and Reprocessing   310
Acceptance and Commitment Therapy   311
Dialectical Behavior Therapy   312
Ethical Issues   316

Using Behavior Therapy with Other Theories   316

Research   317
Review of the Evidence   317
Obsessive-Compulsive Disorder   318
Generalized Anxiety Disorder   318
Phobias   319

Gender Issues   320

Multicultural Issues   321

Group Therapy   322
Social-Skills Training   322
Assertiveness Training   323

Summary   323

Suggested Readings   324

References   325

CHAPTER 9   **Rational Emotive Behavior Therapy   331**
History of Rational Emotive Behavior Therapy   332
Rational Emotive Behavior Theory of Personality   334
Philosophical Viewpoints   334

Factors Basic to the Rational Emotive Behavior Theory of Personality   335
The Rational Emotive Behavior A-B-C Theory of Personality   337

Rational Emotive Behavior Theory of Psychotherapy   339
Goals of Therapy   339
Assessment   340
The Therapeutic Relationship   340
The A-B-C-D-E Therapeutic Approach   343
Other Cognitive Approaches   346
Emotive Techniques   347
Behavioral Methods   349
Insight   349

Psychological Disorders   350
Anxiety Disorder: Ted   350
Depression: Penny   353
Obsessive-Compulsive Disorder: Woman   353
Alcohol and Substance Abuse   354

Brief Therapy   355

Current Trends   355

Using Rational Emotive Behavior Therapy with Other Theories   356

Research   357

Gender Issues   359

Multicultural Issues   361

Group Therapy   361

Summary   362

Suggested Readings   363

References   364

CHAPTER 1 0   # Cognitive Therapy   369

History of Cognitive Therapy   370
Theoretical Influences   371
Current Influences   373

Cognitive Theory of Personality   373
Causation and Psychological Disorders   373
Automatic Thoughts   374
The Cognitive Model of the Development of Schemas   374
Cognitive Schemas in Therapy   375
Cognitive Distortions   377

Theory of Cognitive Therapy   379
Goals of Therapy   379
Assessment in Cognitive Therapy   380
The Therapeutic Relationship   384
The Therapeutic Process   385
Therapeutic Techniques   387

Cognitive Treatment of Psychological Disorders   389
Depression: Paul   389
General Anxiety Disorder: Amy   392
Obsessive Disorder: Electrician   393
Substance Abuse: Bill   396

Brief Cognitive Therapy   398

Current Trends   399
Mindfulness-Based Cognitive Therapy   399
Schema-Focused Cognitive Therapy   400
Treatment Manuals   401

Using Cognitive Therapy with Other Theories   401

Research   402
Research on Depression   403
Research on Generalized Anxiety   404
Research on Obsessional Disorders   405

Gender Issues   406

Multicultural Issues   407

Group Therapy   408

Summary   409

Suggested Readings   410

References   410

CHAPTER **1 1**   **Reality Therapy**   **416**

History of Reality Therapy   417

Personality Theory: Choice Theory   419
Pictures of Reality   419
Needs   420
Choice   420
Behavior   421
Choosing Behavior   422

Theory of Reality Therapy   422
Goals of Reality Therapy   422
Assessment   423
The Process of Reality Therapy   424
Therapist Attitudes   429
Reality Therapy Strategies   430

Psychological Disorders   434
Eating Disorders: Choosing to Starve and Purge: Gloria   434
The Choice to Abuse Drugs: Janet   438
The Choice to Depress: Teresa   440
The Choice to Anxietize: Randy   441

Current Trends   442

Using Reality Therapy With Other Theories   443

Research   443

Gender Issues   444

Multicultural Issues   445

Group Counseling   446

Summary   447

Suggested Readings   448

References   448

CHAPTER **1 2**   **Constructivist Approaches   452**

History of Constructivist Approaches   453
Early Influences   453
George Kelly   454
Milton Erickson   454
Early Family Therapy Approaches   455
Recent Constructivist Approaches   456

Solution-Focused Therapy   457
Views About Therapeutic Change   457
Assessment   458
Goals   458
Techniques   458
Case Example: Rosie   463

Narrative Therapy   466
Personal Construct Therapy   466
Case Example: Barry   467
Epston and White's Narrative Therapy   468
Assessment   468
Goals   469
Techniques of Narrative Therapy   470
Case Example: Terry   472

Current Trends   473

Using Constructivist Theories with Other Theories   474

Research   475

Gender Issues   476

Multicultural Issues   477

Group Therapy   478

Summary   478

Suggested Readings   480

References   480

CHAPTER **1 3**   **Feminist Therapy: A Multicultural
Approach   484**

Gender as a Multicultural Issue   485

History of Feminist Therapy   486

Feminist Theories of Personality   489
Gender Differences and Similarities Across the Lifespan   489
Schema Theory and Multiple Identities   492
Gilligan's Ethic of Care   494
The Relational Cultural Model   495

Theories of Feminist Therapy   497
Goals of Feminist Therapy   497
Assessment Issues in Feminist Therapy   499
The Therapeutic Relationship   499
Techniques of Feminist Therapy   500

Using Feminist Therapy with Other Theories   507
Feminist Psychoanalytic Theory   507

Feminist Behavioral and Cognitive Therapy   508
Feminist Gestalt Therapy   509
Feminist Narrative Therapy   509
Feminist Therapy and Counseling   510

Brief Therapy   510

Psychological Disorders   511
Borderline Disorder: Barbara   511
Depression: Ms. B   513
Posttraumatic Stress Disorder: Andrea   514
Eating Disorders: Margaret   516

Current Trends and Issues   517

Research   519

Gender Issues   520
Feminist Therapy with Men   520
Feminist Therapy with Gay, Lesbian, Bisexual, or Transgendered Clients (GLBT)   522

Multicultural Issues   523

Group Counseling   525

Summary   526

Suggested Readings   527

References   527

CHAPTER 14   Family Therapy   533

Historical Background   534
Early Approaches to Family Counseling   535
Psychoanalytic and Related Influences on Family Therapy   535
The Study of Communication Patterns in Families with Members Having Symptoms of
    Schizophrenia   536
General Systems Theory   537

Bowen's Intergenerational Approach   539
Theory of Family Systems   539
Therapy Goals   542
Techniques of Bowen's Family Therapy   542
An Example of Intergenerational Family Systems Therapy: Ann's family   544

Structural Family Therapy   545
Concepts of Structural Family Therapy   546
Goals of Structural Family Therapy   547
Techniques of Structural Family Therapy   548
Example of Structural Family Therapy: Quest Family   550

Strategic Therapy   553
Concepts of Strategic Therapy   553
Goals   554
Techniques of Strategic Family Therapy   554
An Example of Strategic Therapy: Boy Who Set Fires   557

Experiential and Humanistic Family Therapies   558
The Experiential Therapy of Carl Whitaker   558
The Humanistic Approach of Virginia Satir   559

Integrative Approaches to Family Systems Therapy   560

Theories of Individual Therapy as Applied to Family Therapy   561
Psychoanalysis   561
Adlerian Therapy   562
Existential Therapy   562
Person-Centered Therapy   562
Gestalt Therapy   562
Behavior Therapy   563
Rational Emotive Behavior Therapy   563
Cognitive Therapy   563
Reality Therapy   563
Feminist Therapy   564

Brief Family Systems Therapy   565
The Mental Research Institute Brief Family Therapy Model   565
Long Brief Therapy of the Milan Associates   566

Current Trends in Family Therapy   567
Psychoeducational Approaches   567
Professional Training and Organizations   568
Family Law   568
Medicine   569

Research   569

Gender Issues   572

Multicultural Issues   573

Family Systems Therapy Applied to the Individual   575

Couples Counseling   575

Summary   576

Suggested Readings   576

References   577

CHAPTER **15**   **Other Psychotherapies   582**
Asian Psychotherapies   583
Background   583
Asian Theories of Personality   584
Asian Theories of Psychotherapy   586
Summary   591
References   591

Body Psychotherapies   593
Background   593
Personality Theory and the Body   595
Psychotherapeutic Approaches   597
Summary   600
References   601

Interpersonal Psychotherapy   602
Background   602
Personality Theory   604
Goals   605
Techniques of Interpersonal Therapy   605

An Example of Interpersonal Therapy   610
Other Applications of Interpersonal Therapy   612
Summary   612
References   613

Psychodrama   615
Background   615
Theory of Personality   615
Theory of Psychotherapy   617
Summary   621
References   621

Creative Arts Therapies   622
Art Therapy   623
Dance Movement Therapy   624
Drama Therapy   626
Music Therapy   628
Summary   629
References   629

Summary   630

CHAPTER 16   Comparison and Critique   631

Basic Concepts of Personality   632

Goals of Therapy   635

Assessment in Therapy   635

Therapeutic Techniques   636

Differential Treatment   640

Brief Psychotherapy   641

Current Trends   642
Common Factors Approach   642
Treatment Manuals and Research-Supported Psychological Treatment
    Psychotherapy   643
Postmodernism and Constructivism   643

Using the Theory with Other Theories   645

Research   645
Outcome Research   646
Future Directions   646

Gender Issues   646

Multicultural Issues   649

Family Therapy   650

Group Therapy   650

Critique   653
Psychoanalysis   653
Jungian Analysis   654
Adlerian Therapy   654
Existential Therapy   655
Person-Centered Therapy   655
Gestalt Therapy   656
Behavior Therapy   656

Rational Emotive Behavior Therapy   657
Cognitive Therapy   657
Reality Therapy   657
Constructivist Theories   658
Feminist Therapy   658
Family Systems Therapy   659

Summary   660

References   661

CHAPTER **17**   **Integrative Therapies   662**

Wachtel's Cyclical Psychodynamics Theory   663
An Example of Wachtel's Cyclical Psychodynamic Theory: Judy   665
An Example of Wachtel's Cyclical Psychodynamic Theory: John N.   666
Using Wachtel's Cyclical Psychodynamics Theory as a Model for Your Integrative
Theory   667

Prochaska and Colleagues' Transtheoretical Approach   669
Stages of Change   670
Levels of Psychological Problems   670
Processes of Change   670
Combining Stages of Change, Levels of Psychological Problems, and Processes of
Change   672
An Example of Prochaska and Colleagues' Transtheoretical Approach: Mrs. C   673
Using Prochaska and Colleagues' Transtheoretical Approach as a Model for Your
Integrative Theory   674

Multimodal Therapy   675
Multimodal Theory of Personality   675
Goals of Therapy   677
Assessment   677
Treatment Approach   679
An Example of Lazarus's Multimodal Therapy: Mrs. W   681
Using Lazarus's Multimodal Theory as a Model for Your Integrative Theory   682

Current Trends   683

Research   684

Gender Issues   685

Multicultural Issues   685

Summary   686

Suggested Readings   687

References   688

Glossary   691

Name Index   712

Subject Index   723

Preface

I am pleased to offer the fifth edition of this text that explains psychotherapy and counseling theories, illustrating each using several case examples.

I worked at a university counseling center as a counseling psychologist, and taught graduate students for over 35 years. Both experiences were of immense value to me, professionally and personally. I wanted to write a text that would have extensive case material and include more than one case per chapter. Because many theories of psychotherapy and counseling use different treatment approaches for different psychological disorders, I felt it was important to address differential treatment.

To provide a comprehensive overview of theories of psychotherapy and counseling, I have presented an explanation of concepts, as well as examples of their application, by using case summaries and therapist–client dialogue to illustrate techniques and treatment. I believe that the blending of concepts and examples makes psychotherapy and counseling clearer and more real for the student who wants to learn about the therapeutic process. For most theories, I have shown how they can be applied to individual therapy or counseling for common psychological disorders, such as depression and generalized anxiety disorders. I have also shown how each theory can be applied to group therapy.

Although my name appears on the cover of this book, the chapters represent the expertise of more than 70 authorities on a wide variety of theoretical approaches to psychotherapy and counseling. This is, in essence, a book filled with input from many experts on specific theories. Each has provided suggestions for inclusion of particular content, as well as read chapters at various stages of development. However, I am responsible for the organization and presentation of these theories.

A Flexible Approach to Accommodate Different Teaching Preferences

I realize that many instructors will not assign all chapters and have kept this in mind in preparing the text. Although I have placed theories in the general chronological order in which they were developed, I have written the chapters so that they may be assigned in almost any order, with some exceptions. The chapter on Jungian analysis should follow the chapter on psychoanalysis because of the close relationship between the development of these two theories. Also, Chapter 13, Feminist Therapy, and Chapter 14, Family Therapy, should follow other chapters on major theories because they make use of knowledge presented in previous chapters.

Chapter 2, Psychoanalysis, is the longest and most difficult chapter. To present the modern-day practice of psychoanalysis, it is necessary to explain contributions to psychoanalysis that have taken place since Freud's death, including important ideas of Winnicott, Kohut, and relational theory. Instructors may wish to allow more time for reading this chapter than others. Some may find it helpful to assign this chapter after students have read a few other chapters, especially if members of the class have little familiarity with personality theory.

Comparison and critique of theories are provided in Chapter 16 so that students can learn and understand each theory before criticizing it. Also, because knowledge of theories serves as a basis for making judgments about other theories, it is helpful to have an overview of theories of psychotherapy before describing each theory's strengths and limitations. Knowledge of several theories is important to the understanding of integrative theories, such as Lazarus's multimodal approach, which is discussed in Chapter 17. In this edition, I have presented the chapter on integrating theories after the summary chapter (Chapter 16) of the theories so that students will have a better background to understand integrative theories and be in a position to tentatively design their own integrative approach.

Content of the Chapters

For the major theories presented in the text, basic information about background, personality theory, and theory of psychotherapy provides a means for understanding the application of psychotherapy theory. Understanding the personal life and philosophical influences of a theorist helps to explain how the theorist views human behavior. Knowing a theorist's view of personality provides insight into the theorist's approach to changes in behavior, thoughts, or feelings—his or her theory of psychotherapy.

In presenting theories of psychotherapy, I have discussed goals, assessment, therapeutic relationships, and techniques. Goals show the aspects of human behavior that theorists see as most important. Assessment includes inventories and interviewing approaches as they relate to the theorists' goals. The therapeutic relationship provides the context for the techniques of change, which are illustrated through examples of therapy.

I have also included information on topics relevant to theories of psychotherapy. Research on the effectiveness of each theory is discussed in each chapter. An important issue in the practice of psychotherapy is treatment length and brief approaches as they relate to different methods of treating psychological disorders. I also discuss current issues that each theory is facing, as well as ways in which each theory can be incorporated into or make use of ideas from other theories.

Cultural and gender differences are issues that theories approach differently. An understanding of clients' background is of varying importance to theorists, yet is of profound significance in actual psychotherapy. Each chapter addresses these issues, and Chapter 13, Feminist Therapy, focuses on them in considerable detail so that the student can learn about the interaction of cultural and gender influences and methods of therapeutic change.

Each area of application is presented in a self-contained manner, allowing instructors to emphasize some and de-emphasize others. For example, instructors could choose not to assign the research section to suit their teaching purposes.

I have written an instructor's manual that includes multiple-choice and essay questions. Also, I have provided suggestions for topics for discussion. An alphabetical glossary is included in the textbook.

New to the Fifth Edition

I have made several significant changes to the fifth edition. Many of these changes are designed to make the textbook easier to use for both student and instructor.

Changes Affecting Many Chapters

- Chapter openers have been designed to assist student understanding by providing an overview of the personality theory and the techniques used for the theory chapters. These chapter openers provide an outline of the theory of psychotherapy and counseling that students can refer to in their work. For Chapters 1 and 16, I provide a chapter outline.

- I have added four full new cases and rearranged many existing cases so that the first case presented in the Psychological Disorders section is the longest and most thorough. Some instructors may choose to assign only the first case for their classes to read; others may assign the entire section. This change applies to Chapters 3 through 11, and Chapter 13. The other chapters contain more than one theory and usually have only one case per theory. The name or pseudonym of the client or patient has been added to the cases for ease of reference.

- I have changed the order of the final two chapters. Chapter 16 is now Comparison and Critique and Chapter 17 is now Integrative Therapies. I did this so that students could review and summarize the chapters on different therapies before integrating them. This is a useful step before learning about integration of theories. In Chapter 17, I not only discuss Prochaska's transtheoretical approach, Wachtel's cyclical psychodynamics, and Lazarus's multimodal therapy, but also show students how to make their own integrative therapy. I do this by demonstrating three methods of integrating theory: theoretical integration, the assimilative model, and technical eclecticism.

- I have added material so that instructors may use this textbook with Edward S. Neukrug's *Theories in Action* DVD set. This can be bundled with the textbook if the instructor wishes to do so. *Theories in Action* offers 15-minute video clips of therapist–client role plays, along with an introduction and conclusion that illustrates therapy that I present in Chapters 2 through 12. At the end of each of these chapters, after the chapter summary, is a box that includes a list of the personality theory concepts and the change techniques that are used in the specific *Theories in Action* role play. Additionally, there are four questions for each of the role plays. Two or three of the questions have page numbers so students can easily find a discussion of concepts related to the question. There is a small DVD icon on the page that is referred to by a specific question. I recognize that many instructors will not use the *Theories in Action* DVD, so I have kept this addition as unobtrusive as possible.

- Recently, there has been considerable interest in treatment manuals and evidence-based psychotherapy as well as in identifying common factors of many psychotherapies. I have updated information about *research-supported psychological treatments*. This term is used by the Society of Clinical Psychologists (Division 12 of the American Psychological Association) and replaces the terms *evidence-based psychotherapy* and *empirically supported treatments*. Discussion of research-supported psychological treatments is provided in Chapter 1 and Chapter 16. Tables in each of those chapters list those treatments that are supported by research. Many are cognitive and behavioral, but others include psychodynamic, emotion-focused, and Klerman's interpersonal psychotherapy. I also provide a discussion of the common factors approach to identifying therapeutic skills, which is described in Chapter 1 and continues to be popular.

- "In many of the Therapist-Client dialogues throughout the text, I have spelled out the titles of the speaker for clarification, adding brackets to indicate where this was a modification made to the original excerpted material."

Changes to Individual Chapters

Below is a list detailing significant changes made to several chapters.

- **Chapter 2, Psychoanalysis, and Chapter 3, Jungian Analysis**. These are the two most difficult chapters. I have clarified and rewritten some portions of the text.

- **Chapter 4, Adlerian Therapy**. I have added *creating images* to the group of theoretical techniques.

- **Chapter 8, Behavior Therapy**. I have added negative reinforcement to the Behavior Theory of Personality section to complement positive reinforcement. I have also added a full description of Linehan's Dialectical Behavior Therapy, which is used to treat borderline disorders.

- **Chapter 10, Cognitive Therapy.** In the Current Trends section, I have described in some detail two variations of cognitive therapy: mindfulness-based cognitive therapy and schema-focused cognitive therapy.

- **Chapter 12, Constructivist Approaches**. I have added the concept of assessing motivation to the section on solution-focused therapy. In the narrative therapy section, I have treated personal construct theory and Epston and White's narrative therapy separately. I believe this will provide more clarification for students.

- **Chapter 13, Feminist Therapy: A Multicultural Approach**. This chapter has been greatly revised. I have emphasized multiple identities, such as age and social class, in addition to sections on gender and cultural diversity. Rather than discuss homosexuality, I discuss issues relevant to gay, lesbian, bisexual, and transgendered individuals. Also, I have increased information on the relational and cultural model of therapy.

Many changes and additions have been made in all chapters. More than 375 new references, most quite recent, have been added. Many of these references are new research studies added to the research sections. Other new information is also presented in the Current Trends sections. A variety of specific changes have been made within each chapter.

Student Manual

This text provides a thorough overview of theories of therapy and counseling. To make this material as interesting as possible for students and to help them learn it, I have written a student manual. Case examples with multiple-choice questions put students in the role of a therapist, using the particular theory under discussion.

Chapters of the student manual start with a pre-inventory to help students compare their own views of therapy to the theory. The history of the theory is presented in outline form so that students can summarize the most important influences on the theory or theorist. Significant terms used in the theory of personality and the theory of psychotherapy sections are defined. A portion of a case is presented along with multiple-choice questions on assessment, goals, and techniques. Questions and information are also presented for other sections in the text. Each chapter concludes with a 25-item quiz about the theory.

Acknowledgments

In writing this book, I have received help from more than 70 people in various aspects of the review and preparation for all editions of this book. I would like to thank Dennis Gilbride, Syracuse University; Kurt Emmerling, Carlow University; Laura Hatton, Madonna University; Irwin Badin, Montclair State University; Mary Ann Coupland, Sinte Gleska University; Stacie DeFreitas, University of Houston–Downtown; Julian Melgosa, Walla Walla University; Joy Whitman, DePaul University; and Leonard Tester, New York Institute of Technology, who reviewed the entire manuscript and made useful suggestions for this edition of the book. I would also like to thank the following individuals who reviewed previous editions of this textbook: Emery Cummins, San Diego State University; Christopher Faiver, John Carroll University; David Lane, Mercer University; Ruthellen Josselson, Towson State University; Ellyn Kaschak, San Jose State University; David Dillon, Trinity International University; Beverly B. Palmer, California State University–Dominquez Hills; James R. Mahalik, Boston College; Freddie Avant, Stephen F. Austin State University; Joel Muro, Texas Woman's University; Dorothy Espelage, U of Illinois at Urbana-Champaign; Kelly Wester, University of North Carolina–Greensboro; Linda Perosa, University of Akron; and Carolyn Kapner, University of Pittsburgh.

I am also very appreciative of those individuals who provided suggestions for chapter contents, reviewed the chapter, or did both, for previous editions of this textbook.

Chapter 1: Introduction. E. N. Simons, University of Delaware; John C. Norcross, University of Scranton; Peter E. Nathan, University of Iowa

Chapter 2: Psychoanalysis. Cynthia Allen, private practice; Ann Byrnes, State University of New York at Stony Brook; Lawrence Hedges, private practice; Jonathan Lewis, University of Delaware; Steven Robbins, Virginia Commonwealth University; Judith Mishne, New York University

Chapter 3: Jungian Analysis and Therapy. Amelio D'Onofrio, Fordham University; Anne Harris, California School of Professional Psychology; Stephen Martin, private practice; Polly Young-Eisendrath, private practice; Seth Rubin, private practice

Chapter 4: Adlerian Therapy. Michael Maniacci, private practice; Harold Mosak, Adler School of Professional Psychology; Richard Watts, Sam Houston State University

Chapter 5: Existential Therapy. Stephen Golston, Arizona State University; William Gould, University of Dubuque; Emmy van Deurzen, Regent's College

Chapter 6: Person-Centered Therapy. Douglas Bower, private practice; Jerold Bozarth, University of Georgia; David Cain, private practice; Richard Watts, Sam Houston State University

Chapter 7: Gestalt Therapy. Stephen Golston, Arizona State University; Rich Hycner, Institute for Dialogical Psychotherapy; Joseph Wysong, Editor, *Gestalt Journal*; Gary Yontef, private practice

Chapter 8: Behavior Therapy. Douglas Fogel, John Hopkins University; Alan Kazdin, Yale University; Michael Spiegler, Providence College

Chapter 9: Rational Emotive Behavior Therapy. Albert Ellis, Director, Albert Ellis Institute for Rational Emotive Behavior Therapy; Raymond DiGiuseppe, St. John's University

Chapter 10: Cognitive Therapy. Aaron Beck and Judith Beck, Beck Institute; Denise Davis, Vanderbilt University Medical Center; Bruce Liese, University of Kansas Medical Center

Chapter 11: Reality Therapy. Laurence Litwack, Northeastern University; Robert Wubbolding, Center for Reality Therapy

Chapter 12: Constructivist Approaches. Pamelia Brott, Virginia Polytechnic Institute and State University; Robert Neimeyer, University of Memphis; Richard Watts, Sam Houston State University

Chapter 13: Feminist Therapy. Cyndy Boyd, University of Pennsylvania; Carolyn Enns, Cornell College; Ellyn Kaschak, San Jose State University; Pam Remer, University of Kentucky; Judith Jordan, Wellesley College

Chapter 14: Family Systems Therapy. Dorothy Becvar, private practice; Herbert Goldenberg, California State University

Chapter 15: Other Psychotherapies. Charles Beale, University of Delaware; Ron Hays, Hahnemann University; David K. Reynolds, Constructive Living; Edward W. L. Smith, Georgia Southern University; Adam Blatner, private practice

Chapter 17: Integrative Therapies. Arnold Lazarus, Rutgers University; John C. Norcross; University of Scranton

I also want to thank the following individuals who provided information on research-supported psychological treatments (also known as evidence-based psychotherapy and empirically supported therapy): Martin Antony, Ryerson University; David Barlow, Boston University; Peter Nathan, University of Iowa.

The staff of the Library of the University of Delaware were very helpful in locating resources for this text. I would especially like to thank Susan Brynteson, Director of Libraries, and Jonathan Jeffrey, Associate Librarian, for their assistance.

I additionally want to thank Lisa Sweder, who typed earlier versions of the manuscript. Cynthia Carroll, Elizabeth Parisan, and Alice Andrews also provided further secretarial support and help. Throughout the process of writing this book, I have been fortunate to have the support of John B. Bishop, Professor of Human Development and Family Studies, University of Delaware. In revising this edition, I want to thank Jennie Sharf for updating Chapter 9: Rational Emotive Behavior Therapy. Finally, I wish to thank my family, Jane, Jennie, and Alex, to whom this book is dedicated.

Richard S. Sharf

C H A P T E R 1

Introduction

Outline of Introduction

THEORY
  Precision and Clarity
  Comprehensiveness
  Testability
  Usefulness
PSYCHOTHERAPY AND COUNSELING
THEORIES OF PSYCHOTHERAPY AND COUNSELING
  Psychoanalysis
  Jungian Analysis and Therapy
  Adlerian Therapy
  Existential Therapy
  Person-Centered Therapy
  Gestalt Therapy
  Behavior Therapy
  Rational Emotive Behavior Therapy
  Cognitive Therapy
  Reality Therapy
  Constructivist Therapy
  Feminist Therapy
  Family Therapy
  Other Psychotherapies
  Integrative Therapy
ORGANIZATION OF THE CHAPTERS
  History or Background
  Personality Theories
  Theories of Psychotherapy

Psychological Disorders
  Depression
  Generalized anxiety disorder
  Borderline disorders
  Obsessive-compulsive disorder
  Phobias
  Somatoform disorders
  Posttraumatic stress disorder
  Eating disorders
  Substance abuse
  Narcissistic personality disorder
  Schizophrenia
Brief Psychotherapy
Current Trends
  Treatment manuals
  Research-supported psychological treatments
  Postmodernism and constructivism
Using a Theory with Other Theories
Research
Gender Issues
Multicultural Issues
Group Therapy
ETHICS
MY THEORY OF PSYCHOTHERAPY AND COUNSELING
YOUR THEORY OF PSYCHOTHERAPY AND COUNSELING

Helping another person in distress can be one of the most ennobling human activities. The theories represented in this book all have in common their desire to help others with psychological problems. Through research and the practice of psychotherapy with patients and clients, many different approaches have been developed to alleviate personal misery. In this book, I describe major theories of psychotherapy, their background (history), theories of personality from which they are derived, and applications to practice. To help the reader understand the practice of psychotherapy and counseling, I give many examples of how theories are used with a variety of clients and patients. An overview of the theories and the many ways they can be applied is also described in this chapter.

Theory

Imagine that you have a friend who is depressed. He or she is not motivated to go to class or work, does not spend much time with his or her friends, stays in bed a lot of the time, and does not do the things with you that he or she used to. Then, you suggest your friend seek counseling or psychotherapy. Therefore, you expect the therapist to help your friend with the problems just discussed. What will the counselor or psychotherapist do to help your friend? If the therapist uses one or more theories to help your friend, the therapist will be making use of ideas that have been made clear by clarifying definitions of concepts used in the theory. The theory will be tested to see if it works to help people (some theories have a lot of testing, others have very little). In any case, these theories will have been used by hundreds or thousands of therapists. Many people who use the theories may contribute to the usefulness of the theory. If the therapist does not use a theory to help your friend, the therapist will be relying on intuition and experience from helping other people. These are useful qualities, but without the information provided by experts who have used theories, the therapist is limited in his or her knowledge and strategies.

To understand theories of psychotherapy and counseling, which are based on theories of individual personality, it is helpful to understand the role and purpose of theory in science and, more specifically, in psychology. Particularly important in the development of physical and biological science, theory has also been of great value in the study of personality (Barenbaum & Winter, 2008) and psychotherapy (Gentile, Kisber, Suvak, & West, 2008; Truscott, 2010). Briefly, theory can be described as "a group of logically organized laws or relationships that constitute explanation in a discipline" (Heinen, 1985, p. 414). Included in a theory are assumptions related to the topic of the theory and definitions that can relate assumptions to observations (Fawcett, 1999; Stam, 2000). In this section, criteria by which theories of psychotherapy can be evaluated are briefly described (Fawcett, 1999; Gentile et al., 2008).

Precision and Clarity

Theories are based on rules that need to be clear. The terms used to describe these rules must also be specific. For example, the psychoanalytic term *ego* should have a definition on which practitioners and researchers can agree. If possible, theories should use *operational definitions*, which specify operations or procedures that are used to measure a variable. However, operational definitions for a concept such as *empathy* can be difficult to reach agreement on, and definitions may provide a meaning that is more restricted than desired. A common definition of the concept of empathy, "to enter the world of another individual without being influenced by one's own views and values is to be empathic with the individual," may be clear to some but not provide a definition that is sufficiently specific to be used for research purposes. Along with clear concepts and rules, a theory should be parsimonious, or as straightforward as possible. Constructs such as empathy and unconditional positive regard (terms to be described in Chapter 6, "Person-Centered Therapy") must be related to each other and should be related to rules of human behavior. Theories should explain an area of study (personality or psychotherapy) with as few assumptions as possible.

Comprehensiveness

Theories differ in events that they attempt to predict. In general, the more comprehensive a theory, the more widely it can be applied, but also the more vulnerable it may be to error. For example, all of the theories of psychotherapy and counseling in this book are comprehensive in that they are directed to men and women without specifying age or cultural background. A theory of psychotherapy directed only at helping men change their psychological functioning would be limited in its comprehensiveness.

Testability

To be of use, a theory must be tested and confirmed. With regard to theories of psychotherapy, not only must experience show that a theory is valid or effective, but also research must show that it is effective in bringing about change in individual behavior. When concepts can be clearly defined, hypotheses (predictions derived from theories) can be stated precisely and tested. Sometimes, when hypotheses or the entire theory cannot be confirmed, this failure can lead to development of other hypotheses.

Usefulness

Not only should a good theory lead to new hypotheses that can be tested, but also it should be helpful to practitioners in their work. For psychotherapy and counseling, a good theory suggests ways to understand clients and techniques to help them function better (Truscott, 2010). Without theory, the practitioner would be left to unsystematic techniques or to "reinventing the wheel" by trying new techniques on new patients until something seemed to help. When theories are used, proven concepts and techniques can be organized in ways to help individuals improve their lives. Few therapists work without a theory because to do so would give them no systematic way to assess the client's problem and no way to apply techniques that have been systematically developed and often tested with clients. Theory is the most powerful tool that therapists have to use along with their desire to help troubled clients in an ethical manner.

Neither theories of personality nor theories of psychotherapy and counseling meet all of these criteria. The theories in this book are described not in a formal way but rather in a way to help you understand changes in behavior, thoughts, and feelings. The term *theory* is used loosely, as human behavior is far too complex to have clearly articulated theories, such as those found in physics. Each chapter includes examples of research or systematic investigations that relate to a specific theory of personality and/or theory of psychotherapy and counseling. The type of research presented depends on the precision, explicitness, clarity, comprehensiveness, and testability of the theory.

Psychotherapy and Counseling

Defining *psychotherapy* and *counseling* is difficult, as there is little agreement on definitions and on whether there is any difference between the two. The brief definition given here covers both psychotherapy and counseling.

> Psychotherapy and counseling are interactions between a therapist/counselor and one or more clients/patients. The purpose is to help the patient/client with problems that may have aspects that are related to disorders of thinking, emotional suffering, or problems of behavior. Therapists may use their knowledge of theory of personality and psychotherapy or counseling to help the patient/client improve functioning. The therapist's approach to helping must be legally and ethically approved.

Although this definition can be criticized because not all theories or techniques would be included, it should suffice to provide an overview of the main components in helping individuals with psychological problems.

There have been many attempts to differentiate psychotherapy from counseling. Some writers have suggested that counseling is used with normal individuals and psychotherapy with those who are severely disturbed. The problem with this distinction is that it is difficult to differentiate severity of disturbance, and often practitioners use the same set of techniques for clients of varying severity levels. Another proposed distinction is that counseling is educational and informational while psychotherapy is facilitative (Corsini, 2008). Another attempt at separating counseling and psychotherapy suggests that psychotherapists work in hospitals, whereas counselors work in such settings as schools or guidance clinics. Because the overlap of patient problems is great regardless of work setting, such a distinction is not helpful. Gelso and Fretz (2001) describe a continuum from relatively brief work that is situational or educational on one end (counseling) and long-term, in-depth work seeking to reconstruct personality on the other end (psychotherapy). In between these extremes, counseling and psychotherapy overlap. In this book, the terms *counseling* and *psychotherapy* are used interchangeably, except where they have special meanings as defined by the theorist.

Traditionally, the term *psychotherapy* has been associated with psychiatrists and medical settings, whereas the term *counseling* has been associated with educational and, to some extent, social-work settings. Although there is much overlap, theories developed by psychiatrists often use the word *psychotherapy*, or its briefer form, *therapy*, more frequently than they do *counseling*. In the chapters in this book, I tend to use the term that is used most frequently by practitioners of that theory. In a few theoretical approaches (Adlerian and feminist), some distinctions are made between psychotherapy and counseling, and I describe them. Two theories, psychoanalysis and Jungian analysis, employ the term *analyst*, and in those two chapters I explain the role of analyst as it differs from that of the psychotherapist or counselor.

A related issue is that of the terms *patient* and *client*. *Patient* is used most often in a medical setting, with *client* applied more frequently to educational and social service settings. In this book, the two terms are used interchangeably, both referring to the recipient of psychotherapy or counseling.

Theories of Psychotherapy and Counseling

How many theories of psychotherapy are there? Before the 1950s there were relatively few, and most were derived from Freud's theory of psychoanalysis. Since that time there has been a marked increase in the number of theories that therapists have developed to help people with psychological dysfunctions. Corsini (2001) summarized 69 new and innovative therapies; now there may be a total of more than 400 (Corsini, 2008). Although most of these theories have relatively few proponents and little research to support their effectiveness, they do represent the creativity of psychotherapists in finding ways to provide relief for individual psychological discomfort.

At the same time that there has been an increase in the development of theoretical approaches, there has been a move toward integrating theories, as well as a move toward eclecticism. Broadly, *integration* refers to the use of techniques and/or concepts from two or more theories. Chapter 17 describes three different theories that integrate parts of other theories.

Several researchers have asked therapists about their theoretical orientations (Table 1.1). For example, Prochaska and Norcross (2010) combined three studies in which more than 1,500 psychologists, counselors, psychiatrists, and social workers were asked to identify their primary theoretical orientations (Bechtoldt, Norcross, Wyckoff, Pokrywa, & Campbell, 2001; Bike, Norcross, & Schatz, 2009; Goodyear et al., 2008; Norcross, Karpiak, & Santoro, 2005). Their findings are summarized in Table 1.1, listing major theoretical orientations and the percentage of all therapists identifying with a specific orientation. Generally, those therapists identifying themselves as integrative or eclectic exceed the number identifying with a specific theoretical orientation, but cognitive therapy was a close second. Also, many therapists who identify a primary theory of therapy tend to use techniques from other theories (Thoma & Cecero, 2009).

Table 1.1   Primary Theoretical Orientations of Psychotherapists in the United States

Orientation	Clinical Psychologists	Counseling Psychologists	Social Workers	Counselors
Behavioral	10%	5%	11%	8%
Cognitive	28%	19%	19%	29%
Constructivist	2%	1%	2%	2%
Eclectic/Integrative	29%	34%	26%	23%
Existential/Humanistic	1%	5%	4%	5%
Gestalt/Experiential	1%	2%	1%	2%
Interpersonal	4%	4%	3%	3%
Multicultural	1%	—	1%	1%
Psychoanalytic	3%	1%	5%	2%
Psychodynamic	12%	10%	9%	5%
Rogerian/ Person-Centered	1%	3%	1%	10%
Systems	3%	5%	14%	7%
Other	5%	9%	4%	3%

Sources: Bechtoldt et al., 2001; Bike, Norcross, & Schatz, 2009; Goodyear et al., 2008; Norcross, Karpiak, & Santoro, 2005; Prochaska & Norcross, 2010.

Psychoanalytic theories (those closely related to the work of Freud and his contemporaries) and psychodynamic theories (those having some resemblance to psychoanalytic theories) are a popular theoretical orientation that is subscribed to by therapists from a variety of fields. Cognitive, and to a lesser extent, behavioral methods are popular with a variety of mental health workers. There is some disagreement among studies of therapist preference for theory, due in part to ways in which questions are asked and to changing trends in theoretical preference.

In selecting the major theories to be presented in this book, I have used several criteria. I have consulted surveys such as those summarized here to see which are being used most frequently. Also, I have included theories that have demonstrated that they have a following of interested practitioners by having an organization, one or more journals, national or international meetings, and a developing literature of books, articles, and chapters. Additionally, I have consulted with many therapists and professors to determine which theories appear to be most influential. Ultimately, I tried to decide which theories would be most important for those wishing to become psychotherapists or counselors.

The remaining 16 chapters in this book discuss about 30 different theoretical approaches. Including a number of significant theories provides a background from which students can develop or select their own theoretical approach. Some theories, such as psychoanalysis, have sub-theories that have been derived from the original theory. I have also kept in mind that there is a strong movement toward the integration of theories (using concepts or techniques of more than one theory). To address the topic of integration of theories, I summarize most theories in Chapter 16. In Chapter 17, I present three popular integrative theories. I also show how you can develop your own integrative theory by using different models of theoretical integration. The following paragraphs present a brief, nontechnical summary of the chapters (and theories) in this book to give an overview of the many different and creative methods for helping individuals who are suffering because of psychological problems or difficulties.

Psychoanalysis

Sigmund Freud stressed the importance of inborn drives (particularly sexual) in determining later personality development. Others who followed him emphasized the importance of the adaptation to the environment, early relationships between child and mother, and developmental changes in being absorbed with oneself at the expense of meaningful relationships with others. All of these views of development make use of Freud's concepts of unconscious processes (portions of mental functioning that we are not aware of) and, in general, his structure of personality (ego, id, superego). Traditional psychoanalytic methods require several years of treatment. Because of this, moderate-length and brief therapy methods that use more direct, rather than indirect, techniques have been developed. New writings continue to explore the importance of childhood development on later personality as well as new uses of the therapist's relationship.

Jungian Analysis and Therapy

More than any other theorist, Jung placed great emphasis on the role of unconscious processes in human behavior. Jungians are particularly interested in dreams, fantasies, and other material that reflects unconscious processes. They are also interested in symbols of universal patterns that are reflected in the unconscious processes of people from all cultures. Therapy focuses on the analysis of unconscious processes so that patients can better integrate unconscious processes into conscious awareness.

Adlerian Therapy

Alfred Adler believed that the personality of individuals was formed in their early years as a result of relationships within the family. He emphasized the importance of individuals' contributions to their community and to society. Adlerians are interested in the ways that individuals approach living and family relationships. The Adlerian approach to therapy is practical, helping individuals to change dysfunctional beliefs and encouraging them to take new steps to change their lives. An emphasis on teaching and educating individuals about dealing with interpersonal problems is another characteristic of Adlerian therapy.

Existential Therapy

A philosophical approach to people and problems relating to being human or existing, existential psychotherapy deals with life themes rather than techniques. Such themes include living and dying, freedom, responsibility to self and others, finding meaning in life, and dealing with a sense of meaninglessness. Becoming aware of oneself and developing the ability to look beyond immediate problems and daily events to deal with existential themes are goals of therapy, along with developing honest and intimate relationships with others. Although some techniques have been developed, the emphasis is on issues and themes, not method.

Person-Centered Therapy

In his therapeutic work, Carl Rogers emphasized understanding and caring for the client, as opposed to diagnosis, advice, or persuasion. Characteristic of Rogers's approach to therapy are therapeutic genuineness, through verbal and nonverbal behavior, and unconditionally accepting clients for who they are. Person-centered therapists are concerned about understanding the client's experience and communicating their understanding to the client so that an atmosphere of trust can be developed that fosters change on the part of the client. Clients are given responsibility for making positive changes in their lives.

Gestalt Therapy

Developed by Fritz Perls, gestalt therapy helps the individual to become more aware of self and others. Emphasis is on both bodily and psychological awareness. Therapeutic approaches deal with being responsible for oneself and attuned to one's language, nonverbal behaviors, emotional feelings, and conflicts within oneself and with others. Therapeutic techniques include the development of creative experiments and exercises to facilitate self-awareness.

Behavior Therapy

Based on scientific principles of behavior, such as classical and operant conditioning, as well as observational learning, behavior therapy applies principles of learning such as reinforcement, extinction, shaping of behavior, and modeling to help a wide variety of clients with different problems. Emphasis is on precision and detail in evaluating psychological concerns and then assigning treatment methods that may include relaxation, exposure to a feared object, copying a behavior, or role playing. Its many techniques include those that change observable behavior as well as those that deal with thought processes.

Rational Emotive Behavior Therapy

Developed by Albert Ellis, rational emotive behavior therapy (REBT) focuses on irrational beliefs that individuals develop that lead to problems related to emotions (for example, fears and anxieties) and to behaviors (such as avoiding social interactions or giving speeches). Although REBT uses a wide variety of techniques, the most common method is to dispute irrational beliefs and to teach clients to challenge their own irrational beliefs so that they can reduce anxiety and develop a full range of ways to interact with others.

Cognitive Therapy

Belief systems and thinking are seen as important in determining and affecting behavior and feelings. Aaron Beck developed an approach that helps individuals understand their own maladaptive thinking and how it may affect their feelings and actions. Cognitive therapists use a structured method to help their clients understand their own belief systems. By asking clients to record dysfunctional thoughts and using questionnaires to determine maladaptive thinking, cognitive therapists are then able to make use of a wide variety of techniques to change beliefs that interfere with successful functioning. They also make use of affective and behavioral strategies.

Reality Therapy

Reality therapists assume that individuals are responsible for their own lives and for taking control over what they do, feel, and think. Developed by William Glasser, reality therapy uses a specific process to change behavior. A relationship is developed with clients so that they will commit to the therapeutic process. Emphasis is on changing behaviors that will lead to modifications in thinking and feeling. Making plans and sticking to them to bring about change while taking responsibility for oneself are important aspects of reality therapy.

Constructivist Therapy

Constructivist therapists see their clients as theorists and try to understand their clients' views or the important constructs that clients use to understand their problems. Three types of constructivist theories are discussed: solution-focused, personal construct theory, and narrative. Solution-focused therapy centers on finding solutions to problems by looking at what has worked in the past and what is working now, as well as using active techniques to make therapeutic progress. Personal construct theory examines clients' lives as stories and helps to change the story. Narrative therapies also view clients' problems as stories but seek to externalize the problem, unlike personal construct theory. Frequently, they help clients re-author or change stories, thus finding a new ending for the story that leads to a solution to the problem.

Feminist Therapy

Rather than focusing only on the individual's psychological problems, feminist therapists emphasize the role of politics and society in creating problems for individuals. Particularly, they are concerned about gender and cultural roles and power differences between men and women and people from diverse cultural backgrounds. They have examined different ways that gender and culture affect development throughout the life span (including social and sexual development, child-raising practices, and work roles). Differences in moral decision making, relating to others, and roles in abuse and violence are issues of feminist therapists. By combining feminist therapy with other theories, feminist therapists take a sociological as well as a psychological view that focuses not only on gender but also on multicultural issues. Among the techniques they use are those that help individuals address gender and power inequalities not only by changing client behavior but also by changing societal groups or institutions.

Family Therapy

Whereas many theories focus on the problems of individuals, family therapists attend to interactions between family members and may view the entire family as a single unit or system. Treatment is designed to bring about change in functioning within the family rather than within a single individual. Several different approaches to family therapy have been developed. Some focus on the impact of the parents' own families, others on how family members relate to each other in the therapy hour, and yet others on changing symptoms. Some family systems therapists request that all the family members be available for therapy, whereas others may deal with parents or certain members only. Almost all of the theories in this book can be applied to families. Chapter 14 shows how these theories work with families.

Other Psychotherapies

Five different psychotherapies are treated briefly in Chapter 15, "Other Psychotherapies." *Asian therapies* often emphasize quiet reflection and personal responsibility to others. *Body therapies* work with the interaction between psychological and physiological functioning. *Interpersonal therapy* is a very specific treatment for depression based on a review of research. *Psychodrama* is an active system in which clients, along with group and audience members, play out roles related to their problems while therapists take responsibility for directing the activities. *Creative arts therapies* include art, dance movement, drama, and music to encourage expressive action and therapeutic change. Any of these therapies may be used with other therapeutic approaches.

Integrative Therapy

In Chapter 17, integrative therapists combine two or more theories in different ways so that they can understand client problems. They may then use a wide variety of techniques to help clients make changes in their lives. Prochaska and Norcross's transtheoretical approach examines many theories, selecting concepts, techniques, and other factors that effective psychotherapeutic approaches have in common. Their model for therapeutic change examines client readiness for change, level of problems that need changing, and techniques to bring about change. Paul Wachtel's cyclical psychodynamics combines psychoanalysis and behavior therapy, as well as some other theories. Arnold Lazarus's multimodal therapy uses techniques from many theories to bring about client change but uses social learning theory as a way to view personality. I use each of these three methods as examples of how you and others can construct your own integrative theory.

How different are all of these theories? Therapists and researchers have tried for many years to identify common factors recurring in all therapies (Castonguay & Beutler, 2006; Duncan, Miller, Wampold, & Hubble, 2010; Fiedler, 1950). Isolating common factors in the treatment of many psychological disorders has been complex and difficult. Castonguay and Beutler (2006) in *Principles of Therapeutic Change That Work* examine characteristics of clients and therapists that contribute to client change. Duncan et al. (2010) in *The Heart and Soul of Change: Delivering What Works in Therapy* present many different ways of using the common factors approach with different psychological disorders and addressing different issues such as research. Both books also examine factors such as the quality of the therapeutic relationship and therapist interpersonal and clinical skills. Empathy for clients is an example of a therapist interpersonal skill. Examination of common factors continues to be an active area of interest for some psychologists.

Although each theory in this textbook is treated as a distinct approach, different from others, this presentation disguises the movement toward integration that is found in many, but not all, theories and discussed in Chapter 17. I have tried to emphasize the concepts and techniques that are associated with each theory rather than common factors. When a theory borrows from other theories, such as when cognitive therapy borrows from behavior therapy, I have tended to focus mainly on the techniques that are associated with the original theory. In each chapter, I explain important concepts and techniques that characterize a theory as well as ways to apply the theory to a variety of psychological problems, issues, and situations. In Chapter 16, I compare the theories to each other in several different ways and then critique them. In this way, I summarize the theories so that they can be more easily integrated in Chapter 17.

Organization of the Chapters

For most of the remaining chapters, I follow the same organizational format. The first two sections, on history and personality theory, provide a background for the major section that describes that theory of psychotherapy, in which goals, assessment methods, and techniques are described. Sections that follow describe a variety of areas of application. Case examples are used to show the many ways that theories can be applied. Additionally, important issues such as brief psychotherapy, current trends, using a theory with other theories, and research into the theory are explained. Also, information about how the theory deals with gender and cultural issues and how it can be used in group therapy is provided.

History or Background

To understand a theory of helping others, it is useful to know how the theory developed and which factors were significant in its development. Often the discussion of background focuses on the theorist's life and philosophy, as well as literature and other intellectual forces that contributed to the theorist's ideas about helping others with psychological problems. For example, Freud's ideas about the Oedipus complex (sexual attraction to the other-sex parent and hostility toward the same-sex parent) derive, in a limited way, from Freud's reflections on his own childhood and his intellectual pursuits. However, Freud's work with patients was the most important factor in developing the Oedipus complex. Theorists have grown up in different countries, eras, and have different family backgrounds. All of these factors, as well as theorists' exposure to prominent philosophers, physicians, psychiatrists, or psychologists in their early professional development, have an impact on their theories of psychotherapy. This information helps us to understand how theorists developed their theory of personality and the methods of change or techniques that they use to help patients with personal problems.

Personality Theories

Each theory of psychotherapy is based on a theory of personality, or how theorists understand human behavior. Personality theories are important because they represent the ways that therapists conceptualize their clients' past, present, or future behavior, feelings, and thoughts. Methods of changing these behaviors or thoughts all derive from those factors that theorists see as most important in understanding their patients. The presentations on personality theory in this book differ from those in personality theory textbooks in that the explanations given here are briefer and designed to explain and illustrate concepts that are related to the practice of psychotherapy. In each chapter, the theory of personality provides the foundation for the goals, assessment, and treatment methods of a theory of psychotherapy. Because the concepts that describe each personality theory are essential in understanding the theory, I list these concepts in the first page of each chapter, along with the techniques that are used in each theory of psychotherapy. This list provides a brief overview of the basic concepts of each theory.

Theories of Psychotherapy

For most chapters, this section is the longest and most important. First, I describe the goals or purposes of therapy. What do therapists want to achieve with their clients? What will the clients be like when they get better? What kind of psychological functioning is most important in the theory? All of these questions are implicit in the explanation of a theory's view of goals.

From goals follows an approach to assessment. Some theorists want to assess the relationship of unconscious to conscious processes; others focus on assessing distorted thinking. Some theories attend to feelings (sadness, rage, happiness, and so forth), whereas others specify behaviors of an individual (refusal to leave the house to go outside or sweating before talking to someone). Many theorists and their colleagues have developed their own methods of assessment, such as interview techniques or questions to ask the client, but they also include inventories, rating forms, and questionnaires. All relate to making judgments that influence the selection of therapeutic techniques and are based on the theory of personality discussed in the previous section.

Theorists vary widely in their use of techniques. Those theories that focus on the unconscious (psychoanalysis and Jungian analysis) use techniques that are likely to bring unconscious factors into conscious awareness (for example, using dream analysis). Other techniques focus on changing beliefs (cognitions), accessing and reflecting feelings (emotions), and having clients take actions (behavior). Because techniques of therapy can be difficult to understand, I have used examples to show the therapeutic relevance of methods for changing behavior, emotions, thoughts, or other aspects of oneself. As most theorists have found, helping individuals change aspects of themselves can be difficult and complex. To explain this process further, I have described several psychological disorders to which theories can be applied. I use case studies to illustrate how a theory can be applied to each of a few psychological disorders.

Psychological Disorders

Increasingly, therapists no longer ask, "Which is the best therapy?" but "What is the best therapy for a specific type of client?" To provide an answer to the latter question, I have selected three, four, or five case examples of individual therapy. The first case presented is the most thoroughly developed and the longest. This case, along with the others, illustrates how the theory can be applied to some of the more common diagnostic classifications of psychological disorders listed in the *Diagnostic and Statistical Manual of Mental Disorders*, Fourth Edition–Text Revision (DSM-IV-TR, American Psychiatric Association, 2000). By presenting both a longer case example and several shorter cases, I try to provide both depth and breadth. For individual therapy, there are both advantages and problems in describing how different theories can be applied to common categories of psychological disorders.

The advantage of describing ways in which theories help individuals with a variety of psychological problems is to provide a broader and deeper view of the theory than if no reference to diagnostic classification were made. By examining several case studies or descriptions of treatment, the breadth of theoretical application can be seen by applying it to different situations. Also, some theoretical approaches have devoted particular attention to certain types of disorders, describing specific methods and techniques. The approach of different theories can be assessed by comparing one type of client (for example, a depressed client) with another across several theories. Although it would be extremely helpful if I could say for each therapy, "For this type of disorder, you use this type of treatment from theory A, but for another type of disorder, you use a different treatment from theory A," this is not possible. Perhaps most important, clients do not fit easily into specific categories such as depression, anxiety disorder, and obsessive-compulsive disorder. Individuals often have problems that overlap several areas or diagnostic criteria. Furthermore, problems differ in severity within a particular category, and clients differ due to cultural background, gender, age, motivation to solve their problem, marital situation, the problem that they present to the therapist, and the history of the problem. All of these factors make it difficult for therapists of a given theoretical orientation to say, "I will use this technique when treating these types of patients."

Additionally, practitioners of some theories do not find the DSM-IV-TR classification system (or any other general system) a useful way of understanding clients. Practitioners of some theories see classification systems as a nuisance, required for agency or insurance reimbursement purposes but having little other value. Theories of psychotherapy that make the most use of assessment of diagnostic classification are psychoanalysis, Adlerian therapy, behavior therapy, and cognitive therapy, with cognitive therapy probably making the most extensive use of diagnostic classification information. Although many practitioners of other theories do not use conceptualizations and techniques that warrant use of diagnostic classification systems, they do not treat everyone in the same manner. Instead, they respond to clients based on their own theory of personality and assessment rather than using a classification system.

The main reason for using examples of several psychological disorders for each theory is to enable the reader to develop a greater understanding of the theory through comparison with other theories and through the presentation of diverse applications. To provide a background for understanding common disorders, I give a general description of the major disorders discussed in this book. For every major theory, I present an example of how that theory can be applied to depression. For each theory, except person-centered and feminist therapy, I give an example of how that theory is applied to anxiety disorders. (The reasons that some theories are omitted from these two comparisons are that there either appear to be no appropriate cases for demonstration purposes or that it was important to focus on other disorders.) With the exception of Klerman's interpersonal therapy (Chapter 15) that is designed for treating depression, all theories are used to treat almost all disorders. The other case examples that I use are selected either because they illustrate treatment of a disorder that is frequently treated by a particular theory or because I have found an example that is an excellent illustration of the application of the theory. In the next section, depression and anxiety disorders are described broadly, along with other disorders that are used as examples in this text (Barlow & Durand, 2009).

Depression. Signs of depression include sadness, feelings of worthlessness, guilt, social withdrawal, and loss of sleep, appetite, sexual desire, or interest in activities. With severe depression may come slow speech, difficulty in sitting still, inattention to personal appearance, and pervasive feelings of hopelessness and anxiety, as well as suicidal thoughts and feelings. Major depression is one of the most common psychological disorders and may affect about 16% of the population at some time during their lifetimes (Kessler et al., 2003).

Two types of depression are usually distinguished: unipolar and bipolar. In *bipolar* depression, a manic mood in which the individual becomes extremely talkative, distractible, seductive, and/or active occurs along with episodes of extreme depression. In *unipolar* depression, a manic phase is not present. In discussions on treating depression in this book, distinctions between unipolar and bipolar depression are not frequently made. The psychotherapeutic treatments described here generally apply both to unipolar depression and the depressive phase of bipolar depression.

Generalized anxiety disorder. Excessive worry and apprehension are associated with general anxiety disorders. Individuals may experience restlessness, irritability, problems in concentration, muscular tension, and problems sleeping. Excessive worry about a variety of aspects of life is common, with anxiety being diffuse rather than related to a specific fear (phobia), rituals or obsessions (obsessive-compulsive disorder), or physical complaints (somatoform disorder). These disorders have been characterized as neuroses, as they all are associated with anxiety of one type or another. The term *neurosis* is a broad one and, because of its general nature, is used infrequently in this text; it has been used most frequently by early theorists such as Freud, Jung, and Adler. In general, the term *anxiety disorder* can be said to include nonspecific neuroses or anxiety.

Borderline disorders. More accurately described *as borderline personality disorder*, borderline disorders are one of a number of different personality disorders (such as narcissistic). Personality disorders are characterized as being inflexible, of long duration, and including traits that make social or vocational functioning difficult. They have earned a reputation as being particularly difficult to treat psychotherapeutically.

Individuals with borderline disorders are characterized by having unstable interpersonal relationships. Their view of themselves and their moods can change very rapidly and inexplicably in a short period of time. Behavior tends to be erratic, unpredictable, and impulsive in areas such as spending, eating, sex, or gambling. Emotional relationships are often intense, with individuals with borderline disorders becoming angry and disappointed in a relationship quite quickly. Such individuals have fears of being abandoned and often feel let down by others who do not meet their expectations. Suicide attempts are not unusual.

Obsessive-compulsive disorder. When individuals experience persistent and uncontrollable thoughts or feel compelled to repeat behaviors again and again, they are likely to be suffering from an obsessive-compulsive disorder. *Obsessions* are recurring thoughts that cannot be controlled and are so pervasive as to interfere with day-to-day functioning. Some obsessions may appear as extreme worrying or indecision in which the individual debates over and over again, "Should I do this or should I do that?" *Compulsions* are behaviors that are repeated continually to reduce distress or prevent something terrible from happening. For example, individuals with a compulsion to wash their hands for 20 minutes at a time may believe that this prevents germs and deadly disease. The fear is exaggerated, and the compulsion interferes with day-to-day activity. Individuals with an obsessive-compulsive disorder differ as to whether their symptoms are primarily obsessions, compulsions, or a mixture of the two.

Obsessive-compulsive disorder should be distinguished from *obsessive-compulsive personality disorder*, which refers, in general, to being preoccupied with rules, details, and schedules. Such individuals often are inflexible about moral issues and the behavior of others. Because they insist that others do things their way, their interpersonal relationships tend to be poor. Normally, they do not experience obsessions and compulsions. Although an important disorder, obsessive-compulsive personality disorder is not used as an example in this book.

Phobias. Being afraid of a situation or object out of proportion to the danger of the situation or object describes a phobic reaction. For example, experiencing extreme tension, sweating, and other anxiety when seeing a rat or being at the top of a tall building are reactions that can be debilitating. Phobic individuals go beyond the cautious behavior that most people would experience when seeing a rat or being at the top of a building.

Somatoform disorders. When there is a physical symptom but no known physiological cause, and a psychological cause is suspected, then a diagnosis of somatoform disorder is given. This diagnostic category includes *hypochondria*, which is diagnosed when a person is worried about possibly having a serious disease and there is no evidence for it. *Conversion disorder* is also a type of somatoform disorder. This disorder refers to psychological disturbances that take a physical form, such as paralysis of the legs, when there is no physiological explanation. It is infrequently seen. However, patients with conversion disorder, which Freud called *hysteria,* made up a significant portion of Freud's clientele, and observations about these patients were important in the development of psychoanalysis. In Chapter 2, an example of Freud's treatment of a patient with hysteria is illustrated.

Posttraumatic stress disorder. Extreme reactions to a highly stressful event constitute posttraumatic stress disorder (PTSD). Examples of a stressful event would be being raped, robbed, or assaulted; escaping from a flash flood; or being in military combat. Stress reactions last for months or years and often include physiological symptoms such as difficulty in sleeping or concentrating. Individuals with PTSD may re-experience the event through nightmares or images that remind them of the event. Another aspect of PTSD is attempting to avoid feeling or thinking about the trauma or event.

Eating disorders. Two types of eating disorders are discussed: anorexia and bulimia. *Anorexia* is diagnosed when individuals do not maintain a minimally normal body weight. Such individuals are very afraid of gaining weight and view parts of their body as too big (such as buttocks and thighs), whereas others may see them as emaciated. *Bulimia* refers to binge eating and inappropriate methods of preventing weight gain. Binge eating includes excessive consumption of food at meals or other times, such as eating an entire box of cookies or a half-gallon of ice cream. Inappropriate methods of controlling weight gain include self-induced vomiting, misuse of laxatives or enemas, or excessive fasting or exercise. Individuals with bulimia often are of normal weight. Some individuals have experienced both anorexia and bulimia at various times in their lives.

Substance abuse. When individuals use drugs to such an extent that they have difficulty meeting social and occupational obligations, substance abuse has occurred. Relying on a drug because it makes difficult situations less stressful is called *psychological dependency.* Developing withdrawal symptoms, such as cramps, is called *physiological dependency.* When physiological dependence exists, individuals are said to be *substance-dependent* or addicted. In this text, the term *substance abuse* is used broadly and includes psychological and/or physiological dependence on a variety of drugs such as alcohol, cocaine, marijuana, sedatives, stimulants, and hallucinogens. Because substance abuse is so widespread, many practitioners of theories have devoted significant attention to this area. Examples of treating alcoholism or other drug abuse are found in the chapters on existentialism, REBT, reality therapy, and cognitive therapy.

Narcissistic personality disorder. Showing a pattern of self-importance, the need for admiration from others, and a lack of empathy are characteristics of individuals with a narcissistic personality disorder. They may be boastful or pretentious, inflate their accomplishments and abilities, and feel that they are superior to others or special and should be recognized and admired. Believing that others should treat them favorably, they become angry when this is not done. Also, they have difficulty being truly concerned for others except when their own welfare is involved. Heinz Kohut's self psychology, discussed in Chapter 2, focuses on the development of narcissism in individuals.

Schizophrenia. Severe disturbances of thought, emotions, and behaviors characterize schizophrenia. Individuals may think and speak in illogical fragments that are very disorganized. They may also have delusions, beliefs that exist despite evidence to the contrary, such as the belief (a paranoid delusion) that they are being followed by the director of the Central Intelligence Agency. Hallucinations are prevalent among individuals with schizophrenia and refer to seeing, hearing, feeling, tasting, or smelling things that are not there, such as hearing the voice of Abraham Lincoln. Other symptoms include unusual motions or immobility, extreme lack of energy or emotional response, and inappropriate affect, such as laughing when hearing about the death of a friend. The term *psychosis* is a broader term including schizophrenia and other disorders in which individuals have lost contact with reality.

Although schizophrenia appears somewhat frequently in the population of the world, between 0.2% and 1.5% (Ho, Black, & Andreasen, 2003), I have not focused on psychotherapeutic treatment of schizophrenia, as many researchers believe that this disorder is resistant to most psychotherapeutic techniques and responds better to medication. However, cognitive and behavioral treatments are used in the treatment of schizophrenia with reported success.

The 11 categories of psychological disorders I have just explained may seem complex. In later chapters, as treatment approaches are presented for various disorders, characteristics of these disorders should become clearer. Because the disorders themselves are described only in this section of the book, it may be helpful, when reading about a particular case, to return to this section or consult the glossary for a specific explanation of a disorder.

In this chapter, information about these disorders is presented in summary form. A more in-depth description of these and many other disorders can be found in *the Diagnostic and Statistical Manual of Mental Disorders* (DSM-IV-TR, American Psychiatric Association, 2000), Barlow and Durand (2009), and other textbooks on abnormal psychology. Many practitioners of theoretical approaches use diagnostic categories more superficially and crudely than do investigators of abnormal psychology or psychologists who specialize in the diagnosis or classification of disorders. However, the information provided in this section should help readers understand the different types of problems to which various theoretical approaches can be applied. Additionally, some theories of therapy describe both a typical form of treatment as well as a brief form of treatment.

Brief Psychotherapy

Length of therapy has become an issue of increasing importance to practicing psychotherapists. Because of client demand for services, many agencies such as community mental health services and college counseling centers set limits on the number of sessions that they can provide for clients. Session limits may range broadly from 3 to more than 40, depending on the agency's resources and philosophy. Additionally, health maintenance organizations (HMOs) and insurance companies that reimburse mental health benefits put limits on the number of sessions for which they will pay. Furthermore, clients often seek treatment that will take several weeks or months rather than several years. All of these forces have had an impact on treatment length and the development of brief psychotherapeutic approaches.

Several terms have been used to refer to brief approaches to psychotherapy: brief psychotherapy, short-term psychotherapy, and time-limited therapy. In general, *brief* and *short-term therapies* refer to limits placed on the number of sessions, for example, no more than 20 sessions. *Time-limited therapy* represents a theoretical approach to therapy that takes a certain number of sessions for completion, such as 12, with specific issues being addressed in each phase of the 12-session limit. The approach that most thoroughly addresses the issue of both long-term and brief therapeutic treatments is psychoanalysis. In that chapter, a brief approach to psychoanalysis is discussed, along with traditional long-term methods.

Most of the other theoretical approaches acknowledge the importance of brief psychotherapy and demonstrate under what circumstances these therapies can be applied briefly. For the most part, Jungian, existential, person-centered, and gestalt therapies do not have methodologies that result in treatment length being less than 6 months or a year. Other approaches, such as REBT, behavior, cognitive, and reality therapies, demonstrate how certain types of problems require less therapeutic time than others. Additionally, some varieties of family therapy are designed to be completed in 5 to 10 meetings. For most chapters, the issue of brief psychotherapy is explained from the point of view of the theory. Just as theories have responded to the need to provide brief treatment, theories make other changes in response to new concerns and issues.

Current Trends

Theories are in a continual state of change and growth. Although they may start with the original ideas of a particular theorist, theories are, to varying degrees, influenced by new writings based on psychotherapeutic practice and/or research. Some of the innovations deal with applications to areas such as social problems, education, families, or groups. Other trends reflect challenges to existing theoretical concepts and the development of new ones. Three different trends will be discussed in several chapters: the growth and development of treatment manuals, research-supported psychological treatments (RSPT), and the influence of constructivism on the theory and practice of psychotherapy.

Treatment manuals. Treatment manuals are guidelines for therapists as to how to treat patients with particular disorders or problems. Typically, they describe skills and the sequence of using these skills that therapists should use. Suggestions are given for dealing with frequently encountered questions or problems. A major advantage of treatment manuals is that they specify procedures in a clear manner. Essentially, instructions are given so that therapists know how to conduct therapy with a specific problem. Additionally, treatment manuals provide an opportunity for researchers to investigate the effectiveness of a particular method, because all therapists who use the method in research can be checked to see if they comply with directions. A goal of treatment manuals is to have a specific approach that has been proven to be effective that therapists can use to help clients (Najavits, Weiss, Shaw, & Dierberger, 2000). However, treatment manuals will vary in their content depending on whether the treatment manual is written for a newly developed treatment method or if it is written for treatment methods that have been thoroughly tested. Carroll and Rounsaville (2008) describe a three-stage method for developing treatment manuals depending on how much the therapeutic procedure has been evaluated.

Because psychotherapy is a very complex process, therapists vary greatly as to their opinions about treatment manuals (Norcross, Beutler, & Levant, 2006).

Treatment manuals may focus on technique but not help therapists focus on important working relationships with clients. Also, treatment manuals may be aimed at a few specific problems. What happens when the client has several problems? Individuals are unique, and the way they experience some problems may be different from the way others do. I will discuss the use of treatment manuals in the "Current Trends" section, when appropriate. The theories that are most frequently recognized as having treatment manuals are some brief psychoanalytical approaches and cognitive and behavioral theories. Because treatment manuals are a set of instructions that therapists use for a specific treatment, they can be examined for their validity and can be used in RSPT.

Research-supported psychological treatments. RSPT has previously been known by the terms *evidence-based psychotherapy* and *empirically supported therapy*. The name changes are due to the need to be as clear as possible as to the purpose of RSPT, which is to find out if psychotherapy research supports that the therapy has been effective in providing psychotherapeutic treatment. How research is used to determine whether therapy is effective or not is discussed in the "Research" section. In brief, RSPT must meet strict criteria for thorough research procedures (Chambless et al., 2006; Chambless & Hollon, 1998). Typically, treatments are compared to another treatment or to a no-treatment control group. These therapies must be shown to be effective in comprehensive studies. The psychotherapy that is used must follow the treatment manual and have clear goals and treatment planning. Progress is monitored and followed up for a year or two, or longer, after treatment. RSPT are specific to psychological disorders, such as those described previously, and to specific populations, such as adolescents. RSPT are based on therapeutic treatments that are informed by research (Huppert, Fabbro, & Barlow, 2006; Weisz & Gray, 2008). The methods used for doing outcome research on RSPT are complex but thoroughly described by Nezu and Nezu (2008).

In addition to following treatment manuals, therapists using these treatments must develop good working relationships with clients, be empathic, and help clients maintain motivation to change. Probably the most extensive review of RSPT is *A Guide to Treatments That Work* and research supporting the effectiveness of treatments for many psychological disorders is described in Nathan and Gorman (2007).

As mentioned previously, in this text, I give examples in each chapter of how a specific theory applies to three to five psychological disorders. For several of the disorders, I have used RSPT as examples. RSPT are discussed mainly in Chapter 8, "Behavior Therapy," and Chapter 10, "Cognitive Therapy." Most research-supported therapies use both behavioral and cognitive treatments in combination. The reason that most RSPT are cognitive or behavioral or a combination of both is that these treatments tend to be brief, use treatment manuals, are specific about goals, and make use of research methods. This does not mean that behavioral and cognitive treatments are better than other therapies, only that most other therapies have not been studied in the same way. Some theories such as process experiential therapy (Chapter 7) and short-term psychodynamic therapy for depression (Chapter 2) meet criteria for RSPT. In determining which treatments can be considered to meet criteria for RSPT, I have used *A Guide to Treatments That Work* (Nathan & Gorman, 2007) and *Research Supported*

Table 1.2   Research-Supported Psychological
Treatments Listed by Chapter and
Psychological Disorder

Chapter	Psychological Disorder
Chapter 2. Psychoanalysis	Depression
Chapter 7. Emotion-focused or process experiential therapy	Depression
Chapter 8. Behavior Therapy	Depression, obsessive-compulsive disorder, general anxiety disorder, phobic disorder, posttraumatic stress disorder (eye-movement desensitization and reprocessing), borderline disorder (dialectical behavior therapy)
Chapter 10. Cognitive Therapy	Depression, anxiety, obsessive-compulsive disorders
Chapter 15. Other Psychotherapies (Interpersonal Psychotherapy)	Depression

Psychological Treatments on the Research-Supported Psychological Treatments website of the Society of Clinical Psychology, Division 12, of the American Psychological Association. *Research Supported Psychological Treatments* (2009) lists about 60 different treatments; only 10 are listed in this textbook. Table 1.2 lists the chapters where the RSPT are described along with the psychological disorders with which they are used in this text. These research-supported psychological treatments can also be found in Chapter 16, where they are discussed in more detail.

Postmodernism and constructivism. A very different influence than treatment manuals and RSPT is that of postmodernism (Neimeyer, 2009 ; Neimeyer & Baldwin, 2005). A philosophical position, *postmodernism* does not assume that there is a fixed truth; rather, individuals have constructs or perceptions of reality or truth. This is in reaction to *modernism*, which takes a *rationalist* approach that emphasizes scientific truth and is a reflection of advances in technology and science. Postmodernism reflects a multiculturally diverse world in which psychologists, philosophers, and others have recognized that different individuals can have their own constructs or view of what is real for them.

Related to postmodernism is *constructivism*. Constructivists view individuals as creating their own views of events and relationships in their lives. Constructivist therapists not only attend to the meanings that their patients give to their own problems but also help them see problems as meaningful options that have outlived their usefulness. Constructivist therapists deal with the ways their clients impose their own order on their problems and how they derive meanings from their experiences with others. There are several constructivist points of view. One that is discussed in this text is *social constructionism*, which focuses on the shared meanings that people in a culture or society develop (Neimeyer, 2009). These social constructions are a way that individuals relate to each other. (Two specific social constructionist approaches, solution-focused therapy and narrative therapy, are described in Chapter 12, "Constructivist Approaches.")

Social constructionism: Molly. To make this explanation less abstract, I will use the example of 10-year-old Molly, who was suffering from nightmares and an inability to sleep in her own room (Duncan, Hubble, & Miller, 1997). Molly and her divorced mother had seen two therapists. One had the goal of exploring for sexual abuse and investigating Molly's feelings about her father. This approach had not worked. Rather than take a detailed history and make hypotheses about Molly's problem, the current therapist asked Molly for her solution to the problem. Molly suggested that she could sleep in her own bed and her nightmares may disappear if she could "barricade herself in her bed with pillows and stuffed animals" (Duncan et al., p. 24). Molly tried this and during the course of the third session made the following comment:

> Psychiatrists [therapists] just don't understand you … [the client] also have the solutions, for yourself, but they say, "Let's try this and let's try that" and they're not helping. You know, you're like, "I don't really want to do that." You're asking me what I wanted to do with my room, got me back in my room. *So, what I am saying to all psychiatrists is we have the answers, we just need someone to help us bring them to the front of our head. It's like they're [the solutions] locked in an attic or something.* It's a lot better when you ask a person what they want to do and they usually tell you what they think would help, but didn't know if it was going to help and didn't want to try. (Duncan et al., 1997, p. 25)

Molly's situation is very unusual, as she had a solution in mind. Very few clients have explicit answers to their problems clearly in mind when they seek psychotherapy. However, constructivists frequently assume that careful exploration of the meaning of the problems, combined with respectful negotiation of possible solutions, will yield answers that neither the client nor the therapist could have envisioned at the outset of therapy. Molly's example illustrates the postmodern or constructivist approach to understanding the client's view of reality and valuing it. The constructivist philosophy has had an impact on many theories discussed in this book. When relevant, the constructivist influence on a theory will be discussed in the "Current Trends" section.

Using a Theory with Other Theories

As you read about different theories and how they address issues such as those described in the Current Trends section, you may ask, Could I use this theory with other theories that I have read about? Although 40 or 50 years ago practitioners of various theoretical points of view were often isolated from each other, communicating at conventions and through journals with only those who shared their own theoretical persuasion, increasingly this is no longer the case. Practitioners (as shown previously) have become much more integrative in their work, making use of research and theoretical writings outside their own specific points of view. This section provides some information as to the openness of theories to the ideas of others and the similarity of various theoretical perspectives.

Research

The question "How well does this theory work?" is answered (in part) by the Research section. Theories of psychotherapy differ dramatically in terms of their attitude toward research, type of research done, and the accessibility of the theory for research. Although attitudes are changing, traditionally a number of psychoanalysts and Jungian analysts questioned the value of research in determining the effectiveness of psychotherapy. In general, the more specific the concepts to be measured and the briefer the therapeutic approach, the easier it is to conduct research. However, as is shown shortly, little about research on psychotherapy is easy. Because behavior, cognitive, and REBT therapies use relatively brief and specific methods and goals, there is far more research on the effectiveness of psychotherapy for these theories than for others. It is not possible to conclude on the basis of research that theory x is superior to theory y either in general or for a specific disorder. However, it is possible to show some trends in directions of effectiveness and to highlight the types of research that are currently being done to assess therapeutic benefits.

Evaluation of the effectiveness of theories is a very sophisticated and complex skill that cannot be covered in an introductory text on theories of psychotherapy and counseling, but requires comprehensive coverage (Hill & Lambert, 2004; Mitchell & Jolley, 2010; Nezu & Nezu, 2008). However, a brief overview of important points in conducting psychotherapeutic research can provide some understanding of the factors that need to be considered in trying to determine the advantages of a particular theory of psychotherapy (Kendall et al., 2004).

A major goal of psychotherapy research is to understand how different forms of treatment operate. Another goal is to develop and evaluate research-supported psychological treatments (RSPT) that can be used by therapists. To do this, researchers try to design experiments that control sources of bias within the study so that comparisons can be made. A common method is to compare a group receiving a treatment to one that does not or to another group receiving a different treatment. Measurement of important variables to be studied should take place before and after the treatment, a *pretest-posttest control group design*. Other designs provide ways of studying more than one important variable at a time. When research on the effectiveness of psychotherapy has accumulated either generally or in a specific area, such as depression, it is sometimes helpful to conduct *a meta-analysis*, which is a way of statistically summarizing the results of a large number of studies. In this book, reference is made to meta-analyses as well as to specific studies that are examples of research on the therapeutic effectiveness of a particular theory.

In designing research, attention needs to be given to the type of treatment used, assignment of subjects, therapist characteristics, and measures of therapeutic outcome. Researchers must determine the problem they are going to study, such as depression, and make sure that treatment is focused on this variable. Participants in the study must be assigned to the control and treatment groups using an unbiased system. The treatment provided the participants must represent the treatment to be studied. For example, if behavior therapy is the treatment to be studied, it may be inappropriate to have graduate students administer the treatment. The question would arise, *Is their treatment as effective as that of experienced behavior therapists, and did they carry out the training the way they were supposed to, even if they did receive training?* Also, personal characteristics of the therapist should be controlled for, so that investigators can feel confident that it was the treatment rather than therapist charisma that brought about change. Not only must therapeutic variables be controlled, but also effective measures of outcome must be used.

A number of measures of therapeutic outcome that assess areas such as social and marital adjustment and emotional, cognitive, and behavioral functioning have been developed (Hill & Lambert, 2004). Appropriate measures must be used before, often during, and immediately following treatment, as well as at a later time. For example, some treatments have been found to be effective 1 year after therapy but not 2 years after the therapeutic experience. In general, the longer the follow-up period, the greater the chance that participants in the study will no longer be available for follow-up because of factors such as change of address or death. When evaluating the effectiveness of therapeutic techniques, a variety of statistical methods can be used. Decisions about whether to compare clients with untreated individuals, those who would be expected to be normal, or to look at changes within individuals are all decisions that research investigators must make. In presenting examples of research, I have tried to use those that are representative of research that is related to the theory that is being studied.

Gender Issues

Virtually all theories of psychotherapy discussed in this book have been developed by men (feminist therapy being the major exception). Does this mean that the theories have different assumptions about men and women and their treatment? Furthermore, are there issues that affect women differently than men or specific problems that theories should address, such as rape or eating disorders? Perhaps the theory that has been most frequently criticized for negative values regarding women is psychoanalysis. This theory, as well as others, is discussed in relationship to its assumptions and values about men and women. Not surprisingly, the chapter that most completely addresses the issue of gender is that on feminist therapy, in which the effect of societal values on individuals as they are reflected in therapy is discussed. Another issue regarding gender that is not frequently addressed by theories is that of attitudes and values toward gays, lesbians, bisexual people, and transgendered people. Where there seems to be a clear point of view regarding this issue, I have tried to address it within the appropriate chapter. In general, an assumption I make in this book is that the more one knows about one's own values about gender and those of theories of psychotherapy, the more effective one can be as a therapist with both men and women.

Multicultural Issues

Just as assumptions about the values of theories and therapists about gender are important, so are assumptions about cultural values. Increasingly, therapists deal with clients whose cultural backgrounds are very different from their own. Knowledge of theories of psychotherapy and values about cultural issues that are implicit within them assists therapists in their work with a variety of clients. When examining theories, it is helpful to ask if the values implicit in that theory fit with values of a particular culture. For example, if a culture emphasizes not divulging feelings to others, what implications are there for applying a theory that focuses primarily on understanding feelings?

Theories may reflect the culture and background of the theorist. For example, Sigmund Freud lived in Vienna in the late 19th and early 20th centuries. It is reasonable to ask to what extent the values that are implicit in psychoanalysis are a reflection of his culture and to what extent they can be applied to a current multicultural society. The fact that Freud lived in a society somewhat different from our own does not invalidate his theory but does raise questions about the role of cultural values in theories of psychotherapy. Theorists differ in the attention they pay to cultural issues. For example, Carl Jung and Erik Erikson are noted for their interest in many different societies and cultures. Currently, the theory of psychotherapy that appears most concerned with multicultural issues is that of feminist therapy. In each chapter, I describe writing or research that pertains to the study of multicultural issues for that specific theory of psychotherapy. In recent years, culture has come to include more than race, ethnicity, and national origin (Hays, 2008). Although much of the focus on culture in this book will be on ethnic background, the term *culture*, as used in this textbook, also includes age, disabilities, religion, socioeconomic status, sexual orientation, and gender. Because gender is such a large topic, it is treated separately as described in the section above.

Group Therapy

Group therapy has the advantage of being more efficient than individual therapy because it serves more people at the same time. Also, it offers some benefits that individual therapy does not. Although groups vary in size, they frequently have between 6 and 10 members and 1 or 2 leaders. An advantage of group therapy, when compared with individual therapy, is that participants can learn effective social skills and try out new styles of relating with other members of the group (Corey, 2008). Also, group members are often peers and provide, in some ways, a microcosm of the society that clients deal with daily. Because groups exist to help members with a variety of problems, group members can offer support to each other to explore and work on important problems. Also, groups help individuals become more caring and sensitive to the needs and problems of others. Although most groups are therapeutic in nature, focusing on the development of interpersonal skills or psychological problems, others are more educational in function, teaching clients skills that may be useful in their lives.

Theorists differ as to the value they place on group therapy. Some practitioners of theories view groups primarily as an adjunct to individual therapy (for example, Jungian therapists), whereas others give central importance to group therapy, often suggesting it as a treatment of choice (as do Adlerian, person-centered, and gestalt therapists). For each major theory presented, some specific applications to group therapy are described and illustrated.

Ethics

The basic purpose of psychotherapy and counseling is to help the client with psychological problems. To do this effectively, therapists must behave in an ethical and legal way. Professional organizations for mental health practitioners such as psychiatrists, psychologists, social workers, mental health counselors, pastoral counselors, and psychiatric nurses have all developed codes of ethics that describe appropriate behavior for therapists. These ethical codes are in substantial agreement as to actions that constitute ethical and unethical behavior on the part of the therapist. All practitioners of theories should accept their profession's ethical codes. It is implicit in theories of psychotherapy and counseling that therapists are ethical as they seek approaches to benefit the life situation of their clients.

Although a full discussion of ethics is outside the scope of this book, therapists must be familiar with such issues. For example, an important ethical issue is the prohibition against erotic or sexual contact with clients. A related issue is the appropriateness of touching or holding clients. Ethical codes also discuss limitations on social and personal relationships with clients such as relationships with clients outside of therapy. Confidentiality and the issue of releasing information about clients are also major issues addressed in ethical codes. Other issues include concerns about referrals and record keeping. Competency to practice and to help clients with many different issues can raise ethical dilemmas. Difficult issues, such as the need to protect people a client intends to harm, have required much attention and have complex solutions (Werth, Welfel, & Benjamin, 2009). Several books have been written describing many ethical issues (for example, Corey, Corey, & Callanan, 2011; Welfel, 2010) and deal with them in depth. I discuss ethics only in relation to specific issues that affect certain theories. For example, body psychotherapists (Chapter 15) make significant use of touch, and behavior therapists (Chapter 8) deal with severely psychologically disabled clients who are unable to make decisions for themselves. Although not discussed frequently in this book, legal and ethical behavior on the part of all therapists is essential to the effective practice of all forms of psychotherapy.

My Theory of Psychotherapy and Counseling

For the past 35 years I have seen, on average, about 15 adult and older adolescent clients per week, primarily for individual therapy but also for couples' counseling. In my own work, I have incorporated concepts and techniques from most of the approaches discussed in this book. I have come to have a profound respect for the theorists, practitioners of the theories, and researchers because of their contribution to helping people in distress. I have found that many of the theories discussed in this book have guided me in helping individuals reduce their distress. Although I have biases and preferences for theoretical concepts and techniques, I believe that my profound respect for theories of psychotherapy has kept these biases to a minimum.

After 35 years as a therapist and counselor, I find that I am continually touched by the distress of my clients, concerned about their problems, and excited by the opportunity to help them. Helping others and teaching students about helping others continues to be a value that is exceedingly important to me and does not waiver.

Your Theory of Psychotherapy and Counseling

For readers who are considering this field or planning to become therapists or counselors, this book is an opportunity to become familiar with some of the most influential theories of psychotherapy and counseling. Also, it can be the start of developing your own approach to therapy. I encourage you to be open to different points of view and gradually choose approaches that fit you personally as well as the clientele that you plan to work with. To foster this openness, I have described the theories as thoroughly as possible and have reserved a summary and critique of the theories for Chapter 16. In Chapter 17, I show you three popular ways of integrating theories as well as methods for integrating theories of your choice. For many therapists, the choice of theory is a slowly evolving process, the result of study and, most important, supervised psychotherapy or counseling experience.

Suggested Readings

For each chapter, I have provided a brief list of readings that I think will be most helpful for learning more about the theory. Many readings are at an intermediate rather than an advanced level of complexity, providing more detail on a number of issues that are discussed in each chapter. The following readings are suggestions related to important topics covered in this introductory chapter.

American Psychiatric Association. (2000). *Diagnostic and statistical manual of mental disorders* (4th ed., text revision). Washington, DC: American Psychiatric Association. Known as the DSM-IV-TR, this manual describes the widely accepted classification of psychological and/or psychiatric disorders. Specific criteria for each disorder are listed and explained, along with a thorough explanation of the psychological disorders discussed in this chapter (as well as many other disorders).

Nathan P. E., & Gorman, J. M. (Eds.). (2007). *A guide to treatments that work* (3rd ed.). New York: Oxford University Press. This book serves as a reference for research-supported psychological treatments and the research that supports them. Evidence is provided for psychopharmacological treatment as well as psychotherapies for many different psychological disorders.

Castonguay, L. G., & Beutler, L. E. (Eds.). (2006). *Principles of therapeutic change that work*. New York: Oxford University Press. Research on evidence for common factors for depression, anxiety, personality disorders, and substance abuse is described. Evidence for specific treatment factors is also given.

Lambert, M. (Ed.). (2004). *Bergin and Garfield's handbook of psychotherapy and behavior change* (5th ed.). New York: Wiley. This is a comprehensive volume that describes methods and procedures for research on psychotherapy. Included are evaluations of psychotherapeutic treatment for major theories. Also, research on group and brief psychotherapy and children and adolescents is presented.

Corey, G., Corey, M., & Callanan, P. (2011). *Issues and ethics in the helping professions* (8th ed.). Belmont, CA: Brooks/Cole-Cengage. Chapters in this book cover values in the client–counselor relationship, responsibilities of the therapist, therapeutic competency, and therapist–client relationship issues. Case examples of ethical issues are provided.

References

American Psychiatric Association. (2000). *Diagnostic and statistical manual of mental disorders* (4th ed., text revision). Washington, DC: American Psychiatric Association.

Barenbaum, N. B., & Winter, D. G. (2008). History of modern personality theory and research. In O. P. John, R. W. Robins, & L. A. Pervin (Eds.), *Handbook of personality psychology: Theory and research* (3rd ed., pp. 3–26). New York: Guilford.

Barlow, D. H., & Durand, V. M. (2009). *Abnormal psychology: An integrative approach* (5th ed.). Belmont, CA: Wadsworth Cengage.

Bechtoldt, H., Norcross, J. C., Wyckoff, L. A., Pokrywa, M. L., & Campbell, L. F. (2001). Theoretical orientations and employment settings of clinical and counseling psychologists: A comparative study. *The Clinical Psychologist, 54*(1), 3–6.

Bike, D. H., Norcross, J. C., & Schatz, D. M. (2009). Processes and outcomes of psychotherapists' personal therapy: Replication and extension 20 years later. *Psychotherapy: Theory, Research, Practice, Training, 46*(1), 19–31.

Carroll, K. M., & Rounsaville, B. J. (2008). Efficacy and effectiveness in developing treatment manuals. In A. M. Nezu & C. M. Nezu (Eds.), *Evidence-based outcome research: A practical guide to conducting randomized controlled trials for psychosocial interventions.* (pp. 219–243). New York: Oxford University Press.

Castonguay, L. G., & Beutler, L. E. (Eds.). (2006). *Principles of therapeutic change that work*. New York: Oxford University Press.

Chambless, D. L., Crits-Christoph, P., Wampold, B. E., Norcross, J. C., Lambert, M. J., Bohart, A. C., Beutler, L. E., & Johannsen, B. E. (2006). What should be validated? In J. C. Norcross, L. E. Beutler, & R. F. Levant (Eds.), *Evidence-based practices in mental health: Debate and dialogue on the fundamental questions.* (pp. 191–256). Washington, DC: American Psychological Association.

Chambless, D. L., & Hollon, S. D. (1998). Defining empirically supported therapies. *Journal of Consulting and Clinical Psychology, 66*(1), 7–18.

Corey, G. (2008). *Theory and practice of group counseling* (7th ed.). Belmont, CA: Brooks/Cole-Cengage.

Corey, G., Corey, M., & Callanan, P. (2011). *Issues and ethics in the helping professions* (8th ed.). Belmont, CA: Brooks/Cole-Cengage.

Corsini, R. J. (Ed.). (2001). *Handbook of innovative psychotherapies* (2nd ed.). New York: Wiley.

Corsini, R. J. (2008). Introduction. In R. J. Corsini & D. Wedding (Eds.), *Current psychotherapies* (8th ed., pp. 1–14). Belmont, CA: Brooks/Cole-Cengage.

Duncan, B. L., Hubble, M. A., & Miller, S. D. (1997). *Psychotherapy with "impossible" cases: The efficient treatment of therapy veterans*. New York: Norton.

Duncan, B. L., Miller, S D., Wampold, B. E., & Hubble, M. A. (Eds.). (2010). *The heart and soul of change: Delivering what works in therapy* (2nd ed.). Washington, DC: American Psychological Association.

Fawcett, J. (1999). *The relationship of theory and research* (3rd ed.). Philadelphia: F. A. Davis.

Fiedler, F. E. (1950). A comparison of therapeutic relationships in psychoanalytic, nondirective, and Adlerian therapy. *Journal of Consulting Psychology, 14*, 239–245.

Gelso, C. J., & Fretz, B. R. (2001). *Counseling psychology* (2nd ed.). Fort Worth, TX: Harcourt College Publishers.

Gentile, L., Kisber, S., Suvak, J., & West, C. (2008). The practice of psychotherapy: Theory. In M. Ballou, M. Hill, & C. West (Eds.), *Feminist therapy theory and practice: A contemporary perspective.* (pp. 67–86). New York: Springer .

Goodyear, R. K., Murdock, N., Lichtenberg, J. W., Mcpherson, R., Koetting, K., & Petren, S. (2008). Stability and change in counseling psychologists' identities, roles, functions, and career satisfaction across 15 years. *The Counseling Psychologist, 36*(2), 220–249.

Hays, P. A. (2008). *Addressing cultural complexities in practice: Assessment, diagnosis, and therapy* (2nd ed.). Washington, DC: American Psychological *Association*.

Heinen, J. R. (1985). A primer on psychological theory. *Journal of Psychology, 119*, 413–421.

Hill, C. E., & Lambert, M. J. (2004). Methodological issues in studying psychotherapy processes and outcomes. In M. Lambert (Ed.), *Bergin and Garfield's handbook of psychotherapy and behavior change* (5th ed., pp. 84–135). New York: Wiley.

Ho, B., Black, D. W., & Andreasen, N. C. (2003). Schizophrenia and other psychotic disorders. In R. E. Hales & S. C. Yudofsky (Eds.), *The American psychiatric publishing textbook of clinical psychiatry* (4th ed., pp. 379–438). Washington, DC: American Psychiatric Association.

Huppert, J. D., Fabbro, A., & Barlow, D. H. (2006). Evidence-based practice and psychological treatments. In C. D. Goodheart, A. E. Kazdin, & R. J. Sternberg (Eds.), *Evidence-based psychotherapy: Where practice and research meet* (pp. 131–152).

Washington, DC: American Psychological Association.

Kendall, P. C., Holmbeck, G., & Verduin, T. (2004). Methodology, design, and evaluation in psychotherapy research. In M. J. Lambert (Ed.), *Bergin and Garfield's handbook of psychotherapy and behavior change* (5th ed., pp. 16–43). New York: Wiley.

Kessler, R. C., Berglund, P., Demler, O., Jin, R., Koretz, D., & Merikangas, K. R. et al. (2003). The epidemiology of major depressive disorder: Results from the national comorbidity survey replication (NCS-R). *Journal of the American Medical Association, 289*(23), 3095–3105.

Lambert, M. (Ed.). (2004). *Bergin and Garfield's handbook of psychotherapy and behavior change* (5th ed.). New York: Wiley.

Mitchell, M. L., & Jolley, J. M. (2010). *Research design explained* (7th ed.) Belmont, CA: Cengage Learning.

Najavits, L. M., Weiss, R. D., Shaw, S. R., & Dierberger, A. E. (2000). Psychotherapists' view of treatment manuals. *Professional Psychology, 31*, 404–408.

Nathan, P. E., & Gorman, J. M. (Eds.). (2007). *A guide to treatments that work* (3rd ed.). New York: Oxford University Press.

Neimeyer, R. A. (2009). *Constructivist psychotherapy: Distinctive features*. New York: Routledge.

Neimeyer, R. A., & Baldwin, S. A. (2005). *Personal construct psychotherapy and the constructivist horizon*. New York: Wiley.

Nezu, A. M., & Nezu, C. M. (Eds.). (2008). *Evidence-based outcome research: A practical guide to conducting randomized controlled trials for psychosocial interventions*. New York: Oxford University Press.

Norcross, J. C., Beutler, L. E., & Levant, R. F. (2006). *Evidence-based practices in mental health: Debate and dialogue on the fundamental questions*. Washington, DC: American Psychological Association.

Norcross, J. C., Karpiak, C. P., & Santoro, S. O. (2005). Clinical psychologists across the years: The division of clinical psychology from 1960 to 2003. *Journal of Clinical Psychology, 61*(12), 1467–1483.

Prochaska, J. O., & Norcross, J. C. (2010). *Systems of psychotherapy: A transtheoretical analysis* (7th ed.). Belmont, CA: Wadsworth-Cengage.

Society of Clinical Psychology, Division 12, of the American Psychological Association. (2009). *Research Supported Psychological Treatments* on the Research-Supported Psychological Treatments website.

Stam, H. J. (2000). Theoretical psychology. In K. Paulik & M. R. Rosenzweig (Eds.), *International handbook of psychology* (pp. 551–569). Thousand Oaks, CA: Sage.

Thoma, N. C., & Cecero, J. J. (2009). Is integrative use of techniques in psychotherapy the exception or the rule? Results of a national survey of doctoral-level practitioners. *Psychotherapy: Theory, Research, Practice, Training, 46*(4), 405–417.

Truscott, D. (2010). *Becoming an effective psychotherapist: Adopting a theory of psychotherapy that's right for you and your client.* Washington, DC: American Psychological Association.

Weisz, J. R., & Gray, J. S. (2008). Evidence-based psychotherapy for children and adolescents: Data from the present and a model for the future. *Child and Adolescent Mental Health, 13*(2), 54–65.

Welfel, E. R. (2010). *Ethics in counseling and psychotherapy* (3rd ed.). Belmont, CA: Brooks/Cole-Cengage.

Werth, J. L., Jr., Welfel, E. R., & Benjamin, G. A. H. (Eds.). (2009). *The duty to protect: Ethical, legal, and professional considerations for mental health professionals.* Washington, DC: American Psychological Association.

CHAPTER 2

Psychoanalysis

Outline of Psychoanalysis

FREUD'S DRIVE THEORY
   Drives and Instincts
   Levels of Consciousness
   Structure of Personality
      Id
      Ego
      Superego
   Defense Mechanisms
      Repression
      Denial
      Reaction formation
      Projection
      Displacement
      Sublimation
      Rationalization
      Regression
      Identification
      Intellectualization
   Psychosexual Stages of Development
      Oral stage
      Anal stage
      Phallic stage
      Latency
      Genital stage
EGO PSYCHOLOGY
   Anna Freud
   Erik Erikson
      Infancy: Trust Versus Mistrust (Oral)
      Early childhood: Autonomy versus shame and
      doubt (anal)
      Preschool age: Initiative versus guilt (phallic)
      School age: Industry versus inferiority (latency)
      Adolescence: Identity versus role confusion (genital)
      Young adulthood: Intimacy versus isolation (genital)
      Middle age: Generativity versus stagnation (genital)
      Later life: Integrity versus despair (genital)

OBJECT RELATIONS PSYCHOLOGY
   Donald Winnicott
   Otto Kernberg
KOHUT'S SELF PSYCHOLOGY
RELATIONAL PSYCHOANALYSIS
PSYCHOANALYTICAL APPROACHES
TO TREATMENT
   Therapeutic Goals
   Assessment
   Psychoanalysis, Psychotherapy, and
   Psychoanalytic Counseling
   Free Association
   Neutrality and Empathy
   Resistance
   Interpretation
   Interpretation of Dreams
   Interpretation and Analysis of Transference
   Countertransference
   Relational Responses

Sigmund Freud's contribution to the current practice of psychoanalysis, psychotherapy, and counseling is enormous. Because psychoanalysis was the most influential theory of therapy during the 1930s, 1940s, and 1950s, virtually every major theorist discussed in this book was originally trained in Freudian psychoanalysis. Some theorists totally rejected his ideas, and many developed their own ideas based, in part, on their knowledge of Freud's views of human development and the structure of personality. As new theories were created, it was Freud's theory of psychoanalysis to which they were compared.

For more than 100 years, Freud's views have gathered adherents who have both practiced his theory of psychoanalysis and contributed to the expansion of psychoanalytic theory. From the start, changes in psychoanalytic theory have brought about controversy and disagreement. As a result, psychoanalysis has evolved considerably since Freud's death in 1939. Many of Freud's contributions have been a mainstay of psychoanalytic thought, such as his emphasis on the importance of unconscious processes in human motivation and his concepts of personality (id, ego, and superego). Psychoanalytic writers also accept the importance of early childhood development in determining later psychological functioning. However, they disagree about which aspects of childhood development should be emphasized.

To understand contemporary psychoanalytic thought, it is important to be aware of five different theoretical directions: Freudian drive theory, ego psychology, object relations, self psychology, and relational psychoanalysis. Freud, through the psychosexual stages (oral, anal, and phallic) that occur in the first 5 years of life, stressed the importance of inborn drives in determining later personality development. Ego psychologists attended to the need for individuals to adapt to their environment, as exemplified by Erik Erikson's stages of development that encompass the entire life span. Object relations theorists were particularly concerned with the relationship between the infant and others. They, like Freud, used the term *object* to refer to persons in the child's life who can fulfill needs or to whom the young child can become attached. A different view has been that of self psychologists, who focused on developmental changes in self-preoccupation. Relational psychoanalysis focuses not only on the patient's relationships with others but also on the influence of the patient and therapist on each other. Most psychoanalytic practitioners are aware of these ways of viewing development but differ as to which of them they incorporate in their work. In this chapter, I describe each of these views and show its impact on the practice of psychoanalysis and psychoanalytic therapy.

History of Psychoanalysis

To understand psychoanalysis and Freud's ideas, it is helpful to consider personal and intellectual influences in his own life. Born on May 6, 1856, in the village of Freiburg, Moravia, a small town then in Austria and now a part of the Czech Republic, Sigmund Freud was the first of seven children of Amalia and Jacob Freud. Freud's father had two sons by a former marriage and was 42 when Sigmund was born. When Freud was 4 years old, his father, a wool merchant, moved the family to Vienna to seek more favorable business conditions. In their crowded apartment in Vienna, Freud was given the special privilege of his own bedroom and study. His young mother had high hopes for her son and encouraged his study and schoolwork. He was well versed in languages, learning not only the classical languages—Greek, Latin, and Hebrew—but also English, French, Italian, and Spanish, and he read Shakespeare at the age of 8. In his early schoolwork, he was often first in his class. Later he attended the *Sperlgymnasium* (a secondary school) from 1866 to 1873, graduating summa cum laude (Ellenberger, 1970).

In the winter of 1873, Freud began his medical studies at the University of Vienna and finished his degree 8 years later. Ordinarily, a medical degree was a 5-year program, but his completion was delayed because he spent 6 years working under the supervision of a well-known physiologist, Ernst Brucke, and spent a year (1879–1880) of military service in the Austrian army. During his time with Brucke, he became acquainted with Josef Breuer, 40 years his senior, who introduced him to the complexities of hysterical illness. Because of poor prospects for promotion and financial remuneration, Freud left Brucke's Institute of Physiology and began a residency in surgery. A short time later, in 1883, Freud studied neurology and psychiatry in the large Viennese General Hospital. During that time he worked with patients with neurological disorders; in studying the medical aspects of cocaine, he tried the drug himself, before he was aware of its addictive properties. In 1885, Freud had the opportunity to travel to Paris and spend 4 months with Jean Charcot, a famous French neurologist and hypnotist. At the time, Charcot was studying the conversion reactions of hysterical patients who showed bodily symptoms such as blindness, deafness, and paralysis of arms or legs as a result of psychological disturbance. During that time, Freud observed Charcot using hypnotic suggestion as a way to remove hysterical symptoms. Although Freud was later to question the value of hypnosis as a treatment strategy, his experience in Paris helped him to consider the importance of the unconscious mind and the way in which feelings and behaviors can be influenced to create psychopathological symptoms.

Returning to Vienna, Freud married Martha Bernays in 1886. During their 53 years of marriage, they had six children, the youngest of whom, Anna, was to become a well-known child analyst, making significant contributions to the development of psychoanalysis. During the years immediately following his marriage, Freud began work at a children's hospital and also built a private practice that was slow to develop. At the same time, he continued to read the works of authors in many varied fields.

Information from physics, chemistry, biology, philosophy, psychology, and other disciplines influenced his later thinking. His interest in unconscious processes came not only from his work with Charcot but also from philosophers such as Nietzsche (1937) and Spinoza (1952). The science of psychology was emerging, and Freud had read the works of Wilhelm Wundt and Gustav Fechner. His knowledge of the work of Ludwig Borne, a writer who suggested that would-be writers put everything that occurs to them on paper for 3 days, disregarding coherence or relevance (Jones, 1953), influenced his development of the psychoanalytic technique of free association. Other scientific influences included Darwin's theory of evolution and the biological and physiological research of Ernst Brucke. Throughout many of his writings, Freud made use of scientific models derived from physics, chemistry, and biology (Jones, 1953). His knowledge of science and neurology and his familiarity with the psychiatric work of Pierre Janet and Hippolyte Bernheim were to affect his development of psychoanalysis (Young-Bruehl, 2008).

Although Freud was influenced by other writers and psychiatrists in the development of psychoanalysis, its creation is very much his own. Initially, Freud used hypnosis and Breuer's cathartic method as a means of helping patients with psychoneuroses. However, he found that patients resisted suggestions, hypnosis, and asking questions. He used a "concentration" technique in which he asked patients to lie on a couch with their eyes closed, to concentrate on the symptom, and to recall all memories of the symptom without censoring

SIGMUND FREUD

their thoughts. When Freud sensed resistance, he pressed his hand on the client's forehead and questioned the patient about memory and recall. Later, Freud became less active and encouraged his patients to report whatever came to mind—*free association*. Related to the development of this technique was his discussion with Josef Breuer, his older colleague, who was working with a patient, Anna O., who seemed to be recovering from hysteria by reporting emotional material to Breuer while under hypnosis. Freud used this procedure with other patients, and together Breuer and Freud published *Studies on Hysteria* (1895), in which they hypothesized that symptoms of hysteria resulted from very painful memories combined with unexpressed emotions. The therapeutic task, then, became to bring about a recollection of forgotten events, along with emotional expression. It was Freud's belief, but not Breuer's, that the traumatic events that caused hysteria were sexual and occurred in the patient's childhood.

In part, these beliefs led Freud to undertake a self-analysis of his own childhood and his dreams. As Freud explored his own unconscious mind, he became aware of the importance of biological and particularly sexual drives that were related to suppression of emotion. This realization made him aware of the conflict between the conscious and unconscious aspects of personality. His observations based on his own and patients' dreams were published in *The Interpretation of Dreams* (Freud, 1900).

Although *The Interpretation of Dreams* received relatively little attention from physicians or others, Freud began to attract individuals who were interested in his ideas. Meeting at his home, the Wednesday Psychological Society, started in 1902, gradually grew until in 1908 it became the Vienna Psychoanalytic Society. During these years, Freud published *The Psychopathology of Everyday Life* (1901), *Three Essays on Sexuality* (1905b), and *Jokes and Their Relation to the Unconscious* (1905a). His writings on sexuality drew condemnation, as they were out of step with the times, and Freud was seen as perverted and obscene by both physicians and nonacademic writers. The event that brought Freud and psychoanalysis American recognition was the invitation from G. Stanley Hall to lecture at Clark University in Worcester, Massachusetts, in 1909. This led to a larger audience for books such as *Introductory Lectures on Psycho-Analysis* (1917) and *The Ego and the Id* (1923), which described his approach to personality.

Freud also wrote about the importance of infant relationships with parents. In his books *Three Essays on Sexuality* (1905b) and *On Narcissism: An Introduction* (1914) Freud refined his views on *libido*, the driving force of personality that includes sexual energy. He wrote about autoeroticism, which precedes the infant's relationship to the first object, the mother (Ellenberger, 1970). He found it helpful to differentiate between libidinal (sexual) energies that were directed toward the self and those directed toward the representation of objects in the external world. When an individual withdraws energy from others and directs it toward himself or herself, then narcissism occurs, which, if extreme, can cause severe psychopathology. Freud's writings on early infant relationships and narcissism were the foundation of the work of object relations and self psychology theorists. Freud (1920) revised his theory of drives, which had focused on the importance of sexuality as a basic drive affecting human functioning. Later, he observed the importance of self-directed aggression that occurs in self-mutilation or masochism.

Important in the development of psychoanalysis were not only Freud's writings but also his interactions with other psychoanalysts who were drawn to him. Many of them argued with him, disagreed with him, or broke away from him. Early disciples and important writers were Karl Abraham, Max Eitingon, Sandor Ferenczi, Ernest Jones, and Hans Sachs. Although these disciples stayed relatively loyal to Freud, Alfred Adler (Chapter 4), Carl Jung (Chapter 3), and Otto Rank developed their own theories of psychotherapy and broke their ties with Freud. Later writers who broke with Freud, often referred to as neo-Freudians, focused more on social and cultural factors and less on biological determinants. Objecting to Freud's view of female sexuality, Karen Horney (1937) was concerned with cultural factors and interpersonal relations rather than early childhood traumas. Erich Fromm (1955) differed significantly from Freud by focusing on groups in societies and cultural changes. The neo-Freudian who attracts the most current interest is Harry Stack Sullivan (1953), whose emphasis on interpersonal factors and peer relationships in childhood created added dimensions to psychoanalytic theory. Although these writers present interesting additions and alternatives to psychoanalysis, their thinking is sufficiently different from psychoanalytic theorists presented in this chapter to be beyond its scope.

Freud continued to be productive until his death in 1939 from cancer of the throat and jaw, from which he had suffered for 16 years. At the age of 82, Freud was forced to flee Vienna to escape the Nazi invasion of Austria. Despite his illness and 33 operations on his jaw and palate, Freud was incredibly productive. He made major revisions in his theory of the structure and functioning of the mind, *The Ego and the Id* (1923), highlighting relationships among id, ego, and superego. His prolific work is published in the 24-volume *Standard Edition of the Complete Works of Sigmund Freud*. His life has been described in detail by many writers, most completely by Ernest Jones (1953, 1955, 1957). Jones's work and books by Ellenberger (1970), Gay (1988), Demorest (2005), and Young-Bruehl (2008) either served as resources for this section or are recommended to the interested reader, as is Roazen's (2001) book, which describes contributions of many writers to psychoanalysis.

Just as Freud continued to refine and develop psychoanalysis, so did the psychoanalysts who followed him. A major contribution has been that of his youngest daughter, Anna, who focused on the development of the ego, that part of the Freudian system that deals with the external world of reality. Her student Erik Erikson also examined the individual's interaction with the real world and described stages of development that incorporate the entire life span. Their work is known as *ego psychology*.

Another significant development is that of the object relations school. These theorists focused on the relationship of early childhood development, specifically that of the mother and child. Observations about the relationship between mother and child have been made by Donald Winnicott. Otto Kernberg has made the application to severe disorders, such as borderline personality. Heinz Kohut, the originator of self psychology, drew on object relations theory as well as his own ideas about the childhood development of narcissism. Relational psychoanalysis has focused less on the development of childhood relationships than on many different relationships, including that of patient–therapist. Although many writers have contributed to the development of psychoanalysis, these are among the most important, and their work is described in this chapter after I explain Freud's theory of personality.

Freud's Drive Theory

The concepts of Freudian psychoanalytical theory provide a basic frame of reference for understanding not only his work but also that of other psychoanalytic theorists. Perhaps his most controversial views (both in his own time and now) concern the importance of innate drives, especially sexuality. These drives often express themselves through unconscious processes, a pervasive concept in psychoanalysis, and in sexual stages. Freud identified stages of childhood development—oral, anal, phallic, and latency—that, depending on a person's experience, can have an impact on later psychopathological or normal development. To describe the structure of personality, Freud used three concepts—id, ego, and superego—that are avenues for the expression of psychological energy. Conflicts between them result in neurotic, moral, or objective anxiety and may be expressed through unconscious processes such as verbal slips and dreams. To deal with the emergence of strong biological (id) forces, individuals develop ego defense mechanisms to prevent the individual from being overwhelmed. These concepts are necessary in understanding the application of psychoanalytical therapeutic techniques and are explained in the next paragraphs.

Drives and Instincts

In psychoanalysis, the terms *instincts* and *drives* are often used interchangeably, but the term *drive* is more common. Originally, Freud distinguished between self-preservative drives (including breathing, eating, drinking, and excreting) and species-preservative drives (sexuality). The psychic energy that emanates from sexual drives is known as *libido*. In his early work, Freud believed that human motivation was sexual in the broad sense that individuals were motivated to bring themselves pleasure. However, *libido* later came to be associated with all life instincts and included the general goal of seeking to gain pleasure and avoid pain.

When he was in his 60s, Freud put forth the idea of a *death instinct* that accounted for aggressive drives (Mishne, 1993). These include unconscious desires to hurt others or oneself. Often conflict arises between the life instincts—*eros*—and the death instincts—*thanatos*. Examples of conflict include the love and hate that marriage partners may have for each other. When the hate comes out in destructive anger, then the aggressive drive (*thanatos*) is stronger. Often the two instincts work together, such as in eating, which maintains life but includes the aggressive activities of chewing and biting. Soldiers may express their aggressive drives through socially condoned fighting. Sports provide a more acceptable outlet for physical aggressive expression. Often, libido and aggressive drives are expressed without an individual's awareness or consciousness.

Levels of Consciousness

Freud specified three levels of consciousness: the conscious, the preconscious, and the unconscious. The *conscious* includes sensations and experiences that the person is aware of at any point in time. Examples include awareness of being warm or cold and awareness of this book or of a pencil. Conscious awareness is a very small part of a person's mental life. The *preconscious* includes memories of events and experiences that can easily be retrieved with little effort. Examples might include a previous examination taken, a phone call to a friend, or a favorite dessert that was eaten yesterday. The preconscious forms a bridge from the conscious mind to the much larger *unconscious*, which is the container for memories and emotions that are threatening to the conscious mind and must be pushed away. Examples include hostile or sexual feelings toward a parent and forgotten childhood trauma or abuse. Also included are needs and motivations of which individuals are unaware. Although unconscious motivations are out of awareness, they may still be exhibited in an individual's thoughts or behaviors.

Bringing unconscious material into conscious awareness is a major therapeutic task. It can be done through dream interpretation in which images within the dream may represent various unconscious needs, wishes, or conflicts (Freud, 1900). Slips of the tongue and forgetting are other examples of unconscious expression. When a man calls his wife by the name of a former girlfriend, the name that is uttered may represent a variety of wishes or conflicts. Freud also believed that humor and jokes were an expression of disguised wishes and conflicts (Freud, 1905a). Additionally, when patients repeat destructive patterns of behavior, unconscious needs or conflicts may be represented. For Freud, the concept of the unconscious was not a hypothetical abstraction; it could be demonstrated to be real. In his talks to physicians and scientists, Freud (1917) gave many instances of unconscious material that he had gleaned from his patients' dreams and other behavior. The following is a brief example of unconscious material, symbolizing death, as it was expressed in a patient's dream.

> *The dreamer was crossing a very high, steep, iron bridge, with two people whose names he knew, but forgot on waking. Suddenly both of them had vanished and he saw a ghostly man in a cap and an overall. He asked him whether he were the telegraph messenger … "No." Or the coachman? … "No." He then went on and in the dream had a feeling of great dread; on waking, he followed it up with a fantasy that the iron bridge suddenly broke and that he fell into the abyss.* (Freud, 1917, p. 196)

Attending to unconscious material was crucial for Freud and is central for all psychoanalysts. The techniques that are presented in the section on psychotherapy are generally designed to bring unconscious material into conscious awareness.

Structure of Personality

Freud hypothesized three basic systems that are contained within the structure of personality: the id, the ego, and the superego. Briefly, the id represents unchecked biological forces, the superego is the voice of social conscience, and the ego is the rational thinking that mediates between the two and deals with reality. These are not three separate systems; they function together as a whole.

[handwritten margin note: pleasure principle]

Id. At birth, the infant is all id. Inherited and physiological forces, such as hunger, thirst, and elimination, drive the infant. There is no conscious awareness, only unconscious behavior. The means of operation for the id is the pleasure principle. When only the id is operating, for an infant or an adult, individuals try to find pleasure and avoid or reduce pain. Thus, an infant who is hungry, operating under the pleasure principle, seeks the mother's nipple.

The newborn child invests all energy in gratifying its needs (the pleasure principle). The infant then is said to *cathect* (invest energy) in objects that will gratify its needs. Investment of energy in an object such as a blanket or nipple—*object cathexis*—is designed to reduce needs. The *primary process* is a means for forming an image of something that can reduce the thwarted drive.

The infant's image of the mother's nipple, as it exists to satiate hunger and thirst, is an example of primary process. In adults, the primary process can be seen in the wishful fantasies that appear in dreams or other unconscious material. To distinguish wish or image from reality is the task of the ego.

Ego. The ego must mediate between the world around the infant and the instincts or drives within the infant. By waiting or suspending the pleasure principle, the ego follows the reality principle. For example, the young child learns to ask for food rather than to cry immediately when her needs are not met. This realistic thinking is referred to as the *secondary process*, which is in marked contrast to the fantasizing of the primary process. It is the function of the ego to test reality, to plan, to think logically, and to develop plans for satisfying needs. Its control or restraint over the id is referred to as *anticathexis*. In this way the ego serves to keep us from crying or acting angrily whenever we do not get our way.

Superego. Whereas the id and ego are aspects of the individual, the *superego* represents parental values and, more broadly, society's standards. As the child incorporates the parents' values, the *ego ideal* is formed. It represents behaviors that parents approve of, whereas the *conscience* refers to behaviors disapproved of by parents. Thus, the individual develops a moral code or sense of values to determine whether actions are good or bad. For example, the superego can include powerful values, such as resentment, that may have a strong influence on individuals' political and social life (Wurmser, 2009). The superego is nonrational, seeking perfection and adherence to an ideal, inhibiting both the id and the ego, and controlling both physiological drives (id) and realistic striving for perfection (ego).

When conflicts among the id, ego, and superego develop, anxiety is likely to arise. It is the purpose of the ego and superego to channel instinctual energy through driving forces (cathexes) and restraining forces (anticathexes). The id consists only of driving forces. When the id has too much control, individuals may become impulsive, self-indulgent, or destructive. When the superego is too strong, individuals may set unrealistically high moral or perfectionistic standards (superego) for themselves and thus develop a sense of incompetence or failure. Anxiety develops out of this conflict among id, ego, and superego. When the ego senses anxiety, it is a sign that danger is imminent and something must be done.

In conceptualizing anxiety, Freud (1926) described three types of anxiety: reality, neurotic, and moral. Having an unfriendly person chase after us is an example of reality anxiety; the fear is from the external world, and the anxiety is appropriate to the situation. In contrast, neurotic and moral anxieties are threats within the individual. Neurotic anxiety occurs when individuals are afraid that they will not be able to control their feelings or instincts (id) and will do something for which they will be punished by parents or other authority figures. When people are afraid they will violate parental or societal standards (superego), moral anxiety is experienced. In order for the ego to cope with anxiety, defense mechanisms are necessary.

Defense Mechanisms

To cope with anxiety, the ego must have a means of dealing with situations. Ego defense mechanisms deny or distort reality while operating on an unconscious level. When ego defense mechanisms are used infrequently, they serve an adaptive value in reducing stress. However, if they are used frequently, this use becomes pathological, and individuals develop a style of avoiding reality. Some of the more common ego defense mechanisms are described in the following paragraphs.

Repression. An important defense mechanism, repression is often the source of anxiety and is the basis of other defenses. Repression serves to remove painful thoughts, memories, or feelings from conscious awareness by excluding painful experiences or unacceptable impulses. Traumatic events, such as sexual abuse, that occur in the first 5 years of life are likely to be repressed and to be unconscious. In his work with patients with hysterical disorders, Freud (1894) believed that they had repressed traumatic sexual or other experiences and responded through conversion reactions, such as paralysis of the hand.

Denial. Somewhat similar to repression, denial is a way of distorting or not acknowledging what an individual thinks, feels, or sees. For example, when an individual hears that a loved one has died in an automobile accident, she may deny that it really happened or that the person is really dead. Another form of denial occurs when individuals distort their body images. Someone who suffers from anorexia and is underweight may see himself as fat.

Reaction formation. A way of avoiding an unacceptable impulse is to act in the opposite extreme. By acting in a way that is opposite to disturbing desires, individuals do not have to deal with the resulting anxiety. For example, a woman who hates her husband may act with excessive love and devotion so that she will not have to deal with a possible threat to her marriage that could come from dislike of her husband.

Projection. Attributing one's own unacceptable feelings or thoughts to others is the basis of projection. When threatened by strong sexual or destructive drives or moral imperatives, individuals may project their feelings onto others rather than accept the anxiety. For example, a man who is unhappily married may believe that all of his friends are unhappily married and share his fate. In this way, he does not need to deal with the discomfort of his own marriage.

Displacement. When anxious, individuals can place their feelings not on an object or person who may be dangerous but on those who may be safe. For example, if a child is attacked by a larger child, she may not feel safe in attacking that child and will not reduce her anxiety by doing so. Instead, she may pick a fight with a smaller child.

Sublimation. Somewhat similar to displacement, sublimation is the modification of a drive (usually sexual or aggressive) into acceptable social behavior. A common form of sublimation is participating in athletic activities or being an active spectator. Running, tackling, or yelling may be appropriate in some sports but not in most other situations.

Rationalization. To explain away a poor performance, a failure, or a loss, people may make excuses to lessen their anxiety and soften the disappointment. An individual who does poorly on an examination may say that he is not smart enough, that there is not enough time to study, or that the examination was unfair. Sometimes it is difficult to determine what a real and logical reason is and what is a rationalization.

8 **Regression.** To revert to a previous stage of development is to regress. Faced with stress, individuals may use previously appropriate but now immature behaviors. It is not uncommon for a child starting school for the first time to cling to his parents, suck his thumb, and cry, trying to return to a more secure time. If a college student has two tests the next day, rather than studying she may fantasize about pleasant days back in high school and regress to a more comfortable and more secure time.

9 **Identification.** By taking on the characteristics of others, people can reduce their anxiety as well as other negative feelings. By identifying with a winning team, an individual can feel successful, even though he had nothing to do with the victory. Identifying with a teacher, musician, or athlete may help individuals believe that they have characteristics that they do not. Rather than feel inferior, the individual can feel self-satisfied and worthwhile.

10 **Intellectualization.** Emotional issues are not dealt with directly but rather are handled indirectly through abstract thought. For example, a person whose spouse has just asked for a divorce may wish to dwell on issues related to the purpose of life rather than deal with hurt and pain.

These ego defense mechanisms are ways of dealing with unconscious material that arises in childhood. How and when these defense mechanisms arise depend on events occurring in the psychosexual stages discussed next.

Psychosexual Stages of Development

Freud believed that the development of personality and the formation of the id, ego, and superego, as well as ego defense mechanisms, depend on the course of psychosexual development in the first 5 years of life. The psychosexual oral, anal, and phallic stages occur before the age of 5 or 6; then there is a relatively calm period for 6 years (the latency period), followed by the genital stage in adolescence, which starts at the beginning of puberty. Freud's theory is based on biological drives and the importance of the pleasure principle; thus, certain parts of the body are thought to be a significant focus of pleasure during different periods of development (Freud, 1923). Freud believed that infants receive a general sexual gratification in various parts of the body that gradually becomes more localized to the genital area. The oral, anal, and phallic stages described in the following paragraphs show the narrowing of the sexual instinct in the development of the child.

Oral stage. Lasting from birth to approximately 18 months, the oral stage focuses on eating and sucking and involves the lips, mouth, and throat. Dependency on the mother for gratification—and therefore the relationship with the mother—is extremely significant in the oral stage. The mouth has not only the function of taking in and eating but also holding on to, biting, spitting, and closing. The functions of eating and holding can be related to the development of later character traits referred to as *oral incorporation*, which might include the acquiring of knowledge or things. The functions of biting and spitting can be related to oral aggressive characteristics that might include sarcasm, cynicism, or argumentativeness. On one hand, if, during the oral stage, a child learns to depend too often on the mother, the child may fixate at this stage and become too dependent in adult life. On the other hand, if the child experiences anxiety through inattentive or irregular feeding, the child may feel insecure not only at this early stage but also in adult life.

Anal stage. Between the ages of about 18 months and 3 years, the anal area becomes the main source of pleasure. Exploration of bodily processes such as touching and playing with feces is important. If adults respond to children with disgust toward these activities, children may develop a low sense of self-esteem. During this period, the child develops bowel control, and conflicts around toilet training with parents can develop into personality characteristics in later life, such as an over-concern with cleanliness and orderliness (anal retentive) or disorderliness and destructiveness (anal expulsive). Not only do children establish control over their own bodies, but also they are attempting to achieve control over others.

[handwritten: 18 months- 3 yrs Pleasure]

Phallic stage. Lasting from the age of about 3 until 5 or 6, the source of sexual gratification shifts from the anal region to the genital area. At this age, stroking and manipulation of the penis or clitoris produces sensual pleasure. The concept of castration anxiety comes from the boy's fear that his penis may be cut off or removed. Particularly during the Victorian era, when masturbation was believed to be destructive, parental attempts to stop masturbation may have led the boy to fear the loss of his penis. If he had observed a nude girl, he might have believed that she had already lost her penis. The concept of penis envy refers to girls who wondered why they lacked penises and thought that perhaps they had done something wrong to lose their penises. Freud believed that later personality problems could be attributed to castration anxiety or penis envy. The sexual desire for the parent can lead to the development of the Oedipus complex in boys or the Electra complex in girls (although this latter idea was dropped in Freud's later writings). Named after the ancient Greek playwright Sophocles' play about a young man who becomes king by marrying his mother and killing his father, the *Oedipus complex* refers to the boy's sexual love for his mother and hostility for his father. In this traumatic event, the child eventually learns to identify with the same-sex parent and change from sexual to nonsexual love for the other-sex parent, eventually developing an erotic preference for the other sex. In this way, sexual feelings for the other-sex parent are sublimated. Difficulties in this stage of development may result in later sexual identity problems affecting relationships with the same or other sex.

[handwritten: 3-6 years]

Latency. When the conflicts of the Oedipus complex are resolved, the child enters the latency period. Lasting roughly from the ages of 6 to 12 (or puberty), the latency period is not a psychosexual stage of development because at this point sexual energy (as well as oral and anal impulses) is channeled elsewhere. This force (libido) is repressed, and children apply their energy to school, friends, sports, and hobbies. Although the sexual instinct is latent, the repressed memories from previous stages are intact and will influence later personal development.

[handwritten: 6-12]

Genital stage. Beginning in early adolescence, about the age of 12, the genital stage continues throughout life. Freud concerned himself with childhood development rather than adult development. In the genital stage, the focus of sexual energy is toward members of the other sex rather than toward

[handwritten: 12 yrs]

self-pleasure (masturbation). In contrast to the genital stage, which focuses on others as the sexual object, the three earlier stages (oral, anal, and phallic) focus on self-love.

Freud's theory of psychosexual development has been challenged by other psychoanalytic theorists. Although all psychoanalytic theorists accept the importance of the unconscious and, to a great extent, make use of Freud's concepts of ego, id, and superego, their greatest area of difference concerns his emphasis on drives and psychosexual stages. Other theorists' focus on ego rather than id functioning and on the importance of infant–mother interactions provides the subjects of the next sections.

Ego Psychology

Freud said, "Where there is id, ego shall be." Those who followed Freud found ways to incorporate psychosexual drives (id) with social and nondrive motives (ego). Among the best-known ego psychologists who added to the theoretical model of psychoanalysis were Anna Freud and Erik Erikson. Anna Freud applied psychoanalysis to the treatment of children and extended the concept of ego defense mechanisms. Bringing ego psychology into Freudian developmental theory, Erik Erikson widened the concept of life stages into adulthood and introduced social and nonpsychosexual motives to the stages.

Anna Freud

ANNA FREUD

Anna Freud (1895–1982) studied nursery-school children and provided psychoanalytic treatment at her Hampstead Clinic in London. Her writings reflect her work with both normal and disturbed children (Young-Bruehl, 2008). When evaluating child development, she attended not only to sexual and aggressive drives of children but also to other measures of maturation, such as moving from dependence to self-mastery. The gradual development of various behaviors has been referred to as *developmental lines*. For example, she shows how individuals go from a gradual egocentric focus on the world, in which they do not notice other children, to a more other-centered attitude toward their schoolmates to whom they can relate as real people (A. Freud, 1965). These developmental lines show an increasing emphasis on the ego.

Anna Freud believed that the ego as well as the id should be the focus of treatment in psychoanalysis (Blanck & Blanck, 1986). In *The Ego and the Mechanisms of Defense* (A. Freud, 1936), she describes 10 defense mechanisms that had been identified by analysts at that time, most of which have been discussed in this chapter. To this list she added the defenses "identification with the aggressor" and "altruism." In *identification with the aggressor*, the person actively assumes a role that he or she has been passively traumatized by, and in *altruism* one becomes "helpful to avoid feeling helpless." She wrote also of *defense against reality situations*, a recognition that motivation can come not only from internal drives but also from the external world (Greenberg & Mitchell, 1983). With her experience in understanding child development, she was able to articulate how a variety of defenses developed and recognize not only the abnormal and maladaptive functions of defense mechanisms but also adaptive and normal means of dealing with the external world.

ERIK ERIKSON

Erik Erikson

A student of Anna Freud, Erik Erikson (1902–1994) made a number of contributions to ego psychology, but perhaps most important was his explanation of psychosocial life stages that include adult as well as child development. Starting with Freud's psychosexual stages, he showed their implications for growth and development as the individual relates to the external world. Erikson's eight stages focus on crises that must be negotiated at significant points in life. If these crises or developmental tasks are not mastered, this failure can provide difficulty when other developmental crises are encountered. Unlike Freud's stages, a stage is not completed but remains throughout life. For example, the first stage—trust versus mistrust—begins in infancy; if not encountered successfully, it can affect relationships at any time during the life cycle.

Erikson's eight psychosocial stages are briefly described below. So that comparisons can be made with Freud's psychosexual stages, Freud's stages are listed in parentheses next to Erikson's.

Infancy: Trust versus mistrust (oral). An infant must develop trust in his mother to provide food and comfort so that when his mother is not available, he does not experience anxiety or rage. If these basic needs are not met, non-trusting interpersonal relationships may result.

Early childhood: Autonomy versus shame and doubt (anal). Being able to develop bladder and bowel control with confidence and without criticism from parents is the crucial event in this stage (Erikson, 1950, 1968). If parents promote dependency or are critical of the child, the development of independence may be thwarted.

Preschool age: Initiative versus guilt (phallic). At this stage, children must overcome feelings of rivalry for the other-sex parent and anger toward the same-sex parent. Their energy is directed toward competence and initiative. Rather than indulge in fantasies, they learn to be involved in social and creative play activities. Children who are not allowed to participate in such activities may develop guilt about taking the initiative for their own lives.

School age: Industry versus inferiority (latency). At this point the child must learn basic skills required for school and sex-role identity. If the child does not develop basic cognitive skills, a sense of inadequacy or inferiority may develop.

Adolescence: Identity versus role confusion (genital). During this key stage in Erikson's schema, adolescents develop confidence that others see them as they see themselves. At this point, adolescents are able to develop educational and career goals and deal with issues regarding the meaning of life. If this is not done, a sense of role confusion, in which it is difficult to set educational or career goals, may result.

Young adulthood: Intimacy versus isolation (genital). Cooperative social and work relationships are developed, along with an intimate relationship with another person. If this is not done, a sense of alienation or isolation may develop.

Middle age: Generativity versus stagnation (genital). Individuals must go beyond intimacy with others and take responsibility for helping others develop. If individuals do not achieve a sense of productivity and accomplishment, they may experience a sense of apathy.

Later life: Integrity versus despair (genital). When individuals reach their 60s (or later) and feel that they have not handled their lives well, they may experience a sense of remorse and regret about not having accomplished what they wanted in life. Having passed successfully through life, individuals contribute their accumulated knowledge to others. In her 90s, Joan Erikson, who was married to Erik for 64 years and was intimately involved in his work, added a ninth stage (Erikson, 1997). She proposed a stage called "Disgust: Wisdom" in which those in their 80s and 90s can move toward *gerotranscendence* (Tornstam, 1997) a shift from a materialistic and rational vision to peace of mind and spirituality.

Although these stages encompass the entire life span, Erikson's major contribution to psychoanalytic practice was through his work with adolescents and children (Schultz & Schultz, 2009). He developed several innovative approaches to play therapy, and many counselors and therapists have found his concept of the identity crises of adolescents useful. His work and that of other ego psychologists has provided a conceptual approach that counselors and those who work in a short-term model can apply to their clients by emphasizing ego defenses, current interactions with others, conscious as opposed to unconscious processes, and developmental stages across the life span.

Object Relations Psychology

Theories in Action

Object relations refers to the developing relationships between the child and significant others or love objects in the child's life, especially the mother. The focus is not on the outside view of the relationship but on how the child views, or internalizes consciously or unconsciously, the relationship. Of particular interest is how early internalized relationships affect children as they become adults and develop their own personalities. Examining not merely the interaction between mother and child, object relations theorists formulate the psychological or intrapsychic processes of the infant and child. They are interested in how individuals separate from their mothers and become independent persons, a process referred to as *individuation*. This emphasis on internalized relationships differs markedly from Freud's emphasis on internal drives as they express themselves in psychological stages. Many writers have developed theoretical constructs to explain object relations, described stages of object relations development, and related their work to Freud's drive theory. Among the most influential writers on this subject are Balint (1952, 1968), Bion (1963), Blanck and Blanck (1986), Fairbairn (1954), Guntrip (1968), Jacobson (1964), Kernberg (1975, 1976), Klein (1957, 1975), Mahler (1968, 1979a, 1979b), and Winnicott (1965, 1971). An explanation of their contributions, similarities, and differences goes beyond the scope of this text but is available in St. Clair (2004) and Greenberg and Mitchell (1983).

To provide an overview of object relations psychology, I next describe the contributions of Donald Winnicott and Otto Kernberg. Winnicott explains problems that occur as the child develops in relationship to the mother and others and offers solutions for them. More recently, Kernberg has offered useful insights into the development of object relations as it affects normal behavior and psychological disturbance, especially borderline disorders. A discussion of their contributions provides a broad overview of how early mother–child relationships affect later personality development.

Donald Winnicott

An English pediatrician, Donald Winnicott (1896–1971) did not offer a systematized theory of object relations. However, "his ideas have likely had more influence on the understanding of the common, significant issues met with by psychoanalysts and psychotherapists in their everyday practice than anyone since Freud" (Bacal & Newman, 1990, p. 185). He made many direct observations about the relationship between infant and mother in his work with children and families who had consulted him for assistance with psychological problems (Tuber, 2008; Winnicott, 1965, 1975). His concepts of the transitional object, the good-enough mother, and the true self and false self have been particularly useful in helping therapists work with both children and adults in understanding the importance of early childhood attachment to the mother and its impact on later life.

Gradually, infants move from a state in which they have a feeling of creating and controlling all aspects of the world that they live in to an awareness of the existence of others. Winnicott (Greenberg & Mitchell, 1983; Tuber, 2008) believed that a *transitional object*, such as a stuffed animal or baby's blanket, is a way of making that transition. This transitional object is neither fully under the infant's fantasized control of the environment nor outside his control, as the real mother is. Thus, the attachment to a stuffed rabbit can help an infant gradually shift from experiencing himself as the center of a totally subjective world to the sense of himself as a person among other persons (Greenberg & Mitchell, 1983, p. 195). In adult life, transitional objects or phenomena can be expressed as a means of playing with one's own ideas and developing creative and new thoughts (Greenberg & Mitchell, 1983).

Crucial to the healthy development from dependence to independence is the parental environment. Winnicott (1965) used the term *good enough* to refer to the mother being able to adapt to the infant's gestures and needs, totally meeting needs during early infancy but gradually helping the infant toward independence when appropriate. However, infants learn to tolerate frustration, so the mother needs to be good enough, not perfect. If the mother is too self-absorbed or cold to the infant, does not pick her up, and good-enough mothering does not occur, a true self may not develop. The *true self* provides a feeling of spontaneity and realness in which the distinction between the child and the mother is clear. In contrast, the *false self* can occur when there is not good-enough mothering in early stages of object relations (St. Clair, 2004). When reacting with the *false self*, infants are compliant with their mothers and, in essence, are acting as they believe they are expected to, not having adequately separated themselves from their mothers. In essence, they have adopted their mothers' self rather than developed their own. Winnicott believed that the development of the false self arising from insufficient caring from the mother was responsible for many of the problems he encountered with older patients in psychoanalysis (Bacal & Newman, 1990).

Winnicott's view of therapy was consistent with his view of the object relations approach. He saw the goal of therapy as dealing with the false self by helping the patient feel that she was the center of attention in therapy in a healthy way, and thus repair defective early childhood parenting. A process of controlled regression is used in which the patient returns to the stage of early dependence. To do so, the therapist must sense what being the client is like and be the subjective object of the client's love or hate. The therapist must deal with the irrationality and strong feelings of the patient without getting angry or upset at the patient, encouraging the development of the true self (Winnicott, 1958).

Otto Kernberg

Born in Austria in 1928, Otto Kernberg is a psychoanalyst, a training and supervising analyst, a teacher, and a prolific writer. A current influential theorist, he has attempted to integrate object relations theory and drive theory. A major focus of his work has been on the treatment of borderline disorders and the helpfulness of object relations theory (more so than Freudian drive theory) in understanding patients' problems. Influenced by Margaret Mahler and Edith Jacobson, Kernberg has proposed a five-stage model of object relations that is not described here because of its complexity. An important concept described here is Kernberg's explanation of splitting. This concept (first discussed by Melanie Klein) is then related to Kernberg's view of the borderline disorder.

Splitting is a process of keeping incompatible feelings separate from each other. This is a normal developmental process, as well as a defensive one. It is an unconscious means of dealing with unwanted parts of the self or threatening parts of others. For example, the child who sees a babysitter as all bad because she will not give him candy is splitting. The babysitter is not viewed as a total person but only as bad. Splitting as a defense is seen frequently in psychoanalysis and psychoanalytic psychotherapy, particularly with borderline disorders. Kernberg (1975) gives an example of a patient's use of splitting.

In describing the reason for borderline disorders, Kernberg (1975) states that most patients with a borderline disorder have had a history of great frustration and have displayed aggression during their first few years of life. If a child is frustrated in early life, he may become intensely angry and protect himself by acting angrily toward his mother (and/or father). Rather than being seen as a nurturing or good-enough mother, the mother is seen as threatening and hostile. Because of this early development, such adults may have difficulty integrating feelings of love and anger in their images of themselves and others. In this way, they are likely to "split," or see others, including the therapist, as entirely bad or, sometimes, as entirely good.

It is difficult to convey the complexity and depth of object relations psychology by discussing major concepts of only two of many object relations theorists. Because Winnicott's insights into the interaction between infant and mother have been influential in object relations psychology, they are essential in understanding applications to analysis and psychotherapy (Tuber, 2008). The views of Kernberg are particularly useful in linking early childhood experience with later disturbance in childhood, adolescence, or adulthood. The emphasis of these theorists on early relationships with the mother (and others) is closely related to the developmental aspects of Kohut's self psychology.

Kohut's Self Psychology

Another major development within psychoanalysis has been self psychology, introduced by Heinz Kohut (1913–1981), whose works *The Analysis of the Self* (1971), *The Restoration of the Self* (1977), and *How Does Analysis Cure?* (1984) have elicited a great amount of reaction from critics and followers (St. Clair, 2004). Kohut's work is described in depth by Lessem (2005). A biography of Kohut

(Strozier, 2001) explains the man and his theory. The essence of self psychology is its emphasis on narcissism, not as a pathological condition, but as a partial description of human development. Whereas Freud saw narcissism as an inability to love or relate to others because of self-love or self-absorption, Kohut sees narcissism as a motivating organizer of development in which love for self precedes love for others. Crucial to understanding Kohut's theory are concepts of self, object, and selfobject. Self-absorption (the grandiose self) and the attention of the powerful parent (the idealized selfobject) occur in the course of child development before the age of 4. Difficulty with early developmental stages has an impact on how individuals relate to others and how they view themselves.

The self and related concepts are defined differently by various schools of psychoanalysis. Kohut came to understand the self through an empathic understanding of his patients (described in detail later in this chapter), whereas Winnicott described the individual based on his systematic observations of young children (St. Clair, 2004). Basically, the self is the core or center of the individual's initiative, motivating and providing a central purpose to the personality and responsible for patterns of skills and goals (Wolf, 1988, p. 182). As Kohut's work developed, he made more and more use of the concept of the self and less frequent reference to the concepts of ego, id, and superego. In this respect, his work is further removed from Freud's than are the writings of the ego and object relations psychoanalysts. In infancy, the rudimentary self is made up of an *object*, which is an image of the idealized parent, and a *subject*, the grandiose self that is the "aren't I wonderful" part of the child. The *selfobject* is not a person (a whole love object) but patterns or themes of unconscious thoughts, images, or representations of another. For example, the young child, used to his mother's praise, may respond to other children as if he deserves to play with their toys when he wants to. In this case, the mother's praise serves as the child's "selfobject" (Hedges, 1983; St. Clair, 2004), as the child makes no distinction between himself and his mother in his mental representation of events.

Although acknowledging the role of sexual energy and aggressive drives, Kohut focused on the role of narcissism in child development. He believed, like Mahler, that at the earliest stages infants have a sense of omnipotence, as they do not distinguish themselves from the mother (St. Clair, 2004). When the child's needs are frustrated (for example, he is not fed when he wants to be), he establishes a self-important image, the grandiose self. When the child is fed, he attributes perfection to the admired selfobject, the idealized parental image.

Through a series of small, empathic failures, such as the child not getting what she wants from the parent, a sense of self is developed. A state of tension exists between the grandiose self ("I deserve to get what I want") and the idealized parental image ("My parents are wonderful"). The tension between these two forms the bipolar self. In other words, the child chooses between doing what she expects her parents want her to do (the idealized selfobject) and doing what she wants to do (the grandiose self; Kohut, 1977). When young children do not get what they want, they may burst into a tantrum, a narcissistic rage.

As described to this point, narcissism is a motivating organizer of development, and outbursts are normal. These outbursts are due to the removal of the *mirroring selfobject*. *Mirroring* occurs when the parent shows the child that she is happy with the child. In this way, the grandiose self is supported and the child sees that her mother understands her (reflects the child's image to the child) and incorporates the mirroring parent into the grandiose self. Thus, the parent is viewed, in a sense, as a part of the child, performing the function of mirroring (Patton & Meara, 1992).

When children get stuck at a stage or when the grandiose self or idealized selfobject does not develop normally, problems arise in later life. For example, a child who does not have a responsive (mirroring) mother may be depressed in later life or continually search for love from others that was not supplied at an early age. Some people may never have had a sufficient relationship with parents (idealized selfobject) and may search for the ideal and perfect marriage partner or friend but always experience failure, because no one can meet their standards (St. Clair, 2004).

Psychological disturbances were referred to by Kohut as selfobject disorders or self disorders. Kohut assumed that the problems in developing adequate selfobjects, and thus a strong self, were the rationale for disorders. For example, psychosis is seen as a disorder occurring where there are no stable narcissistic images or no stable idealized object. Thus, individuals may develop delusions to protect themselves against loss of idealized objects (adequate parents; St. Clair, 2004). For those with borderline disorders, the damage to the self may be severe, but defenses are sufficiently adequate for individuals to function (Wolf, 1988). In the case of narcissistic personality disorders, the grandiose self and the idealized selfobject have not been sufficiently integrated into the rest of the personality and self-esteem may be lost (Kohut, 1971).

In his therapeutic approach, Kohut focused particularly on narcissistic and borderline disorders. His approach, in general, was to understand and be empathic with the individual's inadequate or damaged self, which resulted from the inability to have experienced successful development of the grandiose self and the idealized selfobject. In his psychoanalytic work, Kohut found that patients expressed their narcissistic deficits through their relationship with him. How he experienced this relationship (transference) is explained later.

Relational Psychoanalysis

Another perspective on psychoanalysis began with the work of Greenberg and Mitchell (1983) and Mitchell's (1988) *Relational Concepts in Psychoanalysis*. Mitchell and his colleagues saw drive theory as providing a view of personality theory different from that of early relational theories such as object relations and self psychology. Influenced by social constructionists, relational therapists examined their own contributions to patient reactions. They did not believe therapeutic neutrality can be achieved. Rather, they used themselves as an instrument in psychoanalysis and psychoanalytic therapy, reacting to patient statements rather than just observing them.

Greenberg (2001) describes four premises that explain the position of relational psychoanalysis and differentiate it from many other views of psychoanalysis. First, relational psychoanalysts recognize that each analyst or therapist will have a personal influence on the patient based on his or her personality. Second, each analyst–patient pair will be unique. Third, what can happen in treatment is unpredictable and is affected by the interaction between the analyst and patient. Fourth, the analyst is a subjective, not an objective, participant. Detached objectivity does not exist. These four premises describe psychoanalysis in a less authoritarian manner than that described by most drive, ego, object relations, and self psychologists discussed previously. Analysts provide an expertise in developing useful psychoanalytic ideas and in using their own trained ability to self-reflect to help patients change (Mitchell, 1998).

Mitchell (2000) describes four modes of interactions between individuals that illustrate the way relational psychoanalysis views therapeutic relationships. The first mode describes how people relate, in a broad sense, to each other, such as interactions between siblings. The second mode deals with how individuals communicate emotion to each other, such as showing love by holding an infant. The third mode is how individuals view their own various roles, such as being in the role of a daughter or a mother. These perceptions may be conscious or unconscious. The fourth mode is intersubjectivity. In applying *intersubjectivity* to psychoanalysis, both analyst and patient influence each other. Thus, there is a two-person psychology. This is in contrast with the traditional one-person psychology in which the analyst influences the patient, but the patient does not influence the analyst.

Mitchell (1999) describes his work with Connie, a patient whom he had been seeing on a weekly basis. Connie surprised Mitchell by being upset by not being greeted by her name. Rather than believing that this is a symptom of Connie's problem (a one-person view), he examines the situation from the analyst's and patient's view as well as the interaction (a two-person view).

Mitchell's Modes: Connie

A couple of months into the work, Connie surprised me by beginning a session in considerable distress. How did this therapy work, she wanted to know. She felt there was something terribly impersonal about the way I greeted her, without even saying her name, in the waiting room right after the previous, probably anonymous patient had left. I at first felt a little stung by this accusation, particularly because I had been struggling myself with what felt to me to be a distance imposed by her. I began to wonder if I had not unconsciously retaliated by toning down my emotional reactions to her at the beginning and end of our sessions. I do tend sometimes to be pretty businesslike. And my customary way of greeting patients was to acknowledge their presence with a "hello" and invite them into my office without mentioning their names. We explored Connie's experience of these interactions, but she was still angry. I explained that it was just not my customary style to mention people's names when greeting them, either inside or outside the therapy setting. She felt that what she experienced as the anonymity of my manner was intolerable and that, unless I would sometimes mention her name, she would be unable to continue. We agreed that it would not make sense for me to do this mechanically but that I would try to find a way that was genuine for me. And I did. I actually found that I enjoyed saying her name, and her responses to my greetings were warmer than they had been before. I realized that there was something a bit pressured about my "let's get down to work" attitude. I even began to change my manner of greeting and parting from other patients. It seemed to me that Connie and I were working something out related to distance and intimacy, presence and loss, that was not unrelated to her early traumas and deprivations but that was happening in a very live way between us now. A couple of months following our newly fashioned manner of greeting and parting, Connie said that she felt that she had too much to talk about in once-a-week sessions, and she began to come twice weekly. (Mitchell, 1999, pp. 102–103)

Unlike the other approaches to psychoanalysis, the subjectivity and the vulnerability of Mitchell are quite clear. The emphasis on the therapist's subjectivity and self-awareness are typical of the relational approach to psychoanalysis.

Psychoanalysts and psychotherapists differ greatly as to which of these five approaches (drive, ego, object relations, self psychology, and relational) they use to understand their patients. Originally, psychoanalysts used only Freud's drive theory in understanding clients. Those who do so now are usually known as *classical* or *traditional psychoanalysts*. Although some psychoanalysts and psychotherapists use only one of these approaches, more and more analysts are using a combination of psychoanalytic theories. Pine's (1990) approach focuses on four different ways to understand clients. They include the developmental approaches of drive, ego, object-relations, and self psychology but not the more relationship-focused view of relational psychoanalysis. Although not defining the four psychoanalytic theoretical approaches exactly as they have been presented here, Pine (1990) describes how he may switch his approach in understanding patients to any of the four perspectives within a therapy session. How psychoanalysts and psychotherapists understand the early development of their patients has a great impact on how they implement therapeutic techniques.

Psychoanalytical Approaches to Treatment

Although psychoanalysts make use of different listening perspectives from drive, ego, object relations, self psychology, and/or relational psychology, they tend to use similar approaches to treatment. In their goals for therapy, they stress the value of insights into unconscious motivations. In their use of tests and in their listening to patients' dreams or other material, they concentrate on understanding unconscious material. Depending on whether they do psychoanalysis or psychoanalytic therapy, their stance of neutrality and/or empathy toward the patient may vary. However, both treatments deal with the resistance of the patient in understanding unconscious material. Each of these issues is discussed more extensively later in this chapter, as are therapeutic approaches.

Techniques such as the interpretation of transference or of dreams can be viewed from the five perspectives, as can countertransference reactions (the therapist's feelings toward the patient). Applying these perspectives to dream interpretation, to a transference reaction, and to countertransference issues can clarify these different approaches and show several ways that treatment material can be understood.

Therapeutic Goals

Psychoanalysis and psychodynamic psychotherapy are designed to bring about changes in a person's personality and character structure. In this process, patients try to resolve unconscious conflicts within themselves and develop more satisfactory ways of dealing with their problems. Self-understanding is achieved through analysis of childhood experiences that are reconstructed, interpreted, and analyzed. The insight that develops helps bring about changes in feelings and behaviors. However, insight without change is not a sufficient goal (Abend, 2001). By uncovering unconscious material through dream interpretation or other methods, individuals are better able to deal with the problems they face in unproductive, repetitive approaches to themselves and others.

The emphasis in bringing about resolution of problems through exploration of unconscious material is common to most approaches to psychoanalysis. For Freud, increasing awareness of sexual and aggressive drives (id processes) helps individuals achieve greater control of themselves in their interaction with others (ego processes). Ego psychoanalysts emphasize the need to understand ego defense mechanisms and to adapt in positive ways to the external world. For

[handwritten margin notes:]
1) Changes in personality
2) Self-Understand
3) Social History
4) DREAM

object relations therapists, improved relationships with self and others can come about, in part by exploring separation and individuation issues that arise in early childhood. Somewhat similarly, self psychologists focus on the impact of self-absorption or idealized views of parents that may cause severe problems in relating with others in later life, and they seek to heal these early experiences. Relational analysts may have goals similar to object relations analysts and self psychologists. The differences among these approaches are oversimplified here. In clinical work, psychoanalysts may have one or more of these goals in their work with patients.

There are some general goals that many psychoanalytic and psychodynamic therapists have in common (Gabbard, 2004, 2005). Patients should become more adept at resolving unconscious conflicts within themselves. As a result of psychodynamic or psychoanalytic therapy, patients should know themselves better and feel more authentic or real. As a result of understanding their own reactions to other people, patients should have improved relationships with family, friends, and coworkers. Patients should be able, after therapy is completed, to distinguish their own view of reality from real events that have taken place. These goals apply to all systems of psychoanalysis.

Assessment

Because unconscious material is revealed slowly, the process of assessing patients' family history, dreams, and other content continues through the course of analysis or therapy. Some psychoanalysts may use a rather structured approach in the first few sessions by taking a family and social history, whereas others may start therapy or do a trial analysis, using the first few weeks to assess appropriateness for therapy. By applying their understanding of personality development, as described in the prior section, they listen for unconscious motivations, early childhood relationship issues, defenses, or other material that will help them assess their patients' problems.

A few may make use of projective or other tests in their assessment process. Perhaps the most common test used is the Rorschach (Nygren, 2004), which provides ambiguous material (inkblots) onto which patients can project their feelings and motivations. An instrument that was designed specifically to measure concepts within Freudian drive theory is the Blacky Test, a series of 12 cartoons portraying a male dog named Blacky, his mother, father, and a sibling. Examples of dimensions that are measured are oral eroticism, anal expulsiveness, and Oedipal intensity (Blum, 1949). Short and long forms of the Working Alliance Inventory have been developed to assess progress in therapy as it relates to the therapeutic relationship (Busseri & Tyler, 2003; Goldberg, Rollins, & McNary, 2004). Although the Working Alliance Inventory has been used primarily for research purposes, practitioners may find it to be of value in assessment of patients' problems.

Psychoanalysis, Psychotherapy, and Psychoanalytic Counseling

Psychoanalysis, psychoanalytic therapy, and psychoanalytic counseling differ from each other in their length and in the techniques that are used. Usually, psychoanalysis is conducted with a patient lying on a couch and the analyst sitting in a chair behind him. Most commonly, analysands (patients) meet with analysts four times per week, although sometimes it may be two, three, or five times a week. Psychoanalytic therapy takes place in a face-to-face situation, with psychoanalytic therapy meetings occurring one to three times a week. In psychoanalytic counseling, meetings are usually once per week. In general, free association, in which a patient reports whatever thoughts come to her mind, is used less frequently in psychotherapy and counseling than in analysis. In psychoanalysis, analysts are more likely to allow the full exploration of unconscious and early development, which may be counterproductive to those with severe disturbances. In general, when doing psychoanalysis, the therapist speaks less than in a face-to-face psychotherapeutic interaction, offering occasional clarification and interpretation. Most psychoanalysts also do psychotherapy. Although ability to explore unconscious processes and to tolerate less interaction from the therapist is an important consideration in undertaking psychoanalysis, so is cost. A year of four-times-per-week psychoanalysis can cost more than $20,000.

Differentiation between psychoanalytic therapy and psychoanalytic counseling is less clear than between these two and psychoanalysis. In their discussion of psychoanalytic counseling, Patton and Meara (1992) emphasize the working alliance between client and counselor as they explore problems. Like psychotherapists, counselors may make use of suggestion, support, empathy, questions, and confrontation of resistance, as well as insight-oriented interventions in the form of clarification and interpretation (Patton & Meara, 1992). Although some of these techniques are used in many types of counseling and therapy, free association, interpretation of dreams, and transference, as well as countertransference issues, are the cornerstones of psychoanalytic treatment and are discussed next.

Free Association

When patients are asked to free-associate, to relate everything of which they are aware, unconscious material arises for the analyst to examine. The content of free association may be bodily sensations, feelings, fantasies, thoughts, memories, recent events, and the analyst. Having the patient lie on a couch rather that sit in a chair is likely to produce more free-flowing associations. The use of free association assumes that unconscious material affects behavior and that it can be brought into meaningful awareness by free expression. Analysts listen for unconscious meanings and for disruptions and associations that may indicate that the material is anxiety provoking. Slips of the tongue and omitted material can be interpreted in the context of the analyst's knowledge of the patient. If the patient experiences difficulty in free-associating, the analyst interprets, where possible, this behavior and, if appropriate, shares the interpretation with the patient.

Neutrality and Empathy

In traditional psychoanalysis, as compared to relational psychoanalysis, neutrality and empathy are compatible. The analyst wants the patient to be able to free-associate to materials that are affected as little as possible by aspects of the analyst that are extraneous to the patient. For example, discussing the analyst's vacation with the patient or having prominent family pictures in the office may interfere with the analyst's understanding of the patient's unconscious motives, feelings, and behavior. When analysts do disclose about themselves, they think carefully about the impact of this disclosure on the patient. This does not mean that the analyst is cold and uncaring. Rather, the analyst is empathic with the patient's experience and feeling. By understanding the patient's feelings and encouraging free association rather than responding directly to the patient's feelings (anger, hurt, happiness, and so forth), the analyst allows a transference relationship (feelings about the analyst) to develop. Perhaps no analytical theorist stresses the importance of empathy as a means of observing the patient in analysis more than has Kohut. Hedges (1992) gives an example of Kohut's description of empathizing with a patient's very early childhood needs for nurturing, given at a conference shortly before Kohut's death in 1981.

> She lay down on the couch the first time she came, having interrupted a previous analysis abruptly and she said she felt like she was lying in a coffin and that now the top of the coffin would be closed with a sharp click … she was deeply depressed and at times I thought I would lose her, that she would finally find a way out of the suffering and kill herself … at one time at the very worst moment of her analysis [after] … perhaps a year and a half, she was so badly off I suddenly had the feeling—"you know, how would you feel if I let you hold my fingers for awhile now while you are talking, maybe that would help." A doubtful maneuver. I am not recommending it but I was desperate. I was deeply worried. So I moved up a little bit in my chair and gave her two fingers. And now I'll tell you what is so nice about that story. Because an analyst always remains an analyst. I gave her my two fingers. She took hold of them and I immediately made a genetic interpretation—not to her of course, but to myself. It was the toothless gums of a very young child clamping down on an empty nipple. That is the way it felt. I didn't say anything … but I reacted to it even there as an analyst to myself. It was never necessary anymore. I wouldn't say that it turned the tide, but it overcame a very, very difficult impasse at a given dangerous moment and, gaining time that way, we went on for many more years with a reasonably substantial success. (Hedges, 1992, pp. 209–210)

This example is a dramatic and unusual instance of empathy. However, it shows Kohut's understanding and response to his client within an object relations and self psychology context.

Resistance

During the course of analysis or therapy, patients may resist the analytical process, usually unconsciously, by a number of different means: being late for appointments, forgetting appointments, or losing interest in therapy. Sometimes they may have difficulty in remembering or free-associating during the therapy hour. At other times resistance is shown outside therapy by acting out other problems through excessive drinking or having extramarital affairs. A frequent source of resistance is known as transference resistance, which is a means of managing the relationship with the therapist so that a wished or feared interaction with the analyst can take place (Horner, 1991, 2005). A brief example of a transference resistance and the therapist's openness to the patient's perception follows:

> [Patient:] I sensed you were angry with me last time because I didn't give you what you wanted about the feelings in my dream. I could tell by your voice.

> [Therapist:] (Very sure this was a misperception) I don't know what my voice was like, but what is important is how you interpreted what you perceived.

> [Patient:] I was aware of trying to please you, so I tried harder.

[*Therapist:*] I wonder if these concerns have shaped how you've been with me all along.

[*Patient:*] Sure. I don't know what to do in this room. I look for messages. (Horner, 1991, p. 97).

Listening for resistances is extremely important. The decision as to when to interpret the resistance depends on the context of the situation.

Interpretation

To be meaningful to the patient, material that arises from free association, dreams, slips of the tongue, symptoms, or transference must be interpreted to the patient. Depending on the nature of the material, the analyst may interpret sexually repressed material, unconscious ways the individual is defending against repressed memories of traumatic or disturbing situations, or early childhood disturbances relating to unsatisfactory parenting. Analysts need to attend not only to the content of the interpretation but also to the process of conveying it to the patient (Arlow, 1987). The patient's readiness to accept the material and incorporate it into his own view of himself is a significant consideration. If the interpretation is too deep, the patient may not be able to accept it and bring it into conscious awareness. Another aspect of interpretation is the psychological disorder that the patient presents to the therapist. Interpretation in work with individuals with borderline disorders may serve different functions than in less complex disorders (Caligor, Diamond, Yeomans, & Kernberg, 2009). Being attuned to the patient's unconscious material often requires that the analyst be attuned to her own unconscious processes as a way of evaluating the patient's unconscious material (Mitchell, 2000). In general, the closer the material is to the preconscious, the more likely the patient is to accept it.

Interpretation of Dreams

Theories in Action

In psychoanalytic therapy, dreams are an important means of uncovering unconscious material and providing insight for unresolved issues. For Freud, dreams were "the royal road to a knowledge of the unconscious activities of the mind" (Freud, 1900). Through the process of dream interpretation, wishes, needs, and fears can be revealed. Freud believed that some motivations or memories are so unacceptable to the ego that they are expressed in symbolic forms, often in dreams. For Freud, the dream was a compromise between the repressed id impulses and the ego defenses. The content of the dream included the manifest content, which is the dream as the dreamer perceives it, and the latent content, the symbolic and unconscious motives within the dream. In interpreting dreams, the analyst or therapist encourages the patient to free-associate to the various aspects of the dream and to recall feelings that were stimulated by parts of the dream. As patients explore the dream, the therapist processes their associations and helps them become aware of the repressed meaning of the material, thus developing new insights into their problems. Although Freud focused on repressed sexual and aggressive drives, other analysts have used other approaches to dream interpretation and emphasized an ego, object relations, self, or relational approach.

The Dream.
To illustrate three different ways to interpret a dream, Mitchell (1988, pp. 36–38) uses a fragment of a dream. The dreamer is riding a subway, not knowing where, and feeling

physically and mentally burdened. The dreamer has several bags and her briefcase. She lets her attention wander elsewhere and leaves her bags and briefcase to explore whatever has caught her attention. When she returns to her seat, her briefcase is gone and then she is very angry at herself for doing this. A feeling of great terror follows.

Interpretation using Freud's drive model.
There is an emphasis on examining how various drives are represented. Different objects of the dream have different meanings. The underground tunnel is symbolic of the anal drive. The train is a phallic symbol. The briefcase represents castration, and is a vaginal representation. The relational portion of the dream is less important. People are not important for themselves, but they are related to drives and defenses. People in the dream would be objects of desire and punishment. The conflict in the dream is over the missing briefcase and the self-criticism and implied fear of punishment. Having desire (a drive) and what happens as a result of that is an important theme in the drive model interpretation of the dream.

Interpretation using object relations.
The dream is viewed as representing how the dreamer sees herself and how she sees herself in relationship to others. One way she relates to others is through a compulsive loyalty that helps her feel close to others emotionally. Yet there is also a part of her that wants to impulsively pursue her own interests, but this may risk separating herself from others. The fear is that if she pursues her own desires instead of attending to the needs of others, she will not know who she is or how to establish connections with others. This issue could be the major focus of her analytic treatment. In therapy, she may start to see her self differently in terms of the way she relates to others (including the analyst).

Interpretation using self psychology.
The focus is on the patient's sense of self, on who she is as a person, including her fears and feelings. Questions arise as to whether she feels overtaxed with concerns. Perhaps she may be worried about being too impulsive. Or perhaps she is afraid of becoming weaker. The briefcase represents the self that exists and is reflected in her family's view of her. She may have a distorted belief that she has to be responsible in order to be valued by her family. In this way, the loss of the briefcase symbolizes the possibility of losing her sense of who she is as a person.

Depending on the analyst's or therapist's point of view and the nature of the patient's problem and disorder, an analyst or therapist might use any of these means of understanding the unconscious material in a dream. Additionally, an ego psychology approach might reveal a different way of understanding the dream, as would other psychoanalytic approaches that are not covered in this chapter, such as those based on the work of Sullivan or Horney. In interpreting the dream, Mitchell (1988) makes use not only of the dream itself but also of the variations within the recurring dream and, particularly, knowledge of the patient that he has gathered during the several years of analysis.

Interpretation and Analysis of Transference

The relationship between patient and analyst is a crucial aspect of psychoanalytic treatment. In fact, Arlow (1987) believes that the most effective interpretations deal with the analysis of the transference. Learning how to construct interpretations and to assess their accuracy is an important aspect of psychoanalytic training (Gibbons, Crits-Christoph, & Apostol, 2004). Patients work through their early relationships, particularly with parents, by responding to the analyst as they may have with a parent. If there was an emotional conflict in which the patient at age 3 or 4 was angry at her mother, then anger may be transferred to the analyst. It is the task of the analyst to help patients work through their early feelings toward parents as they are expressed in the transference.

Four psychological approaches (drive, ego, object relations, and self psychology) base interpretations of transference on early, unconscious material. The way they differ reflects their special listening perspective. Pine (1990) gives a hypothetical example of four differing interpretations of a female patient's flirtatious behavior with her male analyst. In this example, the woman is described as having had "as a child, a flirtatious sexualized relation to her father of a degree that was intensely exciting to her and who suffered a profound sense of rebuff when she felt she lost him when her mother was near" (p. 5). In the following four hypothetical responses that analysts of differing orientations could make, I include Pine's responses and summarize his explanation:

1. "So, now that your mother has left for her vacation you seem to feel safe in being flirtatious here, too, as you say you've been all day with others. I guess you're figuring that this time, finally, I won't turn away to be with her as you felt your father did." (Drive theory: The sexual drive, the wish to be with the father is interpreted.)

2. "It's not surprising that you suddenly found yourself retelling that incident of the time when your mother was critical of you. I think you were critical of yourself for flirting with me so freely just now, and you brought her right into the room with us so that nothing more could happen between us." (Ego psychology: The focus is on the anxiety aroused from the flirtation and the guilt for flirting; attention is paid to the patient's defense mechanisms.)

3. "Your hope seems to be that, if you continue to get excitedly flirtatious with me, and I don't respond with excitement, you'll finally be able to tolerate your excitement without fearing that you'll be overwhelmed by it." (Object relations: The interpretation relates to dealing with high levels of intensity in an early object relation [parental] experience.)

4. "When those profound feelings of emptiness arise in you, the flirtatiousness helps you feel filled and alive and so it becomes especially precious to you. It was as though when your father turned his attention to your mother, he didn't know that you would wish to be healed by him and not only be sexy with him." (Self psychology: The emphasis is on a painful subjective experience within the grandiose self, with the father turning from the patient toward the mother; Pine, 1990, p. 6)

Although these different approaches may seem subtle, they illustrate that the listening perspectives of the four psychologies are somewhat different, yet all use the interpretive mode. Both Kernberg (with borderline disorders) and Kohut (with narcissistic disorders) integrate transference into their theoretical approaches, as illustrated in the examples of their therapeutic work later in this chapter.

Countertransference

Psychoanalytic therapists approach their reactions to the patient (countertransference) from different viewpoints. Moeller (1977) presents three different positions on countertransference. First, the traditional interpretation of countertransference is the irrational or neurotic reactions of therapists toward the patient. Second, a broader usage of the term refers to the therapist's entire feelings toward the patient, conscious or unconscious (Gabbard, 2004). Eagle (2000) warns that therapists should not assume that all their thoughts and feelings during the therapy hour reflect the patient's inner world. The third view sees countertransference as a counterpart of the patient's transference. In other words, the feelings of the patient affect those of the therapist and vice versa. In this third way of viewing countertransference, the therapist might think, "Am I feeling the way my patient's mother may have felt?" Thus, therapists try to understand (or to empathize with) their patient, their own feelings, and the interaction between the two. A great variety of positions have been taken on countertransference issues.

Relational Responses

Therapists and analysts who follow a relational approach will go beyond the interpretation of countertransference. They are likely to look for issues that affect the therapeutic work. An example of this is seen on p. 46 when Mitchell (1999) and Connie discuss Connie's concern about Mitchell not calling her by her name. When therapists do this, they are using a two-person or intersubjective approach.

Although psychoanalysis, psychoanalytic psychotherapy, and psychoanalytic counseling differ in terms of the length of treatment, whether a couch is used for the patient, and their emphasis on exploring and interpreting unconscious material, they do have much in common. All examine how relationships and/or motivations before the age of 5 affect current functioning in children, adolescents, and adults. In general, their goals are to help patients gain insight into current behaviors and issues and thus enable them to change behaviors, feelings, and cognitions by becoming aware of unconscious material affecting the current functioning. Although projective and objective tests may be used for assessing concerns, most often the analyst's or therapist's theoretical approach to understanding the patient's childhood development provides a way of assessing analytic material. Much of this material may come from free association toward daily events, feelings, dreams, or other events in the patient's life. As the relationship develops, the analyst or therapist observes a transference—the relationship of the patient to the therapist that reflects prior parental relationships—and the countertransference—the therapist's reactions to the patient. Observations about the patient–therapist relationship as well as material coming from dreams and other material are interpreted or discussed with the patient in ways that will bring about insight into the patient's problems.

Psychological Disorders

Finding consensus on how to treat patients with psychoanalysis, psychoanalytic therapy, or psychoanalytic counseling is very difficult. Because of the length of therapy, the emphasis on unconscious material, and the many psychoanalytic writers with varying opinions, it is difficult to describe a specific procedure for each disorder. In this section, I try to illustrate further five different treatment and conceptual approaches by describing cases of each: drive theory (Freud), ego psychology (Erikson), object relations (Kernberg), self psychology (Kohut), and relational psychoanalysis (Mitchell). My emphasis is on presenting the theorists' way of working with disorders that they have written about extensively rather than presenting an overview of treatment for each disorder. An example of Freud's work with a young woman illustrates his conceptualization of sexuality as it relates to hysteria. Many psychoanalysts, such as Anna Freud and Erik Erikson, have applied psychoanalytic principles to treatment of children. I show how Erik Erikson makes use of ego psychology perspectives with a 3-year-old girl with nightmares and anxiety. Otto Kernberg is well known for applying object relations perspectives to borderline disorders, and a case of a man presenting a borderline disorder with paranoid aspects illustrates this. Self psychology has been applied to people with many disorders, but its focus has been on the development of narcissism. Kohut's work with a person with a narcissistic disorder provides insight into his conceptualization of transference in the therapeutic relationship. Freud's and Erikson's brief interventions could be called psychoanalytic counseling, whereas Kernberg's and Kohut's are long term and deeper in nature and come close to fitting the definition of psychoanalytic psychotherapy. Also, I describe a case of depression in which the relational model of psychoanalysis is used in Mitchell's treatment of Sam.

Treatment of Hysteria: Katharina

Much of Freud's early work was with patients who presented symptoms of hysteria, as is documented in five case histories in *Studies on Hysteria* (Breuer & Freud, 1895). The case of Katharina is unusual in that it is extremely brief, basically one contact with the patient, and it took place when Freud was on vacation in the Alps. However, it illustrates several of Freud's approaches to hysterical disorders. In the vast writings on Freud and his contribution to psychoanalysis, his kind concern for his patients is often lost. It is evident in this case, which illustrates the value of unconscious processes and the defense mechanism of repression in dealing with early traumatic sexual events. Although he was later to believe that many of the "facts" reported by patients with hysteria were fantasy, his experience with Katharina does not fit that description. In fact, he says, writing prior to 1895,

> In every analysis of a case of hysteria based on sexual traumas we find that impressions from the pre-sexual period which produced no effect on the child attained traumatic power at a later date as memories when the girl or married woman has acquired an understanding of sexual life. (p. 133)

In the summer of 1893, Freud had gone mountain climbing in the eastern Alps and was sitting atop a mountain when 18-year-old Katharina approached to inquire if he was a doctor; she had seen his name in the visitor's book. Surprised, he listened to her symptoms, which included shortness of breath (not due to climbing the high mountains) and a feeling in her throat as if she was going to choke, as well as hammering in her head. He recorded the dialogue.

"Do you know what your attacks come from?" "No."
"When did you first have them?"
"Two years ago, while I was still living on the other mountain with my aunt. (She used to run a refuge hut there, and we moved here eighteen months ago.) But they keep on happening."
Was I to make an attempt at an analysis? I could not venture to transplant hypnosis to these altitudes, but perhaps I might succeed with a simple talk. I should have to try a lucky guess. I had found often enough that in girls, anxiety was a

consequence of the horror by which a virginal mind is overcome when it is faced for the first time with the world of sexuality.

So I said: "If you don't know, I'll tell you how I think you got your attacks. At that time, two years ago, you must have seen or heard something that very much embarrassed you, and that you'd much rather not have seen."

"Heavens, yes!" she replied, "that was when I caught my uncle with the girl, with Franziska, my cousin." (pp. 126–127)

At this time in his career, Freud was still using hypnosis in treatment, although he ceased doing so shortly after this. The uncle that Freud makes reference to was actually Katharina's father. Because of Freud's wish to protect Katharina's confidentiality, he changed the father's identity to uncle in his case studies (1895) and did not reveal this change until 30 years later. As Katharina talked with Freud, she revealed occasions on which her father had made sexual advances toward her when she was 14, and later she had to push herself away from her father when he was drunk. In her physical reaction to seeing her father having intercourse with Franziska, Freud realized, "She had not been disgusted by the sight of the two people but by the memory which that sight had stirred up in her. And, taking everything into account, this could only be a memory of the attempt on her at night when she had 'felt her uncle's body'" (p. 131). This leads to his conclusion as to why she unconsciously converted her psychological distress to physical symptoms.

So when she had finished her confession I said to her: "I know now what it was you thought when you looked into the room. You thought: 'Now he's doing with her what he wanted to do with me that night and those other times.' That was what you were disgusted at, because you remembered the feeling when you woke up in the night and felt his body."

"It may well be," she replied, "that was what I was disgusted at and that was what I thought."

"Tell me just one thing more. You're a grown-up girl now and know all sorts of things...."

"Yes, now I am."

"Tell me just one thing. What part of his body was it that you felt that night?"

But she gave me no more definite answer. She smiled in an embarrassed way, as though she had been found out, like someone who is obliged to admit that a fundamental position has been reached where there is not much more to be said. I could imagine what the tactile sensation was which she had later learnt to interpret. Her facial expression seemed to me to be saying that she supposed that I was right in my conjecture. (pp. 131–132)

Although this case occurred at a time very different than ours, conversion hysteria such as this does occur. The other cases of hysteria that Freud presents are far more complex but have in common the repression of unwanted sexual memories or traumas and Freud's work in bringing them into conscious awareness.

Childhood Anxiety: Mary

Although psychoanalysis of anxiety disorders with an adult is very different from that of Erikson's work with 3-year-old Mary, many of the conceptual approaches are similar. Mary has just turned 3, is "intelligent, pretty, and quite feminine" (Erikson, 1950, p. 197), has experienced nightmares, and in her playgroup has had violent anxiety attacks. She has been taken by her mother to see Erikson at the suggestion of her physician and has been told that she was coming to see a man "to discuss her nightmares." Although the case is too long to discuss in its entirety here (pp. 195–207), Erikson's gentle sensitivity to Mary is evident throughout the case description. During the first visit with Erikson, she puts her arms around her mother and gradually looks at Erikson. In a few minutes, the mother leaves and Mary takes a doll, which she uses to touch other toys in the room. Finally, with the doll's head, she pushes a toy train onto the floor "but as the engine overturns she suddenly stops and becomes pale" (p. 199). She then leans back against the sofa and holds the doll over her waist, dropping it to the floor. Then she picks it up again, holds it again over her waist, and drops it again; finally, she yells for her mother. Erikson describes his reactions.

> Strangely enough, I too felt that the child had made a successful communication. With children words are not always necessary at the beginning. I had felt that the play was leading up to a conversation. (p. 199)

Erikson goes on to analyze the session.

> In this play hour the dropped doll had first been the prolongation of an extremity and a tool of (pushing) aggression, and then something lost in the lower abdominal region under circumstances of extreme anxiety. Does Mary consider a penis such an aggressive weapon, and does she dramatize the fact that she does not have one? From the mother's account it is entirely probable that on entering the nursery school Mary was given her first opportunity to go to the toilet in the presence of boys. (p. 200)

Erikson is here referring to penis envy, the concept put forth by Freud in which the little girl believes that she has been deprived of a penis and wishes to possess one. However, Erikson attends not only to the psychosexual aspect of Mary's development but also to her psychosocial development. He observes her developing autonomy from her mother during the hour, her initiative in playing with the toys in the playroom, and her aggressiveness in pushing the toys from the shelves with the doll.

In their second meeting, Mary first plays with blocks, making a cradle for her toy cow. Then she pulls her mother out of the room and keeps Erikson in the room. Then Erikson plays a game at Mary's behest and pushes the toy cow through an opening, making it speak. With this, Mary is very pleased and gets her wish to have Erikson play with her. Previously Mary had been pushed away by her father, who had been irritated by her. Erikson sees this event as an episode of "father transference" (p. 204) in which Mary is active in directing Erikson in the play situation, in a way in which she had not been able to do at home.

Suggestions were made to Mary's parents about the need to have other children, especially boys, visit at home. She was allowed to experience her nightmares, which disappeared. In a follow-up visit, Mary was relaxed and interested in the color of the train that Erikson had taken on his vacation. Erikson later found that Mary particularly enjoyed her new walks with her father to the railroad yards, where they watched railroad engines. In commenting, Erikson attends not only to the phallic aspect of the locomotive engine but also to the social interaction with her father that leads to diminishment of anxiety.

Borderline Disorders: Mr. R.

Because Kernberg's writings have influenced the object relations-based treatment of individuals with borderline personality disorders, this section focuses on his approach to these difficult psychological disturbances. In brief, Kernberg sees borderline disorders as the result of extreme frustration and aggression that children experience before the age of 4 (Kernberg, 1975). When young children are intensely and continuously frustrated by one or both parents, they may protect themselves by projecting their feelings of aggression back to the parents and also by distorting their image of their parents (St. Clair, 2004). When this occurs, the parents are seen as potentially threatening and dangerous rather than loving; thus, later love or sexual relationships are likely to be viewed as dangerous rather than nurturing. This results in the development of individuals with borderline disorders who are likely to have difficulty in integrating loving and angry images of themselves and others and thus "split" their reactions into all-good or all-bad views of themselves or others. Much of Kernberg's (1975) approach to treatment revolves around work with the negative transference that the patient directs toward the therapist, structuring therapy so that the patient does not act out negative transference feelings to the therapist. Further, he tries to confront the patient's pathological defenses that reduce the ability to accurately interpret external events.

In understanding Kernberg's approach to personality disorders, it is helpful to be familiar with two terms related to the negative transference. *Transference psychosis* refers to acting out of early angry and destructive relationships that the patient, as a child, had with his parents. Kernberg observes that this transference emerges early in therapy and is usually negative and confusing. *Projective identification* is an early form of projection in which patients take negative aspects of their personality, project them or place them onto another, and then identify with and unconsciously try to control that person. In therapy, the therapist is likely to experience a projective identification as feelings that the patient has and that the therapist now feels. Applying projective identification to therapy, Kernberg (1975, p. 80) states that "it is as if the patient's life depended on his keeping the therapist under control."

In this case, Kernberg's application of negative transference and projective identification is evident in his treatment of a hostile and suspicious patient.

> Mr. R., a businessman in his late forties, consulted because he was selectively impotent with women from his own socioeconomic and cultural environment, although he was potent with prostitutes and women from lower socioeconomic backgrounds; he had fears of being a homosexual and problems in his relationships at work. Mr. R. also was drinking excessively, mostly in connection with the anxiety related to his sexual performance with women. He was the son of an extremely sadistic father who regularly beat his children, and a hypochondriacal, chronically complaining and submissive mother whom the patient perceived as ineffectually attempting to protect the children from father. The patient himself, the second of five siblings, experienced himself as the preferred target of both father's aggression and his older brother's teasing and rejecting behavior. His diagnostic assessment revealed a severely paranoid personality, borderline personality organization, and strong, suppressed homosexual urges. The treatment was psychoanalytic psychotherapy, three sessions per week.

> At one point in the treatment, Mr. R. commented several times in a vague sort of way that I seemed unfriendly and when greeting him at the start of sessions

conveyed the feeling that I was annoyed at having to see him. In contrast to these vague complaints, one day he told me, with intense anger and resentment, that I had spat on the sidewalk when I saw him walking on the other side of the street.

> I asked him whether he was really convinced that, upon seeing him, I had spat; he told me, enraged, that he knew it and that I should not pretend it was not true. When I asked why I would behave in such a way toward him, Mr. R. angrily responded that he was not interested in my motivations, just in my behavior, which was totally unfair and cruel. My previous efforts to interpret his sense that I felt displeasure, disapproval, and even disgust with him as the activation, in the transference, of his relationship with his sadistic father had led nowhere. He had only angrily replied that I now felt free to mistreat him in the same way his father had, just as everybody in his office felt free to mistreat him as well. This time, he became extremely enraged when I expressed—in my tone and gesture more than in my words—my total surprise at the assumption that I had spat upon seeing him. He told me that he had difficulty controlling his urge to beat me up, and, indeed, I was afraid that he might even now become physically assaultive. I told him that his impression was totally wrong, that I had not seen him and had no memory of any gesture that might be interpreted as spitting on the street. I added that, in the light of what I was saying, he would have to decide whether I was lying to him or telling him the truth, but I could only insist that this was my absolute, total conviction. (Kernberg, 1992, pp. 235–236)

Kernberg then discusses the patient's behavior and the patient's reaction to his explanation.

> His attributing to me the aggression that he did not dare to acknowledge in himself—while attempting to control my behavior and to induce in me the aggressive reaction he was afraid of—and, at the time, his attempting to control me as an expression of fear of his own, now conscious, aggression reflect typical projective identification. But rather than interpret this mechanism, I stressed the incompatibility of our perceptions of reality per se, thus highlighting the existence of a psychotic nucleus, which I described to him as madness clearly present in the session, without locating it in either him or me. Mr. R.'s reaction was dramatic. He suddenly burst into tears, asked me to forgive him, and stated that he felt an intense upsurge of love for me and was afraid of its homosexual implications. I told him I realized that in expressing this feeling he was acknowledging that his perception of reality had been unreal, that he was appreciative of my remaining at his side rather than being drawn into a fight, and that, in this context, he now saw me as the opposite of his real father, as the ideal, warm, and giving father he had longed for. Mr. R. acknowledged these feelings and talked more freely than before about his longings for a good relationship with a powerful man. (pp. 236–237)

This excerpt shows Kernberg's view of the powerful anger that can occur in the transference of negative parental experience in early childhood to the therapist. Kernberg also illustrates two concepts related to early object relations in childhood: the transference psychosis and projective identification.

Narcissistic Disorders: Mr. J.

For Kohut, narcissistic personality disorders or disturbances are due to problems in not getting sufficient attention from a parent in early childhood (the grandiose self) or not having sufficient respect for the parents. The cause of narcissistic disorders is the failure to develop positive feelings about the self when the experience of parenting has been disruptive or inadequate. When a child has a perception (usually unconscious) that the parent has been absent, uninterested in the child, or faulty, the child may grow into an adult who sees herself at the center of relationships (Kohut, 1971, 1977).

The inadequate relationships with the mother and/or father are likely to emerge in therapy in two types of transferences: mirroring or idealizing. In the mirroring transference, patients see themselves as perfect and assign perfection to others, especially the therapist. Thus, the mirroring transference is an enactment of early childhood issues that feature the grandiose self. The term mirroring refers to the degree to which the therapist serves the patient's needs by confirming her need for grandiosity through approval and assurance that she is wonderful. In the idealized transference, it is not the patient who is wonderful but the therapist. Patients project their loss of their perfect mother or father onto the therapist.

In therapy, Kohut was attuned to or empathic with the patient's early difficulties in centering all of her attention on the self or on the parent. Therapeutic growth occurs when the patient's needs for attention and admiration from the therapist are replaced by improved relationships with important people in the patient's life. In a sense, the therapist serves as a link so that the patient can move from self-absorption to attention to the therapist rather than to just herself and then later to others. Kohut (1971, 1977, 1984) has developed an extensive set of terms that describe his conceptualization and treatment approach to narcissistic and other disorders.

The case of Mr. J. illustrates Kohut's (1971) approach to narcissistic disorders. A creative writer in his early 30s, Mr. J. was in psychoanalytic psychotherapy with Kohut for several years because of his concern about his productivity and unhappiness. Indications of his grandiosity were his dreams, expressed in Superman terms, in which he was able to fly (p. 169). As treatment progressed, Mr. J. no longer dreamed of flying, but that he was walking. However, in these dreams, he knew that his feet never touched the ground, but everyone else's did. Thus, his grandiosity had diminished, as evidenced by the dreams, but was still present.

In psychoanalysis, seemingly trivial incidents can provide significant material. During one session, Mr. J. reported to Kohut that he carefully rinsed his shaving brush, cleaned his razor, and scrubbed the sink before washing his face. By attending to the arrogant manner in which he presented this material, Kohut was able to move into an exploration of the patient's childhood history, with a focus on the grandiosity of the patient and the lack of maternal attention.

> Gradually, and against strong resistances (motivated by deep shame, fear of over-stimulation, fear of traumatic disappointment), the narcissistic transference began to center around his need to have his body-mind-self confirmed by the analyst's admiring acceptance. And gradually we began to understand the pivotal dynamic position in the transference of the patient's apprehension that the analyst—like his self-centered mother who could love only what she totally possessed and controlled (her jewelry, furniture, china, silverware)—would prefer his material possessions to the patient and would value the patient only as a vehicle to his own aggrandizement; and that I would not accept him if he claimed his own initiative toward the display of his body and mind, and if he insisted on obtaining his own, independent narcissistic rewards. It was only after he had acquired increased insights into these aspects of his personality that the patient began to experience the deepest yearning for the acceptance of an archaic, unmodified grandiose-exhibitionistic body-self which had

for so long been hidden by the open display of narcissistic demands via a split-off sector of the psyche, and that a working-through process was initiated which enabled him ultimately, as he put it jokingly, "to prefer my face to the razor." (pp. 182–183)

Kohut helps Mr. J. in several ways. By recognizing Mr. J.'s need to be mirrored or appreciated, Kohut acknowledges the importance of Mr. J.'s mother's lack of attention. When Kohut discusses his insights with Mr. J., Mr. J. starts to genuinely appreciate Kohut as a person, not just as someone who meets his needs.

Depression: Sam

For Mitchell and other relational analysts, knowledge of family background and attention to unconscious factors are explored in many ways. A significant method is the development of the therapist–patient relationship. This exploration is more evident in the following case study than in the four previous ones. Teyber's (2006) description of methods for developing a relational approach provide some ideas as to how therapists can use relational statements when working with patients. However, Teyber's approach does not provide the psychoanalytic conceptual explanations used by Mitchell and his colleagues that are in the following example.

Sam is an adult male in a long-standing relationship with a woman. Mitchell (1988) describes him as presenting symptoms of depression and compulsive overeating. Sam has a younger sister who was severely brain damaged at birth. Although Sam's father was lively before Sam's sister's birth, he and Sam's mother became depressed because of the sister's problems, family illnesses, and their business failures. Both of Sam's parents became inactive and slovenly. Sam was seen as being the contact person between them and the real world. Mitchell (1988) describes his work with Sam.

> Analytic inquiry revealed that Sam's deep sense of self-as-damaged and his depression functioned as a mechanism for maintaining his attachment to his family. Sam and his family, it gradually became clear, had made depression a credo, a way of life. They saw the world as a painful place, filled with suffering. People who enjoyed life were shallow, intellectually and morally deficient, by definition frivolous and uninteresting. He was drawn to people who seemed to suffer greatly, was extremely empathic with and helpful to them, then would feel ensnared. The closest possible experience for people, he felt was to cry together; joy and pleasure were private, disconnecting, almost shameful.
>
> Sam and his analyst considered how this form of connection affected his relationship with the analyst. They explored various fantasies pertaining to the analyst's suffering, Sam's anticipated solicitous ministrations, and their languishing together forever in misery. In a much more subtle way, Sam's deeply sensitive, warmly sympathetic presence contributed to a sad but cozy atmosphere in the sessions that the analyst found himself enjoying. Sam's capacity to offer this kind of connection was both eminently soothing and somehow disquieting. The analyst came to see that this cozy ambience was contingent on Sam's belief that in some way he was being profoundly helpful to the analyst. The latter was the mighty healer, the one who needed care. This evoked what the analyst came to identify as a strong countertransferential appeal to surrender to Sam's attentive ministrations, which alternated with equally powerful resistances to that pull, involving detachment, manic reversals, and so on. The mechanism of Sam's self-perpetuated depression and the crucial struggle in the countertransference to find a different form of connection was expressed most clearly in one particular session.

He came in one day feeling good, after some exciting career and social successes. As it happened, on that day the analyst was feeling depressed. Although, as far as he could tell, the origins of his mood were unrelated to Sam, Sam's ready solicitations and concern were, as always, a genuine comfort. Early into the session, Sam's mood dropped precipitously as he began to speak of various areas of painful experience and a hopeless sense of himself as deeply defective. The analyst stopped him, wondering about the mood shift. They were able to reconstruct what had happened to trace his depressive response back to the point of anxiety. With hawk-like acuity he had perceived the analyst's depression. He had been horrified to find himself feeling elated and excited in the presence of another's suffering. An immediate depressive plunge was called for. To feel vital and alive when someone else is hurting seemed a barbaric crime, risking hateful retaliation and total destruction of the relationship. His approach to all people he cared about, they came to understand, was to lower his mood to the lowest common denominator. To simply enjoy himself and his life, without constantly toning himself down and checking the depressive pulse of others, meant he hazarded being seen as a traitorous villain and, as a consequence, ending up in total isolation. The analyst asked him in that session whether it had occurred to him that the analyst might not resent his good mood, but might actually feel cheered by Sam's enthusiasm and vitality (which was in fact the case that day). This never had occurred to him, seemed totally incredible, and provoked considerable reflection. Through this and similar exchanges their relationship gradually changed, as they articulated old patterns of integration and explored new possibilities. Sam began to feel entitled to his own experience, regardless of the affective state of others. (Mitchell, 1988, pp. 302–304)

The five case examples give some insight into the complexity of psychoanalysis and psychoanalytic therapy, while illustrating drive, ego, object relations, self psychology, and relational perspectives. Although the disorders presented are different, all cases show the emphasis on unconscious forces and the impact of early childhood development on current functioning. Most of the examples also focus on the transference relationship between patient and therapist. Differences in treatment relate not only to the age and gender of the patient and to the type of psychological disorder but also to the therapist's view of early childhood development that influences interpretations and other approaches to psychoanalytic therapy.

Brief Psychoanalytic Therapy

Because psychoanalysis may require four or five sessions per week over 3 to 8 years (or longer) and psychoanalytic psychotherapy requires meetings at least once a week for several years, many mental health professionals have felt the need to provide briefer therapy. If successful, this would substantially reduce the cost to the patient, provide quicker resolution of psychological distress, provide better delivery of mental health services through shorter waiting lists, and offer more services for more patients. The popularity of brief psychoanalytic therapy is indicated by a variety of approaches (Bloom, 1997; Messer & Warren, 1995). The impetus for brief approaches to psychoanalytic psychotherapy has been the work of Malan (1976) in England. In using a short-term approach, Malan had to deal with issues such as how to select patients, what goals to choose for therapy, and how long treatment should last.

In general, most current short-term psychoanalytic psychotherapies are designed for people who are neurotic, motivated, and focused rather than for those with severe personality disorders as described by Kernberg and Kohut.

The treatment length is usually about 12 to 40 sessions, with several time-limited approaches specifying limits of 12 to 16 sessions. To work in such a short time frame, it is necessary to have focused goals to address. Although short-term therapists use diagnostic or conceptual approaches that are similar to those of long-term therapists, their techniques are not. Where psychoanalysts and psycho-analytic therapists make use of free association, short-term therapists rarely use this technique; rather, they prefer to ask questions, to restate, to confront, and to deal quickly with transference issues. To further describe approaches to brief therapy, I discuss Lester Luborsky's Core Conflictual Relationship Theme Method, based on understanding the transference relationship.

Since 1975, Lester Luborsky and his colleagues have authored more than 70 articles that describe and validate aspects of the Core Conflictual Relationship Theme method. This is a specific method for understanding transference and can be used for short-term psychotherapy (Luborsky & Crits-Christoph, 1998), as well as for difficult issues such as borderline disorder (Drapeau & Perry, 2009) and chronic fatigue (Vandenbergen, Vanheule, Rosseel, Desmet, & Verhaeghe, 2009). Research such as the study of rupture in the working alliance in relation to Core Conflictual Relationship Themes helps to provide more knowledge about how this approach to brief psychoanalytic therapy works (Sommerfeld, Orbach, Zim, & Mikulincer, 2008). Luborsky (1984) and Book (1998) describe the Core Conflictual Relationship Theme method to brief psychotherapy in detail. This method has three phases, all of which deal with the therapist's understanding of the Core Conflictual Relationship Theme.

To determine a patient's Core Conflictual Relationship Theme, a therapist must listen to the patient's discussion or story of Relationship Episodes. Often, the therapist writes down the three important components of a Relationships Episode. These include a Wish, a Response from the Other, and the Response from the Self (Luborsky, 1984). A patient's wish refers to a desire that is expressed in a Relationship Episode. This is determined by listening to what the patient's actual response from the Other person will be (or an anticipated response). The therapist also listens to what the response to the relationship situation will be from the individual (Response from the Self). Sometimes the relationship discussed is a daydream, or it can be an actual situation. A Core Conflictual Relationship Theme is communicated to the patient when the therapist has discussed five to seven Relationship Episodes with the patient. In doing so, the therapist may say to the client, "It seems to me that you want to be in a relationship where ..." (Book, 1998, p. 22).

Book (1998) uses the case of Mrs. Brown to describe the three phases of the Core Conflictual Relationship Theme method. This case is summarized here, focusing on the first phase.

The goal of the first phase, usually the first four sessions, is to help the patient become aware of how the Core Conflictual Relationship Theme plays a role in the patient's relationships. The patient becomes curious about why she may expect others to respond to her in a certain way or why others tend to respond to her in a certain way. For example, Mrs. Brown often kept her accomplishments to herself, believing that others might find them silly or unimportant. Because of this, she tended to distance herself from others in relationships and often felt overlooked and disappointed in her relationships with others. The following excerpt from the second session of therapy shows how the therapist focuses on the Core Conflictual Relationship Theme. In this dialogue, Mrs. Brown discusses her relationship with a coworker, Beth.

[*Patient:*] So Beth and I were discussing who should make the presentations. I said that she should.

[*Therapist:*] Why?

[*Patient:*] She had more experience.

[*Therapist:*] So?

[*Patient:*] She would stand a better chance of getting it through.

[*Therapist:*] If she did the presenting?

[*Patient:*] Yeah. Others would be taken by the way she presents.

[*Therapist:*] And, if you presented?

[*Patient:*] What do you mean?

[*Therapist:*] If you presented, how might others respond (Exploring the Response from the Other)?

[*Patient:*] I don't think I would do such a good job.

[*Therapist:*] In their eyes?

[*Patient:*] Yeah. I figure they would think … it was stupid.

[*Therapist:*] Do you see what you are saying?

[*Patient:*] What? (Perplexed.)

[*Therapist:*] Isn't this exactly what we have been talking about? Isn't it another example of your fear that if you put your best foot forward, that if you attempt to promote yourself and your ideas (her Wish), others will see you and your ideas as stupid and worthless (Response from the Other)?

[*Patient:*] Aha! So I shut up (Response from the Self)? Oh, my goodness. There it is again! I didn't even realize it!

[*Therapist:*] Yes. It is interesting how you rule yourself in this way without even realizing it and short change yourself in the process (Book, 1998, pp. 66–67).

In the first phase of therapy, the therapist focuses on identifying the patient's Core Conflictual Relationship Theme as it relates to her everyday life. Thus, the patient becomes consciously aware of relationship themes in her life that she was not aware of previously. She now will be able to have control over previously unconscious behavior.

During the second phase, usually the 5th through the 12th sessions, the patient works through the Response from Others. This is the major phase of treatment, and during it, the childhood roots of the transference-driven Response from Others are worked through. Here, the therapist interprets how the patient's expectations of Responses from Others are affected by attitudes, feelings, and behaviors that were learned from others in the past. The patient learns how unconscious attitudes from the past affect relationships in the present. In the case of Mrs. Brown, the therapist helped her to understand how her current relationships were affected by her earlier relationship with her father. She had wanted to be praised by her father but rarely received praise or recognition from him. As she realized this, she more willingly shared her achievements with coworkers and family.

Termination is the focus of the third phase, usually the 13th to 16th sessions. This phase allows the therapist and patient to discuss universal themes such as fears of abandonment, separation, and loss. The therapist may also discuss the patient's worries that gains that were made in treatment will not continue. This phase also gives the therapist an opportunity to work through the Core Conflictual Relationship Theme again. Returning to Mrs. Brown, the therapist observed that she was late for her 11th and 12th sessions and was less talkative. After discussing this, the patient and therapist found that Mrs. Brown was acting as if the therapist was losing interest and more interested in the patient who would replace her. This gave the therapist the opportunity to return to the Core Conflictual Relationship Theme that could be related to her father's dismissiveness of her and similar early experiences. In this way, the therapist dealt with transference issues so that Mrs. Brown would be freer to share her achievements with others and be less distant in relationships.

As can be seen from this brief example, the Core Conflictual Relationship Theme method is time limited and very specific in approach. The therapist attends to relationships that the client discusses, listening for a Wish, a Response from the Other, and a Response from the Self. Observations and interpretations made to the patient allow the patient to understand previously unconscious feelings, attitudes, or behaviors and make changes. Important in this method is the understanding of the transference issues that reflect attitudes and behaviors of early relationships as they influence later relationships, especially those with the therapist.

Current Trends

The oldest of all major theories of psychotherapy, psychoanalysis, continues to flourish and thrive. For economic and social reasons, the practice of psychoanalysis is changing. Also, two psychoanalytical issues are receiving attention now: treatment manuals and the two-person versus one-person model. All of these issues are explained more fully.

It seems reasonable to assume that there are more books written about psychoanalysis than about all the other theories covered in this book combined. It would not be unusual for large university libraries to have more than a thousand books on psychoanalysis. Many books continue to be published in this area, with a few publishers specializing in books on psychoanalysis. The vast majority of these writings are not on research but on applying psychoanalytic concepts to treatment issues. Implicit in this work are the discussion and disputation of previous psychoanalytic writers. An issue of debate relates to how far a theorist can revise Freud or diverge from him and still be considered to be within the framework of psychoanalysis. For example, some writers would state that Kohut's self psychology has overstepped the boundaries of psychoanalysis. Due in part to the large number of psychoanalytic therapists and to the emphasis on writing about ideas rather than doing research, there are many divergent perspectives. These appear not only in books but also in many of the psychoanalytic publications: *Contemporary Psychoanalysis, Journal of Applied Psychoanalytic Studies, Journal of the American Psychoanalytic Association, Journal of Psychoanalytic Inquiry, International Journal of Psychoanalysis, Psychoanalytic Dialogues, Psychoanalytic Quarterly, Neuro-Psychoanalysis, Psychoanalytic Study of the Child, Psychoanalytic Review, and Psychoanalytic Psychology.*

The introduction of treatment manuals provides a way to make psychoanalysis more popular and comprehensible to those not directly familiar with it.

Treatment manuals allow psychoanalysts to specify what they do and how they do it. Luborsky (1984) and Book (1998) have specified a 16-session model for the brief psychodynamic therapy described on pages 62–65. Luborsky and Crits-Christoph (1998) spell out in clear detail to students and therapists how the Core Conflictual Relationship method can be used by describing interview strategies along with case illustrations. As treatment manuals become more available to mental health professionals, access to what many consider to be a complex and sometimes arcane model will become more readily available. Psychoanalytic training of new mental health professionals will become easier when they have treatment manuals such as those describing the Core Conflictual Relationship Theme method. Because treatment manuals specify the procedures the therapist must follow in order to practice a particular method, they provide a way for researchers to be more certain that the therapist variable is being controlled in their research. Psychodynamic treatment manuals also make possible comparisons between therapies with more easily definable concepts, such as behavioral and cognitive therapies.

A very different trend has been the interest in a relational model (explained previously) or two-person psychology as contrasted with a one-person psychology. Two-person psychology focuses on how the patient and therapist influence each other. In contrast, one-person psychology emphasizes the psychology of the patient. Two-person psychology is based on the work of postmodern and relational writers such as Mitchell (1997, 1999, 2000). In *Relational Theory and the Practice of Psychotherapy,* Wachtel (2008) describes the current application of the relational model. The two-person approach is a constructivist one in which the analyst pays close attention to his contributions to the patient's reactions. This approach is present in integrative descriptions of psychoanalytic therapy such as *The Psychodynamic Approach to Therapeutic Change* (Leiper & Maltby, 2004). This approach may be helpful as more patients enter psychoanalysis with little knowledge of what psychoanalysis is (Quinodoz, 2001) and from varied socioeconomic and cultural backgrounds. But Chessick (2007) in *The Future of Psychoanalysis* cautions that the focus on the patient–therapist relationship may have been overemphasized and therapists may not focus sufficiently on psychoanalytic principles.

Using Psychoanalysis with Other Theories

Many mental health professionals with a wide variety of theoretical orientations make use of psychoanalytic concepts in understanding their patients. To describe such practitioners, the term *psychodynamic* is used. It generally refers to the idea that feelings, unconscious motives, or drives unconsciously influence people's behavior and that defense mechanisms are used to reduce tension (Leiper & Maltby, 2004). The term psychoanalytic also includes the belief that there are significant stages of development as well as important mental functions or structures such as ego, id, and superego (Robbins, 1989). Often the distinction between the two terms is not clear, and they are sometimes used interchangeably. Gelso and Fretz (1992) use the term *analytically informed therapy* or *counseling* in referring to those practitioners who make use of many of the concepts presented in this chapter but do not rely on analytic treatment methods such as free association and interpretation. Some practitioners use behavioral, cognitive, and/or person-centered techniques while understanding their patients through the use of a psychoanalytic model. Their approach differs from brief analytic psychotherapy in that they use a broader range of techniques.

Just as nonpsychoanalytic practitioners borrow conceptual approaches from psychoanalysis, psychoanalytic practitioners borrow intervention techniques from other theories. In their writings, psychoanalysts tend to focus more on personality-theory issues such as child development, interplay of conscious and unconscious processes, and the psychological constructs of the id, ego, and superego than on specific techniques. In the practice of psychoanalytic therapy or counseling, therapists may make use of existential concepts or gestalt therapy techniques to the extent that they are consistent with understanding the patient's psychological functioning. Blending cognitive therapy and psychoanalysis is an increasing trend (Luyten, Corveleyn, & Blatt, 2005). Owen (2009) has developed an intentionality model of psychotherapy that combines psychoanalysis with cognitive-behavioral techniques that looks for patterns of maladaptive relating and persistent negative moods. Also, person-centered statements that indicate that the therapist understands and empathizes with the patient's experience may be used. In general, the closer the approach to psychoanalysis, where the couch is used, the less likely are psychoanalytic practitioners to use techniques from other theories.

Research

Because psychoanalysis and psychoanalytic therapy are so lengthy and psychoanalytic concepts are so complex and are based on hard-to-define concepts dealing with the unconscious and early childhood development, it has been very difficult to design experiments to test their effectiveness. Moreover, Freud believed that research on psychoanalytic concepts was not necessary because of his confidence in the variety of clinical observations that he and his colleagues had made in their work with patients (Schultz & Schultz, 2009). Another objection to research on psychoanalytic concepts is that when they are taken out of the patient–therapist relationship and subject to laboratory experiments, the same phenomena are not being measured because the artificial experimental situation changes the behavior being measured. Related to this objection is the difficulty in clearly defining theoretical concepts. If psychoanalytic writers cannot agree on the meaning of certain concepts, it is going to be very difficult for researchers to define a concept adequately. Despite these difficulties, many investigators have attempted to measure the effectiveness of psychoanalytic therapy and psychoanalytic constructs. In this section are examples of two long-term, continuing investigations of psychoanalysis and/or psychoanalytic therapy that have assessed their effectiveness in as natural a setting as possible. Specific research relating to the effectiveness of psychodynamic therapy with substance abuse and general anxiety disorder is presented. Additionally, I include a brief overview of the concepts that have been studied as they relate to Freudian drive theory and object relations theory.

Does Psychoanalysis Work? (Galatzer-Levy, Bachrach, Skolnikoff, & Waldron, 2000) answers the question by reviewing seven studies of 1,700 patients receiving psychoanalysis. Most patients received training from graduate students or analysts in training with a background in ego psychology. The authors conclude that "patients suitable for psychoanalysis derive substantial benefits from treatment" (p. 129). They caution that findings made during treatment regarding patient improvement are not always confirmed at the conclusion of treatment. These conclusions appear to be supported by other research (Luborsky et al., 2003). A meta-analysis of 17 studies of brief psychodynamic therapies showed significant improvement across a variety of psychotic disorders when compared to control treatments (Leichsenring, Rabung, & Leibing, 2004). Furthermore, a review of the efficacy of psychoanalytic psychotherapy, primarily focusing on studies that met rigorous criteria that were done in the last 10 years, showed that psychoanalytic psychotherapy could be classified as a possibly efficacious treatment for panic disorder and borderline disorder, as well as drug dependence (Gibbons, Crits-Christoph, & Hearon, 2008). Several studies have shown that short-term psychodynamic treatment of depression can be considered a research-supported psychological treatment (RSPT) (Hilsenroth et al., 2003; Leichsenring & Leibing, 2007).

In a research study extending over 30 years and yielding more than 70 publications, Wallerstein (1986, 1989, 1996, 2001, 2005, 2009) followed 42 patients over the course of treatment, with half assigned to psychoanalysis and half to psychoanalytic psychotherapy. The purpose of this study, conducted at the Menninger Clinic in Topeka, Kansas, was to ask what changes take place in psychotherapy and what patient and therapist factors account for the changes. An unusual aspect of the sample was that the patients came from all over the United States and abroad to receive treatment at the Menninger Foundation. For each patient, most with severe psychological problems, case histories and clinical ratings of patient and therapist behavior and interaction were gathered. Follow-up assessments were made 3 years after treatment and, when possible, 8 years after treatment. The investigators wished to contrast expressive techniques and interpretations designed to produce insight and to analyze resistance and transference—with supportive techniques—designed to strengthen defenses and repress inner conflict. Surprisingly, the investigators found that the distinction between these two approaches became blurred. A major explanation for positive change was the "transference cure," that is, the willingness to change to please the therapist. As Wallerstein (1989) states, the patient is, in essence, saying, "I make the agreed upon and desired changes for you, the therapist, in order to earn and maintain your support, your esteem and your love" (p. 200). In general, the investigators found that change resulted from supportive techniques without patients having always resolved internal conflicts or achieved insights into their problems. Changes resulting from psychoanalysis and psychoanalytic therapy were proportionately similar and in both, supportive approaches were particularly effective.

In another series of studies on psychoanalytic psychotherapy, Luborsky, Crits-Christoph, and their colleagues studied variables that predicted treatment success before treatment and then followed up patients for 7 years after treatment had ceased. In this study (Luborsky, Crits-Christoph, Mintz, & Auberach, 1988), 42 different therapists worked with a total of 111 patients. When differentiating between poorer and better therapy hours, Luborsky et al. (1988) found that in the poorer hours, therapists tended to be inactive, impatient, or hostile, whereas in better hours therapists were more interested, energetic, and involved in the patient's therapeutic work. In describing curative factors, they highlight the importance of a patient's feeling understood by the therapist, which contributed to patients' increasing their level of self-understanding and decreasing conflicts within themselves. They also noted that an increase in physical health accompanied the positive changes in psychotherapy. Another important factor in achieving therapeutic success was the ability of the therapist to help the patient realize and make use of therapeutic gains.

Studying 90 individuals diagnosed with borderline disorder who received a year of treatment, a comparison was made of transference-focused psychotherapy, dynamic supportive treatment, and dialectical behavior therapy (Clarkin, Levy, Lenzenweger, & Kernberg, 2007). Patients in all groups made positive improvements in depression, anxiety, and social functioning. Only transference-focused psychotherapy reduced significant levels of irritability and verbal and direct assault. Transference-focused psychotherapy and dynamic supportive treatment brought about changes in aspects of impulsivity. This study is supportive of the positive effects of psychoanalytically based psychotherapy.

Several researchers have investigated treatments for cocaine dependence. Using data from the National Institute on Drug Abuse Collaborative Cocaine Treatment Study, Crits-Christoph et al. (2008) found psychodynamically oriented psychotherapy was somewhat less effective than individual drug counseling (both groups received group drug counseling). However, both treatments produced major improvements in the decrease of cocaine use. Supportive–expressive psychotherapy was superior to individual drug counseling in changing family/social problems at the 12-month follow-up assessment. In another study of 106 individuals who were dependent on cocaine, drug counseling techniques that focused on decreasing cocaine use were more effective than techniques that helped patients understand reasons for their use (Barber et al., 2008). However, a strong working alliance with low levels of supportive–expressive therapy adherence was associated with moderate to high outcome levels. Studying patients with cocaine-abuse problems, Barber et al. (2001) found that those who received psychoanalytic supportive–expressive therapy treatment and who had strong working alliances with their therapists stayed in treatment longer than did those who did not have strong working alliances. Interestingly, cognitive therapy patients with stronger alliances with therapists did not stay in treatment as long as those with weaker alliances. The findings of these studies are quite complex and show the difficulties in drawing clear conclusions from some psychotherapy research.

Three other investigations examined the effectiveness of psychodynamic therapy for the treatment of generalized anxiety disorder. Crits-Christoph et al. (2004) found that those with a generalized anxiety disorder significantly reduced their symptoms of anxiety and their worrisome thoughts. Crits-Christoph, Connolly, Azarian, Crits-Christoph, and Shappel (1996) found that brief Supportive–Expressive Psychodynamic Therapy showed different patterns of improvement for 29 patients over 16 weeks. After a 1-year follow-up comparing cognitive therapy with analytical therapy, Durham et al. (1999) concluded that cognitive therapy was superior on several variables. Patients with general anxiety disorder made more positive changes in symptoms, significantly reduced medication usage, and were more positive about treatment when they received cognitive therapy than when they received analytic therapy.

Just as measuring change in therapeutic treatment is difficult, so are measurement and validation of a variety of concepts that make up Freud's developmental stages and his propositions concerning defense mechanisms. Schultz and Schultz (2009) review studies on defense mechanisms such as denial, projection, and repression. They also summarize research that attempts to validate the importance of the first 5 years of life in determining later personality characteristics. Research on 4- to 6-year-old boys does not support Freud's concept of the Oedipus complex. Still other research has investigated the existence of oral, anal, and phallic personality types with only limited support for these types, especially the phallic type. More than 2,500 studies have been done to investigate a variety of these and other concepts developed by Freud (Fisher & Greenberg, 1996).

Research related to object relations theory, known as attachment theory, has studied the infant–mother bond and has been plentiful, as attested to by the work of Ainsworth (1982) and Bowlby (1969, 1973, 1980). In research in Uganda and in the United States, Ainsworth and others (for example, Main & Solomon, 1986) have observed four patterns of mother–infant attachment: secure, ambivalent, avoidant, and disorganized. Secure attachment occurs when infants protest when their mothers separate from them but then greet them with pleasure upon return. If their mothers attempt to leave the room, ambivalently anxious babies become insecure and tend to cling to their mothers, and they become agitated when separated. Avoidant infants appear to be independent and may avoid their mothers when they return to the room. Disorganized babies display disoriented or highly unusual patterns of behavior upon their mothers' return. Ainsworth and others have related these types of attachment to the mother to later childhood and adolescent behavior, which may include solitary play, emotional detachment, and problems in relating to others.

Recent psychoanalytic researchers have shown how attachment theory is relevant to psychoanalysis. Target (2005) explains how attachment theory provides an excellent means for understanding early and later emotional relationships of patients as well as traumatic experiences. Viewing the therapist as a secure base and relating this perspective to different attachment styles can help therapists in their psychoanalytic sessions (Eagle & Wolitzky, 2009). In therapy, attachment theory helps to explain the importance of the patients' sense of feeling understood as a part of a secure attachment experience (Eagle, 2003). Rendon (2008) demonstrates how new developments in neurobiology provide more areas for research into attachment concepts. Applying attachment research to psychoanalytic therapy is explained more fully in *Attachment Theory and Research in Clinical Work with Adults* (Obegi & Berant, 2009).

The challenges to researchers in working with psychoanalytic theory include many complex issues and willingness to devote several years or more to a research study (Eagle, 2007; Wallerstein, 2009). The research of Wallerstein, Luborsky, Ainsworth, and Bowlby represents, in most cases, more than 30 years of significant effort from each investigator. Although the work of Ainsworth and Bowlby is not as directly related to psychoanalytic concepts, it can provide evidence for understanding issues and concepts that inform the practice of psychoanalysis.

Gender Issues

More than other theories of psychotherapy, Freud's view of the psychological development of women and his view of women in general have been subject to criticism. As early as 1923, Horney (1967) criticized Freud's concept of penis envy as it showed that women were inferior to men because, during the Oedipal stage, they felt inferior to boys because they did not have penises. In reviewing Freud's writings on female sexuality, Chasseguet-Smirgel (1976) sees Freud's view as a series of lacks: The female lacks a penis, lacks complete Oedipal development, and lacks a sufficient superego because of the lack of castration anxiety, which in boys brings on internalization of society's values. A number of writers (for example, Chodorow, 1978; Sayers, 1986) have criticized Freud for believing that women should be subordinate, in many ways, to men.

Chodorow (1996a, 1996b, 1999, 2004) expresses concern that psychoanalysts will tend to make broad generalizations about women and not pay attention to their individuality. She emphasizes the importance of being open to the varied fantasies and transference and countertransference relationships that exist in client–therapist relationships. This focus on not generalizing and not thinking in universal concepts also reflects the view of Enns (2004) in her critique of Freudian psychoanalysis and object relations psychology.

Object relations theorists have been criticized because of their emphasis on the child–mother rather than the child–parent relationship. Chodorow (1978, 2004) argues that early relationships between mother and daughter and mother and son provide different relational experiences for boys and girls. She compares the mother–father–son triangle, in which the boy must assert himself and repress feelings, to the mother–father–daughter triangle, in which daughters can see themselves as substitutes for the mother and not develop a fully individuated sense of self. Describing her view of how parent–child relationships should change, she says:

> Children could be dependent from the outset on people of both genders and establish an individuated sense of self in relation to both. In this way, masculinity would not become tied to denial of dependence and devaluation of women. Feminine personality would be less preoccupied with individuation, and children would not develop fears of maternal omnipotence and expectations of women's unique self-sacrificing qualities. (Chodorow 1978, p. 218)

Gender issues arise not only in psychoanalytic personality theory but also in the practice of psychoanalytic treatment. Examining why female and male patients may seek therapists of the same or the other gender, Deutsch (1992) and Person (1986) present several views. Female patients may be concerned that male therapists are sexist and cannot understand them, they may want female role models, and they previously may have been able to confide in women. Some women may prefer a male therapist because of their interactions with their fathers, societal beliefs in men as more powerful, and negative attitudes toward their mothers. In a similar fashion, male patients may prefer male or female therapists depending on their prior interaction with their mothers or fathers. Some male patients, also, may have a societal expectation that female therapists are more nurturing than male therapists. Sometimes patients may also be afraid of an erotic feeling toward a therapist of the other sex.

Because gender issues have been discussed and written about widely and psychoanalytic theory has emphasized attention to countertransference feelings, many psychoanalytic practitioners are attuned to gender issues with their patients. However, some writers continue to be concerned about gender bias they believe is contained within psychoanalytic theory itself.

Multicultural Issues

The formulations of psychoanalysis began in Vienna in the 1890s. How appropriate are they then, more than 100 years later, for people in many different societies throughout the world? Clearly, there is disagreement as to whether Freud's view of psychoanalysis can transcend time and geography. In a sense, the developments of ego psychology, object relations, and self psychology may reflect, in a small way, responses to different cultural factors. For example, Freud was most concerned with treating patients with neurosis, especially hysteria. Later theorists such as Kernberg and Kohut addressed the more severe disorders—borderline and narcissistic—that they frequently encountered. Freud's concept of the Oedipal complex may be particularly vulnerable to social and cultural factors. In cultures where the father is available for only brief periods of time, the concept of love for the mother and anger (for boys) toward the father may be different than where the father plays a major role in the child's life. To the extent that object relations psychology deals with early maternal relations, it may be less culture bound. For example, in the first month of life, it is usually common for the infant to be cared for by the mother. However, shortly thereafter, the major relationship the infant has can be with the mother or with a grandmother, aunt, older sister, father, nursery school teacher, or foster parent. In general, cultural and social factors have been less important to psychoanalytic theorists than internal psychological functioning (Chodorow, 1999).

A notable contribution to cultural concerns has been the early work of the ego psychologist Erik Erikson. Many of Erikson's writings (1950, 1968, 1969, 1982) show his interest in how social and cultural factors affect people of many cultures throughout the life span. Of particular interest are his studies of the child-raising practices of Native Americans (the Sioux in South Dakota and the Yurok on the Pacific coast) that gave him a broad vantage point to view cultural aspects of child development. Few other psychoanalytic writers have been as devoted to cross-cultural concerns as Erikson. Although there are cultural differences in ways children separate from their parents in terms of going to school, college, working, and leaving home, object relations theorists, relational theorists, and self psychologists have concentrated on the similarity of developmental issues rather than on cultural differences. Understanding how race and culture interact with psychoanalytic principles in drive, ego psychology, object relations, and relational psychology continues to be an area of study in psychoanalysis (Mattei, 2008).

Reaching out to diverse populations has been a recent thrust of psychoanalytic therapists. Jackson and Greene (2000) show many ways that psychoanalytic techniques, such as transference, can be applied to African American women. Greene (2004) believes that psychodynamic approaches have become more sensitive toward, and therefore more appropriate for, African American lesbians. Thompson (1996) and Williams (1996) discuss how skin color is an important issue to be dealt with in psychodynamic therapy. With African American and Hispanic clients, they point out how client perceptions of self are related to issues of not being sufficiently light or dark colored, particularly in comparison to other family members. They also discuss how skin color can affect the transference relationship with the therapist. When therapists are from a minority culture, this can have an impact on transference relationships and on understanding resistance in dealing with patients from a majority culture. Addressing the appropriateness of psychoanalysis in Arab-Islamic cultures, Chamoun (2005) sees difficulty in the acceptance of psychoanalysis due to conflicts with religious and other cultural values. In *The Crescent and the Couch: Cross-currents Between Islam and Psychoanalysis* (Akhtar, 2008), 18 chapters describe various issues such as sexual values, the structure of the family, and the formation of religious identity that relate to the application of psychoanalysis to individuals who have Islamic beliefs.

Another area of exploration has been the effect of bilingualism on psychoanalysis. Javier (1996) and Perez Foster (1996) discuss how the age at which a language is acquired can affect the reconstruction of early memories. Also, when the therapist speaks only English and the patient speaks another language as her primary language, a variety of transference or resistance issues can result. Both authors describe how the formation of defense mechanisms can be related to language acquisition and the way language can organize experience. In a case study where both therapist and patient shared a similar cultural background (being Hispanic and speaking Spanish), cultural issues were discussed such as the differences in reactions of therapist and patient when therapy was conducted in English versus Spanish (Rodriguez, Cabaniss, Arbuckle, & Oquendo, 2008).

Group Therapy

In trying to help their patients through group therapy, psychoanalytic practitioners attend to unconscious determinants of behavior that are based on early childhood experience. Although group psychoanalysis can be traced to the work of Sandor Ferenczi, a student of Freud's (Rutan, 2003), many of the conceptual approaches to group therapy have taken a drive–ego psychology approach (Rutan, Stone, & Shay, 2007; Wolf, 1975; Wolf & Kutash, 1986), attending to repressed sexual and aggressive drives as they affect the individual's psychological processes in group behavior. Additionally, group leaders observe the use of ego defenses and ways in which Oedipal conflicts affect the interactions of group members and the group leader. As object relations theory has become more influential, some group leaders have focused on issues of separation and individuation as they affect individuals' psychological processes in group interactions. Such leaders may attend to how group participants deal with dependency issues with the group leader and other participants by examining how they react to group pressures and influences. Using the self psychology view of Kohut, group leaders may focus on the ability of patients to be empathic to other group members and to relate in a way that integrates self-concern with concern about others.

A brief insight into the working of psychoanalytic groups is provided by Wolf and Kutash (1986) in their description of different types of resistance group leaders may encounter. Some group members may be "in love with" or attach themselves first to the therapist and then to one and then perhaps another group member. Others may take a parental approach to the group, trying to dominate it; yet others may observe the group rather than participate. Still others may analyze other members of the group but evade examination of themselves. All of these examples divert attention away from the patient's awareness of his own mental processes and the issues he struggles with.

As in individual psychoanalytic therapy, techniques such as free association and interpreting observations based on dreams, resistances, transference, and the working alliance (Corey, 2008; Rutan, Stone, & Shay, 2007) are used. Additionally, group leaders encourage members to share insights and interpretations about other group members. In group, members may be asked to free-associate to their own fantasies or feelings, to free-associate to the material of others (Wolf, 1963), or to free-associate to their own or others' dreams. When group leaders interpret this material, they make hypotheses about the underlying meaning of unconscious behavior (Corey, 2009). In a similar way, when members share their insights about the behaviors of others, group members can learn from these interpretations. If the insight is poorly timed or not accurate, the person to whom it is directed is likely to reject it. Providing dream material, free-associating, and interpreting are often very important aspects of group. When members discuss and interpret someone else's dreams, they may also be learning about important aspects of themselves. As in individual therapy, the working alliance is important. In a small study of psychodynamic group therapy, Lindgren, Barber, and Sandahl (2008) showed how alliance to the group-as-a-whole at the half-way point in therapy was related to the outcome of therapy. Although the leader must attend to a multitude of transference reactions among the group members, between the leader and each of the group members, and between the leader and the group as a whole, group therapy can provide a broader opportunity for individuals to understand how their unconscious processes affect themselves and others than does individual therapy.

Summary

Since the development of psychoanalysis in the late 1800s, psychoanalytic theory has continued to be a powerful force in psychotherapy. Today, many practicing psychoanalysts and psychoanalytic therapists not only make use of Freud's concepts but also incorporate later developments that make use of Freud's constructs of conscious and unconscious. Many incorporate his personality constructs of ego, id, and superego. However, relatively few rely only on his conceptualization of psychosexual stages—oral, anal, phallic, latency, and genital. Ego psychologists, including Anna Freud and Erik Erikson, have stressed the need to adapt to social factors and to assist those with problems throughout stages that encompass the entire life span. Adding to this rich body of theory has been the work of object relations theorists, who have been particularly concerned with childhood development before the age of 3, the way infants relate to people around them, particularly their mothers, and how the disruptions in early relationships affect later psychological disorder. The perspective of self psychology has been on a natural development of narcissism evolving from the self-absorption of infants and on how problems in early child–parent relationships can lead to feelings of grandiosity and self-absorption in later life. Relational psychoanalysts may consider issues raised by all these theorists as well as attention to the existing patient–therapist relationship. In their work, psychoanalytic practitioners may make use of any one or more of these ways of understanding child development.

Although there are a variety of conceptual approaches, most make use of techniques that Freud developed to bring unconscious material into conscious awareness. The technique of free association and the discussion of dreams provide unconscious material that can be interpreted to the patient to give insight into psychological disorders. The relationship between patient and therapist (transference and countertransference concerns) provides important material for therapeutic work. Kernberg (borderline disorders), Kohut (narcissistic disorders), and Mitchell (relational psychoanalysis) have discussed different ways that certain types of patients are likely to experience their relationship with the therapist. Because much has been written about psychoanalytic treatment, there are many ideas as well as disagreements about a variety of therapeutic issues and treatment procedures with different disorders.

Because psychoanalysis and psychoanalytic psychotherapy can be very time consuming, there have been efforts to devise methods other than traditional individual treatment. For example, group therapy can incorporate ideas from drive (Freudian), ego, object relations, self psychology, and relational psychoanalysis. Brief individual psychotherapy also makes use of similar conceptual frameworks; however, the techniques used are more direct and confrontive, and free association is often not a part of this treatment. The various ways of viewing human development and unconscious processes, combined with the development of new approaches to psychotherapy, are indications of the creativity that continues to be a hallmark of psychoanalysis.

Theories in Action DVD: Psychoanalysis

Basic Concepts Used in the Role-Play	Questions about the Role-Play
• Dream exploration • Interpretation • Encouraging insight • Interpretation and wish fulfillment	1. Why is Jeanie's dream a good source of material in psychoanalysis? (p. 51) 2. What insight did Jeanie make about her problems from discussing her problem with Dr. Justice? 3. What did Jeanie discuss with Dr. Justice that makes her a good candidate for psychoanalysis? (Hint: Family issues, see object relations, p. 41) 4. The text discusses five different psychoanalytic personality theories. Which ones would seem to fit Dr. Justice's method of conducting therapy?

Suggested Readings

As theorists create new psychoanalytic concepts, they often develop their own terms to describe them. For the reader who is not familiar with psychoanalytic concepts, this can be confusing and overwhelming. In these suggestions for further reading, I have tried to include materials that are relatively easy to understand without a broad background in psychoanalysis.

Gay, P. (1988). *Freud: A life for our time.* New York: Anchor Books. This is a well-documented biography of Freud. His family, the development of psychoanalysis, his work with patients, and his interactions with his colleagues and followers are described.

Freud, S. (1917). *A general introduction to psychoanalysis.* New York: Washington Square Press. These lectures, which make up volumes 15 and 16 of *The Complete Psychological Works of Sigmund Freud,* were given at the University of Vienna. Because he was addressing an audience that was not familiar with psychoanalysis, Freud presents a clear and readable presentation of the importance of unconscious factors in understanding slips of the tongue, errors, and dreams. Furthermore, he discusses the role of drives and sexuality in neurotic disorders.

Gabbard, G. O. (2004). *Long-term psychodynamic psychotherapy: A basic text*. Washington, DC: American Psychiatric Association. This is a brief, clearly written description of how long-term psychoanalysis is conducted. Excerpts from cases illustrate the methods used in long-term psychodynamic therapy.

McWilliams, N. (2004). *Psychoanalytic therapy*. New York: Guilford. Written for students studying to become psychoanalytic therapists, this is a very practical text that will instruct students about issues they may encounter in practicing therapy.

Horner, A. J. (1991). *Psychoanalytic object relations therapy*. Northvale, NJ: Aronson. In a clear manner, Horner describes stages of object relations development and object relations therapy. Important therapeutic issues such as transference, countertransference, neutrality, and resistance are explained. Several case examples show the application of object relations therapy.

Thorne, E., & Shaye, S. H. (1991). *Psychoanalysis today: A casebook*. Springfield, IL: Charles C. Thomas. A variety of case studies featuring patients with a wide range of disorders illustrate the application of psychoanalysis. Included in the 19 cases are dialogues between patient and therapist.

Teyber, E. (2006). *Interpersonal process in psychotherapy: An integrative model* (5th ed.). Belmont, CA: Wadsworth. This textbook is used to help students learn relational therapeutic skills. Many examples of types of relational responses are given. The book focuses on counselor responses to clients rather than on object relations or relational psychoanalysis.

References

Note: References to Sigmund Freud are from the *Complete Works of Sigmund Freud* published by Hogarth Press, London.

Abend, S. M. (2001). Expanding psychological possibilities. *The Psychoanalytic Quarterly, 70*, 3–14.

Ainsworth, M. D. S. (1982). Attachment: Retrospect and prospect. In C. M. Parkes & J. Stevenson-Hinde (Eds.), *The place of attachment in human behavior* (pp. 3–30). New York: Basic Books.

Akhtar, S. (Ed.). (2008). *The crescent and the couch: Cross-currents between Islam and psychoanalysis*. Lanham, MD: Aronson.

Arlow, J. A. (1987). The dynamics of interpretation. *Psychoanalytic Quarterly, 20*, 68–87.

Bacal, H. A., & Newman, K. M. (Eds.). (1990). *Theories of object relations: Bridges to self psychology*. New York: Columbia University Press.

Balint, M. (1952). *Primary love and psychoanalytic technique*. London: Hogarth Press.

Balint, M. (1968). *The basic fault*. London: Tavistock Publications.

Barber, J. P., Gallop, R., Crits-Christoph, P., Barrett, M. S., Klostermann, S., McCarthy, K. S., & Sharpless, B. A. (2008). The role of the alliance and techniques in predicting outcome of supportive–expressive dynamic therapy for cocaine dependence. *Psychoanalytic Psychology, 25*(3), 461–482.

Barber, J. P., Luborsky, L., Gallop, R., Crits-Christoph, P., Frank, A., Weiss, R. D., Thase, M. E., Connolly, M. B., Gladis, M., Foltz, C., & Siqueland, L. (2001). Therapeutic alliance as a predictor of outcome and retention in the National Institute on Drug Abuse Collaborative Cocaine Treatment Study. *Journal of Consulting and Clinical Psychology, 69*, 119–124.

Bion, W. R. (1963). *Elements of psycho-analysis*. New York: Basic Books.

Blanck, R., & Blanck, G. (1986). *Beyond ego psychology: Developmental object relations theory*. New York: Columbia University Press.

Bloom, B. L. (1997). *Planned short-term psychotherapy* (2nd ed.). Boston: Allyn & Bacon.

Blum, G. S. (1949). A study of the psychoanalytic theory of psychosexual development. *Genetic Psychology Monograph, 39*, 3–99.

Book, H. E. (1998). *How to practice brief psychodynamic psychotherapy: The Core Conflictual Relationship Theme method*. Washington, DC: American Psychological Association.

Bowlby, J. (1969). *Attachment and loss: Vol. 1. Attachment*. New York: Basic Books.

Bowlby, J. (1973). *Attachment and loss: Vol. 2. Separation*. New York: Basic Books.

Bowlby, J. (1980). *Attachment and loss: Vol. 3. Loss, sadness and depression*. New York: Basic Books.

Breuer, J., & Freud, S. (1895). *Studies on hysteria* (Standard Edition, Vol. 2).

Busseri, M., & Tyler, J. D. (2003). Interchangeability of the Working Alliance Inventory and Working Alliance Inventory, short form. *Psychological Assessment, 15*(2), 193–197.

Caligor, E., Diamond, D., Yeomans, F. E., & Kernberg, O. F. (2009). The interpretive process in the psychoanalytic psychotherapy of borderline personality pathology. *Journal of the American Psychoanalytic Association, 57*(2), 271–301.

Chamoun, M. (2005). Islam and psychoanalysis in the Arab-Islamic civilization/Islam et psychanalyse dans la culture Arabo-Musulmane. *Pratiques Psychologiques, 11*(1), 3–13.

Chasseguet-Smirgel, J. (1976). Freud and female sexuality. *International Journal of Psycho-Analysis, 57,* 275–287.

Chessick, R. D. (2007). *The future of psychoanalysis.* Albany: State University of New York Press.

Chodorow, N. J. (1978). *The reproduction of mothering.* Berkeley: University of California Press.

Chodorow, N. J. (1996a). Reflections on the authority of the past in psychoanalytic thinking. *Psychoanalytic Quarterly, 65,* 32–51.

Chodorow, N. J. (1996b). Theoretical gender and clinical gender: Epistemological reflections of the psychology of woman. *Journal of the American Psychoanalytic Association, 44,* 215–238.

Chodorow, N. J. (1999). *The power of feelings: Personal meaning in psychoanalysis, gender, and culture.* New Haven, CT: Yale University Press.

Chodorow, N. J. (2004). Psychoanalysis and women: A personal thirty-five-year retrospect. *Annual of Psychoanalysis, 32,* 101–129.

Clarkin, J. F., Levy, K. N., Lenzenweger, M. F., & Kernberg, O. F. (2007). Evaluating three treatments for borderline personality disorder: A multiwave study. *American Journal of Psychiatry, 164*(6), 922–928.

Corey, G. (2008). *Theory and practice of group counseling* (7th ed.). Belmont, CA: Brooks/Cole.

Crits-Cristoph, P., Connolly, M. B., Azarian, K., Crits-Cristoph, K., & Shappell, S. (1996). An open trial of brief supportive–expressive psychotherapy in the treatment of generalized anxiety disorder. *Psychotherapy, 33,* 418–430.

Crits-Christoph, P., Gibbons, M. B. C., Gallop, R., Ring-Kurtz, S., Barber, J. P., Worley, M., Present, J., & Hearon, B. (2008). Supportive–expressive psychodynamic therapy for cocaine dependence: A closer look. *Psychoanalytic Psychology, 25*(3), 483–498.

Crits-Christoph, P., Gibbons, M. B. C., Losardo, D., Narducci, J., Schamberger, M., & Gallop, R. (2004). Who benefits from brief psychodynamic therapy for generalized anxiety disorder? *Canadian Journal of Psychoanalysis, 12*(2), 301–324.

Demorest, A. (2005). *Psychology's grand theorists: How personal experience shaped professional ideas.* Mahwah, NJ: Erlbaum.

Deutsch, B. G. (1992). Women in psychotherapy. In M. J. Aronson & M. A. Scharfman (Eds.), *Psychotherapy: The analytic approach* (pp. 183–202). Northvale, NJ: Aronson.

Drapeau, M., & Perry, J. C. (2009). The core conflictual relationship themes (CCRT) in borderline personality disorder. *Journal of Personality Disorders, 23*(4), 425–431.

Durham, R. C., Fisher, P. L., Treliving, L. R., Hau, C. M., Richard, K., Stewart, J. B. (1999). One-year follow-up of cognitive therapy, analytic psychotherapy and anxiety management training for generalized anxiety disorder: Symptom change, medication usage, and attitudes to therapy. *Behavioral and Cognitive Psychotherapy, 27,* 19–35.

Eagle, M. N. (2000). A critical evaluation of current conceptions of transference and countertransference. *Psychoanalytic Psychology, 17*(1) 24–37.

Eagle, M. N. (2003). Clinical implications of attachment theory. *Psychoanalytic Inquiry, 23*(1), 27–53.

Eagle, M. N. (2007). Psychoanalysis and its critics. *Psychoanalytic Psychology, 24*(1), 10–24.

Eagle, M., & Wolitzky, D. L. (2009). Adult psychotherapy from the perspectives of attachment theory and psychoanalysis. In J. H. Obegi & E. Berant (Eds.), *Attachment theory and research in clinical work with adults* (pp. 351–378). New York: Guilford Press.

Ellenberger, H. F. (1970). *The discovery of the unconscious.* New York: Basic Books.

Enns, C. Z. (2004). *Feminist theories and feminist psychotherapies: Origins, themes, and variation* (2nd ed.). New York: Haworth.

Erikson, E. H. (1950). *Childhood and society.* New York: Norton.

Erikson, E. H. (1968). *Identity: Youth and crisis.* New York: Norton.

Erikson, E. H. (1969). *Gandhi's truth.* New York: Norton.

Erikson, E. H. (1982). *The life cycle completed.* New York: Norton.

Erikson, E. H. Extended by Erikson, J. M. (1997). *The life cycle completed.* New York: Norton.

Fairbairn, W. R. D. (1954). *An object relations theory of the personality.* New York: Basic Books.

Fisher, S. P., & Greenberg, R. P. (1996). *Freud scientifically reappraised: Testing the theories and therapy.* New York: Basic Books.

Freud, A. (1936). *The ego and mechanisms of defense.* New York: International Universities Press.

Freud, A. (1965). Normality and pathology in childhood: Assessments of development. In *Writings* (Vol. *6*). New York: International Universities Press.

Freud, S. (1894). *The neuropsychoses of defense* (Standard Edition, Vol. *3*).

Freud, S. (1900). *The interpretation of dreams* (Standard Edition, Vol. *4*).

Freud, S. (1901). *The psychopathology of everyday life* (Standard Edition, Vol. *6*).

Freud, S. (1905a). *Jokes and their relationship to the unconscious* (Standard Edition, Vol. *8*).

Freud, S. (1905b). *Three essays on sexuality* (Standard Edition, Vol. *7*).

Freud, S. (1914). *On narcissism: An introduction* (Standard Edition, Vol. *14*).

Freud, S. (1917). *Introductory lectures on psycho-analysis* (Standard Edition, Vols. *15* and *16*).

Freud, S. (1920). *Beyond the pleasure principle* (Standard Edition, Vol. *18*).

Freud, S. (1923). *The ego and the id* (Standard Edition, Vol. *19*).

Freud, S. (1926). *Inhibitions, symptoms and anxiety* (Standard Edition, Vol. *20*).

Fromm, E. (1955). *The sane society*. New York: Holt, Rinehart, and Winston.

Gabbard, G. O. (2004). *Long-term psychodynamic psychotherapy: A basic text*. Washington, DC: American Psychiatric Publishing.

Gabbard, G. O. (2005). *Psychodynamic psychiatry in clinical practice* (4th ed.) Washington, DC: American Psychiatric Publishing.

Galatzer-Levy, R. M., Bachrach, H., Skolnikoff, & Waldron, S. Jr. (2000). *Does psychoanalysis work?* New Haven, CT: Yale University Press.

Gay, P. (1988). *Freud: A life for our time*. New York: Anchor Books.

Gelso, C. J., & Fretz, B. R. (1992). *Counseling psychology*. New York: Harcourt Brace Jovanovich.

Gibbons, M. B. C., Crits-Christoph, P., & Apostol, P. (2004). *Constructing interpretations and assessing their accuracy*. Mahwah, NJ: Lawrence Erlbaum Associates.

Gibbons, M. B. C., Crits-Christoph, P., & Hearon, B. (2008). The empirical status of psychodynamic therapies. *Annual Review of Clinical Psychology, 4*, 93–108.

Goldberg, R. W., Rollins, A. L., & Mcnary, S. W. (2004). The Working Alliance Inventory: Modification and use with people with mental illness in a vocational rehabilitation program. *Psychiatric Rehabilitation Journal, 27*(3), 267–270.

Greenberg, J. R. (2001). The analyst's participation: A new look. *Journal of the American Psychoanalytic Association, 49*, 417–426.

Greenberg, J. R., & Mitchell, S. A. (1983). *Object relations in psychoanalytic theory*. Cambridge: Harvard University Press.

Greene, B. (2004). African American lesbians and other culturally diverse people in psychodynamic therapies: Useful paradigms or oxymoron? *Journal of Lesbian Studies, 8* (1-2) 57–77.

Guntrip, H. (1968). *Schizoid phenomena, object relations and the self*. New York: International Universities Press.

Hedges, L. E. (1983). *Listening perspectives in psychotherapy*. New York: Aronson.

Hedges, L. E. (1992). *Interpreting the countertransference*. Northvale, NJ: Aronson.

Hilsenroth, M. J., Ackerman, S. J., Blagys, M. D., Baity, M. R., & Mooney, M. A. (2003). Short-term psychodynamic psychotherapy for depression: An examination of statistical, clinically significant, and technique-specific change. *Journal of Nervous and Mental Disease, 191*, 349–357.

Horner, A. J. (1991). *Psychoanalytic object relations theory*. Northvale, NJ: Aronson.

Horner, A. J. (2005). *Dealing with resistance in psychotherapy*. Lanham, MD: Aronson.

Horney, K. (1937). *The neurotic personality of our time*. New York: Norton.

Horney, K. (1967). On the genesis of the castration complex in women. In K. Horney, *Feminine psychology* (pp. 37–53). New York: Norton.

Jackson, L. C., & Greene, B. (Eds.). (2000). *Psycho-therapy with African-American women: Innovations in psychodynamic perspective and practice*. New York: Guilford.

Jacobson, E. (1964). *The self and object world*. New York: International Universities Press.

Javier, R. A. (1996). In search of repressed memories in bilingual individuals. In R. M. Perez Foster, M. Moskowitz, & R. A. Javier (Eds.), *Reaching across boundaries of culture and class* (pp. 225–242). Northvale, NJ: Aronson.

Jones, E. (1953). *The life and work of Sigmund Freud: Vol. 1. The formative years and the great discoveries*. New York: Basic Books.

Jones, E. (1955). *The life and work of Sigmund Freud: Vol. 2. Years of maturity*. New York: Basic Books.

Jones, E. (1957). *The life and work of Sigmund Freud: Vol. 3. The last phase.* New York: Basic Books.

Kernberg, O. F. (1975). *Borderline conditions and pathological narcissism.* New York: Aronson.

Kernberg, O. F. (1976). *Object-relations theory and clinical psychoanalysis.* New York: Aronson.

Kernberg, O. F. (1992). *Aggression in personality disorders and perversions.* New Haven: Yale University Press.

Klein, M. (1957). *Envy and gratitude.* New York: Basic Books.

Klein, M. (1975). *Love, guilt and reparation and other works.* London: Hogarth.

Kohut, H. (1971). *The analysis of the self.* New York: International Universities Press.

Kohut, H. (1977). *The restoration of the self.* New York: International Universities Press.

Kohut, H. (1984). *How does analysis cure?* Chicago: University of Chicago Press.

Leichsenring, F., & Leibing, E. (2007). Psychodynamic psychotherapy: A systematic review of techniques, indications and empirical evidence. *Psychology and Psychotherapy: Theory, Research and Practice, 80,* 217–228.

Leichsenring, F., Rabung, S., & Leibing, E. (2004). The efficacy of short-term psychodynamic psychotherapy in specific psychiatric disorders: A meta-analysis. *Archives of General Psychiatry, 61*(12), 1208–1216.

Leiper, R., & Maltby, M. (2004). *The psychodynamic approach to therapeutic change.* Thousand Oaks, CA: Sage.

Lessem, P. A. (2005). *Self psychology: An introduction.* Lanham, MD: Aronson.

Lindgren, A., Barber, J. P., & Sandahl, C. (2008). Alliance to the group-as-a-whole as a predictor of outcome in psychodynamic group therapy. *International Journal of Group Psychotherapy, 58*(2), 163–184.

Luborsky, L. (1984). *Principles of psychoanalytic psychotherapy: A manual for supportive–expressive treatment.* New York: Basic Books.

Luborsky, L., & Crits-Christoph, P. (1998). *Understanding transference: The core conflictual relationship theme method* (2nd ed.). Washington, DC: American Psychological Association.

Luborsky, L., Crits-Christoph, P., Mintz, J., & Auberach, A. (1988). *Who will benefit from psychotherapy? Predicting therapeutic outcomes.* New York: Basic Books.

Luborsky, L., Rosenthal, R., Diguer, L., Andrusyna, T. P., Levitt, J. T., & Seligman, D. A., et al. (2003). Are some psychotherapies much more effective than others? *Journal of Applied Psychoanalytic Studies, 5*(4), 455–460.

Luyten, P., Corveleyn, J., & Blatt, S. J. (2005). *The convergence among psychodynamic and cognitive–behavioral theories of depression: A critical review of empirical research.* Leuven, Belgium: Leuven University Press (Mahwah, NJ: Lawrence Erlbaum).

Mahler, M. (1968). *On human symbiosis and the vicissitudes of individuation.* New York: International Universities Press.

Mahler, M. (1979a). *The selected papers of Margaret S. Mahler: Vol. 1. Infantile psychosis and early contributions.* New York: Aronson.

Mahler, M. (1979b). *The selected papers of Margaret S. Mahler: Vol. 2. Separation-individuation.* New York: Aronson.

Main, M., & Solomon, J. (1986). Discovery of an insecure/disorganized attachment pattern. In T. B. Brazelton & M. W. Yogman (Eds.), *Affective development in infancy.* Norwood, NJ: Ablex.

Malan, D. (1976). *Frontier of brief psychotherapy.* New York: Plenum.

Mattei, L. (2008). Coloring development: Race and culture in psychodynamic theories. In J. Berzoff, L. M. Flanagan, & P. Hertz (Eds.), *Inside out and outside in: Psychodynamic clinical theory and psychopathology in contemporary multicultural contexts* (2nd ed., pp. 245–269). Lanham, MD: Aronson.

McWilliams, N. (2004). *Psychoanalytic therapy.* New York: Guilford.

Messer, S. B., & Warren, C. S. (1995). *Models of brief psychodynamic therapy.* New York: Guilford Press.

Mishne, J. M. (1993). *The evolution and application of clinical theory: Perspectives from four psychologies.* New York: The Free Press.

Mitchell, S. A. (1988). *Relational concepts in psychoanalysis: An integration.* Cambridge: Harvard University Press.

Mitchell, S. A. (1997). *Influence and autonomy in psychoanalysis.* Hillsdale, NJ: Analytic Press.

Mitchell, S. A. (1998). The analyst's knowledge and authority. *Psychoanalytic Quarterly, 67,* 1–31.

Mitchell, S. A. (1999). Attachment theory and psychoanalytic tradition. *Psychoanalytic Dialogues, 9,* 85–108.

Mitchell, S. A. (2000). *Relationality: From attachment to intersubjectivity.* Hillsdale, NJ: The Analytic Press.

Moeller, M. L. (1977). Self and object in countertransference. *International Journal of Psychoanalysis, 58,* 365–374.

Nietzsche, F. (1937). *The philosophy of Nietzsche* (W. Wright, Ed.). New York: Random House.

Nygren, M. (2004). Rorschach comprehensive system variables in relation to assessing dynamic capacity and ego strength for psychodynamic psychotherapy. *Journal of Personality Assessment. Special Issue: Personality Assessment and Psychotherapy, 83*(3), 277–292.

Obegi, J. H., & Berant, E. (Eds.). (2009). *Attachment theory and research in clinical work with adults.* New York: Guilford.

Owen, I. R. (2009). The intentionality model: A theoretical integration of psychodynamic talking and relating with cognitive–behavioral interventions. *Journal of Psychotherapy Integration, 19*(2), 173–186.

Patton, M. J., & Meara, N. (1992). *Psychoanalytic counseling.* New York: Wiley.

Perez Foster, R. M. (1996). Assessing the psychodynamic function of language in the bilingual patient. In R. M. Perez Foster, M. Moskovitz, & R. J. Javier (Eds.), *Reaching across boundaries of culture and class* (pp. 243–263). Northvale, NJ: Aronson.

Person, E. (1986). Women in therapy: Therapist gender as a variable. In H. Meyers (Ed.), *Between analyst and patient* (pp. 193–212). Hillsdale, NJ: Analytic Press.

Pine, F. (1990). *Drive, ego, object, and self. A synthesis for clinical work.* New York: Basic Books.

Quinodoz, D. (2001). The psychoanalyst of the future: Wise enough to dare and to be mad at times. *International Journal of Psychoanalysis, 82,* 235–248.

Rendon, M. (2008). Psychoanalysis, a bridge between attachment research and neurobiology. *The American Journal of Psychoanalysis, 68*(2), 148–155.

Roazen, P. (2001). *The historiography of psychoanalysis.* New Brunswick, NJ: Transaction Publishers.

Robbins, S. B. (1989). Role of contemporary psychoanalysis in counseling psychology. *Journal of Counseling Psychology, 36,* 267–278.

Rodriguez, C. I., Cabaniss, D. L., Arbuckle, M. R., & Oquendo, M. A. (2008). The role of culture in psychodynamic psychotherapy: Parallel process resulting from cultural similarities between patient and therapist. *American Journal of Psychiatry, 165*(11), 1402–1406.

Rutan, J. S. (2003). Sandor Ferenczi's contributions to psychodynamic group therapy. *International Journal of Group Psychotherapy, 53*(3), 375–384.

Rutan, J. S., Stone, W. N., Shay, J .J. (2007). *Psychodynamic group psychotherapy* (4th ed.). New York: Guilford.

Sayers, J. (1986). *Sexual contradictions: Psychology, psychoanalysis and feminism. London:* Tavistock.

Schultz, D. P., & Schultz, S. E. (2009). *Theories of personality* (9th ed.). Belmont, CA: Wadsworth.

Sommerfeld, E., Orbach, I., Zim, S., & Mikulincer, M. (2008). An in-session exploration of ruptures in working alliance and their associations with clients' core conflictual relationship themes, alliance-related discourse, and clients' postsession evaluations. *Psychotherapy Research, 18*(4), 377–388.

Spinoza, B. (1952). *The chief works of Benedict de Spinoza.* New York: Dover Publishing.

St. Clair, M. (2004). *Object relations and self psychology: An introduction* (4th ed.). Belmont, CA: Wadsworth.

Strozier, C. B. (2001). *Heinz Kohut: The making of a psychoanalyst.* New York: Farrar, Straus, & Giroux.

Sullivan, H. (1953). *Conceptions of modern psychiatry.* New York: Norton.

Target, M. (2005). *Attachment theory and research.* Washington, DC: American Psychiatric Association.

Teyber, E. (2006). *Interpersonal process in psychotherapy: An integrative model* (5th ed.). Belmont, CA: Wadsworth.

Thompson, C. (1996). The African-American patient in psychodynamic treatment. In R. M. Pérez Foster, M. Moskowitz, & R. A. Javier (Eds.), *Reaching across boundaries of culture and class* (pp. 115–142). Northvale, NJ: Aronson.

Thorne, E., & Shaye, S. H. (1991). *Psychoanalysis today: A casebook.* Springfield, IL: Charles C. Thomas.

Tornstam, L. (1997). Gerotranscendence: The contemplative dimension of aging. *Journal of Aging Studies, 11*(2), 143–154.

Tuber, S. (2008). *Attachment, play and authenticity: A Winnicott primer.* Lanham, MD: Aronson.

Vandenbergen, J., Vanheule, S., Rosseel, Y., Desmet, M., & Verhaeghe, P. (2009). Unexplained chronic fatigue and core conflictual relationship themes: A study in a chronically fatigued population. *Psychology and Psychotherapy: Theory, Research and Practice, 82*(1), 31–40.

Wachtel, P. L. (2008). *Relational theory and the practice of psychotherapy.* New York: Guilford.

Wallerstein, R. S. (1986). *Forty-two lives in treatment: A study of psychoanalysis and psychotherapy.* New York: Guilford Press.

Wallerstein, R. S. (1989). The psychotherapy research project of the Menninger Foundation: An overview. *Journal of Consulting and Clinical Psychology, 57,* 195–205.

Wallerstein, R. S. (1996). Outcomes of psychoanalysis and psychotherapy of termination and follow up. In E. Nesessian & R. G. Kopff, Jr. (Eds.), *Textbook of Psychoanalysis* (pp. 531–573). Washington, DC: American Psychiatric Press.

Wallerstein, R. S. (2001). The generations of psychotherapy research: An overview. *Psychoanalytic Psychology*, *18*, 243–267.

Wallerstein, R. S. (2005). *Outcome research*. Washington, DC: American Psychiatric Association.

Wallerstein, R. S. (2009). What kind of research in psychoanalytic science? *The International Journal of Psychoanalysis*, *90*(1), 109–133.

Williams, A. C. (1996). Skin color in psychotherapy. In R. M. Pérez Foster, M. Moskowitz, & R. A. Javier (Eds.), *Reaching across boundaries of culture* (pp. 211–224). Northvale, NJ: Aronson.

Winnicott, D. W. (1958). *Collected papers: Through pediatrics to psychoanalysis*. New York: Basic Books.

Winnicott, D. W. (1965). *The maturational processes and the facilitating environment*. New York: International Universities Press.

Winnicott, D. W. (1971). *Playing and reality*. London: Tavistock.

Winnicott, D. W. (1975). Fear of breakdown. *International Review of Psycho-Analysis*, *1*, 103–107.

Wolf, A. (1963). The psychoanalysis of groups. In M. Rosenbaum & M. Berger (Eds.), *Group psychotherapy and group function* (pp. 321–335). New York: Basic Books.

Wolf, A. (1975). Psychoanalysis in groups. In G. M. Gazda (Ed.), *Basic approaches to group psychotherapy and group counseling* (2nd ed., pp. 101–119). Springfield, IL: Charles C. Thomas.

Wolf, A., & Kutash, I. L. (1986). Psychoanalysis in groups. In I. L. Kutash & A. Wolf (Eds.), *Psychotherapist's casebook* (pp. 332–352). San Francisco: Jossey-Bass.

Wolf, E. S. (1988). *Treating the self: Elements of clinical self psychology*. New York: Guilford.

Wurmser, L. (2009). The superego as herald of resentment. *Psychoanalytic Inquiry*, *29*(5), 386–410.

Young-Bruehl, E. (2008). *Anna Freud: A biography*. New Haven, CT: Yale University Press.

CHAPTER **3**

Jungian Analysis and Therapy

Outline of Jungian Analysis and Therapy

THEORY OF PERSONALITY

Levels of Consciousness
  The conscious level
  The personal unconscious
  The collective unconscious
Archetypes
  Symbols
Personality Attitudes and Functions
  Attitudes
  Functions
  Combination of attitudes and functions
  Function strength
Personality Development
  Childhood
  Adolescence
  Middle age
  Old age

JUNGIAN ANALYSIS AND THERAPY

Therapeutic Goals
Analysis, Therapy, and Counseling
Assessment
The Therapeutic Relationship
Stages of Therapy
Dreams and Analysis
  Dream material
  Structure of dreams
  Dream interpretation
  Compensatory functions of dreams
Active Imagination
Other Techniques
Transference and Countertransference

Jung was interested in the spiritual side of individuals, which he felt developed at or after midlife. His writings show a curiosity about patients' conscious and unconscious processes and a caring for the distress of his patients. His therapeutic approach emphasizes ways of helping patients become aware of their unconscious aspects through dreams and fantasy material and thus bring the unconscious into conscious awareness. Such an approach is designed to help individuals realize their unique psychological being. This emphasis on the unconscious can be seen in the explanation of Jung's theory of personality and psychotherapy.

Fascinated by dynamic and unconscious influences on human behavior, Jung believed that the unconscious contained more than repressed sexual and aggressive urges, as Freud had theorized. For Jung, the unconscious was not only personal but also collective. Interpsychic forces and images that come from a shared evolutionary history define the collective unconscious. Jung was particularly interested in symbols of universal patterns, called archetypes, that all humans have in common. In his study of human personality, Jung was able to develop a typology that identified attitudes and functions of the psyche that operate at all levels of consciousness. The constructs that form the basis of his theory came from observations that he made of his own unconscious processes as well as those of his patients.

History of Jungian Analysis and Therapy

National Library of Medicine

CARL JUNG

Theology and medicine, the vocations of Carl Jung's ancestors, are important aspects of Jung's development of analytical psychology and psychotherapy (Bain, 2004; Ellenberger, 1970; Hannah, 1976; Jung, 1961; Shamdasani, 2003). His paternal grandfather was a well-known physician in Basel, Switzerland, and his maternal grandfather was a distinguished theologian with an important position in the Basel Swiss Reformed Church. Additionally, eight of his uncles were pastors; thus, Jung was exposed to funerals and other rituals at an early age. Although his family was not wealthy, his family name was well known in Basel. Like his uncles, his father was a pastor; in later years he questioned his own theological beliefs.

Born in the small village of Kesswil, Switzerland, in 1875, Jung had a rather solitary and often unhappy childhood. During his early years, he was exposed to the mountains, woods, lakes, and rivers of Switzerland. Nature was to be important to him throughout his lifetime. After his first few years of school, Jung became an excellent student. During his childhood Jung had dreams, daydreams, and experiences he did not share with anyone. Seeking refuge in his attic, Jung (1961) recalled making up ceremonies and rituals with secret pacts and miniature scrolls.

After he completed secondary school, Jung enrolled in medicine at the University of Basel in 1895, having secured a scholarship. While at medical school, he continued to study philosophy and to read widely. He experienced a few parapsychological phenomena, such as a table and a knife breaking for no apparent reason, that fed his interest in the spiritual. His 1902 dissertation, *On Psychology and Pathology of So-Called Occult Phenomenon*, dealt in part with the spiritistic experiences of a 15-year-old cousin and readings on spiritism and parapsychology. This interest in parapsychology was to continue throughout his work and was reflected in his theoretical writings.

Throughout his life, Jung read widely in many fields, such as philosophy, theology, anthropology, science, and mythology. He started to learn Latin at the age of 6 and later learned Greek. Philosophically, he was influenced by

Immanuel Kant's view of a priori universal forms of perception. This concept develops the idea that individuals never perceive reality for what it is but have perceptual imperatives that affect what they believe they see, a precursor of the collective unconscious. Another influence was Carl Gustav Carus's idea that there were three levels of the unconscious, including a universal one. Somewhat similar to Carus's work was the description of three levels of unconscious functioning, one of which described a universal unconscious, as explained by Eduard von Hartmann. Both von Hartmann's and Carus's concepts of a universal unconscious influenced Jung's development of the collective unconscious. In the 18th century, Gottfried Leibniz had written about the irrationality of the unconscious, ideas that influenced Jung's concept of the unconscious. Later, Arthur Schopenhauer described irrational forces in individuals that were based on sexuality and ways in which sexuality is repressed in individual behaviors. All of these philosophical concepts can be recognized in Jung's theory of personality.

Jung's intellectual interests were broad and varied. The work of early cultural anthropologists had an impact on many of his theoretical constructs. The cultural anthropologist Johann Bachofen was interested in the social evolution of humanity and the role of symbolism across cultures. Also seeking universality across cultures, Adolf Bastian believed that the similarity of the psychology of individuals could be understood by examining the rites, symbols, and mythology of cultures. In attempting to understand the similarity of mythology and folktales throughout the world, George Creuzer saw the importance of symbolism in stories and viewed the thinking underlying the story as analogical rather than primitive or undeveloped. The emphasis these three writers gave to symbolism in many cultures had a direct impact on Jung's concept of archetypes.

On a more practical level, Jung's training with two psychiatrists, Eugen Bleuler and Pierre Janet, influenced his approach to psychiatry. Jung received psychiatric training at the Burgholzli Psychiatric Hospital in Zurich under the direction of Bleuler. While there, he and Franz Riklin used scientific methodology to further develop and study the word association test, in which people respond to specific words with the first word that comes to them. Finding that some people responded much more quickly or slowly than average to some specific words, Jung believed that these words would then carry special meaning for that person. This finding was to lead to the development of the concept of the complex. Jung believed that a complex, a group of emotionally charged words or ideas, represented unconscious memories that influenced a person's life. In 1902, he took a leave of absence from the hospital to study hypnosis in Paris with Janet. Much of Jung's training was with schizophrenic patients, and he was extremely curious about what "takes place inside the mentally ill" (Jung, 1961, p. 114).

In 1903 he married Emma Rauschenbach, who worked with him in the development of his ideas, was an analyst, and wrote *Animus and Anima* (Jung, E., 1957). Although he does not write very much about his family in his autobiography, *Memories, Dreams, Reflections* (1961), he acknowledged the importance of his family (he had four daughters and a son) in providing balance to his study of his own inner world. This was particularly important during a 6-year period when Jung did little writing or research but devoted time to exploring his unconscious through analyzing his dreams and visions. He says:

> It was most essential for me to have a normal life in the real world as a counterpoise to the strange inner world. My family and my profession remain the base to which I could return, assuring me that I was an actually existing, ordinary person. The

unconscious contents could have driven me out of my wits. But my family, and the knowledge: I have a medical diploma from a Swiss university, I must help my patients, I have a wife and five children, I live at 228 Seestrasse in Kusnacht—these were actualities which made demands upon me and proved to me again and again that I really existed, that I was not a blank page whirling about in the winds of the spirit, like Nietzsche. (Jung, 1961, p. 189)

One of the reasons for the 6 years of suffering (1913–1919) that Jung experienced was the severing of his relationship with Sigmund Freud. Both Freud and Jung had been aware of each other's work through their writings (Aziz, 2007). In March 1907 they talked together for almost 13 hours. During their 6-year relationship they corresponded frequently, and their correspondence has been preserved (McGuire, 1974). Before meeting Freud, Jung had defended psychoanalysis against attacks and was extremely interested in it, having sent a copy of *Psychology of Dementia Praecox* (Jung, 1960d) to Freud, who was impressed by it. Jung's involvement in psychoanalysis is indicated by the fact that he was the first president of the International Psychoanalytic Association. However, Jung had reservations about Freud's psychoanalysis from its inception, as he was to write later: "Before Freud nothing was allowed to be sexual, now everything is nothing but sexual" (Jung, 1954a, p. 84). Further, Jung was interested in the occult and parapsychology, ideas that Freud did not approve of. In fact, Jung was generally rejected by many psychoanalysts because of his interest in spirituality (Charet, 2000). In 1909 they traveled together to lecture at Clark University in Worcester, Massachusetts. On the trip they analyzed each other's dreams. At that time, Jung realized that the theoretical differences between Freud and himself were large, as he found himself interpreting one of his own dreams in a way that Freud would accept, rather than in a way that felt honest and accurate to Jung. Freud saw Jung as his "crown prince," as his successor. In 1910 he wrote to Jung:

> Just rest easy, dear son Alexander, I will leave you more to conquer than I myself have managed, all psychiatry and the approval of the civilized world, which regards me as a savage! That ought to lighten your heart. (McGuire, 1974, p. 300)

The reference to Alexander is a reference to Alexander the Great, with Freud being Philip, Alexander's father.

In 1911 Jung wrote *Symbols of Transformation* (1956), in which Jung described the Oedipus complex not as sexual attraction to an other-sex parent and hostile or aggressive feeling toward the same-sex parent (Freud's view) but as an expression of spiritual or psychological needs and bonds. Jung sensed that this would cost him Freud's friendship, and it probably did. In January 1913 Freud wrote Jung, stating, "I propose that we abandon our personal relations entirely" (McGuire, 1974, p. 539). Jung then resigned his editorship of the *Psychoanalytic Yearbook* and resigned as president of the International Psychoanalytical Association. Although Jung was to credit Freud for many of his ideas, they never saw each other again (Roazen, 2005). This break was difficult for Jung, as he states: "When I parted from Freud, I knew that I was plunging into the unknown. Beyond Freud, after all, I knew nothing; but I had taken the step into darkness" (Jung, 1961, p. 199). Thus, Jung's 6 years of exploration into his own unconscious started.

Following this turbulent period, Jung was extremely productive in his writing, his teaching, and his devotion to psychotherapy and his patients. Furthermore, he traveled frequently. To increase his knowledge of the unconscious, Jung felt it would be valuable for him to meet with people in primitive societies. In 1924 he visited the Pueblo of New Mexico; a year later he stayed with an African tribe in Tanganyika and also traveled to Asia. During these visits he kept diaries of his discussions with people and their shamans. Further exploration of other cultures came about through his friendship with Richard Wilhelm, an expert on Chinese writings and folklore (Stein, 2005). Jung studied alchemy, astrology, divination, telepathy, clairvoyance, fortune telling, and flying saucers to learn more about the mind, particularly the collective unconscious. In the process of learning more about a variety of myths, symbols, and folklore, Jung developed an excellent collection of books on medieval alchemy. His interest in alchemy stemmed from the symbolism that was used throughout the writings of the medieval alchemists. All of these interests represent collective imagery that is related to unconscious functioning. Jung used painting and stonework to express himself symbolically. He built a tower at the end of Lake Zurich that was a private retreat with symbolic meaning for him. Although he added to it in three later renovations, he never installed modern conveniences, as he wanted it to remain a place close to his unconscious.

Jung continued to be productive until his death on June 6, 1961. He had received honorary degrees from Harvard and Oxford and many other honors and awards. Also, he gave many interviews for television, magazines, and visitors. His productivity was enormous, with most of his work published in 20 volumes by Princeton University.

Jungian therapy and ideas related to Jung's theory continue to grow in popularity (Schultz & Schultz, 2009). Interest in Carl Jung's ideas, as represented by the popularity of Jungian associations, has been developing in the United States and throughout the world (Kirsch, 2000). Seminars and educational forums are presented both by local societies and by professional organizations.

Jungian training institutes can be found in the United States and throughout the world. There are more than 2,000 qualified Jungian analysts who are members of the International Association for Analytic Psychology. In the United States there are several training institutes, with somewhat different entrance requirements. Training requires usually more than 300 hours of personal analysis and at least 3 years of training beyond prior professional training. Coursework includes subjects such as the history of religion, anthropology, mythology, fairy tales, and theories of complexes. In addition, trainees are supervised in the analysis of patients. Working with dreams is emphasized in both coursework and therapy.

International meetings of Jungian analysts have been held every 3 years since 1958. Some of the journals that feature Jungian psychology and psychotherapy are *The Journal of Analytical Psychology*, *The Journal of Jungian Theory and Practice*, and *Jung Journal: Culture and Psyche*.

Theory of Personality

Essential to Jung's conception of personality is the idea of unity or wholeness. For Jung this wholeness is represented by the psyche, which includes all thoughts, feelings, and behaviors, both conscious and unconscious. Throughout their lives, individuals strive to develop their own wholeness. Jung viewed the self as both the center and totality of the whole personality. Another aspect of personality includes attitudes of individuals as well as ways they function psychologically. Jung also described the development of psyche in childhood, adolescence, middle age, and old age. Information for this section is drawn from Jung (1961), Harris (1996), Mattoon (1981), Schultz and Schultz (2009), Whitmont (1991), and Jung's collected works.

Levels of Consciousness

Theories in Action

In explaining an individual's personality, Jung identified three levels of consciousness. The concepts of soul, mind, and spirit exist at all levels of consciousness and include cognitions, emotions, and behaviors. The levels of consciousness that are an expression of personality include the conscious, which has as its focus the ego; the personal unconscious, which includes thoughts and memories that can be recalled or brought to a conscious level; and the collective unconscious, derived from themes and material that are universal to the human species. The study of the unconscious and archetypes, images or thoughts that represent universal ways of being or perceiving (described further on page 92), is the focus of much of Jung's writings, as well as those of Jungian analysts. Thus, in this section and in the rest of the chapter, the collective unconscious receives more attention than the conscious.

The conscious level. The conscious level is the only level that individuals can know directly. Starting at birth, it continues to grow throughout life. As individuals grow, they become different from others. This process, referred to as individuation by Jung (1959b, p. 275), has as its purpose the goal of knowing oneself as completely as possible. This can be achieved, in part, by bringing unconscious contents into "relationship with consciousness" (Jung, 1961, p. 187). As individuals increase their consciousness, they also develop greater individuation. At the center of the conscious processes is the ego.

The ego refers to the means of organizing the conscious mind. The ego selects those perceptions, thoughts, memories, and feelings that will become conscious. The organizational structure of the ego provides a sense of identity and day-to-day continuity so that individuals are not a mass of random conscious and unconscious perceptions, thoughts, and feelings. By screening out great amounts of unconscious material (memories, thoughts, and feelings), the ego attempts to achieve a sense of coherence and consistency while at the same time being an expression of individuality.

The personal unconscious. Experiences, thoughts, feelings, and perceptions that are not admitted by the ego are stored in the personal unconscious. Materials stored in the personal unconscious may be experiences that are trivial or unrelated to present functioning. However, personal conflicts, unresolved moral concerns, and emotionally charged thoughts are an important part of the personal unconscious that may be repressed or difficult to access. Often these elements emerge in dreams, as the personal unconscious, and may play an active role in the production of dreams. Sometimes thoughts, memories, and feelings are associated with each other or represent a theme. This related material, when it has an emotional impact on an individual, is called a complex.

It is the emotionality of a complex that distinguishes it from groups of related thoughts that have little emotional impact on the individual. Jung's work with Bleuler on word association led to his development of the concept of complexes. Although Adler (inferiority complex) and Freud (Oedipus complex) developed the construct of the complex in their own theories, Jung integrated the complex into his own thinking.

What distinguishes Jung's writing on complexes from that of other theorists in this book is his emphasis on the archetypal core. Thus, each complex has elements not only from the personal unconscious but also from the collective unconscious. Examples of common complexes with archetypal roots are the mother complex, the father complex, the savior complex, and the martyr complex. Such complexes could be detected from a word association test. An atypical response style was an indication that the individual had an emotional reaction to a word, which, grouped with other thematically related words, may be indicative of a complex. Because individuals are not conscious of complexes, it is the therapist's goal to make complexes conscious. Not all complexes are negative; some may be quite positive. For example, an individual who seeks political office and power may be said to have a Napoleonic complex. Such a complex may lead the individual to accomplish positive social goals for herself and her community. If the search for power cannot be satisfied, the positive complex turns into a negative one or evokes the *transcendent function*, which is a confrontation of opposites, a conscious thought and an unconscious influence. The transcendent function bridges these two opposing attitudes or conditions and in the process becomes a third force usually expressed through an emerging symbol. In a sense, an individual can transcend or rise above a conflict and see it from a different point of view. This is a core concept of Jungian theory and is thoroughly explained by Miller (2004) in his book *The Transcendent Function: Jung's Model of Psychological Growth through Dialogues with the Unconscious*. Clinically, the transcendent function can provide an opportunity for therapeutic growth in dealing with transference (Ulanov, 1997) and other issues. In their therapeutic work, analysts encounter a variety of unconscious complexes that are an important aspect of the therapeutic endeavor. Although attaching importance to complexes, Jungian analysts are particularly interested in the role of the collective unconscious in complexes and in other aspects of an individual's functioning.

The collective unconscious. The concept that most distinguishes Jung's theory of psychotherapy from other theories is that of the collective unconscious, which, in contrast to the personal unconscious, does not contain concepts or thoughts related to a specific person. Images and concepts that make up the collective unconscious are independent of consciousness (Harris, 1996; Whitmont, 1991). The term *collective* denotes materials that are common to all humans and significant to them. The *collective unconscious* refers to "an inherited tendency of the human mind to form representations of mythological motifs—representations that vary a great deal without losing their basic pattern" (Jung, 1970a, p. 228). Because all human beings have similar physiology (brains, arms, and legs) and share similar aspects of the environment (mothers, the sun, the moon, and water), individuals have the ability to see the world in some universally common ways and to think, feel, and react to the differences and commonalities in their environment. Jung was quite clear in stating that he did not believe that specific memories or conscious images were inherited. Rather, it is the predisposition for certain thoughts and ideas that is inherited—archetypes. Archetypes are ways of perceiving and structuring experiences (Jung, 1960b, p. 137). The concept of archetypes is basic to understanding Jungian psychology and is the focus of the next section.

The Most Distinguish (handwritten annotation)

Archetypes

Although they do not have content, archetypes have form. They represent the possibility of types of perceptions (Jung, 1959a, 1959c; Hollis, 2000). Basically, they take a person's reactions and put them into a pattern. Archetypes are pathways from the collective unconscious to the conscious, which may lead to an action. Jung was interested in archetypes that have emotional content and strength and that have endured for thousands of years. For example, the archetype of death carries strong emotions and is a universal experience. There are many archetypes that Jung wrote about, including birth, death, power, the hero, the child, the wise old man, the earth mother, the demon, the god, the snake, and unity. These archetypes are expressed as archetypal images, the content of which is described in the section on symbolism. Those archetypes that Jung considered most important in the composition of the personality are the persona, the anima and the animus, the shadow, and the Self (Shamdasani, 2003). Of these, the persona is the archetype that is the most related to the everyday functioning of the personality, and the Self archetype is the one that is most crucial to proper functioning of the personality.

Persona, meaning *mask* in Latin, is the way individuals present themselves in public. Individuals play various roles—parent, worker, friend. How individuals play these roles depends on how they want to be seen by others and how they believe others want them to act. People vary their personas depending on the situation, acting kindly with a child and defensively with a telemarketer. The persona is helpful in that individuals learn to control feelings, thoughts, and behaviors in specific situations. However, if the persona is valued too highly, individuals become alienated from themselves and shallow; they have difficulty experiencing genuine emotions.

Anima and *animus* represent qualities of the other sex, such as feelings, attitudes, and values. For men, the *anima* represents the feminine part of the male psyche, such as feelings and emotionality. *Animus* is the masculine part of the female psyche, representing characteristics such as logic and rationality. The idea that men and women have a part of the opposite sex within them has a basis in biology. Both sexes produce varying degrees of male and female hormones. Individuals vary as to the extent to which psychological characteristics of the other gender are a part of their personality.

An assumption inherent in the concept of the anima and animus is that women are traditionally emotional and nurturing and that men are traditionally logical and powerful. The anima and animus do not need to be viewed so narrowly. Harding (1970) described how the animus can function differently in different types of women. Emma Jung (1957) described four major archetypes that women may experience as their animus develops. Other writers have also sought to develop the concepts of anima and animus further and modify Jung's thinking (Hillman, 1985). Jung believed that men must express their anima and women their animus in order to have balanced personalities. If individuals do not do so, they run the risk of being immature and stereotypically feminine or masculine. In psychotherapy, exploration of the anima and animus may lead not only to expression of unconscious parts of an individual's personality, but also to the exploration of sexuality of the individual and sexuality in the transference relationship with the therapist (Schaverien, 1996).

The shadow is potentially the most dangerous and powerful of the archetypes, representing the part of our personalities that is most different from our conscious awareness of ourselves. Contained in the *shadow* are unacceptable sexual, animalistic, and aggressive impulses (Shamdasani, 2003). The raw nature of the impulsiveness of the shadow is somewhat similar to Freud's id. Jung believed that men tended to project their own shadow (negative and animalistic feelings) onto other men, causing bad feelings between men. This may explain, in part, the frequency of fights and wars between men. Although they are not manifested physically, Jung believed that women projected shadow impulses onto other women. The persona archetype, expressing itself through social expectations, serves to moderate, or keep in check, the shadow. More broadly, the shadow can be projected on many objects by both sexes.

Although this discussion presents the shadow as a negative archetype, it can have positive aspects. Appropriate expression of the shadow can serve as a source of creativity, vitality, and inspiration. However, if the shadow has been repressed, individuals may feel inhibited, out of touch with themselves, and fearful. For such individuals, the goal of therapy is to help bring their shadow into consciousness.

The Self is energy that provides organization and integration of the personality. The *Self* is the center of the personality (conscious and unconscious) and brings together conscious and unconscious processes. The Self can be seen as similar to the concept of identity formation (Roesler, 2008). For children and individuals who are relatively unindividuated, the Self may be centered in the unconscious, as they may be relatively unaware of their complexes and manifestations of their archetypes. In contrast, the *ego* is the center of consciousness, which has more limited functioning and is a part of the Self (Ekstrom & PDM Task Force, 2007). As individuals become mature and individuated, a stronger relationship develops between the ego and Self.

For Jung, the development and knowledge of the Self are the goals of human life. When individuals have fully developed their personality functions, they are in touch with the Self archetype and are able to bring more unconscious material into consciousness. Because knowledge of the Self requires being in touch with both conscious and unconscious thoughts, there is an emphasis in Jungian analysis on dreams as a way to provide understanding of the unconscious processes. Furthermore, spiritual and religious experiences can bring about further understanding of the unconscious, which can then be brought into conscious awareness. To develop one's personality, therapists help patients move unconscious thoughts and feelings to consciousness.

Symbols. Archetypes are images with form but not content. Symbols are the content and thus the outward expression of archetypes. Archetypes can be expressed only through symbols that occur in dreams, fantasies, visions, myths, fairy tales, art, and so forth. Expressed in a variety of ways, symbols represent the stored wisdom of humanity that can be applied to the future. Jung devoted much effort to understanding the wide variety of symbols found as archetypal representations in different cultures.

Jung's broad knowledge of anthropology, archeology, literature, art, mythology, and world religions provided him with an excellent knowledge of symbolic representations of archetypes. For example, Jung's interest in alchemy (Jung, 1954e, 1957) helped him find symbols that represented archetypes in his patients. Alchemists, who were searching for the philosophers' stone or ways to make gold out of base metals, expressed themselves through abundant symbolic material. Jung was also well versed in mythology and fairy tales, which provided him with more material for understanding symbols. Talking to people in a wide variety of African, Asian, and Native American cultures about spirituality and dreams also helped him to increase his knowledge of symbolism. Jung's curiosity was vast. He sought to understand why so many individuals believed they had seen flying saucers. Through discussion of dreams, myths, and historical references, Jung concluded that the flying saucer represents totality, coming to earth from another planet (the unconscious), and containing strange creatures (archetypes) (Hall & Nordby, 1973, p. 115). In reaching this conclusion, Jung used what he called *amplification*, what he knew about the history and meaning of symbols such as flying saucers. Jung applied amplification to his work with his patients' dreams by learning as much as possible about a particular image within a dream. To amplify the meaning of dreams or other unconscious material, the Jungian analyst must have knowledge of the history and meaning of many symbols for many different cultures.

MANDALA

In his research on myths, alchemy, anthropology, spirituality, and other areas, Jung found that certain symbols tended to represent important archetypes. For example, a common image of the persona is the mask used in drama and in religious ceremonies. The Virgin Mary, Mona Lisa, and other well-known women represent the anima in men. Likewise, the symbols of men as Christ or King Arthur symbolize the animus in women. Evil characters such as the devil, Hitler, and Jack the Ripper may represent the shadow.

A particularly important symbol is that of the *mandala*, which represents the Self. The mandala is a circular form and usually has four sections. Symbolically it represents an effort or need to achieve wholeness. For Jung, it was a symbol for the center of the personality. Four elements can refer to fire, water, earth, and air, the four directions of the winds, or the Trinity and the Holy Mother. These are just some examples of archetypal representations that Jung and others have described.

Personality Attitudes and Functions

By making observations of himself and his patients, Jung was able to identify dimensions of personality that are referred to as personality types. These dimensions have both conscious and unconscious elements. The first dimensions that Jung developed are the attitudes of extraversion and introversion. Later, he developed the functions, those involved in making value judgments—thinking and feeling—and those used for perceiving oneself and the world—sensing and intuiting. Jung combined the attitudes and functions into psychological types, which have been used in the construction of the Myers-Briggs Type Indicator and similar inventories. However, he was careful to talk about these as approximations and tendencies rather than as dogmatic categories. For individuals, one function is usually more developed than others. The least developed of the four functions is likely to be unconscious and expressed in dreams and fantasies, having implications for analytical treatment (Jung, 1971).

Attitudes. *Introversion* and *extraversion* are the two attitudes or orientations in Jung's view of personality. Briefly, extraverted individuals are more concerned with their external world, other people, and other things, whereas introverted people are more concerned with their own thoughts and ideas. Introversion and extraversion are polarities, or opposite tendencies. Not only are individuals capable of being both introverted and extraverted, but they use both attitudes in their lives. As individuals develop, one of the attitudes becomes more dominant or highly developed. The nondominant attitude is likely to be unconscious and influence the person in subtle or unexpected ways. For example, introverts may find themselves attracted to and drawn to extroverts, as extraversion represents an unconscious aspect of themselves. A similar comparison could be made for extroverts. When people who are normally active and outgoing, with an interest in the world around them, become quiet and thoughtful, their introverted attitude, which is unconscious, becomes more active. Although Jung found the attitudes of introversion and extraversion to be useful dimensions of personality, he found them too simple and inadequate to explain differences between individuals (Jung, 1971).

Functions. After about 10 years of struggling with concepts that would add to the personality dimensions of attitudes, Jung designated four functions: thinking, feeling, sensing, and intuition. He explains the conceptualization of the rational functions—thinking and feeling—in this way:

> And so it came about that I simply took the concepts expressed in current speech as designation for the corresponding psychic functions, and used them as my criteria in judging the differences between persons of the same attitude-type. For instance, I took thinking as it is generally understood, because I was struck by the fact that many people habitually do more thinking than others, and accordingly give more weight to thought when making important decisions. They also use their thinking in order to understand the world and adapt to it, and whatever happens to them is subjected to consideration and reflection or at least subordinated to some principle sanction by thought. Other people conspicuously neglect thinking in favor of emotional factors, that is, a feeling. They invariably follow a policy dictated by feeling, and it takes an extraordinary situation to make them reflect. They form an unmistakable contrast to the other type, and the difference is most striking when the two are business partners or are married to each other. It should be noted that a person may give preference to thinking whether he be extraverted or introverted, but he will use it only in the way that is characteristic of his attitude-type, and the same is true of feeling. (Jung, 1971, pp. 537–538)

Thus, both *thinking* and *feeling* require making judgments. When individuals usually use thinking, they are using their intellectual functioning to connect ideas and to understand the world. When they use the feeling function, they are making decisions on the basis of having positive or negative feelings or values about subjective experiences.

Sensation and *intuition* can be considered irrational functions because they relate to perceiving or responding to stimuli. These two functions are not related to evaluation and decision making. Like thinking and feeling, sensing and intuiting represent a polarity. Sensing includes seeing, hearing, touching, smelling, tasting, and responding to sensations that are felt within one's body. It is usually physical, most often conscious, and shows an attention to detail. In contrast, intuition refers to having a hunch or a guess about something that is hard to articulate, often looking at the big picture. Frequently vague or unclear, it is usually unconscious, for example, "I have a bad impression of Joan. I don't know why but I do."

Combination of attitudes and functions.. By combining each of the two attitudes with each of the four functions, eight psychological types can be described

(Schultz & Schultz, 2009). Jung was concerned that individuals would try to put all people into the eight categories. His intent was to help in classifying information. For Jung, each individual had a unique pattern of attitudes and functions that make up his or her personality. The eight psychological types are described briefly here, focusing only on the most important characteristics, with the four functions combined with the introverted attitude in the left-hand column and the four functions combined with the extraverted attitude in the right-hand column (Myers, McCaulley, Quenk, & Hammer, 1998).

Introverted-Thinking: Such individuals like to pursue their own ideas and are not particularly concerned about having these ideas accepted. They may prefer abstract ideas to interaction with others or to making plans.

Introverted-Feeling: Strong feelings may be kept inside, erupting occasionally in forceful expression. Creative artists are likely to express their feelings through their works.

Introverted-Sensation: Such individuals may focus on the perceptions of their world, attending especially to their own psychological sensations. They may prefer artistic and creative expression to verbal communication.

Introverted-Intuition: People of this type may have difficulty communicating their own insights and intuitions because they may themselves have difficulty in understanding their own thoughts and images.

Extraverted-Thinking: Although concerned with the outside world, such individuals may try to impose their own view of the world on others. People who work in science and applied mathematics may use their thinking function to help solve real problems.

Extraverted-Feeling: Interactions with other people can often be emotional at times, but also quite sociable and friendly at other times.

Extraverted-Sensation: Experiencing sensations and participating in exciting activities, such as mountain climbing, are characteristic of this type. They often like to gather data and information and are likely to be practical and realistic.

Extraverted-Intuition: Such people enjoy novelty and promoting new ideas and concepts to others. They may have difficulty sustaining interest in one project.

Although there are many ways of assessing psychological type, the danger of over-assessing or pigeonholing people into eight categories remains. These types can best be seen as a way of understanding how Jung combines the attitudes and functions of personality in explaining individuals' characteristics.

Function strength. Because the four functions represent two polarities, thinking-feeling and sensing-intuition, individuals experience all of the four. However, all are not equally well developed in individuals. The most highly developed function, referred to as the *superior* function, is dominant and conscious. The second most developed function, the *auxiliary* function, takes over when the superior is not operating. The function that is least well developed is referred to as the *inferior* function. Unlike the superior function, which is conscious, the inferior function is repressed and unconscious, appearing in dreams and fantasies. Usually when a rational function (thinking or feeling) is superior, then a nonrational function (sensing-intuiting) will be auxiliary. The reverse is also true.

The concept of function strength or dominance can be an elusive one. Jungian analysts find it helpful to explore the inferior functions of their patients that are expressed in dreams or creative work. The following example illustrates how the inferior function was explored with an individual who was normally an introverted-thinking type. This case not only illustrates the use of Jungian type terminology but also relates it to archetypal material, in this case, the anima.

> A case will illustrate such use of inferior functions. A young engineer who had excelled in school and at college, under pressure from a demanding father, was motivated by drug experiences and peers in the counterculture to drop out of his first job after college for the purpose of exploring "varieties of religious experience." He drifted to the West Coast and lived in various communal situations, where he experimented with his sexual as well as his religious feelings. He eventually tried to exchange his dominant heterosexual adaptation for a homosexual one, but he became a most absurd and unsuccessful homosexual, affecting a mincing, false feminine persona and a whorish attitude that were in comic contrast to his normally reserved and masculine presentation of Self. He became silly and disorganized under the pressure of these experiments, and he was hospitalized for what appeared to be a psychosis. When he asked to see a "Jungian," he was referred from a day treatment center to an analyst.
>
> After some exploration, the analyst concluded that the patient, in his attempt to undo his father's excessive demands, had turned his psyche inside out. He had fled to his inferior functions in an attempt to discover parts of himself that his father could not organize for him. Normally an introverted thinking type with reliable auxiliary extraverted sensation, he had turned first to his relatively inferior introverted intuition, which he explored through drugs and through participation in a religious cult. Then communal life had stimulated his inferior extraverted feeling, which was normally carried by his anima. He became anima-identified, enacting the part of an inferior extraverted feeling woman. To be sure, he was taking revenge on his father by enacting an unconscious caricature of the "feminine" role he had felt himself to have occupied in his original relation to his father. But the entire compensation, witty though it was, was ruining his life and psychotically distorting his personality. Sadly enough, he was really very like the compulsive engineer his father had wanted him to be.
>
> The analyst took the tack of gently supporting the patient's return to adaptation through his superior functions and quietly discouraged the patient from further exploration of his inferior functions. He firmly refused the more floridly "Jungian" feeling-intuitive approach the patient had at first demanded. With this approach, the patient's near-hebephrenic silliness disappeared. He resumed heterosexual functioning, recovered his dominant introverted personality, and sought work in a less ambitious field related to engineering. (Sandner & Beebe, 1982, pp. 315–316)

Although complex, this example illustrates how a Jungian analyst might attend to inferior functions in understanding the client while supporting his introverted attitude and thinking functions.

Personality Development

Because he was more concerned with understanding the unconscious and dimensions of personality than he was with the development of personality, Jung's (1954d) stages of personality are less well developed than those of Freud or Erikson. He divided life into four basic stages: childhood, youth and young adulthood, middle age, and old age. The life stage that he was most interested in and wrote most frequently about is that of middle age.

Childhood. Jung (1954b) believed that psychic energy of children was primarily instinctual—eating, sleeping, and so forth. The parental role is to direct children's energy so that they do not become chaotic and undisciplined. Jung felt that most of the problems of childhood were due to problems at home. If problems of either or both parents could be resolved, then children's disobedient behavior and other problems would be lessened. Fordham (1996) has drawn upon object relations theory as described by Melanie Klein to develop a Jungian approach to child development. Generally, childhood is a time to separate from parents and to develop a sense of personal identity (Schultz & Schultz, 2009).

Adolescence. Adolescents may develop a variety of problems as they are faced with many life decisions, such as choice of schooling and career. Furthermore, they may experience difficulties arising from the sexual instinct, including insecurity while associating with the other sex. As they grow and develop, they may wish that they were children again, with relatively few decisions to make. These conflicts and decision points that adolescents encounter are handled differently, depending on their propensity toward introversion or extraversion. To cope with their problems, adolescents must develop an effective persona to deal with the world based on their own dominant function rather than the one imposed by parental expectations. As they enter the period of young adulthood, individuals discover their own personality and develop an understanding of their own persona.

Middle age. Jung's interest in middle age is probably explained by the fact that he experienced his own midlife crisis, in which he carefully reexamined his own inner being and explored his unconscious life through his dreams and creative work. Furthermore, many of Jung's patients were of middle age, had been successful, and were dealing with questions regarding the meaning of life. As individuals become established in their careers, their families, and their communities, they may be aware of experiencing a feeling of meaninglessness or loss in their lives (Jung, 1954f). In fact, many individuals who wish to become Jungian analysts often do so at middle age rather than in their 20s, a typical age for those seeking training in other psychotherapies. A variety of issues can be encountered at middle age or in the transition from adolescence to middle age. For example, Jung identifies the *puer aeternus*, the man who has difficulty growing out of adolescence and becoming self-responsible, as he is attached unconsciously to his mother. The term *puella aeterna*, where the attachment is to the father, is used for the woman who has difficulty accepting responsibilities of adulthood. Nevertheless, such individuals may be creative and energetic (Sharp, 1998).

Old age. Jung believed that in old age individuals spend more and more time in their unconscious. However, Jung felt that older individuals should devote time to understanding their life experiences and deriving meaning from them (Jung, 1960e). For Jung, old age was a time to reflect and to develop wisdom. Older individuals often thought about the topics of death and mortality, an issue reflected in Jung's writings and dreams (Yates, 1999). For example, Goelitz (2007) describes how dream work with the terminally ill can benefit these patients. A number of Jung's patients were of retirement age (Mattoon, 1981), reflecting his belief that psychological development continues regardless of age.

In Jungian analysis, knowledge and understanding of levels of consciousness and dimensions of personality, as well as changes in psychic energy, are significant. In particular, familiarity in dealing with the unconscious through archetypal material that is produced in dreams, fantasies, and by other means is a central focus. The overview of these elements of Jungian personality theory is related to the process of Jungian analysis and psychotherapy in the next section.

Jungian Analysis and Therapy

Much of Jungian therapy is concerned with bringing unconscious material into consciousness. To accomplish this, assessment is made through the use of projective techniques, objective instruments that measure type, and assessments of dream and fantasy material. The therapeutic relationship is a flexible one, with analysts using their information about their own psyches to guide their patients in bringing the personal and collective unconscious into awareness. To do this, much use is made of dreams, active imagination, and other methods of exploration. Another area of inquiry is transference and countertransference, which refer to an examination of relationship issues that affect the course of therapy. This section provides only a brief discussion of the important aspects of Jungian analysis and psychotherapy.

Therapeutic Goals

From a Jungian point of view, the goal of life is individuation (Hall, 1986). As mentioned, individuation refers to a conscious realization of psychological reality that is unique to oneself. As individuals become aware of their strengths and limitations and continually learn about themselves, they integrate conscious and unconscious parts of themselves. In her brief description of the goals of analysis, Mattoon (1986) describes the goal of Jungian analysis as the integration of the conscious and unconscious to achieve a sense of fullness, leading to individuation.

Goals of Jungian therapy can depend on the developmental stage of the patient (Harris, 1996), whether childhood, adolescent, midlife, or old age. For children, the goal may be to help them in problems that interfere with their Self archetype (normal development). In adolescence and early adulthood there is often a focus on identity and understanding more about one's Self than one's persona. In midlife, goals can shift from pragmatic ones of earning a living and being responsible for a family to less material and more spiritual aspects of one's life. For people 70 or older, seeing life as a whole process and developing serenity are some of the goals of therapy. Of course, individuals may have other goals as well, but these are common ones that are related to stages in the life span.

Analysis, Therapy, and Counseling

Although writers disagree somewhat in their definitions of Jungian analysis, psychotherapy, and counseling, the term *Jungian analyst* is reserved for those who are officially trained at institutions certified by the International Association for Analytical Psychology. In contrasting Jungian psychotherapy with Jungian analysis, Henderson (1982) believes analysis is more intensive than psychotherapy, involving several sessions a week over a long period of time. For Henderson, psychotherapy is briefer, allowing therapists to provide crisis intervention and to meet immediate needs for psychological insight. In contrast, Mattoon (1981) sees no clear distinction between psychotherapy and analysis in terms of method or content. However, she acknowledges that many Jungian analysts believe that analysis deals more with unconscious material, especially dreams, than does therapy. With regard to counseling, Mattoon sees counselors as usually working less with unconscious material than therapists or analysts. Perhaps a reason for this variation in opinion is that Jungian analysts themselves have varied backgrounds (psychology, social work, the ministry, or employment not associated with the helping professions). Many become analysts in their 30s or 40s as a "second career" (Hall, 1986). In general, the more exposure that counselors and psychotherapists have had to Jungian emphasis on the unconscious through their own analysis and specific training, the more likely they are to be comfortable using unconscious materials in their work.

Assessment

The range of assessment methods used by Jungian analysts varies from objective and projective personality tests to the use of their own dreams. Although Jung had few standardized measures of personality available, he used a broad variety of ways of understanding his patients. As diagnostic classification systems were developed (*Diagnostic and Statistical Manual [DSM] II, III, and IV-TR*), there have been some limited attempts to relate Jungian typology to diagnostic categories and many criticisms of the DSM-IV (Ekstrom & PDM Task Force, 2007). When projective tests were being developed, the test developers' familiarity with Jungian psychology had an impact on their design. Perhaps the greatest effort in assessment of Jungian concepts has been that of objective inventories that attempt to measure psychological type. All of these efforts can be traced to Jung's creative approach to assessment.

Jung's description of four methods of understanding patients (word association, symptom analysis, case history, and analysis of the unconscious) can best be put in perspective through understanding his subjective and humane approach to therapy.

> Clinical diagnoses are important, since they give the doctor a certain orientation; but they do not help the patient. The crucial thing is the story. For it alone shows the human background and the human suffering, and only at that point can the doctor's therapy begin to operate. (Jung, 1961, p. 124)

Given this caution, Jung described four methods of learning about patients. First, the word association method that he had developed in his work with Riklin (Jung, 1973) provided a way of locating complexes that might disturb the individual (p. 157) and allowed exploration of the unconscious. Second, hypnosis was used to bring back painful memories. Called *symptom analysis*, Jung felt it to be helpful only for posttraumatic stress disorders. Third, the case history was used to trace the historical development of the psychological disorder. Jung found that this method was often helpful to the patient in bringing about changes of attitude (Jung, 1954a, p. 95). Although this method can bring certain aspects of the unconscious into consciousness, the fourth method, analysis of the unconscious, was the most significant for Jung. To be used only when the conscious contents are exhausted, approaches to its exploration varied, usually including attention to the patient's archetypal material as related in fantasies and dreams. In the following case, Jung gives an example of how he used his own dream about a patient (and thus his unconscious) to further the analysis of the patient. Using and interpreting their own dreams is a method used by some psychoanalytic and Jungian therapists (Spangler, Hill, Mettus, Guo, & Heymsfield, 2009).

> I once had a patient, a highly intelligent woman, who for various reasons aroused my doubts. At first the analysis went very well, but after a while I began to feel that I was no longer getting at the correct interpretation of her dreams, and I thought I also noticed an increasing shallowness in our dialogue. I therefore decided to talk with my patient about this, since it had of course not escaped her that something was going wrong. The night before I was to speak with her, I had the following dream.
>
> I was walking down a highway through a valley in late-afternoon sunlight. To my right was a steep hill. At its top stood a castle, and on the highest tower there was a woman sitting on a kind of balustrade. In order to see her properly, I had to bend my head far back. I awoke with a crick in the back of my neck. Even in the dream I had recognized the woman as my patient.
>
> The interpretation was immediately apparent to me. If in the dream I had to look up at the patient in this fashion, in reality I had probably been looking down on her. Dreams are, after all, compensations for the conscious attitude. I told her of the dream and my interpretation. This produced an immediate change in the situation, and the treatment once more began to move forward. (Jung, 1961, p. 133)

Although Jung used a highly personal approach to understanding clients, his theory of personality has had an impact on the development of two significant projective techniques: the Rorschach Test and the Thematic Apperception Test (TAT). As Ellenberger (1970) states, Hermann Rorschach was interested in Jung's typology, particularly the introversion and extraversion functions as they related to his development of the Rorschach Psychodiagnostic Inkblot Test. Of the several methods that have been used to score the Rorschach, one of the better known ones was developed by Bruno Klopfer, a Jungian analyst. Other Jungian analysts have contributed to the development of the Rorschach, especially McCully (1971). The originator of the TAT, Henry Murray, studied with Jung in Zurich and was involved in starting the first Jungian training institute. With regard to the use of the Rorschach and the TAT, there are wide variations among Jungian analysts, with some preferring one projective test over the other, no test, or objective tests of psychological types.

Three objective measures of types have been developed: the Gray-Wheelwright Jungian Type Survey (GW; Wheelwright, Wheelwright, & Buehler, 1964), the Myers-Briggs Type Indicator (MBTI; Myers, McCaulley, Quenk, & Hammer, 1998), and the Singer-Loomis Inventory of Personality (SLIP; Singer & Loomis, 1984). All instruments give scores on a variety of combinations of the functions and attitudes described on page 93. The GW has been used for more than 50 years by some Jungian analysts, whereas the SLIP has been developed within the last 20 years. By far the most widely known is the MBTI, used by many counselors and helping professionals to assist individuals in understanding how they make decisions, perceive data, and relate to their inner or outer world (Sharf, 2010). The MBTI is often used without relating its concepts to broader

Jungian theory. Both the GW and the MBTI use a bipolar assumption, whereas the SLIP does not (Arnau, Rosen, & Thomson, 2000). For instance, thinking and feeling are opposite ends of a bipolar scale, whereas in the SLIP each function is paired with each attitude to develop eight separate scales. The data these instruments have provided are discussed in the research section of this chapter. Although these instruments are objective measures of Jung's typology, his typology does not relate directly to DSM-IV categories.

The Therapeutic Relationship

Accepting the patient and his psychological disturbance and unconscious processes were essential for Jung. In fact, he was often fascinated by severely disturbed patients who had been hospitalized with psychoses for many years. His colleagues, including Sigmund Freud, sometimes found this perplexing, as they did not share his interest. Jung saw the role of the analyst as using personal experience to help the patient explore his own unconscious. Previous experience as an analysand gives the analyst a respect for the difficult process of exploring the human psyche. The importance of this can be seen by the following quotation:

> The psychotherapist, however, must understand not only the patient; it is equally important that he must understand himself. For that reason the sine qua non is the analysis of the analyst which is called the training analysis. The patient's treatment begins with the doctor. Only if the doctor knows how to cope with himself, and his own problems will he be able to teach the patient to do the same. Only then. In the training analysis the doctor must learn to know his own psyche and to take it seriously. If he cannot do that, the patient will not learn either. (Jung, 1961, p. 132)

Essential to Jung's approach to therapy was his humanness. This can be seen in the concept of the "wounded healer" (Samuels, 2000; Sharp, 1998). The analyst is touched by the patients' pain (angry and hurtful forces represented by the shadow). The analyst's awareness of changes in her own unconscious, as represented by her shadow (for example, through tightening in the stomach), can provide insight into a variety of patients' problems. Such reactions can lead to many choices of interventions by Jungian therapists as they did for Jung himself.

> Naturally, a doctor must be familiar with the so-called "methods." But he must guard against falling into any specific routine approach. In general one must guard against the theoretical assumptions. Today they may be valid, tomorrow it may be the turn of other assumptions. In my analyses they play no part. I am unsystematic very much by intention. To my mind, in dealing with individuals, only individual understanding will do. We need a different language for every patient. In one analysis I can be heard talking the Adlerian dialect, in another the Freudian. (Jung, 1961, p. 131)

Although Jung took what might be called an individualistic and patient-oriented approach to his psychiatric work, he and others have proposed stages of the process of analysis to provide a clearer understanding of analytical work.

Stages of Therapy

To further describe analytic therapy, Jung outlined four stages (G. Adler, 1967, p. 339; Jung, 1954c). These stages represent different aspects of therapy that are not necessarily sequential and not represented in all analyses. The first stage is that of catharsis, which includes both intellectual and emotional confession of secrets. The second, elucidation, or interpretation, borrows from Freud and relies heavily on interpretation of the transference relationship. The third stage makes use of some of the insights of Alfred Adler, who focused on the social needs of individuals and their striving for superiority or power. At this point, there is a need for social education or relating the patient's issues to society. The fourth stage, "transformation" or "individuation," goes beyond the need to be fulfilled socially to focus on individuals' understanding of their unique patterns and their individual personalities.

Theories in Action

Dreams and Analysis

For Jung, dream interpretation was the core of analysis. "Dreams are neither mere reproductions of memories nor abstractions from experience. They are the undisguised manifestation of unconscious creativity" (Jung, 1954a, p. 100). Also, dreams are a symbolic representation of the state of the psyche (Hall, 1986, p. 93). Although dreams were important for Jung, not all dreams were of equal value. He distinguished between "little" and "big" dreams. More common than big dreams, little dreams come from the personal unconscious and are often a reflection of day-to-day activity. "Significant dreams, on the other hand, are often remembered for a lifetime, and not infrequently prove to be the richest jewel in the treasure-house of psychic experience" (Jung, 1960c, p. 290). Images within big dreams are symbols of still unknown or unconscious material. Before discussing the interpretation of dreams, practical considerations in recovering dream material, as well as the structure of dreams, are examined.

Dream material. The sources of dream material are varied. They may include memories of past experiences, important events in the past that were repressed, unimportant daily or past events, and memories of deeply disturbing secrets. Sometimes the dream comes from physical stimuli such as a cold room or a need to urinate. Sources of the dream are not important; what is important is the meaning that the images have for the dreamer (Mattoon, 1981).

To remember dreams and their images is not always easy. Most analysts advise patients to record their dreams on a notepad as soon as possible, even if the dreams are remembered during the middle of the night. A tape recorder may also be used instead of a notepad. Although dreams often are forgotten soon after a person wakes, sometimes they may come into memory shortly after one awakens. As much information about the dream as can be remembered, including small details, should be recorded, as details are often symbolically significant and may turn an otherwise little dream into a significant dream (Harris, 1996). When dreams are fully remembered, they usually follow a particular structure.

Structure of dreams. Although reported dream narratives vary widely in their content, many have four basic elements (Jung, 1961, pp. 194–195). Dream narratives begin with an exposition that describes the place of the dream, the major characters in the dream, the relationship of the dreamer to the situation, and sometimes the time: "I was in a barn with my sister, and a farmer was bringing in a load of hay. It was early evening and we were tired." The second part of the dream is the plot development, an indication of the tension and conflicts developing in the dream: "The farmer was angry at us and wanted us to unload the hay quickly into the barn." The third part is the decisive event, in which a change takes place in the dream: "The farmer's face turned wild and menacing. He got off the tractor and came for us." The last phase of the dream is the conclusion or solution: "My sister and I went out two different open barn doors.

I ran as fast as I could, but the farmer was close on my heels with a hay fork. I awoke breathing rapidly." By learning the full structure of the dream, analysts can make sure that details are not overlooked and that parts are not missing. Of course, sometimes the dreamer can remember only parts or fragments of a dream. Such fragmentary dreams require more caution in interpretation than fully remembered dreams.

Dream interpretation. Jung's goal in dream interpretation was to relate the symbolic meaning of the dream to the conscious situation of the patient (Jung, 1960c). How he approached dream analysis depended on the nature of the dream. Sometimes the images reflected personal associations and other times archetypal associations. Furthermore, he looked for continuity among dream images or patterns of dreams and attended to the subjective or objective meaning of the images within the dream.

Dreams that reveal personal associations are those that relate to the dreamer's own waking life. Such dreams may need to be interpreted not only in terms of the daily events of an individual but also in terms of information about her family, past, friends, and cultural background. Although dreams with personal associations occur much more frequently than those with archetypal associations, the significance of both can be profound.

The following dream, which was related to Jung by an acquaintance, can help illustrate the great significance that Jung attached to dreams. In this case, the dreamer did not see the associations that Jung (1954b) did:

The dreamer was a man with an academic education, about fifty years of age. I knew him only slightly, and our occasional meetings consisted mostly of humorous gibes on his part at what we called the "game" of dream interpretation. On one of these occasions he asked me laughingly if I was still at it. I replied that he obviously had a very mistaken idea of the nature of dreams. He then remarked that he had just had a dream which I must interpret for him. I said I would do so, and he told me the following dream:

He was alone in the mountains, and wanted to climb a very high, steep mountain which he could see towering in front of him. At first the ascent was laborious but then it seemed to him that the higher he climbed the more he felt himself being drawn towards the summit. Faster and faster he climbed, and gradually a sort of ecstasy came over him. He felt he was actually soaring up on wings, and when he reached the top he seemed to weigh nothing at all, and stepped lightly off into empty space. Here he awoke.

He wanted to know what I thought of his dream. I knew that he was not only an experienced but an ardent mountain climber, so I was not surprised to see yet another vindication of the rule that dreams speak the same language as the dreamer. Knowing that mountaineering was such a passion with him, I got him to talk about it. He seized on this eagerly and told me how he loved to go alone without a guide, because the very danger of it had tremendous fascination for him. He also told me about several dangerous tours, and the daring he displayed made a particular impression on me. I asked myself what it could be that impelled him to seek out such dangerous situations, apparently with an almost morbid enjoyment. Evidently a similar thought occurred to him, for he added, becoming at the same time more serious, that he had no fear of danger, since he thought that death in the mountains would be something very beautiful. This remark threw a significant light on the dream. Obviously he was looking for danger, possibly with the unavowed idea of suicide. But why should he deliberately seek death? There must be some special reason. I therefore threw in the remark that a man in his position ought not to expose himself to such risks. To which he replied very emphatically that he would never "give up his mountains," that he had to go to them in order to get away from the city and his family. "This sticking at home does not suit me," he said. Here was a clue to the deeper reason for his passion. I gathered that his marriage was a failure, and that there was nothing to keep him at home. Also he seemed disgusted with his professional work. It occurred to me that his uncanny passion for the mountains must be an avenue of escape from an existence that had become intolerable to him. I therefore privately interpreted the dream as follows: Since he still clung on to life in spite of himself, the ascent of the mountain was at first laborious. But the more he surrendered himself to his passion, the more it lured him on and lent wings to his feet. Finally it lured him completely out of himself: he lost all sense of bodily weight and climbed even higher than the mountain, out into empty space. Obviously this meant death in the mountains.

After a pause, he said suddenly, "Well, we've talked about all sorts of other things. You were going to interpret my dream. What do you think about it?" I told him quite frankly what I thought, namely that he was seeking death in the mountains, and that with such an attitude he stood a remarkably good chance of finding it.

"But that is absurd," he replied, laughing. "On the contrary, I am seeking my health in the mountains."

Vainly I tried to make him see the gravity of the situation. (Jung, 1954b, pp. 60–63)

Six months later he "stepped off into the air." A mountain guide watched him and a young friend letting themselves down on a rope in a difficult place. The friend had found a temporary foothold on a ledge, and the dreamer was following him down. Suddenly he let go of the rope "as if he were jumping into the air," as the guide reported afterwards. He fell on his friend, and both went down and were killed. (Jung, 1970a, p. 208)

In contrast with dream material that has many personal associations, dreams that show archetypal associations contain material that reflects the collective unconscious rather than the personal unconscious. Because archetypes have form, but not content, analysts must use their knowledge of symbolism that is present in mythology, folklore, and religion. With this knowledge, the analyst can expand on the meaning of the material to the patient through the process of amplification.

The following brief example of symbolic dream interpretation comes from a theologian who related a recurring dream to Jung. Using biblical symbolism, information that Jung knew the dreamer was familiar with, Jung relates the dream to the dreamer, but the dreamer chooses not to accept it.

He had a certain dream which was frequently repeated. He dreamt that he was standing on a slope from which he had a beautiful view of a low valley covered with dense woods. In the dream he knew that in the middle of the woods there was a lake, and he also knew that hitherto something had always prevented him from going there. But this time he wanted to carry out his plan. As he approached the lake, the atmosphere grew uncanny, and suddenly a light gust of wind passed over the surface to the water which rippled darkly. He awoke with a cry of terror.

At first this dream seems incomprehensible. But as a theologian the dreamer should have remembered the "pool" whose waters were stirred by a sudden wind, and in which the sick were bathed—the pool of Bethesda. An angel descended and touched the water, which thereby acquired curative powers. The light wind is the pneuma which bloweth where it listeth. And that terrified the dreamer. An unseen presence is suggested, an omen that lives its own life and in whose presence man shudders. The dreamer was reluctant to accept the association with the pool of Bethesda. He wanted nothing of it, for such things are met with only in the Bible, or at most on Sunday mornings as the subjects of sermons, and have nothing to do with psychology. All very well to speak of the Holy Ghost on occasions—but it is not a phenomenon to be experienced! (Jung, 1959a, pp. 17–18)

Another important feature in interpreting dreams is to determine whether the images in the dream are to be treated objectively or subjectively. In an objective interpretation, the objects and people in the dream represent themselves. In a subjective interpretation, each object or person represents a part of the dreamer. For example, a woman who dreams of being in a restaurant and talking to a strange man can view the man in the dream as representing her animus (Jung, 1960a). In general, Jung felt an objective interpretation was usually appropriate when the people in the dream are important to the dreamer. A subjective interpretation may be appropriate when the individuals are not important to the dreamer. When making an objective interpretation, it is often helpful to see if there is a theme among the elements of the dream. For example, a woman who dreams of being in a park with young children and babies crying in the background may connect the young children and babies to the theme of birth. The Jungian analyst may choose to amplify those symbols that are related to a theme and relate them to the patient's life.

Beebe (2005) has written about three different ways of dealing with nightmares or other upsetting dreams. He believes that therapists approach these upsetting dreams differently depending on the type of dream. Some nightmares, often dramatic like movies, symbolize the dreamer's next stage of life. A second type deals with interaction with the shadow archetype of another person. The third is almost the reverse of the second. It is one in which the dreamer experiences the fears and worries of another person. The therapist should work with these dreams differently depending on the category that they fit into.

Where possible, Jungian analysts find it helpful to work with a group or series of dreams. When dreams are difficult to understand, relating them to earlier or later dreams can be helpful. Of significance are dreams that recur or have recurring themes with changing details (Mattoon, 1981). In such cases, archetypal association can be very helpful. As analysts interpret dreams, they try to assess the function of the dream for the dreamer.

Compensatory functions of dreams. Jung believed that most dreams are compensatory and part of the process of regulating the individual's personality (Whitmont, 1991). The question is what the dream does for the dreamer. By bringing unconscious material from the dream into consciousness, the dreamer may be able to determine the purpose of the dream. Dreams may compensate the conscious by confirming, opposing, exaggerating, or in some other way relating to conscious experience. However, not all dreams have a compensatory function. Some dreams may anticipate future events or actions, and others represent traumatic events from the unconscious.

To summarize, the Jungian approach to dreams is quite difficult. There is a vast amount of literature describing symbols in dreams, archetypal representations, and methods for dream interpretation. Although dreams are extremely important in the interpretive process in Jungian analysis, sometimes analysts encounter patients with few dreams. Analysts must be able to use a variety of treatment methods.

Theories in Action

Active Imagination

Jungian analysts often seek a variety of ways to allow new unconscious contents to emerge into consciousness. Active imagination is a way of helping this process. The major purpose is to let complexes and their emotional components emerge from the unconscious to the conscious (Mattoon, 1981, p. 238). Although active imagination can be done verbally or nonverbally, it is often done by carrying on an imaginary conversation with a human or nonhuman figure that may be suggested by a dream or fantasy. This approach is different than passively fantasizing about experiences or images, as it can deepen over time and cover several patient issues. Active imagination is most often done with symbols that represent archetypes such as one's anima or animus or the "wise old man" archetype. To use this approach, patients must have had much experience with analytic therapy, but still it may be difficult to learn. This method is described more fully by Watkins (2000) and Hannah (1981). An illustration of active imagination will help show the dramatic and often emotional aspects of this method.

> A patient in his thirties had a recurrent fantasy in which he felt threatened by a completely veiled dark figure. He had never been able to discover its identity. I asked him to try to concentrate on this figure instead of suppressing it. He did so and in the end could imagine how he took off veil after veil until he discovered that it was a feminine figure. He had to summon up all his courage to undo the last veil covering her face and found with a tremendous shock that the face was that of his mother. It is just the courage needed to proceed with the unveiling and the final shock of discovery that testify to the genuineness of the fantasy and to having contacted a psychic reality. (G. Adler, 1967, p. 366)

Gerhard Adler mentions that other ways of dealing with this recurrent fantasy would be to have a conversation with the figure or to ask for its name. Thus, active imagination is a method in which the ego, the center of consciousness, can relate to the collective unconscious.

In discussing countertransference, Schaverien (2007) describes how the therapist can better understand issues related to countertransference by using active imagery himself or herself. In this way the Jungian analyst allows her imagination to provide a visual or auditory image from her unconscious to her conscious, which she then has an internal dialogue with. When appropriate, she discusses this experience with the patient so that the patient may then use this discussion to bring other material from the unconscious to the conscious.

Other Techniques

Jungian analysts may use a variety of creative techniques to help unconscious processes enter into consciousness. Examples include dance and movement therapy, poetry, and artwork. Patients can use artistic expression without being conscious of what they are creating and provide material with symbolic value. Using the gestalt technique of talking to an imagined person in an empty chair may be another way of accessing unconscious material. A method that is used with both children and adults is the sandtray, a sandbox with small figures and forms that individuals can assign meaning to. Castellana and Donfrancesco (2005) point out that the figures and objects that individuals choose to place in the sandtray represent aspects of one's personality, usually aspects from the patient's unconscious. The variety of approaches that Jungian analysts use depends on their training and the needs of their patients.

Up to this point, discussion of treatment has included methods of accessing the unconscious through dream material, active imagination, and other methods. This discussion has not included examination of the relationship of the analyst and analysand. As in psychoanalysis, an important aspect of Jungian analysis is transference and countertransference. In Jungian analysis, these relationships have specific relevance to Jungian personality theory.

Transference and Countertransference

The source of transference and countertransference is projection, the process in which characteristics of one person are reacted to as if they belong to another object or person. When patients project aspects of themselves or significant others toward the analyst, this is considered transference. When analysts project their unconscious feelings or characteristics onto a patient, it is called countertransference. Both transference and countertransference can be negative, such as when either patient or analyst is frustrated with the course of therapy, and the source of the frustration is characteristic of the individual's experience, such as arguments with parents. Likewise, transference and countertransference can be positive, such as when a warm relationship with the mother is projected onto the other person. One aspect of transference and countertransference that is unique to Jungian analysis is the emphasis on the projection of not only personal experience but also archetypal material from the collective unconscious (Perry, 2008).

Jung's view of transference and countertransference changed considerably throughout his more than 50 years of writings. During the time he was heavily influenced by Freud, he generally agreed with Freud that working with transference issues was an important part of cure in analysis. When Jung devoted his studies to archetypes and their symbols, he began to feel that personal transference was not important in analysis and could be avoided. Later, however, he began to believe that transference had archetypal dimensions and devoted much effort (Jung, 1954e) to describing archetypal material that can be projected onto the therapist.

To illustrate the role of transference and countertransference in Jungian analysis, the following example of a female analyst working with a woman who is experiencing intense anxiety arising from being criticized and belittled by her mother (Ulanov, 1982) demonstrates several important issues. Ulanov describes her patient as lacking self-confidence and having much repressed anger, which is gradually realized as analysis progresses. In the following paragraph, the first sentence summarizes the transference relationship. The rest of the paragraph describes Ulanov's awareness of her own archetypal material and its role in the countertransference process.

> In the transference, she needed now to please me the way she used to try to please mother. The whole mother issue was there with us and I could feel different parts of the mother role in its archetypal form come alive in me at different times. Sometimes I would find myself wanting to react as the good mother the woman never had. Other times her frantic anxiety aroused in me the thought of brusque responses with which to put a swift end to all her dithering. Other times, such as the day the patient greeted me at the door with "I'm sorry" before she even said hello, I wanted to laugh and just get out from under the whole mother constellation. (Ulanov, 1982, p. 71)

Now, Ulanov comments on the patient's separation of the transference from the therapist to better understand her mother's criticism.

The patient's transference took her back into her actual relationship with her mother in the past. Because the patient perceived me as different from her real mother, she could risk facing her repressed angry reactions to her mother. In addition, she came to see how her mother's criticism continued to live in her own belittling attitude toward herself. (Ulanov, 1982, pp. 71–72)

Here Ulanov discusses the role of archetypal material in the patient's transference.

The issue of relating to the mother archetype arose in the midst of all of her personal struggles. For around associations and memories of her real mother, and mixed in with transference feelings to me as a mother figure, appeared images and affects, behavior patterns and fantasies, connected to relating to the archetypal mother. The patient reached to feelings of happy dependence, and which she did not experience with her real negative mother, but which can be an authentic response to the mother image. She reached to a deep sadness that her mother was so anxiously distressed herself that she could not be a secure refuge for her child. Thus she went beyond her own bruises to perceive her mother's damaged state and to feel genuine compassion for her parent. The patient could wonder about where all this led, at moments seeing her mother problem as an important thread in her own destiny, setting her specific tasks to solve. She could accept the relationship now, with all its hurts, as an essential part of her own way of life. (Ulanov, 1982, p. 72)

The patient's transference makes the analyst aware of her own issues and countertransference concerns.

On the countertransference side, I found my patient's material touched issues of my own, experienced with my own mother, some finished, and easy to keep from intruding upon the treatment, others needing more work and attention so that they did not interfere. The life issues around "the mother," good and bad, were posed for me as well, to think about, to feel again, to work on. (Ulanov, 1982, p. 72)

This example shows the interrelationship between transference and countertransference on the part of the patient and therapist. Furthermore, the use of archetypal imagery (the mother) is integrated into comments about the transference and countertransference phenomena.

Taking cues from unconscious or dream materials is a common practice among Jungian psychoanalysts when dealing with transference and countertransference issues. Furthermore, interpretations about archetypal material are frequently used throughout the process of therapy. Jungian therapists may focus more on nontransference-related content and the reality of the content of material in their interpretation of transference than psychoanalysts (Astor, 2001).

Psychological Disorders

Illustrating a Jungian approach to a variety of diagnostic psychopathological concerns is difficult for many reasons. Much of Jungian psychotherapy and analysis takes place over several years and deals with archetypal representations in the unconscious rather than behaviors related to diagnostic classification. Furthermore, some Jungian analysts combine object relations theory or Kohut's self psychology with a Jungian approach to the unconscious, making it difficult to separate Jungian analysis from other approaches. Also, it is difficult to understand a Jungian approach to analysis without knowledge of mythology and folk culture and a familiarity with the wide variety of archetypes referred to by Jungian analysts. Such detailed information is beyond the scope of this text.

Thus, the information about four diagnostic categories that is presented here does not show how all Jungian analysts would work with these disorders, but it illustrates a variety of conceptual and therapeutic approaches.

In an example of depression, a young woman is grieving over the death of her brother and the loss of romantic relationships. Working with dream material and relationships with others is illustrated. The example of anxiety neurosis disorder is used to illustrate how Jung conceptualized patient problems and how he worked therapeutically. By examining unconscious archetypal material, the conceptualization and treatment of borderline and psychotic disorders is illustrated.

Depression: Young Woman

In Jungian therapy, depression is dealt with in unique ways depending on the nature of the dream and other material the patient brings to the session. In this case, a yong woman is grieving over the death of her brother 10 years earlier and the loss of a romantic relationship. Linda Carter (Cambray & Carter, 2004) describes how she views her client's relationship with the "other" (the client's brother and the ex-boyfriend). Carter sees these "others" as possibly being helpful as guiding spirits or intrusive as ghosts. This view expresses the spiritual nature of Jungian analysis. Carter's explanation shows the nature of her relationship with her patient and how she helps the client with her losses of important relationships.

> We come to know the feeling of significant others in our analysands' lives through their implicit conveyance of them. The presence of these "others" may be helpful as guiding spirits or intrusive as ghosts in the analytic field. The memory of an inspiring teacher, for example, may manifest in the analysand's incorporation of mannerisms, gestures or voice tone. On the other hand, the incarnation of a psychotic mother may cause the analysand to experience inexplicable hyperaroused panic via the sympathetic system manifesting as anxiety or hypoaroused dissociation via the parasympathetic system causing shutdown and silence in the session. Through this implicit communication in the analytic hour and in dreams we, too, become well acquainted and respond, often preconsciously, to these embodied "others."
>
> An example of the presence of such an "other" occurred when a patient attended analysis on her brother's birthday. This brother had died 10 years before at 24 and we had been talking a good deal about him in relation to my patient's current romantic interests as they emerged in dreams. During the previous session, she had reported a dream in which a man for whom she had unrequited feelings had fallen out of a tree and died. The centrality of the relationship with her brother and the consequent loss that his death entailed powerfully affected relational, emotional, and career choices. Now this new man had become the center of longing and we discovered multiple resonances between his personality and that of her brother; however, also like her brother, he was unavailable. Subsequently, we discussed the tree as a world axis and the pivotal position that this man had symbolized in her psychic life.
>
> As my analysand reminisced fondly about her brother, his endearing qualities and quirks, I (LC) found myself enjoying his presence through her implicit knowledge of him. I knew much more than factual information, I had a "feel" for what this man had been really like. I got hold of a sense of his charm and flirtatiousness and found myself attracted to him. He was magnetic in personality and my patient

had found it hard to ever say no, even though she was aware of his inclination toward narcissistic manipulation. This pattern had replicated itself in my patient with boyfriends who were charming but emotionally unavailable. To truly develop an intimate relationship, the patient would have to face and grieve the unavailability of her brother and the man in her life who was now the focus of her attention. This process had begun as she was now letting in feelings of sadness and grief. Along with the patient, I felt the excitement of her brother's presence and subsequent gaping loss over not having access to him due first to incest barriers and then to his untimely death. I commented on the aliveness of his presence as she conveyed it and how overwhelming the loss of that presence must be. This brought a watershed of tears that gripped me as well. Implicitly her voice, facial expression, giggles over his humor and tears over his death had fully positioned him between us in the room, giving me the sense that I actually knew and recognized this complex young man. She and I experienced intense togetherness typical of a moment of meeting. We had managed to coordinate implicit knowing of her brother and of each other with explicit factual information and direct interpretation of dream symbols. Letting go of her brother as a core complex eventually opened the patient up to other creative aspects of herself and to other kinds of relational choices. In this sense, the dream imagery predicted a much needed but painful change. (Cambray & Carter, 2004; pp. 136–137)

Anxiety Neurosis: Girl

Jungian analysts differ in the role that their unconscious plays in conceptualizing and treating patients. This case shows how Jung's unconscious was an important part of his work with a woman with an anxiety disorder. Before Jung had heard of the attractive young woman he was to see the next day, he had a dream in which an unknown young girl came to him as a patient. He was perplexed by the woman in the dream and did not understand what was behind her problems. Suddenly he realized that she had an unusual complex about her father. Jung's description of the case shows the importance he attributes to therapists' and patients' spirituality in psychological health.

The girl had been suffering for years from a severe anxiety neurosis.... I began with an anamnesis (case history), but could discover nothing special. She was a well-adapted, Westernized Jewess, enlightened down to her bones. At first I could not understand what her trouble was. Suddenly my dream occurred to me, and I thought, "Good Lord, so this is the little girl of my dream." Since, however, I could detect not a trace of a father complex in her, I asked her, as I am in the habit of doing in such cases, about her grandfather. For a brief moment she closed her eyes, and I realized at once that here lay the heart of the problem. I therefore asked her to tell me about this grandfather, and learned that he had been a rabbi and had belonged to a Jewish sect. "Do you mean the Chassidim?" I asked. She said yes. I pursued my questioning. "If he was a rabbi, was he by any chance a zaddik?" "Yes," she replied, "it is said that he was a kind of saint and also possessed second sight. But that is all nonsense. There is no such thing!"

With that I had concluded the anamnesis and understood the history of her neurosis. I explained to her, "Now I am going to tell something that you may not be able to accept. Your grandfather was a zaddik. Your father became an apostate to the Jewish faith. He betrayed the secret and turned his back on God. And you have your neurosis because the fear of God has got into you." That struck her like a bolt of lightning.

The following night I had another dream. A reception was taking place in my house, and behold, this girl was there too. She came up to me and asked, "Haven't you got an umbrella? It is raining so hard." I actually found an umbrella, fumbled around with it to open it, and was on the point of giving it to her. But what happened instead? I handed it to her on my knees, as if she were a goddess.

I told this dream to her, and in a week the neurosis had vanished. The dream had showed me that she was not just a superficial little girl, but that beneath the surface were the makings of a saint. She had no mythological ideas, and therefore the most essential feature of her nature could find no way to express itself. All her conscious activity was directed toward flirtation, clothes, and sex, because she knew of nothing else. She knew only the intellect and lived a meaningless life. In reality she was a child of God whose destiny was to fulfill His secret will. I had to awaken mythological and religious ideas in her, for she belonged to that class of human beings to whom spiritual activity is demanded. Thus her life took on a meaning, and no trace of the neurosis was left. (Jung, 1961, pp. 138–140)

Jung's reliance on his unconscious awareness of the patient's anxiety allowed him to get to the root of the matter. Having a dream about a patient or an event before meeting the patient or before the event occurred was not unusual for Jung. Such events contributed to his interest in parapsychology.

The occurrence of the first dream before Jung saw the patient can be considered a meaningful coincidence. Jung observed many such coincidences that had no causal connection. He used the term *synchronicity* to describe events that were related in their meaning but not in their cause (Hogenson, 2009; Main, 2007).

Borderline Disorders: Ed

In writing about the borderline process, Schwartz-Salant (1989, 1991) emphasizes the importance of archetypal symbolism. He finds alchemical symbolism to be particularly useful, specifically the notion of *coniunctio*, based on the concept of unity in alchemy. For Schwartz-Salant, borderline patients may be difficult to communicate with, as they may be expressing themselves not through personal feelings but through archetypal themes. Often, the patient presents very concrete associations to dreams that may yield very difficult unconscious material to bring into conscious awareness.

For example, Schwartz-Salant (1991) presents the case of Ed, a bright 38-year-old man who could spend hours contemplating why someone had treated him in a particular way. He was often critical of the morality of his own behavior and that of others. In helping Ed, Schwartz-Salant deals with the coniunctio archetype as represented by Ed's inner couple—two aspects of himself in union with each other. The therapist also saw himself and Ed as a transference couple that desired nonunion and acted at times at cross-purposes. Schwartz-Salant (1991, p. 171) puts it more dramatically: "Whenever I would invoke disharmony by being out of harmony with myself, Ed would become very nasty and have the urge to hit me." Ed improved when patient and therapist could examine the couple within Ed that was at war, but really desired no contact within itself. Ed's individuation increased as he became aware of important archetypal and transference themes.

Psychotic Disorders: Patient

In his early training with Bleuler, Jung had the opportunity to work with many psychotic patients. He was particularly interested in the symbolism that was inherent in their incoherent verbiage. He heard the expression of schizophrenic patients as a verbalization of unconscious material. In his book *The Self in*

Psychotic Process, Perry (1987) gives a case history of a schizophrenic patient who, when most disturbed, was most involved in a quest for "a center." Although not familiar with symbolism, the patient described, over a period of time, a fourfold center, a mandala symbol. In her psychotic processes, Perry saw the themes of death and rebirth as they were related to dealing with parental domination in developing individuation. For Perry, the verbalizations of the psychotic come not from exposure to one's culture but from the collective unconscious. He gives as evidence the spontaneous occurrence of the mandala symbol, not only with this patient but with others. For him, this provides support that the Self is the center of the psyche for all people (Perry, 1987).

Brief Therapy

The length of Jungian analysis varies considerably, depending on the needs of the patient and the approach of the analyst. Analysts who use a developmental approach, combining Jungian theory with object relations theory, are likely to meet two or more times per week, whereas those who follow a more classical model of Jungian analysis may meet once or sometimes twice a week. The duration also varies considerably, sometimes less than a year and often many years. It is not unusual for analysands to leave analysis for a period of time and return later. However, there is not a brief or time-limited approach to Jungian analysis. Harris (1996) suggests that a Jungian frame of reference can be used for brief therapy if the problem is limited in scope.

At times, Jungian analysts may have relatively few contacts with their patients, but that usually occurs when analysis may not be the appropriate treatment. Jung was quite flexible, sometimes using methods that he associated with Adler or Freud or a method that seemed appropriate and expedient to him. In general, Jungian analysts vary as to their flexibility in using methods that are not usually associated with Jungian exploration of the unconscious. Also, some patient problems may indicate that they are not appropriate for Jungian analysis. For example, Jung (1961, p. 135) gives the case of a doctor with whom he decided to terminate therapy because the nature of the dream material revealed to Jung that the patient had the potential of developing a psychosis. In cases such as this, Jungian analysts recognize when exploration of the unconscious will lead not to individuation but to fragmentation of the psyche.

Current Trends

Jung's ideas have become increasingly popular with the public. One reason was Joseph Campbell's television series featuring the importance of myth in modern life. In this series and the book published based on this series (Campbell & Moyers, 1988), Jung's collective unconscious and archetypes are discussed. A best-selling book, *Women Who Run with the Wolves* (Estes, 1992), describes the "wild woman" archetype. Bly's (1990) book *Iron John* discusses the importance of male archetypes. While these books have contributed to making Jungian therapy more popular to the public, there have been two significant ongoing issues affecting the development of Jungian therapy: post-Jungian views and postmodernism.

In describing post-Jungian thought, Samuels (1997) groups analytical writers into three overlapping categories: developmental, classical, and archetypal. The developmental school of Jungian analysis, based in England, combines Jungian thought with that of many of the object relations theorists such as Klein and Winnicott (Solomon, 2008). Fordham's (1996) work is a good example of this theoretical thrust. The classical school makes use of Jung's ideas as he wrote them; it balances developmental issues with archetypal emphasis but tends to neglect transference and countertransference issues (Hart, 2008). The archetypal school, best exemplified by Hillman (1989, 1997, 2004), attends to a wide variety of archetypes rather than emphasizing the persona, anima–animus, and the shadow (Adams, 2008). In *The Archetypal Imagination*, Hollis (2000) shows how imagination can have a healing function that is based in universal (archetypal) roots. The use of many archetypal images is increasingly common among analysts in the United States, as can be seen in the section on gender issues later in this chapter. Archetypal imagery and symbolism are often a subject of discussion at educational seminars for the public.

Postmodern thinking has been brought to Jungian theory by several writers. Haucke (2000) shows how Jungian psychology provides a new look at modern culture in areas as diverse as architecture, hysteria, and psychosis. Other Jungian writers take a postmodern approach to science that is broad and inclusive of Jung's ideas. Beebe (2004) argues that the dialogue between patient and Jungian therapist is an opportunity to test a view of the world and to enlarge that view. Beebe sees the therapeutic dialogue as one in which a world view can be replicated by experience. Wilkinson (2004) takes a more biological point of view, seeing Jungian theory as a valid perspective on the mind–brain–self relationship. These broad views of science find a place for Jungian personality theory and psychotherapy.

Using Jungian Concepts with Other Theories

Jungian therapists often make use of concepts from other theories. Because of Jung's close association with Freud during the early part of his professional life, many similarities between the two theories exist. Jungian analysts often find it helpful to make use of Freud's concepts of child development. Although Jung wrote on this topic, he devoted more effort to other areas. Many Jungians, often referred to as the *developmental* or *British school* of Jungian analysis, have been attracted to the work of attachment theory (Knox, 2009) and object relations theorists who further examine childhood development. Although psychodynamic theories of therapy are most closely related to Jungian analysis, Jungians have also made use of gestalt enactment techniques such as the empty chair, which can bring unconscious material into conscious awareness.

Those who are not Jungian analysts but use object relations or other psychoanalytic theories may find Jung's concept of archetypal forms to be useful and to provide new insights into unconscious behavior. Although the Jungian concept of the personal unconscious corresponds to the psychoanalytic concept of the unconscious, there is no corresponding concept to the collective unconscious. Use of this concept does require knowledge of the archetypal formation of the collective unconscious and archetypal symbols. Morey (2005) warns of the difficulties in trying to integrate object relations and Jungian theory. Easier to integrate are Jung's notions of complexes, which are broader and more comprehensive than the Freudian. Additionally, Jung's emphasis on the second half of life may be of much value to psychodynamic therapists working with older patients. Donahue (2003) uses case examples to show how ego development and human relationship theory can be combined with Jungian therapy.

For mental health professionals who do not make use of psychodynamic concepts in their work, the application of Jung's typology of attitudes and functions may be helpful in providing a means of understanding an individual's personality. The attitudes of introversion and extraversion alert the therapist to attend to the patient's inner and outer world. The Jungian typology also provides insight into how individuals view their world (sensing or intuiting) and how they make judgments or decisions (thinking or feeling). These concepts can be measured through several instruments, including the Myers-Briggs Type Indicator (MBTI) and other inventories, but they do not provide in-depth information obtained in therapy sessions. The MBTI and the attitudes and functions of personality are used widely by many helping professionals. These concepts are relatively easy to understand and do not require the specific training and supervision (usually including personal analysis) that is necessary in working with unconscious material.

Research

Although Jung used word-association tests to study his concept of complexes, he used evidence from myths, folklore, and dreams of patients to confirm his hypotheses about most of his concepts. Perhaps the most thorough review of research on a variety of Jungian concepts and hypotheses was done by Mattoon (1981), who described evidence relevant to many of his constructs. Most of the research related to Jungian thought has been on his typological system—attitudes and functions. There is scattered research but no coherent research efforts on other concepts. An example of research on differences between the dreams of normal and eating-disordered women illustrates research on Jungian concepts. Research on the comparative effectiveness of Jungian analysis and other forms of therapy is not available. Jungian analysis may be the most difficult type of treatment to assess in terms of effectiveness because the therapeutic process is long, outcome and process measures need to deal with concepts related to the personal and collective unconscious, and approaches of Jungian analysts differ widely in terms of style and the integration of other theories. Most of this section concentrates on studies related to Jung's concepts of personality, specifically, attitudes and functions.

Three inventories have been developed to measure not only introversion-extraversion but also the functions of thinking, feeling, sensing, and intuiting: the Gray-Wheelwright Jungian Type Survey (Wheelwright, Wheelwright, & Buehler, 1964), the Myers-Briggs Type Indicator (Myers, McCaulley, Quenk, & Hammer, 1998), and the Singer-Loomis Inventory of Personality (SLIP; Singer & Loomis, 1984; Arnau, Rosen, & Thompson, 2000). In terms of use as a research instrument, the MBTI has received more attention than the other two. For example, the MBTI has sample sizes ranging between 15,000 and 25,000 from which estimates are made about the percentage of women (75%) in the United States who prefer feeling to thinking, and the percentage of men in the United States (56%)

who prefer thinking to feeling. Among Native American and African American high school students, there appears to be a preference for extraversion, sensing, and thinking (Nuby & Oxford, 1998). In a study of 200 Australian and Canadian adults, a motivating feature for extraverts was the social attention that they received as a result of their behavior (Ashton, Lee, & Paunonen, 2002). The MBTI has also been the subject of a study with identical and fraternal twins reared apart (Bouchard, Hur, & Horn, 1998) showing that extraversion, introversion, and thinking-feeling, in particular, are found to be similar in twins reared apart. Relating MBTI typology to Jungian theory, Cann and Donderi (1986) found a correlation between type and recall of "little" and archetypal dreams, with intuitive types recalling more archetypal dreams and introverts recalling more everyday dreams. Regarding dream experiences, Jacka (1991) found that intuitive students view their dreams as more emotionally intense and disturbing than did students who scored high on sensing. Such studies illustrate the wide variety of physical and psychological characteristics that have been related to MBTI type.

Compared to studies relating type to various factors in normal populations, the research on patients is quite sparse. Studying the dreams of 12 anorectic and bulimic patients, Brink and Allan (1992) compared dream content with 11 normal women using a 91-item scale. They found that eating-disordered women had more dream scenarios depicting doom at the end of the dream, attitudes of not being able to succeed, and images of being attacked and watched. Eating-disordered women scored significantly higher than normal women on psychological traits of feelings of ineffectiveness, self-hate, inability to care for themselves, obsession with weight, and anger. The writers suggest that analysts working with eating-disordered women address the mother–daughter wound as a way of moving toward development of the Self. They warned against blaming the patient's mother while exploring the archetypes of the Good Mother and Good Father. In a study of six women diagnosed with anorexia, Austin (2009) suggests that for these women to get better, they needed to deal with their aggressive and self-hating energy that is at the core of anorexia. By becoming more aware of these feelings and by developing life skills, these women could work toward recovery.

Gender Issues

Not only for Jung, but for many Jungian writers and analysts, conceptual issues related to gender have been extremely important. The anima-animus archetypes, which represent other-sex sides of the individual, have been the basis of further inquiry for Jungian writers. Part of the interest, historically, has been due to the fact that many of the early analysts were women. Their writings have been important, as have those of more recent writers who have dealt with feminist and developmental issues related to the animus. Also, leaders of the men's movement have made use of Jungian archetypes in helping men become more aware of themselves. Many of the writings on gender issues reflect not only the desire to help men and women in their search for individuation but also the tension between men and women.

In reviewing the history of Jungian analysis, Henderson (1982) described how various female analysts have made contributions through writing and speaking in areas related to Jungian analysis. Henderson believed that one of the attractions that Jung held for female analysts was "the principal of relationship in which neither sex is limited to playing a stereotyped role" (p. 13). The archetypes of the anima and animus spoke to issues important for both men and women that were not addressed in Freudian theory or in other psychological writings of the 1920s and 1930s. These archetypal concepts can be viewed as supporting the notion of men and women looking at their feminine and masculine sides, respectively. In a narrower sense, however, the concepts of anima and animus have been criticized as reinforcing gender-role stereotypes. In fact, Jung had made statements showing that he viewed men's and women's roles differently: "No one can get around the fact that by taking up a masculine profession, studying and working like a man, woman is doing something not wholly in accord with, if not directly injurious to, her feminine nature" (Jung, 1970b, p. 117). In contrast to this statement was Jung's high regard for female analysts. In describing the need for therapists to have someone to talk to who could give another point of view, Jung says that "women are particularly gifted for playing such a part. They often have excellent intuition and a trenchant clinical insight and can see what men have up their sleeves, at times see also into men's anima intrigues" (Jung, 1961, p. 134). The disparities within his own views and the awareness of discrimination issues affecting women have prompted creative reactions of Jungian therapists.

Addressing male and female aspects of Jungian theory has been a task for several Jungian analysts. In bringing together feminist and archetypal theory, Lauter and Rupprecht (1985) see positive ways in which Jung's ideas can be applied to women. In their *Feminist Archetypal Theory* (1985), they present essays that bring together ideas about the female psyche and concepts from myth, dreams, the unconscious, and therapy. They feel it is important to do not only consciousness-raising about women's issues but also unconsciousness-raising to focus on issues related to women's images and dreams, art, literature, religion, and analysis. In *Jung: A Feminist Revision* (2002), Rowland applies a feminist view to many of Jung's ideas. Her work has helped to develop the influence of feminism in Jungian analysis (Kirsch, 2007). In *Androgyny: The Opposites Within*, Singer (2000) shows how individuals can integrate masculine and feminine aspects of themselves through a discussion of symbols from many cultures.

Pandora, the first mortal woman according to Greek legend, is used by Young-Eisendrath (1997) as a symbol of male–female issues that is a current struggle for North American society. Pandora was created by Zeus as a punishment to men for having stolen fire from Zeus and the other gods. Very beautiful, Pandora is deceitful, manipulating men with her sexual desirability. Young-Eisendrath uses the myth of Pandora to address men's focus on women as sexual objects. She also uses this myth to draw attention to women's focus on beauty that can lead to eating disorders. How to be free of Pandora's curse is the theme of *Gender and Desire: Uncursing Pandora*, which takes a creative approach to understanding gender roles and issues.

Jungian archetypal concepts have also been used to explain men and their issues and development. Bly (1990) and Moore and Gillette (1991, 1992) discuss the needs for ritual and awareness of male archetypes, such as King, Warrior, Magician, and Lover. These writers have led groups to help men get in touch with their own power through myths and stories that present these archetypal forms. As Collins (1993) points out, these writings emphasize male issues at the expense of the feminine side (the anima) that can make men more whole and generally masculine. Collins (1993) feels that male awareness requires appreciation and integration of the Father, Son, and feminine archetypal elements. It is likely writing on gender issues within Jungian theory will continue.

Multicultural Issues

During their training, Jungian analysts are often told, "when you treat the patient, you treat the culture" (Samuels, 1991, p. 18). By this statement, Samuels is referring to the fact that analysts should have knowledge of the culture of the analysand, including myths and folklore. He is also interpreting the statement to mean that by treating the patient, analysts help the patient in some way to positively influence his or her culture. Jung was interested in cultures of all types, as evidenced by his interests in anthropology, mythology, alchemy, religion, and folklore. Because of his interest in the universality of archetypal imagery, he traveled to many countries and continents (the United States, Egypt, and parts of Asia and Africa) to talk to people in nonliterate cultures about their dreams and folklore. However, generalizations that he made about the psychology of various cultures have contributed to criticism of his views as racist.

Jung's interest in religion and spirituality was wide and varied. He learned languages in order to read about religious symbolism as it related to his concept of the collective unconscious. His travels and talk with people of other cultures provided him with material to integrate into his knowledge of mythology, folklore, and religion to relate to his concept of archetypal memory. The type of anthropological investigation that Jung did continues, with analysts and researchers studying dreams and folklore across a wide variety of cultures. For example, Petchkovsky (2000) studied how central Australian aborigines attribute a type of subjectivity to animals and inanimate elements. Petchkovsky, San Roque, and Beskow (2003) report that some indigenous people found the Jungian view of the world to be similar to their own. After investigating a high suicide rate in central Australia, Petchkovsky, Cord-Udy, and Grant (2007) use Jungian theory to attribute the suicide rate to the larger Euro-Australian community as a failed nurturer, especially in relationship to mental health services. Working with a traditional African healer, Maiello (2008) learned of the importance of ancestor reverence in African culture and related this to Jungian views. Michan (2003) traces unresolved conflicts in Mexican personality and culture to themes in ancient Aztec mythology. Krippner and Thompson (1996) show how 16 different Native American societies do not have a distinct separation between the dreamed world and the waking world that Western societies have. In studies like these, cultural experience, whether conscious or unconscious, has been related to Jungian archetypal material and therapy.

Although Jung's intellectual curiosity was vast, his views of cultures could be narrow. In the 1930s and 1940s, Jung often referred to the psychology of races or nations (Martin, 1991). He ascribes psychological characteristics to Protestants, Jews, Swiss, "primitive Africans," and many other groups. During the rise of Nazism, he was attacked by some as being anti-Semitic, partly because of his remarks about the psychology of the Jews. The issues surrounding charges of anti-Semitism are fully explored in a book of essays by Maidenbaum and Martin

(1991). Drob (2005) discusses Jung's view of dream theory in the Kabbala, a book of Jewish mysticism. Joseph (2007) describes how Jung understood material from the Kabbala and how that understanding is different than a religious understanding. Because of the charges against Jung of being racist, Jungian analysts have been careful to point out the full complexity of Jung's thought and not to make generalizations about national or racial characteristics.

The use that Jungian analysts make of knowledge of other cultures can be illustrated by Sullwold's (1971) work with a 6-year-old boy who was often physically destructive with objects and other children and in fact, had just shattered a glass partition in the office of a referring colleague. In her work, Sullwold used a sandtray with a large collection of figures, small buildings, and various other objects. The boy was of Mexican and Native American extraction but had been adopted by Orthodox Jewish parents. Although not aware of his Indian tradition, he had a Native American name, Eagle Eye, which was a name he had given himself at Indian Guides, a boys' organization. In his initial work with the sandtray he used the cowboy and Native American figures, identifying with the Native Americans. In understanding this boy, Sullwold made use of her knowledge of Hopi and Zuni rituals and religion. In her work with the sandtray, Sullwold made observations about archetypal imagery, such as the Great Mother, which were expressed in his playing with animals in the sandtray. Assessing the future of the boy, Sullwold stated the following:

> The continued health of this boy depends on his ability to maintain the strength of his ego and develop ways of using his energies creatively so that the tremendous spiritual and psychic forces in him do not overwhelm him and throw him back into the dark cage of the monsters. (Sullwold, 1971, p. 252)

Thus, Sullwold emphasizes spiritual forces and the importance of the collective unconscious that contribute to the boy's problems. Creative expression is a positive outlet for forces that are out of reach of his conscious processes.

Group Therapy

Group therapy is practiced by only a relatively few Jungian analysts. Those who do so see it as an adjunct to, not as a replacement for, individual analysis. Because of the importance he placed on the individual and the pressures on individuals for conformity from a group, Jung had reservations about group psychotherapy (Sharp, 1998). However, some Jungians see positive values in group therapy. Dream groups, with or without a leader, have been started, some of them online (Harris, 1996). When a group member brings a dream into a group, that can be a focus of discussion, and group members with similar dreams may relate to the presented dream. Also, a dream can be enacted in the group through the use of psychodrama. Some Jungian analysts may make use of active imagination in therapy groups, having participants focus their attention on the imaginal journey of the group member. Additionally, Jungian analysts may wish to use gestalt awareness or other group techniques. Because of the emphasis on individuation, group therapy continues to be an adjunct to, rather than a substitute for, individual analysis.

[handwritten margin notes: "Jungian Arch", "Personality", "Collective Unconscious"]

Summary

Jung paralleled Freud's emphasis on unconscious processes, the use and interpretation of dreams in therapy, and his developmental approach to personality. Perhaps Jung's most original contribution is that of the collective unconscious and archetypal patterns and images that arise from it. Archetypal images are universal; they can be found in the religions, mythologies, and fairy tales of many cultures. Jung, in particular, emphasized the persona (the individual's social role), the anima-animus (the unconscious other-sex side of a man or woman's personality), the shadow (unconscious aspects of the personality that are rejected or ignored by the conscious ego), and the Self (regulating center of the personality). Many other archetypes exist, such as the Wise Old Man, the Great Mother, the lion, and so forth.

The contribution of personality types (introversion-extraversion, thinking-feeling, and sensing-intuiting) is widely known, although their use in analysis varies greatly from analyst to analyst. Although Jung wrote about developmental issues across the life span, he was particularly interested in midlife issues and the role of spirituality in the life of his patients. He often worked with complexes (emotionally charged ideas related to an archetypal image) as they occurred at any time in the person's lifetime, but especially at midlife. Underlying all of Jung's personality constructs and central to his theory is his concern with unconscious processes.

The focus of analysis is that of working with unconscious processes to provide more conscious awareness about them. Although this is done mainly by using dream material, active imagination and fantasy approaches are also used. By recognizing archetypal themes in dreams and other material, analysts help analysands become aware of previously unconscious material. In dealing with issues between the analyst and analysand (transference and countertransference), analysts often use material from the patients' dreams. As therapy progresses, the analysand develops a stronger and more integrated Self.

To be a Jungian analyst, one must receive training at a Jungian institute, which includes information about psychological and psychotherapeutic processes as well as information from the fields of anthropology, mythology, folklore, and other areas of knowledge that would help the analyst work with archetypal symbolism. This training prepares analysts to help their patients individuate and become conscious of their unique psychological reality. Because of the emphasis on individuation, individual treatment is preferred to group therapy. Interest in the concept of unconscious processes continues to grow, as does interest in Jung's approach to psychotherapy.

Theories in Action DVD: Jungian Analysis

Basic Concepts Used in the Role-Play	Questions About the Role-Play
• Dreams as compensation for waking life issues • Relating past and family issues to dreams • The shadow archetype • Integration of shadow-self	1. Why are Carin's dream so important in Jungian analysis? (pp. 100–103) 2. Why is Carin's dream about obese women an example of the personal unconscious rather than the collective unconscious? (p. 100) 3. What is the content of Carin's shadow archetype? Why is it important in Jungian analysis? (pp. 89–90) 4. What ways do Jungians use to access the unconscious that are not used in this role-play? (p. 104)

Suggested Readings

Jung, C. G. (1956). *Two essays on analytical psychology*. New York: Meridian Books. These essays present core Jungian ideas on the personal and collective unconscious. Included also is information on Jung's view of Freud and Adler and three key archetypes (persona and anima and animus), as well as Jung's approach to psychotherapy.

Jung, C. G. (1963). *Memories, dreams, reflections*. New York: Pantheon Books. Written near the end of his life, these autobiographical recollections describe the development of his ideas and his struggles with his unconscious processes. He also discusses his relationship with Freud and his approaches to psychotherapy.

De Laszlo, V. (1990). *The basic writings of C. G. Jung*. Princeton, NJ: Princeton University. Originally published by Random House in 1959, this collection of selected works from Jung includes writings on the psyche, the unconscious, typology, therapy, and human development.

Harris, A. S. (1996). *Living with paradox: An introduction to Jungian psychology*. Pacific Grove, CA: Brooks/Cole. This short book describes the major features of Jungian personality theory and treatment techniques. Current issues in Jungian psychology and its practice are discussed.

Whitmont, E. C. (1991). *The symbolic quest*. New York: Putnam. In this overview, Jung's major ideas are presented, along with clinical material that illustrates them. This is a good introduction to Jungian thought.

References

Adams, M. V. (2008). The archetypal school. In P. Young-Eisendrath & T. Dawson (Eds.), *The Cambridge companion to Jung* (2nd ed., pp. 107–124). New York: Cambridge University Press.

Adler, G. (1967). Methods of treatment in analytical psychology. In B. Wolman (Ed.), *Psychoanalytic techniques* (pp. 338–378). New York: Basic Books.

Arnau, R. C., Rosen, D. H., & Thompson, B. (2000). Reliability and validity of scores from the Singer-Loomis Type Development Inventory. *Journal of Analytical Psychology, 45*, 409–426.

Ashton, M. C., Lee, K., & Paunonen, S. V. (2002). What is the central feature of extraversion?: Social attention versus reward sensitivity. *Journal of Personality and Social Psychology, 83*(1), 245–251.

Astor, J. (2001). Is transference the 'total situation'? *Journal of Analytical Psychology, 46*, 415–430.

Austin, S. (2009). A perspective on the patterns of loss, lack, disappointment and shame encountered in the treatment of six women with severe and chronic anorexia nervosa. *Journal of Analytical Psychology, 54*(1), 61–80.

Aziz, R. (2007). *The syndetic paradigm: The untrodden path beyond Freud and Jung*. Albany: State University of New York Press.

Bain, D. (2004). *Jung: A biography*. Boston: Little, Brown.

Beebe, J. (2004). Can there be a science of the symbolic? *Journal of Analytical Psychology, 49*(2), 177–191.

Beebe, J. (2005). Finding our way in the dark. *Journal of Analytical Psychology, 50*(1), 91–101.

Bly, R. (1990). *Iron John: A book about men*. Reading, MA: Addison-Wesley.

Bouchard, T. J., Jr., Hur, Y. M., & Horn, J. M. (1998). Genetic and environmental influences on the continuous scales of the MBTI. An analysis based on twins reared apart. *Journal of Personality, 66*, 135–149.

Brink, S. J., & Allan, J. A. B. (1992). Dreams of anorexic and bulimic women. *Journal of Analytical Psychology, 37*, 275–297.

Cambray, J., & Carter, L. (2004). Analytic methods revisited. In J. Cambray & L. Carter (Eds.), *Analytical psychology: Contemporary perspectives in Jungian analysis*. (pp. 116–148). New York: Brunner-Routledge.

Campbell, J., & Moyers, B. (1988). *The power of myth*. Garden City, NY: Doubleday.

Cann, D. R., & Donderi, D. C. (1986). Jungian personality typology and recall of everyday and archetypal dreams. *Journal of Personality and Social Psychology, 50*, 1021–1030.

Castellana, F., & Donfrancesco, A. (2005). Sandplay in Jungian analysis: Matter and symbolic integration. *Journal of Analytical Psychology, 50*(3), 367–382.

Charet, F. X. (2000). Understanding Jung: Recent biographies and scholarship. *Journal of Analytical Psychology, 45*, 195–216.

Collins, A. (1993). Men within. *San Francisco Jung Institute Library Journal, 11,* 17–32.

De Laszlo, V. (1990). *The basic writings of C. G. Jung.* Princeton, NJ: Princeton University.

Donahue, B. (2003). *C. G. Jung's complex dynamic and the clinical relationship: One map for mystery.* Springfield, IL: C. C. Thomas.

Drob, S. (2005). Jung's Kabbalistic visions. *Journal of Jungian Theory and Practice, 7*(1), 33–54.

Ekstrom, S., & PDM Task Force. (2007). Review of *Psychodynamic Diagnostic Manual. Journal of Analytical Psychology, 52*(1), 111–114.

Ellenberger, H. F. (1970). *The discovery of the unconscious.* New York: Basic Books.

Estes, C. P. (1992). *Women who run with the wolves.* New York: Ballantine.

Fordham, M. (1996). *Analyst–patient interaction: Collected papers on technique.* New York: Routledge.

Goelitz, A. (2007). Exploring dream work at end of life. *Dreaming, 17*(3), 159–171.

Hall, C. S., & Nordby, V. J. (1973). *A primer of Jungian psychology.* New York: New American Library.

Hall, J. A. (1986). *The Jungian experience: Analysis and individuation.* Toronto: Inner City Books.

Hannah, B. (1976). *Jung: His life's work: A biographical memoir.* New York: Putnam.

Hannah, B. (1981). *Encounters with the soul: Active imagination as developed by C. G. Jung.* Santa Monica, CA: Sigo Press.

Harding, M. E. (1970). *The way of all women.* New York: Putnam.

Harris, A. S. (1996). *Living with paradox: An introduction to Jungian psychology.* Pacific Grove, CA: Brooks/Cole.

Hart, D. L. (2008). The classical Jungian school. In P. Young-Eisendrath & T. Dawson (Eds.), *The Cambridge companion to Jung* (2nd ed., pp. 95–106). New York: Cambridge University Press.

Haucke, C. (2000). *Jung and the postmodern: The interpretation of realities.* London: Routledge.

Henderson, J. L. (1982). Reflections on the history and practice of Jungian analysis. In M. Stein (Ed.), *Jungian analysis* (pp. 3–26). La Salle, IL: Open Court.

Hillman, J. (1985). *Anima: An anatomy of a personified notion.* Dallas, TX: Spring.

Hillman, J. (1989). *A blue fire: Selected writings by James Hillman.* (Introduced and edited by Thomas Moore). New York: Harper & Row.

Hillman, J. (1997). *The soul's code: In search of character and calling.* New York: Warner.

Hillman, J. (2004). *Archetypal psychology.* Putnam, CT: Spring.

Hogenson, G. B. (2009). Synchronicity and moments of meeting. *Journal of Analytical Psychology, 54*(2), 183–197.

Hollis, J. (2000). *The archetypal imagination.* College Station, TX: Texas A & M University Press.

Jacka, B. (1991). Personality variables and attitudes towards dream experiences. *Journal of Psychology, 125,* 27–31.

Joseph, S. M. (2007). Jung and Kabbalah: Imaginal and noetic aspects. *Journal of Analytical Psychology, 52*(3), 321–341.

Jung, C. (1954a). Analytical psychology and education. In *The development of personality,* Collected works (Vol. 17, pp. 63–132). Princeton, NJ: Princeton University Press. (Original work published 1926.)

Jung, C. (1954b). Child development and education. In *The development of personality,* Collected works (Vol. 17, pp. 47–62). Princeton, NJ: Princeton University Press. (Original work published 1928.)

Jung, C. (1954c). Problems of modern psychotherapy. In *The practice of psychotherapy,* Collected works (Vol. 16, pp. 53–75). Princeton, NJ: Princeton University Press. (Original work published 1946.)

Jung, C. (1954d). The development of personality. In *The development of personality,* Collected works (Vol. 17, pp. 165–186). Princeton, NJ: Princeton University Press. (Original work published 1934.)

Jung, C. (1954e). The psychology of the transference. In *The practice of psychotherapy,* Collected works (Vol. 16, pp. 163–322). Princeton, NJ: Princeton University Press. (Original work published 1946.)

Jung, C. (1954f). Psychotherapy today. In *The practice of psychotherapy,* Collected works (Vol. 16, pp. 94–125). Princeton, NJ: Princeton University Press. (Original work published 1945.)

Jung, C. (1956). *Symbols of transformation.* Collected works (2nd ed., Vol. 5). Princeton, NJ: Princeton University Press. (Original work published 1911.)

Jung, C. (1956). *Two essays on analytical psychology.* New York: Meridian Books.

Jung, C. (1957). On the psychology and pathology of so-called occult phenomena. In *Psychiatric studies,* Collected works (Vol. 1, pp. 1–88). Princeton, NJ: Princeton University Press. (Original work published 1902.)

Jung, C. (1959a). Archetypes of the collective unconscious. In *The archetypes and the collective unconscious,* Collected works (Vol. 9, Part 1, pp. 3–42). Princeton NJ: Princeton University Press. (Original work published 1954.)

Jung, C. (1959b). Conscious, unconscious, and individuation. In *The archetypes and the collective unconscious*, Collected works (Vol. 9, Part 1, pp. 275–289). Princeton, NJ: Princeton University Press. (Original work published 1938.)

Jung, C. (1959c). The concept of the collective unconscious. In *The archetypes and the collective unconscious*, Collected works (Vol. 9, Part 1, pp. 42–53). Princeton, NJ: Princeton University Press. (Original work published 1936.)

Jung, C. (1960a). General aspects of dream psychology. In *The structure and dynamics of the psyche*, Collected works (Vol. 8, pp. 235–280). Princeton, NJ: Princeton University Press. (Original work published 1916.)

Jung, C. (1960b). Instinct and the unconscious. In *The structure and dynamics of the psyche*, Collected works (Vol. 8, pp. 129–138). Princeton, NJ: Princeton University Press. (Original work published 1919.)

Jung, C. (1960c). On the nature of dreams. In *The structure and dynamics of the psyche*, Collected works (Vol. 8, pp. 281–297). Princeton, NJ: Princeton University Press. (Original work published 1945.)

Jung, C. (1960d). The psychology of dementia praecox. In *The psychogenesis of mental disease*, Collected works (Vol. 3, pp. 1–152). Princeton, NJ: Princeton University Press. (Original work published 1907.)

Jung, C. (1960e). The stages of life. In *The structure and dynamics of the psyche*, Collected works (Vol. 8, pp. 387–404). Princeton, NJ: Princeton University Press. (Original work published 1930.)

Jung, C. (1961). *Memories, dreams, reflections*. New York: Random House.

Jung, C. (1963). *Memories, dreams, reflections*. New York: Pantheon Books.

Jung, C. (1970a). Symbols and the interpretation of dreams. In *The symbolic life*, Collected works (Vol. 18, pp. 185–266). Princeton, NJ: Princeton University Press. (Original work published 1950.)

Jung, C. (1970b). Women in Europe. In *Civilization in transition*, Collected works (Vol. 10, pp. 113–133). Princeton, NJ: Princeton University Press. (Original work published 1964.)

Jung, C. (1971). *Psychological types*, Collected works (Vol. 6). Princeton, NJ: Princeton University Press. (Original work published 1921.)

Jung, C. (1973). Studies in word association. In *Experimental researches*, Collected works (Vol. 2, pp. 3–479). Princeton, NJ: Princeton University Press. (Original work published 1904.)

Jung, E. (1957). *Animus and anima*. Irving, TX: Spring.

Kirsch, J. (2007). Reading Jung with Susan Rowland. *Jung Journal: Culture & Psyche, 1*(1–2), 13–47.

Kirsch, T. B. (2000). *The Jungians: A comparative and historical perspective*. Philadelphia: Routledge.

Knox, J. (2009). The analytic relationship: Integrating Jungian, attachment theory and developmental perspectives. *British Journal of Psychotherapy, 25*(1), 5–23.

Krippner, S., & Thompson, A. (1996). A 10-facet model of dreaming applied to dream practices of sixteen Native American cultural groups. *Dreaming, 6*, 71–96.

Lauter, E., & Rupprecht, C. S. (1985). *Feminist archetypal theory: Interdisciplinary revisions of Jungian thought*. Knoxville: University of Tennessee Press.

Maidenbaum, A., & Martin, S. A. (1991). *Lingering shadows: Jungians, Freudians, and anti-Semitism*. Boston: Shambhala.

Maiello, S. (2008). Encounter with a traditional healer: Western and African therapeutic approaches in dialogue. *Journal of Analytical Psychology, 53*(2), 241–260.

Main, R. (2007). Synchronicity and analysis: Jung and after. *European Journal of Psychotherapy and Counselling, 9*(4), 359–371. doi:10.1080/13642530701725924

Martin, S. (1991). Introduction. In A. Maidenbaum & S. A. Martin (Eds.), *Lingering shadows: Jungians, Freudians, and anti-Semitism* (pp. 1–15). Boston: Shambhala.

Mattoon, M. A. (1981). *Jungian psychology in perspective*. New York: Free Press.

Mattoon, M. A. (1986). Jungian analysis. In I. L. Kutash & A. Wolf (Eds.), *Psychotherapist's casebook* (pp. 124–143). San Francisco: Jossey-Bass.

McCully, R. (1971). *Rorschach theory and symbolism: A Jungian approach to clinical material*. Baltimore: Williams & Wilkins.

McGuire, W. (Ed.). (1974). *The Freud/Jung letters*. Princeton, NJ: Princeton University Press.

Michan, P. (2003). Analysis and individuation in the Mexican psyche: Culture and context. *Journal of Jungian Theory and Practice, 5*(1), 29–47.

Miller, J. C. (2004). *The transcendent function: Jung's model of psychological growth through dialogues with the unconscious*. Albany, NY: State University of New York Press.

Moore, R., & Gillette, D. (1991). *King, warrior, magician, lover: Rediscovering the archetypes of the mature masculine*. New York: HarperCollins.

Moore, R., & Gillette, D. (1992). *The king within: Accessing the king in the male psyche*. New York: William Morrow.

Morey, J. R. (2005). Winnicott's splitting headache: Considering the gap between Jungian and object relations concepts. *Journal of Analytical Psychology, 50* (3), 333–350.

Myers, J. B., McCaulley, M. H., Quenk, N. L., & Hammer, A. L. (1998). *MBTI Manual: A guide to the development and use of the Myers-Briggs Type Indicator* (3rd ed.) Palo Alto, CA: Consulting Psychologists Press.

Nuby, J. F., & Oxford, R. L. (1998). Learning style preferences of Native American and African American secondary students. *Journal of Psychological Type, 44*, 5–19.

Perry, C. (2008). Transference and countertransference. In P. Young-Eisendrath & T. Dawson (Eds.), *The Cambridge companion to Jung* (2nd ed., pp. 147–170). New York: Cambridge University Press.

Perry, J. W. (1987). *The self in psychotic process* (rev. ed.). Dallas, TX: Spring.

Petchkovsky, L. (2000). "Stream of consciousness" and "ownership of thought" in indigenous people in Central Australia. *Journal of Analytical Psychology, 45*, 577–597.

Petchkovsky, L., Cord-Udy, N., & Grant, L. (2007). A post-Jungian perspective on 55 indigenous suicides in central Australia; deadly cycles of diminished resilience, impaired nurturance, compromised interiority; and possibilities for repair. *Australian e-Journal for the Advancement of Mental Health, 6*(3), 1–14.

Petchkovsky, L., San Roque, C., & Beskow, M. (2003). Jung and the dreaming: Analytical psychology's encounters with aboriginal culture. *Transcultural Psychiatry, 40*(2), 208–238.

Roazen, P. (2005). An interview with Michael Fordham. *Journal of Analytical Psychology, 50*(1), 19–26.

Roesler, C. (2008). The self in cyberspace: Identity formation in postmodern societies and Jung's self as an objective psyche. *Journal of Analytical Psychology, 53*(3), 421–436.

Rowland, S. (2002). *Jung: A feminist revision*. Cambridge, UK: Polity Press.

Samuels, A. (1991). *Psychopathology: Contemporary Jungian perspectives*. New York: Guilford Press.

Samuels, A. (1997). Introduction: Jung and the post-Jungians. In P. Young-Eisendrath & T. Dawson (Eds.), *The Cambridge Companion to Jung* (1st ed., pp. 1–13). Cambridge, UK: Cambridge University Press.

Samuels, A. (2000). Post Jungian dialogues. *Psychoanalytic Dialogues, 10*, 403–426.

Sandner, D. E., & Beebe, J. (1982). Psychopathology and analysis. In M. Stein (Ed.), *Jungian analysis* (pp. 294–334). La Salle, IL: Open Court.

Schaverien, J. (1996). Desire and the female analyst. *Journal of Analytical Psychology, 4*, 261–287.

Schaverien, J. (2007). Countertransference as active imagination: Imaginative experiences of the analyst. *Journal of Analytical Psychology, 52*(4), 413–431.

Schultz, D. P., & Schultz, S. E. (2009). *Theories of personality* (9th ed.). Belmont, CA: Wadsworth.

Schwartz-Salant, N. (1989). *The borderline personality: Vision and healing*. Wilmette, IL: Chiron.

Schwartz-Salant, N. (1991). The borderline personality: Vision and healing. In A. Samuels (Ed.), *Psychopathology: Contemporary Jungian perspectives* (pp. 157–204). New York: Guilford Press.

Shamdasani, S. (2003). *Jung and the making of modern psychology: The dream of a science*. Cambridge, UK: Cambridge University Press.

Sharf, R. S. (2010). *Applying career development theory to counseling* (5th ed.). Belmont, CA: Cengage-Brooks/Cole.

Sharp, D. (1998). *Jungian psychology: My life as an elephant*. Toronto: Inner City Books.

Singer, J. (2000). *Androgyny: The opposites within*. York Beach, ME: Nicolas Hays.

Singer, J., & Loomis, M. (1984). *The Singer-Loomis Inventory of Personality (SLIP)*. Palo Alto, CA: Consulting Psychologists Press.

Solomon, H. M. (2008). The developmental school. In P. Young-Eisendrath & T. Dawson (Eds.), *The Cambridge companion to Jung* (2nd ed., pp. 125–146). New York: Cambridge University Press.

Spangler, P., Hill, C. E., Mettus, C., Guo, A. H., & Heymsfield, L. (2009). Therapist perspectives on their dreams about clients: A qualitative investigation. *Psychotherapy Research, 19*(1), 81–95.

Stein, M. (2005). Some reflections on the influence of Chinese thought on Jung and his psychological theory. *Journal of Analytical Psychology, 50*(2), 209–222.

Sullwold, E. (1971). Eagle eye. In H. Kirsch (Ed.), *The well-tended tree* (pp. 235–253). New York: Plenum.

Ulanov, A. B. (1982). Transference/countertransference: A Jungian perspective. In M. Stein (Ed.), *Jungian analysis* (pp. 68–85). La Salle, IL: Open Court.

Ulanov, A. B. (1997). Transference, the transcendent function, and transcendence. *Journal of Analytical Psychology, 42*, 119–138.

Watkins, M. (2000). Depth psychology and the liberation of being. In R. Brokke (Ed.), *Pathways into the Jungian world: Phenomenology and analytical psychology* (pp. 217–233). New York: Routledge.

Wheelwright, J. B., Wheelwright, J. H., & Buehler, H. A. (1964). *Jungian Type Survey: The Gray Wheelwright Test* (18th revision). San Francisco: Society of Jungian Analysts of Northern California.

Whitmont, E. C. (1991). *The symbolic quest*. Princeton, NJ: Princeton University Press.

Wilkinson, M. (2004). The mind-brain relationship: The emergent self. *Journal of Analytical Psychology, 49*(1), 83–101.

Yates, J. (1999). *Jung on death and immortality*. Princeton, NJ: Princeton University Press.

Young-Eisendrath, P. (1997). *Gender and desire: Uncursing Pandora*. College Station, TX: Texas A & M University Press.

CHAPTER 4

Adlerian Therapy

Outline of Adlerian Therapy

ADLER'S THEORY OF PERSONALITY
  Style of Life
  Social Interest
  Inferiority and Superiority
  Birth Order
ADLERIAN THEORY OF THERAPY AND
COUNSELING
  Goals of Therapy and Counseling
  The Therapeutic Relationship
  Assessment and Analysis
    Family dynamics and constellation
    Early recollections
    Dreams
    Basic mistakes
    Assets

Insight and Interpretation
Reorientation
  Immediacy
  Encouragement
  Acting as if
  Catching oneself
  Creating images
  Spitting in the client's soup
  Avoiding the tar baby
  Push-button technique
  Paradoxical intention
  Task setting and commitment
  Homework
  Life tasks and therapy
  Terminating and summarizing the interview

Although Adler is considered by some to be a neo-Freudian, his views are very different from Freud's. Their similarity is mainly in their belief that the personalities of individuals are formed in their early years, before the age of 6. Beyond that, their views are different in many ways. Adler emphasized the social nature of the individual—that psychological health can be measured by the contribution that individuals make to their community and to society. Adler believed that lifestyle, the way individuals approach living, and their long-term goals can be determined by examining the family constellation, early recollections (memories of incidents from childhood), and dreams. Individuals attempt to achieve competence or a place in the world, but in doing so, they may develop mistaken beliefs that give them a false sense of superiority or a sense of inferiority. Adlerians help their patients develop insight into these beliefs and assist them in achieving goals. Creative strategies for meeting therapeutic goals and helping individuals change their cognitions, behaviors, and feelings are a hallmark of Adlerian psychotherapy and counseling.

Education is important to Adlerians as a part of their approach not only to psychotherapy and counseling but also to child raising, school problems, and marriage and family issues. Adlerians have developed clinics and centers to assist individuals with problems of living in their communities and society. This educational approach is not a new one, as Adler was involved in child guidance clinics in his work in Vienna.

History of Adlerian Theory

ALFRED ADLER

Born on February 7, 1870, Alfred Adler was the second son and third child of six children of middle-class Hungarian-Jewish parents. He was born in Rudolfsheim, Austria, a small village near Vienna. Whereas Freud grew up in a district that was mostly Jewish, Adler's neighborhood was ethnically mixed. He identified more with Viennese than with Jewish culture. He did not concern himself in his writings with anti-Semitism and later as an adult converted to Protestantism (Bottome, 1939; Ellenberger, 1970; Oberst & Stewart, 2003).

Adler's early life was marked by some severe illnesses and traumatic events. Developing rickets, a deficiency of vitamin D, may have affected his self-image. He also suffered from spasms of the glottis that affected his breathing and put him in danger of suffocation if he cried. A severe case of pneumonia when he was 5 was almost fatal. In addition to these illnesses, Adler experienced the death of his younger brother, who died in the bed next to him when Adler was 3. Also, he was almost killed twice in two different accidents outside his home. Although the accuracy of this information may be subject to question, it does suggest an early exposure both to feelings of inferiority—in this case mostly physical inferiority—and a view of life that may have influenced the development of Adler's important concept of social interest.

During his early school years Adler was an average student, having to repeat a mathematics course. Adler's father encouraged him to continue his studies despite his teacher's suggestion to his father that Adler should leave school and learn a trade. Later, Adler became both an excellent mathematics student and a good student overall. Although he improved his academic abilities, he had always had a love for music and had memorized operettas when he was young.

When Adler completed secondary school, he attended the Faculty of Medicine in Vienna in 1888, left for a year of military service, and graduated in 1895. During this time he continued his interest in music and attended political meetings that dealt with the development of socialism. In 1897 Adler married Raissa Epstein, a student from Russia, who had a strong interest in and dedication to socialism.

Adler entered private practice as an ophthalmologist in 1898, later becoming a general practitioner. After a few years in general practice, he became a psychiatrist, believing that he needed to learn about his patients' psychological and social situations as well as their physical processes. This interest in the whole person was to typify his writings and attitude toward psychiatry in his later years.

In 1902 Sigmund Freud invited Adler to join the psychoanalytic circle that Freud was developing. Adler was one of the first four members to do so and remained a member of the Vienna Psychoanalytic Society until 1911. Starting in 1905, he wrote psychoanalytically oriented articles for medical and educational journals, making a particularly important contribution to psychoanalysis at that time through *Studies of Organ Inferiority and Its Psychical Compensation*, published in 1907 (Adler, 1917). Adler's views diverged more and more from psychoanalytic theory, emphasizing the subjectivity of perception and the importance of social factors as opposed to biological drives. In 1911 Adler was president of the Vienna Psychoanalytic Society but left the society with 9 of the 23 members. Although some members of the society attempted reconciliation with Freud, it failed. Adler then formed the Society for Free Psychoanalytic Research or Investigation, which 1 year later was renamed the Society for Individual Psychology. In 1914 Adler, along with Carl Fürtmuller, began the *Zeitschrift für Individual-Psychologie (Journal for Individual Psychology)*.

Adler's work was slowed by the advent of World War I. During a portion of that time, Adler was recalled for military service as a physician in military hospitals. When Austria-Hungary lost the war, famine, epidemics, and other tragedies wracked Vienna. These events seemed to confirm Adler's socialist views. The defeat of Austria, however, did give Adler an opportunity to implement his educational views, as schools and teacher training institutions were overhauled.

In 1926 Adler was very active in publishing papers and giving lectures in Europe and then in the United States. In October 1927 he participated in the Wittenberg Symposium held at Wittenberg College in Springfield, Ohio. After that time he spent more and more time in the United States as a lecturer. In 1935, having foreseen the outbreak of Nazism in Europe, Adler and his wife moved to New York City. Having been appointed to the chair of medical psychology at the Long Island College of Medicine in 1932, Adler maintained his association with this institution. He continued his private practice in the United States and his worldwide lectures. While on a lecture tour in Europe, Adler died of a heart attack in Aberdeen, Scotland, in 1937. Two of his children, Kurt and Alexandra, continued his work as practicing psychotherapists. Adler left a theory of personality and psychotherapy that has had an impressive impact on psychology and psychiatry.

Influences on Adlerian Psychology and Therapy

Before examining Adler's theories of personality and psychotherapy, it will be helpful to explore some of the influences on Adler. Ellenberger (1970, p. 608) shows how Adler was influenced by Kant's desire to find ways to help individuals acquire practical knowledge of themselves and of others, as well as make use of reason in their lives (Stone, 2008). Both Adler and Nietzsche made use of the concept of will to power. For Adler, this concept meant attempts to attain competence, but for Nietzsche it referred to power over others, vastly different from Adler's emphasis on equality. As indicated earlier, Adler was influenced by socialism, more specifically by the ideas of Karl Marx. Adler was appreciative of and in sympathy with the ideas of social equality but objected vigorously to the "enforcement of socialism by violence" by the Bolsheviks (Ansbacher & Ansbacher, 1956). Although others' philosophical writings had an impact on Adler's work, he was also affected by his immediate contemporaries.

In particular, Hans Vaihinger's *The Philosophy of "As If "* (1965) influenced several of Adler's theoretical constructions. His concept of "fictionalism" was to have an impact on Adler's concept of the "fictional goal" (Ansbacher & Ansbacher, 1956). "Fictions" are ideas that do not exist in reality, yet they are useful in helping us deal more effectively with reality, an idea that Kant had written about many years earlier (Stone, 2008). Ansbacher and Ansbacher (1956) give the example of "all men are created equal" as a "fiction." Although this is a statement that can provide guidance in everyday life, it is not a reality. It is a useful fiction for interactions with others, although it may not be "objectively" true. This "philosophy of 'as if'" refers to treating attitudes and values as if they were true (Watts, 1999).

Adler's early association with Freud provided him with the opportunity to have a framework from which to specify and develop his own theory. Between 1902, when Adler joined Freud's society, and 1911, when he left the society, his views had become increasingly different from Freud's. They disagreed on many things: the role of the unconscious, the importance of social issues, and the role of drive theory and biology, to name but a few. The differences of opinion between Freud and Adler were never reconciled (Ansbacher & Huber, 2004). Although Adler would often demonstrate differences between his work and Freud's, he did give credit to Freud for his emphasis on dreams and on unconscious factors. He also credited Freud with having significantly emphasized the importance of early childhood in the development of neurotic and other conflicts that occurred in later life. However, Freud's dislike for Adler's concepts hindered the development of Adlerian thought both in Europe and in the United States.

When he arrived in New York from Vienna, Rudolf Dreikurs, perhaps the most notable adherent of Adlerian theory, had a great deal of difficulty being accepted by psychologists and psychiatrists whose theoretical orientations were Freudian (Griffith & Graham, 2004; Mosak & Maniacci, 2008; Oberst & Stewart, 2003). Dreikurs and his colleagues were creative in their innovations in the application of Adlerian theory. For example, Dreikurs is responsible for the concept of multiple therapy (Dreikurs, 1950), the use of more than one therapist; systematic analysis of early recollections; and creative approaches to psychotherapy. Many Adlerian therapists have worked on novel approaches to group psychotherapy, systems for teaching elementary and high school students, and programs for dealing with delinquency, criminal behavior, drug and alcohol abuse, and poverty. The emphasis that Adler put on the need to improve society has been carried on by his adherents.

Adler's Theory of Personality

Adler's view of personality was broad and open and not only considered the individual as a whole, unified organism but also emphasized the importance of the individual's interaction with the rest of society. This emphasis on the individual as a whole organism was consistent with Adler's view of the individual as a creative and goal-directed individual who was responsible for her own fate (Griffith & Graham, 2004; Sweeney, 2009). In his writings (Ansbacher & Ansbacher, 1970;

Mosak & Maniacci, 2008), Adler examined closely the striving for perfection or superiority of individuals as it conflicted with and complemented the social nature of the individual and society as a whole. This emphasis on the individual and society is in direct contrast to Freud's emphasis on biological needs as a basis for personality theory. By examining the basic concepts underlying Adler's individual psychology, it will be easier to understand the more specific Adlerian concepts such as style of life, social interest, inferiority, and birth order. *Key Concepts*

Style of Life

The style of life determines how a person adapts to obstacles in his life and ways in which he creates solutions and means of achieving goals. Adler believed that the style of life was developed in early childhood (Ansbacher & Ansbacher, 1956, p. 186), allowing children to strive, in individual ways, for perfection or superiority. For example, the child who has been picked on by other children in the neighborhood may develop a style of verbally manipulating other children. This behavior would then compensate for the inferiority that the child had experienced. Adler believed that lifestyle was based on overcoming a series of inferiorities. Most of these would be established by the age of 4 or 5, so that it would be difficult to change one's lifestyle after that time. For Adler, expressions of lifestyles throughout life were elaborations of earlier lifestyles. Using the previous example, the child who develops a style of manipulating other children to get his way may as an adolescent create excellent excuses for late or poorly done work or reasons for missed meetings with friends. As an adult, this individual may find ways to persuade others to buy products or to excuse him for poorly done work. These adult behaviors are the result not of reactions to other adults at a particular point in time but rather of a lifestyle developed at an early age.

Adlerians note that the lifestyle can be understood by observing how individuals approach five major interrelated tasks: self-development, spiritual development, occupation, society, and love (Mosak & Maniacci, 1999; Sweeney, 2009). Adler stated, "The person who performs useful work lives in the midst of the developing human society and helps to advance it" (Ansbacher & Ansbacher, 1956, p. 132). Choice of occupation can be seen as a way of expressing one's lifestyle (Sharf, 2010). For example, the individual who felt bullied as a child may express her lifestyle as an insurance salesperson, persuading and convincing others yet providing a service that helps others in a catastrophe. Lifestyle also has its expression in how individuals deal with friends and acquaintances as well as love. Occupation, society, love, self-development, and spiritual development are not discrete categories, but overlap.

Adlerians have examined lifestyles of different individuals and groups, finding a variety of themes. For example, Mwita (2004) shows how early memories affected Martin Luther King's personality and leadership style as he sought racial and social justice in the civil rights movement. Three memories are discussed, all having to do with racial discrimination. For example, when he was very young he remembered his father being angry and refusing to buy Martin shoes in a shoe store when the clerk asked him and his father to sit in the seats for "colored people." Examining the lifestyles of 30 Jewish Holocaust survivors who attended German universities, White, Newbauer, Sutherland, and Cox (2005) found that many had lifestyle narratives that included valuing education and the arts. The narratives also revealed an emphasis on setting goals and concern about the future. Studying binge drinking, Lewis and Watts (2004) found that college students who drank heavily had lifestyle themes that included being sociable and wanting recognition, yet also resisting rules and regulations. Lifestyle themes vary greatly and there is no universal list that therapists can select from. They must determine themes by listening to the client.

Social Interest

Social interest was discussed extensively in Adler's later work (Ansbacher & Ansbacher, 1970), in his writings on occupation, society, and love. Social interest evolves in three stages: aptitude, ability, and secondary dynamic characteristics (Ansbacher, 1977). An individual has an innate ability or aptitude for cooperation and social living. After the aptitude has been developed, the individual develops abilities to express social cooperation in various activities. As these abilities are developed, secondary dynamic characteristics express themselves as attitudes and interests in a variety of activities that then become a means of expressing social interest. Although Adler viewed social interest as an innate concept, he believed that the parent–child relationship was highly instrumental in developing it.

The first relationship in which social interest arises and is taught is in the mother–child bond. Adler sees the mother's task as developing a sense of cooperation and friendship in her child. By caring deeply for her child, the mother communicates a model of caring to the child. Furthermore, her care for her husband, the child's siblings, and other friends and relatives becomes a model of social interest. If the mother concentrates only on friends and relatives but not her children, or only on her husband but not friends and relatives, then the child's potential for developing social interest may be thwarted. If social interest is truly thwarted, then children may develop an attitude toward others in which they may want to dominate others, use others for their personal gain, or avoid interactions with others. Although the mother–child relationship is the earliest and most significant relationship in the development of social interest, the father–child relationship is also important, and the father should have favorable attitudes toward his family, his occupation, and social institutions. Watts (2003) describes the importance of bonding within the family and attachment to parents in Adlerian theory. According to Adler, the emotional or social detachment or authoritarianism of a parent can bring about a lack of social interest in the child. The relationship between father and mother is an important model for the child. If the marriage is unhappy and the parents actively disagree, an opportunity to develop social interest in the child is missed. Forgiveness between husband and wife is an act of social interest that can lead to improved relationships (McBrien, 2004). The parental relationship can have an impact on the lifestyle of a child by affecting romantic relationships and overall adaptation in later life.

The concept of social interest is so important that Adler used it as a means of measuring psychological health. If a person has little social interest, then that person is self-centered, tends to put down others, and lacks constructive goals. Social interest is important throughout one's entire life. In old age, discouragement and promoting social interest can help in developing meaningful lives even though individuals may no longer be working or raising families (Penick, 2004). Adler, more so than other personality theorists and psychotherapists of his time, had an interest in the problematic development of social interest in criminal and antisocial populations, which he hoped to help through development of social interest (Ansbacher, 1977; Ansbacher & Ansbacher, 1956, pp. 411–417).

Theories in Action

Inferiority and Superiority

While still a member of the Vienna Psychoanalytic Society, Adler tried to explain why a person develops one illness rather than another. He suggested that within individuals, some organs or part of the body are stronger or weaker than others (Oberst & Stewart, 2003). The weaker ones make an individual susceptible to illness or disease. Such organs or parts of the body were inferior at birth, causing an individual to compensate for this inferiority by participating in activities to overcome this inferiority. A classical example is Demosthenes, a stutterer in his youth who became a great orator by practicing speech with pebbles in his mouth. A more common example would be that of an individual who compensates for childhood illness by developing her intellect. Adler suggested that individuals tried to overcome physical inferiorities by psychological adjustments. Adler developed this concept early in his work and largely ignored it in later years. Instead, he focused on how people perceived their social inferiority rather than on their perceptions of physical inferiority.

In a sense, the infant is exposed to inferiority at birth. For Adler, feelings of inferiority were the motivation to achieve and attain in life. Inferiority is not a human weakness unless it develops into an inferiority complex. Children's parents and older siblings are bigger, more powerful, and more independent than the child. Throughout life, individuals struggle to achieve their places in life, striving for perfection and completion. As the child moves from inferiority toward superiority or excellence, three factors may threaten the development of self-confidence and social interest (Ansbacher, 1977): physical disabilities, pampering, and neglect. Physical disabilities may include organ inferiority as described previously, as well as childhood diseases. Pampered children may expect to have things given to them and may not develop an urge to be independent and to overcome inferiorities. Capron's (2004) study of four pampering types (overindulgent, overdomineering, overpermissive, and overprotective) contributes to a more detailed understanding of pampering. Neglected children or those who feel unwanted may try to avoid or escape others rather than overcome their inferiorities. Adler believed that the pampered or spoiled child could, in later life, fail to strive for superiority or to develop social interests.

> Extreme discouragement, continuous hesitation, over sensitivity, impatience, exaggerated emotion, and phenomena of retreat, physical and psychological disturbances showing the signs of weakness and need for support as found in the neurotic, are always evidence that a patient has not yet abandoned his early-acquired pampered style of life. (Ansbacher & Ansbacher, 1956, p. 242)

Although the desire to overcome inferiority and achieve superiority or mastery is normal in individuals and a major goal of life, some inferiority complexes and superiority complexes are not normal. Although the term *inferiority complex* has had several meanings in the development of Adlerian psychology, Adler in his latest writings stated that it is "the presentation of the person to himself and others that he is not strong enough to solve a given problem in a socially useful way" (Ansbacher & Ansbacher, 1956, p. 258). The pervasive feeling that one's abilities and characteristics are inferior to those of other people can take many forms. Individuals may feel less intelligent than others, less attractive, less athletic, or inferior in many other ways. Adler found that neurotic individuals who came to him for psychotherapy often presented an inferiority complex or superiority complex. For Adler, superiority was a means of inflating one's self-importance in order to overcome inferiority feelings. People may try to present themselves as strong and capable to maintain their mistaken feelings of superiority, when actually they are feeling less capable than others. An arrogant person expresses an inferiority complex when he states, "Other people are apt to overlook me. I must show that I am somebody" (Ansbacher & Ansbacher, 1956, p. 260).

> Behind everyone who behaves as if he were superior to others, we can suspect a feeling of inferiority which calls for very special efforts of concealment. It is as if a man feared that he was too small and walked on his toes to make himself seem taller. Sometimes we can see this very behavior if two children are comparing their height. The one who is afraid that he is smaller will stretch up and hold himself very tensely; he will try to seem bigger than he is. If we ask such a child, "Do you think you are too small?" we should hardly expect him to acknowledge the fact. (Ansbacher & Ansbacher, 1956, p. 260)

The superiority complex may be more obvious in children, but neither adults nor children are likely to easily acknowledge their superiority complex. A normal person strives for superiority but does not develop a superiority complex to mask feelings of inferiority. People who demonstrate a superiority complex may often be boastful, self-centered, arrogant, or sarcastic. Such people are likely to feel important by making fun of or demeaning others.

The striving for superiority or competence is a natural and fundamental motivation of individuals, whereas the superiority complex is not. However, in striving for superiority or competence, an individual can do so in a negative or positive direction. Trying to achieve superiority in a negative direction might include trying to achieve wealth or fame through unethical business or political practices. Seeking the goal of superiority in a positive sense might mean helping others through business, social dealings, education, or similar methods. A positive striving for superiority implies a strong social interest. It also requires considerable energy or activity to achieve these goals. In a sense, it is a healthy striving for perfection (Schultz & Schultz, 2009).

Birth Order

In many ways the family is a microcosm of society. For Adler, birth order could have an impact on how a child relates to society and the development of her style of life (Mosak & Maniacci, 2008). Perceived role in the family was more important to Adler than actual birth order itself. Adlerians are often critical of birth-order research that looks only at position in the family. For example, in a family of three children in which the oldest child is 1 year older than the middle child and the middle child is 12 years older than the youngest child, Adlerian therapists might view this family constellation as being more like a family with a younger and older sibling (the first two children) and see the youngest child as being more like the only child in a one-child family. More important is the subjective approach of Adler, which emphasizes the context of a family situation.

Adlerian Theory of Therapy and Counseling

Adlerians tend to vary widely on how they do therapy and counseling (Carlson, Watts, & Maniacci, 2006; Sweeney, 2009; Watts, 2003), and Adlerians make use of many concepts and techniques in their treatment of individuals. In this chapter, I first discuss the goals of counseling versus the goals of psychotherapy, which are seen differently by some Adlerians. Then I use Dreikurs's (1967) four processes of psychotherapy to explain Adlerian psychotherapy and counseling. The first process is the relationship; a cooperative relationship must be maintained throughout therapy. Second, assessment and analysis of client problems include consideration of analysis of early recollections, family constellation, and dreams. Third, interpretation of the comments of clients is an important aspect of Adlerian therapy, particularly as it relates to the goals of therapy. The fourth process, reorientation, takes the insights and interpretations that come from the client–therapist work and helps individuals find alternatives to previously ineffective beliefs and behaviors. Adlerians make use of a large variety of reorienting techniques, and a large sampling of these techniques is presented. These phases often overlap and may not always be used in the order in which they are presented here, but they provide a way of understanding the Adlerian psychotherapy and counseling process.

Goals of Therapy and Counseling

The conceptualization of differences between psychotherapy and counseling has a direct impact on the goals of treatment for Adlerians. Dreikurs (1967) believed that psychotherapy was required if changes in lifestyle were necessary but that counseling was appropriate if changes could be made within a lifestyle. Dreikurs also felt that significant changes should occur in early recollections that were reported in the beginning and end of psychotherapy, reflecting lifestyle changes (Mosak, 1958). In contrast, Dinkmeyer and Sperry (2000) view counseling as concerned with helping individuals change self-defeating behaviors and solve problems more efficiently. Sweeney (2009) believes that if the problem has an immediate nature dealing with relationships, counseling will be appropriate and have an educative or preventative rather than psychological orientation. Generally, if the problem is in only one life task, rather than pervasive throughout the client's life, counseling is sufficient (Manaster & Corsini, 1982). In actual practice, the differentiation between counseling and psychotherapy is rather minor. In general, Adlerians do both counseling and psychotherapy; which they do depends less on their view of the particular issue than on the presenting problem of the client. Implicit in the goals of psychotherapy and counseling is an increase in the client's social interest. Because counseling and psychotherapy overlap and are not clearly distinguished, the following discussion applies to both counseling and psychotherapy.

The Therapeutic Relationship

RESPECT / TRUST →

In trying to achieve a good therapeutic relationship, Adlerians attempt to establish a relationship of respect and mutual trust (Dreikurs, 1967). In order for this relationship to develop, the goals of the patient and the therapist must be similar. If the goals are different, the therapist is likely to experience the patient as resisting progress in therapy. In many cases the therapist educates the patient about appropriate goals for therapy. For example, if the patient does not feel that he can make progress, the therapist must work to encourage the patient that progress is possible and that symptoms, feelings, and attitudes can change. For Dreikurs (1967), anticipation of success in therapy is particularly important in a

Encourag ←

therapeutic relationship. The encouragement process is an important one, continuing throughout the entire process of therapy, and can be helpful in applying a solution-focused approach (Watts, 2000, 2003). As the patient is encouraged to develop goals, it is important to make them explicit. In developing the relationship, the therapist must not only plan goals but also listen and observe as patients present themselves and their goals.

Because the individual is unique, most actions can be considered meaningful (Manaster & Corsini, 1982). How the patient enters the office, sits, phrases questions, and moves his eyes can all be important material. As the therapist stores this information, she is able to decide on later strategies. Often the patient may sabotage therapy by playing games or presenting situations that make therapeutic progress difficult (Manaster & Corsini, 1982). Because patients have had concerns or interpersonal difficulties that bring them to therapy, these problems are likely to occur in the therapeutic relationship. The therapist need not confront the patient with sabotaging therapy but may choose to ignore it or to bring it to the patient's attention in an educational way. In doing the latter, the therapist may help the patient develop insight into self-defeating behaviors.

Empathy

Sabotaging or resisting therapy should not prevent the therapist from being empathic with the patient. Empathy involves attention not only to feelings but also to beliefs. As the patient gradually produces material, the Adlerian develops an understanding of the patient's lifestyle. Empathic responses often reflect the acknowledgment of the lifestyle. For Adlerians, beliefs result in feelings (Dinkmeyer & Sperry, 2000). Statements such as "I must help others," "I need to be the best," "No one else understands me," and "I try hard, but nothing ever works" are examples of beliefs that are often reflective of lifestyles that indicate discouragement with self or others. In response to clients' statements that express these beliefs, Adlerians may respond not only to the feeling but also to the belief itself. For example, Dinkmeyer and Sperry (2000, p. 63) describe how they would respond to a client who has the belief "I must please."

> *Michelle:* I do everything I can to please the boss, but he's never satisfied. I can't figure him out.
>
> *Counselor:* Perhaps what you're feeling is that, if you can't please, there's no point in trying.

The counselor is helping the client identify not only the feeling but the belief— I must please—behind the feeling. To respond only "You're confused" would be to respond only to the feeling and not help Michelle become aware of how her belief that she must please influences the feeling of confusion. If the counselor believes that she has a clear understanding of the client's feelings and beliefs, then an even stronger response to Michelle's comment may be appropriate.

> *Counselor:* Is it possible that you believe that, if you can't please, there is no point in trying? Your boss's failure to recognize your efforts justifies your becoming less cooperative or even quitting.

The statement helps the client become more aware of her intentions. Also, the counselor shows that the client has the power to change the situation by being less cooperative or by quitting. The tentative nature of the counselor's response, "Is it possible …" allows the client to determine if the counselor's response seems accurate and appropriate. The counselor does not impose her understanding of the client's belief on the client.

Assessment and Analysis

Assessment starts as the relationship builds. Adlerians are often likely to be making many observations about the patient in the first session. These observations may become material to be used for comparison for later assessment. Some Adlerians may use informal assessment, whereas others may use projective techniques, lifestyle questionnaires, or standardized interviews. Many of the more formal or detailed methods for collecting information about lifestyle originated with Dreikurs. Other Adlerians have developed a variety of protocols and questionnaires (for example, Clark, 2002; Kern, 1997). Most of these procedures include information about family dynamics and early recollections. Other information, which may come from less formal assessment, includes data from dreams. Additionally, Adlerians often wish to assess not only the problems that the person may be experiencing but also assets, those things in a patient's life that work well for him. These aspects can be considered strengths and can be accessed to bring about a successful outcome in therapy.

Family dynamics and constellation. In assessing the lifestyle of an individual, it is very important to attend to early family relationships—relationships among siblings and parents as well as with friends or teachers (Oberst & Stewart, 2003; Sweeney, 2009). The family represents a microcosm of society; thus, it is here where social interest is developed, frustrated, or thwarted. Although Adlerians may be known for their emphasis on birth order, they are more interested in the dynamics of the siblings with the patient, the dynamics of child–parent interaction within the family, and changes in the family over time. It is the patients' perceptions of their childhood development that form the basis for therapeutic interpretations and interventions that occur in the process of helping the patients reach their goals.

Regarding birth order, several different types of questions are asked (Manaster & Corsini, 1982). The patients are asked to describe their siblings as they remember them. Then the therapist may learn the view that the client has toward others in the family and how the client's lifestyle developed in the family. If a male patient says that his older brother was both brighter and more athletically inclined, it leads the Adlerian to look for what the client felt were his particular strengths and how he dealt with possible feelings of inferiority.

Information about the siblings as an interactive group is also obtained. Ages of the siblings and the number of years separating the siblings are noted. For example, in a family with four children, many possible interactions could be observed. The oldest may protect the youngest, the oldest and next oldest may gang up on the youngest two, or three children may gang up on a fourth. As children go to school and leave home, these interactions may change. Adlerians (Dinkmeyer & Sperry, 2000) have observed that when clients describe themselves as children and as adults, they do so in similar ways. In collecting this data, Adlerians may proceed from one question to the next, or they may test out hypotheses as they move through the data collection. For some, this process may be an hour, for others, 3 or 4 hours.

Comparative ratings of siblings on a number of characteristics are often useful material. For example, Shulman and Mosak (1988) and Sweeney (2009) suggest rating siblings on characteristics such as the hardest worker, the worst temper, the bossiest, the most athletic, the prettiest, the most punished, the most selfish, and the most unselfish. Also, Adlerians may ask about significant events such as serious illness or injury, disciplinary problems in school or in the community, or special accomplishments or achievements. In large families, therapists must decide which siblings or groups of siblings to concentrate on. For example, in a family of nine children, the therapist needs to organize the information so that a lifestyle analysis can be made. Focus may be on relatively few siblings or on groups of siblings.

Parental values, interactions, and relationships with children are important information for Adlerians. Questions about each parent, such as the type of persons the father and mother are or how each separately disciplined the child or other siblings, are asked. Also, information about how the parents got along with each other and how this relationship may have changed at various points in time may be valuable information. If parents divorced, or one parent died, or grandparents lived in the home, adjustments need to be made to assimilate this information in developing a sense of the patient's lifestyle. This provides a view of the patient's perception of himself and how interactions with siblings and family affected his perceptions.

Early recollections. Information from early recollections is essential in helping to determine an individual's lifestyle. Early recollections are the memories of the actual incidents that patients recall.

> It is not important whether the incidents did occur in this way; but it is all important that the patient thinks that it did happen. Members of the same family may remember the same incident; but what they remember of it generally differs greatly, in accordance with their basic outlook on life. (Dreikurs, 1967, p. 93)

In gathering information about early recollections, it is important for Adlerians to get as much detail as possible, and they may ask several questions to do this. According to Adler (1958), memories do not occur by chance. People remember those incidents that have a bearing on their lives. It is not a coincidence that the very few memories that we may have out of thousands of incidents in childhood are related to how we will live our lives. They reinforce and reflect our basic life views. Early recollections are different from reports, which are not valid early recollections. A report would be: "My mother always told me that when I was 3 I liked to play with the neighbor's poodle, which was very friendly and would tolerate my abuse." Obtaining early memories is relatively straight-forward: "Would you try to recall your earliest memories for me? Start with your earliest specific memory, something that happened to you that you can remember, not something that was told to you." After that memory is recalled and the patient seems to be doing it well, it may be sufficient to say, "Try to recall another specific memory, something that happened when you were very young." Adlerians vary as to how many early recollections they use. Adler may have used only one or two with a patient; Dreikurs often obtained 10 or more early recollections from his patients. Usually Adlerian therapists ask for early recollections throughout therapy rather than just at the beginning.

Although Adler believed that more recent remembrances could be useful, he stated that older remembrances, such as those occurring at the age of 4 or 5, were most helpful, as they occur near the beginning of the time when the style of life is crystallized. Examining Adler's analysis of one of his patient's earliest memories is instructive. The patient is a 32-year-old man who experiences anxiety attacks when he starts to work. The anxiety that interferes with his keeping a job also had occurred before examinations at school, as he often tried to stay home from school because he felt tired. Adler (Ansbacher & Ansbacher, 1956, p. 355) described him as "the eldest, spoiled son of a widow." The earliest recollection that the man recalled was the following: "When I was about 4 years old I sat at the window and watched some workmen building a house on the opposite side of the street while my mother knitted stockings." Adler's analysis is as follows: "The pampered child is revealed by the fact that the memory recalls a situation that includes the solicitous mother. But a still more important fact is disclosed: he looks on while people work. His preparation for life is that of an onlooker. He is scarcely anything more than that." Adler concludes by saying, "If he wants to make the best use of his preparation, he should seek some work in which observation chiefly is needed. This patient took up successfully dealing with the objects of arts" (Ansbacher & Ansbacher, 1956, p. 356).

It is helpful when analyzing memories to consider such issues as what the dominant themes for several memories are. Also, the person's situation in the memory can be important. Are individuals participating in the event they describe, or are they observing it, like the man in the situation just mentioned? Also, being aware of the feelings expressed in the memories and their consistency can be useful.

Dreams. In doing an assessment of lifestyle, Adlerians may respond to childhood dreams and to more recent recurrent dreams. Throughout the course of therapy, clients are encouraged to relate dreams to the therapist. Adler believed that dreams were purposeful and that they were often indications of an individual's lifestyle. Also, they could be useful in determining what the individual may like or fear for his future. In Adlerian therapy, symbols do not have fixed meanings in dreams. To understand a dream, one must know the individual dreamer (Mosak & Maniacci, 2008).

Dreikurs's discussion of dreams, along with examples, is quite helpful in understanding how Adlerians understand dreams and interpret them. In one example, Dreikurs explains how dreams can show the patient's attitude toward psychotherapy.

> A patient relates the following dream. He is in a lifeboat with a man looking for rescue. They see a merchant ship and they steer toward it. Then they see a Japanese warship coming from behind the horizon to capture the merchant ship. They decide to steer away from the merchant ship to avoid being captured.
>
> It is obvious that the patient sees some danger in being rescued. The discussion of the dream and the present life situation brings an admission from the patient that he is afraid of getting well. Then he would have to face the danger of life. Losing his symptoms would deprive him of an alibi to withdraw as soon as he felt exposed to situations where his prestige or superiority was threatened. (Dreikurs, 1967, p. 223)

In another example, Dreikurs shows how dreams often can show change or movement in therapy.

> One of my patients had a very peculiar type of dream. All his dreams were rather short and without any action. He did in his dreams what he did in life; he continuously figured out the best way of getting out of a problem, mostly without actually doing anything. He dreamed about difficult situations, figuring out what would happen if he acted in one or the other way, but even in his dreams nothing actually happened. When his dreams started to move and to be active, he started to move in his life, too. (Dreikurs, 1967, p. 226)

Dreikers's emphasis on the temporary nature of dreams is consistent with that of other Adlerians, such as Mosak and Maniacci (2008). Dreams can be used as an assessment of current change and progress. In terms of an assessment of lifestyle, dreams may be used as an adjunct to family constellation and early memories.

Basic mistakes. Derived from early recollections, basic mistakes refer to the self-defeating aspects of an individual's lifestyle. They often reflect avoidance or withdrawal from others, self-interest, or desire for power. All of these are in opposition to Adler's concept of social interest (Dinkmeyer & Sperry, 2000, p. 95).

Although basic mistakes vary for each individual, Mosak and Maniacci (2008, p. 82) provide a useful categorization of mistakes:

1. *Overgeneralizations.* This includes words such as "all," "never," "everyone," and "anything." Examples of overgeneralizations are: "Everyone should like me," "I never can do anything right," or "Everyone is out to hurt me."

2. *False or impossible goals of security.* The individual sees the society as working against him or her and is likely to experience anxiety. Examples are "People want to take advantage of me" and "I'll never succeed."

3. *Misperceptions of life and life's demands.* Examples are "Life is too hard" and "I never get a break."

4. *Minimization or denial of one's worth.* These include expressions of worthlessness such as "I am stupid" or "No one can ever like me."

5. *Faulty values.* This has to do primarily with behavior. Examples are "You have to cheat to get your way" or "Take advantage of others before they take advantage of you."

Although it is helpful to identify basic mistakes, correcting the mistakes can be quite difficult because individuals may have many safeguarding processes that interfere with their correction of mistakes. Manaster and Corsini (1982) give some examples of patients' basic mistakes that show incorrect views of life:

A man who married four times unsuccessfully

1. He does not trust women.

2. He feels alone in life.

3. He is unsure of his success, but won't admit it; he is a smiling pessimist.

An alcoholic nurse

1. She feels she does not belong to the human race.

2. She rejects people, but thinks they reject her.

3. She trusts things more than she does people. (Manaster & Corsini, 1982, p. 102)

According to Manaster and Corsini (1982), people are completely unaware of having these basic views of themselves. Although people may come to therapy for one basic mistake, they may have several interrelated mistakes. In therapy, the therapist attempts to present basic mistakes clearly so that they may be understood and the patient can become aware in future situations when he is about to make a basic mistake.

Assets. Because family constellation, early recollections, dreams, and basic mistakes often lead to finding out what is wrong with the person, it is helpful to look at what is right (Watts & Pietrzak, 2000). Because an analysis of an individual's lifestyle can take several hours, countering discouragement with discussion of the patient's assets can be useful. In some cases, the assets are obvious; in others, the patient is not aware of his assets. Assets can include a number of characteristics: honesty, academic or vocational skills, relationship skills, or attention to family. For example, the sensitive writer who can write about the social injustices of others may have difficulty in social relationships. Applying the asset of sensitivity to others that is present in his writings may be helpful to the patient.

Insight and Interpretation

During the process of analyzing and assessing an individual's family dynamics, early recollections, dreams, and basic mistakes, the therapist interprets the material so that patients can develop insights into their actions. The timing of the interpretations depends on progress toward the patient's goals. Dreikurs (1967, p. 60) emphasizes that interpretations are made in regard to goals and purposes; therapists do not interpret psychological conditions. For Dreikurs, telling patients that they feel insecure or inferior is not useful because these statements do not help patients change their goals and intentions. Adlerians help their patients develop insights into mistaken goals and behaviors that interfere with achieving these goals. When patients develop insights into their behavior, it is helpful to act on these insights. The therapist often expresses interpretations to patients tentatively, because no one can know a patient's inner world or private logic. Suggestions are often in the form of questions or statements that are made tentative with phrases such as "is it possible that," "it seems to me that," and "I wonder if." Patients are less defensive and less likely to argue with the therapist when interpretations are presented this way, and there are fewer obstacles in making insights from the therapist's interpretations.

Interpretations are made throughout the therapeutic process. To illustrate interpretation, it may be helpful to examine a brief case that Adler presents about a young woman suffering from headaches. The case illustrates Adler's attention to family dynamics and to social interest.

> A girl who had been very pretty, spoiled by her mother and ill-used by a drunkard father became an actress and had many love affairs which culminated in her becoming the mistress of an elderly man. Such an obvious exploitation of an advantage indicates deep feelings of insecurity and cowardice. This relationship, however, brought her trouble; her mother reproached her, and although the man loved her, he could not get a divorce. During this time her younger sister became engaged. In the face of this competition, she began to suffer from headaches and palpitations and became very irritable towards the man. (Ansbacher & Ansbacher, 1956, p. 310)

Adler goes on to explain that headaches are produced by feelings of anger. He says that tensions are held in for some time, and they may erupt in a variety of physiological responses. He shows that children and people like the patient who are unsocial in their nature are likely to display their temper. He interprets the girl's behavior in this way:

> The girl's condition was the result of a neurotic method of striving to hasten her marriage, and was not at all ineffective. The married man was greatly worried by her continuous headaches, coming to see me about my patient, and said that he would hurry the divorce and marry her. Treatment of the immediate illness was easy—in fact, it would have cleared up without me, for the girl was powerful enough to succeed with the help of her headaches.
>
> I explained to her the connection between her headaches and the competitive attitude toward her sister: it was the goal of her childhood not to be surpassed by her younger sister. She felt incapable of attaining her goal of superiority by normal

means, for she was one of those children whose interest has become absorbed in themselves, and who tremble for fear that they will not succeed. She admitted that she cared only for herself and did not like the man she was about to marry. (Ansbacher & Ansbacher, 1956, pp. 310–311)

Adler's explanation of the patient's behavior demonstrates the consistency of Adler's interpretations and his emphasis on family constellation and social interest (or lack of it). How to make use of interpretations is the subject of the next section.

Reorientation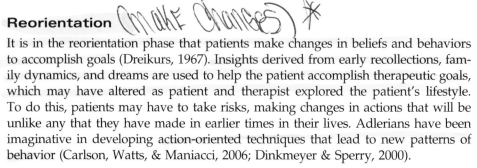

Theories in Action

It is in the reorientation phase that patients make changes in beliefs and behaviors to accomplish goals (Dreikurs, 1967). Insights derived from early recollections, family dynamics, and dreams are used to help the patient accomplish therapeutic goals, which may have altered as patient and therapist explored the patient's lifestyle. To do this, patients may have to take risks, making changes in actions that will be unlike any that they have made in earlier times in their lives. Adlerians have been imaginative in developing action-oriented techniques that lead to new patterns of behavior (Carlson, Watts, & Maniacci, 2006; Dinkmeyer & Sperry, 2000).

Immediacy. Expressing your experience of what is happening at this very moment in therapy defines *immediacy*. The patient communicates, either verbally or nonverbally, something related to the goals of therapy. It may be helpful for the therapist to respond to this. Because it may appear abrupt to the patient, or out of nowhere, it is often helpful to be tentative about this communication. The following is an example of immediacy:

> *Joan:* (is looking at her hands in her lap and softly says to the therapist) I want to tell Harry to listen to me, to pay attention to what I have to say, but he never listens.

> *[Therapist:]* Although you say that you want to have Harry listen to you, your soft voice and downcast glance seem to communicate that you believe you won't be listened to. Is that right?

In this example, the therapist contrasts the verbal and nonverbal behavior, showing that Joan may be preventing herself from improving her relationship with Harry. By adding a question at the end of the therapeutic statement, the therapist allows Joan to respond to the observation.

Encouragement. Encouragement, used throughout the process of Adlerian psychotherapy, is useful in building a relationship and in assessing client lifestyle (Carlson, Watts, & Maniacci, 2006). Emphasizing its importance, Kelly and Lee (2007) see encouragement by the therapist as the primary ingredient in Adlerian counseling. In the reorientation stage, it is helpful to bring about action and change. By focusing on beliefs and self-perceptions, the therapist can help the patient overcome feelings of inferiority and a low self-concept. In the reorientation phase, the individual's willingness to take risks and to try new things is supported. For example:

> *[Patient:]* My work has been frustrating for me. I think I know how I could do it better, but the instructions that my boss gave me make me feel so awkward.

> *[Therapist:]* You seem to have devised a strategy that will be productive and effective. I'd like to hear about it.

In this example, the patient is discouraged at work; the therapist encourages her by referring to her assets and asking for her ideas.

For Adler, encouragement was much more than "Just try harder. I'm sure you can do it." His creativity and humanity are seen in this dramatic example of being encouraging with a young woman with schizophrenia.

> Once I was called in to do what I could for a girl with dementia praecox. She had suffered from this condition for eight years, and for the last two years had been in an asylum. She barked like a dog, spat, tore her clothes, and tried to eat her handkerchief. We can see how far she had turned away from interest in human beings. She wanted to play the role of a dog, and we can understand this. She felt that her mother had treated her as a dog; and perhaps she was saying, "The more I see of human beings, the more I should like to be a dog." When I first spoke to her, on eight successive days, she did not answer a word. I continued to speak to her, and after thirty days she began to talk in a confused and unintelligible way. I was a friend to her and she was encouraged.... When I next spoke to this girl, she hit me. I had to consider what I should do. The only answer that would surprise her was to put up no resistance. You can imagine the girl—she was not a girl of great physical strength. I let her hit me and looked friendly. This she did not expect, and it took away every challenge from her. She still did not know what to do with her reawakened courage. She broke my window and cut her hand on the glass. I did not reproach her, but bandaged her hand. The usual way of meeting such violence, to confine her and lock her in a room, was the wrong way. We must act differently if we wish to win this girl.... I still see this girl from time to time, and she has remained in good health for ten years. She earns her own living, is reconciled to her fellows, and no one who saw her would believe that she had ever suffered from insanity. (Ansbacher & Ansbacher, 1956, pp. 316–317)

As this example shows, encouragement can take courage and creativity on the part of the therapist.

Theories in Action

Acting as if. This technique helps the patient take an action she may be afraid of, often because the patient believes that the action may fail. The patient is asked to "act as if" the action will work (Mosak & Maniacci, 2008). If patients do not want to try a new behavior, Mosak and Dreikurs (1973, p. 60) suggest that they try on a new role the way they might try on a new suit. An attractive suit does not make a person become a new person, but it may give a person a new feeling, perhaps a confident feeling. When working with children, the "as if" technique can be modified by using play, toys, or art materials to encourage children to act as if they are in a pretend situation (Watts & Garza, 2008).

> [*Patient:*] It's hard for me to talk to professors. I need to talk to my math professor; there was a mistake in grading my last exam; but I'm afraid to.
>
> [*Therapist:*] It is hard for you to speak to your professors; but next week I'd like you to talk to your math professor. Act as if you are confident of the discovery of the error and casually explain it to him.

In this situation the patient is given a relatively straightforward task on which to follow through. If the patient is unsuccessful, the therapist will explore what interfered with the "acting as if" experience.

Catching oneself. As patients try to change and implement their goals, they may need to "catch themselves" doing behaviors they desire to change. Because the behavior has been repeated many times in their lifetime, they may need to make an extra effort to "catch themselves." Although they may be initially unsuccessful and catch themselves after they have completed the behavior they wish to change, with practice they are able to catch themselves before they initiate the behavior. As they do this, they learn to make effective changes and see that they are more easily accomplishing their goals. In doing so, they may have an "Aha" response: "Oh, now I see it; now it's clear!" (Sweeney, 2009)

> *Sylvia:* When Alex starts to get angry, I just know that I'm going to walk away into the bedroom and close the door.
>
> *[Therapist:]* You're aware that you start to feel scared and that you want to leave.
>
> *Sylvia:* It seems whenever he gets angry I lock myself in my room.
>
> *[Therapist:]* You might want to try this. When you sense Alex is getting angry, you may catch yourself and say something like, "Alex, I sense you starting to get angry and I'm getting scared. Maybe we can talk this out and I won't go into the bedroom."

Later, when Sylvia experiences an urge to leave the room, she "catches herself," having an insight that she is about to leave the room. She stops herself and then talks to Alex, thus using awareness of her belief to change her behavior.

Creating images. Sometimes therapists might suggest an image to patients that can be used to help them accomplish something. Adler believed that a mental picture of doing something could have much more impact than reminding oneself mentally. For example, if a client wishes to be assertive in getting a roommate to stop smoking in their room, he might picture himself as suave and cool as the roommate submits to his request meekly (Mosak & Maniacci, 2008).

Extending this concept, images can be more than one mental image, but a series of images. Kaufman (2007) suggests that guided visual imagery can be useful in dealing with chronic stress. Visual imagery can be taught to clients to help them cope with different problems that arise. Using the situation of the client who wishes his roommate to stop smoking in the room, the client can be asked to imagine a successful dialogue in which the roommate can be asked to stop smoking in the room. The therapist might model what to say to the roommate first. Then, the client would be asked to imagine what the room looks like, what the roommate looks like, and use the therapist's modeling to cope with the roommate.

Spitting in the client's soup. This phrase comes from the method that children used at boarding schools to get someone else's food by spitting on it. As a technique, the counselor assesses the purpose of a client's behavior and then makes comments that make the behavior less attractive. For example, if a well-to-do mother describes how much she sacrifices in terms of her time and money for her children, the therapist may point out how unfortunate it is that she has no time for her personal life and her need for self-expression. The therapist does not say that the mother cannot continue with her behavior but makes the behavior seem less attractive to the woman.

Avoiding the tar baby. Although the term *tar baby* has come to have racial and other meanings, Adler used *tar baby* to refer to the therapist being careful when discussing a sticky (tar) issue that is both significant for the patient and causes problems for the patient. Some self-defeating behaviors are very difficult to change and may be particularly important to a patient. Although the pattern may be based on faulty assumptions and may not result in meeting goals, the patient may hang on to old perceptions. Further, the patient may try to get the therapist to behave as others do in order to maintain the patient's self-perceptions. For example, a patient who feels worthless may act in annoying ways so that the therapist may be annoyed and thus confirm her perception that she is worthless. The therapist must avoid falling into this trap and thus avoid touching the tar baby. Rather, therapists should encourage behaviors that will lead to greater psychological health instead of commenting on the patient's ineffective perceptions or behavior.

> [*Patient:*] When new coworkers arrive at our store I try to help them, but they tend to ignore me. I notice that you ignore me and don't really listen to me when I talk about my problems.

> [*Therapist:*] You might like me to ignore you, but I'm not. I want to hear more about things that are happening to you at work.

The counselor wants to avoid having the patient see that he is ignoring her. He says that he is not and then goes on to work on patient goals.

Push-button technique. In this technique, developed by Mosak (1985), patients are asked to close their eyes and remember a pleasant incident they have experienced. They are then instructed to attend to the feelings that accompany the pleasant images. Next they are asked to re-create an unpleasant image—it may be of hurt, anger, or failure—and then are asked to create the pleasant scene. By doing this, Adlerians show that patients can create whatever feeling they want just by deciding the subject of their thinking. This technique shows patients that they have the power to change their own feelings.

Paradoxical intention. This strategy has been variously described as "prescribing the symptom" by Adler and as "anti-suggestion" by Dreikurs. In this technique, patients are encouraged to develop their symptoms even more. For example, a young child who sucks his thumb may be told to do it more often. The person who compulsively washes her hands may be told to do it much more frequently. By prescribing the symptom, the therapist makes the patient more aware of the real nature of the situation. Patients then must accept the consequences of their behavior. By accepting the patient's behavior, Adlerians believe that the inappropriate then becomes less attractive to the client. To use this procedure, the therapist should have confidence that when the symptom is prescribed, the patient will have a different perception of the behavior and then choose to change it.

Task setting and commitment. Sometimes patient and therapist plan to take specific actions about problems. When a choice is made, the therapist and patient then determine the best way to implement the choice. It is best if the task is relatively brief and the likelihood of success is high. This would make it easier for the therapist to provide encouragement to the patient. If the patient is not successful, patient and therapist evaluate what about the plan needs to be changed to be more effective.

For example, a patient who is recovering from a back injury may decide to get a job. If she plans to look into want ads, respond to the ads, and then get a job, the therapist may wish to discuss how she will determine which ads to follow up on, what to do if the ads are not sufficient in producing job leads, and how to develop sources. The therapist is likely to focus on the job-search behavior as the task, not the getting of the job. By doing this, the therapist assures that success is more easily obtained by following up on job leads rather than obtaining the actual job, which may take months.

Homework. To help patients in accomplishing tasks, Adlerians often find it helpful to assign homework. The homework is usually something that is relatively easy to accomplish between therapy sessions. Assigning homework is often done carefully so that the therapist is not directing the patient's life. In the previous example, the therapist may suggest that the patient call her hospital social worker about job leads before Tuesday or make three phone calls to prospective employers before the next session. Some homework may be assigned on a week-to-week basis. A child may be told to make her bed just for a week; try it and see what happens. Then the child and the therapist can discuss what to do next.

Life tasks and therapy. As mentioned earlier, Adlerians have identified five main tasks in life: love, occupation, society, self-development, and spiritual development. Manaster and Corsini (1982) suggest testing clients' satisfaction with some of these areas. For example, they ask clients to rate their happiness with their family (husband, wife, or children), satisfaction with work, and satisfaction with friends and community (society). This may identify some issues to work on in therapy that the patient has some difficulty in recognizing. This method can be used throughout therapy to measure change and progress in achieving therapeutic goals.

Terminating and summarizing the interview. Adlerians believe that it is helpful to set clear time limits. With children, sessions may be 30 minutes, and with adults, 45 to 50 minutes. At the end of the session, the therapist does not bring up new material, but, along with the patient, may summarize the interview to provide a clear picture of the counselee's perception of the session. At this point, homework assignments may be discussed, and the client may be encouraged to apply the materials that were discussed in the session to situations as they arise during the week.

These action-oriented approaches are often associated with Adlerian techniques. Although they may be used by other therapists using other theories, they are not often conceptualized in the same way. Adlerians are likely to borrow techniques from other therapies when they feel they will be effective and consistent with Adlerian principles (Carlson, Watts, & Maniacci, 2006; Watts, 2003). Like many other therapists, they may clarify, confront, give emotional support, ask questions, or reassure the patient when they feel that the response is effective. Also, they may give advice if they feel a patient is ready to accept it. Often they find humor is an effective way of making goal-directed changes more palatable (Mosak, 1987). In general, these techniques are illustrative of the action-oriented approach that Adlerians take to assist clients in meeting their therapeutic goals.

Psychological Disorders

Adlerians take a pragmatic approach to psychotherapy and counseling. This can be seen in the four examples described in this section. The use of family constellation and early recollections, along with active interventions, is illustrated in the complex case of a young woman diagnosed with depression. A brief example of an adolescent illustrates an Adlerian approach to general anxiety. An overview of Adlerian conceptualization of borderline and eating disorders is also provided.

Depression: Sheri

Adlerians view people with depression as trying to "overcome inferiority feelings and gain superiority" (Sperry & Carlson, 1993, p. 141), trying very hard to become more effective but failing. In doing so, they lose social interest and become self-absorbed. Dinkmeyer and Sperry (2000) note that depressed individuals often are angry about not getting their own way. Depressed people do not often use the word *angry* in describing themselves. They do not wish to acknowledge anger because then they may have to remedy the situation or confront the individual who is making them angry. Depressed individuals also gain a sense of superiority over others through the way their family and loved ones respond to them—with compassion and concern. This puts the depressed person in the center, experiencing the attention of others and showing little social interest.

Adlerians often help depressed patients develop insight into their distorted and pessimistic perceptions, which were formed in childhood. Further, they work toward helping patients become less self-absorbed and develop social interest by changing beliefs and behaviors. As they move into the reorientation phase of therapy, depressed patients learn to *catch themselves* when they are about to repeat a depressed pattern of behavior. When they catch themselves, they then decide whether to do things differently than they have in the past. The therapist encourages the patient in new beliefs, behaviors, and perceptions. In doing this, the therapist may show the patient how others have a high regard for the patient and that the patient's negative perceptions were based on misperceptions of childhood experiences. Mosak and Maniacci (2008) use the *push-button technique* to show depressed patients that to be depressed means one must choose to be depressed. In this way, depressed patients learn to alter their feelings. These examples illustrate a few approaches Adlerians may take to assist depressed patients in understanding and changing their depressed feelings and beliefs.

To describe an Adlerian approach to depression in more detail, I am summarizing a thorough case study of Sheri by Peven and Shulman (1986, pp. 101–123). In this synopsis, I focus particularly on the use of early recollections and family dynamics in Adlerian psychotherapy. Sheri is a 33-year-old single woman who showed symptoms of neurotic depression. Although she had had psychotherapeutic treatment before, she was in treatment with Peven for 21/2 years. She reported feeling "flawed" by an incestuous relationship that she had had with her father before she was an adolescent. Additional symptoms included feelings of inferiority, difficulty sleeping, diarrhea, and weight loss. Her parents were divorced, and both had remarried. Sheri had an older brother who was married and in business with their father.

The therapist used a number of Adlerian techniques in the first session. For example, she asked what Adler called "The Question"—that is, what Sheri would do with herself if she were symptom-free. Sheri's answers were to "change careers, study something interesting, spend more time with friends, marry, and 'develop myself as a person like taking up painting, reading, and sports'" (p. 102). The therapist listened to Sheri's concern about her incestuous experience with her father and her strong anger toward him. Because she was so angry, the therapist suggested a way in which she could get revenge on her father by taking steps to get more money from him. As Peven says, "Sometimes in the initial interview, I seek to impress new patients, saying or suggesting something novel. I would like them to leave the first interview with something to think about" (p. 103).

After 4 months of therapy, Sheri's depression worsened, and she was referred for medication. She had discussed suicide and had reported uncontrollable crying spells, being very concerned about her symptoms but not ready to examine her issues that were causing depression.

Around this time Peven conducted a formal lifestyle analysis. She interpreted Sheri's lifestyle and presented it to her, along with another therapist, Shulman, in the form of the following summary:

> The younger of two and only girl in a family with a dictatorial czar for a father who was not able to relate to the family except as a dictator. Each family member responded to father's exercise of power in different ways: Mother played the role of an inferior female in order to be less threatening to father and used techniques that caricature femininity in order to establish the territory. Brother imitated father and thus came into conflict with him ("junior czar"), but he was supported by Mother, who indulged him. Sheri imitated Mother both in outward compliance and in an inner resentment. Power over others was the highest value and was achieved by hook or by crook, and females were devalued.
>
> Sheri found herself in an inferior position because of her gender, because of her position as the second-born, and because the family dynamics did not automatically grant family members a worthwhile place. One had to fight or finagle for one's place. Being the youngest and weakest, Sheri discovered that if she submitted to Father, she could be his favorite and thereby achieve some vicarious power.
>
> This was a family in which no human being could trust another and all relationships were competitive. (p. 105)

In addition to this analysis of the family dynamics, early recollections were obtained in the first few months of therapy.

> *Age four.* I'm standing up in my crib. Brother's bed is on another wall. I want a doll that I see across the room, and I can't get it. I cry. I feel frustrated. I am alone in the room.
> *Age two.* I was crawling around on the floor in the living-room. People are there and the TV is going. I am crawling around, stopping, looking around. Everybody else is watching television. I have a feeling of solitude.
> *Age five.* In the house. My parents had gone out of town and were returning. They came in with a dog. I felt real happy. It was exciting and nice to have them back.
> *Age six.* First grade. I beat a neighborhood kid, a boy. He pissed me off, so I grabbed him by the arm and was twirling him around; then I let him go and he bumped his head on a pole. Somebody came and helped him. I stood there feeling very bad, like a criminal. I said to myself, "How could you" (p. 106).

These recollections, according to Peven and Shulman, illustrate Sheri's feelings of alienation from others, along with her frustration in achieving desired goals. She is outside the mainstream of her social network, and her actions lead to little that is useful. In the incident at age 6, she feels bad for hurting someone else. The single happy memory that is reported is one in which she depends on the behaviors of others (when her parents came back with a dog). The therapist presented the following analysis of the early recollections to Sheri:

> I am too small, too hemmed in, to achieve my goals, and there is no one to help me. Surrounded by others, I am still really alone. In my relationship with others, I, at least, want to be the person who acts justly and with consideration so that I can

have some positive feelings about myself. I do not get much positive feeling from others. (p. 106)

From the preceding family dynamics and early recollections, Shulman and Peven determine that Sheri's basic mistakes were the following:

She has been trained to feel negative about herself.
She experiences her goals as impossible to attain and herself as impotent to do anything about it.
The only thing she feels able to do is to suffer and rage at heaven (p. 107).

In receiving the analysis of her lifestyle, Sheri agreed with, or added to, everything that the therapist presented. However, at this time she was not willing to deal with the therapeutic observations.

During much of the first year of therapy, Sheri complained about herself and others. Gradually she began to look at herself. After 2 years of therapy, she began to write to her father and to see him again. At about this time, Sheri decided that she could choose to act and be less depressed.

About a year into therapy, the therapist asked for more early recollections from Sheri. They were different from her earlier recollections. Although they still showed that Sheri found fault with herself, the incidents did not show the rejection that the earlier recollections did.

An example of insight that Sheri developed in the later stages of therapy can be seen in this brief interchange:

[Patient:] I'm sitting with three other people, we are all on vacation, and I get so insecure that other people are getting around me. You know, it's terrible.

[Therapist:] It is neurotic if you want to be the center of attention all the time.

[Patient:] Yes.

[Therapist:] Well, all right, but it isn't that you want to be the center of attention all the time. What's the smile? [Apparently Sheri had a recognition reflex; that is, she had an unconscious, uncontrollable grin on her face. Adlerians consider the recognition reflex a sign of sudden, not quite conscious awareness that an interpretation is correct (Dreikurs, 1967).]

[Patient:] I don't know.

[Therapist:] Dr. Dreikurs used to put it this way: It's a basic mistake if you add the words *only if* so that it comes out "Only if I'm the center of attention do I feel good." If I tell you I like to be the center of attention, that's fine. So what? But I am only happy if I'm the center. That's a neurotic shtick (p. 116; italics in original).

During the latter part of therapy, Sheri is more accepting of the therapist's interpretations, clarifications, and support.

Throughout therapy, Sheri had had several relationships with men, some quite difficult. Toward the end of therapy, she began a longer-lasting relationship. Her depression lifted, and she developed an improved relationship with her father. Although not forgiving him, she no longer dwelled on her feelings of being abused.

Only highlights of this difficult and complex case have been given. However, they illustrate the application of early recollections and family constellation to making therapeutic insights. In addition, a few Adlerian techniques that bring about action have been illustrated.

Generalized Anxiety: Robert

Adlerians view generalized anxiety, tension, sweating, palpitations, and similar bodily symptoms as being indicative of an individual's inability to cope. Often such individuals have experienced failure in their lives. Dealing with difficult decisions is done very hesitantly, if at all. Physiological stress symptoms arise out of the need to avoid defeat or to avoid making poor decisions. Inside, the patient feels inferior and unable to make decisions or to be interested in others. On the outside, the individual may make others aware of the anxiety and may dominate others through the concern that he has for the symptoms of anxiety (Dinkmeyer & Sperry, 2000).

In treatment, encouraging the client becomes very important. The therapist looks for ways to help the individual develop social interest and increase his self-esteem. For the therapist, the symptoms of anxiety are the underlying tar baby that the therapist must avoid sympathizing with or patronizing. Helping the patient develop effective coping strategies and educating the patient in becoming interested in activities around him are important.

A brief example of an adolescent experiencing anxiety and school phobia can help illustrate Adlerian treatment (Thoma, 1959, pp. 423–434). In treating Robert, who had run away from home and left a suicide note, Thoma describes several Adlerian strategies. Robert reported several physical symptoms, including stomachaches. He tried to avoid school, was a poor student, and rarely talked in class because he felt stupid.

He felt distant from his father and saw both of his parents as sick and weak. Emotional feelings were those of hopeless frustration and a resigned weariness. In treating Robert, a school psychologist saw him weekly, but a team of teachers, a counselor, a nurse, and a consulting psychiatrist worked to formulate an approach that would involve professionals in a very significant part of Robert's society-school. Teachers made efforts to involve him in schoolwork and encourage his learning experience. Members of the team helped him assert himself. The psychologist encouraged Robert to disagree with her and to express his opinions. He identified with and was encouraged by male teachers. With this combined encouragement from the entire team, Robert's social interest grew, as evidenced by improved participation in sports events, better relationships with teachers and peers, and improved school attendance.

Eating Disorders: Judy

Adlerians tend to conceptualize eating disorders as situations in which the child is overprotected, overindulged, or overcontrolled by the parents. Usually one and sometimes both of the parents have unrealistic hopes and expectations for the child. This demand for perfection is not challenged by the other parent or by siblings. The young girl develops a compliant attitude, trying to model her parents in order to receive approval: "If I obey you, you should approve of what I do." As the girl gets older, she strives for perfection yet does not believe that she will be able to be perfect. If the family also emphasizes eating or appearance, an eating disorder is even more likely to develop. Rather than rebelling actively, a woman with an eating disorder is more likely to deny body sensations and functions, hunger, and feelings. She will also develop an inability to see herself as others see her (Carlson, 1996, pp. 529–532).

The following brief case example illustrates an Adlerian approach to bulimia (Carlson, 1996). The middle of three girls, Judy is a 17-year-old whose parents expect much from each of their daughters. Judy's older sister tried to be perfect by being good and being effective in school. Judy tried to please her father by trying to become a champion swimmer, but this did not put her in a strong position with her mother. She tried to please her parents with her swimming and academic accomplishments, but as she became a teenager, she found herself unable to achieve the perfection she wanted. She began to gain considerable weight and to purge and binge.

Her early recollections are summarized as follows:

> "Life is a fight and dangerous," "Everyone will give you a hard time unless you can remain perfect," and "People don't treat me the way I should be treated." (p. 531)

Her basic mistakes included not believing that she could develop good relationships with others; being defensive with others, which then gets her into arguments; and feeling like a deprived princess in disguise. Treatment with Judy started with an assessment of her medical condition. The therapist then examined how Judy's beliefs of perfectionism and pessimism caused problems for her. Through encouragement, the therapist helped Judy improve her self-concept and feel more powerful.

Borderline Disorders: Jane

Although psychoanalytic theory views borderline disorder as an arrested level of development, Adlerian theory (Croake, 1989; Shulman, 1982) treats borderline disorder as a style of functioning. From the Adlerian perspective, borderline disorder is found in those who were not only neglected or abused as children but also, at some time, pampered. Due to inappropriate child raising, these individuals take a self-centered view in their interactions with others and do not show a true sense of social interest. Occasionally they may appear to be interested in others, but only when it is to their own advantage (Croake, 1989). Those who are identified as having a borderline disorder generally feel little or no support from others, because they have felt support from their parents in only a random or inconsistent way. Because of this inconsistent support, they continue to seek attention from others, doing this in a maladaptive or manipulative style. If they do not receive enough attention, they may become angry. However, they also continue to try to please others so that they can be noticed by them. From an Adlerian perspective, "Borderline personality disorder is a product of discouragement, poor self-confidence, and pessimism" (Croake, 1989, p. 475).

In treatment of borderline disorders, Adlerian therapists believe that changing borderline behavior requires many sessions to work on goals over and over again, and from different perspectives. Adlerian therapy with borderline disorders features confronting guiding fictions—beliefs about views of themselves and others (Croake, 1989). These guiding fictions often include unreasonable expectations about how others should behave, requiring continual discussion and education from Adlerian therapists. In their therapeutic work, Adlerians help those with borderline disorders to become more flexible in their views of others and more reasonable in their expectations about themselves. Throughout therapy, Adlerians provide unconditional acceptance, encouraging their patients while at the same time examining inappropriate patient behavior. Adlerians try to promote social interest in patients with borderline disorder by encouraging their cooperation with others. The accepting, encouraging, and educative approach of an Adlerian therapist to a patient with a borderline disorder is illustrated in the following brief example.

Jane is a 26-year-old white woman who met the DSM-III-R criteria for borderline personality disorder. Croake (1989) had seen her for more than 45 sessions, often twice a week. Many of the later sessions were multiple therapy sessions with a psychiatric resident. Jane reported early recollections that show a history of sexual abuse. Currently she is having brief, unsatisfactory romantic relationships with men. She is enrolled part-time in college and looking for a job. After discussing an early recollection taking place between the ages of 4 and 6, in which her mother is cooking and she is telling her mother that her stepfather has asked her to pull her pants down, Croake (1989, pp. 478–479) has the following dialogue with her.

[Therapist:] Is it fair to state that you divide people into two groups: those that care about you and those that don't?

Jane: Doesn't everyone?

[Therapist:] No, but I can better understand why you have stormy relationships, while you are enthralled with someone and then get yourself furiously angry with that person.

Jane: I don't know what you mean.

[Therapist:] Perhaps you feel that if someone is nice to you, they like you. If they make a comment that you interpret as critical, you believe that they don't like you anymore.

Jane: Well, it certainly isn't nice for a friend to criticize me (angry affect).

[Therapist:] I'm guessing that you believe I have just criticized you?

Jane: Well, haven't you?

[Therapist:] I was making a comment about your style. I was not putting you down.

Jane: It felt like you were putting me down.

[Therapist:] It would be difficult to always be on guard protecting yourself from possible attack. What did you learn this session?

Jane: I think you were telling me that I get my feelings hurt too easily.

Croake is helping Jane to learn from her behavior and her style of functioning, while at the same time dealing with her anger. He helps her to go beyond her oversimplified, dichotomized thinking. It is not sufficient for him to encourage expression of feelings; he also helps Jane understand the beliefs beneath the feelings. This is illustrated by the last interchange between the therapist and Jane. This very limited dialogue taken from a very complex case provides a glimpse into an Adlerian therapeutic approach to borderline disorders.

Brief Therapy

Adler believed that he could help the patient within 8 to 10 weeks (Ansbacher & Ansbacher, 1970). Because he saw most of his patients twice a week, his total number of sessions would often be fewer than 20, considered brief by most definitions of brief therapy but still typical for many Adlerians (Shlien, Mosak, & Dreikurs, 1962). In a survey of 50 Adlerian therapists, Kern, Yeakle, and Sperry (1989) found that 86% of their clients were seen for less than a year and 53% for less than 6 months. There was a wide variation in the number of sessions, often depending on the severity of the problem.

Adlerians focus on limiting time rather than limiting goals. As Manaster states, "Adlerian therapists attempt full and complete therapy in whatever time is available and in the shortest time possible" (1989, p. 245). Kurt Adler (1989) describes two cases that he treated, seeing each patient twice. Manaster does not believe that diagnostic category is related to length of treatment because it is the "reasoning behind the choice of symptoms," not the symptoms themselves, that determine the length of treatment (1989, p. 247). Being action and goal oriented in their focus on the problem helps Adlerians limit the time needed for therapy (Ansbacher, 1989).

Nicoll (1999) and Bitter and Nicoll (2000) described a method for brief therapy based on Adlerian views of personality theory and therapy. It includes three levels of understanding client behavior as an assessment approach. The brief therapy proceeds in four overlapping stages.

The three levels of understanding include (1) How do I feel? (2) What is the purpose? and (3) Why? Level (1) of assessment includes identifying clients' behaviors and feelings about the behaviors. Level (2) is to determine the purpose or function of the symptoms. Level (3) is to determine the "why," or the rationale or logic that the client uses to make meaning of his life.

These three levels of understanding are then applied to four stages of therapeutic change: Behavioral description of the presenting problem, Underlying rules of interaction assessment, Reorientation of the client's rules of interaction, and Prescribing new behavioral rituals. In getting a Behavioral description, the therapist encourages the client to use action verbs (those ending in -ing) rather than possession verbs such as I am, I have, I suffer because. When listening to the Underlying rules of the interaction that takes place in the narration of the problem, the therapist takes the position of showing the client that she understands the symptoms. Reorientation, or the change process, takes place when the therapist understands the three levels of symptoms. The therapist then shows the client how his rules of interaction can be changed—for example, seeing oneself as competent rather than incompetent. Prescribing new behavioral rituals follows the reorientation process. A client starting to view himself as competent may be asked to make a list of three successes that occur at work at the end of each day.

Current Trends

Adler always had a broad interest in social and educational issues that went beyond individual psychotherapeutic services. Both in Europe and in the United States, Adlerians have been active in developing programs and educational systems within public schools (Mosak and Maniacci, 2008). They have suggested how Adlerian psychology can be helpful to teachers and counselors working in the school system (Carlson, Dinkmeyer, & Johnson, 2008; Lemberger & Milliren, 2008). Partly because of this, they are better known for their work with children and families than with adults. Adlerians believe that they can have a greater impact on society as a whole by working through the educational system than by doing only individual psychotherapy.

Dreikurs and his students and coworkers were responsible for the development of Adlerian psychotherapy and educational ideas in the United States. Training institutes that provide certificates in child guidance, counseling and psychotherapy, and family counseling are spread throughout the United States and

Canada: New York, Chicago, St. Louis, Dayton, Ft. Wayne, Cleveland, Minneapolis, Berkeley, San Francisco, Montreal, and Vancouver. These training institutes grew out of local Adlerian societies in a number of large cities throughout the United States. The North American Society of Adlerian Psychology (NASAP) publishes a quarterly journal, the *Journal of Individual Psychology*, formerly *Individual Psychology*, and a newsletter, *NASAP Newsletter*. For doctoral-level training, there is the Adler School of Professional Psychology, which offers a doctoral degree in clinical psychology. The North American Society of Adlerian Psychology has about 1,200 members. Although this number is small, the number of practicing Adlerians is larger. Furthermore, the influence of Adlerian theory is great, influencing many cognitive, existential, gestalt, reality, and family therapists.

Adlerians have critiqued their own progress, believing that Adlerian psychology cannot stand still but must move in new directions. Mosak (1991) would like to see Adlerians incorporate several areas of scientific psychology into their work, including learning theory, developmental perceptual theory, information related to career decision making, and other life tasks. Because Adlerians attend to social issues, Mosak (1991) would like to see Adlerians more involved in community outreach, poverty, homelessness, discrimination, and women's issues. Watts (2000) shows how Adlerian therapy keeps current with contemporary issues of society such as cultural diversity and spirituality. An example of concern about social issues is the involvement of Adlerians in helping hurricane victims in the United States in 2005. For Adlerian psychology to grow and not disappear into history, new applications are both helpful and necessary.

Using Adlerian Therapy with Other Theories

Just as theorists of psychotherapy have made broad use of Adlerian principles, so do counselors and psychotherapists make use of the concepts and techniques developed by Alfred Adler. Watts (2003) shows how many different approaches can be used with Adlerian therapy. Many therapists have found that the action-oriented and goal-directed approach of Adlerian psychotherapy can provide guidance in their work, particularly in brief therapy. Others find that the collaborative nature of the Adlerian relationship and its emphasis on encouraging the client are helpful guidelines for therapeutic intervention.

From a developmental point of view, the focus on family constellation and birth order gives a broad framework from which to view patients and their interactions with their environment (not only parents but also siblings and others). The uniquely important contribution of early recollections can be used by many therapists and counselors to explore a patient's early development. Additionally, Adler's clarity of purpose of therapy provides therapists and counselors a reminder of the purpose of their work. Adler emphasized the importance of assisting individuals in meeting their goals (Griffith & Graham, 2004; Sweeney, 2009). The focus that Adler put on ascertaining individuals' basic mistakes from their lifestyle helps the therapist focus on the goals of therapy and not be sidetracked by other issues.

Throughout therapy—the development of the relationship, the analysis of lifestyle, interpretation, insight, and reorientation—Adlerians seek to encourage their clients in meeting goals. Somewhat similar to the reinforcement of goals provided by behavior therapists, encouragement helps patients see that there are resolutions to their problems. Encouragement, as conceptualized by

Adlerians, can fit with many types of therapy and counseling (Carlson, Watts, & Maniacci, 2006; Watts & Pietrzak, 2000).

Adlerians actively seek out other theories to integrate into their own work. Active therapies such as narrative (Hester, 2004) and other constructivist therapies (Jones & Lyddon, 2003) are incorporated with Adlerian therapy. Gestalt therapy and Adlerian therapy can offer much to each other (Savard, 2009). Also, brief cognitive and behavioral therapies fit well with Adlerian therapy (Freeman & Urschel, 2003). Attachment theory addresses concepts similar to social interest and ability to complete life's tasks, providing a useful perspective on Adlerian theory (Weber, 2003). The openness to using other theoretical perspectives is a significant characteristic of Adlerian therapy.

Research

Compared with other theories of psychotherapy, relatively little research has been done on Adlerian concepts and the outcome of psychotherapeutic research. One reason so little research has been done on Adlerian psychotherapy is that in general, Adlerians have preferred the case method over research on therapeutic change (Mosak & Maniacci, 2008). Because Adlerians emphasize the subjective nature of the individual, some have been concerned that research that compares groups with each other provides relatively little understanding of Adlerian concepts and therapy. Birth order and social interest are the two areas of Adlerian personality theory that have been studied in most detail and are discussed briefly in terms of their general findings.

Comparing attitudes of parents who attended Adlerian study groups and those who did not, Croake and Burness (1976) observed no differences after four or six sessions of family counseling. However, Lauver and Schramski (1983), in reviewing other studies of Adlerian parent-study groups, found positive changes on measures of attitudes toward child rearing and children, and in becoming less authoritarian and more tolerant in their attitude toward children after participating in study groups. Spence (2009) found that parents using the Systematic Training for Effective Parenting-Teen (STEP-Teen) based on Adlerian principles were able to learn new parenting skills to help them in dealing with their adolescents.

The area of Adlerian psychology that has received the most attention has been that of birth order. The research has focused particularly on first-born, last-born, and only children. A thorough review of this literature may be found in Derlega, Winstead, and Jones (2005) and Schultz and Schultz (2009).

Adler believed that first-borns would attain higher levels of achievement, both academically and professionally, than their siblings. Maddi (1996) reports several studies showing that first-born individuals were overrepresented in the college population compared with their siblings. In a large study of almost 400,000 young men from the Netherlands, Belmont and Marolla (1973) found a positive relationship between birth order and nonverbal intellectual aptitude. In a study of 134 children ages 9 to 13 years, coping resources (family support, peer acceptance, and social support) were highest for first-born or only children and lowest for middle children (Pilkington, White, & Matheny, 1997). Examining perfectionism, Ashby, LoCicero, and Kenny (2003) found nonperfectionists and maladaptive perfectionists were more likely to be middle children than adaptive perfectionists. Fizel (2008) finds support for the finding that maladaptive perfectionists were more likely to be middle children than adaptive perfectionists, and also reports that being the oldest child was associated with adaptive perfection-ism. In a qualitative study of 20 young adult only children, Roberts and Blanton (2001) found that positive aspects of being an only child were no sibling rivalry, enjoying time alone, not having to share parents' financial and emotional re-sources, and developing close relationships with parents. Negative aspects were connecting with peers and worrying about the deaths of their parents. In general, there is some, but not unanimous, support for finding only children and first-borns to be especially responsible individuals.

Adler wrote that the last-born child was likely to be spoiled or pampered by other members of the family. He believed this pampering would make the last-born child more dependent on others and create problems in dealing with difficult life issues. In a review of studies, Barry and Blane (1977) found that last-borns were overrepresented among alcoholics. Longstreth (1970) reported that later-born children were more apprehensive about dangerous activities than were first-borns. First-borns were shown to have the highest number of irrational beliefs about romantic relationships, and last-borns the lowest (Sullivan & Schwebel, 1996). The relationship of birth order issues to personality characteristics is quite complex (Schultz & Schultz, 2009).

In his *Theory and Measurement of Social Interest*, Crandall (1981) quantifies Adler's concept of social interest, finding a positive relationship between social interest and altruism, optimism about the future, and cooperation and empathy. Dinter (2000) finds a relationship between having social interest and a sense of self-effectiveness. Johnson (1997) has related social interest to Adlerian therapy by studying its role in the training of therapists. In a review of studies on social interest, Watkins and Guarnaccia (1999) report that high social interest was re-lated to many positive personal characteristics.

Adlerian research is particularly lacking in studies on psychotherapeutic change. Case studies that focus on the use of early recollections, family constella-tion, or lifestyle development may be helpful. The documentation of the effective-ness of Adlerian action-oriented techniques would also be helpful.

Gender Issues

Early in the development of his theory, Adler was concerned with the role of men and women in society. He saw the relative roles of men and women in early 20th-century Vienna in this way:

> Due to their dominance, men influenced the female position in the division of labor, in the production process, to their own advantage. Men prescribed to women the sphere of life and are in a position to enforce this; they determined forms of life for women that followed primarily the male viewpoint.
>
> As matters stand today, men continuously strive for superiority over women, while women are constantly dissatisfied with the male privileges. (Ansbacher & Ansbacher, 1978, p. 5)

Thus, the male was in a superior role to the female. Both men and women wanted to be superior, or more like the masculine, according to Adler. Neurotic men would focus on "masculinity" rather than their personal development as a way of seeking perfection (Ansbacher & Ansbacher, 1956). He used the term *masculine protest* to refer to a desire among men and women to be superior, to strive to be perfect, a striving away from inferiority toward superiority (Sweeney, 2009). Adler's view was that all individuals should seek to be superior, to do their best. The gender-role expectations of his day were a hindrance to this, and Adler supported the women's rights movement, believing that women should have the right to have an abortion (Ansbacher & Ansbacher, 1978). Adler wrote extensively on gender issues, and his writings have been compiled by Ansbacher and Ansbacher (1978) under the title *Cooperation Between the Sexes*, with a significant part of the book dealing with the myth of women's inferiority. Bottome (1939) suggests that Adler's attitude toward women may be the result, in part, of his interest in Marxism and socialism, which emphasized equality. Also, Adler's wife, Raissa, was interested in these same philosophical and political views, having strong opinions about women's rights. This view of equality has been carried on by Dreikurs and his colleagues (Sweeney, 2009). Adlerians often see Adler as an early feminist or the first prominent psychologist to point out the myth of masculine superiority (Bitter, Robertson, Healey, & Jones Cole, 2009). This does not mean that all Adlerian writings are seen as profeminist. For example, Oswald (2008) reviews three Adlerian texts on parenting, criticizing them for not addressing families headed by same-gender couples.

Multicultural Issues

For Adlerians, to be emotionally healthy means that an individual must develop a social interest extending beyond the immediate family to the individual's broader cultural group. As Newlon and Arciniega (1983) note, many minority groups (Native Americans, Mexican Americans, and African Americans) value social group identity along with individual identity. In therapeutic work with Ubuntu women of South Africa, researchers found that therapeutic interventions based on social interest and belongingness were particularly effective (Brack, Hill, Edwards, Grootboom, & Lassiter, 2003). Studying the practices of a traditional South African healer (a sangoma) who worked in an AIDS clinic, Hill, Brack, Qalinge, and Dean (2008) noted similarities between the sangoma's practices and Adlerian practices. In working with Asian Americans, attending to social interest as well as family environment is important as therapists consider their clients' social and cultural context (Carlson & Carlson, 2000). In another study, the concept of social interest is viewed as one that can be applied to China as well as Europe and North America (Foley, Matheny, & Curlette, 2008) In general, the five scales of the BASIS-A Inventory that measures social interest showed that a sample of individuals throughout China viewed quality of life in a way similar to that of individuals in the United States. Newlon and Arciniega (1983) and Arciniega and Newlon (1983) discuss several social issues that counselors and therapists should be aware of when working with culturally diverse populations.

Language. Within a family, members differ in their fluency and use of their language of origin and English. Paying attention to the individual's use and the role of language for that individual can be helpful in therapy and counseling.

Cultural identity. How individuals label themselves and see themselves can be significant. For example, does an Asian American patient identify herself as American, Asian, or Japanese?

Family dynamics. The issue of birth order often needs to be viewed broadly for minorities. For example, in many Hispanic families, uncles, grandparents, cousins, or friends may play a significant role in child raising. Also, in Mexican American and Native American cultures, the oldest child may be given more responsibility for raising siblings than in some other cultures.

Geographical location. The neighborhood or area in which individuals live and develop can differ within cultural groups. For example, African Americans raised in the southern part of the United States are exposed to a very different culture than those living on the West Coast. Newlon and Arciniega state, "A minority family living in a totally ethnic area views itself differently than a family living in an integrated neighborhood" (1983, p. 9).

This emphasis on social context provides a means for Adlerians to understand different cultural groups. Comparing Adlerian therapy to other theories discussed in this textbook, Sweeney (2009) points out how Adlerian therapy is particularly sensitive to cultural issues.

Group Counseling and Therapy

Adlerian approaches to group counseling and psychotherapy are varied, characterized by educational and creative methods in applying Adlerian principles. Sweeney (2009) explains the varied formats that can be the basis for Adlerian group therapy. Typical of Adlerian groups is the lifestyle group. In this group, members would develop a mini-lifestyle that includes family relationships, comparisons with siblings, and early recollections. The leader and possibly some group members summarize an individual's mistaken perceptions, assets, and goals. The group then can discuss each member's lifestyle in terms of the individual's beliefs and goals. The members help each other develop strategies for change. In such a group, participants may take notes on the lifestyle of each participant.

Dinkmeyer and Sperry (2000) describe a "teleoanalytic workshop" that is designed to help individuals have more effective relationships by activating their social interest. This workshop combines lectures on topics such as social interest, life tasks and challenges, and encouragement and courage. For each topic, exercises help individuals improve their communication skills. The exercises start with people communicating in groups of two, then four, then eight, and then to the larger group. Each exercise involves "presenting oneself to the group in terms of one's strengths, priorities, self-esteem, family atmosphere, family constellation, and assets" (p. 231).

Adlerians have used and modified Moreno's psychodrama technique. Psychodrama is a means of using acting to help individuals solve their problems (Blatner, 2000, 2003). A director or trained psychodrama therapist assists patients in acting out situations or relationships that are problems. Other people—and occasionally the actual people who are part of the patient's problem—play roles in the psychodrama. In this process, the patient moves around the stage, acting out episodes that reflect difficult issues in the patient's life. As they act out their problem and see the problem acted out in front of them, patients develop insights and new strategies for dealing with their issues. Shulman (1971) has developed the Midas technique, in which a group member or leader creates the kind of relationships that the individual would ideally like to have. In "action therapy" (O'Connell, 1975), members act out situations in such a way that people in the group support each other and encourage each other in building self-esteem. This type of social interaction stimulates social interest in the group members.

Summary

Adlerian psychotherapy and counseling make assumptions about individuals that they are part of a larger social system and that they are to be seen subjectively and humanistically. The Adlerian view is developmental in the sense that an individual's lifestyle and views held about the world and about the self are formed before the age of 6. Individuals act on these views and convictions as if they are true. Adlerians emphasize the cognitive nature of individuals, focusing on beliefs that people have about themselves as they interact with their society.

Adlerians understand their patients through the assessment of information about family constellation, early recollections, and dreams. Often conducted through questionnaires and interviews, the lifestyle analysis provides the basis for therapists to help their patients by encouraging them to meet important life goals: love, work, participation in society, self-development, and spiritual development.

The therapeutic process is seen (in part) as educational. Adlerians encourage and assist their patients in correcting their faulty perceptions and their basic mistakes. By doing this, patients learn to cooperate with others and to contribute to society in various ways. Adlerians have developed many innovative action techniques, including paradoxical intention, the push-button technique, and acting as if.

The educational emphasis of Adlerians is seen in their involvement with child guidance centers, marriage counseling, and group counseling. More than most systems of psychotherapy, Adlerians focus on preventive goals to assist people in functioning productively within their social setting. Because the Adlerian approach is pragmatic, they use therapeutic and educational strategies from other theoretical approaches that are consistent with Adler's ideas. Also, Adler's ideas have been used, borrowed, or absorbed by many other theorists in the development of their own theoretical perspectives. Adlerians have always been more concerned about the improvement of society than about ownership of Adlerian thought.

Theories in Action DVD: Adlerian Therapy

Basic Concepts Used in the Role-Play	Questions About the Role-Play
• Inferiority/superiority • Early recollections • Empathy • Focus on problem • Encouraging insight • Acting as if	1. What Adlerian concepts are Shannon's perfectionist tendencies related to? (p. 129) 2. How does Dr. Gilchrist explore the root of Shannon's problems? 3. Why does Dr. Gilchrist suggest that Shannon act as if things are going well? (p. 139) 4. Which methods of changing beliefs can be used that are not discussed in the role-play? (p. 138)

Suggested Readings

Ansbacher, H. L., & Ansbacher, R. (Eds.). (1956). *The individual psychology of Alfred Adler*. New York: Basic Books. The editors have compiled many of Adler's writings into this *volume*. The editorial comments provided by the editors are particularly helpful in understanding how Adler's theory developed.

Ansbacher, H. L., & Ansbacher, R. (Eds.). (1970). *Superiority and social interest.* Evanston, IL: Northwestern University Press. This book is a compilation of Adler's later writings, mainly between 1931 and 1937. Included are Adler's views on psychotherapy, with ideas on conceptualization and treatment of a variety of psychopathological disorders.

Ansbacher, H. L., & Ansbacher, R. (Eds.). (1982). *Cooperation between the sexes.* New York: Norton. This is a compilation of Adler's writings on women and men, love and marriage, and sexuality. It will be of interest to those who would like to learn more about Adler's view on gender issues.

Carlson, J., Watts, R. E., & Maniacci, M. (2006). *Adlerian therapy: Theory and practice.* Washington, DC: American Psychological Association. This is a good description of Adlerian theory of personality and psychotherapy. Information on lifestyle assessment and approaches to therapy and counseling are provided.

Mosak, H. H., & Maniacci, M. P. (2008). Adlerian psychotherapy. In R. J. Corsini & D. Wedding (Eds.), *Current psychotherapies* (8th ed., pp. 63–106). Belmont, CA: Cengage Brooks/Cole. This chapter by Harold Mosak and Michael Maniacci, leading Adlerian scholars, describes historical, theoretical, and applied aspects of Adlerian psychotherapy.

Sweeney, T. J. (2009). *Adlerian counseling and psychotherapy: A practitioner's approach* (5th ed.). New York: Routledge. This is a well-written introduction to Adlerian counseling and psychotherapy featuring sections on Adlerian personality theory, wellness, assessment, encouragement, and therapeutic techniques. Also included are sections on counseling children, career counseling, family therapy, marriage therapy, and group work.

References

Adler, A. (1917). *Study of organ inferiority and its psychical compensation.* New York: Nervous & Mental Disease Publishing Co.

Adler, A. (1958). *What life should mean to you.* New York: Capricorn.

Adler, K. A. (1989). Techniques that shorten psychotherapy. *Individual Psychology, 45,* 62–74.

Ansbacher, H. L. (1977). Individual psychology. In R. J. Corsini (Ed.), *Current personality theories* (pp. 45–85). Itasca, IL: Peacock.

Ansbacher, H. L. (1989). Adlerian psychology: The tradition of brief psychotherapy. *Individual Psychology, 45,* 26–33.

Ansbacher, H. L., & Ansbacher, R. (Eds.). (1956). *The individual psychology of Alfred Adler.* New York: Basic Books.

Ansbacher, H. L., & Ansbacher, R. (Eds.). (1970). *Superiority and social interest by Alfred Adler.* Evanston, IL: Northwestern University Press.

Ansbacher, H. L., & Ansbacher, R. R. (Eds.). (1978). *Cooperation between the sexes.* New York: Anchor Books.

Ansbacher, H. L., & Ansbacher, R. (Eds.). (1982). *Co-operation between the sexes.* New York: Norton.

Ansbacher, H. L., & Huber, R. J. (2004). Adler—psychotherapy and Freud. *Journal of Individual Psychology, 60*(4), 333–337.

Arciniega, M., & Newlon, B. (1983). Cross-cultural family counseling. In O. C. Christensen & T. Schramski (Eds.), *Adlerian family counseling: A manual for counselor, educator and psychotherapist* (pp. 279–292). Minneapolis: Educational Media.

Ashby, J. S., LoCicero, K. A., & Kenny, M. C. (2003). The relationship of multidimensional perfectionism to psychological birth order. *Journal of Individual Psychology, 59*(1), 42–51.

Barry, H., III, & Blane, H. T. (1977). Birth order of alcoholics. *Journal of Individual Psychology, 33,* 62–79.

Belmont, L., & Marolla, E. A. (1973). Birth order, family size, and intelligence. *Science, 182,* 1096–1101.

Bitter, J. R., & Nicoll, W. G. (2000). Adlerian brief therapy with individuals: Process and practice. *Journal of Individual Psychology, 56,* 31–44.

Bitter, J. R., Robertson, P. E., Healey, A. C., & Jones Cole, L. K. (2009). Reclaiming a profeminist orientation in Adlerian therapy. *Journal of Individual Psychology, 65*(1), 13–33.

Blatner, A. (2000). *Foundations of psychodrama: History, theory and practice* (4th ed.). New York: Springer.

Blatner, A. (2003). Not mere players: Psychodrama applications in everyday life. In J. Gershoni (ed.), *Psychodrama in the 21st century: Clinical and educational applications* (pp. 103–115). New York: Springer.

Bottome, P. (1939). *Alfred Adler: A biography.* New York: Putnam.

Brack, G., Hill, M. B., Edwards, D., Grootboom, N., & Lassiter, P. S. (2003). Adler and Ubuntu: Using Adlerian principles in the new South Africa. *Journal of Individual Psychology, 59*(3), 316–326.

Capron, E. W. (2004). Types of pampering and the narcissistic personality trait. *Journal of Individual Psychology, 60*(1), 77–93.

Carlson, J. (1996). Eating disorders (2nd ed.). In L. M. Sperry & J. Carlson (Eds.), *Psychopathology and psychotherapy: From diagnosis to treatment* (pp. 567–596; 2nd ed., pp. 513–537). Washington, DC: Accelerated Development.

Carlson, J., Dinkmeyer, D., Jr., & Johnson, E. J. (2008). Adlerian teacher consultation: Change teachers, change students! *Journal of Individual Psychology, 64*(4), 480–493.

Carlson, J., Watts, R. E., & Maniacci, M. (2006). *Adlerian therapy: Theory and practice.* Washington, DC: American Psychological Association.

Carlson, J. M., & Carlson, J. D. (2000). The application of Alderian psychotherapy with Asian-American clients. *Journal of Individual Psychology, 56*, 214–226.

Clark, A. J. (2002). *Early recollections: Theory and practice in counseling and psychotherapy.* New York, NY: Brunner-Routledge.

Crandall, J. E. (1981). *Theory and measurement of social interest.* New York: Columbia University Press.

Croake, J., & Burness, M. R. (1976). Parent study group effectiveness after four and six weeks. *Journal of Individual Psychology, 32*, 108–111.

Croake, J. W. (1989). Adlerian treatment of borderline personality disorder. *Individual Psychology, 45*, 473–489.

Derlega, V. J., Winstead, B. A., & Jones, W. H. (2005). *Personality: Contemporary theory and research* (3rd ed.). Belmont, CA: Wadsworth.

Dinkmeyer, D., Jr., & Sperry, L. (2000). *Counseling and psychotherapy: An integrated, individual psychology approach.* Upper Saddle River, NJ: Merrill/Prentice-Hall.

Dinter, L. D. (2000). The relationship between self-efficacy and lifestyle patterns. *Journal of Individual Psychology, 56*, 462–473.

Dreikurs, R. (1950). Techniques and dynamics of multiple psychotherapy. *Psychiatric Quarterly, 24*, 788–799.

Dreikurs, R. (1967). *Psychodynamics, psychotherapy, and counseling: Collected papers.* Chicago: Alfred Adler Institute.

Ellenberger, H. F. (1970). *The discovery of the unconscious.* New York: Basic Books.

Fizel, L. (2008). The relationship of birth order to perfectionism. *Dissertation Abstracts International: Section B: The Sciences and Engineering, 69*(5-B), 3265–3265.

Foley, Y. C., Matheny, K. B., & Curlette, W. L. (2008). A cross-generational study of Adlerian personality traits and life satisfaction in mainland China. *Journal of Individual Psychology, 64*(3), 324–338.

Freeman, A., & Urschel, J. (2003). Individual psychology and cognitive-behavioral therapy: A cognitive perspective. In R. E. Watts (Ed.), *Adlerian, cognitive, and constructivist therapies: An integrative dialogue* (pp. 71–88). New York: Springer.

Griffith, B. A., & Graham, C. C. (2004). Meeting needs and making meaning: The pursuit of goals. *Journal of Individual Psychology, 60*(1), 25–41.

Hester, R. L. (2004). Early memory and narrative therapy. *Journal of Individual Psychology 60*(4), 338–347.

Hill, M. B., Brack, G., Qalinge, L., & Dean, J. (2008). Adlerian similarities to a sangoma treating AIDS in South Africa. *Journal of Individual Psychology, 64*(3), 310–323.

Johnson, E. P. (1997). Novice therapists and social interest. *Individual Psychology, 53*, 105–109.

Jones, J. V., Jr., & Lyddon, W. J. (2003). Adlerian and constructivist psychotherapies: A constructivist perspective. In R. E. Watts (Ed.), *Adlerian, cognitive, and constructivist therapies: An integrative dialogue* (pp. 38–56). New York: Springer.

Kaufman, J. A. (2007). An Adlerian perspective on guided visual imagery for stress and coping. *Journal of Individual Psychology, 63*(2), 193–204.

Kelly, F. D., & Lee, D. (2007). Adlerian approaches to counseling with children and adolescents. In H. T. Prout & D. T. Brown (Eds.), *Counseling and psychotherapy with children and adolescents: Theory and practice for school and clinical settings* (4th ed., pp. 131–179). Hoboken, NJ: John Wiley.

Kern, R. (1997). *Lifestyle scale.* Coral Gables, FL: CMTI Press.

Kern, R. M., Yeakle, R., & Sperry, L. (1989). Survey of contemporary Adlerian clinical practices and therapy issues. *Individual Psychology, 45*, 38–47.

Lauver, P. J., & Schramski, T. G. (1983). Research and evaluation of Adlerian family counseling. In O. C. Christensen & T. G. Schramski (Eds.), *Adlerian family counseling* (pp. 367–388). Minneapolis: Educational Media.

Lemberger, M. E., & Milliren, A. (2008). Individual psychology and the schools. *Journal of Individual Psychology, 64*(4), 383–385.

Lewis, T. F., & Watts, R. E. (2004). The predictability of Adlerian lifestyle themes compared to demographic variables associated with college student drinking. *Journal of Individual Psychology, 60*(3), 245–264.

Longstreth, L. E. (1970). Birth order and avoidance of dangerous activities. *Developmental Psychology, 2*, 154.

Maddi, S. R. (1996). *Personality theories: A comparative analysis* (6th ed.). Pacific Grove, CA: Brooks/Cole.

Manaster, G. (1989). Clinical issues in brief psychotherapy: A summary and conclusion. *Individual Psychology, 45*, 243–247.

Manaster, G., & Corsini, R. J. (1982). *Individual psychology*. Itasca, IL: F. E. Peacock.

McBrien, R. J. (2004). Expanding social interest through forgiveness. *Journal of Individual Psychology, 60*(4), 408–419.

Mosak, H. H. (1958). Early recollections as a projective technique. *Journal of Projective Techniques, 22*, 302–311.

Mosak, H. H. (1985). Interrupting a depression: The pushbutton technique. *Individual Psychology, 41*, 210–214.

Mosak, H. H. (1987). *Ha ha and aha: The role of humor in psychotherapy*. Muncie, IN: Accelerated Development.

Mosak, H. H. (1991). Where have all the normal people gone? *Individual Psychology, 47*, 437–446.

Mosak, H. H., & Dreikurs, R. (1973). Adlerian psychotherapy. In R. J. Corsini (Ed.), *Current psychotherapies*. Itasca, IL: Peacock.

Mosak, H. H., & Maniacci, M. (1999). *A primer on Adlerian psychology*. Philadelphia: Brunner/Mazel.

Mosak, H. H., & Maniacci, M. P. (2008). Adlerian psychotherapy. In R. J. Corsini & D. Wedding (Eds.), *Current psychotherapies* (8th ed., pp. 63–100). Belmont, CA: Brooks/Cole.

Mwita, M. (2004). Martin Luther King Jr.'s lifestyle and social interest in his autobiographical early memories. *Journal of Individual Psychology, 60*(2), 191–203.

Newlon, B. J., & Arciniega, M. (1983). Counseling minority families: An Adlerian perspective. *Counseling and Human Development, 16*, 111.

Nicoll, W. G. (1999). Brief therapy strategies and techniques. In R. E. Watts & J. Carlson (Eds.), *Intervention strategies in counseling and psychotherapy* (pp. 15–30). Philadelphia: Accelerated Development.

O'Connell, W. (1975). *Action therapy and Adlerian theory: Selected papers by Walter O'Connell*. Chicago: Alfred Adler Institute.

Oberst, U. E., & Stewart, A. E. (2003). *Adlerian psychotherapy: An advanced approach to individual psychology*. New York: Brunner/Routledge.

Oswald, R. F. (2008). The invisibility of lesbian and gay parents and their children within Adlerian parenting materials. *Individual Psychology, 64*(2), 246–251.

Penick, J. M. (2004). Purposeful aging: Teleological perspectives on the development of social interest in late adulthood. *Journal of Individual Psychology, 60*(3), 219–233.

Peven, D. E., & Shulman, B. H. (1986). Adlerian psychotherapy. In I. L. Kutash & A. Wolf (Eds.), *Psychotherapist's case book* (pp. 101–123). San Francisco: Jossey-Bass.

Pilkington, L. R., White, J. A., & Matheny, K. B. (1997). Perceived coping resources and psychological birth order in school-aged children. *Individual Psychology, 53*, 42–57.

Roberts, L. C., & Blanton, P. W. (2001). "I always knew mom and dad loved me best." Experiences of only children. *Journal of Individual Psychology, 57*, 125–140.

Savard, M. (2009). Critical collaboration: Adlerian therapy and gestalt therapy. *Dissertation Abstracts International: Section B: The Sciences and Engineering, 69*(7-B), 4442–4443.

Schultz, D. P., & Schultz, S. E. (2009). *Theories of personality* (9th ed.). Belmont, CA: Cengage Wadsworth.

Sharf, R. S. (2010). *Applying career development theory to counseling* (5th ed.). Belmont, CA: Cengage Brooks/Cole.

Shlien, J. M., Mosak, H. H., & Dreikurs, R. (1962). Effect of time limits: A comparison of two psychotherapies. *Journal of Counseling Psychology, 9*, 31–34.

Shulman, B. H. (1971). *Contributions to individual psychology*. Chicago: Alfred Adler Institute.

Shulman, B. H. (1982). An Adlerian interpretation of borderline personality. *Modern Psychoanalysis, 7*, 137–153.

Shulman, B. H., & Mosak, H. H. (1988). *Manual for life style assessment*. Muncie, IN: Accelerated Development.

Spence, J. A. (2009). Changes in perception of family environment and self-reported symptom status in adolescents whose parents participate in an Adlerian parent-training intervention. *Dissertation Abstracts International: Section B: The Sciences and Engineering, 69*(9-B), 5794.

Sperry, L. M., & Carlson, J. (1993). *Psychopathology and psychotherapy from diagnosis to treatment*. Muncie, IN: Accelerated Development.

Stone, M. H. (2008). Immanuel Kant's influence on the psychology of Alfred Adler. *Journal of Individual Psychology, 64*(1), 21–36.

Sullivan, B. F., & Schwebel, A. J. (1996). Birth-order position, gender, and irrational relationship beliefs. *Individual Psychology, 52,* 54–64.

Sweeney, T. J. (2009). *Adlerian counseling and psychotherapy: A practitioner's approach* (5th ed.). New York: Routledge/Taylor & Francis Group.

Thoma, E. (1959). Treatment of an adolescent neurotic in a public school setting. In K. A. Adler & D. Deutsch (Eds.), *Essays in individual psychology* (pp. 423–434). New York: Grove Press.

Vaihinger, H. (1965). *The philosophy of "as if."* London: Routledge & Kegan Paul.

Watkins, C. E., Jr., & Guarnaccia, C. A. (1999). The scientific study of Adlerian theory. In R. E. Watts & J. Carlson (Eds.), *Interventions and strategies in counseling and psychotherapy* (pp. 207–230). Philadelphia: Accelerated Development.

Watts, R. E. (1999). The vision of Adler: An introduction. In R. E. Watts & J. Carlson (Eds.), *Interventions and strategies in counseling and psychotherapy* (pp. 1–13). Philadelphia: Accelerated Development.

Watts, R. E. (2000). Adlerian counseling: A viable approach for contemporary practice. *TCA Journal, 28,* 11–23.

Watts, R. E. (Ed.). (2003). *Adlerian, cognitive, and constructivist therapies: An integrative dialogue.* New York: Springer.

Watts, R. E., & Garza, Y. (2008). Using children's drawings to facilitate the acting "as if" technique. *Journal of Individual Psychology, 64*(1), 113–118.

Watts, R. E., & Pietrzak, D. R. (2000). Adlerian "encouragement" and the therapeutic process of solution-focused brief therapy. *Journal of Counseling and Development, 78,* 442–447.

Weber, D. A. (2003). A comparison of individual psychology and attachment theory. *Journal of Individual Psychology 59*(3), 246–262.

White, L. W., Newbauer, J. F., Sutherland, J. H., & Cox, C. C. (2005). Lifestyle strengths of holocaust survivors. *Journal of Individual Psychology, 61*(1), 37–54.

CHAPTER 5

Existential Therapy

Outline of Existential Therapy

EXISTENTIAL PERSONALITY THEORY
- Being-in-the-World
- Four Ways of Being
  - Umwelt
  - Mitwelt
  - Überwelt
  - Eigenwelt
- Time and Being
- Anxiety
- Living and Dying
- Freedom, Responsibility, and Choice
- Isolation and Loving
- Meaning and Meaninglessness
- Self-Transcendence
- Striving for Authenticity
- Development of Authenticity and Values

EXISTENTIAL PSYCHOTHERAPY
- Goals of Existential Psychotherapy
- Existential Psychotherapy and Counseling
- Assessment
  - Initial assessment
  - Dreams as assessment
  - Use of objective and projective tests
- The Therapeutic Relationship
  - Therapeutic love
  - Resistance
  - Transference
  - The therapeutic process
- Living and Dying
- Freedom, Responsibility, and Choice
  - Freedom
  - Responsibility
  - Choice
- Isolation and Loving
- Meaning and Meaninglessness

Based on a philosophical approach to people and their existence, existential psychotherapy deals with important life themes. Rather than prescribing techniques and methods, existential psychotherapy is an attitudinal approach to issues of living. Themes include living and dying, freedom, responsibility to self and others, finding meaning in life, and dealing with a sense of meaninglessness. More than other therapies, existential psychotherapy examines individuals' awareness of themselves and their ability to look beyond their immediate problems and daily events to problems of human existence. Because individuals do not exist in isolation from others, developing honest and intimate relationships with others is a theme throughout existential therapy.

Trained in psychoanalysis, the first existential therapists were European psychiatrists who were dissatisfied with Freud's emphasis on biological drives and unconscious processes. Rather, they were interested in the patients in front of them and what was happening to them, seeing their patients as they really were, not as an extension of a theory. Influenced by 19th-century western European philosophers, they listened to how their patients dealt with anxieties resulting from difficult responsibilities, loneliness, despair, and fears of death. These existential themes, rather than specific approaches (although a few are described), are the focus of this chapter.

History of Existential Thought

Existential psychotherapy developed from the early work of European philosophers. Perhaps the first was Kierkegaard, who wrote of the anxiety and uncertainties in life. Emphasizing subjectivity and the will to power, Nietzsche popularized existential thought in 19th-century Europe. Developing existentialism further, Heidegger and Jaspers worked out sophisticated systems of existential philosophy. A more pessimistic view of existentialism was put forth by the French philosopher Sartre. Additionally, theologians have made important statements that combine elements of their particular beliefs and existentialist philosophy. Also, writers such as Dostoyevski, Camus, and Kafka have dealt with existential themes in their plays, novels, and other writings.

Familiarity with the views of these writers, theologians, and philosophers provides a background for understanding existential psychotherapy. A dictionary of existential therapeutic and philosophical concepts provides a means of getting a brief overview of important existential ideas (van Deurzen & Kenward, 2005).

Existential Philosophers

Søren Kierkegaard, the Danish philosopher, has been called the grandfather of existentialism (Lowrie, 1962), in part because of his opposition to Hegel's emphasis on human rationality. Born in 1813 and living only 42 years, Kierkegaard wrote books, including *The Concept of Dread* and *Either/Or*, that dealt with the conflicts and problems of human existence. Kierkegaard viewed individuals as desiring to be eternal, like God, but having to deal with the fact that existence is temporary. When possible, individuals forget their temporal nature and deal with trivial issues of living. In adolescence, an awareness of one's finiteness emerges, and individuals must deal with the torment, angst, and dread that result, issues of philosophical and personal interest to Kierkegaard. Without this experience, individuals merely go through the motions of living and do not directly confront issues of choice and freedom (Gron, 2004). Dealing with this uncomfortable state is a task of becoming human and a focus of Kierkegaard's work.

The German philosopher Friedrich Nietzsche (1844–1900) emphasized the importance of human subjectivity. He believed that the focus on the rationality of individuals was misleading and that the irrational aspects of human nature played an important role. In particular, he emphasized the dynamics of resentment, guilt, and hostility that individuals attempt to repress (May, 1958a). Nietzsche was concerned that Europeans would express their repressed instincts through self-hatred and aggression rather than through creative means. In his development of the concept of "superman," Nietzsche argued that individuals who allow themselves to develop their "will to power" are creative and dynamic, achieving positions of leadership. By truly realizing their own individual potentialities and courageously living out their own existence, individuals seek to attain Nietzsche's concept of "will to power." Although Kierkegaard's views were based on theology and Nietzsche's on a "life force," both emphasized the subjective and irrational nature of individuals that was to have a direct impact on other existential philosophers and psychotherapists.

Phenomenology, as it was developed by Edmund Husserl (1859–1938), has been part of the evolution of existential psychotherapy. For Husserl, phenomenology was the study of objects as they are experienced in the consciousness of individuals. The methodology of phenomenology includes intuiting or concentrating on a phenomenon or object, analyzing aspects of the phenomenon, and freeing oneself of preconceptions so that the observer can help others understand phenomena that have been intuited and analyzed (Schultz & Schultz, 2009). This approach is used both in therapy and, as is shown later, in the existential method of psychological experimentation. Related to the concept of phenomenology is intentionality, which refers to the process of bringing objects into the mind to intentionally observe the environment. Phenomenological concepts have been important for many gestalt and existential writers.

Perhaps the philosopher who had the most direct impact on the development of existential therapy was Martin Heidegger (1889–1976), who succeeded Husserl as the chair of philosophy at the University of Freiburg. Heidegger's *Being and Time* (1962) has been of particular importance in existential therapy as it emphasizes the awareness of existence, which he calls *Dasein* and is translated as "being-in-the-world." *Dasein* refers to attempting to attain high levels of consciousness and uniqueness by examining oneself, others, and the world. Heidegger distinguishes *Dasein* from *Das Man*, which refers to conventional thinking or going through the motions. When individuals become aware that their existence is a consequence not of choice but of having their existence thrown upon them, they may experience dread and anguish in dealing with an incomprehensible and threatening world. If they deal with this world by conforming to conventional ways of acting and thinking, they are being "inauthentic." Individuals start in a state of inauthenticity, but if they accept the inevitability of death and nothingness and become aware of their moods and feelings, they move toward "authentic" existence. The act of being-in-the-world refers not only to conscious and active awareness of one's own life but also to an active caring about the needs and lives of others in one's world.

A practicing psychiatrist who later became a professor of philosophy, Karl Jaspers (1883–1969) sought to develop a philosophy that would encompass all problems related to the existence of humanity. Influenced by Kierkegaard's writings on the human condition and the philosopher David Hume's work on understanding knowledge, Jaspers saw humanity as being continually confronted with situations involving death, suffering, struggle, and guilt. In dealing

Evolution

with such situations, Jaspers believed that we must find ways to "transcend" them by being-oneself, a state in which we depend on awareness of ourselves and our assertion of ourselves through choices and decisions. This is contrasted with being-there, which refers to knowing the world through observation and experiment. Being-oneself is attained not only through self-awareness but also through communication with others via discussion, education, politics, and other means.

Known widely because of his novels, plays, and articles, Jean-Paul Sartre (1905–1980) dealt with issues concerning the meaning of human existence. Sartre's answer to this problem is that there is no intrinsic reason to explain why the world and humanity should exist; individuals must find a reason. Humanity is freedom, and individuals must choose, within their own and environmental limitations, and decide constantly; they are condemned to be free. Sartre believed that existential psychoanalysis should deal with emotional problems resulting from individuals not acknowledging their original choices. Because one's freedom and nothingness is difficult to face, the psychotherapist must help the patient to confront excuses such as "The reason my life is miserable is because I was born out of wedlock." Sartre emphasizes that, no matter what a person has been, he can choose to be different.

Not only have philosophers contributed to the development of existential thought but also theologians have made important contributions, notably Martin Buber (1878–1965) on existential dialogue, Gabriel Marcel (1889–1973) on trust, and Paul Tillich (1886–1965) on courage. Combining existential philosophy with a Jewish Hasidic perspective, Buber emphasized the *betweenness* of relationships. There is never just an *I*. There is also a *thou*, if the person is treated as a human individual. If the person is manipulated or treated as an object, the relationship becomes *I-it*. From a Catholic perspective, Marcel described the person-to-person relationship, focusing on the being-by-participation in which individuals know each other through love, hope, and faithfulness rather than as objects or as an "it." The Protestant theologian Paul Tillich is best known for his emphasis on *courage*, which includes faith in one's ability to make a meaningful life, as well as a knowledge of and a belief in an existential view of life. These philosophers have emphasized relationships with others and with God, in contrast to Sartre's pessimistic view of the meaning of existence.

Other negative views of the existence of humanity have been expressed by a number of well-known novelists and playwrights, among the most famous of whom are Dostoyevski, Camus, and Kafka. The Russian novelist Fyodor Dostoyevski, in *Notes from Underground*, had his protagonist deal with issues of consciousness and awareness of actions. The French novelist and philosopher Albert Camus, like Sartre, emphasized the absurdity of trying to understand a meaningless world. A similar attitude was displayed much earlier in the writings of Franz Kafka, who presented despairing and frustrating situations that question the meaningfulness of existence. Stories, novels, and plays with existential themes have helped to popularize the philosophical ideas of existentialism.

This brief overview of the philosophical antecedents of existential psychotherapy skims only the surface of important philosophical contributions. As can be seen, there are many divergent views within existentialism. For example, contrast the more optimistic views of the theological philosophers with the pessimistic views of the existential writers. Followers of existential philosophy differ widely as to their view of the impact that various philosophers have made to existentialism. For example, Gelven (1989) believed that Heidegger has made a greater contribution to existentialism than any other philosopher, whereas Cannon (1991) believed that Sartre's contribution to existentialism has been more substantial. However, Medard Boss and Ludwig Binswanger, early existential psychoanalysts, have relied heavily on Heidegger's existential philosophy.

Originators of Existential Psychotherapy

Using ideas from existential philosophy, Binswanger, Boss, and Viktor Frankl were early proponents of existential psychiatry. Their writings do not put forth a clear and articulate theory of psychotherapy (van Deurzen, 2001). Rather, their writings are sometimes poetic and metaphorical. Their concern was the meaning of existence and its ramifications. The contributions of Binswanger, Boss, and Frankl to existential psychotherapy are described in more detail next.

The Swiss psychiatrist Ludwig Binswanger (1881–1966) was interested in many of Freud's ideas about individual drives and motives, but he was more influenced by Heidegger's concepts of being-in-the-world. A major contribution of Binswanger, expressed in *Being-in-the-World* (1975), was his view of *fundamental meaning structure*, which refers to the unlearned ability of individuals to perceive meaning in their world and to go beyond specific situations to deal with life issues. This universal ability to perceive meaning, also called *existential a priori*, provides individuals with the opportunity to develop their way of living and the direction of their lives. By focusing on the patients' views of their world and their present experience, Binswanger was able to help them understand the meaning of their behavior and become their own authentic selves through understanding their relationships with their world, their associates, and themselves (Bühler, 2004).

Another Swiss psychiatrist, Medard Boss (1903–1990), was also quite familiar with Freud, having been analyzed by him in Vienna. Although trained by several psychoanalysts, Boss was also influenced strongly by the philosophy of Martin Heidegger. Integrating existentialism with psychoanalysis in *Psychoanalysis and Daseinsanalysis* (1963), Boss outlines universal themes that individuals incorporate to varying degrees in their being-in-the-world. Boss emphasized that individuals must coexist in the same world and share that world with others. In doing so, individuals relate with varying degrees of openness and clarity to others (spatiality of existence) and do so in the context of time (temporality of existence). The mood of individuals determines how they relate to the world. For example, a sad person is aware of misfortunes, and a happy person is attuned to enjoyable events in relationships. Another important existential theme is guilt, which occurs when we make choices and, in doing so, must reject a variety of possibilities. Guilt for not following through on those possible choices can never be fully relieved. For example, the person who decides to become a lawyer rather than a minister may never fully come to terms with the decision. Finally, by being mortal, individuals have the responsibility to make the most of existence. These existential themes greatly affected Boss's view of his patients and his psychotherapeutic work.

Although having basic views that are consistent with those of Binswanger and Boss, Viktor Frankl, born in Vienna in 1905, expressed and developed his approach to psychotherapy differently. Like Boss and Binswanger, Frankl was also influenced by his study of psychoanalysis. However, his experience in German concentration camps was to affect his development of existential psychotherapy by bringing him in constant contact with existential issues such as guilt and mortality. Important concepts for Frankl (Gould, 1993) deal with the individual's freedom and responsibility for oneself and others. *Logotherapy*, a concept based on the idea that the most fundamental drive for individuals is to understand the meaning of their existence, was developed eloquently in Frankl's popular book *Man's Search for Meaning* (1963/1992) and can be seen in the context of Frankl's life in *Victor Frankl—Recollections: An Autobiography* (1997). Although Frankl made use of specific techniques, his emphasis was not on techniques but on dealing with existential or spiritual questions that focus on the realization of values, the meaning of life, and the meaning of time for the individual (Hillmann, 2004). A journal, the *International Forum for Logotherapy*, contains articles related to techniques of logotherapy and Frankl's view of existential therapy.

Recent Contributors to Existential Psychotherapy

Several contemporary existential psychotherapists have applied existential themes to the practice of psychotherapy. Writing over a period of more than 40 years, Rollo May expanded on existential themes and existential therapy for both the general reader and the professional. Irvin Yalom and James Bugental have written books that are particularly helpful to psychotherapists in their application of existential themes to the practice of psychotherapy (Krug, 2008). Other original concepts come from Laing (1961) and van Deurzen (2001). The work of contemporary existential psychotherapists is used extensively in this chapter.

The best-known contemporary writer on existential psychotherapy, Rollo May (1909–1994) was influenced by the ideas of Binswanger and Boss, but his greatest influence, both personally and professionally, was Paul Tillich, especially through *The Courage to Be* (1952). Throughout May's articles and books, he deals with important existential issues such as anxiety, dealing with power, accepting freedom and responsibility, and developing individual identity. An example of his early work is *The Meaning of Anxiety* (1950, 1977). May's familiarity with anxiety came not only from his readings but also from a 2-year hospitalization for tuberculosis. In *Man's Search for Himself* (1953), May wrote about the anxiety and loneliness that confront individuals in modern society. Two edited books (May, 1961; May, Angel, & Ellenberger, 1958) were important in bringing together related approaches to existential psychology and therapy. As can be seen by the titles, many of his books develop significant existential themes: *Love and Will* (1969), *Power and Innocence* (1972), *The Courage to Create* (1975), and *Freedom and Destiny* (1981). In one of his last books, *The Cry for Myth* (1992), May combined a long-term interest in the classics with his interest in existentialism. May's approach to psychotherapy shows an integration of psychoanalytic concepts with existential themes.

ROLLO MAY

Bernard Gotfryd/Getty Images

Perhaps the most thorough and comprehensive explanation of existential psychotherapy can be found in Yalom's (1980) text. Acknowledging the influence of many of the existential philosophers and psychotherapists mentioned previously in this chapter, Yalom (1931–) presents an in-depth approach to existential psychotherapy by dealing with the themes of death, freedom, isolation, and meaninglessness. His therapeutic approach can be seen in books of his published case studies, *Love's Executioner* (1989) and *Momma and the Meaning of Life* (1999). The frequent use of case material in his textbook, as well as the material in his casebooks, is helpful to psychotherapists who wish to focus their attention on the existential themes of their patients.

Another writer who has brought together approaches to existential therapy is James Bugental (1915–2008). His writings focus on helping patients develop an existential understanding of themselves through a search for authenticity (Bugental, 1978, 1981; Schulenberg, 2003). In his work, he takes a humanistic focus that stresses the ability of individuals to enhance their awareness and to self-actualize. The existential themes he develops are similar to, but not identical to, those of Yalom (Krug, 2008), for example, change, contingency, responsibility, and relinquishment. Bugental's *Psychotherapy Isn't What You Think* (1999) illustrates his therapeutic approach, which focuses on in-the-moment experiences during the therapeutic session.

In addition to the American existentialist writers described in this chapter, two English existentialists have been influential. R. D. Laing (Cooper, 2003) established a therapeutic community in England for severely disturbed patients, based on an existential philosophy that reflects respect for patients. Van Deurzen (formerly known as van Deurzen-Smith) has written *Paradox and Passion in Psychotherapy* (1998), *Existential Counseling and Psychotherapy in Practice* (2001), and *Psychotherapy and the Quest for Happiness* (2009) along with other books. Her work has helped to create an active interest in existential psychotherapy in England, known as the British School of Existential Psychotherapy.

Although there are differences in the existential views of all of these philosophers and therapists, there are many commonalities. The existential approach that is presented in the sections on existential psychology and psychotherapy represents themes that are common to most existential psychotherapists.

Existential Personality Theory

Theories in Action

Existential psychology deals with the dynamic or ever-changing transitions that individuals encounter as they emerge, evolve, and become. To be truly human, individuals must be aware of their own being-in-the-world, asking, "Who will I be? Who am I? Where do I come from?" Human beings are responsible for their own plans and destinies. Existentialism is concerned with how individuals relate to their objective world, to other human beings, and to their own sense of self. Existential psychology emphasizes the importance of time—past and future, but particularly the present—in understanding oneself and one's world. Anxiety results from having to make choices in a world that may often be perceived as hostile or uncaring. The major existential themes described in this chapter follow Yalom's (1980) model and include living and dying; freedom, responsibility, and choice; isolation and loving; and meaning and meaninglessness. How honestly and authentically individuals deal with these themes affects their existential and psychological well-being.

Being-in-the-World

The ability to be consciously aware of themselves and others separates human beings from other species. Boss (1963) and Binswanger (1975) used the term *Dasein*, or *being-in-the-world*, which refers to the ability of individuals to be able to think about and reflect on events and to attribute meaning to them. This concept has also been expressed by Binswanger and others (May, 1958b) as *being-for-itself*, with the implication that people can decide and make choices about many events. Such authors use the phrase "Dasein choosing," which means "the-person-who-is-responsible-for-his-existence choosing" (May, 1958b, p. 41). In describing the full meaning of *human being*, May (1958b) uses the phrase "I-am." To illustrate this experience, May gives an example of a patient in her fourth month of therapy, an illegitimate child of a prostitute, who describes her "I-am" experience in a dream:

> I remember walking that day under the elevated tracks in a slum area, feeling the thought, "I am an illegitimate child." I recall the sweat pouring forth in my anguish in trying to accept that fact. Then I understood what it must feel like to accept, "I am a Negro in the midst of privileged whites," or "I am blind in the midst of people who see." Later on that night I woke up and it came to me this way, "I accept the fact that I am an illegitimate child." But, "I am not a child anymore." So it is, "I am illegitimate." That is not so either: "I was born illegitimate." Then what is left? What is left is this, "I am." This act of contact and acceptance with "I am," once gotten hold of, gave me (what I think was for me the first time) the experience "since I am, I have the right to be." (May, 1958b, p. 43)

For May, this powerful "I-am" experience is important as a precondition for solving the patient's problems. Furthermore, this is an experience of the self and is not related to relationships with the therapist or to society. For May, the "I-am" experience is not like the ego that is the subject in a subject–object relationship but rather the "I am the being who can, among other things, know himself as the subject of what is occurring" (May 1958b, p. 46). Thus, "being" is an experience that is different than ego development. This experience is an ontological experience that refers to the science of being or existence—ontology.

Four Ways of Being

Existentialists identify four ways of being-in-the-world. Human beings exist in the *Umwelt, Mitwelt, Eigenwelt*, and *Überwelt* simultaneously. The *Umwelt* refers to the biological world or the environment. The *Mitwelt* means "with-world" and concerns the area of human relationships. The *Eigenwelt* is the "own-world" and refers to the relationship that individuals have to themselves. *The Überwelt* refers to one's relationship with spiritual or religious values. The first three were introduced by Binswanger; the last has been recently added by van Deurzen.

Umwelt is what we generally think of as the world, objects, the environment, and living beings. All animals and humans have an *Umwelt* that includes drives, instincts, and natural laws and cycles such as sleeping and waking, living and dying. The *Umwelt* is the "thrown world" that individuals and animals are thrown into. Examples of such uncontrollable factors are storms, floods, disease, and aging. Existentialists do not ignore the *Umwelt*, but neither do they view it as the only way of being.

Mitwelt refers to interrelationships that only human beings may have. The instinctual relationships that animals have in mating or the herd instinct belong to the *Umwelt*. For humans, the meaning of relationships with others depends on how much of oneself goes into the relationship. As May states: "The essence of relationship is that in the encounter both persons are changed" (1958b, p. 63). May is referring to the mutual awareness of the other in a human encounter. When the person is treated as an object (an object of ridicule or a sex object), the person is dehumanized and treated as an instrument (*Umwelt*), a way of meeting the needs of the other.

Überwelt was added by van Deurzen-Smith (1997, 1998; Cooper, 2003) to emphasize the importance of beliefs about the world. Often these beliefs are religious or spiritual in nature. For example, wars are often fought based on conflicts of beliefs, such as conflicts between Catholics and Protestants in Northern Ireland. The *Überwelt* is the ideal world, the way the individual wants the world to be.

Eigenwelt, one's "own world," is more than a subjective, inner experience; it is a self-awareness from which we see the world. Implied in the observation "That is a lovely sunset" is the phrase "for me" or "I believe" or "I perceive" (that is a lovely sunset). As May (1958b) points out, Eastern languages, such as Japanese, include the reference to the self ("for me") that is unstated in Western languages. Clearly, the question of the self-knowing itself is a difficult one to grasp, as are the concepts of consciousness and self-awareness.

> Each of these phenomena goes on almost every instant with all of us; they are indeed closer to us than our breathing. Yet, perhaps precisely because they are so near to us, no one knows what is happening in these events. (May, 1958b, p. 64)

Binswanger and May are critical of psychoanalysis and behavioral and cognitive therapies because they deal basically with the *Umwelt* and not the *Eigenwelt*. It is important to emphasize that these four modes of being-in-the-world are always related to each other. At each moment, individuals are in the *Umwelt*, the environment; the *Mitwelt*, human relationships; the *Überwelt*, spiritual values; and the *Eigenwelt*, self-awareness. For example, when a person eats a meal, she is in the biological world in the sense of the physical act of eating, in the realm of human relationships in the sense of relating to others if eating with them or not relating to others if eating alone, possibly saying grace before her meal (spiritual values), and self-aware of her eating activity. Existential analysts are aware that being-in-the-world takes place in the context of time and space. It is time that is of particular interest to existential writers.

Time and Being

Time has attracted the attention of most existentialist writers, many believing that time is at the center of existential issues and can be viewed from several perspectives. In the *Umwelt*, time can be viewed as "clock time" or in terms of space points on a clock or calendar (May, 1958b). In the *Mitwelt*, time has a less quantitative function. For example, one cannot measure how much a person cares about another by the number of years that they have known each other. In the *Überwelt*, time also has a less quantitative function, but individuals vary greatly as to the attention they pay to their religious or belief system. In the *Eigenwelt*, time has little to do with "clock time." When one has an insight or moment of self-awareness, the experience is immediate and profound.

In their work, existential therapists focus on the future, past, and present. The future is an immediate rather than a distant future; it does not allow escape from past or present. The individual is always in a process of self-actualization and moving into an immediate future. To focus on the past, exclusively, is to focus on history and development, the area of the *Umwelt*. May relates the past to the future in this way: *"Whether or not a patient can even recall the significant events of the past depends on his decision with regard to the future"* (1958b, p. 70).

Minkowski (1958) gives an interesting case of a 66-year-old man suffering from psychosis who can think only in the present, and his inability to be future oriented creates his anxiety and depression. An unusual aspect of the case is that Minkowski lived with the patient for 2 months and was able to observe him very frequently. The man was preoccupied with delusions of persecution and felt that everything around him would lead to his demise. He believed that everything had been designed for him and that all residue that he came in contact with would have to be eaten. For example, he saw a clock as hands, springs, screws, and so forth that he would have to eat. The patient's focus on the present and his inability to grasp the future is illustrated by Minkowski's description.

> From the first day of my life with the patient, my attention was drawn to the following point. When I arrived, he stated that his execution would certainly take place that night; in his terror, unable to sleep, he also kept me awake all that night. I comforted myself with the thought that, in the morning he would see that all his fears would be in vain. However, the same scene was repeated the next day and the next, until after three or four days I had given up hope, whereas his attitude had not budged one iota. What had happened? It was simply that I as a normal human being, had rapidly drawn from the observed facts my conclusion about the future. He on the other hand had let the same facts go by him, totally unable to draw any profit from them for relating himself to the same future. I now knew that he would continue to go on, day after day, swearing that he was to be tortured to death that night, and so he did, giving no thought to the present or the past. (Minkowski, 1958, p. 132)

Minkowski points out that the patient's disorder is one of disoriented attitudes toward the future, with the delusions being only one aspect of this. This is different from the usual psychopathological view that would state that the patient is unable to deal with the future because of his delusions. This focus on the role of time in psychotherapy is a significant aspect of existential psychotherapy. In describing mania and depression, Ghaemi (2007) states that mania represents a speeding up of time and depression represents a slowing down of time. Thus patients with mania lack insight into their problems, while depressed patients tend to have insight into their problem. Minkowski's patient has no insight into his problem.

Related to the notion of time is that of timing in psychotherapy. Ellenberger (1958) describes *kairos*, a Greek word referring to the critical point at which a disease is expected to get better or worse. In psychotherapy, the timing of an intervention can be critical. For example, an individual suffering from alcoholism may benefit from suggestions or confrontations about alcoholism only at certain times. Ellenberger (1958) believes that a "surprisingly rapid cure" (p. 120) can occur when a therapist times an intervention appropriately.

Anxiety

For May (1977) as well as other existentialists, anxiety is viewed more broadly than by most other psychotherapy theorists, and it is separated into two major types (May & Yalom, 2005), normal anxiety and neurotic anxiety. A significant subset of normal anxiety—and the focus of attention by existential psychotherapists—is existential anxiety (Cohn, 1997). Although anxiety has physical manifestations, it arises from the basic nature of being. Individuals must confront the world around them, deal with unforeseen forces ("the thrown condition"), and in general develop a place within their world.

For May and Yalom (2005), normal anxiety has three features that differentiate it from neurotic anxiety. First, it is appropriate to the situation that the individual deals with in his life. Second, normal anxiety is not usually repressed. For example, a severe illness may make us come to terms with our death. Third, normal anxiety can provide an opportunity to confront existential dilemmas, such as dying, responsibility, and choices.

Existential anxiety has been the source of interest for a number of existential writers. Tillich (Weems, Costa, Dehon, & Berman, 2004) discusses the relationship of existential anxiety to depression and apprehension. Lucas (2004) sees existential anxiety as deriving from regret for not having made a choice in one's past. This regret may lead one to have a sense of existential guilt for betraying oneself.

In contrast, neurotic anxiety is a reaction that is blown out of proportion or inappropriate for the particular event. For example, the man who is so afraid of disease that he washes his hands several times before and during a meal is experiencing neurotic anxiety. The anxiety is out of proportion to the situation, destructive, and of little value to the patient. Furthermore, the patient may have repressed fears that may be a source of this anxiety. In this example of neurotic anxiety or obsessional neurosis, there is an existential component. The individual is unable to control his anxiety about disease that may lead to his death. The individual compulsively washes his hands rather than dealing with the uncertainty of life. Existential therapists often help their patients develop awareness of their courage to deal with the existential issues that underlie neurotic anxiety.

Living and Dying

A certainty about living is its termination. We do not know how we will die or how long we will live, but awareness of death is inescapable. Individuals may find that close relationships buffer their anxiety about death (Mikulincer, Florian, & Hirschberger, 2004). Although the awareness of death can create dread in individuals, it can also lead toward the development of a creative life (May, 1981). Yalom's (1980) work with cancer patients illustrates how individuals cope with their imminent death. Yalom does not limit his discussion to adults; he cites many studies that show how children deal with death through denial by believing that children do not die, personifying death ("death catches bad children"), and seeing death as a temporary condition or as sleep.

Frankl's 4 years of experience as a prisoner in a concentration camp during World War II gave him a unique perspective on death (Frankl, 1997). On a daily basis, he was faced with choices that could lead to his imminent death.

> Instinctively, I straightened on approaching the officer, so that he would not notice my heavy load. Then I was face to face with him. He was a tall man who looked slim and fit in his spotless uniform. What a contrast to us, who were untidy and grimy after our long journey! He had assumed an attitude of careless ease, supporting his right elbow with his left hand. His right hand was lifted, and with the forefinger of that hand he pointed very leisurely to the right or to the left. None of us had the slightest idea of the sinister meaning behind that little movement of a man's finger, pointing now to the right and now to the left, but far more frequently to the left.
>
> It was my turn. Somebody whispered to me that to be sent to the right side would mean work, the way to the left being for the sick and those incapable of work, who would be sent to a special camp. I just waited for things to take their course, the first of many such times to come. My haversack weighed me down a bit to the left, but I made an effort to walk upright. The SS man looked me over, appeared to hesitate, then put both his hands on my shoulders. I tried very hard to look smart, and he turned my shoulders very slowly until I faced right, and I moved over to that side.
>
> The significance of the finger game was explained to us in the evening. It was the first selection, the first verdict made on our existence or non-existence. For the

great majority of our transport, about 90 per cent, it meant death. Their sentence was carried out within the next few hours. Those who were sent to the left were marched from the station straight to the crematorium. (Frankl, 1992, p. 25)

Such experiences have added to Frankl's appreciation of the meaningfulness of life. He sees death not as a threat but as an urging for individuals to live their lives fully and to take advantage of each opportunity to do something meaningful (Gould, 1993). Thus the awareness of death can lead to creativity and living fully rather than to fear and dread.

In this example, Frankl was dealing with death as a boundary situation, an urgent experience that forces a person to deal with an existential situation (May & Yalom, 2005). Of all boundary situations, death is the most powerful. When one is forced to deal with the imminent death of oneself or a close family member, the individual must live in the present and become more aware of oneself and one's situation. The boundary situation provides deep meaning for the individual.

Because grief and grief counseling is such an important topic for so many counselors, several books provide many perspectives on this topic. In *Staring at the Sun: Overcoming the Terror of Death,* Yalom (2008) gives examples of many people coping with their own mortality and the meaning of death for them. *Existential and Spiritual Issues in Death Attitudes* (Tomer, Eliason, & Wong, 2008) provides 18 chapters on research on issues related to attitudes about death as well as counseling approaches to death. Existential issues such as being-in-the-world, freedom, time, meaning, authenticity, and aloneness as they affect therapy are dealt with in *When Death Enters the Therapeutic Space: Existential Perspective in Psychotherapy and Counselling* (Barnett, 2009).

Freedom, Responsibility, and Choice

Freedom to live our own lives carries with it the responsibility to do so. Existentialists believe that individuals do not enter or leave a structured universe that has a coherent design (May & Yalom, 2005). Rather, in their pursuit of freedom, individuals are responsible for their own world, their life plans, and their choices. Although the terms *freedom, responsibility*, and *choice* may first appear unrelated, they are integrally related, as we are free to choose in what ways we will be responsible for leading our lives and, implicitly, what values are significant to us.

Although freedom appears to be a principle that human beings would value positively, Camus and Sartre see it more negatively. To be truly free, individuals must confront the limits of their destiny. Sartre's position is that individuals are condemned to freedom (1956). They are responsible for creating their own world, which rests not on the ground but on nothingness. In his writings, Sartre gives the feeling that individuals are on their own, like people walking on a thin veneer that could open, leaving a bottomless pit. Sartre believes that our choices make us who we really are.

Responsibility refers to owning one's own choices and dealing honestly with freedom. Sartre uses the term *bad faith* to denote that individuals are finite and limited. For an individual to say, "I can't treat my children well, because I was abused as a child" or "Because I didn't go to a good high school, I can't go to a good college" is to act in *bad faith* by blaming someone else for the problem and not examining one's own limitedness. The person who compulsively hand washes can, from an existential point of view, be seen as acting in bad faith.

Such an individual is choosing a repetitive, compulsive act rather than dealing with the implications of disease and death. Responsibility also includes caring for others and not blaming others for one's problems.

In discussing *freedom*, May (1969) uses the concept *willing* as the process by which responsibility is turned into action. There are two aspects of *willing*: wishing and deciding. May (1969) discusses psychological illness as the inability to wish, which connotes emptiness and despair. Part of the therapeutic task for existential therapists is to mobilize individuals' feelings so that they can wish and then act on choices.

When people have expressed their wishes or desires, they must also choose. This process can lead to panic or to the desire to have someone else make the choice. When people make *choices*, they must also live with the other side of the choice. If Dora decides to marry Fred and be part of a couple, she must live with the decision to stop dating other men. If she decides not to marry Fred, then she must deal with the potential loneliness that may result. The responsibility for choosing can carry great anxiety for individuals, depending both on the situation and on their ability to act in *good faith*.

③ Isolation and Loving

Because we are human, we are alone with our thoughts and our ability to think about our life, past, present, and future, even a therapist or spouse can not completely know us (Cowan, 2009). In discussing isolation, Yalom (1980) differentiates three types of isolation: interpersonal, intrapersonal, and existential. *Interpersonal isolation* refers to distance from others—geographical, psychological, or social. For example, a person with schizophrenia is isolated personally from other individuals due to lack of ability to develop a relationship. *Intrapersonal isolation* occurs when one separates parts of oneself by using defense mechanisms or other methods to be unaware of one's own wishes. The person who focuses on what she should do may be distrusting of her judgment and unaware of her abilities and internal resources. *Existential isolation* is even more basic than either personal or intrapersonal isolation. It refers to being separated from the world. There is a sense of aloneness and isolation that is profound.

Yalom (1980) gives an example of a patient's dream that illustrates the incredible loneliness and dread that come with a sense of existential isolation.

> I am awake and in my room. Suddenly I begin to notice that everything is changing. The window frame seems stretched and then wavy, the bookcases squashed, the door knob disappears, and a hole appears in the door which gets larger and larger. Everything loses its shape and begins to melt. There's nothing there anymore and I begin to scream. (Yalom, 1980, p. 356)

Yalom (1980) uses a phrase that conveys the isolation that comes from being responsible for one's own life: "the loneliness of being one's own parent." Adults are on their own when they take care of themselves and supply their own parental guidance to themselves.

When one is confronted with death, the sense of existential isolation is powerful. Being in an automobile and experiencing crashing into a building is a moment of extreme existential isolation and dread. The feeling of being totally alone and helpless can create a panicky feeling of "nothingness."

Loving relationships are a means of bridging a sense of existential isolation. Buber (1970) emphasizes the importance of the "I–thou" relationship in which two people fully experience the other. Yalom (1980) cautions that such a relationship should be need free. Caring should be reciprocal, active, and a way of fully experiencing the other person. Yalom (1980) speaks of fusion, which occurs when the individual loses a sense of self in the relationship. To avoid existential isolation, individuals may rely on another for a sense of self. The concept of "I-sharing," a positive term, is one that produces a sense of intimacy (Pinel, Long, Landau, & Pyszczynski, 2004). In "I-sharing" a sense of connection or fondness develops when people experience a moment in the same way that another does. This creates a sense of existential connectedness that is in contrast to existential isolation.

Meaning and Meaninglessness

Questions about the meaning of life may haunt people at various times during their lives: Why am I here? What about my life do I find meaningful? What in my life gives me a sense of purpose? Why do I exist? As May and Yalom (2005) point out, human beings need a sense of meaningfulness in their lives. A sense of meaning provides a way of interpreting events that occur to the individual and in the world, and it furnishes a means for the development of values as to how people live and wish to live.

Sartre, Camus, and others have written about the absurdity of life and have dealt fully with the question of meaninglessness. Others, such as Frankl (Hillmann, 2004), have focused on the importance of the development and search for meaning in one's life. Frankl has been concerned that individuals do not look at the spiritual meanings in their lives or beyond material values.

Paradoxically, Yalom has found that people who are terminally ill have found meaning in life far beyond what they had prior to their illnesses. The following is an example of one of Yalom's patients who found meaning in the face of death.

> Eva, a patient who died of ovarian cancer in her early fifties, had lived an extraordinarily zestful life in which altruistic activities had always provided her with a powerful sense of life purpose. She faced her death in the same way; and, though I feel uneasy using the phrase, her death can only be characterized as a "good death." Almost everyone who came into contact with Eva during the last two years of her life was enriched by her. When she first learned of her cancer and again when she learned of its spread and its fatal prognosis, she was plunged into despair but quickly extricated herself by plunging into altruistic projects. She did volunteer work on a hospital ward for terminally ill children. She closely examined a number of charitable organizations in order to make a reasoned decision about how to distribute her estate. Many old friends had avoided close contact with her after she developed cancer. Eva systematically approached each one to tell them that she understood their reason for withdrawal, that she bore no grudge, but that still it might be helpful to them when they faced their own death, to talk about their feelings toward her. (Yalom, 1980, p. 432)

Self-Transcendence

It is the existential nature of human beings to transcend their immediate situation and their self-interest to strive toward something above themselves (May, 1958b; Yalom, 1980). Buber (1961) writes that although human beings begin by asking themselves what they want, what is meaningful for them, they should not end with themselves but should forget themselves and immerse themselves in the world. Boss (1963) remarks that individuals have the capacity for transcending their immediate situation because they have the ability to understand their own being and to take responsibility for being. By using imagination and creativity, individuals transcend their own needs so that they may be aware of others and act responsibly toward them. Human beings can transcend time and space through their imagination. We can think of ourselves in ancient Rome in 100 B.C. or in a far-off galaxy in the year 3000. We can also transcend ourselves and put ourselves in the position of others and feel the distress or happiness that they may experience. As Kierkegaard (1954) writes, imagination is an individual's most important faculty, helping individuals to go beyond themselves and reflect on their being and the being of others.

There are numerous examples of people transcending themselves. News accounts occasionally detail how individuals give up their lives so that others may live. Yalom (1980) gives many examples of individuals who, on becoming aware that they were terminally ill, rather than focus inwardly on their own illnesses, transcended themselves and cared for and helped others who were in distress. In a poignant personal situation, Frankl (1992) illustrates self-transcendence in the face of imminent death.

> On my fourth day in the sick quarters I had just been detailed to the night shift when the chief doctor rushed in and asked me to volunteer for medical duties in another camp containing typhus patients. Against the urgent advice of my friends (and despite the fact that almost none of my colleagues offered their services), I decided to volunteer. I knew that in a working party I would die in a short time. But if I had to die there might at least be some sense in my death. I thought that it would doubtless be more to the purpose to try and help my comrades as a doctor than to vegetate or finally lose my life as the unproductive laborer that I was then. (Frankl, 1992, pp. 59–60)

Frankl (1969) believes that in order to self-realize, it is necessary first to be able to transcend oneself. For Frankl, the *noölogical* (spiritual) dimension that human beings can obtain comes through self-transcendence. In this way, people go beyond their biological and psychological selves to develop values and achieve meaning in their lives. Only when individuals transcend their own being can they become their own true selves.

Striving for Authenticity

Theories in Action

The journey toward authenticity is often a focus of existential therapy (Craig, 2009). Authenticity refers to a "central genuineness and awareness of being" (Bugental, 1981, p. 102) that includes a willingness to face up to the limitations of human existence. Issues related to being authentic relate to moral choices, the meaning of life, and being human.

By contrasting the values, the experiencing, the social interactions, and the thoughts and feelings of authentic individuals with inauthentic individuals, Kobasa and Maddi (1977) explain the concept of authenticity. The values and goals of authentic individuals are very much their own, whereas inauthentic individuals may have goals based on values of others and be less conscious of what is important to them. In social interactions, authentic individuals are oriented toward intimacy, whereas inauthentic individuals are more concerned with superficial relationships. In a broader sense, authentic individuals are concerned about their society and social institutions such as schools and charities, whereas inauthentic individuals are less concerned with them. Authentic individuals, being aware of themselves, are more flexible and open to change than individuals who are inauthentic. The authentic person experiences existential anxiety over issues related to freedom, responsibility, death, isolation, and meaning (Craig, 2009). In contrast, the inauthentic individual experiences guilt about having missed opportunities, as well as cowardice because she has not had the courage to change or make risky decisions. Whereas the authentic person may experience existential crises that produce anxiety, the inauthentic individual is more likely to experience psychopathology and maladaptive means of dealing with crises. Thus, the authentic individual has a genuine awareness of herself and copes with existential questions and crises by experiencing them directly and acting on them.

Development of Authenticity and Values

Because the individual's being is a major focus of existentialist writers, they have not devoted much attention to the development of authenticity and values (Baum & Stewart, 1990). However, May (1966) has described four stages in the development of existential awareness: The first stage is the innocence and openness to experience of the infant. Second, at the age of 2 or 3, children react to the values of the world around them, specifically their parents. Children may respond to parental actions by accepting, demanding, defying, or using. The third stage is the consciousness of oneself as an individual. The fourth is transcendent consciousness, in which individuals can stand outside themselves and be aware of their world and how they relate to it. By not pampering but encouraging independence and accomplishment, parents help children develop values and rely on themselves. Too much dependence on parents can lead to a type of fusion and difficulty in developing self-transcendence. Similarly, Frankl (1969) sees the need for adolescents to be able to be independent and develop their own sense of values, even ones that may conflict with those of their parents. In doing so, they can develop authenticity—a true genuineness and awareness of their being.

The issues of anxiety, living and dying, freedom and responsibility, isolation and loving, and meaning and meaninglessness are dealt with directly in existential therapy. It is these issues rather than specific techniques that are important in helping the patient develop authenticity.

Existential Psychotherapy

Because existential psychotherapy deals with attitudes and thematic concerns, goals focus on issues such as finding a purpose or meaning in life and fully experiencing one's existence. Although assessment instruments are occasionally used (described later in the chapter), it is primarily the therapeutic relationship that allows for the assessment of important existential tasks and themes. In helping their clients, existential therapists deal with resistance and transference issues that may interfere with the development of a real relationship with the client. In working with clients, existential therapists may take a variety of approaches to important existential themes, such as dealing with the death of others or with one's own mortality. Also, clients struggle with being responsible for choices and decisions that come from their freedom in leading their lives. The struggle to be appropriately loving and intimate with others in contrast to struggling with loneliness and isolation is a theme that existential therapists approach through their relationship with the client. Finding meaning in one's life and being able to love others authentically are related issues. How existential therapists approach these major existential themes is the subject of this section.

Goals of Existential Psychotherapy

Authenticity is the basic goal of psychotherapy. In therapy, clients learn how their lives are not fully authentic and what they must do to realize the full capability of their being (Cooper, 2003; Craig, 2009). As Frankl states, "Clients must find a purpose to their existence and pursue it. The therapist must help them achieve the highest possible activation" (1965, p. 54). As an individual develops an awareness of having a task to pursue in life, he will be better able to actualize significant values. Similarly, van Deurzen-Smith (1998) believes that the aim of therapy is to help individuals become authentic and recognize when they are deceiving themselves. Therapy should help clients understand their beliefs and values, have confidence in them, and make choices based on them that can lead to new directions in living. A sense of aliveness comes from therapy as the individual sees life with interest, imagination, creativity, hope, and joy, rather than with dread, boredom, hate, and bigotry.

For May, "the aim of therapy is that the patient experiences *his existence as real*" (1958b, p. 85). The focus is not on curing symptoms but on helping individuals fully experience their existence. Another way of viewing this is that neurotic individuals are overconcerned about their *Umwelt* (the biological world) and not sufficiently concerned with their *Eigenwelt* (their own world). In these terms, the goal of psychotherapy is to help the individual develop his *Eigenwelt* without being overwhelmed by the therapist's *Eigenwelt*. The therapist must be with the patient as he experiences *Eigenwelt*. In learning about the patient, May (1958b) does not ask, "*How* are you?" but rather, "*Where* are you?" May wants to know not just how patients feel and how they describe their problems but how detached patients are from themselves. Do patients seem to be confronting their anxiety, or are they running away from their problems? As May (1958b, p. 85) points out, it is often easier to focus on the mechanism of the behavior rather than the experience in order to reduce anxiety. For example, a patient who reports symptoms of agoraphobia (a fear of being out in public places or outside home) may describe his physical anxiety when he leaves the house and how far he is able to go without attending to the overall dread and anxiety that he experiences because of his limitations. Although the cure of agoraphobia may be a by-product of existential therapy, the goal is to have the individual experience his own existence and become fully alive rather than adjust to or fit cultural expectations.

Existential Psychotherapy and Counseling

Typically, existential therapists and counselors do not make a distinction between the two. Although May writes of existential therapy, he also has written about existential counseling (May, 1989). There seems to be an implication in the writings of existential therapists that counseling is briefer in duration and less intense (meeting once a week rather than two or three times). Furthermore, counseling may focus on specific issues, such as bereavement or confronting one's own death. However, this may be an artificial distinction. Whether called therapy, counseling, or analysis, the work of existential therapists has as its focus existential themes. The issues of death, freedom, responsibility, isolation, and meaninglessness are important, not the techniques or methods used to deal with them. These are often a reflection of the counselor or therapist's being, which is inclusive of the therapist's personal experience and professional training.

Assessment

Rather than attending to diagnostic categories (DSM-IV-TR) and specific behavioral complaints, existential psychotherapists are attuned to existential themes. In the initial presentation of problems, therapists listen for issues related to responsibility, mortality, isolation, and meaninglessness. Later, they may make similar assessments of existential issues in patients' dream material. Furthermore, some therapists use objective tests specifically designed to assess existential themes.

Initial assessment. Not all clients are appropriate for existential counseling and therapy. Those individuals wishing advice and suggestions from the therapist are likely to be frustrated by an existential approach. If a client wants assistance in reducing physical stress but does not wish to attend to broader issues that contribute to this stress, existential therapy is inappropriate. By listening for themes of isolation, meaninglessness, responsibility, and mortality, the therapist ascertains which issues require therapeutic work. Furthermore, the therapist assesses the clients' authenticity—how aware of their problems and responsible for them clients are. The therapist must assess the clients' ability to fully engage with the therapist and to face life issues honestly (van Deurzen-Smith, 1995). In doing so, the therapist will help clients make moral decisions when appropriate (van Deurzen, 1999).

Dreams as assessment. For existential therapists, dreaming, like waking, is a mode of existence or being-in-the-world (Cooper, 2003). Whereas events in one's waking life are connected and shared with other people, dreams have events that are not connected and are special for the dreamer, openings to understanding the dreamer's being (Cohn, 1997). Boss (1977) felt that dreams can help in understanding waking experience and that waking experience can help in understanding dreams. What is important is the client's experience of the dream, not the therapist's interpretation.

In listening to dreams, existential therapists are alert to themes that go beyond the client's conscious experiences and reveal other aspects of being. In her work with Brenda, van Deurzen-Smith focuses on determining the essential meaning of a dream. In one dream, Brenda is running through knee-deep snow with wolves in pursuit. This is followed by a second dream in which:

> She had suddenly found herself on the snow plough, or sledge, which dispersed the wolves but killed the people running through the snow and she felt intense guilt for this when waking up. The guilt was that of her realization that she was trying to escape from her original plight of being a runner through the snow, by joining the public, safe, but ruthless camp. Her guilt reminded her of her aspiration to mean more to others than she had seemed to be able to for the moment. (van Deurzen-Smith, 1988, p. 168)

In her therapeutic work with Brenda, van Deurzen-Smith made frequent use of dream material to assess existential themes that are significant to Brenda.

Yalom (1980) describes research showing how frequently dreams of death occur among individuals in the general population and in those who have recently experienced the death of a friend or loved one. For many individuals, dreams of disease, being chased by someone with a weapon, or encountering a life-threatening storm or fire are not infrequent. For existential therapists, this is often an opportunity to discuss the themes of death and dying.

Use of objective and projective tests. Although most assessment takes place in the interaction between therapist and client, some existential therapists do make use of projective and objective instruments. Some therapists have used the Rorschach and the Thematic Apperception Test (TAT) to assess existential themes. For example, Murray's TAT (1943) assesses the needs of abasement, affiliation, dominance, and play, which have an indirect relationship to existential themes.

More directly related to existential concepts are objective tests that have been developed to measure specific themes. Based on Frankl's concern about meaninglessness in life, the Purpose in Life Test (PIL; Crumbaugh & Henrion, 1988) is a 20-item scale that surveys individuals' views of life goals, the world, and their death. Measuring the degree to which individuals actively experience their feelings and have an authentic sense of self-awareness, the Experiencing Scale (Gendlin & Tomlinson, 1967) can be used to assess a commitment to the therapeutic process. Templer's Death Anxiety Scale contains items referring to cancer, heart disease, war, and so forth, that reflect cultural and personal views (Beshai & Naboulsi, 2004). The Silver Lining Questionnaire, which measures whether being positive about illness is a delusion or existential growth, has been validated by Sodergren, Hyland, Crawford, and Partridge (2004), and its factor structure supported by McBride, Dunwoody, Lowe-Strong, and Kennedy (2008). In general, these instruments, when used, are more applicable to research on existential themes than to psychotherapeutic use.

The Therapeutic Relationship

The focus of existential therapy is that of two individuals being-in-the-world together during the length of the therapy session. This authentic encounter includes the subjective experience of both therapist and client, which takes place during the present. The therapist's attitude toward the patient, referred to by Yalom (1980) as therapeutic love, is central to other therapeutic issues, including transference and resistance. The process of existential therapy, which has the therapist–patient relationship as a major focus, differs among existential therapists. For example, Bugental (1987) describes an approach that features a developing and deepening relationship with the client and an exploration of the inner self. These issues are described in more detail in the following paragraphs.

Therapeutic love. The therapeutic relationship is a special form of the I–thou relationship (Buber, 1970). Yalom writes of the relationship as a "loving friendship" (1980, p. 407) that is nonreciprocal. In other words, the client may experience the therapist in a variety of ways, but the therapist strives to develop a genuine caring encounter that does not encumber the client's growth with the therapist's personal needs. In a sense, the therapist is in two places at once, authentic with herself and authentically open to the client (Buber, 1965; Yalom, 1980).

By truly caring for the client, the therapist helps intimacy between client and therapist to grow. Even though the client may be angry, hostile, untruthful, narcissistic, depressed, or unattractive in other ways, there should be a feeling of authentic love for the client (Sequin, 1965). As the therapeutic relationship develops, clients experience an atmosphere of true openness and sharing with the therapist. Bugental (1987) gives an example of the intimate sharing that can take place with a client when the therapist is truly authentic. In this example, Betty explores the pain in the relationship with her father, which changed when she grew older.

> [Client:] I know I keep coming back to the pendant my father gave me when I had my seventh birthday party, and I don't know just what it means to me, but it's been in my thoughts again today.
>
> [Therapist:] Uh-huh.
>
> [Client:] I wore the pendant today. See? (It hung about her neck and she pulls it forward toward therapist.)
>
> [Therapist]: Yes. It's very nice.
>
> [Client:] It's just a child's present, I know, but … (weeps).
>
> [Therapist:] But?
>
> [Client:] But it means so much to me. (Still weeping) It … it … it's as though….
>
> [Therapist:] Mmmmm.
>
> [Client:] … as though he … (sobs) he loved me then. He loved me then; I know he did (crying strongly).
>
> [Therapist:] He loved you then.
>
> [Client:] Yes, he loved me then (crying eases; voice drops, becomes more reflective). But then I … but then I … what did I do? I did something so that he stopped loving me and was angry all the time. What did I do? (Crying again, a protesting tone)
>
> [Therapist:] (Tone low, intent) What you did made him stop loving you?
>
> [Client:] (Crying stopping, eyes unfocused, searching inwardly) Yes … (deeply seeking). Yes, what was it? What did I do? Oh!
>
> [Therapist:] (Silent, waiting)
>
> [Client:] I think I know (fresh sobs, face miserable). (Pause, hardly aware of anything but inner thoughts and feelings.)
>
> [Therapist:] (Silent, breathing slowed)
>
> [Client:] I know (quietly, firmly, resignedly). I know: I became a woman!

> In that moment a door opened inside of Betty, and she became aware of so much that she had known but not let herself know for so very long. That awareness within her was so much larger than she could ever reduce to words. In that enlarged inner vision is the healing/growth dynamic. In that recognition there was no need for words for several moments. Therapist and client were very close emotionally; their heads and bodies bent toward each other; they do not touch though they might well have. A time of true intimacy. (Bugental, 1987, p. 44)

Resistance. Resistance, from an existential point of view, occurs when a client does not take responsibility, is alienated, is not aware of feelings, or otherwise is inauthentic in dealing with life. Resistance is rarely directed at the therapist but is a way of dealing with overwhelming threats, an inaccurate view of the world, or an inaccurate view of self. Expressed in resistance are not only the fears of clients but also their own courageous way of dealing with themselves and their world.

Clients display resistance in the therapy hour by whining, complaining, talking about insignificant material, being seductive with the therapist, or otherwise being inauthentic. The therapist attempts to establish a real and intimate relationship with the client, being supportive of the client's struggle with such issues (van Deurzen, 2001). Schneider (2008) sees resistance as blockages to potentially important material. He is cautious or tentative and may discuss the issue indirectly rather than directly. An example of a cautious comment would be "I wonder if I'm pushing too hard right now" (p.77).

Transference. As Cohn (1997) points out, too great a focus on the transference relationship interferes with an authentic relationship with the client. Bugental (1981) recognizes that some resistances "are acted out through the transference" (p. 145). He believes that it is important to recognize when the client's attention implicitly or explicitly focuses on the therapist. For example, if the client continually praises the therapist inordinately for her help, the therapist may explore how this behavior is an acting out of relationship issues with the client's mother or father. Then the client and therapist can make progress in the process of developing a real and authentic relationship. In this way the therapist is focusing on what is happening in therapy in the present rather than attending to unconscious content as a psychoanalyst would (Davis, 2007).

The therapeutic process. Throughout the therapeutic process, existential therapists are fully present and involved with their clients. If they become bored, look forward to the end of the hour, or lose their concentration on the client, the therapists are not achieving an authentic encounter with their clients. Although existential therapists would agree on the importance of the authentic therapeutic encounter, the process in which therapists proceed varies, as they encounter issues that inhibit the development of authenticity. In dealing with them, they may disclose their own feelings and experiences when doing so helps clients fully develop their own sense of authenticity. In the movement toward authenticity, therapists explore important existential themes such as living and dying; freedom, responsibility, and choice; isolation and loving; and meaninglessness.

Living and Dying

As Yalom has observed, "Death anxiety is inversely proportional to life satisfaction" (1980, p. 207). When an individual is living authentically, anxiety and fear of death decrease. Yalom notes two ways that individuals choose to deny or avoid issues of dying: belief in their own specialness and belief in an ultimate rescuer who will save them from death. Recognizing these issues helps the therapist deal directly with issues of mortality. Such issues may confront those who are grieving, those who are dying, and those who have attempted suicide. Ways that existential therapists work with these issues are described in this section.

Yalom (1980) shows the many ways that individuals try to support a view that they are invulnerable, immortal, and will not die. The notion of narcissism emphasizes the specialness of the individual and the belief that he is invulnerable to illness and death. Coming to grips with death may be gradual or sudden.

> Jan had breast cancer that had spread to her brain. Her doctors had forewarned her of paralysis. She heard their words but at a deep level felt smugly immune to this possibility. When the inexorable weakness and paralysis ensued, Jan realized in a sudden rush that her "specialness" was a myth. There was, she learned, no "escape clause." (Yalom, 1980, p. 120)

Another defense against our own mortality is a belief in an ultimate rescuer. When patients develop a fatal illness, they must confront the fact that no one will save them. Often, they may become frustrated and angry with physicians who cannot perform magic, and they cannot believe that the doctor will fail them. Other examples of the "ultimate rescuer" are people who live their lives for others: spouse, parent, or sibling. They invest all of their energy in an interpersonal relationship that cannot save them when they are dying.

Dealing with grief is a common therapeutic task of the therapist. The loss may be that of a parent, a spouse, a child, a friend, or a pet. Existential therapists deal openly with grief and emotions such as ambivalence, guilt, and anger. Furthermore, Yalom (1980) shows how individuals confront their own deaths when dealing with the deaths of loved ones. Often dreams show material that deals not only with the death of the loved one but also fear of one's own death. In dealing with death, therapists must be aware of their own belief systems and their own fears and anxieties. If the therapist chooses to deny her own anxieties regarding death, it is likely that she may avoid the issue of death when working with a client.

To deal with suicidal patients is to deal with those who may choose death over life. Van Deurzen-Smith (1988) gives the example of Susan, a 17-year-old who had taken an overdose of sleeping tablets. She felt misunderstood, ridiculed, and hopeless. Van Deurzen-Smith views Susan's suicide attempt in brave and courageous terms rather than cowardly ones. Susan valued her action and was offended by those who discounted the importance of her attempt, felt sorry for her, or lectured her. Van Deurzen-Smith's approach was to help Susan confront her own existence.

> Existential work with Susan meant confirming those aspects of her outlook on life that were based on her discovery of hard realism while helping her to reach a more constructive conclusion in her thinking about those facts. It was no good pretending that life could be easy and that people would end up understanding her. Her recognition of life as basically rough and of people as basically unfair was one of her greatest discoveries and personal realities. She needed to get some credit for daring to look at life in such a way. Moreover she needed to be reminded that if she had the courage to brave death, all on her own, then surely she would have the courage to brave life as well. At least she had no illusions left, so she would now be able to move forward without the paralysis of constant disappointments. (1988, p. 35)

The therapist takes a caring yet forthright approach to Susan's life and death. She helps Susan accept full responsibility for taking the right to live and the right to die. In this example, the therapist's and client's attitudes toward life and death are significant; specific techniques are not.

Although there are many group techniques and exercises for helping individuals become aware of their mortality, Yalom (1980) prefers to deal directly with the individual issues rather than use techniques. However, methods such as guided fantasies, in which people imagine their death and their funeral, may be helpful. Other exercises have included talking with people who are elderly or terminally ill or writing one's own obituary or epitaph (May & Yalom, 2005). Whatever approach is used to help individuals deal with their own fears and anxieties about death can help them develop a fuller experience of being-in-the-world.

Freedom, Responsibility, and Choice

Frequent themes in counseling and psychotherapy are choices and decisions that clients must make. The existential therapist sees a client as being thrown into the world with the opportunity to make purposeful and responsible choices. The existential point of view allows clients to experience their freedom of being in the world and its inherent responsibilities.

Freedom. The existential therapist sees freedom as an opportunity to change, to step away from the client's problems, and to confront oneself (Fabry, 1987). Despite what may have happened in the past—child abuse, traumatic incidents, financial deprivation—clients have the freedom to change their lives and find meaning in their lives (van Deurzen, 2009). This is why many existential therapists prefer to work in the present rather than dwell on the past. They may talk about the past as it affects the present, but the focus is on the client's freedom to change. Although it can be exhilarating, this freedom to change can be terrifying as well. For example, Yalom describes Bonnie, who is in a restrictive 20-year marriage to a husband who made all of her decisions. She was terrified of being alone.

> Though her husband was unspeakably restrictive, she preferred the prison of her marriage to, as she put it, the freedom of the streets. She would be nothing, she said, but an outcast, a soldier in the army of misfit women searching for the occasional stray single man. Merely asking her, in the therapy hour, to reflect on the separation was sufficient to bring on a severe bout of anxious hyperventilation. (Yalom, 1980, p. 139)

It is not unusual for adolescents to complain about their family and their lack of freedom in not being able to come and go as they please, not being able to smoke, and so forth. Rather than empathize with the restrictiveness that adolescents feel and help them to develop assertiveness, the existential therapist would assist adolescents in discovering their ability to make their own choices (van Deurzen, 2001).

Responsibility. With freedom comes responsibility (Schneider, 2008). Therapists encounter vast differences in their clients' willingness to accept responsibility for themselves and their current situations. Clients may often blame parents, bosses, spouses, or others for their difficulties. In assisting the client in becoming more responsible, the therapist assumes that clients have created their own distress. Therapy progresses as clients identify their own role in their problems and stop blaming their parents, spouses, or others. Therapists' comments about responsibility are made at appropriate points, bearing in mind timing, or *kairos* (Ellenberger, 1958), the critical point at which to intervene.

In working with Betty (a different client than the Betty described on page 179), Yalom (1989) found that he was becoming bored and irritated with her. Betty was an obese, lonely woman in her 30s who constantly externalized her problems. She complained about work, the sterile California culture, people's attitudes toward her obesity, and her inability to lose weight because she had inherited obesity. She would come into the therapy hour and complain, tell stories, and try to present objective reasons as to why she was depressed. Yet she presented a joking and falsely gay facade. In the following crucial intervention,

Yalom persists in confronting Betty's pretense and refusal to take responsibility for her own condition, even though Betty resists.

> "I'm really interested in what you said about being, or rather pretending to be, jolly. I think you are determined, absolutely committed, to be jolly with me."
>
> "Hmmmm, interesting theory, Dr. Watson."
>
> "You've done this since our first meeting. You tell me about a life that is full of despair, but you do it in a bouncy 'aren't-we-having-a-good-time?' way."
>
> "That's the way I am."
>
> "When you stay jolly like that, I lose sight of how much pain you're having."
>
> "That's better than wallowing in it."
>
> "But you come here for help. Why is it so necessary for you to entertain me?"
>
> Betty flushed. She seemed staggered by my confrontation and retreated by sinking into her body. Wiping her brow with a tiny handkerchief, she stalled for time.
>
> "Zee suspect takes zee fifth."
>
> "Betty, I'm going to be persistent today. What would happen if you stopped trying to entertain me?"
>
> "I don't see anything wrong with having some fun. Why take everything so ... so ... I don't know—You're always so serious. Besides, this is me, this is the way I am. I'm not sure I know what you're talking about. What do you mean by my entertaining you?"
>
> "Betty, this is important, the most important stuff we've gotten into so far. But you're right. First, you've got to know exactly what I mean. Would it be O.K. with you if, from now on in our future sessions, I interrupt and point out when you're entertaining me—the moment it occurs?"
>
> Betty agreed—she could hardly refuse me; and I now had at my disposal an enormously liberating device. I was now permitted to interrupt her instantaneously (reminding her, of course, of our new agreement) whenever she giggled, adopted a silly accent, or attempted to amuse me or to make light of things in any distracting way.
>
> Within three or four sessions, her "entertaining" behavior disappeared as she, for the first time, began to speak of her life with the seriousness it deserved. She reflected that she had to be entertaining to keep others interested in her. I commented that, in this office, the opposite was true: the more she tried to entertain me, the more distant and less interested I felt.
>
> I was less bored now. I looked at the clock less frequently and once in a while checked the time during Betty's hour. Not, as before, to count the number of minutes I had yet to endure, but to see whether sufficient time remained to open up a new issue. (Yalom, 1989, pp. 97–98, 99)

This was a turning point in therapy for Betty. She began the process of losing a considerable amount of weight, developed relationships with men, and took responsibility for her own life. By making responsible choices, Betty was able to alleviate her depression and to be more open and honest with herself and others.

Choice. In describing the process of choice, May (1969) delineates the process as wishing, willing, and deciding. Some individuals are so depressed that they have few wishes, and in such a case the therapist must help the individual become more aware of feelings. Other clients may avoid wishing by acting impulsively or compulsively. In other words, they act but do not think about what they want. By "willing," individuals project themselves onto a point at which they will be able to decide. Willing involves the ability to change and to decide. When the individual decides, action follows. Implicit in this process is the responsibility for one's own wishing, willing, and deciding. This responsibility may be felt strongly by clients when they find themselves panicked in deciding important issues such as whether to leave an unsatisfactory job or to get married.

When dealing with choices, the existential therapist recognizes the importance of client decision making as opposed to therapist decision making (Cooper, 2003). The following example illustrates succinctly how Bugental deals with a client's indecisiveness.

Thelma's daughter wants to date a boy that Thelma does not like. The daughter, 17, insists that she can handle her own affairs and that Thelma is babying her. Thelma wants to avoid being overprotective and wants to keep her daughter's affection; yet she is frankly concerned about the reputation of the boy with whom her daughter wants to go. She tells me (the therapist) about this at some length, pauses and seems about to change the subject.

[*Therapist:*] So what will you do?

[*Patient:*] Do? What can I do?

[*Therapist:*] That's a good question, what can you do?

[*Patient:*] I can't do a thing; she's going to go, and that's it.

[*Therapist:*] So you decided to let her go with John?

[*Patient:*] I haven't decided. She's the one who has decided.

[*Therapist:*] No, you've decided too. You've chosen to let her go with John.

[*Patient:*] I don't see how you can say that. She's insisting.

[*Therapist:*] That's what she's doing; what you're doing is accepting her insistence.

[*Patient:*] Well, then I won't let her go. But she'll be unhappy and make life hell for me for a while.

[*Therapist:*] So you've decided to forbid her to go with John.

[*Patient:*] Well, isn't that what you wanted? What you said I should do?

[*Therapist:*] I didn't say that you should do anything. You have a choice here, but you seem to be insisting that either your daughter is making a choice or that I am.

[*Patient:*] Well, I don't know what to do.

[*Therapist:*] It is a hard choice.

And so Thelma begins to confront her choice. It should be evident that this same procedure would have been followed whether Thelma had first concluded to deny her daughter permission to go with the boy or had given the permission. (Bugental, 1981, pp. 345–346)

Issues of freedom, responsibility, and choice are intimately related. Experiencing a sense of freedom can cause clients to fear or to welcome the responsibility that falls upon them for the choices that they make in their own lives. As seen in the case of Betty, by taking responsibility for themselves, clients decrease the isolation and loneliness in their own lives.

Isolation and Loving

Individuals enter the world alone and leave the world alone. An awareness of the individual's relationships with others constitutes an integral part of existential treatment. Exploring feelings of loneliness and isolation is an important aspect of a therapeutic relationship. As adults grow away from their families, issues of developing new and loving relationships exist. Those who come to therapy often show an inability to develop intimacy with others. The most severe categories of psychological disturbance—paranoia and schizophrenia—show an extreme isolation in which the patient may be unable to communicate to others on the most basic levels. For the existential therapist, the challenge is to bring intimacy and therapeutic loving into the relationship to affect the loneliness of the client.

Yalom's (1980) concept of therapeutic love, described on page 178, deals directly with the loneliness of the client. Each of the examples in this section shows, to some degree, the intimate interaction with the client. Such intimacy, as in the case of Betty on page 179, can stimulate clients to have the courage to change their lives so that intimacy with others can develop. In writing about therapists' love, Bugental (1981) cautions that dependency can develop and the patient may not establish intimacy with others, only with the therapist. He gives the example of Kathryn, who made frequent phone calls, requested special meetings, and presented several crises. By setting limits, he was, with difficulty, able to stabilize the relationship. The therapeutic relationship is not a reciprocal one, as the client receives love but does not have to give it. In that sense, it can be an inaccurate representation of the relationships that the client seeks, which requires loving and giving from both individuals. Therapists communicate that along with the sense of loving and intimacy that comes with genuine caring, reciprocal giving relationships increase the meaningfulness of life.

Meaning and Meaninglessness

Helping clients—and people in general—find meaningfulness in their lives has long been a concern of Frankl (1969, 1978, 1992, 1997). As Hillmann (2004) shows, meaning is a basic concept throughout Frankl's thoughts on therapy and is the key to the mentally healthy self. If an individual searches for the meaning of life, he will not find it.

Meaning emerges as one lives and becomes concerned with others. When individuals focus too much on themselves, they also lose a perspective on life. For Frankl, helping a patient who is self-absorbed by searching for causes of anxiety and disturbance only makes the person more self-centered. Rather, for Frankl (1969), the solution is to look toward events and people in which the client finds meaning.

In concentrating on the importance of values and meaning in life, Frankl has developed an approach called *logotherapy* (Hillmann, 2004; Schulenberg, Hutzell, Nassif, & Rogina, 2008). Four specific techniques help individuals transcend themselves and put their problems into a constructive perspective: attitude modulation, dereflection, paradoxical intention, and Socratic dialogue. In *attitude modulation*, neurotic motivations are changed to healthy ones. For example, motivations to take one's life are questioned and replaced by removing obstacles that interfere with living responsibly. In *dereflection*, clients' concerns with their own problems are focused away from them. For example, clients who experience sexual performance difficulties may be asked to concentrate on the sexual pleasure of the partner and to ignore their own. Similarly, *paradoxical intention* requires that patients increase their symptoms so that attention is diverted from them by having them view themselves with less concern and often with humor. (An example of paradoxical intention is shown in the next section.) Guttmann (1996) considers *Socratic dialogue* to be the main technique in logotherapy. It can be used to guide clients to find meaning in their lives, assess current situations, and become aware of their strengths. Discussed more fully in Chapters 9 and 10, it is a series of questions that help clients arrive at conclusions about beliefs or hypotheses, guided in part by therapist perceptions of the client's misunderstandings. These techniques help patients become less self-absorbed and develop meaning in their lives through concern with other events and people.

Some existential therapists object to Frankl's approach, which appears to them to emphasize techniques over existential themes (Yalom, 1980). They prefer to help individuals become more fully aware of meaning in their lives by looking for issues that interfere with the process of finding meaning. As the therapist and the patient engage in their relationship, and as the therapist works authentically at creating a caring atmosphere, those issues that trouble the client are shared and meaningfulness emerges from their work together.

These themes—living and dying; freedom, responsibility, and choice; isolation and loving; and meaning and meaninglessness—are interrelated. They all deal intimately with issues concerning the client's existence or being-in-the-world. Engaging the client, showing therapeutic love, and involving oneself with the client are all ways of entering the client's world. They show clients that they are not alone and that they can be aided in their struggle with existential themes.

Psychological Disorders

As may be clear at this point, existential therapists conceptualize and treat psychological disorders by focusing on existential themes, not on psychodiagnostic categories. However, it is helpful to see how existential therapists apply their treatment approach to a variety of different disorders. The first is a case of existential anxiety, supervised by Emmy van Deurzen (2009) that describes the existential anxiety of a mother (the patient) and her son. The focus is on existential issues in dealing with anxiety. In working with depressed patients, Bugental (1976, 1987) discusses depression in terms of the "dispirited condition" and suggests three phases for working with such patients. With a patient with a borderline disorder, Yalom focuses on the importance of "engagement" to work with such individuals who feel isolated from others. Often paradoxical intention has been applied to individuals with obsessive-compulsive disorders. Lukas (1984) helps a patient "step outside herself" and be more aware of her own being by changing her approach to compulsive behavior. With a man who abuses alcohol, Bugental (1981) raises the importance of taking responsibility for one's own life and ceasing self-blaming behaviors. Although different existential themes are associated with various disorders in these examples, these themes are not specific to the disorders, as several existential themes may arise in any of the disorders that are discussed here.

Anxiety: Nathalie and Her Son

Anxiety disorders often include many existential issues. In this case of Nathalie and her son, Jason, a mother faces the existential issues that arise from her son's friendship with Adam, and Adam's suicide. Existential anxiety appears to be very present in this case along with some symptoms of generalized anxiety disorder. Both Nathalie and her son are faced with choices to make as to how to deal with Adam's suicide. Weighing heavily on Nathalie's mind are questions about her and her son's responsibility to Adam and his family. Contrasting with her responsibility to Adam and his family is her responsibility to her son. In dealing with the death of Adam, both mother and Jason face the important issue of existential authenticity.

> Nathalie was the client of someone whose therapeutic practice I supervised. She was a lady in her forties with a son of 17. Nathalie was in psychotherapy because of her agoraphobia, which for a while had kept her completely house-bound, as she would have severe panic attacks as soon as she ventured outdoors. Her phobia had much subsided and she was coming to therapy sessions unaccompanied by the time that a new development struck her down with a fresh attack of anxiety. This time it was generalized anxiety and it was clearly triggered by a specific event.
>
> Nathalie's son, Jason, had been involved in a nasty series of bullying events, which involved a boy, Adam, who used to be his friend when they were younger. The school had disciplined Jason and his friends who were seen to be ganging up on Adam after Adam's parents complained to the school. None of this made any difference and the boys had carried on pestering Adam until Adam was found hanging in his room, having left a letter in which he stated that his life was not worth living. His death thus appeared to be directly related to the bullying. Nathalie's son Jason was almost certainly involved in this and he had been questioned by the police. He had denied any responsibility, as had his friends. They had been let off the hook. Then, just a couple of days after attending Adam's funeral, Jason broke down and told his mother that he and his friends had repeatedly taunted Adam and had threatened to torture him even further if he told on them again. It was clear to Jason that Adam's suicide had been directly motivated by the gang's threats. Jason was only a peripheral member of the gang but he knew that three of the other boys had actually attacked Adam on his way home from school the day that he killed himself. The same boys had now threatened him with similar violence if he told the police of what he knew had gone on. The police in fact were already aware of these events, but as Adam's death was a clear case of suicide they had left the school to discipline the boys. Jason had not however told the truth when questioned and he felt dreadfully guilty and in a quandary over how to act.
>
> Nathalie was frozen with horror to discover that her son had been involved in acts that had led to another boy's death. She had known Adam all his life and felt a tremendous sense of responsibility for what had happened to him. She became frantic with dread. She could not speak up because it would harm Jason and the other boys. She could not remain silent because that would be condoning what she saw as criminal behaviour. In fact she could not face the idea that her son was part of a gang capable of such behaviour. Paralysed with anxiety she fell back into her old symptoms and remained ensconced in her house, cancelling her therapy sessions several times. When she finally did come back to therapy, she avoided telling her therapist what had happened to make her so upset. She merely said it wasn't safe to go out since Adam, a friend of Jason's, had died. This seemed a mysterious statement that the therapist at first left unchallenged. (van Deurzen, 2009, pp.137–138)
>
> What Nathalie was experiencing was intense existential anxiety. She was aware of the dangers of living and at the same time aware of her own responsibility in confronting these dangers. Her previous attitude of hiding away from danger until it became impossible to be safe anywhere was still with her, but she could no longer give in to it. Here she was being offered an opportunity to live bravely and speak up and yet she was once again trying to evade the challenge. Now she had a choice to either encourage Jason to speak up and perhaps be punished, or to remain silent and cover up what had really happened. She knew evasion was not really an option as it led to renewed paralysis not just in her but in her son as well. Before long she

accepted that to discuss her dilemma openly with the therapist would be a step in the right direction. She told her therapist that she was only able to do this when she saw that her therapist would not pathologize or diminish her experience.

It was clear that Nathalie was inexperienced at solving moral dilemmas because she had previously denied and avoided them. But it now became possible to help her see that the avoidance of such challenges placed her in a cul-de-sac from where she could see no way forward. Facing this challenge bravely was the only way to go to retrieve her freedom of movement. She knew that overcoming her agoraphobia had required her to face her fear and go out to do the very things she dreaded most. She knew therefore that facing these problems in living would equally make her stronger and that with this new strength she would stand the best chance of finding a solution to her predicament.

She agreed to look at the issues directly. She thought at first that she was mainly concerned about Jason. She worried that his chances of succeeding in his exams would be wrecked if he owned up to the part he had played in Adam's drama. She acknowledged that this seemed a catastrophe to her, because Jason was usually so clever and made her proud of him. His successes made up for her personal lack of academic prowess and this mattered greatly to her. She had pulled out of her education when she was 17 and she feared that the same would now happen to Jason. The psychotherapist initially pursued the line that Nathalie might envy Jason's potential success, suggesting that Nathalie might have a wish to destroy his chances of passing his exams, so that he would not surpass her. (p. 138)

What emerged in the next session was that Nathalie felt that if she let Jason keep hiding away from the truth of his own actions, he would remain a passive bystander forever. He would in other words become like herself: afraid to stand up and be counted. This was the real moral dilemma: was she strong enough to stand up and be counted and teach her son to do the same? This was the question she needed to answer in action. The endless debate about whether or not it mattered to let people know about what had really happened to Adam had become irrelevant. It was by then a publicly recognized fact that the bullying had been an important contributing factor to Adam's suicide. Of course it still mattered to tell the truth. It mattered to Adam's family to know the truth and it mattered to Jason and Nathalie to take a truthful stance rather than a cowardly and self-protective stance. Later on, as Nathalie found the courage to say these things to her son she discovered that Jason felt the same. He actually wanted to recover his self-respect by owning up to what he had done and what he knew others had done. He feared the consequences of his silence more than the consequences of speaking out. There was also the issue of doing his duty by his dead friend. It was interesting that both Jason and his mum had at times pretended that Jason could not speak up because it would implicate the other friends. They now found that the idea of protecting friends was not a convincing story, as Adam, a dead friend, needed protecting more than anyone. In the end it was clear that Jason could come clean without attracting particular punishment or even directly implicating anyone else. It also became obvious that such an act would be morally correct and emotionally corrective. When Jason did own up and took his reprimands calmly, this increased his self-esteem and gained him approval from many. He still had to manage his relationship with the old gang, who now banned him, but he found that this was not a major loss and probably an advantage. Nathalie was very proud of him and somewhat reluctantly took some of the credit for helping him to be truthful. She sensed that both she and her son had reclaimed their self-esteem by being truthful. Jason's passing his exams rather more successfully than expected immensely gratified her. Her fate and that of Jason were intrinsically linked. Passing the test of truth together strengthened their relationship. They could now think of themselves and each other as people who were able to do the right thing. This did enough for Nathalie's self-confidence to help her out of the impasse of anxiety and back into the flow of life. (pp. 139–140)

Depression: Catherine

In his work with depressed patients, Bugental (1987) prefers to refer to their condition as dispirited. To him, dispiritedness refers to blocks to intending or wishing. The depressed or dispirited person feels that there is nothing worth doing or bothering with. There may be a desire to be still, be alone, and not participate in the world.

In dealing with dispiritedness, Bugental suggests three phases that underlie his therapeutic approach. First, when patients casually report inactivity or joke about their depression, the therapist deals directly with this detachment by bringing it to the patient's awareness. Second, as people become less detached, the therapeutic process involves calling attention and reducing the guilt or blame patients feel for their own depression or dispiritedness. Third, clients are helped to accept their own dispiritedness and to sense it. When this happens, they are likely to feel existential anxiety, fears of death, meaninglessness, or aloneness. Therapy then deals with issues of responsibility and choices.

Although not using Bugental's model, van Deurzen-Smith (1988) uses a remarkably similar approach with Catherine, a young woman who had been diagnosed as having a postpartum depression. She had felt hopeless and unable to care for her baby. Her husband and her mother suggested that Catherine go away for a while and rest—in essence, disengage. This is exactly what Catherine did not want to do, and it made the problem worse. Catherine felt more alive when she resisted her husband and her mother than when she gave in. First, Catherine was helped to acknowledge her depression and then to deal with her disillusionment about having a baby. The therapist helped Catherine to accept her exhaustion and her disappointment and to rediscover her enjoyment and desire to be with her baby. In essence, the therapist was helping Catherine to recover her lost desire and motivation to fully experience mothering a child. Although not strictly following Bugental's three phases, there is an increased engagement as Catherine "moved from depression to anxiety" (p. 55) while gaining insights about herself and her baby. As van Deurzen-Smith says, "anxiety was a sign of her engagement with life and expressed her readiness for its inevitable crises" (p. 55). As Catherine accepted her responsibilities for her baby, she grew more confident and dealt self-assuredly with her husband and her mother. Having a sense of direction and will helped her to live authentically.

Borderline Disorder: Anna

In working with a young woman whom he diagnosed as having a borderline disorder, Yalom (1980) helped her to "bridge the gulf of isolation" (p. 396) that she experienced with others. Anna had been hospitalized after she had tried to kill herself, and she appeared to be very bitter and isolated.

In her treatment, Anna profited from her participation in group therapy. She had been critical of herself for being phony and for not having real feelings. Often she felt she did not belong and that other people had close relationships that she would not be able to have. In group, she was encouraged to enter the world of the other group members, to be open to their experience and to her own. During one group meeting, Anna was able to become involved with several members, "weeping with and for one of them" (p. 396). Yalom points out that it was important not only for her to have this experience but also to examine the experience and comment on what it had been like. Anna said that she had felt alive and involved and unaware of her usual feeling of isolation.

Dealing with individuals with borderline disorder is long and complex work. The point of this example is to show that clients with borderline personality disorders can be helped when they can engage in a meaningful way with others. In this example, Yalom approaches the conceptualization and treatment of a person with a borderline disorder by focusing on the theme of isolation.

Obsessive-Compulsive Disorder: Female Patient

Frankl (1969, 1992, 1997) developed logotherapy as a means of helping clients deal with meaning in their lives. In working with clients with obsessive-compulsive disorders, he developed paradoxical intention, which essentially helps clients get outside themselves in order to deal with their problem. Paradoxical intention forces clients to attribute new meaning to events in their lives (Hillmann, 2004). Thus a feared object may no longer appear fearful. When clients have trust in the therapist, a sense of humor about themselves, and an ability to distance themselves from their problems, they are more likely to experience a positive reaction to paradoxical intention. Unlike the approach of many existential therapists, who focus on existential themes in the lives of clients, the approach of logotherapy is brief and active (Guttmann, 1996; Schulenberg et al., 2008).

In the following example of her work with a patient who compulsively looked at herself in the mirror many times during the day, Lukas (1984) not only makes paradoxical suggestions but also participates in the paradoxical intervention herself.

> One of my patients had mirror compulsion that prompted her to run to a mirror up to 20 times a day to make sure that her hair was sufficiently well-groomed. She resisted paradoxical intention until I offered to participate with her in a game of "hair rumpling": We would see who could rumple our hair more thoroughly by attacking it with all ten fingers. Afterwards we ran hand in hand around the block, all the while paradoxically intending to show all passers-by just how wildly our hair "stood on end." When someone passed us without paying any attention, we roughed up our hair a bit more because it obviously was not disheveled enough. This game won the cooperation of the patient who up to then had resisted all paradoxical formulations. Of course, no one paid any attention to us. Who nowadays cares whether someone's hair is well-groomed? My patient realized this and was able to overcome her compulsion to go to the mirror by paradoxically wishing, "Let my hair stand on end. Let it be a mess!" After eight weeks her mirror compulsion was gone. (Lukas, 1984, p. 24)

In using paradoxical intention, Lukas feels that it is important to show that she can identify with her clients and that she takes their problems seriously. By participating with them in the practice of paradoxical intention, she finds that they are likely to accept her intervention, even though it may seem ridiculous at first (p. 83).

Alcoholism: Harry

Theories in Action

A common existential theme among drug and alcohol abusers is their refusal to take responsibility for their own lives. Bugental (1981, p. 340) points out that such individuals may blame themselves rather than take responsibility for their own behaviors. If therapists allow and support the blaming behaviors of clients, they may introduce an iatrogenic complication. Iatrogenic refers to making matters worse. In the following example, Bugental (1981) confronts Harry's self-blaming and focuses on the need for him to take responsibility. Recognizing that Harry uses blame to avoid responsibility, Bugental persists in explaining Harry's actions to him.

> Harry was very guilty and ashamed this Tuesday morning, as he was from time to time after he had a drinking bout over the weekend. "So, I did it again! Tied one on, swung my weight around the house, had Leah and the kids terrified. Oh, I'm the big man all right. Just let me get a snoot full and...."
>
> I interrupted him, "You really sound pretty enthusiastic when you get going on cussing yourself out."
>
> "Well, hell, I'm just no damned good. I'm to blame for every lousy thing that's wrong with my family. Why Leah puts up with an eight ball like me is...."
>
> "You're just no good, huh?"
>
> "That's right. I never was any count. My father told me I made mother sick with worry. If I was any good, I'd ... I'd...."
>
> "Well, there's really nothing to feel badly about, is there?"
>
> "What do you mean?"
>
> "Well, you're no good and never have been any good. So plainly it's not your responsibility. Somebody else messed you up: God or your parents, but you don't have to carry the load."
>
> "What? I'm taking the blame, aren't I? What do you want?"
>
> "Sure, you're taking the blame and dodging the responsibility."
>
> "It's the same thing."
>
> "Is it? I don't think so. I've heard you take the blame a dozen times, and all I can see that it does is pay a little emotional bill for your drunk. Then the next time you can't deal with things you can get drunk again and pay the bill with blaming yourself and do it all over. You've never taken responsibility for yourself, only blame."
>
> "Well, what's the difference?"
>
> "Just this: If you took responsibility for the feeling you had before you started to drink, if you took responsibility for starting to drink, if you took responsibility for the way you treat Leah and the kids when you're loaded—instead of blaming it on the alcohol.... If you took it on yourself to know what you were doing at each of those points, what do you think would happen?"
>
> "I wouldn't do it. But, hell, I don't think about it that way. I just get kind of wound up, and I figure a drink would relax me and then before I know it...."
>
> "That's the point: 'Before you know it....' You're not taking responsibility. All you do is sing the 'Ain't I bad!' song so you can do it all over again."
>
> Harry did not get a sweeping insight this time, but we did get two points of importance before his awareness so that we could refer to them again and again in the future: (a) he used blame to avoid responsibility; (b) if he accepted responsibility, he would find that he was fully aware of what he was doing and probably could not slide through the dismal sequence again. In dealing with these recognitions, Harry came to make his first really sincere efforts to inquire into the sources of his needs to get drunk periodically. (Bugental, 1981, pp. 339–340)

Brief Therapy

Because existential therapy represents an attitude toward living and toward the client, to speak of brief existential therapy is to imply that existential therapy is far more systematic than it really is. Many existential therapists have a background in psychoanalysis, which, when combined with existential attitudes, is usually practiced in an in-depth manner. Although preferring a longer-term model, Bugental has proposed an outline for short-term existential humanistic therapy (Bugental, 2008). Frankl's logotherapy is also another short-term approach that often requires less than a few months of treatment. Additionally, pastors and counselors who work with crises such as death of a loved one or loss of a job often use a brief existential approach with their clients.

In his model of short-term therapy, Bugental (2008) suggests three principles in deriving a short-term approach to existential therapy. First, the client's self-discovery rather than insight or suggestions by the therapist is key. Second, the client should be helped to develop his abilities to search for solutions to his own problems. Third, short-term therapy should not be conducted in a way that would interfere with long-term existential therapy, should the client ever seek it out. These principles guide the following six phases of short-term existential therapy, which have a defined goal of treatment.

Phase 1. Assessment: The therapist should determine if the goal of therapy is explicit. Also, the therapist should assess that the client is capable of taking an existential approach to examining the problem and is psychologically strong enough to conduct this search (will not be overwhelmed by emotions such as anger and depression).

Phase 2. Identify the concern: Contract with the client to work on a specific objective that is expressed briefly and clearly.

Phase 3. Teaching the searching process: The client is guided to focus on the present and then to focus on the energy and feelings around the problem. Although resistances are identified, they are not to be worked through.

Phase 4: Identifying resistance: Rather, resistances are used to identify cues to the conflicts that the patient is dealing with.

Phase 5: The therapeutic work: Both therapist and client should maintain awareness that the therapy is limited by time. The goal of therapy should be maintained, although other issues can be discussed as they relate to the goal.

Phase 6: Termination: The time limit should be observed. The last session should assess what has been accomplished in therapy, what remains to be done, and how to do it.

This short-term model provides a means for maintaining an existential approach within a limited focus. The problem could focus on one or two existential issues that could include living and dying, freedom, responsibility, choice, isolation, loving, or finding meaning in life. Problems such as grief, a divorce, or loss of a job may fit a short-term model as they represent a finite problem that is occurring in the present. However, sometimes existential brief therapy may lead to a realization that longer-term existential therapy is required.

Frankl (1969, 1992) and his colleagues (Fabry, 1987; Lukas, 1984) have developed a different short-term approach. Because logotherapy makes use of techniques of attitude modulation, dereflection, and paradoxical intention (as explained on page 185), an active and challenging approach is used. Furthermore, many logotherapists use a Socratic dialogue in assisting clients in finding meaning in their lives. Although logotherapy is used with traditional psychological disorders, particularly obsessive-compulsive neurosis, it is used specifically for noögenic neuroses, when clients experience little meaning in their lives, such as when they have too much leisure or abuse drugs. Such an approach may take only a few sessions or require several months of meetings (Hillmann, 2004).

Counselors, nurses, social workers, and clergy often do short-term crisis counseling. Common crises include dying, the death of a loved one, the loss of a job, sudden illness, a divorce, and similar life milestones. By combining helping skills with a knowledge of existential themes, these mental health professionals may not only be empathic to the pain of their clients but also be able to help them examine their lives from different points of view.

Current Trends

Interest in existential therapy is strongest in Europe. The International Federation for Daseinsanalyse has members from many countries, as does The International Collaborative for Existential Counsellors and Psychotherapists. The Society for Existential Analysis, formed in England in 1988, sponsors an annual conference and a journal. Other organizations are the Eastern European Association for Existential Psychotherapy based in Lithuania and the South American Existential Association based in Columbia. Existential training programs are available in Albania, Austria, the Czech Republic, Demark, England, Ireland, Italy, Poland, Romania, Sweden, and the United States, as well as other countries (Emmy van Deurzen, personal communication, October 1, 2005; August 28, 2009). Because most existential therapists (and most therapists in general) had a psychoanalytic orientation in the 1930s and 1940s, much existential writing reflects this background. However, in more recent years, psychotherapists with backgrounds in person-centered psychotherapy, gestalt therapy, Jungian therapy, feminist therapy, and some cognitive and behavioral approaches have been able to integrate existential attitudes into their work. Because the dissemination of existentialism takes place through supervision, demonstrations, and reading rather than in systematic research, it is extremely difficult to assess its current impact.

Although the growth of existential therapy is informal, this is not true of Frankl's logotherapy. His writings have been extremely popular, with *Man's Search for Meaning* (1992) selling millions of copies. Also, the Viktor Frankl Institute of Logotherapy publishes a journal, *The International Forum for Logotherapy*. Viktor Frankl not only wrote widely but also spoke throughout the world. There are a number of logotherapy centers, with several active ones in Germany and South America. Because of the emphasis on the spirit in Frankl's writings, many clergy and religious workers find his writings and therapeutic approach consistent with their views that spirit is the key to self.

With its emphasis on phenomenology, the client's subjective experience, existential therapy is consistent with certain aspects of postmodern thought. By emphasizing authenticity, existential therapists help their clients be aware of their own view of reality (such as views on death or responsibility) and not deny their views. Rather than being hindered by techniques that may derive from their own perception of reality, existential therapists concentrate on the client's subjective experience. *Mindfulness*, an approach derived from Buddhist writings focusing on awareness of physical, cognitive, and affective responses in the present moment, is an important current topic in therapy and is highly consistent with the existential focus on the process of client experience and the concept of authenticity (Claessens, 2009; Nanda, 2009). Mindfulness is compatible with postmodern thought because it helps patients become aware of their own view of reality.

Using Existential Therapy with Other Theories

The value of existential psychotherapy is that it deals with assumptions underlying psychotherapy in general. Because there are no specific techniques (with the exception of a few techniques used by logotherapists), existential psychotherapists must have a background in other psychotherapeutic modalities. With expertise in the use of one or more theoretical approaches to respond to clients' problems, the therapist is then able to attend to existential themes. As May and Yalom (2005) point out, most therapies deal with the client in relationship to the biological or environmental world (Umwelt) or relationships with others (Mitwelt), but few deal with the individual's relationship to his or her self (Eigenwelt) or with the spiritual self (Überwelt) (van Deurzen-Smith, 1997, 1998). It is this emphasis on self-awareness and self-relatedness that distinguishes existential therapy from other therapies. But recent work shows how existential therapy can be integrated with other therapies. Bornstein (2004) describes how cognitive therapy and existential therapy can be combined in treating patients who have problems with being too dependent on others. Wolfe (2008) illustrates how existential themes and cognitive-behavioral methods can be integrated in the treatment of anxiety disorders. Because both relational psychoanalysis and existential therapy emphasize the therapeutic relationship, both are compatible to apply in combination when working with patients (Portnoy, 2008). Existential therapists may also find that the expressive approach of gestalt therapy that uses a variety of experiential techniques provides a means of integrating these two therapies (Kondas, 2008). *Existential-Integrative Psychotherapy* (Schneider, 2008) describes way of using existential themes with a variety of theories to build an existential-integrative approach that helps the therapist make use of existing theories in her work. As the case examples have shown, existential therapists apply a variety of listening skills, confrontive techniques, and other ways of responding while being aware of a variety of existential themes. To do this presupposes that existential psychotherapists have developed counseling skills first, before they integrate their existential philosophy and attitudes.

Research

Because existential psychotherapy makes use of techniques and practices of other theories, it is very difficult to study its effectiveness. Most overviews of existential therapy tend to combine it with person-centered, gestalt, and experiential therapies under the "humanistic" label (Elliott, 2001, 2002). A few studies that have tried to assess whether existential goals were realized in group therapy are discussed here. More common are studies that relate existential themes such as death, anxiety, and meaning to therapeutic issues and individual characteristics. All of these studies use traditional methods of assessment such as interviews and objective tests. An overview of the research in all of these areas is given in this section.

There seems to be some support for the conclusion that existential themes can be addressed and dealt with successfully in group therapy. In studying the progress of four groups of bereaved spouses, Yalom and colleagues (Lieberman & Yalom, 1992; Yalom & Lieberman, 1991; Yalom & Vinogradov, 1988) found modest improvement in psychological functioning when they were compared with untreated control bereaved individuals. The investigators implied there was an increasing existential awareness in the experimental group. They suggest that the most helpful roles that leaders could take were in attending to existential issues and themes such as the group members' sense of identity and their responsibility for their future lives. Other studies have examined internal versus external control to assess increasing self-responsibility as a result of group therapy. For example, van der Pompe, Duivenvoorden, Antoni, and Visser (1997) examined the impact of experiential existential group therapy on physiological measures of breast cancer patients. They found positive changes in endocrine and immune functions in a small group of 50- to 70-year-old patients which were not found in a waiting-list control group. Another study examined the effectiveness of cognitive-existential group therapy in women with early-stage breast cancer (Kissane et al., 2003). The patients reported improved family functioning, better coping skills, and increased self-growth. Recurrence of cancer for some of the women negatively affected therapeutic gains. Although research studies measuring changes in existential themes in group therapy are few, the review of research by Page, Weiss, and Lietaer (2002) suggests that participants in existential group therapy improve in their evaluations of themselves.

Concerns with death as a general issue and, more specifically, the loss of a loved one have been the subject of a variety of investigations. In a study of college students who were grieving the death of a family member, Edmonds and Hooker (1992) found that grief can have positive aspects by bringing about growth in existential concerns. In a study of 188 individuals over the age of 65 who had recently lost their spouses, Fry (2001) found that personal meaning, religiosity, and spirituality were more important in predicting psychological well-being than factors such as social support and physical health. In therapy with older adult couples, Lantz and Raiz (2004) report that the therapy focused on existential activities that included holding, telling, mastering, and honoring. Studying terminally ill advanced-state cancer patients, Lichtenthal et al. (2009) reported that closeness to death was not associated with increased existential distress or mental disorders. Rather, these patients were more likely to acknowledge being terminally ill and were more apt to desire the end of their lives. These findings would seem to be consistent with the observations of Yalom and his colleagues in their work with bereaved spouses.

An existential issue of particular concern to Viktor Frankl is that of meaninglessness, or what he refers to as existential vacuum. To assess this concept, Crumbaugh (1968) and Crumbaugh & Henrion (1988) have developed the Purpose-in-Life Test (PIL). This instrument has been used both with clients and in research on meaninglessness. Using the PIL with 48 married couples, McCann and Biaggio (1989) found that those individuals who scored high on the PIL also reported higher levels of sexual enjoyment in their marriages than those with low scores on the PIL. In a study of spirituality in college students, French and Joseph (1999) found a relationship between religiosity and existential well-being as measured by the PIL. In their study of college students who had experienced the death of a relative or friend within the previous 3 years, Pfost, Stevens, and Wessels (1989) found that those who scored low on the PIL (having little meaning in their lives) reported more anger in response to the death of a friend or relative than did those who scored high on the PIL. Reporting on family members who cared for elderly relatives with Alzheimer's disease, Farren, Keene-Hagerty, Salloway, and Kupferer (1991) concluded that caregivers respond to their experience with their relatives by valuing positive aspects of the experience and by searching for meaning in their caregiving. Paid caregivers working in a mental health homeshare program who had been working in their job for more than 2 years scored higher on the PIL than those working less than 2 years (Rhoades, 1999). The PIL provides a way of measuring the dimension of meaninglessness–meaningfulness in a variety of individuals and situations.

Gender Issues

Existential therapists tend to see the themes that have been discussed in this chapter as universal, applying to men and women, and may not concentrate on biological and social factors that affect men and women differently. Biological factors affecting women's existential themes are pregnancy, birth, miscarriage, and unwanted pregnancy. The case of Catherine (p. 189), who suffered from a postpartum depression, is such an example.

Cultures and societies may differ in the sex-role expectations placed on men and women. However, it is clear that sex-role stereotypes do affect the way individuals deal with existential themes. A contribution of humanistic psychology, which includes existentialism, is the encouragement for women, as well as men, to realize their potential to self-actualize and rise above stereotyping (Serlin & Criswell, 2001). Because many societies expect women to be subservient to men, women must deal with how to make choices authentically. In contrast, men may feel that they have been given too much responsibility and may hide from it. Brown (2008) emphasizes the importance of feminist writings on the need to empower women and to look at the variety of roles they play or their many identities. Being aware of clients' gender-role stereotypes can often help the therapist to identify those existential issues the client fears. For gay and lesbian individuals, greater social support, a religious orientation, and existential well-being predicted greater self-esteem (Yakushko, 2005). In addition to gender-role concerns, there are societal problems, such as a homophobic attitude, that present great existential challenges.

Multicultural Issues

To what extent does existential philosophical thought, which has a western European history, represent universal values? Young and Morris (2004) see religion as a universal cultural value that shows that cultures have much in common. In *Existential Psychology: East-West,* Hoffman, Yang, Kaklauskas, Francis and Chan (2009) also show how religious values influence the challenges and opportunities people have in their lives that allow existential therapy to apply existential themes to a great variety of religious and cultural experiences. Some differences do exist between Eastern and Western thought; for example, many Eastern religions tend to look at the universe as a whole and focus less on the separation between humans and other living and nonliving things than does existential philosophy. Loy (1996) describes the commonalities inherent in Buddhism and existentialism showing how both work toward transcendence of dependence and hostility and deal with somewhat similar topics. In working with African Americans, Rice (2008) sees existential issues such as freedom, meaning, being, and choice as issues that are important for both African Americans and Caucasian Americans. On the other hand, Comas-Díaz (2008) believes that the emphasis on spirituality among Latinas and Latinos influences the way they view the healing or therapeutic process, which may be different than the way people from other cultures react to therapy. In discussing cross-cultural counseling, Vontress (2003) and Vontress and Epp (2001) point out that clients and counselors are members of the same universal culture and must deal with a variety of existential themes. In general, existential psychotherapy seems to strike universal chords, as evidenced by the popularity of Frankl's logotherapy throughout the world.

Because existential therapy emphasizes individuals' responsibility and their struggle with mortality and isolation, sociocultural factors may be overlooked. Examining cultural values and existential themes provides a perspective that existential philosophy itself does not. Vontress and Epp (2001) describe *cultural anxiety*, which refers to the anxiety that individuals experience when they move to or visit a new culture. This could refer to visiting a country that uses a different language from our own or moving to a neighborhood where individuals share a culture that is different from our own. Cultural anxiety, like existential anxiety, can lead to physical symptoms such as headaches. Studying existential themes as they relate to cultural values of different groups serves to widen the application of existential therapy. Recognizing the external pressures of discrimination and oppression can help therapists increase their understanding of the forces that have an impact on existential themes and crises.

Van Deurzen-Smith (1988) finds that existential counseling is particularly relevant for work with cross-cultural issues and that existential themes can provide guidance for working with crisis situations. She gives the example of Gabriel, a young man from Africa who came to England to study. At home, he was a prominent member of his society and was treated with respect. In England, he became very confused by the expectations of fellow students, stopped attending classes, and was doubting his decision to come to England. He felt isolated from his country and alone and was experiencing cultural anxiety.

> To remain in contact with his homeland and culture he had begun to prolong the daily rituals of cleansing himself of the influence of his new environment. The rituals involved the use of water and one day he unintentionally provoked a minor flood in the residential hall of the college. (pp. 31–32)

Gabriel denied responsibility for the flooding and explained that his ancestors had made the flood happen because they disapproved of his new way of life. Hearing this explanation, administrators and students questioned Gabriel's sanity, as they made judgments about his behavior based on their own cultural experience. Van Deurzen-Smith explained the existential counseling approach that was used with Gabriel.

> What was needed was in the first place that the counselor grasped his isolation and the essential cultural miscommunication that had been taking place. Gabriel had not had a fair chance of fully presenting the situation from his own perspective. In the second place he lacked the plain and simple comprehension of what people were trying to get him to do. An explanation of Western notions of personal responsibility and honour went a long way toward easing the situation for him. He had felt accused, when he was only asked not to deny his part in an event. He had felt offended in his honour when people rejected his mention of his ancestors as the origin of all this. Western dismissal of magical thinking seemed like a personal affront.

While he needed to be understood from his perspective he also needed to be told about the perspective that he misunderstood himself. (p. 33)

In essence, what van Deurzen-Smith did was to help Gabriel transcend his immediate situation and look at it from a perspective outside himself. Further, she was able to understand Gabriel's issues from the point of view of the existential theme of isolation and then deal with his crises in the new culture.

Group Counseling and Psychotherapy

Group counseling and psychotherapy can be an excellent format to deal with existential issues (May & Yalom, 2005; Saiger, 2008). Corey (2008) sees the purpose of an existential group as helping people make a "commitment to a lifelong journey of self-exploration" (p. 218). The atmosphere of a group helps individuals search inside themselves and attend to their own subjective experience while sharing these experiences with others who have similar goals. In this way, meaningful issues and questions can be dealt with and respected. This section briefly addresses from the point of view of group therapy the four major existential themes discussed in this chapter: living and dying; freedom, responsibility, and choice; isolation and loving; and meaning and meaninglessness.

Living and Dying

A group format provides an excellent opportunity to deal with issues regarding living life fully and purposefully with awareness and authenticity. In his approach to existential group work, Corey asks, How meaningful is your life? How would you answer this if you knew you were about to die? Have you made decisions that you have not acted on? A group is a safe place for people to express sadness about change, difficulties in changing, and fears of death and incompleteness. Elizabeth Bugental (2008) describes a group process for older individuals and illustrates how they bring wisdom through a broad perspective on life to the group process.

Freedom, Responsibility, and Choice

In a group, individuals are responsible for their own existence, actions, and miseries. When existential therapists observe group members viewing themselves as victims and as helpless, they point out that the group members are not taking responsibility for their own lives (Corey, 2008).

Yalom sees clients as "born simultaneously: each starts out in the group on an equal footing" (1980, p. 239). For Yalom, the group is an excellent place for individuals to become aware of their own responsibility through the feedback of the members and the leader. In groups, patients can learn how their behavior is viewed by others, how they make others feel, how their behavior influences others' opinions of them, and how their behavior in group influences their own opinions of themselves. In a group, members have not only responsibility for themselves but also an obligation for the functioning of the group. In this way, a group becomes a small social system (Yalom, 1980). It is the leader's task to be aware of group processes, to encourage members to act appropriately in group, and to discuss the matter of members' participation in group.

Isolation and Loving

A group experience provides the opportunity to develop close and real relationships with others. Individuals can learn to be themselves and to be authentic, and they find that it is a rewarding experience. The ways of relating that are learned in group can be applied to people outside the group so that a sense of intimacy can develop. The development of intimacy is illustrated by the following example of Eve, who had been passive and a peripheral member of a group for 6 months.

> I asked Eve if she could try to engage any of the members. She compliantly went around the group and discussed, in a platitudinous manner, her feelings toward each person. "How would you rank," I asked, "your comments to each member on a one-to-ten risk-taking scale?" "Very low," she ventured, "about two to three." "What would happen," I said, "if you were to move up a rung or two?" She replied that she would tell the group that she was an alcoholic! This was, indeed, a revelation—she had told no one before. I then tried to help her open herself even more by asking her to talk about how she felt coming to the group for so many months and not being able to tell us that. Eve responded by talking about how lonely she felt in the group, how cut off she was from every person in the room. But she was flushed with shame about her drinking. She could not, she insisted, be "with" others or make herself known to others because of her drinking.
>
> I turned Eve's formula around (here the real therapeutic work began): *she did not hide herself because she drank, but she drank because she hid herself!* She drank because she was so unengaged with the world. Eve then talked about coming home, feeling lost and alone, and at that point doing one of two things: either slumping into a reverie where she imagined herself very young and being cared for by the big people, or assuaging the pain of her lostness and loneliness with alcohol. Gradually Eve began to understand that she was relating to others for a specific function—to be protected and taken care of—and that, in the service of this function, she was relating only partially. (Yalom, 1980, p. 394)

Group often serves as a way to engage with others and to develop a sense of intimacy that individual therapy cannot provide.

Meaning and Meaninglessness

The group experience allows individuals to reexamine their values and compare them with the values of others in the group. An emphasis on examining the meaning of life can be an important focus of existential group therapy (Saiger, 2008). Often group members challenge the values of another member, forcing that person to deal with her sense of identity and her purpose in life (Corey, 2008). When values are present in a group but unexamined, group members are likely to confront and challenge. In such a way, group members and leaders can be supportive yet confrontational as individuals search for a purpose and meaning in their lives.

Because they deal with important life issues, existential groups tend to meet for a year or more and to be emotionally intense. As the leader fosters sincere relationships among participants, caring and concern are developed for other participants. By being themselves (being authentic), leaders encourage members to challenge themselves and others to bring about personal growth.

Summary

Existential therapy is an attitude toward life, a way of being, and a way of inter-acting with oneself, others, and the environment. Rooted in 19th-century western European philosophy, existential philosophy was applied to psychotherapy by the Swiss psychiatrists Ludwig Binswanger and Medard Boss. Other existential psychotherapists, both in the United States and in Europe, have examined a variety of issues as they affect the human experience.

Existential therapists, in their focus on individuals' relationships with themselves, others, and the environment, are concerned with universal themes. In this chapter, the existential themes provide a means of conceptualizing personality and of helping individuals find meaning in their lives through the psychotherapeutic process. All individuals are "thrown" into the world and ultimately face death. How they face their own deaths and those of others is an important concern of existential therapists. Individuals are seen not as victims but as responsible for their own lives, with the ability to exercise freedom and make choices. Dealing with the anxiety that can evolve from these concerns is an aspect of existential therapy. Forming relationships with others that are not manipulative but intimate is a goal of existential therapy that often arises from a sense of isolation and loneliness. Finding a sense of meaning in the world has been a particular concern of Viktor Frankl and those who use his logotherapeutic techniques. Most existential psychotherapists take an attitudinal or thematic approach to therapy and do not focus on techniques, although Frankl does describe some specific existential techniques.

Exploring existential themes is done in group therapy. In existential group therapy, there is an emphasis not only on relationships between members of the group but also on individuals' experience of their own sense of themselves. Existential issues transcend culture and gender, although certain biological and social realities are encountered differently, depending upon one's gender or cultural identification.

Theories in Action DVD: Existential Therapy

Basic Concepts Used in the Role-Play

- Choice
- Responsibility
- Authenticity
- Search for authentic life
- Search for meaning
- Empathy

Questions About the Role-Play

1. Which existential issues emerge as Betty changes her profession from the police department to the counseling profession? (p. 168)
2. How is Betty's mother's illness an existential issue? How does it help her grow?
3. In what ways has Betty developed authenticity? (p. 174)
4. Compare the case of Harry on page 190 and Bugental's attention to taking responsibility to Neukrug's therapeutic approach to Betty. How are they similar? How are they different?

Suggested Readings

Yalom, I. D. (1980). *Existential psychotherapy*. New York: Basic Books. This excellent book, the source for some of the material in this chapter, deals in depth with existential themes that are covered only briefly here. Yalom uses many clinical examples to illustrate existential themes.

Yalom, I. D. (1989). *Love's executioner*. New York: Basic Books. In this selection of 10 case studies, Yalom demonstrates his existential approach to psychotherapy. The cases are engaging and fully developed.

Yalom, I. D. (1999). *Momma and the meaning of life: Tales of psychotherapy*. New York: Basic Books. Six cases taken from Yalom's therapeutic work. Well written and interesting reading.

Bugental, J. F. T. (1987). *The art of the psychotherapist*. New York: Basic Books. Norton. Bugental describes his own in-depth approach to psychotherapy. The book is clear and well organized.

Deurzen, E. Van. (2009). *Psychotherapy and the quest for happiness*. London: Sage. This book deals with many of life's difficult issues. As the title suggests, the book examines what life's goals should be and whether happiness is a valid goal. The book is one that students who wish to learn more about using existential theory will find helpful.

Deurzen, E. Van. (2001). *Existential counselling and psychotherapy in practice* (2nd ed.). Thousand Oaks, CA: Sage. This is an excellent overview of existential psychotherapy by one of the most current active and representative existential therapists.

Deurzen, E. Van, & Kenward, R. (2005). *Dictionary of existential counseling*. London: Sage. This book gives brief definitions of philosophical and therapeutic terms. Included are brief explanations of contributions of existential philosophers and therapists.

Frankl, V. (1992). *Man's search for meaning*. Boston: Washington Square Press. This very popular book, in its 26th edition, is an autobiographical account of Frankl's own search for meaning during his experience in World War II Nazi concentration camps. Additionally, he describes his development of logotherapy and its basic approaches.

References

Barnett, L. (Ed.). (2009). *When death enters the therapeutic space: Existential perspectives in psychotherapy and counselling*. New York: Routledge/Taylor & Francis Group.

Baum, S. M., & Stewart, R. B. (1990). Sources of meaning through the lifespan. *Psychological Reports, 67,* 3–14.

Beshai, J. A., & Naboulsi, M. A. (2004). Existential perspectives on death anxiety. *Psychological Reports, 95*(2), 507–513.

Binswanger, L. (1975). *Being-in-the-world: Selected papers of Ludwig Binswanger*. London: Souvenir Press.

Bornstein, R. F. (2004). Integrating cognitive and existential treatment strategies in psychotherapy with dependent patients. *Journal of Contemporary Psychotherapy, 34*(4), 293–309.

Boss, M. (1963). *Psychoanalysis and daseinanalysis*. New York: Basic Books.

Boss, M. (1977). *Existential foundations of medicine and psychology*. New York: Aronson.

Brown, L. S. (2008). Feminist therapy as a meaning-making practice: Where there is no power, where is the meaning? In K. J. Schneider (Ed.), *Existential-integrative psychotherapy: Guideposts to the core of practice* (pp. 130–140). New York: Routledge/Taylor & Francis Group.

Buber, M. (1961). The way of man according to the teachings of Hasidism. In W. Kaufman (Ed.), *Religion from Tolstoy to Camus* (pp. 425–441). New York: Harper Torchbooks.

Buber, M. (1965). *The knowledge of man* (M. Friedman & R. O. Smith, Trans.). New York: Harper Torchbooks.

Buber, M. (1970). *I and thou* (W. Kaufman, Trans.). New York: Scribner's.

Bugental, E. K. (2008). Swimming together in a sea of loss: A group process for elders. In K. J. Schneider (Ed.), *Existential-integrative psychotherapy: Guideposts to the core of practice* (pp. 333–342). New York: Routledge/Taylor & Francis Group.

Bugental, J. F. T. (1976). *The search for existential identity: Patient–therapist dialogues in humanistic psychotherapy*. San Francisco: Jossey-Bass.

Bugental, J. F. T. (1978). *Psychotherapy and process: The fundamentals of an existential-humanistic approach*. Reading, MA: Addison-Wesley.

Bugental, J. F. T. (1981). *The search for authenticity: An existential-analytic approach to psychotherapy* (Rev. ed.). New York: Holt, Rinehart & Winston.

Bugental, J. F. T. (1987). *The art of the psychotherapist*. New York: Norton.

Bugental, J. F. T. (1999). *Psychotherapy isn't what you think: Bringing the psychotherapeutic engagement into the living moment*. Phoenix, AZ: Zeig, Tucker.

Bugental, J. F. T. (2008). Preliminary sketches for a short-term existential-humanistic therapy. In K. J. Schneider (Ed.), *Existential-integrative psychotherapy: Guideposts to the core of practice* (pp. 165–168). New York: Routledge/Taylor & Francis Group.

Bühler, K. (2004). Existential analysis and psychoanalysis: Specific differences and personal relationship between Ludwig Binswanger and Sigmund Freud. *American Journal of Psychotherapy, 58*(1), 34–50.

Cannon, B. (1991). *Sartre and psychoanalysis*. Wichita: University Press of Kansas.

Claessens, M. (2009). Mindfulness and existential therapy. *Existential Analysis, 20*(1), 109–119.

Cohn, H. W. (1997). *Existential thought and therapeutic practice: An introduction to existential psychotherapy*. London: Sage.

Comas-Díaz, L. (2008). Latino psychospirituality. In K. J. Schneider (Ed.), *Existential-integrative psychotherapy: Guideposts to the core of practice* (pp. 100–109). New York: Routledge/Taylor & Francis Group.

Cooper, M. (2003). *Existential therapies*. Thousand Oaks, CA: Sage.

Corey, G. (2008). *Theory and practice of group counseling* (7th ed.). Belmont, CA: Brooks/Cole.

Cowan, E. G., Jr. (2009). On existential aloneness: The earthly pilgrimage. In L. Hoffman, M. Yang, F. J. Kaklauskas, & A. Chan (Eds.), *Existential psychology: East-West* (pp. 275–297). Colorado Springs, CO: University of the Rockies Press.

Craig, M. (2009). To be or not to be: Understanding authenticity from an existential perspective. *Existential Analysis, 20*(2), 292–298.

Crumbaugh, J. C. (1968). Cross validation of Purpose-in-Life Test based on Frankl's concept. *Journal of Individual Psychology, 24*, 74–81.

Crumbaugh, J. C., & Henrion, R. (1988). PIL Test: Administration, interpretation, uses, theory and critique. *The International Forum for Logotherapy Journal of Search for Meaning, 11*, 76–88.

Davis, T. (2007). The relevance of the Freudian concept of "transference" to existential psychotherapy. *Existential Analysis, 18*(2), 348–357.

Deurzen, E. Van. (1999). Common sense or nonsense: Intervening in moral dilemmas. *British Journal of Guidance and Counselling, 27*, 581–586.

Deurzen, E. Van. (2001). *Existential counselling and psychotherapy in practice* (2nd ed.) Thousand Oaks, CA: Sage.

Deurzen, E. Van. (2009). *Psychotherapy and the quest for happiness*. London: Sage.

Deurzen, E. Van, & Kenward, R. (2005). *Dictionary of existential psychotherapy and counselling*. London: Sage.

Deurzen-Smith, E. Van. (1988). *Existential counseling in practice*. Newbury Park, CA: Sage.

Deurzen-Smith, E. Van. (1995). *Existential therapy*. London: Society for Existential Analysis.

Deurzen-Smith, E. Van. (1997). *Everyday mysteries: Existential dimensions of psychotherapy*. London: Routledge.

Deurzen-Smith, E. Van. (1998). *Paradox and passion in psychotherapy: An existential approach to therapy and counselling*. Chichester, UK: Wiley.

Edmonds, S., & Hooker, K. (1992). Perceived changes in life meaning following bereavement. *Omega Journal of Death and Dying, 25*, 307–318.

Ellenberger, H. F. (1958). A clinical introduction to psychiatric phenomenology and existential analysis. In R. May, E. Angel, & H. F. Ellenberger (Eds.), *Existence: A new dimension in psychiatry and psychology* (pp. 92–124). New York: Basic Books.

Elliott, R. (2001). Hermeneutic single-case efficacy design: An overview. In K. J. Schneider, J. F. T. Bugental, & J. F. Pierson (Eds.), *The handbook of humanistic psychology* (pp. 315–324). Thousand Oaks, CA: Sage.

Elliot, R. (2002). The effectiveness of humanistic therapies: A meta-analysis. In D. J. Cain & J. Seeman (Eds.), *Humanistic psychotherapies: Handbook of research and practice* (pp. 57–82). Washington, DC: American Psychological Association.

Fabry, J. B. (1987). *The pursuit of meaning* (rev. ed.). Berkeley, CA: Institute of Logotherapy Press.

Farren, C. J., Keene-Hagerty, E., Salloway, S., & Kupferer, S. (1991). Finding meaning: An alternative paradigm for Alzheimer's disease family caregivers. *Gerontologist, 31*, 483–489.

Frankl, V. (1965). *The doctor and the soul*. New York: Bantam Books.

Frankl, V. (1969). *The will to meaning: Foundations and applications of logotherapy*. New York: New American Library.

Frankl, V. (1978). *The unheard cry for meaning*. New York: Simon & Schuster.

Frankl, V. (1992). *Man's search for meaning: An introduction to logotherapy*. Boston: Beacon Press. (Original work published 1963.)

Frankl, V. (1997). *Viktor Frankl—Recollections: An autobiography*. New York: Plenum.

French, S., & Joseph, S. (1999). Religiosity and its association with purpose in life, and self-actualisation. *Mental Health, Religion and Culture, 2*, 117–120.

Fry, P. S. (2001). The unique contribution of key existential factors to the prediction of psychological well-being of older adults following spousal loss. *Gerontologist, 41*, 69–81.

Gelven, M. (1989). *A commentary on Heidegger's Being and Time* (Rev. ed.). De Kalb: Northern Illinois University Press.

Gendlin, E. T., & Tomlinson, T. M. (1967). The process conception and its measurement. In C. R. Rogers, E. T. Gendlin, D. J. Kiesier, & C. B. Truax (Eds.), *The therapeutic relationship and its impact: A study of psychotherapy with schizophrenics* (pp. 109–131). Madison: University of Wisconsin Press.

Ghaemi, S. N. (2007). Feeling and time: The phenomenology of mood disorders, depressive realism, and existential psychotherapy. *Schizophrenia Bulletin, 33*(1), 122–130.

Gould, W. B. (1993). *Viktor E. Frankl: Life with meaning.* Pacific Grove, CA: Brooks/Cole.

Gron, A. (2004). The embodied self: Reformulating the existential difference in Kierkegaard. *Journal of Consciousness Studies, 11*(10–11), 26–43.

Guttmann, D. (1996). *Logotherapy for the helping professional: Meaningful social work.* New York: Springer.

Heidegger, M. (1962). *Being and time* (J. Macquarrie & E. Robinson, Trans.). New York: Harper & Row. (Original work published 1927.)

Hillmann, M. (2004). *Viktor E. Frankl's existential analysis and logotherapy.* New York: Wiley.

Hoffman, L., Yang, M., Kaklauskas, F. J., & Chan, A. (Eds.). (2009). *Existential psychology: East-West.* Colorado Springs, CO: University of the Rockies Press.

Kierkegaard, S. (1954). *Fear and trembling and the sickness unto death* (W. Lowrie, Trans.). Garden City, NY: Doubleday. (Original work published 1843.)

Kissane, D. W., Bloch, S., Smith, G. C., Miach, P., Clarke, D. M., & Ikin, J. et al. (2003). Cognitive-existential group psychotherapy for women with primary breast cancer: A randomized controlled trial. *Psycho-Oncology, 12*(6), 532–546.

Kobasa, S. C., & Maddi, S. R. (1977). Existential personality theory. In R. J. Corsini (Ed.), *Current personality theories* (pp. 243–276). Itasca, IL: Peacock.

Kondas, D. (2008). Existential explosion and gestalt therapy for gay male survivors of domestic violence. *Gestalt Review, 12*(1), 58–74.

Krug, O. T. (2008). A comparative study of James Bugental and Irvin Yalom, two masters of existential psychotherapy. *Dissertation Abstracts International: Section B: The Sciences and Engineering, 68*(11-B), p. 7668.

Laing, R. D. (1961). *Self and others.* Harmondsworth, England: Penguin.

Lantz, J., & Raiz, L. (2004). Existential psychotherapy with older adult couples: A five-year treatment report. *Clinical Gerontologist, 27*(3), 39–54.

Lichtenthal, W. G., Nilsson, M., Zhang, B., Trice, E. D., Kissane, D. W., Breitbart, W., & Prigerson, H. G. (2009). Do rates of mental disorders and existential distress among advanced stage cancer patients increase as death approaches? *Psycho-Oncology, 18*(1), 50–61.

Lieberman, M. A., & Yalom, I. (1992). Brief group psychotherapy for the spousally bereaved: A controlled study. *International Journal of Group Psychotherapy, 42,* 117–132.

Lowrie, W. (1962). *Kierkegaard* (2 vols.). New York: Harper. (Original work published 1938.)

Loy, D. (1996). *Lack and transcendence: The problem of death and life in psychotherapy, existentialism, and Buddhism.* Atlantic Highlands, NJ: Humanities Press.

Lucas, M. (2004). Existential regret: A crossroads of existential anxiety and existential guilt. *Journal of Humanistic Psychology, 44*(1), 58–70.

Lukas, E. (1984). *Meaningful living.* Berkeley, CA: Institute of Logotherapy Press.

May, R. (1950). *The meaning of anxiety.* New York: Ronald Press.

May, R. (1953). *Man's search for himself.* New York: Dell.

May, R. (1958a). The origins and significance of existential movement in psychology. In R. May, E. Angel, & H. E. Ellenberger (Eds.), *Existence: A new dimension in psychiatry and psychology* (pp. 3–36). New York: Basic Books.

May, R. (1958b). Contributions of existential psychotherapy. In R. May, E. Angel, & H. E. Ellenberger (Eds.), *Existence: A new dimension in psychiatry and psychology* (pp. 37–92). New York: Basic Books.

May, R. (1961). *Existential psychology.* New York: Random House.

May, R. (1966). *Psychology and the human dilemma.* New York: Norton.

May, R. (1969). *Love and will.* New York: Norton.

May, R. (1972). *Power and innocence: A search for the sources of violence.* New York: Norton.

May, R. (1975). *The courage to create.* New York: Norton.

May, R. (1977). *The meaning of anxiety* (Rev. ed.). New York: Norton.

May, R. (1981). *Freedom and destiny.* New York: Norton.

May, R. (1989). *The art of counseling.* New York: Gardner.

May, R. (1992). *The cry for myth.* New York: Norton.

May, R., Angel, E., & Ellenberger, H. (Eds.). (1958). *Existence: A new dimension in psychiatry and psychology.* New York: Basic Books.

May, R., & Yalom, I. (2005). Existential psychotherapy. In R. J. Corsini & D. Wedding (Eds.), *Current psychotherapies* (7th ed., pp. 269–298). Belmont, CA: Brooks/Cole.

McBride, O., Dunwoody, L., Lowe-Strong, A., & Kennedy, S. M. (2008). Examining adversarial growth in illness: The factor structure of the Silver Lining Questionnaire (SLQ-38). *Psychology & Health, 23*(6), 661–678.

McCann, J. T., & Biaggio, M. K. (1989). Sexual satisfaction in marriage as a function of life meaning. *Archives of Sexual Behavior, 18,* 59–72.

Mikulincer, M., Florian, V., & Hirschberger, G. (2004). The terror of death and the quest for love: An existential perspective on close relationships. In J. F. Greenberg, S. L. Koole, & T. Pyszczynski (Eds.), *Handbook of experimental existential psychology* (pp. 287–304). New York: Guilford.

Minkowski, E. (1958). Findings in a case of schizophrenic depression (B. Bliss, Trans.). In R. May, E. Angel, & H. F. Ellenberger (Eds.), *Existence: A new dimension in psychiatry and psychology* (pp. 127–138). New York: Basic Books.

Murray, H. H. (1943). *Thematic Apperception Test manual.* Cambridge, MA: Harvard University Press.

Nanda, J. (2009). Mindfulness: A lived experience of existential-phenomenological themes. *Existential Analysis, 20*(1), 147–162.

Page, R. C., Weiss, J. F., & Lietaer, G. (2002). Humanistic group therapy. In D. J. Cain & J. Seeman (Eds.), *Humanistic psychotherapies: Handbook of research and practice* (pp. 339–368). Washington, DC: American Psychological Association.

Pfost, K. S., Stevens, M. J., & Wessels, A. B. (1989). Relationship of purpose in life to grief experience in response to the death of a significant other. *Death Studies, 13,* 371–378.

Pinel, E. C., Long, A. E., Landau, M. J., & Pyszczynski, T. (2004). I-sharing, the problem of existential isolation, and their implications for interpersonal and intergroup phenomena. In J. F. Greenberg, S. L. Koole, & T. Pyszczynski (Eds.), *Handbook of experimental existential psychology* (pp. 352–368). New York: Guilford.

Pompe, G. Van Der, Duivenvoorden, H. J., Antoni, M. H., & Visser, A. (1997). Effectiveness of a short-term group psychotherapy program on endocrine and immune function in breast cancer patients: An exploratory study. *Journal of Psychosomatic Research, 42,* 453–466.

Portnoy, D. (2008). Relatedness: Where existential and psychoanalytic approaches converge. In K. J. Schneider (Ed.), *Existential-integrative psychotherapy: Guideposts to the core of practice* (pp. 268–281). New York: Routledge/Taylor & Francis Group.

Rhoades, D. R. (1999). *Caregiver meaning and self-actualization: A homeshare provider study.* Dissertation Abstracts International, Section A: *Vol. 59*(7-A): 2366.

Rice, D. L. (2008). An African American perspective: The case of Darrin. In K. J. Schneider (Ed.), *Existential-integrative psychotherapy: Guideposts to the core of practice* (pp. 110–121). New York: Routledge/Taylor & Francis Group.

Saiger, G. M. (2008). Some thoughts on the existential lens in group psychotherapy. In G. M. Saiger, S. Rubenfeld, & M. D. Dluhy (Eds.), *Windows into today's group therapy: The National Group Psychotherapy Institute of the Washington School of Psychiatry* (pp. 153–168). New York: Routledge/Taylor & Francis Group.

Sartre, J. P. (1956). *Being and nothingness* (H. E. Barnes, Trans.). New York: Philosophical Library.

Schneider, K. J. (Ed.). (2008). *Existential-integrative psychotherapy: Guideposts to the core of practice.* New York: Routledge/Taylor & Francis Group.

Schulenberg, S. E. (2003). Approaching terra incognita with James F. T. Bugental: An interview and an overview of existential-humanistic psychotherapy. *Journal of Contemporary Psychotherapy, 33*(4), 273–285.

Schulenberg, S. E., Hutzell, R. R., Nassif, C., & Rogina, J. M. (2008). Logotherapy for clinical practice. *Psychotherapy: Theory, Research, Practice, Training, 45*(4), 447–463.

Schultz, D. P., & Schultz, S. E. (2009). *Theories of personality* (9th ed.). Belmont, CA: Wadsworth.

Sequin, C. (1965). *Love and psychotherapy.* New York: Libra.

Serlin, I., & Criswell, E. (2001). Humanistic psychology and women: A critical-historical perspective. In K. J. Schneider, J. F. T. Bugental, & J. F. Pierson (Eds.), *The handbook of humanistic psychology* (pp. 26–36). Thousand Oaks, CA: Sage.

Sodergren, S. C., Hyland, M. E., Crawford, A., & Partridge, M. R. (2004). Positivity in illness: Self-delusion or existential growth? *British Journal of Health Psychology, 9*(2), 163–174.

Tillich, P. (1952). *The courage to be.* New Haven, CT: Yale University Press.

Tomer, A., Eliason, G. T., & Wong, P. T. P. (Eds.). (2008). *Existential and spiritual issues in death attitudes*. New York: Lawrence Erlbaum.

Vontress, C. E. (2003). *On becoming an existential cross-cultural counselor*. Needham Heights, MA: Allyn and Bacon.

Vontress, C. E., & Epp, L. R. (2001). Existential cross-cultural counseling: When hearts and cultures share. In K. J. Schneider, J. F. T. Bugental, & J. F. Pierson (Eds.), *The handbook of humanistic psychology* (pp. 371–388). Thousand Oaks, CA: Sage.

Weems, C. F. , Costa, N. M., Deho C., & Berman S. L. (2004). Paul Tillich's theory of existential anxiety: A preliminary conceptual and experimental examination. *Anxiety, Stress, and Coping, 17*(4), 383–389.

Wolfe, B. E. (2008). Existential issues in anxiety disorders and their treatment. In K. J. Schneider (Ed.), *Existential-integrative psychotherapy: Guideposts to the core of practice* (pp. 204–216). New York: Routledge/Taylor & Francis Group.

Yakushko, O. (2005). Influence of social support, existential well-being, and stress over sexual orientation on self-esteem of gay, lesbian, and bisexual individuals. *International Journal for the Advancement of Counselling, 27*(1), 131–143.

Yalom, I. D. (1980). *Existential psychotherapy*. New York: Basic Books.

Yalom, I. D. (1989). *Love's executioner*. New York: Basic Books.

Yalom, I. D. (1999). *Momma and the meaning of life: Tales of psychotherapy*. New York: Basic Books.

Yalom, I. D. (2008). *Staring at the sun: Overcoming the terror of death*. San Francisco: Jossey-Bass.

Yalom, I. D., & Lieberman, M. A. (1991). Bereavement and heightened existential awareness. *Psychiatry, 54*, 334–345.

Yalom, I. D., & Vinogradov, S. C. (1988). Bereavement groups: Techniques and themes. *International Journal of Group Psychotherapy, 38*, 419–446.

Young, M. J., & Morris, M. W. (2004). Existential meanings and cultural models: The interplay of personal and supernatural agency in American and Hindu ways of responding to uncertainty. In J. F. Greenberg, S. L. Koole, & T. Pyszczynski (Eds.), *Handbook of experimental existential psychology* (pp. 215–230). New York: Guilford.

Person-Centered Therapy

Outline of Person-Centered Therapy

PERSON-CENTERED THEORY OF
PERSONALITY
    Psychological Development
    Development and Conditionality
    Self-Regard and Relationships
    The Fully Functioning Person
A PERSON-CENTERED THEORY OF
PSYCHOTHERAPY
    Goals
    Assessment

The Necessary and Sufficient Conditions for
Client Change
    Psychological contact
    Incongruence
    Congruence and genuineness
    Unconditional positive regard or acceptance
    Empathy
    Perception of empathy and acceptance
The Client's Experience in Therapy
    Experiencing responsibility
    Experiencing the therapist
    Experiencing the process of exploration
    Experiencing the self
    Experiencing change
The Process of Person-Centered Psychotherapy

First called nondirective therapy, later client-centered therapy, and currently person-centered therapy, this therapeutic approach, developed by Carl Rogers, takes a positive view of individuals, believing that they tend to move toward becoming fully functioning. Rogers's work represents a way of being rather than a set of techniques for doing therapy. Emphasizing understanding and caring rather than diagnosis, advice, and persuasion, Rogers believed that therapeutic change could take place if only a few conditions were met. The client must be anxious or incongruent and in contact with the therapist. Therapists must be genuine, in that their words, nonverbal behavior, and feelings agree with each other. They must also accept the client and care unconditionally for the client. Furthermore, they must understand the client's thoughts, ideas, experiences, and feelings and communicate this empathic understanding to the client. If clients are able to perceive these conditions as offered by the therapist, Rogers believed that therapeutic change will take place.

Rogers applied the core concepts of genuineness, acceptance, and empathy to a variety of human behaviors. He was committed to the group process as a positive means for bringing about personal change and trusted in the growthful characteristics of group members. Other areas of application included marriage and couples counseling, education, and administration. Especially in his later life, Rogers was committed to applying person-centered concepts to deal with international conflicts and to promote world peace. Person-centered therapy changed and grew, as did Carl Rogers's approach to personality and psychotherapy.

History of Person-Centered Therapy

Born in a suburb of Chicago (Oak Park) in 1902, Carl Rogers was the fourth of six children (five were boys). Rogers (1961) describes his parents as loving, affectionate, and in control of their children's behavior. Because both parents were religious fundamentalists, the children learned that dancing, alcohol, cards, and theater were off-limits to them. When Carl was 12, his father, a prosperous civil engineer and contractor, moved the family to a farm west of Chicago.

Much of Rogers's adolescent life was spent in solitary pursuits. Because he attended three different high schools and commuted long distances to each one, he did not participate in extracurricular activities. Reading adventure stories and agricultural books occupied much of his time. In the summers, he spent long hours operating farm equipment in the fields (Kirschenbaum, 2009). His interest in agriculture, as shown by raising farm animals and collecting and breeding a specific type of moth, led him to pursue agriculture as a career at the University of Wisconsin. However, because of his participation in religious conferences, particularly one in China, he shifted his career goals to the ministry (Rogers, 1961). In China, Rogers questioned the religious views that he had learned as a child and broadened his conception of religion.

Upon graduation from Wisconsin, he married Helen Elliott and went to New York City to study at the Union Theological Seminary. After completing 2 years there, he transferred to Columbia University Teachers College to study clinical and educational psychology; he received his Ph.D. in clinical psychology in 1931. Perhaps one reason for pursuing psychology instead of the ministry was Rogers's reluctance to tell others what they should do. He did not feel he should be in a field where he must profess a certain set of beliefs (Mearns & Thorne, 2007).

Person-centered therapy can be divided into four stages or phases. The first, a developmental stage, includes Rogers's early professional years. His nondirective stage marked the beginning of his theoretical development and his emphasis

Courtesy of Dr. Natalie Rogers

CARL ROGERS

on understanding the client and communicating that understanding. The third stage, client-centered, involved more theoretical development of personality and psychotherapeutic change, as well as a continued focus on the person rather than on techniques. The fourth stage, person-centered, goes beyond individual psychotherapy to include marriage counseling, group therapy, and political activism and change. The gradual formation of these stages and Rogers's contribution to psychotherapy is discussed next.

His first position was in the child study department at the Society for the Prevention of Cruelty to Children in Rochester, New York. During the first 8 of his 12 years in Rochester, he was involved in diagnosing and treating delinquent and underprivileged children who were referred by the courts and social agencies (Rogers, 1961). His early work was influenced by psychoanalytic concepts, but gradually his view changed as he realized "that it is the client who knows what hurts, what directions to go, what problems are crucial, what experiences have been buried" (Rogers, 1961, pp. 11–12). During his time in Rochester, he wrote *The Clinical Treatment of the Problem Child* (1939) and trained and supervised social workers and psychologists.

In 1940, Rogers moved to Columbus, Ohio, to start an academic career in clinical psychology at Ohio State University. Due mainly to his successful book, he was offered the rank of full professor. While Rogers was at Ohio State University, he entered the second stage (nondirective) of his theoretical approach (Holdstock & Rogers, 1977). When giving a paper at the University of Minnesota in 1940, he became aware that his views on psychotherapy were a new contribution to the field. His focus was on the client's taking responsibility for himself. Important was the therapist's relationship with clients, which established trust and permission for clients to explore their feelings and themselves and thus take more responsibility for their lives. Reflection of the client's feelings and clarifications that led to an understanding of client feelings were the essence of Rogers's therapy at this point. Questions were used rarely, because they might interfere with the client's personal growth. The Minnesota lecture and his book *Counseling and Psychotherapy* (1942a) were controversial—enthusiastically received by some, criticized vehemently by others (Mearns & Thorne, 2007).

How did Carl Rogers come to develop this new nondirective approach? During his work with children in Rochester, Rogers was influenced by a seminar led by Otto Rank. Additionally, a social worker at the Rochester clinic, Elizabeth Davis, and a student of Rank's, Jessie Taft, shared their interpretation of Rank's ideas, which were to have considerable impact on Rogers's thinking (DeCarvalho, 1999). Rank, who had previously broken away from Freud's psychoanalytic approach, did not focus on ego and id but rather was struck by the creativity of individuals. For Rank, the goal of therapy was to help individuals accept their uniqueness and responsibility for their lives. To achieve this goal of self-empowerment and expression, the therapist needed to take a role as a nonjudgmental helper rather than as an expert or authority (Rank, 1945). Unlike psychoanalysts, Rank emphasized not techniques or past history but rather the uniqueness of the individual and the need to attend to that individual's experience.

Adler's theoretical views had less direct influence on Rogers's therapy. Rogers and Adler shared an emphasis on the value of the individual and the need for good relationships with others. Both believed that individuals should be viewed holistically and as persons who can develop creatively and responsibly. Watts (1998) believes that Adler's concept of social interest may have had a strong impact on Rogers's development of core conditions.

Self-actualization

A concept that has been important to the development of person-centered therapy has been that of self-actualization (Bohart, 2007a; Gillon, 2007; Levitt, 2008; Mearns & Thorne, 2007). Originated by Kurt Goldstein (1959), self-actualization implies that individuals seek and are capable of healthy development, which leads to full expression of themselves. Goldstein's writings were furthered by Maslow (1968, 1987), who developed humanistic psychology. Not a therapist, Maslow focused on the needs and characteristics of "normal" individuals and wrote about love, creativity, and "peak experiences"—the state in which an individual might feel pure relaxation or, more commonly, intense excitement. Maslow (1987) stressed significant aspects of being human, including freedom, rationality, and subjectivity. In writing about human needs, Maslow (1987) wrote not only of the need to satisfy physiological needs, such as hunger and thirst, and security and safety needs, but also the importance of searching for belongingness, love, self-esteem, and self-actualization. For Maslow, self-actualization meant to become all that one can be and thus to live a life that brings meaning and accomplishment. Maslow's positive view of humanity is congruent with Rogers's in that both take a positive and optimistic view of humanity, called *humanism*.

Additionally, Rogers's views of humanity and therapy have been affected by existentialist writers (Cooper, O'Hara, Schmid, & Wyatt, 2007). Both existentialism and person-centered therapy stressed the importance of freedom, choice, individual values, and self-responsibility. Although much existentialist writing deals with anxiety and difficult human experiences such as meaningfulness, responsibility, and death—a more pessimistic view than that of Rogers—writers such as Buber and May have much in common with person-centered therapy. Rogers and May (Kirschenbaum & Henderson, 1989) had an active correspondence that contrasts Rogers's positive humanistic views with May's more negative existentialist ones. Additionally, Rogers valued the views of Martin Buber on the "I–thou" dialogue and the impact of human relationships on individuals (Cissna & Anderson, 1997). Rogers shares the existentialist emphasis on being in the present and understanding the clients' phenomenological world.

Although the influences of Rank, Adler, and existential and humanistic thinkers can be seen in Rogers's writings, many of his early writings are quite practical and reflect his therapeutic experience. *Counseling and Psychotherapy* (1942a) describes the nature of the counseling relationship and the application of nondirective approaches. His view of the processes of counseling, as well as extensive excerpts from his therapy with Herbert Bryant, illustrate his therapeutic style during his nondirective stage. Rogers fully enters the subjective state of his client, feeling what it is like to be Herbert Bryant.

Client Centered Therapy

In 1945, Rogers left Ohio State for the University of Chicago, where he continued to develop his theory and to conduct research into its effectiveness. His client-centered stage began with the publication of *Client-Centered Therapy: Its Current Practice, Implications, and Theory* (1951). In this book, client-centered therapy was extended to include a theory of personality and applications to children, groups, leadership training, and teaching. The concept of reflection of feelings and incongruity between the experiencing self and the ideal self were fully discussed, as were the clients' and counselors' growth in the therapeutic process. In a detailed analysis of Rogers's recorded interviews between 1940 and 1986, Brodley (1994) showed that Rogers was more theoretically consistent in the third phase (client-centered) than in the nondirective phase, as almost all (96%) of his responses to clients were "empathic following responses," whereas earlier he had made more interventions from his own, rather than a client's, frame of reference.

While at the University of Chicago, Carl Rogers was both professor of psychology and director of the university counseling center. During this time he was involved in training and research with graduate students and colleagues. His work was recognized by the American Psychological Association in 1956 with the Distinguished Scientific Contribution Award. Both this award and the publication of *Client-Centered Therapy* brought Rogers considerable recognition within and outside the United States.

Rogers's scholarly accomplishments can serve to mask the intensity and earnestness of his approach to therapy. While at the University of Chicago, he was in an intense therapeutic relationship with a young woman (Rogers, 1972). In his work with her, Rogers found it difficult to separate his own "self" from the client's. Although he sought help from his colleagues, he felt that the intensity was too much. One morning, after making a referral for the client, he walked out of his office and, with his wife, left Chicago for 6 weeks. Occasionally, Rogers's writings are personally revealing, presenting not only his therapeutic responses but also comments about his internal feelings, thus providing further insight into his work.

In 1957, Rogers took a position at the University of Wisconsin, where he was first affiliated with the Department of Psychology and later the Department of Psychiatry. He found his work at the psychology department to be agonizing, and he was frequently in conflict with his colleagues (Mearns & Thorne, 2007; Sanders, 2004a). While there he undertook an ambitious research project (Rogers, Gendlin, Kiesler, & Truax, 1967) to study the impact of psychotherapy on hospitalized patients with schizophrenia. The study was marked by many difficulties and conflicts and had few significant findings. Dissatisfied with his position at the University of Wisconsin, Rogers left in 1963 for the Western Behavioral Science Institute, which was devoted to the study of interpersonal relationships.

Before leaving Wisconsin, Rogers published *On Becoming a Person* (1961), which brought him even more recognition than his earlier works. Written for both psychologists and nonpsychologists, the book is personal and powerful, describing his philosophy of life and his view of research, teaching, and social issues. Marking the beginning of the person-centered stage, this book went beyond approaches to therapy to consider issues that affected all individuals. While at the Western Behavioral Sciences Institute in La Jolla, California, he devoted energy to encounter groups (Rogers, 1970) and to education (Rogers, 1969).

In 1968 Rogers, along with others, formed the Center for Studies of the Person, where Rogers called himself "resident fellow." The center became a base of operations for Rogers to become involved in worldwide travel and global issues. His *Carl Rogers on Personal Power* (1977) is concerned with how person-centered principles can be applied to people of different cultures and to bring about political change. Often, Rogers (Barrett-Lennard, 1998) led workshops with disputing parties, such as South African Blacks and Whites and Protestants and Catholics from Northern Ireland. Political change continued to take a considerable amount of Rogers's energy and interest, as indicated in *A Way of Being* (1980). Recently revealed, Rogers had also been involved with the Central Intelligence Agency as a consultant or advisor on mental health (Demanchick & Kirschenbaum, 2008). During the last decade of his life, Rogers returned to spirituality, which had been a part of his early life (Mather, 2008). Traveling, writing, and working tirelessly, Rogers continued to show enthusiasm and a desire to learn until his death in February 1987 at the age of 85.

Person-centered therapy continues to attract international interest, as contributors to person-centered work come from many different countries. Mearns

(2003) believed that the person-centered approach predominated over others in England. The British Association for the Person-Centred Approach and the World Association for Person-Centered and Experiential Psychotherapy and Counseling have been active and have memberships exceeding 1,000 people. The journal *Person-Centered and Experiential Psychotherapy* has been published in England since 2002. In the United States, a newsletter, *Renaissance*, is sponsored by the Association for the Development of the Person-Centered Approach, an organization with about 150 members worldwide that sponsors training, workshops, and international conferences. In addition, the Center for Studies of the Person in La Jolla offers workshops and training seminars and maintains the Carl Rogers Memorial Library.

Person-Centered Theory of Personality

Personality Theory

Rogers had a strong personal interest in helping people change and grow. Before setting out to develop a theory of personality, Rogers (1959) devoted his effort to presenting his ideas of therapeutic change in an organized way. His theory of personality can be seen as a way of broadening his theory of therapy to include normal as well as abnormal behavior and of outlining individual growth toward becoming fully functioning. Additionally, Rogers examined forces that interfered with the development of functioning fully and those that promote it. By closely attending to the factors that determine improving relationships between people, Rogers was able to describe a model of relating that went beyond individual therapy. Only a few of Rogers's writings deal primarily with personality theory (Holdstock & Rogers, 1977; Rogers, 1959), as much of his effort was devoted to helping individuals grow and change in individual therapy, groups, and in society.

Psychological Development

From birth onward, individuals experience reality in terms of internal and external experiences. Each person is biologically and psychologically unique, experiencing different social, cultural, and physical aspects of the environment. As infants develop, they monitor their environment in terms of degrees of pleasantness and unpleasantness. Differentiation is made between a variety of bodily senses, such as warmth and hunger. If parents interfere with this process, such as urging children to eat when they are not hungry, children can have a difficult time in developing "organismic sensing" or trusting in their reactions to the environment (Holdstock & Rogers, 1977).

POSITIVE REGARD

As children develop an awareness of themselves, their need for positive regard from those around them develops. As they grow older, they manage their own physical needs more effectively, and the need for positive regard from others increases. Such needs include being loved by others, being emotionally and/or physically touched, and being valued or cared for (Schultz & Schultz, 2009).

Individuals' perceptions of the positive regard they receive from others have a direct impact on their own self-regard. If children believe that others (parents, teachers, friends) value them, they are likely to develop a sense of self-worth or self-regard. Additionally, children, in interaction with others, experience satisfaction from meeting the needs of others as well as their own needs. Although needs for positive regard and self-regard are essential, individuals have many experiences that do not foster these conditions.

Development and Conditionality

Throughout their lives, individuals experience conditions of worth, the process of evaluating one's own experience based on the beliefs or values of others that may limit the development of the individual. For Rogers, conditions of worth led to an incongruence between a person's experience of self and interactions with others. To get the conditional positive regard of others, individuals may discount their own experience and accept the values or beliefs of others. People who do not listen to their own beliefs and values but act to please others so that they may feel loved are operating under conditions of worth and are likely to experience anxiety as a result.

When there is conditional regard, individuals may lose touch with themselves and feel alienated from themselves. In order to deal with conditional regard, they can develop defenses that result in inaccurate and rigid perceptions of the world, for example, "I must be kind to all others, regardless of what they do to me, so that they will care for me." Such an individual is likely to experience anxiety because of the conflict between the need to have a positive self-concept and the need to please others. Additionally, individuals may experience anxiety because the values of one group and the values of another are both incongruent with the individual's own sense of self.

The greater the incongruence between an individual's experiences and her self-concept, the more disorganized her behavior is likely to be. Thus, when the view of self and the experiences are in extreme conflict, psychosis may result. In general, Rogers classifies behavior along a continuum of severity, depending on the strength of distortion. Some common defenses include rationalization, fantasy, projection, and paranoid thinking (Holdstock & Rogers, 1977). Often defenses such as rationalization are quite common and minor, as in the following example. Alberta believes "I am a competent salesperson," but she experiences "I have been fired from my job." She then rationalizes, "I wouldn't have been fired if my boss didn't dislike me." Thus, Alberta ignores her rude behavior to customers and rationalizes her behavior. In this case, there is a conflict between view of self and experience.

To counter the conditions of worth that an individual experiences, Rogers believed that there must be unconditional positive regard from some others so that a person's self-regard can be increased. Often, individuals seek out others who appreciate them rather than judge them and who behave in a warm, respectful, and accepting way. Although individuals may not experience unconditional positive regard with their family or friends, it is essential that the therapist provide these conditions.

Self-Regard and Relationships

An important part of Rogers's (1959) personality theory is the nature of personal relationships. In describing the process of an improving relationship, Rogers emphasizes congruence, the process of the therapist or listener in accurately experiencing and being aware of the communication of another person. Relationships improve when the person being listened to feels understood, empathically listened to, and not judged. The individual feels a sense of unconditional positive regard and a feeling of being heard by the other person. This relationship can be called congruent because the therapist or listener is able to understand and communicate the psychological experience of the other, being "in tune" with the other person. Sometimes individuals are incongruent within themselves, such as when one's facial expression or voice tone does not match one's words. The listener who perceives incongruence in the behavior of the speaker may choose to communicate this perception by saying, "You say that you are glad that your parents got a divorce, yet you sound sad." Thus, relationships improve to the extent that the listener perceives and communicates the other's present experience.

✳The Fully Functioning Person

Because Rogers viewed human development as a positive movement or growth, a view of the fully functioning person is consistent with his theory (Rogers, 1969). To become fully functioning, individuals must meet their need for positive regard from others and have positive regard for themselves. With these needs met, an individual can then experience an optimal level of psychological functioning (Bohart, 2007a, b; Gillon, 2007).

Rogers's view of what constitutes congruence and psychological maturity includes openness, creativity, and responsibility. According to Rogers (1969), a fully functioning person is not defensive but open to new experiences without controlling them. This openness to congruent relationships with others and self allows an individual to handle new and old situations creatively. With this adaptability, individuals experience an inner freedom to make decisions and to be responsible for their own lives. As part of being fully functioning, they become aware of social responsibilities and the need for fully congruent relationships with others. Rather than being self-absorbed, such individuals have needs to communicate empathically. Their sense of what is right includes an understanding of the needs of others as well as of themselves.

Rogers saw the goal of being a fully functioning person as an ideal to strive toward that was not attainable by any one individual. He believed that, in effective relationships, individuals moved toward this goal. It was his goal as a family member, as a group leader, and as an individual therapist to grow to become a congruent, accepting, and understanding person, and in that way he would be able to help others around him do the same.

A Person-Centered Theory of Psychotherapy

The development of Rogers's theory of psychotherapy came about as a result of his experience as a therapist, his interaction with colleagues, and his research on the therapeutic process. He believed that the goals of therapy should be to help individuals become congruent, self-accepting persons by being more aware of their own experiences and their own growth. Assessment was seen as a part of the therapeutic process, appraising the individual's current awareness and experiencing. Psychological change was brought about through a genuine, accepting, and empathic relationship, which was perceived as such by the client. How clients and counselors experience this therapeutic process is a part of Rogers's psychotherapeutic conceptualization of personality change.

Goals

The goals of therapy come from the client, not the therapist. Clients move away from phoniness or superficiality to become more complex in that they more deeply understand various facets of themselves. With this comes an openness to

✳

Goals Clients want @ Goal Setting

experience and a trusting of self "to be that self which one truly is" (Kierkegaard, 1941), as well as acceptance of others. Goals should be to move in a self-directed manner, being less concerned about pleasing others and meeting the expectations of others. As a consequence of becoming more self-directed, individuals become more realistic in their perceptions, better at problem solving, and less defensive with others. Thus, the therapist does not choose the client's counseling goals but rather helps develop a therapeutic atmosphere that can increase positive self-regard so that the client can become more fully functioning.

Assessment

Although there is some disagreement among person-centered therapists as to whether psychodiagnosis is appropriate in therapy, most person-centered writers believe that psychodiagnosis is not necessary (Bozarth, 1991). Boy and Pine (1989, 1999) consider psychodiagnosis to be inconsistent with understanding the client in a deep and meaningful way. For Seeman (1989), psychodiagnosis is helpful only when there is a need to assess physiological impairment that affects psychological functioning. Interestingly, Rogers (Kirschenbaum, 2009) used diagnostic procedures in his early work but later abandoned them to focus on the functioning of the client. For most person-centered therapists, assessment takes place as the therapist empathically understands the experience and needs of the client.

Although assessment for diagnostic purposes has little or no role in person-centered therapy, there are times when testing may be appropriate. Bozarth (1991) suggests that testing may be used when clients request it, particularly for vocational counseling. Also, there may be times when either client or therapist finds that it is helpful to use a reference that is external to the client to assist in decision making or for other purposes. Basically, Bozarth believes that the test information needs to fit within the context of the client–counselor relationship. For example, it would be inappropriate for a person-centered therapist to rely on a test to make a decision for the client; decision making is the client's responsibility. The Art Stimulus Apperceptive Response Test developed by Schor (2003) can be used to facilitate the counseling process. This projective technique has pictures and artistic images that help clients overcome distractions that limit their creativity and affect their development of authenticity.

Although Rogers questioned the value of diagnostic or assessment instruments, he recognized their value for research. He developed a process scale (Rogers & Rablen, 1958) to measure stages of the therapeutic process. Others (Carkhuff, 1969; Hamilton, 2000; Truax & Carkhuff, 1967) have developed scales to measure therapeutic conditions in the client–counselor relationship. Such scales have been important in the development of methods of teaching helping skills (Carkhuff, 1987; Egan, 2010). Most person-centered therapists believe that such scales should be used for research purposes but not when doing therapy.

6 Conditions for Change

1) Psychological contact

2) Incongruence

3) Congruence Genuine

4) Unconditional positive regard or acceptance

5) Empathy

The Necessary and Sufficient Conditions for Client Change

The core of person-centered therapy is the six necessary and sufficient conditions for bringing about personality or psychotherapeutic change (Gillon, 2007; Kalmthout, 2007; Rogers, 1957, 1959). Drawing from his clinical experience, Rogers felt that if all six of the following conditions were met, change would occur in the client.

Theories in Action

6) Perception or Empathy/acceptance

1. *Psychological contact.* There must be a relationship in which two people are capable of having some impact on each other. Brodley (2000) describes the

concept of *presence*, which refers to the therapist not just being in the same room with the client but also bringing forth her abilities to attend to and be engaged by the client.

2. *Incongruence.* The client must be in a state of psychological vulnerability, that is, fearful, anxious, or otherwise distressed. Implied in this distress is an incongruence between the person's perception of himself and his actual experience. Sometimes individuals are not aware of this incongruence, but as they become increasingly aware, they become more open to the therapeutic experience.

3. *Congruence and genuineness.* In the therapeutic relationship, the therapist must genuinely be herself and not "phony." Congruence includes being fully aware of one's body, one's communication with others, being spontaneous, and being open in relationships with others (Cornelius-White, 2007). In addition, congruence incorporates being able to be empathic and to offer unconditional positive regard to the client (Wyatt, 2000). Rogers (1966) defines *genuineness* (similar to congruence) as follows.

> Genuineness in therapy means that the therapist is his actual self in his encounter with his client. Without facade, he openly has the feelings and attitudes that are flowing in him at the moment. This involves self-awareness; that is, the therapist's feelings are available to him—to his awareness—and he is able to live them, to experience them in the relationship and to communicate them if they persist. The therapist encounters his client directly, meeting him person to person. He is being himself, not denying himself. (p. 185)

As Rogers clarifies, genuineness does not mean that the therapist discloses all of her feelings to the client. Rather, the therapist has access to her feelings and makes them available, where appropriate, to further the therapeutic relationship. Genuineness by itself is not a sufficient condition; a murderer may be genuine but not meet other conditions. The following is an example of a therapist responding genuinely.

[Client:] I'm lost, totally lost. I've got no direction.

[Therapist:] You're feeling lost and not sure where to go. I sense your despair, and feel I'm here to be with you, to be here with you in this tough time.

The therapist expresses herself openly. She genuinely feels for the client, is aware of her feelings, and expresses her desire to be there for the client.

Theories in Action

4. *Unconditional positive regard or acceptance.* The therapist must have no conditions of acceptance but must accept and appreciate the client as is (Bozarth, 2007; Rogers, 1957). Hurtful, painful, bizarre, and unusual feelings, as well as good feelings, are to be accepted by the therapist. Even when the client lies, the therapist accepts, and eventually the client is likely to confront his own lies and admit them to the therapist (Brice, 2004). Acceptance does not mean agreement with the client but rather refers to caring for the person as a separate individual. By accepting but not agreeing with the client, the therapist is not likely to be manipulated. Clearly, therapists do not always feel unconditional positive regard for their clients, but it is a goal toward which they strive.

By appreciating clients for being themselves, the therapist makes no judgment of people's positive or negative qualities. Conditions of worth imposed on the client by others are not fostered by the therapist. As the client values the unconditional positive regard of the therapist, there is an increase of positive self-regard within the client. Bozarth (2007) views unconditional positive regard as the primary condition of therapeutic change.

An example of Rogers's warmth or unconditional positive regard for a young, depressed patient with schizophrenia is given in the following excerpt. At the conclusion of a session, Rogers asks the patient if he wants to see him next Tuesday. Not getting an answer, Rogers replies with this suggestion.

[Therapist:] I'm going to give you an appointment at that time because I'd sure like to see you then. *(Writing out appointment slip)*
(Silence of 50 seconds)

[Therapist:] And another thing I would say is that—if things continue to stay so rough for you, don't hesitate to have them call me. And if you should decide to take off, I would very much appreciate it if you would have them call me and—so I could see you first. I wouldn't try to dissuade you. I'd just want to see you.

[Client:] I might go today. Where, I don't know, but I don't care.

[Therapist:] Just feel that your mind is made up and that you're going to leave. You're not going to anywhere. You're just—just going to leave, hm? *(Silence of 53 seconds)*

[Client:] *(muttering in discouraged tone)* That's why I want to go, 'cause I don't care what happens.

[Therapist:] Huh?

[Client:] That's why I want to go, 'cause I don't care what happens.

[Therapist:] M-hm, M-hm. That's why you want to go, because you really don't care about yourself. You just don't care what happens. And I guess I'd just like to say—I care about you. And I care what happens. *(Silence of 30 seconds) (Jim bursts into tears and unintelligible sobs.)*

[Therapist:] *(tenderly)* Somehow that just—makes all the feelings pour out. *(Silence of 35 seconds)*

[Therapist:] And you just weep and weep and weep. And feel so badly. *(Jim continues to sob, then blows nose and breathes in great gasps.)*

[Therapist:] I do get a sense of how awful you feel inside. You just sob and sob. *(Jim puts his head on desk, bursting out in great gulping, gasping sobs.)*

[Therapist:] I guess all the pent-up feelings you've been feeling the last few days just—just come rolling out. *(Silence of 32 seconds, while sobbing continues)*

[Therapist:] There's some Kleenex there, if you'd like it—Hmmm. *(sympathetically)* You just feel kind of torn to pieces inside. *(Silence of 1 minute, 56 seconds)* (Rogers et al., 1967, p. 409)

The caring and warmth for the patient, Jim, are evident. The voice tone and words must be congruent within the therapist to be perceived as caring from the therapist. Statements such as those Rogers makes reduce the isolation that the patient feels by expressing acceptance and stressing caring.

5. *Empathy.* To be empathic is to enter another's world without being influenced by one's own views and values (Freire, 2007; Rogers, 1975). To do so, individuals must have sufficient separateness so that they do not get lost in the perceptual world of the other person. Rogers has eloquently described the process of empathy.

The way of being with another person which is termed empathic has several facets. It means entering the private perceptual world of the other and becoming thoroughly at home in it. It involves being sensitive, moment to moment, to the changing felt meanings which flow in this other person, to the fear or rage or tenderness or confusion or whatever, that he/she is experiencing. It means temporarily living in his/her life, moving about in it delicately without making judgments, sensing meanings of which he/she is scarcely aware, but not trying to uncover feelings of which the person is totally unaware, since this would be too threatening. It includes communicating your sensings of his/her world as you look with fresh and unfrightened eyes at elements of which the individual is fearful. It means frequently checking with him/her as to the accuracy of your sensing, and being guided by the responses you receive. You are a confident companion to the person in his/her inner world. By pointing to the possible meanings in the flow of his/her experience you help the person to focus on this useful type of referent, to experience the meanings more fully, and to move forward in the experiencing. (Rogers, 1975, p. 4)

For Rogers, empathy is a process. Early in his career he ceased using the phrase "reflecting the client's feelings" because it had been misunderstood by a number of practitioners. Some mistook Rogers to mean that the therapist was to repeat what the client has said verbatim or to repeat the last words. Because of this, Rogers preferred to speak about an empathic attitude rather than about reflecting or empathic listening (Rogers, 1975). Zimring (2000) adds that empathy helps clients grow and change their way of being rather than helping clients find some hidden inner truth.

The following example is taken from a transcript of a session with Jim, the same client described previously. In this example, Rogers's attitude of empathy toward Jim in his depressed state is clearly evident.

[Client:] No. I just ain't no good to nobody, never was, and never will be.

[Therapist:] Feeling that *now, hm*? That you're just no good to yourself, no good to anybody. Never will be any good to anybody. Just that you're completely worthless, huh?—Those really are lousy feelings. Just feel that you're no good at *all, hm*?

[Client:] Yeah. (*muttering in low, discouraged voice*) That's what this guy I went to town with just the other day told me.

[Therapist:] This guy that you went to town with really told you that you were no good? Is that what you're saying? Did I get that right?

[Client:] M-hm.

[Therapist:] I guess the meaning of that if I get it right is that here's somebody that meant something to you and what does he think of you? Why he's told you that he thinks you're no good at all. And that just really knocks the props out from under you. (*Jim weeps quietly.*) It just brings the tears. (*Silence of 20 seconds*)

[Client:] (*rather defiantly*) I don't care though.

[Therapist:] You tell yourself you don't care at all, but somehow I guess some part of you cares because some part of you weeps over it. (*Silence of 19 seconds*)

[Therapist:] I guess some part of you just feels, "Here I am hit with another blow, as if I hadn't had enough blows like this during my life when I feel that people don't like me. Here's someone I've begun to feel attached to and now he doesn't like me. And I'll say I don't care. I won't let it make

any difference to me—But just the same the tears run down my cheeks."
(Rogers et al., 1967, p. 404)

6. *Perception of empathy and acceptance*. It is not sufficient for the therapist to unconditionally accept and empathically understand the client. The client must also perceive in some way that she is being understood and accepted. Communication of empathy and acceptance can be verbal or nonverbal, but it needs to be natural and not forced or artificial. By reading aloud any of the therapist comments in the previous examples, the reader can hear the difference between a stilted expression and a genuine expression. When the conditions of genuineness, acceptance, and empathy are communicated and perceived, then, Rogers believed, therapeutic change will take place.

In commenting on the relationships among the concepts of genuineness, acceptance, and empathy, Bozarth (1996) reviews Rogers's writings on these three conditions. Bozarth concludes that *"Genuineness and Empathic Understanding are viewed as two contextual attitudes for the primary conditions of change, i.e., Unconditional Positive Regard"* (p. 44). Ultimately, Bozarth believes that these are one condition and should be viewed as the attitude that the therapist holds in therapy.

Other writers have discussed different aspects of person-centered therapy, but always the six conditions remain as the core. For example, Patterson (Myers & Hyers, 1994), among many other writers, has talked about the need for specificity or concreteness when communicating an empathic attitude to clients. He believes that counselors should encourage their clients to be specific in describing their problems and that counselors themselves should be specific in responding to their clients, avoiding generalizations and labels. Most books that describe methods of helping relationships (such as Egan, 2010) emphasize specificity as well as Rogers's concepts of genuineness, acceptance, and empathy.

The Client's Experience in Therapy

When clients come to therapy, they are usually in a state of distress, feeling powerless, indecisive, or helpless. The therapeutic relationship offers them an opportunity to express the fears, anxieties, guilt, anger, or shame that they have not been able to accept within themselves. When the six necessary and sufficient conditions are met, they will be better able to accept themselves and others and to express themselves creatively. In the process of therapy, they will experience themselves in new ways by taking responsibility for themselves and their process of self-exploration, leading to a deeper understanding of self and to positive change. In the sections that follow, excerpts from the case of Mrs. Oak (Rogers, 1953, 1961) are used to illustrate clients' experiencing in therapy.

Experiencing responsibility. In therapy, clients learn that they are responsible for themselves both in the therapeutic relationship and more broadly. Although clients may at first be frustrated or puzzled by the therapist's emphasis on the client's experience, person-centered therapists believe that clients soon come to accept and welcome this.

Experiencing the therapist. Gradually, the client comes to appreciate the empathy and nonconditional positive regard of the therapist. There is a feeling of being cared for and being fully accepted (Rogers, 1953). The experience of being truly cared for assists clients in caring more deeply for themselves and for others and is illustrated by Mrs. Oak at the beginning of her 30th hour with Rogers.

[*Client:*] Well, I made a very remarkable discovery. I know it's—(*laughs*) I found out that you actually care how this thing goes. (*Both laugh*) It gave me the feeling, it's sort of well—"maybe I'll let you get in the act," sort of thing. It's—again you see, on an examination sheet, I would have had the correct answer, I mean but it suddenly dawned on me that in the—client–counselor kind of thing, you actually care what happens to this thing. And it was a revelation, a—not that. That doesn't describe it. It was a—well, the closest I can come to it is a kind of relaxation, a—not a letting down, but a—(*pause*) more of a straightening out without tension if that means anything. I don't know.

[*Therapist:*] Sounds as though it isn't as though this was a new idea, but it was a new experience of really feeling that I did care and if I get the rest of that, sort of a willingness on your part to let me care.

[*Client:*] Yes. (Rogers, 1961, p. 81)

Although Mrs. Oak finds it difficult to describe the experience of being cared for, she finds ways of doing so. Rogers empathically responds to this new experience and accepts her caring.

③ **Experiencing the process of exploration.** The caring and empathy of the therapist allow the client to explore fearful or anxiety-producing experiences. These attitudes allow for the client to change and develop (Kalmthout, 2007). By exploring feelings that are deeply felt rather than feelings that should be sensed, the client can experience a feeling of total honesty and self-awareness. Contradictions within oneself can be explored, such as, "I love my daughter, but her violent anger toward me makes me really question this." In the following example, Mrs. Oak comments on her exploration process at the close of her 30th session.

[*Client:*] I'm experiencing a new type, a—probably the only worthwhile kind of learning, a—I know I've—I've often said what I know doesn't help me here. What I meant is, my acquired knowledge doesn't help me. But it seems to me that the learning process here has been—so dynamic, I mean, so much a part of the—of everything, I mean, of me, that if I just get that out of it, it's something, which, I mean—I'm wondering if I'll ever be able to straighten out into a sort of acquired knowledge what I have experienced here.

[*Therapist:*] In other words, the kind of learning that has gone on here has been something of quite a different sort and quite a different depth; very vital, very real. And quite worthwhile to you in and of itself, but the question you're asking is: Will I ever have a clear intellectual picture of what has gone on at this somehow deeper kind of learning level?

[*Client:*] M-hm. Something like that. (Rogers, 1961, pp. 85–86)

Mrs. Oak struggles to put into words her nonintellectual learning experience, and Rogers helps her clarify her sense of exploration through his empathic response.

④ **Experiencing the self.** With self-exploration comes the realization that the deepest layers of personality are forward moving and realistic (Rogers, 1953). As individuals deal with their angry and hostile feelings, they gradually encounter positive feelings about themselves and others. They are "getting behind the mask" (Rogers, 1961, p. 108). In essence, they are exploring who they really are and their inner world, as well as dropping pretenses about who they should be. In the following example from the 35th session with Mrs. Oak, there is, in her self-expression, a positive direction.

> [*Client:*] Yeah. Well, I have the feeling now that it's okay, really. … Then there's something else—a feeling that's starting to grow; well, to be almost formed, as I say. This kind of conclusion, that I'm going to stop looking for something terribly wrong. Now I don't know why. But I mean, just—it's this kind of thing. I'm sort of saying to myself now, well, in view of what I know, what I've found—I'm pretty sure I've ruled out fear, and I'm positive I'm not afraid of shock—I mean, I sort of would have welcomed it. But—in view of the places I've been, what I learned there, then, also kind of, well, taking into consideration what I don't know, sort of, maybe this is one of the things that I'll have to date, and say, well, now, I've just—I just can't find it. See? And now without any—without, I should say, any sense of apology or covering up, just sort of simple statement that I can't find what at this time, appears to be bad.
>
> [*Therapist:*] Does this catch it? That as you've gone more and more deeply into yourself, and as you think about the kind of things that you've discovered and learned and so on, the conviction grows very, very strong that no matter how far you go, the things you're going to find are not dire and awful. They have a very different character.
>
> [*Client:*] Yes, something like that. (Rogers, 1961, p. 101)

Rogers is empathic with Mrs. Oak's awkwardly worded experience of being herself. His empathic response more clearly articulates her struggle within herself.

(5) **Experiencing change.** As the client struggles, as Mrs. Oak does, there is a sense of progress, even when the client may still feel confused (Kalmthout, 2007). Clients bring up some issues, discuss them and sense them, and move on to others. The therapist's warm presence allows the client to deal with issues that may be upsetting and difficult.

When the client has sufficient positive self-regard, he is likely to bring up the prospect of stopping therapy. Because the therapeutic relationship has been a deep one, the client and counselor may experience a sense of loss. Discussion of the ending process may take a few sessions, and the period between sessions may be lengthened to help the client deal with the loss of a significant therapeutic relationship.

The encounter between client and therapist is deeply felt by the client, although this may occur very gradually. The therapist's genuineness, acceptance, and empathy help facilitate the client's positive self-exploration, while at the same time helping the client deal with disturbing thoughts and feelings. Because of the deep personal involvement of clients—in the relationship and the intense search for an inner self—clients are likely to experience the relationship in different ways than the facilitative and empathic therapist. Clients may experience their own change in a deeply felt manner, including a wide range of emotions, whereas therapists experience caring and empathy for clients.

The Process of Person-Centered Psychotherapy

After participating in and listening to many interviews, Rogers (1961) was able to describe seven stages of therapeutic progress that ranged from being closed, not open to experience, and not self-aware, to the opposite—openness to experience, self-awareness, and positive self-regard. Because the stages are somewhat difficult to differentiate and combine several aspects of therapeutic growth, I describe here some of the changes that Rogers believed took place as a result of therapeutic relationships, rather than list the stages themselves. In describing the stages, Rogers noted that individuals could be quite far along in dealing openly and congruently with some issues but less open to others. Important aspects of the therapeutic process include changes in feelings, willingness to communicate them, openness to experience, and intimacy in relating to others.

When individuals are at beginning stages of openness to change, they are not likely to express feelings or take responsibility for them. Gradually, they may come to express their feelings with decreasing fear about doing so. At the higher stages, they will be able to experience and readily communicate feelings to the therapist.

Throughout the therapeutic process, individuals come to be more internally congruent, that is, more aware of their own feelings. Some individuals may be so lacking in awareness that they find it difficult or impossible to initiate the therapeutic process. They may have rigid views of themselves that cut them off from relationships with others, including the therapist. With progress in therapy, individuals come to understand how they have contributed to their own problems and may not blame others for them. Experiencing genuineness, acceptance, and empathy from the therapist leads to changes in how the individual relates to others. There is greater openness to intimacy, including more spontaneous and confident interactions with others.

As clients progress, not evenly or neatly, but gradually through stages of therapeutic progress, they come closer to Rogers's description of the fully functioning person. Sharing their fears, anxiety, and shame in the presence of the therapist's genuine caring helps individuals trust their own experience, feel a sense of richness in their lives, become physiologically more relaxed, and experience life more fully (Rogers, 1961).

Psychological Disorders

Rogers believed that his six necessary and sufficient conditions for change applied to all psychological disorders. Regardless of the client's disorder, if the therapist is genuine, has unconditional positive regard, and is empathic with the client, improvement in psychological disorders takes place. Some critics have remarked that person-centered therapists apply the same approach to all clients. In response, person-centered therapists reply that they use a different approach with each client, reflecting the uniqueness of the client's humanness. Although some person-centered therapists may diagnose a client's disorder, it is usually for the purpose of insurance reimbursement or agency requirements.

In this section, illustrations of the application of person-centered therapy are given for depression, grief and loss, and borderline disorders. The example of Rogers's therapy with a depressed client helps illustrate his style. Therapy with a 7-year-old boy whose father was killed in an accident shows the broad range of person-centered therapy. In describing approaches to treating patients with a borderline disorder, a therapist builds upon Rogers's theory of person-centered psychotherapy to suggest new approaches to treating these difficult clients.

Depression: Graduate Student

In dealing with all psychological disorders, Rogers was empathic with the deep feelings within his clients. Often he helped them become aware of strong feelings that were below surface awareness. With depressed people, feelings of sadness, hopelessness, despair, and discouragement were present. However, Rogers was also empathic with the inner strength within an individual and helped clients take responsibility for their own decisions and judgments.

In the following example, Rogers (1961) helps a young female graduate student become aware that she is responsible for her own life and her own choices. The woman had considered suicide and was concerned with many problems. Part of her concerns were that she wanted others to tell her what to do and was bitter that her professors were not sufficiently guiding or educating her. This segment is drawn from a therapeutic session near the end of therapy and concludes with a commentary by Rogers.

> [Client:] Well now, I wonder if I've been going around doing that, getting smatterings of things, and not getting hold, not really getting down to things.
>
> [Therapist:] Maybe you've been getting just spoonfuls here and there rather than really digging in somewhere rather deeply.
>
> [Client:] M-hm. That's why I say—(*slowly and very thoughtfully*) well, with that sort of a foundation, well, it's really up to me. I mean, it seems to be really apparent to me that I *can't depend on someone else* to give me an education. (*Very softly*) I'll really have to get it myself.
>
> [Therapist:] It really begins to come home—there's only one person that can educate you—a realization that perhaps nobody else can give you an education.
>
> [Client:] M-hm. (*Long pause—while she sits thinking*) I have all the symptoms of fright. (*Laughs softly*)
>
> [Therapist:] Fright? That this is a scary thing, is that what you mean?
>
> [Client:] M-hm. (*Very long pause—obviously struggling with feelings in herself*)
>
> [Therapist:] Do you want to say any more about what you mean by that? That it really does give you the symptoms of fright?
>
> [Client:] (*Laughs*) I, uh—I don't know whether I quite know. I mean—well it really seems like I'm cut loose (*pause*), and it seems that I'm very—I don't know in a vulnerable position, but I, uh, I brought this up and it, uh, somehow it almost came out without my saying it. It seems to be—it's something I let out.
>
> [Therapist:] Hardly a part of you.
>
> [Client:] Well, I felt surprised.
>
> [Therapist:] As though, "Well for goodness sake, did I say that?" (*Both chuckle*)
>
> [Client:] Really, I don't think I've had that feeling before, I've—uh, well, this really feels like I'm saying something that, um is a part of me really. (*Pause*) Or, uh, (*quite perplexed*) it feels like I sort of have, uh, I don't know. I have a feeling of strength, and yet, I have a feeling of—realizing it's so sort of fearful, of fright.

[Therapist:] That is, do you mean that saying something of that sort gives you at the same time a feeling of, of strength in saying it, and yet at the same time a frightened feeling of what you have said, is that it?

[Client:] M-hm, I am feeling that. For instance, I'm feeling it internally now—a sort of surging up, or force or outlet. As if that's something really big and strong. And yet, uh, well at first it was almost a physical feeling of just being out alone, and sort of cut off from a—a support I had been carrying around.

[Therapist:] You feel that it's something deep and strong, and surging forth, and at the same time, you just feel as though you'd cut yourself loose from any support when you say it.

[Client:] M-hm. Maybe that's—I don't know—it's a disturbance of a kind of pattern I've been carrying around, I think.

[Therapist:] It sort of shakes a rather significant pattern, jars it loose.

[Client:] M-hm. *(Pause, then cautiously, but with conviction),* I think—I don't know, but I have the feeling that then I am going to begin to do more things that I know I should do.… There are so many things that I need to do. It seems in so many avenues of my living I have to work out new ways of behavior, but—maybe—I can see myself doing a little better in some things.

I hope that this illustration gives some sense of the strength which is experienced in being a unique person, responsible for oneself, and also the uneasiness that accompanies this assumption of responsibility. To recognize that "I am the one who chooses" and "I am the one who determines the value of an experience for me" is both an invigorating and a frightening realization. (pp. 120–122)

Grief and Loss: Justin

Theories in Action

Person-centered therapists do not diagnose or suggest, they empathize with the individual experiencing grief. If the person is talking about an issue not related to grief, they stay with the client's concern and follow the client's change in topic.

In the following example, Donna Rogers (not related to Carl Rogers) is helping 7-year-old Justin, a kindergarten student. Donna is a graduate student working in an elementary school. Justin has been referred by his teacher for counseling because he is acting angrily, fighting with others, and not willing to change his behavior (Rogers & Bickham, 1995). His father, who had a history of alcohol abuse, had been killed in an auto accident about 4 months before. Also, there had been some violence in the family. Justin has just started to deal with the loss of his father. This is the third counseling session. In this brief excerpt, Ms. Rogers is empathic with Justin's statements. He moves from feeling hated and being aware of being mean to others to physical problems with his ear, to a feeling of hearing screaming in his head, to his father's death, to his locked-up tears. Ms. Rogers' responses facilitate his expression of his experience (Rogers & Bickham, 1995, pp. 96–97).

Justin: Like everybody on the playground, it seems like they hate me. Because how mean I've been 'cause, how mean I been to everybody.

Donna: You've really been mean to your friends.

Justin: Uh, huh. Like I don't know how rough I play but I play rough with them. And I don't know 'cause they don't tell me.

Donna: Maybe it would be easier if they told you that you were hurting them, and that might stop you.

Justin: I will stop.

Donna: You will stop.

Justin: Because they're my friends. And now I don't have that many friends because they're not my friends no more because I was playing rough with them, they didn't tell me. And no people, only one person on the bus likes me, that is Christopher.

Donna: It's really hard, hard not having anybody to talk to and to play with. And maybe all this stuff bottled up inside of you maybe could be relieved a little if you had some friends to help you.

Justin: I don't feel good either. And I still ain't going to that hospital thing because I don't want to tell my Mom 'cause I don't want to go to that hospital thing. I keep on hurting, we don't have no pills. And my ear is stopped up and I can't even hear out of it. And I went to the doctor about it. And I still cannot hear out of it 'cause gook got clogged up in there. My Mamma, we don't have very much of those things you clean out your ears. My Mom finally bought some but she doesn't use them very much. So, um, things get clogged up in there a lot, behind my ear drum. It like soaks through my ear drum, that's how watery it is, it soaks through my ear drum. Just like inside my ear drum.

Donna: Sounds like you have stuff that's keeping you from hearing very good.

Justin: I can only hear out of this ear. I know I can't hear out of this ear because when I cover this ear, I cannot hear very loud. And when I cover this ear, I can hear loud. Because it seems like it's echoing in there. It echoes in there when I cover this ear.

Donna: You've got this stuff inside of you that, that is all bottled up and won't come out and it's like you have a lot of noise in your head. It's real confusing. A lot of things going on. It hurts.

Justin: I have been having like inside of this ear. It seems like something is in that gook and it's saying, it's screaming in there. It's like screaming inside that gook.

Donna: You have someone screaming inside your head.

Justin: Because it seems like in that gook that someone is screaming because they don't want to be drowned in that gook. And it's screaming, it hurts my head.

Donna: It hurts when someone's screaming inside.

Justin: And it's echoing and only in this ear.

Donna: They're afraid that maybe they can't get out.

Justin: Yea. Like they're trying to get out, out of that ear and they can't.

Donna: Like they're trapped, and they don't know what to do.

Justin: Like I am.

Donna: You feel trapped. Like you don't have anywhere to turn.

Justin: My dad died, and it's been hard for me and my Mom and all them. I felt like, it seems like I cannot cry and because I can make other people cry with my songs about him, see I was on the bus and singing this song and these two girls crying 'cause it was so pretty on that, and I didn't 'cause it was hard for me to cry, 'cause my tears were up, it felt like my tears were locked up in there, like down here in here, it felt like it was locked up in a cage.

Donna: There's all these things inside of you …

Justin: That's locked up.

Donna: Yea. And they can't come out. Even though sometimes you want them to.

Justin: It seems like the key is lost to all of them.

Donna: The key is lost.

Borderline Disorder: Woman

In treating patients with borderline symptoms, Swildens (1990) applies the person-centered approach to three phases of therapy. Because Swildens sees the self-concept of a person with a borderline disorder as lacking cohesion, continuity, and adequate defenses, he believes therapy must proceed slowly and carefully. In the first phase of therapy, the therapist tries to develop trust with the client and to prevent acting out, such as destructive behavior toward self or others. The therapist is likely to focus on diffuse feelings of anxiety, and empathic responses are likely to be limited and not penetrate too deeply into the client's sense of self. Empathy is directed at understanding the client's fears without trying to describe or explain them to the client. Understanding acting-out behavior, rather than getting involved in resulting conflicts, is important.

In the second phase, the therapist tries to understand the unsafe situations that clients find themselves in and works with clients in finding ways to survive stress. In dealing with the client's splitting (seeing people or events as all-good or all-bad), Swildens suggests using statements that have an "as well as" pattern, which expands the client's frame of reference. This can best be illustrated in an example.

> A 40-year-old woman constantly saw one or the other of her friends in diabolical terms. In a therapeutic session, she once again reported how cunning and mean one of her friends had been and how hard and relentless she had felt in this situation. The therapist responded with "Hard and relentless as well as vulnerable and sensitive … like your friend who is not only sly and unreliable but who has also been affectionate and caring toward you." This "as well as" confrontation was accepted with tears in her eyes and resulted in the client correcting her judgment. (Swildens, 1990, p. 630)

In the third phase, the therapist is not as concerned with acting out or fits of rage but more with helping clients accept their own oversensitivity and lack of stability. Attention is paid to helping clients understand their feelings of being vulnerable and defenseless. Also, help in processing day-to-day decisions is important.

> *[Client:]* It is hard to choose: Should I rent the small house in Alkmaar or should I rather wait until something bigger presents itself in the country?
>
> *[Therapist:]* Small in the city or something bigger in the country … does the choice have any other consequences for you?

[*Client:*] Yes, and I must give it some serious thinking: Anonymity and perhaps loneliness, or many people I can get to know ... both possibilities have their pros and cons. (Swildens, 1990, pp. 632–633)

In his work, Swildens takes an existential as well as a person-centered approach to help clients with borderline disorders reduce their anxiety and deal with their fears. He highlights the importance of a positive and nonthreatening relationship with the client. Being empathic, congruent, and accepting is approached somewhat differently in the three phases of counseling.

Brief Therapy

In person-centered therapy, the client plays a major role in determining the length of therapy and its termination. Being empathic and accepting of the client's distress means that the therapist understands the client's concerns as deeply as possible and, if possible, avoids artificial limits on therapy. However, genuineness also requires that the therapist sets limits with the client if the client's demands seem unreasonable, such as requesting therapy 5 days a week. Typically, person-centered therapists see their clients once a week for a few weeks to a few years. In general, person-centered therapists do not use a brief therapy model.

Current Trends

Of the several issues now facing person-centered therapy, three diverse issues and trends are discussed here. One area of particular importance during the latter part of Rogers's life that is still important for person-centered therapists is the application of person-centered principles to international concerns of conflict and peace. The issue of eclecticism and the incorporation of other theoretical modes by therapists has been a source of debate among person-centered therapists. Training programs, which are found mostly in Europe, have developed approaches that deal with these and other issues that are important in person-centered therapy.

Societal Implications

As Rogers's writings (1951, 1961, 1970, 1977, 1980) became known worldwide, he received invitations to discuss his philosophy of life and his views of psychotherapy with large audiences throughout the world. Rogers's (1970) work with groups has been applied to improve cross-cultural communications and to ease political tensions. Even when he was over 80, he led intense workshops in South Africa with Black and White participants and facilitated groups that included militant Protestants and Catholics from Northern Ireland. He also led workshops in Brazil, France, Italy, Japan, Poland, Mexico, the Philippines, and the Soviet Union. His impact in these countries has been such that colleges, universities, and clinics throughout the world continue to teach and practice his principles. Cilliers (2004) describes how person-centered groups continued to be used in South Africa into the 21st century.

Rogers taught and practiced psychotherapy when there was great political tension between the Soviet Union and the United States, as well as many other significant national and international conflicts, terrorism, local wars, and threats of nuclear conflict. In his work with people in political conflict, such as those in Northern Ireland, Rogers applied the principles of genuineness, acceptance, and empathy in large groups. This work was extremely dangerous. In Northern Ireland, factions talking with each other could be seen as traitors to the cause and assassinated. However, Rogers felt that if individuals could extend their powers of understanding to the pain, fears, and anxieties of their political opponents, then tension among enemies should lessen. As an example of the application of person-centered principles to Black and White South Africans in exile, Saley and Holdstock (1993) report that person-centered discussions were successful in breaking down barriers toward intimacy and self-disclosure despite fears of political persecution. Cilliers (2004) shows how these discussions are effective in changing the political climate in governmental groups in South Africa. Such work has continued after Rogers's death, some of it sponsored by the Carl Rogers Institute for Peace in La Jolla, California, which tries to bring local and national leaders together to work through real and potential crisis situations.

Theoretical Purity versus Eclecticism

Rogers's theoretical constructs can present a dilemma for the person-centered therapist (Sanders, 2004b). On the one hand, person-centered therapy describes six necessary and sufficient conditions for therapeutic change to which therapists should adhere. On the other hand, Rogers took an antidogmatic approach and said that "he would rather help the psychologist or psychotherapist who prefers a directive and controlling form of therapy to clarify his or her aims and meanings, than convince him or her of the person-centered position" (Hutterer, 1993, p. 276). Rogers was very open to the beliefs of others, yet he was also very committed to his own person-centered views. Those who practice person-centered therapy are often faced with decisions about whether to apply other types or styles of therapy. Sanders (2004b) recognizes that there are a number of therapies that are related to person-centered therapy but not identical to it. His book *The Tribes of the Person-Centred Nation: An Introduction to the Schools of Therapy* (2004b) includes chapters on classical client-centered therapy (as described in this chapter), focusing-oriented therapy, experiential person-centered therapy, and existential approaches to therapy.

Training Trends

Training in the person-centered model has been problematic for students wishing to learn this approach. This model has not been as popular in the United States as it has been in Europe. In the United States only the Chicago Counseling Center offers a formal training program. Mearns (1997a, 1997b) describes a model for training developed at Scotland's University of Strathclyde that focuses on individual dynamics. Shared responsibility between student and faculty for training is related to the person-centered focus on self-actualization. Self-acceptance is developed through the unconditional positive regard of the faculty. In keeping with a person-centered approach, the curriculum is individualized, as is the evaluation and assessment of participants. Much of the progress in the program is based on self-assessment of participants. About 35 different training programs are offered in Great Britain. Other formal training programs are offered in France, Germany, Greece, the Slovak Republic, and Switzerland, as well as other countries.

Using Person-Centered Therapy with Other Theories

All the theorists discussed in this book recognize the importance of the client–counselor relationship and the need for the therapist to want to help the client. However, there is disagreement on the application of genuineness, acceptance, and empathy. For example, theorists such as Frankl and Haley, who apply paradoxical treatments, can be accused of not being genuine with their clients. Others such as Ellis or Kohut (Kahn & Rachman, 2000) may experience empathy for their clients but may not show it the way Rogers does. Cognitive and behavioral therapists may accept their clients but try to change their behavior. However, almost all theorists draw on the principles of genuineness, acceptance, and empathy in their work. A special section of the journal *Psychotherapy: Research, Practice, and Training*, entitled *Special Section: The Necessary and Sufficient Conditions at the Half Century Mark (2007, Volume 44 (3))* features 12 articles that discuss the contribution of Carl Rogers's necessary and sufficient conditions for client change. The consensus of the authors appears to be that Rogers's contribution has had a lasting effect on the practice of psychotherapy, and that his conditions for change are very helpful but not necessary or sufficient for change.

Particularly during early stages of therapy, other theorists are likely to listen empathically to the worries and concerns of their patients. They show genuineness and congruence by not being interrupted in their work and by giving the client full attention, both verbally and nonverbally, and do not criticize or ridicule the client. All of these actions are consistent with Rogers's principles.

In their application of person-centered therapy to clients, some person-centered therapists may draw on other theories, especially existential and gestalt therapies. Existential therapists are concerned with the human condition, being in the present, and experiencing the self, and in that way they share values that were important to Carl Rogers (Sanders, 2004a). Gestalt therapy, which also has a strong existential basis, emphasizes experiencing current awareness in a more bodily and active way than does person-centered therapy. O'Leary (1997) demonstrates how the person-centered focus on the client–therapist relationship can be integrated with the emphasis that gestalt therapy gives to self-support and interdependence. Greenberg's (Elliott, Watson, Goldman, & Greenberg, 2004) process-experiential and emotion-focused therapies use person-centered therapy as a basis for developing a good relationship with a client and then use gestalt therapy to help clients experience events and issues in their lives.

In general, person-centered therapists are more likely to make use of theories that emphasize "knowing" the client rather than cognitive and behavioral therapies that are more directive in nature. However, Tausch (1990) describes situations in which person-centered therapists may wish to make use of behavioral methods such as relaxation strategies. Other writers have addressed the issue of integration with other therapies (Sanders, 2004b) and, more specifically, with cognitive behavioral therapy (Keijsers, Schaap, & Hoogduin, 2000). As mentioned on page 227, Sanders (2004b) describes focusing-oriented, experiential, and existential therapies, which he believes have much in common with person-centered therapy. Farber and Brink (1996) have assembled a series of chapters that discuss some of Rogers's cases from client-centered, psychoanalytic, cognitive, behavioral, and other points of view, giving insights as to how other theories may be integrated with the person-centered point of view. In using other theories, most person-centered therapists ask, "To what extent are these other theoretical concepts consistent with the necessary and sufficient conditions of Rogers?"

Research

At the same time that Rogers was advocating a humanistic and phenomenological approach to helping clients, he also believed that it was necessary to use research methods to validate the effectiveness of psychotherapeutic concepts and the outcome of psychotherapy. Rogers was a pioneer in therapy research, as can be seen in his early advocacy (Rogers, 1942b) of recording sessions of psychotherapy for training and research purposes. Throughout his career, Rogers (1986) believed that research would test person-centered hypotheses, add to theoretical explanations, and provide a deeper understanding of individuals' personality and of psychotherapy. In general, there have been two types of research on person-centered therapy: tests of the importance of genuineness, acceptance, and empathy (the core conditions) for therapeutic change and studies comparing the effectiveness of person-centered therapy with other theories.

Research on the Core Conditions

For more than 30 years, there has been research on the role of empathy, genuineness, and acceptance in therapeutic change. At first, research focused on developing scales for measuring Rogers's core concepts. Later, there was criticism of this work. Although recent studies have not been abundant, they have examined the core conditions, particularly empathy, from a variety of perspectives.

Early research on the core conditions concluded that therapists who are genuine, empathize accurately with their clients, and are accepting and open are effective in bringing about therapeutic change (Truax & Carkhuff, 1967; Truax & Mitchell, 1971). In their research review, Truax and Mitchell cite more than 30 studies that use scales to measure accurate empathy, nonpossessive warmth, and genuineness. The typical approach in many of these investigations was for raters to listen to tapes of therapy and rate therapists' responses to clients' statements on previously developed rating scales. In a later review, Beutler, Crago, and Arezmendi (1986) concluded that there was no clear evidence that genuineness, acceptance, and empathy were necessary and sufficient conditions for client change.

In explaining the criticisms of research that used rating scales to measure the effectiveness of the core conditions, Barkham and Shapiro (1986) describe four major problems with the methodological approach of the early studies. First, ratings included the rater's view of the amount of the core condition, not the client's. Second, early studies tended to use a 4-minute segment rather than the whole session for the ratings. Third, listening to audiotapes does not account for the nonverbal communication of core conditions. Fourth, the ratings scales were criticized for not being sufficiently specific. Also, there has been criticism for not paying sufficient attention to the occurrence of empathy, genuineness, or acceptance in the early, middle, or late stages of therapy.

As a partial answer to such criticisms, Barkham and Shapiro (1986) studied 24 client–counselor pairs at various phases of therapy. They found that clients felt that counselors were more empathic in later sessions, whereas counselors believed that they were themselves more empathic in the initial sessions of counseling. There were also differences between how clients and counselors defined empathy. For some categories, statements that were interpretation, exploration, reflection, advisement, and reassurance were considered to be empathic. This study highlights the complexity of the concept of empathy and suggests that it is not unitary.

Another view of empathy is provided by Bachelor (1988), who studied how clients perceive empathy. Analyzing the descriptions of empathic perceptions of 27 clients who were participating in therapy, she was able to specify four different client perceptions of empathy: cognitive, affective, sharing, and nurturing. Cognitive-style clients perceived empathy when their innermost experience or motivation was understood. Affective-style clients experienced empathy when the therapist was involved in the client's feeling state. Sharing empathy was perceived when the therapist disclosed opinions in her life that were relevant to the client's problem. Less frequent than the others, nurturant empathy was sensed when the therapist was attentive and provided security and support. Bachelor's study suggests that empathy should be seen in a variety of ways rather than as one dimension. An instrument that may prove helpful in the study of clients' perception of core conditions in therapy is the Client Evaluation of Counselor Scale (Hamilton, 2000).

The Effectiveness of Person-Centered Therapy

Over the last 25 years, outcome research on client-centered therapy has been sporadic. Early research was done by Rogers et al. (1967) on a small group of patients with schizophrenia. Since that time there have been other studies on similar hospitalized patients, as well as on a variety of other clinical populations. A detailed review of research comparing client-centered therapy with other therapies shows common findings and recent trends in research (Kirschenbaum & Jourdan, 2005). Examples of typical outcome studies are illustrated here.

While Rogers was at the University of Wisconsin, he conducted an in-depth study of 28 patients with schizophrenia, half of whom were in a control group. The investigators were interested in the effect of Rogers's core conditions on the process of hospitalization and the length of hospital stay, which is described in a lengthy book (Rogers et al., 1967). In brief, the investigators found that those patients who received high degrees of empathy, warmth, and genuineness spent less time in the hospital than those who received lower conditions. This was also found to be true in a follow-up study 9 years later (Truax, 1970). Unfortunately, few differences were found between the patients who received high core conditions and the control group that was not treated. Patients who received lower levels of empathy, warmth, and genuineness spent more days in the hospital than did the control group or those receiving high core conditions. Although there was some support for the importance of the core conditions in several of the analyses, the patients receiving high levels of core conditions made disappointingly small gains relative to the control group.

In a study focused on the working alliance (therapeutic relationship), person-centered therapy was compared to process-experiential therapy (an approach using aspects of person-centered and gestalt therapy) in the treatment of 34 depressed patients (Weerasekera, Linder, Greenberg, & Watson, 2001). Few differences were found between the two treatment methods, but in the midphases of the 16- to 20-session therapy, the process-experiential group did have higher working alliance scores than the person-centered clients.

Another study was done with 209 African American women who tested positive for HIV (Szapocznik et al., 2004). A type of brief family therapy and a referral to community services were compared with a person-centered therapy approach. The family therapy approach, Structural Ecosystems Therapy, helped to reduce psychological distress and family-related hassles more than person-centered therapy or referral to outside agencies. No differences were found among the three treatments in producing family support. Women who were most distressed at the start of treatment received the most relief in their distress.

Reviewing studies that compared client-centered or nondirective therapy to either control groups or other therapies, Kirschenbaum and Jourdan (2005) describe research done from the 1970s through 2005, both in Europe and the United States. They also discuss common factors in therapeutic success, such as the therapeutic alliance and Rogers's core conditions. Interestingly, the vast majority of recent research on client-centered therapy has been done in Belgium and Germany, with relatively little taking place in the United States, whereas in the 1960s and 1970s most research was in the United States. Calculating effect sizes for 18 studies, Greenberg, Elliott, and Litaer (1994) found positive changes between pretreatment and posttreatment for all studies, with most studies using follow-up measures between 3 months and 1 year after treatment completion. When client-centered therapy is compared to a wait-list or no-treatment control, all studies showed more powerful effect sizes for client-centered therapy. However, when person-centered therapy was compared to cognitive or behavioral therapy in five studies, there were slightly stronger effect sizes, differences that favored the behavioral and cognitive treatments. Comparing client-centered therapy to two different types of dynamic therapy, client-centered therapy had more positive results in one case, but there were no differences in another.

While Greenberg and his colleagues (1994) studied experiential therapies specifically, other investigations have included the entire range of therapies in their analyses. Weisz, Weiss, Alicke, and Klotz (1987) and Weisz, Weiss, Han, Granger, and Morton (1995) have conducted meta-analyses on the effectiveness of treatments with adolescents and children. If both investigations are combined, they examined 26 studies in which person-centered therapy was used. They found a lower effect size (less effectiveness), in general, for person-centered therapy than behavioral, cognitive, parent training, or social skills interventions. Using a sample of 5,613 patients, few differences were found whether cognitive-behavior therapy, person-centered therapy, or psychodynamic therapy was used (Stiles, Barkham, Mellor-Clark, & Connell, 2008). Another study compared cognitive analytic therapy to person-centered therapy and cognitive therapy; the findings showed all produced clinical improvement (Marriott & Kellett, 2009). Following 697 patients over a 5-year period, Gibbard and Hanley (2008) reported that person-centered therapy was more effective than a wait-list control sample for individuals with anxiety and depression, who had problems of short or longer duration.

Rather than ask which therapy is best, it is helpful to ask who benefits best from which types of therapy. In reviewing several studies, Greenberg et al. (1994) suggest that client-centered therapy may be particularly helpful to clients who are resistant or, more technically, high in reactance—that is, high on a measure of dominance and low on a measure of submissiveness. Greenberg et al. (1994) suggest that those who are low in reactance do better in gestalt therapy than in client-centered therapy. Other variables besides reactance have been examined to determine who can best benefit from client-centered therapy; however, the results are not clear (Greenberg et al., 1994). There continues to be a need for research that studies client characteristics and therapist performance to learn more about the effective aspects of client-centered therapy.

Gender Issues

Although some writers (Bozarth & Moon, 2008) believe that incorporating gender explicitly into person-centered theory adds on to Rogers's necessary and sufficient conditions and violates Rogers's view of what person-centered theory consists of, others take different points of view. Wolter-Gustafson (2008) believes that being empathic with issues that reflect the context of gender would help individuals to fully accept one another and to improve communications with each other. By examining male–female therapist–client pairings, Proctor (2008) shows that therapists can better understand the role of gender and power in person-centered therapy. Additionally, by better understanding gender and power issues, therapists can be effective in helping violent men change their behavior (Weaver, 2008). Addressing issues of masculinity can help therapists provide a male-sensitive approach to their clients (Gillon, 2008) When therapists are able to prevent their values from interfering with understanding their clients, they can help adolescents grow in their development of sexual identity formation (Lemoire & Chen, 2005).

Multicultural Issues

Especially in the last 20 years of his life, Rogers (1977) was motivated to apply person-centered ways of thinking and being to all cultures, as can be seen in his chapter in *Carl Rogers on Personal Power*, "The Person-Centered Approach and the Oppressed." In order to promote cross-cultural communication, Rogers conducted large workshops in Northern Ireland, Poland, France, Mexico, the Philippines, Japan, the Soviet Union, and other countries.

Several authors have pointed out similarities between person-centered and Eastern thought, giving perspectives on person-centered therapy. Rogers wrote that Taoism influenced his development of person-centered therapy (Moodley & Mier, 2007). Miller (1996) points out how Taoist philosophy emphasizes that individuals need to be receptive to their own being. Person-centered therapists strive for that in their work and indirectly communicate this to clients. Similarly, Buddhist psychology, like person-centered therapy, emphasizes openness to other experience (Harman, 1997; Wang, 2003). Thus, in Eastern therapy the self is viewed as a process rather than a fixed being. In this process individuals learn to accept and trust themselves. Singh and Tudor (1997) take a broader approach in which they define race, culture, and ethnicity as a basis for discussing Rogers's six conditions for change from the viewpoint of culture. They give examples of how person-centered concepts can be applied to Sikh and Moslem clients.

Western ways of knowing have been called egocentric, some non-Western ways, sociocentric (O'Hara, 1997). O'Hara (1997) talks of visiting a community workshop in Brazil in 1977 with Carl Rogers. Typically, Rogers would be empathic with a group member, an example of an egocentric approach. O'Hara, however, describes empathy from a sociocentric point of view. An impasse had occurred in the community in which group members could not agree on whether Rogers should give a formal presentation. On the third day, three group members reported dreams that dealt with this impasse. That night a representative of the African-Brazilian religion Macumba performed rituals that indirectly unlocked the group's impasse. This experience relaxed the group and was seen as richer than a formal talk by Rogers. In this way, empathy emerged from the group with shared perceptions of an experience rather than relying on Rogers's view of the impasse. In this situation, Rogers's approach was consistent with a postmodern framework, as he did not impose his perception on others but rather let theirs develop.

Rogers's belief in the core conditions of genuineness, acceptance, and empathy as a way of relating socially and politically can be seen as a set of cultural values. Some writers have questioned their universality and the appropriateness of the person-centered approach for clients of all cultures. Psychotherapy is either unknown or carries strong negative social stigma in many cultures. When individuals from some Asian cultures seek therapy, it may be as a last resort, and they are likely to seek direction or advice that will be immediate, not gradual (Chu & Sue, 1984). In cultures where individuals learn to respect and take direction from authority, the transition to a less directive person-centered approach may be difficult (Wang, 2003). Also, many cultures focus on familial and social decision making rather than on individual empowerment, as does Rogers. However, the person-centered view of responding to clients from different cultures emphasizes the importance of empathic listening (Lago, 2007). Glauser and Bozarth (2001) summarize the person-centered approach in these comments about counseling and culture.

> What a counselor says or does in a session must be based on the counselor's experience of the client in the relationship and the client's perception of the experience, not on the counselor's perception of the racial identity or culture of the client. (p. 144)

Group Counseling

Rogers had a strong belief in and commitment to the power of groups, both those designed for personal growth and those designed to ease conflicts between people of different ethnic or national groups. Since the 1960s, Rogers believed deeply in the power of individuals to help each other grow through the group process, as indicated in his *Carl Rogers on Encounter Groups* (1970). Person-centered groups continue to be an important means for helping individuals who have personal problems (Schmid & O'Hara, 2007).

The same philosophy that Rogers had toward individual therapy was directed toward the process of *facilitating* (a word he preferred to leading) groups (Rogers, 1970). Like the individual, the group was an organism with its own direction that could be trusted to develop positively. This trust could be extended to the goals of the group, which were to arise from the group members, not from the facilitator. Rather than lead, the facilitator's goal was to facilitate core conditions so that individuals may become more genuine, accepting, and empathic with each other so that leadership, in the sense of direction, became less necessary. Yet at the same time, Rogers (1970) recognized the need for the facilitator to make the atmosphere in a group psychologically safe for each member.

The role of the core conditions of person-centered therapy is evident in Rogers's (1970) writings on group process. Individuals are accepted for themselves regardless of whether they wish to commit to the group, participate, or remain silent. For Rogers, empathic understanding is key: The facilitator tries to understand what an individual is communicating at the moment within the group. As a result, Rogers rarely made comments about the group process. He preferred that group members do this themselves. However, some group facilitators feel that process comments reflect an empathic understanding of the group feeling. For Rogers, it was important to be aware of his own feelings, impulses, and fantasies, to trust them, and to choose to react to them through interaction with participants. Having applied his philosophy to many groups, Rogers was able to articulate a process that he believed most groups went through in their development.

When the core conditions were met in the group, trust would develop and a process similar to the one summarized here would take place (Rogers, 1970, pp. 14–37). At first there would be confusion among group members about what to do or who is responsible for movement in the group. Along with this, resistance to exploring personal issues and a sense of being vulnerable might occur. Then group members could disclose past feelings, which were safer to express than current feelings.

As trust developed in the group, members would become more likely to expose their inner selves, which might include discussion of negative feelings about themselves, other members, or the group leader. Gradually the material would become personally more meaningful and reflect immediate reactions to people within the group.

As interpersonal interaction became more meaningful, Rogers observed changes within the group. As honesty developed among members, communication became deeper, with honest positive and negative feedback given to others in the group. As members became closer and more genuinely in contact with each other, they were able to express and experience more positive feelings and closeness within the group. This often resulted in behavior change, less affectation or fewer mannerisms, new insights into problems, and more effective ways of dealing with others. Such changes occurred in interaction with group members and with other people who were significant in their lives.

Recognizing the power of the group process, Rogers also was aware of the risks and dangers. He was concerned that positive changes might not last as long as members would like. Also, relationships within the group that could be quite positive and warm might threaten intimate relationships outside the group, such as with a spouse or parents. For some individuals, sharing deep feelings and thoughts with group members could lead to feeling vulnerable and exposed at the end of the group or workshop. Although Rogers discusses these risks, his trust in the positive healing power of the group process was strong, causing him to believe that the risks were minimal and that the prospects of positive personal growth outweighed potential hazards.

Summary

Essential to the person-centered approach of Carl Rogers is the belief that individuals are able to develop an ability for self-understanding, for changing their behaviors and attitudes, and for fully being themselves. Individuals integrate positive self-regard (an attitude of confidence) in part from receiving positive regard (warmth, caring, and affection) from others. When individuals receive conditions of worth (limited caring or conditional affection) from others, they may develop a lack of confidence or lack of self-regard, which can result in anxiety, defensiveness, or disorganized behavior.

To help individuals with relatively low self-regard who are experiencing psychological stress, Rogers believed that providing the core conditions of person-centered therapy would bring about positive change. By being empathic to the individuals' experience (offering a complete and accurate understanding of the client's concern), by accepting and respecting the individuality of the person, and by being genuine (saying what is truly felt), therapists can help the client become a more fully functioning person. To do this, the client must be able to perceive the empathy, acceptance, and genuineness that are offered by the therapist.

Along with this humanistic approach to therapy, Rogers had a deep commitment to research and was involved in several early studies to assess the effectiveness of the core conditions of person-centered therapy. Although Rogers continued to value research, as he grew older his interest turned to issues other than individual psychotherapy and its evaluation.

When Rogers left academic life in 1964, he devoted attention to a variety of issues. One important area for Rogers was encounter groups and his belief in the power of groups of people to work together to bring about positive change for the individual members. Other areas of interest included couples counseling, teaching, and supervision. During the last decade of his life, Rogers applied concepts of person-centered therapy to bring about political change and world peace and to alleviate suffering among individuals who were involved in political conflict. To do this, Rogers traveled to many countries to facilitate small and large groups of individuals in conflict. By communicating empathy, acceptance, and genuineness for others, Rogers believed that group leaders could help group members to experience and incorporate these conditions into their lives. Rogers's caring for others, his warmth, and his continual emphasis on being empathic to the experience of others epitomize his work and are the essence of person-centered therapy.

Theories in Action DVD: Person-Centered Counseling

Basic Concepts Used in the Role-Play	Questions About the Role-Play
• Congruence • Unconditional positive regard • Empathic understanding • Reflecting	1. How does Dr. Neukrug's empathic understanding help Jose with his concerns about his mother and brother? 2. Are the six necessary and sufficient conditions for client change discussed on pages 214 to 217 being met in this therapeutic example? 3. How does Dr. Newkrug show unconditional positive regard for Jose? (p. 215) 4. In what ways does the therapeutic approach of Donna with Justin on pages 223 to 225 seem similar to and different than that of Dr. Neukrug with Jose?

Suggested Readings

Kirschenbaum, H. (2009). *The life and work of Carl Rogers*. Alexandria, VA: American Counseling Association. This is both a historical and a therapeutic overview of Carl Rogers. It describes early influences on his life as well as the many contributions he made to the field of psychotherapy.

Rogers, C. R. (1951). *Client-centered therapy*. Boston: Houghton Mifflin. Rogers's view of the process of therapy and the conditions under which change takes place is described, along with applications to groups, teaching, and individual therapy.

Rogers, C. R. (1961). *On becoming a person.* Boston: Houghton Mifflin. In one of his best-known books, Rogers provides autobiographical comments as well as his view of psychotherapy. He also addresses broader questions such as the place of research and the applications of client-centered principles for education, family life, and interpersonal relations.

Rogers, C. R. (1980). *A way of being.* Boston: Houghton Mifflin. Published when Rogers was 78, this book describes changes in events and thoughts over Rogers's life. Of particular interest are his views on the therapist's role in social and political issues.

References

Bachelor, A. (1988). How clients perceive therapist empathy: A content analysis of "received" empathy. *Psychotherapy, 25,* 227–240.

Barkham, M., & Shapiro, D. A. (1986). Exploratory therapy in two-plus-one sessions: A research model for studying the process of change. In G. Lietaer, J. Rombauts, & R. Van Balen (Eds.), *Client-centered and experiential psychotherapy in the nineties* (pp. 429–445). Leuven, Belgium: Leuven University Press.

Barrett-Lennard, G. T. (1998). *Carl Rogers' helping system: Journey and substance.* London: Sage.

Beutler, L. E., Crago, M., & Arezmendi, T. G. (1986). Research on therapist variables in psychotherapy. In S. L. Garfield & A. E. Bergin (Eds.), *Handbook of psychotherapy and behavior change* (3rd ed., pp. 257–310). New York: Wiley.

Bohart, A. C. (2007a). The actualizing person. In M. Cooper, M. O'Hara, P. F. Schmid, & G. Wyatt (Eds.), *The handbook of person-centred psychotherapy and counselling* (pp. 47–63). New York: Palgrave Macmillan.

Bohart, A. C. (2007b). Taking steps along a path: Full functioning, openness, and personal creativity. *Person-Centered and Experiential Psychotherapies. 6*(1), 14–16.

Boy, A. V., & Pine, G. J. (1989). Psychodiagnosis: A person-centered perspective. *Person-Centered Review, 4,* 132–151.

Boy, A. V., & Pine, G. J. (1999). *A person-centered foundation for counseling and psychotherapy* (2nd ed.). Springfield, IL: Charles C. Thomas.

Bozarth, J. (2007). Unconditional positive regard. In M. Cooper, M. O'Hara, P. F. Schmid, & G. Wyatt (Eds.), *The handbook of person-centred psychotherapy and counselling* (pp. 182–193). New York: Palgrave Macmillan.

Bozarth, J. D. (1991). Person-centered assessment. *Journal of Counseling and Development, 69,* 458–461.

Bozath, J. D. (1996). A theoretical reconceptualization of the necessary and sufficient conditions for therapeutic change. *The Person-Centered Journal, 3,* 44–51.

Bozarth, J. D., & Moon, K. A. (2008). Client-centered therapy and the gender issue. *Person-Centered and Experiential Psychotherapies, 7*(2), 110–119.

Brice, A. (2004). Lies: Working person-centeredly with clients who lie. *Person-Centered Journal, 11*(1–2), 59–65.

Brodley, B. T. (1994). Some observations of Carl Rogers's behavior in therapy interviews. *Person-Centered Journal, 1,* 37–48.

Brodley, B. T. (2000). Personal presence in client-centered therapy. *Person-Centered Journal, 7,* 139–149.

Carkhuff, R. R. (1969). *Helping and human relations.* New York: Holt, Rinehart & Winston.

Carkhuff, R. R. (1987). *The art of helping* (6th ed.). Amherst, MA: Human Resource Development Press.

Chu, J., & Sue, S. (1984). Asian/Pacific-Americans and group practice. In L. E. Davis (Ed.), *Ethnicity in social group work practice* (pp. 23–36). New York: Haworth.

Cilliers, F. (2004). A person-centered view of diversity in South Africa. *Person-Centered Journal, 11*(1–2), 33–47.

Cissna, K. N., & Anderson, R. (1997). Carl Rogers in dialogue with Martin Buber: A new analysis. *Person-Centered Journal, 4,* 4–13.

Cooper, M., O'Hara, M., Schmid, P. F., & Wyatt, G. (2007). *The handbook of person-centred psychotherapy and counselling.* New York: Palgrave Macmillan.

Cornelius-White, J. (2007). Congruence. In M. Cooper, M. O'Hara, P. F. Schmid, & G. Wyatt (Eds.), *The handbook of person-centred psychotherapy and counselling* (pp. 168–181). New York: Palgrave Macmillan.

DeCarvalho, R. J. (1999). Otto Rank, the Rankian circle in Philadelphia, and the origins of Carl Rogers' person-centered psychotherapy. *History of Psychology, 2,* 132–148.

Demanchick, S. P., & Kirschenbaum, H. (2008). Carl Rogers and the CIA. *Journal of Humanistic Psychology, 48*(1), 6–31.

Egan, G. (2010). *Essentials of skilled helping: Managing problems, developing opportunities.* (9th ed.). Belmont, CA: Wadsworth.

Elliott, R., Watson, J. C., Goldman, R. N., & Greenberg, L. S. (2004). *Learning emotion-focused therapy: The process-experiential approach to change.* Washington, DC: American Psychological Association.

Farber, B. A., & Brink, D. C. (Eds.). (1996). *The psychotherapy of Carl Rogers: Cases and commentary.* New York: Guilford.

Freire, E. S. (2007). Empathy. In M. Cooper, M. O'Hara, P. F. Schmid, & G. Wyatt (Eds.), *The handbook of person-centred psychotherapy and counselling* (pp. 194–206). New York: Palgrave Macmillan.

Gibbard, I., & Hanley, T. (2008). A five-year evaluation of the effectiveness of person-centred counselling in routine clinical practice in primary care. *Counselling & Psychotherapy Research, 8*(4), 215–222.

Gillon, E. (2007). *Person-centred counselling psychology: An introduction.* London: Sage.

Gillon, E. (2008). Men, masculinity and person-centered therapy. *Person-Centered and Experiential Psychotherapies., 7*(2), 120–134.

Glauser, A. S., & Bozarth, J. D. (2001). Person-centered counseling: The culture within. *Journal of Counseling and Development, 79*, 142–147.

Goldstein, K. (1959). *The organism: A holistic approach to biology derived from psychological data in man.* New York: American Book. (Original work published 1934.)

Greenberg, L. S., Elliott, R. K., & Litaer, G. (1994). Research on experiential therapies. In A. E. Bergin & S. L. Garfield (Eds.), *Handbook of psychotherapy change* (4th ed., pp. 509–539). New York: Wiley.

Hamilton, J.-C. (2000). Construct validity of the core conditions and factor structure of the Client Evaluation of Counselor Scale. *Person-Centered Journal, 7*, 40–51.

Harman, J. L. (1997). Rogers' late conceptualization of the fully functioning individual: Correspondences and contrasts with Buddhist psychology. *Person-Centered Journal, 4*, 23–31.

Holdstock, T. L., & Rogers, C. R. (1977). Person-centered theory. In R. J. Corsini (Ed.), *Current personality theories* (pp. 125–152). Itasca, IL: Peacock.

Hutterer, R. (1993). Eclecticisms: An identity crisis for person-centered therapists. In D. Brazier (Ed.), *Beyond Carl Rogers* (pp. 274–284). London: Constable.

Kahn, E., & Rachman, A. W. (2000). Carl Rogers and Heinz Kohut: A historical perspective. *Psychoanalytic Psychology, 17*, 294–312.

Kalmthout, M. V. (2007). The process of person-centred therapy. In M. Cooper, M. O'Hara, P. F. Schmid, & G. Wyatt (Eds.), *The handbook of person-centred psychotherapy and counselling* (pp. 221–231). New York: Palgrave Macmillan.

Keijsers, G. P. J., Schaap, C. P. D. R., & Hoogduin, C. A. L. (2000). The impact of interpersonal patient and therapist behavior on outcome in cognitive-behavioral therapy: A review of empirical studies. *Behavior Modification, 24*, 264–297.

Kierkegaard, S. (1941). *The sickness unto death.* Princeton, NJ: Princeton University Press.

Kirschenbaum, H. (2009). *The life and work of Carl Rogers.* Alexandria, VA: American Counseling Association; Ross-on-Wye, England: PCCS Books.

Kirschenbaum, H., & Henderson, V. L. (Eds.) (1989). *Carl Rogers: Dialogues.* London: Constable.

Kirschenbaum, H., & Jourdan, A. (2005). The current status of Carl Rogers and the person-centered approach. *Psychotherapy: Theory, Research, Practice, Training, 42*(1), 37–51.

Lago, C. (2007). Counselling across difference and diversity. In M. Cooper, M. O'Hara, P. F. Schmid, & G. Wyatt (Eds.), *The handbook of person-centred psychotherapy and counselling* (pp. 251–265). New York: Palgrave Macmillan.

Lemoire, S. J., & Chen, C. P. (2005). Applying person-centered counseling to sexual minority adolescents. *Journal of Counseling & Development, 83*(2), 146–154.

Levitt, B. E. (Ed.). (2008). *Reflections on human potential: Bridging the person-centered approach and positive psychology.* Ross-on-Wye, England: PCCS Books.

Marriott, M., & Kellett, S. (2009). Evaluating a cognitive analytic therapy service; practice-based outcomes and comparisons with person-centred and cognitive-behavioural therapies. *Psychology and Psychotherapy: Theory, Research and Practice, 82*(1), 57–72.

Maslow, A. H. (1968). *Toward a psychology of being* (rev. ed.). New York: Van Nostrand Reinhold.

Maslow, A. H. (1987). *Motivation and personality* (3rd ed.). New York: Harper & Row.

Mather, R. (2008). Hegel, Dostoyevsky and Carl Rogers: Between humanism and spirit. *History of the Human Sciences, 21*(1), 33–48.

Mearns, D. (1997a). Central dynamics in client-centered therapy training. *Person-Centered Journal, 4*, 31–43.

Mearns, D. (1997b). *Person-centered counseling training*. London: Sage.

Mearns, D. (2003). The humanistic agenda: Articulation. *Journal of Humanistic Psychology, 43*(3), 53–65.

Mearns, D., & Thorne, B. (2007). *Person-centred counselling in action*. (3rd ed.). London: Sage.

Miller, M. J. (1996). Some comparisons between Taoism and person-centered therapy. *Person-Centered Journal, 3*, 12–14.

Moodley, R., & Mier, S. (2007). Cultural diversity, therapist openness and Carl Rogers: An interview with Nat Raskin. *Person-Centered and Experiential Psychotherapies, 6*(2), 141–151.

Myers, J. E., & Hyers, D. A. (1994). The philosophy and practice of client-centered therapy with older persons: An interview with C. H. Patterson. *Person-Centered Journal, 1*, 49–54.

O'Hara, M. (1997). Relational empathy: Beyond modernist egocentrism to postmodern contextualism. In A. C. Bohart & L. S. Greenberg (Eds.), *Empathy reconsidered: New directions in psychotherapy* (pp. 295–320). Washington, DC: American Psychological Association.

O'Leary, E. (1997). Towards integrating person-centered and Gestalt therapies. *Person-Centered Journal, 4*, 14–22.

Proctor, G. (2008). Gender dynamics in person-centered therapy: Does gender matter? *Person-Centered and Experiential Psychotherapies. 7*(2), 82–94.

Rank, O. (1945). *Will therapy, truth and reality*. New York: Knopf.

Rogers, C. R. (1939). *The clinical treatment of the problem child*. Boston: Houghton Mifflin.

Rogers, C. R. (1942a). *Counseling and psychotherapy*. Boston: Houghton Mifflin.

Rogers, C. R. (1942b). The use of electrically recorded interviews in improving psychotherapeutic techniques. *American Journal of Orthopsychiatry, 12*, 429–434.

Rogers, C. R. (1951). *Client-centered therapy: Its current practice, implications, and theory*. Boston: Houghton Mifflin.

Rogers, C. R. (1953). Some of the directions evident in therapy. In O. H. Mowrer (Ed.), *Psychotherapy: Theory and research*. New York: Ronald Press.

Rogers, C. R. (1957). The necessary and sufficient conditions of therapeutic personality change. *Journal of Consulting Psychology, 21*, 95–103.

Rogers, C. R. (1959). A theory of therapy, personality and interpersonal relationships as developed in the client-centered framework. In S. Koch (Ed.), *Psychology: A study of science: Formulations of the person and the social context* (pp. 184–256). New York: McGraw-Hill.

Rogers, C. R. (1961). *On becoming a person*. Boston: Houghton Mifflin.

Rogers, C. R. (1966). Client-centered therapy. In S. Arieti (Ed.), *American handbook of psychiatry* (Vol. 3, pp. 183–200). New York: Basic Books.

Rogers, C. R. (1969). *Freedom to learn: A view of what education might become*. Columbus, OH: Charles E. Merrill.

Rogers, C. R. (1970). *Carl Rogers on encounter groups*. New York: Harper & Row.

Rogers, C. R. (1972). *Becoming partners: Marriage and its alternatives*. New York: Delacorte Press.

Rogers, C. R. (1975). Empathic: An unappreciated way of being. *Counseling Psychologist, 5*, 2–10.

Rogers, C. R. (1977). *Carl Rogers on personal power*. New York: Delacorte.

Rogers, C. R. (1980). *A way of being*. Boston: Houghton Mifflin.

Rogers, C. R. (1986). Carl Rogers on the development of the person-centered approach. *Person-Centered Review, 1*, 257–259.

Rogers, C. R., Gendlin, G. T., Kiesler, D. V., & Truax, C. (Eds.). (1967). *The therapeutic relationship and its impact: A study of psychotherapy with schizophrenics*. Madison: University of Wisconsin Press.

Rogers, C. R., & Rablen, R. A. (1958). *A scale of process in psychotherapy*. Unpublished manuscript.

Rogers, D., & Bickham, P. J. (1995). A child's journey through loss. *Person-Centered Journal, 2*, 94–103.

Saley, E., & Holdstock, L. (1993). Encounter group experiences of black and white South Africans in exile. In D. Brazier (Ed.), *Beyond Carl Rogers* (pp. 201–216). London: Constable.

Sanders, P. (2004a). History of client-centred therapy and the person-centred approach: Events, dates and ideas. In P. Sanders (Ed.), *The tribes of the person-centred nation* (pp. 1–20). Ross-on-Wye, UK: PCCS Books.

Sanders, P. (Ed.). (2004b). *The tribes of the person-centred nation*. Ross-on-Wye, UK: PCCS Books.

Schmid, P. F., & O'Hara, M. (2007). Group therapy and encounter groups. In M. Cooper, M. O'Hara, P. F. Schmid, & G. Wyatt (Eds.), *The handbook of person-centred psychotherapy and counselling* (pp. 93–106). New York: Palgrave Macmillan.

Schor, L. (2003). A person-centered approach to the use of projectives in counseling. *Person-Centered Journal, 10*, 39–48.

Schultz, D. P., & Schultz, S. E. (2009). *Theories of personality* (9th ed.). Belmont, CA: Wadsworth.

Seeman, J. (1989). A reaction to "Psychodiagnosis: A person-centered perspective." *Person-Centered Review, 4*, 152–156.

Singh, J., & Tudor, K. (1997). Cultural conditions of therapy. *Person-Centered Journal, 4*, 32–46.

Stiles, W. B., Barkham, M., Mellor-Clark, J., & Connell, J. (2008). Effectiveness of cognitive-behavioural, person-centred, and psychodynamic therapies in UK primary-care routine practice: Replication in a larger sample. *Psychological Medicine, 38*(5), 677–688.

Swildens, J. C. A. G. (1990). Client-centered psychotherapy for patients with borderline symptoms. In G. Lietaer, J. Rombauts, & R. Van Balen (Eds.), *Client-centered and experiential psychotherapy in the nineties* (pp. 623–635). Leuven, Belgium: Leuven University Press.

Szapocznik, J., Feaster, D. J., Mitrani, V. B., Prado, G., Smith, L., & Robinson-Batista, C., et al. (2004). Structural ecosystems therapy for HIV-seropositive African American women: Effects on psychological distress, family hassles, and family support. *Journal of Consulting and Clinical Psychology, 72*(2), 288–303.

Tausch, R. (1990). The supplementation of client-centered communication therapy with other valid therapeutic methods: A client-centered necessity. In G. Lietaer, J. Rombauts, & R. Van Balen (Eds.), *Client-centered and experiential psychotherapy in the nineties* (pp. 447–455). Leuven, Belgium: Leuven University Press.

Truax, C. B. (1970). Effects of client-centered psychotherapy with schizophrenic patients: Nine years pre-therapy and nine years post-therapy hospitalization. *Journal of Consulting and Clinical Psychology, 3*, 417–422.

Truax, C. B., & Carkhuff, R. R. (1967). *Toward effective counseling and psychotherapy.* Chicago: Aldine.

Truax, C. B., & Mitchell, K. M. (1971). Research on certain therapist interpersonal skills in relation to process and outcome. In A. E. Bergin & S. L. Garfield (Eds.), *Handbook of psychotherapy and behavior change: An empirical analysis* (pp. 299–344). New York: Wiley.

Wang, C.-C. (2003). Cultural influences vs. actualizing tendency: Is the person-centered approach a universal paradigm? *Person-Centered Journal, 10*, 57–69.

Watts, R. E. (1998). The remarkable parallel between Rogers's core conditions and Adler's social interest. *Journal of Individual Psychology, 54*, 4–9.

Weaver, L. (2008). Facilitating change in men who are violent towards women: Considering the ethics and efficacy of a person-centered approach. *Person-Centered and Experiential Psychotherapies, 7*(3), 173–184.

Weerasekera, P., Linder, B., Greenberg, L., & Watson, J. (2001). The working alliance in client-centered and process-experiential therapy of depression. *Psychotherapy Research, 11*, 221–233.

Weisz, J. R., Weiss, B., Alicke, M. D., & Klotz, M. L. (1987). Effectiveness of psychotherapy with children and adolescents: A meta-analysis for clinicians. *Journal of Consulting and Clinical Psychology, 55*, 542–549.

Weisz, J. R., Weiss, B., Han, S. S., Granger, D. A., & Morton, T. (1995). Effects of psychotherapy with children and adolescents revisited: A meta-analysis of treatment outcome studies. *Psychological Bulletin, 117*, 450–468.

Wolter-Gustafson, C. (2008). Casting a wider empathic net: A case for reconsidering gender, dualistic thinking and person-centered theory and practice. *Person-Centered and Experiential Psychotherapies, 7*(2), 95–109.

Wyatt, G. (2000). The multifaceted nature of congruence. *Person-Centered Journal, 7*, 52–68.

Zimring, F. (2000). Empathic understanding grows the person. *Person-Centered Journal, 7*, 101–113.

CHAPTER 7

Gestalt Therapy: An Experiential Therapy

Outline of Gestalt Therapy: An Experiential Therapy

GESTALT THEORY OF PERSONALITY
Gestalt Psychology and Gestalt Therapy
Contact
Contact Boundaries
Contact Boundary Disturbances
Awareness
The Present
THEORY OF GESTALT PSYCHOTHERAPY
Goals of Therapy
The Therapeutic Relationship
Assessment in Gestalt Psychotherapy
Therapeutic Change

Enhancing Awareness
Awareness statements and questions
Emphasizing awareness
Enhancing awareness through language
Awareness through nonverbal behavior
Awareness of self and others
Enhancing awareness of feelings
Awareness through self-dialogue
Awareness through enactment
Awareness through dreams
Awareness outside of therapy: homework
Awareness of avoidance
Integration and Creativity
Risks

There are several experiential therapies. Although they differ in approach, they all share a focus on the client's experiencing events in the present. Rather than talk about the problem, the client, at times, experiences the problem by feeling it internally, talking it out, or re-enacting it. Eugene Gendlin (1996) has developed "focusing," which is a method that guides individuals to quietly become aware of their inner selves. By being in touch with their inner selves, patients are able to resolve internal issues and make positive changes in their lives. In contrast, Alvin Mahrer (2005) has the client and therapist sitting near each other, both faced in the same direction with their eyes usually closed. The client narrates a climactic moment in her life and the therapist joins in the emotional discussion of this. As they do this, the client develops a sense of peace and understanding leading to therapeutic change in each session. Gestalt therapy, which is the most popular and well-known experiential therapy, focuses on making change as a result of growing awareness of self and others. Leslie Greenberg has developed process-experiential therapy and a similar but more integrative approach, emotion-focused therapy (Elliott & Greenberg, 2007; Pos & Greenberg, 2008). The emotion-focused approach is quite similar to gestalt therapy, but emotion-focused therapy integrates the specific principles of Rogers's person-centered therapy in its approach whereas gestalt therapy does not (Leslie Greenberg, personal communication, December 5, 2005). Because gestalt therapy is used much more widely throughout the world than other experiential therapies, this chapter will explain and illustrate gestalt therapy.

Gestalt therapy is concerned with the whole individual, who is viewed as more than the sum of her behaviors. The term *gestalt* refers to the dynamic organization of a whole that comprises two or more related parts. A phenomenological method that values human experience as the source of data, gestalt therapy emphasizes the patient's and the therapist's experience of reality. It is an existential approach in that it stresses the responsibility of individuals for themselves and their ability to determine their own present experience. In gestalt therapy, as in other experiential therapies, issues dealing with the past or future are brought into the present. The general goal of gestalt therapy is awareness of self, others, and the environment that brings about growth and integration of the individual.

Gestalt therapy emphasizes having an appropriate boundary between self and others. The boundary must be flexible enough for meaningful contact with others but firm enough for the individual to experience a sense of autonomy. When an individual is not clear about the boundary between self and others, a disturbance of contact and awareness can occur, which may result in psychopathology. Approaches to therapy focus on being responsible for oneself and being attuned to one's language, nonverbal behaviors, emotions, and conflicts within oneself and with others. Gestalt therapists have developed creative experiments and exercises to facilitate self-awareness that they use in an empathic relationship with the client. Along with individual therapy, group therapy has been an important part of gestalt treatment. Both modalities assist the individual in resolving conflicts with self and others and in dealing with problems from the past that have emerged into the present.

History of Gestalt Therapy

In learning about gestalt therapy, it is helpful to understand both its developer, Fritz Perls, and the various psychological and psychotherapeutic theories that influenced his thinking (Clarkson & Mackewn, 1993). Although he was trained in psychoanalysis, other psychological theories and philosophical approaches led to his development of a therapeutic system that is very different from psychoanalysis.

Frederick S. (Fritz) Perls (1893–1970) originated, developed, and popularized gestalt therapy. He was born in Berlin, the youngest of three children, to older middle-class German Jewish parents. His family was affected by the rise of

Fritz Perls

Nazism, and his eldest sister was killed in a concentration camp (Shepard, 1975). Both Perls and his younger sister describe him as being a problem child who was in trouble at home and at school, failed the seventh grade twice, and was asked to leave school. For a short time he worked for a merchant before returning to school at age 14. Later he studied medicine and, at 23, left school to volunteer in World War I as a medic, first as a private and later as an officer.

After he obtained his medical degree in 1920, he worked as an assistant to Kurt Goldstein at the Institute for Brain Injured Soldiers. Perls was influenced by Goldstein, who viewed the soldiers with brain injuries from a gestalt psychology perspective, focusing on the perceptions that the soldiers had of themselves and their environment. While he was at the institute in Frankfurt, Perls met several people who were to have great impact on his later work, including his future wife, Laura, 12 years younger than he.

Perls trained as a psychoanalyst at the Vienna and Berlin Institutes of Psychoanalysis. His training analyst was Wilhelm Reich, who was to become particularly influential in the development of Perls's ideas about gestalt therapy. Perls was also influenced by analysts Helene Deutsch, Otto Fenichel, and Karen Horney. During this time, he also met Adler, Jung, and Freud. In 1934, because of the rise of Nazism, Perls left Germany for South Africa.

He established the South African Institute for Psychoanalysis in 1935. While in South Africa he met Jan Smuts, author of *Holism and Evolution* (1926), which had an influence on Perls's development of gestalt psychotherapy. After 12 years in South Africa, he left for New York City. Along with Paul Goodman and Laura Perls, he established the New York Institute for Gestalt Therapy in 1952. After 9 years in New York, Perls moved to or visited a variety of cities and countries and established gestalt training centers in Miami, San Francisco, Los Angeles, Israel, Japan, and Canada. Between 1964 and 1969 he was an associate psychiatrist in residence at the Esalen Institute. In 1969 he moved to Cowichan Lake on Vancouver Island, British Columbia, where he initiated the establishment of a therapeutic community. He died about 6 months later in 1970.

The development of gestalt therapy and Perls's movement away from psychoanalysis can be seen in the dramatic contrast between his early and later writings. While in South Africa, Perls wrote *Ego, Hunger and Aggression* (1969a) (originally published in 1947), which combined his ideas about the whole organism with traditional ideas of psychoanalysis. He also focused on the hunger instinct, which he related to psychological functioning (Lobb, 2007). In eating and in psychological functioning, people bite off what they can chew (food, ideas, or relationships), then chew and digest (think about and receive physiological or psychological nourishment). What Perls called "mental metabolism" represents psychological functioning in gestalt therapy. In this book he describes *concentration-therapy*, which was the early term for gestalt therapy that had as its goal "waking the organism to a fuller life" (Perls, 1969a). Although she is not given credit in the book, Laura Perls wrote several of the chapters. In 1951 Perls, along with Ralph F. Hefferline and Paul Goodman (1951/1994), wrote *Gestalt Therapy: Excitement and Growth in the Human Personality*, which consists of two parts. The first describes the theory of gestalt therapy; the second has exercises designed to develop awareness of the senses and the body (Stoehr, 2009).

Perls's later works are more informal in style. *Gestalt Therapy Verbatim* (1969b) includes a section on the theory of gestalt therapy, along with questions from participants in a seminar and Perls's answers. Most of the book is made up of verbatim transcripts of Perls's work with individuals who attended weekend training sessions on dreams, as well as those in a 4-week intensive workshop. Perls's autobiography, *In and Out of the Garbage Pail* (1969c), is very informal, interspersed with poetry, humor, and comments about his work. After his death, two books that he was working on were published. The first, *The Gestalt Approach* (1973), included theoretical material about gestalt therapy as well as transcripts from films. The second book, *Legacy from Fritz* (1975), finished by Patricia Baumgardner, includes transcripts from films of Fritz Perls working with individuals in group training seminars. The abundant case material contained in the last four books gives excellent examples of Perls's style of working with individuals in a group training format.

After Perls's death, gestalt therapy continued to grow, and there are more than 100 gestalt therapy institutes throughout the world, with many in the United States. The European Association for Gestalt Therapy is an association of individual gestalt therapists, training institutes, and national associations. One of its roles is to set standards for practice. These standards are used in 41 European countries and by more than 120,000 gestalt therapists. The Association for Advancement of Gestalt Therapy is a major international organization for gestalt therapy. Forums for the development of the theory and practice of gestalt therapy are *The International Gestalt Journal*, the *Gestalt Review*, the *British Gestalt Journal*, and the *Gestalt Journal of Australia and New Zealand*. Also, meetings as well as conferences have provided the opportunity for presentations on recent developments in gestalt therapy. (Gary Yontef, personal communication, October 18, 2009).

Influences on the Development of Gestalt Therapy

Although trained as a psychoanalyst and influenced by Freud's theoretical work, Perls took advantage of the intellectually rich city of Frankfurt when he was a medical student and practicing psychiatrist. He was influenced by Wilhelm Reich's ideas on verbal and nonverbal behavior and attracted to Sigmund Friedlander's work on creative difference. Work with Kurt Goldstein introduced Perls to the application of gestalt psychology to therapeutic treatment. From a more theoretical and philosophical point of view, his development of gestalt therapy was influenced by Lewin's field theory, phenomenology, and existentialism. On a more personal level, his wife, Laura, a practicing gestalt therapist, writer, and teacher, made an invaluable contribution to gestalt therapy. These various influences are the intellectual underpinnings of Perls's development of gestalt therapy.

Wilhelm Reich was particularly influential, both as his training analyst and through his writings. Reich paid attention to the linguistic, facial, and body positions of his patients. Rather than view libido as energy inherent in childhood sexuality, Reich saw libido as excitement that was apparent in an individual. The defenses that individuals applied to repress their libido he called *body armor*. For Reich, therapy involved helping individuals become less rigid by attending to tensions in their language and body awareness. In his later introduction for *Ego, Hunger and Aggression* (1969a), Perls paid a special tribute to Reich's "bringing down to earth the psychology of resistances" (p. 5), which Reich did by attending to bodily awareness within individuals.

The work of the philosopher Sigmund Friedlander had an impact on Perls's concept of polarities. Friedlander believed that every event was related to a zero-point from which opposites can be differentiated. This zero-point was a balance point from which an individual could move creatively in either direction.

Perls (1969a, p. 15) states: "By remaining alert in the centre, we can acquire a creative ability of seeing both sides of an occurrence and completing an incomplete half." When an individual is too far on one side or the other of an external or an internal need, there is a tendency to need to balance it or move to the center. In his work, Perls was often involved in helping individuals achieve a sense of balance, centeredness, or control over their needs.

Perls was influenced by Kurt Goldstein, not only through working with him at the Institute for Brain Injured Soldiers but also through Goldstein's (1939) writings. Goldstein believed that behavior is made up of performances (voluntary activities, attitudes, feelings) and processes (bodily functions). Like Friedlander, Goldstein believed that organisms moved in a direction to balance their needs. In doing so, they came to terms with environmental pressures. In this process, they strived for "self-actualization" (Bowman & Nevis, 2005).

Perls (1969a) found Goldstein's view of anxiety as arising from the fear of the possible outcome of future events to be relevant to gestalt therapy. Also, anxiety could lead to the separation of parts of the personality from the whole person, bringing about a splitting of the personality. Another contribution of Goldstein, as well as of the semanticist Alfred Korzybski, was the emphasis on precision in language in therapy. In his work with brain-damaged soldiers, Goldstein observed their inability to think abstractly and, therefore, to use language fully.

Field theory (Parlett & Lee, 2005) was developed by Kurt Lewin and several other gestalt psychologists. Similar to gestalt psychology, field theory studies an event by looking at the whole field of which an event is a part. The relationship of the parts to each other and to the whole is the object of the study. This is a descriptive approach rather than one of classification. Field theory takes a phenomenological approach in that the field is defined by the observer. To understand an event, one must know the observer's way of viewing the event. An example of using field theory to make hypotheses is the Zeigarnik effect; Zeigarnik hypothesized and found that unfinished tasks could be remembered better than finished tasks because of tension remaining within the field (Woodworth & Schlosberg, 1954).

The phenomenological approach that was inherent in the work of Reich, Friedlander, Lewin, and Goldstein, as well as in that of gestalt psychologists, has had an impact on the development of Perls's gestalt therapy. The phenomenological perspective holds that an individual's behavior can be understood only through studying his perceptions of reality. Phenomenologists study both the perceptions and the process of perceiving. The environment is seen as something that exists apart from the observer but is known through the observer's perspective (Watzlawick, 1984). The focus on, and the enhancing of, awareness was an important aspect of Perls's therapeutic approach, which was perhaps most impressed upon him by his work with Wilhelm Reich. From a phenomenological point of view, Perls was interested in not only the patient's awareness but also the entire field—the therapist's awareness of the interaction of the patient and therapist (Watzlawick, 1984).

Perls viewed gestalt therapy as one of three existential therapies, along with Binswanger's Daseinanalysis and Frankl's logotherapy. Because existentialism is rooted in phenomenology, existentialists focus on the direct experience of existence, joys and suffering, and relationships with others. The existentialist's concept of authenticity has some similarity to the gestalt concept of awareness in that both include an honest appraisal and an understanding of oneself. The existential emphasis on individual responsibility for actions, feelings, and thoughts is consistent with that of gestalt therapy. The existential writer Martin Buber also influenced the development of gestalt therapy through his concept of the significance of the "I–thou" relationship (Doubrawa & Schickling, 2000; Harris, 2000). Like gestalt therapy, existentialism focused on the present rather than the past or future. Although it is difficult to judge the impact of existentialism on gestalt therapy, there are many similarities between the two.

On a more personal level, Laura Posner Perls made an essential contribution to gestalt psychotherapy. Bloom (2005) considers her to be very important in the development of gestalt therapy. Born near Frankfurt, Germany, in 1905, she married Fritz Perls in 1930 and received the D.Sc. degree from the University of Frankfurt in 1932. She was influenced by Max Wertheimer and the existentialists Paul Tillich and Martin Buber (Humphrey, 1986). Not only did she contribute to Fritz Perls's first book, *Ego, Hunger and Aggression*, but she also participated in the discussions leading to his second major book, *Gestalt Therapy*. Laura became involved in the New York Institute for Gestalt Therapy, founded in 1952, both leading training groups and providing leadership of the institute, until her death at age 85 in 1990. Although they were physically separated for most of the last 15 years of Fritz's life, they kept in contact, discussing issues related to gestalt therapy. Because she published very little, her contribution to gestalt therapy is difficult to assess. One contribution of her work was her respect for the maintenance of marital and other relationships, in contrast to the work of her husband, who focused on awareness rather than the development of relationships (Rosenblatt, 1988).

Gestalt Theory of Personality

Awareness and relationships with self and others are the major emphases of gestalt personality theory. Many of the concepts that are important in gestalt psychotherapy have their basis in gestalt psychology concepts such as figure and ground. Gestalt personality theory attends to the contact between the individual and others or objects that immediately affect the individual. There is a focus on the boundaries between individuals and their environment, as well as the depth of contact with self and others. Gestalt personality theory emphasizes the importance of the individual being aware of oneself and one's environment in terms of the senses, bodily sensations, and emotional feelings. The attention to being in contact with oneself and others and the awareness of self and others takes place in the present rather than the past or future. These somewhat vague concepts are described in more detail here.

Gestalt Psychology and Gestalt Therapy

Gestalt psychology was first developed by Max Wertheimer and later by Wolfgang Kohler and Kurt Koffka. Essentially, gestalt psychology is based on the view that psychological phenomena are organized wholes rather than specific parts. Gestalt psychologists principally studied visual and auditory perception and viewed learning as a perceptual problem in which individuals attempt to discover a correct response in their perceptual field (Shane, 2003). In doing so, individuals experience the "Aha!" response, or "Now I see it" or "Now, I understand it; it's all come together for me!" Some properties of a phenomenon cannot be observed by looking at its parts but occur only when individuals view the

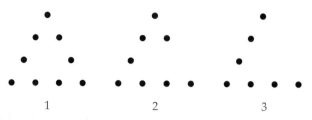

FIGURE 7.1   Stages of completeness in triangles

entirety. For example, a student learning algebra may know formulas, but only when these formulas are brought together is she able to arrive at the solution to the problem.

In gestalt psychology, the "field" can be viewed in terms of "figure" and "ground." The figure is what stands out, and the ground is the background. For example, when you look at Triangle 1 in Figure 7.1, that is the figure; the rest of the page and your surroundings are the ground. The triangle, page, and surroundings make up the field (Parlett & Lee, 2005). Figures differ in their strength and goodness of form. The series of dots in Triangle 1 is perceived as a triangle. The dots in Triangle 2 are an incomplete gestalt but can also be perceived as a triangle. The third series of dots is a very weak gestalt that can be viewed as two lines, an angle, or a triangle. Gestalt psychologists have developed gestalt laws, or laws of perception, to explain how individuals see phenomena such as these series of dots. In fact, Boring (1950) lists more than 114 laws.

Although therapists have applied these concepts to feelings and bodily sensations, gestalt psychologists did not (Wallen, 1970). In fact, gestalt psychologists have been quite critical of the loose and inaccurate ways in which Perls applied gestalt psychology to gestalt psychotherapy (Henle, 2003; Shane, 2003). Sherrill (1986, p. 54) states: "Gestalt therapists see close kinship between the two gestalt systems; gestalt psychologists deny any meaningful similarity."

Despite the criticisms of gestalt psychologists about the applications of gestalt psychological concepts to gestalt therapy, concepts of figure and ground are important in understanding the theoretical rationale of gestalt therapy. When figures are incomplete or unclear, they are forced into a background that may be distracting for the individual (Polster & Polster, 1973, p. 30). For example, a boy who is afraid of snakes is unable to bring the concept of snakes fully into the foreground or to make a complete figure. When the boy can touch snakes and be unafraid, then the figure is complete.

Wallen (1970) cites three kinds of interferences in developing a complete gestalt, or clear figure against the ground. First, individuals may have poor perceptual contact with others and with themselves. An example would be looking away from a friend when one is talking to her. Second, a complete gestalt is thwarted when expression of needs is blocked. Wanting to express affection to a friend but refraining from doing so is an illustration. Third, repressing feelings or perceptions can prevent the formation of a complete gestalt. Inability to express psychological hurt after someone has insulted an individual may interfere with the development of a full gestalt experience. Such an individual is likely to feel anxious, experience some muscular tension in the stomach, or otherwise be unable to complete the gestalt.

The therapist then works to assist individuals in becoming aware of their tensions, thus completing the gestalt so that the figure is full and complete. In doing so, the therapist helps the patient develop improved contact with people in his world. Taking risks and removing blocks to experiences help individuals discover their own boundaries.

Contact ⤳ Levels of Contact

"Contact is the lifeblood of growth, means for changing oneself, and one's experience of the world" (Polster & Polster, 1973, p. 101). Contact differs from fusion, as contact exists when a sense of separateness is maintained. In fusion, there is no separateness. Although contact is a quality that occurs with other persons and objects, rarely are people aware of the contact they have with others. With contact can come a sense of self as well as a sense of impingement on a boundary. Difficulties in contact are many for children with autism; gestalt therapy can be used to help children develop their contact with others (Audet & Shub, 2007). For Polster and Polster (1973), the challenge for most individuals is how to maintain lively, productive contact with people and things without losing a sense of identity (being fused).

Although much contact is ordinary and occurs frequently during an individual's day, contact episodes in gestalt therapy can be powerful and meaningful. The following excerpt gives an example of the power of therapeutic contact.

> Witness the experience of a lovely young woman, 20 years old, in the center of a group telling about already having been a drug addict and prostitute and, four years earlier, having had a child who had been given up for adoption. Now she was on a new track in life, helping young addicts and going through college herself. In a peak poignant moment, she turned to one of the men in the group and asked him to hold her. He nodded, and after some hesitation, she went over to him and he held her. At this point she let go and cried. After her crying subsided, she looked up, alarmed about what the other women in the group might feel about her being held and being the center of focus in the room. I said that perhaps she could teach the other women something about how to be held. She was obviously at home being held and showed a fluid grace and welcoming quality which wouldn't hurt anyone to learn. For a while, then, she felt calm, remaining in the man's arms but still tuned in to the reactions of the women in the group, who were actually very moved emotionally and were unjudging. She then asked one of the more attractive and guiding women whether she would hold her. The drama was of such force that it was almost inevitable that the woman would indeed want to hold her. She walked over to where the girl was seated and took her into her arms. At this point the final letting go came, and the girl cried more deeply than before. When she was done, her tension had left, she felt unselfconscious and altogether at one with the group. (Polster & Polster, 1973, pp. 104–105)

Levels of contact have been described by Perls (1969b, 1969c, 1970) as five layers of neuroses. To become psychologically mature, individuals must strip off each of the five layers: phony, phobic, impasse, implosive, and explosive. Each layer's removal reveals increasingly impactful contact with the environment.

1. The *phony* layer refers to reacting to others in unauthentic or patterned ways. Examples are "How are you?" and "Have a nice day." More substantial examples include trying to be nice to someone so they will buy something from you.

2. At the *phobic* layer is an avoidance of psychological pain. For example, we may not want to admit to ourselves that an important relationship is over.

3. *Impasse* is the point at which we are afraid to change or move. We may feel very little, only a sense of being stuck. Perls (1970, p. 25) gives an example of a marriage in which the partners are no longer in love; they have ideas of what the other should be but no ideas of what the other is really like. They blame each other and are at an impasse. Individuals feel little internal or external support. This is a particularly significant level for making therapeutic change.

4. At the *implosive* level we experience our feelings, start to become aware of the real self, but may do little about the feelings.

5. Contact with the *explosive* layer is authentic and without pretense. For Perls it was necessary to experience the explosive to become truly alive and authentic. The example of the young woman on page 247 illustrates the experiencing of the explosive layer.

Contact Boundaries

Contact boundaries are the process of connecting to or separating from other or objects. More specifically, *I-boundaries* are those that distinguish between one person and another, a person and an object, or the person and a quality of the person (Polster & Polster, 1973, pp. 107–108). I-boundaries are formed by an individual's life experiences. Polster and Polster distinguish vantage points from which I-boundaries can be described: body-boundaries, value-boundaries, familiarity-boundaries, and expressive-boundaries.

Body-boundaries are those that may restrict sensations or place them off limits. Polster and Polster (1973, pp. 115–116) describe a man with a complaint of impotence who was at first aware only of head movements and became more and more aware of a trembling sensation in his legs that led to a sense of peacefulness in his body. Thus, his body-boundary was extended.

Value-boundaries refer to values we hold that we are resistant to changing. When a man who holds antiabortion values must deal with the unwanted pregnancy of an unmarried 17-year-old daughter, value boundaries may be challenged, possibly changed, or possibly reinforced.

Familiarity-boundaries refer to events that are often repeated but may not be thought about or challenged. Examples include going to the same job every day, taking the same route to work every day, or interacting in a stereotyped way with an associate. If an individual loses a job or experiences the rejection of a marriage partner, the challenge to familiarity-boundaries can be devastating.

Expressive-boundaries are learned at an early age. We learn not to yell, not to whine, not to touch, and so forth. In the United States, men have often been taught not to cry. For a man to be in contact with important others, it may be necessary to extend his expressive-boundary.

Contact Boundary Disturbances

Occasionally the boundary between self and others becomes vague, disintegrates, or is otherwise disturbed (Clarkson, 2004). Sometimes an individual keeps out nourishing and helpful aspects of objects or others. In one sense, the individual is out of balance, and needs are not being met. If the contact with objects or

Boundary- Resmicrs Us

others is resisted, the interaction with the object or other may follow one of these five patterns: introjection, projection, retroflection, deflection, and confluence (Polster & Polster, 1973).

Introjection refers to swallowing whole or accepting others' views without reviewing them. For example, children often take their parents' opinions as fact rather than as values. As children grow older, they introject their parents' views less frequently. Doing so may be appropriate at some times, but not at others. Introjection can be healthy or pathological, depending on the circumstances.

Projection refers to the dismissing or disowning of aspects of ourselves by assigning them to others. Often feelings of guilt or anger may lead individuals to project blame onto someone else. By doing so, the individual may feel better temporarily, but full contact with others is reduced. In projection, aspects of the self are attributed to others, thus extending the boundary between self and others. Blaming a professor for failing an exam for which an individual did not study is an example of projection.

Retroflection consists of doing to ourselves what we want to do to someone else, or it can refer to doing things for ourselves that we want others to do for us. The statement "I can do it myself" when we want others to help us is an example of retroflection. Although this behavior is designed to make us feel self-sufficient, we may feel alone and cut off from others. In retroflection, a function that is originally directed from an individual toward others changes directions and returns to the individual. In an extreme example, suicide becomes a substitute for murder. More symbolically, biting one's nails can be a substitute for aggression toward others or biting off their heads. In this way, the nail biter symbolically treats himself as he wants to treat others.

Deflection refers to varying degrees of avoidance of contact. The person who does not get to the point, who is overly polite, or talks constantly is deflecting—avoiding contact. Other examples include talking about something rather than talking to someone or substituting mild emotions for strong ones. Particularly at the beginning of the therapeutic process, it is common for patients to deflect—to describe their problems abstractly or as if they belong to another person, or to include irrelevant details. Avoiding physical contact is an example of deflecting contact.

Confluence occurs when the boundary between one's self and others becomes muted or lessened. In relationships there may be a perception that both individuals have the same feelings and thoughts, when in fact the individuals have become less aware of their own feelings and values. People who feel a strong need to be accepted may experience confluence; they relinquish their true feelings and opinions for the acceptance of others. Thus, knowing how they truly feel or think is difficult for them.

O'Leary (1997) compares confluence with empathy. In doing so, she draws person-centered and gestalt therapy closer together. Healthy confluence can be experienced as empathy toward individuals or groups. Unhealthy confluence may serve to isolate individuals from others, as they agree with others without unconditional positive regard or understanding. Clients can experience the healthy expression of confluence by therapists as empathic understanding. O'Leary et al. (1998) show how person-centered gestalt groups can be useful by modeling and teaching empathy, confluence, and other gestalt approaches in training therapists.

Gestalt therapists assume that contact is healthy and necessary for satisfactory psychological functioning. Introjection, projection, retroflection, deflection, and confluence are ways of diminishing, avoiding, or otherwise resisting contact. In judging whether these are used in a healthy or unhealthy way, Frew (1988) uses two major criteria. He wants to know if individuals are aware of what they are doing and how their particular style works for them. Also, he wants to assess whether the style lets individuals meet their current needs. Awareness of what they are doing and how their needs are being met is an indication of the degree of contact they have with their boundaries with other people and other things. Both in individual and group therapy, gestalt therapists are attuned to how individuals avoid psychological contact with themselves or with others.

Awareness

Awareness of oneself is an important part of gestalt personality theory, referring to contact within individuals themselves, as well as with others and objects (Clarkson, 2004). Polster and Polster (1973) identify four types of awareness: (1) *Awareness of sensations and actions* pertains to sensing through seeing, hearing, touching, or other senses and then expressing oneself through movement or vocal expression; (2) *awareness of feelings* concerns awareness of both emotional feelings and physical feelings such as sweaty palms or shortness of breath; (3) *awareness of wants* refers to awareness of desires for future events to take place, such as to graduate from college or to win the lottery; and (4) *awareness of values and assessments* concerns larger units of experience than those mentioned, including how one values others, social and spiritual issues, and other assessments of events related to these. *Awareness* refers to what is happening now rather than what is remembered.

To be fully aware is to be in contact with one's boundaries. In the following description of Tom, Polster and Polster (1973) give an example of how a patient is helped to become more aware of sensations and actions, feelings, and wants. It helps illustrate the value gestalt therapists place on the development of awareness.

A simple example of following awarenesses from moment to moment is this illustration from a therapy session. The session started with Tom's awareness of his tight jaw and moved through several intermediate steps to a loosening up of his speaking mannerisms and then to the recovery of some childhood memories. Tom, a minister, felt that he could not pronounce words as he would like to. His voice had a metallic tone and he turned out his words like a brittle robot. I noticed an odd angle to his jaw and asked him what he felt there. He said he felt tight. So I asked him to exaggerate the movements of his mouth and jaw. He felt very inhibited about this and described his awareness first of embarrassment, then stubbornness. He remembered that his parents used to nag him about speaking clearly and he would go out of his way not to. At this point he became aware of tightness in his throat. He was speaking with muscular strain, forcing out his voice rather than using the support which his breathing could give him. So, I asked Tom to bring more air into his speech, showing him how to coordinate speaking with breathing by using a little more air and by trying to feel the air as a source of support. His coordination was faulty, though so faulty, as to border on stuttering. When I asked him whether he had ever stuttered, he looked startled, became aware of his coordination troubles, and then remembered what he had until then forgotten that he had stuttered until he was six or seven. He recalled a scene from a day when he had been three or four years old; his mother was phoning from some distant place and was asking him what he wanted. He tried to say, "ice cream," but his mother misunderstood and thought he said, "I scream" and took it to mean that he was going to scream at his brother and she became infuriated with him. He recalled still another scene. His mother was in the bathroom and he heard what at first he thought was her laughter. He was startled when he realized it was not laughter at all; she was crying hysterically. Tom remembered once again the horrible feeling of incongruity. As he recounted the story he also became aware of his own feelings of confusion both in being misunderstood by his mother and by misunderstanding her. Having recovered the old sensations, his speech became more open and his jaw softened too. He felt relieved and renewed. (Polster & Polster, 1973, pp. 212–213)

Theories in Action

The Present

Prior and future events are seen through the present. The present is also important because only here can an individual's bodily and sensory systems be seen. Yontef (2007) sees many advantages of focusing on the immediate moment so that the patient can experience self-acceptance, feel awareness of the moment, and a commitment to what emerges. When a patient talks about an event, the individual is distanced from the event and is not in the present. Although the present is most important, past history and future plans are also considered. gestalt therapists often assess ways in which the past and future are stated in the present.

One way of examining how the past affects the present is through the concept of *unfinished business* (Joyce & Sills, 2001). This refers to feelings from the past that have been unexpressed but are dealt with in the present. The feelings may be of anger, hatred, guilt, fear, and so forth, or they may be memories or fantasies that are still within the individual. Sometimes unfinished business may take the form of an obsession with money, sex, or some other issue. By working through unfinished business, individuals are completing a gestalt. When closure has been accomplished, the preoccupation with the past is completed. Handlon and Fredericson (2007) discuss a similar concept, *unfinished pleasures*, being able to complete something that is enjoyable that has been left undone so one can experience the joy of the activity.

In the last case, Tom brings the past into the present. His tight jaw reminds him of being nagged by his parents about speaking clearly. It brings him back to unfinished business about his mother's misinterpretation of his attempt to say "ice cream" and his feeling of incongruity when he realized his mother was not laughing but crying. Moving the past into the present enabled Tom to feel a sense of relief. The unfinished business was finished. Notice in this example that Tom does not talk *about* his mother but rather feels the situation in the therapy hour. As Yontef and Jacobs (2011) point out, it is important to be in the present where emotions and nonverbal behavior can be attended to, so that the past can be brought into the present.

Theory of Gestalt Psychotherapy

Gestalt therapy has as its basic goal the development of growth and personal integration through awareness. This is done through the establishment of a good therapeutic relationship. Given this goal, the therapeutic role is different from that in other therapies, with an emphasis on the present and utilization of awareness. In gestalt therapy, much assessment is through the therapist's moment-to-moment observation of the patient. Many observations provide a useful overview of the problem for both patient and therapist. Resulting from this assessment are procedures to enhance the patient's awareness, both verbal and nonverbal. Integrating approaches to awareness takes creativity and experience.

Goals of Therapy

Perls (1969b, p. 26) stated that the goal of therapy is to help individuals mature and grow. Implied in this definition (Passons, 1975) is the emphasis on self-responsibility, helping patients depend on themselves rather than on others (Perls, 1969b). Therapy should assist patients in seeing that they can do much more than they think they can. Thus, patients become more self-aware and move toward self-actualization.

Implicit in the goal of maturity and growth is that of achieving integration. Perls (1973, p. 26) stated, "The man who can live in concernful contact with his society, neither being swallowed up by it nor withdrawing from it completely, is the well integrated man." Integration implies that a person's feelings, perceptions, thoughts, and body processes are part of a larger whole (Gary Yontef, personal communication, September 1, 1998). When a person is not fully integrated, there are voids and the individual is likely to experience contact boundary disturbances. Perls (1948) believed that the integration of previously alienated parts was an extremely important goal of psychotherapy.

Basic to maturity, growth, and integration is the development of awareness (Yontef & Jacobs, 2011). Perls (1969b, p. 16) put it this way: "Awareness per se—by and of itself—can be curative." He believed that with full awareness the organism or individual would regulate itself and function optimally. Fully aware individuals are aware of their environment, are responsible for their choices, and accept themselves.

Zinker (1978, pp. 96–97) outlines in more detail the ways in which gestalt therapy helps individuals become more fully aware of themselves and their environment.

- Individuals develop fuller awareness of their bodies, feelings, and environment.
- Individuals own their own experiences rather than projecting them onto others.
- Individuals learn to be aware of their own needs and skills in order to satisfy themselves without violating the rights of others.
- Fuller contact with sensations (smelling, tasting, touching, hearing, and seeing) allows individuals to savor all aspects of themselves.
- Rather than whining, blaming, or guilt making, individuals experience their power and ability to support themselves.
- Individuals become sensitive to their surroundings yet are able to protect themselves from those parts of the environment that may be dangerous.
- Responsibility for actions and consequences is a part of greater awareness.

As therapy progresses (Zinker, 1978), individuals gradually feel more comfortable in experiencing their own energy and using it in a productive and complete way. These are general goals of gestalt therapy. By feeding back observations and encouraging the client to become more aware, the therapist helps clients achieve their goals.

Gestalt therapy is particularly appropriate for individuals who are inhibited. Examples are people who are overly socialized or feel restrained or constricted in some way. Those who are perfectionistic, phobic, or feel depressed may be inhibiting their awareness of themselves and others. Shepherd (1970) warns that as individuals get in touch with themselves and experience dissatisfaction with conventional goals or relationships, they may find themselves frustrated with much social interaction and find less in common with others who do not share their growth or awareness.

The Therapeutic Relationship

For gestalt therapy to be effective, a good therapeutic relationship is important. Gestalt therapists have been influenced by the work of Carl Rogers, Martin Buber, and more recently, the concepts found in intersubjectivity theory, an approach related to self psychology. All of these focus on ways to understand the client and to communicate this understanding to the client. Gestalt interventions (to be described later) are used within the context of the client–therapist relationship.

Being attuned to the client's experience was essential for Carl Rogers. Gestalt therapists concur, agreeing with Rogers's emphasis on empathy. Being genuine and showing the client that you understand is an important aspect of therapy (Elliott & Greenberg, 2007). The empathic responding of the therapist provides continuing support to the client. Additionally, clients support themselves through their own motivation for therapy, intelligence, and commitment to therapy (Yontef, 1995).

To bring about growth through awareness, a meaningful relationship with the therapist is essential (Yontef, 2007; Yontef & Jacobs, 2011). Buber's (1965) discussion of the I–thou relationship has been important in understanding the gestalt view of a dialogic relationship. The dialogue exists to meet or understand the other person, not to do something to the person. In this dialogue, the individual becomes fully aware of the other person while still being aware of his or her own separate existence. The dialogue occurs; it is not directed toward an outcome. In the dialogue the therapist is genuine yet focused on the patient's needs. The dialogic relationship is fully described by Hycner and Jacobs (1995), who are influenced by the work of Buber and intersubjectivity theorists. Intersubjectivity theorists have written within the framework of psychoanalysis to emphasize the importance of a two-way relationship between patient and therapist.

Assessment in Gestalt Psychotherapy

Traditionally, gestalt therapy has not addressed itself in a systematic way to diagnosis or assessment. Typically, gestalt therapists are attending to moments in therapy that include patients' bodily movements, feelings, sensations, or other content. Joyce and Sills (2001) recommend a diagnostic approach to gestalt therapy in which client and therapist work to identify problems that can be addressed. They have designed a brief "client assessment sheet" that assesses broad units of patients' awareness and disturbances of contact boundaries. Yontef (1988) states that gestalt therapy by itself does not provide sufficient diagnostic information to help patients with serious problems such as narcissistic or borderline disorders. He believes that developmental insights drawn from object relations and intersubjectivity theory provide a background that can be integrated with the application of gestalt therapeutic processes. Yontef (2001) illustrates this as he describes childhood issues for individuals with schizoid functioning (difficulty in developing emotional bonds with others). Because gestalt therapists differ in how they integrate other therapies into their work, gestalt approaches to assessment differ widely.

Gestalt therapists can use a cyclical approach to assessment (Clarkson, 2004). Melnick and Nevis (1998) explain how the experiencing cycle can be used to diagnose types of disorders by attending to five phases: sensation/awareness, mobilization, contact, resolution/closure, and withdrawal.

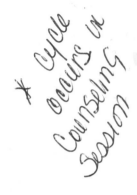

Sensation/awareness involves taking in experience through the senses. Patients with a borderline disorder often have difficulty maintaining relationships because of distorted intake of sensations.

Mobilization refers to moving from awareness to forming a desire or want. Individuals with phobias and other anxieties may avoid actions or events rather than move toward an action. A person who wants to visit Paris from the United States may not do so because of fear of flying. Such individuals may be reluctant to take actions to act on wants.

Contact produces emotional arousal and implies contact with self and others. The individual who functions histrionically may be very emotional but may not be aware of his feelings or be able to relate well emotionally to others. He may need to slow down and become more aware of not just raw feelings but also feelings about self and others.

Resolution/closure takes place as individuals disengage from an experience. Individuals with posttraumatic stress disorder have difficulty moving from a traumatic event (such as a robbery or a rape) to other events. Gestalt therapists help such individuals acknowledge that they must resolve the problem and find ways to express feelings about the problem to develop closure.

Withdrawal takes place as the experiencing cycle draws to a close and moves toward other contact experiences. In a sense, it is the end of the resolution/closure phase. Just as those with posttraumatic stress are likely to have difficulty with resolution/closure, so are they apt to experience difficulty with withdrawal. It is difficult for such individuals to move on to other experiences.

Although gestalt therapists are making greater and greater use of traditional diagnostic categories and need to do so for administrative and insurance reimbursement purposes, they also are able to use a variety of approaches to conceptualize and assess. Because many gestalt therapists use other therapeutic systems such as relational forms of psychoanalysis (Jacobs, 2005) as part of the assessment process, assessment techniques of gestalt therapists are likely to be varied.

Therapeutic Change

In gestalt therapy, both patient and therapist are fully present, allowing for the development of a fully functioning I–thou relationship. The therapist's nondefensive posture and awareness of self and of the patient provide an atmosphere for change (Yontef & Fuhr, 2005). Change occurs by exploring the patient's wishes (Yontef & Jacobs, 2011). If there is frustration, the therapist investigates it. If a patient is reluctant to follow a suggestion for exploration by the therapist, the therapist gently explores the reluctance rather than pushing the patient to follow the therapist's instructions. Beisser (1970) notes that the process of change is a paradoxical one, stating: *"Change occurs when one becomes what he is, not when he tries to become what he is not"* (p. 77).

When patients reach an impasse in therapy and have difficulty changing, Perls (1969b) has suggested that the patient be stuck and stay with the feeling of no progress. Perls believed that some people are unable to make progress in therapy because they are afraid of what might happen. A patient might say, "If I really look at my friendship with Harry, there won't be any friendship, and I won't have any friends." The gestalt therapist helps the patient to experience the blockage and to experiment with, or fantasize about, what would happen if the patient explores his relationship with Harry. Working through such an impasse is an important part of the change process in gestalt therapy.

The change process can be further articulated by examining Miriam Polster's (1987) description of a three-stage sequence of integration. In the first stage, *discovery*, patients may get a new view of themselves or of an old problem or situation. In the second stage, *accommodation*, patients learn that they have choices and can try out different behaviors. In this process, therapeutic support is particularly important. In the third stage, *assimilation*, patients progress from choosing and trying out new behaviors to learning how to make changes in their environment. At this point they are apt to act assertively in obtaining what they want from others. Although patients do not move neatly through these three stages, and some may not fully experience each stage, Polster's model for client growth does provide an overview of the change process.

Theories in Action

Enhancing Awareness

The purpose of this section is to show different ways that gestalt therapists use to bring about changes in client awareness within the context of a therapeutic relationship. Gestalt therapists may use techniques such as cognitive and behavioral methods, but they are used as an experiment to help the patient learn by doing something different. In focusing on the goal of achieving patient awareness, gestalt therapists have developed many exercises and experiments to bring about client growth. Exercises are specific techniques that are used in group or individual counseling. Experiments are innovations of the therapist that grow out of the struggles patients have when they encounter an impasse or have difficulty in achieving awareness. When applied in therapy, exercises become experiments as the client learns new ways of learning or of achieving awareness. Some methods are relatively simple, involving commenting on or emphasizing awareness. Others involve enhancing awareness through verbal or nonverbal behaviors. Some exercises and experiments increase awareness of self; others increase awareness of other people. The dialogue with oneself, often using another chair, is a means of becoming aware of different parts of oneself. *Enacting*—that is, playing out parts of oneself or others—can be a dramatic gestalt experiment to bring about change. Gestalt therapists have been creative in how they deal with dreams as a means of furthering awareness. Gestalt therapists also make use of homework to encourage growing awareness throughout the patient's life, not just in the therapeutic session.

Awareness statements and questions. Sometimes awareness can be enhanced by relatively straightforward questions (Passons, 1975, p. 61). For example, if a patient is talking about her phone conversation with her mother, the therapist may simply say, "What are you aware of now?" to focus on what is happening to the patient in the present. Sometimes the therapist may focus the awareness a little more closely, as in "Mel, can you be aware of what you are doing when you are sitting in this chair?" or the therapist may go a step further and use a statement that starts with "I am aware that you" (Passons, 1975, p. 63); thus, "Mel, I'm aware that as you sit in the chair you're looking at your knees." Sometimes it may be appropriate to ask the patient to use a sentence such as "Now I am aware" to bring about more awareness; for example, "Mel, as you sit there looking at your knees, could you use the phrase, 'Now I am aware that' and finish it and go right into another phrase, such as 'Now I'm aware of the dictionary on your desk, now I am aware of the lamp behind you'?" and so forth. Such statements and questions can be used relatively easily in the course of therapeutic work.

Emphasizing awareness. Sometimes it is helpful simply to ask a client to repeat a behavior, as in "Please wring your hands together again." In gestalt terms, this makes the figure clearer and more separate from the ground. Similarly, requesting that the patient "stay with" the feeling he is experiencing may sharpen awareness by bringing the figure to the foreground. Exaggeration of a behavior also emphasizes the patient's present awareness. For example, it may be appropriate to ask a son who is being critical of his mother to emphasize the critical tone in his voice, thus making him more in touch with the critical quality within his voice. Levitsky and Perls suggest the phrase "May I feed you a sentence?" (1970, p. 148). This remark lets the therapist pick out a particular portion of the present encounter that the therapist would like the patient to increase awareness of. Reversal is a similar but opposite approach from exaggeration in increasing awareness (Levitsky & Perls, 1970, p. 146). In this technique, a patient who is usually soft-spoken might be asked to increase the loudness of her voice and to sound brash. In this manner, awareness of her soft-spokenness is enhanced.

Enhancing awareness through language. Words that are likely to give the patient responsibility for himself and his growth are to be preferred over indirect and vague words. For example, changing pronouns such as *it* and *you* to *I* brings responsibility for the situation to the individual. Passons gives the following example.

> [*Patient:*] I didn't have very many dates this year. Next year it will be different.
>
> [*Therapist:*] It will be different? Who are you talking about?
>
> [*Patient:*] Me, I'll be different.
>
> [*Therapist:*] What will you do differently? (1975, p. 78)

In this situation, the therapist helps the patient take responsibility for getting dates rather than waiting for dates to happen.

Some verbs distract from the patient's ability to increase awareness and responsibility. Passons gives three common examples of these (1975, pp. 81–87):

> *"Can't versus won't."* Often the use of *can't* gives the patient the feeling that he is unable to do something, when it is more accurate to say "I won't," meaning, "I choose not to do this for any of various reasons."
>
> *"Need versus want."* Usually a list of wants is much longer than a list of needs. It is helpful to use the word *want,* as in "I want to be popular," rather than "I need to be popular." The former is more accurate, less urgent, and less anxiety provoking.
>
> *"Have to versus choose to."* Like *need,* *have to* implies an urgency, demand, and anxiety that *choose to* does not. *Choose to* gives the patient responsibility for the choice.

Just as experimenting with different verbs can be helpful, changing questions to statements is often useful in emphasizing the responsibility of the patient.

Some questions are really declarations rather than questions. They diminish patient responsibility, thus limiting patient awareness.

> *[Patient:]* You know me, don't you think I'd be better off if I didn't go to school next year?
>
> *[Therapist:]* You may have given your own answer. Change that question around to a statement and let's see what you have to say.
>
> *[Patient:]* Going to school next year is not right for me. Not now, anyhow. (Passons, 1975, p. 91)

These are some of the more common examples of language that diminishes awareness and responsibility. When appropriate, gestalt therapists may help patients develop self-awareness by listening carefully to language usage.

Awareness through nonverbal behavior. Attending to nonverbal behavior can be particularly helpful for the gestalt therapist. Passons gives four reasons for attending to nonverbal behaviors in therapy (1975, pp. 101–102). First, each behavior is an expression of a person at a given moment. Second, people generally are more attuned to listening to what they are saying rather than noticing what they are doing with their bodies. Third, nonverbal behaviors are usually spontaneous, whereas verbal behaviors are often thought out in advance. Fourth, nonverbal and verbal expressions match in individuals who function in an integrated way. Parts of the body that therapists may respond to include mouth, jaw, voice, eyes, nose, neck, shoulders, arms, hands, torso, legs, feet, and the entire body.

> *[Client:]* The pressure is really on for getting into college. It seems like there's nothing I can do without college.
>
> *[Therapist:]* And how do you respond to all this pressure?
>
> *[Client:]* I'm not as excited about college as everyone else is, so I'm not doing much about it. (Folds arms across chest.)
>
> *[Therapist:]* Jo Anne, could you concentrate on your arms and hold them there?
>
> *[Client:]* O.K.
>
> *[Therapist:]* What do you feel in them?
>
> *[Client:]* They're kind of tight … sort of like I'm holding on.
>
> *[Therapist:]* Holding onto what?
>
> *[Client:]* To me. If I don't, they'll shove me all over the place. They don't know how I can hold on. (Passons, 1975, pp. 117–118)

Passons (1975) comments that Jo Anne is resisting pressures for fear others will point her in a direction that may not be right for her. As she becomes more aware of her investment in her resistance, she may find out why she is objecting to going to college. A clearer decision between going to college and not going to college may result.

Awareness of self and others. Sometimes individuals can understand themselves and others by "becoming" the other person. This approach is often used in racial relations workshops in which people of different races may be asked to play each other's roles. Asking a patient to be his mother and say what his mother would say if the patient came in at 2 in the morning is often more helpful than asking the patient, "What would your mother think if you came in at

2:00 A.M.?" In this way the patient develops a fuller awareness of the differentiation between himself and others.

Sometimes it is also helpful for patients to be more aware of parts of themselves, such as feelings or nonverbal behavior (Passons, 1975). For example, a patient may say, "Sometimes I can be so cold to Marcie." The therapist may reply, "Be that cold self with coldness in your voice, and talk to Marcie as if she were here." Sometimes a therapist may wish to employ a similar technique with a body part. For example, a client who is pointing his finger at the therapist while he talks to her may hear from the therapist, "Let me hear what that finger has to say. It's pointing at me vigorously. Please put some words to it, if you can." In a vast variety of situations like these, therapists may choose to have clients split off a part of themselves or become someone else in order to become more aware of themselves.

Enhancing awareness of feelings. Attending to emotions in gestalt therapy is particularly important because emotions provide energy to mobilize a person and provide an orientation to those aspects of the environment that are important to the person (Passons, 1975). Although gestalt therapists may respond empathically to expressed feelings, they have also developed exercises they frequently use to further the expression of feelings. Polster and Polster discuss how feelings are sometimes directed against the wrong person or not expressed well (1973, p. 226). They give the example of Phyllis, whose resentment and anger toward her boss were out of proportion to his influence in her life. Phyllis received little satisfaction by expressing her resentment toward her boss in therapy. A more creative approach was needed to help Phyllis overcome her impasse with regard to angry feelings about her boss.

> One day I realized that Phyllis was a person who needed a lot of special attention and I asked her whether she was accustomed to getting it. She remembered two men she had been in love with who had really given her "star" treatment. In both cases, though, she wound up abruptly rejected. After the second time she realized she had never permitted herself to get the special treatment she wanted. And so I asked her, in fantasy, to express herself to these two men. In doing so she was able to get out of the complex of rage, loss, grudge and resolve which she had previously been left with and around which she had organized such a substantial chunk of her life. By talking to these men in her fantasy, Phyllis aired her unfinished feelings. Following this deeply moving experience, she grew calm and no longer felt the sharp resentment towards her boss. She was able, finally, to reduce him to a more appropriate level of importance in her life. Phyllis had moved—out of the neurotic system in which she had made her boss the center and into a system which was more organically suited to her feelings. (Polster & Polster, 1973, p. 227)

Awareness through self-dialogue. Because integrated functioning is an important goal of gestalt therapy, gestalt therapists attend to those aspects of the individual that are not integrated. Polster and Polster see each individual as a "never-ending sequence of polarities" (1973, p. 61). Conflict in polarities often results from introjection. For example, if a person introjects parental religious values that are different from religious values that she identifies as her own, it is often useful to project the parental values outward so that they can be dealt with. By having dialogues between opposite tendencies, increased integration results and patient self-criticism is likely to decrease.

The conflict between the *top dog* and the *underdog* is that between the righteous, moralistic, and demanding person, often seen as the "critical parent," versus the helpless, weak, and passive side of the individual (Strümpfel & Goldman, 2002).

These two parts of us struggle constantly for control. The top dog tells us what we should do, and the underdog procrastinates and puts off doing. The underdog can be more powerful than the top dog because it can interfere with achieving therapeutic change. Such conflicts lend themselves to dialogues within oneself.

Self-dialogues can be done by having an individual take each role of the polarity and express it from her chair. However, it is more common to use the two-chair method. Used either in individual or group therapy, the individual takes one role in one chair (for example, the top dog) and plays the other role (for example, the underdog) in another chair. As the individual changes roles, she moves to the other chair. The therapist may call attention to what has been said or how it was said. In this way the therapist helps the patient get in touch with the feeling that she may have been denying. Aspects of the patient are experienced rather than talked about. Dialogues can be used in diverse situations such as one part of the body versus the other (one hand versus the other), or a dialogue can be between a patient and another person or between the self and an object such as a building or an accomplishment. For a therapist, working with such dialogues requires experience and training.

Elliott et al. (2004) describe the empty-chair or two-chair approach in working with the critical self (top dog) in great detail. They separate two-chair work into six sections to show how the therapist recognizes when to initiate the two-chair work and how to start the two-chair dialogue. They then discuss how to make the split deeper and move to partial resolution. They explain how to soften the critical self and then work toward full resolution of the conflict. Not only do they show how to work with internal self-criticism, but they also illustrate how to use the two-chair technique in working with problems that the client has with other people.

The example below uses a portion of a therapist's dialogue with Lynn to illustrate how the therapist moves from a comment Lynn makes to introducing the two-chair technique and initiating it with her (Elliott et al., 2004).

Theories in Action

> *Lynn:* I want to be myself and express what I feel. (p. 222)

This statement alerts the therapist that Lynn is expressing her experiencing self. The therapist goes on to reflect Lynn's experience using the person-centered approach described in Chapter 6.

> *Therapist (gently):* Yeah, it's like being yourself and saying what you want is really difficult for you.
>
> *Lynn:* Yeah, you really hit the spot. (sobbing)
>
> *[Therapist:]* Yeah, just take a breath.
>
> *Lynn:* You really touched something when you said "be myself."
>
> *[Therapist:]* I guess there's a feeling of closing yourself down.
>
> *Lynn:* Yeah, it really worries me, too. Like don't I have self-respect?
>
> *[Therapist:]* Yeah, that is the other side talking, but there's something about, that it's bad to be yourself.
>
> *Lynn:* Yeah, it's bad to speak my mind, because (sniff), and I know it comes from my parents saying it, and then also getting it from Jim (her husband). I have a hard time, you know; even though it is in my mind, I want to express it, but (pause) I hold back. (p. 224)

At this point, the client is being critical of herself. The therapist recognizes the split between the critical and passive sides of Lynn. The therapist now goes on to show Lynn how to use the two chairs in such a way that the flow of therapy is not interrupted.

> [*Therapist (gently):*] Why don't we try something? Can you come over here for a second? (points to a chair the therapist has placed directly across from the client)
>
> *Lynn:* Sure. (moves to critic chair)
>
> [*Therapist:*] You are kind of saying this is how you hold yourself back, how you restrain yourself, so maybe we could work with how you do that. Can you try doing that, actually kind of put whoever is pushing her back here, if it's your parents, or Jim, or you, making it hard to be yourself, whatever feels right. Hold her back. Stop her from being herself. (p. 225)

Now Lynn consents to using the two chairs. The therapist moves the second chair facing Lynn's chair. In a two-chair dialogue, the therapist encourages the client to be specific in enacting the problem. Lynn can then experience how she controls and criticizes herself. Lynn talks to the therapist using her critical self.

> *Lynn:* Don't say those things, don't make people laugh at you. If you say that, people will laugh at you. You don't know anything!
>
> [*Therapist:*] Tell her, "You don't know what you are talking about."
>
> *Lynn:* Yeah, you're no good, what comes out of your mouth is senseless, it doesn't count, it's just stupidity. You're stupid and you don't make any sense.
>
> [*Therapist:*] OK, can you switch? (Client moves to experiencer chair.) How do you feel when she tells you that?
>
> *Lynn (as experiencer):* Uh, you're wrong. (p. 226)

Lynn gets involved in the dialogue quickly. This allows the therapist to continue the dialogue and to help Lynn become aware of feelings underlying her critical self.

> [*Therapist:*] You feel she is wrong, that leaves you feeling dismissed, hurt. (pause) Stay with whatever is happening inside.
>
> *Lynn:* I want to say how I feel.
>
> [*Therapist:*] You want to say what you feel, what you want. Tell her what you feel.
>
> *Lynn:* I feel that I do count... (p. 227)

In this brief dialogue, the therapist helps Lynn to separate two important parts of herself and experience these two aspects of herself. When using the two-chair technique, therapists are careful to assess the client's readiness to work in this way. If clients find the two-chair dialogue frightening or unhelpful, therapists often move back to a discussion of the problem.

Awareness through enactment. Dramatizing some part of the patient's existence is the basis of enactment. A patient who says that he feels like a wimpy little dog might be asked to act like a wimpy little dog, to whine, to paw at the therapist, and to lower his head. Enactment may be of a previous experience or of a characteristic, like wimpy. When done in groups, the enactment may involve several group members. Enactment is a bold approach to awareness and must be done in a way that helps patients become more aware of characteristics or unfinished business, not to embarrass them. In the next example, Miriam Polster describes an enactment concerning trust of women.

> For example, in one workshop, there was a huge bear of a man who looked the modern equivalent of Falstaff, a gigantic frame, a large belly, a ruddy face, and a hearty manner. In spite of his huge bulk and a physical power so grand that he dominated the visual quality of the workshop scene, Hal was silent most of the time. When he did speak, he spoke with darting glances, a great self-protective hunching of his shoulders, and addressing no one in particular. A look of fear was in his face and a sense of vagueness and nondirection in his demeanor. Hal looked as though he feared an attack at any moment. When asked about his silence, he said that he had great difficulty in dealing with bossy women, especially when they are in the role of authority. He said he would not turn his back on one, that he wouldn't trust one to be behind him. Thus, Hal expressed his resistance in his silence, his distrust, and his hunched shoulders. I let him use his hunched shoulders, his silence and his distrust. First, I got up and walked behind Hal and asked him what it was like for him now that I was behind his back. He was sitting on the floor. When he turned around to confront me, he put his hands down, as though crouching. So, the resistance moved into a crouch. I walked around again, searching for a way we could use his silent, distrustful crouch. This time I climbed on top of his back, crouching on top of him, and I asked Hal what he could do with me. He was free for a whole range of reactions, including flicking me off like a cigarette ash. If I had sensed that was the direction in which his energized resistance would go, I would not have gotten up on him. But he said, "Well, I could ride you around the room." He had chosen his own medicine. Riding me around the room put him in control. Even though it looked like the woman was on top, Hal had flipped the sense of dominance over to himself. He also proceeded to turn a threatening situation into a playful one, using his strength, developing great delight and a sense of union within himself, with me, and with the group, which had become aroused by seeing him ignited. The roars and the fun confirmed his power. For me it was like a jolly ride on an elephant. Hal was the mover, determining much of the speed, direction and playfulness. By the time we got back to our original places and I got off his back, he was able to laugh and say in new freshness that he no longer felt cautious with me and expected he would be heard from during the rest of the workshop, which indeed he was, becoming a central figure in the group. Thus through accentuating and mobilizing his resistance, Hal unharnessed its power, making it unique and timely to our interaction. Instead of being dominated by a woman, he could dominate; instead of maintaining a stalemate of inaction, filling it with suspicion and projection, he entered an actual contest which had its own rich detail and unpredictable outcome. (1973, pp. 55–56)

In this example, Miriam Polster illustrates confidence in gestalt awareness techniques, as well as a playful sense of humor. Out of context, such behavior from a therapist seems odd and inappropriate. Within the context of gestalt therapy, it is therapeutically consistent and helpful to Hal in dealing with issues concerning trusting women, as awareness is enhanced through words, bodily positioning, and movement.

Awareness through dreams. For Perls, dream work was one of the best ways to promote personal integration. Perls (1970) saw the dream as possibly the most spontaneous expression of an individual. Perls's method was not to interpret the dream but to have the patient relive the dream in the present and to play various parts of it. By playing the various persons and objects in the dream, the patient is identifying with parts of the self that have been alienated. Perls would often use the two-chair technique to have the patient play out parts of the dream, which would then have a dialogue with each other.

Enright (1970, p. 121) gives the example of a restless, manipulative woman who dreamed of walking down a crooked path in a forest of straight trees. He asked her to become one of these trees. This made her feel more serene and deeply rooted. She was able to take these feelings back into her current life and experience the lack of them and the possibilities of accomplishing them. When she became the crooked path, she became teary-eyed and experienced the crookedness in her own life and the possibilities of straightening out, if she chose.

Enright, in Gaines (1979), gives an example of Perls's work with dreams.

> The first time I ever saw him do dream work was in that group. It was very touching, there, this gray-haired fellow, somewhat depressed, 55-year-old psychologist had had a dream about seeing some friends off at a railroad station. Fritz had him go through the dream as himself, as the friends, and as the railroad train. None of it seemed to produce very much. Then Fritz said, "Be the station."
>
> [Patient:] What do you mean, "Be the station"?
>
> Fritz: Just describe the station, only keep saying, "I."
>
> [Patient:] Well, I'm old and dilapidated, not very well cared for, and actually out of date. Please come and go and use me and pay no attention to me. (And he started to cry.)
>
> I was very touched by that, feeling it as part of me, also, I guess. (Gaines, 1979, p. 135)

Another creative approach to dream work is taken by Zinker (1971, 1978, 1991). Rather than have an individual play objects or people in a dream, he has group members do so. This method has the individual first work through the dream, and then a group experiment is devised so that other members of the group as well as the dreamer can profit from playing parts in the dream. Members of the group act out themes that may be particularly appropriate to them. The dreamer experiences the process and progress of the dream, changing action in the dream when appropriate. The dreamer may serve as a director or coach at times or experiment with different outcomes. In Perls's method, the audience participates mainly through observation (and occasional participation), whereas in Zinker's approach the entire group is active in the dream interpretation.

 Awareness outside of therapy: homework. Homework can be assigned that puts individuals in a position of confronting areas that are blocking their emerging awareness. In some cases, individuals are asked to write dialogues between parts of themselves or between parts of their body. Others may be asked to find information or do a specific task that fits congruently with the therapeutic process. As individuals' awareness develops in therapy, they may be ready for more difficult assignments that may help them in becoming more aware of themselves and others, which in turn can provide more material for therapeutic work.

 Awareness of avoidance. When feelings are present in a person, yet the person is not aware of them, the individual is in the process of avoiding them. Avoidance is an active process, not a passive one. An individual may be expending energy to avoid feelings such as happiness, loneliness, fear, or sadness. Expression of feelings is often viewed as doing, whereas avoiding may be seen as not doing by non-gestalt therapists. From a gestalt point of view, an individual who is avoiding is working to adjust herself. Helping patients own their feelings and experience awareness regarding a number of issues may help in reintegrating avoided feelings.

Approaches such as emphasizing awareness, enhancing awareness through language or nonverbal behavior, and self-dialogues can be helpful in assisting people to become aware of their avoidance behaviors.

Integration and Creativity

Because the gestalt focus on the whole person is so broad, all the parts—verbal behavior, nonverbal behavior, emotional feelings—are all attended to and integrated. The approaches to awareness that are described the previous section can be used at any time in the course of therapy.

> Everything the person disowns can be recovered, and the means of this recovery is understanding, playing, becoming these disowned parts, and by letting him play and discover that he already has all this (which he thinks only others can give him), we increase his potential. (Perls, 1969b, p. 37)

Thus, techniques are not done in isolation; they are all directed toward the integration of the whole person. How this is done often depends on the disturbance of the contact boundary. For example, if a person projects anger onto someone or something else, it may be important to attend to the language process. Does the individual use *you* or *it* instead of the more responsible *I*? When a projection is recognized, it then can be accepted, modified, assimilated, and thus integrated. Other boundary disturbances (introjection, retroflection, deflection, and confluence) require different approaches to the integration of the whole person. The creative process by which integration of awarenesses takes place is difficult to describe, and the approaches are boundless in number.

> This woman came in for a first session. She's separated from her husband and is in great mourning about it. She cries a lot. So, she's crying also in the office, but she looks like she's also a spunky woman. But, she's crying in a way that will never give her any kind of satisfaction, or release, or even appreciation of the dimensions of her loss. So, I asked her, instead of trying to stop herself from crying, to see if she could put some words to her crying. A very simple thing that many gestalt therapists would do. I don't remember exactly what words she wound up saying, but as she said it she burst into crying, not just dripping. She then said, "Where am I gonna put all this love that's inside of me?" And I said to her, [speaking in a most reverent tone] "The whole world is dying for it." That just changed the whole tone of her experience. The realization that what she has inside, there's a place for it, all over the world. That it doesn't have to be stuck inside her chest. (Hycner, 1987, p. 55)

The therapeutic process is doubly unique. The unique creative process of the therapist as a person interacts with the unique creative process of the patient (Lobb & Amendt-Lyon, 2003). Erving Polster gives a brief example of the creativity, awe, and aliveness that can take place in therapy.

Polster's reverence for his client is clear. His statement "The whole world is dying for it" comes from his being, his experience, his interaction, and care for the patient. Not fitting into any of the approaches to awareness described previously, it is a creative, spontaneous, and moving comment that changes the tone of the therapy hour at that point. Such a statement is consistent with Buber's "I–thou" relationship or the importance that gestalt therapists attach to the therapeutic relationship.

Risks

Just as gestalt therapy can bring about powerful change through awareness, it also can be misused. George Brown, a prominent gestalt therapist, has said (1988, p. 37): "Of all the therapies, gestalt has the most potential for somebody really being cruel and hurting other people." He warns about therapists being enchanted by the techniques of gestalt therapy without being skeptical of themselves and without having a clear grasp of gestalt theory. Attending to ethics and ethical issues is an important aspect of gestalt therapy (Bernhardtson, 2008). Yontef (1987) worried about the use of "gestalt therapy and," referring to therapists who use portions of gestalt therapy with other theories of therapy without grounding their work in the theory of gestalt therapy. To avoid misuse of gestalt therapy, preparation is paramount.

In discussing preparation to be a gestalt therapist, Resnick (1984) believes therapists should have three parts to their training: personal therapy, academic preparation, and supervision. The therapy should be intensive enough to form a relationship between the beginning therapist (the patient) and the therapist, with self-dialogue an important part of the therapy. The academic preparation should include study of personality theories, theories of psychotherapy, and diagnosis. Supervision should include cognitive and experiential supervision by several gestalt therapists. Such training helps ensure that the therapist is experienced, well grounded in theory, and ethical. The spontaneity of gestalt techniques can be deceptive, erroneously implying that whatever the therapist feels or senses is appropriate. The examples in the following section provide a context for approaches to awareness and integrative techniques in therapy.

Psychological Disorders

Although some gestalt therapists make use of diagnostic categories as shown on page 253, many do not. The methods gestalt therapists use often reflect actions and statements the client makes in the present. In this section, examples are shown of gestalt therapists helping clients with depression, anxiety, posttraumatic stress disorder, and substance abuse. One way of dealing with depression as it emerges in the therapy hour is presented. A therapeutic response to anxiety and staying with anxious feelings when the client wishes to digress is also shown. A gestalt approach to treating posttraumatic stress disorder by reliving the past and completing unfinished business is illustrative of a type of treatment for this disorder. Attending to an addict who has been in recovery for 15 years and having him put words to bodily changes shows an example of a gestalt approach to addiction treatment. These approaches have much in common, using different ways of enhancing patient awareness.

Depression: Woman

Although depression is seen by many non-gestalt therapists as a diagnostic category, gestalt therapists are apt to see the degree of depression fluctuate throughout the session. In the following case, Strümpfel and Goldman (2002) show how two-chair work can be used. The client is a 27-year-old woman who is depressed. Not only is her husband a compulsive gambler, but his father was one also. The client feels responsible for her husband and abandoned by him when he goes out to gamble. On two occasions before starting therapy, the client had left her husband. Her family's response was that "a good wife 'stands by her man'" (p. 207). Here, the therapist uses the two-chair technique to help the client deal with her self-criticism (her top dog). In this excerpt, a shift (softening of the critic or harsh top dog) begins to take shape. (Microinterventions are identified throughout in brackets.)

[Client:] I feel I don't count, that I don't know anything, that I am stupid.

[Therapist:] OK, come back over here (to critic chair). Make her feel stupid. [dramatizing]

[Client:] You don't count, you're stupid, you are worthless.

[Therapist:] Again, make her not count. [exaggeration]

[Client:] You're stupid. It doesn't matter what you say, there's no meaning to what you say; you just don't know anything.

[Therapist:] OK, come back to this chair. How do you feel when she puts you down and ridicules you? [encouraging emotional expression]

[Client:] Oh (sigh), I just feel like she is right and that is just the way it is.

[Therapist:] Do you notice when you say this that your shoulders kind of hunch and you slump in your chair. Hunch over like that some more. What is it like to feel so hopeless? [repetition]

[Client:] It hurts when you talk to me like this (sobbing).

[Therapist:] Yeah, it hurts when she talks to you like this. What do you want from her? [encouraging emotional expression]

[Client:] I want you to accept me unconditionally. I want you to listen to me.

Later in the dialogue,

[Therapist:] Now change back over here (to critic chair). She says she wants to feel she counts and she wants to be heard, accepted. What do you say?

[Client:] Okay, um, yes that is fair. [beginning of softening of critic]

[Therapist:] So, what are you saying, that you understand her need?

[Client:] (crying) Um, yeah, I'm sorry. You don't deserve to be treated like that. [elaboration of softening]

In this dialogue, the therapist helps the client move beyond her feelings of hopelessness to access her primary feelings of sadness and loneliness and accompanying need for approval. Identification and validation of these emotions help to strengthen the self, which allows her to stand up to her critical self. Later in the dialogue, when the client moves into the other chair, her critical self softens and becomes more accepting. As the dialogue ends, the client is beginning to access underlying needs for nurturance.

By the end of the 16-week therapy, the client was no longer depressed and did not feel guilty or responsible when her husband gambled. She showed significant improvement in her self-esteem and interpersonal relationships. (pp. 208–209)

Anxiety: Man

Like treating depression, treating anxiety is done as it occurs in the session. In this example, Naranjo (1970) responds to an expression of anxiety by staying in the moment, despite the patient's attempt to avoid the therapist's requests. Naranjo's comments at the end of the excerpt are instructive in that they deal with the patient's avoiding responsibility for his feeling of gratitude to the therapist.

> *[Patient:]* My heart is pounding. My hands are sweating. I am scared. I remember the time when I worked with you last time and....
>
> *[Therapist:]* What do you want to tell me by going back to last week?
>
> *[Patient:]* I was afraid of exposing myself, and then I felt relieved again, but I think that I didn't come out with the real thing.
>
> *[Therapist:]* Why do you want to tell me that now?
>
> *[Patient:]* I would like to face this fear and bring out whatever it is that I am avoiding.
>
> *[Therapist:]* O.K. That is what you want now. Please go on with your experiences in the moment.
>
> *[Patient:]* I would like to make a parenthesis to tell you that I have felt much better this week.
>
> *[Therapist:]* Could you tell me anything of your experience while making this parenthesis?
>
> *[Patient:]* I feel grateful to you, and I want you to know it.
>
> *[Therapist:]* I get the message. Now please compare these two statements: "I feel grateful," and the account of your well-being this week. Can you tell me what it is you felt that makes you prefer the story to the direct statement of your feeling?
>
> *[Patient:]* If I were to say, "I feel grateful to you," I would feel that I still have to explain.... Oh! Now I know. Speaking of my gratefulness strikes me as too direct. I feel more comfortable in letting you guess, or just making you feel good without letting you know my feeling.

Because of his ambivalence, the patient has avoided expressing and taking responsibility for his feeling of gratitude. In an attempt to please the therapist rather than becoming aware of his desire for the therapist to be pleased, the patient has acted out his feelings instead of disclosing them (Naranjo, 1970, pp. 57–58).

Posttraumatic Stress Disorder: Holocaust Survivor

Traumatic incidents and the behavior resulting from them can be seen in gestalt therapy terms like *unfinished business* (Serok, 1985). In this conceptualization, events from the past prevent the individual from developing full awareness in the present. These events from the past demand energy and affect the quality of the person's life. As Perls, Hefferline, and Goodman (1951) point out, a traumatic moment may actually be a series of frustrated or dangerous moments in which the feelings of tension and the dangerous explosiveness are very high. When "unfinished business" is not resolved, an individual may display irrelevant reactions such as compulsive behaviors, weariness, or self-defeating activity that interferes with daily life.

In treating a survivor of the Holocaust, Serok (1985) used re-created and guided fantasy to help a 40-year-old woman, married and the mother of three children. The woman complained of anxiety and depression, with difficulty functioning in most areas of her life, including sexual activity. At the age of about 5, her mother gave her to an aunt to prevent Nazis from taking her. Much of the therapeutic work focused on replaying the separation, at the age of 5, from her mother. The entire situation was explored: the hall where the separation took place, the other captives, the guards with their weapons, and the dogs next to the guards. At times Serok suggested talking to the guards to ask why she was being treated so badly. At other times the patient walked around the therapy room, recalling further details of the scene. Later therapy focused on separation from the aunt and other people in her early experience. As a result of a year and a half of treatment, the patient began to have more control over her energy and to experience full expression in motherhood, personal grooming, education, and sexuality. Dealing with such trauma can be exhausting for both patient and therapist, and it requires considerable commitment to the therapeutic process.

Substance Abuse: Mike

Gestalt therapy has been applied to all phases of addiction problems. Since denial is an important defense in addiction, gestalt techniques can help substance abusers become more aware of themselves and their relationships with others. Clemmens (1997) describes important themes that are dealt with in the recovery process: trust, shame, confidence, and boredom. These themes may be dealt with when the individual is first becoming drug-free and years later as the individual continues the recovery progress.

In the following example, Clemmens (1997) shows how gestalt therapy can be used with an addict who has been in recovery for 15 years. Mike is dealing with issues related to feeling out of touch with his family and hurting his relationship with them. Clemmens attends to Mike's bodily awareness.

> Mike is a recovering addict of fifteen years who came to therapy complaining of feeling "out of touch with myself." He wondered if he were depressed. I noticed by looking at Mike's chest and stomach that his breathing was shallow and slow. This made him look stiff as he spoke about his life and family. I told Mike the way in which I perceived his breathing. He was surprised (as many clients are when I comment on their physical behavior) and asked, "What does that mean?" I answered that I wasn't sure what it meant, but believed he might learn by experimenting with his breathing.
>
> Mike agreed to do this and initially took deeper breaths, eventually filling up his chest and stomach on each inhale and emptying out of each exhalation. As he did so, Mike began to shudder and shake. I asked him if he could stay with this experience. After a few minutes, Mike began to modulate his breathing in a more rhythmic way. The sound that he made was like a moaning. Mike's chin shook and he began to cry. I asked him if there were words for his crying and he said, "I'm not sure." I suggested his words from the beginning of the session, "I feel so out of touch." He tried saying these words three times, each filling his chest and tearing up, and then added, "And in so much pain … That's it. I feel so out of touch and so sad about my life." We spent the rest of the session defining what about himself and others Mike was out of touch with. (Clemmens, 1997, p. 148)

Clemmens and Matzko (2005) describe a gestalt conceptualization of treatment of drug abuse that differs depending on the severity of drug abuse. They also describe an approach to therapy with clients with drug dependency issues that includes attention to client functioning, experiencing the problem in the present, understanding the experiences that occur in the session, and actively participating in the session with the client.

Brief Therapy

Typically, gestalt therapists meet with their patients once a week. When sessions are less often than once a week, there is a danger that patients do not make use of material developed in the sessions and do not develop a relationship with the therapist. Then again, if sessions are held too often, there is the danger that patients regress and do not deal with their current problems. Some gestalt therapy may be brief or short-term.

An interesting approach to brief therapy has been applied to gestalt therapy by Houston (2003). She uses questionnaires that clients fill out before seeing the therapist. In her book *Brief Gestalt Therapy*, she describes a six- to eight-session model and issues that are dealt with in the beginning, middle, and end of therapy. Additionally, she explains homework or experiments that help individuals stay active in working on their problems when not in the therapist's office. Houston's model makes use of almost all of the methods described in this chapter.

Current Trends

There is a continuing trend in gestalt therapy to focus on relationship issues with clients and to use softer rather than abrupt or abrasive methods in helping clients bring issues into the present (Yontef & Jacobs, 2011). Although Perls was known for using creative and strong approaches in his gestalt demonstrations, current gestalt therapists are concerned with the impact of techniques on their continuing therapeutic relationships with clients. Particularly, they examine and address the difficulties in the relationship and the nature of the relationship itself (Gary Yontef, personal communication, October 18, 2009).

As mentioned at the beginning of this chapter, Greenberg and his colleagues (Elliott et al., 2004; Elliott & Greenberg, 2007; Greenberg, 2008) have developed emotion-focused therapy, previously called process-experiential or experiential therapy. Emotion-focused therapy combines the relationship-building aspects of person-centered therapy with the attention to emotion and active phenomenological awareness experiments of gestalt therapy. The work of Greenberg and his colleagues presents a focus on understanding client emotions and communicating understanding that is not found in Perls's therapeutic dialogues. Their move toward a relationship-focused, less confrontive style is also typical of many current gestalt therapists. This approach is described in a comprehensive and clear manner in *Learning Emotion-Focused Therapy: The Process Experiential Approach to Change* (Elliott et al., 2004).

Another area of recent interest has been that of shame, particularly among gestalt therapists with a psychodynamic orientation. Jacobs (1996) believes that shame created in childhood can affect a sense of independence as well as interpersonal relationships. Jacobs demonstrates how shame emerges and can be dealt with in the therapeutic relationship. Philippson (2004) has addressed shame from a theoretical point of view as it relates to gestalt therapy and also as it relates to the application of gestalt theory. In general, these writers address the importance of therapists being aware of their own feelings of shame and being aware of when shame may be inadvertently introduced into therapeutic or therapist training situations.

Some writers have looked at diverse topics of interest and related them to principles of gestalt therapy. Many theories of therapy have incorporated the topic of mindfulness. Mindfulness focuses on awareness by helping clients (in this article, children) attend to internal and external experiences in the present (Fodor & Hooker, 2008). Another recent topic in psychological literature is that of forgiveness. Harris (2007) demonstrates ways for working with forgiveness in gestalt therapy. From a scientific perspective , neourobiology has been used to try to understand how individuals perceive themselves (Brownell, 2009). Applying quantum physics, O'Neill (2008) has shown how Lewin's and other psychologists' concepts of field theory can be expanded to apply to gestalt therapy.

Using Gestalt Psychotherapy with Other Theories

Gestalt therapists are cautious about using gestalt approaches to awareness with other theories. Yontef (1987) has been critical of those who combine elements of gestalt therapy with elements of other theoretical systems without integrating gestalt concepts fully into their work. Because some therapists have gone beyond the constructs of the theory of gestalt therapy, Yontef worries that gestalt therapy as a whole will be hurt by those who use a variety of techniques without a clear understanding of boundary disturbances and the need for an integrated approach to the patient.

Several gestalt therapists see the value of integrating gestalt therapy with psychodynamically derived therapy. For example, Philippson (2001) shows that relational psychoanalysis offers important insights for gestalt therapists in understanding both the contacting process and its development. He believes that perspectives from this theory about the patient's childhood development add to concepts such as contact and gestalt formation. Similarly, Breshgold and Zahm (1992) see a compatibility between self psychology and gestalt therapy, in that both have a relational perspective. They find that self psychology can help gestalt therapists by making them more aware of the developmental needs they are meeting in their work with their patients. Cannon (2009) believes that combining existential psychoanalysis with gestalt helps the patient by focusing some of the therapeutic work on the present. Savard (2009) describes how Adlerian and gestalt therapies can be better understood through a detailed comparison of each. Ginger (2008) and Tobin (2004) illustrate how a behavioral approach, eye movement desensitization and reprocessing (EMDR, described in Chapter 8), can be used with gestalt therapy. Writings that combine developmental concepts from psychoanalytically oriented theory with awareness approaches of gestalt therapy are likely to continue to be important in the future.

Research

In some ways gestalt therapy is a highly experimental approach, with therapists frequently creating experiments for their patients to try. However, these individualistic experiments do not lend themselves to reproducible scientific research. As Perls et al. (1951, p. 8) say, "We must, for instance, face the fact that we blandly commit what to the experimentalist is the most unpardonable of sins: *we include the experimenter in the experiment!*" They assert that many researchers are a part of and affect their experiment, whether they wish to admit it or not.

Their own emphasis on individual experimentation can be seen by the fact that half of their book, *Gestalt Therapy*, is a series of experiments for individuals to test the validity of principles of gestalt therapy themselves. These experiments include exercises such as sharpening the sense of one's body, integrating awareness, and focusing on concentrating. These exercises are the precursors of experiments that gestalt therapists use with their patients in helping them explore previously unknown aspects of themselves.

In terms of published and verifiable research, there is relatively little. *The International Gestalt Journal, The Gestalt Review*, and the *British Journal of Gestalt Therapy* publish very little research, and experimental studies are scattered throughout other psychological journals. There are two main reasons for the lack of published research: Treatments cannot be planned but occur spontaneously, and the therapeutic interaction between patient and therapist is very complex, so that measuring it is very difficult (Fagan & Shepherd, 1970, p. vii). Despite these difficulties, research has been done in a variety of areas. I will examine studies that compare gestalt therapy with other approaches, specific techniques (especially use of the empty chair), and contact boundary disturbances.

Research comparing gestalt therapy with other approaches or with no treatment has been done with a variety of psychological disorders. Strümpfel and Courtney (2004) provide a thorough review of research on disorders that include depression, personality disorders, psychosomatic problems, and drug abuse. They also review follow-up studies that range from 4 months to 3 years. Gestalt therapy, in general, provides significant improvement when compared with a waiting-list control or no treatment. Wagner-Moore (2004) also reviews empirical research providing evidence for the positive changes that take place in using two-chair techniques. Often compared with cognitive-behavioral methods or client-centered therapy, all of the therapies tend to provide similar results, although any of the treatments may have some advantages in certain situations.

Examples of some typical studies are described here. In a study comparing treatment of snake phobia with 23 participants, Johnson and Smith (1997) found that participants who received the empty-chair gestalt dialogue approach did as well as those receiving systematic desensitization. Both groups improved more than nontraditional control participants. In a study on depression, Greenberg and Watson (1998) showed that process-experiential therapy (using both gestalt and person-centered therapy) was as effective with depression as person-centered therapy. Process-experiential therapy produced quicker changes by the middle of therapy than person-centered therapy. This study was replicated by Goldman, Greenberg, and Angus (2000), who showed similar findings, but greater improvement in reducing depressive symptoms for process-experiential therapy. Studying 43 patients with major depression using an 18-month follow up questionnaire, Ellison, Greenberg, Goldman, and Angus (2009) found that emotion-focused therapy (similar to process-experiential and gestalt therapy) reduced depression more than person-centered therapy. Treatment gains appeared to be helped by use of gestalt techniques. Another study on depression compared process-experiential and cognitive-behavioral psychotherapy, studying 66 clients who received 16 sessions of psychotherapy (Watson, Gordon, Stermac, Kalogerakos, & Steckley, 2003). Both treatments helped clients improve self-esteem, find relief from distress, and improve attitudes toward self and others. Those receiving process-experiential therapy reported fewer interpersonal problems than those receiving cognitive-behavioral therapy. These studies have been used to show that process-experiential therapy can be considered a research-supported psychological treatment.

Watson and her colleagues have studied differences in the therapeutic relationship (working alliance) between process-experiential therapy and cognitive-behavioral therapy. In general, cognitive therapists asked more questions whereas process-experiential therapists provided more support to clients. Comparing low-alliance sessions (more difficult client–therapist relationship issues) with high-alliance sessions, both types of therapists provided more support in low-alliance sessions (Watson & McMullen, 2005). In another study of the therapeutic relationship, no differences were found between process-experiential and cognitive-behavioral therapists on their levels of empathy, acceptance, and congruence (Watson & Geller, 2005). However, clients of process-experiential therapists felt they were more highly regarded by their therapists than did clients of cognitive-behavioral therapists.

The empty-chair technique has been a focus of a series of research studies by Leslie Greenberg. He and his students and colleagues have assessed the effectiveness of the empty-chair technique in conflict resolution (Strümpfel & Courtney, 2004). For example, Clarke and Greenberg (1986) compared a cognitive problem-solving group, a gestalt group that featured use of the empty chair, and a waiting-list control group. Clients were seen for two sessions, and pretests and posttests of indecision and stages of decision making were made. Although both counseling approaches were more effective than no treatment in facilitating decision making, the affective (gestalt) intervention was more effective than the cognitive-behavioral approach. Clarke and Greenberg suggest that the gestalt approach may have been more successful than the cognitive-behavioral approach in maintaining a focus on the decision problems. Much of Greenberg's research has shown that the empty-chair technique was helpful to patients by reducing their self-criticism and increasing their self-understanding (Elliott et al., 2004). The empty-chair technique also proved to be more helpful than a psychoeducational group in facilitating forgiveness and helping clients let go of emotional injuries (Greenberg, Warwar, & Malcolm, 2008). The empty-chair technique was also more successful in diminishing specific and global symptoms than was the psychoeducational group. The empty-chair technique has been particularly appropriate for research because, more than most gestalt experiments, it can be specified and controlled. Greenberg and his colleagues have developed a model of how individuals process emotions that adds to the understanding of gestalt therapy and emotion-focused therapy. This model has predicted positive effects when applying emotion-focused therapy (Pascual-Leone & Greenberg, 2007).

Gender Issues

In discussing gender differences in gestalt therapy, it is useful to note that both men and women have been involved in the leadership and development of gestalt therapy. Laura Perls was active from the inception of gestalt therapy, writing chapters of early books on gestalt therapy. Her leadership of the New York Institute for Gestalt Therapy had a powerful effect on the many gestalt therapists she trained. Although difficult to ascertain, the fact that many of those who supervised new therapists and led workshops were women has helped gestalt therapy maintain an appreciative and balanced approach to gender issues.

In a general sense, men and women are apt to react differently to the gestalt approach of developing awareness and growth in individuals. Men and women may react to therapeutic issues such as transference and countertransference, abuse, and relationship issues differently (Amendt-Lyon, 2008). For women, gestalt therapy can be empowering, helping them be aware of a sense of power-fulness as well as blocks to powerfulness that create tension, often due to societal restrictions and expectations. When women develop a sense of empowerment and a full awareness of their abilities after participation in gestalt therapy, they may have to develop new ways to deal with societal expectations that are rela-tively unchanged. To the extent that men are taught to hide their feelings, not show emotions, and repress rather than deal with difficult experiences, gestalt therapy can provide an opportunity to become aware of blocks to functioning in roles as lover, father, coworker, and so forth. However, men who become more aware of their feelings, nonverbal behaviors, and other aspects of themselves may have to explore appropriate social contexts for self-expression.

Miriam Polster has addressed the societal limitations that exist for women be-cause of the lack of female heroes. In *Eve's Daughters* (1992), she points out that tra-ditionally heroes are men, with women either being heroines in the sense of supporters of men or having negative characteristics, such as Helen of Troy, who was beautiful but deceptive. Polster states that the image of a hero comes from wit-nessing and telling an act that is so outstanding that people repeat the story from generation to generation. Women's heroism can include involvement in civil rights, child advocacy, and scientific accomplishments. As a part of the heroic quest, Pol-ster believes that women should be helping other women along their way rather than helping the male hero in his quest. As women achieve heroic feats, they dis-play a combination of support, knowledge, and power that enables other women to achieve. Polster urges a new view of heroism, a neoheroism, viewing women's heroic accomplishments on a par with those of men. Polster's work is unusual in gestalt writings, as it emphasizes societal empowerment and awareness as well as the development of individual awareness.

Gestalt therapists have also attended to concerns of gay and lesbian clients. Methods for helping lesbian couples include use of gestalt experiments and tech-niques as well as being concerned with community, political, and family-of-origin issues (Brockmon, 2004). Dealing with gay male survivors of domestic violence, Kondas (2008) shows ways of helping clients by addressing the con-cepts of implosion and explosion in gestalt therapy. Iaculo and Frew (2004) de-scribe the process of revealing one's homosexuality to others as paralleling the gestalt contact cycle. The client–therapist relationship is described as crucial to helping gay clients with the process of coming out.

Multicultural Issues

Gestalt therapy can be effective in working with culturally diverse populations in several ways (Wheeler, 2005). The gestalt therapist can use gestalt experiments to help individuals deal with and perceive their own culture. Also, because the patient–therapist relationship focuses on the present, there is an opportunity for the therapist to bridge cross-cultural barriers by responding to issues that they perceive are interfering with the patient–therapist relationship and that may have a cultural base. For example, a White therapist perceiving an Asian Ameri-can client as reticent may say, "Can you put words to your soft voice?" This may enable the patient to verbalize her concerns about being understood by a White therapist. A dialogue between the patient's perceptions of herself in Asian and American cultures may help bring a cultural conflict to greater awareness. At times, such dialogues or other gestalt experiments may be carried out in the patient's native language or vernacular. Joyce and Sills (2001) provide several suggestions for therapists to attend to their own cultural perceptions when dealing with cultural issues. In general, sensitivity to the patient's immediate experience also includes sensitivity to the patient's culture.

From another perspective, gestalt therapy can create problems in working with people from different cultures. Because gestalt therapy can arouse deep emotions, this can be problematic for people whose cultural traditions discourage expression of emotion (Joyce & Sills, 2001). In many cultures, displaying emotionality, particularly for men, can be seen as a display of weakness and vulnerability. Some cultures have traditions that make interactions with various family members limited and proscribed. For example, in many Asian cultures, the way one interacts with older family members, particularly parents, is often with respect and deference to authority. To display anger toward them, even in a dialogue, can be disturbing for individuals.

Some gestalt writers have viewed the relationship of society or culture to gestalt therapy in a broad sense. Staemmler (2005) attends to the way communication differs across cultures. He describes how gestalt therapists can examine their own inconsistencies in communicating with clients from different cultures. Raising the questions How do we treat a wounded society? and How do we apply gestalt therapy to social needs? Slemenson (1998) reflects on far-reaching issues that pertain to Argentina but could have implications for other countries as well. These comments suggest that gestalt therapists should be sensitive not only to the awareness that individuals have about their own selves but also to how cultural factors can affect awareness of self, family, friends, acquaintances, and people in society as a whole.

Group Therapy

Group therapy has always been a common intervention in gestalt therapy. In the 1960s and 1970s, gestalt therapists were better known for their work in groups than for work with individuals. The types of groups can be divided into three kinds: hot seat, where individuals work with a therapist and the audience observes; process groups, where attention is paid to current group processes; and a variation of process groups, process-thematic groups, where in addition to attending to process, themes that involve the entire group may be acted out. In a survey of 251 gestalt therapists, Frew (1988) found that 70% were currently using groups in their practice. Of these, 4% reported using the hot-seat approach primarily or exclusively; the majority (60%) indicated that they use a variety of leadership models with their groups. Group therapy continues to be an important approach to treatment, providing an opportunity for members to improve their interactions with others (Feder, 2006; Schoenberg, Feder, Frew, & Gadol, 2005).

The hot-seat approach was popularized by Perls and also by James Simkin; it has been used less and less since the 1970s. In this approach, one group member works from a few minutes to as many as 40 minutes with a leader. During this one-to-one work, audience members do not participate. Later they may talk about how they were affected by the observed work. Each member of the group has an opportunity to work one-to-one before a second round is started. Some gestalt therapists using the hot-seat method have incorporated group dynamics into their approach and use a combination of a group process and a hot-seat approach. Perls (1969b) believed that the hot-seat approach was superior to individual therapy and that audience members learned through their observation of those on the hot seat.

In explaining gestalt group process, Kepner (1994) describes personal growth as a boundary phenomenon that results from contact between the individual and others. Gestalt process groups may include experiments and exercises to further group awareness. Kepner describes three developing stages of a gestalt therapy group. The first, identity and dependence, involves setting limits and boundaries for the group. This includes modeling approaches that will be used in the group and encouraging interpersonal contact among the group members. In the second stage, influence and counterdependence, group members deal with influence, authority, and control of the group. The group leader, as well as individual group members, may be challenged, and open differences of opinions may be expressed. Also, roles in the group are differentiated from the person. For example, if scapegoating appears in the group and a person becomes designated as a "victim," the leader can differentiate the role from the person. In the third stage, intimacy and interdependence, a sense of closeness between group members is developed. Kepner believes that it takes a group a year or two of being together to function consistently at this third stage. At this point the leader is a consultant who makes relatively few interventions. Not all groups reach this third stage, where processing can be fast and respectful, even though issues of grief and pain are dealt with. This structure is not a format for leading a group but rather a description of processes that Kepner has observed.

Zinker (1978) finds that group members often work on themes that occur in everyday life, such as family conflicts, grief, aspirations, and unfinished life traumas. As in his approach to dream work, Zinker (1978) may have group members act out an issue or theme to bring it into the present. Such experiments may be spontaneous, involving all group members. Whether working with themes or with group processes, Zinker (1994) believes that group awareness develops from here-and-now statements such as "You're hunched up and your shoulders are near your ears," "Joan, your jaw tightened when John said...." To facilitate the group awareness process further, Zinker (1994) suggests such group behaviors as looking at people when you speak to them and using their names, being aware of your own body and other people's body language, speaking directly to people and not about them, not intruding when other people are in the middle of working on an issue, speaking in the first person, converting questions into statements, and respecting the needs and values of others. These values illustrate the emphasis on the here-and-now approach of gestalt therapists.

Because of the intensity brought about by the approaches illustrated by Kepner's and Zinker's process and theme work, gestalt therapists have attended to issues of therapeutic safety. Feder (1994, 2006) believes that the most important variable regarding group safety is the therapist's approach. Being caring, respectful of group members, and flexible helps ensure that group members experience healing of contact boundary disturbances rather than damage to them. Screening prospective group members also helps ensure that the group process will be effective and that members will not damage or be damaged in the process. Feder has found it helpful to use a "safety index," in which he asks members of the group to assign a number between 0 and 10 to the level of safety that they are experiencing. He often asks the group to review the current safety level and check current experiences of members. Establishing whether members have had prior relationships with each other can also help ensure the safety of the group. Opportunities to participate in and later co-lead a gestalt therapy group are useful in helping the beginning group therapist experience a sense of safety in group leadership.

Summary

Although the developer of gestalt therapy, Fritz Perls, was trained as a psychoanalyst, his method of psychotherapy evolved into a very different approach. Perls was influenced by phenomenology and existentialism in his emphasis on the whole person. The theory and research of field theory and gestalt psychology helped him to develop a terminology for his theory of psychotherapy. He was able to use gestalt psychology concepts of figure and ground to talk about the awareness that individuals had of themselves, others, and objects in their surroundings. The emphasis on bringing the past or future into the present is an extremely important concept in gestalt psychotherapy. Gestalt therapy examines the ways in which individuals are in good or poor contact with themselves and others and observes contact boundary disturbances, including introjection, projection, retroflection, deflection, and confluence. They also look for polarities, or opposites, that individuals experience. This view of the individual then influences the practice of psychotherapy.

Gestalt therapists focus on the importance of awareness in the growth and integration of the whole person. They assess individuals' contact boundary disturbances, including their here-and-now verbal and nonverbal behavior. Gestalt therapists assist their patients in enhancing awareness by attending to their nonverbal behaviors and awareness of sensations and feelings in the context of a caring relationship. Methods include dialogues with the self and acting out polarities and contact boundaries. Dreams are an important part of the therapeutic experience for many gestalt therapists, with objects and people in dreams being representations of the individual. Gestalt experiments and exercises are used in individual and group therapy to bring about a deeper awareness of oneself. Experience with gestalt techniques, training, and supervision are necessary in order to help therapists become aware, integrate their experiences, and grow and mature as therapists.

Theories in Action DVD: Gestalt Therapy

Basic Concepts Used in the Role-Play	Questions About the Role-Play
• Pointing out nonverbal response • Empathy • Unfinished business • Empty chair technique • Exaggeration technique • "I" statement • Clarification	1. What ways does Dr. Neukrug use to make Jill aware of different parts of herself? (p. 255) 2. What does Jill's talk to her mother in the empty chair do for her that talking about her mother does not do? (p. 259) 3. How does Jill move toward completing "unfinished business" with her feelings about her mother? (p. 251) 4. On page 264, the text discusses risks of gestalt therapy. Does the therapy that Dr. Neukrug is doing with Jill seem riskier than existential or person-centered therapy? Explain.

Suggested Readings

Polster, E., & Polster, M. (1973). *Gestalt therapy integrated: Contours of theory and practice.* New York: Brunner/Mazel. This excellent book covers present awareness, figure and ground, contact-boundary, and gestalt experiments. The case illustrations are very well written.

Passons, W. R. (1975). *Gestalt approaches in counseling.* New York: Holt, Rinehart & Winston. Gestalt experiments and exercises for both individual and group counseling are described systematically and illustrated with examples.

Clarkson, P. (2004). *Gestalt counselling in action* (3rd ed.). London: Sage. This brief book gives an overview of gestalt counseling with several case examples. There is a focus on the healthy contact cycle and its application to counseling.

Elliott, R., Watson, J. C., Goldman, R. N., & Greenberg, L. S. (2004). *Learning emotion-focused therapy: The process-experiential approach to change.* Washington, DC: American Psychological Association. Although emotion-focused therapy and the process-experiential approach are described rather than gestalt therapy, the methods are very similar to gestalt therapy. This empirically supported treatment is described in detail. Readers will learn many ways to use the two-chair method.

Perls, F. (1969). *Gestalt therapy verbatim.* Moab, UT: Real People Press. The beginning of the book includes lectures by Perls and answers to questions from the audience. The second part includes verbatim transcripts of Perls doing dream work, seminars, and weekend workshops.

References

Amendt-Lyon, N. (2008). Gender differences in Gestalt therapy. *Gestalt Review, 12*(2), 106–121.

Audet, L. R., & Shub, N. (2007). Contact and the phenomena of autism. *Gestalt Review, 11*(3), 217–236.

Baumgardner, P. (1975). *Legacy from Fritz.* Palo Alto, CA: Science and Behavior Books.

Beisser, A. R. (1970). The paradoxical theory of change. In J. Fagan & I. L. Shepherd (Eds.), *Gestalt therapy now* (pp. 77–80). Palo Alto, CA: Science and Behavior Books.

Bernhardtson, L. (2008). Gestalt ethics: A utopia? *Gestalt Review, 12*(2), 161–173.

Bloom, D. (2005). Laura Perls in New York City: A community recalls its leader during the centenary of her birth. *International Gestalt Journal, 28*(1), 9–23.

Boring, E. G. (1950). *A history of experimental psychology.* New York: Appleton-Century-Crofts.

Bowman, C. E., & Nevis, E. C. (2005). The history and development of Gestalt therapy. In A. L. Woldt & S. M. Toman (Eds.), *Gestalt therapy: History, theory, and practice* (pp. 3–20). Thousand Oaks, CA: Sage.

Breshgold, E., & Zahm, S. (1992). A case for the integration of self psychology developmental theory into the practice of Gestalt therapy. *Gestalt Journal, 15,* 61–94.

Brockmon, C. (2004). The fish is in the water and the water is in the fish: A perspective on the context of gay and lesbian relationships for Gestalt therapists. *Gestalt Review, 8*(2), 161–177.

Brown, G. (1988). The farther reaches of Gestalt therapy: A conversation with George Brown. *Gestalt Journal, 11,* 33–50.

Brownell, P. (2009). Executive functions: A neuropsychological understanding of self-regulation. *Gestalt Review, 13*(1), 62–81.

Buber, M. (1965). *Between man and man.* New York: Macmillan.

Cannon, B. (2009). Nothingness as the ground for change: Gestalt therapy and existential psychoanalysis. *Existential Analysis, 20*(2), 192–210.

Clarke, K. M., & Greenberg, L. G. (1986). Differential effects of the Gestalt two-chair intervention and problem solving in resolving differential conflict. *Journal of Counseling Psychology, 33,* 11–15.

Clarkson, P. (2004). *Gestalt counselling in action* (3rd ed.). London: Sage.

Clarkson, P., & Mackewn, J. (1993). *Fritz Perls.* London: Sage.

Clemmens, M. C. (1997). *Getting beyond sobriety: Clinical approaches to long-term recovery.* San Francisco: Jossey-Bass.

Clemmens, M. C., & Matzko, H. (2005). Gestalt approaches to substance use/abuse/dependency: Theory and practice. In A. L. Woldt & S. M. Toman (Eds.), *Gestalt therapy: History, theory, and practice* (pp. 279–300). Thousand Oaks: Sage.

Doubrawa, E., & Schickling, U. (2000). The politics of the I–Thou. *Gestalt Journal, 23,* 19–37.

Elliott, R., & Greenberg, L. S. (2007). The essence of process-experiential/emotion-focused therapy. *American Journal of Psychotherapy, 61*(3), 241–254.

Elliott, R., Watson, J. C., Goldman, R. N., & Greenberg, L. S. (2004). *Learning emotion-focused therapy: The process-experiential approach to change.* Washington, DC: American Psychological Association.

Ellison, J. A., Greenberg, L. S., Goldman, R. N., & Angus, L. (2009). Maintenance of gains following experiential therapies for depression. *Journal of Consulting and Clinical Psychology, 77*(1), 103–112.

Enright, J. B. (1970). Awareness training in the mental health professions. In J. Fagan & I. L. Shepherd (Eds.), *Gestalt therapy now* (pp. 263–273). Palo Alto, CA: Science and Behavior Books.

Fagan, J., & Shepherd, I. L. (1970). *Gestalt therapy now.* Palo Alto, CA: Science and Behavior Books.

Feder, B. (1994). Safety and danger in the Gestalt group. In B. Feder & R. Ronall (Eds.), *Beyond the hot seat* (pp. 41–52). New York: Brunner/Mazel.

Feder, F. (2006). *Gestalt group therapy: A practical guide.* Metairie, LA: Gestalt Institute Press.

Fodor, I. E., & Hooker, K. E. (2008). Teaching mindfulness to children. *Gestalt Review, 12*(1), 75–91.

Frew, J. (1988). The practice of Gestalt therapy in groups. *Gestalt Journal, 11,* 77–96.

Gaines, J. (1979). *Fritz Perls: Here and now.* Millbrae, CA: Celestial Arts.

Gendlin, E. T. (1996). *Focusing oriented psychotherapy.* New York: Guilford.

Ginger, S. (2008). Enriching Gestalt therapy through EMDR. *International Journal of Psychotherapy, 12*(2), 13–20.

Goldman, R., Greenberg, L. S., & Angus, L. E. (2000, June). Results of the York II comparative study testing the effects of process-experiential and client-centered therapy for depression. Paper presented at the 31st annual meeting of the Society for Psychotherapy Research, Chicago.

Goldstein, K. (1939). *The organism.* New York: American Book.

Greenberg, L. J., Warwar, S. H., & Malcolm, W. M. (2008). Differential effects of emotion-focused therapy and psychoeducation in facilitating forgiveness and letting go of emotional injuries. *Journal of Counseling Psychology, 55*(2), 185–196.

Greenberg, L. S. (2008). The clinical application of emotion in psychotherapy. In M. Lewis, J. M. Haviland-Jones, & L. F. Barrett (Eds.), *Handbook of emotions* (3rd ed., pp. 88–101). New York: Guilford Press.

Greenberg, L. S., & Watson, J. (1998). Experiential client-centered relationship conditions and process experiential interventions. *Psychotherapy Research, 8,* 210–224.

Handlon, J. H., & Fredericson, I. (2007). Unfinished pleasures. *Gestalt Review, 11*(2), 130–135.

Harris, E. S. (2000) God, Buber and the practice of Gestalt therapy. *Gestalt Journal, 23,* 39–62.

Harris, E. S. (2007). Working with forgiveness in Gestalt therapy. *Gestalt Review, 11*(2), 108–119.

Henle, M. (2003). Gestalt psychology and Gestalt therapy. *International Gestalt Journal, 26*(2), 7–22.

Houston, G. (2003). *Brief Gestalt therapy.* London: Sage.

Humphrey, K. (1986). Laura Perls: A biographical sketch. *Gestalt Journal, 7,* 5–11.

Hycner, R. (1987). An interview with Erving and Miriam Polster. *Gestalt Journal, 10,* 27–66.

Hycner, R., & Jacobs L. (1995). *The healing relationship in Gestalt therapy. A dialogic/self psychological approach.* Highland, NY: Gestalt Journal Press.

Iaculo, G., & Frew, J. E. (2004). Relational support in the gay coming-out process. *Gestalt Review, 8*(2), 178–203.

Jacobs, L. (1996). Shame in the therapeutic dialogue. In R. Lee & G. Wheeler (Eds.), *The voice of shame: Silence and connection in psychotherapy.* San Francisco: Jossey-Bass.

Jacobs, L. (2005). The inevitable intersubjectivity of selfhood. *International Gestalt Journal, 28*(1), 43–70.

Johnson, W. R., & Smith, E. W. L. (1997). Gestalt empty-chair dialogue vs. systematic desensitization in the treatment of phobia. *Gestalt Review, 1,* 150–162.

Joyce, P., & Sills, C. (2001). *Skills in Gestalt counselling and psychotherapy.* London: Sage.

Kepner, E. (1994). Gestalt group process. In B. Feder & R. Ronall (Eds.), *Beyond the hot seat* (pp. 5–24). New York: Brunner/Mazel.

Kondas, D. (2008). Existential explosion and Gestalt therapy for gay male survivors of domestic violence. *Gestalt Review, 12*(1), 58–74.

Levitsky, A., & Perls, F. (1970). The rules and games of Gestalt therapy. In J. Fagan & I. L. Shepherd (Eds.), *Gestalt therapy now* (pp. 140–149). Palo Alto, CA: Science and Behavior Books.

Lobb, M. S. (2007). Ego, hunger and aggression: Do we bite in the same way as in the 50s? A contribution to the development of the concept of aggression in Gestalt therapy theory and practice. *Gestalt Review, 11*(3), 239–243.

Lobb, M. S., & Amendt-Lyon, N. (Eds.). (2003). *Creative license.* New York: Springer-Verlag Wien.

Mahrer, A. R. (2005). Experiential therapy. In R. J. Corsini & D. Wedding (Eds.), *Current psychotherapies* (7th ed., pp. 439–474). Belmont, CA: Brooks-Cole Thomson.

Melnick, J., & Nevis, S. M. (1998). Diagnosing in the here and now: A Gestalt therapy approach. In L. S. Greenberg, J. C. Watson, & G. Lietaer (Eds.), *Handbook of experiential therapy* (pp. 428–447). New York: Guilford.

Naranjo, C. (1970). Present-centeredness: Technique, perception, and ideal. In J. Fagan & I. L. Shepherd (Eds.), *Gestalt therapy now* (pp. 47–69). Palo Alto, CA: Science and Behavior Books.

O'Leary, E. (1997). *Confluence versus empathy. Gestalt Journal, 20,* 137–154.

O'Leary, E., Purcell, U., Mc Sweeney, E., O'Flynn, D., O'Sullivan, K., Keane, N., & Barry, N. (1998). The Cork person centred Gestalt project: Two outcome studies. *Counselling Psychology Quarterly, 11*(1), 45–61.

O'Neill, B. (2008). Relativistic quantum field theory: Implications for Gestalt therapy. *Gestalt Review, 12*(1), 7–23.

Parlett, M., & Lee, R. G. (2005). Contemporary Gestalt therapy: Field theory. In A. L. Woldt & S. M. Toman (Eds.), *Gestalt therapy: History, theory, and practice* (pp. 41–63). Thousand Oaks, CA: Sage.

Pascual-Leone, A., & Greenberg, L. S. (2007). Emotional processing in experiential therapy: Why "the only way out is through." *Journal of Consulting and Clinical Psychology, 75*(6), 875–887.

Passons, W. R. (1975). *Gestalt approaches in counseling.* New York: Holt, Rinehart & Winston.

Perls, F. S. (1948). Theory and technique of personality integration. *American Journal of Psychotherapy, 2,* 572–573.

Perls, F. S. (1969a). *Ego, hunger and aggression.* New York: Vintage. (Original work published 1947.)

Perls, F. S. (1969b). *Gestalt therapy verbatim.* Moab, UT: Real People Press.

Perls, F. S. (1969c). *In and out of the garbage pail.* Moab, UT: Real People Press.

Perls, F. S. (1970). Four lectures. In J. Fagan & I. L. Shepherd (Eds.), *Gestalt therapy now* (pp. 14–38). Palo Alto, CA: Science and Behavior Books.

Perls, F. S. (1973). *The Gestalt approach.* Palo Alto, CA: Science and Behavior Books.

Perls, F. S., Hefferline, R. F., & Goodman, P. (1951/1994). *Gestalt therapy.* Highlands, NY: Gestalt Journal Press.

Philippson, P. (2001). *Self in relation.* Highland, NY: Gestalt Journal Press.

Philippson, P. (2004). The experience of shame. *International Gestalt Journal, 27*(2), 85–96.

Polster, E., & Polster, M. (1973). *Gestalt therapy integrated.* New York: Brunner/Mazel.

Polster, M. (1987). Gestalt therapy: Evolution and application. In J. K. Zeig (Ed.), *The evolution of psychotherapy* (pp. 312–325). New York: Brunner/Mazel.

Polster, M. (1992). *Eve's daughters: The forbidden heroism of women.* San Francisco: Jossey-Bass.

Pos, A. E., & Greenberg, L. S. (2008). Emotion focused therapy. In K. Jordan (Ed.), *The quick theory reference guide: A resource for expert and novice mental health professionals* (pp. 285–298). Hauppauge, NY: Nova Science Publishers.

Resnick, R. (1984). Gestalt therapy East and West: Bicoastal dialogue, debate or debacle? *Gestalt Journal, 7,* 13–32.

Rosenblatt, D. (1988). What has love got to do with it? *Gestalt Journal, 9,* 63–76.

Savard, M. (2009). Critical collaboration: Adlerian therapy and Gestalt therapy. *Dissertation Abstracts International: Section B: The Sciences and Engineering, 69* (7–B), 4442.

Schoenberg, P., Feder, B., Frew, J., & Gadol, I. (2005). Gestalt therapy in groups. In A. L. Woldt & S. M. Toman (Eds.), *Gestalt therapy: History, theory, and practice* (pp. 219–236). Thousand Oaks, CA: Sage.

Serok, S. (1985). Implications of Gestalt therapy with post traumatic patients. *Gestalt Journal, 8,* 78–89.

Shane, P. (2003). An illegitimate child: The relationship between Gestalt psychology and Gestalt therapy. *International Gestalt Journal, 26*(2), 23–46.

Shepherd, I. L. (1970). Limitations and cautions in the Gestalt approach. In J. Fagan & I. L. Shepherd (Eds.), *Gestalt therapy now* (pp. 234–238). Palo Alto, CA: Science and Behavior Books.

Shepard, M. (1975). *Fritz.* Sagaponack, NY: Second Chance Press.

Sherrill, R. E. (1986). Gestalt therapy and Gestalt psychology. *Gestalt Journal, 9,* 53–66.

Slemenson, M. (1998). Gestalt therapy in Argentina: Revolution, evolution, and contributions. *Gestalt Review, 2,* 123–130.

Smuts, J. C. (1926). *Holism and evolution.* New York: Macmillan.

Staemmler, F. (2005). Cultural field conditions: A hermeneutic study of consistency. *British Gestalt Journal, 14*(1), 34–43.

Stoehr, T. (2009). Perls, Hefferline, and Goodman: Gestalt therapy—An afterword. *Gestalt Review, 13* (1), 82–95.

Strümpfel, U., & Courtney, M. (2004). Research on Gestalt therapy. *International Gestalt Journal, 27*(1), 9–54.

Strümpfel, U., & Goldman, R. (2002). Contacting Gestalt therapy. In D. J. Cain & J. Seeman (Eds.), *Humanistic psychotherapies: Handbook of research and practice.* (pp. 189–220). Washington, DC: American Psychological Association.

Tobin, S. (2004). The integration of relational Gestalt therapy and EMDR. *International Gestalt Journal, 27*(1), 55–82.

Wagner-Moore, L. E. (2004). Gestalt therapy: Past, present, theory, and research. *Psychotherapy: Theory, Research, Practice, Training, 41*(2), 180–189.

Wallen, R. (1970). Gestalt therapy and Gestalt psychology. In J. Fagan & I. L. Shepherd (Eds.), *Gestalt therapy now* (pp. 8–13). Palo Alto, CA: Science and Behavior Books.

Watson, J. C., & Geller, S. M. (2005). The relation among the relationship conditions, working alliance, and outcome in both process-experiential and cognitive-behavioral psychotherapy. *Psychotherapy Research, 15*(1–2), 25–33.

Watson, J. C., & McMullen, E. J. (2005). An examination of therapist and client behavior in high- and low-alliance sessions in cognitive-behavioral therapy and process experiential therapy. *Psychotherapy: Theory, Research, Practice, Training, 42*(3), 297–310.

Watson, J. C., Gordon, L. B., Stermac, L., Kalogerakos, F., & Steckley, P. (2003). Comparing the effectiveness of process-experiential with cognitive-behavioral psychotherapy in the treatment of depression. *Journal of Consulting and Clinical Psychology, 71*(4), 773–781.

Watzlawick, P. (1984). *The invented reality.* New York: Norton.

Wheeler, G. (2005). Culture, self, and field: A Gestalt guide to the age of complexity. *Gestalt Review, 9*(1), 91–128.

Woodworth, R., & Schlosberg, H. (1954). *Experimental psychology.* New York: Holt, Rinehart, & Winston.

Yontef, G. (2007). The power of the immediate moment in Gestalt therapy. *Journal of Contemporary Psychotherapy, 37*(1), 17–23.

Yontef, G. M. (1987). Gestalt therapy 1986: A polemic. *Gestalt Journal, 10*, 41–68.

Yontef, G. M. (1988). Assimilating diagnostic and psychoanalytic perspectives into Gestalt therapy. *Gestalt Journal, 11*, 5–32.

Yontef, G. M. (1995). Gestalt therapy. In A. S. Gurman & S. B. Meisser (Eds.), *Essential psychotherapies: Theory and practice* (pp. 261–303). New York: Guilford.

Yontef, G. M. (2001). Psychotherapy of schizoid process. *Transactional Analysis Journal, 31*, 723.

Yontef, G. M., & Fuhr, R. (2005). Gestalt therapy theory of change. In A. L. Woldt & S. M. Toman (Eds.), *Gestalt therapy: History, theory, and practice* (pp. 81–100). Thousand Oaks, CA: Sage.

Yontef, G. M., & Jacobs, L. (2011). Gestalt therapy. In R. J. Corsini & D. Wedding (Eds.), *Current psychotherapies* (9th ed., pp. 342–382). Belmont, CA: Brooks/Cole-Cengage.

Zinker, J. (1971). Dream work as theater: An innovation in Gestalt therapy. *Voices, 7*, 2.

Zinker, J. (1978). *Creative process in Gestalt therapy.* New York: Brunner/Mazel.

Zinker, J. (1991). Creative process in Gestalt therapy: The therapist as artist. *Gestalt Journal, 14*, 71–88.

Zinker, J. (1994). The developmental process of a Gestalt therapy group. In B. Feder & R. Ronall (Eds.), *Beyond the hot seat* (pp. 55–77). New York: Brunner/Mazel.

Behavior Therapy

Outline of Behavior Therapy

BEHAVIOR THEORY OF PERSONALITY
  Classical Conditioning
  Operant Conditioning
  Social Cognitive Theory
  Positive Reinforcement
  Negative Reinforcement
  Extinction
  Generalization
  Discrimination
  Shaping
  Observational Learning
    Attentional processes
    Retention processes
    Motor reproduction processes
    Motivational processes
    Self-efficacy
THEORIES OF BEHAVIOR THERAPY
  Goals of Behavior Therapy
  Behavioral Assessment
    Behavioral interviews
    Behavioral reports and ratings
    Behavioral observations
    Physiological measurements

General Treatment Approach
Systematic Desensitization
    Relaxation
    Anxiety hierarchies
    Desensitization
Imaginal Flooding Therapies
In Vivo Therapies
Virtual Reality Therapy
Modeling Techniques
    Live modeling
    Symbolic modeling
    Role playing
    Participant modeling
    Covert modeling
Self-Instructional Training: A Cognitive Behavioral Approach
Stress Inoculation: A Cognitive Behavioral Approach
    The conceptual phase
    Skills acquisition
    Application
Eye-Movement Desensitization and Reprocessing
Acceptance and Commitment Therapy
Dialectical Behavior Therapy

[handwritten note at top: Like therapy or white paper]

uilt on scientific principles of behavior developed over the last 100 years, behavior therapy began in the late 1950s. Many of the first therapeutic approaches were based on Pavlov's concept of classical conditioning and Skinner's work on operant conditioning. This research, along with studies on observational learning, provided a background for the development of psychotherapeutic behavioral techniques. Behavior therapists have been able to apply basic principles such as reinforcement, extinction, shaping of behavior, and modeling to help clients. The application of scientific method can be seen in the detailed assessments that behavior therapists use.

In behavior therapy there has been a general trend from working only with observable events, such as screaming, to working with unobservable events, such as the learning that takes place by watching someone do something. More recently, many therapists have combined behavioral approaches with cognitive ones that attend to the client's thoughts. In this chapter, illustrations that combine behavioral strategies to treat a variety of specific disorders are provided. Because behavior therapy includes so many methods, not all can be described here.

History of Behavior Therapy

[handwritten: John Watson]
[handwritten: B. F. Skinner]

Unlike other theories of psychotherapy, behavior therapy has its roots in experimental psychology and the study of the learning process in humans and animals. Although a few physicians used approaches that are remarkably similar to behavior therapy as it is practiced today, there was no systematic study of behavior that led to principles of behavior change until the work of Ivan Pavlov (Farmer & Nelson-Gray, 2005; Wolpe, 1990). Pavlov's observations about the salivation of dogs before receiving food led to the study and development of classical conditioning (also called respondent conditioning). Influenced by Pavlov's conditioning experiments, John Watson applied these concepts to human behavior. Another important approach to learning is operant conditioning, developed by B. F. Skinner, which examines how environmental influences affect or shape the behavior of individuals. Both classical and operant conditioning study observable behaviors that operate outside the individual. In contrast, social cognitive theory, developed by Albert Bandura, deals with internal or cognitive processes and attempts to explain how individuals learn through observations or perceptions of their environment. These three approaches (operant and classical conditioning and social learning theory) are described in more detail in this chapter, as is the current status of behavior therapy.

Classical Conditioning *(Pavlov)*

While studying the digestive process of dogs, Pavlov observed that dogs would salivate before food was put on their tongues (Hyman, 1964). On closer observation, he concluded that the dogs had learned from environmental events, such as a sound or the sight of food, that they were about to be fed. He was able to present a neutral stimulus, such as a sound or a light (the conditioned stimulus, CS), for a second or two before presenting the food (the unconditioned stimulus, UCS) to the dog. The dog's salivation at the sight of food (the UCS) was the unconditioned response (UCR). After the CS (light or tone) was presented together with the UCS (food), the CS (by itself) would produce salivation, the conditioned response (CR), from the dog. Thus, the learned behavior was the conditioned response (CR) to the presentation of a conditioned stimulus (CS).

National Library of Medicine

IVAN PAVLOV

Classical conditioning could be applied to a variety of species (including humans) and types of behavior. For example, Pavlov was able to pair a black square with a previously conditioned stimulus, a beat of a metronome, and demonstrate second-order or higher-order conditioning. Other experimentation dealt with how long an animal might respond to the conditioned stimulus (CS) without the presentation of the unconditioned stimulus before the CS (a light) would fail to evoke a CR (salivation) and the CR would be extinguished. In this way, scientific findings regarding the learning process began to develop. As research into classical conditioning and other behavioral principles has increased, investigators have found that the principles are quite complex. For example, classical conditioning does not always occur with pairings such as those described in this section.

In the early 1900s, John Watson, an experimental psychologist at Johns Hopkins University, was impressed by Pavlov's research. He appreciated the objectivity of the approach, which called for studying directly observable stimuli and responses without resorting to internal mental processes, such as thoughts or imagery (Watson, 1914). In a famous study (Watson & Rayner, 1920), Watson explained how an emotional reaction could be conditioned in a child by using a classical conditioning model. Investigators had noted that Albert, an 11-month-old boy, would show fear and appear startled when he heard a loud noise. Albert also played comfortably with a white rat. However, when the sound was presented immediately before Albert saw the white rat, he became afraid. After seven pairings of the sound and the rat over a 1-week period, Albert cried when the rat was presented alone (Beck, Levinson, & Irons, 2009). Watson's work (1914, 1919), which was based on research such as the study of Albert, was to have an impact on many other psychologists.

Mowrer and Mowrer (1938) were intrigued by classical conditioning principles and applied them to bed-wetting in their New Haven Children's Center, where they developed a urine alarm system that paired bladder tension with an alarm. When the child would go to sleep and urination began, the urine would seep through the cloth, closing an electric circuit and sounding an alarm. After this had happened several times, the bladder tension alone would arouse the child before urination could occur. Variations of this method have been used for more than 70 years (Spiegler & Guevremont, 2010) in a process that takes 6 to 12 weeks to stop bed-wetting.

(margin handwritten note: (OBJECTIVITY) APPROACH)

Operant Conditioning

Whereas classical conditioning focuses on the antecedents of behavior (the presentation of the CS before the UCS), operant conditioning focuses on antecedents and consequences of behaviors. Based on the early work of E. L. Thorndike and B. F. Skinner, operant conditioning (also known as *instrumental conditioning*) laid the groundwork for much of what constitutes behavior therapy today. This work formed the basis for the application of principles of behavior to a wide variety of problems, especially those dealing with severe mental disabilities such as schizophrenia and autism.

Working at about the same time as Pavlov, Edward L. Thorndike (1898, 1911) was using controlled experimental procedures to study learning. Rather than studying reflex behavior, as Pavlov had done, he was interested in the learning of new behaviors. Using cats as subjects, he would place food outside a cage and observe how a cat would try to escape and find the food by releasing a latch. The first escape from a box occurred in a trial-and-error fashion. Later the cat would be able to escape from the box more and more quickly. Recording the time taken to press the latch, Thorndike plotted a learning curve. From his experiments and observations, Thorndike was able to derive the Law of Effect, that "consequences that follow behavior help learning" (Kazdin, 2001, p. 17). In essence, the correct response (for example, touching the lever) was strengthened, and incorrect responses (biting at the bars of the cage) were weakened or lessened. Besides the Law of Effect, Thorndike derived many other principles of behavior from his experiments, emphasizing the importance of the adaptive nature of learning for animals to survive and function well.

The name most associated with operant conditioning is B. F. Skinner (1904–1990). Whereas Thorndike had seen classical and operant conditioning as being quite similar, Skinner saw many differences. Basically, _operant conditioning_ is a type of learning in which behavior is altered by systematically changing consequences. An example of this is the pigeon in a Skinner box, a small chamber in which a pigeon can peck at a lighted key. The experimenter controls the amount of food the pigeon receives (reinforcement), and the pigeon's "pecks" are automatically recorded. By selectively reinforcing a green light rather than a red light, the pigeon can learn to peck at the green light and not the red light. Although much of Skinner's work was with laboratory animals, he extended his principles of operant conditioning to human behavior as well.

Skinner's (1953) attempt to apply operant conditioning principles to complex human behavior drew much attention. He wrote of the relevance of operant conditioning for government, education, business, religion, psychotherapy, and a variety of human interactions. His novel, _Walden Two_ (1948), shows how operant conditioning can provide the basis for an ideal community. Much of the controversy over Skinner's views dealt with critics' objections to the application of limited laboratory findings to prescriptions for living.

Social Cognitive Theory

Whereas classical and operant conditioning focus on overt behavior, actions that people can directly observe, social cognitive theories focus on the study of covert behaviors, those that take place within the individual and cannot be observed (or at least not easily). These include physiological responses (such as blood pressure and muscle tensions), thinking (observing, remembering, imagining), and feeling (emotions such as sadness and anger). The term _cognitive-behavioral_ is often used to describe theorists who consider both overt and covert behaviors in their research and psychotherapy. One particularly significant contribution to this field has been the research of Albert Bandura, which can be traced to earlier investigators such as Mary Cover Jones.

A student of Watson, Jones (1924) described the treatment of a 3-year-old boy, Peter, who was afraid of rabbits. Jones's treatment of Peter illustrates two important aspects of social learning theory: observation and modeling. Peter's fears were treated by having him observe children who enjoyed their play with a rabbit and served as models for Peter. In this way, Peter could observe that rabbits did not need to be frightening. Later, Jones put a caged rabbit into a room, at some distance from Peter, while he was eating his favorite food. Over a period of days, Jones brought the rabbit closer and closer, always making sure that Peter was comfortable with the rabbit. At the end of this treatment, Peter was able to

Yvonne Hemsey/Contributor/Getty Images News/Getty Images

B.F. SKINNER

OVERT:
actions that can be OBSERVE

COVERT
actions that take place w/in Individual cannot BE observed.

play with and pat the rabbit. In this example, Jones worked with both Peter's overt and covert behavior.

Initiated in the 1960s by Albert Bandura, social cognitive theory, formerly called social learning theory, emphasizes the role of thoughts and images in psychological functioning (Bandura, 2007). Bandura proposed a *triadic reciprocal interaction system* involving the interactions among the environment; personal factors including memories, beliefs, preferences, predictions, anticipations, and self-perceptions; and behavioral actions (Martin, 2004). These three factors operate interactively, with each affecting the other two. An important aspect of Bandura's theory is that individuals learn by observing others. At the center of this triad is the self-system, a set of cognitive structures and perceptions that regulate behavior (Bandura, 1978, 1997, 2000). These cognitive structures include self-awareness, self-inducements, and self-reinforcement that can influence thoughts, behaviors, and feelings. Related to these is the concept of self-efficacy, which deals with how well people perceive that they are able to deal with difficult tasks in life (Bandura, 1986). Associated with a strong sense of self-efficacy is the ability to accomplish significant tasks, learn from observation, believe that one can succeed, and have a low level of anxiety.

Although classical conditioning and operant conditioning are important components of behavior therapy as it is practiced today, a blend of cognitive and behavioral approaches is more representative of current practice, particularly for people who are not living in institutions. The flexibility provided by theorists such as Bandura provides many ways for viewing psychological disorders.

Current Status of Behavior Therapy

Before the 1960s, behavior therapy was not well accepted within psychology, social work, education, or psychiatry. Since the 1970s, behavior therapy has been applied to a great number of areas such as business and industry, child raising, improving athletic performance, and enhancing the lives of people in nursing homes, psychiatric hospitals, and other institutions. Furthermore, behavior therapy has been better understood as a process in which patient and therapist, in many cases, collaborate to improve psychological functioning. In behavior therapy, the relationship with the client is valued, just as it is in other therapies.

Increased acceptance of behavior therapy has come about as a result of the growth in numbers of behavioral practitioners and their publications. The Association for Behavioral and Cognitive Therapies was founded in 1966 and in 2009 had more than 4,000 members. Although this organization was established in the United States, behavior therapy societies are found in a number of countries. With the increased interest in behavior therapies has come the establishment of many journals devoted to behavior therapy. Important journals include *Behavioral Disorders, Therapy, Behavioral Technology Today, Behavior Modification, The Behavior Therapist, Behavior Therapy, Behaviour Research and Therapy, Behavioural and Cognitive Psychotherapy, Behavioral Interventions, Child and Family Behavior Therapy, Cognitive and Behavioral Practice, Cognitive Therapy and Research, Journal of Applied Behavior Analysis, Journal of Behavior Therapy and Experimental Psychiatry, Journal of Psychopathology and Behavioral Assessment,* and *Journal of Rational-Emotive and Cognitive-Behavior Therapy.* All but two of the journals have been established since 1970. Almost all of these journals demonstrate the close relationship between research and the practice of behavior therapy.

ALBERT BANDURA

Behavior Theory of Personality

Unlike most theories of psychotherapy described in this book, behavior therapy does not have a comprehensive personality theory from which it is derived. Learning theories have been developed to explain personality, but few have been integrated into the practice of behavior therapy. For example, Dollard and Miller (1950) translated psychoanalytic concepts into learning theory terminology, based in part on the work of Hull (1943). Mowrer (1950) suggested two important learning processes to explain psychological disorder: the tendency to find a solution to a problem and learning based on expectations and beliefs. A social learning theory that stresses behavior potential, expectancies, reinforcement value, and situational factors has been developed by Rotter (1954). Eysenck's (1970) theory of traits is based on underlying behaviors that focus on introversion-extraversion and stability-neuroticism. Believing that people's behaviors are consistent across time but may differ depending upon the nature of the situation, Mischel (1973) has stressed the importance of competencies, personal constructs, values, and self-regulating systems in personality development. Although these theories have had relatively little impact on the practice of behavior therapy, Bandura's social learning theory (discussed previously) has had an impact on behavior therapy through the practice of modeling and the emphasis on self-observation. The important principles that underlie most of these theories are those developed through research on classical and operant conditioning and on observational learning.

Basic principles of behavior, especially those derived from operant conditioning, describe reinforcement, the process in which the consequences of behavior increase the likelihood that a behavior will be performed again. Lack of reinforcement can bring about extinction of behavior. Through a variety of processes, behavior can be shaped, narrowed (discrimination), broadened (generalized), or otherwise changed. Another key principle of basic learning is that of learning through observation. Implicit in the study of behavior is that behavior has antecedents (events occurring before the behavior is performed) and consequences (events occurring after a behavior is performed) (Spiegler & Guevremont, 2010). An important aspect of behavior therapy is the attention paid to each specific situation. Examples in this chapter show therapeutic and other situations that illustrate these basic principles of behavior.

Positive Reinforcement

A positive event presented as a consequence of a person's performing a behavior is called *positive reinforcement*. When a positive event follows a behavior, and that behavior increases in frequency, the event is a positive reinforcer (Spiegler & Guevremont, 2010). If you say "Thank you" to a friend who brings you a sandwich, your expression of thanks is a positive reinforcer for the act of your friend that increases the chance that your friend will do something like this for you or someone else in the future. If the friend does something positive for you again, you have observed positive reinforcement, which is different from a reward— something given to or awarded to someone for doing something. Rewards do not necessarily increase the probability that the frequency of a response following a favorable event will increase, whereas a positive reinforcer does.

Positive reinforcement is considered to be one of the most widely used behavior therapy procedures because of its effectiveness in bringing about positive

Theories in Action

changes in behavior and its compatibility with cultural values (Groden & Cautela, 1981). Intermittent positive reinforcement is longer lasting than continuous positive reinforcement. *Intermittent reinforcement* can be given at time intervals (an interval schedule) or after a certain number of correct responses (ratio reinforcement).

Kazdin (2001) gives a brief example from Kirby and Shields (1972) of the use of social reinforcement with a seventh-grade boy who is doing poorly in school and not doing his work. In this example, praise is used as a positive reinforcer and is provided on an intermittent schedule of reinforcement in which the ratio of correct responses to praise became greater and greater. (Praise was frequent at first but tapered off later.)

> For example, in one program, praise was used to alter the behavior of a 13-year-old boy named Tom in a seventh-grade classroom (Kirby & Shields, 1972). Tom was of average intelligence but was doing poorly on his class assignments, particularly the arithmetic assignments. Also, he rarely paid attention to the lesson and constantly had to be reminded to work. Praise was used to improve his performance on arithmetic assignments. Each day in class, after he completed the arithmetic assignment, he was praised for correct answers on his arithmetic worksheet. At first, every couple of responses were praised, but the number of correct problems required for praise was gradually increased. The praise consisted merely of saying, "Good work," "Excellent job," and similar things. (p. 160)

Negative Reinforcement

Like positive reinforcement, negative reinforcement increases a behavior. It should not be confused with punishment, which decreases or weakens a behavior. In negative reinforcement an undesirable consequence of a behavior is removed, which increases the likelihood that a behavior will be repeated. For example, if you are waiting in the rain for a friend to meet you and you have an umbrella with you, you open it up. The umbrella keeps the rain off of you. The next several times you carry an umbrella with you, you are more likely to use it if the rain is of the same intensity increasing the likelihood of a positive behavior (Spiegler & Guevremont, 2010).

Extinction

When reinforcers are withdrawn or not available, individuals stop performing a behavior. *Extinction* is the process of no longer presenting a reinforcer. Examples of extinction include ignoring a crying child, working without being paid, or not responding to someone who is talking to you. Parents may use the basic principle of extinction when dealing with a child. On the one hand, for example, if a child grabs her mother's pants and pulls, the mother may choose to ignore the behavior and let it extinguish. If she responds to the child warmly, she runs the risk of positively reinforcing the pants-grabbing behavior. On the other hand, appropriate behavior can be extinguished when it is desirable to reinforce the behavior. For example, if a father reads a magazine while his son is playing productively and quietly and does not attend to the son, there is a danger of extinguishing the child's appropriate play.

Generalization

When behavior is reinforced, it may generalize to other behavior. Reinforcement increases the chances that ways of responding to one type of stimulus will transfer to similar stimuli. Thus, when one encounters a difficult problem in dealing with someone, if the solution had been effective, that way of interacting with people will generalize to other situations. By learning how to deal with one angry person, individuals learn how to deal with that same person in different situations and with different individuals who are angry. To use another example, if a child is praised for doing well on an arithmetic test, then she may not only work harder on her arithmetic problems but also generalize this behavior to other subjects. Just as it is important to be able to generalize from one experience to others, it is important to be able to discriminate among different situations.

Discrimination

The ability to be able to react differently, depending upon the stimulus condition that is presented, is extremely important for individuals. To use an example, drivers must be able to discriminate between red and green traffic lights. If they are color blind, they must learn to discriminate based upon the position of the light. In social interactions, children soon learn how to act differently around bullies as opposed to friends and may act differently with a substitute teacher than with their regular teacher. Individuals may also make subtle distinctions, responding differently to the statement "You look very nice today," depending on who has said it and in what tone of voice. In brief, discrimination comes about as certain responses are reinforced and others are ignored and thus extinguished.

Shaping

When a therapist shapes a client's behavior, reinforcement, extinction, generalization, and discrimination are involved. In shaping, there is a gradual movement from the original behavior to the desired behavior by reinforcing approximations of the desired behavior. For example, shaping occurs when parents reinforce their toddler's attempt to walk. First, the child is praised for walking while holding on to a parent's hand, later for walking while holding on to the furniture, later for taking a few steps without holding on to anything, and later for walking from one end of the living room to the other. As each new target is reached, the child is no longer praised for reaching the previous target.

Observational Learning

In describing social cognitive theory, Bandura (1977, 1997) states that reinforcement is not sufficient to explain learning and personality development. He believes that much learning takes place through observing and modeling the actions of others. For example, children may learn by watching parents, friends, television, or movies, or by reading. In the process of learning, behavioral processes are important, as are cognitive processes that symbolically code observations and memories (Bandura, 1986, 1989a). Bandura describes the processes that explain observational learning as having four basic functions: attention, retention, motor reproduction, and motivation.

Attentional processes. Important in the observational process is the attending process itself, as well as the persons and/or situations that are being observed. It is not enough to see something; to observe, one must perceive it accurately. For example, if a student watches a professor who is lecturing, he may attend to what is being presented in varying degrees.

Additionally, the pattern of associations (Bandura, 1989a) that an individual has with the model or situation being observed greatly influences attention. Strong associational patterns with parents make them important models for children to observe. Models vary in terms of their interpersonal attractiveness and interest. Advertisers take advantage of this fact by using athletes or other celebrities who attract the attention of a large proportion of the audience of potential customers. In doing so, advertisers want the star to draw attention to the product, not to himself.

Retention processes. For observation to be successful, a model's behavior must be remembered. In proposing a cognitive system for recalling the observed model, Bandura describes *imaginal* coding and verbal coding. *Imaginal* coding refers to mental images of events, such as picturing two friends having talked to each other yesterday. *Verbal coding*, sometimes called *self-talk*, refers to subvocal descriptions of events. For example, a person who is trying to master golf may say to herself, "I grip the putter with my hands in an interlocking grip." Bandura believes that verbal coding is particularly effective in retaining observed events because it can be easily stored. For observation to be effective, the memories of the situation must be directed toward performing behaviors.

Motor reproduction processes. It is one thing to observe and remember the behaviors of a model and quite another to translate what is observed into action. Imitating the way a baseball player puts on a hat is relatively simple, requiring little rehearsal to perform the action correctly. Hitting a baseball the way a star athlete does is another matter. Extremely quick and accurate perceptual and motor skills are needed to imitate highly skilled behavior. Even if someone has a degree of success in imitating modeled behavior, there is no guarantee that the modeled behavior will be maintained for a significant period of time.

Motivational processes. If an individual observes and puts into action modeled behavior, it is likely to be continued only if it is reinforced. A person is likely to use a particular hitter's stance only if the behavior leads to success. Incentives can be important in modeling. For example, if a math teacher's presentation of fractions reinforces the student's success with fractions, the student is likely to model the behavior of the math teacher and use the teacher's method to solve fraction problems.

Bandura argues that reinforcement does not have to be external but can be internal—that is, come from individuals themselves. He describes two types of internal reinforcement: vicarious and self-reinforcement. *Vicarious* reinforcement refers to observing someone getting reinforced for performing an action and concluding that performing the same behavior will bring about a reinforcement. *Self-reinforcement* occurs when people set standards for themselves and reinforce themselves for meeting their expectations, as an athlete may on accomplishing a particular goal.

 Self-efficacy. According to Bandura (1989b, 1997), *self-efficacy* is the individual's perception of her ability to deal with different types of situations. People with high self-efficacy expect success, which often leads to success itself, whereas those with low self-efficacy have self-doubts about their abilities to accomplish tasks; thus, the chance of successful outcome may be lower, and self-esteem will be lowered. Those who have high self-efficacy are likely to have imaginal coding and verbal coding that reflect success. In other words, a student with a high

[handwritten margin note: Self-Efficacy 4 major Sources]

[handwritten margin note: Paper: Performance Accomplishments]

sense of self-efficacy can visualize herself doing well on an exam and can think confidently about her upcoming exam.

In describing the acquisition of self-efficacy, Bandura (1989b, 1997) believes that self-efficacy comes from four major sources: performance accomplishments, vicarious experiences, verbal persuasion, and lowering emotional arousal. *Performance accomplishments* refer to the fact that past successes are likely to create expectations and a resulting high sense of efficacy. *Vicarious experiences* mean opportunities to observe someone else and say, "I can do that" or, for those with low self-efficacy, "I don't think I can do that." *Verbal persuasion* refers to the impact that encouragement or praise from parents, friends, or others can have on expectations of performance. Lowering powerful anxiety (*emotional arousal*) will allow individuals to perform more accurately and calmly, leading to a stronger sense of self-efficacy. Of these four sources of self-efficacy, Bandura believes that the strongest factor is an individual's performance accomplishments.

Despite the many theories of behavior and its impact on personality, basic for most behavior therapists are the principles of reinforcement and observational learning. They have been used in a variety of ways to develop techniques to help individuals change covert and overt behavior.

Theories of Behavior Therapy

[handwritten margin note: Assessments]

There are no overriding theories of behavior therapy; rather, techniques have been developed that are consistent with basic principles of behavior. Goals of behavior therapy are situationally specific, depending on the desired behavior change. Similarly, assessment focuses on reports and observations of client behaviors in real and simulated situations. With this information, behavior therapists use a variety of techniques, such as systematic desensitization, which can reduce fears and anxieties. Sometimes behavior therapists work with the actual situation in which an event has occurred; other times, they may have the client imagine an event. Additionally, behavior therapists have developed a variety of strategies to model and teach new behaviors. By combining behavioral approaches with self-instruction and other cognitive techniques, some therapists have developed additional creative approaches to help clients cope more effectively with their problems.

Goals of Behavior Therapy

[handwritten margin note: Target Behaviors]

A distinguishing feature of behavior therapy is its emphasis on the specificity of goals. Early in their work with patients, behavior therapists focus on changing *target behaviors*—that is, behaviors that can be defined clearly and accurately. They identify the actions or events that explain why an individual persists in a certain behavior. Often clients have several problems, and the therapist and client decide together which problem needs to be treated first. Examples of target behaviors include ceasing smoking, decreasing fighting among children, increasing class attendance, and decreasing checking to see if outside doors in a home are all locked. Behavior therapists work with a variety of goals and target behaviors (Miltenberger, 2008).

Frequently, behavior therapists perform a *functional analysis*. They evaluate (assess) the behavior and the antecedents and consequences associated with it (assessment). They identify causes (antecedents) of the behavior or reasons the patient uses the behavior. The therapist makes hypotheses about what factors contribute

to controlling the behavior. Information from the functional analysis guides the choice of the behavioral interventions (Miltenberger, 2008). The functional analysis provides a way to further specify goals. Behavior therapists may not always perform an explicit functional analysis, but they do perform assessments.

Selecting appropriate goals is done as part of a thorough assessment. As behavior therapists learn more about the antecedents and consequences of the behavior, they are more able to help the client identify specific goals. As assessment continues, clients are able to explore, with the help of the therapist, possible advantages and disadvantages of goals, how the goals can be achieved, and the likelihood of doing so. Assessment is a process that continues throughout behavior therapy and after it ends. Measurement of change as it relates to achieving goals is a continuing part of behavior therapy and functional analysis. The detailed approach to assessment as it relates to progress toward goals is described in the next section.

Behavioral Assessment

Assessing specific behaviors rather than broader characteristics or traits is the hallmark of behavioral assessment. The emphasis is on determining the unique details of a client's problem and situation. Thus, diagnostic categories (DSM-IV-TR) may not be a part of behavioral treatment for some behavior therapists. The emphasis on behavioral assessment is current rather than past behavior and on sampling specific discrete behaviors. For example, a college student having difficulty in scheduling his homework might be asked to keep a list of his activities during the day and the evening. Behavior therapists gather information from clients with behavioral interviews, reports and ratings, and observations of client behavior, among other ways (Spiegler & Guevremont, 2010). They are likely to use several of these methods, not one or two.

Behavioral interviews. The initial behavioral interview is an essential part of the assessment process. Understanding the problem in behavioral terms is essential. For example, if the client says he has difficulty in schoolwork, the therapist may want to know what his grades are, in which courses he is experiencing difficulty, and the nature of that difficulty. By asking about the antecedents and consequences of specific behavior, the therapist assesses information about the target behavior. For example, when and in which course does the client procrastinate on his work? In the process of doing this, the behavior therapist will also tell the client what other information has to be gathered.

Many of the questions that behavioral therapists ask have to do with finding details about the target behavior. They make good use of *what, when, where, how,* and *how often* (Spiegler & Guevremont, 2010, p. 85). An abbreviated example follows:

> [*Therapist:*] *What* brings you here today?
>
> [*Patient:*] I feel depressed.
>
> [*Therapist:*] *When* did you first start to feel depressed?
>
> [*Patient:*] About three months ago. I just felt down. It was hard to get up out of bed.
>
> [*Therapist:*] How often has it occurred since then?
>
> [*Patient:*] Well it happened three months ago and then twice more.
>
> [*Therapist:*] *When* does your depression occur?
>
> [*Patient:*] I feel it in the mornings; it's worse then.

In this way, the behavior therapist finds out more about the problem. As she does so, the therapist shows concern that the patient is upset about the problem.

Behavioral reports and ratings. An efficient way of assessing the changes the client wishes to make is to use written instruments developed to assess problem behaviors. Self-report inventories, often quite brief, ask clients to rate themselves on a 5- or 7-point scale or answer "yes" or "no" to items. Self-report inventories have been designed to assess depression, fear, anxiety, social skills, health-related disorders, sexual dysfunction, and marital problems.

Also valuable are checklists and rating scales that parents, teachers, peers, or others complete to describe the client's behavior. When checklists and rating scales are used in this way, it is important that there be *interrater reliability*—that is, close agreement among raters about their observations of the same behavior of the individual.

Behavioral observations. Besides self-reports and others' ratings, direct observational procedures can be used. By having clients record the number of times they perform a target behavior, immediate records can be kept. Also, diaries that indicate the date, time, place, and activity during which related behaviors occur can be useful. One problem with having clients record their own behavior is that reactivity can result. *Reactivity* refers to change in clients' behavior caused by knowing that behavior is being recorded or observed. In some situations, reactivity can be useful in achieving desired behavior change.

To prevent reactivity, therapists may use naturalistic or simulated observation. *Naturalistic observation* means that observers record the frequency, duration, and/or strength of target behaviors; for example, observers may record the social interactions of 3-year-old children in a nursery school. *Simulated observation* means a situation is set up for monitoring behavior, for example, with microphones and one-way mirrors, so that more accurate data can be obtained than in a natural situation. Because both natural and simulated observation can be time consuming, therapists sometimes use role playing by requesting that the client enact the behavior, such as a problematic relationship with a parent.

Physiological measurements. As a measure of stress or fear, therapists may use a variety of measures of physical functioning. Common measures include blood pressure, heart rate, respiration, and skin electrical conductivity. Occasionally, behavior therapies are used specifically to change physiological symptoms, such as when the goal of therapy is to lower high blood pressure.

Although assessment is done particularly at the beginning of therapy, interviewing to assess maintaining conditions of the target behavior continues throughout the therapeutic process. Additionally, self-report measures and natural, simulated, or role playing observation can be used at any time in the therapeutic process. By gathering this information, assessment of maintaining conditions is made and changes in target behaviors can be measured.

General Treatment Approach

Behavioral therapists have developed a variety of methods based on behavioral principles to reduce fear and anxiety and to change other behaviors. One of the first and one of the most significant approaches is Wolpe's desensitization method, which makes use of relaxation and gradual imaginal strategies. Some approaches use intense imaginal strategies; others work in the actual environment that causes anxiety. Yet other techniques include modeling the behavior of others. By combining behavioral and cognitive approaches, Donald Meichenbaum has created stress management approaches. Each of these is described more fully here.

JOSEPH WOLPE

Systematic Desensitization

Developed by Joseph Wolpe (1958), systematic desensitization was designed to treat patients who presented with extreme anxiety or fear toward specific events, people, or objects, or had generalized fears. The basic approach is to have clients replace their anxious feelings with relaxation. The first step is to teach the client relaxation responses that compete with and replace anxiety. Second, the events that make the client anxious are assessed and arranged by degrees of anxiety. The third step is to have the client imagine anxiety-evoking situations while being relaxed. Repeated in a gradual manner, so that relaxation is paired with thoughts of events that had previously evoked anxiety, the client is systematically desensitized to situations that had previously created anxiety.

Excerpts from the case of Miss C. illustrate the three major procedures of systematic desensitization: relaxation, hierarchy construction, and desensitization (Wolpe, 1990).

Relaxation. The process of progressive relaxation was first developed by Jacobson (1938). Basically it involves tensing and relaxing muscle groups, including arms, face, neck, shoulders, chest, stomach, and legs, to achieve deeper and deeper levels of relaxation. In work with his patients, Wolpe (1990) would ask them to devote 10 to 15 minutes twice a day to relaxation. Wolpe often used five or six sessions to teach relaxation. In introducing this technique to Miss C., he probably started in the following way.

> I am now going to show you the essential activity that is involved in obtaining deep relaxation. I will again ask you to resist my pull at your wrist so as to tighten your biceps. I want you to notice very carefully the sensations in that muscle. Then I will ask you to let go gradually as I diminish the amount of force exerted against you. Notice, as your forearm descends, that there is decreasing sensation in the biceps muscle. Notice also that the letting go is an activity, but of a negative kind—it is an "uncontracting" of the muscle. In due course, your forearm will come to rest on the arm of the chair, and you may then think that you have gone as far as possible—that relaxation is complete. But although the biceps will indeed be partly and perhaps largely relaxed, a certain number of its fibers will still, in fact, be contracted. I will then say to you, "Go on letting go. Try to extend the activity that went on in the biceps while your forearm was coming down." It is the act of relaxing these additional fibers that will bring about most of the emotional effects we want. Let's try it and see what happens. (p. 156)

Relaxation proceeded in this way, with different sessions addressing different parts of the body. Continued relaxation practice throughout the course of therapy was important so that a state of relaxation could be paired with imagined anxious situations.

Anxiety hierarchies. Obtaining detailed and highly specific information about events that cause a client to become anxious is the essence of constructing an anxiety hierarchy. Often several hierarchies representing different fears are constructed. After describing the events that elicit anxiety, clients then list them in order from least anxiety evoking to most anxiety evoking. This is often done by assigning a number from 0 to 100 to each event. In this way a *subjective units of discomfort scale* (SUDs) is developed, with 0 representing total relaxation and 100 representing extremely high anxiety. These units are subjective and apply only to the individual. As systematic desensitization progresses, events that originally had high SUDs ratings have lower SUDs ratings.

Wolpe (1990, p. 166) describes Miss C. as a 24-year-old art student seeking treatment primarily because she had failed exams due to her extreme anxiety. Further interviewing revealed that Miss C. was anxious not only about examinations but also about being watched or scrutinized by others, being criticized or devalued by others, and seeing others disagreeing or arguing. A brief hierarchy based on the latter concern that was developed by Miss C. with Wolpe's help is listed below along with the SUDs. (Many lists are longer, with more than 10 items.)

Discord between other people

1. Her mother shouts at a servant (50)

2. Her younger sister whines to her sister (40)

3. Her sister engages in a dispute with her father (30)

4. Her mother shouts at her sister (20)

5. She sees two strangers quarrel (10)

Having established a hierarchy like this one, Wolpe is ready to start the process of desensitization.

Desensitization. Although the relaxation process may not be fully mastered, the desensitization procedures can start (Wolpe, 1990). During the first desensitization session, the therapist asks clients, after they are relaxed, how many SUDs they are experiencing. If the level is too high, above 25, relaxation is continued. The first scene presented is a neutral one, such as a flower against a background. This provides an opportunity for the therapist to gauge how well the client is able to imagine or visualize. Then the therapist proceeds in a way similar to that of Wolpe in his work with Miss C., as shown next. First, he has her imagine a neutral scene, then one from her hierarchy of her fear of examinations, and then number 5, from the discord hierarchy.

> [Therapist:] I am now going to ask you to imagine a number of scenes. You will imagine them clearly and they will interfere little, if at all, with your state of relaxation. If, however, at any time you feel disturbed or worried and want to draw my attention, you can tell me so. As soon as a scene is clear in your mind, indicate that by raising your left index finger about 1 inch. First, I want you to imagine that you are standing at a familiar street corner on a pleasant morning watching the traffic go by. You see cars, motorcycles, trucks, bicycles, people, and traffic lights, and you hear the sounds associated with all these things. (After a few seconds the patient raises her left index finger. The therapist pauses for 5 seconds.)

> [Therapist:] Stop imagining that scene. By how much did it raise your anxiety level while you imagined it?

> Miss C.: Not at all.

> [Therapist:] Now give your attention once again to relaxing. (There is again a pause of 20–30 seconds, with renewed relaxation instructions.)

> [Therapist:] Now imagine that you are home studying in the evening. It is May 20, exactly a month before your examination. (After about 15 seconds Miss C. raises her finger. Again she is left with the scene for 5 seconds.)

[Therapist:] Stop that scene. By how much did it raise your anxiety?

Miss C.: About 15 units.

[Therapist:] Now imagine the same scene again—a month before your examination.

At this second presentation the rise in anxiety was five SUDs and at the third it was zero. The numbers given vary with the individual and with the scene. When the initial figure is over 30, repetition is unlikely to lower it. But there are exceptions. There are also occasional patients in whom an initial rise of 10 is too great to be diminished by repetition.

Having disposed of the first scene of the examination hierarchy, I could have moved on to the second. Alternatively, I could have tested Miss C.'s responses in another area, such as the discord hierarchy, which I did.

[Therapist:] Imagine you are sitting on a bench at a bus stop and across the road are two strange men whose voices are raised in argument. (This scene was given twice. After the patient reported on her response to the last presentation, I terminated the desensitization session.)

[Therapist:] Relax again. Now I am going to count up to five and you will open your eyes, feeling calm and refreshed. (Wolpe, 1990, pp. 173–174)

After the end of 17 desensitization sessions, Wolpe reports that Miss C. was able to be relaxed while imagining any items from each of the four hierarchies and to be relaxed in the actual situations themselves. Four months later Miss C. took her examinations without being anxious and passed them.

Although Wolpe's approach to desensitization is typical, there are variations. Some therapists have used pleasant thoughts as a substitute for deep muscle relaxation. Although commonly used with anxiety, desensitization has also been used in working with anger, asthmatic attacks, insomnia, nightmares, problem drinking, speech disorders, and other problems (Spiegler & Guevremont, 2010). Because it is a lengthy process compared to other behavioral procedures (discussed in the next sections), desensitization is used much less frequently than it was in the 1970s (Hazel, 2005). Wolpe explains the application of systematic desensitization, regardless of the type of response used to compete with different emotions, as *counterconditioning*, drawing a parallel between desensitization and classical conditioning. However, other principles of behavior can be used to describe this process as well. Note that both physical behaviors (tensing parts of the body) and covert behaviors (imagination of scenes) are used to bring about change. In systematic desensitization, a gradual exposure to anxiety-producing situations is produced through use of imagined scenes. Other techniques make use of dramatic scenes of anxiety-producing situations.

Imaginal Flooding Therapies

Whereas the process of systematic desensitization is a gradual one, flooding is not. In imaginal flooding, the client is exposed to the mental image of a frightening or anxiety-producing object or event and continues to experience the image of the event until the anxiety gradually diminishes. The exposure is not to the actual situation but to an image of a frightening situation such as being mugged or being in an airplane.

The basic procedure in imaginal flooding is to develop scenes that frighten or induce anxiety in the client and then have the client imagine the scene fully and indicate the SUDs. Then the client is asked to imagine the scene again in the same session and in future sessions, indicating the SUDs. With continual exposure, the SUDs should be reduced to a point where discomfort is no longer experienced. For illustration purposes, a simplified example of treating Al, who is afraid of riding on elevators, is described below. Al is asked to imagine these scenes:

1. The client rides on an elevator with his mother from the fourth floor of a four-story building to the first floor.

2. The client rides an elevator from the top floor of a four-story building to the first floor, with no one else in the elevator.

3. The client rides in an elevator alone from the 30th floor of a 30-story building to the basement.

After Al indicates his SUDs ratings to each of these situations, the therapist has him imagine the situations until they no longer create anxiety. Then the therapist would have Al imagine another scene. In an actual therapeutic situation, more scenes may be used and elevators that were familiar to Al would be imagined. Often relaxation exercises are practiced before flooding to make the imagery more real and, after the flooding, to return to a low level of anxiety (Keane, Fairbank, Caddell, & Zimering, 1989).

Another imaginal flooding approach is implosive therapy, developed by Thomas Stampfl (1966). In *implosive therapy*, the scenes are exaggerated rather than realistic, and hypotheses are made about stimuli in the scene that may cause the fear or anxiety. Stampfl (1970) makes use of the client's description of the scene as well as a psychoanalytic interpretation of the scene. However, it is rarely used now.

Imaginal flooding (including implosive therapy) is not widely used for several reasons. Possibly, the high level of anxiety the client is exposed to will not be reduced. Also, flooding and implosive therapies can be quite unpleasant for clients, who must re-experience anxiety. Because clients are given the option of participating in either of these therapies, they are able to decide if the approach would be too unpleasant or uncomfortable (Spiegler & Guevremont, 2010). Although like desensitization, flooding involves imaginal presentation of anxiety-producing events, there are times when behavior therapists prefer to use actual situations.

In Vivo Therapies

Environmen

The term *in vivo* refers to procedures that occur in the client's actual environment. Basically, the two types of in vivo therapy are those in which the client approaches the feared stimuli gradually (similar to systematic desensitization) and those in which the client works directly with the feared situation (similar to imaginal flooding). With the graduated approach, clients often learn and practice relaxation techniques that will compete with the exposure to anxious situations. In some cases, other competing responses, such as pleasant images, are also used to compete with the anxiety experienced in the actual situation. A client choosing a graduated approach to reducing fears and anxiety would discuss with therapists which situations are likely to arouse varying degrees of anxiety, establishing a hierarchy or list of events. For example, given Al's fear of elevators, a list such as the following may be produced.

1. Walk to an elevator door in the presence of the therapist.

2. Watch as the therapist presses the button to open the elevator door.

3. The client presses the elevator button while the therapist watches.

4. Therapist and client walk into the elevator and back out again on the same floor.

5. The therapist holds the elevator door while the client walks around inside the elevator.

6. The therapist and client take the elevator one flight and exit.

7. The client and therapist ride up and ride down one flight in the elevator.

8. The client and therapist go up two flights together and back again, and so forth.

9. The client rides up one flight by himself, to be met by the therapist.

10. The client rides up two flights, three flights, and so forth by himself.

If at any time the client is tense, the therapist has the client perform relaxation procedures. Advancement from one step to the next occurs only when the client is comfortable. When the client is able to perform these activities in the presence of the therapist, he is asked to do similar work on his own, riding in elevators daily. The length of therapy will depend on the severity of the anxiety.

In intense in vivo exposure therapy, the exposure is to a strongly feared situation. Before starting the exposure, the therapist assures the client that the therapy is effective, that the therapist will be there with the client, and that some emotional distress will be experienced (Spiegler & Guevremont, 2010). To return to the elevator example, the therapist would ride up and down an elevator with Al for half an hour or more at a time. Sessions with the therapist would continue until reported anxiety is low. At that point, the therapist would wait at a floor while Al rides up and down an elevator. Additionally, Al would be asked to ride on elevators several times each day. In this way, the anxious response to elevators is extinguished, and a nonanxious response to elevators is reinforced.

Virtual Reality Therapy

First started in the 1980s and 1990s, virtual reality therapy is therapy that takes place in a computer-generated environment (North, North, & Burwick, 2008; Wiederhold & Wiederhold, 2005). Typically, the client can interact with this environment by using a joystick, a headband, a glove with physiological sensors, or a similar device. These devices give information to the computer about the client. In this way, a client could "walk" or "drive" a car in a simulated manner. Occasionally, "mixed" or "augmented" systems might be used, such as driving a simulated car where there are actual engine sounds and smells. A major challenge for virtual reality therapies is cost. Sometimes screens are from head to foot or taller and may be built in a semicircle or full circle. Software and programming are complex so that they can take the client's feedback and change computer settings and visual and audio feedback quickly (North et al., 2008; Wiederhold & Wiederhold, 2005).

Typically, virtual reality therapy is used for the treatment of anxiety disorders, especially phobias. Specific anxiety disorders include panic disorder, agoraphobia, claustrophobia, social phobia or anxiety, obsessive-compulsive disorder, and posttraumatic stress disorder (PTSD). Some of the more common phobias that have been treated with virtual reality therapy include fears of flying (Krijn et al., 2007; Price & Anderson, 2007), driving, speaking in public (Wallach, Safir, & Bar-Zvi, 2009), heights, spiders, closed spaces (Malbos, Mestre, Note, & Gellato,

2008), and a variety of medical procedures (Wiederhold & Wiederhold, 2005). Virtual reality therapy has also been used with eating disorders. In one system, clients can match current self-image and ideal self-image using two-dimensional and three-dimensional figures of various sizes (Riva et al., 2003). As virtual reality devices become faster and more accurate in simulating reality, as well as less expensive, virtual reality therapies are likely to be used in more mental health applications. Recent studies have focused on posttraumatic stress due to exposure to military trauma. Virtual reality exposure to combat conditions for American soldiers fighting in Iraq has shown preliminary evidence to suggest its effectiveness in reducing posttraumatic stress (Reger & Gahm, 2008; Rizzo, Reger, Gahm, Difede, & Rothbaum, 2009). Evidence for the effectiveness of virtual reality therapy has been reported for anxiety disorders (including phobias). In a meta-analysis of 13 studies focused on anxiety disorders, virtual reality therapy showed a small effect size favoring it over in vivo therapy (Powers & Emmelkamp, 2008). In another meta-analysis of 21 studies including anxiety disorders and phobias, virtual reality therapy led to decreases in symptoms of anxiety (Parsons & Rizzo, 2008). The authors suggest more work needs to be done to determine the role of feeling that virtual reality therapy is like real life and the role of demographic factors in the success of virtual reality therapy.

To give a clearer example of virtual reality therapy, let us return to Al and his fear of riding in elevators. We could use a visual system in which Al wears goggles with a computer screen in place of the lenses, or we could have him enter a room filled with screens that show the lobby of a building with elevators. With sensors attached to his legs, Al could walk through the simulated lobby, press a simulated elevator button, and enter an elevator in the simulated building. In the simulated elevator, lights would indicate which floor the elevator was stopping at. This procedure could be very expensive. It would be less expensive, and probably less effective, to have Al follow a similar path, but by using a joystick instead of walking. Either of these procedures could be used many times until Al is ready to try in vivo exposure. In vivo exposure should not take long, as Al has had this virtual exposure to elevators.

Whether behavior therapists use imaginal, virtual, or in vivo approaches, or graduated or intense approaches, behavior therapy depends on both the therapist's assessment of target behaviors and the patient's preference. If the anxiety is very great and the patient is fearful, the patient may elect a more graduated approach. In some cases, patients may prefer an intense approach to reduce their discomfort more quickly. Usually, in vivo approaches often provide quicker relief than imaginal approaches, as they are direct and do not rely on the client's ability to imagine events. However, some fears, such as fears of lightning or earthquakes, lend themselves to imaginal and, possibly, virtual reality procedures.

Modeling Techniques

The therapeutic use of modeling is based chiefly on the work of Bandura (1969, 1971, 1976, 1977, 1986, 1997, 2007). Modeling as a therapeutic technique occurs when a client observes the behavior of another person and makes use of that observation. Learning how the model performs the behavior and what happens to the model as a consequence of learning the behavior are both a part of the technique.

In behavior therapy, the five basic functions of modeling (Spiegler & Guevremont, 2010, p. 267) are teaching, prompting, motivating, reducing anxiety, and discouraging.

Modeling can occur by teaching through demonstration—for example, watching someone throw a baseball or peel an apple. Modeling can serve as a prompt, such as when a child struts like a drum major, imitating his behavior. By reinforcing modeling behavior, people can motivate others to perform that behavior, such as when a parent makes a game of cleaning a room, so that the child can see how the task can be enjoyable. Anxiety reduction can occur as a result of modeling, such as when a child goes into the water after having watched another child do so, thus reducing a fear of the water. Last, an individual can be discouraged from continuing behavior, such as when a smoker watches a graphic film of a patient smoking and gradually dying from lung cancer. In this section, these five functions are combined to varying degrees in live, symbolic, participant, and covert modeling.

Live modeling. Basically, *live modeling* refers to watching a model, sometimes the therapist, perform a specific behavior. Often the modeling is repeated a number of times, and then, after having observed the modeling, the client repeats the observed behavior several times. In Jones's (1924) study cited earlier, Peter's fear was reduced by observing other children modeling nonanxious behavior as they played with a rabbit.

Symbolic modeling. Often a live model is not available or would be inconvenient, so symbolic modeling is used. Common examples of symbolic modeling are films or videotapes of appropriate behavior; individuals are observed indirectly rather than in person. Other examples include photographs, picture books, and plays. For example, children's books about a child going to a hospital for an operation serve as symbolic modeling and can reduce a child's anxiety about surgery.

Self-modeling. Sometimes it is helpful to videotape a client performing the target behavior in a desired way (Dowrick, 1991; Dowrick, Tallman, & Connor, 2005). By filming a child interacting in a socially appropriate way with other children and then showing that film to the child, the child can observe himself modeling socially appropriate behavior and replace inappropriate behavior with the newly learned social skills.

Participant modeling. Sometimes it is helpful for the therapist to model a behavior for the client and then guide the client in using the behavior—participant modeling. If a client is afraid of climbing ladders, the therapist can model the behavior by first climbing the ladder. Then, using an adjoining ladder, the therapist can help the client climb a ladder while offering encouragement and physical support when necessary.

Covert modeling. Sometimes, when a model cannot be observed, it may be helpful to have a client visualize a model's behavior. In this process, covert modeling, the therapist describes a situation for the patient to imagine. Krop and Burgess (1993) give an example of covert modeling with a 7-year-old deaf girl who was sexually abused by her stepfather. As a result of the abuse, the girl was inappropriately touching males (in the crotch area), engaging in other inappropriate sexual behavior, and having tantrums. In using covert modeling, Krop and Burgess had the girl imagine another little girl named Sara who felt good about making decisions not to throw tantrums and instead to interact appropriately with other children. Several scenes involved taking constructive action rather than acting out in a negative way.

Modeling, whether symbolic or live, is often used with other behavioral strategies to bring about change. In particular, modeling is frequently used in situations that involve interpersonal communication. Wolpe (1990) and many other behavior therapists have modeled appropriate assertive behavior with clients who are overly polite, have difficulty expressing negative feelings, or feel they do not have a right to express feelings. Because assertiveness skills are different, depending on the situation, behavior therapists often model and have their clients practice a variety of situations (Spiegler & Guevremont, 2010). Although assertiveness is perhaps the most common social skill to which behavior therapists have applied modeling, other social skills such as playing, negotiating, and dating are appropriate for modeling techniques. Such modeling behavior can also be used in cognitive-behavioral approaches that require individuals to observe events and then tell themselves how to perform appropriately.

Self-Instructional Training: A Cognitive-Behavioral Approach

DONALD
MEICHENBAUM

Self-instruction is one of several methods of self-management. In his approach to self-management, Meichenbaum emphasizes the instructions that an individual gives to herself (Spiegler & Guevremont, 2010). Developed by Donald Meichenbaum (Meichenbaum, 1974; Meichenbaum & Goodman, 1971), self-instructional training is a way for people to teach themselves how to deal effectively with situations that had previously caused difficulty. The basic process is that the therapist models appropriate behavior, the client practices the behavior (as in participant modeling), and then the client repeats the instructions to herself. Self-instructional training can be applied to a great variety of behaviors, such as anxiety, anger, eating problems, and creative difficulties.

In applying self-instructional training to assertive behavior, the therapist would first model appropriate behavior, such as how to confront a roommate who borrows shirts. After modeling the behavior, the client would role play appropriate responses to the roommate with the therapist. Then the client would develop and repeat instructions to himself. "He has borrowed my shirt again. I will say to him now: 'Please do not wear my clothing without asking me. There are times when I will be glad to let you wear my shirts, but ask me first, please.'" In this simple example, the client could repeat this self-instruction several times to himself and then use it, or variations of it, at appropriate times with his roommate. Often used with children, self-instructional training can include the use of taped instructions, either by the client or the therapist, that the client listens to and practices. Additionally, the client may wish to keep records using a worksheet or practice the behavior in a variety of situations or with different people.

Stress Inoculation: A Cognitive-Behavioral Approach

Another self-management method developed by Meichenbaum (1985, 1993, 2007) is stress inoculation training (SIT). Just as an inoculation to prevent measles puts a little stress on a person's biological system to prevent the development of measles, so giving individuals an opportunity to cope with relatively mild stress stimuli successfully allows them to tolerate stronger fears or anxieties. Underlying the SIT program is Meichenbaum's view that individuals deal with stressful behaviors by changing their beliefs about the behaviors and the statements they make to themselves about their way of dealing with stress. The SIT program is a broad-ranging one, including information giving, relaxation training, cognitive restructuring, problem solving, behavioral rehearsals, and other cognitive and behavioral techniques. To illustrate Meichenbaum's three-stage model for stress inoculation training, I use the example of Ben, who has been robbed and badly beaten when walking home from work, and outline how SIT would be used with him in the conceptual phase, the skills-acquisition phase, and the application phase.

The conceptual phase. In the first phase, information is gathered and the client is educated about how to think about the problem. As Ben presents the situations and concerns that cause stress, the therapist points out that cognition and emotions, not the events themselves, create, maintain, and increase stress. Attention is paid to observing self-statements about the stressful or fearful situation and monitoring stressful behaviors that result. Using a log or diary throughout the therapeutic process is often recommended.

Ben would learn that his fear of walking to work is based on self-statements such as "I am going to be robbed again," "I know there is someone out there who is going to get me again," and "If I am attacked, I will be helpless." The therapist and Ben would go over his inner dialogue, and he would be asked to keep a record of stressful thoughts, feelings, and behaviors. This sets the stage for developing ways to cope with his fears.

Skills acquisition phase. To cope with the fear and stress, a variety of cognitive and behavioral skills are taught, including relaxation training, cognitive restructuring, problem-solving skills, and self-reinforcement instructions. To cope with stress, relaxation techniques such as those developed by Wolpe (1990) and Jacobson (1938) are taught, so that relaxation responses compete with fearful and anxious responses. Cognitive restructuring refers to changing negative thoughts to coping thoughts. Ben might replace "I'm afraid and can't do anything" with "When I am afraid, I will pause a moment" and "I can't handle this" with "Take this one step at a time and breathe slowly and comfortably." Problem solving includes rehearsing mentally how one is going to handle a situation. Ben might say to himself, "I will change the situation by gathering information about it; I can plan alternate routes; I can walk with people; I can manage my fear." Self-reinforcement is used by giving positive self-statements such as "I am walking to work, and I am doing well" and "I am almost at work, and I feel comfortable; I'm doing better than I did yesterday." Depending on the situation, therapists using SIT would teach their clients a variety of coping skills to deal with stressful situations.

Application phase. When clients have learned coping skills, they are then ready to put them into use in actual situations. First, Ben would mentally rehearse going to work while using the statements that have been developed. The more accurately Ben can visualize the scenes that take place while he is walking to work, the better he will be able to use previously developed coping strategies. When these skills have been mastered, Ben would be given homework assignments regarding what to do while walking to work. These would be gradual, such as practicing the coping statements while walking with a group of people, later practicing them while walking 30 feet behind the people, and so forth.

Like most other therapeutic methods, SIT does not always proceed smoothly, and relapse prevention (dealing with setbacks in treatment) should be a part of SIT (Meichenbaum, 1985). For example, Marlatt and Gordon (1985) have suggested that treatment can include planned failure experiences so that coping responses can be developed. Although stress inoculation training can focus on a few specific target behaviors, it is designed to generalize to other client behaviors as well. In this way, a client develops a feeling of self-efficacy as he is better able to cope with a variety of stressful events as they occur. This is possible because relaxation, cognitive restructuring, problem-solving skills, and self-reinforcement skills have been developed, practiced, and proven to be successful. Ben can apply these skills in situations as diverse as dealing with client pressures for delivery of merchandise at work, his father's insistence that Ben be a more conscientious son, and his brother's late-night alcoholic tirades. Meichenbaum (1993) describes many different applications of SIT, including dealing with general stress, anger, anxiety, and pain with psychiatric patients, athletes, medical patients, machine operators, and alcohol abusers.

In both behavioral therapy and cognitive-behavioral therapy, goals are very specific, but techniques are varied (Meichenbaum, 2007). Treatment can focus on changing behavior through imagining fearful or anxious scenes or through confronting them in a natural situation. The approach can be graduated or sudden, depending on the client's preference. Often modeling appropriate behavior can bring about therapeutic change, as can combining behavioral techniques with cognitive approaches, such as instructing oneself as to how to cope with a given situation. In the actual practice of therapy, these techniques are rarely used alone but can be combined into various treatment packages, depending on the behavioral assessment.

Psychological Disorders

Behavioral approaches to therapy depend on a number of factors, such as assessment, research, and client preference. A thorough assessment including observation, where possible, and rating instruments often influences techniques that are to be used. Furthermore, in the treatment of some disorders, research has shown some behavioral methods to be more effective than others. When several methods are likely to be equally effective, therapists give their clients a choice, such as to use graduated or intense exposure. In employing these behavioral techniques, these therapists are able to provide positive change in the lives of their patients.

The following cases represent a diverse set of approaches to behavioral treatment. In treating generalized anxiety disorders, a specific approach is used with a behavioral focus on progressive muscle relaxation and worry behavior prevention. In the treatment of a case of depression, relaxation techniques, time management, assertiveness, and cognitive-behavioral approaches are used. For obsessive-compulsive disorders, a behavioral treatment called exposure and response prevention, requiring intense treatment, is explained and illustrated. Exposure is illustrated as a treatment for phobias. These cases show different perspectives on assessing and treating psychological disorders. Underlying all of these approaches is an emphasis on assessment, specificity of target behaviors, changing behaviors, and creative and adaptive methodology.

Generalized Anxiety Disorder: Claire

After reviewing and analyzing research, Brown, O'Leary, and Barlow (2001) as well as others, have developed a manual for the treatment of generalized anxiety.

This approach combines cognitive therapy (described in Chapter 10) with several components of behavior therapy. This procedure consists of 12 to 15 meetings. Meetings are weekly, except for the last two, which are biweekly. The outline of this approach is described in Table 8.1. The table lists the treatment techniques to be used in each session. Techniques are addressed at various points during the sessions. For example, progressive muscle relaxation is taught and then practiced or reviewed in Sessions 3 through 13. Worry behavior prevention is introduced in Session 9 and then addressed in the remainder of the meetings. Problem solving and time management are discussed in the final two sessions. Monitoring and changing thoughts is addressed at the beginning of the therapy. Because cognitive techniques are addressed more thoroughly in Chapter 10, this case example will focus on demonstrating the behavioral techniques (especially progressive muscle relaxation and worry behavior prevention).

Table 8.1 Outline of Generalized Anxiety Disorder Treatment Protocol

Session 1
Patient's description of anxiety and worry
Introduction to nature of anxiety and worry
Three-system model of anxiety
Overview of treatment (e.g., importance of self-monitoring, homework, regular attendance)
Provision of treatment rationale
Homework: Self-monitoring

Session 2
Review of self-monitoring
Review of nature of anxiety, three-system model
Discussion of the physiology of anxiety
Discussion of maintaining factors in GAD
Homework: Self-monitoring

Session 3
Review of self-monitoring forms
Rationale for 16-muscle-group progressive muscle relaxation (PMR)
In-session PMR with audiotaping for home practices
Homework: Self-monitoring, PMR

Session 4
Review of self-monitoring forms, PMR practice
In-session 16-muscle-group PMR with discrimination training
Introduction to role of cognitions in persistent anxiety (e.g., nature of automatic thoughts, solicitation of examples from patient)
Description and countering of probability overestimation cognitions
Introduction to Cognitive Self-Monitoring Form
Homework: Self-monitoring (anxiety, cognitive monitoring, and countering), PMR

Session 5
Review of self-monitoring, PMR, probability overestimation countering
In-session 8-muscle-group PMR with discrimination training
Description and countering of catastrophic cognitions
Homework: Self-monitoring (anxiety, cognitive monitoring, and countering), PMR

Session 6
Review of self-monitoring, PMR, cognitive countering (probability overestimation, decatastrophizing)
In-session 8-muscle-group PMR with discrimination training; introduction of generalization practice
Review of types of anxiogenic cognitions and methods of countering
Homework: Self-monitoring (anxiety, cognitive monitoring, and countering), PMR

Session 7
Review of self-monitoring, PMR, cognitive countering
In-session 4-muscle-group PMR, introduction to worry exposure (e.g., imagery training, hierarchy of worry spheres, in-session worry exposure)
Homework: Self-monitoring (anxiety, cognitive monitoring, and countering), PMR, daily worry exposure

(Continued)

Table 8.1 Outline of Generalized Anxiety Disorder Treatment Protocol (Continued)

Session 8

Review of self-monitoring, PMR, cognitive countering, worry exposure practices

Introduction of relaxation-by-recall

Review of rationale for worry exposure

In-session worry exposure

Homework: Self-monitoring (anxiety, cognitive monitoring, and countering), worry exposure, relaxation-by-recall

Session 9

Review of self-monitoring, cognitive countering, worry exposure, relaxation-by-recall

Practice relaxation-by-recall

Introduction of worry behavior prevention (e.g., rationale, generation of list of worry behaviors, development of behavior prevention practices)

Homework: Self-monitoring (anxiety, cognitive monitoring, and countering), worry exposure, worry behavior prevention, relaxation-by-recall

Session 10

Review of self-monitoring, cognitive countering, worry exposure, worry behavior prevention, relaxation-by-recall

Introduction to cue-controlled relaxation

Homework: Self-monitoring (anxiety, cognitive monitoring, and countering), worry exposure, worry behavior prevention, cue-controlled relaxation

Session 11

Review of self-monitoring, cognitive countering, worry exposure, worry behavior prevention, cue-controlled relaxation

Practice cue-controlled relaxation

Introduction to time management or problem solving

Homework: Self-monitoring (anxiety, cognitive monitoring, and countering), worry exposure, worry behavior prevention, cue-controlled relaxation

Session 12

Review of self-monitoring, cognitive countering, worry exposure, worry behavior prevention, cue-controlled relaxation

Generalization of relaxation techniques

Time management or problem-solving practice

Homework: Self-monitoring (anxiety, cognitive monitoring, and countering), worry exposure, worry behavior prevention, cue-controlled relaxation, time management/problem-solving practice

Session 13

Review of self-monitoring, cognitive countering, worry exposure, worry behavior prevention, cue-controlled relaxation, time management/problem-solving practice

Practice of cue-controlled relaxation

Review of skills and techniques

Discussion of methods of continuing to apply techniques covered in treatment

Source: Brown, O'Leary, & Barlow, 2001, p. 177.

Claire is a married woman who has many worries, including worrying about her husband when he is traveling away from home for work and her son, who is playing football in high school. Claire first participates in a careful and detailed assessment to make sure that she fits the criteria for generalized anxiety disorder. The interview focuses on the nature of her worries and her experience of tension and anxiety. The first two therapy sessions are spent describing the nature of anxiety and the three-system model (physiological, cognitive, and behavioral), as well as reviewing treatment and giving homework.

In the third session the therapist explains the relaxation procedures to Claire and the time that it will take. When Claire raises concern about the amount of time, the therapist explains the rationale for the relaxation procedure.

[*Client:*] I know that I have to set aside time for homework, but 30 minutes sounds like a lot to me.

[*Therapist:*] It may be that sense of time pressure adds to your anxiety. Put it to yourself this way: By completing the relaxation every day, you're doing something that will help you physically and emotionally. All the other things that are going on in your life that have that "have to get done by such-and-such time" can wait. If you try to fit the relaxation in between several things on your daily agenda, you will most likely feel pressured to get it done and over with. So you won't feel relaxed at all! Make sure that you do the relaxation exercise at a time when you won't feel rushed or pressured by other responsibilities.

The procedure entails tensing and then releasing or relaxing your muscles. By tensing, you can accentuate the feeling of release, as well as discriminate when you might be unconsciously tensing your muscles during the day. Tensing your muscles shouldn't produce pain, but rather a sensation of tightness or pressure. You'll progress in sequence by tensing and releasing your lower and upper arms, lower and upper legs, abdomen, chest, shoulders, neck, face, eyes, and lower and upper forehead.

Be certain to practice in the beginning in quiet, nondistracting places. Concentration is a key element in learning how to relax, so you'll need to be in an environment where you can focus your attention completely on the sensation of tensing and releasing your muscles. This means no phone, TV, radio, or kids around during the exercise, but be sure not to fall asleep. Loosen or remove tight clothing, eyeglasses, contact lenses, shoes, belts, and the like. This exercise should be practiced twice a day for 30 minutes each time, for the following week.

Now I'll turn on the audiotape and record the relaxation procedure that I'll have you do to my voice in the session. You can use the audiotape at home for your practices.

The therapist then administers the relaxation procedure and discusses it at the end, to see how the client reacted to it. The therapist will continue to monitor the client's use of the relaxation procedures during the rest of the sessions.

In Session 9, Claire and the therapist work on worry behavior prevention. Claire will identify some behaviors that she will prevent herself from doing during the week. The therapist introduces worry behavior prevention in this way:

[*Therapist:*] As I've mentioned several times in our earlier meetings together, part of the treatment program involves identifying certain behaviors and activities that you may either be doing or avoiding that serve to relieve your anxiety in the short term. What happens, however, is that those behaviors actually reinforce your worry and anxiety in the long term, so that they are counterproductive. Today I'd like to generate a list of some of those behaviors that you might be doing, or activities that you may be avoiding, due to anxiety and worry. Some examples of such behaviors and activities include avoiding certain parts of the newspaper (like the health section or the obituaries), cleaning the house several times, being early for appointments, etc. Let's come up with some for you, Claire.

[*Client:*] I think the most obvious behavior is my total avoidance of my son's football games. He's been begging me to go to the homecoming game and I would really like to, because it's a big day for the team and there's a lot of pageantry about it. But it'll be tough to do, that I know for sure.

[*Therapist:*] So that's one activity. What is your anxiety about going to the game, from 0 to 8?

[*Client:*] Around a 7.

[*Therapist:*] What other things can we put on the list? How about not cleaning for a few days?

[*Client:*] Umm, that would also be around a 6 or 7. (Brown, O'Leary, & Barlow, 2001, pp. 192–193)

The therapist and Claire continue in this way to make a hierarchy. The therapist then summarizes what they have examined and suggests that Claire try the lowest item on the list.

[*Therapist:*] We have a few things that can comprise the list. Here it is: Going to the homecoming game, 7. Not cleaning for a few days, 6 to 7. Not having your husband call home at all, 6. Not cleaning the bathroom at all one day, 5. Not making the bed one morning, 4. Cleaning the bathroom only once one day, 3. Your husband calls only before leaving, 2.

For this week, you can begin the last item on the hierarchy—namely, having your husband call only when leaving work. Rate your anxiety during the day each week when you know he's not going to call until later, and then rate your anxiety after he calls. Let me know how this goes. If you find yourself worrying about him during the day, be sure to implement your cognitive strategies and the relaxation-by-recall to help you to control your worry and anxiety. (pp. 202–203)

The treatment manual for generalized anxiety disorder (Brown, O'Leary, & Barlow, 2001) is quite complex and structured. In the examples shown above, there is considerable attention to detail. Where needed, the therapist persuades the client what to do as well as offering a clear explanation for the procedures, such as relaxation. Although the manual is clear on how to proceed, the therapist must be well trained to deal with the specific concerns that the client presents.

 ## Depression: Jane

In general, behavioral therapists seek to reinforce patients' activities and social interactions. Because depressed patients are usually passive, behavioral interventions try to give them a sense of control and options for positive change. To bring about these changes, therapists start with an assessment of moods by asking patients to rate their moods and record pleasant and aversive events. Additionally, a large number of scales such as the Hamilton Rating Scale for Depression and the Beck Depression Inventory assess feelings of guilt, sadness, and failure and changes in appetite, sleeping, health, sex, and other behaviors. With this information, therapists can then set and plan realistic goals with their patients. A general assumption in behavior therapy is that changes in behavior bring about changes in thoughts and feelings.

With this emphasis on behavior, therapists help their patients increase daily activities, which may include more social contact or work productivity. They may develop a contract that provides for rewards such as meals, magazines, or time to do pleasurable things. Additionally, they may include social-skills training such as modeling appropriate behavior, role playing, and behavioral rehearsal and generally finding ways to increase pleasant social interactions while decreasing unpleasant ones.

Many of these techniques are illustrated here in therapy with Jane, a 29-year-old divorced mother with children ages 7 and 5 (Hoberman & Clarke, 1993). Jane complained of crying spells and frequent absences from work. She was worried about her older child's school performance and was upset about her ex-husband's failure to provide child support. The therapist's observation of depression was supported by a score indicating severe depression on the Beck Depression Inventory.

Assessment and treatment for Jane's depression began simultaneously. She was asked to write her sad and anxious feelings daily. Also, she filled out a 320-item Unpleasant Events Schedule to identify reasonable goals. The first target behavior that was attacked was that of lateness. By making a self-change plan, she was better able to estimate the time she needed to get herself and her children ready to leave for school and work and thus to diminish those times that she was late. Additionally, she learned relaxation techniques and used them to relax in a variety of situations, such as dealing with difficulties with her children.

Because problems with her children were creating tension, therapy changed from a focus on Jane's self-management to participating in a child-management program. By being better able to manage her children, Jane experienced a feeling of increased self-control. Following from this was the development of time-management skills and an increase in participation in pleasant events. As a part of this work, Jane agreed to participate in two pleasant events per day for a week. To develop her sense of self-esteem and to help her to become more assertive, the therapist assigned exercises from books on self-esteem and assertiveness.

As a result of these activities, Jane's mood and work performance improved substantially. Her score on the Beck Depression Inventory dropped dramatically. Additionally, she role played a variety of ways of dealing with her son's disruptive behavior. Her sense of self-efficacy developed as she increased her control over her children and began to take courses at a local community college.

Obsessive-Compulsive Disorder: June

As noted earlier, behavior therapy is characterized by a dedication to measurement of the effectiveness of outcomes of therapeutic procedures. This is particularly true of exposure and ritual prevention (EX/RP), which features the prevention of compulsive rituals or maladaptive behavioral responses. As a result of research, investigators (Franklin & Foa, 2007, 2008; Riggs & Foa, 2007; Simpson et al., 2008; Simpson, Zuckoff, Page, Franklin, & Foa, 2008) have concluded that EX/RP is effective in more than 70% of patients diagnosed with obsessive-compulsive disorders, and EX/RP is used with both those who may have obsessive thoughts (such as the thought that they will get AIDS from touching a public toilet seat) and compulsions (such as washing one's hands many times per day). Basically, EX/RP consists of exposure for an hour or two at a time to situations that provoke discomfort. Also, individuals are asked to refrain from following through on rituals, like hand washing. Usually, situations that produce distress are graded from moderate to severe, with the moderate ones presented earlier in treatment.

When using EX/RP, therapists need 4 to 6 hours of appointments to identify cues that cause distress, rituals, and avoidance. Detailed information about the symptoms is important, including a history of the more important ones. Often rating schedules, daily logs, and brief assessment instruments are also used. When logs of daily activities are kept, SUDs are recorded for the activities, thoughts, and rituals that evoke anxiety. Treatment is intense; where possible, meetings are 5 days a week for a period of 3 weeks, and less frequent thereafter. Home visits or outside work may also be required. Additionally, assistance from friends and relatives is extremely helpful.

A few excerpts from the case of June, a 26-year-old married woman with obsessions and compulsions regarding cleanliness, are presented (Riggs & Foa, 1993). June requires 45 minutes in the shower and washes her hands about 20 times a day. In treatment planning, the therapist makes use of both imaginal and in vivo exposure, as indicated by the following example.

> [Therapist:] OK, now. I want to discuss our plan for each day during the first week of therapy. We need to expose you both in imagination and in reality to the things that bother you, which we talked about in our first sessions. As I said already, we'll also limit your washing. The scenes you will imagine will focus on the harm that you fear will happen if you do not wash. The actual exposures will focus on confronting the things that contaminate you. Restricting your washing will teach you how to live without rituals. In imagination you will picture yourself touching something you're afraid of, like toilet seats, and not washing and then becoming ill. We can have you imagine going to a doctor who can't figure out what's wrong and can't fix it. That's the sort of fear that you have, right?
>
> June: Yes, that and Kenny getting sick and it being my fault.
>
> [Therapist:] OK, so in some scenes you'll be sick and in others Kenny will get sick. Should I add that other people blame you for not being careful? Is this what you're afraid of?
>
> June: Yes, especially my mother.
>
> [Therapist:] OK. We'll have her criticize you for not being careful enough. Can you think of anything else we should add to the image?
>
> June: No, that's about it.
>
> [Therapist:] We can compose the scenes in detail after we plan the actual exposure. Let's review the list of things you avoid or are afraid to touch to make sure that we have listed them in the right order. Then we'll decide what to work on each day. OK?
>
> June: OK. [June went over the list, which included such items as trash cans, kitchen floor, bathroom floor, public hallway carpet, plant dirt, puddles, car tires, dried dog "dirt," and bird "doo." Changes were made as needed.]
>
> [Therapist:] Good. Now let's plan the treatment. On the first day we should start with things that you rated below a 60. That would include touching this carpet, doorknobs that are not inside bathrooms, books on my shelves, light switches, and stair railings. On the second day, we'll do the 60- to 70-level items, like faucets, bare floors, dirty laundry, and the things on Ken's desk. [The therapist continued to detail Sessions 3 to 5 as above, increasing the level of difficulty each day.] In the second week we will repeat the worst situations like gutters, tires, public toilets, bird doo, and dog dirt, and we'll also find a dead animal to walk near and touch the street next to it. (Riggs & Foa, 1993, pp. 225–226)

In vivo exposure often requires time and creativity from the therapist. The following example shows how the therapist uses humor and persuasion to get the patient to participate in an unattractive activity.

> *[Therapist:]* It's time to do the real thing now. I looked for a dead animal by the side of the road yesterday and I found one about a mile away. I think we should go there.
>
> *June:* Yuck, that's terrific. Just for me you had to find it.
>
> *[Therapist:]* Today's our lucky day. You knew we were going to have to find one today anyhow. At least it's close.
>
> *June:* Great.

Humor is encouraged and can be quite helpful if the patient is capable of responding to it. It is important that the therapist not laugh at but rather with the patient.

> *[Therapist:]* [Outside the office]. There it is, behind the car. Let's go and touch the curb and street next to it. I won't insist that you touch it directly because it's a bit smelly, but I want you to step next to it and touch the sole of your shoe.
>
> *June:* Yuck! It's really dead. It's gross!
>
> *[Therapist:]* Yeah, it is a bit gross, but it's also just a dead cat if you think about it plainly. What harm can it cause?
>
> *June:* I don't know. Suppose I got germs on my hand?
>
> *[Therapist:]* What sort of germs?
>
> *June:* Dead cat germs.
>
> *[Therapist:]* What kind are they?
>
> *June:* I don't know. Just germs.
>
> *[Therapist:]* Like the bathroom germs that we've already handled? (Riggs & Foa, 1993, p. 228)

Phobic Disorder: Six-Year-Old Girl

Considerable research has been done on a wide variety of phobic disorders including fears of animals, flying, heights, blood, medical procedures, and social phobias. The method that has been found to be most effective is that of exposure (Antony & Swinson, 2000; Hirai, Vernon, & Cochran, 2007; Ollendick, Davis, & Sirbu, 2009). In their treatment manual, Antony and Swinson (2000) suggest that exposure be frequent, predictable, and prolonged. Where possible, exposure should be done in vivo rather than through imagery, but in fears such as lightning and earthquakes, this is rarely possible. Typically, exposure is done gradually rather than by flooding the patient with the feared object. There are some specific techniques used for certain phobias, such as blood phobia, that are different from the typical treatment for other phobias. Other techniques, such as modeling and planned practice, can be helpful as well. The example below includes both modeling and practice in an environment where the individual is exposed to the feared object.

The treatment of a 6-year-old girl who had a phobia of balloons illustrates the application of modeling techniques and exposure (Johnson & McGlynn, 1988). The child's mother had noticed that her daughter avoided situations in which there might be or were balloons. She also had nightmares about balloons. The therapist used a model of a girl playing with balloons. Gradually, the patient became less fearful. Then the young girl who was the model in the videotape helped the patient become less fearful of balloons by playing with them in the room. She asked the patient to imitate her behaviors. Later, the therapist served as the model, playing with the balloons. Before treatment was to be stopped, the mother reported that the little girl could come in contact with balloons and not be anxious. A follow-up 2 years later showed that the little girl was no longer phobic of balloons.

Brief Therapy

Because of its emphasis on changing actions, many behavior therapy approaches tend to be relatively brief. However, many factors influence length of therapy. In general, the more difficult target behaviors are to specify and the more there are of them, the longer the treatment will take. Also, if a fear or anxiety is very strong and there are ways to avoid an object of fear—for example, by not flying on airplanes—then more sessions may be required. Such resources as financial backing and supportive friends and family members can help increase the opportunity of achieving various target behaviors. Some types of treatment strategies take longer than others: imaginal approaches may require more sessions than in vivo techniques, and gradual methods may take more sessions than intensive methods. Each individual's problem has unique features that may vary over time, making treatment length difficult to predict.

However, there are some general guidelines as to the length of the process for different types of disorders. Treatment of obsessive-compulsive disorders may require five appointments a week for 3 weeks or so and then weekly follow-up for several more months. Depression and generalized anxiety may take several months of weekly meetings, but length may depend on ability to assess, define, and treat target behaviors. Additionally, if in vivo work is done outside the therapist's office, more than an hour a week is often needed. More so than many other therapists, behavior therapists are likely not to meet on a weekly basis but rather to have several sessions a week at the beginning of therapy for assessment and in vivo treatments, followed by weekly, biweekly, or monthly follow-up sessions. When behavior therapy is combined with cognitive therapy (Chapter 10), which is often the case, treatment may be longer.

Current Trends

Because behavior therapy can be applied across the full age spectrum from infants through the elderly, many varied problems have been addressed. Advances in research and application bring new ideas. Many have been documented and illustrated in treatment manuals. New applications such as eye-movement desensitization, acceptance and commitment therapy, and dialectical behavior therapy are being developed. Ethical issues regarding involuntary patients have evoked concern on the part of behavior therapists and others. Because much has been written about each of these areas, they are briefly summarized in this section.

Eye-Movement Desensitization and Reprocessing

Relatively new, eye-movement desensitization and reprocessing (EMDR) was developed by Francine Shapiro in 1987 (1997, 1999, 2001; Shapiro & Forrest, 2004; Shapiro, Kaslow, & Maxfield, 2007). It was first designed for individuals with posttraumatic stress disorder, but it has been applied more broadly since then. This method uses a combination of cognitive and behavioral techniques. First a behavioral assessment is done, imaginal flooding is used, and cognitive restructuring, somewhat similar to that of Meichenbaum, follows.

In explaining EMDR, Shapiro (2001; Leeds & Shapiro, 2000; Shapiro & Forrest, 2004) describes eight phases. Luber (2009) provides a variety of scripted protocols for work with different psychological disorders, age groups, couples, and group work. *EMDR and the Art of Psychotherapy with Children* (Adler-Tapia & Settle, 2008) is a comprehensive approach to applying EMDR to children. The first three phases are an introduction to behavioral assessment. In the first phase, the therapist takes a client history and tries to determine if the client will be able to tolerate the stress that EMDR may bring about. In the second phase, the therapist explains how EMDR works and how the client may feel between sessions as a result of EMDR. In the third phase, the therapist gathers baseline data before desensitizing the client. Typically, the client is asked to select a memory and to assign a subjective unit of discomfort (SUD) in which 10 is the highest distress possible and 0 is the lowest.

With this preparation done, the therapist moves to the desensitization phase, which is the longest one. At this point, the therapist asks the client to think of the traumatic image and to notice feelings attached to it as the therapist moves her hand. The client concentrates on the image and feelings as the therapist moves her hand back and forth as rapidly as possible. Usually the therapist holds two fingers up with her palm facing the client about 12 inches from the client's face. About 15 to 30 bilateral eye movements make a set. After the set, the therapist tells the client to let go and take a breath. Then the client describes his feelings, images, sensations, or thoughts. The therapist may ask, "What are you experiencing now?" Although the most common approach, eye movements are not the only way of activating this information-processing system. Therapists may use hand taps or repeat verbal cues. This desensitization process continues until near the end of the session or when the SUD rating drops to 0 or 1.

After the client has been desensitized, the fifth phase is to increase the positive cognition. This stage is called installation because a new positive thought is installed. In this phase, the positive cognition is linked to the original memory by asking the individual to focus on the positive cognition and the desired target behavior. At this point, eye movements are done to enhance the connection.

When the positive cognition is installed, the client moves to the sixth phase and performs a body scan. Here, he scans his body from head to toe, trying to find any tension or discomfort. If discomfort is located, it is targeted with successive sets of eye movements until the tension is diminished.

In the last two phases, the client returns to an emotional equilibrium. Between sessions, the client is asked to maintain a log of distressing thoughts, images, or dreams. If they occur, the client is told to apply the self-soothing or relaxation exercises he has learned. Then the entire process is re-evaluated and reviewed. Typically EMDR takes four to six sessions for a single target to be reached, but the sessions usually run 90 to 120 minutes.

As EMDR has grown in popularity, more than 50,000 mental health professionals have been trained in the system. However, evidence for it has been questioned. Hertlein and Ricci (2004) reviewed 16 studies on EMDR using rigorous criteria for effective research designs. The authors judged all of the studies as not meeting the appropriate criteria used to determine the efficacy of EMDR. Reviewing conclusions of a meta-analysis that he and others had done, Taylor (2004) believed that exposure therapy was superior to both EMDR and relaxation therapy in the treatment of posttraumatic stress disorder in several ways. However, Taylor also finds that EMDR was effective in treating posttraumatic stress disorder. In a meta-analysis of 38 randomized controlled trials, both EMDR and trauma-focused cognitive behavioral therapy were found to be more effective in treating posttraumatic stress disorder than stress management and other therapies (Bisson et al., 2007). Also finding support for EMDR, Maxfield (2007) discusses research relating neurobiological changes to EMDR. Shapiro (1999) has raised questions about how similar the EMDR treatment in some studies is to the method that she has described. Further, she points out that the eye-movement part of the procedure is only one of many parts of her complex method. She suggests that the name, eye movement desensitization and reprocessing, may have caused some psychologists to have misconceptions about this complex procedure. Clinicians continue to report good results with their clients, which contributes to the popularity of EMDR among therapists (R. Shapiro, 2005a, 2005b). Much research has shown that EMDR is a research-supported psychological treatment; however, the need to use rapid eye movements continues to be questioned.

Acceptance and Commitment Therapy

A relatively new approach, acceptance and commitment therapy (ACT) uses behavioral techniques in combination with an emphasis on clients' use of language to alleviate client distress (Blackledge, Ciarrochi, & Deane, 2009; Eifert & Forsyth, 2005; Hayes & Strosahl, 2005). Hayes and his colleagues believe many emotional problems develop as clients use ineffective methods, such as avoidance, to control their emotions. Rather than having clients focus on avoiding a feeling, they help clients accept a feeling, event, or situation. Clients can then look at their thoughts and feelings rather than look from them. They help clients clarify values and commit to behaviors that fit with these values. Manuals (Luoma, Hayes, & Walser, 2007) and transcripts (Twohig & Hayes, 2008) are helpful to those wishing to learn ACT.

To illustrate their approach, Blackledge and Hayes (2001) use the case of Mark, a young college student who has had a history of problems that affect his dating relationships with women. As a therapeutic goal, they want the client to accept and experience fearful or painful thoughts, clarify his values, and commit to changing behaviors. In Mark's case, he "needed to learn to recognize his negative self-evaluations simply as words rather than truths, and to stop avoiding the anxiety and fear he experienced in response to intimacy" (p. 248).

One of the first steps in ACT is "creative hopelessness." The therapist reviews with the client the ways the client has taken to solve the problem and examines why they have not worked. This helps the client be open to suggestions the therapist makes that may not seem, at first, to make sense to the client. Mark describes solutions he has tried, such as not asking women out anymore to avoid anxiety about being rejected. The therapist responds by suggesting that anxiety is not the problem.

Therapy then continues by focusing on aspects of the client's experience other than the feeling of anxiety. For example, Mark is asked to close his eyes and focus on the physical sensations in his body for several minutes, repeating this several times. His physical feelings are identified as "mind stuff" by the therapist rather than the "truth" about how he feels. Then Mark sees his thoughts as thoughts rather than the truth about how he fears dating women. In this way the negative emotion is defused.

Other defusion strategies may be used as well. For example, Mark feels ashamed because of his lack of sexual experience. The therapist does not attempt to talk Mark out of these thoughts but instead says, "Thank your mind for that thought" or "Those are interesting words" (p. 251). Later in therapy, when Mark has a disturbing thought, he is asked to picture himself in front of a stream. He then is asked to place the thought on a leaf and focus on his breathing.

Another diffusion exercise is used when Mark says, "I'm worthless" (p. 251). The therapist and Mark repeat the phrase over and over until the phase has no meaning. You may want to try this yourself with a similar phrase, saying it out loud. Notice how the phrase sounds different the first time as compared to the 30th time you say it. Mark noted that the phrase had lost its literal meaning after many repetitions.

In the fifth and final session, Mark reports his commitment to the behavior. He has asked out two women and has experienced little anxiety asking them out on the date or being with them on the date.

Most examples are more complex. Mark did not need to evaluate what he wanted, but many clients do. Furthermore, many clients have several problems rather than one. This example does, however, illustrate the effect of language on behavior and how a focus on both can be used to bring about therapeutic change.

Hayes and his colleagues have written more than 70 books and articles on acceptance and commitment therapy. Some of the articles focus on the philosophical basis of ACT, especially relational frame theory (RFT), which provides an underlying rationale for ACT. Relational frame theory focuses on how language is learned through interacting with the environment (Hayes, 2008; Levin & Hayes, 2009). Others focus on specific psychological problems such as posttraumatic stress (Orsillo & Batten, 2005), alcohol dependence (Heffner, Eifert, Parker, Hernandez, & Sperry, 2003), depression and anxiety (Twohig & Hayes, 2008), and disorders of children and adolescents (Greco & Hayes, 2008).

Dialectical Behavior Therapy

Dialectical behavior therapy (DBT) was developed by Marsha Linehan in the 1980s as a result of her work with patients with suicidal intentions. She later developed it into a therapy that has been used primarily with patients diagnosed with borderline disorder (Linehan, 1993a, 1993b; Linehan & Dexter-Mazza, 2008). These patients present difficulties that challenge therapists more than almost any other psychological disorder. Patients with borderline disorder present with severe mood swings and impulsive behavior such as drug abuse, sexual acting out, and self-damaging behavior. They may see relationships as either all good or all bad, including the relationship with the therapist. To work with these patients using DBT requires at least a year of both individual and group therapy, as well as phone consultations. Furthermore, therapeutic work needs to be comprehensive and sophisticated to accomplish what other therapies have not.

Linehan views borderline personality disorder as having biological and environmental components (Linehan, 1993a, b; Linehan, McDavid, Brown, Sayrs, & Gallop, 2008). Her biosocial theory examines genetics, prenatal conditions, and other factors that may influence how people regulate their emotions and respond to problems in their environment. Her theory suggests that individuals with borderline personality disorder experience a great deal of *emotional vulnerability*, resulting in intense emotional reactions that are difficult for the individual to manage. Individuals with borderline personality disorder generally also have experienced *invalidating environments*. These may include neglect from parents or other caregivers, abuse, or abandonment. Such experiences may lead to people having a poor self-image, being self-critical, lacking trust in others, and having poor problem-solving skills. Linehan theorizes that borderline personality disorder arises from the interaction between emotional vulnerability and invalidating environments.

Dialectical behavior therapy may be best described by the title words: *dialectical* and *behavior*. *Dialectical* refers to the fact that in an argument there is an assertion and a position that opposes the assertion. To resolve the argument, a *synthesis* that incorporates the assertion and the opposition will help to move past the argument and resolve it (Spiegler & Guveremont, 2010). For patients with borderline symptoms, this provides a way to reduce symptoms and find meaning in their lives by balancing acceptance and change. *Behavior* refers to the need to use behavioral methods to change self-destructive behaviors (such as careless driving or cutting one's arms). Different therapeutic methods are applied in individual and group therapy. Additionally, phone consultations are made with individuals in crisis.

Individual therapy. The first part of individual therapy in DBT is to assess the client's problems and to assess her ability to follow through in meeting therapeutic goals. Both therapist and client must agree on the goals, target behaviors, and techniques to be used. The client must agree to attend individual and group sessions. This is important, as dropout from treatment of borderline personality disorder has a reputation for being high. The therapist may also disclose supervision arrangements and issues dealing with availability to the client in a crisis. The therapist then decides which of four stages to start with.

In DBT, the four stages are in order of degree of importance to the goal of keeping the client alive. Therapists may change from one stage to another depending on the nature of the problems the patient presents. Since patients with borderline symptoms often experience crises, changing stages can be frequent. The stages are described here.

Stage 1. Life-threatening behaviors such as suicide attempts, risk-taking behaviors such as driving recklessly, and intent to harm self or others must be the first priority. Assuring safety is important because self-destructive behaviors are common in individuals with a borderline personality disorder.

Stage 2. Attention is paid to behaviors that may interfere with therapy. Because of the difficulty of treatment and the lack of success of treatment for many individuals with borderline personality disorder, it is important to keep the patient in therapy. In Stage 2, clients work on experiencing strong emotions with less and less disturbance. They also learn to deal with problems in their environment in a more effective way.

Stage 3. Clients work on ways to increase their quality of life and decrease their problematic responses to daily events. For example, they try to reduce symptoms of anxiety and depression. Dealing with substance abuse may be an issue in Stages 1 and 2, but making reductions in drug dependence continues in Stage 3. Attention is paid to relationships with family, friends, and coworkers.

Stage 4. Clients make changes in their lives to adapt to problems around them. Attention is paid to finding more happiness, a greater sense of freedom, and the development of spirituality. Work is done to develop skills in handling problems with others and with unanticipated events.

Therapeutic skills. In DBT, certain skills are used in individual therapy but may be used in group as well when appropriate. These skills include validation and acceptance strategies, problem-solving and change strategies, and dialectical persuasion.

Validation and acceptance strategies. Clients with borderline personality disorder often present behaviors that may be harmful to themselves. The therapist should communicate empathy toward the client rather than point out the harmfulness of the behavior. The therapist can point out to the client that the behavior serves a function to reduce stress or to help in some way, even if the behavior causes other problems. For example if a client drinks alcohol to the point that she gets sick and can't walk, the therapist may say to her : "When you are very upset, drinking seems to help you relax, and it would be helpful to reduce your stress, which you do by drinking. Perhaps there are other ways to achieve the goal of relaxation." In this response, the client's behavior is accepted, and a suggestion is made to examine possible changes.

Problem-solving and change strategies. Many different behavioral and problem-solving techniques can be used so that patients with borderline personality disorder can change behavior that has interfered with their life goals. Sometimes the therapist may wish to use positive reinforcement or modeling techniques to help clients achieve their goals. Meichenbaum's self-instructional training and stress inoculation (pp. 299–300) provide a means for accomplishing cognitive restructuring. For certain problems, especially related to phobias or obsessive-compulsive disorders, therapists may wish to use exposure and ritual prevention (p. 306). Other behavioral and cognitive techniques can be used as well.

Dialectical persuasion. *Dialectical* was explained above as trying to find a resolution between two extremes. Using *dialectical persuasion,* the therapist accepts the client but gently tries to persuade the client to use a more effective method to bring about change. This is done by pointing out inconsistencies in actions, beliefs, and values. The client is helped to change behavior to fit with values and beliefs. In the following example, dialectical persuasion is used with a 23-year-old woman who cuts her arms to relieve stress.

> [*Client:*] After I left my boyfriend at his house, and came back to my room, I was so angry, that I cut myself again. But it wasn't that bad. And I felt better afterward, relieved.

> [*Therapist:*] So then, if I understand you correctly, if your 12-year-old cousin were to be very angry at someone, you would cut her arm to reduce the stress.

> [*Client:*] I would not!

> [*Therapist:*] Why wouldn't you?

> [*Client:*] It would hurt her. I wouldn't do that to her.

[Therapist:] What would you do then?

[Client:] I would comfort her. Tell her to look at it in perspective with other things that she had done. Tell her to calm herself. She has a cat she loves to cuddle. I would suggest that.

[Therapist:] Those are good ideas. Are there any of those ideas you can use with yourself?

In this way, the therapist points out inconsistencies in the client's behavior without directly confronting the client. The client then starts to develop some alternative ways to change her behavior.

Group skills training. Along with individual therapy, clients participate in 2 to 3 hours of group skills training per week for a year or more. The group leader would not be the client's individual therapist. The group leader follows a manual that includes handouts for clients. The group focuses, especially at first, on Stages 1 and 2: life-threatening behaviors and behaviors that interfere with individual therapy. Although some of the techniques described above may be used by the group leader, the skills that are taught are core mindfulness, interpersonal effectiveness, emotional regulation, and distress tolerance.

Core mindfulness skills. As the word "core" implies, these skills are basic to DBT and are taught throughout the course of training. These skills are based on Buddhist principles and techniques. The focus is on being in the present, not judging yourself, and paying attention. Participants learn about three states of mind:
Reasonable mind: thinking rationally or logically, using facts.
Emotional mind: thinking emotionally, distorted thoughts, determined by mood.
Wise mind: a melding or synthesis of the reasonable and emotional mind.
These three concepts are used to understand and evaluate the thoughts and behaviors of the participants.

Interpersonal effectiveness skills. Clients learn skills, such as problem solving and assertiveness, to get what they want while maintaining relationships and not alienating others. They also learn how to examine those things they desire to do and those they "have to do" so they are not overwhelmed with having too much to do.

Distress-tolerance skills. Typically, clients with borderline personality disorder have low tolerance for stress. Clients learn to tolerate stress or emotional discomfort. They learn to distract themselves when they are upset and then to find ways to soothe or decrease the emotional upset. To make changes, they may use cognitive restructuring and think of pros and cons of what to do next.

Dialectical behavior therapy has been shown to meet the criteria for evidence-based practice for work with people with borderline disorders (Lindenboim, Comtois, & Linehan, 2007; Linehan & Dexter-Mazza, 2008). For example, DBT was found to be more effective in treating women diagnosed with borderline disorder and substance abuse than nonbehavioral therapies (Harned et al., 2008). In a study of women with borderline personality disorder and high irritability, both medication and DBT were found to be helpful in reducing irritability, aggression, depression, and self-injury (Linehan et al., 2008). Also, a small study shows the potential of DBT for reducing symptoms for women with binge eating disorder or bulimia (Chen et al., 2008). Examining how well participants practiced skills taught in the group skills component, Lindenboim, Comtois, and Linehan (2007) found that most participants practiced most of the skills on most days of the week. Many other studies show the effectiveness of DBT (Linehan & Dexter-Mazza, 2008). Dialectical behavior theory is considered to be a research-supported psychological treatment.

Ethical Issues

Although ethical issues are important for all mental health practitioners, regardless of their profession or theoretical orientation, behavior therapists have been particularly concerned about ethical issues (Bailey & Burch, 2005; Spiegler & Guevremont, 2010). First, there is a general public misperception of behavior modification, with some people thinking that behavior therapy is something that people do to others against their will. Second, behavior therapy can be applied to a broader group of patients than any other theory of psychotherapy discussed in this book. For populations such as infants, and developmentally delayed, autistic, and severely psychotic patients, behavior therapy is often the only appropriate approach. For many of these people or their families, behavior therapy can help promote independent decision making by giving them choices about goals and ways to attain them (Spiegler & Guevremont, 2010). However, behavior therapists may often work with clients who cannot or will not give their permission for therapeutic change. Bailey and Burch (2005) give examples of ethical dilemmas dealing with clients with autism, developmental disabilities, and other concerns where clients may not be able to give permission for therapy.

With young children (Evans, 2008), individuals with severe learning disabilities, and psychotic patients, informed consent is usually not possible. However, partial consent can sometimes be obtained, such as a patient with schizophrenia who, during a period of lucidity, agrees to treatment. When possible, individuals participate in treatment selection, even though consent of a legal guardian is often necessary. In institutions, an ethics committee is used to approve involuntary treatment. Sensitivity to both legal and ethical issues has characterized the practice of behavior therapy for more than 40 years.

Using Behavior Therapy with Other Theories

For some problems, behavior therapists may draw on other theories, but for others their approach may be strictly behavioral. With young children and nonverbal institutionalized adults, behavior therapists use techniques that are almost entirely behavioral. Also, with patients who have a single phobic reaction, for example, to snakes, behavioral treatments such as exposure may be used exclusively. With many other problems such as conduct disorders, depression, anxiety, and eating disorders, however, behavior therapists often make use of cognitive strategies as well. If they can conceptualize a technique, such as the gestalt empty-chair technique, from a behavioral point of view, they may use it. Because behavior therapists usually do not apply only one technique to a patient but rather use treatment packages, they may make use of cognitive or other strategies in their treatment approach.

Other therapists may draw techniques from behavior therapy either knowingly or unknowingly. An early influential book by Dollard and Miller (1950), *Personality and Psychotherapy*, explains psychoanalysis from a reinforcement learning theory point of view that saw neurosis as behavior learned in childhood. In their approach to therapy, Adlerian psychotherapists have often incorporated behavioral techniques. Also, Albert Ellis changed the name of rational-emotive therapy to rational emotive behavior therapy, acknowledging the important role of behavioral techniques in his work. In his approach to cognitive therapy, Aaron Beck makes selective use of behavioral techniques.

When a client and therapist are talking to each other, certain behavioral principles are likely to be at work. The therapist may reinforce the client's verbal behavior by smiling, showing interest, nodding, and verbally responding. In many therapeutic approaches, when the client talks of having made therapeutic progress, the therapist is likely to comment on the client's statement and praise it, thus providing positive reinforcement. Furthermore, when the therapist appears calm in the face of the patient's anxiety, the therapist is modeling nonanxious behavior. Although many theorists do not conceptualize the role of the therapist as model and reinforcer, behavioral therapists are well aware of that role.

Research

More than any other therapy, behavior therapy's effectiveness has been studied with many different populations and a variety of disorders. It is not possible to review the results of several hundred studies here, so I give a broad view of research findings and discuss an early important study comparing psychodynamic and behavior therapy, as well as studies (meta-analyses) that compare the findings of many studies. Discussion of the therapeutic effectiveness for the treatment of obsessive-compulsive, generalized anxiety disorders, and phobias is also provided.

Review of the Evidence

By comparing the results of many studies, meta-analyses provide a means of drawing inferences about therapeutic effectiveness from a wide range of research. In some cases, meta-analyses are limited to certain age groups or disorders; in other cases, all studies are included. In a study that examined almost 400 evaluations of psychotherapy, Smith and Glass (1977) concluded, after they had statistically integrated and analyzed the research, that "the typical therapy client is better off than 75% of untreated individuals" (p. 751). No differences were found between the effectiveness of behavioral therapies and that of other therapies. In a more restrictive meta-analysis with an improved design, Shapiro and Shapiro (1982) examined 143 studies that were completed in a 5-year period. Most of the studies were of behavioral treatments, some were of cognitive therapy, and a few were psychodynamic. In general, they found more improvement for behavioral and cognitive therapies than for psychodynamic. However, they also found more improvement with cognitive therapies than with systematic desensitization, the most common of the behavioral methods studied. In a meta-analysis of 74 studies that included more than 3,400 patients, Grawe, Donati, and Bernauer (1998) found that behavioral and cognitive-behavioral treatments were superior to client-centered and psychodynamic therapy and control groups. In treatments featuring social-skills training, stress inoculation, and problem solving, this was true in at least 75% of the comparisons. Currently, most research studies focus on specific disorders rather than studying all types of problems at once.

Obsessive-Compulsive Disorder

Most investigations of behavioral treatment of obsessive-compulsive disorders have studied the effectiveness of exposure and ritual prevention approaches. In a meta-analysis of 19 studies of treatment for obsessive-compulsive disorder, therapist-guided exposure was shown to be more effective than therapist-assisted self-exposure, and in vivo exposure with imagination was better than in vivo exposure alone (Rosa-Alcázar, Sánchez-Meca, Gómez-Conesa, & Marín-Martínez, 2008). Patients taking medications at follow-up did as well as those receiving EX/RP. In a study with 122 patients receiving 12 weeks of EX/RP, those receiving EX/RP alone or with medications reported more improvement than those receiving medications alone (Foa et al., 2005). When cognitive therapy was compared with EX/RP for 59 patients, cognitive therapy showed a slightly greater, but not significantly so, recovery rate after a 3-month follow-up (Whittal, Thordarson, & McLean, 2005). When examining recovery rates, EX/RP tends to produce improvement in 60% to 75% of patients, but only about 25% are symptom free at the end of treatment (Fisher & Wells, 2005). Franklin and Simpson (2005) point out when it is helpful to use both medication and EX/RP. Continued interest in both cognitive and EX/RP treatments for obsessive-compulsive disorder is likely to make this an area of research.

Other research on obsessive-compulsive disorder has examined various aspects of treatment. For example, twice-weekly sessions have been shown to be as effective as daily sessions (Abramowitz, Foa, & Franklin, 2003). Another study examined cognitive/behavior therapy for obsessive-compulsive disorder that was administered over the telephone, finding it effective and to have a relatively low dropout rate (Taylor et al., 2003). One study compared cognitive therapy to EX/RP and found no differences between the two in terms of the process of change for obsessions and compulsions (Anholt et al., 2007). However, the authors conclude that reduction of compulsions rather than obsessions is the process by which both cognitive therapy and EX/RP produce change. When types of patient problems are identified, patients with hoarding symptoms tend to have poorer recovery rates than those with contamination compulsions, harming compulsions, intrusive unacceptable thoughts, and the need to keep objects symmetrical (Abramowitz et al., 2003). Such studies expand information about types of treatment and details regarding treatment effectiveness.

Generalized Anxiety Disorder

A meta analysis of 10 studies that examined cognitive behavioral therapy for generalized anxiety disorder showed that cognitive-behavioral therapy significantly reduced worry, especially for younger adults when compared to older adults (Covin, Ouimet, Seeds, & Dozois, 2008). These results were maintained over 6-month and 12-month follow-up. Regarding the use of specific change techniques, Brown et al. (2001) suggest cognitive strategies based on their review of outcome studies of patients with generalized anxiety disorder. They suggest that worry exposure, identifying basic worries, and practicing imagining them vividly for 25 to 30 minutes, after which clients generate alternatives as to the worst possible outcome, can be effective treatment. Additionally, time management (which includes delegating responsibility, being assertive, and adhering to agendas) and problem solving are effective treatments for generalized anxiety.

Several studies have examined different populations or specific aspects of the treatment described by Brown et al., (2001). For older adults, treatment for generalized anxiety disorder that includes motivation and education, relaxation, exposure, and sleep management has been found to be helpful (Stanley, Diefenbach, & Hopko, 2004). Another study of 134 older adults showed that cognitive behavior therapy, when compared to enhanced usual care, helped to decrease symptoms of depression and improve general mental health for older patients with general anxiety disorder (Stanley et al., 2009). Although most treatment of generalized anxiety disorder focuses on individual therapy, group treatment taking 14 sessions with four to six members has shown improvements over a 2-year period. The group treatment focused on re-evaluating positive beliefs about worry, problem solving, and cognitive exposure (Dugas et al., 2003). In a sample of 36 female college students, cognitive-behavioral therapy alone or combined with interpersonal psychotherapy (Chapter 15, pp. 602–614) decreased the rate of general anxiety disorder relapses (Rezvan, Baghban, Bahrami, & Abedi, 2008). When acceptance-based therapy that incorporated mindfulness as a treatment, symptoms of generalized anxiety disorder decreased after therapeutic treatment (Roemer, Orsillo, & Salters-Pedneault, 2008).

Phobias

Research has studied the effectiveness of behavioral therapy for the treatment of a variety of phobias as a group, as well as study-specific phobias, such as social phobias and spider phobias. A meta-analysis of 33 studies of treatment found that exposure therapy was much more effective than no therapy for a variety of phobias (Wolitzky-Taylor, Horowitz, Powers, & Telch, 2008). But in vivo therapy outperformed imaginal exposure and virtual reality therapy at the conclusion of therapy, but not after follow-up. Several sessions of treatment were marginally more effective than single-session treatments. However, in a study of 196 children aged 7 to 16 with a variety of phobias, Ollendick et al. (2009) found that one session of exposure treatment for phobia was superior to education support treatment, which was superior to a no-treatment control condition for reducing symptoms of phobia.

For extreme shyness or social phobia, Feske and Chambless (1995) in their meta-analysis found that cognitive-behavioral treatment when combined with exposure therapy is not more effective than exposure therapy alone. A study of 295 patients compared group cognitive-behavioral therapy alone, medication with the therapy, medication alone, and a placebo group. After 14 weeks of treatment, all approaches were better than the placebo treatment, but no differences were found among the treatments for social phobia (Davidson et al., 2004). Despite improvement, many patients still had some symptoms of social phobia. In another study with 325 patients, exposure therapy was compared to exposure therapy with medication, and to medication alone (Haug et al., 2003). After a 1-year follow-up, patients treated with exposure therapy alone showed further improvement whereas the other treatments showed a tendency to lose effectiveness over time.

Using technology, new behavioral treatments for social phobia are being developed. In a study of 36 patients, virtual reality therapy was used for social phobia (Klinger et al., 2005). Four virtual reality treatments were created to help patients deal with their anxiety: performance, intimacy, scrutiny, and assertiveness. This treatment proved to be effective, as did group cognitive therapy. In another study, handheld computers were used as a diary for monitoring anxiety, as well as providing assistance in relaxation, cognitive restructuring, and controlling anxiety (Przeworski & Newman, 2004). In a small preliminary study, this method showed promise as an intervention technique.

Several investigations have concerned the alleviation of spider phobias. Öst and colleagues have studied the effectiveness of exposure treatment, individually or in group, to videotapes or manuals. In one study, patients were first given a self-help manual to deal with spiders; if that worked, they were considered finished with the study (Öst, Stridh, & Wolf, 1998). If that was not sufficient, they watched a video on dealing with spiders. If that was not sufficient, group therapy and, finally, individual therapy were offered. Although it was clear that group and individual therapy were more effective than the manual or video treatment, the stepwise approach to phobia represents an efficient use of therapeutic resources. Virtual reality therapy was used in another study where patients experienced the illusion of physically touching a virtual spider (Hoffman, Garcia-Palacios, Carlin, Furness, & Botella-Arbona, 2003). Using eight spider-phobic and 28 nonclinically phobic individuals, the virtual reality approach where patients had the illusion of touching a spider was more effective than when the virtual reality program was presented without the virtual touching experience. A 33-month follow-up study was done with 45 patients who received three 45-minute sessions of live graded exposure, computer-aided vicarious exposure, or a progressive relaxation treatment (Gilroy, Kirkby, Daniels, Menzies, & Montgomery, 2003). At follow-up, both exposure treatments showed the maintenance of improvement, whereas the relaxation treatment did not. An Internet-based self-help treatment of spider phobia of one 3-hour session on the Internet was found to reduce fear of spiders almost as effectively as treatment that consisted of exposure to live spiders (Andersson et al., 2009). Exposure, virtual reality therapy, and other treatments are also being applied to phobias of other animals such as mice, snakes, and bats.

In this section I have been able to give only a brief overview of research on obsessive-compulsive disorders, generalized anxiety disorders, and phobias. Considerable research also exists on behavioral treatment of depression, alcoholism, schizophrenia, posttraumatic stress disorders, panic disorder, sexual dysfunction, and other disorders. As behavior therapists refine their approaches, they use research studies to determine which treatment works best for patients who demonstrate certain characteristics. As this research has become more sophisticated, care in planning precise and accurate studies has become even more important.

Gender Issues

Although value issues enter into behavior therapy, as they do in all therapies, the terms and techniques are free of reference to gender. In terms of the relationship between therapist and client, behavior therapists focus on change, working with the client to develop and achieve behavioral goals. Allowing the client to choose among several treatments emphasizes the equality between therapist and client. Two important principles of behavior therapy—operant conditioning and observational learning—provide a way of viewing the impact of external factors related to gender on individuals.

Operant conditioning provides a means of looking at external factors that affect individuals' behavior (Worell & Remer, 2003). For example, in treating a woman who reports being depressed, a therapist may observe that her husband

and parents reinforce only her housekeeping skills, not her intellectual ones. The therapist may help the woman identify events or activities that are potential reinforcers, such as writing for a newspaper. As her writing develops, active behavior increases and depressive behavior decreases. By writing articles, other aspects of her behavior also increase in frequency; thus, reinforcement for writing may generalize to increased social behavior with friends or activity relating to social issues. Therapists may note how certain external events that others may consider reinforcing (praise for housework) are not reinforcing for the client but instead attempt to reinforce gender-stereotyped behavior.

Bandura's (1977, 1997) description of observational learning offers a way of assessing gender issues as they affect individual lives. People may not recognize who the models are in their lives. More specifically, Bussey and Bandura (1999) show how gender development affects relationships and social change. For example, adolescents may try to shape their bodies and appearance by observing actors. They may purge food to keep thin or do excessive weight lifting to develop a muscular body. Improved social behavior may come from observing the behavior of individuals who are friendly and humorous rather than those who are physically attractive. Behavior therapists may attend to the appropriateness of models for bringing about behavior change as it relates to traditional and nontraditional gender-role behavior.

As Spiegler and Guevremont (2010) point out, behavior therapists need to continue to attend to issues of diversity. A review of 4,635 articles from three behavior therapy journals showed that few articles (Sigmon et al., 2007) were focused on gender issues, such as comparison of treatments by gender. An implication of this article is that there is a need for behavior therapists to attend actively to gender issues; avoiding gender bias is insufficient.

Multicultural Issues

Because behavior therapy is an active approach, designed to implement change, many therapists have seen it as being consistent with meeting the needs of clients with diverse cultural backgrounds. Challenging this assumption, Hays (2009) gives 10 steps for cognitive-behavior therapists to be culturally competent in their practice. Furthermore, in *Addressing Cultural Complexities in Practice* (Hays, 2008), she addresses many issues such as working with culturally diverse groups, dealing with people living in poverty, working with people living in poverty, and addressing issues of people for whom English is a second language.

The emphasis that behavior therapy places on empiricism leading to a functional analysis has been seen by Tanaka-Matsumi and Higginbotham (1996) as an asset for helping people from many cultures. Cross-cultural behavioral therapists take vague expressions of distress that may be commonly used in a culture and specify them in behavioral terms. In doing this, the therapist may ask the client to express her problem; then the therapist gives his model of the problem. Next the therapist and client identify variables that are antecedents and consequences of the behavior. Cross-cultural knowledge is helpful in understanding behavior. For example, in Balinese and Hawaiian cultures, speaking with entities from the spirit world may be a part of a person's life and should not be confused with symptoms of schizophrenia (Tanaka-Matsumi & Higginbotham, 1996). Also, symptoms of dementia may vary across cultures (Shah, Dalvi, & Thompson, 2005). Knowing how individuals cope within a particular cultural norm can be helpful (Spiegler & Guevremont, 2010). In some cultures, the expression of anger in public is considered inappropriate. Knowing this can help a therapist identify appropriate antecedents and consequences of behavior.

When developing treatment strategies, knowledge of cultural norms can be very helpful (Marlow, 2004). Collaborating with a client from a different culture in choosing strategies becomes very important. For example, Higginbotham and Streiner (1991) developed a model for preventing misuse of prescription medication by attending to cultural beliefs regarding drug efficacy and related issues. In her study of five African American women with posttraumatic stress disorder (PTSD), Feske (2001) described the need to address transportation and child care for therapy to be successful. As a general approach to the use of behavior therapy in individuals from different cultures, Tanaka-Matsumi and Higginbotham (1996) make several suggestions. The therapist should be aware of culture-specific definitions of what constitutes deviant behavior. Similarly, knowledge of what roles individuals can play in their culture that are considered acceptable is important. In some cultures, certain individuals, such as priests, may be considered the only ones to give assistance to psychological disturbance, and the type of assistance may be limited by cultural norms. To put this in behavioral terms, cultural groups differ on what activities are reinforced and when group or individual behavior is reinforced. For example, in some cultures, teachers may reinforce the performance of their entire class as a group; in others it may be more appropriate to reinforce individual performance.

Group Therapy

A variety of group programs have been used for most psychological disorders. Sometimes groups are supplementary to individual therapy; at other times they are the only treatment. Some procedures have been developed to be used in involuntary situations, such as a classroom or ward of a psychiatric hospital (Spiegler & Guevremont, 2010), but many have been developed for clients who choose treatment. Important in any type of behavioral group therapy is that the clients share, to some degree, compatible target behaviors. For example, a behavioral group could focus on anxiety reduction. Even though the specific target behaviors of individual members varied, techniques used to bring about change would be similar. In this section, two specific types of behavioral group therapy are explained: social-skills groups and assertiveness groups.

Social-Skills Training

Different social-skills training programs have been applied to a wide variety of populations, such as children (LeCroy, 2007) and individuals diagnosed with recent onset of psychosis (Lecomte et al., 2008). Rose and LeCroy (1991) present a general approach to social-skills training that incorporates features that many behavioral therapists use: orienting group members to social skills and training them by teaching role playing skills. Next, group members develop the specifics of problem situations that they will role play, such as dealing with a coworker who tries to get the client to do her work. When the group has developed and discussed their problem situations, each person is asked to keep a diary of what happens when the situation occurs during the week. In group, members develop goals for dealing with their situation, and they and other members propose how they can meet these goals.

When specific behavioral goals are developed for group members, they then begin to implement change. Modeling is an important step in change, with either a therapist or another group member role playing how to deal effectively with the problem situation. After observing others model how to behave in the situation, the client then practices the situation and receives feedback from other group members as to what might be done differently, as well as feedback about what was done well. If the client has difficulty in practicing the situation, the therapist or another group member may coach a client by giving suggestions during the role play itself. Homework is given so that the individual can apply what has been learned and practice it in a real situation. For example, a client might practice newly learned ways of dealing with colleagues' impositions in the work setting itself. A record can be kept of this activity, and the consequences of the client's new behavior can be discussed in the group. By providing feedback to each other, group members give positive reinforcement to each other and are likely to develop a sense of camaraderie and support. Through their interactions with other group members, even though the focus is on behavior outside the group, group members are likely to increase their social skills.

Assertiveness Training

Similar to social-skills training groups, assertiveness training groups are designed for those who have difficulty in asking for what they want or who have difficulty in expressing negative feelings, such as anger and disagreement. In designing an approach to assertiveness, Alberti and Emmons (2008) have suggested important goals of assertiveness training. One of the first goals, learning how to identify and discriminate among assertive, aggressive, and passive behaviors, is addressed through teaching the differences between these behaviors through demonstration or role play. Another goal is to teach individuals that they have the right to express themselves while at the same time respecting the rights of others. A key goal is to learn assertiveness skills, which are demonstrated, practiced, and tried out in real situations. Meeting the goal of applying assertiveness skills successfully is accomplished through homework that is practiced between sessions, with feedback provided by members and group leaders.

Because teaching, demonstrating, and modeling are behavioral strategies that can be applied as easily to a group as to an individual, the use of group therapy with social skills and assertiveness issues is particularly appropriate. Groups provide members an opportunity to practice situations with different group members and to get feedback from several people rather than just one. Reinforcement from peers as well as from the leader can often be quite powerful. Assertiveness training can be applied to a variety of concerns, such as working with cultural issues with Palestinian Arab citizens of Israel (Dwairy, 2004), Iraqi individuals with social phobia (Al-Kubaisy & Jassim, 2003), and with women's sexual issues (Walen & Wolfe, 2000).

Summary

Behavior therapy has developed from a strong scientific base, starting with Pavlov's early work on classical conditioning. Other major psychological research that has influenced the development of behavior therapy has been Skinner's operant conditioning and Bandura's work on observational learning. From their research, basic behavioral principles have been developed that have broad application for therapeutic practice. These include both positive and negative reinforcement, extinction of unwanted behavior, shaping of desired behavior, and modeling. Attention to precision and detail is evident in the specific behaviors used in assessing individuals' behavior through such measures as self-report, role playing, observation, interviewing, and behavior ratings.

Basic principles of behavior derived from classical conditioning, operant conditioning, and modeling directly affect the development of behavioral therapeutic approaches. One of the first methods used to help individuals was Wolpe's systematic desensitization procedure, a gradual process of introducing relaxation to reduce fear and anxiety. Other methods use intense and prolonged exposure to the feared stimulus and may use in vivo procedures, in which the client deals with anxiety in the natural environment. Virtual reality techniques simulate a natural environment. Modeling techniques using role playing and other methods have been derived from observational learning. Recently, therapists have combined methods from behavior therapy with those from cognitive therapy to produce comprehensive procedures, such as Meichenbaum's stress inoculation training. Other methods include eye-movement desensitization and reprocessing (EMDR), acceptance and commitment therapy (ACT), and dialectical behavior therapy (DBT). Application of a particular method depends on careful assessment and often includes several treatments (a treatment package) rather than the application of just one method.

As a result of a number of research studies, specific procedures have been tested for a variety of disorders, as shown in the research section. Examples of differential behavior treatment are given for depression, obsessive-compulsive disorder, anxiety, and phobias. Unlike other therapies, behavior therapy can also be applied to those with severe intellectual disabilities or severe psychiatric disorders and to very young children. The versatility of behavior therapy and its emphasis on the creative application of scientific methodology to a wide variety of psychological disturbances are its hallmarks.

Theories in Action DVD: Behavior Therapy

Basic Concepts Used in the Role-Play	Questions About the Role-Play
Systematic desensitization Identifying short- and long-term goals Relaxing Rating fear responses Being very specific about items in the hierarchy Developing hierarchy Moving up the hierarchy Reinforcing client Encouraging small steps	1. In what ways is systematic desensitization of Rayneer's fear of driving similar to and different from behavior therapy used in any one of the case studies described on pages 292 to 294? 2. Why is attention to minute detail important in desensitizing Rayneer's fear of driving? 3. Why does Dr. Thompson use positive reinforcement when doing desensitization of Rayneer's fear of driving? (p. 285) 4. How is behavior therapy as described in the text different from that demonstrated in the Theories in Action DVD?

Suggested Readings

Spiegler, M. D., & Guevremont, D. C. (2010). *Contemporary behavior therapy* (5th ed.). Belmont, CA: Wadsworth. This highly readable text gives examples and exercises to explain important behavioral principles and treatment strategies. Included are chapters on cognitive-behavioral therapy and applications to medicine and community psychology, as well as approaches for working with a wide variety of clients.

Barlow, D. H. (Ed.). (2007). *Clinical handbook of psychological disorders: A step-by-step treatment manual* (4th ed.). New York: Guilford. Each of the 16 chapters describes research and practical approaches to dealing with different disorders and includes a case example.

References

Abramowitz, J. S., Foa, E. B., & Franklin, M. E. (2003). Exposure and ritual prevention for obsessive-compulsive disorder: Effects of intensive versus twice-weekly sessions. *Journal of Consulting and Clinical Psychology, 71*(2), 394–398.

Adler-Tapia, R., & Settle, C. (2008). *EMDR and the art of psychotherapy with children.* New York: Springer.

Alberti, R. E., & Emmons, M. L. (2008). *Your perfect right: A guide to assertive living* (9th ed.). Atascadero, CA: Impact.

Al-Kubaisy, T. F., & Jassim, A. L. (2003). The efficacy of assertive training in the acquisition of social skills in Iraqi social phobics. *Arab Journal of Psychiatry, 14*(1), 68–72.

Andersson, G., Waara, J., Jonsson, U., Malmaeus, F., Carlbring, P., & Öst, L. (2009). Internet-based self-help versus one-session exposure in the treatment of spider phobia: A randomized controlled trial. *Cognitive Behaviour Therapy, 38*(2), 114–120.

Anholt, G. E., Kempe, P., de Haan, E., van Oppen, P., Cath, D. C., Smit, J. H., & van Balkom, A. J. L. M. (2007). Cognitive versus behavior therapy: Processes of change in the treatment of obsessive-compulsive disorder. *Psychotherapy and Psychosomatics, 77*(1), 38–42.

Antony, M. M., & Swinson, R. P. (2000). *Phobic disorders and panic in adults: A guide to assessment and treatment.* Washington, DC: American Psychological Association.

Bailey, J. S., & Burch, M. R. (2005). *Ethics for behavior analysts: A practical guide to the behavior analyst certification board guidelines for responsible conduct.* Mahwah, NJ: Lawrence Erlbaum.

Bandura, A. (1969). *Principles of behavior modification.* New York: Holt, Rinehart & Winston.

Bandura, A. (1976). Effecting change through participant modeling. In J. D. Krumboltz & C. E. Thoresen (Eds.), *Counseling methods* (pp. 248–265). New York: Holt, Rinehart & Winston.

Bandura, A. (1977). *Social learning theory.* Englewood Cliffs, NJ: Prentice-Hall.

Bandura, A. (1978). Reflections on self-efficacy. In S. Rachman (Ed.), *Advances in behaviour research and therapy* (Vol. 1, pp. 237–269). Oxford: Pergamon.

Bandura, A. (1986). *Social foundations of thought and action: A social cognitive theory.* Englewood Cliffs, NJ: Prentice-Hall.

Bandura, A. (1989a). *Social cognitive theory.* In R. Vasta (Ed.), Annals of child development (Vol. 6, pp. 1–60). Greenwich, CA: JAI Press.

Bandura, A. (1989b). Regulation of cognitive processes through perceived self-efficacy. *Developmental Psychology, 25,* 729–735.

Bandura, A. (1997). *Self-efficacy: The exercise of control.* San Francisco: W. H. Freeman.

Bandura, A. (2000). Social cognitive theory: An agentic perspective. *Annual Review of Psychology, 52,* 1–26.

Bandura, A. (2007). Albert Bandura. In G. Lindzey, & W. M. Runyan (Eds.), *A history of psychology in autobiography* (Vol. IX, pp. 43–75). Washington, DC: American Psychological Association.

Bandura, A. (Ed.). (1971). *Psychological modeling: Conflicting theories.* Chicago: Aldine Atherton.

Barlow, D. H. (Ed.). (2007). *Clinical handbook of psychological disorders: A step-by-step treatment manual* (4th ed.). New York: Guilford.

Beck, H. P., Levinson, S., & Irons, G. (2009). Finding little Albert: A journey to John B. Watson's infant laboratory. *American Psychologist, 64*(7), 605–614.

Bisson, J. I., Ehlers, A., Matthews, R., Pilling, S., Richards, D., & Turner, S. (2007). Psychological treatments for chronic post-traumatic stress disorder: Systematic review and meta-analysis. *British Journal of Psychiatry, 190*(2), 97–104.

Blackledge, J. T., Ciarrochi, J., & Deane, F. (Eds.). (2009). *Acceptance and commitment therapy: Contemporary theory, research and practice.* Bowen Hills, QLD, Australia: Australian Academic Press.

Blackledge, J. T., & Hayes, S. C. (2001). Emotion regulation in acceptance and commitment therapy. *Journal of Clinical Psychology, 57,* 243–255.

Brown, T. A., O'Leary, T. A., & Barlow, D. H. (2001). Generalized anxiety disorder. In D. H. Barlow, *Clinical handbook of psychological disorders* (3rd ed., pp. 154–208). New York: Guilford.

Bussey, K., & Bandura, A. (1999). Social cognitive career theory of gender development and differentiation. *Psychological Review, 106*, 676–713.

Chen, E. Y., Matthews, L., Allen, C., Kuo, J. R., & Linehan, M. M. (2008). Dialectical behavior therapy for clients with binge-eating disorder or bulimia nervosa and borderline personality disorder. *International Journal of Eating Disorders, 41*(6), 505–512.

Covin, R., Ouimet, A. J., Seeds, P. M., & Dozois, D. J. A. (2008). A meta-analysis of CBT for pathological worry among clients with GAD. *Journal of Anxiety Disorders, 22*(1), 108–116.

Davidson, J. R. T., Foa, E. B., Huppert, J. D., Keefe, F. J., Franklin, M. E., & Compton, J. S. et al. (2004). Fluoxetine, comprehensive cognitive behavioral therapy, and placebo in generalized social phobia. *Archives of General Psychiatry, 61*(10), 1005–1013.

Dollard, J., & Miller, N. E. (1950). *Personality and psychotherapy*. New York: McGraw-Hill.

Dowrick, P. W. (1991). *Practical guide to using video in the behavioral sciences*. New York: Wiley.

Dowrick, P. W., Tallman, B. I., & Connor, M. E. (2005). Constructing better futures via video. *Journal of Prevention & Intervention in the Community, 29*(1–2), 131–144.

Dugas, M. J., Ladouceur, R., Léger, E., Freeston, M. H., Langolis, F., & Provencher, M. D. et al. (2003). Group cognitive-behavioral therapy for generalized anxiety disorder: Treatment outcome and long-term follow-up. *Journal of Consulting and Clinical Psychology, 71*(4), 821–825.

Dwairy, M. (2004). Culturally sensitive education: Adapting self-oriented assertiveness training to collective minorities. *Journal of Social Issues, 60*(2), 423–436.

Eifert, G. H., & Forsyth, J. P. (2005). *Acceptance and commitment therapy for anxiety disorders: A practitioner's treatment guide to using mindfulness, acceptance, and values-based behavior change strategies*. Oakland, CA: New Harbinger.

Evans, I. M. (2008). Ethical issues. In M. Hersen & D. Reitman (Eds.), *Handbook of psychological assessment, case conceptualization, and treatment, vol 2: Children and adolescents*. (pp. 176–195). Hoboken, NJ: John Wiley & Sons.

Eysenck, H. J. (1970). *The structure of human personality* (3rd ed.). London: Methuen.

Farmer, R. F., & Nelson-Gray, R. O. (2005). The history of behavior therapy. In R. F. Farmer & R. O. Nelson-Gray (Eds.), *Personality-guided behavior therapy* (pp. 33–49). Washington, DC: American Psychological Association.

Feske, U. (2001). Treating low-income and African American women with posttraumatic stress disorder: A case series. *Behavior Therapy, 32*, 585–601.

Feske, U., & Chambless, D. L. (1995). Cognitive behavioral versus exposure only treatment for social phobias: A meta-analysis. *Behavior Therapy, 30*, 695–720.

Fisher, P. L., & Wells, A. (2005). How effective are cognitive and behavioral treatments for obsessive-compulsive disorder? A clinical significance analysis. *Behaviour Research and Therapy, 43*(12), 1543–1558.

Foa, E. B., Liebowitz, M. R., Kozak, M. J., Davies, S., Campeas, R., & Franklin, M. E. et al. (2005). Randomized, placebo-controlled trial of exposure and ritual prevention, clomipramine, and their combination in the treatment of obsessive-compulsive disorder. *American Journal of Psychiatry, 162*(1), 151–161.

Franklin, M. E., & Foa, E. B. (2007). Cognitive behavioral treatment of obsessive-compulsive disorder. In P. E. Nathan & J. M. Gorman (Eds.), *A guide to treatments that work* (3rd ed., pp. 431–446). New York: Oxford University Press.

Franklin, M. E., & Foa, E. B. (2008). *Obsessive-compulsive disorder*. New York: Guilford Press.

Franklin, M. E., & Simpson, H. B. (2005). Combining pharmacotherapy and exposure plus ritual prevention for obsessive compulsive disorder: Research findings and clinical applications. *Journal of Cognitive Psychotherapy, 19*(4), 317–330.

Gilroy, L. J., Kirkby, K. C., Daniels, B. A., Menzies, R. G., & Montgomery, I. M. (2003). Long-term follow-up of computer-aided vicarious exposure versus live graded exposure in the treatment of spider phobia. *Behavior Therapy, 34*(1), 65–76.

Grawe, K., Donati, R., & Bernauer, F. (1998). *Psychotherapy in transition*. Seattle, WA: Hogrefe & Huber.

Greco, L. A., & Hayes, S. C. (2008). *Acceptance and mindfulness treatments for children and adolescents: A practitioner's guide*. Oakland, CA: New Harbinger.

Groden, G., & Cautela, J. R. (1981). Behavior therapy: A survey of procedures for counselors. *Personnel and Guidance Journal, 60*, 175–179.

Harned, M. S., Chapman, A. L., Dexter-Mazza, E. T., Murray, A., Comtois, K. A., & Linehan, M. M. (2008). Treating co-occurring axis I disorders in recurrently suicidal women with borderline personality disorder: A 2-year randomized trial of dialectical behavior therapy versus community treatment by experts. *Journal of Consulting and Clinical Psychology, 76*(6), 1068–1075.

Haug, T. T., Blomhoff, S., Hellstrom, K., Holme, I., Humble, M., & Madsbu, H. P. et al. (2003). Exposure therapy and sertraline in social phobia: 1-year follow-up of a randomised controlled trial. *British Journal of Psychiatry, 182*(4), 312–318.

Hayes, S. C. (2008). Climbing our hills: A beginning conversation on the comparison of acceptance and commitment therapy and traditional cognitive behavioral therapy. *Clinical Psychology: Science and Practice, 15*(4), 286–295.

Hayes, S. C., & Strosahl, K. D. (2005). *A practical guide to acceptance and commitment therapy.* New York: Springer Science.

Hays, P. A. (2008). *Addressing cultural complexities in practice: Assessment, diagnosis, and therapy* (2nd ed.). Washington, DC: American Psychological Association.

Hays, P. A. (2009). Integrating evidence-based practice, cognitive–behavior therapy, and multicultural therapy: Ten steps for culturally competent practice. *Professional Psychology: Research and Practice, 40*(4), 354–360.

Hazel, M. T. (2005). Visualization and systematic desensitization: Interventions for habituating and sensitizing patterns of public speaking anxiety. (Doctoral dissertation). *Dissertation Abstracts International Section A: Humanities and Social Sciences, 66*(1–A), 30.

Heffner, M., Eifert, G. H., Parker, B. T., Hernandez, D. H., & Sperry, J. A. (2003). Valued directions: Acceptance and commitment therapy in the treatment of alcohol dependence. *Cognitive and Behavioral Practice, 10*(4), 378–383.

Hertlein, K. M., & Ricci, R. J. (2004). A systematic research synthesis of EMDR studies: Implementation of the platinum standard. *Trauma, Violence, & Abuse, 5*(3), 285–300.

Higginbotham, H. N., & Streiner, D. (1991). Social science contribution to pharmaco-epidemiology. *Journal of Clinical Epidemiology, 44* (suppl. 2), 73S–82S.

Hirai, M., Vernon, L. L., & Cochran, H. (2007). Exposure therapy for phobias. In D. C. S. Richard & D. L. Lauterbach (Eds.), *Handbook of exposure therapies* (pp. 247–270). Burlington, MA: Elsevier.

Hoberman, H. M., & Clarke, G. N. (1993). Major depression in adults. In R. T. Ammerman & M. Hersen (Eds.), *Handbook of behavior therapy with children and adults* (pp. 73–90). Boston: Allyn & Bacon.

Hoffman, H. G., Garcia-Palacios, A., Carlin, A., Furness, T. A., III, & Botella-Arbona, C. (2003). Interfaces that heal: Coupling real and virtual objects to treat spider phobia. *International Journal of Human-Computer Interaction, 16*(2), 283–300.

Hull, C. L. (1943). *Principles of behavior.* New York: Appleton-Century-Crofts.

Hyman, R. (1964). *The nature of psychological inquiry.* Englewood Cliffs, NJ: Prentice-Hall.

Jacobson, E. (1938). *Progressive relaxation.* Chicago: University of Chicago Press.

Johnson, J. H., & McGlynn, F. D. (1988). Simple phobia. In M. Hersen & C. G. Last (Eds.), *Child behavior therapy case book* (pp. 43–53). New York: Plenum.

Jones, M. C. (1924). A laboratory study of fear: The case of Peter. *Pedagogical Seminary, 31*, 308–315.

Kazdin, A. E. (2001). *Behavior modification in applied settings* (6th ed.). Belmont, CA: Wadsworth.

Keane, T. M., Fairbank, J. A., Caddell, J. M., & Zimering, R. T. (1989). Implosive (flooding) therapy reduces symptoms of PTSD in Vietnam combat veterans. *Behavior Therapy, 20*, 245–260.

Kirby, F. D., & Shields, F. (1972). Modification of arithmetic response rate and attending behavior in a seventh-grade student. *Journal of Applied Behavior Analysis, 5*, 79–84.

Klinger, E., Bouchard, S., Légeron, P., Roy, S., Lauer, F., & Chemin, I. et al. (2005). Virtual reality therapy versus cognitive behavior therapy for social phobia: A preliminary controlled study. *CyberPsychology & Behavior, 8*(1), 76–88.

Krijn, M., Emmelkamp, P. M. G., Ólafsson, R. P., Bouwman, M., van Gerwen, L. J., Spinhoven, P., Schuemie, M. J., & van der Mast, C. A. P. G. (2007). Fear of flying treatment methods: Virtual reality exposure vs. cognitive behavioral therapy. *Aviation, Space, and Environmental Medicine, 78*(2), 121–128.

Krop, H., & Burgess, D. (1993). The use of covert modeling in the treatment of a sexual abuse victim. In J. R. Cautela & A. J. Kearney (Eds.), *Covert conditioning casebook* (pp. 153–158). Pacific Grove, CA: Brooks/Cole.

Lecomte, T., Leclerc, C., Corbière, M., Wykes, T., Wallace, C. J., & Spidel, A. (2008). Group cognitive behavior therapy or social skills training for individuals with a recent onset of psychosis: Results of a randomized controlled trial. *Journal of Nervous and Mental Disease, 196*(12), 866–875.

LeCroy, C. W. (2007). Problem-solving and social-skills training groups for children. In T. Ronen & A. Freeman (Eds.), *Cognitive behavior therapy in clinical social work practice* (pp. 285–300). New York: Springer.

Leeds, A. M., & Shapiro, F. (2000). EMDR and resource installation: Principles and procedures for enhancing current functioning and resolving traumatic experience. In J. Carlson & L. Sperry (Eds.), *Brief therapy with individuals and couples* (pp. 469–534). Phoenix, AZ: Zeig, Tucker, and Theisen.

Levin, M., & Hayes, S. C. (2009). ACT, RFT, and contextual behavioral science. In J. T. Blackledge, J. Ciarrochi, & F. P. Deane (Eds.), *Acceptance and commitment therapy: Contemporary theory, research and practice.* (pp. 1–40). Bowen Hills, QLD, Australia: Australian Academic Press.

Lindenboim, N., Comtois, K. A., & Linehan, M. M. (2007). Skills practice in dialectical behavior therapy for suicidal women meeting criteria for borderline personality disorder. *Cognitive and Behavioral Practice, 14*(2), 147–156.

Linehan, M. M. (1993a). *Skills training manual for treating borderline personality disorder.* New York: Guilford.

Linehan, M. M. (1993b). *Cognitive-behavioral treatment of borderline personality disorder.* New York: Guilford.

Linehan, M. M., & Dexter-Mazza, E. T. (2008). *Dialectical behavior therapy for borderline personality disorder.* New York: Guilford Press.

Linehan, M. M., McDavid, J. D., Brown, M. Z., Sayrs, J. H. R., & Gallop, R. J. (2008). Olanzapine plus dialectical behavior therapy for women with high irritability who meet criteria for borderline personality disorder: A double-blind, placebo-controlled pilot study. *Journal of Clinical Psychiatry, 69*(6), 999–1005.

Luber, M. (Ed.). (2009). *Eye movement desensitization and reprocessing (EMDR) scripted protocols: Basics and special situations.* New York: Springer.

Luoma, J. B., Hayes, S. C., & Walser, R. D. (2007). *Learning ACT: An acceptance and commitment therapy skills-training manual for therapists.* Oakland, CA: New Harbinger.

Malbos, E., Mestre, D. R., Note, I. D., & Gellato, C. (2008). Virtual reality and claustrophobia: Multiple components therapy involving game editor virtual environments exposure. *CyberPsychology & Behavior, 11*(6), 695–697.

Marlatt, G., & Gordon, J. (Eds.). (1985). *Relapse prevention: Maintenance strategies in the treatment of addictive behavior.* New York: Guilford.

Marlow, C. (2004). The evidence-based practitioner: Assessing the cultural responsiveness of research. In H. E. Briggs & T. L. Rzepnicki (Eds.), *Using evidence in social work practice: Behavioral perspectives* (pp. 257–272). Chicago: Lyceum Books.

Martin, J. (2004). Self-regulated learning, social cognitive theory, and agency. *Educational Psychologist, 39*(2), 135–145.

Maxfield, L. (2007). Current status and future directions for EMDR research. *Journal of EMDR Practice and Research, 1*(1), 6–14.

Meichenbaum, D. (1974). Self-instructional training: A cognitive prosthesis for the aged. *Human Development, 17,* 273–280.

Meichenbaum, D. (1985). *Stress inoculation training.* New York: Pergamon.

Meichenbaum, D. (1993). Stress inoculation training: A 20-year update. In P. M. Lehrer & R. L. Woolfolk (Eds.), *Principles and practice of stress management* (2nd ed., pp. 373–406). New York: Guilford.

Meichenbaum, D. (2007). Stress inoculation training: A preventative and treatment approach. In P. M. Lehrer, R. L. Woolfolk, & W. E. Sime (Eds.), *Principles and practice of stress management* (3rd ed., pp. 497–516). New York: Guilford.

Meichenbaum, D., & Goodman, J. (1971). Training impulsive children to talk to themselves: A means of developing self-control. *Journal of Abnormal Psychology, 77,* 115–126.

Miltenberger, R. G. (2008). *Behavior modification: Principles and procedures* (4th ed.). Belmont, CA: Thomson Wadsworth.

Mischel, W. (1973). Toward a cognitive social learning reconceptualization of personality. *Psychology Review, 80,* 730–755.

Mowrer, O. H. (1950). *Learning theory and personality dynamics.* New York: Ronald Press.

Mowrer, O. H., & Mowrer, W. M. (1938). Enuresis: A method for its study and treatment. *American Journal of Orthopsychiatry, 8,* 436–459.

North, M. M., North, S. M., & Burwick, C. B. (2008). *Virtual reality therapy: A vision for a new paradigm.* Hauppauge, NY: Nova Science.

Ollendick, T. H., Davis, T. E., III, & Sirbu, C. (2009). Specific phobias. In D. McKay & E. A. Storch (Eds.), *Cognitive-behavior therapy for children: Treating complex and refractory cases* (pp. 171–199). New York: Springer.

Ollendick, T. H., Öst, L., Reuterskiöld, L., Costa, N., Cederlund, R., Sirbu, C., Davis, T. E., III, & Jarrett, M. A. (2009). One-session treatment of specific phobias in youth: A randomized clinical trial in the United States and Sweden. *Journal of Consulting and Clinical Psychology, 77*(3), 504–516.

Orsillo, S. M., & Batten, S. V. (2005). Acceptance and commitment therapy in the treatment of posttraumatic stress disorder. *Behavior Modification, 29*(1), 95–129.

Öst, L. G., Stridh, B. M., & Wolf, M. (1998). A clinical study of spider phobia: Prediction of outcome after self-help and therapist-directed treatments. *Behavior Research and Therapy, 36*, 17–35.

Parsons, T. D., & Rizzo, A. A. (2008). Affective outcomes of virtual reality exposure therapy for anxiety and specific phobias: A meta-analysis. *Journal of Behavior Therapy and Experimental Psychiatry, 39*(3), 250–261.

Powers, M. B., & Emmelkamp, P. M. G. (2008). Virtual reality exposure therapy for anxiety disorders: A meta-analysis. *Journal of Anxiety Disorders, 22*(3), 561–569.

Price, M., & Anderson, P. (2007). The role of presence in virtual reality exposure therapy. *Journal of Anxiety Disorders, 21*(5), 742–751.

Przeworski, A., & Newman, M. G. (2004). Palmtop computer-assisted group therapy for social phobia. *Journal of Clinical Psychology, 60*(2), 179–188.

Reger, G. M., & Gahm, G. A. (2008). Virtual reality exposure therapy for active duty soldiers. *Journal of Clinical Psychology, 64*(8), 940–946.

Rezvan, S., Baghban, I., Bahrami, F., & Abedi, M. (2008). A comparison of cognitive-behavior therapy with interpersonal and cognitive behavior therapy in the treatment of generalized anxiety disorder. *Counselling Psychology Quarterly, 21*(4), 309–321.

Riggs, D. S., & Foa, E. B. (1993). Obsessive compulsive disorder. In D. H. Barlow (Ed.), *Clinical handbook of psychological disorders* (pp. 189–239). New York: Guilford.

Riggs, D. S., & Foa, E. B. (2007). Treating contamination concerns and compulsive washing. In M. M. Antony, C. Purdon, & L. J. Summerfeldt (Eds.), *Psychological treatment of obsessive-compulsive disorder: Fundamentals and beyond* (pp. 149–168). Washington, DC: American Psychological Association.

Riva, G., Alcãniz, M., Anolli, L., Bacchetta, M., Bañs, R., & Buselli, C. et al. (2003). The VEPSY updated project: Clinical rationale and technical approach. *CyberPsychology & Behavior, 6*(4), 433–439.

Rizzo, A., Reger, G., Gahm, G., Difede, J., & Rothbaum, B. O. (2009). Virtual reality exposure therapy for combat-related PTSD. In P. J. Shiromani, T. M. Keane, & J. E. LeDoux (Eds.), *Post-traumatic stress disorder: Basic science and clinical practice.* (pp. 375–399). Totowa, NJ: Humana Press.

Roemer, L., Orsillo, S. M., & Salters-Pedneault, K. (2008). Efficacy of an acceptance-based behavior therapy for generalized anxiety disorder: Evaluation in a randomized controlled trial. *Journal of Consulting and Clinical Psychology, 76*(6).

Rosa-Alcázar, A. I., Sánchez-Meca, J., Gómez-Conesa, A., & Marín-Martínez, F. (2008). Psychological treatment of obsessive-compulsive disorder: A meta-analysis. *Clinical Psychology Review, 28*(8), 1310–1325.

Rose, S. D., & Lecroy, C. W. (1991). Group methods. In F. H. Kanfer & A. P. Goldstein (Eds.), *Helping people change* (4th ed., pp. 422–454). New York: Pergamon.

Rotter, J. B. (1954). *Social learning and clinical psychology.* Englewood Cliffs, NJ: Prentice-Hall.

Shah, A., Dalvi, M., & Thompson, T. (2005). Is there a need to study behavioral and psychological signs and symptoms of dementia across cultures? *International Psychogeriatrics, 17*(3), 513–518.

Shapiro, D. A., & Shapiro, D. (1982). Meta-analysis of comparative therapy outcome studies: A replication and refinement. *Psychological Bulletin, 92*, 581–604.

Shapiro, F. (1997). *EMDR in the treatment of trauma.* Pacific Grove, CA: EMDR.

Shapiro, F. (1999). Eye movement desensitization and reprocessing (EMDR) and the anxiety disorders: Clinical and research implication of an integrated psychotherapy treatment. *Journal of Anxiety Disorders, 13*, 35–67.

Shapiro, F. (2001). *Eye movement desensitization and reprocessing: Basic principles, protocols, and procedures* (2nd ed.). New York: Guilford.

Shapiro, F., & Forrest, M. S. (2004). *EMDR: The breakthrough therapy for overcoming anxiety, stress, and trauma.* New York: Basic Books.

Shapiro, F., Kaslow, F. W. , & Maxfield, L. (2007). *Handbook of EMDR and family therapy processes.* Hoboken, NJ: John Wiley.

Shapiro, R. (2005a). *EMDR solutions: Pathways to healing.* New York: Norton.

Shapiro, R. (2005b). The two-hand interweave. In R. Shapiro (Ed.), *EMDR solutions: Pathways to healing* (pp. 160–166). New York: Norton.

Sigmon, S. T., Pells, J., Edenfield, T. M., Hermann, B. A., Schartel, J. G., LaMattina, S. M., & Boulard, N. E. (2007). Are we there yet? A review of gender comparisons in three behavioral journals through the 20th century. *Behavior Therapy, 38*(4), 333–339.

Simpson, H. B., Foa, E. B., Liebowitz, M. R., Ledley, D. R., Huppert, J. D., Cahill, S., Vermes, D., Schmidt, A. B., Hembree, E., Franklin, M., Campeas, R., Hahn, C., & Petkova, E. (2008). A randomized, controlled trial of cognitive-behavioral therapy for augmenting pharmacotherapy in obsessive-compulsive disorder. *American Journal of Psychiatry, 165*(5), 621–630.

Simpson, H. B., Zuckoff, A., Page, J. R., Franklin, M. E., & Foa, E. B. (2008). Adding motivational interviewing to exposure and ritual prevention for obsessive-compulsive disorder: An open pilot trial. *Cognitive Behaviour Therapy, 37*(1), 38–49.

Skinner, B. F. (1948). *Walden two*. New York: Macmillan.

Skinner, B. F. (1953). *Science and human behavior*. New York: Free Press.

Smith, M. L., & Glass, G. V. (1977). Meta-analysis of psychotherapy outcome studies. *American Psychologist, 32*, 752–760.

Spiegler, M. D., & Guevremont, D. C. (2010). *Contemporary behavior therapy* (5th ed.). Belmont, CA: Wadsworth.

Stampfl, T. G. (1966). Implosive therapy. Part 1: The theory. In S. G. Armitage (Ed.), *Behavioral modification techniques in the treatment of emotional disorder* (pp. 12–21). Battle Creek, MI: VA Hospital Publications.

Stampfl, T. G. (1970). Implosive therapy: An emphasis on covert stimulation. In D. J. Levis (Ed.), *Learning approaches to therapeutic behavior change* (pp. 182–204). Chicago: Aldine.

Stanley, M. A., Diefenbach, G. J., & Hopko, D. R. (2004). Cognitive behavioral treatment for older adults with generalized anxiety disorder: A therapist manual for primary care settings. *Behavior Modification, 28*(1), 73–117.

Stanley, M. A., Wilson, N. L., Novy, D. M., Rhoades, H. M., Wagener, P. D., Greisinger, A. J., Cully, J. A., & Kunik, M. E. (2009). Cognitive behavior therapy for generalized anxiety disorder among older adults in primary care: A randomized clinical trial. *Journal of the American Medical Association, 301*(14), 1460–1467.

Tanaka-Matsumi, J., & Higginbotham, H. N. (1996). Behavioral approaches to counseling across cultures. In P. B. Pedersen, J. G. Dragerns, W. J. Lonner, & J. E. Trimble (Eds.), *Counseling across cultures* (4th ed., pp. 266–292). Thousand Oaks, CA: Sage.

Taylor, S. (2004). Efficacy and outcome predictors for three PTSD treatments: Exposure therapy, EMDR, and relaxation training. In S. Taylor (Ed.), *Advances in the treatment of posttraumatic stress disorder: Cognitive-behavioral perspectives* (pp. 13–37). New York: Springer.

Taylor, S., Thordarson, D. S., Spring, T., Yeh, A. H., Corcoran, K. M., & Eugster, K. et al. (2003). Telephone-administered cognitive behavior therapy for obsessive-compulsive disorder. *Cognitive Behaviour Therapy, 32*(1), 13–25.

Thorndike, E. L. (1898). Animal intelligence: An experimental study of the associative process in animals. *Psychological Review: Monograph Supplement* (No. 8).

Thorndike, E. L. (1911). *Animal intelligence: Experimental studies*. New York: Macmillan.

Twohig, M. P., & Hayes, S. C. (2008). *ACT verbatim for depression and anxiety: Annotated transcripts for learning acceptance and commitment therapy*. Oakland, CA: New Harbinger.

Walen, S., & Wolfe, J. L. (2000). Women's sexuality. J. R. White & A. S. Freeman (Eds.), *Cognitive-behavioral group therapy for specific problems and populations* (pp. 305–330). Washington, DC: American Psychological Associates.

Wallach, H. S., Safir, M. P., & Bar-Zvi, M. (2009). Virtual reality cognitive behavior therapy for public speaking anxiety: A randomized clinical trial. *Behavior Modification, 33*(3), 314–338.

Watson, J. B. (1914). *Behavior: An introduction to comparative psychology*. New York: H. Holt.

Watson, J. B. (1919). *Psychology from the standpoint of a behaviorist*. Philadelphia: Lippincott.

Watson, J. B., & Rayner, R. (1920). Conditioned emotional reactions. *Journal of Experimental Psychology, 3*, 1–14.

Whittal, M. L., Thordarson, D. S., & Mclean, P. D. (2005). Treatment of obsessive-compulsive disorder: Cognitive behavior therapy vs. exposure and response prevention. *Behaviour Research and Therapy, 43*(12), 1559–1576.

Wiederhold, B. K., & Wiederhold, M. D. (2005). *Virtual reality therapy for anxiety disorders: Advances in evaluation and treatment*. Washington, DC: American Psychological Association.

Wolitzky-Taylor, K. B., Horowitz, J. D., Powers, M. B., & Telch, M. J. (2008). Psychological approaches in the treatment of specific phobias: A meta-analysis. *Clinical Psychology Review, 28*(6), 1021–1037.

Wolpe, J. (1958). *Psychotherapy by reciprocal inhibition*. Stanford, CA: Stanford University Press.

Wolpe, J. (1990). *The practice of behavior therapy* (4th ed.). New York: Pergamon.

Worell, J. H., & Remer, P. (2003). *Feminist perspectives in therapy: Empowering diverse women* (2nd ed.). New York: Wiley.

CHAPTER 9

Rational Emotive Behavior Therapy

Outline of Rational Emotive Behavior Therapy

RATIONAL EMOTIVE BEHAVIOR THEORY OF
PERSONALITY
    Philosophical Viewpoints
        Responsible hedonism
        Humanism
        Rationality
    Factors Basic to the Rational Emotive Behavior
    Theory of Personality
        Biological factors
        Social factors
        Vulnerability to disturbance
    The Rational Emotive Behavior A-B-C Theory of
    Personality
        Rational belief: pleasant activating event
        Rational belief: unpleasant activating event
        Irrational belief: unpleasant activating event
        Disturbances about disturbances
        Interrelationship between A, B, and C
        Musts
        Low frustration tolerance
        Anxiety
RATIONAL EMOTIVE BEHAVIOR THEORY OF
PSYCHOTHERAPY
    Goals of Therapy
    Assessment

The Therapeutic Relationship
The A-B-C-D-E Therapeutic Approach
    A (Activating event)
    C (Consequences)
    B (Beliefs)
    D (Disputing)
    E (Effective)
Other Cognitive Approaches
    Coping self-statements
    Cost-benefit analysis
    Psychoeducational methods
    Teaching others
    Problem solving
Emotive Techniques
    Imagery
    Role playing
    Shame-attacking exercises
    Forceful self-statements
    Forceful self-dialogue
Behavioral Methods
    Activity homework
    Reinforcements and penalties
    Skill training
Insight

Rational emotive behavior therapy (REBT) was developed in the 1950s by Albert Ellis, a clinical psychologist, as a result of his dissatisfaction with his practice of psychoanalysis and with person-centered therapy. He originated an approach that he believed would be more effective and efficient in bringing about psychotherapeutic change. His approach is primarily a cognitive one, although it has significant behavioral and emotive aspects.

Essential to his theory is his A-B-C model, which is applied to understanding personality and to effecting personality change. This model holds that individuals respond to an activating event (A) with emotional and behavioral consequences (C). The emotional and behavioral consequences are not only caused by the activating event (A), but partly by the individual's belief system (B). When the activating event (A) is a pleasant one, the resulting beliefs are likely to be innocuous. However, when the activating events are not pleasant, irrational beliefs may develop. These irrational beliefs (B) often cause difficult emotional and behavioral consequences (C).

A major role of the therapist is to dispute (D) these irrational beliefs (B) by challenging them through a variety of disputational techniques. Also, a number of other cognitive, emotive, and behavioral techniques are used to bring about therapeutic change. Although this outline of REBT is relatively simple, the practice of REBT is not. Assessing, disputing, and changing irrational beliefs require familiarity with assessment of implicit irrational beliefs and knowledge of a wide variety of cognitive, emotive, and behavioral techniques for individuals, families, and groups.

History of Rational Emotive Behavior Therapy

Albert Ellis, the founder and developer of REBT, was born in Pittsburgh in 1913 and moved to New York City 4 years later. He grew up in New York, did all his schooling there, founded a training institute there, the Institute for Rational Living (later the Albert Ellis Institute) in 1959, and lived and worked there until his death in 2007 at the age of 93. During his childhood, Albert, the oldest of three children, was often sick and was hospitalized nine times, mainly for problems related to kidney disease. As a result, Ellis developed a pattern of taking care of himself and being self-responsible. Making his breakfast and lunch and getting to school by himself are early indicators of the self-sufficiency that was to be a trademark of Ellis's approach to education and professional life. His father, a businessman, was often away from home, and Ellis described his mother as neglectful of her family (Weiner, 1988, p. 41). In looking back at his childhood, Ellis stated: "I invented rational emotive behavior therapy naturally, beginning even back then, because it was my tendency" (Weiner, 1988, p. 42). But during his adolescence, Ellis was quite shy with girls. Using a method that foreshadows REBT, he made himself talk to 100 girls at the Bronx Botanical Gardens during a 1-month period. Although he was not successful in getting a date, this method helped Ellis decrease his fear of rejection. Also shy about speaking in front of groups, Ellis used a similar approach to overcome this fear, so much so that he later came to enjoy public speaking.

Ellis received his undergraduate degree at the City College of New York in 1934. Between graduation from college and entering graduate school at the age of 28, he wrote novels and worked as a personnel manager in a small business. After obtaining his Ph.D. in 1947 at Columbia University, he started work at a New Jersey mental hygiene clinic while receiving analysis from Richard Hulbeck, a psychiatrist, who was later to supervise Ellis in his early psychoanalytic work. In the 1940s Ellis published several articles on personality assessment

ALBERT ELLIS

questionnaires. Later he was to publish and speak frequently on sex, love, and marital relationships (Ellis, 1986a). His popular books, *Sex Without Guilt* (1958), *The Encyclopedia of Sexual Behavior* (1961), and *The Art and Science of Love* (1965) sold well and influenced marriage and family therapy, as well as many individual Americans.

While practicing psychoanalysis and psychoanalytic therapy between 1947 and 1953, Ellis became increasingly dissatisfied with it. He felt that although some clients felt better, they rarely improved in a way that would help them be symptom free and more in control of their lives. Having been interested in philosophy since the age of 16, Ellis returned to philosophy to determine ways to help individuals change their philosophical point of view and combat self-defeating behavior (Ellis, 2005b). In 1956, at the American Psychological Association annual convention, Ellis gave his first paper on rational therapy, his term then for REBT (Ellis, 1999b). He later regretted using the term *rational therapy*, because many psychologists misinterpreted it as meaning therapy without emotion. That was not Ellis's intention, and he spent time trying to clarify and explain his position. Although other psychologists were developing other direct methods of dealing with clients at about the same time, none made such consistent and pronounced efforts in explicating their point of view as did Ellis.

Although Ellis was an adjunct professor of psychology at three universities, he devoted his energy to his practice of individual and group REBT and the training of therapists at the Albert Ellis Institute in New York. Established in 1959, the nonprofit institute provides workshops, therapist training, and individual and group psychotherapy. Ellis also initiated the *Journal of Rational-Emotive Behavior and Cognitive-Behavior Therapy*. Ellis was unusually active, working 7 days a week from about 9:00 A.M. into the evening, even into his 90s. His work week included more than 70 individual (half-hour) therapy sessions, four group therapy sessions, supervision of therapists in REBT, and public lectures. In addition, he wrote several articles, chapters of books, or books each year (Ellis, 1992c; Ellis, 2004b; Ellis, 2004d; Weiner, 1988). Ellis' final book was a graduate-level textbook, *Personality Theories: Critical Perspectives* (Ellis, Abrams, & Abrams, 2009).

Ellis was extremely productive in professional organizations and in the publication of books and articles. He was a fellow of many divisions of the American Psychological Association and of many other professional therapy and sex education organizations, and received a number of awards from these organizations for his leadership and contributions to the field. Not only did he serve as a consulting or associate editor of more than a dozen professional journals, but he also wrote nearly 800 articles and 75 books, the more recent ones on REBT. Particularly significant is *Reason and Emotion in Psychotherapy* (1962), which presented the theory and practice of REBT. His *Humanistic Psychotherapy: The Rational-Emotive Approach* (1973) shows the humanistic aspect of REBT. Ellis has also written a significant number of books for the public, most notably *A New Guide to Rational Living* (1997), written with Robert Harper. Now in its third edition, it shows how individuals can apply the concepts (Ellis, 2004b) of REBT to their own lives. *How to Make Yourself Happy and Remarkably Less Disturbable* (1999a) suggests how to use REBT to deal with anxiety, depression, and anger. *Rational Emotive Therapy: It Works for Me—It Can Work for You* (Ellis, 2004c) describes Ellis's background and then illustrates how REBT can help the reader with her own problems.

Rational Emotive Behavior Theory of Personality

Ellis's theory of personality is based not only on psychological, biological, and sociological data but also on philosophy. His philosophical approach features responsible hedonism and humanism, which, combined with a belief in rationality, influenced his personality theory. Ellis was interested in biological, social, and psychological factors that make individuals vulnerable to psychological disturbances that are cognitive, behavioral, and emotional in nature. It is particularly the cognitive factors that Ellis emphasizes, attending to the irrational beliefs that help create disturbances in individuals' lives. By understanding how Ellis views irrational beliefs, it is easier to understand his therapeutic interventions.

Philosophical Viewpoints

As a high school student, Ellis enjoyed the study of philosophy. He was interested particularly in the Stoic philosophers and was influenced by Epictetus, a Roman philosopher who said, "People are disturbed not by things, but by their view of things" (Dryden, 1990, p. 1). He was also affected by European philosophers who dealt with the issues of happiness and rationality, such as Baruch Spinoza, Friedrich Nietzsche, and Immanuel Kant, as well as Arthur Schopenhauer's concept of "the world as will and idea" (Ellis, 1987b, p. 160). The writings of more modern philosophers, including John Dewey, Bertrand Russell, and Karl Popper (a philosopher of science), influenced Ellis to emphasize cognition in his development of REBT (DiGiuseppe, 2010; Dryden & Ellis, 2001; Ellis, 1973, 1987a, 1991a, 1994a, 1996b, 1996c, 2003f, 2008). The philosophical underpinnings of REBT include responsible hedonism, humanism, and rationality.

Long-Term pleasure

Responsible hedonism. Although hedonism refers to the concept of seeking pleasure and avoiding pain, responsible hedonism concerns maintaining pleasure over the long term by avoiding short-term pleasures that lead to pain, such as drug abuse and alcohol addiction. Ellis believes that people are often extremely hedonistic but need to focus on long-range rather than short-range hedonism (Dryden & Ellis, 2001; Ellis, 1985, 1987a, 1988, 2001c, 2001d; Ellis & Dryden, 1997; Walen, DiGiuseppe, & Wessler, 1980). Although REBT does not tell people what to enjoy, its practitioners believe that enjoyment is a major goal in life. This point of view does not lead to irresponsible behavior because individuals with a responsible attitude toward hedonism think through the consequences of their behavior on others as well as on themselves. Manipulating and exploiting others is not in the long-range interest of individuals. An example of Ellis's attention to hedonism is his work directed at irrational beliefs that people have regarding sexuality that interfere with their experience of sexual pleasure. His many books on the subject are a way of promoting responsible hedonism.

Humanism. Practitioners of REBT view human beings as holistic, goal-directed organisms who are important because they are alive (Dryden, 1990, p. 4). This position is consistent with that of ethical humanism, which emphasizes human interests over the interests of a deity, leading to misinterpretations that Ellis is against religion. He has stated, "It is not religion, but religiosity, that is a cause of psychopathology. Religiosity is an absolutistic faith that is not based on fact" (Ellis, 1986a, p. 3). Ellis (1986b, 2000) believes that accepting absolute notions of right and wrong, and of damnation if one acts wrongly, without thinking them through leads to guilt, anxiety, depression, and other psychological dysfunctions.

Ellis (Ellis, 2004b; Ellis & Dryden, 1997; Ziegler, 2003) believes that individuals preferably should have unconditional self-acceptance (USA). They should accept that they make mistakes, that they have worth, and that some of their own assets and qualities are stronger than other assets that they or others possess. "Thus, Adolf Hitler may be equal in humanity to Mother Teresa, but in terms of their compassion toward human beings, the latter far outscores the former" (Ellis & Dryden, 1997, p. 205). To achieve USA, individuals need to work at this; otherwise, they may blame themselves for being "worthless" or "no good." An extension of this view is that people can be perceived as good in themselves because they exist (Ellis, 2001e; Ziegler, 2000). Abhorring discrimination against anyone based on traits such as race, sex, or intellect, Ellis believes that individuals should be accepted for themselves, a concept similar to Carl Rogers's "unconditional positive regard" (Dryden, 1998; Ellis, 1962, 1973, 1993, 2001c; Ellis & Dryden, 1997; Ziegler, 2003). Thus, Ellis believes that both the therapist and the client should rate or criticize their deeds, acts, or performances but not their essence or themselves. Acceptance of the client while not liking aspects of his behaviors is consistent with the philosophy of REBT.

Rationality. *Rationality* refers to people using efficient, flexible, logical, and scientific ways of attempting to achieve their values and goals (Dryden & Neenan, 2004; Ellis, 1962, 1973, 1999a, 2001c, 2005b; Wilson, 2010), not to the absence of feelings or emotions. Therapy with REBT shows individuals how they can get more of what they want from life by being rational (efficient, logical, and flexible). This means that they may reexamine early parental or religious teachings or beliefs they had previously accepted. As this is done, they develop a new philosophy of life that leads to increased long-range happiness (responsible hedonism).

These philosophies, which have been abbreviated here, are communicated to clients to help them not only alleviate current problems but also develop a philosophy of life that will help them deal with problems as they present themselves.

Factors Basic to the Rational Emotive Behavior Theory of Personality

Ellis has recognized a number of factors that contribute to an individual's personality development and personality disturbances, including strong biological and social aspects that present a challenge to the therapist to help change. Depending on biological and social factors, individuals are varyingly vulnerable to emotional disturbance, which is explained by Ellis's A-B-C theory of personality described in the next section.

Biological factors. Impressed by the power of biological factors in determining human personality, Ellis has said, "I am still haunted by the reality, however, that humans … have a strong biological tendency to needlessly and severely disturb themselves, and that, to make matters much worse, they also are powerfully predisposed to unconsciously and habitually prolong their mental dysfunctioning and to fight like hell against giving it up" (Ellis, 1987a, p. 365). Writing that individuals have powerful innate tendencies to hurt themselves or to think in irrational ways, Ellis (1976) believes that individuals have inborn tendencies to react to events in certain patterns, regardless of environmental factors that may affect events, by damning themselves and others when they do not get what they want. Additionally, Ellis (1962) believes that certain severe mental disturbances are partly inherited and have strong biological components. For example, schizophrenia is illustrative of biological limitations that inhibit thinking clearly and logically.

PAPER (checkmark)

Social factors. Interpersonal relationships in families, peer groups, schools, and other social groups have an impact on the expectations that individuals have of themselves and others (Ellis, 2003e). They are likely to define themselves as good or worthwhile, depending on how they see others reacting to them. If they feel accepted by others, they are likely to feel good about themselves. Individuals receiving criticism from parents, teachers, or peers are likely to view themselves as bad or worthless or in other negative ways. From a rational emotive behavior perspective, individuals who feel worthless or bad about themselves are often caring too much about the views and values of others. According to Ellis, social institutions such as schools and religions are likely to promote absolutist values that suggest the proper ways of relating to others in terms of manners, customs, sexuality, and family relationships (Ellis, 1962, 1985a, 2001c; Ellis & Dryden, 1997; Ellis & Harper, 1997). Individuals often are faced with dealing with the "musts" and "shoulds" they have incorporated from their interactions with others. For example, if an individual believes she absolutely must pray twice a day, that belief has been partly learned through religious training. Ellis does not say that this value of praying is inappropriate; rather, he encourages individuals to question their absolutist "musts" and "shoulds."

Vulnerability to disturbance. Depending on social and biological factors, individuals vary as to how vulnerable they are to psychological disturbance. They often have goals to enjoy themselves when alone or in social groups, to enjoy an intimate sexual relationship with another, to enjoy productive work, and to enjoy a variety of recreational activities (Dryden & Ellis, 2001, 2003). Opposing these desires are dysfunctional beliefs that thwart their ability to meet or enjoy these goals. Ellis (1987a, pp. 371–373) gives several examples of irrational beliefs that are indicators of individuals who are disturbed or disrupted in meeting their goals:

Theories in Action

Irrational Beliefs About Competence and Success—"Because I strongly desire to get A's in all subjects, I absolutely 'must' get all A's at all times and do perfectly well."

Irrational Beliefs About Love and Approval—"Because I strongly desire to be loved by Sarah, I absolutely 'must' always have her approval."

Irrational Beliefs About Being Treated Unfairly—"Because I strongly desire Eric to treat me considerately and fairly, he absolutely 'must' do so at all times and under all conditions, because I am always considerate and fair to him."

Irrational Beliefs About Safety and Comfort—"Because I strongly desire to have a safe, comfortable, and satisfying life, I 'must' find life easy, convenient, and gratifying at all times."

These represent just a few examples of irrational beliefs. According to Ellis, the more frequently these beliefs occur, the more an individual may be vulnerable to psychological disturbance. Whether these beliefs come from biological or social factors is immaterial; they are disruptive to the individual who would lead a happy life. How such beliefs are established within an individual's system of thinking is the subject of the next section.

The Rational Emotive Behavior A-B-C Theory of Personality

The focus of rational emotive behavior personality theory is the A-B-C model of personality. Individuals have goals that may be supported or thwarted by activating events (As). They then react, consciously or unconsciously, with their belief system (B), by which they respond to the activating event with something such as, "This is nice." They also experience the emotional or behavioral consequence of the activating event. This system works well for individuals when the activating events are pleasant and support their goals. When the activating events no longer support their goals, there is potential for disturbance in this system. The potential exists for the belief system to be irrational or dysfunctional, which can lead to further disturbances.

When individuals believe something must happen as they wish, emotional disturbance occurs. This is particularly true when tolerance for frustration is low (Harrington, 2007). Although these concepts appear simple, they can, when fully developed, become quite complex (Dryden, DiGiuseppe, & Neenan, 2003; Dryden & Ellis, 2001, 2003; Ellis, 1962, 2001c, 2004a; Ellis & Dryden, 1997). To illustrate these principles, here is Kelly, who has a goal to become a psychologist and a subgoal to do well on her psychology examination.

Rational belief: pleasant activating event. The A-B-C theory of personality functions well and, for most people, goes unnoticed when the activating events are pleasant. When Kelly receives an A on her psychology exam (activating event), her belief (B) in her ability to do well on the psychology exam and to become a psychologist is supported. The consequence is an emotional experience of pleasure and a behavioral anticipation of the next psychology examination, an activating event.

Rational belief: unpleasant activating event. When the activating event is unpleasant, many different beliefs and consequences can result. If Kelly fails her psychology exam, the activating event (A), she may experience a belief (B) such as "This is too bad; I don't like to fail a test." She may experience a healthy emotional consequence of feeling frustrated by her performance on the test. She may also choose to study hard for the next test (an upcoming activating event) so that she will not experience this behavioral consequence again.

Irrational belief: unpleasant activating event. When individuals do not experience activating events in a way that is congruent with their belief systems (B), they may react with irrational beliefs (IBs). Rather than saying, "It is unfortunate, it is too bad," they may say, "I ought to have, I should, I must, I have to, have my goals fulfilled." Furthermore, they may say, "If my goals are not fulfilled, it is awful," "I can't stand it," "I'm a terrible person," and so forth. It is these irrational beliefs that contribute to emotional disturbance. They are usually followed by emotional consequences such as "I feel depressed and hopeless" or "I am extremely angry." Behavioral consequences may be avoidance, attack, or a whole range of inappropriate reactions. When Kelly fails her psychology exam (A, an activating event), she may react by believing, "I have to have an A on the exam" or "I am a worthless person because I didn't get an A." She may experience an unhealthy emotional consequence, such as deep despair, a sense of worthlessness, and a choice not to study for other courses—a behavioral consequence.

Disturbances about disturbances. Ellis believes that individuals largely upset themselves through their belief systems. They can become disturbed about the consequences resulting from an unfortunate activating event. People may disturb themselves by turning a disturbed consequence into a new activating event. Kelly may continue by saying, "I feel depressed and worthless!"—a new activating event. The new belief that follows is "That is really awful!" This leaves her with a new consequence in which her feelings of worthlessness and upset are even greater. This new upset (new C) can become a third activating event, such as "I am the most worthless person in the world," and the cycle can continue ad infinitum. Thus, Kelly was depressed about her examination performance but became depressed and upset about being depressed. She criticized herself for doing poorly on the exam, felt depressed because she criticized herself, then criticized herself for being overly critical, and then criticized herself for not seeing that she is being critical, and then for not stopping being critical. She can further say, "I am more critical than others, and I'm more depressed than others, and nothing can be done about how hopeless I am." In such a way, individuals can be overwhelmed by their irrational belief systems.

Interrelationship between A, B, and C. Although the A-B-C personality theory may appear rather simple, Ellis has explained the variety of interactions among A, B, and C. Activating events, beliefs, and consequences can each have components that are emotional, behavioral, or cognitive. Furthermore, each of these (A, B, and C) can influence and interact with each other. Ellis and his colleagues (Browne, Dowd, & Freeman, 2010; Ellis, 2001c, 2001e) describe how cognition, emotions, and behaviors affect one another and combine into a set of dysfunctional philosophical assumptions leading to emotional disturbance.

Musts. Implicit in individuals' consequences are musts, such as "I must do well on the exam," "I must get an A in the course," "I must become a psychologist," and so forth. Ellis (2001e, 2008) states that musts not only are intellectual and cognitive but also have elements that are highly emotional and others that are behavioral. Musts are a part of goals, activating events, beliefs, and ineffective consequences. Ellis (1962) lists 12 musts that he believes are common to many individuals, examples of which follow:

I must be loved by everyone I know.
I must be competent, adequate, and achieving in all respects to be worthwhile.
Some people are wicked and must be severely blamed and punished for what they have done.
It is awful when things don't go the way I want them to.
Things must go the way I want them to.
I must worry about dangerous things that I cannot control.
I must rely on someone stronger than myself.
I must become worried about other people's problems.
I must find the right solution to my problems.

Dryden (1990) and Ellis (1985a, 1991a) divide these irrational beliefs into three categories: demands about self, demands about others, and demands about the world and/or life conditions. Ellis has developed the term *musturbation* for all types of must statements. Musturbating develops irrational beliefs and leads to emotional disturbance. For Kelly to say, "I must get an A on my exam, or I will be a worthless person, and no one will ever respect me" is an example of an irrational belief that can lead to her becoming anxious, fearful, panicky about exams, and physically tense.

Low frustration tolerance. Individuals who cannot tolerate frustration easily are more likely to be disturbed than those who can (Harrington, 2005). Such statements as "That's too difficult," "I can't take the pressure," and "I'm too frightened to do it" are examples of low frustration tolerance. A personal philosophy maintaining that one should not have to do anything unpleasant or uncomfortable can lead to frustration in obtaining goals. If Kelly is frustrated easily by her poor performance on one exam, she may give up on her goal of becoming a psychologist and develop anxiety, depression, and so forth.

Anxiety. Related to the concept of low frustration tolerance to disturbance is anxiety. Ellis (2003a, b) describes two types of anxiety—discomfort anxiety and ego anxiety. In discomfort anxiety, individuals' comfort level is threatened and they must get what they want (low frustration tolerance). In ego anxiety, individuals' sense of self-worth is threatened and they feel that they must perform well. In both discomfort and ego anxiety, individuals have a belief that if they don't get or do what they want, the results will be awful or catastrophic. Kelly may experience discomfort anxiety if she does not get an A, which she badly wants, on her exam. She may feel ego anxiety if she does not get an A because her sense of worth may be threatened.

2 Types Anxiety:
1.) Discomfort
2.) Ego
Key Concepts

The A-B-C theory of personality is also the central focus for personality change. The next section describes therapeutic approaches to activating events, beliefs, and emotional and behavioral consequences.

Rational Emotive Behavior Theory of Psychotherapy

A characteristic of REBT is its combination of philosophical change with cognitive, behavioral, and emotive strategies to bring about both short-range and long-range change. The emphasis on cognition has its antecedents in Adlerian psychotherapy, which has a strong focus on individuals' beliefs. The goals of REBT stress the use and adoption of the A-B-C theory of personality. Although assessment instruments are used, the A-B-C theory is the core of assessment as well as of psychotherapy. Rational emotive behavior therapists vary their approach to the development of the relationship with a client, but all acknowledge the importance of acceptance of the client as an individual. The core approach to REBT is to dispute irrational thoughts; however, many other cognitive, emotive, and behavioral approaches are used to bring about change and meet clients' goals.

Core Approach

Goals of Therapy

The general goals of REBT are to assist people in minimizing emotional disturbances, decreasing self-defeating self-behaviors, and becoming more self-actualized so that they can lead a happier existence (Ellis, 2003d, 2004b, 2005b). Major subgoals are to help individuals think more clearly and rationally, feel more appropriately, and act more efficiently and effectively in achieving goals of living happily. Individuals learn to deal effectively with negative feelings such as sorrow, regret, frustration, and annoyance. They deal with unhealthy negative feelings such as depression, anxiety, and worthlessness by using an effective rational emotive behavior philosophy.

For Ellis (1990b, 2004d, 2008), the philosophy of REBT distinguishes it from other cognitive therapies and makes it more efficient and elegant. Although REBT helps individuals minimize or remove emotional disturbances, it is the teaching of philosophical change that prevents individuals from redisturbing themselves with overwhelming irrational thoughts. The A-B-C philosophy can help clients see when they are creating new symptoms or re-creating previous ones. The global goals of REBT can be applied to specific client goals through the use of A-B-C personality theory (DiGiuseppe, 2007; Dryden & Ellis, 2001, 2003; Dryden & Neenan, 2004).

Assessment

REBT assessment is of two overlapping types. The first is assessment of cognition and behaviors that are sources for the problems, as well as themes of cognition, emotions, and behaviors. The second is the use of the A-B-C theory of personality to identify client problems. Both of these methods, but especially the latter, continue throughout the therapeutic process. This assessment is driven by hypotheses that therapists make as they listen to their clients.

3 main Forms

In addition to therapy-oriented assessment, a wide variety of scales and tests can be used to assess client concerns (Macavei & McMahon, 2010). DiGiuseppe (1991, pp. 152–153) lists several instruments, such as the Millon Clinical Multiaxial Inventory II and the Beck Depression Inventory, that are used at the Albert Ellis Institute. Harrington (2005) believes that the Frustration-Discomfort Scale can be used to distinguish self-esteem from frustration intolerance when working with clients. Also, rating forms such as the REBT Self-Help Form (Dryden, Walker, & Ellis, 1996), on which clients enter their activating events and consequences, help determine important irrational beliefs (see Figure 9.1). Clients then dispute the irrational beliefs that apply and replace them with effective rational beliefs. Such a form can have both diagnostic and therapeutic purposes. By using a wide variety of assessment procedures, rational emotive behavior therapists not only assess activating events, emotions, and irrational beliefs but also assess cognitive flexibility, social problem-solving skills, and the client's reasons for maintaining symptoms.

The A-B-C assessment usually starts from the beginning of the first session and continues throughout therapy. Therapists listen while clients describe feelings and behaviors (consequences) that they feel are caused by specific experiences (activating events). As the client describes problems, therapists listen to the beliefs the clients have about the activating event. Therapists differ as to how long they will listen to descriptions of emotional and behavioral problems before determining irrational beliefs. As the therapeutic process continues, therapists may revise or hear new irrational beliefs (Bernard & Joyce, 1984).

The Therapeutic Relationship

Solve the Clients Immediate Problem

The process of assessment and the development of a therapeutic relationship are often closely related in REBT. Ellis believed that the best way to develop a therapeutic relationship is to help solve the client's immediate problem (Ellis, 2004d; Ellis & Dryden, 1997). After asking the client what he wishes to discuss, Ellis then identifies the activating events, irrational beliefs, and emotional and behavioral consequences. He may do this for two or three sessions and then possibly work on larger, or other, issues. Clients see and hear that they are being listened to and responded to. Ellis suggests that this is a type of advanced empathy in which the therapist understands the basic philosophies that underlie client communications. Clients not only feel understood but also sense that therapists understand their feelings better than they do.

REBT Self-Help Form

A (ACTIVATING EVENT)

```

```

- Briefly summarize the situation you are disturbed about
  (what would a camera see?).
- An *A* can be *internal* or *external, real,* or *imagined.*
- An *A* can be an event in the *past, present,* or *future.*

IBs (IRRATIONAL BELIEFS)

D (DISPUTING IBs)

To identify IBs, look for:

- DOGMATIC DEMANDS
  (musts, absolutes, shoulds)
- AWFULIZING
  (It's awful, terrible, horrible)
- LOW FRUSTRATION TOLERANCE
  (I can't stand it)
- SELF/OTHER RATING
  (I'm/he/she is bad, worthless)

To dispute ask yourself:

- Where is holding this belief getting me?
  Is it *helpful* or *self-defeating*?
- Where is the evidence to support the
  existence of my irrational belief? Is it
  consistent with reality?
- Is my belief *logical*? Does it follow from
  my preferences?
- Is it really *awful* (as bad as it could be)?
- Can I really not *stand* it?

FIGURE 9.1   REBT Self-help form

Reprinted with permission from Windy Dryden and Jane Walker. Copyright © 1992.
Revised by The Albert Ellis Institute, 1996.

Although students hearing or watching films of Ellis for the first time are
sometimes put off by his direct and assertive style, clients often experience his
style differently.

Group members frequently reported feelings of warmth and respect toward Al.
When questioned by us, group members reported that he demonstrated his caring
by his many questions, his complete attention to their problems, advocating an

C (CONSEQUENCES)

Major unhealthy negative emotions:

Major self-defeating behaviors:

Unhealthy negative emotions include:
- Anxiety
- Depression
- Rage
- Low Frustration Tolerance
- Shame/Embarassment
- Hurt
- Jealousy
- Guilt

RBs (RATIONAL BELIEFS)

E (NEW EFFECT)

New healthy
negative emotions:

New constructive
behaviors:

To think more rationally, strive for:

- NONDOGMATIC PREFERENCES
  (wishes, wants, desires)
- EVALUATING BADNESS
  (it's bad, unfortunate)
- HIGH FRUSTRATION TOLERANCE
  (I don't like it, but I can stand it)
- NOT GLOBALLY RATING SELF OR
  OTHERS (I—and others—are fallible
  human beings)

Healthy negative emotions include:

- Disappointment
- Concern
- Annoyance
- Sadness
- Regret
- Frustration

FIGURE 9.1   *(Cont'd)*

accepting and tolerant philosophy and teaching them something immediate that they could do to reduce their pain. (Walen et al., 1980, p. 32)

Ellis is also seen as a mentor to therapists (Johnson, DiGiuseppe, & Ulven, 1979). Of 150 Fellows and Associate Fellows at the Albert Ellis Institute, 75% considered Ellis to be a mentor. Those who considered Ellis a mentor found him to be an effective teacher who offered acceptance, support, and encouragement.

The relationship between client and therapist is important in REBT (Dryden, 2009a). Those rational emotive behavior therapists who have outlined stages of psychotherapy (Dawson, 1991; DiGiuseppe & Bernard, 1983) have rapport building and relationship issues as their first stage. With patients who are unfamiliar with

REBT or psychotherapy, rational emotive behavior therapists often introduce the purpose of therapy before working on problems. When working with children, rational emotive behavior therapists may proceed slowly and cautiously in developing a relationship before teaching REBT methods (Bernard & Joyce, 1984).

The A-B-C-D-E Therapeutic Approach

The core of REBT is the application of the A-B-C philosophy to client problems. Often this approach is used in the first and subsequent sessions. Where possible, therapists prefer to explain and make explicit each of the three aspects. In addition, therapeutic interventions require the use of D and E. There are three basic types of disputation (D): detecting irrational beliefs, discriminating irrational from rational beliefs, and debating irrational beliefs. When beliefs have been actively and successfully disputed, clients will experience E, a new effect—a logical philosophy and a new level of affect appropriate to the problem. In working with the A-B-C-D-E model, therapists can experience issues and difficulties in application to their clients. The paragraphs that follow provide some examples of the issues involved in applying each of the five parts of the model. Most of the material in this section comes from Walen et al. (1980).

A (activating event). The activating event can be divided into two parts: what happened and what the patient perceived happened. Often it is helpful to ask for specifics to confirm an activating event. For example, the activating event "My grade in geology is terrible" combines an event with a perception and an evaluation. To ascertain the activating event, the therapist might ask, "What are your grades on your geology exams at this point?" Getting a clear and active picture of the activating event, while avoiding unnecessary detail and vagueness, is quite helpful. Occasionally, clients present too many activating events, and therapists need to focus on only a few. Therapists also need to be alert as to when a previous consequence becomes an activating event. Sometimes it is possible to change an activating event, such as avoiding a possible confrontation, but doing so may not help clients deal with their irrational behavior or make more than temporary changes.

C (consequences). Clients often start the first therapy session with their consequences—"I feel very depressed." Sometimes inexperienced therapists can have difficulty in discriminating between beliefs and consequences. One difference is that feelings cannot be disputed—they are experiences—whereas beliefs can be disputed. When dealing with feelings, clients may be unclear about their emotions, mislabel them, or exaggerate them. Often, but not always, consequences can be changed by altering beliefs. However, clients must be willing for those consequences to occur. For example, if a woman wishes to feel better about herself in her work, she should be willing to change angry feelings about her boss that are debilitating.

B (beliefs). As discussed earlier, there are two types of beliefs—rational and irrational. Irrational beliefs are exaggerated and absolutistic, lead to disturbed feelings, and do not help individuals attain their goals. Rational beliefs generate adaptive and healthy emotions and behaviors (David, Freeman, & DiGiuseppe, 2010; Szentagotai & Jones, 2010). Being familiar with typical irrational beliefs (Ellis, 1962, 1994c) can be helpful in learning to identify beliefs so that they can be disputed.

Theories in Action

D (disputing). A common and important approach in REBT is to teach the A-B-C philosophy to clients and then to dispute irrational beliefs (Ellis, 2003d). Disputing has three parts: detecting, discriminating, and debating irrational beliefs. The therapist first detects irrational beliefs in the client and helps the client detect irrational beliefs in his perceptions. Irrational beliefs may underlie several activating events; for example, a client may experience stress on the job because he feels that everyone should be impressed by his abilities. Detecting the irrational belief "Others must find me intelligent and witty" is the first part of disputing. Discriminating irrational from rational beliefs is the next step. Being aware of *musts, shoulds, oughts*, and other unrealistic demands helps the client learn which beliefs are rational and which are not. A major emphasis in REBT is debating irrational beliefs. The therapist questions the client: "Why must you do everything better than everyone else at work?" "Why must you know everything that is going on in the office?" Debating irrational beliefs helps clients change their beliefs to rational ones, which diminishes their emotional discomfort.

Several strategies of disputing or debating irrational beliefs can be used: the lecture, the Socratic debate, humor, creativity, and self-disclosure (Dryden, 1990, pp. 52–54). Using the lecture approach (or, better, mini-lecture), the therapist gives the client an explanation of why her irrational belief is self-defeating. Obtaining feedback from the client that she understands what has been explained is important. A simple "yes" or "no" from the client is insufficient. In the Socratic style, the therapist points out the lack of logic and the inconsistencies in the client's belief, encouraging argument from the client, so that the client does not just accept the therapist's point of view and instead thinks for herself. Individuals should understand that humor is directed at their irrationality, not at them. By using humor and creative approaches, such as stories and metaphors, the therapist can maintain a relationship in which the client is open to change and not argumentative. Therapists' self-disclosure about how they themselves have used the A-B-C method to deal with their own irrational beliefs can also be helpful. Increased familiarity with disputing the irrational beliefs of clients can lead to the development of new strategies.

E (effective). When clients have disputed their irrational beliefs, they are then in a position to develop an effective philosophy. This philosophy, following the A-B-C model, helps individuals develop rational thoughts to replace inappropriate irrational thoughts. This new effective philosophy can bring about more productive behaviors, minimize feelings of depression and self-hatred, and bring about satisfying and enjoyable feelings.

The A-B-C-D-E model illustrated. The following transcript features a therapist using disputation techniques within the A-B-C-D-E model. In his work with an older Australian adolescent boy, Bernard provides some guiding comments to illustrate which aspects of the A-B-C-D-E model are being used.

Assessment of feeling and activating event:

[*Client:*] Boy, am I down.

[*Therapist:*] What are you feeling?

[*Client:*] Don't know … sorta rotten … sick, like someone kicked me in the stomach.

[*Therapist:*] Did someone?

[*Client:*] Well, I did what we said last week. I went to the disco at my school last night. I went over my little speech that we did last week about how to ask Jane for a dance. I didn't feel as uptight 'cause I had something to say. And so I finally went over to Jane and before I could even ask her she walked away to dance with someone else. And she ignored me for the rest of the night.

Empathic reflection of feelings by practitioner:

[*Therapist:*] Sounds like you feel depressed because Jane didn't dance with you and you really want her to like you. Is that about it?

[*Client:*] Yeah.

Assessment of the ABC relationship:

[*Therapist:*] Well, can you explain using the ABC method why you are still fairly upset?

[*Client:*] Starting with C, I guess I am sorta depressed. And A was Jane dancing with this other guy.

Assessment of behavioral consequence:

[*Therapist:*] Good, how did you react then?

[*Client:*] That was it! I just gave up. Didn't dance, didn't talk to her. I just waited around outside until my dad picked me up.

Assessment of cognition:

[*Therapist:*] Okay, what about B? What is B again?

[*Client:*] B are my thoughts … especially those … I can't remember …

[*Therapist:*] Irrational?

[*Client:*] Right. Rational and irrational thoughts about A.

[*Therapist:*] Okay, now what are you thinking about A? See if you can focus on some of the nutty things you might be saying.

(*reflective pause*)

[*Client:*] Well, I sorta feel embarrassed. You know, she must not like me at all. She probably thinks I'm a jerk. I hate it when she did it. Makes me feel like a dill.

[*Therapist:*] See if you can start your sentences with I'm thinking.

[*Client:*] I'm thinking what a dill I am … and I'm thinking how much I want her.

[*Therapist:*] How much?

[*Client:*] More than anything.

Practitioner summarizes ABC assessment data:

[*Therapist:*] Okay, that's great, Mark. You've done some good thought detection. You are feeling down and depressed not because you were rejected, but because you keep saying to yourself that you can't stand being rejected. You also are probably saying not only how much you want her, but that you'll die if you don't get her. And finally, as is your way, you are putting yourself down, down, down, down, down, lower and lower, to square zero, and even lower, because of what happened.

[Client:] Uh-huh.

Practitioner guides client toward solving problem—the D E link:

[Therapist:] Well, how does the good book say we can think our way out of misery?

[Client:] I can see on your wall … that's right … D. I can challenge my thoughts.

[Therapist:] Where shall you start?

[Client:] Huh?

[Therapist:] It seems to me that you can start to feel better by challenging and changing any one of three thoughts. That you are a dill because you have been rejected. That you need Jane to be happy. That you can't stand it when you are rejected. Shall I pick one?

[Client:] Okay.

[Therapist:] How about, and we've discussed this before, your tendency to put yourself down and rate yourself zero because of some personal failure?

[Client:] I know I shouldn't do it. I know it's stupid to say I'm a dill because I do other things well.

[Therapist:] Like?

[Client:] I work well with my Dad's horses, and I'm pretty good at working with machines.

[Therapist:] Good. So you can never be a dill. Ever! And when you catch yourself saying you're a dill or some other lousy thing, say to yourself something like "While I don't like it when I fail, it doesn't matter all that much; I do other things well."

[Client:] It's nutty to put myself down for what I do wrong.

[Therapist:] That's the message! Now how about nutty thought number two: That you must have the lovely, glamorous and scintillating Jane. Come on Tarzan, why must you have her? (Bernard & Joyce, 1984, pp. 89–91)

In this example Bernard uses Socratic dialogue to dispute Mark's irrational beliefs. He also uses brief lectures with analogies to explain concepts to Mark. A reference is made in the dialogue to a wall chart the therapist uses to help the client understand the A-B-C model. The disputational method represents the major cognitive approach used in REBT. However, there are several others. Some are described here; more are explained in *Better, Deeper, and More Enduring Brief Therapy* (Ellis, 1996a), *How to Think and Intervene Like an REBT Therapist* (Dryden, 2009a), and *Rational Emotive Behaviour Therapy: Distinctive Features* (Dryden, 2009b).

Other Cognitive Approaches

Rational emotive behavior therapists apply a number of cognitive techniques that help individuals develop new rational beliefs. Many of these are used as an adjunct to, and in support of, disputing techniques. Their variety illustrates the creativity of rational emotive behavior therapists and invalidates a misunderstanding that some have had that rational emotive behavior therapists employ only disputing techniques.

Coping self-statements. By developing coping statements, rational beliefs can be strengthened. For example, an individual who is afraid of public speaking may write down and repeat to himself several times a day statements such as "I want to speak flawlessly, but it is all right if I don't," "No one is killed for giving a poor speech," and "I am an articulate person."

Cost-benefit analysis. This method is particularly helpful for individuals who have addictions and/or low frustration tolerance. Individuals who are addicted to smoking may be asked to make lists of the advantages of stopping smoking and the disadvantages of continuing smoking. They are then instructed to think seriously about these advantages and disadvantages 10 or 20 times a day. This activity gives them good reasons for overcoming the addiction (Ellis, 1991b; Ellis & Velten, 1992).

Psychoeducational methods. When the session is over, REBT does not stop. Ellis and his colleagues have published a variety of self-help books that they recommend to their clients. For example, Knaus (2008) has written a workbook for anxious clients: *The Cognitive Behavioral Workbook for Anxiety: A Step-by-Step Program.* Listening to audiotapes that teach the principles of REBT is often recommended, as is listening to audiotapes of the client's therapy session. By doing so, the client is able to better remember points made by the therapist during the session (Ellis & Harper, 1997).

Teaching others. Ellis recommends that clients teach their friends and associates, when appropriate, the principles of REBT. When others present irrational beliefs to the clients, Ellis suggests that clients try to point out rational beliefs to their friends. Trying to persuade others not to use irrational beliefs can help the persuader to learn more effective ways of disputing her own irrational beliefs (Bard, 1980; Ellis, 1991b).

Problem solving. By helping people expand their choices of what they want to do and be, REBT helps them choose rational thoughts, feelings, and actions rather than be guided by their dogmatic irrational beliefs. Rational emotive behavior therapists help their clients figure out and arrive at viable options by dealing with both practical problems (finding a job) and emotional problems—problems about having practical problems (fretting and worrying about getting a job). In working with problems about practical problems, therapists often make use of the specifics of the A-B-C theory of personality (Ellis, 1991b, 2001c, 2001e).

A common thread that runs throughout most of these cognitive strategies is assigning homework activities that are learned in the session and practiced throughout the client's week. Many of the techniques such as coping self-statements may take only a few minutes a day. The repeated use of such methods is consistent with Ellis's view that irrational beliefs are quite entrenched in individuals (Dryden & Ellis, 2001, 2003; Ellis, 1996a).

Emotive Techniques

Like other strategies, emotive techniques are both used in the session and assigned as homework. Some techniques such as imagery and visualization can be viewed as cognitive, emotive, or behavioral. When the emphasis is on emotional aspects, imagery becomes an emotive method of treatment. Role playing also has cognitive, emotional, and behavioral components and is used to get at the strong consequences that accompany irrational beliefs. Ellis believes that strong or powerful approaches are necessary to change irrational beliefs. Examples include shame-attacking exercises, forceful self-statements, and forceful self-dialogue. All of these techniques are used with the full acceptance of the therapist. The therapist not only accepts clients but also tries to communicate this acceptance so that clients accept themselves.

Imagery. Imagery is often used in REBT to help clients change their inappropriate feelings to appropriate ones. For example, a man may vividly imagine that, if he is rejected by a woman he wishes to date, he will be terribly depressed afterward, be unable to think about anything else, and be very angry at himself. The therapist then would have him keep the same negative image and work on feeling the healthy emotions—disappointment and regret about the woman's wish not to go out with him—without feeling depressed and angry at himself. Imagining asking the woman for a date, being turned down, and working on experiencing healthy rather than unhealthy negative emotions can help reduce depression and feelings of inadequacy. Preferably, such techniques should be practiced once a day for several weeks (Dryden & Ellis, 2001, 2003).

Role playing. Rehearsing certain behaviors to elicit client feelings often can bring out emotions the client was not previously aware of. For example, by role playing a situation in which a woman asks a man for a date, the woman can be aware of strong fears she did not know she had. Repeated role playing of the situation gives the individual a chance to feel better about her social skills and change inappropriate emotional self-statements (Ellis, 1986c).

Shame-attacking exercises. The purpose of these exercises is to help clients feel unashamed when others may disapprove of them. Although the exercise can be practiced in a therapy session, it is done outside therapy. Examples include minor infractions of social conventions, such as talking loudly to a store clerk or engaging strangers in conversations. Asking silly questions to receptionists or teachers is another example. Such exercises are continued until one stops feeling sorry and disappointed about others' disapproval and ceases putting oneself down and feeling ashamed. Such exercises must be legal and not harmful for others. Inappropriate examples would be calling a 911 emergency number and leaving a false message or directing traffic in the middle of a street while playing the role of a police officer.

Forceful self-statements. Statements that combat "musturbating" beliefs in a strong and forceful manner can be helpful in replacing irrational beliefs with rational beliefs. If a client has told himself that it is awful and terrible to get a C on an examination, this self-statement can be replaced by a forceful and more suitable statement such as "I want to get an A, but I don't have to!" Ellis often uses obscenities as a way of providing more force to a statement (Dryden & Ellis, 2001, 2003; Ellis, 2001b).

Forceful self-dialogue. In addition to single self-statements, a dialogue with oneself, somewhat similar to the Socratic dialogue on page 344, can be quite helpful. Arguing strongly and vigorously against an irrational belief has an advantage over therapist–client dialogue in that all of the material comes from the client. Taping such dialogues, listening to them over and over again, and letting listeners determine if one's disputing is really powerful can help clients impress themselves with their own power (Ellis, 1986c; Ellis, Gordon, Neenan, & Palmer, 1997).

Behavioral Methods

Rational emotive behavior therapists make use of a wide variety of behavioral therapeutic approaches such as those described in Chapter 8. These would include systematic desensitization, relaxation techniques, modeling, operant conditioning, and principles of self-management. Most behavioral techniques are carried out as homework. REBT has developed some new behavioral techniques in recent years (Ellis, 2003f). Three behavioral methods frequently used by rational emotive behavior therapists are activity homework, reinforcements and penalties, and skill training (Ellis, 1985, 1986c; Ellis & Dryden, 1997).

Activity homework. To combat client demands and musts, therapists may make assignments that reduce irrational beliefs. When clients are in a situation where they feel others should treat them fairly, the therapist may suggest that they stay in the uncomfortable situation and teach themselves to deal with hard or uncomfortable tasks. For example, rather than quitting a job, a client may work with an unreasonable boss and listen to unfair criticism but mentally dispute the criticism and not accept the boss's beliefs as her own irrational beliefs. Other situations might include asking someone for a date or making an attempt to fail at a task, such as writing a report poorly (Ellis, 1962). Clients often observe that when they do such tasks, they are anxious or self-conscious at first but are able to comprehend the irrational beliefs underlying their emotions.

Reinforcements and penalties. When people accomplish a task, it is useful for them to reward themselves. For example, a shy person who has an extended conversation with three sales clerks may reward himself by reading a favorite magazine. Individuals who fail to attempt a task may penalize themselves. Ellis (1986c) gives the example of burning a $100 bill. Such a self-penalty can quickly encourage clients to complete agreed-upon assignments.

Skill training. Workshops and groups often teach important social skills. For example, assertiveness training workshops can be helpful for those who are shy and find it difficult to have their needs met by other people (Ellis, 1991b). Workshops on communication skills, job-interviewing skills, and other social and work-related skills can supplement individual REBT.

Although these techniques are divided into cognitive, emotive, and behavioral techniques, in actual practice some techniques fall into two or three of those categories. For example, Ellis (1987c) made frequent use of humor in his application of a variety of methods and asks patients to learn songs he had written that challenge irrational beliefs in a whimsical, nonthreatening way. Decisions as to which techniques to employ come with experience in listening to clients discuss their irrational beliefs. Often the techniques previously described follow disputational techniques. As therapists evaluate how well clients handle various assignments and suggestions, they then revise and reassign other techniques or methods. As therapy progresses, clients often develop insight into their problems.

Insight

Not only does REBT stress cognitive insight, but also it emphasizes emotional insight that can lead to behavioral change. Changing unhealthy feelings and behaviors usually requires three types of insight. The first level of insight is acknowledging that disturbances come not only from the past but also from irrational beliefs that individuals bring to activating events. Thus, individuals up-set themselves by their irrational beliefs about past occurrences. The second level of insight has to do with how individuals continually reindoctrinate themselves with the same kind of irrational beliefs that originated in the past. Thus, irratio-nal beliefs can take on lives of their own and continue, even though the original activating event has been forgotten. The third level of insight refers to accepting the first two levels of insight with the realization that knowledge of these insights does not automatically change people. Awareness of irrational beliefs is not suffi-cient; active challenging of irrational beliefs and development of rational beliefs, using knowledge of the A-B-C theory of personality, is essential. For Ellis, changes that occur through the acquisition of all three insights represent elegant change. Thus, individuals not only have changed feelings, thoughts, and beliefs but also know how they have done so and why (Ellis, 2002; Ellis, 2003d).

Psychological Disorders

In REBT, treatment is based on assessment of goals, activating events, beliefs, and consequences rather than on diagnostic categories. However, in a recent text, Dryden (Dryden, 2009c) outlines the REBT perspective on some of the most com-mon emotional problems individuals face today. For those individuals who are severely disturbed (psychotic, borderline, or obsessive-compulsive), Ellis (1991b, 2001b, 2002) believed that the cause is most likely to include a biochemical disorder as well as environmental stress. He found that medication, along with REBT and much patience, helps improve the emotional disturbances of individuals with these diagnoses. In this section I provide examples of the treatment of anxiety with adults and of depression with a 14-year-old girl that demonstrate disputing, cognitive, behavioral, and emotive approaches to treatment. I also discuss the treatment of obsessive-compulsive disorder and alcohol and substance abuse.

Anxiety Disorder: Ted

Ellis often applies disputational strategies along with other cognitive, behavioral, and emotive approaches to individuals with anxiety disorders that may include panic or physical symptoms. He believes that significant improvement can be obtained in a few weeks and that therapy can be completed in 10 to 20 sessions (Ellis, 1992a).

.How Ellis uses REBT for anxiety disorder can be illustrated by the case of Ted, a 38-year-old African American man who has been married for 10 years and has two young children. Referred by his physician because of pseudo–heart attacks (really panic attacks), Ted has complained of chest pains, particularly when riding a train from Jersey City to Manhattan or vice versa. Ellis's approach was to obtain a brief family history and to administer several tests, including the Millon Clinical Multiaxial Inventory II. Ted's only high score on this instrument was on the anxiety scale. In the first session, after determining Ted's symptoms and obtaining family background, Ellis deals with Ted's "shoulds, oughts, and musts." In the following brief segment from the first session, Ellis challenges Ted's "musts" and explains his irrational beliefs.

> [Therapist:] Well, if we can help you to change your ideas and attitudes about taking trains and about having a heart attack, that will really help you and you won't need medication. You see, you said you were a

perfectionist. So you're first making yourself anxious about doing things perfectly well. "I must do well! I *must* do well!" Instead of telling yourself, "*I'd like* to do well, but if I don't, F … it! It's not the end of the world." You see, you're rarely saying that. You're saying, "I've *got* to! I've got to!" And that will *make* you anxious—about your work, about sex, about having a heart attack, or about almost anything else. Then, once you make yourself anxious, you often tell yourself, "I *must* not be anxious! I must not be anxious!" That will make you *more* anxious—anxious about your anxiety. Now, if I can help you to accept *yourself* with your anxiety, first, and stop horrifying yourself about it; if we can help you, second, to give up your perfectionism—your demandingness—then you would not keep making yourself anxious. But you're in the habit of demanding that things *have* to go well and that, when they don't, you *must* not be anxious about them. "I must not be anxious! I must be sensible and sane!" That's exactly how people make themselves anxious—with rigid, forceful shoulds, oughts, and musts.

[*Client:*] Like yesterday. Yesterday was my worst day in a long time.

[*Therapist:*] Yes, because?

[*Client:*] What I did is when I was going to the train, I said: "I need to put something in my mind."

[*Therapist:*] To distract yourself from your anxiety that you expected to have when you got on the train?

[*Client:*] Yes. I said, "I am going to buy some sports things for the children." So I went to one of the stores and I bought some things, and as soon as I got on the train I started deliberately reading. Ten minutes after I was on the train, I still didn't have any anxiety. I was okay. But then I remembered and I said, "Jesus, I feel okay." At that moment, I started feeling panicked again.

[*Therapist:*] That's right. What you probably said to yourself was, "Jesus, I feel okay. But maybe I'll have another attack! Maybe I'll get an attack!" You will if you think that way! For you're really thinking, again, "I must not get another attack! What an idiot I am if I get another attack!" Right?

[*Client:*] Yes. (Ellis, 1992a, pp. 39–40)

Later in the first session, Ellis continues to dispute Ted's irrational beliefs of having an attack on the train. He also suggests self-statements that will be useful when riding the train.

[*Therapist:*] So suppose you do have an attack on the train? What's going to happen to you then?

[*Client:*] Something will happen to me.

[*Therapist:*] What?

[*Client:*] Most of the time I've said to myself, "Okay, nothing will happen. Because I know that whatever I have is not a heart problem—it's a mental problem, and I create it myself." So I then relax. But what's getting to me is that I have to deal with the same thing every day. Every day I have to deal with it.

[*Therapist:*] I know. Because you're saying, "I *must* not be anxious! I must not be anxious!" Instead of, "I don't *like* being anxious, but if I am, I am!" You see, you're terrified of your own anxiety.

[*Client:*] That's exactly what it is!

[*Therapist:*] Okay. But anxiety is only a pain in the ass. That's all it is. It doesn't kill you. It's only a pain. Everybody gets anxious, including you. And they live with it!

[*Client:*] It's a big pain in the ass!

[*Therapist:*] I know. But that's all it is. Just like—well, suppose you lost all the money you had with you. That would be a real pain, but you wouldn't worry about it too much, because you know you'd get some more money. But you're making yourself terrified. "Something awful will happen. Suppose people see I'm so anxious! How terrible!" Well, suppose they do.

[*Client:*] I don't care about that.

[*Therapist:*] Well, that's good. Most people are afraid of that and it's good that you're not.

[*Client:*] When I walk to the train, I know that I am going to start feeling anxious.

[*Therapist:*] You know it because you're afraid of it happening. If you said to yourself strongly and really believed, "F… it! If it happens, it happens!" Then it won't even happen. Every time you say, "I must not be anxious! I must not be anxious!"—then you'll be anxious. (Ellis, 1992a, p. 45)

In the remainder of the first session and in the second session, Ellis continued to go over and over the essentials of REBT, pointing out ways in which the client upset himself. He gets quickly to the central problem for Ted and helps him to do something about attacks on the train. The following comments are taken from the third therapy session and indicate that Ted has been working hard and successfully to apply the principles of REBT.

"I'm feeling better. Whatever I'm feeling, like anxiety, is not it. I'm creating it. Whatever I'm feeling I can make it go away in a couple of minutes and if I get upset about my anxiety, I can talk to myself about that.

"When I get to the train I'm not that anxious…. Like this morning, I completely forgot about it until I was on the train. Then I remembered and started saying to myself, 'It's nice to be feeling the way I'm feeling now.' It doesn't bother me anymore…. And last week, a couple of days, I'm going home, I fall asleep on the train, and I wake up at my station and I said to myself, 'Whatever happened a couple of months ago is gone.'

"And even in my work I don't feel anxious. I am working better than before without getting that, uh, anxiety to make everything fast and quick. I can pace myself better than before…. Another thing I learned to do: not to upset myself about the others in my office who act badly. If I got upset, they're going to act the same way.

"Before I thought my anxiety meant something was physically wrong. Now I see that I'm creating that sick feeling. Two or three minutes later, I am okay. Two weeks ago it would have taken me fifteen minutes to be less anxious. Now it takes me two or three minutes and there are days when I don't feel panic.

"The other day I got to the train when it was almost full, and I couldn't sit down and read and distract myself. But it didn't bother me and I didn't wait for another train as I used to have to do…. I can talk to myself and say, 'Look, whatever anxiety you feel, you created it. And you can uncreate it.'" (Ellis, 1992a, p. 51)

This was Ted's third and last individual session with Ellis. After this he attended Friday-night workshops at the Albert Ellis Institute. He also participated in several 4-hour workshops. Both Ted and his wife reported that he has held the gains that he has made, has lost his panic about trains, and was rarely anxious or angry at the office.

Depression: Penny

In working with depressed clients, rational emotive behavior therapists apply as many of the cognitive, emotive, and behavioral techniques as seem appropriate. In the example that follows, the emphasis is on cognitive techniques applied with Penny, a 14-year-old student with a hearing loss. She felt hopeless, not as good as her brothers, and nervous when they were not around. Feeling her childhood had been ruined because she had not done the risky things that her brothers had done, Penny felt ineffective and her schoolwork was suffering. The following excerpt shows how Marie Joyce used REBT to challenge and change Penny's irrational beliefs.

> The main focus of therapy was in teaching her rational emotive behavior ways of challenging her irrational beliefs, and altering her causal attributions regarding her unhappiness. She acquired a new causal attribution belief: "It is possible to do something about my unhappy feelings and I am the one who can do something about them." In addition, she learned that factors under her control, namely the learning of disputational skills and encouraging herself to make an effort, were major influences over what would happen to her in the future and how she would feel. The main irrational beliefs she learned to dispute were "I must have my brothers' love and approval at all times" and "I must perform well in my schoolwork at all times or I am a failure."
>
> Penny was taught to distinguish between herself and her performance and learned to stop rating herself globally. Homework exercises helped her to rehearse exactly what she would say to people when asked to do something she did not want to try (e.g., riding a surfboard in heavy surf). Other in-session rehearsals of rational self-talk, for dealing with schoolwork "catastrophes" worse than she had feared or imagined, reduced her exaggerated evaluations of events such as getting poor marks. Humorous exaggerations by the practitioner helped her to put her perceptions into a new perspective. (Bernard & Joyce, 1984, pp. 310–311)

After eight sessions she was feeling happier and doing her schoolwork without rating herself globally on her performance level. Changes in Penny reported by her mother included improved self-acceptance, new positive perceptions of her teachers, and improvements in the independence and organization of her schoolwork.

Obsessive-Compulsive Disorder: Woman

Ellis (1991b, 1994b, 2001b) believes there is a strong biological component to obsessive-compulsive disorders. He attributes this disorder to deficient neurotransmitters (especially serotonin). Although Ellis suggests medication, he also works with individuals who demand absolute and perfect certainty. His approach to those with obsessive-compulsive disorders is to show them that perfect certainty does not exist and to challenge their belief systems. The following is a brief description of a woman with an obsessive-compulsive disorder to whom Ellis has applied REBT.

> I see one now who has both the need for certainty and also awfulizes about her child being switched for another child right after she gave birth. She demands a 100% guarantee that her child wasn't switched, which, of course, she can't have. Although

I show her that there's no evidence that the child was switched and only a one-in-a-billion chance that it was, and although the child looks just like her, she still insists that it may have been switched and is panicked about the "horror" of such a possibility.

I then try elegant REBT and show her that, even if the child had been switched, it would not be so bad, because she has OCD (obsessive-compulsive disorder), her mother is schizophrenic, and several of her other close relatives are borderline personalities. So if she got the wrong baby, it might well turn out to be less disturbed than if she got the right one! Finally, after weeks of strongly using REBT with her, I am getting her to accept uncertainty, and she is becoming much less obsessed about the highly unlikely baby switching. (Ellis, 1991b, pp. 21–22)

Alcohol and Substance Abuse

Ellis and his colleagues have devoted considerable attention to the treatment of alcohol and substance abuse. In their book *Rational-Emotive Treatment of Alcoholism and Substance Abuse*, Ellis, McInerney, DiGiuseppe, and Yeager (1988) explain an REBT theory of addiction and specific REBT cognitive, emotive, and behavioral techniques to assist those with substance abuse problems. Their approach to treatment of alcohol or drug abusers starts by establishing a persuasive therapeutic relationship with the client and setting achievable goals. Clients are taught how to dispute their dysfunctional thoughts about drinking or abusing drugs. An example of how abusers can dispute irrational beliefs about inevitability and hopelessness regarding drinking is shown here.

> *Irrational Belief:* "Because I *must* not drink again and I did what I must not do, it's hopeless. I'll *always* be a drunk and never be able to stop drinking."
>
> *Disputing:* "How can you prove that anything *always* will exist and *never* will be changeable?"
>
> *IB:* "But look how many times I tried to abstain and didn't. Doesn't that prove that I *can't* do so?"
>
> *Disputing:* "No, it merely proves that you haven't done it yet and that it is *very difficult* to do so. But *very difficult* doesn't mean *impossible*. Unless you *think* it is and thereby *make* it practically impossible."
>
> *Answer:* "Maybe you're right. I'll think about that." (Ellis et al., 1988, p. 74)

When clients have been able to demonstrate some control over addictive behavior, later phases of REBT shift to "self-management of cognitive, emotional, behavioral, and situational triggers for substance abuse" (Ellis et al., 1988, p. 107). Final treatment stages are devoted to helping clients use practical problem solving to continue their abstinence (a common goal but not the only goal of therapy) and to understand underlying irrational beliefs that are major contributors to alcohol and drug abuse. Ellis and other therapists have studied reasons for addiction. A common explanation for addiction, according to Ellis (1992d), is that of low frustration tolerance, a concept suggesting that addicts cannot bear much discomfort over the short term. Ellis has suggested a six-step model to explain addiction that is related to emotional disturbance. According to Ellis (1992d), when the REBT theory of addictive drinking is understood, therapists and abusers can use it to undo thoughts, feelings, and behaviors involved in addiction. This can be done in individual therapy or in self-help groups. Bishop (2000) applies REBT to individual clients using many of the methods described by Ellis et al. (1988).

An alternative self-help organization to Alcoholics Anonymous (AA), Self-Management and Rational Training (SMART) differs in several ways from AA. Most notably, it does not rely on a higher power or require religious or spiritual beliefs from members (Ellis & Velten, 1992). Also, it uses a model based on REBT to help those who abuse alcohol to recover from addiction. Ellis does not deny that Alcoholics Anonymous is helpful. On the contrary, he believes that it has been helpful to many people and that a number of its approaches are consistent with REBT.

Brief Therapy

In general, REBT is a brief therapeutic intervention, with many individuals being helped in 5 to 12 sessions (Ellis, 1992a, 1996a). Providing more data, DiGiuseppe (1991) reported a study at the Albert Ellis Institute of 731 clients that found that the mean number of sessions was 16.5 and the median was 11 sessions. About 25% had 23 sessions or more. For Ellis himself, most sessions were only half an hour in length. This is not typical of other rational emotive behavior therapists.

In *Better, Deeper, and More Enduring Brief Therapy* (1996a), Ellis addresses how REBT can be applied in less than 20 sessions. He describes methods that he believes are appropriate to brief but less deep and intensive therapy as well as deeper and more intensive methods of brief therapy. Included in the latter are three of Ellis's favorite methods: disputing, accepting the worst possibilities, and anti-whining philosophies. Ellis, however, also includes a wider variety of other techniques than he has in his previous work, incorporating work of other theorists.

Ellis's approach to therapy is to bring about change as soon as possible. As he said, "I have a gene for efficiency whereas Sigmund Freud had a gene for inefficiency, as most analysts do" (Palmer, 1994, p. 7). He worked with out-of-town clients when they visited New York or talked to them over the phone. He has had hundreds of clients who have seen him for only one session (Ellis, 1996a; Dryden & Ellis, 2003). Also, Ellis offered the Friday Night Workshop in which he demonstrated REBT with volunteer individuals who bring up problems in public. He compiled data on those who have been a part of this workshop, and it shows that many of them significantly benefited from a single session in public workshops. Live public workshops continue to be held at the Albert Ellis Institute, led by experienced REBT therapists, with the participation of audience volunteers.

Current Trends

From its inception in the early 1950s, the A-B-C theory of REBT has grown and developed, becoming more complex and thorough yet maintaining its strong cognitive focus (David et al., 2010; Ellis, 2003c). In fact, in an interview conducted in 2005, Ellis proposed adding an "F" to the A-B-C-D-E model—forcefully agreeing with and applying new rational beliefs to strengthen E (effect), the effect of disputation (Bernard, 2009, p. 70). Ellis has emphasized emotive and behavioral aspects of the model, as well as its humanistic and existential elements. Also, Ellis has been very open to incorporating new techniques and applying them to help clients change their irrational beliefs. For example, he used hypnosis occasionally for more than 50 years when it would seem to add to REBT (Ellis,

2001b). Ellis (1996c) also used gestalt experiential techniques to act out and change irrational beliefs.

Ellis (2000, 2001a, 2001b, 2002) has incorporated constructivism into his theory. Because he takes a determined and focused point of view, exploring irrational beliefs, his approach would appear to be rationalist (Guterman, 1996). He listens to clients and understands their problems as they relate to A-B-C theory. The "rational" in rational emotive behavior therapy would imply that he uses reasoning from his own point of view to understand his clients. However, Ellis (1997) argued that his position is more constructivist than rationalist. Clients react differently to REBT techniques, and he observed that individual clients perceive their problems in unique ways. Ellis was aware that his approach may have had flaws, and he sought them out. As mentioned, he was open to incorporating new, creative techniques for helping clients. Ellis' openness to seeing clients in different ways is consistent with the constructivist point of view of seeing the world through the client's constructs.

Given Ellis' extremely central and active role in the development of REBT theory, technique, and research, future directions for REBT in the period following Ellis' death are uncertain. The recent publication of Dryden's three books, however, demonstrates continued activity and interest in REBT following Ellis' death (Dryden, 2009a, 2009b, 2009c). Dryden and David report in their review of the current status of REBT theory and research that REBT has distinctive theoretical and practical features which will continue to attract practitioners, researchers, and clients (Dryden & David, 2008).

Using Rational Emotive Behavior Therapy with Other Theories

As long as techniques from other theories fit into the consistent A-B-C model of personality, REBT makes use of them. Because Frankl's existential therapy (logotherapy, Chapter 5) has somewhat similar philosophies, logotherapy can be seen as enhancing REBT (Hutchinson & Chapman, 2005). Adelman (2008) combines REBT and constructivism (Chapter 12) to treat adolescent substance abusers. Most frequently, REBT practitioners use a wide variety of techniques described in Chapters 8 and 10. Other techniques, such as the gestalt empty-chair approach, have been adopted as an emotive technique in REBT. The models of Meichenbaum (Chapter 8) and Beck (Chapter 10) are most consistent with REBT. Ellis's REBT and Beck's cognitive therapy are seen by many therapists as rather similar to each other. However, Ellis (2003f, 2005a) has argued that there are differences between the two approaches and points out the strengths of REBT. Taking the other side of the argument, Padesky and Beck (2003, 2005) emphasize the strengths of cognitive therapy.

The technique most central to REBT is that of disputation. When disputation is used, it can change the therapeutic relationship. For example, disputing a client's irrational beliefs and responding only to a client's feelings or experience (Carl Rogers) are not consistent. Furthermore, disputational techniques require training and confidence on the part of the therapist; some other cognitive techniques are learned more quickly. Therapists who combine REBT with other theoretical approaches must contend with the forcefulness inherent in REBT.

Research

Rational emotive behavior therapy has been the subject of about 300 studies. Many studies have compared REBT with other therapeutic systems or with a variety of control or treatment groups. In addition, research on REBT concepts and instruments has measured irrational beliefs. In this section, I provide an overview of outcome studies and their findings, along with issues related to doing research on REBT. Also, I give an example of research that is typical of an outcome study examining REBT and present some studies examining irrational beliefs and other important concepts in REBT.

Three related reviews have examined 158 outcome studies comparing REBT with other treatments or control groups. In the first study, DiGiuseppe and Miller (1977) examined 22 published articles. In reviewing 47 later studies, McGovern and Silverman (1984) found that REBT was significantly more effective than other therapies or control groups in 31 of 47 studies. In the studies where REBT was not superior, there were usually no significant differences. Reviewing 89 studies between 1982 and 1989, Silverman, McCarthy, and McGovern (1992) found that REBT was significantly more effective than other therapies or control groups in 49 of the studies. In most of the other 40 studies, differences between groups were not significant. In some cases, REBT was used in combination with other therapy techniques, and in those cases the combination was the most effective. A separate meta-analysis of 191 studies compared the efficacy and methodological quality of REBT treatment outcome research before 1990 and from 1990 to 2003 and found methodological quality was consistent for both time periods and that REBT was at least as effective as other empirically supported treatments during both time periods (Ford, 2009). A study of REBT, cognitive therapy, and pharmacotherapy found that all three treatments made changes in reducing irrational beliefs (Szentagotai, David, Lupu, & Cosman, 2008). After a 6-month follow-up, REBT was found to decrease symptoms of depression for clients with major depressive disorder (David, Szentagotai, Lupu, & Cosman, 2008).

In a meta-analysis of 70 REBT outcome studies, Lyons and Woods (1991) compared REBT to control groups, cognitive behavior modification, behavior therapy, and other psychotherapies. They found that REBT showed a significant improvement over control groups and initial measures of dysfunction. Improvement was also related to therapists' experience and the length of therapy. However, they note a system problem in this type of research: It is very difficult to assess how much of REBT as developed by Ellis is actually being used. In some cases, therapists may use a combination of REBT with other methods or use a different version of REBT. Furthermore, REBT makes use of many cognitive and behavioral strategies. Separating the effectiveness of REBT and cognitive therapy is quite difficult. However, Lyons and Woods (1991) note that the most stringently conducted studies comparing REBT with other treatment modes demonstrated the effectiveness of REBT procedures. This occurred when the measures of change were relatively unrelated to the treatment being used. For example, changes were found in physiological measures of stress, as well as changes in irrational beliefs. The latter would be expected because it is taught as a part of REBT.

REBT is often used with children and adolescents. Meta-analytic techniques were applied to 19 studies that met stringent criteria for having appropriate experimental designs (Gonzalez et al., 2004). REBT was found to be helpful for both children and adolescents, especially in reducing the number of disruptive events. The researchers also found that children benefited more than adolescents. The longer therapy lasted, the greater were the effects of REBT. Surprisingly, non-mental health professionals produced more change than mental health professionals. REBT has been further adapted as an educational intervention (often referred to as REBE, rational emotive behavior education, or REE, rational emotive education). A meta-analytical review of 26 studies found that REBE/REE reduced irrational beliefs and dysfunctional behaviors in the classroom and was more effective for children and adolescents than for young adults (Trip, Vernon, & McMahon, 2007). Banks and Zionts (2009) show how REBT can be used with emotionally disturbed children and adolescents. Both Vernon (2009) and Wilde (2008) outline practical and specific REBT techniques that can be effectively used with children and adolescents in individual, small group, and classroom settings.

In critiquing outcome research, Haaga, Dryden, and Dancey (1991) are concerned with how well therapists in research studies actually represent REBT. They examine four criteria: adherence to the theory (how well the therapist performs behaviors prescribed by the treatment); purity (the portion of therapists' behaviors that would be considered positive adherence to the theory); differentiability (how well uninformed observers can tell what theory they are observing); and quality (how well the therapist performed the therapy). Although these constructs can be measured, they are difficult to measure, and many studies have not attended to them. However, without doing so, it is difficult to know whether one is really comparing REBT with another theory. Haaga and Davison (1991) also expressed concern about ignoring differences between REBT and other cognitive therapies in research. In reviewing the psychometric characteristics of measures of irrational beliefs frequently used in studies of REBT, Terjesen, Salhany, and Sciutto (2009) found considerable variability in reliability and validity among the sample. The authors discuss the implications of these findings for the development of future measures of irrational beliefs as well as recommend assessment instruments for REBT practitioners.

In addition to studies of therapeutic outcome, several investigations have examined concepts within REBT. For example, Woods, Silverman, and Bentilini (1991) found a strong relationship between suicidal contemplation and irrational beliefs in 800 college and high school students. A significant relationship between irrational beliefs and problems with drinking was found in a sample of 203 college students (Hutchinson, Patock-Peckham, Cheong, & Nagoshi, 1998). Studying 240 undergraduates, Harran and Ziegler (1991) found a strong relationship between irrational beliefs and reports of hassles and problems in the lives of the undergraduates. Ziegler and Leslie (2003) replicated Harran and Ziegler's findings using a group of 192 college students. Ziegler and Leslie also found that students who scored higher on awfulizing and low frustration tolerance reported more concern about hassles than did those who scored lower on awfulizing and low frustration tolerance. This is consistent with Ellis's view that those with high irrational beliefs tend to "awfulize" or "catastrophize." REBT has also been used with anger management for seventh graders with behavior management problems. Compared to a control group, the anger management program produced fewer office referrals for the students in the program and increased their level of rational thinking (Sharp, 2004). These studies help relate irrational beliefs to measures of physiological stress and psychological concepts.

Gender Issues

Regardless of client gender, rational emotive behavior therapists examine the irrational beliefs of their clients and work with cognitive, behavioral, and emotive methods to bring about healthy psychological functioning. The nature of the irrational beliefs is often different for males and females, as individuals accept a number of societal expectations as irrational beliefs that they *must* accommodate. Several rational emotive behavior writers have identified societal and other issues that therapists often address when working with women.

Rational emotive behavior therapy can help women examine their beliefs and philosophies and work through emotional and practical problems (Wolfe, 1985, 1993). It teaches women how to define their problems, identify factors affecting feelings and actions, alter their behavior, and move toward greater self-acceptance (Wolfe & Russianoff, 1997). Wolfe and Naimark (1991) believe that therapists should encourage their female clients to challenge sex-role stereotypes in their relationships with men, with family, and in community activities. Wolfe and Fodor (1996) discuss these issues, the development of greater self-acceptance, and others as they pertain to "upper"-class women. Methods have been developed for helping women with sexual problems through the use of group therapy (Walen & Wolfe, 2000; Wolfe, 1993). Muran and DiGiuseppe (2000) have developed a guide for helping women suffering from rape trauma. Wolfe (1985) lists several types of groups that have been developed at the Albert Ellis Institute to help women with these issues, including women's assertiveness, effectiveness, sexuality, life-cycle change, career entry, weight and stress management, mother–daughter communications, and all-women therapy groups.

Women are subject to a number of gender-role socialization messages that promote irrational beliefs (Wolfe & Naimark, 1991). For example, women may receive a gender-role message such as "Nice, sweet girls get husbands." An associated irrational belief is "I must not act assertively in front of men. I must not put my desires first" (Wolfe & Naimark, 1991, p. 270). Another example is "For women, work is nice, but love is better." The irrational belief behind that socialization message is "I must not take my work too seriously" (p. 269). Wolfe and Naimark list several gender-role socialization messages and irrational beliefs along with common emotional and behavioral consequences, as well as ways in which both men and women may react when women do not behave according to gender-role expectations.

The following example illustrates how an REBT therapist deals with irrational beliefs regarding guilt over being raped (Zachary, 1980, pp. 251–252). Particularly in the last two statements of the therapeutic dialogue, irrational beliefs are dealt with. Conceptually, the therapist has applied the A-B-C-D-E theory to the woman's discussion of the traumatic event in this first session of therapy.

> [*Client:*] So I'm finding myself feeling really awkward at parties and in groups of people, and I just don't like sex as much as I used to. I think it has to do with the rape a year and a half ago, but I'm not sure of the connection.
>
> [*Therapist:*] You're feeling that your current problems are related to being raped.
>
> [*Client:*] Uh huh. It was a guy I accepted a date with, but I barely knew him. He drives me out to a really deserted place, raped me, and left me out there. I hitched back into town, went to the police station, and had a

medical exam. I even got myself a lawyer, but he told me that since I had accepted a date with the guy I wouldn't have a snowball's chance in hell of proving rape, so I dropped the whole thing.

[*Therapist:*] And what do you think about all of that now?

[*Client:*] Well, I go back and forth about it. Sometimes I think I should have prosecuted and other times I think it was better to drop it. I mean, the police, the lawyer, they acted like I was asking for it by going out with the guy, and it would have been more humiliating to pursue it.

[*Therapist:*] So you're continuing to go over and over it in your mind and you're vacillating back and forth about what would have been the best thing to do.

[*Client:*] Yes, I think about it a lot. It's really pretty distracting.

[*Therapist:*] So you're thinking that there must have been a perfectly right thing to do and you continue to torture yourself with that thought.

[*Client:*] Uh-huh. I even think that maybe I could have avoided being raped.

[*Therapist:*] How could you have done that?

[*Client:*] I don't know exactly. He said he had a knife, but I never actually saw it. Maybe he didn't. Maybe I could have screamed or fought harder or tried to run away, but I was afraid he might stab me.

[*Therapist:*] So at the time, you believed that he had a knife and would really hurt you or even kill you if you didn't give in.

[*Client:*] Yes, but I don't know now if he would have. And it was just my word against his. He told the police that I had seduced him and they seemed to believe him. Even my lawyer seemed to question my story.

[*Therapist:*] And how do you feel?

[*Client:*] This sounds crazy, but I feel guilty and ashamed of myself, like less of a person. He raped me and I feel guilty!

[*Therapist:*] So you're feeling guilty, ashamed and devalued as a person. And you're telling yourself that you should have fought him away at the time and you should have stuck by your story. Mostly you seem to be telling yourself that it's all your fault and that you're less of a person because you were raped and didn't do the right thing.

[*Client:*] Yes, that's all true, but what do we do with that?

[*Therapist:*] We begin by examining the beliefs you have, disputing them, and, hopefully eventually allowing you to put the incident to rest. Let's begin right now by looking at your belief that there is a perfectly right thing that you could have done at the time. (Zachary, 1980, pp. 251–252)

In this session and in ensuing ones, Zachary helped the client gain insight into her irrational belief that she should have done something other than what she did when raped. The focus of therapy then turned to the current rumination about the rape rather than the rape itself. Zachary dealt with the irrational belief that individuals (specifically the client) can be devalued by what other people do to them (the rapist, police officers, and lawyers). After 4 months of therapy, the client was able to let go of the rape incident and to respond satisfactorily socially and sexually.

Multicultural Issues

Rational emotive behavior therapists listen carefully for the cultural values and issues of their clients. They do not plunge into Socratic disputation of irrational beliefs before establishing an understanding of cultural issues. For example, Ellis (1991b) describes his work with a Mormon woman who was pregnant and undecided as to whether she would marry her non-Mormon lover. She had considered having an abortion. If she did, she faced excommunication from her religion. Knowledge of the client's culture often determines the therapist's actions. In another situation, a Mormon therapist describes how he used the Qur'an with REBT to treat a 24-year-old Muslim woman who suffered from posttraumatic stress disorder (Nielsen, 2004). Ellis (1991b) has treated a number of Chinese, Japanese, and other Asian clients. Although he attends to their family values, he finds that he uses an approach that is similar to his work with clients from the United States (Ellis, 2002). REBT has been suggested as a tool to provide competent, culturally sensitive therapeutic services to elderly African American individuals (Sapp, McNeely, & Torres, 2007).

Rational emotive behavior therapy emphasizes self-sufficiency as opposed to dependency on the support of others. Many Asian and African cultures, for example, promote interdependence rather than independence, stressing reliance on the family and the individual's community rather than self-reliance (Sapp, 1996). Such issues may cause REBT therapists to modify their assessment of clients' irrational beliefs. This, then, affects their decision as to which beliefs are irrational and warrant disputation. For clients who are used to being told what to do—because of cultural customs or other reasons—therapists need to be certain that clients participate actively rather than passively when Socratic dialogue or other disputational techniques are used. Studying Spanish-speaking populations in Colombia, Costa Rica, El Salvador, Spain, and the United States, Lega and Ellis (2001) found some cultural differences in irrational beliefs as measured by a Spanish version of the Attributes and Beliefs Inventory. REBT has been applied successfully in international settings, such as Hong Kong (Si & Lee, 2008), India (Lakhan, 2009), Iran (Zare, Shafiabadi, Sharifi, & Navabinejad, 2007); and Romania (David, 2007; David, et al., 2008; Szentagotai, et al., 2008).

Group Therapy

Although REBT can be applied in 2-day rational encounter marathons, 9-hour intensive groups with 10 to 20 participants, public demonstrations of real therapy with audiences as large as 100, and structured self-acceptance groups (Dryden, 1998), only traditional group therapy is described here (Ellis, 1992b). These groups usually have between 6 and 10 members and meet once a week for 2 to 3 hours. The goal of the REBT group is to show clients how they are assessing, blaming, and damning themselves for their behavior. The group also endeavors to help them stop devaluing other people and evaluate only their behaviors, not their self- or personhood. They are instructed to try to change or avoid difficulties that they encounter within themselves and with others. The process of doing this combines a directive educational function on the part of the therapist with a discussion of group processes.

Therapists purposefully lead the group in "healthy" rather than "unhealthy" directions (Ellis, 1992b). By organizing the group in a structured way, they see that no one is neglected or monopolizes the group. Therapists discuss the progress and lack of progress of individual group members as well as the results of their previously assigned homework or their failure to complete their homework. Also, they may make statements in the group that refer to both inside and outside behaviors. For example, they may say, "Johanna, you speak so low here that we can hardly hear what you say. Do you act the same way in social groups? If so, what are you telling yourself to make yourself speak so low?" (Ellis, 1992b, p. 69). Often the leaders agree with the group member on cognitive or emotive or behavioral exercises to be done both in the group and outside the group. Where appropriate, they give brief lectures on important aspects of REBT. Most of the group time is spent on individual problems that group members bring to the group, but some time is spent examining how group members relate to each other.

For groups to be successful, group members need to work together to help each other apply REBT principles (Dryden, 1998; Ellis, 1992b). Ellis wants group members to participate appropriately, neither to monopolize the group nor to be too passive. If an individual does not speak up in the group, the group therapist may give an assignment to speak at least three times about other people's issues in the group meeting. If a group member consistently comes late to the group or is absent, Ellis or group members may raise this issue and discuss it in terms of A-B-C theory and examine self-defeating behavior that results from being late. If group members give only practical advice to other members instead of disputing their irrational beliefs, Ellis and the group members will point this out. If a group member rarely completes homework assignments, irrational beliefs such as "It's too hard" and "It should be much easier" are disputed. Thus, REBT techniques are used for both group process and individual problems that are issues in the group.

Summary

Rational emotive behavior therapy asserts that it is not only events themselves that disturb people but also their beliefs about the events. This view leads to an approach to psychotherapy that stresses cognitive aspects of personality theory and therapeutic intervention yet also makes use of emotive and behavioral components. The philosophical assumptions are humanistic, hedonistic, and rational (self-helping and society helping). The focus is on individuals and their potential to overcome irrational (self-defeating) beliefs and to be responsible for their own lives. *Rationality* does not refer to an absence of emotion; rather, it refers to individuals' ability to use reason to guide their lives and to diminish the impact of irrational (dysfunctional) beliefs on their lives. *Responsible hedonism* refers to the concept of individuals seeking happiness over the long term, in contrast to short-term hedonism, which, in the case of alcoholism, for example, can lead to long-term difficulties. The notable contribution that Ellis has made to the treatment of sexual problems as well as his commitment to sex education through his writings is an example of his emphasis on increasing human happiness.

Rational emotive behavior therapy applies cognitive, emotive, and behavioral approaches to changing irrational beliefs. A major method for working with irrational beliefs is disputing, which involves detecting, discriminating, and debating irrational beliefs. The stronger emphasis on understanding the A-B-Cs of the development of one's irrational beliefs distinguishes REBT from other cognitive and behavioral therapies. However, REBT also uses other cognitive strategies, such as repeated constructive statements about oneself, audiotapes, and psycho-educational materials. Methods that employ imagery along with emotions, exercises that attack beliefs that are shameful, and forceful self-dialogue are some of the emotive methods REBT uses. Behavioral methods include homework outside the session, skill training, and reinforcement of desired behavior. Rational emotive behavior therapists make use of a large number of techniques, primarily from other cognitive and behavioral therapies, as well as creative ones that they devise on their own, to help clients deal with strongly entrenched irrational beliefs.

Rational emotive behavior therapists are tolerant of their clients and fully accept them. It is their behavior that they dispute by challenging, confronting, and convincing the clients to practice activities in and out of therapy that will lead to constructive changes in thinking, feeling, and behaving. An active therapy, REBT includes insights about irrational beliefs and about becoming aware of how individuals harm themselves through absolutist beliefs and then uses these insights to make constructive changes in their lives.

Theories in Action DVD: REBT

Basic Concepts Used in the Role-Play	Questions About the Role-Play
• Activating event • Belief about activating event • Consequences • Disputing • Effect • Teaching A-B-Cs • Suggesting alternative beliefs • Distinguishing musts and needs from wants • Homework • Catching irrational beliefs	1. When helping Rebekah deal with her beliefs about her breakup of a relationship, does Dr. Allen teach or do psychotherapy? Explain. 2. What are Rebekah's irrational beliefs about her relationship? (p. 366) 3. How does Dr. Allen show Rebekah how to dispute these irrational beliefs? (p. 344) How comfortable would you be using disputing with a client? Explain. 4. Do all individuals with anxiety have irrational beliefs? Explain.

Suggested Readings

Ellis, A. (1973). *Humanistic psychotherapy: The rational-emotive approach*. New York: McGraw-Hill. Written for the public and the profession, this book shows both the humanistic and the active approach typical of REBT. It shows how the A-B-C model can be applied to therapy.

Ellis, A., & Harper, R. A. (1997). *A new guide to rational living* (3rd ed.). North Hollywood: Wilshire Books. Written for the public, this self-help book helps individuals recognize their irrational beliefs and overcome emotional disturbances. Suggestions for changing beliefs and homework to bring about change are given.

Dryden, W. (2009). *How to think and intervene like an REBT therapist*. New York: Routledge. This book, geared toward novice therapists, demonstrates how experienced therapists use REBT interventions with clients. There are many examples of therapist/patient dialogues, as well as illustrations of typical beginner errors.

Ellis, A. (1996). *Better, deeper, enduring brief therapy: The rational emotive behavior therapy approach*. New York: Brunner/Mazel. This book gives a good perspective on how to apply REBT to a variety of client problems. These include anger, low frustration tolerance, and irrational beliefs. Since REBT is a brief approach, many of the concepts can be applied to REBT in general, but Ellis does address specific issues dealing with brief therapy.

Dryden, W., & Ellis, A. (2003). *Albert Ellis live!* London: Sage. Other than an introductory chapter describing REBT, this book consists of five demonstration sessions that Ellis had with audience members. Each chapter is followed by a dialogue and includes Dryden's comments on Ellis's responses.

David, D., Lynn, S. J., & Ellis, A. (Eds.). (2010). *Rational and irrational beliefs: Research, theory, and clinical*

practice. New York: Oxford University Press. This book is written for psychotherapy practitioners, students, and academic psychologists. It focuses on the key theoretical construct of REBT, irrational and rational beliefs, and the relationship of irrational beliefs to psychopathology and rational beliefs to emotional health. The book describes the A-B-C-D-E model and contains a comprehensive review of both research and theory.

References

Adelman, R. (2008). Methods of reconstruction with adolescent substance abusers: Combining REBT and constructivism. In J. D. Raskin & S. K. Bridges (Eds.), *Studies in meaning 3: Constructivist psychotherapy in the real world* (pp. 183–200). New York: Pace University Press.

Banks, T., & Zionts, P. (2009). REBT used with children and adolescents who have emotional and behavioral disorders in educational settings: A review of the literature. *Journal of Rational-Emotive & Cognitive Behavior Therapy, 27*(1), 51–65.

Bard, J. (1980). *Rational-emotive therapy in practice.* Champaign, IL: Research Press.

Bernard, M. E. (2009). Dispute irrational beliefs and teach rational beliefs: An interview with Albert Ellis. *Journal of Rational-Emotive & Cognitive Behavior Therapy, 27*(1), 66–76.

Bernard, M. E., & Joyce, M. R. (1984). *Rational-emotive therapy with children and adolescents.* New York: Wiley.

Bishop, F. M. (2000). *Managing addictions: Cognitive and behavioral techniques.* Holmes, PA: Aronson.

Browne, C. M., Dowd, E. T., & Freeman, A. (2010). Rational and irrational beliefs and psychopathology. In D. David, S. J. Lynn, & A. Ellis (Eds.), *Rational and irrational beliefs: Research, theory, and clinical practice* (pp. 149–171). New York: Oxford University Press.

David, D. (2007). Quo vadis CBT? Trans-cultural perspectives on the past, present, and future of cognitive-behavioral therapies: Interviews with the current leadership in cognitive-behavioral therapies. *Journal of Cognitive and Behavioral Psychotherapies, 7*(2), 171–217.

David, D., Freeman, A., & DiGiuseppe, R. (2010). Rational and irrational beliefs: Implications for mechanisms of change and practice in psychotherapy. In

D. David, S. J. Lynn, & A. Ellis (Eds.), *Rational and irrational beliefs: Research, theory, and clinical practice* (pp. 195–217). New York: Oxford University Press.

David, D., Lynn, S. J., & Ellis, A. (Eds.). (2010). *Rational and irrational beliefs: Research, theory, and clinical practice.* New York: Oxford University Press.

David, D., Szentagotai, A., Lupu, V., & Cosman, D. (2008). Rational emotive behavior therapy, cognitive therapy, and medication in the treatment of major depressive disorder: A randomized clinical trial, posttreatment outcomes, and six-month follow-up. *Journal of Clinical Psychology, 64*(6), 728–746.

Dawson, R. (1991). REGIME: A counseling and educational model for using RET effectively. In M. E. Bernard (Ed.), *Using rational-emotive therapy effectively: A practitioner's guide* (pp. 111–132). New York: Plenum.

DiGiuseppe, R. (1991). A rational-emotive model of assessment. In M. E. Bernard (Ed.), *Using rational-emotive therapy effectively: A practitioner's guide* (pp. 151–172). New York: Plenum.

DiGiuseppe, R. (2007). Rational emotive behavioral approaches. In H. T. Prout & D. T. Brown (Eds.), *Counseling and psychotherapy with children and adolescents: Theory and practice for school and clinical settings* (4th ed., pp. 279–331). Hoboken, NJ: John Wiley.

DiGiuseppe, R. (2010). Rational emotive behavior therapy. In Kazantzis, N., Reinecke, M. A., & Freeman, A. (Eds.), *Cognitive behavior therapy: Using theory and philosophy to strengthen science and practice.* New York: Guilford.

DiGiuseppe, R., & Bernard, M.E. (1983). Principles of assessment and methods of treatment with children: Special considerations. In A. Ellis & M. E. Bernard (Eds.), *Rational-emotive approaches to the problems of childhood* (pp. 45–86). New York: Plenum.

DiGiuseppe, R., & Miller, N. J. (1977). A review of outcome studies on rational-emotive therapy. In A. Ellis & R. Grieger (Eds.), *Handbook of rational-emotive therapy* (pp. 72–95). New York: Springer.

Dryden, W. (1990). *Rational-emotive counseling in action*. London: Sage.

Dryden, W. (1998). *Developing self-acceptance groups: A brief, educational, small group approach*. New York: Wiley.

Dryden, W. (2009a). *How to think and intervene like an REBT therapist*. New York: Routledge.

Dryden, W. (2009b). *Rational emotive behaviour therapy: Distinctive features*. New York: Routledge.

Dryden, W. (2009c). *Understanding emotional problems: The REBT perspective*. New York: Routledge.

Dryden, W., & David, D. (2008). Rational emotive behavior therapy: Current status. *Journal of Cognitive Psychotherapy, 22*(3), 195–209.

Dryden, W., DiGiuseppe, R., & Neenan, M. A. (2003). *Primer on rational-emotive therapy*. (2nd ed.). Champaign, IL: Research Press.

Dryden, W., & Ellis, A. (2001). Rational emotive behavior therapy. In K. S. Dobson (Ed.), *Cognitive-behavioral therapies* (2nd ed., pp. 295–348). New York: Guilford.

Dryden, W., & Ellis, A. (2003). *Albert Ellis live!* London: Sage.

Dryden, W., & Neenan, M. (2004). *Counselling individuals: A rational emotive behavioural handbook* (4th ed.). London: Whurr.

Dryden, W., Walker, J., & Ellis, A. (1996). *REBT self-help form*. New York: Albert Ellis Institute.

Ellis, A. (1958). *Sex without guilt*. New York: Lyle Stuart.

Ellis, A. (1961). *The encyclopedia of sexual behavior*. New York: Hawthorn.

Ellis A. (1962). *Reason and emotion in psychotherapy*. Secaucus, NJ: Lyle Stuart.

Ellis, A. (1965). *The art and science of love*. New York: Lyle Stuart.

Ellis, A. (1973). *Humanistic psychotherapy: The rational-emotive approach*. New York: McGraw-Hill.

Ellis, A. (1976). The biological basis of human irrationality. *Journal of Individual Psychology, 32*, 145–168.

Ellis, A. (1985). *Overcoming resistance: Rational-emotive therapy with difficult clients*. New York: Springer.

Ellis, A. (1986a). Awards for distinguished professional contributions. *American Psychologist, 41*, 380–397.

Ellis, A. (1986b). Do some religious beliefs help create emotional disturbance? *Psychotherapy in Private Practice, 4*, 101–106.

Ellis, A. (1986c). Rational-emotive therapy. In I. L. Kutash & A. Wolf (Eds.), *Psychotherapist's casebook* (pp. 277–287). San Francisco: Jossey-Bass.

Ellis, A. (1987a). The impossibility of achieving consistently good mental health. *American Psychologist, 42*, 364–375.

Ellis, A. (1987b). On the origin and development of rational-emotive therapy. In W. Dryden (Ed.), *Key cases in psychotherapy* (pp. 148–175). New York: New York University Press.

Ellis, A. (1987c). The use of rational humorous songs in psychotherapy. In W. E. Fry, Jr., & W. A. Salameh (Eds.), *Handbook of humor and psychotherapy* (pp. 265–286). Sarasota, FL: Professional Resource Exchange.

Ellis, A. (1988). *How to stubbornly refuse to make yourself miserable about anything—yes, anything!* New York: Carol Publishing.

Ellis, A. (1991a). The philosophical basis of rational-emotive therapy (RET). *Psychotherapy in Private Practice, 8*, 97–106.

Ellis, A. (1991b). Using RET effectively: Reflections and interview. In M. E. Bernard (Ed.), *Using rational-emotive therapy effectively* (pp. 1–33). New York: Plenum.

Ellis, A. (1992a). Brief therapy: The rational-emotive method. In S. H. Budman, M. F. Hoyt, & S. Friedman (Eds.), *The first session in brief therapy* (pp. 36–58). New York: Guilford.

Ellis, A. (1992b). Group rational emotive and cognitive-behavioral therapy. *International Journal of Group Psychotherapy, 42*, 63–80.

Ellis, A. (1992c). My early experiences in developing the practice of psychology. *Professional Psychology: Research and Practice, 23*, 7–10.

Ellis, A. (1992d). The rational-emotive theory of addiction. In J. Trimpey, L. Trimpey, P. Tate, M. Sullivan, & L. V. Fox (Eds.), *Rational recovery self-help network: Official manual for coordinators and advisors*. Lotus, CA: Rational Recovery Self-Help Network.

Ellis, A. (1993). *Psychotherapy and the value of a human being* (rev. ed.). New York: Institute for Rational Emotive Therapy.

Ellis, A. (1994a). General semantics and rational emotive therapy. In P. D. Johnston, D. D. Bourland, Jr., & J. Klein (Eds.), *More E-prime: To be or not II* (pp. 213–240). Concord, CA: International Society of General Semantics.

Ellis, A. (1994b). Rational emotive behavior therapy approaches to obsessive-compulsive disorder (OCD). *Journal of Rational-Emotive and Cognitive-Behavior Therapy, 12*, 121–141.

Ellis, A. (1994c). *Reason and emotion in psychotherapy* (rev. 2nd ed. updates). New York: Kensington.

Ellis, A. (1996a). *Better, deeper, and more enduring brief therapy: The rational emotive behavior therapy approach.* New York: Brunner/Mazel.

Ellis, A. (1996b). *My philosophy of psychotherapy.* New York: Albert Ellis Institute for Rational Emotive Behavior Therapy.

Ellis, A. (1996c). The humanisms of rational emotive behavior therapy and other cognitive behavior therapies. *Journal of Humanistic Education and Development, 35,* 69–88.

Ellis, A. (1997). Postmodern ethics for active-directive counseling and psychotherapy. *Journal of Mental Health Counseling, 10,* 211–225.

Ellis, A. (1999a). *How to make yourself happy and remarkably less disturbable.* Atascadero, CA: Impact.

Ellis, A. (1999b). Why rational-emotive therapy to rational emotive behavior therapy? *Psychotherapy: Theory, Research, Practice, Training, 36,* 154–159.

Ellis, A. (2000). Spiritual goals and spiritual values in psychotherapy. *Journal of Individual Psychology, 56,* 277–284.

Ellis, A. (2001a). A continuation of the dialogue on issues in counseling in the postmodern era. *Journal of Mental Health Counseling, 22,* 97–106.

Ellis, A. (2001b). Changing the use of hypnosis in my practice. In S. Kahn & E. Fromm (Eds.), *Changes in the therapist* (pp. 165–172). Mahwah, NJ: Erlbaum.

Ellis, A. (2001c). *Overcoming destructive beliefs, feelings, and behaviors: New directions for rational emotive behavior therapy.* Amherst, NY: Prometheus Books.

Ellis, A. (2001d). Reasons why rational emotive behavior therapy is relatively neglected in the professional and scientific literature. *Journal of Rational-Emotive and Cognitive Behavior Therapy, 19,* 67–74.

Ellis, A. (2001e). *Feeling better, getting better, and staying better.* Atascadero, CA: Impact.

Ellis, A. (2002). *Overcoming resistance* (rev. ed.). New York: Springer.

Ellis, A. (2003a). Discomfort anxiety: A new cognitive-behavioral construct (Part I). *Journal of Rational-Emotive & Cognitive Behavior Therapy, 21*(3–4), 183–191.

Ellis, A. (2003b). Discomfort anxiety: A new cognitive-behavioral construct (Part II). *Journal of Rational-Emotive & Cognitive Behavior Therapy, 21*(3–4), 193–202.

Ellis, A. (2003c). Early theories and practices of rational emotive behavior therapy and how they have been augmented and revised during the last three decades. *Journal of Rational-Emotive & Cognitive Behavior Therapy, 21*(3–4), 219–243.

Ellis, A. (2003d). Helping people get better rather than merely feel better. *Journal of Rational-Emotive & Cognitive Behavior Therapy, 21*(3–4), 169–182.

Ellis, A. (2003e). The relationship of rational emotive behavior therapy (REBT) to social psychology. *Journal of Rational-Emotive & Cognitive Behavior Therapy, 21* (1), 5–20.

Ellis, A. (2003f). Similarities and differences between rational emotive behavior therapy and cognitive therapy. *Journal of Cognitive Psychotherapy, 17*(3), 225–240.

Ellis, A. (Ed.). (2004a). *Expanding the ABCs of rational emotive behavior therapy.* New York: Springer.

Ellis, A. (2004b). How my theory and practice of psychotherapy has influenced and changed other psychotherapies. *Journal of Rational-Emotive & Cognitive Behavior Therapy, 22*(2), 79–83.

Ellis, A. (2004c). *Rational emotive behavior therapy: It works for me—it can work for you.* Prometheus Books, Amherst, NY: Prometheus Books.

Ellis, A. (2004d). Why rational emotive behavior therapy is the most comprehensive and effective form of behavior therapy. *Journal of Rational-Emotive & Cognitive Behavior Therapy, 22*(2), 85–92.

Ellis, A. (2005a). Discussion of Christine A. Padesky and Aaron T. Beck, "Science and philosophy: Comparison of cognitive therapy and rational emotive behavior therapy." *Journal of Cognitive Psychotherapy. Special Issue: Cognitive Psychotherapy and Irritable Bowel Syndrome, 19*(2), 181–185.

Ellis, A. (2005b). Why I (really) became a therapist. *Journal of Clinical Psychology, 61*(8), 945–948.

Ellis, A. (2008). Rational emotive behavior therapy. In K. Jordan (Ed.), *The quick theory reference guide: A resource for expert and novice mental health professionals* (pp. 127–139). Hauppauge, NY: Nova Science Publishers.

Ellis, A., & Dryden, W. (1997). *The practice of rational-emotive therapy.* New York: Springer.

Ellis, A., & Harper, R. A. (1997). *A new guide to rational living* (3rd ed.). North Hollywood, CA: Wilshire Books.

Ellis, A., & Velten, E. (1992). *When AA doesn't work for you: A rational guide for quitting alcohol.* New York: Barricade Books.

Ellis, A., Abrams, M., & Abrams, L. D. (2009). *Personality theories: Critical perspectives.* Thousand Oaks, CA: Sage.

Ellis, A., Gordon, J., Neenan, M., & Palmer, S. (1997). *Stress counselling: A rational emotive behavior approach*. London: Cassell.

Ellis, A., McInerney, J. E., DiGiuseppe, R. A., & Yeager, R. (1988). *Rational-emotive treatment of alcoholism and substance abuse*. New York: Pergamon.

Ford, P. W. (2009). Effect of methodological improvements and study quality on REBT treatment outcome research since 1990: A meta-analysis. *Dissertation Abstracts International: Section B: The Sciences and Engineering, 69* (12–B), 7809.

Gonzalez, J. E., Nelson, J. R., Gutkin, T. B., Saunders, A., Galloway, A., & Shwery, C. S. (2004). Rational emotive therapy with children and adolescents: A meta-analysis. *Journal of Emotional and Behavioral Disorders, 12*(4), 222–235.

Guterman, J. T. (1996). Doing mental health counseling: A social constructivist revision. *Journal of Mental Health Counseling, 18*, 228–252.

Haaga, D. A. F., & Davison, G. C. (1991). Disappearing differences do not always reflect healthy integration: An analysis of cognitive therapy and rational-emotive therapy. *Journal of Psychotherapy Integration, 1*, 287–303.

Haaga, D. A. F., Dryden, W., & Dancey, C. P. (1991). Measurement of rational-emotive therapy in outcome studies. *Journal of Rational-Emotive and Cognitive-Behavior Therapy, 9*, 73–88.

Harran, S. M., & Ziegler, D. J. (1991). Cognitive appraisal of daily hassles in college students displaying high or low irrational beliefs. *Journal of Rational-Emotive and Cognitive-Behavior Therapy, 9*, 265–271.

Harrington, N. (2005). It's too difficult! Frustration intolerance beliefs and procrastination. *Personality and Individual Differences, 39*(5), 873–883.

Harrington, N. (2007). Frustration intolerance as a multidimensional concept. *Journal of Rational-Emotive & Cognitive Behavior Therapy, 25*(3), 191–211.

Hutchinson, G. T., & Chapman, B. P. (2005). Logotherapy-enhanced REBT: An integration of discovery and reason. *Journal of Contemporary Psychotherapy, 35*(2), 145–155.

Hutchinson, G. T., Patock-Peckham, J. A., Cheong, J., & Nagoshi, C. T. (1998). Irrational beliefs and behavioral misregulation in the role of alcohol abuse among college students. *Journal of Rational Emotive and Cognitive Behavior Therapy, 16*, 61–74.

Johnson, W. B., Digiuseppe, R., & Ulven, J. (1979, 1999). Albert Ellis as mentor: National survey results. *Psychotherapy, 36*, 305–313.

Knaus, W. J. (2008). *The cognitive behavioral workbook for anxiety: A step-by-step program*. Oakland, CA: New Harbinger.

Lakhan, R. (2009). Review of the effectiveness of counselling. *Journal of the Indian Academy of Applied Psychology, 35*(1), 166–167.

Lega, L. I., & Ellis, A. (2001). Rational emotive behavior therapy (REBT) in the new millennium: A cross-cultural approach. *Journal of Rational-Emotive and Cognitive-Behavioral Therapy, 19*, 201–222.

Lyons, L. C., & Woods, P. J. (1991). The efficacy of rational-emotive therapy: A quantitative review of the outcome research. *Clinical Psychology Review, 11*, 357–369.

Macavei, B., & McMahon, J. (2010). The assessment of rational and irrational beliefs. In D. David, S. J. Lynn, & A. Ellis (Eds.), *Rational and irrational beliefs: Research, theory, and clinical practice* (pp. 115–147). New York: Oxford University Press.

McGovern, T. E., & Silverman, M. S. (1984). A review of outcome studies of rational-emotive therapy from 1977–1982. *Journal of Rational Emotive Therapy, 2*, 7–18.

Muran, E., & Digiuseppe, R. (2000). Rape trauma. In F. M. Dattilio & A. S. Freeman (Eds.), *Cognitive-behavioral strategies in crisis intervention* (2nd ed., pp. 150–165). New York: Guilford.

Nielsen, S. L. (Ed.). (2004). A Mormon rational emotive behavior therapist attempts Qur'anic rational emotive behavior therapy. In R. P. Scott & A. E. Bergin, (Eds.), *Casebook for a spiritual strategy in counseling and psychotherapy* (pp. 213–230). Washington, DC: American Psychological Association.

Padesky, C. A., & Beck, A. T. (2003). Science and philosophy: Comparison of cognitive therapy and rational emotive behavior therapy. *Journal of Cognitive Psychotherapy, 17*(3), 211–224.

Padesky, C. A., & Beck, A. T. (2005). Response to Ellis' discussion of "Science and philosophy: Comparison of cognitive therapy and rational emotive behavior therapy." *Journal of Cognitive Psychotherapy. Special Issue: Cognitive Psychotherapy and Irritable Bowel Syndrome, 19*(2), 187–189.

Palmer, S. (1994). In the counsellor's chair: Stephen Palmer interviews Dr. Albert Ellis. *The Rational Emotive Behavior Therapist, 2*, 6–15.

Sapp, M. (1996). Irrational beliefs that can lead to academic failure for African American middle school students who are academically at risk. *Journal of Rational-Emotive and Cognitive-Behavior Therapy, 14*, 123–134.

Sapp, M., McNeely, R. L., & Torres, J. B. (2007). Dying a "good" death, the desire to die, and rational-emotive behavior therapy: Focus on aged African Americans and Hispanics/Latinos. In L. A. See (Ed.), *Human behavior in the social environment from an African-American perspective* (2nd ed., pp. 695–713). New York: Haworth Press.

Sharp, S. R. (2004).. Effectiveness of an anger management training program based on rational emotive behavior theory (REBT) for middle school students with behavior problems. (Doctoral dissertation). *Dissertation Abstracts International Section A: Humanities and Social Sciences*, 64 (10–A), 3595.

Si, G., & Lee, H. (2008). Is it so hard to change? The case of a Hong Kong Olympic silver medalist. *International Journal of Sport and Exercise Psychology*, 6(3), 319–330.

Silverman, M. S., McCarthy, M. L., & McGovern, T. (1992). A review of outcome studies of rational emotive therapy from 1982–1989. *Journal of Rational-Emotive and Cognitive-Behavioral Therapy*, 10, 111–186.

Szentagotai, A., & Jones, J. (2010). The behavioral consequences of irrational beliefs. In D. David, S. J. Lynn, & A. Ellis (Eds.), *Rational and irrational beliefs: Research, theory, and clinical practice* (pp. 75–97). New York: Oxford University Press.

Szentagotai, A., David, D., Lupu, V., & Cosman, D. (2008). Rational emotive behavior therapy versus cognitive therapy versus pharmacotherapy in the treatment of major depressive disorder: Mechanisms of change analysis. *Psychotherapy: Theory, Research, Practice, Training*, 45(4), 523–538.

Terjesen, M. D., Salhany, J., & Sciutto, M. J. (2009). A psychometric review of measures of irrational beliefs: Implications for psychotherapy. *Journal of Rational-Emotive & Cognitive Behavior Therapy*, 27(2), 83–96.

Trip, S., Vernon, A., & McMahon, J. (2007). Effectiveness of rational-emotive education: A quantitative meta-analytical study. *Journal of Cognitive and Behavioral Psychotherapies*, 7(1), 81–93.

Vernon, A. (2009). Applying rational-emotive behavior therapy in schools. In R. W. Christner & R. B. Mennuti (Eds.), *School-based mental health: A practitioner's guide to comparative practices* (pp. 151–179). New York: Routledge.

Walen, S., & Wolfe, J. (2000). Women's sexuality. In J. R. White & A. S. Freeman (Eds.), *Cognitive-behavioral group therapy: For specific problems and populations* (pp. 305–329). Washington, DC: American Psychological Association.

Walen, S., DiGiuseppe, R., & Wessler, R. L. (1980). *A practitioner's guide to rational-emotive therapy*. New York: Oxford University Press.

Weiner, D. N. (1988). *Albert Ellis: Passionate skeptic*. New York: Praeger.

Wilde, J. (2008). Rational-emotive behavioral interventions for children with anxiety problems. *Journal of Cognitive and Behavioral Psychotherapies*, 8, 133–141.

Wilson, D. S. (2010). Rational and irrational beliefs from an evolutionary perspective. In D. David, S. J. Lynn, & A. Ellis (Eds.), *Rational and irrational beliefs: Research, theory, and clinical practice* (pp. 63–72). New York: Oxford University Press.

Wolfe, J. L. (1985). Women. In A. Ellis & M. Bernard (Eds.), *Clinical applications of rational-emotive therapy* (pp. 101–127). New York: Plenum.

Wolfe, J. L. (1993). *What to do when he has a headache*. New York: Hyperion.

Wolfe, J. L., & Fodor, I. G. (1996). The poverty of privilege: Therapy with women of the "upper" classes. *Women and Therapy*, 18, 73–89.

Wolfe, J. L., & Naimark, H. (1991). Psychological messages and social context: Strategies for increasing RET's effectiveness with women. In M. E. Bernard (Ed.), *Using rational-emotive therapy effectively: A practitioner's guide* (pp. 265–301). New York: Plenum.

Wolfe, J., & Russianoff, P. (1997). Overcoming self-negation in women. *Journal of Rational-Emotive and Cognitive-Behavior Therapy*, 15, 81–92.

Woods, P. J., Silverman, E. G., & Bentilini, J. M. (1991). Cognitive variables related to suicidal contemplation in adolescents with implications for long range prevention. *Journal of Rational-Emotive and Cognitive-Behavior Therapy*, 9, 215–245.

Zachary, I. (1980). RET with women: Some special issues. In R. Grieger & J. Boyd (Eds.), *Rational-emotive therapy: A skills based approach* (pp. 249–264). New York: Van Nostrand.

Zare, M., Shafiabadi, A., Sharifi, H. P., & Navabinejad, S. (2007). The efficacy of rational emotive behavioral group therapy and psychodrama in modifying emotional expression styles. *Journal of Iranian Psychologists*, 4(13), 25–41.

Ziegler, D. J. (2000). Basic assumptions concerning human nature underlying REBT personality theory. *Journal of Rational and Emotive and Cognitive Behavior Therapy*, 18, 67–86.

Ziegler, D. J. (2003). The concept of psychological health in rational emotive behavior therapy. *Journal of Rational-Emotive & Cognitive Behavior Therapy*, 21 (1), 21–36.

Ziegler, D. J., & Leslie, Y. M. (2003). A test of the ABC model underlying rational emotive behavior therapy. *Psychological Reports*, 92(1), 235–240.

Cognitive Therapy

Outline of Cognitive Therapy

COGNITIVE THEORY OF PERSONALITY
  Causation and Psychological Disorders
  Automatic Thoughts
  The Cognitive Model of the Development
  of Schemas
  Cognitive Schemas in Therapy
  Cognitive Distortions
    All-or-nothing thinking
    Selective abstraction
    Mind reading
    Negative prediction
    Catastrophizing
    Overgeneralization
    Labeling and mislabeling
    Magnification or minimization
    Personalization
THEORY OF COGNITIVE THERAPY
  Goals of Therapy
  Assessment in Cognitive Therapy
    Interviews
    Self-monitoring
    Thought sampling
    Scales and questionnaires

The Therapeutic Relationship
The Therapeutic Process
  Guided discovery
  The three-question technique
  Specifying automatic thoughts
  Homework
  Session format
  Termination
Therapeutic Techniques
  Understanding idiosyncratic meaning
  Challenging absolutes
  Reattribution
  Labeling of distortions
  Decatastrophizing
  Challenging all-or-nothing thinking
  Listing advantages and disadvantages
  Cognitive rehearsal
Mindfulness-Based Cognitive Therapy
Schema-Focused Cognitive Therapy

Cognitive therapy, a system developed by Aaron Beck, stresses the importance of belief systems and thinking in determining behavior and feelings. The focus of cognitive therapy is on understanding distorted beliefs and using techniques to change maladaptive thinking while also incorporating affective and behavioral methods. In the therapeutic process, attention is paid to thoughts that individuals may be unaware of and to important belief systems.

Working collaboratively with clients, cognitive therapists take an educational role, helping clients understand distorted beliefs and suggesting methods for changing these beliefs. In doing so, cognitive therapists may give clients assignments to test out new alternatives to their old ways of solving their problems. As the therapist gathers data to determine therapeutic strategies, clients may be asked to record dysfunctional thoughts and to assess their problems through brief questionnaires developed for a variety of different psychological disorders. In their approach to treatment, cognitive therapists have outlined types of maladaptive thinking and specific treatment strategies for many psychological disturbances, including depression and anxiety disorders.

History of Cognitive Therapy

Although several theories of psychotherapy emphasize cognitive aspects of treatment, cognitive therapy is associated with the work of Aaron Beck. Born in 1921, Beck received his bachelor's degree from Brown University and his doctor of medicine degree from Yale University in 1946. From 1946 to 1948 he served an internship and residency in pathology at the Rhode Island Hospital in Providence. Following that experience, he was a resident in neurology, then later in psychiatry at the Cushing Veterans Administration Hospital in Framingham, Massachusetts. Also, he was a fellow in psychiatry at the Austen Riggs Center in Stockbridge, Massachusetts. In 1953, he was certified in psychiatry by the American Board of Psychiatry and Neurology. In 1956, he graduated from the Philadelphia Psychoanalytic Institute. He joined the faculty of the Department of Psychiatry of the Medical School of the University of Pennsylvania, where he is now Professor Emeritus. His early research on depression (Beck, 1961, 1964) led to publication of *Depression: Clinical, Experimental, and Theoretical Aspects* (1967), which discussed the importance of cognition in treating depression. Since then he has authored or co-authored more than 500 articles and 25 books related to cognitive therapy and the treatment of a variety of emotional disorders. His daughter, Judith S. Beck, a psychologist, is currently director of the Beck Institute for Cognitive Therapy and Research near Philadelphia, Pennsylvania, and Aaron Beck is the president.

Originally a practicing psychoanalyst, Beck (2001) observed the verbalizations and free associations of his patients. Surprised that his patients experienced thoughts they were barely aware of and did not report as a part of their free associations, he drew his patients' attention to these thoughts. Appearing quickly and automatically, these thoughts or cognitions were not within the patients' control. Often these automatic thoughts that patients were unaware of were followed by unpleasant feelings that they were very much aware of (Beck, 1991). By asking patients about their current thoughts, Beck was able to identify negative themes, such as defeat or inadequacy, which characterized their view of past, present, and future.

Having been trained as a psychoanalyst, Beck compared his observation of automatic thoughts to Freud's concept of the "preconscious." Beck (1976) was interested in what people said to themselves and the way they monitored

Courtesy of Aaron Beck

AARON BECK

themselves—their own internal communication system. From the internal communications within themselves, individuals formed sets of beliefs, an observation reported earlier by Ellis (1962). From these important beliefs, individuals formulated rules or standards for themselves, called schemas, or thought patterns that determine how experiences will be perceived or interpreted. Beck noticed that his patients, particularly those who were depressed, used internal conversations that communicated self-blame and self-criticism. Such patients often predicted failure or disaster for themselves and made negative interpretations where positive ones would have been more appropriate.

From these observations, Beck formulated the concept of a negative cognitive shift, in which individuals ignore much positive information relevant to themselves and focus instead on negative information about themselves. To do so, patients may distort observations of events by exaggerating negative aspects, looking at things as all black or all white. Comments such as "I never can do anything right," "Life will never treat me well," and "I am hopeless" are examples of statements that are overgeneralized, exaggerated, and abstract. Beck found such thinking, typical of individuals who are depressed, to be automatic and to occur without awareness. Many of these thoughts developed into beliefs about worthlessness, being unlovable, and so forth. Such beliefs, Beck (1967) hypothesized, were formed at earlier stages in life and became significant cognitive schemas. For example, a student who has several exams coming up in the next week may say to herself, "I'll never pass, I can't do anything right." Such an expression is a verbalization of a cognitive schema indicating a lack of self-worth. The student may express such a belief despite the fact that she is well prepared for her exams and has done well previously in her schoolwork. Thus, the beliefs persist despite evidence that contradicts them.

Although Beck's early work focused on depression, he applied his concepts of automatic thoughts, distorted beliefs, and cognitive schemas to other disorders. For example, he explained anxiety disorders as dominated by threat of failure or abandonment. From observations of patients and going over transcripts of sessions, Beck identified cognitive schemas that were common to people with different types of emotional disorders and developed strategies for treating them.

Theoretical Influences

Although much of Beck's theory of cognitive psychotherapy is based on observations from his clinical work, he and his colleagues have also been somewhat influenced by other theories of psychotherapy, cognitive psychology, and cognitive science. Because of his training as a psychoanalyst, Beck drew some concepts from psychoanalysis into his own work. Furthermore, there are similarities between cognitive therapy and the work of Albert Ellis and Alfred Adler, notably their emphasis on the importance of beliefs. Also, George Kelly's theory of personal constructs and Jean Piaget's work on the development of cognition play a role in understanding cognitions in personality. Attempts to develop computer models of intellectual thinking, an aspect of cognitive science, also contributed to the continuing development of cognitive psychotherapy.

Psychoanalysis and cognitive therapy share the view that behavior can be affected by beliefs that individuals have little or no awareness of. Whereas Freud hypothesized about unconscious thoughts, Beck has focused on automatic thoughts that can lead to distress. It was Freud's theory that anger, when turned inward, becomes depression that started Beck on his path for understanding the process of depression. Thus, Freud's theories of psychological disorders became the starting point from which cognitive therapy developed. This fact is not readily apparent, as the cognitive view of personality and techniques of psychotherapeutic change are very different from those of psychoanalysis.

More similar in theory and practice are the ideas of Adler, who emphasized the cognitive nature of individuals and their beliefs. Although Adlerians have focused on the development of beliefs, more so than Beck, they also have created a number of strategies to bring about changes in perceptions. Both Adler and Beck share an active approach to therapy, using specific and direct dialogue with patients to bring about change.

Similarly, Albert Ellis (1962) has used active and challenging approaches to confront irrational beliefs. Both Beck and Ellis challenge their patients' belief systems through direct interaction. They believe that by changing inaccurate assumptions, clients can make important changes to overcome psychological disorders. Although there are clear differences, which are discussed later, the commonalities between Beck's and Ellis's systems have served to strengthen the impact of cognitive therapies on the field of psychotherapy, both through the writings of the two theorists and the extensive research on the effectiveness of both approaches.

Although not as directly related to cognitive therapy as the work of psychotherapists, Kelly's theory of personal constructs explores the role of cognitions in personality development. Describing his basic construct of personality, Kelly (1955) said, "A person's processes are psychologically channelized by the way in which he anticipates events" (p. 46). Seeing constructs as individual, dichotomous, and covering a finite range of events, Kelly believed that individuals have a system of personal constructs that express their views of the world. For example, "smart-stupid" may be a personal construct, a way we view our acquaintances and friends. Not all people would construe events in this way, and some may have other constructs such as "strong-weak" that explain the way they see others. There is a resemblance between Kelly's personal constructs and Beck's schemas, in that both describe ways of characterizing individuals' systems of beliefs. Also, both theorists share an emphasis on the role of beliefs in changing behavior.

A very different approach to studying cognition was taken by Piaget, who was interested in the way individuals learn. In his studies of children's intellectual skills, Piaget (1977) described four major periods of cognitive development: sensorimotor, preoperations, concrete operations, and formal operations. The sensorimotor stage occurs from birth to age 2 and describes the learning that takes place when infants learn by touching, seeing, hitting, screaming, and so forth. The preoperations stage (ages 2 to about 7) includes basic intellectual skills like adding and subtracting. In the third stage, concrete operations, ages 7 to 11, children are better able to tell fantasy from reality and do not have to see an object to imagine manipulating it. They can deal with the concept of adding 4 tigers to 3 tigers, but they cannot add 4z to 7z. This ability takes place in the fourth stage, formal operations, and requires abstract learning. In discussing the implication of Piaget's theory for psychotherapy, Ronen (1997, 2003) has described how it can be helpful to match psychotherapeutic techniques of cognitive therapy with the individual's stage of cognitive development.

A broad and developing area of research that has the potential to contribute much to the cognitive theory of psychotherapy is cognitive science. Basically, cognitive science is interested in understanding how the mind works and in developing models for intellectual functioning. Involving such fields as cognitive psychology, artificial intelligence, linguistics, neuroscience, anthropology, and philosophy, cognitive science provides many perspectives on human intellectual processing. In cognitive psychology, researchers have studied how individuals make choices, remember facts, learn rules, remember events selectively, and learn differentially (Stein & Young, 1992).

Current Influences

Research in cognitive psychology and related fields is important in advancing new techniques in cognitive therapy. As is shown later, outcome research is an important part of the development of new methods and the testing of the effectiveness of cognitive therapy. This research is published widely in cognitive therapy journals such as *Cognitive Behaviour Therapy, Cognitive Therapy and Research, Journal of Cognitive Psychotherapy,* and *Cognitive and Behavioral Practice.* Additionally, research studies are published in a variety of behavior therapy and other psychological journals. Information from this work is used in teaching individuals at training centers for cognitive therapy in the United States. In particular, the Beck Institute for Cognitive Therapy and Research in Bala Cynwyd, Pennsylvania, has a large program devoted to training therapists and bringing in visiting scholars to participate in research and clinical activities. Another 10 centers for cognitive therapy are located in the United States. Started in 1959, cognitive therapy has become increasingly popular, perhaps due to the specificity of its techniques and the positive results of outcome research.

Cognitive Theory of Personality

Cognitive therapists are particularly concerned with the impact of thinking on individuals' personalities. Although cognitive processes are not considered to be the cause of psychological disorders, they are a significant component. In particular, automatic thoughts that individuals may not be aware of can be significant in personality development. Such thoughts are an aspect of the individual's beliefs or cognitive schemas, which are important in understanding how individuals make choices and draw inferences about their lives. Of particular interest in understanding psychological disorders are cognitive distortions, inaccurate ways of thinking that contribute to unhappiness and dissatisfaction in the lives of individuals.

Causation and Psychological Disorders

As Beck (1967; Clark, Beck, & Alford, 1999; Wills, 2009) has said, psychological distress can be caused by a combination of biological, environmental, and social factors, interacting in a variety of ways, so that there is rarely a single cause for a disorder. Sometimes early childhood events may lead to later cognitive distortions. Lack of experience or training may lead to ineffective or maladaptive ways of thinking, such as setting unrealistic goals or making inaccurate assumptions (Beck, Freeman, Davis, & Associates, 2004). At times of stress, when individuals anticipate or perceive a situation as threatening, their thinking may be distorted. It is not the inaccurate thoughts that cause the psychological disorder; rather, it is a combination of biological, developmental, and environmental factors (Beck & Weishaar, 1989). Regardless of the cause of the psychological disturbance, automatic thoughts are likely to be a significant part of the processing of the perceived distress.

Theories in Action

Automatic Thoughts

As mentioned previously, the automatic thought is a key concept in Beck's cognitive psychotherapy. Such thoughts occur spontaneously, without effort or choice. In psychological disorders, automatic thoughts are often distorted, extreme, or otherwise inaccurate. For example, Nancy put off applying to department stores for a job as an assistant buyer. Unhappy with her job as a sales clerk, she had such thoughts as "I'm too busy now," "When the holiday season is over, I will apply for a job," and "I cannot get time off to go to other stores to get job applications." Recognizing these thoughts as excuses, Nancy, with the help of her therapist, identified automatic thoughts related to job seeking, such as "I won't present myself well" and "Other people will be better than me." By talking with Nancy about her thought processes, the therapist was able to generate several automatic thoughts. By organizing these automatic thoughts, the therapist was able to articulate a set of core beliefs or schemas.

The Cognitive Model of the Development of Schemas

Cognitive therapists view individual beliefs as beginning in early childhood and developing throughout life (Figure 10.1). Early childhood experiences lead to basic beliefs about oneself and one's world. These beliefs can be organized into cognitive schemas. Normally, individuals experience support and love from parents, which lead to beliefs such as "I am lovable" and "I am competent," which in turn lead to positive views of themselves in adulthood. Persons who develop psychological dysfunctions, in contrast to those with healthy functioning, have negative experiences that may lead to beliefs such as "I am unlovable" and "I am inadequate." These developmental experiences, along with critical incidents or traumatic experiences, influence individuals' belief systems. Negative experiences, such as being ridiculed by a teacher, may lead to conditional beliefs such as "If others don't like what I do, I am not valuable." Such beliefs may become basic to the individual as negative cognitive schemas.

Young (Kellogg & Young, 2008; Young, 1999; Young, Rygh, Weinberger, & Beck, 2008; Young, Weinberger, & Beck, 2001) has identified common maladaptive schemas that can lead to the development in childhood of many psychological disorders. Early *maladaptive schemas* are ones that individuals assume to be true about themselves and their world. These schemas are resistant to change and cause difficulties in individual's lives. Usually these schemas are activated by a change in one's world, such as a loss of a job. When these conditions occur, individuals often react with strong negative emotions. These schemas often result from previous dysfunctional childhood interactions with family members. Through these belief systems that children develop, they start to view reality in ways that cause problems in functioning internally or with others. Such schemas are likely to continue through adolescence and adulthood.

In studying early maladaptive schemas, Young (1999) has identified 18, which he has classified into the following five domains: disconnection and rejection,

(paper)
5 Domains

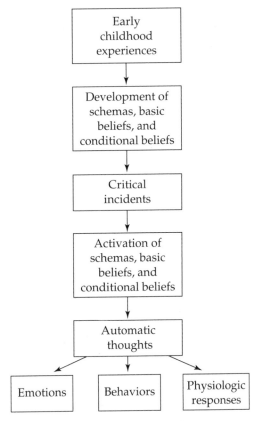

FIGURE 10.1   The Cognitive Developmental Model.
From "Brief Therapy, Crisis Intervention and the Cognitive Therapy of
Substance Abuse," by B. S. Liese, 1994, *Crisis Intervention*, 1, 11–29.
Copyright © 1994 by Harwood Academic Publishers. Reprinted by permission.

impaired autonomy and performance, impaired limits, other directedness, and
over-vigilance and inhibitions. *Disconnection and rejection* refer to an individual's
belief that needs for security, caring, acceptance, and empathy may not be met in
a predictable way. *Impaired autonomy and performance* are schemas that suggest
individuals can't handle their responsibilities well, or function independently,
and that they have failed and will continue to do so. *Impaired limits* refer to schemas concerning difficulty in respecting the rights of others, in being cooperative,
and in restraining one's own behavior. *Other directedness* deals with putting the
needs of others before one's own needs in order to be loved. *Overvigilance and
inhibition* are beliefs that one must suppress feelings and choices or meet high
expectations of performance. Worry and anxiety often result. Individuals are
rarely aware of the development of these early maladaptive schemas.

Cognitive Schemas in Therapy

How patients think about their world and their important beliefs and
assumptions about people, events, and the environment constitute cognitive

schemas. There are two basic types of cognitive schemas: positive (adaptive) and negative (maladaptive). What can be an adaptive schema in one situation may be maladaptive in another. Freeman (1993) gives an example of a schema that can be both positive and negative, depending on the circumstance.

> Allen was a 67-year-old male. He had recently retired as chief executive officer of a large international firm. He had worked himself up in the company from the lowest level as a high school student to the chief position over a period of 50 years. In his retirement, he was physically healthy, had a great deal of money, good marital and family relationships, and a circle of friends. When he came for therapy he was, however, moderately to severely depressed. The operative schemas that drove him to success—that is, "I am what I do or produce," "One is judged by others by one's productivity," and "If one isn't working, one is lazy/worthless" were now contributing to his depression. The schemas were the same, but the effect on his life was far different. (p. 60)

In describing schemas, Beck and Weishaar (1989) note that schemas develop from personal experience and interaction with others. Some of the schemas are associated with cognitive vulnerability or a predisposition to psychological distress. For example, patients who are depressed may have negative schemas such as "I can't do anything right," "I won't amount to anything," and "Other people are much more adept than I." In this way, cognitive vulnerability can be seen in distorted or negative schemas.

Schemas can be viewed across dimensions other than positive-negative. *Active* (versus inactive) *schemas* refer to schemas occurring in everyday events; inactive schemas are triggered by special events (Freeman & Diefenbeck, 2005). *Compelling* (versus noncompelling) *schemas* are those that were learned when young and are reinforced by family members and society (C. A. Diefenbeck, personal communication, January 2, 2006). *Changeable* (versus unchangeable) *schemas* are ones that are not too difficult to change. *Religious schemas* tend to be relatively unchangeable and quite compelling. In his book *Prisoners of Hate*, Beck (1999) writes about the strength of religious beliefs that support genocide. Active-inactive, compelling-noncompelling, and changeable-unchangeable are useful dimensions for therapists to attend to as clients present concerns. Noticing changes in affect can also be useful.

When a patient presents a negative schema, the therapist may note a cognitive shift. For each psychological disorder, particular cognitive distortions are likely to be present. By diagnosing the disorder, the therapist can understand how the client integrates data and acts in accordance with the data. Thus, an anxious client may perceive a threat while driving home and take a prescribed route that may include alternates in case traffic jams or accidents are seen ahead. By observing the client describing this situation, the therapist may perceive an affective shift that indicates that the client has made a cognitive shift. Signals of such a shift may be facial or bodily expressions of emotion or stress. When such an event takes place in therapy, the cognitive schema may be emotional or "hot." In such a case, the therapist is likely to follow up the "hot" cognition with a question such as "What were you thinking just now?" Working with and evoking active hot cognitions in a session can be very helpful in dealing with negative cognitive schemas (C. A. Diefenbeck, personal communication, January 2, 2006).

In further describing schemas, Clark, Beck, and Alford (1999) list five types of schemas: cognitive-conceptual, affective, physiological, behavioral, and motivational. *Cognitive-conceptual schemas* provide a way for storing, interpreting, and making meaning of our world. Core beliefs are cognitive-conceptual schemas. *Affective schemas* include both positive and negative feelings. *Physiological schemas* are those that include perceptions of physical functions, such as a panic reaction that could include hyperventilating. *Behavioral schemas* are actions that are taken, such as running away when scared. *Motivational schemas* are related to behavioral schemas in that they often initiate an action. Examples of motivational schemas include the desire to avoid pain, to eat, to study, and to play. These schemas can be adaptive or maladaptive.

[handwritten margin note: 5 TYPES OF Schemas]

Cognitive Distortions

An individual's important beliefs or schemas are subject to cognitive distortion. Because schemas often start in childhood, the thought processes that support schemas may reflect early errors in reasoning. Cognitive distortions appear when information processing is inaccurate or ineffective. In his original work with depression, Beck (1967) identified several significant cognitive distortions that can be identified in the thought processes of depressed people. Freeman (1987) and DeRubeis, Tang, and Beck (2001) have discussed a variety of common cognitive distortions that can be found in different psychological disorders. Nine of these are described here: all-or-nothing thinking, selective abstraction, mind reading, negative prediction, catastrophizing, overgeneralization, labeling and mislabeling, magnification or minimization, and personalization.

All-or-nothing thinking. By thinking that something has to be either exactly as we want it or it is a failure, we are engaging in all-or-nothing, or dichotomous, thinking. A student who says, "Unless I get an A on the exam, I have failed" is engaging in all-or-nothing thinking. Grades of A– and B then become failures and are seen as unsatisfactory.

[handwritten margin note: @ PAPER]

Selective abstraction. Sometimes individuals pick out an idea or fact from an event to support their depressed or negative thinking. For example, a baseball player who has had several hits and successful fielding plays may focus on an error he has made and dwell on it. Thus, the ballplayer has selectively abstracted one event from a series of events to draw negative conclusions and to feel depressed.

Mind reading. This refers to the idea that we know what another person is thinking about us. For example, a man may conclude that his friend no longer likes him because he will not go shopping with him. In fact, the friend may have many reasons, such as other commitments, not to go shopping.

Negative prediction. When an individual believes that something bad is going to happen, and there is no evidence to support this, this is a negative prediction. A person may predict that she may fail an exam, even though she has done well on exams before and is prepared for the upcoming exam. In this case, the inference about failure—the negative prediction—is not supported by the facts.

Catastrophizing. In this cognitive distortion, individuals take one event they are concerned about and exaggerate it so that they become fearful. Thus, "I know when I meet the regional manager, I'm going to say something stupid that will jeopardize my job. I know I will say something that will make her not want to consider me for advancement" turns an important meeting into a possible catastrophe.

Overgeneralization. Making a rule based on a few negative events, individuals distort their thinking through overgeneralization. For example, a high school sophomore may conclude: "Because I do poorly in math, I am not a good student." Another example would be the person who thinks because "Alfred and Bertha were angry at me, my friends won't like me, and won't want to have anything to do with me." Thus, a negative experience with a few events can be generalized into a rule that can affect future behavior.

Labeling and mislabeling. A negative view of oneself is created by self-labeling based on some errors or mistakes. A person who has had some awkward incidents with acquaintances might conclude, "I'm unpopular. I'm a loser" rather than "I felt awkward talking to Harriet." In labeling and mislabeling in this way, individuals can create an inaccurate sense of themselves or their identity. Basically, labeling or mislabeling is an example of overgeneralizing to such a degree that one's view of oneself is affected.

Magnification or minimization. Cognitive distortions can occur when individuals magnify imperfections or minimize good points. They lead to conclusions that support a belief of inferiority and a feeling of depression. An example of magnification is the athlete who suffers a muscle pull and thinks, "I won't be able to play in the game today. My athletic career is probably over." In contrast, an example of minimization would be the athlete who would think, "Even though I had a good day playing today, it's not good enough. It's not up to my standards." In either magnification or minimization, the athlete is likely to feel depressed.

Personalization. Taking an event that is unrelated to the individual and making it meaningful produces the cognitive distortion of personalization. Examples include "It always rains when I am about to go for a picnic" and "Whenever I go to the shopping center, there is always an incredible amount of traffic." People do not cause the rain or the traffic; these events are beyond our control. Furthermore, when people are questioned, they are able to give instances of how it does not always rain when they have planned an outdoor function and that they do not always encounter the same level of traffic when shopping. For example, traffic is usually heavier at certain times of day than at others, and if one chooses to shop at a particular time, there will be more or less traffic.

If they occur frequently, such cognitive distortions can lead to psychological distress or disorders. Making inferences and drawing conclusions from a behavior are important parts of human functioning. Individuals must monitor what they do and assess the likelihood of outcomes to make plans about their social lives, romantic lives, and careers. When cognitive distortions are frequent, individuals can no longer do this successfully and may experience depression, anxiety, or other disturbances. Cognitive therapists look for cognitive distortions and help their patients understand their mistakes and make changes in their thinking.

Theory of Cognitive Therapy

In what is characterized as a collaborative relationship, cognitive therapists work together with their clients to change thinking patterns, as well as behaviors that interfere with the clients' goals. The establishment of a caring therapeutic relationship is essential. Cognitive therapy emphasizes a careful approach to detail and the role of the thinking process in behavioral and affective change. In setting goals, cognitive therapists attend to faulty beliefs that interfere with individuals achieving their goals. This is reflected in assessment methods that require individuals to monitor, log, and indicate in a variety of ways their cognitions, feelings, and behaviors. A characteristic of cognitive therapy is that the therapist and client collaborate to reach the patient's goals by using a format that allows for feedback and discussion of client progress. Although therapeutic techniques used to bring about change include cognitive, affective, and behavioral elements, the cognitive approaches to changing automatic thoughts and cognitive schemas are emphasized here.

Goals of Therapy

The basic goal of cognitive therapy is to remove biases or distortions in thinking so that individuals may function more effectively. Attention is paid to the way individuals process information, which may maintain feelings and behaviors that are not adaptive. Patients' cognitive distortions are challenged, tested, and discussed to bring about more positive feelings, behaviors, and thinking. To remove biases or distortions in thinking, therapists attend not just to automatic thoughts but also to the cognitive schemas that they represent. Thus, changing cognitive schemas is an important goal of cognitive therapy.

Changing cognitive schemas can be done at three different levels (Beck et al., 2004). The most limited type of change is *schema reinterpretation*. Here an individual recognizes the schema but avoids or works around it. For example, a perfectionistic person might not change the perfectionism, but rather work as an inspector where these traits are valued and reinforced. In *schema modification* an individual makes some but not total changes in the schema. Beck et al. (2004) give an example of a person with paranoia who makes changes to trust some people in certain situations but continues to be careful in trusting people in general. The highest level of schema change is *schematic restructuring*. For example, a person with paranoia who became trusting of others would have restructured his significant cognitive schema. Such a person would believe that others would be trustworthy and not likely to attack him. These three levels of schema change provide a way to examine goals in cognitive therapy.

Generally, when establishing goals, cognitive therapists focus on being specific, prioritizing goals, and working collaboratively with clients. The goals may have affective, behavioral, and cognitive components, as seen by this example from Freeman, Pretzer, Fleming, and Simon (1990):

> Frank, a depressed salesman, initially stated his goal for therapy as, "to become the best that I can be." When stated in that way, the goal is quite vague and abstract. It also was clearly unmanageable, considering that Frank was so depressed that he could not manage to revise his résumé or do household chores. After considerable discussion, Frank and his therapist agreed on more specific goals including "feel less depressed and anxious, decrease amount of time spent worrying, and actively hunt

for a job (revise resumé, actively search for job openings, complete applications for appropriate openings, etc.)." (pp. 10–11)

The clearer and more concrete the goals, the easier it is for therapists to select methods to use in helping individuals change their cognitive schemas and also their feelings and behaviors. Clients can present a number of difficult issues when presenting their concerns. Judith Beck (2005) gives eight examples of dealing with unclear or problematic goals. For example, she describes Thomas, who feels too helpless to set goals. He responds "I don't know" to many of the therapist's questions about his goals. The therapist decides to help Thomas with small goals, such as throwing away trash at home and cleaning the kitchen. These goals fit within a core belief that the therapist was able to ascertain after a few sessions—that Thomas felt he was capable of very little and would fail at things he tried (pp. 135–137). This brief example shows how cognitive therapists work specifically on goals, seeing them in the context of cognitive schemas.

Assessment in Cognitive Therapy

Careful attention is paid to assessment of client problems and cognitions, both at the beginning of therapy and throughout the entire process, so that the therapist may clearly conceptualize and diagnose the client's problems. As assessment proceeds, it focuses not only on the client's specific thoughts, feelings, and behaviors but also on the effectiveness of therapeutic techniques as they affect these thoughts, feelings, and behaviors. Specific strategies for assessment have been devised for many different psychological disorders, such as anxiety and depression (J. S. Beck, 1995, 2005; Whisman, 2008; Wills, 2009). In this section, I describe ways cognitive therapists use assessment techniques, including client interviews, self-monitoring, thought sampling, the assessment of beliefs and assumptions, and self-report questionnaires (Beck et al., 2004; Whisman, 2008).

Interviews. In the initial evaluation, the cognitive therapist may wish to get an overview of a variety of topics while at the same time creating a good working relationship with the client. The topics covered are similar to those assessed by many other therapists and include the presenting problem, a developmental history (including family, school, career, and social relationships), past traumatic experiences, medical and psychiatric history, and client goals. Therapists may use previously developed structured interviews (Beck et al., 2004) or nonstructured interviews. Freeman et al. (1990) emphasize the importance of getting detailed reports of events. They caution against asking biased questions such as "Didn't you want to go to work?" and suggest instead "What happened when you did not get to work?" In assessing thoughts, therapists may need to train their clients to differentiate between thoughts and feelings and to report observations rather than make inferences about the observations. Accuracy of recall is encouraged (although clients are not expected to remember all details) and is preferred to guesses about past events. Sometimes in vivo interviews and observations may be of particular help. For example, if a client suffers from agoraphobia, the therapist may meet the client at home and walk outside with the client, making observations and assessments in the interviewing process.

Keeping notes of patients' experiences, emotions, and behaviors is very helpful. Judith Beck (1995) has developed a Cognitive Conceptualization Diagram (Figure 10.2) to organize patient data. The therapist starts at the bottom half of the diagram, taking each situation one at a time. For example, Fred has been

Pt's Initials: Therapist's Name:

Pt's Diagnosis: Axis I: Axis II:

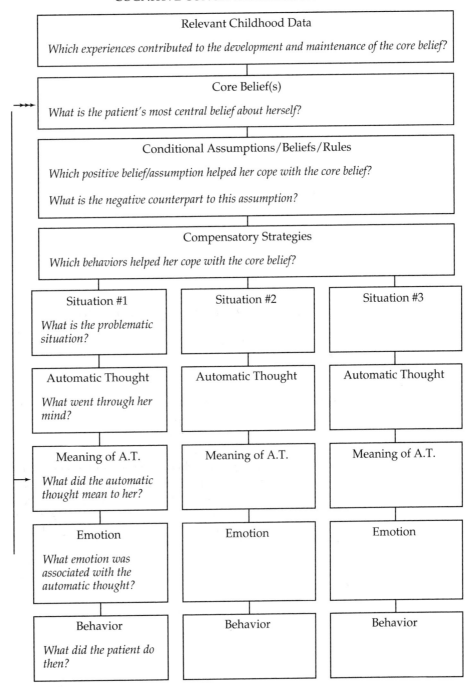

FIGURE 10.2 Cognitive Conceptualization Diagram.

From *Cognitive Therapy: Basics and Beyond*, Guilford Press, 1995.
Copyright © 1995 by J. S. Beck. Reprinted by permission.

very frightened of presenting at his senior recital at college. He is afraid he will sing off key and embarrass himself in front of the music faculty. Under Situation #1, the therapist would write "Presenting at a recital. Evaluated by 3 music professors." The therapist then helps Fred in determining the automatic thought and writes it in the box below "Situation #1"—"The professors will think I'm terrible." Then they determine the "Meaning of A. T.," which for Fred is "I fold under pressure." The "Emotion" is "anxiety." His "Behavior" is "Singing the song he will present, 5 times." As the therapist and Fred continue, they will discuss at least two more situations in the same way. Each time, the therapist and Fred determine the automatic thoughts, their meaning, the emotion relevant to the situation, and the behavior.

When the therapist has enough information to assess core beliefs, she will integrate information she has about Fred's "Relevant Childhood Data" with information from the material she has just gathered to determine Fred's "Core Beliefs." Then she uses "if-then" phrases to determine "Conditional Assumptions/ Beliefs/Rules." For Fred, his "Core Belief" may be "I'm not good enough." His "Conditional Assumptions/Beliefs/Rules" may be "If I have to be on my own, I'll screw up." This is a negative assumption. A positive assumption would be "When I'm with others (e.g., singing in a chorus), I'm OK." The final box is "Compensatory Strategies." Fred's are "practice, practice, practice" and "keep telling my girlfriend how nervous I am." This information then becomes material the therapist uses when developing change strategies. Although the interview is probably the most important way to gather information, cognitive therapists also ask clients to gather specific information on their own.

Self-monitoring. Another method used to assess client thoughts, emotions, and behaviors outside the therapist's office is self-monitoring. Basically, clients keep a record of events, feelings, and/or thoughts. This could be done in a diary, on an audiotape, or by filling out a questionnaire. One of the most common methods is the Dysfunctional Thought Record (DTR) (Beck, Rush, Shaw, & Emery, 1979). Sometimes called a thought sheet, the DTR has one column in which the client describes the situation, a second in which the client rates and identifies an emotion, and a third to record her automatic thoughts. Clients may practice using the DTR (Figure 10.3) in therapy so that they get used to recording automatic thoughts and rating the intensity of feelings. Use of the DTR provides material for discussion in the next session and an opportunity for clients to learn about their automatic thoughts.

Theories in Action

Thought sampling. Another method for obtaining information about cognitions is thought sampling (Blankstein & Segal, 2001). Having a tone sound at a random interval at home and then recording thoughts is one way to get a sample of cognitive patterns. Clients may then record their thoughts in a tape recorder or notebook. Freeman et al. (1990) give an example of how thought sampling can be productive in therapy.

> A middle-aged factory foreman had made good progress in therapy by using DTRs to identify dysfunctional cognitions related to episodes of anger and depression and then "talking back" to the cognitions. However, he began to experience a vague, depressed mood that seemed not to be related to any clear stimuli. He was unable to identify situations or cognitions related to the depressed mood, and therefore was asked to use a thought sampling procedure to collect additional data. When he returned for his next

DYSFUNCTIONAL THOUGHT RECORD (Example)

Directions: When you notice your mood getting worse, ask yourself, "What's going through my mind right now?" and as soon as possible jot down the thought or mental image in the Automatic Thought column.

Date/ Time	Situation	Automatic Thought(s)	Emotion(s)	Alternative Response	Outcome
	1. What actual event or stream of thoughts, or daydreams, or recollection led to the unpleasant emotion? 2. What (if any) distressing physical sensations did you have?	1. What thought(s) and/or image(s) went through your mind? 2. How much did you believe each one at the time?	1. What emotion(s) (sad, anxious, angry, etc.) did you feel at the time? 2. How intense (0-100%) was the emotion?	1. (optional) What cognitive distortion did you make? (e.g., all-or-nothing thinking, mind-reading, catastrophizing.) 2. Use questions at bottom to compose a response to the automatic thought(s). 3. How much do you believe each response?	1. How much do you now believe each automatic thought? 2. What emotion(s) do you feel now? How intense (0-100%) is the emotion? 3. What will you do? (or did you do?)
2/2	Thinking about Mark's not calling me.	He must not care. (90%)	Sad (90%)	Jumping to conclusions 1. He didn't call when he said he would but he was affectionate the last time we were together. 2. Maybe he's been busy at work or just forgot. 3. The worst is he'll never call again and I'd survive. Best is he'd call right now. Most realistic is he'll call in a day or two. 4. Believing he must not care makes me feel devastated. Realizing I might be wrong makes me feel more hopeful. 5. I should go ahead and call him myself. 6. If Joan was in this situation I'd tell her to go ahead and call him. (75%)	1. A.T. = 70% 2. Sad = 60% 3. I will call him after work tonight.

Questions to help compose an alternative: (1) What is the evidence that the automatic thought is true? Not true? (2) Is there an alternative explanation? (3) What's the worst that could happen? Could I live through it? What's the best that could happen? What's the most realistic outcome? (4) What's the effect of my believing the automatic thought? What could be the effect of changing my thinking? (5) What should I do about it? (6) If _____ was in the situation and had this thought, what would I tell him/her?
(friend's name)

FIGURE 10.3 Dysfunctional Thought Record.

From Cognitive Therapy: Basics and Beyond, Guilford Press, 1995. Copyright © 1995 by J. S. Beck. Reprinted by permission.

therapy session, a review of the cognitions he had recorded revealed constant ruminative thoughts centering on the theme of "I'm too tired to ..." It gradually became clear that these ruminative thoughts were responsible for his decreased motivation to deal with problems actively and for his increased depression. (p. 41)

Thought sampling can be useful in getting data that is related to specific situations, such as work and school. However, thought sampling can interrupt the client's activity and may become irritating. Also, thoughts irrelevant to the client's problems may be recorded.

Scales and questionnaires. In addition to these techniques, previously developed self-report questionnaires or rating scales can be used to assess irrational beliefs, self-statements, or cognitive distortions (Whisman, 2008). Structured questionnaires have been developed for specific purposes, such as the Beck Depression Inventory (Beck, Ward, Mendelson, Mock, & Erbaugh, 1961), the Scale for Suicide Ideation (Beck, Kovacs, & Weissman, 1979), the Dysfunctional Attitude Scale (Weissman, 1979), and the Schema Questionnaire (Young & Brown, 1999). Questionnaires such as these are usually brief and can be administered at various points in therapy to monitor progress. For example, the Beck Depression Inventory consists of 21 items, with each containing four choices expressing degrees of sadness, dislike, guilt, crying, worthlessness, and similar items. Each choice is brief, with most being less than eight words long. Additionally, psychological inventories such as the Minnesota Multiphasic Personality Inventory may be used for similar purposes.

When gathering data from clients, especially raw data that include automatic thoughts, it is often helpful for the therapist to try to infer themes or cognitive schemas represented by the cognitions. As data are reported from session to session, different cognitive schemas, or insights into them, may develop. Schemas can be seen as hypotheses that the client and counselor are continually testing. Progress can be assessed as patients complete homework, fill out questionnaires, and report automatic thoughts. With progress should come a decrease in the number of cognitive distortions, increased challenges to automatic thoughts, and a decrease in negative feelings and behavior.

The Therapeutic Relationship

Theories in Action

Goal Oriented

Beck's (1976; Wills, 2009) view of the client–therapist relationship is that it is collaborative. The therapist brings an expertise about cognitions, behaviors, and feelings to guide the client in determining goals for therapy and means for reaching these goals. The clients' contributions to therapy are the raw data for change (thoughts and feelings). They participate in the selection of goals and share responsibility for change. The assessment process is a continually evolving one. As new data are gathered, the therapist and client may develop new strategies. In some ways, the therapeutic process can be seen as a joint scientific exploration in which both therapist and client test new assumptions. In this process, the therapist may use listening skills that focus on the client's feelings, somewhat similar to the approach of Carl Rogers, to further understand the client's concerns and to develop the relationship. However, the client also takes responsibility for progress by completing assigned homework outside of the office. Although the cognitive therapist is open to the feedback, suggestions, and concerns of the client, the process of therapy is specific and goal oriented.

STRUCTURED

The Therapeutic Process — STRUCTURED

More so than many other theories of therapy, cognitive therapy is structured in its approach. The initial session or sessions deal with assessment of the problem, development of a collaborative relationship, and case conceptualization. As therapy progresses, a guided discovery approach is used to help clients learn about their inaccurate thinking. Other important aspects of the therapeutic process are methods to identify automatic thoughts and the assignment of homework, which is done throughout therapy. As clients reach their goals, termination is planned, and clients work on how they will use what they have learned when therapy has stopped. As therapeutic work progresses, clients move from developing insight into their beliefs to moving toward change. Particularly with difficult and complex problems, insight into the development of negative cognitive schemas is important. All of these aspects of the therapeutic process are described more fully here.

Guided discovery. Sometimes called Socratic dialogue, guided discovery helps clients change maladaptive beliefs and assumptions. The therapist guides the client in discovering new ways of thinking and behaving by asking a series of questions that make use of existing information to challenge beliefs.

> [*Client:*] I've been afraid that when I report to my new job on Monday, people will think I can't do the work.
>
> [*Therapist:*] What does that tell you about the assumptions that you are making?
>
> [*Client:*] Like I'm mind reading, like I know in advance what's going to happen.
>
> [*Therapist:*] And what assumptions are you making?
>
> [*Client:*] That I know what my new colleagues will think of me.

The three-question technique. A specific form of the Socratic method, the three-question technique consists of a series of three questions designed to help clients revise negative thinking. Each question presents a way of inquiring further into negative beliefs and bringing about more objective thinking.

1. What is the evidence for the belief?
2. How else can you interpret the situation?
3. If it is true, what are the implications?

A brief example of this technique shows how it is an extension of the Socratic method and how it can help individuals change their beliefs. Liese (1993) gives an example of a physician using the three-question technique with a patient with AIDS.

> *Dr.:* Jim, you told me a few minutes ago that some people will scorn you when they learn about your illness. (reflection) What is your evidence for this belief?
>
> *Jim:* I don't have any evidence. I just feel that way.
>
> *Dr.:* You "just feel that way." (reflection) How else could you look at the situation?
>
> *Jim:* I guess my real friends wouldn't abandon me.
>
> *Dr.:* If some people did, in fact, abandon you, what would the implications be?
>
> *Jim:* I guess it would be tolerable, as long as my real friends didn't abandon me. (Liese, 1993, p. 83)

Specifying automatic thoughts. An important early intervention is to ask the client to discuss and to record negative thoughts. Specifying thoughts using the Dysfunctional Thought Record (Figure 10.3) and bringing them into the next session can be helpful for work in future sessions. An example of automatic thoughts and helping a patient understand them is given here.

> During the first session, I had asked my client how often he thought that he had negative thoughts. His response was that he had them at times, but only infrequently. Given his Beck Depression Inventory of 38, my thinking was that he would have many, many more. He estimated no more than two to three a day. As a homework assignment I asked him to record as many of his thoughts as possible. I estimated that he probably had several negative thoughts a day, and that by the end of the week he would probably have 50 thoughts recorded. He quickly responded: "I'll never be able to do it. It would be too hard for me. I'll just fail." My response was to indicate that he already had three and only needed 47 more. (Freeman et al., 1990, pp. 12–13)

Homework. Much work in cognitive therapy takes place between sessions so that skills can be applied to real-life settings, not just the office (J. S. Beck & Tompkins, 2007). Specific assignments are given to help the client collect data, test cognitive and behavior changes, and work on material developed in previous sessions. If the client does not complete the homework, this fact can be useful in examining problems in the relationship between client and therapist or dysfunctional beliefs about doing homework assignments (J. S. Beck, 2005). Generally, homework assignments are discussed and new ones developed in each session.

Session format. Although therapists may have their own format that they adapt for different client problems, there are certain topics to be dealt with in the therapy session (J. S. Beck, 1995). The therapist checks on the client's mood and how he is feeling. Usually, the therapist and client agree on an agenda for the therapy session based, in part, on a review of events of the past week and on pressing problems that may have emerged. Also, the therapist asks for feedback about the previous session and concerns or problems that the client may have about issues that have occurred since the last meeting. The therapist and client review homework and collaborate to see how the client could get more out of it. Usually, the major focus of the session is on the concerns the client raised at the beginning of the therapy hour. Having dealt with specific items, new homework is assigned relevant to the client's chief concerns. Feedback from the client about the session is an important element of the collaborative relationship between therapist and client.

Termination. As early as the first session, termination may be planned. Throughout treatment, therapists encourage patients to monitor their thoughts or behaviors, report them, and measure progress toward their goals. In the termination phase, the therapist and client discuss how the client can do this without the therapist. Essentially, clients become their own therapists. Just as clients may have had difficulties in accomplishing tasks and may have relapsed into old thought patterns or behaviors, they work on how to deal with similar issues and events after therapy has ended. Commonly, the frequency of therapy sessions tapers off, and client and therapist may meet every 2 weeks or once a month.

Although issues occur in therapy that may require changes in the therapeutic process described here, the specificity of the therapeutic approach, the emphasis on thoughts, and the use of homework are typical. Throughout the process of therapy, a number of strategies are used to bring about changes in thoughts, behaviors, and feelings. Some of these are discussed next.

Therapeutic Techniques

A wide variety of cognitive techniques are used in helping clients achieve their goals. Some of the techniques focus on eliciting and challenging automatic thoughts, others on maladaptive assumptions or ineffective cognitive schemas. The general approach in cognitive therapy is not to interpret automatic thoughts or irrational beliefs, but to examine them through either experimentation or logical analysis. An example of an experiment would be to ask a client who feels that no one will pay attention to her to initiate a conversation with two acquaintances and observe how they attend or fail to attend to her. An example of questioning a client's logic would be, when the client says "I can never do anything right," to ask "Have you done anything right today?" Cognitive therapists also use techniques to help clients with feelings and behaviors. Some of the techniques used in assisting clients with feelings are described in Chapter 6, and those used to help clients change behaviors are explained in Chapters 8 and 9. Many different cognitive therapy techniques are described by Freeman (1987), Dattilio and Freeman (1992), Leahy (2003), J. S. Beck (1995, 2005), and Ledley, Marx, and Heimberg (2005). *The New Handbook of Cognitive Therapy Techniques* (McMullin, 2000) describes more than 35 different techniques. Barlow (2007) illustrates techniques used for a variety of disorders in the *Clinical Handbook of Psychological Disorders*. The following section explains eight common strategies for helping clients change unhelpful thought patterns.

Understanding idiosyncratic meaning. Different words can have different meanings for people, depending on their automatic thoughts and cognitive schemas. Often it is not enough for therapists to assume that they know what the client means by certain words. For example, depressed people are often likely to use vague words such as *upset, loser, depressed,* or *suicidal*. Questioning the client helps both therapist and client to understand the client's thinking process.

> *[Client:]* I'm a real loser. Everything I do shows that I'm a real loser.
>
> *[Therapist:]* You say that you're a loser. What does it mean to be a loser?
>
> *[Client:]* To never get what you want, to lose at everything.
>
> *[Therapist:]* What is it that you lose at?
>
> *[Client:]* Well, I don't exactly lose at very much.
>
> *[Therapist:]* Then perhaps you can tell me what you do lose at, because I'm having difficulty understanding how you are a loser.

Challenging absolutes. Clients often present their distress through making extreme statements such as "Everyone at work is smarter than I am." Such statements use words like *everyone, always, never, no one,* and *all the time*. Often it is helpful for the therapist to question or challenge the absolute statement so that the client can present it more accurately, as in the following example:

> *[Client:]* Everyone at work is smarter than me.
>
> *[Therapist:]* Everyone? Every single person at work is smarter than you?

[*Client:*] Well, maybe not. There are a lot of people at work I don't know well at all. But my boss seems smarter; she seems to really know what's going on.

[*Therapist:*] Notice how we went from everyone at work being smarter than you to just your boss.

[*Client:*] I guess it is just my boss. She's had a lot of experience in my field and seems to know just what to do.

Reattribution. Clients may attribute responsibility for situations or events to themselves when they have little responsibility for the event. By placing blame on themselves, clients can feel more guilty or depressed. Using the technique of reattribution, therapists help clients fairly distribute responsibility for an event, as in this example:

[*Client:*] If it hadn't been for me, my girlfriend wouldn't have left me.

[*Therapist:*] Often when there is a problem in a relationship, both people contribute to it. Let's see if it is all your fault, or if Beatrice may also have played a role in this.

Labeling of distortions. Previously, several cognitive distortions such as all-or-nothing thinking, overgeneralization, and selective abstraction were described. Labeling such distortions can be helpful to clients in categorizing automatic thoughts that interfere with their reasoning. For example, a client who believes that her mother always criticizes her might be asked to question whether this is a distortion and whether she is "overgeneralizing" about her mother's behavior.

Decatastrophizing. Clients may be very afraid of an outcome that is unlikely to happen. A technique that often works with this fear is the "what-if" technique. It is particularly appropriate when clients overreact to a possible outcome, as in this case:

[*Client:*] If I don't make dean's list this semester, things will be over for me. I'll be a mess; I'll never get into law school.

[*Therapist:*] And if you don't make dean's list, what would happen?

[*Client:*] Well, it would be terrible, I don't know what I would do.

[*Therapist:*] Well, what would happen if you didn't make dean's list?

[*Client:*] I guess it would depend on what my grades would be. There's a big difference between getting all B's and not making dean's list and getting all C's.

[*Therapist:*] And if you got all B's?

[*Client:*] I guess it wouldn't be so bad, I could do better the next semester.

[*Therapist:*] And if you got all C's?

[*Client:*] That's really not likely, I'm doing much better in my classes. It might hurt my chances for law school, but I might be able to recover.

Challenging all-or-nothing thinking. Sometimes clients describe things as all or nothing or as all black or all white. In the previous example, the client is not only catastrophizing about grades but also dichotomizing the idea of making or not making the dean's list. Rather than accept the idea of dean's list versus not dean's list, the therapist uses a process called *scaling*, which turns a dichotomy into a continuum. Thus, grades are seen as varying in degree; the client will respond differently to the possibility of getting a 3.0 rather than a 3.25 than to the possibility of dean's list or not dean's list.

Listing advantages and disadvantages. Sometimes it is helpful for patients to write down the advantages and disadvantages of their particular beliefs or behaviors. For example, a student can write down the advantages of maintaining the belief "I must make dean's list" and the disadvantages of such a belief. This approach is somewhat similar to scaling, as listing the advantages and disadvantages of a belief helps individuals move away from an all-or-none position.

Cognitive rehearsal. Use of imagination in dealing with upcoming events can be helpful. A woman might have an image of talking to her boss, asking for a raise, and then being told, "How dare you even talk to me about this subject?" This destructive image can be replaced through cognitive rehearsal. The woman can imagine herself talking to her boss and having a successful interview in which the boss listens to her request. The cognitive rehearsal can be done so that the woman presents her request in an appropriate way, with the boss not granting the request in one instance and the boss granting the request in another. The therapist asks her to imagine the interview with the boss and then asks the patient questions about the imagined interview.

Other useful cognitive strategies follow a similar pattern. They question the client's cognitive schemas and automatic thoughts. In addition to cognitive techniques, cognitive therapists may use behavioral techniques such as activity scheduling, behavioral rehearsal, social-skills training, bibliotherapy, assertiveness training, and relaxation training (discussed in other chapters). In the practice of psychotherapy, many of these techniques are used at different times in the therapeutic process to bring about change in cognitions, feelings, and behavior.

Cognitive Treatment of Psychological Disorders

Cognitive therapists have probably developed explanations and specific treatments for more psychological disorders than has any other therapeutic approach. Particularly for depression and general anxiety, two disorders described here, they have provided a detailed approach to treatment and have been able to test these approaches through the application of outcome research and to determine that they are research-supported psychological treatments. Other disorders discussed here include obsessional thinking and substance abuse. Because the type of cognitive distortions that patients experience can vary within each disorder, and because there are many cognitive techniques, the examples given here are not meant to represent a universal application of cognitive therapy to each of these four disorders. Additionally, the treatment descriptions highlight only major approaches to cognitive therapy with these problems, as a full account goes beyond the scope of this book.

Depression: Paul

Beck's (1967) initial application of cognitive therapy was to depression. More writing and research have been devoted to depression in cognitive therapy than to any other disorder. Clark, Beck, and Alford (1999) have thoroughly described the rationale for cognitive therapy as treatment for depression in *Scientific Foundations of Cognitive Theory and Therapy of Depression*. Five practical applications to the treatment of depression make thorough use of Beck's treatment approach: *Essential Components of Cognitive-Behavior Therapy for Depression* (Persons, Davidson, & Tompkins, 2001), *Cognitive Therapy for Bipolar Disorder* (Lam, Jones, Hayward, & Bright, 1999), *The Prevention of Anxiety and Depression* (Dozois & Dobson, 2004), *Adapting Cognitive Therapy for Depression* (Whisman, 2008), and *Cognitive Therapy for Suicidal Patients: Scientific and Clinical Applications* (Wenzel, Brown, & Beck, 2009).

Many conceptualizations of depression include the cognitive triad, which provides a framework for the application of cognitive and other strategies. The term *cognitive triad* refers to the negative view that depressed people have about themselves, their world, and their futures. In terms of self-perception, depressed people see themselves as worthless, lonely, and inadequate. In a similar way, they view their world as one that makes difficult demands and presents obstacles that keep them from meeting their goals. When they look at the future, depressed people see a dismal view; their problems can get only worse, and they will not be successful. With such perceptions, depressed people are likely to be indecisive, hopeless, tired, and apathetic. Their cognitive distortions may include those discussed earlier: all-or-nothing thinking, catastrophizing, overgeneralization, selective abstraction, mind reading, negative prediction, personalization, labeling and mislabeling, and magnification or minimization.

Many of the cognitive distortions described in this chapter, as well as common cognitive therapy techniques, are used in the course of treating depression. In this section, I describe treatment strategies suggested by Liese and Larson (1995) in their detailed approach to the treatment of depression with Paul. In their approach, they establish a collaborative therapeutic relationship leading to conceptualization of Paul's problems, which includes assessment of his basic beliefs and cognitive schemas. They then educate Paul by presenting important information that is relevant to his basic beliefs. Additionally, they apply the Socratic method, the three-question technique, and the Daily (Dysfunctional) Thought Record to help Paul make changes in thoughts and behaviors.

Conceptualizing Paul's problems includes a psychiatric diagnosis, determination of his current problems, a history of his childhood development, and a profile of his basic beliefs and automatic thoughts. Paul is a 38-year-old lawyer who recently found out he has AIDS. He had been sad, had difficulties sleeping and concentrating, and had been extremely anxious. According to Liese and Larson (1995), he was experiencing a major depressive episode of moderate severity. An only child, Paul was expected to perform well in school and did so. As a result of relationships with parents and at school, Paul developed two significant beliefs about himself: "I am lovable only when I please others" and "I am adequate only when others love me" (p. 18).

Paul sought love and approval through promiscuous sexual relationships with other men. This behavior reflected his attempts to "avoid feeling lonely" (p. 18). When he entered therapy, his behavior was reflected in certain basic beliefs.

"Now, I'm really unlovable and defective."
"I have disappointed everyone who matters to me."
"I deserve AIDS because of my behavior." (p. 18)

The therapist shared his diagnosis with Paul. Sensitive to Paul's sadness and fear, the therapist was empathic with Paul's feelings. However, Paul was surprised to discover the high degree of structure in cognitive therapy. During his second session Paul commented that the structure made therapy seem "kind of impersonal." With a great deal of encouragement from the therapist, Paul was able to admit (to the therapist): "You seem more concerned about problem solving than you are about me as a person." They discussed this belief, and Paul learned from his therapist that such beliefs reflect mind reading. Paul eventually realized from his therapist's spontaneous warmth and empathy that his therapist genuinely cared about him. He further learned that therapeutic structure would contribute substantially to defining problems and resolving them (p. 19).

To help Paul with his depression, the therapist used the Socratic method (guided discovery). In this way Paul could realize that his life was not over.

[Therapist:] How are you feeling today? (open question)

Paul: Pretty depressed.

[Therapist:] You seem depressed. (reflection) What have you been thinking about? (open question)

Paul: My life seems wasted at this point.

[Therapist:] What do you mean by "wasted"? (open question)

Paul: It seems like nothing matters anymore.

[Therapist:] "Nothing." (reflection) … (long pause) Can you think of anything that does matter? (open question)

Paul: (long pause) Curt is important, I guess.

[Therapist:] You only "guess"? (reflection/question)

Paul: Okay, Curt really is important.

[Therapist:] What else is important to you? (open question)

Paul: I guess my friends are still important to me.

[Therapist:] What makes your friends important to you? (open question)

Paul: They really seem to care about me.

[Therapist:] When you consider your importance to Curt and your friends, what thoughts do you have? (open question)

Paul: Well, I guess my life isn't completely wasted.

[Therapist:] And how do you feel when you think your life is not wasted? (open question)

Paul: Somewhat less upset.

In this dialogue, the therapist has begun to help Paul feel emotional relief simply by guiding him to think about his important relationships with Curt and his friends. The Socratic method facilitates Paul's ability to discover his own positive thoughts, resources, and strengths rather than having the therapist advise or dispute maladaptive thoughts (pp. 21–22).

To deal further with the issue of feeling that his life is wasted, the therapist uses the three-question technique.

[Therapist:] You told me a few minutes ago that your life was wasted. (reflection) What is your evidence for this belief? (question #1)

Paul: I don't have any evidence. I just feel that way.

[Therapist:] You "just feel that way." (reflection) *How else* could you look at the situation? (question #2)

Paul: I guess my life isn't wasted if I'm still important to Curt.

[Therapist:] If, in fact, you weren't important to Curt, what would the *implications* be? (question #3)

Paul: I guess it might be tolerable if my friends didn't abandon me.

In this brief interaction, Paul's therapist helps him to become more objective about his own worth. In fact, when Paul realizes that his life has some meaning, he begins to experience emotional relief (p. 23).

> Paul's therapist had him complete at least two DTRs daily when Paul first began therapy. At that time Paul had reported feeling extremely depressed. Hence, "entering counseling" was written in the *situation* column and "depression" was written in the *emotions* column. Paul revealed that his *automatic thoughts* about counseling were: "It's hopeless. I won't benefit from this." These were written in the automatic thoughts column. The therapist helped Paul, using the Socratic method, to identify *rational responses* to his belief "It's hopeless." With prompting, Paul proposed the alternative, more adaptive thoughts: "In fact, I can't say for sure that there is no hope." "Maybe there is some hope for me." (p. 24)

Additionally, Paul's therapist used homework that included filling out a weekly activity schedule. Through this cognitive therapy approach, Paul was able to become less depressed and find more meaning in his life. Implicit in this example is the attention to a detailed assessment of negative automatic thoughts. A great variety of cognitive strategies are used, many more than are presented in this chapter, for changing the depressive thoughts and behaviors of clients suffering from different variations of depression (Persons, Davidson, & Tompkins, 2001; Whisman, 2008).

General Anxiety Disorder: Amy

In applying the cognitive triad to anxiety, Beck, Emery, and Greenberg (1985) discuss the role of threat. Individuals may view the world as dangerous, where catastrophes may occur or people may hurt them. This threat can be applied to the self, where individuals are afraid to assert themselves or to try to overcome a threat or danger. This outlook carries over into their view of the future, in which they believe that they will be unable to deal with events that they perceive will be dangerous. Anxious people are likely to perceive an event as risky and their abilities as minimal.

Freeman and Simon (1989) identify the significant cognitive schema of anxiety as that of *hypervigilance*. Individuals with this schema usually have a history of being alert to their surroundings. Some may be very aware of who is sick, the weather, road conditions, or the looks on persons' faces. Less anxious people may perceive such environmental factors but do not have automatic thoughts that indicate that these situations are threats to them. They have an accurate assessment of risk and danger, not a hypervigilant one.

In assessing the cognitive distortions of anxious individuals, Freeman et al. (1990) note that catastrophizing, personalization, magnification and minimization, selective abstraction, arbitrary inference, and overgeneralization are common. When anxious clients catastrophize, they dwell on extreme potential negative consequences. They may assume that if something harmful could potentially happen, there is a great likelihood that it will. In the following example, the client's cognitive distortion of catastrophizing is countered by the therapeutic intervention of decatastrophizing. By using the Socratic method, the therapist is able to have the client describe her fears in detail and then counters the fears by asking, "What is the worst that could happen?"

> Amy came into treatment for her fears of eating and drinking in public that were severely limiting her life. As she was planning to go out for coffee with some friends (including Sarah, a woman she did not know well), she had been able to identify the thought, "What if I get upset and really start shaking?" She and the therapist explored the likelihood of that happening and concluded that it was possible (because that had happened before) but not very likely (because she had been quite anxious in a number of situations but had not had a severe shaking episode in a long time). The therapist then moved on to explore the worst possible scenario by asking, "Well, let's just say that you did get so upset that you shook harder than you ever have before. What's the worst that could happen?" Amy replied, "Sarah might notice and ask what's the matter with me." The therapist then asked, "And if she did notice and ask you, what's the worst that would happen next?" This time Amy thought for a second and answered, "Well, I'd be terribly embarrassed, and Sarah would proba-bly think I was weird." Once more, the therapist asked, "And what's the worst that could happen then?" After thinking some more, Amy replied, "Well, Sarah might not want to have any more to do with me, but the other people they are my friends and probably would understand." Finally, the therapist asked, "And if that did happen?" Amy concluded, "I'd feel embarrassed, but I do have plenty of good friends, so I'd live without Sarah as a friend. Besides, if she's that narrow minded, who needs her anyway?" (Freeman et al., 1990, p. 144)

In this example, negative thoughts are identified and modified through questioning. Sometimes therapists may use imagery or actual behavior to challenge fears. Often cognitive therapists use the behavioral technique of relaxation training, together with other cognitive methods, to reduce individuals' stress or anxiety.

Obsessive Disorder: Electrician

Chapter 8 describes a cognitive-behavioral approach, exposure and ritual preven-tion, for treating obsessive-compulsive disorders that combine obsessions with compulsive rituals (such as checking a car door 20 times to see if it is locked). Most individuals with obsessive thoughts (those that clients continually worry about) tend to seek out certainty in situations that others usually believe to be safe. For example, a physically healthy person who obsesses may worry repeat-edly about getting cancer, whereas other individuals who do not obsess would not worry continually about a low-risk event but rather address the issue by hav-ing a physical examination once every year or two.

In describing automatic thoughts that are typical of individuals with obsessive-compulsive problems, Beck, Freeman, and Associates (2004) list a num-ber of typical automatic thoughts.

1. "What if I forget to pack something?"
2. "I better do this again to be sure I got it right."
3. "I should keep this old lamp because I might need it someday."
4. "I have to do this myself or it won't be done correctly" (p. 313).

Underlying these automatic thoughts are assumptions that Beck et al. (2004) believe that individuals who have obsessive thoughts make about themselves and their world.

"There are right and wrong behaviors, decisions, and emotions" (p. 313).

"To make a mistake is to be deserving of criticism" (p. 314).

"I must be perfectly in control of my environment as well as of myself," "Loss of control is intolerable," and "Loss of control is dangerous" (p. 314).

"If something is or may be dangerous, one must be terribly upset by it" (p. 314).

"One is powerful enough to initiate or prevent the occurrence of catastrophes by magical rituals or obsessional ruminations" (p. 315).

Many of these thoughts fit into a similar view of issues that are relevant to obsessive-compulsive disorder described by Taylor, Kyrios, Thordarson, Steketee, and Frost (2002) and Purdon (2007). These include overestimation of threat, intolerance of uncertainty, responsibility, perfectionism, mental control, and overimportance of thoughts.

Overestimation of threat. People with obsessive-compulsive disorder may overestimate the chances that terrible things may occur. For example, a person may believe she faces many dangers in her life. One method for dealing with this is to examine the meaning of the thought for the person rather than the content.

Intolerance of uncertainty. Having a belief that one should know for certain about what will happen is a common belief of people with obsessive-compulsive disorders. For example, they may think "If I can't predict what will happen when I go on vacation, I must be doing something wrong." Tracking the need to know what will happen on vacation and the time spent in trying to know is an approach clients may find helpful and not think of on their own.

Responsibility. Some individuals feel that it is their responsibility to protect themselves and others from harm. They may believe that if they do not clean up very carefully after themselves, someone may be harmed by their germs. There are several methods that may be effective. One is to examine what would happen if others were as responsible as the client.

Mental control. People with obsessive-compulsive disorder may feel that they must control impulsive thoughts or bad things might happen. For example, if someone is flying on an airplane and can't control their thoughts that the plane must crash, he may have a belief that he is going crazy. One method is to suggest that clients alternate days trying to control their thoughts and then compare the results (Clark, 2004).

Perfectionism. Believing that problems have a perfect solution and mistakes can not be made is a view of perfectionism that people with obsessive-compulsive disorder may have. For example, "If I cannot answer all items on the math test correctly, I am a failure." Finding out who the client admires and asking about this person's mistakes or perfect behavior can be a useful method to deal with perfectionism.

Overimportance of thoughts. This refers to the view that thoughts can cause or be responsible for actions (fusing thoughts and actions). "If one thinks that someone may die, that could come true" is an example. A method of helping clients address fusing thoughts and actions is discussed in the next section.

While this model is one way of viewing obsessive-compulsive disorder, there are others. Researchers have examined the variety of beliefs that are common in obsessive-compulsive disorder. They also have used a variety of methods to counter these beliefs.

For people with obsessions, guilt often follows from not doing what one should or must. For such individuals, reassurance is almost never sufficient and alleviates anxiety only for the moment, not over the long term. Although there are several methods for dealing with obsessive thinking, one specific example characterizes a cognitive approach: the thought–action fusion model. This approach attempts to counter the avoidance that individuals use in trying to deal with obsessional thoughts.

Several writers have discussed the problem of fusing actions and thoughts. Wells (1997) has continued the work of Rachman (1997) and Wells and Matthews (1994) that describes how individuals with obsessive thoughts tend to equate them with actions. For example, a person who has a thought about harming a child may think that he is going to harm the child. This fusion of thought and actions can also be applied to past actions. If I think I have done something bad in the past, I probably did it. Thus, if I felt that I harmed a child in the past, I may feel that I did it. Needleman (1999) gives an example of Carlos, who believed he may have hit someone with his car when he did not. The therapist created an experiment in which Carlos held a hammer over his therapist's thumb and repeated the thought "I'm going to smash her thumb as hard as I can" (p. 220). Reluctantly, Carlos agreed to it and was able to separate an intrusive thought from an intention.

Wells (1997) makes several suggestions about how to conceptualize and help individuals who fuse their thoughts and feelings. The basic goal of this therapy is to help the patient see the thoughts as irrelevant for further action and to develop a detached acceptance of intrusive thoughts. In gathering data about these thoughts, Wells has developed a modified version of the Dysfunctional Thought Record for obsessive-compulsive disorder.

Wells describes several methods for defusing thoughts from actions and events. One of the first steps is to help the patient increase his awareness of when thought–action fusion is taking place. He uses a similar approach in helping patients defuse thoughts and events. In the following, he uses a Socratic dialogue to help a man distinguish between thoughts and events at work.

[*Therapist:*] How long have you been checking the power sockets at work?

[*Patient:*] About three years.

[*Therapist:*] Have you ever discovered that you forgot to switch them off?

[*Patient:*] No. I go around systematically and switch them off. But that doesn't stop me driving back to work to check.

[*Therapist:*] So even though you have many experiences telling you that your doubting thoughts are not true, you still believe that they are. What makes you believe that?

[*Patient:*] I don't know. Perhaps I haven't switched them off properly.

[*Therapist*]: When you check is there any evidence for that?

[*Patient:*] No.

[*Therapist:*] Yet you continue to check and continue to have a problem. So how helpful is your checking in overcoming your problem?

[*Patient:*] Obviously it's not helping at all.

[*Therapist:*] So why don't you stop checking?

[Patient:] I'd be too uncomfortable. I would ruin my weekend.

[Therapist:] What do you mean by uncomfortable?

[Patient:] I'd be dwelling on the possibility that I'd not turn things off.

[Therapist:] So you'd still be responding as if your thoughts were true. What if you responded to your thoughts differently, could that help?

[Patient:] Well, I already tell myself that it's stupid to think these things.

[Therapist:] Does that stop you dwelling on the thought?

[Patient:] No. I go through my switching off routine in my head to see if I can remember all of it.

[Therapist:] So you're still acting as if your thought is true. It sounds as if it might cause its own problems.

[Patient:] Sometimes it makes me feel better, but if I can't clearly remember switching off some of the appliances, it means I'll feel worse and I'll end up checking.

[Therapist:] So how useful is your behavioural or mental checking in the long run?

[Patient:] I can see it probably doesn't help. But I'd feel worse if I didn't check.

[Therapist:] OK. We can explore that possibility in a minute. But I think we should do something about your strategies for dealing with your thoughts. It sounds as if your checking may be generating more doubts and keeping your problem going. (Wells, 1997, pp. 254–255)

Wells (1997) and Clark (2004) use several other cognitive strategies to help patients defuse their thoughts from actions and events. They also make use of the exposure and ritual prevention strategies described on page 306–308 in Chapter 8. Clark (2004) finds Socratic questioning, guided discovery, and homework to be quite helpful. Several models of addressing obsessive-compulsive disorder that are developing from research on cognitive therapy, and are described on page 405.

Substance Abuse: Bill

The application of cognitive therapy to substance abuse is thorough and complex, described in detail in *Cognitive Therapy of Substance Abuse* (Beck, Wright, Newman, & Liese, 1993). Therapists (Liese & Beck, 2000; Liese & Franz, 1996; Newman, 2008) discuss advances in the cognitive treatment of substance abuse. Although the treatment of drug-abusing patients follows a cognitive model that is somewhat similar to the treatment of other disorders, there are significant differences. The therapeutic relationship may be difficult because patients may not enter treatment voluntarily, may be involved in criminal activities, may have negative attitudes about therapy, and may be unwilling to be honest about their drug usage. Also, patients may not voluntarily disclose drug abuse. Sometimes they may refuse to discuss their substance abuse and focus on other problems such as depression (Newman, 2008). Therapists should ask not only about usage but also about the severity of urges to use (J. S. Beck, 2005). When setting goals, therapists focus not only on being drug free but also on how this will solve other problems, such as financial and work problems. Particular issues unique to substance abuse are those of dealing with cravings due to withdrawal symptoms and a lack of the pleasure that was previously provided by the drug. Of importance is the focus on the individual's belief system, which is described in more detail here.

Those who abuse drugs tend to hold three basic types of beliefs: anticipatory, relief-oriented, and permissive (Beck et al., 1993). *Anticipatory beliefs* refer to an expectation of reinforcement, such as "When I see Andy tonight, we'll get high. Great!" *Relief-oriented* beliefs often refer to the removal of symptoms due to psychological or physiological withdrawal. *Permissive* beliefs are those that refer to the idea that it is all right to use drugs. Examples include "I can use drugs, I won't get addicted" and "It's OK to use ... everybody else does." These permissive beliefs are self-deceiving and can be considered rationalizations or excuses. Permissive beliefs are especially common. McMullin (2000) lists several, along with therapeutic comments that can be used to counter client statements. "A couple of drinks are good for me" (p. 363) can be countered by "When was the last time you had two drinks of anything?" (p. 364). The major focus of cognitive therapy is to challenge and change a variety of beliefs.

To change the belief system of drug abusers, Beck et al. (1993) suggest six methods: assessing beliefs, orienting the patient to the cognitive therapy model, examining and testing addictive beliefs, developing control beliefs, practicing activation of these new beliefs, and assigning homework (p. 170). Assessment of such beliefs comes from questions such as "How do you explain ...?" and "What are you thinking about?" (p. 170). To further assess beliefs, Beck and his colleagues have developed drug-related questionnaires, such as the Craving Beliefs Questionnaire, Beliefs About Substance Abuse, and Automatic Thoughts About Substance Abuse. After a thorough assessment of beliefs, the patient can then be oriented to the specific cognitive model of addiction.

Belief systems related to drug abuse tend to become firm and entrenched. Such beliefs, including "Marijuana is great," "You can't get off heroin," and "Nothing beats a cocaine high," can be examined and tested by questions such as "What is your evidence for that belief?", "How do you know that your belief is true?", and "Where did you learn that?" (Beck et al., 1993, p. 177). To develop a system of control beliefs, or new beliefs, to replace previous dysfunctional ones, therapists use the Socratic method, as in this example dealing with cocaine use:

> [*Therapist:*] Bill, you now seem less dead set in believing that nothing is as much fun as getting high.
>
> *Bill:* I'm not sure what to believe now.
>
> [*Therapist:*] What do you mean?
>
> *Bill:* Well, I still think that getting high with my friends was lots of fun, but maybe it wasn't the perfect high I made it out to be.
>
> [*Therapist:*] Bill, what else could you have done with your friends that would have been fun?
>
> *Bill:* Well, I don't know about these guys, but with other friends in the past I could have gone to a baseball game, or played racquetball, or done something like sports or something.
>
> [*Therapist:*] What else?
>
> *Bill:* I guess there are lots of things ... but none seems as exciting as doing cocaine.
>
> [*Therapist:*] Let's try to think of some more things. What gave you the biggest thrill before you began using cocaine?
>
> *Bill:* Well, I was an adventurous guy. When I was much younger I would go camping and hiking and rock climbing, but I'm in no shape for that now.
>
> [*Therapist:*] What do you mean when you say "I am in no shape for that"?

Bill: I guess I'm just skeptical that I would enjoy that kind of thing anymore. It's just been so long since I last did it.

[Therapist:] What would it take for you to try doing those things again?

Bill: I guess I'd just have to do them.

[Therapist:] What were some of the feelings you had in the past when you would go camping or hiking or climbing?

Bill: I felt great … really alive!

[Therapist:] How did that feeling compare to the cocaine high?

Bill: (pause) … I guess, in some ways it was better.

[Therapist:] What do you mean?

Bill: Well, I really earned the high I got from those activities. There were no short cuts then. It was a super feeling.

[Therapist:] So perhaps you now have a control belief to replace the old addictive belief. "I can experience a super high without using cocaine."

Bill: Yes, I just need to remember that thought. (Beck et al., 1993, pp. 179–180)

After control beliefs have been developed, they then must be practiced. Sometimes therapists use flash cards to reinforce the beliefs, including messages such as "Getting wasted can get me busted" or "When I smoke crack, I have no control of my life." Clients fantasize a craving for the drug and then use control beliefs to counter the craving. Accompanying the practice in using control beliefs within the session is that of assigning homework to be done outside therapy. Control beliefs are practiced in high-risk situations, such as being around friends who use the drug.

Although changing the belief system is essential in cognitive therapy of drug abuse, other issues are also addressed. Therapists help their clients deal with concerns such as reactions of family members or financial issues. Stress from work or from friends who abuse drugs can also add to the patient's problems. Additionally, when working with substance abuse, therapists teach clients methods for preventing and dealing with lapses in treatment. Individuals learn to deal with a single slip so that they will not give themselves permission to have many (relapse) (C. A. Diefenbeck, personal communication, January 2, 2006). Throughout the process of drug treatment, Socratic methods are used frequently, as are other techniques that help drug abusers change distorted beliefs.

Although this section has focused on disorders of depression, generalized anxiety, obsessive thinking, and substance abuse, cognitive therapy has been applied to many other concerns. Some examples are agoraphobia, posttraumatic stress disorder, grief, bulimia and anorexia, obesity, narcissism, borderline personality disorder, schizophrenia, multiple personality, and chronic pain. Books and articles describe each of these disorders and give examples of common cognitive distortions likely to be present as well as specific cognitive techniques.

Brief Cognitive Therapy

For many disorders, such as depression and anxiety, cognitive therapy tends to be brief, usually between 12 and 20 sessions. When possible therapists may see patients twice a week for the first month and then weekly for the next several months. A number of factors influence the length of psychotherapy, such as the client's willingness to do homework, the range and depth of problems, and how long the client has had the problem. For narcissistic, borderline, and other personality disorders, treatment often takes between 18 and 30 months, with meetings two or three times a week during the beginning of therapy. Other factors, such as therapists' style and experience and potential for relapse, may also affect the length of cognitive therapy.

Current Trends

Cognitive therapy is a very active area of practice and research. Some therapists and researchers have developed new directions in the application of cognitive therapy that are related to the work of Aaron Beck. Mindfulness-based cognitive therapy is an eight-session group approach designed to help individuals who have had major depression prevent relapse. Another approach designed for individuals with personality disorders and other severe psychological problems is that of schema-focused cognitive therapy that assesses and changes significant cognitive schemas. There are treatment manuals or guides for these approaches. Additionally, I have listed treatment manuals for using cognitive therapy for many other psychological disorders.

Mindfulness-Based Cognitive Therapy

Cognitive therapists have added mindfulness meditative techniques to their treatment strategies for a variety of disorders (Teasdale, Segal, & Williams, 2003). Mindfulness meditation is discussed further in Chapter 8 in the description of acceptance and commitment therapy (p. 311) and in Chapter 15 in the section on Asian therapies (p. 583). Mindfulness-based stress reduction uses a Buddhist philosophy to help people relate more effectively to thoughts and feelings. It does not focus on changing the content of thoughts or feelings (Salmon et al., 2004). Mindfulness-based cognitive therapy is similar in that it does not focus on changing the content of thoughts and feelings, but it differs because it is designed for a specific audience.

Mindfulness-based cognitive therapy is a specific method of group training used with individuals with depression (usually major depression) to prevent relapse (Barnhofer et al., 2009; Crane, 2009; Segal, Teasdale, & Williams, 2004; Segal, Williams, & Teasdale, 2002; Williams, Teasdale, Segal, & Kabat-Zinn, 2007). This approach focuses on how to help clients change the way they attend to their negative thoughts (and feelings and bodily sensations). To do this, they decenter their thoughts. *Decentering* refers to understanding that thoughts are just thoughts, not reality (Spiegler & Guevremont, 2010). For example if you think "I am lazy," that is not an accurate self-description; it is a thought. By practicing mindfulness, you can become removed or distanced from the thought and not engaged in the thought. If a depressed person becomes more aware or mindful of thoughts like this, the individual can see this as a signal that depression could be initiated. By becoming aware of such thoughts, individuals can prevent their relapse into depression (Spiegler & Guevremont, 2010).

Mindfulness-based cognitive therapy is an eight-week group training program that consists of 2-hour sessions (Segal et al., 2002; Segal et al., 2004). A focus of this program is not controlling thoughts but giving up control of thoughts, feelings, and bodily sensations. By accepting these thoughts, feelings, and sensations change, clients produce change and prevent relapsing into depression. The first four sessions are used to teach and practice how to attend to thoughts, feelings, and bodily sensations and not evaluate them. The last four sessions are used to attend to shifts in mood by using mindfulness techniques. Clients are taught to notice how their thoughts can affect how they feel emotionally and physically. Using homework, clients are taught to apply these techniques in their daily lives. Additionally, they may ask family members to help with these methods so that they may better prevent or interrupt a relapse into depression. Limited research has shown that mindfulness-based cognitive therapy has been helpful in preventing the reoccurrence of major depression (Evans et al., 2008; Fresco et al., 2007; Kuyken et al., 2008; Segal et al., 2004).

Schema-Focused Cognitive Therapy

Developed by Jeffrey Young and his colleagues (Kellogg & Young, 2008; Riso, du Toit, Stein, & Young, 2007; Young, 1999; Young & Brown, 1999; Young et al., 2008), schema-focused cognitive therapy is derived from and complementary to Beck's cognitive therapy. However, it differs in several ways. Schema-focused cognitive therapy has been developed for individuals with personality disorders such as borderline disorders, as well as difficult problems such as eating disorders, childhood abuse, and substance abuse. In schema-focused cognitive therapy, there is more emphasis on the client–therapist relationship. Also, the therapist is more likely to explore schemas that developed in early childhood than in traditional cognitive therapy (Spiegler & Guevremont, 2010). In working with schemas from childhood, therapists are likely to make use of gestalt experiential techniques as described in Chapter 7.

As described earlier (p. 374), schemas are themes or ways of thinking that comprise a set of beliefs about oneself, others, and the environment. Young (1994) describes five major core beliefs that may emerge in childhood and create difficulties leading to severe psychological disorders. These include abandonment/instability, mistrust/abuse, emotional deprivation, defensiveness/shame, and social isolation/shame that are described here.

Abandonment/instability. There is difficulty in developing trusting relationships, as others are viewed as unstable or unreliable.

Mistrust/abuse. Individuals may expect that others may want to hurt, abuse, ridicule, or manipulate them.

Emotional deprivation. Others may disappoint the client by not meeting their need for emotional support by providing sufficient caring or protection.

Defensiveness/shame. Individuals may feel bad, unlovable, or inferior, which may result in being sensitive to criticism, rejection, or blame. They may be self-conscious about these characteristics.

Social isolation/shame. There may be a sense of being alone, of not belonging to a group or community, and generally being different from others.

There may be other schemas than these, but these are common ones. Typically, these schemas started in childhood and continue into adulthood. When these schemas are activated by thoughts or perceptions of events, individuals may feel anxious or depressed, which may show themselves in psychological disorders.

One of the first tasks of the therapist is to do an assessment of the specific schemas of the client to determine the themes of problems important to the client. To do this, the therapist must first identify the schemas that are causing problems. Second, the therapist activates the schema by using imagery or role playing. Often the subject of the imagery or role playing is a disturbing incident that took place in childhood. These schemas are then dealt with in the change phase of therapy. Third, the therapist conceptualizes the schemas or themes of the client as well as the feelings and actions that the client shows when the schema is activated. Last, the therapist describes the assessment of the schemas or themes to the client. This then sets the stage for therapeutic change.

In general, the therapist uses the same cognitive and behavioral techniques that have been described in this chapter. There are a few special techniques that the therapist may use directly related to working with schemas. One example is an experiential or gestalt type of technique, *schema dialogue*, in which the client role plays the "voice" or message of the schema. After this, the client can role play or articulate their "voice" or healthy response to the schema. The gestalt two-chair technique is used with the client playing the role of the message of the schema in one chair and the healthy response to the schema in the other chair. Another technique is the *life review* in which the therapist asks the client to show evidence to support or refute the schema. These and other schema-focused techniques may be used in addition to other cognitive therapy techniques. Evaluation of schema-focused therapy is somewhat limited, but some studies provide support for this approach (Lobbestael, van Vreeswijk, & Arntz, 2007, 2008; Riso et al., 2007).

Treatment Manuals

Several books, many of them treatment manuals, describe how cognitive therapy can be applied to specific populations and to disorders. Some have covered the application of cognitive therapy to eating disorders, *Treating Bulimia Nervosa and Binge Eating: An Integrated Metacognitive and Cognitive Therapy Manual* (Cooper, Todd, & Wells, 2009). Other books cover the application of cognitive therapy to personality disorders, such as *Cognitive Therapy for Personality Disorders: A Guide for Clinicians* (Davidson, 2008). Because of their specificity, recommending specific interviewing strategies, protocols, and questionnaires, these serve as treatment manuals. *Cognitive-Behavioral Therapy for Bipolar Disorder* (Lam et al., 1999) and *Bipolar Disorder: A Cognitive Therapy Approach* (Newman, Leahy, Beck, Reilly-Harrington, & Gyulai, 2001) show specific ways for dealing with the depressive and manic phases of bipolar depression. Related to treatment of depression is a manual for working with suicidal patients, *Cognitive Therapy for Suicidal Patients: Scientific and Clinical Applications* (Wenzel et al., 2009). Cognitive therapy has also been applied to psychoses, as illustrated by *A Casebook of Cognitive Therapy for Psychoses* (Morrison, 2001), *Cognitive Therapy of Schizophrenia* (Kingdon & Turkington, 2005), and *Schizophrenia: Cognitive Theory, Research, and Therapy* (Beck, Rector, Stolar, & Grant, 2009). Because of the popularity of cognitive therapy and the number of individuals undertaking research studies, more books about applications to specific psychological disorders are likely to be written in the future.

Using Cognitive Therapy with Other Theories

Because cognitive therapy has both behavioral and affective components, it draws on other theories, especially behavior therapy and REBT. When using cognitive therapy, many behavioral treatments are incorporated, such as in vivo exposure, positive reinforcement, modeling, relaxation techniques, homework, and graded activities. Cognitive therapy shares with behavior therapy the emphasis on a collaborative relationship with the client and the use of experimentation in trying behavioral and cognitive homework. The term *cognitive-behavioral* is used to describe therapists that combine techniques from Chapter 8 (behavioral) with those from Chapter 9 (cognitive) and this chapter (cognitive). While drawing from behavior therapy for their work, cognitive therapists also attend to the feelings and moods of the client, incorporating empathic aspects of person-centered therapy. To further integrate the client's experiential and affective experiences into therapy, Fodor (1987) suggests using gestalt enactment techniques such as the empty chair or awareness exercises. Also, the gestalt approach to imagery uses emotional responses as a way of accessing cognitions to provide an overview of beliefs and to help clients be aware of painful affect (Edwards, 1989). By using behavioral and gestalt methods, cognitive therapists make their therapeutic treatments more flexible and more effective in dealing with the noncognitive aspects of individuals' problems.

Cognitive therapy shares with rational emotive behavior therapy (REBT) many techniques and strategies, but there are some important differences. Whereas REBT challenges irrational beliefs, cognitive therapy helps clients change beliefs into hypotheses they can contest. Another important difference is that cognitive therapy approaches psychological disorders differentially by identifying cognitive schemas and distortions as well as behaviors and feelings that are common to each disorder, whereas REBT focuses on methods to change irrational beliefs themselves regardless of the nature of the psychological disorder. Although they differ as to the philosophical approach to psychological disturbances, both cognitive and REBT practitioners are likely to make use of Socratic and disputational methods in dealing with clients' belief systems.

Originally developed because of Beck's dissatisfactions with psychoanalytic therapy, cognitive therapy uses some psychoanalytic constructs. Both cognitive and psychoanalytic therapies believe that behavior can be influenced by beliefs. However, psychoanalysis emphasizes the importance of unconscious beliefs, whereas cognitive therapy focuses on the conscious belief system. The concept of automatic thoughts in cognitive therapy bears a similarity to the preconscious of psychoanalysis.

Not only do cognitive therapists draw on a variety of other theories in their work but also other theorists have drawn heavily on cognitive therapy. Behavior therapy and cognitive therapy share an emphasis on detailed assessment and experimenting with methods of change. Additionally, Adlerian therapists and rational emotive behavior therapists emphasize Beck's cognitive methods in their approach and make use of many of the cognitive strategies discussed in this chapter. Also, therapists using other theories may not use detailed cognitive assessment in their work but may examine their clients' cognitive distortions and use cognitive techniques, such as decatastrophizing, to help bring about change. Because cognitive therapy, which was started in the 1960s, has become popular quickly, the integration of it into other therapies is likely to continue.

Research

For many years there has been great interest in studying the effectiveness of cognitive therapy, particularly in contrast with behavior, psychodynamic, and psychopharmacological treatments. Butler and J. S. Beck (2001) reviewed

14 meta-analyses on cognitive therapy that included 325 studies and 9,138 individuals. The meta-analyses included several psychological disorders and had many findings, the most significant being that cognitive therapy provided help to those who received treatment as contrasted to those who received a placebo or other control condition. Without doubt, the greatest amount of effort has been devoted to research on depression. Several meta-analyses on research into effective methods of treating depression are presented here, as are two studies comparing cognitive therapy with other treatments. Additionally, research on the effectiveness of cognitive therapy as treatment for generalized anxiety and obsessional disorders is described. The review of research in this section is very brief and does not explore the application of cognitive therapy to other psychological disorders. Treatment for all three of these disorders is considered to be research-supported psychological treatment.

Research on Depression

Much attention has been given to studying the effectiveness of Beck's cognitive therapeutic approach to depression, as can be seen by several meta-analyses that evaluate it. In a meta-analysis examining 58 investigations, Robinson, Berman, and Neimeyer (1990) found that depressed clients benefited considerably from psychotherapy, with gains comparable to pharmacotherapy. Gloaguen, Cottraux, Cucherat, and Blackburn (1998) reviewed 72 studies of adults using randomized clinical trials. They concluded that cognitive therapy helped patients significantly better when compared to waiting lists, antidepressants, and miscellaneous therapies. Cognitive therapies for depression did not produce significantly better results than behavior therapy. Studying adolescents, cognitive therapy was found to be superior to wait-list, relaxation, and supportive therapy at the conclusion of treatment and in 6- to 12-week follow-ups in 13 studies (Reinecke, Ryan, & DuBois, 1998). Additionally, a large-scale study—Treatment for Adolescents with Depression Study (TADS)—has shown that combining pharmacological treatment with cognitive and behavioral methods can be effective in helping depressed adolescents (Ginsburg, Albano, Findling, Kratochvil, & Walkup, 2005). This conclusion is shared by Aaronson, Katzman, and Gorman (2007), who reviewed many studies and concluded that medication and psychotherapy were more effective than either alone. Cognitive methods that were helpful in treating depression included mood monitoring, identifying cognitive distortions, and developing realistic counterthoughts (Rohde, Feeny, & Robins, 2005). Cognitive therapy for depressive symptoms has shown similar patterns of change in reducing unwanted behaviors and helping patients return to a normal or less depressed state (Bhar et al., 2008).

The application of cognitive therapy to depression continues to be a widely investigated topic. For example, depressed patients who did assigned psychotherapy homework were found to improve much more than patients who did little or no homework (Burns & Spangler, 2000). Interestingly, severity of depression did not seem to be a factor in whether or not patients did homework. What else might be responsible for improvement in cognitive therapy? Tang and DeRubeis (1999) found that gains in the treatment of cognitive therapy for depression were often the result of significant changes in thinking about problems related to depression that occurred in the previous session. Beevers & Miller (2005) reported that individuals who had participated in cognitive therapy (as compared to family therapy) were able to deal more effectively with negative thoughts and not necessarily become depressed by the thoughts. Another study (Teasdale et al., 2001) suggests that relapse can be reduced by training patients to be intentional rather than automatic in the way they process unwanted thoughts. Rather than change their beliefs, they can label them as "events in the mind." In a study of 35 moderately to severely depressed patients, relapse was also shown to be reduced by developing and using cognitive therapy techniques (Strunk, DeRubeis, Chiu, & Alvarez, 2007).

Comparisons have been made with other theories of therapy. Comparing person-centered therapy with cognitive therapy in a sample of 65 French patients, Cottraux et al. (2009) found that patients in cognitive therapy were retained in therapy longer and showed better long-term improvement on global measures than those in person-centered therapy. Also, those in cognitive therapy showed earlier improvements in feeling hopeful and acting less impulsively than those in person-centered therapy. Both REBT and cognitive therapy have been shown to bring about changes in automatic thoughts, dysfunctional attitudes, and irrational beliefs (a REBT concept; Szentagotai, David, Lupu, & Cosman, 2008). Also, both cognitive therapy and REBT were found to be much more cost effective than pharmacotherapy in a sample of Romanian patients with a major depressive disorder (Sava, Yates, Lupu, Szentagotai, & David, 2009). Comparing cognitive therapy to pharmacotherapy, combining the two was more effective than using either one alone with a sample of 120 adults with a major depressive disorder (Shamsaei, Rahimi, Zarabian, & Sedehi, 2008). Discussing cognitive therapy and interpersonal psychotherapy, Weissman (2007) concludes that both remain the two therapies that are most often tested in studies of unipolar depression.

Research on Generalized Anxiety

In their review of the effectiveness of cognitive therapy with patients who have symptoms of generalized anxiety disorder, Hollon and Beck (1994) conclude that cognitive therapy is successful in reducing individuals' perception of threat and reducing levels of distress. They report that cognitive therapy has been more effective than behavioral or pharmacological therapy, especially in maintaining therapeutic change over time. One reason that cognitive therapy may be superior to behavioral therapy in working with generalized anxiety disorders is that there are few specific target behaviors for behavioral therapy to focus on, whereas cognitive therapy can focus on distorted cognitions regarding beliefs related to threat. However, a meta-analysis of five studies that compared cognitive therapy with relaxation therapy found that both helped in the treatment of generalized anxiety disorder (Siev & Chambless, 2007). A meta-analysis of 16 studies on the treatment of general anxiety disorder showed that cognitive behavior therapy was significantly more effective than a wait-list condition (Gould, Safren, Washington, & Otto, 2004). Also, combining cognitive therapy with behavior therapy was more effective than behavior therapy alone. The treatment focused on helping patients tolerate uncertainty, challenge erroneous beliefs about worry, and improve their approach to solving problems that contributed to anxiety. A review of efficacy of generalized anxiety disorder and other anxiety disorders gives evidence for the effectiveness of cognitive therapy (McManus, Grey, & Shafran, 2008).

Further insight into differential effectiveness between behavior therapy and cognitive behavior therapy can be seen in a study by Butler, Fennell, Robson, and Gelder (1991). They provided individual treatment lasting between 4 and 12 sessions to 57 patients who met the criteria for generalized anxiety disorder.

Those who received behavior therapy were treated with muscle relaxation and, where possible, made a hierarchy of anxious stimuli to which they were exposed in vivo. For the cognitive behavior therapy sample, patients kept records of dysfunctional thoughts and developed skills to examine the thoughts and to formulate alternatives to them that could be tested in subsequent homework. The authors report a clear advantage of cognitive-behavioral over behavior therapy, because cognitive techniques, more so than behavioral ones, tend to help individuals by dealing with ways of thinking that promote anxiety as well as the consequences of anxiety (the latter is the focus of behavior therapy).

Research on Obsessional Disorders

As described in Chapter 8, exposure and ritual prevention has been shown to be effective for dealing with obsessive-compulsive disorders. Abramowitz (1997), reviewing studies that compared cognitive techniques to exposure and ritual prevention, found cognitive techniques to be at least as effective as exposure. These approaches overlap somewhat, so it is difficult to separate them. When there are obsessions or ruminations but no compulsive or ritualistic behavior, the appropriate treatment method is less clear. In a study of 35 outpatients with obsessive-compulsive symptoms, those who received cognitive therapy in addition to exposure therapy were less likely to drop out of treatment than those who received exposure treatment alone (Vogel, Stiles, & Götestam, 2004). Clark (2005) believes that cognitive therapy can be useful in supplementing exposure therapy in the treatment of obsessive-compulsive disorder. This is confirmed by Whittal, Robichaud, Thordarson, and McLean (2008), who did a 2-year follow-up study comparing group cognitive therapy to group exposure plus response prevention. Most scores on the Yale-Brown Obsessive Compulsive scale were lower for the exposure plus response prevention group than for cognitive therapy. Another study compared two pairs of twins with obsessive-compulsive disorder and found that exposure plus ritual prevention helped to decrease obsessive-compulsive symptoms whether or not it was combined with cognitive-behavior therapy (Twohig, Whittal, & Peterson, 2009). Described next is an exploratory study that uses several single-subject studies to make recommendations for further research and therapy.

In treating obsessive ruminations, Salkovskis and Westbrook (1989) suggest that obsessions can be divided into obsessional thoughts and cognitive rituals. Using a method somewhat similar to exposure and ritual prevention, they suggest methods for preventing clients from engaging in cognitive rituals. Following up on a preliminary study by Salkovskis and Westbrook, Freeston et al. (1997) studied 29 patients with obsessive thoughts but not compulsive rituals. They used procedures similar to those of Salkovskis and Westbrook, finding that the treatment was effective in patients after a 6-month follow-up. A manual (McGinn & Sanderson, 1999) combines the work on exposure/ritual prevention and Beck's and Salkovskis's approach to cognitive restructuring in treating obsessive-compulsive symptoms.

Although I have given examples of research studies evaluating the effectiveness of cognitive therapy with depression, generalized anxiety disorder, and obsessive thinking, cognitive therapy has been evaluated with many other disorders. Particularly, much research has recently been done on the effectiveness of cognitive therapy in treating individuals with attention deficit disorder with hyperactivity (McDermott, 2009), panic disorder (Otto, Powers, Stathopoulou, & Hofmann, 2008), agoraphobia, and posttraumatic stress (Butler & Beck, 2001; Hollon, 2003). Another major focus of cognitive therapy has been treatment for drug and alcohol abuse (Newman, 2008), and cigarette smoking (Perkins, Conklin, & Levine, 2008). Severe disorders such as schizophrenia have also been the subject of research, but less extensively than other psychological concerns (Beck et al., 2009; Beck, Rector, Stolar, & Grant, 2009; Sensky, 2005). Other research areas include evaluating the effectiveness of cognitive therapy with children, couples, and families.

Gender Issues

In addressing the application of cognitive therapy to women, Davis and Padesky (1989) and Dunlap (1997) describe how gender issues can be incorporated in dealing with women's concerns. Similarly, Bem's (1981) gender schema theory can be used to comprehend how gender schemas interact with other schemas in understanding psychological problems. In their analysis of cognitive distortions that are common to women, Davis and Padesky (1989) describe issues related to valuing oneself, feeling skilled, and feeling responsible in relationships, concerns that may occur in issues of body image, living alone, relationships with partners, parenting roles, work issues, and victimization. For Davis and Padesky, the advantage of cognitive therapy is that it teaches clients to help themselves and to take responsibility for recognizing negative self-schemas that interfere with being autonomous and powerful. With regard to treating women who are depressed, Piasecki and Hollon (1987) and Dunlap (1997) describe the challenge of using cognitive therapy to help women dispute their thoughts and beliefs while at the same time recognizing the value of their own views. Because cognitive therapy is active and structured, therapists need to be careful not to take too much power or responsibility in the therapeutic contract.

Cognitive therapy can also be helpful to men because of several features, including an emphasis on problem solving (Mahalik, 2005). Men may be more comfortable with cognitive therapy's emphasis on thoughts rather than emotions. This is likely to be particularly true of men who are reluctant to express themselves emotionally. Also, men who are experiencing gender role conflicts may prefer, as some research evidence suggests (Mahalik, 2005), a cognitive approach to treatment. Traditionally socialized men also may prefer the structured and action-oriented approach of cognitive therapy to others described in this text.

Cognitive therapy has also been applied to gay and lesbians (Martell, 2008; Martell, Safren, & Prince, 2004) who are dealing with issues of "coming out" (who to tell about being gay, how to tell, and when to tell), depression, anxiety, and relationship issues. Martell et al. (2004) combine cognitive therapy with behavior therapy in the treatment of a wide variety of problems. They also provide resources for therapists working with gay and lesbian clients. Books about sexuality and the coming-out process can be particularly helpful to gay men who are dealing with coming out to others to learn about the gay subculture and to integrate their own beliefs about sexuality. Because there is much misinformation about being gay and potential shame about being gay, the therapeutic process may proceed gradually, with the client taking responsibility for whom, when, and how to tell about being gay (Martell, 2008). Because of societal discrimination against gays and lesbians, it is important to have insights about the cognitive and behavioral treatment of psychological disorders as it impacts gay and lesbian clients.

Multicultural Issues

Just as gender values and beliefs can be seen in cognitive therapy as gender schemas, so can cultural values and beliefs be viewed as cultural schemas. Because cognitive therapists emphasize a collaborative relationship with their clients, they are likely to be able to ascertain values and beliefs that interfere with effective psychological functioning. Such beliefs can affect how patients perceive therapy and the therapist. Attending to spiritual beliefs of clients and their values that are a part of their statements about themselves can be an important part of cognitive therapy. Hodge (2008) illustrates this by applying spiritual values important to Islamic clients and beliefs important to Christian clients when using cognitive therapy. However, other beliefs such as Buddhist philosophy can also enrich the methods that cognitive therapists use (Dowd & McCleery, 2007). Some cultural groups may be more likely to deal with certain cultural issues than others. For many Latinos and Latinas, spiritual issues are important. These issues must be dealt with respectfully and not assumed to be symptoms of the problem (Kohn-Wood, Hudson, & Graham, 2008). In the United States, African Americans as well as other cultural groups may encounter discrimination in the workplace and other aspects of their lives. Respecting the experience of discrimination and working to help the client overcome it can be an important aspect of the therapeutic experience (Kohn-Wood et al., 2008). Also, cognitive therapy focuses not only on the belief system but also on behaviors and feelings, providing a broad framework to deal with multicultural issues. Such an approach often counteracts the stigma of mental illness that people who are not familiar with the culture of psychotherapy may possess. For many people, the active approach of cognitive therapy in which suggestions can be given during the first session may be quite attractive.

In their writings, cognitive therapists have focused more on treatment of specific psychological disorders and research on the effectiveness of treatment than they have on cultural issues. Some literature exists on psychotherapeutic approaches with different minority groups. Group cognitive therapy for African American women with panic disorder had similar recovery rates to those of White Americans (Carter, Sbrocco, Gore, Marin, & Lewis, 2003). In large-scale studies such as the Treatment for Adolescents with Depression Study (TADS; Sweeney, Robins, Ruberu, & Jones, 2005), care was taken to include samples of African American and Latino adolescents. For depressed adolescents in Puerto Rico, both cognitive therapy and Klerman's interpersonal process therapy (Chapter 15) were more successful in reducing depressive symptoms than a waiting-list control group (Rosello & Bernal, 1999). The researchers note that both treatments were changed slightly to fit with Puerto Rican cultural values. However, interpersonal process therapy seemed to fit the adolescents' cultural values better than cognitive therapy, as the former brought about changes in self-concept and adaptability, whereas cognitive therapy did not. Dowd (2003) suggests that to be more open to other cultures, cognitive therapists may need to listen more carefully to their clients, spend time in other cultures, or possibly learn another language. Sometimes it is necessary to use an interpreter in therapy, as the client and counselor may not be able to speak each other's language.

Working this way can be effective. However, it is often necessary to use trained interpreters, as untrained interpreters can summarize either client or therapist, not translate accurately, or respond for the patient instead of translating what the patient says (d'Ardenne & Farmer, 2009). As cognitive therapy's popularity spreads, so do its application to individuals of different cultures and the need to be responsive to cultural issues.

Group Therapy

In cognitive group therapy, therapeutic change comes not as a result of insights that arise from group interaction but as a result of clients making use of change strategies that are consistent with the cognitive model. White (2000b) uses this description to explain the cognitive approach:

> To gain a better understanding of yourselves, we want to be able to track your ongoing thoughts, feelings, behaviors. This is what's called using the cognitive model. The more you are able to recognize these immediate reactions on your part, your experience will probably make more sense to you and you'll be able to determine where you want to make changes. (p. 4)

The cognitive approach to each group session tends to center on specific, structured, and problem-oriented changes. Thus, it would be appropriate before each session to use a measure of change, such as the Beck Depression Inventory, to monitor alternatives and symptoms. Similarly, cognitive interventions in group tend to be specific and, as is shown next, to emphasize practicing cognitions and behaviors. Some cognitive groups may use a specific type of technique, such as problem solving, whereas others may be designed to help people with the same disorder, such as depression.

A method of applying cognitive group therapy to depression is somewhat illustrative of the general approach taken to group therapy by cognitive therapists (White, 2000a). For cognitive group therapy to be successful, group cohesiveness and a task focus must be present. *Cohesiveness* refers to looking forward to relating to other members, to thinking about them between sessions, and having compassion for the other members. A task focus is one that seeks to resolve problems. To bring about task focus and cohesion, the therapist should model participation and collaboration. This therapist may take a directing role, not in the sense of telling group members what to do but in the sense of organizing the group. Some cognitive group therapists conduct the group standing and write notes on a blackboard. The themes likely to emerge and be dealt with by patients and therapist are loss (loss of energy, loss of appetite, loss of relationships), anger or irritability, and guilt about not meeting responsibilities.

Free (2007) has developed a manual for a psychoeducational approach to cognitive group therapy. The program consists of 25 sessions with five modules and each module having four to six sessions that last about an hour each. The manual provides information about the administration of the program, including PowerPoint slides. The five psychoeducational modules are described here.

Module One: Surface beliefs and processes. This module includes group basics, discussion of thinking and feeling, logical errors, use of appropriate logic, and countering logical errors.

Module Two: Beneath the surface: Exploring your negative belief system. Included is a general model of emotional, behavioral, and personality disorders. Also, identifying negative schema content using the vertical arrow method is explained. Description of advanced vertical arrows and subjective units of disturbance follow. Then, making sense of beliefs by categorizing beliefs and making cognitive maps is discussed. Last, participants make sense of their beliefs in developing a cognitive diagnosis.

Module Three: Testing your beliefs. In this section beliefs can be changed and participants learn about and apply adversarial analysis. Next participants challenge their beliefs using an investigative approach. Then participants learn how to do a scientific analysis. This is followed by learning ways to consolidate information.

Module Four: Changing your thinking and feeling. Participants learn about countering and participating in an adversarial debate. Other topics are propositional perceptual shift, emotional shift, and schema content shift. Learning how to rebalance schemas and how to use imagery with schemas follows. Negative schema injury is discussed, as is strong nurturing-self imagery.

Module Five: Changing your counterproductive behavior. Included in this behavioral section are selecting behavior to change, making a behavioral self-change plan, problem solving, cognitive-behavioral rehearsal, and maintaining gains.

In Free's (2007) psychoeducational cognitive approach to group described here, several common elements appear. Assessment is specific, with behaviors and cognitions targeted for change. The first four modules focus on cognitive change, the last module focuses on behavioral change. Group members collaborate with the therapist to suggest new ways of thinking about situations and new behaviors to try out. Experimenting with new alternatives to old problems, both within and outside of the group, is an important aspect of group cognitive therapy.

Summary

Developed by Aaron Beck from his observations about the impact of patients' belief systems on their psychological functioning, cognitive therapy examines the effect of maladaptive thinking on psychological disorders while at the same time acknowledging the importance of affect and behavior on psychological functioning. As cognitive therapy has developed, it has continued to draw on psychological research into individuals' belief systems and the study of how people process information from their environment. An important aspect of cognitive therapy is the automatic thoughts, thoughts that individuals may not be aware of, but that make up their belief systems, called *cognitive schemas*.

In his work with patients, Beck identified cognitive distortions that affect individuals' feelings, thoughts, and beliefs, such as all-or-nothing thinking, overgeneralization, and catastrophizing. To change these beliefs, a thorough assessment is given by attention to distortions inherent in certain thoughts. To further the process of assessment in therapy, Beck and his colleagues have developed a number of instruments for different psychological disorders that assess relevant cognitions and behaviors.

In their therapeutic approach, cognitive therapists collaborate with their clients to assess and change behaviors. Often in the therapeutic process, the therapist may take an instructional role, using techniques such as guided discovery and Socratic dialogue to identify maladaptive beliefs and help clients develop insights into their beliefs. Within the session, therapists often go over homework, examine current beliefs, and develop alternatives. As well as using behavioral and affective approaches, cognitive therapists make use of techniques such as decatastrophizing, labeling distortions, and cognitive rehearsal.

More than other theories, cognitive therapy has identified particular distorted beliefs that are typical of each of several psychological disorders. Of all the disorders, depression has received the most attention, as it was the focus of Beck's early therapy and research. Just as there has been much emphasis on specific approaches to each psychological disorder, researchers have studied the effectiveness of a variety of cognitive approaches to many common psychological disorders, often comparing cognitive treatments to behavioral and pharmacological approaches.

Theories in Action DVD: Cognitive Therapy

Basic Concepts Used in the Role-Play	**Questions About the Role-Play**
• Monitoring thoughts • Generalizing from thoughts • Overgeneralization • Catastrophizing • Cognitive schemas • Automatic thoughts • Choosing new thoughts • Homework	1. How does Karen generalize from her early life experiences to her current relationship with John? 2. How are Karen's automatic thoughts different from her cognitive schemas? (p. 374) 3. How might the Dysfunctional Thought Record described on page 382 help Karen with her problems of loss? 4. What is the nature of the therapeutic relationship in cognitive therapy? (p. 384) How typical of cognitive therapy is Dr. McAuliffe's relationship with Karen? Explain.

Suggested Readings

Beck, J. S. (1995). *Cognitive therapy: Basics and beyond.* New York: Guilford. Written by Aaron Beck's daughter, Judith, this is an excellent overview of cognitive therapy. Diagrams and case examples add to the clarity of this book.

Beck, J. S. (2005). *Cognitive therapy for challenging problems: What to do when the basics don't work.* New York: Guilford. This book follows up on the previous book (Beck, 1995). Judith Beck gives many suggestions and uses examples to help therapists deal with problems that occur in cognitive therapy.

Wills, F. (2009). *Beck's cognitive therapy: Distinctive features.* New York: Routledge/Taylor & Francis

Group. Divided into two parts, the first part describes Beck's theory of cognitive therapy. The second part describes ways to apply cognitive therapy to client problems.

Freeman, A., & Dattilio, F. M. (1992). *Comprehensive casebook of cognitive therapy.* New York: Plenum. A brief explanation of treatment strategy along with a case history are given for about 30 different psychological disorders and/or patient populations. The case examples are particularly helpful in understanding a cognitive therapy conceptualization of psychological dysfunction.

References

Aaronson, C. J., Katzman, G.P. & Gorman, J. M. (2007). Combination pharmacotherapy and psychotherapy for the treatment of major depressive and anxiety disorders. In P. E. Nathan & J. M. Gorman (Eds.), *A guide to treatments that work* (3rd ed.). New York: Oxford University Press.

Abramowitz, J. S. (1997). Effectiveness of psychological and pharmacological treatment of obsessive compulsive disorder: A quantitative review. *Journal of Consulting and Clinical Psychology, 65,* 44–52.

Barlow, D. (Ed.). (2007). *Clinical handbook of psychological disorders: A step-by step treatment manual* (4th ed.). New York: Guilford.

Barnhofer, T., Crane, C., Hargus, E., Amarasinghe, M., Winder, R., & Williams, J. M. G. (2009). Mindfulness-based cognitive therapy as a treatment for chronic depression: A preliminary study. *Behaviour Research and Therapy, 47*(5), 366–373.

Beck, A. T. (1961). A systematic investigation of depression. *Comprehensive Psychiatry, 2,* 162–170.

Beck, A. T. (1964). Thinking and depression. 2. Theory and therapy. *Archives of General Psychiatry, 10,* 561–571.

Beck, A. T. (1967). *Depression: Clinical, experimental, and theoretical aspects.* New York: Hoeber.

Beck, A. T. (1976). *Cognitive therapy and the emotional disorders.* New York: International Universities Press.

Beck, A. T. (1991). Cognitive therapy: A 30-year retrospective. *American Psychologist, 46,* 368–375.

Beck, A. T. (1999). *Prisoners of hate: The cognitive basis of anger, hostility, and violence.* New York: HarperCollins.

Beck, A. T. (2001). Biography of Aaron T. Beck, M.D. *The Corsini Encyclopedia of Psychology and Behavioral Science* (3rd ed., pp. 177–178). New York: Wiley.

Beck, A. T., & Weishaar, M. (1989). Cognitive therapy. In A. Freeman, K. M. Simon, L. E. Beutler, & H. Arkowitz (Eds.), *Comprehensive handbook of cognitive therapy* (pp. 21–36). New York: Plenum.

Beck, A. T., Emery, G., & Greenberg, R. L. (1985). *Anxiety disorders and phobias: A cognitive perspective.* New York: Basic Books.

Beck, A. T., Freeman, A., Davis, D. D., & Associates. (2004). *Cognitive therapy of personality disorders* (2nd ed.). New York: Guilford.

Beck, A. T., Kovacs, M., & Weissman, A. (1979). Assessment of suicidal intention: The Scale for Suicidal Ideation. *Journal of Consulting and Clinical Psychology, 47,* 343–352.

Beck, A. T., Rector, N. A., Stolar, N., & Grant, P. (2009). *Schizophrenia: Cognitive theory, research, and therapy.* New York, NY: Guilford Press.

Beck, A. T., Rush, A. J., Shaw, B. F., & Emery, G. (1979). *Cognitive therapy of depression.* New York: Guilford.

Beck, A. T., Ward, C. H., Mendelson, M., Mock, J. E., & Erbaugh, J. K. (1961). An inventory for measuring depression. *Archives of General Psychiatry, 4,* 561–571.

Beck, A. T., Wright, F. D., Newman, C. E., & Liese, B. (1993). *Cognitive therapy of substance abuse.* New York: Guilford.

Beck, J. S. (1995). *Cognitive therapy: Basics and beyond.* New York: Guilford.

Beck, J. S. (2005). *Cognitive therapy for challenging problems: What to do when the basics don't work.* New York: Guilford.

Beck, J. S., & Tompkins, M. A. (2007). Cognitive therapy. In N. Kazantzis & L. L'Abate (Eds.), *Handbook of homework assignments in psychotherapy: Research, practice, prevention* (pp. 51–63). New York: Springer.

Beevers, C. G., & Miller, I. W. (2005). Unlinking negative cognition and symptoms of depression: Evidence of a specific treatment effect for cognitive therapy. *Journal of Consulting and Clinical Psychology, 73*(1), 68–77.

Bem, S. L. (1981). Gender schema theory: A cognitive account of sex typing. *Psychological Review, 88,* 354–364.

Bhar, S. S., Gelfand, L. A., Schmid, S. P., Gallop, R., DeRubeis, R. J., Hollon, S. D., Amsterdam, J. D., Shelton, R. C., & Beck, A. T. (2008). Sequence of improvement in depressive symptoms across cognitive therapy and pharmacotherapy. *Journal of Affective Disorders, 110*(1–2), 161–166.

Blankstein, K. R., & Segal, Z. V. (2001). Cognitive assessment: Issues and methods. In K. S. Dobson (Ed.), *Handbook of cognitive behavioral therapies* (2nd ed., pp. 40–85). New York: Guilford.

Burns, D. D., & Spangler, D. L. (2000). Does psychotherapy homework lead to improvements in depression in cognitive-behavioral therapy or does improvement lead to increased homework compliance? *Journal of Consulting and Clinical Psychology, 68,* 46–56.

Butler, A. C., & Beck, J. S. (2001). Cognitive therapy outcomes: A review of meta-analyses. *Journal of the Norwegian Psychological Association, 38,* 698–706.

Butler, G., Fennell, M., Robson, P., & Gelder, M. (1991). Comparison of behavior therapy and cognitive behavior therapy in the treatment of generalized anxiety disorder. *Journal of Consulting and Clinical Psychology, 59,* 167–175.

Carter, M. M., Sbrocco, T., Gore, K. L., Marin, N. W., & Lewis, E. L. (2003). Cognitive-behavioral group therapy versus a wait-list control in the treatment of African American women with panic disorder. *Cognitive Therapy and Research, 27*(5), 505–518.

Clark, D. A. (2004). *Cognitive-behavioral therapy for obsessive compulsive disorder.* New York: Guilford.

Clark, D. A. (2005). Focus on "cognition" in cognitive behavior therapy for OCD: Is it really necessary? *Cognitive Behaviour Therapy, 34*(3), 131–139.

Clark, D. A., Beck, A. T., & Alford, B. A. (1999). *Scientific foundations of cognitive theory and therapy of depression*. New York: Wiley.

Cooper, M., Todd, G., & Wells, A. (2009). *Treating bulimia nervosa and binge eating: An integrated meta-cognitive and cognitive therapy manual*. New York: Routledge/Taylor & Francis Group.

Cottraux, J., Note, I. D., Boutitie, F., Milliery, M., Genouihlac, V., Yao, S. N., Note, B., Mollard, E., Bonasse, F., Gaillard, S., Djamoussian, D., de Mey Guillard, C., Culem, A., & Gueyffier, F. (2009). Cognitive therapy versus Rogerian supportive therapy in borderline personality disorder: Two-year follow-up of a controlled pilot study. *Psychotherapy and Psychosomatics*, *78*(5), 307–316.

Crane, R. (2009). *Mindfulness-based cognitive therapy: Distinctive features*. New York: Routledge.

D'Ardenne, P., & Farmer, E. (2009). Using interpreters in trauma therapy. In N. Grey (Ed.), *A casebook of cognitive therapy for traumatic stress reactions* (pp. 283–300). New York: Routledge/Taylor & Francis Group.

Dattilio, F. M., & Freeman, A. (1992). Introduction to cognitive therapy. In A. Freeman & F. M. Dattilio (Eds.), *Comprehensive casebook of cognitive therapy* (pp. 3–12). New York: Plenum.

Davidson, K. (2008). *Cognitive therapy for personality disorders: A guide for clinicians* (2nd ed.). New York: Routledge/Taylor & Francis Group.

Davis, D., & Padesky, C. (1989). Enhancing cognitive therapy with women. In A. Freeman, D. M. Simon, L. E. Beutler, & H. Arkowitz (Eds.), *Comprehensive handbook of cognitive therapy* (pp. 535–558). New York: Plenum.

DeRubeis, R. J., Tang, T. Z. & Beck, A. T. (2001). Cognitive therapy. In K. S. Dobson (Ed.), *Handbook of cognitive-behavioral therapies* (2nd ed., pp. 349–392). New York: Guilford.

Dowd, E. T. (2003). Cultural differences in cognitive therapy. *Behavior Therapist*, *26*(2), 247–249.

Dowd, T., & McCleery, A. (2007). Elements of Buddhist philosophy in cognitive psychotherapy: The role of cultural specifics and universals. *Journal of Cognitive and Behavioral Psychotherapies*, *7*(1), 67–79.

Dozois, D. J. A., & Dobson, K. S. (2004). *The prevention of anxiety and depression: Theory, research, and practice*. Washington, DC: American Psychological Association.

Dunlap, S. J. (1997). *Counseling depressed women*. Louisville, KY: Westminster John Knox Press.

Edwards, D. J. A. (1989). Cognitive restructuring through guided imagery: Lessons from Gestalt therapy. In A. Freeman, K. M. Simon, L. E. Beutler, & H. Arkowitz (Eds.), *Comprehensive handbook of cognitive therapy* (pp. 283–298). New York: Plenum.

Ellis, A. (1962). *Reason and emotion in psychotherapy*. New York: Lyle Stuart.

Evans, S., Ferrando, S., Findler, M., Stowell, C., Smart, C., & Haglin, D. (2008). Mindfulness-based cognitive therapy for generalized anxiety disorder. *Journal of Anxiety Disorders*, *22*(4), 716–721.

Fodor, I. G. (1987). Moving beyond cognitive-behavior therapy: Integrating Gestalt therapy to facilitate personal and interpersonal awareness. In N. S. Jacobson (Ed.), *Psychotherapists in clinical practice* (pp. 190–231). New York: Guilford.

Free, M. L. (2007). *Cognitive therapy in groups: Guidelines and resources for practice*. (2nd ed.). Chichester, United Kingdom: John Wiley.

Freeman, A. (1987). Cognitive therapy: An overview. In A. Freeman & V. Greenwood (Eds.), *Cognitive therapy: Applications in psychiatric and medical settings* (pp. 19–35). New York: Human Science Press.

Freeman, A. (1993). A psychological approach for conceptualizing schematic development for cognitive therapy. In K. T. Kuehlwein & H. Rosen (Eds.), *Cognitive therapy in action* (pp. 54–87). San Francisco: Jossey-Bass.

Freeman, A., & Dattilio, F. M. (1992). *Comprehensive casebook of cognitive therapy*. New York: Plenum.

Freeman, A., & Diefenbeck, C. A. (2005). Personality disorders. In S. M. Freeman, & A. Freeman (Eds.), *Cognitive behavior in nursing practice* (pp. 239–269). New York: Springer.

Freeman, A., & Simon, K. M. (1989). Cognitive therapy of anxiety. In A. Freeman, K. M. Simon, H. Arkowitz, & L. Beutler (Eds.), *Handbook of cognitive therapy* (pp. 347–365). New York: Plenum.

Freeman, A., Pretzer, J., Fleming, B., & Simon, K. M. (1990). *Clinical applications of cognitive therapy*. New York: Plenum.

Freeston, M H., Ladouceur, R., Gagnon, F., Thibodeau, N., Rhéaume, J., Letarte, H., & Bujold, A. (1997). Cognitive-behavioral treatment of obsessive thoughts: A controlled study. *Journal of Consulting and Clinical Psychology*, *65*(3), 405–413.

Fresco, D. M., Moore, M. T., van Dulmen, M. H. M., Segal, Z. V., Ma, S. H., Teasdale, J. D., & Williams, J. M. G. (2007). Initial psychometric properties of the experiences questionnaire: Validation of a self-report measure of decentering. *Behavior Therapy*, *38*(3), 234–246.

Ginsburg, G. S., Albano, A. M., Findling, R. L., Kratochvil, C., & Walkup, J. (2005). Integrating cognitive behavioral therapy and pharmacotherapy in the treatment of adolescent depression. *Cognitive and Behavioral Practice*, *12*(2), 252–262.

Gloaguen, V., Cottraux, J., Cucherat, M., & Blackburn, I. (1998). A meta-analysis of the effects of cognitive therapy in depressed patients. *Journal of Affective Disorders, 49*, 59–72.

Gould, R. A., Safren, S. A., Washington, D. O., & Otto, M. W. (2004). A meta-analytic review of cognitive-behavioral treatments. In R. G. Heimberg, C. L. Turk, & D. S. Mennin (Eds.), *Generalized anxiety disorder: Advances in research and practice* (pp. 248–264). New York: Guilford Press.

Hodge, D. R. (2008). Constructing spiritually modified interventions: Cognitive therapy with diverse populations. *International Social Work, 51*(2), 178–192.

Hollon, S. D. (2003). Does cognitive therapy have an enduring effect? *Cognitive Therapy and Research, 27*(1), 71–75.

Hollon, S. D., & Beck, A. T. (1994). Cognitive and cognitive-behavioral therapies. In A. E. Bergin & S. L. Garfield (Eds.), *Handbook of psychotherapy change* (4th ed., pp. 428–466). New York: Wiley.

Kellogg, S. H., & Young, J. E. (2008). Cognitive therapy. In J. L. Lebow (Ed.), *Twenty-first century psychotherapies: Contemporary approaches to theory and practice.* (pp. 43–79). Hoboken: John Wiley & Sons Inc.

Kelly, G. A. (1955). *The psychology of personal constructs.* New York: Norton.

Kingdon, D. G., & Turkington, D. (2005). *Cognitive therapy of schizophrenia.* New York: Guilford.

Kohn-Wood, L., Hudson, G., & Graham, E. T. (2008). Ethnic minorities. In M. A. Whisman (Ed.), *Adapting cognitive therapy for depression: Managing complexity and comorbidity* (pp. 351–372). New York: Guilford Press.

Kuyken, W., Byford, S., Taylor, R. S., Watkins, E., Holden, E., White, K., Barrett, B., Byng, R., Evans, A., Mullan, E., & Teasdale, J. D. (2008). Mindfulness-based cognitive therapy to prevent relapse in recurrent depression. *Journal of Consulting and Clinical Psychology, 76*(6), 966–978.

Lam, D. H., Jones, S. H., Hayward, P., & Bright, J. A. (1999). *Cognitive therapy for bipolar disorder: A therapist's guide to concepts, methods, and practice.* New York: Wiley.

Leahy, R. L. (2003). *Cognitive therapy techniques: A practitioner's guide.* New York: Guilford.

Ledley, D. R., Marx, B. M., & Heimberg, R. G. (2005). *Making cognitive therapy work: Clinical process for new practitioners.* New York: Guilford.

Liese, B. S. (1993). Coping with AIDS: A cognitive therapy perspective. *Kansas Medicine, 94*, 80–84.

Liese, B. S., & Beck, A. T. (2000). Back to Basics: Fundamental cognitive therapy skills for keeping drug-dependent individuals in treatment. In J. J. Boren, L. S. Onken, & J. D. Blaine (Eds.), *Beyond the therapeutic alliance: Keeping drug-dependent individuals in treatment.* National Institute on Drug Abuse Research Monograph. Washington, DC: Government Printing Office.

Liese, B. S., & Franz, R. A. (1996). Treating substance-use disorders with cognitive therapy: Lessons learned and implications for the future. In P. M. Salkovskis (Ed.), *Frontiers of cognitive therapy* (pp. 470–508). New York: Guilford.

Liese, B. S., & Larson , M. W. (1995). Coping with life-threatening illness: A cognitive therapy perspective. *Journal of Cognitive Psychotherapy: An International Quarterly, 9*, 18–24.

Lobbestael, J., van Vreeswijk, M., & Arntz, A. (2007). Shedding light on schema modes: A clarification of the mode concept and its current research status. *Netherlands Journal of Psychology, 63*(3), 76–85.

Lobbestael, J., Van Vreswijk, M. F., & Arntz, A. (2008). An empirical test of schema mode conceptualizations in personality disorders. *Behaviour Research and Therapy, 46*(7), 854–860.

Mahalik, J. R. (2005). Cognitive therapy for men. In G. E. Good & G. R. Brooks (Eds.), *The new handbook of psychotherapy and counseling with men*: *A comprehensive guide to settings, problems, and treatment approaches* (rev. ed., pp. 217–233). San Francisco: Jossey-Bass.

Martell, C. R. (2008). Lesbian, gay, and bisexual women and men. In M. A. Whisman (Ed.), *Adapting cognitive therapy for depression: Managing complexity and comorbidity* (pp. 373–393). New York: Guilford Press.

Martell, C. R., Safren, S. A., & Prince, S. E. (2004). *Cognitive-behavioral therapies with lesbian, gay, and bisexual clients.* New York: Guilford Press.

McDermott, S. P. (2009). Cognitive therapy for adults with ADHD. In T. E. Brown (Ed.), *ADHD comorbidities: Handbook for ADHD complications in children and adults* (pp. 399–414). Arlington, VA: American Psychiatric Publishing.

McGinn, L. K., & Sanderson, W. C. (1999). *Treatment of obsessive-compulsive disorder.* Northvale, NJ: Aronson.

McManus, F., Grey, N., & Shafran, R. (2008). Cognitive therapy for anxiety disorders: Current status and future challenges. *Behavioural and Cognitive Psychotherapy.* 36(6), 695–704.

McMullin, R. E. (2000). *The new handbook of cognitive therapy techniques.* New York: Norton.

Morrison, A. P. (2001). *A casebook of cognitive therapy for psychosis.* New York: Brunner-Routledge.

Needleman, L. D. C. (1999). *Cognitive case conceptualisation: A guidebook for practitioners*. Mahwah, NJ: Erlbaum.

Newman, C. F. (2008). Substance use disorders. In M. A. Whisman (Ed.), *Adapting cognitive therapy for depression: Managing complexity and comorbidity* (pp. 233–254). New York: Guilford Press.

Newman, C. F., Leahy, R., Beck, A. T., Reilly-Harrington, N., & Gyulai, L. (2001). *Bipolar disorder: A cognitive therapy approach*. Washington, DC: American Psychiatric Press.

Otto, M. W., Powers, M. B., Stathopoulou, G., & Hofmann, S. G. (2008). Panic disorder and social phobia. In M. A. Whisman (Ed.), *Adapting cognitive therapy for depression: Managing complexity and comorbidity* (pp. 185–208). New York: Guilford Press.

Perkins, K. A., Conklin, C. A., & Levine, M. D. (2008). *Cognitive-behavioral therapy for smoking cessation: A practical guidebook to the most effective treatments*. New York: Routledge/Taylor & Francis Group.

Persons, J. B., Davidson, J., & Tompkins, M. A. (2001). *Essential components of cognitive-behavior therapy for depression*. Washington, DC: American Psychological Association.

Piaget, J. (1977). *The development of thought: Equilibration of cognitive structures*. New York: Viking.

Piasecki, J., & Hollon, S. D. (1987). Cognitive therapy for depression: Unexplicated schemata and scripts. In N. Jacobson (Ed.), *Psychotherapists in clinical practice: Cognitive and behavioral perspectives* (pp. 121–152). New York: Guilford.

Purdon, C. (2007). Cognitive therapy for obsessive-compulsive disorder. In M. M. Antony, C. Purdon, & L. J. Summerfeldt (Eds.), *Psychological treatment of obsessive-compulsive disorder: Fundamentals and beyond.* (pp. 111–145). Washington, DC: American Psychological Association.

Rachman, S. (1997). A cognitive theory of obsessions. *Behaviour Research and Therapy, 35*, 793–802.

Reinecke, M. A., Ryan, N. E., & DuBois, D. L. (1998). Cognitive-behavior therapy depression and depressive symptoms during adolescence: A review and meta-analysis. *Journal of the American Academy of Child and Adolescent Psychiatry, 37*, 1006–1007.

Riso, L. P., du Toit, P. L. , Stein, D. J., & Young, J. E. (2007). *Cognitive schemas and core beliefs in psychological problems: A scientist-practitioner guide*. Washington, DC: American Psychological Association.

Robinson, L. A., Berman, J. S., & Neimeyer, R. A. (1990). Psychotherapy for the treatment of depression: A comprehensive review of controlled outcome research. *Psychological Bulletin, 108*, 30–49.

Rohde, P., Feeny, N. C., & Robins, M. (2005). Characteristics and components of the TADS CBT approach. *Cognitive and Behavioral Practice, 12*(2), 186–197.

Ronen, T. (1997). *Cognitive developmental therapy with children*. New York: Wiley.

Ronen, T. (2003). *Cognitive-constructivist psychotherapy with children and adolescents*. New York: Kluwer Academic/Plenum Publishers.

Rosello, J., & Bernal, G. (1999). The efficacy of cognitive-behavioral and interpersonal treatments for depression in Puerto Rican adolescents. *Journal of Consulting and Clinical Psychology, 67*, 734–745.

Salkovskis, P. M., & Westbrook, D. (1989). Behaviour therapy and obsessional ruminations: Can failure be turned into success? *Behaviour Research and Therapy, 27*, 149–160.

Salmon, P., Sephton, S., Weissbecker, I., Hoover, K., Ulmer, C., & Studts, J. L. (2004). Mindfulness meditation in clinical practice. *Cognitive and Behavioral Practice, 11*(4), 434–446.

Sava, F. A., Yates, B. T., Lupu, V., Szentagotai, A., & David, D. (2009). Cost-effectiveness and cost-utility of cognitive therapy, rational emotive behavioral therapy, and fluoxetine (Prozac) in treating clinical depression: A randomized clinical trial. *Journal of Clinical Psychology, 65*(1), 36–52.

Segal, Z. V., Teasdale, J. D., & Williams, J. M. G. (2004). Mindfulness-based cognitive therapy: Theoretical rationale and empirical status. In S. C. Hayes, V. M. Follette, & M. M. Linehan (Eds.), *Mindfulness and acceptance: Expanding the cognitive-behavioral tradition* (pp. 45–65). New York: Guilford Press.

Segal, Z. V., Williams, J. M. G., & Teasdale, J. D. (2002). *Mindfulness-based cognitive therapy for depression: A new approach to preventing relapse*. New York: Guilford Press.

Sensky, T. (2005). The effectiveness of cognitive therapy for schizophrenia: What can we learn from the meta-analyses? *Psychotherapy and Psychosomatics, 74*(3), 131–135.

Shamsaei, F., Rahimi, A., Zarabian, M. K., & Sedehi, M. (2008). Efficacy of pharmacotherapy and cognitive therapy, alone and in combination in major depressive disorder. *Hong Kong Journal of Psychiatry, 18*(2), 76–80.

Siev, J., & Chambless, D. L. (2007). Specificity of treatment effects: Cognitive therapy and relaxation for generalized anxiety and panic disorders. *Journal of Consulting and Clinical Psychology, 75*(4), 513–522.

Spiegler, M. D., & Guevremont, D. C. (2010). *Contemporary behavior therapy* (5th ed.). Belmont, CA: Wadsworth.

Stein, D. J., & Young, J. E. (Eds.). (1992). *Cognitive science and clinical disorders*. San Diego: Academic Press.

Strunk, D. R., DeRubeis, R. J., Chiu, A. W., & Alvarez, J. (2007). Patients' competence in and performance of cognitive therapy skills: Relation to the reduction of relapse risk following treatment for depression. *Journal of Consulting and Clinical Psychology*, 75(4), 523–530.

Sweeney, M., Robins, M., Ruberu, M., & Jones, J. (2005). African-American and Latino families in TADS: Recruitment and treatment considerations. *Cognitive and Behavioral Practice*, 12(2), 221–229.

Szentagotai, A., David, D., Lupu, V., & Cosman, D. (2008). Rational emotive behavior therapy versus cognitive therapy versus pharmacotherapy in the treatment of major depressive disorder: Mechanisms of change analysis. *Psychotherapy: Theory, Research, Practice, Training*, 45(4), 523–538.

Tang, T. Z., & Derubeis, R. J. (1999). Sudden gains and critical sessions in cognitive-behavioral therapy for depression. *Journal of Consulting and Clinical Psychology*, 67, 894–904.

Taylor, S., Kyrios, M., Thordarson, D. D., Steketee, G., & Frost, R. O. (2002). Development and validation for an instrument measuring intrusions and beliefs in obsessive-compulsive disorder. In R. Frost & G. Steketee (Eds.), *Cognitive approaches to obsessions and compulsions: Theory, assessment, and treatment.* (pp. 118–138). Amsterdam: Elsevier/Pergamon.

Teasdale, J. D., Segal, Z. V., & Williams, J. M. G. (2003). Mindfulness training and problem formulation. *Clinical Psychology: Science and Practice*, 10(2), 157–160.

Teasdale, J. P., Scott, J. S., Moore, R. G., Hayhurst, H., Pope, M., & Paykel, E. S. (2001). How does cognitive therapy prevent relapse in residual depression? Evidence from a controlled trial. *Journal of Consulting and Clinical Psychology*, 69, 397–357.

Twohig, M. P., Whittal, M. L., & Peterson, K. A. (2009). Treatment of monozygotic twins with obsessive compulsive disorder using cognitive therapy and exposure with ritual prevention. *Behavioural and Cognitive Psychotherapy*, 37(4), 475–480.

Vogel, P. A., Stiles, T. C., & Götestam, K. G. (2004). Adding cognitive therapy elements to exposure therapy for obsessive compulsive disorder: A controlled study. *Behavioural and Cognitive Psychotherapy*, 32(3), 275–290.

Weissman, A. (1979). *The Dysfunctional Attitudes Scale*. Philadelphia: Center for Cognitive Therapy.

Weissman, M. M. (2007). Cognitive therapy and interpersonal psychotherapy: 30 years later. *American Journal of Psychiatry*, 164(5), 693–696.

Wells, A. (1997). *Cognitive therapy of anxiety disorders: A practice manual and conceptual guide*. New York: Wiley.

Wells, A., & Matthews, G. (1994). *Attention and emotion. A clinical perspective*. Hove, UK: Erlbaum.

Wenzel, A., Brown, G. K., & Beck, A. T. (2009). *Cognitive therapy for suicidal patients: Scientific and clinical applications*. Washington, DC: American Psychological Association.

Whisman, M. A. (Ed.). (2008). *Adapting cognitive therapy for depression: Managing complexity and comorbidity*. New York: Guilford Press.

White, J. R. (2000a). Depression. In J. R. White & A. S. Freeman (Eds.), *Cognitive-behavioral group therapy for specific problems and populations* (pp. 29–62). Washington, DC: American Psychological Association.

White, J. R. (2000b). Introduction. In J. R. White & A. S. Freeman (Eds.), *Cognitive-behavioral group therapy for specific problems and populations* (pp. 3–25). Washington, DC: American Psychological Association.

Whittal, M. L., Robichaud, M., Thordarson, D. S., & McLean, P. D. (2008). Group and individual treatment of obsessive-compulsive disorder using cognitive therapy and exposure plus response prevention: A 2-year follow-up of two randomized trials. *Journal of Consulting and Clinical Psychology*, 76(6), 1003–1014.

Williams, M., Teasdale, J., Segal, Z., & Kabat-Zinn, J. (2007). *The mindful way through depression: Freeing yourself from chronic unhappiness*. New York: Guilford Press.

Wills, F. (2009). *Beck's cognitive therapy: Distinctive features*. New York: Routledge/Taylor & Francis Group.

Young, J. E. (1999). *Cognitive therapy for personality disorders: A schema-focused approach* (3rd ed.). Sarasota, FL: Professional Resource Press.

Young, J. E., & Brown, G. (1999). Young Schema Questionnaire. In J. E. Young (Ed.), *Cognitive therapy for personality disorders: A schema-focused approach* (rev. ed., pp. 63–76). Sarasota, FL: Professional Resources Press.

Young, J. E., Rygh, J. L., Weinberger, A. D., & Beck, A. T. (2008). *Cognitive therapy for depression*. New York, NY: Guilford Press.

Young, J. E., Weinberger, A. D., & Beck, A. T. (2001). Cognitive therapy for depression. In D. H. Barlow (Ed.), *Clinical handbook of psychological disorders: A step-by-step treatment manual* (3rd ed., pp. 264–308). New York: Guilford.

Reality Therapy

Outline of Reality Therapy

PERSONALITY THEORY: CHOICE THEORY

Pictures of Reality

Needs

Choice

Behavior

Choosing Behavior

THEORY OF REALITY THERAPY

Goals of Reality Therapy

Assessment

The Process of Reality Therapy

Friendly involvement

Exploring total behavior

Evaluating behavior

Making plans to do better

Commitment to plans

Therapist Attitudes

Don't accept excuses

No punishment or criticism

Don't give up

Reality Therapy Strategies

Questioning

Being positive

Metaphors

Humor

Confrontation

Paradoxical techniques

Reality therapy is designed to help individuals control their behavior and make choices, often new and difficult ones, in their lives. It is based on choice theory, which assumes that people are responsible for their lives and for what they do, feel, and think. Reality therapy was developed by William Glasser, who was disenchanted with psychoanalysis, believing that it did not teach people to be responsible for their behavior but to look to their past to blame others for it. Reality therapy developed from Glasser's work with difficult and hard-to-reach populations, for example, female adolescent delinquents. He refined the ideas behind reality therapy by using a scientific model called control theory. Glasser's development of reality therapy was based, in some ways, on deficits that he saw in psychoanalysis. He felt that the relationship with the client should be involved and friendly, with appropriate self-disclosure from the therapist, rather than distant, as he perceived the relationship in psychoanalysis. By having clients commit to therapy and explore their behavior, Glasser felt that he could bring about changes in thinking and feeling. Although talking about feelings was acceptable, it was not to be a major focus of therapy. He wanted to help clients choose to make changes in their lives and stick to those choices. In doing so, he would not accept excuses from clients. Rather, he worked hard to help them take control over their lives.

His work has had impact on people in many fields. Teachers, school counselors, and school administrators have found applicable to education the ideas expressed in *Schools Without Failure* (1969), *Control Theory in the Classroom* (1986a), *The Quality School* (1998b), *Choice Theory: A New Psychology of Personal Freedom* (1998a), *Counseling with Choice Theory* (2000a), *Warning: Psychiatry Can Be Dangerous to Your Mental Health* (2003), *and Eight Lessons for a Happier Marriage.* (Glasser & Glasser, 2007). Drug and alcohol abuse counselors, corrections workers, and others dealing with institutional populations have found reality therapy to be attractive and appropriate in their work with difficult populations. This chapter explains the concepts of choice theory and reality therapy and illustrates how they can be applied to a variety of problems and populations.

History of Reality Therapy

Courtesy of William Glasser

WILLIAM GLASSER

Born in 1925, William Glasser was educated in Cleveland and earned an undergraduate degree in chemical engineering at 19. At 28 he had completed the program at Case Western Reserve University medical school. His psychiatric residency was done at the Veterans Administration Center in Los Angeles and the University of California at Los Angeles. He became board certified at 36. Glasser's dissatisfaction with the traditional psychoanalytic training he received became the seeds of the development of reality therapy. Frustrated with these teachings, he expressed his dissatisfactions to G. L. Harrington, who was his clinical supervisor in his third year of residency and was supportive of Glasser. Harrington served as a mentor for Glasser during the next 7 years.

In 1956 Glasser became a consulting psychiatrist at a state institution for delinquent adolescent girls. Although staff members were initially resistant to Glasser's suggestions for changing discipline and teaching practices, they found his approach to be helpful. In *Reality Therapy*, Glasser (1965) showed how a focus on friendliness and responsibility was helpful to the girls, not only while they were at the school but also after they left. Glasser was able to reach a group of individuals who, at first, were resistant to change. His work included individual and group therapy, as well as staff training. He developed a specific program for girls who abused drugs at the Ventura School for Girls.

In 1962 his mentor, Harrington, took charge of a ward of the Veterans Administration Neuropsychiatric Hospital in West Los Angeles. This unit housed chronic and regressed patients suffering from psychosis. Until Harrington's arrival, the patients had been taken care of, but no therapy was provided. Patients were discharged at a rate of about two per year. Harrington, who had questioned traditional psychoanalytic principles and had been influential in Glasser's development of reality therapy, used a similar active approach that encouraged patients to take more responsibility for their own behavior. With this approach, a unit that held more than 210 patients with an average of 17 years of confinement had a discharge rate of 45 patients the first year, 85 the second, and 90 the third (Glasser & Zunin, 1979).

As Glasser's success at the Ventura School for Girls became known, he began to consult in the California school system. His *Schools Without Failure* (1969) has had an impact on the administration of schools and the training of teachers, not just in the United States but in other countries as well. He had been concerned that schools did not do enough to prevent students from developing a "failure identity." He believed schools could be changed to help students find a sense of control over their lives and have successful learning experiences by developing a success-oriented philosophy that would motivate students to perform well and be involved in their work. Designed to remove failure from the curriculum, this therapy helped students become more responsible in their behavior in a way that would minimize the amount of discipline needed at school.

In 1986 Glasser's *Control Theory in the Classroom* continued and expanded upon his earlier work on education while introducing ideas from choice theory (explained next). *The Quality School* (1998b) applies ideas from choice theory to the management and administration of schools. Written for teachers, *Every Student Can Succeed* (Glasser, 2000b) shows how teachers can apply choice theory to many teaching issues, such as dealing with the disruptive student. These applications have been developed at Glasser's Education Training Center, an outgrowth of the William Glasser Institute in California.

In 1977 Glasser was introduced to the ideas of William Powers through his book *Behavior: The Control of Perception* (1973). Glasser applied the ideas of Powers to help people make choices as they attempted to control their lives (Glasser, 1985). Powers's work led to Glasser's *Stations of the Mind* (1981), a rather technical application of control theory to human lives. A less technical book that individuals can make use of in their own lives is *Control Theory: A New Explanation of How We Control Our Lives* (1985), originally published as *Take Effective Control of Your Life* (1984). These books provide information to the reader and/or therapist for applying ideas from control theory to reality therapy.

In his 1998 book, *Choice Theory: A New Psychology of Personal Freedom*, Glasser changed the focus from control theory to choice theory. One reason is that Glasser makes use of only some aspects of Powers's (1973, 1999) control theory and does not want to have readers believe that reality personality theory is the same as Powers' broader-ranging theory of control. Another reason is that some people have misunderstood control as meaning that people should be controlling of others. That was far from Glasser's intention, which was to promote self-control so that individuals could increase their ability to make and act on responsible choices. *Counseling with Choice Theory* (2000a) is a book of examples of cases from Glasser's practice showing how choice theory can be applied to many types of problems. *The Language of Choice Theory* (Glasser & Glasser, 1999) helps clients use choice theory in their own lives. These books, along with *Getting Together and*

Staying Together (Glasser & Glasser, 2000) and *Eight Lessons for a Happier Marriage* (Glasser & Glasser, 2007), demonstrate Glasser's emphasis on relationship problems and how choice theory can help them. His book *Warning: Psychiatry Can be Hazardous to Your Mental Health* (2003) is critical of the use of medication for dealing with personal problems, as Glasser believes medications interfere with individuals making positive choices in their lives and taking responsibility for their lives.

Personality Theory: Choice Theory

Theories in Action

Although Glasser had developed reality therapy without the benefit of information about control theory, his explication of Powers's (1973) formulation of control theory, described in *Stations of the Mind* (1981), made explicit and specific the ideas implicit in reality therapy (Glasser, 1961, 1965). In describing control theory, Glasser makes frequent use of metaphors from engineering and physical science. These metaphors are helpful, as the control aspects of the models are relatively easy to understand when contrasted with the complexity of problems in controlling human behavior.

Glasser (1981) uses the analogy of a thermostat to explain human behavior. A thermostat in a house perceives or senses the actual physical qualities of the temperature in the house. When the heat reaches a certain level, the thermostat "instructs" the heating system to shut off. In this way, a thermostat "controls" the temperature of the home. Human beings operate in a somewhat analogous manner. Like a thermostat, individuals sense the world outside themselves. These perceptions are processed in the brain, and individuals choose how to respond to these perceptions. This is done in "comparing stations" or "comparing places." The brain then organizes or reorganizes this behavior, resulting in thoughts, actions, and feelings. This system is described in more detail in this chapter, with particular emphasis on how individuals behave in adaptive and maladaptive ways.

Pictures of Reality

Glasser (1981, p. 126) makes the point that we do not live "to any extent in the real world." Individuals may have perceptions of reality, but they cannot know reality itself. For example, that you are reading this book in a chair is a perception of reality that few would argue with. However, it is still a perception, and people's perceptions of reality often differ. As an example, Glasser (1981) cites Marie Antoinette's statement during the French Revolution to peasants who wanted bread, "Let them eat cake" (p. 115). Marie Antoinette perceived the real world as being a place where, if the peasants could not get bread, they could get cake. The peasants' perception of the real world was, of course, that they were starving and there was no food anywhere. If I say to someone "Get real" or "Why don't you face reality?" I am asking them why their perceptions of reality are not the same as my perceptions. We often become interested in others' perceptions of realities in order to satisfy our own needs. This concept of pictures of reality is consistent with the postmodern constructivist position discussed in Chapter 1. For Glasser, perceptions of reality, rather than reality itself, determine behavior—actions, thoughts, and feelings. Wubbolding and Brickell (2009) believe that this concept may not have enough emphasis in reality therapy. They discuss the importance of helping clients examine when they can control events and when they cannot control events.

Needs

According to Glasser (1985), we develop pictures in our heads to satisfy innate needs. As needs are met, we store pictures of people, objects, or events that satisfy us. The pictures are stored in what Glasser refers to as the quality world. Glasser (1985, p. 21) estimates that 80% or more of the perceptions that are stored are visual, which is why he refers to them as pictures. The pictures do not have to be rational. For example, a woman with anorexia may have a picture of herself as fat, while friends and family see her as emaciated. Alcohol abusers may view their use of alcohol in pictures in which alcohol satisfies needs. For alcoholics to change, they must change the picture about their drinking from a constructive event to a destructive event. In marriages, couples need to find ways to make their pictures of events compatible. If they cannot, they should be able to tolerate or compromise with the spouse's pictures. The quality world, where the pictures are stored, is the world we live in where our desires are satisfied (Sohm, 2004). Glasser (1998a) also refers to this as the all-we-want world. It contains our expectations, our core beliefs, and our opportunities to fulfill our needs.

Glasser (Wubbolding, 2004) describes five basic, essential psychological needs: survival, belonging, power, freedom, and fun. The survival need refers to taking care of oneself by eating, drinking, seeking shelter, and resisting illness. The need for belonging includes the need to love, to share, and to cooperate and is found in all cultures (Wubbolding, 2005). This need is met by friends, family, pets, plants, or objects such as a stamp collection or antique cars. The need for power and to be better than others often conflicts with our need for belonging. For example, our need to be powerful in a marriage conflicts with the need to be loved by one's spouse. Glasser (1985, 1998a; Glasser & Glasser, 2000) believes that it is not insufficient love that destroys relationships but the power struggle, the inability of husbands and wives to give up their power and negotiate compromises. The need for freedom refers to how we wish to live our lives, how we wish to express ourselves, whom we wish to associate with, what we wish to read or write, how we wish to worship, and other areas of human experience. In a totalitarian society, the dictator's need for power conflicts with individuals' need for freedom and choice. If an individual has a need for freedom that is so strong that she has no significant relationships with others, then the need for belongingness is not met and the individual is likely to feel lonely. Although the need for fun is not as strong a need as that for survival, power, freedom, or belonging, it is still an important one. Fun may include laughing, joking, sports activities, reading, collecting, and many other areas of one's life. All five of these needs are met through our perceptions, our pictures in our heads.

Choice

When describing psychological problems, Glasser does not use adjectives such as *depressed, angry, anxious,* or *panicky.* Rather, he uses the verb form of these words to emphasize action and the choice implied in taking the action: *depressing, angering, anxietizing, phobicing,* and so forth. People do not become miserable or sad; rather, they choose to be miserable or sad. In Glasser's view, a feeling of sadness may occur immediately after an event. For example, if a friend dies, we may feel sad or depressed. After a brief period of time, we choose to depress, that is, to maintain the feeling of depression. Glasser believes that when people say, "I am choosing to depress" rather than "I am depressed," they are less likely to choose to depress and therefore less likely to feel depressed.

Behavior

Glasser defines behavior as "all we know how to do, think, and feel" (1985, p. 88). For Glasser, the behavioral system has two parts: The first contains organized behaviors that we are familiar with. The second part, which is constantly being reorganized, is the creative component of behavior. As new pictures and perceptions arise, there is often a need for the reorganization of behaviors. As Glasser (1985, p. 90) states, "Driven by our ever-present needs, we require a large supply of behaviors to deal with ourselves and the world around us." The creativity may range from something very positive, such as a contribution to art or music, to something quite negative, such as suicide or bulimia.

✱ 4 Components

Four components make up "total behavior": doing, thinking, feeling, and physiology. *Doing* refers to active behavior such as walking, talking, or moving in some way. Behaviors may be voluntary or involuntary. For example, when I read a book, I may without thinking about it adjust my sitting position to get more light. *Thinking* includes both voluntary and involuntary thoughts, including daydreams and night dreams. *Feelings* include happiness, satisfaction, dismay, and many others that may be pleasurable or painful. *Physiology* refers to both voluntary and involuntary bodily mechanisms, such as sweating and urinating. These four components are important in understanding Glasser's view of human behavior.

Wheels

Glasser (1990) uses a diagram of a car, Figure 11.1, to show how humans behave. In this analogy, the individual's basic needs (survival, belonging, power, freedom, and fun) make up the engine. The vehicle is steered by the individual's wants. The rear wheels are feelings and physiology. These are not steered, and we have less control over feelings and physiology than we do over the front wheels (doing and thinking). Doing and thinking direct our behavior, just as the front wheels of a car determine its direction. According to choice theory, it is difficult to directly change our feelings or physiology (the rear wheels) separately from our doing or thinking (the front wheels). However, we are able to change what we do or think in spite of how we feel. For Glasser, the key to changing behavior lies in choosing to change our doing and thinking, which will change our emotional and physiological reactions.

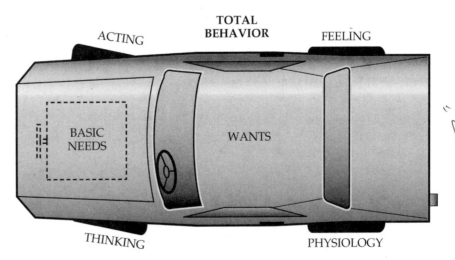

"metaphor"

FIGURE 11.1 The Reality Therapy Car.
*The Reality Therapy Car is reprinted by permission of
The William Glasser Institute, Chatsworth, CA.*

Choosing Behavior

If we have control over our behavior, why would we choose behavior that makes us miserable? Glasser (1985) gives four reasons why individuals may choose to depress, to be anxious, or to be otherwise psychologically miserable. First, by choosing to depress or to anxietize, individuals can keep their angering under control. More control and power over others is gained by depressing than by angering. Angering can lead to violence and prison, whereas choosing to depress does not. Second, people may choose to depress or to anxietize in order to get others to help them. This helps meet the need for belonging, and sometimes for power. As Glasser says (1998, p. 81), "Depressing is a way we ask for help without begging. It is probably the most powerful help-me information we can give to another person." Third, individuals may choose pain and misery to excuse their unwillingness to do something more effective. It is often difficult to choose pictures that will lead to effective behavior. If a man has chosen to depress because he has been fired from a job, it is easier to choose to avoid searching for a job and to choose to feel fearful than it is to make the effort to find a new job. Fourth, choosing to depress or to anxietize can help individuals gain powerful control over others. When an individual chooses to depress, others must do things for that person—offer comfort and encouragement, look after the person, and perhaps provide food and housing. These four reasons explain why it is not an easy task for a therapist to help a client change from choosing to depress or anxietize to more effective behaviors.

Just as it would seem difficult at first glance to understand why individuals would choose to depress or to anxietize, it is difficult to understand why they would choose to act "crazy." Glasser (1985, 2000a) views "crazy" behavior as a type of creativity that those of us who are "sane" would not do in a similar situation. For Glasser, hallucinations, delusions, and anorectic behavior are creative. People choose such "crazy" behavior if they are desperate enough because it gives them some control over their lives. Glasser does not view "crazy" behavior as mental illness. For example, if someone chooses to kill a movie star, that is a creative "crazy" idea for which the individual is responsible and for which that person should be punished according to the law. The view of choice theory on the legal question of an insanity defense is that criminals should not be tried until they have enough control over their lives to stand trial. When they have that control, then they should take responsibility for their actions.

Theory of Reality Therapy

More than many other theories, reality therapy is specific in its goals and procedures. Goals of reality therapy emphasize fulfilling needs by taking control over choices in life. Assessment is integrated into reality therapy and is based on the principles of choice theory. The conduct of reality therapy requires both attention to the relationship and specific procedures to bring about change. In bringing about change, reality therapists use strategies such as questioning, being positive, humor, confrontation, and paradoxical techniques.

Goals of Reality Therapy

 The general goal of reality therapy is to help individuals meet their psychological needs for belonging, power, freedom, and fun in responsible and satisfying ways. The counselor works with the client to assess how well these needs are being met and what changes should take place to meet them. For Glasser (1965), the more severe the symptom, the more the client has been unable to fulfill her needs. In helping individuals meet their needs, Glasser (1965, 1985, 2000a) emphasizes that individuals must behave responsibly and in such a way that they do not interfere with others in pursuing their needs. In helping people meet their needs more effectively, reality therapy takes an educational approach. Unconscious processes and dreams play almost no role in reality therapy. The counselor ascertains how realistic the wants of clients are and whether their behavior (doing, thinking, feeling, and physiology) is helping them realize their wants. Clients, not counselors, determine what they want, although counselors help clients assess their total behaviors and needs and develop ways to meet them.

Assessment

An integral part of reality therapy, assessment takes place throughout the therapeutic process. Glasser does not directly address the issue of assessment; rather, he focuses on assessment as a means of producing change in client behavior. Reality therapists do not often use objective and projective tests. However, three different instruments have been developed to measure the strength of basic needs: the Basic Needs Self Assessment (Mickel & Sanders, 2003); the Contextual Needs Assessment (Brown & Swenson, 2005); and the Students Need Survey (Burns, Vance, Szadokierski, & Stockwell, 2006) are used to measure how well schools follow choice theory principles. Also, a client goal report form has been developed by Geronilla (1989). Informal discussion or report forms can be used to assess client needs and wants, client pictures, total behaviors, or choices.

By asking clients what they want, counselors begin to establish goals of therapy and understand the motivation for therapy. Wubbolding (1988) suggests that if counselors continue to pursue client wants—what they "really want"—then they are uncovering needs that clients wish to fulfill (p. 33). In this way, counselors assess clients' needs for belonging, power, freedom, and fun. Thus, needs are met by closing the gap between what clients want from the environment and what they perceive or what picture they are getting.

Reality therapists also assess total behaviors. Although this can be done with a report form, the assessment of behaviors often takes place as clients talk about their physical feelings, emotional feelings, thoughts, and what they are doing. For example, in working with a young man who was assigned to a maximum-security unit in a prison, Corry (1989) described the behavioral choices that Everett was making within his correctional unit and how these behaviors were providing him with his wants—release from prison.

- **Doing**—Assaulting inmates over disagreements; attacking child molesters and rapists; confronting correctional officers—verbal defiance; making shanks (prison-made knives)
- **Thinking**—Hate, anger, bitterness, failure, fear
- **Feeling**—Powerless and defeated
- **Physiology**—Tense, agitated, on edge (Corry, 1989, p. 67)

[handwritten margin note: Assess "Total Behavior"]

Counseling with Everett included discussion of value judgments and his total behavior. He was able to state that none of his basic needs were being met by these behaviors. Corry continued to ask Everett what he really wanted. Corry and Everett chose to explore the need for fun. Everett was asked which pictures he had in his head to meet his need for fun. He talked about the desire to work out, read, and draw. He was able to make changes in his total behaviors that resulted in his move to a less restrictive cell block. After these changes, Corry made the following assessment of Everett's total behavior:

- **Doing**—Reading, drawing, working out, playing basketball
- **Thinking**—More positively, hopefully, skeptically
- **Feeling**—Less angry and defeated, a little successful
- **Physiology**—Less tense (Corry, 1989, p. 69)

In this example, the counselor continues to assess total behavior so that future changes can be planned and accurate evaluation can be achieved. In this difficult case, the counselor continued to integrate an assessment of total behavior into her counseling treatment. This integration of assessment and treatment is typical in reality therapy.

Another aspect of assessment is that of listening for choices. Because choice theory views behavior as a constant attempt to control perceptions, counselors view behavior as volitional, a choice to control. For example, if a client says, "I'm depressed because my girlfriend won't talk to me and doesn't want to see me," the counselor may hear, "I am choosing to depress now because my girlfriend doesn't want to see or talk to me." Depending on appropriateness, the counselor may choose to respond or not respond to the client's statement. However, reality therapists listen for choices and control that are implicit in clients' statements. A full working knowledge of choice theory helps the counselor determine which needs to meet first and which total behaviors to try to help the client change.

Listen

The Process of Reality Therapy

Glasser conceptualizes reality therapy as a cycle of counseling that is made up of the counseling environment and specific procedures that lead to change in behavior. Throughout counseling, a friendly relationship is established; in later phases the friendliness is combined with firmness. This relationship helps facilitate change through the application of specific procedures. Wubbolding (1991, 1996a, 2000, 2010) has taken Glasser's work and developed a more specific model that describes the counseling process. Called WDEP, it refers to W = wants, D = direction and doing, E = evaluation, and P = planning. Each of these refers to a cluster of activities that client and counselor engage in. This well-developed model is used in training reality therapists. To describe WDEP goes beyond the scope of this book. In general, its formulation is similar to Glasser's (1986b), but it gives more specific direction to the counselor.

WDEP = Counseling Process

In the following section, a description of the process of reality therapy provides a brief introduction to reality therapy. Wubbolding's four basic phases are indicated in parentheses.

Establish a friendly environment. The establishment of an environment that shows the concern and helpfulness of the counselor initiates the reality therapy process and continues throughout it.

The client's wants, needs, and perceptions are explored. (W = wants)

The client's total behavior, especially the doing aspect of total behavior, is explored. (D = direction and doing; E = evaluation)

Plans are made to improve the behavior. (P = planning)

A client's commitment to plans is obtained.

Theories in Action

① **Friendly involvement** . Reality therapy begins with a counselor making a sincere effort to build a relationship with a client that will sustain itself through the length of treatment. Glasser (1972) feels that the counselor must show that he cares about the client and is willing to talk about anything that both client and counselor consider worth changing. As Bassin (1993, p. 4) states: "The reality therapist is warm, friendly, personal, optimistic, and honest." This attitude helps the client confide and trust in the counselor. In doing so, the client is able to meet a basic need for belonging (Glasser, 1981) that helps sustain the therapeutic relationship. As a part of this involvement, the counselor should be prepared to disclose information about himself when appropriate. Likewise, using the first-person pronouns *I* and *me* encourages involvement with the client (Bassin, 1993). Even at the beginning of the relationship, the counselor focuses on actions rather than feelings. However, the counselor listens to how clients feel about problems in their lives—that is a part of being involved with the client.

In his explanation of the process of reality therapy, Wubbolding (1988) describes in some detail suggestions for developing a friendly and involved relationship with the client. He speaks first of the importance of attending behaviors: sitting in an open, receptive position, maintaining appropriate eye contact, and occasionally paraphrasing the client. Important conditions for therapeutic relationships include courtesy, enthusiasm, and genuineness. For reality therapy to be successful, these should be coupled with determination that positive change can take place and that rules and responsibilities should be adhered to. Wubbolding does not see a contradiction between courtesy and enthusiasm on one hand and firmness and obeying rules and regulations on the other. When clients break rules, as may often happen in settings such as schools, hospitals, and correctional facilities, the reality therapist does not judge or condemn the behavior but views it as the clients' way of meeting their needs. When appropriate, the counselor at the beginning of the relationship shares personal information to illustrate that she, too, is vulnerable.

Friendly involvement and development of the relationship can be illustrated by describing Alan's counseling experience. Alan is a 20-year-old Chinese American college student whose parents were born in Taiwan. He is in his second semester of his sophomore year at a local university. He complains that he does not like his major and has few friends. The friends he does have are from high school rather than those he met at the university, as he has been living at home and driving home from school when his classes are over. He would like to date, but has not done so. Recently, he reports feeling generally depressed and unhappy since he broke up with Eleanor, his girlfriend of 10 months. Glasser (2000a) believes that problems in relationships often lead individuals to pursue therapy.

In the first session, the therapist listens carefully to Alan. As he listens, the theme of being fearful and inactive arises several times.

Alan: I don't seem to be able to do anything. I'm stuck in the mud. I can't get out.

Counselor: Sounds like you want to get unstuck. Maybe we can get a tow truck to pull you out. I'm not a truck, but I can help you get unstuck.

Alan: You think things can get better?

Counselor: I do. There seem to be a lot of things that you want, and we can work together on how to get them.

The counselor uses some mild humor when talking to Alan. Further, he shows his own involvement through his willingness to help the client get unstuck. His use of *I* is evident. The counselor mentally retains Alan's use of the metaphor "I'm stuck in the mud" for later work.

Toward the end of the first session, Alan puts his complaints in terms of wants, needs, and perceptions. He wants to find a career path that will be satisfying. He wants to have friends who he feels care for him and do not use him only for rides back and forth to the university. He wants to start dating and to feel more comfortable when he is with women, as he has become more anxious with women since breaking up with Eleanor. In terms of needs, he wants to feel a greater sense of belongingness through friendships and dating. He would like to feel more powerful in interactions with others and to initiate and maintain conversations with men and women. The counselor is aware that there seems to be little fun in Alan's life. When he asks, "What would you be doing if you were living the way you wish?" Alan is able to describe his goals to the counselor, which include activities that he finds fun, such as sports. Besides talking about having good friendships and a career choice, he also talks about wanting to play tennis, swim, and work on cars. The counselor helps Alan explore his perceptions to see if his wants are being met and then starts the process of helping Alan meet his needs.

Exploring total behavior. As shown on page 421, total behavior consists of doing, thinking, feeling, and physiology. Reality therapists believe that change in one's life or control over one's life occurs through doing. In fact, this aspect of reality therapy is so important that the first book of case studies illustrating reality therapy was called *What Are You Doing?* (N. Glasser, 1980). Reality therapists want to know what clients are doing now. For example, if a client's parents abused alcohol, it may be helpful to examine how parental alcoholism has affected problems now. However, the focus is on choices that confront the adult children of alcoholics now rather than blaming parents for past behavior. In determining "what clients are doing," it is helpful to ask specific questions: What happened? Who was there? When did it happen? What happened after you said this? These questions help clarify clients' pictures or perceptions of what they are doing. In future aspects of the reality therapy process, the counselor focuses on planning that involves doing behaviors that meet the needs of the client. This should bring about changes in the clients' pictures or perceptions, as well as feelings.

When Alan talked about what he was doing, his activities during the day followed a pattern. He described a recent day at school in the following way:

Alan: I leave home at about 8:30 and drive to school.

Counselor: Do you drive alone?

Alan: No. Yesterday I came in with Paul. I usually drive with him on Thursday.

Counselor: What do you do in the car?

Alan: We listen to the radio. We usually don't talk.

Counselor: And what do you do next?

Alan: I park the car and then I go to my sociology class, then my English class. Then I have lunch.

Counselor: Where do you eat and who do you have lunch with?

Alan: I usually eat over in the cafeteria near my English class. I always bring a bag lunch from home. I generally eat it in about 15 minutes, then I do some studying for my next class at 1:00.

The counselor hears what Alan is doing, with whom, where, and when. For Alan these are unsatisfactory behaviors because they do not meet his need for belongingness, power, or fun. The counselor continues to talk about other parts of Alan's life and to find out what he is doing. The theme of doing solitary behaviors continues throughout the discussion with the counselor.

③ **Evaluating behavior.** Encapsulated in the word *evaluation* is the word *value.* Clients are asked to make value judgments about their behavior. By skillfully asking questions, counselors can help clients self-evaluate. It is the client who makes the value judgments, not the counselor. Sometimes clients evaluate their behavior casually or with little thought. It is helpful for the client and counselor to evaluate behavior thoroughly and to assess the consequences of the behavior. Wubbolding (1988, pp. 50–56) suggests the following questions:

Does your behavior help you or hurt you? For example, a high school student who has been disciplined for leaving class before the teacher has dismissed him might say, "My behavior helps me, I leave class when I want to so that I can smoke." By following this question up, the counselor can help the client assess whether the opportunity to smoke a cigarette is worth the consequences of the penalty involved in leaving class. This question helps clients assess the effectiveness of their actions in a variety of circumstances.

By doing what you're doing, are you getting what you want? This question helps clients specifically evaluate their behaviors and see if they are really worthwhile. It clarifies the previous question and makes it easier to evaluate behaviors. For example, by leaving class to smoke, the high school student may be getting only a little bit of what he wants.

Are you breaking the rules? This question helps clients examine their needs and wants in comparison with those of others. For rule breakers, this question makes them aware of what they are doing.

Are your wants realistic and attainable? Assessing the reality of wants can help clients determine whether to persist in a particular behavior. Returning to our example of the smoker, he may determine that it is not realistic for him to leave class whenever he wants to smoke.

How does it help to look at it like that? This gives clients a different way of viewing behavior. In our example, a smoker may view differently leaving class whenever he wants; it may also help him to look at his relationships with the teachers and administrators in the school.

Questions such as these help clients assess the effectiveness of their current behaviors. When asked by a counselor who has a genuine concern about the client, these questions can provoke a thoughtful interchange. They are questions that help clients take responsibility for their choices.

Alan's counselor helped him evaluate his behavior by asking some of these questions. Questions such as "Are you breaking rules?" do not apply to him, but other questions do.

Counselor: Is it helpful to you to eat lunch alone?

Alan: No, it isn't. I feel lonely and I guess I don't really enjoy the time at lunch.

Counselor: What is it that you're doing with your time?

Alan: I'm reading some articles for English. I think I could do something better.

Counselor: You're not getting what you want?

Alan: No. There are people I could talk with. I'd enjoy that more.

Making plans to do better. When behavior has been evaluated, the next question is what to do about it (Bassin, 1993; Glasser, 1981; Wubbolding, 2000). Plans consist of doing specific behaviors that are often very detailed in nature. For example, if my plan is to get up at 5:30 tomorrow morning, I should know if I have an alarm clock, where I will put it, what time I will set it for, whom I will wake up if I get up that early, and so forth. Plans should fulfill a physiological or psychological need (belonging, power, freedom, and fun). When developing plans, they should be simple and attainable. Reality therapists assist clients in developing plans that are likely to be successful.

The responsibility for the plan should depend on the client, not someone else. A poor plan would be "I'll get up at 5 A.M. tomorrow if my brother wakes me up." The client should have control over getting up at 5 A.M. Plans should also be positive in the sense of doing something rather than not doing something. Instead of saying, "I'm not going to smoke tomorrow," it would be better to say, "I will be working on three specific projects that I look forward to doing so that I can control my urge to smoke." Often an individual chooses repetitive plans. For example, the choice to exercise four times a week requires repetitive planning. If the exercise is enjoyable and does not depend on others to participate, the chances for its success are increased. Also, if I plan to exercise tomorrow rather than in 2 weeks, my chances for successfully completing my exercise plan are improved.

In choosing a plan to meet his need for belongingness, Alan and his counselor developed several plans, one of which was to eat lunch with a friend on Mondays, Wednesdays, and Fridays before class. They discussed which friends to ask, where to meet each of the possible friends, and what to do if a friend was not available. Furthermore, they discussed what to talk about with the friend. When Alan became unsure of what to talk about with certain friends, he and the counselor role played specific examples of conversations they might have. They talked about which friend to talk to about football, which to talk to about movies, and which to talk to about the election for governor. Plans were made for having lunch with someone in 2 days.

Commitment to plans. When making a commitment to a plan, it is important that the plan be feasible. Reality therapists may use a verbal or written contract to ensure commitment. An advantage of a written contract is that it makes clear what is going to be done. Also, it is helpful to talk about consequences if the plan is not carried out as agreed.

Alan and his counselor developed a written contract, specifying that Alan would contact Joe and Pedro and make plans for lunch. For many people, a contract sounds like an involved legal document. For the counselor and Alan, the contract was a few sentences on a piece of paper written toward the end of the counseling hour. They discussed consequences if Alan did not follow through on the plan. They decided, as a consequence, that Alan would drive Paul to school each day for a week rather than share the driving as they had before.

Therapist Attitudes

The following are attitudes that counselors adopt when handling difficulties in exploring total behavior, evaluating the behavior, making plans, and committing to plans. These three aspects of the process reflect the realization of reality therapists that change requires effort and does not come without work.

The following attitudes taken by reality therapists add to the counseling environment:

No excuses for failure to follow through on plans are accepted.
The counselor does not criticize, argue with, or punish the client.
The counselor does not give up on the client, but persists.

Don't accept excuses. As Wubbolding (1988) points out, to ask "Why?" is to invite excuses. Excuses should be ignored, and the counselor should go on to focus on carrying out other plans. Expressing confidence in clients that they will be able to make future changes is helpful. Discussing why they did not make the change they wanted to make will take the focus away from clients' control over their own lives. There are sometimes legitimate reasons why clients cannot follow through on plans. Most of these have to do with circumstances beyond the client's control. For example, Alan's plans to have lunch with friends does depend somewhat on his friends' behavior. If Joe does not meet Alan as planned, the counselor can comment that Alan followed through with his part of the plan as much as was possible and praise him for doing so. If Alan says, "I forgot to call Joe and make lunch plans," however, the counselor does not ask, "Why didn't you call him?" because that would be asking for excuses. Rather, the counselor talks about new plans for meeting friends for lunch.

No punishment or criticism. If a client fails to follow through on a plan, the client receives the consequences. If a parolee violates parole, that individual is punished by the legal system. It is not appropriate for the counselor to criticize, punish, or argue with an individual who has not followed through on the procedures of reality therapy, as it will damage the therapeutic relationship. In fact, a very important part of Glasser's view of education and therapy is that criticism is destructive to the entire educational and therapeutic process. Sometimes it is necessary to criticize, but it should be done sparingly and with a focus on the person's behavior rather than negative comments about the person. Glasser distinguishes between consequences for misbehavior and punishment that humiliates the person.

If Alan fails to meet with friends for lunch as he planned, it is helpful to examine what the consequences were for not completing his plans. Then the counselor and Alan can start again in reevaluating the plans and making new ones. Perhaps plans that involve meeting friends after class rather than lunch would be better. Later, with more success, Alan could make plans for lunch with friends.

Don't give up. Change is not an easy process. For clients who have previously made ineffective choices, to gain effective control over their choices is difficult. If the client is arrested for drunken driving, has an alcoholic binge, purges food, or otherwise reverts to ineffective behavior, the counselor must not give up on the client. The process of exploring behavior, evaluating it, making plans, and committing to plans is recycled, and the client and counselor reevaluate. When there is success, the reality therapist praises, encourages, or otherwise rewards the client.

The tasks that Alan had set for himself, with the help of his counselor, were reasonable. His problems were quite simple in contrast with those who are incarcerated or have drug or alcohol problems. He was able to develop several plans that led to his developing new friends at the university with whom he could play tennis and work on cars. Furthermore, he was introduced to women through mutual friends. He was able to feel comfortable on a date. As he began to meet his needs for belonging, power, and fun, the necessity for planning dropped away. After 4 months of counseling once a week, he met twice more with the counselor every other week to talk about progress in his academic and social life. Because Alan was making good progress, the tone of the sessions was light. The atmosphere was friendly, sometimes sharing stories, sometimes receiving praise from the counselor for his success in meeting his goals.

The relative simplicity and easy success of Alan's case should not lead to the conclusion that reality therapy is simple or easy to employ. Techniques that reality therapists often use to help individuals to control their own behavior, particularly when the change process is difficult, are described in the next section.

Reality Therapy Strategies

Reality therapy is not a technique-focused psychotherapy system. In fact, Glasser (1965) believes that transcripts, tape recordings, and observing a series of sessions through a one-way mirror would be of relatively little help to new therapists in understanding reality therapy unless they have had previous experience with doing some form of psychotherapy. The relationship and the friendly involvement with the client that are required of reality therapists make it difficult to look at small pieces of reality therapy and learn from them. However, reality therapists do tend to use certain psychotherapeutic techniques more than others (Wubbolding & Brickell, 1998). The ones that are more commonly used are described here: questions, being positive, metaphors, humor, confrontation, and paradoxical intention.

Questioning. As can be seen from the discussion of the process of counseling on pages 424 to 429, questions play an important role in exploring total behavior, evaluating what people are doing, and making specific plans. Wubbolding (1988) suggests that questions can be useful to reality therapists in four ways: to enter the inner world of clients, to gather information, to give information, and to help clients take more effective control (pp. 162–164). When reality therapists help clients explore their wants, needs, and perceptions, they do so by asking clients what they want and follow the question with more questions to determine what they really want. They also ask clients what they are doing and what their plans are. These questions help the reality therapist understand the inner world (the wants, needs, and perceptions) of clients.

Reality therapists often develop different ways of asking questions about the inner world of clients so that the questions do not become repetitive or mechanistic. When gathering information to explore total behavior or to help clients make plans, it is useful to ask specific questions such as "When did you leave the house?", "Where did you go?", "Did you carry out your plan?", and "How many stores did you visit?" Wubbolding (1988, p. 163) also believes that questions can give information in a subtle way. For instance, in asking a client,

"What do you want to do tonight to change your life for the better?", information is provided. There is an implicit message: "You have control over your life and an immediate plan can help you take even better charge of your life."

In this way, a message is delivered that helps clients focus on their own behavior, evaluate that behavior, and make plans. This use of questioning is related to the use of paradox, which is discussed on page 432. Last, questioning helps clients choose which perceptions to focus on, which behaviors to do, and how to evaluate them. Questions give clients choice and, through choice, control over how they are to change their lives. However, Wubbolding (1996b) cautions that therapists should not overuse questions but integrate them with reflective and active listening, sharing of perceptions, and other statements.

Being positive. The reality therapist focuses on what the client can do. Opportunities are taken to reinforce positive actions and constructive planning. Positive statements are made to statements of misery and complaint. For example, if a client says, "I am angry about what Mary said to me today," the reality therapist does not respond, "Has this been happening to you for a long time?" or "You're feeling angry that Mary doesn't treat you well." The reality therapist might respond, "What are you going to do so that you will not choose to anger at Mary?" The emphasis of the counselor's questions is on positive actions.

In *Positive Addiction*, Glasser (1976) discusses the potential strength that individuals have. A positive addiction is not easy to obtain but requires practice and repetition. The most common positive addictions are running and meditating. Glasser (1984, p. 229) says, "It [positive addiction] gives you easy access to your creativity. This in turn can provide you with a small, but still significant, amount of additional strength to help deal with any problems you may have in your life." People who have developed negative addictions such as drug, nicotine, or alcohol addiction may find positive addictions such as running, swimming, meditation, Zen, yoga, or some combination to contribute to their creative process. Like a negative addiction, positive addictions bring discomfort to the individual if they are withdrawn. To develop a positive addiction, the activity must be noncompetitive; be accomplished with minimal mental effort; be done alone; have physical, mental, or spiritual value; and be done without self-criticism (Glasser, 1976, p. 93). For a small proportion of clients, the choice of a positive addiction may be a part of reality therapy.

Related to being positive are two other qualities (Wubbolding & Brickell, 1998): seeing everything as an advantage and communicating hope. Wubbolding and Brickell show how what could be seen negatively can be reframed positively. An ex-offender who had been fired from nine jobs in 10 months was told that he was "very skilled at *locating* jobs" (p. 47). Reality therapists often work with ex-offenders, drug abusers, and others. To do so it is important to instill in clients the belief that there is hope for their future. They may do this, in part, by discussing choices and plans. Rapport (2004) has developed a questionnaire and information sheet to help individuals learn about positive addiction and to assess themselves to see if they have one.

Metaphors. Attending to and using the client's language can be helpful in communicating understanding to a client through use of her language (Wubbolding & Brickell, 1998). For example, if a client says, "When he left, it was like the roof fell on me," the therapist might say, "What does it feel like when the roof falls on your body?" If the client says, "When I got an A on that math exam, the whole world seemed brighter," the therapist may respond, "What is it like in that light and sunshine?" In essence, the therapist is talking in a way that is congruent with the client's personal perceptions.

Humor. Because of the friendly involvement that reality therapists try to develop with their clients, humor fits in rather naturally. Therapists sometimes have the opportunity to laugh at themselves, which encourages clients to do the same (Glasser & Zunin, 1979). This can take the pressure off client disappointment if plans are not realized. Because fun is a basic need, according to reality therapy, it can sometimes be met to a small degree in the therapy session itself. When the therapist and client can share a joke, there is an equalizing of power and a sharing of a need (fun). To the extent that humor can create a greater sense of friendly involvement, it also helps to meet the client's need for belongingness. Of course, humor cannot be forced. Some therapists may use humor rarely, others in one type of situation, and yet other therapists in another type.

Confrontation. Because reality therapists do not accept client excuses and do not give up easily in their work, confrontation is inevitable. Helping clients to make plans and to commit to plans for behaviors that are difficult to change means that often plans are not carried out as desired. In confronting, the therapist can still be positive in dealing with client excuses. Not accepting them is a form of confrontation. The therapist does not criticize or argue with the client but rather continues to work to explore total behavior and to make effective plans.

Confrontation can occur in any aspect of reality therapy. To give an example, let us return to the case of Alan. If Alan were to say, "I didn't get around to meeting anyone after class this week. I guess it really doesn't matter to me," the reality therapist can confront this in several ways. One response would be "You've said before that it really does matter, that you're lonely, and you want to develop friendships. I think it really does matter to you." The counselor could also say, "Yes, I guess it doesn't matter to you. What does matter to you?" The purpose of the latter statement would be to get the client to confront his own excuses and choose to say that making plans to improve friendships is important. How one chooses to confront a client is a matter of personal style.

Paradoxical techniques. In reality therapy, making plans and getting clients to commit to plans can generally be done directly. However, clients at times are resistant to carrying out plans they make. Paradoxical techniques are those that give contradictory instructions to the client (Wubbolding & Brickell, 1998). Positive change can result from following any of the options given by the therapist. For example, clients who are obsessively concerned with not making mistakes at work may be directed to make mistakes. If the client tries to make mistakes, as the therapist suggests, then the client has demonstrated control over the problem. If the client resists the counselor's suggestion, then the behavior is controlled and eliminated. Paradoxical techniques are both unexpected and difficult to use. Reading this section on paradoxical techniques makes it easy to understand why the practice of reality therapy can be complex and why Glasser believes that at least two years of training are needed to do reality therapy. The following paragraphs explain paradox within choice theory, illustrate types of paradoxical interventions, and give warnings about the dangers of paradox.

By re-examining perceptions, needs, and total behavior in the context of choice theory, paradoxes implicit in choice theory can be illustrated. Individuals want to have control over their perceptions, see themselves as intelligent and successful, and so forth. Wanting a perception does not change it. Wanting to see someone as attractive rather than unattractive does not usually work. Paradoxically, the perception of someone's attractiveness may change if an individual becomes more familiar with and more friendly with that person. The behavior may change the perception more easily than the individual can change one perception to another. Also, there are paradoxes in fulfilling needs. Needs are often in conflict with one another. By supervising a friend who is fixing a car, an individual may sacrifice the need for belongingness for the need for power. Also, our needs (Glasser, 1981, 1990) cannot be fulfilled directly; needs are met through our perceptions or pictures of our wants. Other paradoxes occur in our total behaviors. Individuals pay more attention to feeling and thinking in their everyday lives, but it is "doing" that brings about change (Wubbolding, 1988, p. 78). Feelings are changed not by talking about feelings but by doing or changing behaviors. If a person who depresses starts becoming active with others, the feeling of depression is likely to change.

Two types of paradox will be described below: reframing and prescriptions (Wubbolding & Brickell, 1998). These paradoxical instructions help clients feel that they are in control and that they choose their behavior. To choose to feel more depressed means that an individual can also choose to feel less depressed.

Reframing helps individuals change the way they think about a topic. Reframing can help a client see a behavior that was previously undesirable as desirable.

> In counseling a young man whose hand was "frozen" into a fist (with no physiological basis), I suggested that he hold it up for all to see rather than hide it under his arm, as was his habit. We both laughed and were able to see humor in what had been only a "serious" problem for him. I suggested that he try to feel proud of his temporary handicap, and that if he hid it, no one would know when he overcame it. I asked, "Why not use it to show people you can conquer difficulties?" He was able to reframe the problem in a two-fold manner: from seriousness to humor and from a shameful event to a positive, attention-getting tool (Wubbolding, 1988, p. 83).

If a young man says that he is upset because a young woman refused his invitation to dinner, this can be reframed by commenting on the young man's strength in asking the woman out for dinner and for weathering rejection. Reframing helps individuals look at their behavior as a choice. This leads to a greater sense of control.

Paradoxical prescriptions refer to instructing the client to choose a symptom. For example, if a person is concerned about blushing, he can tell others how much he blushes and how often. If a person is choosing to depress, she can be told to schedule the depression—to depress at certain times. These instructions give individuals a means of controlling their behavior, an important aspect of control theory.

Paradoxical treatments are complex and can be confusing. Training and familiarity are essential before using them. Weeks and L'Abate (1982) found that involvement and safety are key concepts in using paradoxical interventions. Such interventions should not be used with individuals who are dangerous (suicidal) or destructive (sociopathic). Confusing paradoxical instructions can make people who have paranoid ideation more suspicious and less trusting. Furthermore, they state that paradox should not be employed in crises, such as loss of a loved one, a job, or similar events. Although powerful and potentially dangerous, paradoxical interventions are illustrative of the creative approaches that reality therapists take to help their clients put more control in their lives.

Psychological Disorders

More than almost any other theorist, Glasser uses case examples throughout his writing to illustrate choice theory and reality therapy. Two books edited by his first wife, Naomi Glasser, *What Are You Doing?* (1980) and *Control Theory in the Practice of Reality Therapy* (1989), and his more recent book *Counseling with Choice Theory* (Glasser, 2000a) are the sources for most of the examples used in this section. These books provide many good examples of how reality therapy can be used with a wide variety of psychological problems. The following examples deal with eating disorders, drug abuse, depression, and anxiety disorders. For each case, the same systematic process of the aspects of reality therapy is used. Choice theory offers differing explanations for treatment of the disorders.

Eating Disorders: Choosing to Starve and Purge: Gloria

Theories in Action

Glasser's (1989) view of eating disorders is that they are an addiction. For Glasser, "An addiction is a behavior we choose that we can do easily, that does not depend on others, and that consistently gives us immediate pleasure, or we believe will soon give us pleasure" (p. 300). However, those addicted to food (bulimics and anorectics) are unlike other addicts in that they cannot give up their addiction completely; otherwise, they will starve. What they must do, then, is to restrict their eating. By starving themselves, they may find that there is great pleasure in starvation or purging. Such behavior gives them control over their own lives so that they can defy their families and others they see as controlling them. Glasser states: "They do this by saying directly or indirectly 'very thin is right' and 'all you who want me to eat and be fat are wrong'" (p. 300). In the next case, Gloria has given up most of her eating-disordered behaviors and has stopped purging. However, she is still stomach-aching. For Glasser this eating disorder-related behavior, stomach-aching, accomplishes three things. First, the individual restrains the anger against others. Second, stomach-aching is an acceptable way to ask for help. Third, stomach-aching helps Gloria get out of situations she fears. In this conceptualization, Glasser is looking at eating-disordered behavior as a self-destructive and creative choice. In this case, Geronilla (1989) helps Gloria choose more effective behaviors to take control over her life.

Gloria is a 32-year-old single woman who is employed as an assistant to a state senator. She has a bachelor's degree in English and has previously worked as a journalist. She has been able to stop most, but not all, eating disorder-related behaviors at this point. The focus of reality therapy with Gloria is on interpersonal matters: dating relationships and dealing with her boss, coworkers, and family. Another concern is Gloria's self-image. Gloria was seen for 18 sessions: The first two were a week apart, the others were 2 to 4 weeks apart. In the first session, Geronilla works on developing a relationship with Gloria. As soon as possible, she has the client share her wants and perceptions, so that they can discuss the client's needs. The following excerpt shows Geronilla's work with Gloria's perceptions and needs.

> At first sessions I am willing to listen to symptoms so that I get a good idea of the function that they play in the client's life, but I try to keep this to a minimum. As soon as I can, I present a notebook entitled, "My Picture Album," which has each of the needs on a separate page in a clear plastic cover. I talk about the needs and

I relate them to my own life. I have a picture of my family that I slide into the clear plastic cover to demonstrate how we move pictures into our internal album.

[Therapist:] Where do you get your loving/belonging need met?

Gloria: My parents are pretty good to me, but I need other relationships. I really don't have a bunch of close friends. I think the one friendship I have at work is destructive.

[Therapist:] How about anyone else at work?

Gloria: I work with married women who drive Mercedes or BMW's because their husbands make good money, and I drive a Honda. They even pointed it out at lunch the other day. I feel pressure to buy a more expensive car, even though I don't want to do that.

[Therapist:] Do you feel they are imposing their values on you?

Gloria: Yes. And I don't like it. I don't want to be like them, anyway. I have always been the type to carry my own weight and not count on someone supporting me.

[Therapist:] Sounds to me as if you don't get much of your love and belonging need met at work.

Gloria: You can say that again.

[Therapist:] Let's take a look at your other needs. How about power? Do people listen to you, give you approval, and put you in charge of doing things?

Gloria: That's pretty low, too. Not much at work at all.

[Therapist:] How about fun?

Gloria: Most of the things I do are by myself, like reading.

[Therapist:] Would you like to be more social in your fun?

Gloria: Yes. (Geronilla, 1989, pp. 260–261)

Geronilla goes on to assess Gloria's needs and perceptions. She does not focus on the eating disorder itself. In the third session, Geronilla helps Gloria evaluate her behaviors. This excerpt illustrates how she does that.

[Therapist:] So what do you want to be? Get a picture in your head and describe that person to me. Let's go through the four wheels of the behavioral car. [See page 421 for an explanation.]

Gloria: I want to be open and approachable. I want to say "hello" to everyone I meet. I want to be patient and helpful, but know when to draw the line. I don't want to be taken advantage of in professional and business life. Someone people would both like to work around and socialize with. Just a pleasant person.

[Therapist:] Describe how that person thinks.

Gloria: That person believes that people are basically good. All people are on the same level. People that you deal with are appreciative of what you do for them. If people would take the time to get to know me, they would be appreciative of me.

[Therapist:] How would that person feel on the inside?

Gloria: Fulfilled and happy all the time. Nothing gnawing away.

[Therapist:] How would that person's body feel?

Gloria: Like calm water on a lake. No ripples. Smooth.

[*Therapist:*] Sounds like you have a good picture of the person you would like to be.

Gloria: Yes, I'm beginning to see what you mean: I can become the person I want to be if I try. (Geronilla, 1989, pp. 268–269)

In the fourth session Gloria and the therapist talk about owning behavior. They discuss ways of planning new behavior that will be more effective. The planning focuses on more effective behavior in dealing with Gloria's boss.

[*Therapist:*] Do you want to talk about owning your own behavior?

Gloria: Owning it? What do you mean?

[*Therapist:*] Things and/or people don't cause you to be upset. You cause this reaction.

Gloria: That's a lot of responsibility.

[*Therapist:*] Yes, that is a biggie! Do you want to be upset?

Gloria: No.

[*Therapist:*] Would you like to feel better about your boss?

Gloria: Yes.

[*Therapist:*] Let's look at one of the instances in which you upset yourself when he does something incompetent. What are some of the things you say to yourself that keep you upset?

Gloria: When I am listening to his speech, I say things like, "He is taking up all my time; if only he weren't such a wimp!"

[*Therapist:*] What are you feeling?

Gloria: I'm mad at her [Bessie, a coworker] for her misbehavior and at him for being incompetent.

[*Therapist:*] What are you doing?

Gloria: I am sitting there in a very closed position with my arms folded across my chest, while he is walking back and forth and looking at me instead of at her.

[*Therapist:*] How is your body when he is giving this speech?

Gloria: Uptight, and my stomach is slightly upset.

[*Therapist:*] What would you like to do to change the way you feel?

Gloria: I'd prefer to handle the whole situation myself. I'd tell Bessie off.

[*Therapist:*] Do you want to take over everything he is incompetent in doing?

Gloria: No. He is being paid a big salary. He should do it.

[*Therapist:*] What else could you do to get yourself less excited?

Gloria: I could imagine myself in his shoes and not wanting people to be angry with me.

[*Therapist:*] So it would be helpful if you could think about how other people feel instead of just about yourself?

Gloria: Yes. (Geronilla, 1989, pp. 271–273)

In this way, the therapist helps Gloria decide on and picture behaviors that will be more effective in dealing with her boss.

In the following dialogue from Session 6, Geronilla (1989) assists Gloria in planning to be more socially active. This excerpt also illustrates the involvement or self-disclosure that is common among reality therapists. Also, at the end of this excerpt Geronilla explicitly deals with the important reality therapy principle of not taking excuses from the client.

> *Gloria:* I don't know, I'm really out of practice. I hate it. Going to my friends' is like going to a cocoon. They eat and vegetate all weekend. I went to a home interior party last week, and I thought going to that was a big deal. Boy, how I have deteriorated! It was a big deal; before, it was easier to stay home than get in my car and go. I'd like to be more social. There are a lot of social opportunities in the next several weeks that I should take advantage of.
>
> *[Therapist:]* Do you want to take advantage of them?
>
> *Gloria:* Yes.
>
> *[Therapist:]* How can you make sure you get to them all?
>
> *Gloria:* I don't know.
>
> *[Therapist:]* Do you have a pocket calendar?
>
> *Gloria:* Yes.
>
> *[Therapist:]* Do you write down your social events in it?
>
> *Gloria:* No, not usually.
>
> *[Therapist:]* I don't know about you, but I tend to forget things unless I mark them down. I'm more likely to do it if I mark it down. It is easy to sit and vegetate. But the more things I can schedule, the more things I am likely to do. I remember when I used to force myself to go out for an hour a day.
>
> *Gloria:* You were the anti-social type? (Shocked.)
>
> *[Therapist:]* I wouldn't say I was totally anti-social, but I just wasn't the extrovert that I am today. I was never your cheerleading type in high school. It was in college that I decided that I wasn't going to meet "Mr. Right" in my room in the dorm. That's when I made up my mind to go out for at least an hour a day. It was a lot easier to stay in my room than go out. I found a schedule of social events and marked them down.
>
> *Gloria:* I was O.K. in college. I always had a lot of friends. Why is this hitting me after 30? I guess I don't have the exposure to people that I used to.
>
> *[Therapist:]* Exposure and proximity are important factors, but are we going to let them get in the way and be an excuse?
>
> *Gloria:* No. That is a good idea. I'll start to mark them down. (Geronilla, 1989, p. 276)

In the 13th session the therapist comments that she wanted to focus on doing rather than on the behaviors of feeling, thinking, or physiology. In this session the therapist praises Gloria for her commitment to her plans and reinforces the fact that Gloria is making changes for Gloria, not for the therapist.

> *Gloria:* You confronted me last time, and I went home and ate. I upset myself because I wasn't doing the things I needed to do. I've been giving a lot of lip service. I really needed to think about if it was worth working for.

We talked about the two sides, the pleasure and the pain of almost everything. I told Gloria that I did not see her as she saw herself. Coincidentally, we had been at a party together at which she had been socializing well. I encouraged her to try to relax and be herself and not to worry about critical people, because she did not need them. She was making excellent progress, I thought.

> *Gloria:* I had class on the weekend, but I interacted at every break and meal break. Monday I went out to eat with Joe. Tuesday I went to Nautilus and talked to guys there. Wednesday I went out for a drink with two guys from work. I initiated it. Thursday I made two calls and went to exercise. Saturday I took a friend to celebrate her birthday. Sunday I went out to friends' to see their new baby.
>
> *[Therapist:]* How did you feel about everything you did?
>
> *Gloria:* Good, real good.
>
> *[Therapist:]* I think you did a fabulous job.
>
> *Gloria:* I figured I should after the last session.
>
> *[Therapist:]* Are you doing it for me or for you? If you're doing it for me, you missed the point. (Geronilla, 1989, p. 290)

At the end of therapy (the 18th session), Gloria brought the therapist a note titled "WHAT DO I WANT?" In that note she included the following paragraphs that summarize her progress with her eating disorder.

> I feel good about me. I feel like I have something I can grasp now. I don't know how I got to the place where I was when I was anorexic and bulimic. Somewhere I got the idea that thin was the answer to all my problems—it would fill my dance card and make me win friends and influence people. The funny thing was my social life came to a halt when I started doing the dieting thing. I couldn't believe it. I plan on staying out.
>
> I know now that I have a technique to accomplish what I want to do with my life. If I don't do it, it will be my own fault. I never wanted to take responsibility for my own happiness before, but now I feel better that I am responsible for it. It is too important to leave in the hands of others. (Geronilla, 1989, p. 298)

This example illustrates how reality therapy can be used with an eating disorder. Throughout the therapy, the therapist emphasizes a friendly and involved relationship with the client. The therapist explores the wants, needs, and perceptions of the client and evaluates total behavior. An example is given of how specific plans for small situations are made.

The Choice to Abuse Drugs: Janet

Reality therapy has been used widely as a treatment for drug abuse. Glasser (1981, 1985) has used choice theory to explain addiction. Briefly, individuals usually are in control of their lives when they feel good. An important exception to this is the use of drugs. Drugs often give a quick burst of pleasure that may make individuals feel ecstatic but are an indication that their lives are very much out of control. In making use of Powers's control theory, Glasser (1985) describes the differential effect of opiates, marijuana, alcohol, and cocaine on individuals. Opiates such as heroin and morphine act on the control system to make individuals feel pleasure. Marijuana and LSD seem to act like pleasure filters, making things that individuals perceive look or sound better. However, LSD does not always make things seem better; in fact, things can often appear quite frightening. Because of its unpredictability, LSD is rarely addictive. By contrast, alcohol gives individuals a powerful sense of control when in fact they are out of control. Glasser (1985, p. 123) states: "This action is unique; no other drug acts to increase the sense of control that is actually being lost." Cocaine and, to a much lesser extent, caffeine and nicotine give individuals a sense of control in a different way. They energize the behavioral system so that individuals using cocaine can act as if they can do anything. Cigarettes and coffee, in a much milder way, also can give an individual a small feeling of energy. For example, many individuals feel better when they start their day with a cigarette or a cup of coffee. Thus, all of these drugs act in different ways to interfere with individuals' controlling their own lives.

Glasser singles out alcohol as being a particularly insidious drug. His view of how alcohol takes control over people's lives is informative.

> I believe that alcohol will always be an integral, accepted, even glorified part of our culture, while other drugs will not, because alcohol is supportive of the cultural ideal—taking control of your life. The fact that alcohol is the single most destructive force in our culture that causes people to lose control is not recognized and will not be recognized, because of how it acts. The culture, or at least the culture presented by the mass media, sees it as a positive force, which it may be if it is used in delicate moderation.
>
> Supported by the media, our culture rarely assumes that "real" men and women will not exceed the very fine line between enhancing and losing control. Alcohol is the get-things-done, take-control drug, and to deal with it well is a sign of strength and maturity. Because it enhances the sense of control, we welcome it instead of fearing it as we should. (Glasser, 1985, p. 132)

In treating alcoholism, Glasser (1981) says that counselors and others must be brutal enough to help the alcoholic see that something is wrong. He believes that Alcoholics Anonymous is particularly helpful because members make individuals take responsibility for their alcoholism by standing up and admitting they are alcoholics. Further, individuals must repeat the stupid things they do while drunk. By doing so they are taking control of and responsibility for their behaviors.

In treating Janet, a 16-year-old high school student who had abused a wide variety of drugs, Abbott (1980) used the principles of reality therapy to help her give up drugs and later become a highly successful college student. He worked very hard to develop a good relationship with her, directly showing his concern and caring for her. The focus of treatment was not on drug use but on her decision making and the responsibility for dealing with situations in her life that would be more successful. He would continually ask Janet, "Now that this has happened, what are you going to do?" If she was truant from school, he would ask her what she was going to do about graduation requirements. Her behavior was sporadic; she ran away from home on several occasions. Each time Abbott (1980, p. 270) would ask a version of the questions "Are you happy with the way your life is going now?", "What is happening as a result of your behavior?", and "Will it accomplish your goals in life?" Janet's behavior was unpredictable. Throughout, Abbott did not give up on Janet (an important reality therapy principle). Despite her many relapses, he was there to help her to take control of her life and not to accept excuses from her.

The Choice to Depress: Teresa

Micah

According to Glasser (1985, p. 48), individuals do not feel depressed; rather, they choose to depress, or they display depressing behavior. Getting involved in an active, doing behavior helps individuals change from depressing behaviors and feelings of misery to a feeling of greater control that is accompanied by more positive feelings, more positive thoughts, and greater physical comfort.

Glasser (2000a) focuses on the importance of choice in his work with Teresa, a 40-year-old woman who is very depressed. Immediately, he noticed a woman who was "neat, clean, and attractive despite the fact that she was at least sixty pounds overweight" (p. 129). He was impressed by her total lack of energy. His task with her was to show her that she was choosing to depress and that she could make other choices. He anticipated resistance:

> I was determined not to ask Teresa to tell me her story and, especially not to ask her how she felt. I had to try to convince her that she was making ineffective choices in her life, knowing full well that my claim that she was making choices, especially choosing to depress, would be the furthest thing from her mind. If I couldn't begin to convince her on her first visit, there was little chance of any measurable progress. (Glasser, 2000a, p. 129)

Teresa was surprised when Glasser did not want to hear her story about her husband leaving her with children and no money. She was initially puzzled by Glasser's questions about making choices. His kindness and friendliness allowed her to accept his seemingly odd questions. Teresa tried to show Glasser that her plight was hopeless, but he continued to focus on choice. Finally, Teresa makes a choice that Glasser sees as a positive move away from choosing to depress.

> "But I had a marriage, I was somebody. I'm nobody now. Just a poor woman with kids on welfare, and they're going to take that away in a year."
>
> "I'll admit your life was a lot better than it is now, but you're still alive. And if you're still alive, you can still choose to have a life. The only person who can stop you from making better choices right now is you. As long as you choose to depress, you no longer have a life."
>
> "But what else can I choose? I just can't go home and choose to be happy."
>
> "That's right, you can't separate choosing how you feel from choosing what you do. They go together. But you can go home and spend the rest of the day saying to yourself: *Teresa, face it. Good or bad, happy or sad, you're choosing everything you do all day long.*"
>
> I didn't explain total behavior to Teresa, but this is connecting acting to feeling. It worked. She caught on.
>
> "But what difference will that make? I'll still have the same lousy life."
>
> "What do you choose to do all day that keeps your life the same?"
>
> "I sit home, watch my soaps, and eat. That's what I do. That's what a lot of women like me do. I know quite a few of them from the neighborhood. Most of them are just like me. Too old for love, too young to die."
>
> "But not too old to start making better choices."
>
> "OK, like what?"
>
> In print that "like what" seems cynical, but it didn't come out that way at all. She really wanted to know.
>
> "All right, let's start with one. What could you choose to do tomorrow that would be better than today?"
>
> "I could choose not to sit around all day."

"No, that won't work. It'd be like trying to choose not to eat so much. I'm not looking for you to choose not to do anything. I'm looking for you to start to choose to do
something better than you're doing now. Something active, so that you have to get
up and get going."

Then she said something that made us both smile. She was getting it.

"I could choose to clean the house. It's a mess."

"That'd be great, but will you do it?"

"I'll do it. I will."

"What you just said and, I guess, the way you said it reminds me of something. Did
you ever see the movie, *My Fair Lady?*"

"I did, the play and the movie. I was married. I had money then."

"Remember when Eliza started to speak correctly? Higgins and Pickering danced and
sang. Do you know some of the words to that song?"

She gave me a look that said she didn't remember.

"They sang, 'She's got it, by Jove, I think she's got it.' Or something like that. Teresa I
think you've got it. So tell me, what do you know about everything you do? What do
we all do before we do anything?"

"Choose it, by Jove I think we choose it."

"Will you call me after you clean the house? In fact, anytime you choose to do
anything all week, call me and leave a message on my machine. Leave your number,
and I'll find the time to call you back. Can you come next week at the same time?"
(Glasser, 2000a, pp. 134–136)

Glasser illustrates several aspects of reality therapy in this dialogue. He is
friendly and positive throughout. He focuses on "choosing to" and does not accept "choosing not to" as an alternative. Teresa makes a plan to clean her house
(to do better) and he helps her make a commitment to do these plans by asking
her to call him at his office.

The Choice to Anxietize: Randy

Choice theory provides a conceptualization of anxiety, similar to that of depression, which helps the reality therapist examine those aspects of an individual's
life that are not under control. This conceptualization provides a way of examining behaviors and then developing plans to improve upon them. Glasser (1985)
provides a summary of a person experiencing the physical symptoms of anxiety
and interprets his symptoms by using choice theory.

Randy was a highly intelligent college student, who, as an undergraduate, made almost straight A's. He continued his success through the first year of the graduate
school of business, but in his final year he became suddenly incapacitated with fear
and anxietying. He chose to anxious so strongly that he could not sit through an entire class. If he forced himself to stay, he increased his anxietying to the point where
he felt total panic, as if he were doomed to die immediately unless he left the room.
His stomach became queasy, his hands sweated, heart pounded, his ears buzzed, and
his mouth became so dry that he could not speak coherently. Although he was easily
able to do "A" work on all assignments, he could not pass the course unless he took
the final exam in class, so he was stymied. In his album he had the picture of becoming a highly successful business executive. In the real world he was suddenly a non-
successful graduate student. The last thing he thought was that he was choosing
what he was doing.

Randy saw himself as excessively shy and unattractive, and believed that no
matter how well he did in school, no one would hire him. If he succeeded in school,
he would have to face the real world and possibly find out that he could never be the

successful business executive of his album. But he enjoyed his academic success too much to drop out of school, so he took control by failing to go to class and anxietying if he went. Through these behaviors he gained painful control over his anger at not being attractive and gregarious. He was also able to ask for help with the school problems that his behavior was causing. When he learned through counseling to take more effective control, he finished school with honors. Maintaining this control and continuing to work very hard, in a few years he became vice-president of a very successful company. (Glasser, 1985, p. 64)

Using choice theory to conceptualize individuals' problems provides a consistent framework for reality therapists. Although the disorders described are different, the choice theory approach, whether with drug abuse or eating disorders, examines ways in which individuals can maintain control over their environment. Methods for bringing about change—whether direct plans or paradoxical techniques—are means of changing thoughts and feelings by developing and following through with a plan of action.

Current Trends

Since Glasser coined the term *reality therapy* in 1962 (O'Donnell, 1987), the popularity of reality therapy has grown rapidly. In 1967 the Institute for Reality Therapy was founded in Los Angeles, and in 1968 a special branch for training teachers in the use of reality therapy, the Educators' Training Center, was started. In 1975 the Institute for Reality Therapy (now known as the William Glasser Institute) began to certify reality therapists. Currently, more than 7,800 people are certified to use reality therapy. In 1981 the group of certified reality therapists had grown so large that an international organization was created; it has annual conventions in different cities. Nine different regions have been established, with each region represented on the board of directors of the institute. The important functions of the institute are to train and certify practitioners and instructors of reality therapy and to provide continuing education for current reality therapists.

To become certified in reality therapy, individuals must participate in a training program that lasts at least 18 months (William Glasser Institute, 2000). The training includes a week of intensive training followed by a 6-month supervised practicum. If recommended by the supervisor, the trainee may attend an advanced week of training. This is then followed up by another 6-month practicum period. The supervisor of this practicum may recommend the individual to be invited to certification week, where the trainee is asked to demonstrate and apply an understanding of choice theory and reality therapy. Once certified, individuals are referred to as reality therapy certified (RTC) because many who are certified are not counselors or therapists and do not wish to violate state licensure or certification laws. To advance from the first training workshop to a senior faculty position typically takes more than 5 years.

In 1987 Glasser developed a certification program for certified reality therapists so that they could become qualified as senior faculty. These instructors must submit a videotape on reality therapy and choice theory approved by Robert E. Wubbolding, the Director of Training for the William Glasser Institute. Certification of reality therapists and instructors allows the director of training to have a means of assuring that those who call themselves reality therapists have demonstrated adequate skills, especially in practicing the WDEP system of reality therapy (Robert E. Wubbolding, personal communication, September 12, 2009).

Using Reality Therapy with Other Theories

The procedures that make up reality therapy are quite specific. Although there is latitude for using other procedures derived from a variety of theories of psychotherapy, techniques must fit within the reality therapy framework (Wubbolding, 2000). Because reality therapy focuses on doing, techniques from behavior therapy are likely to be most compatible. Praise is important in reality therapy and comparable to the term *positive reinforcement* in behavior therapy. Role playing and modeling are other behavior therapy techniques that are consistent with methods used to help clients carry out plans in reality therapy. Although reality therapy is not a problem-solving approach, there are times when it is helpful to use behavioral problem-solving techniques with clients. The strategic therapy of Milton Erickson, which uses paradoxical techniques, is consistent with reality therapy (Palmatier, 1990), as is the constructivist approach. The cognitive therapies such as those of Adler (Petersen, 2005) and Ellis's rational emotive behavior therapy (Ellis, 1999) have active components that can be used by reality therapists in their work. Frankl's existential view of meaning and being able to choose and being responsible for choices one makes is quite similar to Glasser's philosophy of choice theory (Manchester, 2004). During the development of a friendly relationship with a client, some reality therapists have found the empathic listening approach of Carl Rogers to be helpful. Knowledge of a variety of theories helps reality therapists to augment their skills while adhering to reality therapy procedures.

Those who are not reality therapists may find the principles of choice theory and reality therapy to be useful. The notion that clients have control over their behavior—that they choose solutions, ineffective though they may be, to problems—can be a useful concept for integrative therapists. By thinking of clients as having control over their lives, counselors can develop strategies that can provide constructive change. The idea of planning and committing to plans is consistent with a variety of cognitive and behavioral treatments. Although the aspects of reality therapy that include "don't accept excuses," "don't criticize or argue," and "don't give up easily" are particularly appropriate to some of the difficult populations (juvenile and adult offenders and drug and alcohol abusers) that reality therapists encounter, such advice is consistent with many theoretical approaches.

Research

Research has not been a major focus of Glasser's work with choice theory and reality therapy. Rather, he has focused on doing—implementing reality therapy in human services and educational institutions. He has pointed to clear changes that have occurred in his work at the Ventura School for Girls that significantly reduced the recidivism rate. He has also pointed to the significant changes that Harrington made in the release rates of hospitalized patients at a veterans hospital in Los Angeles. The case studies edited by his first wife (N. Glasser, 1980, 1989) illustrate, for him, the effectiveness of reality therapy with a large variety of psychological problems.

A number of studies and dissertations (Litwack, 2007; Wubbolding, 2000) have been done in several different countries throughout the world. Typical of the educational studies are those that compare reality therapy with another treatment with elementary, junior high, high school, or college students. In a study in Korea, a small sample (11) of middle school girls responded positively to reality group counseling compared with a control group of 12 students (Kim & Hwang, 1996). Improvements were found in locus of control, motivation for achievement, and discipline. A reality therapy program was developed for Korean college students who were addicted to the Internet (Kim, 2007). This program was found to reduce the Internet addiction level of university students (Kim, 2008). Reality therapy has been used widely in Korea. Selecting 43 studies that measured self-esteem and locus of control from 250 that studied reality therapy and choice theory in educational institutions, Kim and Hwang (2006) performed a meta-analysis. For the 43 studies, in general, individuals receiving reality therapy in group treatment had greater self-esteem and higher locus of control scores than did those in control groups. A very different population was studied in Nigeria—empty nester retirees. Reality therapy, cognitive coping behavior training, and their combination were found to be more effective than a control group in helping the retirees (Chima & Nnodum, 2008). These studies show some ways of investigating the effectiveness of reality therapy.

Wubbolding (2000) reviewed research using reality therapy with individuals with addiction and depression as well as studies of juvenile and adult offenders. Aggressive behavior has been a specific area of attention in reality therapy research. In one study, male domestic violence perpetrators were divided into two groups of 15. One group received 12 weeks of group reality therapy treatment. The other received 12 weeks of structured cognitive behavioral therapy. The men who participated in the reality therapy group made a significant change on a scale of self-control over violence, whereas the other men did not (Gilliam, 2004). No significant differences were found across a variety of psychological and social measures. In a study of 23 females and 22 males who participated in a 21-session program for domestic violence based on reality therapy concepts and reality therapy for the families, there was very little or no reported violence for female offenders, whereas some violence was reported with males (Rachor, 1995). Another study addressed victims of bullying. In Korea, a 10-session reality therapy group program was used to increase responsibility and reduce victimization among children being bullied (Kim, 2006) . Research such as that described here is important because it focuses on populations that are often underrepresented in other studies. Although some research on reality therapy is published in the *International Journal of Reality Therapy* and reality therapy is the subject of some doctoral dissertations, the amount of research is quite limited. Because Glasser's approach is pragmatic and oriented toward helping others in the educational and social service systems bring about change, research has not been a priority. Furthermore, the training of certified reality therapists does not include research training.

Gender Issues

In reality therapy, clients present to therapists those parts of their lives that are out of control. Reality therapists help their clients explore how satisfying their current behavior is to others and to themselves. Ideally, this is done irrespective of gender. The counselor does not decide what should be changed. In reality therapy, both men and women learn that they have the power to control their own lives. Historically, it can be argued that this issue has been a greater concern for women than for men.

Depending on one's viewpoint, reality therapy can be seen as enhancing the power of women to control their lives or thwarting them in trying to attain control. In working with battered women, Whipple (1985) states that abused women are not able to meet their needs for belonging, power, freedom, and fun and that their survival needs are threatened. Whipple (1985) shows how the procedures that make up reality therapy can be applied to battered women in helping them meet their basic needs. From a feminist therapy perspective, Ballou (1984) points out that in holding individuals responsible for their behavior, historical and social discrimination is ignored. Furthermore, reality therapy, like other therapies, has neglected the need for social change and for reducing sexism in women's environment. Although the feminist therapy point of view is critical of reality therapy for not focusing on external events, there are areas of agreement between feminist therapy and reality therapy. Both emphasize the therapeutic relationship and the importance of accepting, but not agreeing with, the client's value system. Ballou's article was examined 22 years later by Linnenberg (2006), who believes that many of her comments are still applicable, but some progress has been made. He feels that the emphasis on multiculturalism in recent years has helped reality therapy, although reality therapy has not directly addressed multiculturalism. Ballou (2006) concurs with Linnenberg's analysis and emphasizes the importance of critical self-reflection.

Silverberg (1984) believes that reality therapy is a particularly appropriate treatment for men. He argues that historically men have been more reluctant than women to seek therapy, to explore feelings, and to make insights about their behavior. He believes that the emphasis that reality therapy gives to development of self-control, autonomy, and independence are particularly appealing to men. Further, the emphasis on specific behaviors and on productivity in sessions that have planning as a component would be appropriate for men whose outlook toward life is achievement oriented. Men who have a negative feeling toward examining their feelings and emotions may find reality therapy an attractive approach. Threadgall (1996) believes that reality therapy is appropriate for gay men and emphasizes the importance of commitment to therapy and to plans.

Multicultural Issues

Because of its emphasis on individuals' choices and control over their own lives, reality therapy can be seen both positively and negatively from a multicultural point of view. A criticism of reality therapy is that it does not take into account environmental forces such as discrimination and racism that affect people from different cultures. Because of discrimination and racism, individuals' attempts to make certain social and economic choices, such as friendships or employment interviews, can be limited. Nevertheless, reality therapists respect individual cultural differences. The reality therapist does not decide which behaviors the client should change. Thus, clients decide on the changes they wish to make that are consistent with their own cultural values. Although cultures vary in how they view the basic needs of survival, belonging, power, freedom, and fun, exploring these needs and individuals' wants and perceptions can apply across cultures. Discussing what clients are doing and what they would like to change is also consistent across most cultures. When making plans with clients, reality therapists consider not only the effect of the plan on individual clients but also how the plans will affect the people who are important to them as well as society as a whole. Although use of reality therapy with clients of different cultures can be helpful, it is still important for counselors to have knowledge of the cultures they are working with. Wubbolding (2000) summarizes issues important in working with individuals from many different cultural backgrounds.

Several writers have used reality therapy with a wide variety of people from different cultures: African Americans, Koreans, Malaysians, Native Americans, and students living in Hong Kong. Mickel (2005) states that reality therapy can be integrated with an approach that represents African-centered family therapy. Okonji, Osokie, and Pulos (1996) report that a sample of 120 African American Job Corps students preferred reality therapy to person-centered counseling after watching simulated counseling sessions on video. Working with Native Americans, therapists can use the Rule of Six that states that for a particular situation there are six possible interpretations (Mottern, 2003). The Rule of Six is very consistent with choice theory because of its emphasis on responsibility for choices. Reality therapy can also be used with individuals from Cape Verde, islands off of West Africa (Sanchez & Thomas, 2000). Reality therapy can help Cape Verdeans integrate their Cape Verdean culture, their African culture, and their Creole language into their quality world. Renna (2000) describes a pilot project that uses choice theory to help bring Israeli and Palestinian students together. In discussing how choice theory and reality therapy can be applied to Koreans, Cheong (2001) emphasizes the need to be more empathic and to use less direct questioning than may be necessary with Americans. In Malaysia, a country with a large Muslim population, reality therapy is seen as appropriate because it is consistent with an Islamic perspective (Jusoh & Ahmad, 2009). However, Jusoh, Mahmud, and Ishak (2008) found that although reality therapy is appealing to Malaysian counselors, they need more access to training to increase their skills in applying reality therapy. Not only is reality therapy seen as consistent with an Islamic perspective, it is also seen as consistent with a Judaic perspective as addressed by Talmudic Law (Barr, 2009). The variety of uses that reality therapy has had for people of different cultures should be encouraging for those wishing to adapt reality therapy to a specific cultural group.

Group Counseling

Commonly used in junior high and high schools, reality therapy groups have also been used with parent groups, substance abusers, mentally limited adults, and incarcerated adolescents and adults. Although used with a great variety of groups, the same basic model that is applied to individual counseling is appropriate for groups. The emphasis on what group members are doing is key to reality therapy groups. Discussion of past behavior and excuses for current behavior are cut off by the group leader and by other participants. Plans are made by each group member, and the actual carrying out of these plans is followed up by the participants and leaders. Usually each participant takes a certain amount of group time; then the leader moves on to another member.

Bassin (1993) suggests that a group can be an excellent follow-up to individual reality therapy. Having some knowledge of reality therapy, an individual can help other members of the group in understanding principles of choice theory and reality therapy. Likewise, an individual can get suggestions and support from others when bringing in a problem to the group. Corey (2008) describes the use of group reality therapy in more detail, including the role and functions of the group leader, as well as the actual practice of reality therapy in groups.

Wubbolding (2000) suggests that needs of group members can be met throughout group meetings. The first need to be met is that of belonging, so that group members can feel included in the group. Total behavior can be addressed by discussing ineffective and effective actions, thoughts, and feelings. Later, when anxiety, conflict, and resistance arise, power needs of group members are discussed. This can lead to group members feeling more powerful as they address specific actions to change. Level of commitment to plans for changing thinking and actions is assessed, and encouragement is given so that plans can be followed. Group members assist each other in making plans to meet needs. Needs for fun and freedom may be discussed in latter stages of the group.

Summary

Reality therapists help individuals control their own lives more effectively. Clients are helped to see choices where they thought they had none. For example, a depressed person is taught to understand that she is choosing depressing behavior. An integral part of reality therapy is the personality theory that it is based on choice theory. Glasser has applied his theories to a wide variety of educational and human services settings.

Choice theory explains how and why people behave. The real world is distinguished from the perceived world, which forms the basis for determining the wants of individuals. Individuals develop pictures of what they want, which will meet, to varying degrees, the basic needs of survival, belonging, power, freedom, and fun. Based on pictures of what they want, individuals behave. This behavior is referred to as total behavior, as it has four components: doing, thinking, feeling, and physiology. Although reality therapy deals with all of these, the focus is on changing doing.

Reality therapy can best be described as a cycle of counseling that intertwines the counseling environment or relationship with procedures that lead to change. Developing a friendly relationship with the client that shows that the therapist is interested starts at the beginning of therapy and continues throughout. The reality therapist uses procedures that will establish the wants, needs, and perceptions of the client. The clients' total behavior, with a focus on what they are doing, is examined in terms of the clients' needs and values. This is done so that the therapist can help clients design plans to change ineffective behavior. It is not enough to make plans; the therapist may contract with clients or otherwise get a commitment for clients to carry out the plans. As a part of the counseling environment or relationship, the therapist is friendly yet firm, not accepting excuses yet not criticizing or arguing with the client. Reality therapists often work with individuals with difficult problems, such as substance abuse, criminal behavior, or psychotic behavior. A principle of reality therapy is that the therapist does not give up on the client.

High school guidance counselors, alcohol and drug abuse counselors, social workers, and others working with juvenile or adult offenders have been attracted to Glasser's emphasis on responsibility and control. Glasser's concern about the educational system, discipline within the school, and school management has had an impact on thousands of teachers, guidance counselors, and school administrators. Workshops for counselors, teachers, and others have been designed to apply principles of choice theory and reality therapy.

 ## Theories in Action DVD: Reality Therapy

Basic Concepts Used in the Role-Play	Questions About the Role-Play
• Reflection focused on understanding problem • Examine needs • Ask about wants • Clarify wants • Ask about evaluating choices • Push client to evaluate wants • Challenge clients to evaluate choices • Focus on new choices—"Doing" • Planning	1. How does Dr. Gilchrist help Todd to take responsibility for his choices that concern socializing with others? 2. How does Dr. Gilchrist form a working relationship with Todd? (p. 425) 3. How is choice theory applied to Todd's problem? (pp. 419–423)? 4. Compare and contrast the use of reality therapy in the case of Gloria (pp. 434–438) with the use of reality therapy in the case of Todd in the *Theories in Action* DVD.

Suggested Readings

Glasser, W. (1998). *Choice theory: A new psychology of personal freedom.* New York: HarperCollins. Glasser replaces control theory with choice theory. He focuses on applications to marriage, family, school, and work.

Glasser, W. (1965). *Reality therapy: A new approach to psychiatry.* New York: Harper & Row. Although many of the concepts in this book have been modified, the basic principles of reality therapy still pertain. Glasser's writings include many case examples, making his work easy to read and understand.

Glasser, W. (2000). *Counseling with choice theory.* New York: HarperCollins. Each chapter is a case study or a continuation of a case study that illustrates Glasser's use of choice theory with a variety of

relationship problems. The style is interesting and easy to follow.

Wubbolding, R. (2000). *Reality therapy for the 21st century.* Philadelphia: Brunner-Routledge. Wubbolding describes the basics of choice theory and how to use reality therapy with individuals, groups, and families. He describes the history of reality therapy, use with individuals from a variety of cultures, and research supporting the effectiveness of reality therapy.

Wubbolding, R. E. (1988). *Using reality therapy.* New York: Harper & Row. Focusing on the application of reality therapy, Wubbolding explains techniques such as the use of paradox, questioning, and ways to implement reality therapy. Applications to marriage and family counseling are also included.

References

Abbott, W. J. (1980). Banking on your interests. In N. Glasser (Ed.), *What are you doing?* (pp. 270–280). New York: Harper & Row.

Ballou, M. (1984). Thoughts on reality therapy from a feminist. *Journal of Reality Therapy, 4,* 28–32.

Ballou, M. (2006). Critical self-reflection necessary but not sufficient. *International Journal of Reality Therapy, 26*(1), 27–28.

Barr, Y. (2009). Reality therapy and the Talmud. *International Journal of Reality Therapy, 29*(2), 31–35.

Bassin, A. (1993). The reality therapy paradigm. *Journal of Reality Therapy, 12*, 3–13.

Brown, T., & Swenson, S. (2005). Identifying basic needs: The contextual needs assessment. *International Journal of Reality Therapy, 24*(2), 7–10.

Burns, M. K., Vance, D., Szadokierski, I., & Stockwell, C. (2006). Student needs survey: A psychometrically sound measure of the five basic needs. *International Journal of Reality Therapy, 25*(2), 4–8.

Cheong, E. S. (2001). A theoretical study on the application of choice theory and reality therapy in Korea. *International Journal of Reality Therapy, 22*(2), 8–11.

Chima, I. M., & Nnodum, B. (2008). Efficacy of reality therapy and cognitive coping behaviour training in handling adjustment problems of empty-nester retirees. *Nigerian Journal of Guidance & Counselling, 13* (1), 190–200.

Corey, G. (2008). *Theory and practice of group counseling* (7th ed.). Belmont, CA: Thomson, Brooks/Cole.

Corry, M. A. (1989). Value judgments sometimes don't come easily. In N. Glasser (Ed.), *Control theory in the practice of reality therapy* (pp. 64–82). New York: Harper & Row.

Ellis, A. (1999). Rational emotive behavior therapy as an internal control psychology. *International Journal of Reality Therapy, 19*(1), 4–11.

Geronilla, L. S. (1989). Starved for affection. In N. Glasser (Ed.), *Control theory in the practice of reality therapy* (pp. 255–304). New York: Harper & Row.

Gilliam, A. (2004). The efficacy of William Glasser's reality/choice theory with domestic violence perpetrators: A treatment outcome study. (Doctoral dissertation). *Dissertation Abstracts International: Section B: The Sciences and Engineering, 65*(1–B).

Glasser, N. (Ed.). (1980). *What are you doing? How people are helped through reality therapy*. New York: Harper & Row.

Glasser, N. (Ed.). (1989). *Control theory in the practice of reality therapy: Case studies*. New York: Harper & Row.

Glasser, W. (1961). *Mental health or mental illness?* New York: Harper & Row.

Glasser, W. (1965). *Reality therapy: A new approach to psychiatry*. New York: Harper & Row.

Glasser, W. (1969). *Schools without failure*. New York: Harper & Row.

Glasser, W. (1972). *The identity society*. New York: Harper & Row.

Glasser, W. (1976). *Positive addiction*. New York: Harper & Row.

Glasser, W. (1981). *Stations of the mind*. New York: Harper & Row.

Glasser, W. (1984). *Take effective control of your life*. New York: Harper & Row.

Glasser, W. (1985). *Control theory: A new explanation of how we control our lives*. New York: Harper & Row.

Glasser, W. (1986a). *Control theory in the classroom*. New York: Harper & Row.

Glasser, W. (1986b). *The control theory–reality therapy workbook*. Canoga Park, CA: Institute for Reality Therapy.

Glasser, W. (1989). Control theory in the practice of reality therapy. In N. Glasser (Ed.), *Control theory in the practice of reality therapy: Case studies* (pp. 1–15). New York: Harper & Row.

Glasser, W. (1990). *The basic concepts of reality therapy* [chart]. Canoga Park, CA: Institute for Reality Therapy.

Glasser, W. (1998a). *Choice theory: A new psychology of personal freedom*. New York: HarperCollins.

Glasser, W. (1998b). *The quality school* (rev. ed.). New York: Harper & Row.

Glasser, W. (2000a). *Counseling with choice theory*. New York: HarperCollins.

Glasser, W. (2000b). *Every student can succeed*. Chatsworth, CA: William Glasser Institute.

Glasser, W. (2003). *Warning: Psychiatry can be hazardous to your mental health*. New York: HarperCollins.

Glasser, W., & Glasser, C. (1999). *The language of choice theory*. New York: HarperCollins.

Glasser, W., & Glasser, C. (2000). *Getting together and staying together*. New York: HarperCollins.

Glasser, W., & Glasser, C. (2007). *Eight lessons for a happier marriage*. New York: Harper Paperbacks.

Glasser, W., & Zunin, L. M. (1979). Reality therapy. In R. Corsini (Ed.), *Current psychotherapies* (2nd ed., pp. 302–339). Itasca, IL: F. E. Peacock.

Jusoh, A. J., & Ahmad, R. (2009). The practice of reality therapy from the Islamic perspective in Malaysia and variety of custom in Asia. *International Journal of Reality Therapy, 29*(2), 3–7.

Jusoh, A. J., Mahmud, Z., & Ishak, N. M. (2008). The patterns of reality therapy usage among Malaysian counselors. *International Journal of Reality Therapy, 28*(1), 5–14.

Kim, J. (2006). The effect of a bullying prevention program on responsibility and victimization of bullied children in Korea. *International Journal of Reality Therapy, 26*(1), 4–8.

Kim, J. (2007). A reality therapy group counseling program as an Internet addiction recovery method for college students in Korea. *International Journal of Reality Therapy, 26*(2), 3–9.

Kim, J. (2008). The effect of a R/T group counseling program on the Internet addiction level and self-esteem of Internet addiction university students. *International Journal of Reality Therapy, 27*(2), 4–12.

Kim, R. I., & Hwang, M. G. (1996). "Making the world I want"—Based on reality therapy. *Journal of Reality Therapy, 16*, 26–35.

Kim, R. I., & Hwang, M. G. (2006). A meta-analysis of reality therapy and choice theory group programs for self-esteem and locus of control in Korea. *International Journal of Choice Theory, 1*(1), 25–30.

Linnenberg, D. M. (2006). Thoughts on reality therapy from a pro-feminist perspective. *International Journal of Reality Therapy, 26*(1), 23–26.

Litwack, L. (2007). Research review: Dissertations on reality therapy and choice therapy—1970–2007. *International Journal of Reality Therapy, 27*(1), 14–16.

Manchester, K. (2004). The needs within the meaning. *International Journal of Reality Therapy, 24*(1), 45–46.

Mickel, E. (2005). African-centered family therapy in transition: Healing cycle as an answer to terrorism. *International Journal of Reality Therapy, 24*(2), 33–37.

Mickel, E., & Sanders, P. (2003). Utilizing CLSI and BNSA to improve outcomes: Perceptions of the relationship between the basic needs and learning styles. *International Journal of Reality Therapy, 22*(2), 44–47.

Mottern, R. (2003). Using the Rule of Six and traditional American Indian learning stories to teach choice theory. *International Journal of Reality Therapy, 23*(1), 27–33.

O'Donnell, D. J. (1987). History of the growth of the Institute for Reality Therapy. *Journal of Reality Therapy, 7*, 2–8.

Okonji, J. M. A., Osokie, J. N., & Pulos, S. (1996). Preferred style and ethnicity of counselors by African American males. *Journal of Black Psychology, 22*, 329–339.

Palmatier, L. L. (1990). Reality therapy and brief strategic interactional therapy. *Journal of Reality Therapy, 9*, 3–17.

Petersen, S. (2005). Reality therapy and individual or Adlerian psychology: A comparison. *International Journal of Reality Therapy, 24*(2), 11–14.

Powers, W. T. (1973). *Behavior: The control of perception.* Hawthorne, NY: Aldine.

Powers, W. T. (1999). PCT, HPCT, and internal control psychology. *International Journal of Reality Therapy, 19*(1), 12–16.

Rachor, R. (1995). An evaluation of the First Step passages in domestic violence. *Journal of Reality Therapy, 14*, 29–36.

Rapport, Z. (2004). Positive addiction: Self-evaluation and teaching tools. *International Journal of Reality Therapy, 24*(1), 43–44.

Renna, B. (2000). Israel and Palestine. *International Journal of Reality Therapy, 19*(2), 24–28.

Sanchez, W., & Thomas, D. M. (2000). Quality world and Capeverdians: Viewing basic needs through a cultural/historical lens. *International Journal of Reality Therapy, 20*(1), 17–21.

Silverberg, R. A. (1984). Reality therapy with men: An action approach. *Journal of Reality Therapy, 3*, 27–31.

Sohm, S. (2004). Quality world awareness: Placing people into the quality world. *International Journal of Reality Therapy, 23*(2), 39–40.

Threadgall, R. A. (1996). Counselling homosexual men. *Journal of Reality Therapy, 15*, 39–43.

Weeks, G. R., & L'Abate, L. (1982). *Paradoxical psychotherapy: Theory and practice with individuals, couples, and families.* New York: Brunner/Mazel.

Whipple, V. (1985). The use of reality therapy with battered women in domestic violence shelters. *Journal of Reality Therapy, 5*, 22–27.

William Glasser Institute (2000). *Programs, policies and procedures manual.* Chatsworth, CA: William Glasser Institute.

Wubbolding, R. E. (1988). *Using reality therapy.* New York: Harper & Row.

Wubbolding, R. E. (1991). *Understanding reality therapy.* New York: HarperCollins.

Wubbolding, R. E. (1996a). *Reality therapy training* (9th ed.). Cincinnati, OH: Center for Reality Therapy.

Wubbolding, R. E. (1996b). Professional issues: The use of questions in reality therapy. *Journal of Reality Therapy, 16*, 122–127.

Wubbolding, R. E. (2000). *Reality therapy for the 21st century*. Philadelphia: Brunner-Routledge.

Wubbolding, R. E. (2004). Professional school counselors and reality therapy. In B. Erford (Ed.), *Professional school counseling: A handbook of theories, programs, and practices* (pp. 211–218). Austin, TX: CAPS Press.

Wubbolding, R. E. (2005). The power of belonging. *International Journal of Reality Therapy*, 24(2), 43–44.

Wubbolding, R. E. (2010). *Reality therapy*. Washington, American Psychological Association.

Wubbolding, R. E., & Brickell, J. (1998). Qualities of the reality therapist. *Journal of Reality Therapy*, *18*, 47–49.

Wubbolding, R. E., & Brickell, J. (2009). Perception: The orphaned component of choice therapy. *International Journal of Reality Therapy*, 29(2), 50–54.

Constructivist Approaches

Outline of Constructivist Approaches

SOLUTION-FOCUSED THERAPY

Views about Therapeutic Change

Assessment

Goals

Techniques of Solution-Focused Therapy
Forming a collaborative relationship
Complementing
Pretherapy change
Coping questions
The miracle question
Scaling questions
Assessing motivation
Exception-seeking questions
Formula first session tasks
"The message"

NARRATIVE THERAPY

Personal Construct Theory
Setting
Characterization
Plot
Theme

Epston and White's Narrative Therapy

Assessment

Goals

Techniques of Narrative Therapy
Externalizing the problem
Unique outcomes
Alternative narratives
Positive narratives
Questions about the future
Support for client stories

As shown in previous chapters, many theorists apply postmodern thinking or a constructivist point of view to their therapeutic approaches. However, some therapies are identified primarily as constructivist. I will describe three in this chapter: solution-focused therapy and two types of narrative therapy: personal construct theory and Epston and White's narrative therapy. Constructivist approaches are relatively new, and I will describe current trends for each approach as well as recent research. Additionally, I will explain gender and multicultural issues for each.

Both solution-focused therapy and narrative therapies attend to the client's way of viewing problems and situations. Neither therapy brings in its own theory of development or personality to the clients' problems; rather, the clients' problems stimulate the therapists' approach to helping the clients. Developed by Steve de Shazer and Insoo Kim Berg, solution-focused therapy concentrates on new solutions for a problem rather than on the origin of the problem. The therapy is brief and attends to implementing solutions. Narrative therapy examines patients' stories to learn how they view their lives. Constructivist therapists like Robert Neimeyer use an approach that looks at a person's life the way one might analyze a drama. A specific approach developed by David Epston and Michael White helps individuals and families change their stories with problems to stories with more positive outcomes. All three therapies use creative techniques to help their clients see their own lives in different ways.

History of Constructivist Approaches

This section focuses on the philosophical and psychological thinking that provided an opportunity for constructivist theories of psychotherapy to develop. Early philosophical thinking such as the work of Epictetus and Immanuel Kant, as well as of psychologists such as Piaget, shows how attending to the perception of reality rather than trying to define reality itself influenced constructivist theories of therapy. The work of George Kelly has probably had the single greatest impact on constructivist approaches to therapy because of his belief that each individual uses different psychological constructs to view the world. The psychiatrist Milton Erickson was well known for his creative approaches to understanding clients and helping them change. While Erickson did not identify with constructivism, his creative ways of viewing and understanding his patients continue to intrigue therapists. A number of other theorists associated with family therapy have studied communication patterns, especially as they can be applied to solving people's problems. The contributions of Steve de Shazer and Insoo Kim Berg to solution-focused therapy are explained. Briefly, I will describe the narrative therapeutic approach of personal construct theory using Robert Neimeyer's work as an example. Michael White and David Epston, along with their narrative approach to helping clients, are also described. The work of these individuals provides some of the background for understanding the development of solution-focused and narrative therapies.

Early Influences

Early philosophers and psychologists who have had an influence on the development of constructivist therapies believed that perceptions of reality are important in understanding people's actions. For example, the ancient Greek philosopher Epictetus felt that it was not reality that disturbed people but their views of reality (Neimeyer & Stewart, 2000). The German philosopher Immanuel Kant, writing in the late 1700s, described the human mind as transforming and coordinating data that individuals sense and then integrating this data into thought. Thus, it is the human mind that helps us to determine what we know. Hans Vaihinger (1965), discussed previously as having influenced Alfred Adler (Chapter 4), described "fictionalisms," which are ideas that do not exist in reality but help individuals to deal more effectively with reality. Thus, Vaihinger believed that the mind could create constructs that individuals would use to see the world. The linguist Alfred Korzybski, writing in the first half of the 20th century, examined how individuals present their perceptions as reality. For example, I may say, "Joan is an alcoholic" rather than "I believe Joan drinks so much that she creates problems for herself." In the first sentence, I am not identified as the perceiver, whereas in the second sentence, I am identified as perceiving that I think that Joan has a problem rather than implying that my view of reality is reality. Swiss psychologist Jean Piaget studied how the growth of children and their exposure to increasingly difficult intellectual material affected the way they learn and view their world. These diverse ways of understanding the importance of viewing one's world have had an impact on the work of George Kelly as well as on the development of solution-focused and narrative therapies.

George Kelly

Born on a farm in Kansas, George Kelly (1905–1967) was an only child who was raised by religious parents committed to helping others. He studied a number of subjects before becoming a psychologist. Most of his teaching was done at Ohio State University, where he taught for 19 years and refined his theory of personality. Kelly believed that like scientists, people construct hypotheses and test them against their view of reality. He is known for the development of the *personal construct*, which is a way of viewing events (Fransella & Neimeyer, 2005; Schultz & Schultz, 2009). Kelly developed the Role Construct Repertory Test (known as the Reptest) to measure dichotomies that were important in a person's life. In the Reptest, an individual lists dichotomies of constructs, such as "religious—not religious," "not athletic–athletic," "smart–dumb" as they apply to important people in the client's life. The client then rates individuals on each concept. There are no objective scoring methods. However, the Reptest helps individuals uncover important dichotomies in their lives and understand constructs that are important to their lives (Neimeyer, 2009). Kelly also developed a therapeutic technique called "fixed role therapy" in which clients act out the constructs of an imaginary person to demonstrate how to use new constructs that would be more useful than previous ones (Neimeyer & Baldwin, 2005). Kelly's work on personal constructs has had a broad impact on therapists using solution-focused, narrative, and some other constructivist therapies. Kelly died in 1967 after a relatively short academic career.

Milton Erickson

Milton Erickson (1901–1980) was born in Wisconsin. As a young man, he suffered from polio and was to deal with physical pain in his lifetime, especially in old age. As a practicing psychiatrist in Arizona, he saw many patients in his small brick home. Hearing of his work, many therapists, such as Haley (1973) and Zeig (1985), talked to him about his work and reported his cases. In his use of hypnotic techniques, he would join with patients to gain their trust so that he could set about using direct or indirect suggestions.

Erickson was known for his extraordinary way of looking at a patient, listening to the patient, and hearing and seeing aspects of the patient that others would not see. He was also known for being courteous and able to bypass resistance that patients may have to therapy. Because of this, patients would not experience a loss of control as they talked of their problems. In his later work, he used indirect suggestions more frequently and hypnosis less frequently. The suggestions would often puzzle other therapists, as they would not see aspects of the individual that Erickson saw. In a discussion between Jay Haley and John Weakland (Zeig, 1985), Haley reports Erickson's work with a young woman suffering from psychosis. She reported that young men were floating overhead. Erickson has her

> put those young men in the closet in his office so they wouldn't interfere with her school teaching. And then when she was going to leave the city, she said, "What if I have psychotic episodes in the other city?" and he said, "Why don't you put them in a manila envelope and send them to me?" And so she sent him her psychotic episodes in a manila envelope. (Zeig, 1985, p. 590)

She proceeded to send him manila envelopes, which he kept in a drawer in case she returned. There were many more recorded cases of Erickson's use of suggestions, both direct and indirect. His emphasis on understanding the communication style (and important constructs) of the patient has had a great impact on those who practice solution-focused, narrative, and other forms of constructivist therapy. Like solution-focused therapy, Erickson was focused on finding solutions to the patient's problem rather than being concerned with the history of the problem.

Early Family Therapy Approaches

In 1952, Gregory Bateson (1904–1980) started the Palo Alto project, which had as its goal the study of communication. Bateson was particularly interested in the direct meaning of a message as well as its hidden or unnoticed meaning (Nichols, 2008). For example, when a parent says to a child "Go to bed," the direct message is that it is time for the child to go to her bedroom. The hidden message is "I am in charge and I am telling you to go to your bedroom." The next year, Bateson was joined by John Weakland and Jay Haley. They and others studied a variety of communication patterns, including the words of patients with schizophrenia. In 1956, they published a view of how problems in communication could cause schizophrenia, described in more detail in Chapter 14, "Family Therapy." This article describes methods of communication, not methods of therapy, as Bateson was more interested in studying people than changing them.

In 1959, Don Jackson (1920–1968) founded the Mental Research Institute, which had as a goal developing ways to help people change using a brief therapy model. This group included John Weakland and Jay Haley, as well as a number of others. In their work, they were influenced by Milton Erickson's problem-solving approach to therapy as well as the study of communication done at the Palo Alto project. Members of the Mental Research Institute had a great impact on several theories of family therapy and many theorists and therapists.

Recent Constructivist Approaches

Constructivist approaches do not have one founder. Rather, there are many people who have contributed to several different constructivist approaches. Steve de Shazer and Insoo Kim Berg are noted as two of the leading developers of solution-focused therapy along with their colleagues. Both social workers, and married to each other, they helped this approach grow through their work at the Brief Family Therapy Center in Milwaukee, Wisconsin. Many theorists such as Greg and Robert Neimeyer developed Kelly's personal construct theory into personal construct therapy, a type of narrative therapy. A different approach to narrative therapy was developed by Michael White in Australia and David Epston in New Zealand, along with many other colleagues throughout the world.

STEVE DE SHAZER

Steve de Shazer. De Shazer (1940–2005) is considered the primary developer of solution-focused therapy. He was very much influenced in his development of solution-focused therapy by the work of Milton Erickson and the Mental Research Institute. As he developed his theory, he continued to keep in contact with John Weakland and others associated with the Mental Research Institute. In developing his theory, he mapped out communication patterns of clients. He also used a method in which therapists would step outside of the therapy room to consult with colleagues who had been watching the therapy proceed. Some of his influential writings include *Keys to Solutions in Brief Therapy* (1985), *Clues: Investigating Solutions in Brief Therapy* (1988), and *Words Were Originally Magic* (1994). He gave workshops throughout the world on using solution-focused therapy and continued to work on the development of the theory until his death in 2005.

INSOO KIM BERG

Insoo Kim Berg. Born in Korea, Berg (1937–2007) was a leading theoretician of solution-focused therapy and was an active clinician. She was executive director of the Brief Family Therapy Center in Milwaukee. Some of her accomplishments included applying solution-focused therapy to alcoholism, marital therapy, and services for poor people. Her books include *Working with the Problem Drinker: A Solution-Focused Approach* (Berg & Miller, 1992), *Family Based Services: A Solution-Focused Approach* (1994), and a practical text: *Interviewing for Solutions* (De Jong & Berg, 2008).

MICHAEL WHITE

Michael White. Working at the Dulwich Centre in Adelaide, South Australia, White (1948–2008) developed narrative therapy along with many others. He started out as an electrical and mechanical draftsman but later became a social worker to help others. Many of his writings appeared in the quarterly *Dulwich Centre Newsletter*. Like de Shazer, he was influenced by the work of Bateson and the Mental Research Institute. He was particularly interested in how people view their world (Nichols, 2008), which led to his approach of understanding people's stories and externalizing people's problems. He has written several books including *Narrative Means to Therapeutic Ends* (White & Epston, 1990), *Reauthoring Lives: Interview and Essays* (1995), and *Maps of Narrative Practice* (2007).

DAVID EPSTON

David Epston. Living in New Zealand, David Epston is codirector of the Family Therapy Centre in Auckland, New Zealand. One of his unique contributions has been the suggestions of "leagues." Leagues are groups of clients who are addressing the same problem and may be in contact with each other through writing. Epston is the archivist for some of these leagues and collects letters and tapes of how clients have battled certain problems. Another idea that he frequently uses with clients is to send letters to them after he has met with them to help through support of their stories and their suggestions. Along with *Narrative Means to Therapeutic Ends* (White & Epston, 1990), which he coauthored with Michael White, he has written *Playful Approaches to Serious Problems: Narratives with Children and their Families* (Freeman, Epston, & Lobovits, 1997) and *Biting the Hand that Starves You: Inspiring Resistance to Anorexia/Bulimia* (Maisel, Epston, & Borden, 2004).

Solution-Focused Therapy

A postmodern, social constructivist approach, solution-focused brief therapy is concerned with how individuals (or a family) view solutions to problems. This therapeutic method is less interested in why or how a problem arose than in possible solutions. De Shazer (1985, 1991, 1994) uses the metaphor of a lock and key to explain this therapeutic approach. Client complaints are like locks on doors that have not been opened. De Shazer and Berg (Berg, 1994; De Jong & Berg, 2008; Metcalf, 2001) do not want to focus on why the lock is the way it is or why the door won't open; rather, they want to help the family look for the key to the problem. Not wanting to get bogged down in reasons or excuses for the problem, they want to find ways to reduce current dissatisfaction and unhappiness. Thus, they focus on the solution. Although they listen to the client's complaint, they attend particularly to the expectations individuals have of possible changes and solutions. Limiting the number of sessions to about 5 to 10, they create an expectation of change. Compared to other brief therapies (such as cognitive therapy), solution-focused therapy is very brief. A study of 160 clients reported that the average number of sessions for solution-focused therapy was two and the average for cognitive therapy was five (Rothwell, 2005).

Views About Therapeutic Change

Solution-focused therapists view clients as wanting to change, and therapists do their best to help bring about change (De Jong & Berg, 2008). Because solutions are different for each client, it is particularly important to involve clients in the process of developing solutions. It is helpful to focus on the solution rather than the problem. In this way, individuals can find exceptions to the problem, which then leads to solutions. Clients do not get bogged down in negative thinking about the problem. By taking one step at a time and making small changes, larger changes can be made. Solution-focused therapists do not diagnose or look for negative aspects of the client; rather, they look for what is working. Solution-focused therapy takes advantage of client strengths and gives a positive view of the future and ways to find solutions to a variety of problems (Kelly, Kim, & Franklin, 2008).

Solution-focused therapy is very practical. The therapist examines whether a problem needs changing. If there is a solution to the problem, the therapist identifies the solution the client is using and compliments the client for using it (de Shazer, 1985). If the approach that the therapist is taking does not seem to be working, then the therapist is flexible and tries something else. When clients have a problem, they are likely to react by doing more of what they are doing. Subtly getting clients to stop what they are doing or to do something else can be helpful in bringing about change (de Shazer, 2005).

Assessment

Unlike many other therapies, solution-focused therapy is not concerned with making diagnostic categorizations; rather, the therapist assesses openness to change (O'Connell, 2005; Sklare, 2005). The therapist is interested in finding out how motivated the client is to change and if the client knows what she wants to change. Related questions are, Can the client recognize when change is taking place? and What obstacles does the client need to deal with to make change? Readiness to make change and finding out if the client knows how to make changes are also questions that are relevant to assessment in solution-focused therapy. These questions are important because solution-focused therapy focuses on specific issues and therapists may prioritize them with the client. The focus is positive, looking at changing problems in clients' lives. Change starts with smaller problems leading to bigger changes.

De Shazer (1985) made extensive use of mapping the sequence of behaviors within families, couples, and individuals. This mapping is often referred to as mindmapping. *Mindmaps*, which are diagrams or outlines of the session, are made during or after the session and used for the therapist to focus on organizing the goals and solutions to the problems. Mindmaps may also be used when therapists take a break to get consultation from colleagues or supervisors. Therapists can take a break at any appropriate point in the session to discuss issues with others or to have time to think about what to do next. The techniques that are used are related to each other and to the problems and solutions. Therefore, planning what to do next may take considerable thought.

Goals

In solution-focused therapy, it is important that goals be clear and concrete (De Jong & Berg, 2008; Kelly, Kim, & Franklin, 2008). In the beginning of therapy, questions make the goals clearer. It is also important that these goals be small so that several small goals can be met rather quickly. Information about exceptions and about "miracles" helps develop specific goals. By finding out what would be different in one's life, problems are solved. How well these small goals are being met is evaluated at several points during therapy. Often the client is asked to rate progress on the goals on a scale from 0 to 10. One technique that relates directly to feedback about progress on goals is "the message." Messages, written or oral, are explicit and given to the client at the end of the session. These include compliments about progress or other aspects of the therapy. They may also include suggestions that will help the clients to solve their problems. All of these techniques, which are described further in the next section, are directly related to achieving goals.

Techniques LANGUAGE

Solution-focused therapists use many different techniques to help their clients find ways to solve their problems. The most common ones are described here. Most basic is to form a collaborative working relationship. One way of doing this is by complimenting the client. Change is the focus of therapy, and examining pretherapy change is one of the first things that solution-focused therapists do. Coping questions and the miracle question help clients start to make changes. Sometimes it is helpful to assess the client's motivation to determine the best therapeutic strategy. A key question is to find out about exceptions to the problem. When completing the first session, it is helpful to use the "formula first session task," which focuses on changes that will take place in the next week. "The message" is a parting message given to clients to help them find solutions to their problems during the next week. All of these methods help the therapist, in different ways, work with the client to find solutions to the problem.

Forming a collaborative relationship. Therapists listen carefully to what clients want to change. Asking about what has changed between the time that the appointment was made and the first session is a way to both acknowledge the client's power to change on her own and to focus the session on change. As in most therapies, counselors wish to be empathic with the client. Lipchik (2009) describes her own solution-focused therapy as increasingly respectful of clients through her years of practice. Solution-focused counselors may become more empathic and respectful with clients through active listening, feeling reflections, goal setting, focusing on the present, and asking questions (O'Connell, 2005). Labeling the problem is often helpful. O'Connell uses the metaphor of the problem island and the solution island. It is often helpful to go back and forth between the two. As therapy progresses, more time is spent on the solution island. The therapist assesses when it is appropriate, in terms of client readiness, to go to the solution island.

Complimenting. One way to make progress in moving from the problem to the solution is to compliment the client (Berg & De Jong, 2005; De Jong & Berg, 2008). This is a method that is positive and helps clients feel more encouraged. It is often helpful in the first session. Berg and De Jong discuss three types of complimenting: direct, indirect, and self-compliments. *Direct compliments* are based on observations of actions that clients have found to be successful. They then bring the client's success with the action to his attention. *Indirect compliments* come from asking clients questions that are similar to points of view of family and friends. *Self-complimenting* refers to asking questions in a way that clients need to answer by talking about success or their abilities. Complimenting helps clients become more focused on and open to making changes.

Pretherapy change. Solution-focused therapists examine change that has taken place even before the client arrives at the therapist's office. The act of making an appointment is a positive indicator for change. Asking "What have you done since you called for the appointment that has made a difference in your problem?" (de Shazer, 1985) sets a tone for a focus on solutions and change. In this way, the therapist focuses on the client's own abilities to bring about change rather than the therapist giving the client solutions. By taking the answer to this question and amplifying it and developing it, the therapist has material to use to move toward solutions to the problem.

Coping questions. By finding out how clients cope, therapists can build on their coping skills even when clients' problems seem very difficult. Generally, it is better for the therapist to use "When" rather than "If." For example, "When you move up on the scale from 3 to 5 ..." is better than "If you move up the scale from 3 to 5 ..." The use of "When" suggests that changes are bound to happen (Berg, 1994). The question "How did you do it?" (Berg, 1994) empowers the client by helping him think about resources and methods he used to deal with a difficult situation. Berg gives a brief example of a social worker using this question with a mother from a difficult family background raising her own child.

Worker: So, how did you figure out that that you wanted to be a different kind of mother to your baby than your mother was to you? Where did you learn to do that?

[Client:] Well, I watched other people, read magazines, watched T.V. programs, and I think about it all the time.

Worker: You are a very thoughtful person. Have you always been that way, or is it something you learn to do?

[Client:] I had to learn myself. Nobody taught me how to do it.

Worker: That's fantastic. I'm sure some day, your baby will learn that from you. (Berg, 1994, p. 115)

Theories in Action

The miracle question. This is one of the most important techniques in solution-focused therapy. The standard question was developed by Steve de Shazer (1988):

> Imagine when you go to sleep at night a miracle happens and the problems we've been talking about disappear. As you were asleep, you didn't know that a miracle had happened. When you woke up, what would be the first signs for you that a miracle had happened?

De Jong and Berg (2008) suggest that this question be given slowly so that the client can think about it and discuss her preferred future. By answering this question, the client is laying out goals for change. Sometimes clients are thrown off by this question or give a response like "I would win the lottery and have $50 million," so the therapist can ask the question again in a briefer form. If the client says, "I would be refreshed and not tired when I wake up," the therapist may reply, "What else?" In solution-focused therapy, "What else?" is a frequently used phrase, as it helps the client to come up with more goals or potential solutions. The miracle question can also be used to follow up on a discussion of an event, such as, "If your interview went well, what would it be like when you got home?" Asking how the miracle would affect significant others would be helpful as well: "If your interview went well, how do you think your husband would react?" Miracle questions may be about how the client would feel or how the client would think.

Theories in Action

Scaling. Scaling is used frequently in many aspects of solution-focused therapy. Scaling questions help clients set goals, measure progress, or establish priorities for taking action. O'Connell (2005) gives several examples of scaling questions.

> On a scale of one to ten, with ten representing the best it can be and zero the worst, where would you say you are today?
> Would staying where you are on the scale be good enough for now, given all the pressures on you?
> What do you need to do, or not do, to prevent you from going down the scale?
> What was happening at the time when you were higher? (p. 53)

Assessing motivation. Clients need to be motivated, at least to some degree, in order to make changes. Scaling questions are often used to assess the motivation for change. Scaling is used frequently in the following example of a client dealing with panic attacks.

Counsellor: On a scale of zero to ten, ten being you would do anything to overcome these panic attacks and zero being you would really love to but you don't think you will do anything, where would you put yourself today?

[*Client:*] Three.

Counsellor: Will three be good enough to make a start?

[*Client:*] No. I feel I tried everything and nothing works. I've almost given up hope that it could get any better.

Counsellor: So although you've had a lot of setbacks you've managed to keep trying? Some people would have completely given up. How have you kept going?

[*Client:*] We've always been fighters in my family. My mum taught me to keep at it when things weren't going well.

Counsellor: So if she was here she would say keep fighting?

[*Client:*] Yes.

Counsellor: Where would you need to get to on the scale before you felt you had a chance of fighting off the panic attacks?

[*Client:*] Five.

Counsellor: How will you know when you've got to five?

[*Client:*] If I could relax more. I feel so tense most of the time, it keeps giving me headaches and then I feel like giving up.

Counsellor: How would you go about being relaxed enough to feel you were getting to five?

[*Client:*] I don't know.

Counsellor: When the sun comes out for you and you feel less tense than usual what has helped to make you better?

[*Client:*] When I'm on my own and I can listen to my own music.

Counsellor: Anything else?

[*Client:*] I like Fridays when I don't have to go to work. I can lie in and potter around a bit.

Counsellor: Does that mean that if this Friday you put on your music and had an easy start to the day, you'd possibly feel a five and more able to fight back against the panic attacks?

[*Client:*] I think so.

Counsellor: If you're a three today, what would help to get you to be a four?
(O'Connell, 2005, p. 56)

The counselor uses scaling questions to elicit estimates of motivation from the client. When asking the client to quantify the level of motivation, the counselor is also asking questions that elicit ideas of behaviors that the client will do that are partial solutions to the problem.

Exception-seeking questions. In solution-focused therapy, questions that ask when the problem did not occur are important. Asking about a time when the client did something that made a difference in the problem is very helpful. Often exception-seeking questions follow directly from a miracle question. Sklare (2005) gives examples: "Can you recall a time when this miracle took place even a little?" and "Could you tell me when this miracle has already happened?" (p. 44). Therapists often follow exception-seeking questions up with "What else?" questions. Therapists frequently compliment the client for using ingenuity and creativity in developing solutions for the problem. Therapists are careful not to be condescending when doing so. The solutions that therapists have heard then become solutions that can be planned and developed to be used in the next week.

Formula first-session task. Solution-focused therapists not only want to emphasize the importance of change, they also want to show that change is inevitable. Near the end of the first session, the therapist can change the orientation of the client from the present to the future. De Shazer (1985, p. 137) developed this question that the therapist asks the client: *"Between now and next week I would like you to observe, so that you can describe to me next time, what happens in your/ pick one: family, life, marriage, relationship/that you want to continue to have happen?"* Notice that the therapist does not ask if something happens, but what happens. There is the expectation that change will happen. This question is asked after the client has expressed her concerns and views of the situation. In this way the client feels understood before making changes (Bertolino & O'Hanlon, 2002). When the client comes to the second session, the client is asked what did happen and what she observed.

"The message." Many solution-focused therapists will stop the session 5 to 10 minutes early to give the client a written message as feedback about the session (O'Connell, 2005). When possible, the therapist may consult with a supervisor or colleagues who are watching the session to determine the content of the message or to discuss other aspects of the therapist's work with the client. This message is somewhat similar to the invariant prescription given by family therapists using methods developed by the Milan associates, as explained on page 566. The message given at the end of a session of solution-focused therapy is more straightforward than the invariant prescription and is frequently used with one client rather than with a family. In the message, the client is given positive feedback. A summary of the client's achievements follows this. A bridge is then made to relate the client's change to the goals that have been developed. Then tasks or suggestions are given to the client. These may be ones where the client is asked to notice positive change (an observational task), times when the expanded problem is handled better, or times when something they want to have happen happens. Sometimes clients will be asked to try a different task or to try a pretend task [a behavioral task] (De Jong & Berg, 2008; O'Connell, 2005). De Jong and Berg (2008) give descriptions of common messages that are given to clients depending on the issues being addressed. For example, a different message would be given to a client who is highly motivated but who does not have well-formulated goals from that given to a client who has well-formulated goals but has done little to achieve them.

Sklare (2005) gives an example of a message with Pedro, a 12-year-old boy who has been suspended from school frequently. The task is written out and a copy is given to Pedro. First the counselor gives positive feedback to Pedro, complimenting him for changes, and then makes a statement to bridge from the compliment to the task.

Compliments

I'm real impressed with how smart you are, with your ability to know what it is you have to do. I am really impressed with how much you care about improving your attitude and your behavior in school. Your efforts today in not throwing a fit with your teacher when she reminded you about your work demonstrate your ability to control yourself. I'm also amazed with your creativity in figuring out a way to at least let yourself know that you know the answers to your teacher's questions even if you are not called on. Your thoughts about not wanting to be suspended show that you respect your mom, grandparents, and yourself a whole lot. Being on the Honors Team in September shows that you know what it takes to be successful, by doing your work and saving your talking time for the lunchroom, the halls, and in related arts and still being able to hang with your friends. You know what to do and how to do it.

Bridging statement

Because of your desire to improve in school,

Task

I want you to notice the times and what you are doing to move you up to a 6 this week. (p. 85)

All of these techniques are often used in the first session of therapy. They may be used in subsequent sessions as well. In the second and other sessions, therapists are careful to follow up on changes that the client has made. They look for successes even if they are relatively small. They use scaling to evaluate the client's gains and help the client to become used to scaling so that the client can continue this behavior when therapy is terminated. Always it is the client, not the therapist, who gets credit for change. Sometimes the miracle question is revised or applied to new problems. Reframing a statement to see positive change is another technique used. Other techniques are used as needed as the therapist remains flexible to work with the problems that the client presents (O'Connell, 2005).

Case Example: Rosie

The following case shows how being positive, complimenting, and using the miracle question can be used with a client with difficult problems. These techniques are used along with scaling and the exception question to show how a therapist might integrate all of these techniques. In this hypothetical case, Cheryl (the therapist) starts by trying to understand the problem and being empathic with it.

Cheryl: How can I be of assistance?

Rosie: Well, I've got some big problems. First thing—I'm pregnant again. I already have two babies, two little girls who are 3 and 2 [years old], and I have two boys who are in school. I'm going crazy with all I have to do, and I'm afraid that my two boys are gonna be put in a foster home again because I have trouble getting them to school in the morning. They don't wanna get up in the morning. They just wanna lay around and watch TV. They say school won't do them any good, and they can make more delivering goods for their uncles.

Cheryl: "Delivering goods"?

Rosie: Yeah, drugs I think. I tell them that is no good and they're gonna get into trouble, but they don't listen to me. I feel better when they're in school, because at least then they can't be with Lamar and Brian [the uncles]. But they won't get up and I'm so tired because I'm pregnant again.

Cheryl: (empathically) Wow, I can see you really have your hands full. Handling four kids by yourself is really tough to start with, but to be pregnant on top of all that …

Rosie: Yeah, it is, and I don't want my boys to be taken away again. But they fight me on school, and I'm so tired with everything I have to do and being pregnant. (De Jong & Berg, 2002, pp. 13–14)

The interview continues as Cheryl gathers information about Rosie and her involvement with prostitution, child welfare needs, and her pregnancy. Then the therapist moves to a different topic where she is able to introduce the "miracle" question. Rosie does not answer the question initially and in a useful way. The therapist is patient and keeps asking. Notice the solutions that start to emerge in the last two client statements.

Cheryl: So you have several big problems—getting your boys to school, getting enough money, being pregnant and very tired. Let me ask you a different kind of question about these; it's called the miracle question. (pause) Suppose that you go to bed as usual tonight and, while you've been sleeping, a miracle happens. The miracle is that the problems you've been telling me about are solved! Only you're sleeping, and so do not know right away that they've been solved. What do you suppose you would notice tomorrow morning that would be different—that would tell you, wow, things are really better!

Rosie: (smiling) That's easy; I would have won the lottery—$3 million.

Cheryl: That would be great, wouldn't it. What else would you notice?

Rosie: Some nice man would come along who has lots of money and lots of patience with kids, and we get married. Or I wouldn't have so many kids and I would finish high school and I would have a good job.

Cheryl: OK, that sounds like a big miracle. What do you imagine would be the first thing that you would notice which would tell you that this day is different, it's better, a miracle must have happened?

Rosie: Well, I would get up in the morning before my kids do, make them breakfast, and sit down with them while we all eat together.

Cheryl: If you were to decide to do that—get up before them and make them breakfast—what would they do?

Rosie: I think maybe they would come and sit down at the table instead of going and turning on the TV.

Cheryl: And how would that be for you?

Rosie: I'd be happier because we could talk about nice things, not argue over TV. And my babies won't start crying over all the fighting about the TV.

Cheryl: What else? What else would be different when the miracle happens? (De Jong & Berg, 2002, pp. 14–15)

The therapist then asks an implicit exception question. She wants to know what the exceptions are to the problem by asking in the first statement, "Are there times already, say in the last two weeks, which are like the miracle which you have been describing, even a little bit?" In this segment Rosie describes the exceptions to the problems and then how she copes with the problem in answer to Cheryl's question, "How did you manage that, reading to four kids?"

Cheryl: Rosie, I'm impressed. You have a pretty clear picture of how things will be different around your house when things are better. Are there times already, say in the last two weeks, which are like the miracle which you have been describing, even a little bit?

Rosie: Well, I'm not sure. Well, about four days ago it was better.

Cheryl: Tell me about four days ago. What was different?

Rosie: Well, I went to bed about ten the night before and had a good night of sleep. I had food in the house, because I had gone to the store and to the food pantry on Saturday. I had even set the alarm for 6:30 and got up when it rang. I made breakfast and called the kids. The boys ate and got ready for school and left on time. (*remembering*) One even got some homework out of his backpack and did it—real quick—before he went to school.

Cheryl: (*impressed*) Rosie, that sounds like a big part of the miracle right there. I'm amazed. How did all that happen?

Rosie: I'm not sure. I guess one thing was I had the food in the house and I got to bed on time.

Cheryl: So, how did you make that happen?

Rosie: Ah, I decided not to see any clients that night and I read books to my kids for an hour.

Cheryl: How did you manage that, reading to four kids? That seems like it would be really tough.

Rosie: No that doesn't work—reading to four kids at the same time. I have my oldest boy read to one baby, because that's the only way I can get him to practice his reading; and I read to my other boy and baby.

Cheryl: Rosie, that seems like a great idea—having him read to the baby. It helps you, and it helps him with his reading. How do you get him to do that?

Rosie: Oh, I let him stay up a half hour later than the others because he helps me. He really likes that. (De Jong & Berg, 2002, p. 15)

The following segment uses scaling questions to address the problem and Rosie's view of its level of severity for her.

Cheryl: I'd like you to put some things on a scale for me, on a scale from 0 to 10. First, on a scale from 0 through 10, where 0 equals the worst your problems have been and 10 means the problems we have been talking about are solved, where are you today on that scale?

Rosie: If you had asked me that question before we started today, I would have said about a 2. But now I think it's more like a 5.

Cheryl: Great! Now let me ask you about how confident you are that you can have another day in the next week like the one four days ago—the one which was a lot like your miracle picture. On a scale of 0 to 10, where 0 equals no confidence and 10 means you have every confidence, how confident are you that you can make it happen again?

Rosie: Oh, … about a 5.

Cheryl: Suppose you were at a 6; what would be different?

Rosie: I'd have to be sure that I always had food in the house for breakfast for the kids. (De Jong & Berg, 2002, p. 16)

The use of these techniques is positive and focused on finding the solution. Berg and Dolan (2001), in *Tales of Solutions: A Collection of Hope-Inspiring Stories*, have assembled a collection of cases that illustrate how solution-focused therapy can offer hope to people who may be suffering from social, economic, political, or psychological difficulties. In *Solution-Focused Brief Therapy in Schools: A 360-Degree View of Research and Practice*, Kelly, Kim, and Franklin (2008) show how solution-focused therapy can be applied to elementary and high school students as well as be taught to teachers to use in the classroom. In *The Art of Solution-Focused Therapy*, Connie and Metcalf (2009) present readings from experienced solution-focused practitioners on their views of using solution-focused therapy with their clients. O'Connell (2005), in *Solution-Focused Therapy*, explains how solution-focused therapy can be integrated with other therapies.

Narrative Therapy

Narrative therapists attend to their clients' stories that contain problems. Telling the same story from different points of view or emphasizing different aspects of these stories enables clients to work through problems in their lives (Neimeyer, 2009). Neimeyer (2009) and other constructivist therapists (Raskin & Bridges, 2008) have examined personal problems the way one might analyze a story and then used a variety of techniques to apply what is broadly called personal construct therapy. A specific method of narrative therapy developed by Michael White and David Epston will be discussed later.

Personal Construct Therapy

Just as we learn to analyze novels in English classes by attending to the setting, characters, plot, and themes, so do personal construct therapists analyze client stories. They also attend to other aspects of stories, but these are the most basic concepts. These concepts will be explained, and then I will give an example of personal construct therapy.

Setting. Where and when the story takes place is the setting of a story. The story can occur in an indoor or outdoor setting or be an actual experience, an image, or a dream. The setting provides a background for the characters to act out the plot. It can be described in great detail or with broad brushstrokes. It can take place in seconds or years.

Characterization. The people (or actors) in the story are called characters. Frequently, the client is the *protagonist* or central character. There are also *antagonists* (the people in conflict with the protagonist), as well as supporting characters. The personality and motive of the characters can be described by the client *(narrator)* directly or may emerge in the telling of the story. Sometimes clients may tell a story, at other times they may act part of it out by being a character or by using a technique such as the gestalt two-chair (or empty-chair) approach (Neimeyer, 2000, 2009).

Plot. Learning what has happened is the role of the plot. As the plot unfolds, we follow the actions of the characters in the setting of the narrative. A plot may have several episodes or actions. Sometimes the therapist helps the client put the episodes together in a manner that is coherent to the client. Often clients may tell the story more than once and different plots or views of the plot develop. Also, with repeated retelling of the story, plots with difficult problems (problem-saturated) may develop new solutions.

Themes. The reasons things happen in the story are referred to as *themes*. What is the meaning for the storyteller? What is the client's emotional experience in telling the story? What does the client see as significant in the story? It is the clients' understanding of the story, not the therapist's, that is the focus of the therapist. Sometimes clients may have an emotional understanding, a cognitive understanding, a spiritual understanding, or some combination of these. Therapists may use different techniques to help clients understand the themes of their stories.

Case Example: Barry

In the following example, Neimeyer (2000) tells the story of Barry and Matt, a father and son, who witnessed parts of a suicide-murder of two family members. A goal for Neimeyer was to have Barry and Matt describe their perceptions of the event and the details that stayed with them. Barry and Matt describe the setting, characters, and plot. As they do this, the theme emerges, as does their understanding of the event.

> Coming home from work early one day, Barry heard his wife, Lisa, call their 4-year-old daughter, Carrie, back to the bedroom. Two gunshots then exploded the relative tranquility of the house, the crack being clearly distinguishable from the musical background of the videogame that 15-year-old Matt was playing in a room down the hall. Running frantically into the bedroom, Barry saw Lisa standing over Carrie's broken and bleeding body. As he shouted, "What have you done?" Lisa leveled the gun at Barry's own torso and pulled the trigger. The impact of the shot to his chest slammed him against the wall, but he remained standing and lunged at her to remove the gun from her grip. Matt then ran into the room and assisted in tearing the gun from his mother's hand, as both men turned and knelt to render help to Carrie. Lisa then fell face forward onto the floor and died, apparently from the previously undiscovered second shot to her own chest.
>
> Seeing them only 1 month after this tragedy, I confronted several urgent therapeutic tasks, among which was helping both Barry and Matt develop a coherent account of the traumatic event and struggle with the apparently unanswerable questions of why Lisa took such desperate action. A turning point came in our fourth session, as I guided them through a step-by-step accounting of the scene of violence, with special attention to the vivid details that had captured their attention at the time. As each emotionally recounted his own perceptions, one image in particular—absent from previous more synoptic tellings—emerged. On first entering the murder-suicide scene, Barry vividly recalled his wife's impassive expression as she looked him in the eyes and shot him. In strong contrast, he described her "enraged and contorted" visage on seeing Matt enter the room, an expression he said he had never before seen in any human face. Matt confirmed the latter image, and the two worked together with only occasional prompting by me to formulate a rendering of Lisa's emotions, intent, and motives adequate to account for this powerful discrepancy. What emerged was a story of sexual betrayal anchored in abusive experiences in Lisa's own childhood and reenacted in subsequent relationships prior to the reactivation of similar themes in her marriage to Barry. With this much more complex narrative in view for the first time, Lisa's possible motivation to coldly punish Barry by killing those he loved, and her rage at the children for not supporting her story of abuse, was opened for the mutual consideration of both survivors. Both left the

session feeling that their grieving, although complicated by this interpretation, had somehow been moved forward through active exploration of the details of the episode and the alternative, if disturbing "readings" of family relationships it suggested. (Neimeyer, 2000, pp. 218–219)

Although an unusually dramatic story, this case shows how the telling and retelling of a story can help individuals deal with such issues as grief and to understand them in new and helpful ways. In this story, the setting (the bedroom) provides a focus for the characters (Barry, Matt, Lisa, and Carrie). The plot (the murder, attempted murder, and suicide) provide an opportunity for different themes to emerge. In the retelling of the story by Barry and Matt, themes of rage and betrayal are related to earlier themes in Lisa's life, giving new understandings of the story and helping Barry and Matt deal with the deaths of Lisa and Carrie.

Therapists have used a number of different approaches to narrative therapy to help clients solve problems by telling, retelling, and re-examining parts of their stories. Many personal constructivist therapists have examined different ways to use a narrative approach to study personality, which has produced a number of ways of using narrative therapy with clients (Adelman, 2008; Hoyt, 2008; Raskin & Bridges, 2008). Perhaps the most well-known approach is the narrative approach of White and Epston.

Epston and White's Narrative Therapy

Listening to their clients' stories and focusing on the importance of the stories and alternative ways of viewing them characterize the work of Michael White and David Epston (Epston & White, 1992; Freeman, Epston, & Lobovits, 1997; Maisel, Epston, & Borden, 2004; White, 1995, 1997, 2007; White & Epston, 1990, 1994; Zimmerman & Dickerson, 2001). The work of Michael White and David Epston reflects the influence of postmodernism and the views of those theorists associated with the Mental Research Institute. The key to change in families (or individuals) is the reauthoring or retelling of stories. They use techniques such as externalizing, searching for unique outcomes, and exploring alternative narratives or stories to help their clients bring about changes in their lives. They also use creative methods to support their clients in making changes by writing letters, giving certificates, or providing letters from former clients as a way of making their stories more permanent. Additionally, they ask clients to look into the future to help clients maintain therapeutic changes.

White and Epston take a social constructionist view of the world. They are interested in how their clients perceive events and the world around them. They know that some family members are likely to have different views than other family members, which can lead to conflict and problems. The narratives or stories that are people's lives represent political, cultural, economic, religious, and social influences. When these stories are problem oriented or negative, they often affect the attitude of the clients or family. White and Epston (1990) are concerned with fully understanding and valuing the story of their clients.

Assessment

Narrative therapists do not diagnose or try to find why the problem occurred; rather, they listen for how the client's story develops so that they may develop a new alternative. To do this they use maps of the story (White, 2007). They often write down what the client is saying so that they have a map of how the story proceeds. The focus is on how the problem influences the person or how the person's life affects the problem. Assessment may start with asking about what the client would like to happen in therapy. Then as the client(s) talk(s) about the influence of the problem on the family and the difficulties that result, the therapist records this and follows the discussion. A question such as "When did you first notice the problem entered your life?" moves away from blaming the client to externalizing the problem. To facilitate this exploration, the therapist may ask questions such as "How is it that you avoid making mistakes that most people with similar problems usually make?" and "Were there times in the recent past when this problem may have tried to get the better of you, and you didn't let it?" (Nichols, 2008, p. 384). These questions help the family or individual see that they are competent and resourceful. Such questions also point out to clients that the problems are not their lives and do not necessarily dominate their lives. Such questions encourage the development of positive unique outcomes.

Goals

Like Neimeyer, Epston and White try to help their clients see their lives (stories) in ways that will be positive rather than problem saturated. They help their clients shape meaning from the characters and plots in their stories so that they can overcome their problems. They believe in the power of words to affect the way individuals see themselves and others. By phrasing a client's problem in such a way that he can see alternatives or avenues open to him, the client becomes ready to pursue a resolution for his problem.

The following example of 8-year-old Samuel (Freeman et al., 1997, pp. 57–58) shows different ways of construing Samuel's problem and setting goals for Samuel.

> Samuel's parents say that *"Samuel is very self-centered. He has no patience. When he can't have just what he wants, exactly when he wants it, he throws a fit."* (p. 57)
>
> Samuel puts the problem differently. He says: *"I hate school. The stuff they want me to do is boring, I'd rather play my own games. The teacher and the other kids don't like me because I won't pretend to be interested. If they get in my face, I get in theirs."* (p. 57)
>
> A therapist also takes a problem-oriented view of Samuel's behavior, *"Samuel has an abbreviated attention span. He should be further evaluated for attention deficit hyperactivity disorder. Samuel cannot contain his anxiety well for his age. Samuel regresses to a narcissistic and grandiose stage of development in social situations that require age-appropriate cooperation."* (pp. 57–58)

Freeman et al. (1997) see this issue from a positive point of view. In their positive approach to the problem, they put the problem outside of the individual (externalizing it). They use questions that can have productive answers rather than making statements such as those of Samuel, his parents, and the therapist. They raise the following questions:

> *"Is Samuel the type of young person who can be very clear about what he wants and expects? Do Temper and Impatience get the better of him when he perceives an injustice, or when events don't follow the lead of his vivid imagination? Has this interfered with his peace of mind? Has it affected his reputation with the teachers and other kids? What do his own games offer that elicit his interest?"* (p. 58)

These questions may help the client and his parents view the problem differently and develop goals for Samuel. They offer hope to the family that new solutions can be achieved.

Techniques of Narrative Therapy

The techniques that narrative therapists use have to do with the telling of the story. They may examine the story and look for other ways to tell it differently or to understand it in other ways. In doing so, they find it helpful to put the problem outside of the individual or family, thus externalizing it. They look for unique outcomes, positive events, which are in contrast to a problem-saturated story. They often find that it is helpful to explore alternative narratives or stories. Asking about positive narrative stories in the client's life that have good alternatives also helps to lead to satisfaction with outcomes of other problems. Questions about the future help clients continue positive gains. Therapists also look for ways that family, friends, and others can support clients. By far, the most frequent type of therapeutic response from therapists is questions. Questions help to develop the story and to lead to discovery of new ways to deal with problems.

Theories in Action

Externalizing the problem. In narrative therapy, the problem becomes the opponent, not the child or the family with which the problem is associated. The family may work together to combat the problem. Thus, in the example of Samuel presented earlier, "Temper" and "Impatience" are the oppressors that the family will work against. This places the problem outside of the family and makes it a separate entity, not a characteristic of the individual. Samuel does not have a bad temper; rather, Temper is interfering with Samuel. Thus, the therapist might ask, "What do you think Temper's purpose is in upsetting Samuel?" This counters the parents' assumption that Samuel is the problem. This paves the way for finding different solutions rather than blaming Samuel for the problem. The therapist can then deconstruct a problem or story and then reconstruct or reauthor a preferred story. The therapist can help the family work together to defeat a problem rather than hold on to their own stories of the problem (Nichols, 2008).

Unique outcomes. When narrative therapists listen to a story that is full of problems, they look for exceptions to the stories (Nichols, 2008). They try to find moments in the story when the family worked well together or the problem started to dissolve by asking opening-space questions. These questions reveal exceptions that are seen as *sparkling moments* or as *unique outcomes*. These moments may consist of thoughts, feelings, or actions that are different from those found in the problem that family members have. By focusing on these unique outcomes, narrative therapists start to explore the influence the family may have over the problem. This can begin a new story.

Alternative narratives. Exploration of strengths, special abilities, and aspirations of the family and the person with the problem is the focus of the alternative narrative or story. Therapists comment on the positive aspects of what the identified patient or family is doing and develops them into a new way of viewing the problem. They may ask questions such as "Can you think of a time when you did not go along with Temper's requests? How were you able to trust your own view? What does this tell you about how you handle yourself?" The therapist might also ask, "How did you accomplish that positive goal? What was different that you said to yourself?" In this way, the narrative therapist helps clients see strengths by telling their stories about themselves in a more powerful and positive way.

Positive narratives. Narrative therapists not only examine problem-saturated stories, but they also look for stories about what is going well. Sometimes clients are so focused on or stuck in problem-saturated stories that it is difficult for them to see any positive stories (things that they are doing well). Clients may ignore these positive stories, but therapists may ask for them so that they can point out to the client how she has come up with effective ways to solve some problems. Such positive stories can give clients a sense of empowerment.

Questions about the future. As change takes place, therapists can assist the client in looking into the future and at potentially positive new stories. The therapist can help the client see her resourcefulness by asking, "If the problem were to continue next week, what meaning would it have for you?" The therapist may also ask, "Now that you know new things about yourself, how will you deal with Anger in the future?" Such questions help therapeutic changes continue beyond the termination of therapy.

Support for client stories. To emphasize the stories that clients tell and to help the therapeutic effect of reauthoring the stories, narrative therapists use letters, Web pages, certificates, leagues, and the involvement of others to help new changes stay with the client (Epston, 2009; Maisel et al., 2004; Marner, 2000; Schneider, Austin, & Arney, 2008; Steinberg, 2000). Letters written by the therapist summarize the session and externalize the problem. Such letters are positive and highlight the client's strengths. They focus on the unique outcomes of exceptions to the problem. Direct quotes from the session may be used. Also, questions or comments that the therapist thought about after the session can be included. Letters are mailed between sessions and at the end of therapy. Clients often report rereading the letters to help them to continue to make progress on the problem. Certificates, usually used with children, help to mark change and foster pride in having made changes.

Leagues have been initiated to develop support from others for clients. For example, there are anti-anorexia/bulimia leagues in Auckland, New Zealand; Vancouver, Canada; and Atlanta, Georgia, in the United States. Such leagues may have newsletters that contain letters from clients that include parts of their stories about how they fight Anorexia and Bulimia. Leagues may be run by one therapist or by several therapists and clients. They may use an archive of letters from clients about how they successfully battled Anorexia, Anger, Depression, or some other problem. These leagues provide support for clients who can learn about the stories of other clients with similar problems and can give encouragement to battle the problem that the client and others have in common. For example, a therapist may refer a client to Web pages that contain archives of a league to get more support in battling the problem.

Support for client stories can also come from parents, siblings, friends, or others. In family therapy, a therapist may ask questions such as "Mother, how do you see Jennie overcoming Anger?" or "Dad, how do teachers see Jennie fighting Anger at school?" These questions support the client's stories and provide ways to have several people supporting client change. From a narrative point of view, the client has a receptive audience to applaud or appreciate her progress.

Although narrative therapists may use a variety of other approaches related to understanding the client's story, all focus on how the client can look differently at her story to bring about a new sense of hope or accomplishment. Family and others work with the client to bring about a new narrative that fights the externalized "problem."

Case Example: Terry

The following example is a description by David Epston of his work with 12-year-old Terry (a Caucasian New Zealander) and his mother Dorothy. David Epston met with Terry and his mother eight times over an 8-month period. In this excerpt describing the first session, David externalizes the problem for Terry by attacking Guilt and Compulsions.

"He's overloaded with guilt," Dorothy summarized after sharing her concerns about her son, Terry. She had just told David of Terry's hand washing, excessive worrying, daily vomiting on the way to school, and hysterical responses to viewing people kiss on TV and to "dirt" in general.

Dorothy, still undecided about its merit, told of an attempt that she and Terry's older sister had made to disrupt his screaming demands to put cushions over their eyes when people on TV were kissing. They had, with exaggerated good humor and a bit of teasing thrown in, refused to comply with his demands. Their policy behind such a practice was that "it was better to be open with him so he felt okay about it." Terry nicknamed their tactics as "teasing"; when asked by David if he considered "teasing" to be benevolent or malevolent, he assured David that it was "benevolent."

David asked what effect "benevolent teasing" had on the problem. Terry was quick to say, "I'm making headway with the compulsions and it (benevolent teasing) has been helping me along." David speculated, "Your mum and your sister could have thought they were upsetting you rather than strengthening you?"

"Not really," replied Terry.

David asked for further information. "You knew it was for your own good? How?"

"Yeah, they were laughing and they weren't shouting. They didn't have frowns on their faces."

David wondered aloud to Terry, "Do you think that you saw the joke of it all? Do you think Guilt and Compulsions don't like to be made fun of?"

Terry replied sagely, "Yeah, but I like them to be made fun of because then it is a lot easier to talk about them. And you just think, 'They are silly thoughts and I can fight them off.'"

David, thinking that everyone had stumbled onto something outstanding, asked a question to confirm this and to contribute to his on-going process of reviewing his ideas, "When your mother and older sister benevolently tease you—you can fight off the thoughts and be stronger?" Terry answered in the affirmative.

Picking up on Dorothy's initial comment that Terry was "overloaded with guilt," David double-checked with Terry, "Is it okay for me to call it Guilt?" When Terry concurred, David took the liberty of personifying the problem: "Do you mind my saying that Guilt has a voice and kind of speaks to you?"

"No," said Terry.

"I'm asking you this because Chris, who had a run-in with similar sorts of problems—he was sixteen at the time by the way—gave me his consent to tell you what he found out—that Guilt talked to him and told him to do things," David continued. "What does Guilt say to you Terry?"

Terry replied by speaking through the voice of Guilt: "You have to be perfectly clean. Your hands have to be all nice and clean. They're not meant to be dirty."

David couldn't help getting angry hearing Guilt's demands on Terry's hands, and could not stop himself from telling Terry about his feelings: "I get quite angry just thinking about it!"

Terry went on in further detail about the demands, still mimicking the voice of Guilt: "The thoughts you are having at the moment are nasty and malicious. You are not meant to have them. You are strange and inhuman. You are the only one who has them. You are abnormal!"

Earlier David had promised Terry that he would not get overly excited or angry about things, so he had to control his rising anger at the ludicrous lies that Guilt was telling Terry. (Freeman et al., 1997, pp. 278–279.)

In the following segment, Epston continues to externalize the problem, but he also provides support for the client's stories. He reads out loud a letter he had written to a successful client, Chris. In this way, he takes a positive story from someone else and uses it to encourage Terry.

David formed the opinion that Terry was "quite a smart character" and his mother smiled and nodded in agreement. He assumed that Terry was, in fact, a smarter person than Guilt was taking him for. So he asked him, "Why do you think Guilt lies that way? What are its purposes in having you spend all your time obsessed and compelled?"

Terry replied thoughtfully, "Well, it's trying to help me get my mind off things I don't want to think about—that I'm scared of thinking. It's trying to help me not think about things, but it is hurting me really."

This answer confirmed David's opinion about Terry's overall smartness and his knowledgeable relationship with the problem. It reminded him of similarly knowledgeable thoughts of Chris. David read out loud a letter he had written to Chris, which Chris had donated to the "archives" of The Anti-Habit League for just such a purpose.

Dear Chris,
Chris, you told me you aren't worrying so much about your schoolwork. I marveled at this. You told me that "worrying isn't helping" and for that reason you dropped it and yet your effort level has stayed the same. Chris, do you think your compulsions have tricked you and almost betrayed you into their grip? What promises did they make to suck you in? Did they promise you everlasting happiness if you wiped your bum clean, or washed your body spic-and-span? Do you think these are childish ideas or do you think there is any truth in them? Before, you thought, "They were just weird things I did." Now it seems you are seeing through the tricks that Guilt was playing on you. (Freeman et al., 1997, p. 280)

Epston continues to build an alternative story of Terry's life. For example, he asks Terry's mother about the qualities in Terry that would have predicted he could overcome his adversities. At the third meeting, Terry brought a letter to Epston in which he says, *"After only one visit, the shell of guilt that had covered me crumbled and light and freedom came to me again. I started making new friends and with my old friends started tying the tethers back together which over time had been left to rot and slowly decay"* (p. 285). In their eighth and last meeting, Epston presents a "diploma in imperfection" to Terry that reiterates the positive story that is now a part of Terry's life. This certificate illustrates another way of supporting the client's new story. This example shows how several different techniques can be implemented in narrative therapy.

Current Trends

Both solution-focused and narrative therapies continue to be of great interest to therapists. Both have had a significant impact on the practice of couples, family, and individual therapy. However, narrative therapy has been especially popular in the treatment of children's psychological problems.

Solution-focused therapy is often used in settings where it may be difficult to have more than five or six sessions. Social workers and guidance counselors (Kelly, Kim, & Franklin, 2008; Sklare, 2005) find that they can use it not only when the number of sessions is limited, but also when the length of sessions may be less than half an hour. Solution-focused therapy continues to attract interest among a variety of practitioners. In 2002, the Solution-Focused Brief Therapy organization was started.

Narrative therapists explore many aspects of relationships. White (2007) uses *definitional ceremonies* to further develop a story. To do this he might bring in friends or relatives of the client to be *outside witnesses* to tell about how they experience their lives in a way that helps further the client's narrative in a positive way. The outside witnesses could include former clients of the therapist or other professionals. How power affects individuals' stories and their problems is one area of study (Brown, 2007b; Combs & Freeman, 2004). Another approach to narrative therapy examines the different views that the client can have in telling a story. For example, Leo described the relationship with his ex-partner from the point of view of a stalker, revenger, and dreamer (Hermans, 2004). Narrative therapists are likely to explore a number of different ways of working with stories in therapy.

Using Constructivist Theories with Other Theories

It is common for therapists with many theoretical perspectives to incorporate the idea of listening to the client's story or need to solve problems and not force a theoretical orientation onto a client where it may not fit. O'Connell (2005) shows how solution-focused therapy can be integrated with person-centered and cognitive and behavioral therapies. He also shows how some solution-focused techniques and philosophies can be used with many therapies, such as person-centered therapy and cognitive behavioral therapy.

Since clients tell their stories in all therapies, it is not surprising that many therapies address how narrative therapy ideas and issues of narrating affect their work. In *The Handbook of Narrative and Psychotherapy* (Angus & McLeod, 2004), several chapters describe how ideas from narrative research and therapy can be integrated into Luborsky's Core Conflictual Relationship Therapy (described in Chapter 2 of this book), cognitive therapy (Chapter 10), and experiential or gestalt therapy (Chapter 7). Interest in client stories is an important concept that narrative therapy shares with Alfred Adler (Chapter 4), who focuses on the early memories of clients. Adler also shared an egalitarian attitude toward clients with narrative therapy (Hester, 2004). Adelman (2008) shows how rational emotive behavior therapy can be combined with personal construct therapy to help those with substance abuse problems. Creative arts therapy, such as art therapy (van der Velden & Koops, 2005) and drama therapy (Novy, Ward, Thomas, Bulmer, & Gauthier, 2005), provides a way to add other means of expression besides telling a story using narrative in therapy. Narrative therapists vary greatly in terms of how much they make use of other theories in their work.

Research

Because constructivist therapies are relatively new, research on them is somewhat limited. Neimeyer and Stewart (2000) provide an overview of research on solution-focused, narrative, and other constructivist psychotherapies. In the paragraphs below, I report on research pertaining specifically to solution-focused therapy and narrative therapy.

Although it is a relatively new approach to therapy, solution-focused therapy has been the subject of a few studies. Kim (2008) reviewed 22 outcome studies of solution-focused therapy. Small effect sizes were found on measures of externalizing behavior problems, internalizing behavior problems, and family and relationship problems. A 4-year follow-up study with 190 patients who had received solution-focused therapy showed that more than 80% of the patients reported being abstinent or successfully controlling their drinking (de Shazer & Isebaert, 2003). In China, solution-focused therapy used with medication for the treatment of obsessive-compulsive disorder was more successful than the medication alone (Fang-Ru, Shuang-Luo, & Wen-Feng, 2005). In Finland, both solution-focused therapy and short-term psychodynamic therapy produced more benefits during the first year of follow-up research than did long-term psychodynamic psychotherapy (Knekt et al., 2008). However, long-term psychodynamic psychotherapy was superior to both short-term therapies when measured 3 years after the therapy was over. In another study in Finland, solution-focused therapy was more effective in reducing smoking when compared with short-term psychodynamic psychotherapy, but there were no differences in other lifestyle changes such as weight gain and alcohol consumption (Knekt, Laaksonen, Raitasalo, Haaramo, & Lindfors, 2009). These studies are typical of current studies used to examine the effectiveness of solution-focused therapy.

Other studies have examined aspects of the process of solution-focused therapy such as the role of hope, therapeutic gains, and the importance of the working alliance. In a study of hope with clients who had depressive symptoms, Bozeman (2000) showed that those clients who were exposed to three solution-focused therapy techniques had higher levels of hope than did those who received a more traditional past-focused treatment plan. However, depression scores did not improve significantly in either group. Examining change between sessions, Reuterlov, Lofgren, Nordstrom, Ternstrom, and Miller (2000) report treatment-related gains between sessions of solution-focused therapy with 129 clients. Another study replicated these findings, reporting that clients who showed gains between sessions increased these gains at the end of the session (De Vega & Beyebach, 2004). However, both studies reported that when clients saw few gains at the beginning of therapy, they were not likely to see many improvements by the end of therapy. Some critics of solution-focused therapy believe that not enough attention is paid to the client–therapist relationship. In a comparison with brief interpersonal therapy, both therapies produced positive change. However, the working alliance was found to be associated with positive change only for brief interpersonal therapy (Wettersten, Lichtenberg, & Mallinckrodt, 2005). It is likely that solution-focused therapy will be a continued focus of process and outcome therapy studies.

Because of the unique nature of narrative therapy and personal construct therapy, it is difficult to assess its effectiveness because each person or family's story is different. Two meta-analyses examined 22 and 27 studies using personal construct therapy (Holland, Neimeyer, Currier, & Berman, 2007; Metcalfe, Winter, & Viney, 2007). Both studies found that personal construct therapy compared favorably with a no-treatment control group, but few differences were found when it was compared with another psychotherapeutic treatment. In studying families that discontinue narrative therapy without discussing it with their therapist, Hoper (1999) reports that most families did so because they were pleased with their experience and the improvements that resulted. Those that dropped out of therapy and were not pleased often had unrealistic expectations of therapy and wanted more advice from an expert on their children's problems. Another study focused on innovative moments in narrative therapy by comparing five cases with good outcomes and five with poor outcomes (Matos, Santos, Gonçalves, & Martins, 2009). Two types of therapeutic change stood out: when the clients re-conceptualized the problem, and when they had new experiences. Although much research on narrative therapy is limited, one line of research has been quite comprehensive.

Perhaps the most concentrated area of study has been the use of narrative therapy for Hispanic children and adolescents. In working with inner-city Hispanic children and adolescents, therapists have used stories of Hispanic role models to help young people with behavior problems (Malgady & Costantino, 2003). Much of the therapy includes ethnic and cultural narratives as well as role playing that is related to cultural stories. The treatment method has been group therapy (sometimes with parents) delivered primarily to Puerto Rican and Mexican American children and adolescents, but also to those from Central America. For young children, folk tales were effective narratives. For older children, stories of heroes were more effective. One-year follow-up studies showed that culturally based narratives were more effective than stories unrelated to Hispanic culture. There were also gender differences, with older boys preferring sports figures as models and females appreciating role models that had elements of family and home values in their narratives. In general, treatment was effective with conduct problems, phobias, and anxiety, less so with depression. The research reported by Malgady and Costantino (2003) includes several studies with different age groups and different Hispanic backgrounds.

Gender Issues

From one point of view, gender should not be an issue for solution-focused and narrative therapists as they listen to the stories of patients. Solution-focused therapy can be used to both help women see the role of social injustice in their problems as well as empower women to use abilities that they have but may have overlooked (O'Connell, 2005). In *Divorced, Without Children: Solution-Focused Therapy with Women at Midlife*, Castaldo (2008) describes the pressures of a "marrying, mothering world" (p. 3). In describing solution-focused therapy for women who are divorced without children, Castaldo demonstrates how to help women find their own solutions and to resist the pressures of the solutions of therapists, friends, or relatives. This enables women to feel comfortable and positive about their choices. In general, solution-focused therapy helps women determine their own goals rather than the counselor's or significant others' goals.

In narrative therapy, the patient's gender is one element of the story, sometimes a minor element, which therapists work with as they help their clients solve their problems. However, Laura Brown (2000), a feminist therapist, points out that social factors such as violence, sexism, and racism influence individuals depending on their gender, thus affecting their stories. Other feminist therapists have examined the influence of society in narratives women develop about their bodies and eating disorders (Brown, 2007a, b; Epston & Maisel, 2009; Jasper, 2007). In her book *Integrating Spirit and Psyche: Using Women's Narratives in Psychotherapy*, Henehan (2003) gives many brief examples of positive stories of women that can relate to a variety of different issues that women may experience. Addressing coming-out issues of parents of gays and lesbians, Saltzburg (2007) describes how narrative therapy can help families re-author or take a new perspective in dealing with gay and lesbian children. In one sense, the setting of the story becomes especially important, as it may have an impact on the client as it regards his or her gender. Nylund and Nylund (2003) view narrative therapy as a way of helping men better understand how cultures support women's oppression and men's sense of entitlement and dominance. This perspective can better help men understand the impact of these factors on their relationships. The comments of feminist therapists (discussed in Chapter 13) and others on constructivist therapies, such as solution-focused and narrative therapies, provide another view of these methods of therapy.

Multicultural Issues

For constructivist theories, the client's background or culture influences how she presents her story. In solution-focused therapy, language is an important component. Yeung (1999) points out how it is difficult to use the miracle question and some other solution-focused therapy techniques with clients speaking Chinese languages because of differences between the English phonetic and the Chinese pictograph sign systems, which result in different language structures. Presenting another point of view, Lee and Mjelde-Mossey (2004) show how solution-focused therapy can be appropriate for East Asian cultures where family harmony and reverence for family elders is important. Solution-focused therapy helps individuals to use their strengths to deal with different views of the world that family members and others have. Solution-focused therapy can also be seen as an approach that will meet the approval of many cultures because support and advice is provided rather than analysis of problems and focus on feelings or pathology (Lee, 2003).

In narrative therapy, the client's culture has an impact on the client's story. This can be seen in the case of a female Korean-Japanese college student struggling with ethnic identity issues (Murphy-Shigematsu, 2000). Common themes in narratives of African Americans are spirituality, ritual, the power of words, and dreams, which Parks (2003) sees as curative factors in narrative therapy. Narrative therapy can be used in helping African caregivers of family members diagnosed with HIV/AIDS rewrite their story so that they can feel more helpful, hopeful, and stronger as they provide care for their relatives (Ngazimbi, Hagedorn, & Shillingford, 2008). *Testimony therapy* is an African-centered therapy that focuses on stories of the African experience in the United States (Akinyela, 2005, 2008). Like narrative therapy, testimony therapy makes use of telling stories to help individuals resolve their problems. For multiracial individuals, it is helpful for both the client and the constructivist therapist to address the role of race in society, and how they view race (Priest & Nishimura, 2008). As mentioned in the research section, using folktales and other stories can be helpful in psychotherapeutic work with Hispanic youth (Malgady & Costantino, 2003). Constructivist therapists are concerned with understanding all aspects of their clients, and culture often makes a significant contribution to the stories and the progress of therapy.

Group Therapy

In solution-focused therapy and narrative therapy, there is a close parallel between the methods used in individual therapy and those used in group therapy. In solution-focused therapy, the focus is brief and on taking action to deal with future problems that may arise (Banks, 2005; Corey, 2008). O'Connell (2005) believes that the support of group members helps to raise self-esteem. Further, he feels that a solution-focused approach produces more group energy toward solving problems than does a problem-oriented focus. He also believes that taking small steps toward a solution creates a positive momentum toward change that group members receive enthusiastically.

Telling stories in groups is a universal human activity. Applying this activity to therapy would seem to be a natural extension of storytelling. As mentioned before, Malgady and Costantino (2003) and others have used narrative therapy with Hispanic children and adolescents. Narrative therapy has also been used with incarcerated young men to help them develop a sense of identity and a point of view about issues affecting them. They can move from problem-saturated stories to ones that show a future for them (Tahir, 2005). Stories are the basis of plays. *Narradrama* is the combination of drama therapy and narrative therapy in which individuals can act out their stories (Dunne, 2003). Group work in narrative therapy tends to vary widely depending on the age, culture, or problem of the individuals.

Summary

This chapter contains descriptions of three constructivist psychotherapies. Constructivist approaches offer a view of understanding clients and applying therapeutic techniques more from the client's frame of reference than do other theories. Solution-focused, personal construct, and narrative therapy try to understand the client's story. In essence, they listen to the client's theory of his personality.

Solution-focused therapists are concerned with not how or why a problem arose, but in solutions to problems. Forming a collaborative relationship is the first step in producing change. Complimenting a client helps in this process and leads to openness to change. Solution-focused therapists also ask about changes that have taken place prior to the first session of therapy (pretherapy change). Asking about how clients cope with problems helps clients see that they can make effective changes in their lives. They use techniques such as exception finding and the miracle question to help find solutions to a problem. They rate progress in solving a problem by using a technique called scaling. They are positive in their approach and look for ways to compliment and motivate clients as they pursue solutions to problems. "The message" is also used to give a client support and instruction for change during the week. This fits with the formula first-session task that implies that change is inevitable. Many of these techniques are phrased as questions.

Personal construct therapists, who use a narrative approach, are concerned with the stories in clients' lives that are full of problems. They help clients see their lives in ways that remove the problems. As novels are concerned with the setting, characterization, plot, and themes, so are clients' descriptions of their lives and problems. There are different approaches to personal construct therapy. An example of Neimeyer's work that focuses on a traumatic family event is given in the text.

Epston and White's narrative therapy helps clients reconstruct their stories. Like solution-focused therapists, they look for exceptions in the stories, times when things went well. They explore alternative narratives that show clients' strengths and special abilities. To do this, they may externalize the problem by presenting the problem, such as Temper, as something outside of the client that needs to be conquered. Narrative therapists explore positive stories (client stories with good outcomes), and ask questions that look into the future so that clients can carry therapeutic gains into their future life. They also offer support for client stories by using letters to clients, letters from former clients, and support from family members and others to bring about positive changes. Unlike solution-focused therapy, there are several different views of how to apply narrative therapy.

Theories in Action DVD: Solution-Focused Therapy

Basic Concepts Used in the Role-Play

- Pretherapy change
- Respectful curiosity, empathy (Forming a collaborative relationship)
- Looking for exceptions (Exception-seeking questions)
- Identifying clients' strengths and resources (Coping questions)
- Affirming client's strengths and weaknesses (Complimenting)
- Miracle questions
- Scaling
- Focusing on small changes
- Summarizing

Questions About the Role-Play

1. Why does Dr. Grothaus ask about pretherapy change when no other therapy uses this technique on a regular basis?
2. What does Dr. Grothaus intend to do by asking Latanya what would happen if you woke up tomorrow morning and a miracle occurred and your problem had disappeared? (p. 460)
3. What is achieved in solution-focused therapy by asking Latanya to rate herself on a 1 to 10 scale on how successful she has been in meeting her goal of dating? (pp. 460, 461)
4. Compare and contrast the approaches used in solution-focused therapy with those used in narrative therapy.

Theories in Action DVD: Narrative Therapy

Basic Concepts Used in the Role-Play

- Naming (Externalizing the problem)
- Empathy
- Exception to problem (Unique outcome)
- Suggesting new story (Alternative outcome)
- Building new outcome (Question about the future)
- Building new story, Empowering (Positive narrative)

Questions About the Role-Play

1. Why does Dr. Milliken externalize Sean's depression by calling it Darkness? (p. 470)
2. Does externalizing a problem seem appropriate for adults like Sean, or does it seem more appropriate for children?
3. How does the therapeutic approach to Terry on pages 472–473 seem similar to or different from that used by Dr. Milliken with Sean?
4. Does narrative therapy seem too gimmicky or artificial? Explain.

Suggested Readings

De Jong, P., & Berg, I. K. (2008). *Interviewing for solutions* (3rd ed.). Pacific Grove, CA: Brooks/Cole–Cengage. This book is written for the student wanting to learn how to do solution-focused therapy. Examples illustrate this approach. Protocols that illustrate a way of articulating specific solution-focused techniques are also given. This is a very thorough introduction to solution-focused therapy.

O'Connell, B. (2005). *Solution-focused therapy* (2nd ed.). London: Sage. Solution-focused therapy is presented in a sequential way with clear explanations of techniques and many examples. A Frequently Asked Questions section, as well as portions of the book for those just starting to use solution-focused therapy, is helpful.

Angus, L. E., & McLeod, J. (Eds.). (2004). *The handbook of narrative and psychotherapy: Practice, theory, and research*. Thousand Oaks, CA: Sage. This collection of views on narration and narrative therapy provides a way to read about current trends in narrative therapy as well as view ideas about storytelling that influence narrative therapy.

Neimeyer, R. A. (2009). *Constructivist psychotherapy: Distinctive features*. New York: Routledge. Divided into theory and practice sections, this book describes Neimeyer's view of personal construct theory. There are many examples and case illustrations.

White, M. (2007). *Maps of narrative practice*. New York: Norton. Michael White describes what he sees as the six core areas of narrative psychotherapy: externalizing conservation , re-authoring conversation, remembering conversations, definitional ceremonies, unique outcome conversations, and scaffolding conversations. These areas are illustrated with many case examples and maps of his conceptualizations. This book represents his last update of his view of narrative therapy.

References

Adelman, R. (2008). Methods of reconstruction with adolescent substance abusers: Combining REBT and constructivism. In J. D. Raskin & S. K. Bridges (Eds.), *Studies in meaning 3: Constructivist psychotherapy in the real world* (pp. 183–200). New York: Pace University Press.

Akinyela, M. M. (2005). Testimony of hope: African-centered praxis for therapeutic ends. *Journal of Systemic Therapies*, 24(1), 5–18.

Akinyela, M. M. (2008). Once they come: Testimony therapy and healing questions for African American couples. In M. McGoldrick & K. V. Hardy (Eds.), *Re-visioning family therapy: Race, culture, and gender in clinical practice* (2nd ed., pp. 356–366). New York: Guilford.

Angus, L. E., & McLeod, J. (Eds.). (2004). *The handbook of narrative and psychotherapy: Practice, theory, and research*. Thousand Oaks, CA: Sage.

Banks, R. (2005). Solution-focused group therapy. *Journal of Family Psychotherapy*, 16(1–2), 17–21.

Berg, I. K. (1994). *Family based services: A solution-focused approach*. New York: Norton.

Berg, I. K., & De Jong, P. (2005). Engagement through complimenting. *Journal of Family Psychotherapy*, 16 (1–2), 51–56.

Berg, I. K., & De Shazer, S. (1993). Making numbers talk: Language in therapy. In S. Friedman (Ed.). *The new language of change: Constructive collaboration in psychotherapy* (pp. 5–24). New York: Guilford.

Berg, I. K., & Dolan, Y. (Eds.). (2001). *Tales of solutions: A collection of hope-inspiring stories*. New York: Norton.

Berg, I. K., & Miller, S. D. (1992). *Working with the problem drinker: A solution-focused approach*. New York: Norton.

Bertolino, B., & O'Hanlon, B. (2002). *Collaborative, competency-based counseling and therapy*. Boston: Allyn & Bacon.

Bozeman, B. N. (2000). The efficacy of solution-focused therapy techniques on perceptions of hope in clients with depressive symptoms. *Dissertation Abstracts International, August, Vol. 6* (2–B): 1117.

Brown, C. (2007a). Discipline and desire: Regulating the body/self. In C. Brown & T. Augusta-Scott (Eds.), *Narrative therapy: Making meaning, making lives* (pp. 105–131). Thousand Oaks, CA: Sage.

Brown, C. (2007b). Situating knowledge and power in the therapeutic alliance. In C. Brown & T. Augusta-Scott (Eds.), *Narrative therapy: Making meaning, making lives* (pp. 3–22). Thousand Oaks, CA: Sage Publications.

Brown, L. S. (2000). Discomforts of the powerless: Feminist construction of distress. In R. A. Neimeyer & J. D. Raskin (Eds.), *Construction of disorder: Meaning-making frameworks for psychotherapy* (pp. 207–308). Washington, DC: American Psychological Association.

Castaldo, D. D. (2008). *Divorced, without children: Solution focused therapy with women at midlife.* New York: Routledge.

Combs, G., & Freeman, J. (2004). A poststructuralist approach to narrative work. In L. E. Angus & J. McLeod (Eds.). *The handbook of narrative psychotherapy: Practice, theory, and research* (pp. 137–155). Thousand Oaks, CA: Sage.

Connie, E., & Metcalf, L. (Eds.). (2009). *The art of solution-focused therapy.* New York: Springer.

Corey, G. (2008). *Theory and practice of group counseling* (7th ed.). Belmont, CA: Brooks/Cole.

De Jong, P., & Berg, I. K. (2008). *Interviewing for solutions* (3rd ed.). Pacific Grove, CA: Brooks/Cole–Cengage.

De Shazer, S. (1985). *Keys to solution in brief therapy.* New York: Norton.

De Shazer, S. (1988). *Clues: Investigating solutions in brief therapy.* New York: Norton.

De Shazer, S. (1991). *Putting differences to work.* New York: Norton.

De Shazer, S. (1994). *Words were originally magic.* New York: Norton.

De Shazer, S. (2005). *More than Miracles: The State of the Art of Solution-focused Therapy.* Binghamton, NY: Haworth Press.

De Shazer, S., & Isebaert, L. (2003). The Bruges model: A solution-focused approach to problem drinking. *Journal of Family Psychotherapy, 14*(4), 43–52.

De Vega, M. H., & Beyebach, M. (2004). Between-session change in solution-focused therapy: A replication. *Journal of Systemic Therapies, 23*(2), 18–26.

Dunne, P. (2003). Narradrama: A narrative action approach with groups. In D. J. Wiener & L. K. Oxford (Eds.), *Action therapy with families and groups: Using creative arts improvisation in clinical practice* (pp. 229–265). Washington, DC: American Psychological Association.

Epston, D. (2009). The legacy of letter writing as a clinical practice: Introduction to the special issue on therapeutic letters. *Journal of Family Nursing, 15*(1), 3–5.

Epston, D., & Maisel, R. (2009). Anti-anorexia/bulimia: A polemics of life and death. In H. Malson & M. Burns (Eds.), *Critical feminist approaches to eating dis/orders* (pp. 210–220). New York: Routledge.

Epston, D., & White, M. (1992). *Experience, contradiction, narrative, and imagination: Selected papers of David Epston and Michael White, 1989–1991.* Adelaide, South Australia: Dulwich Centre Publications.

Fang-Ru, Y., Shuang-Luo, Z., & Wen-Feng, L. (2005). Comparative study of solution-focused brief therapy (SFBT) combined with paroxetine in the treatment of obsessive-compulsive disorder. *Chinese Mental Health Journal, 19*(4), 288–290.

Fransella, F., & Neimeyer, R. A. (2005). George Alexander Kelly: The man and his theory. In F. Fransella (Ed.), *The essential practitioner's handbook of personal construct psychology* (pp. 3–13). New York: Wiley.

Freeman, J., Epston, D., & Lobovits, D. (1997). *Playful approaches to serious problems: Narrative therapy with children and their families.* New York: Norton.

Haley, J. (1973). *Uncommon therapy: The psychiatric techniques of Milton H. Erickson, M. D.* New York: W. W. Norton.

Henehan, M. P. (2003). *Integrating spirit and psyche: Using women's narratives in psychotherapy.* New York: Haworth Pastoral Press.

Hermans, H. J. M. (2004). *The innovation of self-narratives: A dialogical approach.* In L. E. Angus & J. McLeod (Eds.), *The handbook of narrative and psychotherapy: Practice, theory, and research* (pp. 175–192). Thousand Oaks, CA: Sage.

Hester, R. L. (2004). Early memory and narrative therapy. *Journal of Individual Psychology, 60*(4), 338–347.

Holland, J. M., Neimeyer, R. A., Currier, J. M., & Berman, J. S. (2007). The efficacy of personal construct therapy: A comprehensive review. *Journal of Clinical Psychology, 63*(1), 93–107.

Hoper, J. H. (1999). Families who unilaterally discontinue narrative therapy: Their story, a qualitative study. *Dissertation Abstracts International, January, Vol. 60* (6–B): 2945.

Hoyt, M. F. (2008). Everyday constructivism. In J. D. Raskin & S. K. Bridges (Eds.), *Biennial conference of the Constructivist Psychology Network, 12th, July 2006, San Marcos, CA* (pp. 295–328). New York: Pace University Press.

Jasper, K. (2007). The blinding power of genetics: Manufacturing and privatizing stories of eating disorders. In C. Brown & T. Augusta-Scott (Eds.), *Narrative therapy: Making meaning, making lives* (pp. 39–58). Thousand Oaks, CA: Sage.

Kelly, M. S., Kim, J. S., & Franklin, C. (2008). *Solution-focused brief therapy in schools: A 360-degree view of research and practice.* New York: Oxford.

Kim, J. S. (2008). Examining the effectiveness of solution-focused brief therapy: A meta-analysis. *Research on Social Work Practice, 18*(2), 107–116.

Knekt, P., Laaksonen, M. A., Raitasalo, R., Haaramo, P., & Lindfors, O. (2009). Changes in lifestyle for psychiatric patients three years after the start of short- and long-term psychodynamic psychotherapy and solution-focused therapy. *European Psychiatry,* June 22, 2009 (no pages).

Knekt, P., Lindfors, O., Härkänen, T., Välikoski, M., Virtala, E., Laaksonen, M. A., Marttunen, M., Kaipainen, M., Renlund, C., & Helsinki Psychotherapy Study Group. (2008). Randomized trial on the effectiveness of long- and short-term psychodynamic psychotherapy and solution-focused therapy on psychiatric symptoms during a 3-year follow-up. *Psychological Medicine, 38*(5), 689–703.

Lee, M. Y. (2003). A solution-focused approach to cross-cultural clinical social work practice: Utilizing cultural strengths. *Families in Society, 84*(3), 385–395.

Lee, M. Y., & Mjelde-Mossey, L. (2004). Cultural dissonance among generations: A solution-focused approach with East Asian elders and their families. *Journal of Marital & Family Therapy, 30*(4), 497–513.

Lipchik, E. (2009). A solution-focused journey. In E. Connie & L. Metcalf (Eds.), *The art of solution focused therapy.* (pp. 45–63). New York: Springer.

Maisel, R., Epston, D., & Borden, A. (2004). *Biting the hand that starves you: Inspiring resistance to anorexia/bulimia.* New York: Norton.

Malgady, R. G., & Costantino, G. (2003). Narrative therapy for Hispanic children and adolescents. In A. E. Kazdin & J. R. Weisz (Eds.), *Evidence-based psychotherapies for children and adolescents* (pp. 425–435). New York, NY: Guilford.

Marner, T. (2000). *Letters to children in family therapy: A narrative approach.* Philadelphia: Kingsley.

Matos, M., Santos, A., Gonçalves, M., & Martins, C. (2009). Innovative moments and change in narrative therapy. *Psychotherapy Research, 19*(1), 68–80.

Metcalf, L. (2001). Solution-focused therapy. In R. J. Corsini (Ed.), *Handbook of innovative therapy* (2nd ed.). New York: Wiley.

Metcalfe, C., Winter, D., & Viney, L. (2007). The effectiveness of personal construct psychotherapy in clinical practice: A systematic review and meta-analysis. *Psychotherapy Research, 17*(4), 431–442.

Murphy-Shigematsu, S. (2000). Cultural psychiatry and minority identities in Japan: A constructivist narrative approach to therapy. *Psychiatry: Interpersonal and Biological Processes, 63,* 371–384.

Neimeyer, R. A. (2000). Narrative disruptions in the construction of the self. In R. A. Neimeyer & J. Raskin (Eds.), *Constructions of disorder* (pp. 207–242). Washington, DC: American Psychological Association.

Neimeyer, R. A. (2009). *Constructivist psychotherapy: Distinctive features.* New York: Routledge.

Neimeyer, R. A., & Baldwin, S. A. (2005). Personal construct psychotherapy and the constructivist horizon. In F. Fransella (Ed.), *The essential practitioner's handbook of personal construct psychology* (pp. 235–243). New York: Wiley.

Neimeyer, R. A., & Stewart, A. E. (2000). Constructivist and narrative psychotherapies. In C. R. Snyder & R. E. Ingram (Eds.), *Handbook of psychological change* (pp. 337–357). New York: Wiley.

Ngazimbi, E. E., Hagedorn, W. B., & Shillingford, M. A. (2008). Counseling caregivers of families affected by HIV/AIDS: The use of narrative therapy. *Journal of Psychology in Africa, 18*(2), 317–324.

Nichols, M. P. (2008). *Family therapy: Concepts and methods* (8th ed.). Boston: Allyn and Bacon.

Novy, C., Ward, S., Thomas, A., Bulmer, L., & Gauthier, M. (2005). Introducing movement and prop as additional metaphors in narrative therapy. *Journal of Systemic Therapies, 24*(2), 60–74.

Nylund, D., & Nylund, D. A. (2003). Narrative therapy as a counter-hegemonic practice. *Men and Masculinities, 5*(4), 386–394.

O'Connell, B. (2005). *Solution-focused therapy* (2nd ed.). London: Sage.

Parks, F. M. (2003). The role of African American folk beliefs in the modern therapeutic process. *Clinical Psychology: Science and Practice, 10*(4), 456–467.

Priest, R., & Nishimura, N. (2008). Counseling multiracial clients in context: A constructivist approach. In J. D. Raskin & S. K. Bridges (Eds.), *Studies in meaning 3: Constructivist psychotherapy in the real world* (pp. 253–271). New York: Pace University Press.

Raskin, Jonathan D. , & Bridges, S. K. (Eds.). (2008). *Studies in meaning 3: Constructivist psychotherapy in the real world.* New York: Pace University Press.

Reuterlov, H., Lofgren, T., Nordstrom, F., Ternstrom, A., & Miller , S. D. (2000). What is better? A preliminary investigation of between session change. *Journal of Systemic Therapies, 19,* 111–115.

Rothwell, N. (2005). How brief is solution-focused brief therapy? A comparative study. *Clinical Psychology & Psychotherapy, 12*(5), 402–405.

Saltzburg, S. (2007). Narrative therapy pathways for reauthoring with parents of adolescents coming out as lesbian, gay, and bisexual. *Contemporary Family Therapy: An International Journal, 29*(1–2), 57–69.

Schneider, B., Austin, C., & Arney, L. (2008). Writing to wellness: Using an open journal in narrative therapy. *Journal of Systemic Therapies, 27*(2), 60–75.

Schultz, D. P., & Schultz, S. E. (2009). *Theories of personality* (9th ed.). Belmont, CA: Wadsworth Cengage.

Sklare, G. B. (2005). *Brief counseling that works: A solution-focused approach for school counselors and administrators* (2nd ed.). Thousand Oaks, CA: Corwin Press.

Steinberg, D. (2000). *Letters from the clinic: Letter writing in clinical practice for mental health professionals.* London: Routledge.

Tahir, L. (2005). The evolving systems approach and narrative therapy for incarcerated male youth. In D. B. Wallace (Ed.), *Education, arts, and morality: Creative journeys* (pp. 85–101). New York: Kluwer.

Vaihinger, H. (1965). *The philosophy of "as if."* London: Routledge & Kegan Paul.

Van der Velden, I., & Koops, M. (2005). Structure in word and image: Combining narrative therapy and art therapy in groups of survivors of war. *Intervention: International Journal of Mental Health, 3*(1), 57–64.

Wettersten, K. B., Lichtenberg, J. W., & Mallinckrodt, B. (2005). Associations between working alliance and outcome in solution-focused brief therapy and brief interpersonal therapy. *Psychotherapy Research, 15*(1–2), 35–43.

White, M. (1995). *Reauthoring lives: Interviews and essays.* Adelaide, South Australia: Dulwich Centre Publications.

White, M. (1997). *Narratives of therapists' lives.* Adelaide, South Australia: Dulwich Centre Publications.

White, M. (2007). *Maps of narrative practice.* New York: Norton.

White, M., & Epston, D. (1990). *Narrative means to therapeutic ends.* New York: Norton.

White, M., & Epston, D. (1994). *Experience, contradiction, narrative, and imagination.* Adelaide, South Australia: Dulwich Centre Publications.

Yeung, F. K. C. (1999). The adaptation of solution-focused therapy in Chinese culture: A linguistic perspective. *Transcultural Psychiatry, 36,* 477–489.

Zeig, J. K. (Ed.). (1985). *Ericksonian Psychotherapy: Structures* (Vol. *1*). New York: Brunner/Mazel.

Zimmerman, J. L., & Dickerson, V. C. (2001). Narrative therapy. In R. J. Corsini (Ed.), *Handbook of innovative therapy* (2nd ed., pp. 415–426). New York: Wiley.

Feminist Therapy: A Multicultural Approach

Outline of Feminist Therapy

FEMINIST THEORIES OF PERSONALITY

Gender Differences and Similarities Across the Lifespan
    Childhood
    Adolescence
    Adulthood
Schema Theory and Multiple Identities
Gilligan's Ethic of Care
The Relational Cultural Model

THEORIES OF FEMINIST THERAPY

Goals of Feminist Therapy
Assessment Issues in Feminist Therapy
The Therapeutic Relationship
Techniques of Feminist Therapy
    Cultural analysis
    Cultural intervention
    Gender-role analysis
    Gender-role intervention
    Power analysis
    Power intervention
    Assertiveness training
    Reframing and relabeling
    Therapy-demystifying strategies

USING FEMINIST THERAPY WITH OTHER THEORIES

    Feminist Psychoanalytic Theory
    Feminist Behavioral and Cognitive Therapy
    Feminist Gestalt Therapy
    Feminist Narrative Therapy

More than other theories of psychotherapy, feminist therapy examines not only psychological factors that lead to individuals' problems but also sociological influences, such as the impact of gender roles and multicultural background on individual development. Increasingly, feminist therapy attends to issues of women around the world and women who are members of minority groups. Feminist therapists also see their work as being helpful to children and men. Feminist therapists recognize the importance of the different ways that men and women develop throughout the lifespan, including differences in social and sexual adolescent development, child-raising practices, and work roles. Feminist theories of personality examine issues such as gender schemas, the importance of relating to others, and multiple identities that represent an individual. An issue of importance to feminist therapists is developing a social and cultural explanation for women's overrepresentation in certain psychological disorders, such as depression and eating problems. Interventions in feminist therapy deal with helping people understand the impact of gender roles and power differences in society and, in some cases, helping them make changes in social institutions that discriminate against or hurt them. Consistent with their emphasis on societal and group issues has been the evolution from the political feminist movement and consciousness-raising groups of the 1960s and 1970s to the current interest in working with both men and women from many cultures and with groups such as families and women's therapy groups.

Gender as a Multicultural Issue

Gender can be viewed broadly as a multicultural issue. Ethnicity and gender can be viewed as cultural issues along with language, religion, sexual orientation, age, and socioeconomic situations (Ivey, D'Andrea, Ivey, & Simek-Morgan, 2006). All of these multicultural issues can be viewed from a sociological perspective. A theoretical approach to psychotherapy for one of these issues is likely to have much in common with an approach to another of these issues. Specifically, awareness of cultural values and the need for social action is likely to be a commonality.

There are many meanings and views of gender (Stewart & McDermott, 2004). The term *intersection of multiple identities* refers to the many forces that affect the way that gender is seen. Erikson's view of identity (described in Chapter 2) adds to the meaning of gender in the sense that individuals see themselves in relation to various social groups and institutions. Also, gender provides a way of viewing power and its effect on individual relationships. This can be at work, in romantic relationships, in educational institutions, and a variety of other situations. *Gender* typically has been used to understand differences between men and women. However, gender also is used to understand "individual differences among men and among women" (Stewart & McDermott, 2004, p. 522). *Gender* also helps researchers to understand social institutions such as marriage. These ways of studying gender can be combined to get a full view of gender as it relates to individual lives.

Both therapists and clients differ as to their awareness of these issues. Ivey et al. (2006) present a broad five-stage approach to awareness of multicultural issues. These range from being naive or unaware of the importance of cultural differences to integrating cultural awareness into a positive sense of self. Most work on stages of cultural awareness has been done in the area of racial awareness. Helms (Helms & Cook, 1999) has described models of racial identity for culturally different groups and for Whites. Others have expanded this work for people of other racial identities (Slattery, 2004). Typically, this approach has not been used for awareness of gender identity, although it could.

Feminist therapy has included many variables such as ethnicity and social class into theories of feminist therapy (Hays, 2008). The main reason for this is that there are many more issues than gender that impact each other. For example, Native Americans may come from a vast array of tribal heritages where religion and indigenous heritage are important. Additionally, many individuals are multicultural and may speak more than one language, an important factor in therapy. In fact, most individuals can be viewed as having a multicultural background. For example, relatively few individuals in the United States have had all four grandparents who share very similar cultural backgrounds. Feminist therapists, particularly recently, have been very aware of the importance of ethnicity, social class, gender orientation, disabilities, and other characteristics when they help their clients with problems.

Feminist therapists have emphasized the importance of social action and empowering their clients, in addition to using psychotherapy techniques specific to feminist therapy based on other theories. This emphasis on social action and empowering clients reflects a view summarized as "the person is political," which recognizes the effect of social and political institutions on individuals. Many feminist therapists use techniques of power analysis, intervention, assertiveness training, and other techniques to help their clients. These techniques can be applied to people from diverse ethnic and racial backgrounds. More than other psychotherapy theorists, feminist therapists address the issue of ethnic and racial background. In this chapter, the case examples that I present will illustrate more cultural diversity than in other chapters.

History of Feminist Therapy

Unlike other theories of psychotherapy discussed in this book, feminist therapy represents the work and effort of not just one or a few theorists but of many women from a variety of academic disciplines who share the basic belief that women are valuable and that social change to benefit women is needed (Ballou, Hill, & West, 2008; Brown, 2008b, 2008c, 2010; Enns, 2004; Evans, Kincade, Marbley, & Seem, 2005). Acting on their observations of the social history of the treatment of women, both currently and in the past, feminists and feminist therapists worked together to bring about change, often in groups called *consciousness-raising (CR) groups*. They were also critical of psychotherapy, particularly psychoanalysis, as it was practiced by male therapists on female patients. Feminist therapy developed as women combined their professional training with feminist values. Although all dealt with the impact of social forces on women, feminist therapists differed in the degree and manner in which they dealt with societal as well as personal change (Enns, 2004; Kaschak, 1981).

An early critic of the mental health system, Chesler (1972, 1997, 2005) has been, in many ways, responsible for having mental health practitioners re-examine their therapeutic relationships with women. In particular, she has been critical of the relationship between the female patient and the male therapist, which she described as patriarchal; the therapist is the expert, and the woman submits to his wisdom (Brown, 2010). Chesler argued that women were misdiagnosed because they did not conform to gender-role stereotypes of male therapists and thus received higher rates of treatment and hospitalization than were warranted. Furthermore, she pointed out the destructiveness of sexual relations between female patient and male therapist and the severe damage due to this unethical behavior. In her book *Women and Madness* (1972, 2005) Chesler gives many examples of sexism in psychotherapy and counseling. In an article 25 years later, Chesler (1997) describes gains and problems that reflect the influence of awareness of issues raised by feminist therapists.

Feminist theorists have been critical of gender-biased values and propositions inherent in psychoanalysis, yet others find it to be useful. Some female psychoanalysts such as Helen Deutsch (1944) added to orthodox Freudian psychoanalytic theory without challenging many of its basic principles. Others such as Karen Horney (1966) differed with Freud on several significant issues. For example, she did not subscribe to the belief in penis envy. Rather, she promoted the idea of womb envy in men as representing an overcompensation for feeling inferior to women because of their ability to give birth. Furthermore, she suggested that it was not sexual energy that was the motivating force for women but envy of men's power, because women lack power in comparison to men. Other writers (Eichenbaum & Orbach, 1983) have tried to integrate psychoanalysis and feminist psychotherapy by criticizing sexist aspects of psychoanalysis. Chodorow (1989, 1996, 1999) has used an object relations perspective to provide insight into the differential development of males and females based on women's primary role in mothering and has also been critical of sexist aspects of Freudian psychoanalysis. The relational cultural model described on page 495 that was developed at the Stone Center is based on a psychodynamic view of human relations. Although other feminist writers such as Brown (1994) and Kaschak (1992) have been critical of several psychotherapeutic approaches, psychoanalysis has been both subject to feminist criticism and an important influence in feminist therapy approaches.

At the same time that female therapists were concerned about sexism in the practice of psychotherapy, women were voicing concerns about social and personal rights. Such organizations as the National Organization for Women provided an opportunity to deal with political issues, such as laws and hiring practices that unfairly discriminated against women. Consciousness-raising groups developed as a means to end isolation among women and to bring about social change (Enns, 2004; Matlin, 2008). These groups served primarily an educational function to develop concern about the connection between personal and political issues and to bring about changes in U.S. society. In the mid-1970s the focus of consciousness-raising groups started to shift from political and social to personal change, but it never lost sight of the interrelationship between social and personal concerns. Issues such as dealing with gender-role stereotyping in the workplace or in the greater society became topics of discussion (Kravetz, 1987). These groups promoted open discourse and were run without leaders. From the development and use of consciousness-raising groups, it was relatively easy to move into therapy groups with a professional leader who would help women deal with internal and external personal issues. Equality of women within the consciousness-raising groups carried over to the role of the leader, who was expected to be open about her skills, limitations, and values while providing direction and expertise for group members (Kaschak, 1976). A characteristic that all feminist therapy, whether individual or group, had in common was the feminist analysis of discrimination against women (Kaschak, 1981). In this way, women clients became aware of how their problems were similar to those of other women.

In describing characteristics of feminist and nonfeminist therapists, Enns (2004) makes a distinction between radical and liberal feminist therapy and between these two approaches to therapy and nonsexist therapy. Nonsexist therapy is distinguished from radical or liberal feminist therapy in that nonsexist therapy does not focus on social change, anger, or power issues but on the therapist's awareness of his or her own values and on an egalitarian approach when working with clients. However, radical and liberal feminist therapy have much in common, such as their emphasis on the political nature of the individual and the role of social institutions. Both recognize the importance of anger as an appropriate response to social pressures and that psychopathology is a result of individual development and societal discrimination. Both support the examination of the difference in power between therapist and client and the use of self-disclosure in therapy.

Distinguishing between radical and liberal feminist therapists, Enns (2004) indicates that the difference is often in the degree to which they participate in and challenge social issues. For example, radical feminist therapists become involved in changing social issues, whereas liberal feminist therapists may or may not opt to do so. Also, therapist self-disclosure is very useful in radical feminist therapy to eliminate exploitation of the patient, but liberal feminist therapists may use it less often. In terms of the gender of therapists, radical feminist therapists are more likely to believe that men cannot be feminist therapists because they cannot serve as role models for women or validate their experience as women. However, men can be profeminist and can incorporate feminist values in their work. In contrast, liberal feminist therapists believe that men can be trained to work as feminist therapists (Baird, Szymanski, & Ruebelt, 2007). The distinction between radical and liberal feminist therapists is not always clear, and some feminist therapists prefer not to use labels for themselves.

With the emergence of the third wave of feminism (Enns, 2004) and other approaches to feminism such as queer theory and lesbian feminism, views of feminist therapy have been affected. Third-wave feminism reflects the opinions of younger feminists. Third-wave feminists have been critical of the lack of action taken by older feminists. Being involved in changing how society deals with HIV/AIDS, violence against women, economic crises, and other political and social issues has been a major approach of third-wave feminists. They recognize that the nature of oppression changes and is not constant in society. Furthermore, they recognize that what one group of individuals sees as oppression another group may not. Also, third-wave feminists are concerned with body image issues that relate to eating disorders and self-criticism. The issue of race and culture is yet another concern of third-wave feminism.

Concern about women of color and women throughout the world has been an issue for many writers (Enns, 2004). Women of color have had an increasing influence on the practice of feminist therapy. Also, feminist therapy has been integrated with the practice of therapy in many different countries. African American and Latina women have pointed out that racism was an important issue to non-White women and that racism existed in the feminist point of view. Lerner (1979) observed,

> White society has long decreed that while "woman's place is in the home," Black woman's place is in the white woman's kitchen. No wonder that many Black women define their own "liberation" as being free to take care of their own homes and their own children, supported by a man with a job. (p. 81)

Hurtado (1996) has noted that the issues of White women tended to be more individual (unequal divisions of labor in the household, inequality with personal interactions with men) and private than those of culturally diverse women, which are more public. Such public issues include desegregation, affirmative action, poverty, and prison reform. Women in different countries have also identified issues that apply to their circumstances, which were different than those faced by middle-class White American women. To differentiate their views from traditional feminists, some feminists identifying with other cultural groups preferred terms such as *womanist* and *femaleist*. In "Multicultural Feminist Therapy: Theory in Context," Barrett et al. (2005) show how examining culture along with women's experience contributes to a full explanation of human experience that is relevant to many different groups.

Most recently, some feminist therapists have paid attention to factors related to the emphasis on cultural diversity that has just been described. These factors include issues of feminists living in countries that had previously been colonized by other countries, the acceptance of men as feminist therapists, and spirituality. Feminist therapists have viewed countries, especially those in South America, Africa, and parts of Asia that were previously colonies of European countries, as being colonized not only as countries, but also as being colonized psychologically. This has led to a patriarchal experience, as individuals in previously patriarchal countries are not treated as equals to the colonizing country. Along with this change has come a renewed acceptance of men as feminist therapists (Brown, 2009b, 2010). Comas-Díaz (2008) has written about the importance of spirituality for Latinos and Latinas, as well as for individuals living in other cultures. Spirituality has not yet received much attention in feminist therapies (Berliner, 2007). These three issues are examples of concerns that feminist therapists address as they deal with social and political issues that interfere with the psychological development of all peoples.

Feminist Theories of Personality

Because the study of women's personality is relatively recent (most of it being done after 1970) and is conducted by many investigators rather than one specific theorist, theoretical ideas for the most part have not accumulated clear and substantial research support. In this section, I summarize some of the different social roles that men and women are often taught in childhood, adolescence, and adulthood. This should provide a background from which to understand theoretical approaches to personality development. One such approach is gender schema theory, which examines the degree to which individuals use gender-related information to analyze the world around them. Gender schema is put in the context of other identities individuals have. Also, many psychologists have studied the relative importance of interpersonal relationships for women and men. Carol Gilligan and Judith Jordan take different approaches in describing the development of women's personalities and the role of relationships in this development. These theoretical concepts provide insight as to how feminist therapists approach psychotherapy with their male and female clients.

Gender Differences and Similarities Across the Lifespan

Research on gender-related characteristics is extensive, especially for children, but also includes research on many biological, psychological, and sociological or environmental factors. In discussing the study of gender, Hare-Mustin and

Marecek (1988) describe two biases in the approach to gender: *Alpha bias* refers to separating women and men into two categories, which has the dangers of treating women as separate and unequal and of furthering male–female stereotypes. *Beta bias* treats men and women as identical and ignores real differences between the lives of women and the lives of men. Hare-Mustin and Marecek caution both researchers and therapists to be sensitive about exaggerating either differences or similarities between men and women. In this section, I focus on differences in the social development of men and women, thus running the risk of alpha bias, over-generalizing about differences (Brown, 2010). The information in this section is condensed from an extensive discussion of gender differences in Crawford and Unger (2004) and Matlin (2008).

Before discussing gender differences in development and experiences, it will be useful to discuss gender similarities. Hyde (2005) points out that people often focus on gender differences. However, after reviewing 46 meta-analyses, Hyde reports that males and females are similar on many psychological variables. Although men are often reported to be better in math than women, and women better than men in language skills, Hyde reports that their ability levels are quite similar to each other. In terms of communication styles, there are also few differences between males and females. Examining social and personality variables, men and women do not differ very much on variables such as leadership, anxiety, gregariousness, self-esteem, and assertiveness. Areas where Hyde reported differences were in males being more aggressive, having greater motor skills in areas like throwing distances, and in approaches to sexuality. However, there are differences in certain areas of life that women and men experience growing up.

Childhood. Even before birth, there are gender preferences for children. In reviewing the literature on this topic, Matlin (2008) shows that in many cultures men especially, but also women, have a clear preference for a son rather than a daughter. This is particularly true in Asia, where selective abortion of female children is known. If one or both parents have a strong preference for a male child and a daughter is born, it is possible that these preferences may affect parental child-raising attitudes. The behavior of male and female infants is quite similar. However, adults' treatment of infants shows gender differences. Adults select clothing and toys for young children often based on gender-role expectations. By the way they and other children are dressed, play, and learn about life through stories and television, children begin to adopt different gender-role expectations.

In elementary school children, sex segregation is common. Boys prefer playing with boys to playing with girls, especially when play is physically active and competitive (Edwards, Knoche, & Kumuru, 2001). During these years there is pressure to unlearn behaviors associated with the other sex. In other words, girls may be taunted or teased for being a "tomboy," and boys may be called "sissy." Due in part to the devaluing of gender stereotype characteristics, friendships between boys and girls that may have been common at the age of 3 become increasingly uncommon at the age of 7 (Gottman & Parker, 1987). Interactions with parents, teachers, and other adults often encourage independence and efficacy in boys and nurturing and helplessness in girls (Crawford & Unger, 2004). Even though some parents may consciously choose not to impart gender-role expectations to their children, children communicate gender-role preferences through their preferences for play, toys, and stereotyped expectations based on gender, which can come from peers, television, movies, and so forth.

Adolescence. Gender-role pressures tend to be more severe in adolescence than in any other period because of physiological and sociological factors. In general, puberty provides more conflict for girls than for boys because of how society views the female body and the role of female sexuality (Matlin, 2008). Girls and/or their parents sometimes respond negatively to the onset of menstruation (most commonly between the ages of 11 and 13). Similarly, breast development, because others can easily observe it, may be the subject of embarrassment for girls and teasing by boys. Girls often become well aware of the need to be thin and to be seen as physically attractive. Although different peer groups (friends at church or synagogue, female athletes, close friends) may have slightly different expectations, exposure to expectations of women's appearance through magazines and television can have profound effects. For African American female adolescents, the experience may be different because African American women tend not to be featured in teen magazines. Dating becomes an important factor in female personality development, with females being valued for their appearance whereas males are valued for achievements as well as appearance. Females often learn to compete against other girls for the attention of boys, whereas boys may be focused more broadly on academic and athletic accomplishments. Girls, not boys, must learn to regulate sexual activity. Use of contraception and the consequences of teenage pregnancy are usually a much greater problem for the adolescent girl than for the boy. For adolescent females who are beginning to discover their lesbian identity, it is often difficult to find positive role models in the media. Also, the experience of coming out to parents can vary widely; sometimes parents are supportive and at other times dramatically rejecting.

With growing independence, conflicts between parents and teenage adolescents are frequently different for mother–daughter, mother–son, father–daughter, and father–son pairs (Crawford & Unger, 2004; Matlin, 2008), as gender-role stereotypes affect parental expectations. Although adolescent–parental relationships are important, for adolescent heterosexual women it is the emphasis on the need to develop relationships (particularly with men) and thus to be valued for their appearance that carries over into women's experience in adulthood.

Adulthood. Because there are so many variations in the ways that men and women deal with a complex array of issues, it is difficult to concisely describe women's or men's adult development. However, among the important issues that have a special impact on women, here I address mothering, work, midlife issues, and violence.

Motherhood includes not only biological changes but also changes in social roles. Not only do physiological changes occur because of pregnancy, but also decisions about work, marital roles, and issues regarding physical self-image occur differently, depending upon a woman's social class, race, and sexual orientation. Adjustment depends upon a variety of factors, especially the relationship to the child and husband or partner. Married women who decide not to have children are often under considerable social pressure to do so. Controlling the decision to have children requires dealing with sexual issues such as contraception and possibly abortion. Women, more than men, are given the responsibility for raising children in American society and are likely to receive blame if children are not raised properly. Cultural practices and views vary widely and affect approaches to child raising (Crawford & Unger, 2004; Matlin, 2008).

Work is often quite different for married women than for married men. Although some men share in housework, women usually do 60% to 70% of it

(Matlin, 2008). Housework includes not only physical management of the house, meal preparation, and laundry but also relating to others—taking care of a husband, children, and possibly aged parents. In their paid work, women make up 97% of secretaries and administrative assistants, whereas men account for 86% of engineers and architects and 70% of physicians (U.S. Department of Labor, 2007). Women are also likely to earn considerably less than men (Sharf, 2010). Although traditional women's professions such as teaching, social work, and health occupations have status because they require skill and dedication, their pay is lower than many high-status occupations in which men are predominant. Furthermore, in applying for a job and in the actual work itself, women are more likely than men to experience discrimination and sexual harassment (Sharf, 2010). Although legislation has brought changes in societal awareness of discrimination, attitudes and behaviors tend to be slower to change.

The aging process can be quite different for women than for men. A part of aging for women is menopause, which is often seen as being a time in which women change negatively in physical and psychological ways. Some women may feel devalued as their children leave home or their role in child care decreases significantly. To the extent that much of society values women in a relational or caring role, this change can be difficult. However, for some women it is an opportunity to achieve and be active. For women, insufficient income can be a particular problem. In summary, aging women are likely to be seen more negatively than men and to experience more financial hardship than men. However, the ability of aging women to develop friendships because of their involvement in nurturing activities is likely to help them deal effectively with children leaving home, the death of husbands, and other losses.

Although most women expect to be able to make decisions about issues of mothering, working, and aging in their lives, violence is very different. Violence to women occurs at all age levels. For children, child abuse and incest can have terrible consequences for their later psychological development. In adolescence and adulthood, women may be victims of date rape, stranger rape, or wife battering (Crawford & Unger, 2004; Matlin, 2008). Statistics tend to underreport acts of violence because victims may fear being further victimized through physical intimidation or being blamed for provoking the incident. As Matlin points out, women who experience violence often report anxiety and depression as well as many physiological problems.

In discussing women's development, I have mentioned only some major differential impacts of physiological changes and social attitudes on women. In putting forth a theory of personality development for women, feminist theorists have drawn on a variety of these lifespan issues. People vary greatly in their response to perceived gender differences due to cultural and other variables. Both men and women differ in the degree to which they apply gender-role stereotyping to themselves and others. This variation in gender-role stereotyping is a part of schema theory.

Schema Theory and Multiple Identities

As discussed in Chapter 10, schemas are cognitive concepts referring to ways of thinking. These are core beliefs that individuals hold and are assumptions about how individuals see the world. From a multicultural feminist point of view, beliefs about how men and women view each other and how individuals of various cultural backgrounds view others of different cultural backgrounds is an important area of study and an issue that therapists may focus on. First I will examine gender schemas and then cultural schemas using Helms's (Helms & Cook, 1999) racial identity model. Last, I will describe Hays's (2008) description of the multiple identities that comprise an individual. She uses the acronym ADDRESSING to describe these many identities.

Gender schemas can be applied to all levels of development. As Bem (1993) has observed, children learn not only society's views of gender but also to apply those views to themselves. For example, they learn that girls wear dresses, boys do not; girls may wear lipstick and nail polish, boys do not; and boys are called *handsome* and girls are called *pretty*. Adolescents, in particular, are likely to be highly gender focused as they become concerned about the physical attractiveness of the other sex and of themselves. Adults who are gender focused are more likely to view behaviors of associates as "unmanly" or "unfeminine" than those who use other schemas in attributing characteristics to associates. Bem (1987) believes that gender is one of the strongest schemas, or ways of looking at society. She is concerned that a strong gender schema is a very limiting way to view oneself and others. Differentiating between the necessity for children to learn about physiological sex differences and the stereotyping of gender-role behaviors, Bem proposes that parents help their children learn other schemas, such as those focused on individual differences or cultural relativism. An *individual differences* schema emphasizes the variability of individuals within a group. For example, when the young child says, "Harry is a sissy because he likes to paint," a parent might point out that both boys and girls paint and enjoy it. The *cultural relativism* schema refers to the idea that not everyone thinks the same way and that people in different groups or cultures have different beliefs. Fairy tales, which often contain many gender-role stereotypes, can be explained as beliefs that reflect a culture that is different than our current culture (if the child is old enough to understand this concept). Schema theory has applications not only for child raising but also for how clients view themselves and others in therapy. By observing their own gender schemas and those of their clients, therapists can become aware of patterns of thinking that may be hampering progress in therapy.

Although not described as a schema theory, Helms's (Helms, 1995; Helms & Cook, 1999) racial identity model examines individuals' beliefs about their own culture as it relates to other cultures. Helms has developed stages of racial identity for people of color as well as White Americans. These stages reflect how beliefs about oneself and the culture of others may go through changes. As individuals hear stories about people from different cultures, they use input from self and others to evaluate these and to develop beliefs or stereotypes about other cultures. The stages that Helms describes are ones that show a developing understanding of cultural diversity and the discarding of racism. In this way, individuals' schemas regarding culture may change at various times during their lives.

Attending to more variables than gender and ethnicity, Hays (2008) uses the acronym ADDRESSING to describe many of the multiple identities an individual may have:

Age—How do age or generational issues affect the person?
Disability that is acquired—How does the disability effect relationships with family or caregivers?
Disability that is developmental—How does the disability affect relationships at different points in the person's life?

Religion—What are a person's upbringing and current beliefs?

Ethnicity—What are the meanings of the racial or ethnic identity in the communities that the person lives in?

Social class—Socioeconomic status may be defined by occupation, income, education, marital status, gender, ethnicity, or community.

Sexual orientation—What is the sexual orientation of the individual? Gay, lesbian, bisexual, or transgendered?

Indigenous heritage—Is being indigenous a part of one's heritage? If so, how?

National origin—What is the national origin and primary language of the individual?

Gender or sex—What are the person's gender roles and expectation?

These are common identities individuals have; some may have more identities. In a patriarchal culture (such as the United States), some individual will have privileges, such as being Caucasian and male, while others (being African American and female) are likely to experience disadvantages. Being short or overweight can be seen as identities that are disadvantages. Feminist therapists continue to view gender as a very important identity. However, they recognize that individuals have other identities therapists should be aware of.

Gilligan's Ethic of Care

Newscom

CAROL GILLIGAN

Although Freud and Erikson, as well as other theorists, wrote about the importance of human relationships for women in the formation of their identity, Gilligan (1977, 1982) commented on the values that traditional psychology has placed on women's concern about relationships. She was concerned that traits such as compassion and care, which define the "goodness" of women, were viewed as a deficit in their moral development and that women's caretaking roles were devalued in favor of the development of individuality and achievement. Working with Lawrence Kohlberg, who had conceived a stage model of moral development that she found less applicable for women than for men, Gilligan undertook a series of studies on women's moral development. Briefly, she viewed Kohlberg's (1981) model as one of morality of justice and her own as one of morality of care and responsibility. This difference can be seen in the comparison of the comments of two 8-year-old children, Jeffrey and Karen, who were both asked to describe a situation where they were not sure what the correct approach should be. Where Jeffrey uses an ordering system to resolve a conflict between desire and duty, Karen uses a relationship system that includes her friends. Jeffrey thinks about what to do first; Karen is concerned about who is left out (Gilligan, 1982, pp. 32–33).

Jeffrey

When I really want to go to my friends and my mother is cleaning the cellar, I think about my friends, and then I think about my mother, and then I think about the right thing to do. (But how do you know it's the right thing to do?) Because some things go before other things.

Karen

I have lots of friends and I can't always play with all of them, so everybody's going to have to take a turn, because they're all my friends. Like if someone's all alone, I'll play with them. (What kinds of things do you think about when you are trying to make that decision?) Um, someone all alone, loneliness.

Gilligan's writings have prompted much attention. In summarizing more than 20 years of research on Gilligan's hypotheses, Hyde (Hyde, 2005; Jaffee & Hyde,

2000) suggests that most research studies have shown few gender differences either for dilemmas created for studies or for actual life dilemmas. Gilligan has been misinterpreted as suggesting that the care and responsibility approach was superior to the morality of justice approach, something that she has denied. Others have criticized her research for not including comparable situations in which both men's and women's moral development can be assessed, for not using well-defined procedures for scoring moral development, and for focusing on sex differences without considering the impact of social class or religion. Hare-Mustin and Marecek (1988) question whether lack of power rather than gender creates an ethic of care and responsibility. This broad debate on men's and women's moral thinking has provided a forum for viewing gender differences. Gilligan helps us look at moral decision making in more flexible ways and pays attention to factors that show that both men and women use a care orientation. Furthermore, Gilligan (2008) examines the potential for care and attachment that occurs in human development. In summary, a major contribution of Gilligan is to show that making moral judgments is based not only on rational judgments but also on valuing caring and relationships when men and women make moral decisions.

The Relational Cultural Model

Started at the Stone Center at Wellesley College in Wellesley, Massachusetts, relational cultural therapy has developed over more than 30 years, with its name changing from self-in-relation theory to relational theory and then to relational cultural theory. These changes reflect the growing emphasis on applying this theory to women of different cultures. The central focus of relational cultural theory is being responsive to and being responded to when dealing with others (Jordan, 2010; West, 2005). A major concern is disconnectedness that occurs in relationships with others. These disconnections usually represent failures in being understood by others. Contributing to disconnections in relationships is power. If a more powerful person is not empathic with a less powerful person, then the less powerful person cannot be herself in the relationship and may hold back aspects of herself. By not being able to express oneself openly, one can feel pain and a sense of isolation. When a person is cared about, then she can feel that she matters. Not only are power differences important on the individual level, but they are also important on the broader social and political level. At the social or political level, individuals or cultural groups who have never been discriminated against can feel a sense of connection if they are listened to and responded to (Jordan, 2003, 2010).

Previously disenfranchised individuals can feel a sense of power in a positive sense, not in the sense of feeling power over someone. There is a sense of mutual empowerment from both parties, whether individual, social, or political. This mutual empowerment has five features: zest, action, knowledge, a sense of worth, and desire (West, 2005).

Zest is a positive feeling of energy coming from positive or mutually empathic interactions.

Action is positive as it comes from empathic interactions between or among people listening to each other.

Knowledge is gained through nonjudgmental listening to others.

A sense of worth comes from trusting relationships and feeling that one's thoughts and feelings are valued.

Desire is a wish to have more empowering connections or relationships.

When relational cultural therapists work with clients, they seek to develop high-quality relationships that the client will have with others. This often starts with the therapeutic relationship itself (Jordan, 2010). Fostering independence may occur, but it is not the major focus. Safety is a feature of positive relationships both with the therapist and others. Relational cultural therapy moves from disconnection to authenticity and mutual trust. As a result, a sense of empowerment as described above develops.

This theoretical approach is based on the work of Jean Baker Miller (1986, 1991), who saw women as the subordinate group in society who developed characteristics that helped them cope with this subordination (Enns, 2004). She saw women (and minorities and poor people) as relegated to providing personal services for the dominant groups (generally White males). When those who are subordinate behave with intelligence or independence, they may be seen as abnormal and criticized for this behavior. To please the dominant group, subordinates develop characteristics that include passivity, dependency, lack of initiative, and inability to act. Those who are subordinate must be able to interpret the verbal and nonverbal behaviors of those who are dominant (men). In this way, women have developed "feminine intuition." As a result of being in a subordinate position, women may feel less important than men and strive to improve their relationships with both men and women by attending to the emotional and physical needs of others and by helping them develop their strength and improve their well-being (mothering or nursing). These observations led to the desire to help women and individuals from diverse cultures develop a sense of relatedness and empowerment.

Recognizing the many cultural differences that individuals experience, relational cultural therapy focuses on developing relational resilience and relational competence. *Relational resilience* refers to growing in a relationship and being able to move forward despite setbacks (Jordan, 2010). When growth is supported, individuals move forward more readily. Relational resilience also concerns recognizing when relationships are not mutual and moving on from them. It is important to recognize whom one can trust and to feel safe with those people. *Relational competence* is somewhat similar. It refers to being able to be empathic toward self and others. It also includes the ability to participate in and build a sense of strength in a community. This goes beyond self-interest. This is consistent with the feminist principle that the personal is political. Working for social change to move beyond racism, classism, heterosexism, and sexism are aspects of relational competence.

All three theories—schema theory, Gilligan's moral development theory, and relational cultural theory—seek to value women and cultural diversity. Schema theory and relational cultural theory examine the ways individuals think and what they believe. This provides a way of examining beliefs that foster or interfere with ways individuals see their world. Gilligan's theory is the only one of the three to be extensively researched; the other theories are ideas developed over time by initiators of the theories. Although Gilligan's theory has not been shown to differentiate men's ways of relating from women's, it has shown the importance of caring in moral judgments. Relational cultural theory shows ways that therapists can empower individuals not just to change themselves but also to make social and political change.

Theories of Feminist Therapy

More than any other theoretical approach discussed in this book, feminist therapy looks at sociological (social) factors that affect human development. The goals of feminist therapy are characterized by an emphasis on appreciating the impact of political and social forces on women and culturally diverse groups, an open and egalitarian relationship between client and therapist, and an appreciation of the female and culturally diverse perspectives on life. This view has led to criticism of the current psychological classification system, DSM-IV-TR, and to suggestions for other approaches to assessment. Almost all feminist therapists combine feminist therapy with other theoretical approaches. However, certain methods associated with feminist therapy recognize the impact of social forces on individuals and provide a way to make individuals more effective in dealing with society. Examples of techniques that help individuals deal with social discrimination are those that focus on gender role, power, and assertiveness. A broad understanding of the purpose of feminist therapy can be gained by examining the therapeutic goals that feminist therapists value.

Goals of Feminist Therapy

Feminist therapists believe that goals of therapy should include not only changes in one's own personal life but also changes in society's institutions (Brown, 2010; Enns, 2004). A number of feminist writers (Ballou & West, 2000; Enns, 2004; Gilbert, 1980; Kaschak, 1981; Rawlings & Carter, 1977; Russell, 1984; Worell & Remer, 2003) have expressed considerable agreement in their basic views of the goals of therapy. In this section, I summarize the goals of feminist therapy as described by Sturdivant (1980), Enns (2004), and Brown (2010).

1. *Therapy for change, not adjustment*, is a basic goal of feminist therapy. Symptom removal (adjustment), a traditional goal of therapy, is appropriate only if it will not interfere with women's development and growth. For example, prescribing only medications to a woman who has complained of headaches and depression due to marital conflicts would be inappropriate because it treats only the symptom. Recognizing how life circumstances, pain, and symptoms are related can bring about change rather than adjustment. For example, dealing with a marital conflict and helping a woman express and assert herself would be an appropriate means of helping headaches go away. Change that takes place would include new skill development and involvement in social change.

2. *Self-nurturance and self-esteem* in feminist therapy refers to taking care of oneself and meeting one's own needs. Being aware of one's own needs is an aspect of self-nurturance. Self-esteem requires a move away from being dependent on external sources of self-esteem (what others think) to self-esteem based on one's own feeling about oneself. For women, this may mean liking themselves despite how others (friends, family, and the media) tell them how they should look, act, or think.

3. *Balancing instrumental and relational strengths* is a goal of effective feminist therapy. Clients should become more independent and take actions in their lives but also develop meaningful relationships with others. Becoming more expressive, facilitative, and caring with friends and family cannot be at the expense of meeting one's own needs. Sometimes improving the quality of interpersonal relationships may threaten a marriage if the partner is not willing to change also. A goal of feminist therapy is not just to improve relationships with friends and family but also to pay particular attention to the quality of relationships with women (Jordan, 2003, 2010).

4. *Body image and sensuality* are often defined for women by the media and by men, as society puts great importance on physical attractiveness for women. The goal of feminist therapy is to help individuals accept their body and their sexuality and not to use the standards of others to criticize their physicality. Sexual decisions should be made by individuals without coercion from others.

5. *Affirming diversity* refers to valuing cultural differences of clients. This includes acknowledging multiple identities such as class, age, race, and power (Hays, 2008). This may mean learning about different cultural groups such as lesbians and Native Americans. Although women share many common issues and goals, women's lives are shaped by many different experiences coming from diverse cultural, linguistic, religious, economic, and sexual orientation backgrounds. At times, feminist therapists deal with conflicts between feminist values and cultural norms, such as homophobic attitudes that run counter to feminist values. For White heterosexual feminist therapists, this may mean being aware of White privilege and heterosexual privilege, which represent unearned entitlements.

6. *Empowerment and social action* are key goals in feminist therapy. Often expressed as "the person is political," this goal is dissimilar from those of other therapies. It emphasizes the need for women to be aware of gender-role stereotyping, sexism, and discrimination and then to work toward changing this treatment (Ballou & West, 2000). For Brown (2010), empowerment is an important goal of feminist therapy. A common double question she asks of herself is: "What are the power dynamics in this situation? Where am I taking patriarchal assumptions for granted as true?" (p. 30). Being an advocate for one's client who is being discriminated against or being oppressed would be consistent with the goal of empowerment. Also, often therapists can help clients reduce self-blame by pointing out how the problem comes from forces outside the client, such as in sexual harassment or rape. Encouraging clients to be involved in political action groups such as the National Organization for Women that work to change federal and state laws that adversely effect women is an effective way to empower clients. Similarly, working to effect change on a more informal level, such as by confronting a male colleague who has treated a female supervisee in a sexist manner, is also supported. Implicit in this goal is the recognition that society brings about psychopathology through discriminatory practices that affect women. Social action is applied not only to women but to culturally diverse groups that may be underserved, underrepresented, or discriminated against.

Underlying assumptions of these goals are that female and culturally diverse points of view are accepted, that relationships between people should be equal (that men should not dominate women, nor women dominate men), and that people of all cultural backgrounds exist in a political and diverse social system that can be discriminatory. These views also influence the diagnosis and treatment of psychological problems.

Assessment Issues in Feminist Therapy

Because feminist therapists value a sociological and political perspective on psychological problems, cultural diversity, equality with their clients, and the female perspective on life, they have been critical of the major diagnostic system (DSM-IV-TR) and its earlier versions. They have criticized classification systems because they have been developed primarily by White male psychiatrists, many with a psychoanalytic perspective, to be used for diagnosing and reporting mental disorders for all people (Brown, 2010; Eriksen & Kress, 2005). Also, many feminist therapists have pointed out that classification systems focus on psychological symptoms and not the social factors that cause them. Rawlings and Carter (1977) are concerned that a de-emphasis on sociological factors that produce rape and child abuse diminishes the respect that therapists have for clients. Further, diagnostic labeling is criticized because it encourages adjustment to social norms, reinforcing stereotypes rather than questioning social injustices. Laura Brown (1994) succinctly describes the power of naming diagnostic categories in this way: "If you call it a skunk, you will assume that it smells" (p. 130). As an alternative to the DSM-IV-TR, McAuliffe, Eriksen, and Kress (2005) describe a constructivist approach to diagnosis that examines four aspects of human functioning. Their CPSS model examines these aspects of persons' lives: *Context*, life *Phase*, constructive *Stage*, and personality *Style*. The purpose of the model is to promote client strength, self-awareness, and the ability to confront oppressive social forces. Because of their criticism of traditional diagnostic categories, feminist therapists have been more concerned with exploring strong feelings, such as anger, and bringing about both individual and societal change (Brown, 2010; Enns, 2004). However, Roades (2000), acknowledging these weaknesses in classification systems, also accepts the wide use of classification systems. She describes gender differences in the prevalence of anxiety, depression, substance abuse, and other disorders for men and women. Feminist therapists assess the cultural context of client problems, obtaining information about the client's power or lack of it, so that clients are not blamed for their problems.

The Therapeutic Relationship

For feminist therapists, the therapeutic relationship is the key to successful therapy. For Jordan (2010), it is the core of her view of therapy, as described in *Relational-Cultural Therapy*. Therapy can be viewed as a healing relationship. First, the therapeutic relationship must be safe enough for the client to explore her concerns. Clients often come to therapy with relationship strategies that disconnect them from others. In relational cultural therapy, the therapist shows respect for how the client has communicated in these relationships and does not confront them directly but appreciates their necessity and how threatening it is to give them up. A gradual discussion of relationships leads to the style of relating that is more nuanced and more effective. With therapy comes a greater freedom of expression and more confidence in dealing with feelings in relationships. This can then lead to building relationships with others and connecting with others in a way that empowers the client. By examining social factors that are destructive, the client can be empowered to work with others to bring about change. Skills are learned that help the client relate empathically with others and, working with others, to bring about social change. These relationship skills come from an effective therapeutic relationship. In relational cultural therapy, mutual empathy helps to facilitate change because both client and therapist develop mutual respect. Some feminist therapists use relational cultural therapy, whereas others use other models of feminist therapy. However, all feminist therapists believe the therapeutic relationship to be critical to therapeutic success. Additionally, many feminist therapists use a variety of techniques in their work.

Techniques of Feminist Therapy

Because feminist therapists may combine feminist approaches with any of the theories discussed in this book, here I describe only some techniques that are either unique to feminist therapy or particularly relevant to the goals of feminist therapy. In a later section, I explain how feminist therapy and other theoretical approaches may be integrated. A number of writers have described feminist therapy techniques that can be applied to women (and men) and that recognize the importance of both psychological and sociological factors.

First I will describe three approaches that are often used together. In conceptualizing a client's concerns, counselors often use cultural analysis, gender-role analysis, and power analysis. This provides a basis for making cultural interventions, gender-role interventions, and power interventions. The therapist is not limited to these three categories and may choose to analyze disabilities, religion, or other identities. Additionally, feminist therapists may make use of assertiveness training, reframing and relabeling, and demystifying strategies. The primarily cognitive and behavioral approach of Worell and Remer (2003) is the major source for this discussion. Although group techniques are used widely in feminist therapy, they are described in a later section.

Cultural analysis. Feminist therapy maintains that the problems that individuals discuss in counseling should be seen in the context of culture. In analyzing culture as it relates to a client, feminists examine several issues (Worell & Remer, 2003). Therapists may ask to what extent do the issues of the dominant culture that the client lives in affect the definition of the problem? For example, in the United States the culture is White, Western, and heterosexual dominant. This affects the way issues such as rape and spouse battering are seen. Incidence of issues provides information about the culture. Rape is primarily done by men to women. How individuals identify the problem is significant. For example, women may blame themselves for being raped. Myths about issues also may exist in the society, such as beliefs that African Americans are not as intelligent as Whites or do not want to work. Examining these issues provides a way of analyzing the impact of a culture on the nature of a problem.

Cultural intervention. There are many ways to acknowledge and work with cultural problems that are a significant aspect of individuals' problems. Rabin in *Understanding Gender and Culture in the Helping Process* (2005) takes a narrative perspective, which is described in Chapter 12. By analyzing aspects of clients' lives or stories focusing on issues that arise from a cultural analysis, a therapist can be sensitive to cultural issues affecting a client. Understanding the client's culture can then help therapists make interventions that require the use of lawyers, social agencies, families, or others. Suggestions are informed through the therapist's understanding of the client's concerns.

An example of a female Somalian refugee who has emigrated to Australia will help to illustrate a cultural intervention (Babacan & Gopalkrishnan, 2005). The therapist in this example tries to help Ms. M. unburden herself of issues and helps her to validate her experience. The trusting relationship helps to empower Ms. M. and to help her build her confidence and seek to make progress in addressing her problem. The counselor uses a narrative approach in her work with Ms. M.

Ms. M. is a 28-year-old Muslim woman who fled Somalia with her 8-year-old son after witnessing her husband being killed by an armed gang. Her sister also was killed and her sister's husband was missing, leaving her to care for her sister's four children. After living in a refugee camp for 2 years, Ms. M. was resettled in Australia. She was reassigned from a male counselor to a female counselor, in part because Ms. M. had difficulty opening up to a strange male from a different culture.

> In telling her story, Ms. M. revealed that she had been raped in the camp by a person in charge and could not disclose it to anyone as he had threatened to stop her resettlement if she were to tell anyone. She had not had the opportunity to debrief with anyone and felt extremely "dirty and unclean." This related to her cultural understanding of morality and sex out of wedlock. She also felt that she was somehow to blame for this. Her belief that she was "dirty" was reinforced by arriving in a hostile environment where she was confronted with overt racism as a black woman in a predominantly white environment. Further, the support group was constantly forcing Ms. M. to learn English, to assimilate, and to convert to Christianity. This was a source of tension and further fear for Ms. M. She felt unsafe and responded through withdrawal, retreat, and a diminished will to live (Babacan & Gopalkrishnan, 2005, p. 157).

In helping Ms. M., the counselor needed to understand being a woman in the Somalian culture, examining the interaction between the individual and the culture. The counselor gathered factual information about Somalia and its history. Because Ms. M. was careful about trusting the counselor, being empathic with Ms. M.'s situation was received slowly. After a year, Ms. M. was able to stop her panic attacks and be able to better attend to the problems in her family. She also became more interested in events going on in her daily life. The counselor was culturally empathic. She examined issues such as how reality is understood in Somalian culture, as dualistic or holistic. She grasped how Ms. M. viewed morality as it related to her values and choices. Views on relationships with others such as elders and men were also understood by the counselor. The counselor used a feminist counseling strategy to help Ms. M. see that the rape was not her fault and that she was not dirty. She helped Ms. M. use other support networks besides a church-based charity. In 2 years, Ms. M. was able to develop proficiency in English and enroll in a university engineering program. Knowledge of Ms. M.'s culture helped the counselor intervene to slowly assist Ms. M. with her difficulties.

Gender-role analysis. To understand the impact of gender-role expectations on them, clients can participate in a gender-role analysis (Worell & Remer, 2003). Although this gender-role analysis can be modified, depending on the needs of the client, the steps provide a way of clearly identifying a sequential approach. The approach is illustrated by the case of Carla, who is depressed because she is constantly fighting with her parents and as a result feels stupid and incompetent.

To use a gender-role analysis with Carla, the therapist would have her first identify various gender-role messages that she had experienced during her life. For example, Carla's father has told her that women should raise children and keep house. Her mother has told her not to argue with her father, to let him be the boss, and to be more understanding of him. Second, the counselor helps the client identify positive and negative consequences of gender-related messages. Carla tells the counselor that she feels she really cannot be effective in her studies or in her job because she believes work is not important for women and she is reluctant to suggest new methods for improving her work to her boss. Third, the counselor and the client identify the statements clients make to themselves based on these gender-role messages. For example, Carla has said to herself, "I really shouldn't worry about work. It shouldn't be very important to me anyway, so I won't talk to my boss." Fourth, the counselor and client decide which messages they want to change. In Carla's case, after discussing many of her internalized messages about gender roles, she decides to change the message that "work should not be important to me." Last, the client and counselor develop a plan to implement the change and then follow through. Carla writes, "My work is important to me and I want to be able to speak to my clients with more authority, speaking louder and more firmly." Carla then follows through with this change in her behavior. At the next session, she discusses the results of her attempt to change her speaking behavior.

In this hypothetical example, the client learns how assumptions about the way women should behave in society have negatively affected her view of herself and her performance. By identifying her gender-role messages, she is then able to implement a change. In a real counseling situation, there would be many messages to analyze and more complex goals to reach.

Gender-role intervention. Often feminist therapists respond to a client's comments or problems by understanding the impact of gender-role and other social expectations on the client. They may not go through the process of gender-role analysis described previously, but they do provide the client insights about social issues as they affect the client's psychological problem. Russell (1984, p. 76) describes this as the skill of social analysis, which "provides a rationale, that is a cognitive framework for the skill of positive evaluation of women." Following is an example of a gender-role intervention with a woman who has been separated from her husband and has not worked for 20 years.

> *Doreen:* Now on top of all my other problems, I have to worry about getting a job. I'm not qualified to do any kind of work, and just the thought of looking for work is absolutely petrifying. Offices today are so complicated with computers and new machines. I could never learn to use them.
>
> *Counselor B:* Well, Doreen, I agree that trying to get a job can be a pretty tough proposition, especially when some employers discriminate against older women. However, that kind of discrimination is not legal, and other employers are aware of the benefits of maturity in their employees. We can work together on looking for all the positive things you can offer an employer and plan how you can best present this.

Comment: Counselor B is using social analysis to indicate that sexist and age-linked discrimination does exist, that the client may need to be prepared for it, and that this is inherently not only unfair but invalid. The counselor is encouraging the client to combat such attitudes by clearly enunciating the positive claims that refute them. Individual action is proposed at this stage, but conceivably social action might be contemplated at a later point in the counseling process. (Russell, 1984, pp. 85–86)

The emphasis on society's discrimination toward women rather than on Doreen's hesitancy toward working is an important aspect of this approach. The counselor helps the client to think positively, so that she can attain her goals.

Power analysis. Traditionally, White men have had more power than women and non-White men in many countries; as a result they have made and enforced decisions about family, work, laws, and social relationships. Brown (2010) categorizes power into four types: somatic power, interpersonal power, interpsychic power, interpersonal/social-contextual power, and spiritual/existential power.

Somatic power A person is aware of one's physical senses, such as eating, drinking, sex, comfort, and rest. The body is experienced as a safe place and is accepted for what it is, not for what it should be.

Intrapersonal/intrapsychic power If an individual knows what she thinks and feels, this would be an indication of power. Such a person would be flexible, but not suggestible. She would focus on the present, not dwell on the past or future. She would have powerful emotions and the ability to take care of her emotions so they don't harm herself or others.

Interpersonal/social-contextual power By being interpersonally effective, such an individual would have a desired impact on others. She would be able to have good relationships with others and leave relationships if they prove harmful.

Spiritual/existential power Such a person would be able to make meaning out of her life. She would be able to integrate her heritage and culture in a way that helps her understand herself better. Being aware of the social factors that she deals with and interacting with them rather than being overwhelmed by them would be an aspect of spiritual/existential power.

Brown uses these categories to assess power issues with her clients. These four ways of examining power help her to know how to work with her clients and help them to be more effective in their lives. This is one approach to analyzing power; there are others.

By increasing clients' awareness of the differences between the power of men and women in society, therapists can then help them make changes where their lack of power has previously prevented change (Worell & Remer, 2003). To illustrate power analysis, I use the case of Rose, who has been feeling stressed when her husband comes home in the evening. Two weeks ago, after he had been drinking, they had a fight about his going out alone at night without her. Angry at her, he punched her in the stomach and hit her head against the wall.

The first step of power analysis is to have the client choose a definition that fits for her and to apply it to different kinds of power. Rose wants the power to express herself to her husband and to do something about his inappropriate behavior. For her, this may mean investigating legal, physical, or psychological ways to be powerful. Second, because men and women may have different access to legal, financial, physical, or other types of power, this issue is discussed. The counselor and

Rose talk about her finances, the value of separate checking accounts, self-defense lessons, and the advantages and disadvantages of consulting a lawyer. Third, different ways that power can be used to bring about change are discussed. Will Rose use indirect and helpless ways of having power by pleading with her husband to stop drinking, or will she consult a lawyer and be clear about what behaviors she will or will not tolerate from her husband? Fourth, clients examine gender-role messages that interfere with their use of power. Because Rose had earlier learned that wives listen to their husbands and help them when they are distressed, she decides to challenge this message. Finally, clients may use a variety of power strategies in appropriate situations. In this case, Rose decides to insist that her husband seek help for his drinking immediately and then move in with a friend if he does not. In this example, the client learns that she can change depressed or anxious feelings in herself by acting in an appropriately powerful way.

Power intervention. Power analysis is a technique that requires planning and follow-up in counseling. Often, a therapist can strengthen a client's sense of self through reinforcing her statements or through giving information. Empowering a client can occur in the course of therapeutic discussion and does not need to be planned.

In the following example, Bonnie Burstow (1992), using an unusual approach, empowers a client whose father has acted incestuously with her. The client is angry at her father but wondering if she should forgive him.

> [Client:] Bonnie, I really hate his guts. Like I mean, REALLY HATE. I don't know how I'm ever going to be able to forgive him. . . . Do you think I have to?
>
> Bonnie: I want to be clear about this. No, Doris, you don't have to. As far as I am concerned, you don't have to forgive him now. You don't have to forgive him ever. Hating him doesn't make you any less valuable a human being, and it is perfectly natural. Of course you hate him! Why wouldn't you hate someone who crept up on you and molested you night after night!
>
> [Client:] I feel like spitting every time I think of him.
>
> Bonnie: Feel like spitting now?
> (A spitting exercise ensues.)
>
> Bonnie: How do you feel now?
>
> [Client:] Funny. Good funny. Like I really did something, though it's a bit weird. . . .
>
> Bonnie: How do you feel when you think of your father?
>
> [Client:] Let me see. I am more aware of hating his guts. And I feel a wee bit stronger. I also feel somewhat better about hating his guts. Like it's giving me something. It feels nice to hate.
>
> Bonnie: Of course it does. So, it's okay to hate his guts?
>
> [Client:] Well, it's okay for now. But what if I continue to hate his guts 20 years from now?
>
> Bonnie: Then you continue to hate his guts.
>
> [Client:] Oh, I know. But aren't we supposed to forgive?
>
> Bonnie: Sure. We're also supposed to darn men's socks, cook their meals and accept being sexualized.

[Client:] You mean it's not okay to forgive?

Bonnie: No. I mean it's not mandatory.

[Client:] I see what you mean. I'm glad you said that. 'Cause you know, it is more a matter of "should" than "want." I don't actually want to forgive him. I want to. . . .

Bonnie: Yeah?

[Client:] I want to . . . SPIT ON HIM. (laughter) (Burstow, 1992, pp. 140–141)

In this example, Burstow legitimates her client's anger and encourages her to express it. The anger and sense of power are important, whereas forgiveness is an optional societal message that does not need to be resolved at the moment. Therapists try to help clients become more powerful while at the same time being careful not to use therapy to meet their own needs to be more powerful (Veldhuis, 2001).

Assertiveness training. Because women often do not feel powerful, they may not act in an assertive manner and thus may give up some control over their lives. Feminist therapists see laws and gender-role expectations as contributing to the need for women to be assertive because the rules have historically prevented women from being treated with equality.

Assertiveness skills can be taught to clients so that they feel less depressed, angry, frustrated, or helpless in situations where they give their rights to others. To understand assertiveness, it is helpful to distinguish between assertive behavior and passive or aggressive behavior (Jakubowski, 1977). Assertiveness refers to standing up for one's rights without violating the rights of others. Assertive behavior is a clear and direct (no sarcasm or humor) statement or request. Aggressiveness refers to insisting on one's rights while violating the rights of others. Making fun of, dominating, or belittling another person is aggressive behavior. Passive or nonassertive behavior means giving up one's rights and doing what others may want.

Statement: I borrowed a mirror from your desk drawer. I hope you don't mind.

Assertive: Please don't take things from my desk drawer. If you want to borrow something, I'll probably be able to help you out. Just ask.

Aggressive: Don't go through my drawers and leave my things alone!

Passive: I don't mind.

There are many different ways of acting assertively, and situations vary. For example, being assertive with a parent is often quite different than being assertive with a friend, boss, or teacher. Clients often find it helpful to practice assertiveness by role playing. The counselor and client may take turns playing the roles of the client and the other person. By trying different strategies, including different aggressive, assertive, and passive behaviors, the client can practice a situation that is anticipated.

However, assertiveness can be seen as a male construction (Crawford, 1995). Thus, while a man's assertive behavior may be seen as firm or authoritative, a woman's could be seen as pushy or stubborn. Reviewing research on the perception of women's assertive behavior, Enns (2004) suggests that on some occasions, women's assertive behavior may be seen as less acceptable than men's by both men and women.

Reframing and relabeling. The term *reframing* refers to changing "the frame of reference for looking at an individual's behavior" (Worell & Remer, 2003, p. 80). In feminist therapy, it usually means a shift from blaming oneself to looking at society for an explanation. Reframing is often used to help individuals understand how societal pressures can add to their problem. For example, a woman who is feeling depressed because she believes that she is overweight would be helped to look at the societal pressures in the media and in social values that reinforce thinness as a goal for women. As a result of reframing this situation, she might relabel her problem from "depression" to "feeling overwhelmed by and angry at pressures to be thin."

Therapy-demystifying strategies. Feminist therapists try to have an open and clear relationship with their clients so that inequities of power in society are not re-created in the therapeutic relationship. Therapy should not be a mysterious process or one in which the therapist is more powerful than the client; rather, it should be egalitarian (Brown, 2010). For example, if therapists call their clients by their first names, then they introduce themselves with a first name. Two important ways to demystify therapy are providing information to the client and using appropriate self-disclosure when working with therapeutic issues.

Therapy is demystified by providing information about the process of therapy and by sharing some of the skills of therapy. At the beginning of therapy, feminist therapists describe their theoretical orientation, relevant personal values, and rights the client has as a consumer of therapy (Worell & Remer, 2003). Brown (2010) gives her new clients a five-page explanation of how she does therapy. Items that may be included in such an explanation are the session fee, session time, length of therapy, and possible therapeutic goals. Clients must agree to these before counseling can continue. Additionally, feminist therapists may teach relevant counseling skills such as assertiveness, ways to control behaviors, and ways to increase choices. Also, feminist therapists encourage their clients to give information regarding the impact the therapist is having. In these ways, the therapist helps the client understand, as clearly as possible, the process and purpose of therapy.

Another means of demystifying therapy is self-disclosure. Brown and Walker (1990) describe many ways self-disclosure can be helpful to the client's growth. In general, self-disclosure is given to help the client in his growth, not for the therapist to share her pain or for the therapist to say, "This is how I became successful, and if you follow my example, you can, too." Self-disclosure that the counselor initiates shows that the counselor is a real person, thus equalizing the relationship. Self-disclosure should feel appropriate to the counselor and educative for the client. Russell (1984) gives the following example of appropriate self-disclosure by the counselor regarding marital issues.

> *Eileen:* I want my husband to be my best friend and favorite companion as well as provider and lover. I am interested in everything that he does, and he should likewise be interested in my activities. If you don't share your life together totally, what is the point of being married?
>
> *Counselor B:* The kind of marriage you're describing reminds me of my own ideas about marriage when I was first married. I really resented anything my husband did without me, and I remember making some terrible scenes because he wasn't home punctually from a golf game or he planned to attend some sporting events with his friends without consulting me. It still embarrasses me to think about my ranting and raving! I had to learn to

give him some more space in our relationship and to enjoy my own space. Now, I wouldn't give up my own activities for the world! And, you know, our marriage is a lot happier than when I was insisting on total sharing.

Comment: Counselor B is disclosing information about herself at a fairly intimate level, information about herself that reveals her own inadequacies and limitations, but as it relates to events in the past that have been subsequently resolved, the riskiness of the disclosure is curtailed. Counselor B is disclosing an experience that she perceives to be parallel to that of the client. She is indicating that she resolved the situation in a particular way and this may also work for the client. Counselor B is therefore indicating that she was in the same situation as the client but managed to move beyond it. In this way, the counselor is addressing both the egalitarian goals and the alternative expansion goals of the self-disclosure. (Russell, 1984, pp. 160–161)

Self-disclosure and giving information about the therapeutic process help make the client more powerful and responsible for her growth. These techniques discourage dependency on the therapist and provide a model for independent behavior with others. Likewise, the other techniques previously discussed— cultural analysis and intervention, gender-role analysis and intervention, and power analysis and intervention—show how empowerment and focus on political and social issues are essential components of multicultural feminist therapy. Assertiveness training and reframing and relabeling also help clients deal with social forces that interfere with the issues that brought them to therapy. These techniques are not the only ones that feminist therapists use, but they are often used in fostering individuals' growth.

Using Feminist Therapy with Other Theories

As discussed previously, feminist therapy is often used in conjunction with other theories of psychotherapy. In describing how feminist therapy can be integrated with other theories, Worell and Remer (2003) mention several points. They look for sources of bias in the theory by examining its historical developments, key psychotherapuetic concepts, sexist use of language and labels, and bias in diagnosis and therapeutic techniques. They also try to eliminate sexist components to see if the theory is still compatible with feminist principles. The major principles, as stated earlier, are that political and social factors influence people's lives, that egalitarian relationships are important, and that the perspective of women must be valued. Although feminist therapists who have integrated feminist therapy with other theories have not incorporated Worell and Remer's (2003) principles explicitly, they have done this implicitly, as these themes are important in feminist therapy. In the following sections, I have chosen to describe psychoanalysis, behavioral and cognitive therapy, gestalt therapy, and narrative therapy as they have been changed to be consistent with the feminist therapy perspective and have received more attention than other theories from feminist writers.

Feminist Psychoanalytic Theory

Complaints about gender bias have taken place within the field of psychoanalysis itself, as discussed in Chapter 2. Feminist psychoanalytic theorists have criticized the Freudian description of women as passive, masochistic, and dependent. They have also criticized the concept of penis envy and have suggested womb envy (Horney, 1966) and breast envy (Eichenbaum & Orbach, 1983), as infants have more contact with breasts than with penises. Critics of psychoanalytic theory have felt that equality between therapist and client can be negatively affected by the need to develop a transference relationship with the patient, thus precluding therapist self-disclosure (Daugherty & Lees, 1988). The focus on mother–child relationships in object relations theory tends to limit emphasis on political and social factors as they affect the individual's development.

However, some feminist therapists have pointed out that psychoanalysis can be a very appropriate technique for helping women. Understanding the influence of gender on conscious and unconscious aspects of women can provide insight in the practice of psychodynamic therapy with women who are survivors of abuse (Walker, 2009). As Hayden (1986) has shown, psychoanalytic therapy can free women from symptoms to become more active and independent. By examining Oedipal issues, psychoanalysis explores how people deal with and learn gender identities and how male domination can develop in society (Enns, 2004). Furthermore, by examining the role of the unconscious in repression, psychoanalysis can provide insights on why gender roles are so powerful and difficult to change. Chodorow (1989) has pointed out that psychoanalysis can be helpful in understanding how the role of mother can contribute to women being devalued and dominated by men.

Related to the psychoanalytic object relations approach are several views on the relationship in therapy. The relational cultural model of the Stone Center that has been previously discussed (pages 495-496 Jordan, 2010) has been an approach to revalue the role relationships with family and others. In *Relational Psychotherapy: A Primer*, DeYoung (2003) makes use of relational psychoanalysis, Kohut's self psychology, and the Stone Center's relational cultural psychotherapy in her development of a psychoanalytically based approach to using the relationship in psychotherapy. Jordan's (2010) description of relational cultural therapy has more emphasis on social influences on the client than on mother–child relationships than psychoanalytically based approaches. Efforts to extend the integration of psychodynamic and feminist therapies have been made in applications to African American women, taking into account cultural considerations that most psychodynamic therapists do not (Greene, 1997). Even though a psychoanalytic viewpoint does provide some insights into women's issues, some concepts have been criticized.

Feminist Behavioral and Cognitive Therapy

Some of the criticisms of cognitive behavioral therapies are that they tend to ignore social and political factors that affect clients (Enns, 2004). People who are homeless, battered, or poor may not have the financial resources or social support to use some cognitive and behavioral methods. Also, therapist values about how clients should change may not take into account the client's social or cultural background. Additionally, cognitive behavioral therapies may not attend to clients' cultural assumptions about rationality that are implicit in such therapies.

To make cognitive and behavioral therapies more compatible with feminist therapy, Worell and Remer (2003) have suggested changing labels that stress the pathology of people, focusing on feelings, and integrating ideas about gender-role and cultural socialization. Rather than use negative or pathological labels such as *distortion*, *irrationality*, or *faulty thinking*, Worell and Remer (2003) suggest that clients explore ideas based on gender-role generalizations that appear to be distorted or irrational. For example, rather than label the thought that "women's place is in the home" as irrational, the therapist should explore the actual rewards and punishments for living out this stereotyped belief. By focusing on feelings, particularly angry ones, that arise as a result of gender-role limitations or discrimination, women can be helped to feel independence and gain control over their lives. To help women with social-role issues, gender-role and power analysis can be useful in exploring ways of dealing with societal pressures that interfere with women's development. Wyche (2001) believes cognitive and behavior therapies are particularly relevant for women of color because they focus on the present, providing clients methods to use in handling current problems. Working with individuals who have been sexually abused as children, Cohen (2008) shows how feminist and emotion-focused (gestalt) therapies can be integrated into cognitive-behavioral therapy.

Feminist Gestalt Therapy

In reviewing the compatibility of gestalt therapy and feminist therapy, Enns (2004) sees several ways that the two meet similar goals. Both have as goals the increase of awareness of personal power. Gestalt therapists suggest words such as *won't* rather than *can't*, or *want* rather than *need*. By changing "I should do this" to "I choose to do this," therapists encourage independence and build a feeling of power. Feminist therapists also value the expression of anger as a response to discrimination and external limitations. Thus, techniques such as the empty chair encourage clients to say "I'm angry at you" rather than "I am angry at him." Because of the emphasis on awareness of self and choices, women can learn of options that they may not previously have considered. Options develop when one says "I choose to" rather than "I have to." By combining awareness of social and political discrimination with methods of empowerment, gestalt therapeutic approaches meet many of the goals of feminist therapy.

Enns (2004) also cautions that some aspects of gestalt therapy do not fit well with feminist therapy. Because gestalt therapy tends to focus exclusively on taking responsibility for one's own behavior, the social, economic, and political factors that also influence independence and choice may be ignored. Such methods as cultural, gender-role, or power analysis may be viewed as blaming the environment rather than taking responsibility for one's own choices and development. Also, some gestalt therapists may not recognize the importance of relationships in the lives of many women and focus almost exclusively on the development of self-reliance.

Feminist Narrative Therapy

Recently many feminist and multicultural therapists have been attracted to using narrative therapy with their clients because narrative therapists examine how their clients view gender and culture as these concepts relate to their stories rather than using theories that may make value generalizations about culture and gender. Narrative therapy can help therapists avoid preconceived notions of gender and culture (Gremillion, 2004). Because social or cultural influences are so powerful in eating disorders, narrative approaches provide a means to examine these influences and to make changes in the clients' views of themselves as they relate to their culture (C. Brown, 2007; C. G. Brown, Weber, & Ali, 2008). Rabin (2005) gives examples from a variety of cultures to show some very different ways that individuals view culture and gender in their own lives. In some societies, storytelling is a very import way to deal with problems and to make changes.

Tafoya (2005) gives an example of a 13-year-old Apache (a Southwestern Native American tribe in the United States) girl who is not ready for and does not care about an upcoming puberty ceremony. Tamara is rebellious, failing school, smoking at home, and has a boyfriend. She is attracted to an urban culture that is different from her own. Her mother brings Tamara to a counselor. Tamara is resistant to being there. In the first few minutes of the first session, the therapist tells Tamara and her mother about a young Pueblo girl who went to a boarding school and then when she came home was lazy and wouldn't help with chores. Because the girl won't help at home, her grandmother sends her to get some vegetables. When she is picking the vegetables, a masked figure from a folklore tale chases her home with long whips. Tamara and her mother both can relate to this tale. They look at each other and laugh. Tamara says, "I'm not really that bad, am I?" (p. 298). The daughter now can talk in a more open and relaxed way about her problems at home. Many cultures make use of stories to teach and illustrate acceptable and nonthreatening ways of changing behavior.

Psychoanalysis, behavioral and cognitive therapies, gestalt therapy, and narrative therapies are not the only therapeutic approaches to individuals that have integrated feminist therapy principles. However, they do provide ways to show how feminist therapy principles and attention to cultural issues are compatible with a variety of therapies. Adding feminist therapy perspectives to other therapies often provides a view of culture and gender that most other therapies do not address. A number of other theories of therapy, including Jungian therapy (Rowland, 2003) and person-centered therapy (Brown, 2007; Enns, 2004), have examined feminist therapeutic value systems as to their compatibility with these approaches. To integrate theories of psychotherapy with feminist therapy, Worell and Remer's (2003) method of feminist transformation of counseling theories can be helpful, as can Brown's (2010) view of integrating therapies with feminist therapy.

Feminist Therapy and Counseling

Because of the egalitarian approach of feminist therapists to their work, most do not differentiate between counseling and psychotherapy. However, Russell (1984) sees psychotherapy as "an intensive process of remediation of psychological dysfunction or adjustment to psychic stressors" (p. 13), whereas counseling is more developmental, educational, or preventive. Because feminist therapy is often integrated with another theory of psychotherapy or counseling, the terminology of the other theory, such as psychoanalysis, behavioral or cognitive therapy, or gestalt therapy, may influence whether *counseling* or *psychotherapy* is the term used.

Brief Therapy

The length of feminist therapy often depends on with which other theory or theories it is integrated. Because much of feminist therapy takes an action-oriented approach in helping clients confront societal and political issues, there may be an emphasis on working efficiently and quickly. Adding to the brevity of many feminist therapeutic approaches is the use of therapy and support groups that supplement the work of individual therapy. From the perspective of empowering clients to take more control over their lives, long-term therapy is seen by some feminist therapists as allowing clients to blame themselves or to feel dependent on a therapist. However, certain issues such as incest and rape may require a year or more of therapy. A short-term approach has been developed for relational cultural therapy, where the client is active in treatment and the therapy is specific in focus (Jordan, Handel, Alvarez, & Cook-Nobles, 2004). In keeping with a relational cultural model, termination is not final; the client may return as needed.

Psychological Disorders

In the discussion of the following four cases, the feminist therapeutic approach shows the importance of gender roles and social forces in psychotherapy. As described earlier, feminist therapists often avoid DSM-IV-TR categories, as they feel that classification systems may represent male cultural stereotypes of women and do not emphasize the significance of sociological factors in women's roles (Eriksen & Kress, 2005). For consistency, the DSM-IV-TR system is used in this chapter as it is in the others. The discussion of four disorders focuses on feminist therapy and features the techniques described earlier in this chapter, recognizing that feminist therapy is often used in combination with other theories. The disorders illustrated have been identified in the DSM-IV-TR as particularly common to women: borderline personality disorders, depression, posttraumatic stress disorders, and eating disorders. In the case of Barbara, relational cultural therapy is used to help Barbara deal with sexual abuse and lack of trust of others. Relational cultural therapy is also used with an African American woman experiencing depression in graduate school. Empowerment is an important issue in the treatment of a gang rape that resulted in posttraumatic stress disorder. Narrative therapy is applied to anorexia and a brief example is described.

Borderline Disorder: Barbara

Categorization by psychological disorder can be difficult. Feminist therapists often describe how using a diagnostic labeling system can stigmatize people inappropriately and may reflect society's biases regarding gender and cultural diversity. In the case of Barbara, she has been previously diagnosed as being schizophrenic, having bipolar disorder, and being depressed (Jordan, 2010). I will use the category of borderline disorder because of the emphasis on unstable personal relationships. Illustrated in this case is the emphasis on the importance of the therapeutic relationship. Judith Jordan (2010) uses the relational cultural method in her work with Barbara. The case illustrates how a therapist deals with angry and volatile behavior from a client. The emphasis on equality in the relationship and demystifying therapy is representative of feminist therapy.

> Barbara was a 24-year-old, well-educated White woman who had seen six therapists before she began treatment with me. Each therapy had an unhappy demise, often following an impasse where Barbara felt unseen, unheard, and angry. She had initiated the ending of all but two of these treatments. In those two cases, her therapists "gave up" and suggested she was not treatable. Barbara had been diagnosed at various

times as schizophrenic, borderline, and bipolar. She led an extremely isolated life. At the time I began treating her, she was hospitalized for a failed suicide attempt.

Barbara came to me with a modicum of hope (she had heard I was a little less "rigid" than some of the other therapists), but she held no great expectations. Early on she decided that I was not much better than the other clinicians she had seen. The early weeks of treatment were characterized by long silences, occasional talking about her previous therapists and some genuine expressions of fear that this would be no more helpful than anything else she had tried. I did not press her to give up her fears, acknowledged it had been a hard road, and told her that while I could not guarantee that I would understand her any better than the others, I was committed to trying. But I also suggested she had no real reason to trust me.

One day she came to a session with fresh blood on her shirt, having recently scratched her arm. She wanted to know if I would "fire" her. I said her self-injury was very difficult for me to see. She wondered in a challenging way if I was worried about what my colleagues would think when they saw someone coming into my office with blood dripping down her arm. I hesitated and agreed that the thought had crossed my mind, but that I also could see she was in real pain and needed to be able to communicate that to me. She looked at first triumphant (at my admission of personal concern about my "reputation") but then genuinely relieved (perhaps that I had spoken a piece of truth about myself that she knew anyway). We then had a truly collaborative conversation about how she might be able to really let me know her pain and whether she could trust my response.

Soon after this incident, Barbara began to talk about childhood sexual abuse at the hands of an uncle and how no one, particularly her mother, had believed her when she attempted to tell them about it. She had not revealed this abuse in any of her previous therapies. Following her disclosure, she became extremely agitated and again mute. I allowed her distance. When she began to speak again, it was to criticize almost everything about me: "You aren't strong enough. You're too detached. You're not available when I need you. You're wishy-washy. You don't really care about me. You are among the worst of the therapists I have seen." I sometimes felt reactive, and sometimes I was defensive. Once I got angry and told her how frustrated I felt, that I was trying so hard to be there for her and nothing I did seemed good enough. Then I had to apologize for blaming her. I worried about her sometimes when I was at home, and I told her so. Then I regretted telling her.

Despite my own difficulty practicing what I preached (responsive, nondefensive presence with her connections and disconnections), slowly we navigated our way through her pain, isolation, and terror. And it was largely around the failures and, paradoxically, the increasing closeness with her subsequent leaps into angry isolation that we began to experience movement and shifts. After 2 years of a highly volatile therapy, things began to settle down. The prevailing relational images that told her any increasing vulnerability on her part would lead to abuse and violation by others began to shift. She could begin to entertain the possibility that if she showed her "real" feelings, she would be responded to empathically and cared about. Her reactivity began to alter so that when the inevitable empathic failures happened, she could feel angry and disappointed rather than alarmed, terrified, or rageful.

Barbara's life was taking shape, too. After years of working in marginal and poorly paid positions, she landed a high-level job, realized she was attracted to women, and started dating a kind and caring woman. She began to bring humor into the therapy, and the two of us laughed together over some of the predicaments we had lived through. I developed incredible respect for the ways she had learned to keep herself safe and the ways she had helped us stay in relationship. My realness was important to her. She was incredibly sensitive to inauthenticity and "playing games," and she felt there was "a lot of that in most therapies." Eventually I "got" that she needed to be vigilant to my lapses in empathy; each failure on my part made her feel unsafe, as if she was too vulnerable and about to be further injured by me. Together we worked on ways to achieve safety so that both of us did not feel whiplashed. Toward the end of therapy when we reflected together on how the therapy had been, she commented on my willingness to be vulnerable with her. She felt that had made a real difference; it made me less dangerous to her. When I acknowledged my limitations instead of "setting limits" for her, she felt respected. She wondered, "Isn't it ironic that when you showed yourself as most fallible and vulnerable, I had the most trust in you? You didn't always get it right . . . and often it took awhile for you to get it at all, but you almost always came back, trying and clearly imperfect. That made you feel safe to me. (Jordan, 2010, pp. 53–55)

Depression: Ms. B

From a feminist therapist's perspective, women have many reasons to be twice as likely as men to experience depression. Because women are often taught to be dependent on men, to be helpless, and to please others, they may experience depression because they feel an inability to control their lives and assert themselves. An emphasis on personal appearance and on being valued in terms of how they are perceived by men can contribute to a sense of powerlessness. If a woman experiences personal violence, sexual assault, or discrimination in the workplace, depression can result from a feeling of inability to control one's own environment. Many other factors such as pregnancy, childbirth, and homemaking can affect women in positive and negative ways, depending on their attitudes and those of others close to them (Roades, 2000; Wells, Brack, & McMichen, 2003). Although depression may be partly the result of genetics and hormonal changes, Worell and Remer (2003) believe that gender-role expectations and social discrimination contribute greatly to depression at varying times during the lifespan.

In the following case, Turner (1997) describes her work with a young African American woman who has started graduate school. Ms. B is depressed because of her poor performance in school and feeling cut off from her family. Turner uses the relational cultural model of the Stone Center (Jordan, 2010) to explain Ms. B's feeling invisible in a White graduate school. Also, Turner attends to Ms. B's feelings of shame and fear of telling her parents about her difficulties at school. Turner helps empower Ms. B by focusing on connections and relations with mentors, study groups, organizations, and family.

Ms. B is a young Black woman in her twenties pursuing an advanced graduate degree. She had not had previous counseling and, until recently, had not experienced any serious setbacks or difficulties. She is one of several siblings, the younger daughter of a low-income intact family. One of her brothers has an advanced professional degree, but she will be the first woman in her family to do so. She presented with issues of deflated self-esteem, low grades and "hot off the press" news from her dean that the school wanted to "counsel her out of the program" by the end of the current semester. She had failed all her tests and didn't seem to be making a good fit at the school, according to most of her teachers. She was shocked in light of her past high achievement in college and her motivation to succeed. She appeared not only defeated but depressed and agitated. She was not suicidal, but very down on herself and very frustrated. She told me that she studied religiously, knew the material, but just couldn't perform when she was expected to.

At a closer look, I discovered that she was cut off from any source of emotional, academic, or social support. She studied alone and never conversed with any of her teachers or school staff. She couldn't tell her family because she thought it would destroy them. In short, no one knew what I knew about this discrepancy between preparation and performance! She felt shame, embarrassment and a profound sense of failure in letting herself and her family down. There were a handful of Black women and men and a few more White women in her class. She didn't feel she could confide in any of them, and whenever anyone in her class asked how she was doing, she always responded, "OK."

I saw Ms. B for a little over a year. I was able to connect with her around her profound isolation and guilt-laden feelings by helping her to better see her role and that of significant others in hiding important parts of herself from people all around her. Basic to this was her inner feeling of not being accepted as a legitimate member of her school environment. This inner feeling caused intense anxiety and somatic symptoms. She fostered a perception of not "belonging" or "being valued" which, as it turned out, was shared by a few at the school, but not by everyone. She did have to leave the school for a term; however, she is now re-enrolled there. This time, she has identified and sought out mentors, study groups, an active Black organization, and a greater sense of "entitlement" to study there as a Black woman. I'm happy to say that this activity is also reflected in her grades. She has learned to use a number of stress reduction techniques to move past the anxiety blocks and to relax more. She also knows now that her family loves and respects her, no matter what happens, because she freed herself up to share some of the pressure she felt about being the first woman in her family to achieve professional status. This pressure was tied in with her internal fears about losing her place with them, and in a sense "leaving them behind." On an affective level, this fear contributed to her depressed feelings, while on a cognitive level she wanted to believe that they would still love her as they always had. Because she felt vulnerable to a "perceived loss," her academic pursuits had been conflicted and inhibited. (Turner, 1997, pp. 83–84)

Posttraumatic Stress Disorder: Andrea

The term *posttraumatic stress disorder* refers to the fears, anxieties, and stresses an individual experiences after being victimized. In that sense, the term focuses on the victim rather than the perpetrator. A common cause of women's posttraumatic stress disorder is rape (Worell & Remer, 2003). In dealing with rape victims, Burstow (1992) suggests that feminist therapists must first invite the woman to express the feelings she has experienced and then to empathize with these feelings both from a personal point of view and from a broader social and political point of view. She suggests that having the client describe the trauma in the present tense can be quite effective. However, the therapist should also empathize with the humiliation and terror that the woman may be feeling but not expressing, as well as her desire to flee from her feelings. The therapist helps the client to be in touch with her feelings and to express them. Burstow also talks about discussing the client's rights, such as the right to go out alone at night without being raped. In *Cultural Competence in Trauma Therapy: Beyond the Flashback*, Brown (2008a) shows how important it is to attend to the client's multiple identities, including gender, culture, social class, sexual orientation, spiritual beliefs, and other identities. Brown stresses attending to influences of dominant group culture, as well as attending to the therapist's own identity and culture when working with individuals who have experienced trauma.

In the following example, Greenspan (1983) describes counseling with a woman who, before being gang-raped, functioned well and had few problems. In her work with Andrea, Greenspan responds to her client in ways similar to those described by Burstow. She empathizes with the client's feelings of rage, hate, and helplessness, but she also helps Andrea to develop a sense of identity and power, to do something positive with her outrage.

> The potentially disastrous consequences of not possessing a healthy fear of men was painfully illustrated by Andrea's story. Andrea was an intelligent and creative woman, fiercely devoted to her independence. She was single and supported herself as a carpenter and artist. She prided herself on her fearlessness, physical strength, and lack of physical intimidation. One evening, her car broke down and had to be towed. She visited with a friend nearby until around midnight. Then, rather than take the subway, she decided that she would try to hitch a ride. She was picked up by two men who took her for a long ride, brought her to a house, threw her on a bed, and called several of their friends. For the next several hours, Andrea was raped at knife point by seven different men. In between rapes, the man with the knife would urge her to tell him how much she enjoyed it. Afterward, she was blindfolded, taken for another ride, and dropped off on the street in an unknown neighborhood.
>
> No woman recovers from an experience like this very easily. The climb back is hazardous and full of pain. For the first few days, Andrea was numb—she could feel nothing at all. Like many rape victims, she told no one what had happened to her. Prior to the rape, Andrea had always kept a firm lid on her feelings. But her instinct for survival now told her that she would have to get to the bottom of what she felt. With just a little encouragement from me, her feelings came gushing out in great torrents; terror, rage, shame, helplessness, and vulnerability overwhelmed her. She saw a rapist in every car. She distrusted men and wanted nothing to do with them—including the male friends she had known before the rape. She was ashamed of her body, which felt numb and dead. She wanted to kill or maim or castrate the men who had raped her. (Greenspan, 1983, pp. 273–274)

Therapy had to help Andrea turn her losses into gains: to offer her a new basis for a sense of identity and power as a woman.

One of the best ways to do this was to work with Andrea's newly found sense of outrage. This burning outrage was like nothing else she had ever experienced. She simply could not understand how any person was capable of doing what these men had done to her. Like all victims, she could not help asking, "Why me?" But beyond this, she wanted to know: "Why any woman? Why do men rape? How will I ever feel strong and free again?" Andrea's fierce outrage was like a bomb exploding in her head. It, more than anything else, motivated her to piece her world back together again. Her consciousness was open in a way that it had not been before. In this lowest point of Andrea's life, therapy could help her make use of this openness, for it was her greatest strength in the task of surviving and recovering with a renewed sense of her power in the world.

Andrea's consciousness of herself after the rape contained the seeds of a very powerful new awareness: that her fate as a woman was inextricably bound to the fate of women as a whole: that she could not be the exceptional free spirit as long as women as a group remained oppressed. This new awareness was the bridge to a new basis for her sense of power as a woman. With her consciousness raised, Andrea came to understand that her post-rape emotions of terror, rage, and powerlessness were supreme exaggerations of the "normal" way that women feel in our society, whether consciously or unconsciously. She saw that her old brand of freedom before the rape was, in part, a denial of these feelings and an escape into a pseudo-haven which did not really exist. At the same time, she saw that none of this meant that she had to feel terrorized or helpless all of her life—that in unity there was strength;

that there was a different way to feel powerful in concert with women with whom she now closely identified. (Greenspan, 1983, pp. 278–279)

The emphasis on the social and political activity of the client is part of the feminist therapist's approach to rape. Thus, rape is seen not as a problem of one woman but of all women.

Eating Disorders: Margaret

Society's socialization practices and messages are an important focus of feminist therapists when dealing with anorexia, bulimia, or obesity. As Matlin (2008) shows, women's dissatisfaction with their bodies differs depending on cultural background. Upper- and middle-class heterosexual women of European ancestry tend to be particularly dissatisfied with their appearance. However, eating disorders can be a problem for non-Western women as well (Nasser & Malson, 2009). Feminist therapists have addressed the many cultural pressures that lead to the development of eating disorders (Malson & Burns, 2009). Narrative therapists take an interesting and powerful approach to anorexia and bulimia. As described in Chapter 12, narrative therapists externalize the disorder. In their book, *Biting the Hand that Starves You*, Maisel, Epston, and Borden (2004) describe anorexia and bulimia as an enemy trying to kill young women that the therapist and client must deal with. They describe their task and their book this way:

> In addressing these questions, our intention is not to understand a/b (anorexia/bulimia) as much as to undermine and subvert it. This, then, is a book about fighting words, terrifying anti-a/b deeds and thrilling anti-a/b possibilities for the lives of therapists, individuals struggling with a/b, and the communities in which they reside. A/b is our sworn antagonists in these life-or-death duels. The purpose of this book is to help those whose lives have been captured by a/b (referred to as "insiders") to know, beyond all doubt, their enemy from their friend—to know who will treacherously betray them and who will be faithful and constant. (p. 1)

In their work with eating disorders, they help women listen to the meanings and ideas that have interfered with the development of their sense of worth. The clients must come to develop a sense of moral outrage at how anorexia or bulimia has hurt them. The therapist cannot do this for them. The outrage may be at past sexual, physical, or emotional abuse. Sometimes the anger is at ideas of what it means to be a good or desirable woman or at those who have been critical of the woman's appearance or other aspects of her. When the client understands these outrages, she may then feel a welling up of anger. This is expressed by a client, Margaret, in the following letter to Anorexia:

> *To the Voice of Anorexia,*
> Tonight I spoke to my therapist about how I have never been angry at you and, as a consequence, I began to question the idea that I didn't have the right to be angry at you. It didn't hit me till after I got home how much you had influenced my thinking about anger and how much you supported the ridiculous lie that "good girls don't get mad." Well, I got some news for you, anorexia, I am mad. I'm more than mad. I'm outraged at your injustice! I hate you and everything you stand for. I wish for one second you could be solid and touchable so I could smash you with all my might. You took so much from me and almost took my very life. I thank god that doctors were there to revive me from your clutches. For years you had me believing, in spite of my doctors saying that it was your starvation of me that stopped my heart,

that they were wrong and it was my very heart that was defective and bad. It makes me ill when I realize you actually made me believe that and think that if I continued to listen to you, you would make my heart strong.

You are such a ***** liar. I now know why you never wanted me to be mad or angry. It had nothing to do with securing my goodness but everything to do with not wanting me to see you for what you are—absolute and total evil. If I saw that clearly, I would have stood up to you long ago. Get the ****** out of my life and leave me alone! I don't have room for you in my life any longer.

In absolute anger and hatred of you, anorexia,

Margaret (p. 157)

In this narrative approach to eating disorders, women examine cultural and gender values by externalizing the problem. Power analysis and intervention are an important aspect of feminist therapy. The description of the therapist's views of anorexia and bulimia are powerful ways of helping the client. Margaret's letter shows power in working to overcome a life-threatening disorder. The analysis of power is done differently than that described by Worell and Remer (2003), by helping the client analyze her own power, as she tells her story of fighting anorexia. The power intervention is made by the client as she sees what she must do to smash anorexia.

Because of their diverse backgrounds, feminist therapists use a variety of approaches toward clients with depression, borderline disorders, posttraumatic stress disorder, and eating disorders, as well as other conditions. What distinguishes feminist therapies from other therapies is the emphasis on cultural and gender-role issues, power differences between people, and the need to look at social and political change in addition to individual psychological change.

Current Trends and Issues

Because feminist therapy is relatively recent, starting in the 1970s, and because there are many contributors rather than one leader, it is moving in many different directions. In doing so, feminist postmodern writers have shown how social constructionism can give power to individuals of different genders and cultures. Feminist therapists have also been concerned about determining standards of competency and ethics, as well as how best to train feminist therapists. An issue that was present at the beginning of the development of feminist therapy is that of feminist activism. Each of these issues, described in the next paragraphs, has received the attention of many feminist therapists.

Social constructionism has been an important force within feminist therapy and has been a major focus of postmodern thinking (Enns, 2004; Worell & Remer, 2003). Feminist therapists have questioned the traditional ways that males have viewed situations and events. Feminist therapy provides a way of examining issues that affect children's rights, minorities, and women from a social constructionist view that gives rather than removes power from these groups (Gergen, 2001). Feminist therapists focus on power relationships between groups and seek to help those who are disenfranchised. Social constructionism has helped feminist therapists be more sensitive to cultural diversity, as can be seen in this chapter by the attention given to multicultural issues. Feminist therapists are very careful not to make generalizations about issues related to the race, class, ethnicity, age, and sexual orientation of their clients, but to value the stories and lives of their clients. Narrative therapy, mentioned in several places in this chapter, is a therapeutic example of a social constructionist approach.

Having focused primarily on the lives of White middle-class women, feminist therapists have turned their attention to issues that affect women from diverse cultural backgrounds. Since the early 1990s, many books, journals, and comprehensive articles on feminist therapy have included chapters or sections on issues dealing with women from varying cultures and classes (Brown, 1994, 2010; Enns, 2004; Jordan, 2010; Mirkin, Suyemoto, & Okun, 2005; Worell & Remer, 2003). These writings have led to the discussion of how social and cultural issues within particular societies interact with gender issues to provide insights into working with women from different groups. Additionally, feminist therapists have shown that feminist therapy is not for women only; it can also be concerned with men (Brown, 2010) and families (Silverstein & Goodrich, 2003). As feminist therapists reach out to the needs of various populations, the issue of how best to train feminist therapists becomes crucial.

Much of the training of feminist therapists has been informal. However, through their teaching and training, feminist therapists have integrated issues such as sexual exploitation of therapy clients, domestic violence, sexual abuse of children, and sexual harassment into teaching, supervision, and community service (Worell & Remer, 2003). Additionally, a few institutes or centers, such as the Stone Center at Wellesley College, offer training in feminist therapy. Related to the issue of training for feminist therapists is how to decide when a person is qualified to be called a feminist therapist.

As Brown and Brodsky (1992) point out, there has been a need to regulate the term *feminist therapy* to provide for ethical behavior by those who call themselves feminist therapists. Feminist therapists have been active in addressing complex ethical issues confronting those who practice feminist therapy, as well as other mental health practitioners (Roffman, 2008). Issues that are addressed include analysis of power dynamics, overlapping relationships, self-disclosure, and a variety of other important ethical concerns. Although most other psychotherapy theories have not examined ethical issues from a theoretical perspective, feminist therapists have done so by examining gender roles and power issues in relationships with clients (Vasquez, 2003). Providing help to clients has not been limited to therapeutic services; feminist therapists have also been concerned with broader societal issues.

Although feminist therapists have varied opinions on the importance of social action and the practice of feminist therapy, these issues continue to be important (Enns, 2004). In recent years, there has been a trend away from group therapy and dealing with social issues toward concerns about personal changes through individual therapy. However, social change through involvement in local and national groups continues. In their review of the activities of feminist therapists and social change, Ballou and West (2000) describe several ways of taking social action, such as providing services to women's shelters and centers, leading community support groups, changing public policy by preventing environmental disease and global damage to the environment, and working with organizations to promote day care, antiviolent attitudes toward women, and fair access to medical treatment. When feminist therapists have particular expertise, such as working with battered women, they may often apply their knowledge to issues affecting such institutions as the courts or shelters rather than limit their activities to individual therapy.

The issues that feminist therapists are concerned with are related to issues of fair and equal treatment of all clients. Because feminist therapy has grown rapidly, the development of theory, standards for training, and ethical concerns continue to present new and problematic issues. These are made more complex as feminist therapists integrate different theories of psychotherapy into their practices.

Research

Very little research compares the effectiveness of feminist therapies with other approaches to therapy because most feminist therapists integrate other theories of therapy into their approach. Studies evaluating feminist therapy with battered women, incarcerated women, and women with eating disorders are reviewed. Research on issues that are important to feminist therapists are also studied, including self-disclosure, mutuality, and therapists' views of their own ethnicity. Also, new directions in research that will provide more information about feminist therapeutic interventions are discussed.

One study compared group feminist treatment with individual therapy in assisting 60 women who had been battered by their spouses (Rinfret-Raynor & Cantin, 1997). Both approaches to helping the women were effective. The researchers found that the women were able to make effective use of social networks and organizations to reduce the domestic violence they encountered. Therapy also helped to empower the women to use their own resources.

Another study examined the treatment of women with eating disorders. The investigators examined both symptoms of bulimia and of depression. Comparing group short-term cognitive therapy to short-term group relational cultural therapy, both treatments helped to reduce binge eating, vomiting, and depression at follow-up (Tantillo & Sanftner, 2003).

Another study examined the effectiveness of a time-limited therapy group for women in prison who were survivors of childhood sexual abuse (Cole, Sarlund-Heinrich, & Brown, 2007). Compared to a control group, women who participated in brief group therapy reduced their trauma-related scores on one measure. They also did not increase their number of symptoms as did women in the prison control group.

Mutuality was the subject of another investigation. Mutuality refers to the ability of two people to respect each other and to be open to being changed by others. In a sample of college women and men, low mutuality with parents predicted dissatisfaction with one's body for men and women. For women, low mutuality with romantic partners predicted body dissatisfaction (Sanftner, Ryan, & Pierce, 2009).

Self-disclosure and egalitarian relationships are important aspects of feminist therapy. The Feminist Self-Disclosure Inventory (FSDI) was developed to study how different therapists approach these topics (Simi & Mahalik, 1997). Five different factors were measured by the FSDI: therapist background, promoting liberatory feelings, promoting egalitarianism, therapist availability, and empowering the client. Results from 143 female therapists indicated that the 41 feminist therapists differed from 34 psychoanalytic/dynamic therapists and 68 other therapists on their use of self-disclosure. Feminist therapists were more likely than the other therapists to create an egalitarian relationship in therapy. They also were more likely to encourage the client in choosing a role model in the course of therapy. With regard to their own personal self-disclosure, feminist therapists were more likely than other therapists to tell their clients of their own sexual orientation.

A pilot study of feminist family therapists examined the influence of therapists' ethnicity on the way that they practiced feminist therapy (Mittal & Wieling, 2004). The therapists described problems of integrating ethnic values and feminist values in their therapy. Whether they saw themselves in a majority or minority status was reported to be a factor in the way that they approached therapy. They also discussed concerns they had when they worked with families whose ethnicity was different than their own.

Examining the role of values in research on women, Hoshmand (2003) discussed methodological issues that suggest using qualitative research, which included an examination of the values being examined in the study. She pointed out the need for research on women. Examples of needed research are research with lesbian women, women's perceptions of gender equality, sexual abuse, battering, women from minority groups, and outcome studies on feminist therapy. With regard to outcome studies, studying the effectiveness of therapy with women from different cultures could be very helpful.

Gender Issues

To this point, the discussion of feminist therapy has focused mainly on applications to women. Feminist therapy also has applications for treatment of men. Additionally, because of its focus on gender-role issues, it has probably addressed issues of gay, lesbian, bisexual, and transgendered clients more than other theories.

Feminist Therapy with Men

From a feminist therapy perspective, it is not sufficient to be nonsexist in work with clients; it is also important to help them within the perspective of gender roles (Nutt & Brooks, 2008; Worell & Johnson, 2000). When counselors do not examine gender stereotypes with male clients, they may be supporting traditional views of men and women. For that reason, the assessment and therapeutic intervention of feminist therapy discussed in this chapter can be helpful to men. Brown (2010) addresses power issues as they relate to men and sees feminist therapy as being very appropriate for treatment of males.

In *A New Psychotherapy for Traditional Men*, Brooks (1998) sees a parallel between his suggestions and feminist therapy. He sees, in the way that feminist therapists do, the need to focus on the political and social impact of culture on men.

> I have come to believe that psychotherapy with traditional men is much more complicated than simply adding a few new techniques to one's therapy repertoire. Much as feminist therapy requires a fundamental change in one's ideas about the roots of

women's problems and the processes of psychotherapy, a perspective on traditional men also requires that we therapists consider the many ways in which we interact with client problems. We cannot be apolitical; if we are not part of the solution, we are part of the problem. We are agents of a gendered culture and must be gender-aware therapists. To accomplish this, we probably will need to change ourselves, to reconsider our previous comfort with a very solid barrier between clients and therapists, and to rethink any ideas about a rigid boundary between therapy and the larger culture. We will need to consider the intersection between psychotherapy and social action as we endeavor to create new social contexts and environments. (Brooks, 1998, pp. xiv, xv)

Several problems that men have can be treated from a feminist therapy approach. For example, Brooks (1998, 2003; Nutt & Brooks, 2008) has discussed men's difficulty in experiencing emotional pain. Also, the societal emphasis on achievement and performance can oppress men to maintain a "masculine" role (Feder, Levant, & Dean, 2007; Levant & Wimer, 2009; Levant, Wimer, Williams, Smalley, & Noronha, 2009). When dealing with alcohol or drug problems, men may be reluctant to confront their feelings and unacceptable thoughts and choose to express themselves through alcohol or drug abuse (Brooks, 1998). In general, difficulties in developing relationships and being aware of one's own feelings are issues that lend themselves to the application of feminist therapy.

In describing feminist therapy with male clients, Ganley (1988) has identified several issues and techniques for dealing with men that reflect a feminist therapeutic perspective. When men are having difficulty integrating the need for relationships and the need to achieve, Ganley suggests that gender-role analysis can be helpful in understanding the conflict between relationship and achievement aspects of a man's life. With issues of intimacy avoidance, feminist therapists may use gender-role analysis to understand the social rewards of avoiding intimate relationships. In contrast, a nonfeminist therapist might focus on abandonment by the mother or rejection by a spouse. Because feminist therapy encourages self-disclosure in both the client and therapist, the therapist may model self-disclosure and reinforce self-disclosure on the part of the client. Additionally, participation in therapy groups can help men disclose their feelings.

Another issue is that of anger, which may be expressed through inappropriate behaviors such as drugs or fighting rather than constructively through discussion of angry feelings (Brooks, 2003; Feder et al., 2007). Related to this issue is dealing with disappointment or rejection. Feminist therapists may help male clients find other feelings besides anger to deal with disappointments encountered in relationships or work. Not only is gender-role analysis helpful in dealing with these issues, but also power analysis may be useful in helping men understand male–female relationships in terms of the lack of power that society gives to women. Brooks (2003) addresses the additional challenges that occur when the therapist is working with clients with different cultural backgrounds that represent different male value systems about gender, power, and other issues.

In addition to the use of gender-role analysis and power analysis with emotional issues, Ganley (1988) has suggested several skills that feminist therapists can help men learn so that they may deal better with relationships, work issues, and other problems. Because men have often been taught to listen so that they may take action or make suggestions, feminist therapists may teach listening skills to their clients that will help them understand the feeling behind the message as well as its content. Because men may have been socialized to believe that they are more powerful than women, men may need to learn how to work collaboratively and collegially with women rather than being competitive or dominant. In teaching problem-solving skills, feminist therapists may focus on listening, brainstorming, negotiation, and compromise skills rather than directing or ordering skills. Related to skills that focus on cooperation are attitudes and beliefs about women that can be confronted and brought to men's attention to help them understand different ways some men and women communicate with each other. By modeling open and collaborative relationships with male clients, feminist therapists can help their male clients improve their relationships with others.

Feminist Therapy with Gay, Lesbian, Bisexual, or Transgendered Clients (GLBT)

Because of their emphasis on societal values and sex-role expectations, feminist therapists have paid particular attention to work with lesbians, but they have also applied their approaches to gay men. In writing about lesbian women, many writers believe that a common problem for lesbians is coping with a homophobic and heterosexist culture. *Homophobia* refers to the dislike, fear, or hatred of gay, lesbian, bisexual, or transgendered (GLBT) people; *heterosexism* is the concept that being heterosexual is inherently better than being GLBT. Homophobia and heterosexism include societal beliefs that are held by both GLBT and heterosexual people, such as ideas that gay, lesbian, bisexual, or transgendered are less psychologically healthy than heterosexuals, being gay is a developmental disorder, lesbian women hate men, and lesbian women are masculine in appearance (Reynolds, 2003). One of the goals of feminist therapy with GLBT clients is to help counter such myths. Thus, feminist therapists focus on social factors such as legal, political, religious, and psychological discrimination rather than psychological factors such as determining the underlying causes of being gay, lesbian, bisexual, or transgendered or trying to convert gay, lesbian, bisexual, or transgendered individuals to heterosexuality. Because societal messages are usually quite anti-GBLT, it is particularly important for therapists to be aware of their own internal homophobic and heterosexist messages.

In writing about feminist therapy approaches to gay and lesbian people, Brown (1988, 2000) addresses the issues of gender-role socialization, dealing with homophobia, working with "coming-out" issues, and dealing with other social factors that affect gays and lesbians. Feminist therapists assess how their clients value or view their sexual preference and how that view may have changed over time. A gender-role analysis can be particularly helpful with lesbians and gay men so that they can understand the impact of social influences on their own development. Analyzing the culture, particularly society's shaming of lesbians and gay men (Brown, 2000), can also be useful. In these ways clients can see how they lower their own self-esteem by criticizing themselves for hurting their families or being fixated on homosexuality. Coming out—telling others that one is gay, lesbian, bisexual, or transgendered—can be viewed as a process rather than an event. Helping individuals deal with criticism or abuse and telling others about their sexuality can be an important aspect of feminist therapy with GLBT clients. In addition to confronting societal discrimination against gay, lesbian, bisexual, or transgendered people, feminist therapists may help their lesbian and gay clients deal with racial or cultural discrimination and biases due to low socioeconomic background. To do this, therapists must have knowledge about lesbian, gay, bisexual, and transgendered issues as well as about their own reactions to these issues (Bieschke, Perez, & DeBord, 2007; Morrow, 2000).

Halstead (2003) presents a case of Tisha, an African American woman, whose parents are college professors, and Laura, raised in a White Catholic working-class family, who sought counseling when trying to make decisions about having a commitment ceremony. In dealing with this case, Halstead found that she was continually checking her own assumptions about race, class, homophobia, and gender. In discussing who to invite to the commitment ceremony, many complex questions were raised about which family members might be disruptive and which individuals in their extended families did not know that they were lesbians. Whether or not to make vows in public was discussed, as both Laura and Tisha were concerned about the meaning that the words would have for them. In discussing the commitment ceremony, both women looked into their future and their desire to have a child together. They considered questions such as "How will a mixed-race child of two lesbians fare in this culture?" (p. 45), as well as other questions about whether or not lesbians could be good parents and how well will the community and their families provide emotional support for their child or children. This case illustrates many complex issues about negative societal attitudes toward GLBT individuals that arise in counseling GLBT individuals that are different from those which heterosexuals confront.

Multicultural Issues

Feminist therapists have addressed issues affecting women of color (and, to a lesser extent, men of color) in more depth and with more consistency than have other psychotherapy theorists. Although feminist therapy was originally based on issues affecting middle-class White women, since the 1990s attention has been paid to women from a variety of cultures: Native American, Asian American, Hispanic/Latina, and African American women (Enns, 2004). Brown (2009b) and Park (2008) have described the importance of cultural competence in dealing with women of color and the racism or discrimination they have encountered in their lives. More specifically, Brown (2008a, 2009a) has explained how therapists can develop cultural competence when working with individuals that have experienced trauma. Although White feminists have often felt that women from a variety of ethnic groups have more in common with each other than with men from their group, this belief has not been shared by all ethnic minority women, many of whom have felt discrimination along with men (Comas-Diaz, 1987). Because of their awareness of the sociological variable of gender, feminist therapists have extended this awareness to culture.

As illustrated in this chapter, any of the techniques of feminist therapy can be applied or extended to cultural issues. When feminist therapists conduct gender-role analyses of their clients, they also include factors such as ethnic background, class, and relationships with parents and grandparents. When working with women of a different racial group, feminist therapists may share experiences with the client but also acknowledge differences (Enns, 2004). Bibliotherapy with writings by feminists of a particular culture or using examples of women based on myth, legend, or history can also be helpful. In working with South Asian women who are survivors of domestic violence, therapists may use feminist principles such as attending to the social context of the problem and empowering women to take control of their lives, but not use the term *feminist therapy* (Kallivayalil, 2007). Eating disorders are concerns that have been addressed with Asian American women (Yokoyama, 2007). Racism and specific parts of the body along with body shape and weight are issues discussed in a multicultural approach to treatment. Other effective therapeutic interventions with women of color can include support groups or self-help networks of women from a specific culture or community. Some interventions may be more internal, such as focusing on women's spiritual needs. A psychospiritual approach attends to religious issues, as illustrated in a case study of a Latina client, to bring about positive change (Comas-Díaz, 2008). For Muslim women, religion often plays a significant part in their lives. Ali (2009) shows how feminist therapy can be used to help deal with psychological problems rather than to confront the Muslim culture. Using a variety of ways of learning about the culture of one's clients becomes extremely important in the same way that being informed about gender issues of clients is important.

Feminist therapists have also stressed the impact of the attitudes of the therapist on the client (Worell & Remer, 2003). In exploring this issue, Greene (1986) lists three major problems that the White therapist must consider: bigotry, color blindness, and paternalism. *Bigotry* refers to conscious or unconscious views about ethnic deficits that may affect the way the therapist sees the client. *Color blindness*—meaning attempting to ignore racial differences—may prevent therapists from understanding the client's experience of discrimination. *Paternalism* refers to a therapist who takes responsibility for the discrimination that the client may have received in the past. It is saying, in essence, "I'm not like other White people who have let you down. I won't." This attitude may make it difficult for the client to explore personal issues herself. These three guidelines can be useful for White therapists in understanding their potential impact upon clients of color.

A more specific approach to African American women by an African American feminist therapist (Childs, 1990) illustrates a sensitivity to both gender and race. In her first contact with African American female clients, Childs conveys the idea that the client does not have to submit to the therapist; rather, the therapist will examine the client's strengths and capabilities and work with them. After discussing the purpose of therapy and estimating its duration, the therapist may encounter the rage, anger, and grief that stem from an African American client's sense of betrayal and depression over being denied her ability, rights, and sense of competence. Childs points out that these strong feelings are a natural response to the client's having repressed her own feelings. This experience of anger or rage can lead to more creative self-expression and does not jeopardize therapy, as it is not taken out on the client herself or on the therapist. Discussions in therapy include dealing with the stigma of being African American and being female. Childs helps the client feel independent and creative and not compare herself with others. In this process, the client may find it helpful to read African American feminist literature to understand racial and gender discrimination as it has affected African American women. Additionally, participating in a support group consisting of African American women can decrease the sense of alienation and increase the sense of belongingness.

Feminist therapists have applied feminist therapy to different populations of African American women. Alcohol and substance abuse are problems that have been addressed for African American women (Rhodes & Johnson, 1997). In discussing treatment of incarcerated African American women, Brice-Baker (2003) examines how prisons resemble dysfunctional families. In general, attention to Afrocentric values and beliefs as well as stereotypes can be very helpful in counseling African American women (Hall & Greene, 2003). Few (2007) suggests that Black feminist theory provides a unique culturally sensitive perspective in understanding African American women and issues that they deal with such as the balancing of gender and racial consciousness. Combining sensitivity to gender and sensitivity to racial or cultural societal factors is likely to be a continuing trend of feminist therapy.

Group Counseling

Because feminist therapy developed from the consciousness-raising (CR) groups of the 1970s, group treatments have been an important part of feminist therapy. Consciousness-raising groups, usually with 4 to 12 members, dealt with women's roles and experiences in a culture that was often perceived as discriminatory toward women. These groups were leaderless, noncompetitive, and emotionally supportive—characteristics that the participants would like to see in larger society (Worell & Remer, 2003). Often meeting in people's homes, the groups discussed a variety of topics related to social gender roles. The CR groups were often responsible for services for women such as rape crisis centers, women's counseling centers, shelters for battered women, and women's health centers (Enns, 2004). In this way, social activism and personal awareness of the impact of gender roles on women were combined.

Since the emergence of CR groups, groups have been designed for women at various life stages and for women with a variety of concerns. Women's groups have sometimes focused on specific issues such as agoraphobia, homelessness, alcoholism, sexual abuse, sexual concerns, battering, work stress, eating disorders, and relationship problems. Additionally, women's groups have been designed for subgroups of women: African Americans, Native Americans, Hispanics, lesbians, pregnant teenagers, working women with families, women raising their children at home, and many other groups. Unlike CR groups, these groups usually have a paid professional leader. Feminist therapists encourage the use of all-female groups, not only because of the need to discuss specific issues such as those listed previously but also to explore their commonalities, affirm each other's strengths, and understand the similar concerns of women (Kravetz, 1978). When men are included in groups, they may do more initiating and directing than women and may be more frequently listened to than women (West & Zimmerman, 1985). Additionally, women may be less likely to discuss topics such as body image and sexuality in mixed groups and less likely to develop trusting and close female relationships within the group (Walker, 1987). Specific issues that women have, as well as their styles of relating, have produced not only groups of all women working on specific topics but also specific techniques for dealing with women's issues.

For individual and group therapy alike, gender-role issues are an important aspect of treatment that can be approached in a variety of ways (DeChant, 1996). Group leaders can ask, "What did it mean to you to be female or male growing up?" "What happens when you don't follow general gender-role norms?" or "How have you learned about roles of men and women?" (Brown, 1986, 1990). Groups for adolescent women can address issues such as identity and sexual development while also attending to the importance of relationships with peers (Sweeney, 2000). For college women, relationship issues using the relational-cultural model (Jordan, 2003, 2010) can be combined with a problem-solving, solution-focused approach to deal with immediate client problems (Quinn & Dunn-Johnson, 2000). The relational cultural approach to group therapy has also been used with female juvenile offenders to build relationships with other females while attending to problematic behaviors (Calhoun, Bartolomucci, & McLean, 2005). Issues addressed in group concern not only family and peer relationships but also issues with group leaders and other group members.

Should group members have contact with each other outside the group? Feminist group therapy supports the growth of women's power in relationships. The relationship is itself highly valued. However, in many approaches to group therapy, members are told not to have contact with other members outside the group. By avoiding contact with other group members, no hidden alliances can form and all members are aware of issues affecting other group members. In contrast to this view, Rittenhouse (1997) supported out-of-group contact by members of a female-survivors-of-abuse group. After analyzing group process notes, she concludes that establishment of relationships outside of the group is helpful when issues of isolation, trust, and relationships are so important. Because of its emphasis on empowerment and political change, feminist therapists' view of out-of-group behavior of clients may differ from that of other group therapists.

Summary

Whereas most theories of psychotherapy focus on individual development, feelings, thoughts, or behaviors, feminist therapy incorporates societal variables by examining the impact of gender and cultural differences on women (and men). Significantly, feminist therapists have also examined the interaction of gender and ethnic variables (as well as other social factors) as they affect personal development throughout childhood, adolescence, and adulthood. Feminist theories of personality are new and not complete but offer interesting insights into psychological characteristics of men and women. Schema theory provides a means of examining the role of gender and culture in people's behavior. More recently, feminist therapists have examined such factors as religion and disabilities as they seek to understand their clients. Gilligan's work in moral development emphasizes the importance of relationships in making ethical decisions. The ways in which women and men learn different styles of relating have been the subject of the work of relational cultural therapists. The theme of unequal power emerges in views of how gender roles affect women's development across the lifespan. Feminist therapists have also addressed the impact of violence toward women on personality development.

Feminist therapists have developed techniques they integrate with other theories that are consistent with their philosophical view of therapy. This view recognizes the importance of political and social factors on individuals, values a female perspective of society and the individual, and works toward egalitarian relationships. Feminist therapy interventions examine gender, cultural, and power differences with their clients and help them bring about change. Sometimes this is done through assertiveness training or relabeling or reframing ways of viewing events. Furthermore, many feminist therapists have found diagnostic classification to be unhelpful to their clients and have relabeled client problems in a more positive manner. Disorders such as depression, borderline diagnoses, eating disorders, and posttraumatic stress that occur more frequently with females than with males have been discussed in this chapter. Although feminist therapy has focused on women's issues, feminist therapists have also applied their approach, combined with other theoretical perspectives, to men, children, and culturally diverse populations.

Suggested Readings

Brown, L. S. (2010). *Feminist therapy*. Washington, DC: American Psychological Association. Many issues that bring feminist therapy and theory together are discussed. The explanation of feminist therapy is clear and concise. The frequent use of case material helps illustrate the applications of feminist therapy.

Jordan, J. V. (2010). *Relational-cultural therapy*. Washington, DC: American Psychological Association. Jordan describes the relational cultural approach of the Stone Center in Wellesley, Massachusetts, that she and her colleagues have developed over a number of years. Using excellent case studies, she explains how feminist therapy can be used to make the relationship between client and therapist a helpful one that can empower the client and bring about positive change.

Enns, C. Z. (2004). *Feminist theories and feminist psychotherapies: Origins, themes, and variations* (2nd ed.). New York: Haworth. The history of feminist therapy and its principles and variations are summarized. Many types of feminist therapy are also

described. Many of the chapters are devoted to feminist therapy and cultural issues and concerns.

Worell, J., & Remer, P. (2003). *Feminist perspectives in therapy: Empowering diverse women*. Hoboken, NJ: Wiley. Topics such as assessment and therapeutic approaches are explained in some detail. Culture, gender-role, and power issues are described along with therapeutic approaches to them. Also, approaches to depression, sexual assault, abuse, and working with lesbian and ethnic minority women are described.

Rabin, C. L. (Ed.). (2005). *Understanding gender and culture in the helping process: Practitioners' narratives from global perspectives*. Belmont, CA: Thomson Wadsworth. Using narrative therapy to help people from many different cultures, the chapters illustrate a very diverse set of issues that people face where the cultural and gender concerns represent complex social values. The case examples that are in most chapters are enlightening.

References

Ali, S. R. (2009). Using feminist psychotherapy with Muslim women. *Research in the Social Scientific Study of Religion, 20*, 297–316.

Babacan, H., & Gopalkrishnan, N. (2005). Posttraumatic experiences of refugee women. In C. L. Rabin (Ed.), *Understanding gender and culture in the helping process: Practitioners' narratives from global perspectives* (pp. 68–83). Belmont, CA: Thomson Wadsworth.

Baird, M. K., Szymanski, D. M., & Ruebelt, S. G. (2007). Feminist identity development and practice among male therapists. *Psychology of Men & Masculinity, 8*(2), 67–78.

Ballou, M., & West, C. (2000). Feminist therapy approaches. In M. Biaggio & M. Hersen (Eds.), *Issues in the psychology of women* (pp. 273–297). New York: Kluwer/Plenum.

Ballou, M., Hill, M., & West, C. (Eds.). (2008). *Feminist therapy theory and practice: A contemporary perspective*. New York: Springer.

Barrett, S. E., Chin, J. L., Comas-Diaz, L., Espin, O., Greene, B., & McGoldrick, M. (2005). Multicultural feminist therapy: Theory in context. *Women & Therapy, 28*(3–4), 27–61.

Bem, S. L. (1987). Gender schema theory and the romantic tradition. In P. Shaver & C. Hendrick (Eds.), *Sex and gender* (pp. 251–271). Newbury Park, CA: Sage.

Bem, S. L. (1993). *The lens of gender: Transforming the debate on sexual inequality*. New Haven, CT: Yale University Press.

Berliner, P. M. (2007). *Touching your lifethread and revaluing the feminine: A process of psychospiritual change*. South Bend, IN: Cloverdale Books.

Bieschke, K. J., Perez, R. M., & DeBord, K. A. (2007). *Handbook of counseling and psychotherapy with lesbian, gay, bisexual, and transgender clients* (2nd ed.). Washington, DC: American Psychological Association.

Brice-Baker, J. (Ed.). (2003). Incarcerated African American women. In L. B. Silverstein & T. J. Goodrich (Eds.), *Feminist family therapy: Empowerment in social context* (pp. 241–252). Washington, DC: American Psychological Association.

Brooks, G. R. (1998). *A new psychotherapy for traditional men.* San Francisco: Jossey-Bass.

Brooks, G. R. (2003). Helping men embrace equality. In L. B. Silverstein & T. J. Goodrich (Eds.), *Feminist family therapy: Empowerment in social context* (pp. 163–176). Washington, DC: American Psychological Association.

Brown, C. (2007). Talking body talk: Merging feminist and narrative approaches to practice. In C. Brown & T. Augusta-Scott (Eds.), *Narrative therapy: Making meaning, making lives* (pp. 269–302). Thousand Oaks, CA: Sage.

Brown, C. G., Weber, S., & Ali, S. (2008). Women's body talk: A feminist narrative approach. *Journal of Systemic Therapies, 27*(2), 92–104.

Brown, L. S. (1986). Gender-role analysis: A neglected component of psychological assessment. *Psychotherapy, 23,* 243–248.

Brown, L. S. (1988). Feminist therapy with lesbians and gay men. In M. Dutton-Douglas & L. E. Walker (Eds.), *Feminist psychotherapies: Integration of therapeutic and feminist systems* (pp. 206–227). Norwood, NJ: Ablex.

Brown, L. S. (1990). Taking account of gender in the clinical assessment interview. *Professional Psychology, 21,* 12–17.

Brown, L. S. (1994). *Subversive dialogues: Theory in feminist therapy.* New York: Basic Books.

Brown, L. S. (2000). Dangerousness, impotence, silence, and invisibility: Heterosexism in the construction of women's sexuality. In C. B. Travis & J. W. White (Eds.), *Sexuality, society, and feminism: Psychology of women* (pp. 273–297). Washington, DC: American Psychological Association.

Brown, L. S. (2007). Empathy, genuineness—and the dynamics of power: A feminist responds to Rogers. *Psychotherapy: Theory, Research, Practice, Training, 44*(3), 257–259.

Brown, L. S. (2008a). *Cultural competence in trauma therapy: Beyond the flashback.* Washington, DC: American Psychological Association.

Brown, L. S. (2008b). Feminist therapy. In J. L. Lebow (Ed.), *Twenty-first century psychotherapies: Contemporary approaches to theory and practice* (pp. 277–306). Hoboken, NJ: John Wiley.

Brown, L. S. (2008c). Feminist therapy as a meaning-making practice: Where there is no power, where

is the meaning? In K. J. Schneider (Ed.), *Existential-integrative psychotherapy: Guideposts to the core of practice* (pp. 130–140). New York: Routledge.

Brown, L. S. (2009a). Cultural competence. In C. A. Courtois & J. D. Ford (Eds.), *Treating complex traumatic stress disorders: An evidence-based guide* (pp. 166–182). New York: Guilford.

Brown, L. S. (2009b). Cultural competence: A new way of thinking about integration in therapy. *Journal of Psychotherapy Integration, 19*(4), 340–353.

Brown, L. S. (2010). *Feminist therapy.* Washington, DC: American Psychological Association.

Brown, L. S., & Brodsky, A. M. (1992). The future of feminist therapy. *Psychotherapy, 29,* 51–57.

Brown, L. S., & Walker, L. E. A. (1990). Feminist therapy perspectives on self-disclosure. In G. Stricker & M. Fischer (Eds.), *Self-disclosure in the therapeutic relationship* (pp. 135–154). New York: Plenum.

Burstow, B. (1992). *Radical feminist therapy.* Newbury Park, CA: Sage.

Calhoun, G. B., Bartolomucci, C. L., & McLean, B. A. (2005). Building connections: Relational group work with female adolescent offenders. *Women & Therapy, 28*(2), 17–29.

Chesler, P. (1972). *Women and madness.* New York: Doubleday.

Chesler, P. (1997, November/December). Women and madness: A feminist diagnosis. *Ms.,* 36–42.

Chesler, P. (2005). *Women and madness.* (rev.) New York, NY: Palgrave Macmillan.

Childs, E. K. (1990). Therapy, feminist ethics, and the community of color with particular emphasis on the treatment of Black women. In H. Lerman & N. Porter (Eds.), *Feminist ethics in psychotherapy* (pp. 195–203). New York: Springer.

Chodorow, N. J. (1989). *Feminism and psychoanalytic theory.* New Haven, CT: Yale University Press.

Chodorow, N. J. (1996). Theoretical gender and clinical gender: Epistemological reflections of the psychology of women. *Journal of the American Psychoanalytic Association, 44,* 215–238.

Chodorow, N. J. (1999). *The power of feelings: Personal meaning in psychoanalysis, gender, and culture.* New Haven, CT: Yale University Press.

Cohen, J. N. (2008). Using feminist, emotion-focused, and developmental approaches to enhance cognitive-behavioral therapies for posttraumatic stress disorder related to childhood sexual abuse. *Psychotherapy: Theory, Research, Practice, 45*(2), 227–246.

Cole, K. L., Sarlund-Heinrich, P., & Brown, L. S. (2007). Developing and assessing effectiveness of a time-limited therapy group for incarcerated women survivors of childhood sexual abuse. *Journal of Trauma & Dissociation, 8*(2), 97–121.

Comas-Diaz, L. (1987). Feminist therapy and Hispanic/Latina women. *Women and Therapy, 6,* 39–62.

Comas-Díaz, L. (2008). Our inner Black Madonna: Reclaiming sexuality, embodying sacredness. *Women & Therapy, 31*(1), 5–20.

Crawford, M. (1995). *Talking difference: On gender and language.* New York: Sage.

Crawford, M., & Unger, R. (2004). *Women and gender: A feminist psychology* (4th ed.). Boston: McGraw-Hill.

Daugherty, C., & Lees, M. (1988). Feminist psychodynamic therapies. In M. A. Dutton Douglas & L. E. Walker (Eds.), *Feminist psychotherapies* (pp. 68–90). Norwood, NJ: Ablex.

DeChant, B. (Ed.). (1996). *Women and group psychotherapy: Theory and practice.* New York: Guilford.

Deutsch, H. (1944). *The psychology of women: A psychoanalytic interpretation.* New York: Grune & Stratton.

DeYoung, P. A. (2003). *Relational psychotherapy: A primer.* New York: Brunner-Routledge.

Edwards, C. P., Knoche, L., & Kumuru, A. (2001). Play patterns and gender. In J. Worell (Ed.), *Encyclopedia of women and gender.* San Diego: Academic Press.

Eichenbaum, L., & Orbach, S. (1983). *Understanding women: A feminist psychoanalytic approach.* New York: Basic Books.

Enns, C. Z. (2004). *Feminist theories and feminist psychotherapies: Origins, themes, and variations* (2nd ed.). New York: Haworth.

Eriksen, K., & Kress, V. E. (Eds.). (2005). *Beyond the DSM story: Ethical quandaries, challenges, and best practices.* Thousand Oaks, CA: Sage.

Evans, K. M., Kincade, E. A., Marbley, A. F., & Seem, S. R. (2005). Feminism and feminist therapy: Lessons from the past and hopes for the future. *Journal of Counseling & Development. 83*(3), 269–277.

Feder, J., Levant, R. F., & Dean, J. (2007). Boys and violence: A gender-informed analysis. *Professional Psychology: Research and Practice, 38*(4), 385–391.

Few, A. L. (2007). Integrating Black consciousness and critical race feminism into family studies research. *Journal of Family Issues, 28*(4), 452–473.

Ganley, A. L. (1988). Feminist therapy with male clients. In M. A. Dutton-Douglas & L. E. Walker (Eds.), *Feminist psychotherapies: Integration of therapeutic and feminist systems* (pp. 186–205). Norwood, NJ: Ablex.

Gergen, M. (2001). *Feminist reconstructions in psychology: Narrative, gender, and performance.* Thousand Oaks, CA: Sage.

Gilbert, L. A. (1980). Feminist therapy. In A. Brodsky & R. T. Hare-Mustin (Eds.), *Women and psychotherapy* (pp. 245–265). New York: Guilford.

Gilligan, C. (1977). In a different voice: Women's conception of self and morality. *Harvard Educational Review, 47,* 481–517.

Gilligan, C. (1982). *In a different voice.* Cambridge, MA: Harvard University Press.

Gilligan, C. (2008). *Exit-voice dilemmas in adolescent development.* New York: Analytic Press.

Gottman, J. M., & Parker, J. G. (Eds.). (1987). *Conversations of friends: Speculations on affective development.* New York: Cambridge University Press.

Greene, B. (1986). When the therapist is White and the patient is Black: Considerations for psychotherapy in the feminist heterosexual and lesbian communities. In D. Howard (Ed.), *The dynamics of feminist therapy* (pp. 41–65). Binghamton, NY: Haworth Press.

Greene, B. (1997). Psychotherapy with African American women: Integrating feminist and psychodynamic models. *Smith College Studies in Social Work, 67,* 299–322.

Greenspan, M. (1983). *A new approach to women and therapy.* New York: McGraw-Hill.

Gremillion, H. (2004). Unpacking essentialisms in therapy: Lessons for feminist approaches from narrative work. *Journal of Constructivist Psychology, 17*(3), 173–200.

Hall, R. L., & Greene, B. (2003). Contemporary African American families. In L. B. Silverstein & T. J. Goodrich (Eds.), *Feminist family therapy: Empowerment in social context* (pp. 107–120). Washington, DC: American Psychological Association.

Halstead, K. (2003). Over the rainbow: The lesbian family. In L. B. Silverstein & T. J. Goodrich (Eds.), *Feminist family therapy: Empowerment in social context* (pp. 39–50). Washington, DC: American Psychological Association.

Hare-Mustin, R. T., & Marecek, J. (1988). The meaning of difference: Gender theory, post-modernism, and psychology. *American Psychologist, 43,* 445–464.

Hayden, M. (1986). Psychoanalytic resources for the activist feminist therapist. *Women and Therapy, 5,* 89–94.

Hays, P. A. (2008). *Addressing cultural complexities in practice: Assessment, diagnosis, and therapy* (2nd ed.). Washington, DC: American Psychological Association.

Helms, J. E. (1995). An update of Helm's White and People of Color racial identity models. In J. G. Ponterotto, J. M. Casas, L. A. Suzuki, & C. M. Alexander (Eds.), *Handbook of multicultural counseling* (pp. 181–198). Thousand Oaks, CA: Sage.

Helms, J. E., & Cook, D. A. (1999). *Using race and culture in counseling and psychotherapy: Theory and process.* Needham Heights, MA: Allyn & Bacon.

Horney, K. (1966). *New ways in psychoanalysis.* New York: Norton.

Hoshmand, L. T. (2003). Value choices and methodological issues in research with women. In M. Kopala & M. A. Keitel (Eds.), *Handbook of counseling women* (pp. 546–556). Thousand Oaks, CA: Sage.

Hurtado, A. (1996). *The color of privilege: Three blasphemies on race and feminism.* Ann Arbor, MI: University of Michigan Press.

Hyde, J. S. (2005). The gender similarities hypothesis. *American Psychologist, 60*(6), 581–592.

Ivey, A. E., D'Andrea, M., Ivey, M. B., & Simek-Morgan, L. (2006). *Counseling and psychotherapy: A multicultural perspective* (6th ed.). Boston: Allyn & Bacon.

Jaffee, S. & Hyde, J. (2000). Gender differences in moral orientation: A meta-analysis. *Psychological Bulletin, 26,* 703–726.

Jakubowski, P. A. (1977). Assertion training for women. In E. I. Rawlings & D. K. Carter (Eds.), *Psychotherapy for women* (pp. 147–190). Springfield, IL: Charles C. Thomas.

Jordan, J. V. (2003). Relational-cultural therapy. In M. Kopala & M. A. Keitel (Eds.), *Handbook of counseling women* (pp. 22–30). Thousand Oaks, CA: Sage.

Jordan, J. V. (2010). *Relational-cultural therapy.* Washington, DC: American Psychological Association.

Jordan, J. V., Handel, M., Alvarez, M., & Cook-Nobles, R. (2004). Applications of the relational model to time-limited therapy. In J. V. Jordan, M. Walker, & L. M. Hartling (Eds.), *The complexity of connection: Writings from the Stone Center's Jean Baker Miller Training Institute* (pp. 250–269). New York: Guilford.

Kallivayalil, D. (2007). Feminist therapy: Its use and implications for South Asian immigrant survivors of domestic violence. *Women & Therapy, 30*(3–4), 109–127.

Kaschak, E. (1976). Sociotherapy: An ecological model for psychotherapy with women. *Psychotherapy: Theory, Research, and Practice, 13,* 61–63.

Kaschak, E. (1981). Feminist psychotherapy: The first decade. In S. Cox (Ed.), *Female psychology: The emerging self* (pp. 387–400). New York: St.Martins.

Kaschak, E. (1992). *Engendered lives.* New York: Basic Books.

Kohlberg, L. (1981). *The philosophy of moral development: Essays on moral development* (Vols. 1–2). San Francisco: Harper & Row.

Kravetz, D. (1978). Consciousness-raising groups in the 1970s. *Psychology of Women Quarterly, 3,* 168–186.

Kravetz, D. (1987). Benefits of consciousness-raising groups for women. In C. Brody (Ed.), *Women's therapy groups: Paradigms of feminist treatment* (pp. 55–66). New York: Springer.

Lerner, G. (1979). *The majority finds its past: Placing women in history.* New York: Oxford Press.

Levant, R. F., & Wimer, D. J. (2009). The new fathering movement. In C. Z. Oren & D. C. Oren (Eds.), *Counseling fathers* (pp. 3–21). New York: Routledge.

Levant, R. F., Wimer, D. J., Williams, C. M., Smalley, K. B., & Noronha, D. (2009). The relationships between masculinity variables, health risk behaviors and attitudes toward seeking psychological help. *International Journal of Men's Health, 8*(1), 3–21.

Maisel, R., Epston, D., & Borden, A. (2004). *Biting the hand that starves you: Inspiring resistance to anorexia/bulimia.* New York: Norton.

Malson, H., & Burns, M. (Eds.). (2009). *Critical feminist approaches to eating dis/orders.* New York: Routledge.

Matlin, M. W. (2008). *The psychology of women* (6th ed.). Belmont, CA: Wadsworth.

McAuliffe, G., Eriksen, K., & Kress, V. E. (2005). A developmental, constructivist model for developmental assessment (which includes diagnosis of course). In K. Eriksen & V. E. Kress (Eds.), *Beyond the DSM story: Ethical quandaries, challenges, and best practices* (pp. 187–205). Thousand Oaks, CA: Sage.

Miller, J. B. (1986). *Toward a new psychology of women.* Boston: Beacon Press. (Original work published 1976.)

Miller, J. B. (1991). The development of women's sense of self. In J. V. Jordan, A. G. Kaplan, J. B. Miller, I. P. Stiver, & J. L. Surrey (Eds.), *Women's growth in connection* (pp. 11–26). New York: Guilford.

Mirkin, M. P., Suyemoto, K. L., & Okun, B. F. (Eds.). (2005). *Psychotherapy with women: Exploring diverse contexts and identities.* New York: Guilford.

Mittal, M., & Wieling, E. (2004). The influence of therapists' ethnicity on the practice of feminist family therapy: A pilot study. *Journal of Feminist Family Therapy, 16*(2), 25–42.

Morrow, S. L. (2000). First do no harm: Therapist issues in psychotherapy with lesbian, gay and bisexual clients. In M. R. Perez, K. DeBord, & K. J. Biescke (Eds.), *Handbook of counseling and psychotherapy with lesbian, gay, and bisexual clients* (pp. 137–156). Washington, DC: American Psychological Association.

Nasser, M., & Malson, H. (2009). Beyond western dis/orders: Thinness and self-starvation of other-ed women. In H. Malson & M. Burns (Eds.), *Critical feminist approaches to eating dis/orders* (pp. 74–86). New York: Routledge.

Nutt, R. L., & Brooks, G. R. (2008). Psychology of gender. In S. D. Brown & R. W. Lent (Eds.), *Handbook of counseling psychology* (4th ed., pp. 176–193). Hoboken, NJ: John Wiley.

Park, S. M. (2008). Feminist therapies: Working with diverse women. In C. Negy (Ed.), *Cross-cultural psychotherapy: Toward a critical understanding of diverse clients* (2nd ed., pp. 327–361). Reno, NV: Bent Tree Press.

Quinn, K., & Dunn-Johnson, L. (2000). Women's empowerment and wellness group: An integration of solution-focused and relational models. In K. A. Fall & J. E. Levitov (Eds.), *Modern applications to group work* (pp. 133–158). Huntington, NY: Nova Science.

Rabin, C. L. (Ed.). (2005). *Understanding gender and culture in the helping process: Practitioners' narratives from global perspectives*. Belmont, CA: Thomson Wadsworth.

Rawlings, E. I., & Carter, D. K. (1977). Feminist and nonsexist psychotherapy. In E. I. Rawlings & D. K. Carter (Eds.), *Psychotherapy for women* (pp. 49–76). Springfield, IL: Charles C. Thomas.

Reynolds, A. L. (2003). Counseling issues for lesbian and bisexual women. In M. Kopala & M. A. Keitel (Eds.), *Handbook of counseling women* (pp. 53–73). Thousand Oaks, CA: Sage.

Rhodes, R., & Johnson, A. (1997). A feminist approach to treating alcohol and drug addicted African-American women. *Women and Therapy, 20*, 23–37.

Rinfret-Raynor, M., & Cantin, S. (1997). Feminist therapy for battered women: An assessment. In G. K. Kantor & J. L. Jasinski (Eds.), *Out of darkness: Contemporary perspectives on family violence* (pp. 219–234). Thousand Oaks, CA: Sage.

Rittenhouse, J. (1997). Feminist principles in survivor's groups: Out of group contact. *Journal for Specialists in Group Work, 22*, 111–119.

Roades, L. A. (2000). Mental health issues for women. In M. Biaggio & F. M. Hersen (Eds.), *Issues in the psychology of women* (pp. 251–272). New York: Kluwer/Plenum.

Roffman, E. (2008). Ethics and activism: Theory—identity politics, conscious acts, and ethical aspirations. In M. Ballou, M. Hill, & C. West (Eds.), *Feminist therapy theory and practice: A contemporary perspective* (pp. 109–125). New York: Springer.

Rowland, S. (2003). Jung: A feminist revision. *Journal of Analytical Psychology, 48*(1), 119–121.

Russell, M. (1984). *Skills in counseling women*. Springfield, IL: Charles C. Thomas.

Sanftner, J. L., Ryan, W. J., & Pierce, P. (2009). Application of a relational model to understanding body image in college women and men. *Journal of College Student Psychotherapy, 23*(4), 262–280.

Sharf, R. S. (2010). *Applying career development theory to counseling* (5th ed.). Belmont, CA: Brooks/Cole—Cengage.

Silverstein, L. B., & Goodrich, T. J. (2003). *Feminist family therapy: Empowerment in social context*. Washington, DC: American Psychological Association.

Simi, N. L., & Mahalik, J. R. (1997). Comparison of feminist versus psychoanalytic/dynamic and other therapists on self-disclosure. *Psychology of Women Quarterly, 21*, 465–483.

Slattery, J. M. (2004). *Counseling diverse clients: Bringing context into therapy*. Belmont, CA: Brooks/Cole—Thomson.

Stewart, A. J., & McDermott, C. (2004). Gender in psychology. *Annual Review of Psychology, 55*, 519–544.

Sturdivant, S. (1980). *Therapy with women*. New York: Springer.

Sweeney, M. L. (2000). The self-image of adolescent females: A group exploration. In K. A. Fall & J. E. Levitov (Eds.), *Modern applications to group work* (pp. 66–96). Huntington, NY: Nova Science.

Tafoya, N. (2005). Native American women: Fostering resiliency through community. In M. P. Mirkin, K. L. Suyemoto, & B. F. Okun (Eds.), *Psychotherapy with women: Exploring diverse contexts and identities* (pp. 297–312). New York: Guilford.

Tantillo, M., & Sanftner, J. (2003). The relationship between perceived mutuality and bulimic symptoms, depression, and therapeutic change in group. *Eating Behaviors, 3*(4), 349–364.

Turner, C. W. (1997). Clinical applications of the Stone Center theoretical approach to minority women. In J. V. Jordan (Ed.), *Women's growth in diversity: More writings from the Stone Center* (pp. 74–90). New York: Guilford.

U.S. Department of Labor. (2007). *Employed and experienced and unemployed persons by occupation, sex, and race. Table 1* (pp. 209–214). Data from the Current Population Survey. Washington, DC: Bureau of Labor Statistics.

Vasquez, M. J. T. (2003). Ethical responsibilities in therapy: A feminist perspective. In M. Kopala & M. A. Keitel (Eds.), *Handbook of counseling women* (pp. 557–573). Thousand Oaks, CA: Sage.

Veldhuis, C. B. (2001). The trouble with power. *Women and Therapy 23*(27), 37–38.

Walker, L. J. S. (1987). Women's groups are different. In C. M. Brody (Ed.), *Women's therapy groups* (pp. 3–12). New York: Springer.

Walker, M. (2009). Counselling survivors of abuse: Feminism, psychodynamic psychotherapy and ethics. In L. Gabriel & R. Casemore (Eds.), *Relational ethics in practice: Narratives from counselling and psychotherapy* (pp. 166–177). New York: Routledge.

Wells, M., Brack, C. J., & McMichen, P. J. (2003). Women and depressive disorders. In M. Kopala & M. A. Keitel (Eds.), *Handbook of counseling women* (pp. 429–457). Thousand Oaks, CA: Sage.

West, C. K. (2005). The map of relational-cultural theory. *Women & Therapy*, *28*(3–4), 93–110.

West, C., & Zimmerman, D. H. (1985). Gender, language, and discourse. In T. A. van Dijk (Ed.), *Handbook of discourse analysis in society* (pp. 103–124). London: Academic Press.

Worell, J., & Johnson, D. (2001). Therapy with women: Feminist frameworks. In R. K. Unger (Ed.), *Handbook of the psychology of women and gender* (pp. 317–329). New York: Wiley.

Worell, J., & Remer, P. (2003). *Feminist perspectives in therapy: Empowering diverse women* (2nd ed.). New York: Wiley.

Wyche, K. F. (2001). Sociocultural issues in counseling women of color. In R. K. Unger (Ed.). *Handbook of the psychology of women and gender* (pp. 330–340). New York: Wiley.

Yokoyama, K. (2007). The double binds of our bodies: Multiculturally informed feminist therapy considerations for body image and eating disorders among Asian American women. *Women & Therapy*, *30*(3–4), 177–192.

Family Therapy

Outline of Family Therapy

THE STUDY OF COMMUNICATION PATTERNS IN FAMILIES WITH MEMBERS HAVING SYMPTOMS OF SCHIZOPHRENIA
- Double bind
- Marital schism and marital skew
- Pseudomutuality

General Systems Theory
- Feedback—negative and positive
- Homeostasis

BOWEN'S INTERGENERATIONAL APPROACH

Theory of Family Systems
- Differentiation of self
- Triangulation
- Nuclear family emotional systems
- Family projection process
- Emotional cutoff
- Multigenerational transmission process
- Sibling position
- Societal regression

Therapy Goals

Techniques of Bowen's Family Therapy
- Evaluation interview
- Genograms
- Interpretation
- Detriangulation

STRUCTURAL FAMILY THERAPY

Concepts of Structural Family Therapy
- Family structure
- Family subsystems
- Boundary permeability
- Alignments and coalitions

Goals of Structural Family Therapy

Techniques of Structural Family Therapy
- Family mapping
- Accommodating and joining
- Enactment
- Intensity
- Changing boundaries
- Reframing

STRATEGIC THERAPY

Concepts of Strategic Therapy

Goals

Techniques of Strategic Family Therapy
- Straightforward tasks
- Paradoxical tasks

EXPERIENTIAL AND HUMANISTIC FAMILY THERAPIES
- The Experiential Therapy of Carl Whitaker
- The Humanistic Approach of Virginia Satir

INTEGRATIVE APPROACHES TO FAMILY SYSTEMS THERAPY

THEORIES OF INDIVIDUAL THERAPY AS APPLIED TO FAMILY THERAPY
- Psychoanalysis
- Adlerian
- Existential
- Person-Centered
- Gestalt
- Behavioral
- Rational Emotive Behavior
- Cognitive
- Reality
- Feminist

BRIEF FAMILY SYSTEMS THERAPY
- The Mental Research Institute Brief Family Therapy Model
- Long Brief Therapy of the Milan Associates

CURRENT TRENDS
- Psychoeducational Approaches
- Professional Training and Organizations
- Family Law
- Medicine

In discussing treatment of family problems, two terms are used in this chapter: *family therapy* and *family systems therapy. Family therapy* is psychotherapeutic treatment of the family to bring about better psychological functioning. Most of the preceding chapters illustrate a particular psychotherapeutic approach, and ways in which each of these theories can be applied to a therapy with families are described briefly in this chapter on pages 561 to 564. *Family systems therapy* is a type of family therapy that concentrates on the interactions of family members and views the entire family as a unit or system. Treatment is designed to understand and bring about change within the family structure. Family systems therapy is the topic of much of this chapter.

Of the many different family systems therapy approaches, this chapter focuses on four: intergenerational, structural, strategic, and experiential. The intergenerational approach of Murray Bowen examines the impact of the parents' interaction with their own family of origin as it affects their interaction with their children. Salvador Minuchin's structural approach is concerned with how family members relate to each other in the therapy hour and at home. Emphasizing the need to bring about change in the family, Jay Haley's strategic approach is directed at bringing about change in symptoms. The experiential family system therapies emphasize the unconscious and affective processes of families and therapists in their work.

Because many family therapists use more than one of these four approaches, ways of integrating them are also described. Additionally, other family systems therapists have devoted attention to brief family systems therapy and to integrating educational information and therapy when working with families.

Because family systems therapists address family dynamics and not individual personalities, this chapter requires a different outline than the others. Rather than sections on theories of personality and psychotherapy, it contains separate sections describing the family systems approach and the application of technique to each of four theories: intergenerational, structural, strategic, and experiential. Each of the four sections describes how theorists understand the family, their goals for treatment, their treatment approach, and a case example. Later sections describe the application of other theories to family therapy, brief family therapy, current trends and innovations, research, gender issues, cultural issues, and the application of family therapy to individuals and couples counseling. First, however, is a brief history of family therapy and general systems theory.

Historical Background

The current practice of family therapy has its roots in a variety of theoretical, practical, and research approaches to helping children, married couples, and individuals with family problems. In understanding family therapy as it is now, it will be helpful to learn about the contribution of child guidance clinics and marriage counseling in helping families cope with problems. From both theoretical and in-depth perspectives, Freud and other psychoanalysts contributed to the understanding of families through their emphasis on the impact of early childhood events on adulthood and through their own psychotherapeutic work with children. Also, early research on schizophrenic children and adolescents as part of family systems led to the concepts and ideas that are widely used in the current practice of family therapy. Another important addition to family therapy comes from outside the social sciences: general systems theory. It examines the interactions and processes of parts of a whole in areas such as engineering, biology, economics, politics, sociology, psychology, and psychotherapy. A familiarity with these diverse applied and theoretical approaches is helpful in understanding the development of theoretical approaches to family therapy.

Early Approaches to Family Counseling

Formal marriage counseling has been available since the 1930s. Before that time, informal counseling was probably provided by friends, doctors, clergy, and lawyers. The first centers for marriage counseling were opened in Los Angeles by Paul Popenoe and in New York City by Abraham and Hannah Stone (Goldenberg & Goldenberg, 2008). By the 1940s, 15 centers devoted to marriage or family issues had been established to help families in the community. These clinics dealt with problems such as infidelity, divorce, child raising, financial problems, communication problems, and sexual incompatibilities. In general, most marital therapy was brief and problem focused, taking into consideration the personality and role expectations of each member of the couple as well as their communicating and decision-making patterns (Cromwell, Olson, & Fournier, 1976). A common practice in the 1930s and 1940s was for different therapists to see individuals separately (Goldenberg & Goldenberg, 2008). In the 1950s, conjoint therapy, in which both members of the couple were seen together by one therapist, became more common. As marriage counseling developed, it focused more and more on attending to and working with the marriage relationship and less on the individual personality issues of each client. During the 1930s and 1940s and into the 1950s, problems with children were often left to child guidance clinics, although they might be discussed in marriage counseling (Mittelman, 1948).

Because of the prevailing psychoanalytic view in the 1930s and 1940s that emotional disorders began in childhood, the treatment of children's problems was seen as an excellent way of preventing mental illness in later life (Goldenberg & Goldenberg, 2008). Usually the parents were treated separately from the children. Often mothers were seen as the cause of the problem, with little attention given to fathers. The focus was primarily on treatment of the child and secondarily to help the mother deal with negative feelings that may affect child raising and to help her learn new attitudes or approaches. Levy (1943) wrote about the negative impact of maternal overprotection on children, and Fromm-Reichmann (1948) was concerned about the impact of the schizophrenogenic mother (dominating, rejecting, and insecure) on children.

In the 1950s, there was a shift from blaming parents for children's problems to helping parents and children relate better to each other. For example, Cooper (1974) addressed positive goals of parental involvement so that progress with the child in therapy could develop and parents could make changes in the child's environment to help the child improve.

Psychoanalytic and Related Influences on Family Therapy

Although focusing mainly on work with individuals, several early theorists contributed to the development of family therapy treatment. In his individual work, Sigmund Freud treated both children and adolescents and attended to processes related to early childhood development in all of his patients. Another early contributor to family therapy was Alfred Adler, who observed the development of social interest within the family and initiated child guidance clinics in Vienna. Harry Stack Sullivan (1953) was concerned with not only intrapsychic factors but also interpersonal relationships within the family and with others. Some of his observations had a direct influence on later family therapists. The person considered the initiator of family therapy and work with families as a unit is Nathan Ackerman. A child psychiatrist who was trained in psychoanalysis, Ackerman initially used the traditional model in which the psychiatrist saw the child and the social worker saw the mother. In the mid-1940s, however, he started to see the entire family for both diagnosis and treatment. He was aware of conscious and unconscious issues within the individual and the family, as well as issues that affected the family as a whole. As a result, he often attended to nonverbal cues such as facial expression, posture, and seating arrangements as a way of assessing family problems. In his therapeutic approach, Ackerman was open, honest, and direct, encouraging families to share their own thoughts and feelings as he did. In his work with families, he became emotionally involved with the family while at the same time looking for unconscious themes (Nichols, 2008). Many family therapists were drawn to his engaging style and his active approach to therapy. However, his writings (Ackerman, 1966a, 1966b) do not provide a clear, systematic approach for therapists who wish to follow his method.

The Study of Communication Patterns in Families with Members Having Symptoms of Schizophrenia

During the 1950s, several research groups studied communication patterns within families that had a member suffering from schizophrenia. From this work emerged concepts that describe dysfunctional ways of relating within a family: the double bind, marital schism, marital skew, and pseudomutuality.

Double bind. Working in Palo Alto, Bateson, Jackson, Haley, and Weakland (1956) studied how families with children who had symptoms of schizophrenia functioned and maintained stability. They observed the double bind, in which a person receives two related but contradictory messages. One message may be relatively clear, the other message unclear (often nonverbal), creating a "no-win" paradox. Bateson et al. (1956) give a classic example of a mother giving a nonverbal message that says "go away," followed by a message that says "come closer, you need my love," and then "you're interpreting my messages in the wrong way" (Goldenberg & Goldenberg, 2008).

> A young man who had fairly well recovered from an acute schizophrenic episode was visited in the hospital by his mother. He was glad to see her and impulsively put his arm around her shoulders, whereupon she stiffened. He withdrew his arm and she asked, "Don't you love me anymore?" He then blushed and she said, "Dear, you must not be so easily embarrassed and afraid of your feelings." (Bateson et al., 1956, p. 259)

Bateson et al. report that, following this interaction, the patient became violent and assaultive upon returning to the ward. No matter how the patient would respond to his mother, he would be wrong. Bateson and his colleagues believed that if individuals were continually exposed to these types of messages, they would eventually lose the ability to understand their own and others' communication patterns and would develop schizophrenic behavior.

Marital schism and marital skew. In their work with individuals who had been hospitalized with schizophrenia, Lidz and his colleagues found unusual patterns of family communications between parents and their children (Lidz, Cornelison, Fleck, & Terry, 1957). They reported two particular types of marital discord in families with members with schizophrenia: marital schism and marital skew. In *marital schism*, parents preoccupied with their own problems tended to undermine the worth of the other parent by competing for sympathy and support from the children. For example, if the father did not value the mother, he would be afraid the child would grow up like the mother, and so the mother would be devalued. In *marital skew*, the psychological disturbance of one parent tends to dominate the home. The other parent, accepting the situation, implies that the home is normal and that everything is fine, thus distorting reality to the children. This puts imbalance in the marriage and places pressure on the children to try to normalize the family and balance the marriage. In both of these situations, but particularly in marital schism, a child is in a bind; by pleasing one parent, he might displease the other.

Pseudomutuality. Another early researcher of families with members with symptoms of schizophrenia was Lyman Wynne. He and his colleagues observed that in families of children with symptoms of schizophrenia, there was often a conflict between the child's need to develop a separate identity and to maintain intimate relationships with troubled or emotional family members. In this concept, called *pseudomutuality*, there is an appearance of open relationships that serves to conceal distant relationships within the family (Wynne, Ryckoff, Day, & Hirsch, 1958). Where roles are used to keep harmony in the family rather than have open interactions, family members may relate in limited or superficial ways to each other and to other people. From Wynne's point of view, heightened emotional expression in families coping with schizophrenia contributes to problems within the family (Wahlberg & Wynne, 2001). Thus, the interaction between individuals, not the person's own psychological functioning, is seen as having a role in the development of schizophrenia.

The findings of Bateson, Lidz, and Wynne and their colleagues all relate to communication patterns that the participants are unaware of and that create stress in marriages and in child raising. Their observations, although based on parents of schizophrenic children, also applied to other families (Okun & Rappaport, 1980). These findings were to have a significant impact on the development of approaches to family therapy with many types of problems. Complex patterns of communicating and interacting could be clarified, to some degree, by examining general systems theory, which viewed each system as a part of a larger system.

General Systems Theory

Significant contributions to family systems theory came from outside the social sciences (Greene, 2008). Norbert Wiener (1948), a mathematician who played an important role in the development of computers, wrote of feedback mechanisms that were essential in the processing of information. Von Bertalanffy's (1968) work in biology and medicine explored the interrelationships of parts to each other and to the whole system. When his general theoretical approach is applied to family therapy, a family cannot be understood without knowing how the family functions as a whole unit. From a systems theory perspective, each family is a part of a larger system, a neighborhood, which is again a part of a larger system, a town, and so forth. Individuals are wholes that comprise smaller systems, organs, tissues, cells, and so forth. If any part of a system changes, the whole system reflects a change. Important concepts in understanding general systems theory are feedback and homeostasis, which deal with ways in which systems and their units function.

Feedback. The term *feedback* refers to the communication pattern within the units of a system. There are two basic patterns of communication: linear and circular.

$$A \rightarrow B \rightarrow C \rightarrow D$$

Linear Causality

Circularity

FIGURE 14.1 Linearity and circularity in a system.

The linear approach is diagrammed in Figure 14.1; it shows that communication occurs in a single direction, moving from A to B to C to D. In a system with circular feedback, each unit may change and thus affect any of the other units. In the example in Figure 14.1, a change in E can trigger a change in F, G, or H, which then can trigger another change, and so forth. To put the concept of circularity into a family context, a mother may feel that her drug dependence is caused by her son's insolent behavior. The son may feel his behavior toward his mother is influenced by her drug abuse. In this way, the feedback of the mother affects the feedback of the son, and the feedback of the son affects the feedback of the mother. In family systems theory, the circular interaction is observed, and blame is not placed on either mother or son.

Related to circular interaction is the idea in family systems therapy that the emphasis is on process rather than content. Family systems therapists focus on what is happening in the present rather than what happened or the sequence of events that led up to an event, as in the linear causality sequence diagrammed in Figure 14.1. A husband may describe a family's problem from a linear and content perspective: "When my wife had a stroke, I thought that we all had to pitch in at home in running the house." A process-oriented approach that looks at the interrelationships of the members of the family would focus on circularity in the present: "My wife is in the chair most of the day. Helen comes home from school, leaves her books, goes out, and doesn't come home until after dinner. I am angry at Helen for not helping. I wish that my wife would do more. She seems to think that I don't do enough." In this way, the relationships of each of the three family members are seen to interact from the husband's perspective, and more information is learned by examining the processes of family interactions than from only the content of the interaction.

Related to the idea of complexity in a family system is that of underlying *equifinality*, which implies that there are many different ways to get to the same destination. In Figure 14.1, there are many different paths from E to H. To return to the example of the three-person family, there are many ways that the family can relate to each other and to change the system to create more stability.

Homeostasis. In general, systems have a tendency to seek stability and equilibrium, referred to as *homeostasis* (Goldenberg & Goldenberg, 2008). An example of homeostasis is a thermostat used to regulate temperature so that a house does not become too hot or cold. Likewise, a family system attempts to regulate itself so that stability and equilibrium can be maintained. The process by which this equilibrium is achieved is feedback from units within the system. In a family, new information brought into a system affects its stability. In the previous example, if Helen comes home at 2 A.M., this information is likely to affect her relationship with each of her parents and to some degree their relationship with each other.

There are two basic types of feedback: negative and positive. (Note that in systems theory the meanings of *negative* and *positive* feedback differ from their common meanings of "negative" and "positive feedback." In systems theory, positive and negative feedback are related to changing the system or maintaining stability in the system, respectively.) In *positive feedback*, change occurs in the system; in *negative feedback*, equilibrium is achieved. For example, if Helen's father talks with Helen about why she is late and works with her to reduce the behavior that causes disequilibrium, negative feedback affects the family system. If instead he gets angry and yells at her, she may stay out late more often, and the system is changed through the use of positive feedback processes. In this brief example, positive feedback is seen as having an unhelpful impact on a family. Depending on the nature of the change that occurs, positive feedback may also be helpful.

Although early psychoanalytic therapy, child guidance, and marriage counseling tended to focus on the individual, family therapy has focused on the entire family as the context of the problem. Research with families of children with schizophrenia and application of general systems theory to family therapy has been instrumental in the development of family therapy. The focus is no longer on the identified patient, the person the parents believe needs help.

In the following sections, four approaches to family systems therapy are presented: Bowen's intergenerational approach, Minuchin's structural theory, Haley's strategic approach, and Satir's and Whittaker's experiential approaches. Because family therapists often use several approaches to family systems therapy, as well as individually oriented approaches, integrating family therapy approaches is discussed.

Bowen's Intergenerational Approach

MURRAY BOWEN

Murray Bowen's (1913–1990) early work with children with schizophrenia and their families at the Menninger Clinic was highly influential in his development of a system of family therapy (Bowen, 1960). His approach to systems theory is different from that of other family therapy theorists, emphasizing the family's emotional system and the history of this system as it may be traced through the family dynamics of the parents' families and even grandparents' families. He was interested in how families projected their own emotionality onto a particular family member and that member's reaction to other family members (Titelman, 2008). Preferring to work with parents rather than the whole family, Bowen (1978) saw himself as a coach, helping parents to think through ways they can behave differently with each other and their children to bring about less destructive emotionality in the family.

Theory of Family Systems

Bowen's theory of family systems is based on the individual's ability to differentiate his own intellectual functioning from feelings. This concept is applied to family processes and the ways that individuals project their own stresses onto other family members. In particular, Bowen examined the triangular relationship between family members such as the parents and a child. How individuals cope with the stress put on them by the way other family members deal with their anxieties is an important issue for Bowen. He is particularly concerned with the ways children may distance themselves emotionally, and also physically, from their families. One of the most significant aspects of Bowen's theory is how families can transmit over several generations psychological characteristics that affect the interaction of dysfunctional families. Bowen's view of multigenerational transmission and family interactions provides an original way of viewing the family. Eight concepts form the core of his system of family therapy.

Differentiation of self. Being able to differentiate one's intellectual processes from one's feeling processes represents a clear differentiation of self. Bowen recognizes the importance of awareness of feelings and thoughts, particularly the ability to distinguish between the two. When thoughts and feelings are not distinguished, fusion occurs. A person who is highly differentiated (Bowen, 1966) is well aware of her opinions and has a sense of self. In a family conflict, people who are able to differentiate their emotions and intellects are able to stand up for themselves and not be dominated by the feelings of others, whereas those whose feelings and thoughts are fused may express a pseudoself rather than their true values or opinions. For example, in a family with 10- and 12-year-old girls, the 10-year-old may have a mind of her own and be clearer about what she will and will not do (differentiated) than the 12-year-old (fused). The 12-year-old who is not able to express herself accurately (pseudoself) may cause problems in relating that affect the whole family. If there is poor differentiation, triangulation is likely to take place.

Triangulation. When there is stress between two people in a family, they may be likely (Bowen, 1978) to bring another member in to dilute the anxiety or tension, which is called *triangulation*. When family members are getting along and are not upset, there is no reason to bring a third person into an interaction. Bowen believes that when there is stress in the family, the least-differentiated person is likely to be drawn into the conflict to reduce tension (Goldenberg & Goldenberg, 2008). Triangulation is not limited to the family, as friends, relatives, or a therapist may be brought into a conflict.

For Bowen (1975), a two-person system was unstable, and when there is stress, joining with a third person reduces the tension in the relationship between the original two people. The larger the family, the greater the possibility for many different interlocking triangles. Stepfamilies are likely to have many possibilities for triangles (Cauley, 2008). One problem could involve several triangles, as more and more family members are brought into the conflict. Bringing a third family member into a conflict (triangulation) does not always reduce the stress in the family. Stress reduction depends, in part, on the differentiation level of the members involved. For example, if two children who are arguing bring in a third member of the family (brother, mother, or uncle), the tension between the two children diminishes if the other person does not take sides and helps to solve the problem. If the person becomes excited or acts unfairly, however, stress between the two children may continue (Nichols, 2008). From a therapeutic point of view, it is very important that the therapist triangulates in a clear and differentiated way with a couple while attending to patterns of triangulation in the family.

Nuclear family emotional systems. The family as a system—that is, the nuclear family emotional system—is likely to be unstable unless members of the family are each well differentiated. Because such differentiation is rare, family conflict is likely to exist. Bowen (1978) believed that spouses are likely to select partners with similar levels of differentiation. If two people with low levels of differentiation marry, it is likely that as a couple they will become highly fused, as will their family when they have children.

Family projection process. When there are relatively low levels of differentiation in the marriage partners, they may project their stress onto one child—the family projection process. In general, the child who is most emotionally attached to the parents may have the least differentiation between feelings and intellect and the most difficulty in separating from the family (Papero, 1983, 2000). For example, a child who refuses to go to school and wants to stay home with his parents can be considered to have fused with his parents. How intense the family projection process is depends on how undifferentiated the parents are and on the family's stress level (Bitter, 2009). The "problem child" can respond to the stress of his undifferentiated parents in a variety of ways.

Emotional cutoff. When children receive too much stress because of overinvolvement in the family, they may try to separate themselves from the family through emotional cutoff. Adolescents might move away from home, go to college, or run away. For younger children and adolescents, it may mean withdrawing emotionally from the family and going through the motions of being in the family. Their interaction with parents is likely to be brief and superficial. A child experiencing an emotional cutoff may go to her room not so much to study but to be free of the family conflict. Such a child may deal with everyday matters but withdraw when emotionally charged issues develop between parents. In general, the higher the level of anxiety and emotional dependence, the more likely children are to experience an emotional cutoff in a family (Titelman, 2008).

Multigenerational transmission process. In his approach to work with families, Bowen (1976) looked not just at the immediate family but also at previous generations (Kerr, 2003). As mentioned previously, he believed that spouses with similar differentiation levels seek each other out and project their stress and lack of differentiation onto their children. If Bowen's hypothesis was correct, then after six or seven generations of increasingly fused couples, an observer could find highly dysfunctional families who are vulnerable to stress and to lack of differentiation between thoughts and feelings. Naturally, Bowen recognized that spouses do not always marry at their own exact level of differentiation. In the concept of the multigenerational transmission process, the functioning of grandparents, great-grandparents, great-aunts, great-uncles, and other relatives may play an important role in the pathology of the family. To give an example, a great-grandfather who was prone to emotional outbursts and experienced depression may affect the function of the grandmother, who in turn affects the functioning of the father, who may in turn have an impact on the psychological health of the child. Other issues besides differentiation affect family functioning.

Sibling position. Bowen believed that birth order had an impact on the functioning of children within the family. Relying on the work of Toman (1961), he believed that the sibling position of marriage partners would affect how they perform as parents. Concerned less with actual birth order than with the way a child functioned in the family, Bowen felt that how one behaved with brothers and sisters had an impact on how one acts as a parent. For example, an oldest brother may have taken care of his younger brother and sister in his family and thus may take on a role of responsibility with his children. This might be particularly true if his wife did not take much responsibility with her siblings, as could be the case if she is the youngest child (Bitter, 2009).

Societal regression. Bowen extended his model of family systems to societal functioning. Just as families can move toward undifferentiation or toward individuation, so can societies. If there are stresses on societies, they are more likely to move toward undifferentiation. Examples of stresses could be famine, civil uprisings, or population growth. To extend Bowen's model to societies, leaders and policymakers should distinguish between intellect and emotion when making decisions and not act on feelings alone.

Bowen's theory of family structure goes beyond the immediate family system to cross generations. His interest was in how the personality of individuals affects other members in the family. He was particularly interested in the individual's ability to differentiate intellectual processes from feelings and the impact of this individual's ability on other family members. These views bear a direct relationship to his beliefs about the goals of family therapy.

Therapy Goals

In attending to the goals of therapy, Bowen was interested in the impact of past generations on present family functioning. As he set goals in working with families, he listened to the presenting symptoms and, even more important, to family dynamics as they relate to differentiation of family members and to triangulation. More specifically, he sought to help families reduce their general stress level and to find ways to help family members become more differentiated and meet their individual needs as well as family needs (Kerr & Bowen, 1988).

Techniques of Bowen's Family Therapy

In Bowen's system of family therapy, an evaluation period precedes therapeutic intervention. The process of taking a family history is aided by the use of a genogram, a diagram of the family tree that usually includes the children, parents, grandparents, aunts and uncles, and possibly other relatives. In bringing about family change, Bowen used interpretation of his understanding of intergenerational factors. In his writings, Bowen (1978) saw himself as a coach, helping his patients analyze the family situation and plan strategies for events that are likely to occur. In this work, he often focused on detriangulation, a way of changing patterns of dealing with stress. The effectiveness of coaching, interpreting, and detriangulating depends on effective evaluation of family history.

Evaluation interview. Characteristic of Bowen's therapeutic work are objectivity and neutrality. Even in the initial telephone contact, Bowen (Kerr & Bowen, 1988) warned against being charmed into taking sides in the family or in other ways becoming fused with the nuclear family emotional system. The family evaluation interviews can take place with any combination of family members. Sometimes a single family member can be sufficient if that person is willing to work on differentiating his own feelings and intellectual processes rather than blaming other family members.

In taking a family history, Bowen attended to triangles within the family and to the level of differentiation within family members. Because there is usually an identified patient, Bowen family therapists listen for ways in which family members may project their own anxieties onto that patient. How that patient responds to the family is also important. Is he emotionally cut off from other family members? In taking the family history, the therapist attends to relationships within the family, such as sibling position, but also relationships within the parents' families of origin. Because intergenerational patterns can get complex, therapists may use a genogram to describe family relationships.

Genograms. The genogram is a method of diagramming families and includes significant information about families, such as ages, sex, marriage dates, deaths, and geographical locations. Genograms not only provide an overview of the extended family but also may suggest patterns of differentiation that reach back into a family of origin and beyond. A genogram provides the opportunity to look for emotional patterns in each partner's own extended family. As Magnuson and Shaw (2003) show, genograms can be used for couples and families with issues such as intimacy, grief, and alcoholism, and for identifying resources within the family. Diagrams, as well as genograms, can serve specific purposes in family therapy (Butler, 2008).

In the accompanying example, a small illustration of a family, including parents and children, is shown. In genograms, males are represented by squares and females by circles, and their current ages are noted inside the figures. The person who is the object of the genogram is indicated by a double circle or square. In this oversimplified example, the genogram is of a 45-year-old female whose husband is 46, whose two sons are 10 and 9, and whose daughter is 4 years old.

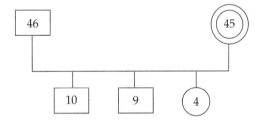

Interpretation. Information from genograms is often interpreted to family members so that they can understand dynamics within the family. By maintaining objectivity, the therapist is able to see patterns within the current family that reflect patterns in the family of origin. To do so, it is important that therapists themselves be well differentiated so that they ask thinking questions rather than feeling questions and avoid being drawn into triangles with their patients. One way that Bowen (1978) kept objective enough to make astute interpretations was by having the conversation directed to him rather than from one family member to another.

Detriangulation. When possible, Bowen tried to separate parts of a triangle directly. When dealing with family problems, he often saw the parents or one of the parents. He then worked with them on ways to develop strategies to deal with the impact of their own emotional stress on the identified patient or other family member. In general, Bowen preferred to work with the healthiest member of the family, the person who was most differentiated, so that that person could make changes in various stressful family relationships.

A hallmark of Bowen's work was the calm manner with which he tried to deal with the emotionality that exists between family members. His goal was to reduce anxiety as well as resolve symptoms, which he did by looking at self-differentiation not only within the individual and the family but also within the family of the parents. To do so he used tools such as a genogram and discussed the relationships that went beyond the nuclear family to aunts, uncles, and grandparents. An illustration of his approach will help demonstrate his method.

An Example of Intergenerational Family Systems Therapy: Ann's family

Two very important concepts in Bowen's theory are those of triangulation and multigenerational issues. In this example, Guerin and Guerin (1976) report the case of Catholic parents living in New York City with their three adopted children, two boys and a girl. The identified patient is the daughter, who the parents felt was acting inappropriately. Philip Guerin describes the family as a child-focused family. In his conceptualization of the case, different sets of triangles are important.

> Whenever I see a child-focused family, I automatically assume a set of four potential triangles: the central nuclear triangle of mother, father and symptomatic child; two auxiliary nuclear family triangles, one involving a parent, the symptomatic child, and an asymptomatic sibling, the other an intersibling triangle among three of the children; and finally a triangle over three generations involving a grandparent, a parent, and the symptomatic child. There are many other possibilities, but these are the most frequently encountered clinically. (p. 91)

For this family, both the family triangles and the fusion within the nuclear family and the families of origin are important. Guerin and Guerin (1976) see the relationship of fusion within the family and intergenerational issues in this way.

> As the marriage is worked on, and the marital fusion unfolds, the process inevitably involves a tie into the extended family. The interlocking character of the three generations comes into view. Pieces of all three of those generations must be worked on at different times, depending on what's going on in the present time frame with the family. Success and progress don't mean that the symptoms and the dysfunction just disappear; instead symptoms will reappear over time in all three generational levels of the family. (pp. 93–94)

Although the therapist has met with the parents by themselves, with just the daughter, and with the whole family, this excerpt of a session 6 months into therapy is only with the parents. The therapist comments on a three-generational triangulation that revolves around Ann's concern that her mother is playing favorites with her children. Guerin makes comments that encompass Ann, her mother, and each of Ann's children.

> *Ann:* Well, she'll ask how the children are, and I'll start to tell her. Then she gets to talk about things like she tells me how Richie is her favorite, and that she really can't help it, and then I ask her to please try and keep that to herself and not show it to the other two children. I don't think it's a good idea to have a favorite grandchild when you have three, and she knows that I definitely disapprove of something like that. (Ann begins to develop one aspect of the three-generational triangulation in this family.)
>
> *Dr. G:* Do you have some kind of principle that your kids should be equal in the eyes of their grandmother? (Therapist challenges Ann's position.)

Ann: But, you don't realize, it's not practical.

Dr. G: Are you trying to protect your kids from not being the favorite or from being the favorite?

Ann: Well, because I was the favorite in my house over my sister, and then I was faced with the same problem myself with the boys and Susan, and I kind of feel it's not a good thing. (The generational repeat surfaces.)

Dr. G: How is she going to go around pretending that Richard is not her favorite? (Therapist continues to challenge.)

Ann: Well, she said it Saturday night in front of him. I kind of appreciated it as something she has been feeling for a long time; and usually she sneaks it in without directly saying it. So Saturday night when she said it, I said, "Why?" She wants to take Richie to the ballet for Christmas, and she doesn't want to take the other two anyplace, and I won't let her do that because I don't feel it's fair. She hasn't taken any of them any place in eight years, and I know that they would really be hurt. So I suggested if you take one someplace that you take the other two too, not necessarily to the same thing, but that you follow up with Eddie and Susan some place. Then she takes Eddie into it and completely leaves Susan out. Then I go through the same thing nicely, you know, I really think it's better to take all three, some time at least. It doesn't have to be all the time.

Dr. G: What would happen if she took Richard, the kids would start complaining? (Therapist moves to concretize the process.)

Ann: Yes.

Dr. G: Eddie and Susan would start complaining that Richard is going on a trip with Grandmother, and she likes Richie better?

Ann: She told Richie that.

Dr. G: If they complain, tell them to go to your mother. Would they like that? (Therapist suggests surfacing the process in the family.) (Guerin & Guerin, 1976, pp. 105–106)

The therapist makes comments that deal with the three-generational triangles that exist in the family. By doing so, Ann is encouraged to think about the impact of her relationship with her mother and children rather than respond emotionally to her mother. The problem of "playing favorites with the three children" is discussed, and the mother is encouraged to question the triangles and to consider removing herself from the relationship between her mother and each of the children. Although this is only a small sample of dialogue, it illustrates triangulation and multigenerational issues that are important in Bowen's theory of family systems.

Structural Family Therapy

Structural therapy, developed by Salvador Minuchin, helps families by dealing with problems as they affect current interactions of family members. Of particular interest are boundaries between family members. Are members too close or too distant? What is the nature of relationships within the family? Therapeutic approaches emphasize changing the nature and intensity of relationships within the family both inside and outside the therapy session.

Concepts of Structural Family Therapy

How families operate as a system and their structure within the system are the focus of Minuchin's work (Bitter, 2009; Minuchin, 1974; Minuchin, Colapinto, & Minuchin, 2007). By attending to the organization of the family and the rules and guidelines family members use to make decisions, Minuchin forms an impression of the family. Although family members differ in the power they have in making decisions, the ways family members work together are indications of the degree of flexibility or rigidity within the family structure. Minuchin uses concepts such as boundaries, alignments, and coalitions to explain family systems.

Family structure. For Minuchin (1974), the structure of the family refers to the rules that have been developed over the years to determine who interacts with whom. Structures may be temporary or long-standing. For example, two older brothers may form a coalition against a younger sister for a short period of time or for several years. It is Minuchin's view that there should be a hierarchical structure within the family, with the parents having more power than the children and older children having more responsibilities than younger children. Parents take different roles; for example, one parent may be the disciplinarian, and the other may provide sympathy to the children. Eventually children learn the rules of the family about which parent behaves in what way and to which child. When new circumstances develop, such as one of the children going off to college, the family must be able to change to accommodate this event. Being aware of family rules, and thus the structure, is important for therapists in determining the best way to help dysfunctional families change. Within the family system are subsystems that also have their own rules.

Family subsystems. For a family to function well, members must work together to carry out functions. The most obvious subsystems are those of husband–wife, parents–children, and siblings. The purpose of the husband–wife or marital subsystem is to meet the changing needs of the two partners. The parental subsystem is usually a father–mother team but may also be a parent and/or another relative who is responsible for raising children. Although the same people may be in the marital subsystem and the parental subsystem, their roles are different, although overlapping. In sibling subsystems, children learn how to relate to their brothers or sisters and, in doing so, learn how to build coalitions and meet their own needs, as well as deal with parents. Other subsystems may develop, such as when the oldest child learns to make dinner for the family when the mother or father is drunk. Thus, a child–parent subsystem develops. Such alliances may arise depending on the roles, skills, and problems of the individual members. Who does what and with whom depends on boundaries that are not always clearly defined.

Boundary permeability. Both systems and subsystems have rules as to who can participate in interactions and how they can participate (Minuchin, 1974). These rules of interaction, or boundaries, vary as to how flexible they are. Permeability of boundaries describes the type of contact that members within family systems and subsystems have with each other. A highly permeable boundary would be found in enmeshed families, whereas nonpermeable or rigid boundaries would be found in disengaged families. For example, if a seventh-grade child who had previously been performing well in school brings a note home from a teacher saying that he is failing English, the child may be told by his father not to let this happen again, to change his behavior, and that there will be no further discussion of this issue. In this case, the boundaries are rigid and the family is relatively *disengaged* from the child. In an *enmeshed* family, the father, mother, brother, and sister may inquire about the child's grades. The siblings may tease, the father may be distressed, and the mother may check frequently during the week to see if the child is doing his homework. During dinner the parents may discuss this event with the entire family so that there is little separation between family members. In general, boundaries refer to how a family is organized and follows the rules; they do not address the issue of how family members work together or fail to work together.

Alignments and coalitions. In responding to crises or dealing with daily events, families may have typical ways that subsystems within the family react. *Alignments* refer to the ways that family members join with each other or oppose each other in dealing with an activity. *Coalitions* refer to alliances between family members against another family member. Sometimes they are flexible and sometimes they are fixed, such as when a mother and daughter work together to control a disruptive father. Minuchin uses the term *triangle* more specifically than does Bowen to describe a coalition in which "each parent demands that the child side with him against the other parent" (Minuchin, 1974, p. 102). Thus, power within the family shifts, depending upon alignments and coalitions.

In the family system, power refers to who makes the decisions and who carries out the decisions. Being able to influence decisions increases one's power. Thus, a child who aligns with the most powerful parent increases her own power. Because certain decisions are made by one parent and other decisions by the other parent, power shifts, depending on the family activity. In an enmeshed family, power is not clear, and children may ask one parent permission to do something, even if the other parent has said "no."

When the family's rules become inoperative, the family becomes dysfunctional. When boundaries become either too rigid or too permeable, families have difficulty operating as a system. If the family does not operate as a hierarchical unit, with parents being the primary decision makers and the older children having more responsibility than younger children, confusion and difficulty may result. Alignments within the family may be dysfunctional, such as parents who are arguing over money both asking the oldest child to agree with them (triangulation). Whereas Bowen was particularly interested in family function across generations, Minuchin is more concerned with the current structure of the family, especially as he sees it within the therapeutic transaction.

Goals of Structural Family Therapy

By making hypotheses about the structure of the family and the nature of the problem, structural family therapists can set goals for change (Aponte & Van Deusen, 1981). Working in the present with the current family structure, structural family therapists try to alter coalitions and alliances to bring about change in the family. They also work to establish boundaries within the family that are neither too rigid nor too flexible. By supporting the parental subsystem as the decision-making system that is responsible for the family, therapists work to help the family system use power in a way that functions well. The techniques that family therapists use to bring about these changes are active and highly attuned to family functioning.

Techniques of Structural Family Therapy

The structural approach to family therapy is to join with the family and to focus on current and present happenings. To do this, structural therapists may often use "maps" that provide a shorthand description of boundaries and subsystems as they have an impact on the family. By accommodating to family customs, the therapist can act like a member of the family to improve the understanding of family interactions and to gain acceptance. By having a family enact a problem in the treatment session, the therapist can experience the interactions within subsystems. Suggestions can then be made for changing the power structure and boundaries within the family. Bringing about change by increasing the intensity of interventions and reframing problems is among the approaches to therapeutic change that are described.

Family mapping. Whereas Bowen uses the genogram to show intergenerational patterns of relating, Minuchin uses diagrams to describe current ways that families relate. For example, the concept of boundaries is extremely important in structural therapy. Figure 14.2 shows lines that represent different types of boundaries within families. These symbols, along with others described by Minuchin (1974), allow the therapist to symbolically represent the organization of the family and determine which subsystems contribute most actively to a problem (Umbarger, 1983). Maps of family interaction allow therapists to better understand repeated dysfunctional behavior so that strategies for modification can be applied.

Accommodating and joining. To bring about change within a family, Minuchin (1974) believes that it is important to join a family system and accommodate to its way of interacting. By using the same type of language and telling amusing stories relevant to the family, he seeks to fit in. One example of joining the family is *mimesis*, which refers to imitating the style and content of a family's communications. For example, if an adolescent sprawls on his chair, the family therapist may do likewise. Similarly, structural therapists use tracking to follow and make use of symbols of family life. For example, if an enmeshed family uses the phrase "our life is an open book," a structural therapist may attend to issues in which family members are too deeply involved in each others' activities and may later make use of the "open book" metaphor as a way of helping families clarify their boundaries. By joining a family system, a structural therapist not only has a good understanding of the family's systemic operation but also is in a good position to make changes in it.

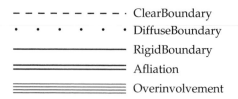

FIGURE 14.2   Minuchin's symbols for family mapping.

Reprinted by permission of the publishers from *Families and Family Therapy*, by Salvador Minuchin, pp. 53, 117–119, Cambridge, MA: Harvard University Press. Copyright © 1974 by the President and Fellows of Harvard College.

Enactment. By instructing the family to act out a conflict, the therapist can work with problems as they appear in the present rather than as they are reported. This allows the therapist to understand the family's coalitions and alliances and then to make suggestions for changing the family system. For example, the therapist may give specific instructions for the family to enact an argument about not doing homework. Having seen the argument enacted, the therapist is more aware of boundaries and coalitions and thus is prepared to make powerful interventions.

Intensity. How a suggestion or message is given is extremely important. By repeating the message, changing the length of time of a particular interaction, or other means, change can be facilitated (Minuchin & Fishman, 1981). For example, if parents are overprotective, the therapist may suggest that parents not nag the child about his homework, not ask as many questions about school, and not monitor how his allowance is spent. Although these messages differ, they all stress that the child be given more responsibility. Intensity can be achieved in enactment by having the family draw out an interaction or repeat it. As the therapist becomes familiar with the family's style of interacting and its boundaries, more suggestions for change develop.

Changing boundaries. As the therapist observes the family interacting either in an enactment or in general presentation, the therapist uses *boundary marking* to note boundaries in the family. To change boundaries, therapists may rearrange the seating of the family members and change the distance between them. They may also wish to unbalance the structure so that power within a subsystem changes. For example, in an enmeshed family, where children have too much power, the therapist may decide to side with one of the parents to give that person power in dealing with the child. If the husband is indecisive, the therapist may reinforce his suggestions and agree with him. It is the therapist's conscious choice as to which family member to agree with, affiliate with, or exclude from an interaction. In dealing with family systems, the therapist can also interpret events to change the power structure and mode of interaction within the family.

A creative way to address boundary issues is to use the Family Boundaries Game (Laninga, Sanders, & Greenwood, 2008). This is a life-size board game in which members of the family become game pieces, like a rook in chess. This game provides an opportunity for family members to learn their roles in the family and to follow rules in the family as well as take turns in their interaction with other family members. This game also promotes change in the family members and in their relationships to each other.

Reframing. There are several ways to see an event or situation or to reframe it. The therapist may wish to give a different explanation so that a constructive change can occur in a family situation. Writing about anorexia, Minuchin, Rosman, and Baker (1978) suggest a number of ways of reframing an anorectic girl's behavior. By labeling behavior as "stubborn" and not as "sick," the adolescent no longer is the sole source of the problem, as a family can deal with stubbornness in several ways, whereas "sickness" makes the problem the adolescent's and one that is out of her control. Because parents are likely to see anorexia as the child's problem, reframing allows the family therapist to present anorexia as a family problem that can be approached by changing subsystems, boundaries, and coalitions.

Example of Structural Family Therapy: Quest Family

In this example the therapist pays attention to the structure of the family and the family subsystems. The mother, Jane, is 43 and the father, Paul, is 45. Paul is a doctor of internal medicine and Jane takes care of the four children. Amy is 18 and Ann is 16. Paul and Jane took Jason, 6, and Luke, 4, into their home as foster children, as they had been badly abused by their father (Bitter, 2009). Later Jane and Paul decided to adopt Jason and Luke. Paul and Jane are seeking family therapy because of the boys' disruptive behavior. The boys have stolen food, clothes, and money from the family, fight each other a lot, and recently Jason tried to set Luke on fire. In this fictitious example, the therapist develops an alliance with the father in order to develop a stronger subsystem within the family that consists of the boys and Paul. He helps Paul become more active in the family. The therapist asks Paul rather than Jane to take care of the boys when they are fighting and he supports Paul's change of the boundaries. He observes the alliance between Paul and Jane and makes comments about their relationship. Later, he brings in the girls to talk about their father's role in the family, thus observing the family subsystem of Paul, Amy, and Ann. Also, the therapist has Ann and Amy talk to Jason and Luke to change the boundaries so that helpful changes in the boys' behavior are more likely to take place.

Amy and Ann sit together next to their father and across from the two empty chairs placed close to Jane for the boys. Jason and Luke are up and moving around. Addressing Paul first, the therapist begins the session.

> [Therapist:] You know, Paul, I think that Jane was used to raising little girls, and she probably knows a lot about that, but she seems almost lost when it comes to little boys.
>
> Paul: With these two boys, I think we all are lost. [therapist nods] Amy and Ann were pretty easy to raise.
>
> [Therapist:] Yes, but at least you know what it is like to be a boy, and you have some idea about how a father raises boys. Or do you? How was it for your father and you?
>
> Paul: Well, he was a surgeon with a large practice. My mother largely raised me. I admired my father when I was growing up, and I wanted to be like him, but I didn't really know a lot about him until I went to medical school.
>
> [Therapist:] So you are away from the house just like your father was. You know, Paul, I don't think that is going to work so well with these two boys. They seem to need a lot more attention—really, some direct care and input from you.
>
> Paul: You mean spend more time with them?
>
> [Therapist:] Yes, but also to teach them things and to help them learn how to handle life and difficulties in a new way. How was it for Jason and Luke before they came to live with you?
>
> Paul: Both of the boys were hurt a lot in some really awful ways. Some of what they do to each other and even to pets and other people, they had done to them. Jason likes to be the boss of Luke, and Luke sometimes goes along with it and sometimes not. Jason is very loud, and he will enforce his desires. Luke is quieter, and I often see him becoming a victim in relation to Jason. Jason doesn't like to be held or tucked in—not even a story or a

song at bedtime. These are things I used to always do with Amy and Ann. And yet, as much as Jason can sometimes push you away, he cannot stand to be alone. He always needs someone engaged with him.

Just as the therapist is about to ask another question, a small fight breaks out between the boys. Jane immediately gets up with the intention of making both of the boys sit down in the circle.

[*Therapist:*] Jane, I wonder if you would let Paul handle this. I would like to see how it goes. (Jane slowly sits back down.)

Paul asks Amy and Ann if they would mind sitting by their mother. Without speaking, both of the young women move. Paul gets up and takes each boy by the arm and directs them to chairs next to him. In a voice that seems calm but controlled and quite firm, Paul says, "Sit there and don't move." The boys quiet down almost immediately and sit there, looking at each other, then their Dad, and then back at each other.

[*Therapist:*] How did that go?

Jane: It won't last.

[*Therapist:*] Nothing lasts. But, Paul, how was that for you? (Paul stays silent.) Did you notice that they seemed to listen to you and do as you asked?

Paul: Jane's right. It won't last.

[*Therapist:*] Maybe not. But something needed to happen, and you got it to happen.... I am wondering if you and Jane could have a talk about what things Jason and Luke need to learn, what they need to handle, and which of you might be best able to get these essential messages across to them.

Paul and Jane identify a number of concerns from the boys' use of violence to resolve conflict to the special needs they will have related to education. Paul mentions sports, fishing, and camping. Jane wants music lessons for the boys—perhaps the violin. Paul suggests taking them to work with him occasionally. Jane is interested in developing a love of the arts (museums, galleries, etc.). Both parents think Jason and Luke should take part in the work of the household, but Paul means working out in the yard and Jane means cleaning their rooms and the bathroom.

The sequences of their conversation seem to follow a fixed pattern: Paul suggests something he feels is important for the boys' growth and development or to bring them into the family more fully. Jane acknowledges what he says, but then immediately advances an idea of her own—almost as a substitute for what Paul is suggesting. Paul starts to speak, and then Jane makes reference to what they always did with the girls. "And it worked." Paul then falls silent for a while before bringing up another possibility or responding to Jane's ideas.

[*Therapist:*] I think the way this conversation is going, Jane, that there must be a right way to help Jason and Luke, and Paul does not seem to know what it is unless you guide him?

Jane: I just want him to be more involved with the boys.

[*Therapist:*] Probably won't happen if none of the things he wants to do with them is considered acceptable. Why don't you like his ideas?

Jane: There's just so much to be done, and what he wants seems more like ... well, play.

[Therapist:] I don't know if that's true. It's like I was saying before: I think you know a lot about raising Ann and Amy. You did a nice job with them, but boys are harder. They need something different, maybe something that only Paul can give them, like how to be a gentle, caring man in the company of both women and other men.

Jane: So you're saying that taking them to baseball games or fishing or to work with him is enough?

[Therapist:] It may not be enough, but it's a good start. (turning to Paul) Tell me again what it was like for you with your father. Did you go to baseball games or fishing?

Paul: Not much. My father was very busy. But I always wanted to go. And when he said that we could go, I would get very excited—even though most of the time, he would have to cancel. I would be very disappointed, but I tried to understand. He did important work.

[Therapist:] So do I understand that you would not want to disappoint Jason or Luke?

Paul: That's right. If I say I am going to do something with them, I would make sure I showed up for it.

[Therapist:] I don't know, but that sounds pretty important to me too. (turning to Jane) What was it like for you, Jane, with your mother and father?

Jane: My mother ran everything. My father was a beat cop. He was a good one, well respected, but when he came home, he was always tired. He wanted to read the paper or watch TV. It was Mom who made sure that we had music lessons, were exposed to the arts, and took part in after-school activities. She signed us up, and she got us there.

[Therapist:] How was your father with your brother?

Jane: They didn't have much of a relationship. Dad would help Joey whenever he could, but Joey was clearly Mom's favorite, and she let him get away with everything. He's really pampered—even to this day.

[Therapist:] So you're not exactly sure what it looks like when a man gets involved in raising his sons.

Jane: No. I guess not.

[Therapist:] Amy, I am wondering what it was like when you were younger? Did your mother make space for you and Ann to have time with your Dad or did you, too, have to raise a ruckus to get him to spend time with you?

Amy: I think we had time with Dad—not as much time as we had with Mom, of course—but we had time. Ann would often fix him breakfast in bed, and they would sit and talk. And he would always read to us before bed at night. He took us fishing once and to a ball game or two, but we really weren't into that.

Ann: What I remember most is the vacations we would take. Sometimes, we would camp out, but a lot of the times it was these long car trips to see national monuments or historic sites. Dad knew a lot about different places and history. And Mom would have us all singing in the car or playing car games.

The therapist asks Amy and Ann if they would have a conversation with Jason and Luke about what their childhood was like, to sort of catch the boys up and let them know ways in which they could all be happier together. The therapist asks Amy and Ann: "What, for example, do the two of you know that might help a 6- and a 4-year-old boy find places in the family?" For some time, Amy and Ann talk with Jason while Luke listens. Occasionally, Jane wants to interject something, but the therapist holds up her hand and keeps the conversation among the four children. Amy and Ann talk about very concrete things they used to do when they were young children—each individually with different parents and in pairs or as a family. As they talk, they start to sound both nostalgic and excited. Ann often asks, "Is that something you would like to do too?" Jason almost always responds in the affirmative with Luke nodding. A different kind of connection is forming (Bitter, 2009, pp. 179–181).

Strategic Therapy

JAY HALEY

Concerned with treating symptoms that families present, Haley (1923–2007) takes responsibility for what occurs in treatment and designs approaches for solving family problems. By focusing on the problem, strategic therapists design the best way to reach the family's goals. In developing his approach, Jay Haley was influenced by Milton Erickson (Haley, 1973), who was known for his use of hypnotic and paradoxical techniques. At the Mental Research Institute (MRI) in Palo Alto, California, Haley, with Don Jackson and John Weakland, emphasized problem solution rather than insight as a goal of therapy. Additionally, Haley's work with Minuchin was important in developing a theoretical approach to family systems. Although Haley's theory of family systems is not as developed as Minuchin's, his approach to treatment as described in detail in his writings (Haley, 1963, 1971a, 1971b, 1973, 1976, 1979, 1984, 1996; Haley & Richeport-Haley, 2007) is the focus of this section.

Concepts of Strategic Therapy

Like Minuchin, Haley observes the interaction among family members, attending particularly to power relationships and to the ways parents deal with power. Viewing relationships as power struggles, Haley (1976) is interested in understanding how relationships are defined. Thus, a communication from one person to another is an act that defines the relationship (Haley, 1963). When a mother says to her son, "Your room is messy," she is not only reporting on the state of the room but also commanding the son to clean it up. If the son does not clean up the room, he is engaging in a power struggle with his mother. Important to Haley, as well as to Minuchin, is the concept of hierarchy, in which the parents are in a superior position to the children in terms of making decisions and adhering to family responsibilities. Like Minuchin, he is concerned with family triangles such as those in which one parent is overinvolved with the child and the other is underinvolved.

What separates structural from strategic approaches is the attention given by strategic family therapists to symptoms. For Haley, symptoms are an unacknowledged way of communicating within the family system, usually when there is no other solution to a problem. For strategic therapists, the symptom is often a metaphor (Madanes, 1981) for a way of feeling or behaving within the family.

Contained in a metaphorical message are an explicit element (such as "my stomach hurts") and an implicit element ("I feel neglected"; Brown & Christensen, 1999). For example, the child who says "I have a stomach ache" may be communicating pain that his mother feels in an interaction with her husband. In listening to a symptom being described, strategic therapists look for the message being communicated as a metaphor of the symptom. They recognize that the symptom may be an ineffective attempt to solve the problem.

Goals

Consistent with the emphasis on working with the system is the value placed on choosing goals (Keim, 2000). Although the therapist may ask family members why they have come and what they want to accomplish, the therapist ultimately decides on the goal. Such goals may be intermediate as well as final and must be concrete and not vague. The goal to reduce anxiety must be stated in such a way that the therapist knows which family members are experiencing anxiety, in what way, and in which situations. There must be sufficient information so that therapists can plan strategies to reach goals. For example, if a daughter is anxious because her completion of chores at home is met by criticism from her parents, the therapist might have an intermediate goal of having just the father make requests, and later have another intermediate goal of having the mother and father agree on the chores they want their daughter to do. For each goal, specific methods for accomplishing them are designed by the therapist. In recent years, strategic therapy has focused more on helping family members show love and caring in interventions and less on power in the family relationships (Keim, 2000; Nichols, 2008).

Techniques of Strategic Family Therapy

Because the presenting problem is the focus of strategic therapy, tasks to alleviate the problem or symptom are its cornerstone. Having family members complete tasks is important for three reasons (Haley, 1976). First, tasks change the way people respond in therapy. Second, because therapists design the task, their role is important, and they likely to be listened to. Third, whether or not tasks are completed, information about the family is obtained. When working with a task, strategic family therapists must select ones that are appropriate to the family, design them, and help the family complete them (Haley, 1976, 1984; Haley & Richeport-Haley, 2007). Generally, tasks are of two types: straightforward tasks, where the therapist makes directions and suggestions to the family, and paradoxical tasks for families that may resist change.

Straightforward tasks. When strategic family therapists judge that the family they are trying to help is likely to comply with their suggestions, they may assign a straightforward task. By talking with the family and observing family boundaries and subsystems, the therapist will be able to help the family accomplish its goals (Madanes, 1981). Sometimes suggestions can consist of relatively simple advice to families, but more often families require suggestions to change a variety of ways members interact with each other (Papp, 1980). Just because tasks are assigned does not mean that each member of the family will be cooperative.

To gain cooperation from family members, Haley (1976) suggests several ways to ensure they complete tasks. Before suggesting tasks, therapists should explore what the family has done to solve the problem so they do not make suggestions that have been tried and failed. By examining what happens if the problem is not solved, then, family members are more likely to appreciate the importance of doing something about the problem. When tasks are assigned, they should be relatively easy to accomplish, clearly explained, and fit the ability level of the children as well as the adults who will complete the task. In strategic family therapy, the therapist is clearly the expert, and she may make use of her status as the expert to get the family to comply with her instructions. Designing tasks, particularly metaphorical tasks, takes experience and confidence.

Because tasks are designed for each unique situation, general guidelines are insufficient for developing tasks. Some of the unique features of straightforward directives can be seen in these examples from Brown and Christensen (1999):

> A peripheral father and his daughter were asked to do something that the mother would not be interested in, thus reducing the likelihood of the mother's interference.
>
> A conflictual couple was asked to return to a place, such as a restaurant or park, that had been pleasant during their courting period. The focus on positive experiences can change the affect of the relationship.
>
> Parents who had concerns about a local mall frequented by their daughter were asked to visit the mall and see for themselves what it was like. (pp. 93–94)

Sometimes therapists give a family a task that is a metaphor for the way the therapist believes members need to behave in order to alleviate the symptom. In such cases, family members are not aware of the purpose of the tasks. Sometimes tasks can be given to solve relatively simple problems that are a metaphor for much more difficult and complex problems. In the following example, Brown and Christensen (1999) tell how helping a daughter stop writing bad checks can be a task that deals with improving the relationship between mother and daughter while increasing the daughter's independence.

> Take, for example, the case of a depressed 19-year-old brought into treatment because she did nothing but sit around the house and cry. Learning that the girl had been sexually abused by her father several years earlier, the therapist redefined the girl's depression as anger toward her mother. The therapist believed that the anger was there because the mother had allowed (by not stopping it) the abuse of the daughter. The anger (rage) was never expressed because it was so volatile and explosive that the daughter feared losing her mother completely. The daughter and mother were far too over-involved with each other. The mother admitted that she needed her daughter and did not want her to leave home. The daughter resented her mother's wish but did nothing to change it because she was afraid that any disagreement would end in an explosion of the relationship. Although neither would discuss these issues with the other, the mother complained that her daughter would write bad checks on the mother's account. While the therapist chose not to deal directly with the problems of incest and leaving home, the issue of bad checks could be dealt with as a metaphor for the more serious issues because all the same dynamics were present. The therapist got the mother and daughter to argue about the checks as a metaphor for those other issues. At the end of the discussion, the therapist directed the daughter to get a separate account and directed the mother not to pay the daughter's bills. (Brown & Christensen, 1999, pp. 94–95)

By assigning metaphorical tasks, the therapist was able to help the daughter develop autonomy through her responsibility for her own checking account and to decrease hostility between mother and daughter by reducing the mother's over-involvement in the daughter's activities. By successfully completing this task, other tasks involved in separation issues between mother and daughter may be more easily resolved in the future. Sometimes, however, straightforward tasks, whether they are metaphorical or direct, may not be sufficient to bring about change.

Paradoxical tasks. Basically, paradoxical suggestions are those that ask the family to continue the behavior for which they are requesting help, but in such a way that whether they comply or not, positive change will result. In a sense, the therapist is trying to get the family to decide not to do what they have been asked to do. Families are often confused by why the therapist is not asking them to change. Use of paradoxical directives takes experience and confidence on the part of the therapist, and they are used only when the family resists straightforward suggestions.

Weeks and L'Abate (1982) discuss several types of family behavior that may be appropriate for paradoxical interventions. When family members fight among themselves, argue, or contradict each other's statements, they may not be providing sufficient support for the use of straightforward tasks, or parents may not be sufficiently responsible to help children carry them out. When children and adolescents challenge or do not listen to their parents, it may be difficult for parents to make use of straightforward suggestions.

In describing the use of paradoxical tasks, Papp (1980, 1984) has suggested three steps: redefining, prescribing, and restraining. The first step is to redefine the symptom in terms of the benefits it provides for the family. As Goldenberg and Goldenberg (2008) suggest, anger can be called love, suffering can be seen as self-sacrifice, and distancing can be used as a way of reinforcing closeness. In prescribing the symptom, the family is encouraged to continue what they have been doing because if they do not there will be a loss of benefits to the family. Thus, an angry child may be asked to continue to be angry and throw tantrums. In prescribing the symptom, the therapist must be clear and sincere in the rationale. When the family starts to show improvement, the therapist tries to restrain the growth or change in order to keep the paradox working. For example, a couple who argue frequently and has been told to argue over kitchen chores may report that they are fighting less. Rather than reinforce the change, the strategic family therapist may caution the couple to be careful; otherwise, one or the other might lose the powerful position relative to the other. In doing this, the therapist never takes credit for the change or acts sarcastically. Throughout the process of using paradoxical tasks, the therapist shows concern for the family and, when change occurs, may express surprise but also hope that change can take place.

Because paradoxical tasks are by their very nature confusing, a few examples of tasks that Brown and Christensen (1999) have used in their work will serve as illustrations.

> A fiercely independent single parent who is reluctant to give her son more autonomy was asked to do even more for him, lest she experience the anxiety of being on her own.
>
> A wife who tried to leave her husband but couldn't was urged to stay with her husband because he needed someone to take care of him.
>
> A couple whose only contact occurred when they argued were to increase their bickering so that they would be closer to each other. (pp. 98–99)

Although these examples describe paradoxical tasks, they do not explain the process of using them in therapy. A more complete example shows how a therapist incorporates paradoxical tasks into therapy.

An Example of Strategic Therapy: Boy Who Set Fires

In this example of helping a family consisting of a mother and five children, Madanes (1981) makes use of a paradoxical intervention, for the mother is concerned because her 10-year-old son is setting fires. As shown in the third paragraph, Madanes sees the boy's behavior metaphorically. By setting fires, he helps his mother by making her feel angry instead of depressed. In prescribing the task, Madanes changes the relationship between mother and son so that the boy can help her because he is an expert on fires.

> A mother consulted because her 10-year-old son was setting fires. He was a twin and the oldest of five children. The family had many other serious problems. The father had just left them and moved to another city. The mother was not receiving any financial support from him. She was Puerto Rican, did not speak English, and did not know how to go about obtaining the help she needed. The mother would not leave the boy alone for a minute for fear that he would set the house on fire.
>
> In the first interview, the therapist gave the boy some matches and told him to light one and asked the mother to do whatever she usually did at home when she caught him lighting a match. The therapist then left the room to observe from behind the one-way mirror. The boy reluctantly lighted a match, and the mother took it and burned him with it.
>
> By providing a focus for her anger, the boy was helping his mother. He was someone whom she could punish and blame. He made her feel angry instead of depressed and in this way helped her to pull herself together in spite of all her troubles.
>
> The therapist told the child that she was going to teach him how to light matches properly. She then showed him how one closes the match box before lighting the match and how, after the match burns, one carefully puts it in the ashtray. She then asked the mother to light a fire with some papers in an ashtray and to pretend to burn herself. The son had to help her by putting out the fire with some water that the therapist had brought into the office for this purpose. The boy had to show his mother that he knew how to put out fires correctly. As all this was going on, the other children were allowed to look but not to participate in any other way. After the fire was put out, the therapist told the boy that he now knew how to light fires and to put them out correctly. She emphasized to the mother that now she could trust him because he knew about fires. The therapist then asked the mother to set aside a time every evening for a week when she would get together with the boy and she would light a fire and pretend to burn herself and he would help her to put it out. The other children were only allowed to participate as spectators.
>
> The interaction between mother and son was changed so that, instead of helping his mother by providing a focus for her anger, the son was helping her in a playful way when she pretended to burn herself. Before, the boy had been helping the mother by threatening her with fires. Now he was helping her because he was an expert on fires. Before the therapy, the child had been special in the family because he was setting fires; after the therapeutic intervention, he was special because he was an expert on fires. When the boy was unpredictably lighting fires, he was in a superior position to the mother. When he set fires under direction, he was beneath her in the hierarchy. (Madanes, 1981, pp. 84–85)

In following up the family, Madanes reports that the boy stopped lighting fires after this session. In later sessions, Madanes discussed different ways of putting out fires with the boy and told his mother that he should be allowed the privilege of lighting fires, a privilege the other children did not have. Other family therapists have taken somewhat different approaches to deal with juvenile firestarting (Barreto, Boekamp, Armstrong, & Gillen, 2004).

Each strategic family therapy intervention is different, depending on the therapist's observations of the family structure. Interventions, whether they are straightforward or paradoxical, are thought out clearly and carefully. When therapists first start to use such interventions, it is suggested that they do so under supervision so that they can discuss their observations of family power struggles and coalitions.

Experiential and Humanistic Family Therapies

Both experiential and humanistic family therapists see dysfunctional behavior as the result of interference with personal growth. For families to grow, communication between family members and self-expression of individuals must both be open, while appreciating the uniqueness and differences between family members. In setting goals for therapy, both therapist and the family take responsibility (Goldenberg & Goldenberg, 2008). This section briefly describes the experiential approach of Carl Whitaker and the humanistic approach of Virginia Satir. Although both therapists contributed to the development of family therapy over a period of more than 40 years, their work is somewhat idiosyncratic and their theoretical approaches are not articulated as well as the other theories presented in this chapter.

The Experiential Therapy of Carl Whitaker

Carl Whitaker (1912–1995) saw theory as a hindrance in clinical work and preferred an intuitive approach, using the therapist's own resources. Characteristic of his approach is the use of countertransference (his own reactions to clients). Not only do clients grow and change in therapy; so do therapists. Because clients and therapists affect each other, each takes on the role of patient and therapist at various moments in therapy. This interaction fosters the goal of interpersonal growth among family members (and therapists).

In his intuitive approach to families, Whitaker (1976) listened for impulses and symbols of unconscious behavior. Sometimes he responded consciously to feelings or family members' ways of relating; at other times he would be unaware of why he was responding the way he was. Relating symbolically, he often suggested clients fantasize about an experience. This may lead to understanding the absurdity of a situation. Situations are viewed in ways that emphasize choice and experience rather than sickness or pathology.

Whitaker's insight into family processes can be seen when he spoke to a 16-year-old girl who just concluded an angry and tearful interaction with her father. He had just tried to set limits on her behaviors, such as when she comes home too late at night. In this situation, Whitaker (Napier & Whitaker, 1978) acted spontaneously to address issues of which the girl is unaware.

Carl: "What I thought threw you, pushed you so hard, was your father's *painful reasonableness.* You were mocking him, remember?" Claudia nodded slightly. "And I thought you were doing it to avoid crying or to get your old man to come out of hiding and react to you in some way." Carl shifted slightly in his chair, leaning forward. His unlit pipe was balanced carefully in his hand, and the hand was resting on his knee. "But what your dad did was give you a lecture about how he was your father and how you had to obey the rules of the house. He had lots of very real feelings, but he kept them all covered. I think that was what threw you, that he wouldn't admit what he was feeling, that he kept trying to be reasonable, trying to be a father rather than a person." Then Carl paused, and Claudia waited for him to finish. Finally: "It was the process of Dad's *destroying his own feelings*, his own personhood, that I thought got you so upset. And it was appropriate for you to get upset. I think it's a very serious problem." (pp. 69–70)

Whitaker's response to Claudia reflected his attention to the entire family and the impact of father and daughter on each other. He saw their relationship in ways that Claudia did not. Although Whitaker's approach is spontaneous, it is also structured.

Whitaker and Keith (1981) described the beginning, middle, and ending phases of therapy. In the beginning phase, there is a battle for taking initiative in developing a structure, such as determining who is going to be present at the therapy sessions. In the middle phase, Whitaker worked actively on family issues, bringing in extended family when appropriate. To bring about change, he used confrontation, exaggeration, or absurdity. When he picked up an absurdity in the patient, he built upon it until the patient recognized it and could change her approach. The ending phase of therapy deals with separation anxiety on the part of the family (and therapist) and the gradual disentanglement from each other's lives. Throughout the therapeutic process, Whitaker's style was marked by energy, involvement, and creativity. His approach is described in detail by Connell, Mitten, and Bumberry (1999).

The Humanistic Approach of Virginia Satir

Known for her creativity and warmth, Virginia Satir (1916–1988) attended to the feelings of family members and worked with them on day-to-day functioning and their own emotional experiences in the family. With individuals and families, she focused on developing a sense of strength and self-worth and bringing flexibility into family situations to initiate change (McLendon, 2000; Nichols, 2008). Noted for her communication skills, Satir worked on helping family members develop theirs. An example is her outline for effective communication within the family (Satir, 1972): Use the first person and express what you feel; use "I" statements that indicate the taking of responsibility, such as "I feel angry"; family members must level with each other; and one's facial expression, body position, and voice should match.

One of Satir's contributions to family communications was the identification of five styles of relating within the family (Satir, 1972): the *placater*, weak and tentative, always agreeing; the *blamer*, finding fault with others; the *superreasonable*, detached, calm, and unemotional; the *irrelevant*, distracting others and not relating to family processes; and the *congruent communicator*, genuinely expressive, real, and open. Satir's emphasis on communication style influenced her selection of therapeutic interventions.

From the beginning of her work, Satir always met with the entire family, helping them to feel better about themselves and each other. One approach was a *family life chronology* in which the history of the family's development was recorded. This chronology included how spouses met, how they saw themselves in relationship with their siblings, and their expectations of parenting. The children were also included and asked to contribute by saying how they saw their parents and family activities. This information, as well as her observations about the imbalances within the family system, helped her attend to blockages in the system and intervene in ways that would facilitate each family member's growth. One way to accomplish this was *family reconstruction*, an experiential approach including guided fantasy, hypnosis, psychodrama, and role playing. Additionally, she used *family sculpting*, in which family members were physically molded into characteristic poses representing a view of family relationships. Using these methods, she would have a family enact events in the family's life.

A glimpse into Satir's concern and caring about family members can be seen in this interaction with Coby, the middle child and only boy of five children. A brief dialogue with Coby is followed by Satir's explanation of her own experience at the time, illustrating her compassion and her attention to feelings within the family.

> *Virginia:* Let me see now if I hear you. That if your father—if I'm hearing this—some way that he brings out his thought…. He gets over-angry, you feel, or something like that?
>
> *Coby:* Yes, ma'am.
>
> *Virginia:* Some way—and you're saying if he could find some way to treat that differently—is that what you hope for?
>
> *Coby:* Well, yes, ma'am, but you know, he loses his temper too easy.
>
> *Virginia:* I see.
>
> *Coby:* If he can hold it back and try to talk to us instead of yelling and screaming and everything.
>
> *Virginia:* I see. So sometimes you think your father thinks you do something, and then you don't do it, and then you don't know how to tell him or he doesn't hear you, or something like that? Is that what you're saying? (Satir & Baldwin, 1983, pp. 34–36)

Satir describes her observations of her response to Coby. She responds to both his verbal and nonverbal messages. Her empathy for the boy and his relationship with his father typifies Satir's sensitive response to families.

> Here I was aware of the love this child had for his father. And that said to me that if a father could inspire that kind of love, there was also much gentleness underneath and that what must be coming off was his defense against feeling that he didn't count. I saw all of that in this little interchange. Listening to Coby, I also knew that he would not take the risk of talking the way he did so quickly if there wasn't some leeway for the rule of freedom to comment. And he also told me that his father was not always angry, and that there was a whimsical quality to his anger. This reinforced for me the feeling that the father was struggling for power and that he was often unaware of what he was doing. He wanted to be the head of the family but he wasn't and felt weak. (Satir & Baldwin, 1983, p. 35)

Therapists who trained with Satir were often deeply affected by her humanistic approach, which emphasized individual growth and self-worth. Although she died in 1988, her work continues to have an impact on many family therapists.

Integrative Approaches to Family Systems Therapy

The current practice of family therapy reflects a creative approach on the part of family therapists who integrate transgenerational, structural, strategic, experiential, and many other family therapies. As McDaniel, Lusterman, and

Philpot (2001) show, the majority of family therapists make use of more than one theory. Although this chapter has covered four approaches to family therapy, there are others as well, such as brief family therapy, illustrated in the next section. Additionally, each theory described in this book (with the exception of Jungian psychotherapy) has been adapted to families, as will be shown in an upcoming section.

Because many therapists come to family therapy after having been trained as individual therapists, they are likely to combine their training with family systems therapy. Often the approaches they use are influenced by their own personalities and the patient population they work with, as well as their prior training. For example, social workers who must do crisis intervention are likely to use briefer techniques such as strategic therapy rather than psychoanalytic or transgenerational approaches. Therapists often find that they cannot always work with the family system or even a family subsystem. At times they may need to work with the patient alone, a view recognized by many theories of family therapy (Nichols, 2008).

Integrative approaches to family therapy are becoming increasingly common, and several therapists have described ways they incorporate various approaches. Several reasons for this integrative trend can be identified (Lebow, 1997). Distinctions between individual and family therapy are less definitive. Therapists may mix individual, couple, and family sessions in treatment. There is currently a greater focus on use of concepts rather than theory. Thus, "differentiation" (Bowen), "enactment" (Minuchin), and genograms may be used by therapists of many orientations. Also, as integrative approaches emerge, no single one dominates. As will be shown in the research section, research does not support one approach more than others. Typically, integrative approaches are theoretically sound in that a rationale is given for using combinations of theories of family therapies.

Theories of Individual Therapy as Applied to Family Therapy

Proponents of each theory covered in this text so far have applied its approach to couples and families. The exception is Jungian therapists, who occasionally do couples counseling but rarely apply their work to families, as they tend to focus on individuals becoming more individuated. In the following paragraphs, I will provide a summary of how each theory approaches personality and therapeutic change to help families. I will not introduce new concepts but rather show how the theory tends to work with families.

Psychoanalysis

The work of Nathan Ackerman, discussed on page 535, continues to have an impact on the practice of psychoanalytic family therapy. His theoretical orientation is that of drive and ego theory combined with an active and a confrontive approach to families. Currently, the object relations point of view has great influence in psychoanalytic work with families. Object relations family therapists make observations about the nurturing or caring that family members provide for each other. They provide a safe environment so that family members can deal with issues that are hurtful. Often object relations family therapists attend to concerns that involve attachment and separation from the parents. Interpreting past behavior and therapeutic resistance is often a part of the repertoire of psychoanalytic family therapists.

Adlerian Therapy

Adlerians have always valued family therapy. In fact, Alfred Adler had conducted 32 child-guidance clinics in Vienna before leaving for the United States. Often, Adlerians take an educational point of view, teaching parents how to deal with difficulties at home. Sometimes this is done in one or two sessions. For example, they may suggest that parents give information to a child, observe how the child acts, and then allow the child to receive the consequences of the behavior. With conflict within the family, members are taught to resolve conflicts by developing mutual respect for each other, pinpointing the issue, and reaching agreement on how to handle the problem. Such practical approaches are typical of Adlerian family therapy.

Existential Therapy

In existential family therapy, therapists focus not only on the relationship between individuals but also on the awareness that individuals have of themselves and their own being in the world. In work with couples, existential therapists may ask partners to take turns at being the observer in a session so that they can become more aware of their partner's inner world and their own. Another approach would be to ask each partner to keep a secret diary during the course of therapy to make entries about the private world of each member of the couple. A similar approach can be applied in family therapy with older children.

Person-Centered Therapy

As in individual therapy, empathy is a central component of person-centered family therapy. Therapists try to understand, at the deepest possible level, the conflict between family members. Family therapists may empathize not only with individual members of the family but also with the relationship issues at hand. When not all family members are present for a session, the therapist could also be empathic with an absent family member. An example of this is "I understand how you might be disappointed in Martha for not listening to you, but I wonder if she were with us now, if she might feel that she didn't have an opportunity to respond."

Gestalt Therapy

As in individual therapy, gestalt family therapists are quite active. They observe how individuals in the family cause boundary disturbances for each other. The focus is very much on the present, using techniques described in Chapter 7. Gestalt family therapists help individuals in the family become aware of their patterns of interactions. Often family members are unaware of their own needs and the needs of other family members. Gestalt family therapists often comment on relationships within the family and the therapist's relationship with the family. They may focus on sensations, listening, watching, or touching to achieve the awareness of boundaries so that appropriate separation and integration can be achieved.

Behavior Therapy

A popular behavioral approach is that of behavioral parent training. In this method, parents apply behavioral and experimental methods to change the behavior of the identified patient. They may first establish a baseline of the child's behavior they wish to change in order to determine its nature and frequency. When the behavior has been observed and measured, parents try behavioral techniques they have been taught by the therapist. For example, a child who screams excessively may be given privileges, such as watching a television program after the usual bedtime, if screaming behavior decreases. This contract can be negotiated, and progress on it can be recorded. In general, parents learn how to make a careful and detailed assessment of the problem and then use specific strategies to modify the contingencies of reinforcement in their child or children.

Rational Emotive Behavior Therapy

The goals of REBT for families are to help members see that they disturb themselves by their irrational beliefs. By learning about their irrational beliefs and giving them up, family members find that they can still have their wishes, preferences, and desires. Family members are taught techniques similar to those taught to individual clients. These techniques follow the A-B-C-D-E therapeutic approach: A (activating event), B (beliefs), C (consequences), D (disputing), E (effect). The therapist uses disputing and a variety of other cognitive and behavioral techniques to help families deal with crises and situations that occur in the present and could occur in the future. Ellis believed that each family member is responsible for his or her own actions and should assume that responsibility. REBT therapists take a teaching focus, emphasizing principles of nondisturbance and self-help that can be applied to families. Therapists often use disputing of *shoulds* and *musts* more than other family therapists using different theories.

Cognitive Therapy

Education is a significant part of cognitive family therapy. Cognitive family therapists often assess individuals' cognitive distortions. They attend to the automatic thoughts and cognitive schemas of individuals so that they can make therapeutic interventions. They may suggest changing distorted beliefs such as "My husband can't do a thing right with the children" to an alternate version, such as "My husband doesn't talk to the children when he arrives home." In this way, beliefs are changed from blaming or hurtful to descriptive. Frequently, therapists may have to deal with anger and other disruptive emotions before they can make such interventions. A common distortion in families is that of mind reading, in which family members may make comments such as "You're late just because you knew that it would make me angry." Therapists challenge mind reading by showing, for example, that there can be a number of reasons for being late. Although such interventions are made in therapy, many suggestions can be made to each family member about what to do outside of the session to bring about family change.

Reality Therapy

In recent years, marriage counseling and family therapy have become a particular interest of William Glasser. Reality therapists often observe the choice systems of different family members and how they interact and connect with each other. Attention is paid not just to the shared feelings but also to the wants and values of each family member. After an assessment of wants and needs, suggestions are made to focus on doing things together to promote family harmony. However, reality therapists also recognize the need for family members to develop their life separately from other members of the family. Reality family therapists may ask the child what activities she likes and how much of the activity she is doing. This way, reality family therapists can assess how well the family relationship is meeting the child's needs. Suggestions may be made to do activities that bring about interaction. For example, a father walking to the park with a daughter is a better activity than watching television together. Attention is paid to activities the family does as a group, as small groups, and separately so that these activities will meet needs of family members separately and together.

Feminist Therapy

Family therapy is a very important area of study for feminist therapists, as indicated by the publication of the *Journal of Feminist Family Therapy*. The approach is not on how to help the unfortunate woman who has been mistreated by a "bad" man. Rather, feminist therapists look at political and social factors that provide insight into how family members react to each other. The focus is not on attaching blame or rescuing people but on how gender and power issues affect clients. Feminist therapists are aware of how their own gender can affect their work with different family members, depending on their gender-role expectations and stereotypes. Information may be given about gender role, language usage, and other related activities. Feminist therapists also attend to issues of cultural and racial identity. They may integrate gender-role and power interventions with other theoretical approaches.

Approaches to family therapy are often quite different from each other. Psychoanalytic family therapists may emphasize early relationships of both children and parents in their work. Adlerians may focus on relationships of siblings and family members as well as the need to educate. In contrast, existential therapists focus on knowing oneself and being self-aware. Person-centered therapists are empathic with their clients, while gestalt therapists attend to events happening in the therapeutic hour and are likely to use enactment activities. More structured in approach are behavioral, rational emotive behavioral, and cognitive therapists, whose assessments may be quite systematic along with their interventions into the behaviors and thoughts of families. Although emphasizing doing, as behavior therapists do, reality therapists focus on meeting individual needs and wants and on the different choices that family members make. In contrast to all of these approaches, feminist family therapists look at the impact of society on the family and the internalization of gender and power roles. None of these approaches examines the family as a system in the way that Bowen, Minuchin, Haley, Whitaker, and Satir do. These therapists focus more on the family as one system than as a group of individuals. Brief family therapists also see the family as a system, but they may conduct fewer sessions than other family systems therapists and their interventions may be quite unusual or powerful.

Brief Family Systems Therapy

By attempting to make interventions in a short period of time, innovators of brief family systems therapy have developed approaches that are practical, clear as to method, and related to the presenting problem. However, they desire to produce not just temporary change in the family to solve a pressing problem, *first-order change*, but a lasting change in the family system, *second-order change*. Because these approaches use powerful interventions, they often use therapy teams, some members of which observe behind a one-way mirror and may enter the therapy room, on occasion, or confer with the therapist during a break in the session. Two of these brief approaches are described here: the Brief Therapy Project at the Mental Research Institute in Palo Alto, which has been involved in training, theory development, and research since 1967; and the long brief therapy approach based in Milan, Italy.

The Mental Research Institute Brief Family Therapy Model

Based in part on the work of Gregory Bateson, Don Jackson, Jay Haley, and Milton Erickson, the Mental Research Institute (MRI) approach to brief therapy emphasizes resolving problems and relieving symptoms (Nardone & Watzlawick, 2005). A special section of the *Journal of Systemic Therapies* (Volume 23, Issue 4, December 2004) describes current research and training programs. Lasting fewer than 10 sessions, MRI brief therapy is a structured approach to problem resolution, similar to Haley's strategic system. However, it differs in that it does not make use of Minuchin's structural concepts of power and hierarchy within the family, which Haley does.

Particularly important to MRI brief family therapists are communication patterns, such as those that are complementary or symmetrical. In *complementary relationships*, one person is superior while the other is inferior or submissive. In a *symmetrical relationship*, there is equality between partners. However, a symmetrical message can be escalated in such a way that one angry remark is met with an angrier remark, which in turn is met with an even angrier remark, so that fighting continues until one partner is ready to concede. The way such an argument continues depends on what is termed each partner's *punctuation*, which is based on the idea that each partner believes what he or she said is caused by the other partner. This is reminiscent of the dialogue between children who are arguing about who started an argument: "You did it!" "No, you did it!" In such circular interaction, there is no reason to look for a starting point; rather, attention is paid to the double binds that exist in family communication (Weakland, 1976).

In their approach to therapy, MRI brief therapists make use of many of the techniques described in the section on Haley's strategic approach: reframing, relabeling, and paradoxical interventions. In approaching their work with families, they try to get a clear view of the problem and devise a way to change the parts of the system that maintain the problem (Segal, 1987). In seeking to make changes, they look for small changes and encourage patients to progress slowly. As therapy progresses, the family's way of viewing its problems and its communication style is gradually restructured. Arguments and disagreements are avoided while working with the family. Each type of problem requires a different approach.

In the following example, based on work with 10 families in which the husband suffered a heart attack but refused to exercise or change his diet, Segal (1982) worked with the wives to change solutions from ineffective ones to productive ones. Staying within a five-session limit, the therapist attempted to change the system so that the husband's behavior would be adaptive. Observing that the wives nagged and argued to change their husband's behavior, instructions were given to the wives. In one case, a wife was told to tell her husband to live out his life in any way he wanted to no matter how short it might be. She was instructed to take control over her life and to go over life insurance and estate planning with her husband. Furthermore, she was asked to call life insurance agencies and have them call back at a time when she would not be at home but her husband would. After 2 weeks of dealing with her husband this way, he participated in rehabilitation exercises and watched his diet.

Long Brief Therapy of the Milan Associates

Based on the work of the MRI theorists and Haley's strategic model, an approach has been developed that focuses on differences in the ways family members behave, relate, and perceive events. This approach is difficult to describe because it has changed over time, and members of the group, based in Milan, Italy, have evolved different views. This approach continues to develop, making use of solution-focused and narrative therapy techniques described in Chapter 12 (Rhodes, 2008). The original work was described as "long brief therapy" because it had relatively few sessions, about 10, but met monthly for a few hours with the family rather than weekly (Tomm, 1984). Of note are two creative approaches to family interventions developed by different members of the Milan group. An intervention developed by Boscolo and Cecchin, termed *circular questioning*, was designed to bring out differences in the way family members saw events and relationships by asking them the same question (Athanasiades, 2008). For example, they might ask various family members (Boscolo, Cecchin, Hoffman, & Penn, 1987), How bad was the arguing this week? Who is the closest to the other? Who is most upset by Andy's not eating? Such questions help family members expand their perspective on issues and find new ways to understand their problems and find new solutions.

Another innovative technique has been designed by Selvini-Palazzoli to help in situations where parents and children collude in a dysfunctional way. Using the *invariant prescription*, Selvini-Palazzoli gives the parents a written prescription that the family is to follow after being interviewed. This prescription is designed to create clear boundaries between parents and children (Selvini-Palazzoli, Cirillo, Selvini, & Sorrentino, 1989). Developed from research done by Giuliana Prata and Mara Selvini-Palazzoli, the invariant prescription relies on paradoxical intervention. The invariant prescription is similar to "the message" used in solution-focused therapy, described in Chapter 12 on page 462. "The message" is used in individual therapy and focuses mainly on solutions to a problem rather than boundaries.

The following case explains how Selvini-Palazzoli et al. (1989) used the invariant prescription in their work. Helping a married couple with three adolescent daughters, one of whom had attempted suicide, the therapist tried to determine the type of "game" that was going on in the family. After the fifth session, they found a way to keep the adolescent girls from meddling in their parents' concerns. Having separated the children from the parents in the therapist's offices, they gave the parents the following message in writing.

> Keep everything that has been said during this session absolutely secret from everyone. Should your daughters ask questions about it, say that the therapist has ordered everything to be kept only between her and the two of you. On at least two occasions between now and your next scheduled appointment, you are to "disappear" from home before dinner without any forewarning. Leave a note worded as follows: "We shall not be in tonight." Each time you go out, pick some place to meet where you are reasonably sure no one will recognize you. If, when you get back home, your daughters ask you where on earth you've been, simply smile and say: "That concerns only the two of us." Each of you is also to keep a sheet of paper, well out of everyone's sight, on which to jot down personal observations on how each of your daughters has reacted to her parents' unusual behavior. At our next meeting, which will again be with only the two of you, each of you will read your notes out loud. (p. 16)

The therapists reported that at the next meeting, a month later, the parents had carried out their orders, and the identified patient had improved her behavior. After three more sessions with only the parents attending, relationships between the parents and among the three daughters improved.

The creative approaches of the Milan Group go beyond the techniques that have been described. In general, their work diverges somewhat from Haley's strategic approach, but it is similar in its emphasis on dealing with interventions within the family system. Their use of sessions spaced at monthly intervals emphasizes the importance of the tasks given to the family and gives them time to make changes.

Current Trends in Family Therapy

The field of family therapy, including family systems therapy, is a quickly growing, very diverse area. Most theorists that are discussed in this book integrate family therapy into psychotherapeutic practice. Trends discussed in this section include the impact of educational approaches to families on family therapy. As family therapy has grown as a profession, organizational groups and training centers have developed, and family therapists have increasingly become involved in the legal system. Also, advances in medicine have had an impact on family therapy.

Psychoeducational Approaches

Since the beginning of family therapy, therapists have been interested in helping families with a child with schizophrenia. Although other family therapists have often seen the family as the cause or at least an impediment to good family functioning, the psychoeducational approach of Anderson, Reiss, and Hogarty (1986) takes what would appear to be a more traditional approach to support and educate the family to deal with the schizophrenic patient. They use a 1-day "survival skills workshop" to teach family members about schizophrenia and its prognosis, psychobiology, and treatment. By teaching families information about schizophrenia, they help them learn what they can do to assist the identified patient. Additionally, they schedule regular family sessions, often continuing for more than a year, to help the families deal with a child with schizophrenia.

Increasingly, efforts are being made to design psychoeducational programs for families of patients with varied cultural backgrounds such as Hispanic/Latino families (Weisman, 2005) and rural Chinese families (Ran et al., 2003). Other psychoeducational programs have attended to reducing expressed emotion in family members of individuals with schizophrenia (Lefley, 2009). By reducing expressed emotion around individuals with schizophrenia, family members can help them maintain stability and cope with their chaotic thoughts (Nichols, 2008). These psychoeducational approaches are often quite intensive, as they are designed to help families with severely disabled and distressed members.

A number of programs have been developed to teach families coping and communication skills (Nichols, 2008). Skills and communication training have three different goals: to teach the family how to deal with the identified patient; to teach the whole family how to communicate, problem solve, or negotiate conflict more effectively; or to enhance already adequate functioning. These programs may be designed for a variety of family issues, such as premarital counseling, marital relationships, parent–adolescent relationships, children of divorce, and families of drug abusers. The theoretical orientation of these programs varies, as they have been offered by psychoanalytic, Adlerian, person-centered, gestalt, cognitive, behavioral, rational emotive behavioral, reality, and feminist therapists. Although some of the approaches to teaching families how to function more effectively may be more educational than psychoeducational, they are among the many treatment alternatives offered to families.

Professional Training and Organizations

As the field of family therapy has grown, so has the need to set standards for training and practice. Started in 1942, the American Association for Marriage and Family Therapy (AAMFT) serves as a credentialing body for the field of family therapy by setting requirements for membership and working with state and federal governments in the development of licensing laws. With a membership of more than 24,000, AAMFT offers continuing education and training to its members through conferences and the *Journal of Marital and Family Therapy*. Also, the American Family Therapy Association (AFTA), started in 1977, allows researchers, clinicians, and trainers to exchange ideas about family therapy. Increasingly, graduate schools in counseling, social work, and psychology offer course work and supervision in family therapy. Also, the AAMFT credits master's degree and doctoral programs that specialize in marital and family therapies. Training centers not affiliated with universities offer advanced training in family therapy.

Family Law

Knowledge of the legal system as it relates to families can be extremely important for family therapists (Goldenberg & Goldenberg, 2008). Issues such as confidentiality, child abuse laws, and dealing with dangerous clients make family therapists vulnerable to malpractice suits. Occasionally, family therapists may be called upon to give expert testimony in court on issues involving custody, disposition of juvenile offenders, and hospitalization or incarceration. Making assessments and writing reports for families involved in custody and divorce cases may be increasingly common, as more and more child custody and visitation disputes are brought to the court system. To perform these activities, therapists need to be informed about the law and be willing to work closely with attorneys.

Medicine

As there have been advances in pharmacology or biological psychiatry, there has been an increasing trend for patients and families to see the root of the problem as a "chemical imbalance." This has led to a trend toward a medicalization of social deviance, which some family therapists question (Prosky & Keith, 2003). When there are problems in a family, such as a child becoming aggressive, a relatively easy solution is to have the child take a prescribed medication. By doing so, the answer to the problem is clear cut, requiring no behavioral or attitudinal change on the part of the family. Medical advances in treating childhood psychological problems have been remarkable. However, family therapists believe that both psychological and biological approaches need to be considered when working with children.

As family therapy has grown, so have the issues about which it has been concerned. With growth has come the development of professional organizations, training centers, and journals, as well as the need to be prepared to deal with legal situations. The growth of different therapeutic approaches to families, whether through psychoeducation or the application of a variety of therapeutic interventions, has caused therapists to be selective and to integrate family systems therapy and other approaches as they continue to be developed.

Research

Research in family therapy is a wide and active area of study with diverse methodology as can be seen in *Research Methods in Family Therapy* (Sprenkle & Piercy, 2005). Research in family therapy makes use of a wide range of assessment instruments to measure the outcome of family therapy (Sanderson et al., 2009). A number of reviews of research on family therapy have found family therapy to be useful for a variety of problems and to be at least as effective as other types of therapy (Friedlander & Tuason, 2000; Nichols, 2008; Stratton, 2007). Recently, efforts have been made to evaluate family therapies as to their ability to meet the standards of research supported therapy (RST) (Lefley, 2009; Lefley, 2009; Northey, 2009). Some RST family therapies are cognitive, behavioral, or cognitive-behavioral. Although most studies of family therapy do not completely define family therapy and may not be measuring specific family therapeutic approaches, some research supports the effectiveness of Bowenian, behavioral, MRI, structural, the Milan group, and psychoeducational approaches. Studies of the effectiveness of these therapies and some of their key concepts are discussed in this section.

Bowen's intergenerational approach to family therapy continues to draw interest from both practitioners and researchers. Important to Bowen's theory is his concept of differentiation. A review of the literature shows a significant relationship between lack of differentiation and chronic anxiety, marital satisfaction, and psychological distress (Miller, Anderson, & Keala, 2004). Little support was found for the belief that individuals with the same levels of differentiation marry each other. A recent study supports Bowen's view that decreasing emotional reactivity (increasing differentiation) toward one's parents helps in reducing psychological stress (Bartle-Haring & Probst, 2004). Another study supports Bowen's view that the concept of differentiation has an impact on how individuals perceive stress in their lives (Murdock & Gore, 2004). Emotional cutoff is another important concept in Bowen's theory. McKnight (2003) reports that if mothers are emotionally cut off from their own mothers or fathers, then they are likely not to function as well in their own family. Mothers' emotional cutoff from their parents was not related to their teenagers' cutoff. Studying concepts such as differentiation and emotional cutoff helps to further clarify the accuracy of Bowen's intergenerational family therapy.

A review of a variety of therapies for family and marital therapy reports that many of the studies have focused on behavioral treatments (Northey, Wells, Silverman, & Bailey, 2003). Most research on behavioral family therapy has studied the effectiveness of training parents to produce specific changes in the child (Spiegler & Guevremont, 2010). This approach is called behavioral parent training, behavioral child management, or parent management training. Behavioral studies are more likely to meet the stringent criteria for effectiveness required by many researchers. A behavioral approach, integrative behavioral couple therapy, combines methods for enhancing emotional acceptance with traditional behavioral approaches. Two-year follow-up studies have shown integrative behavioral couple therapy to be effective, and, on several variables, to be more effective than traditional couple therapies (Baucom, Atkins, Simpson, & Christensen, 2009; Christensen, Atkins, Yi, Baucom, & George, 2006). Infidelity is a significant problem that couples therapy addresses. Baucom, Gordon, Snyder, Atkins, and Christensen (2006) have developed a model for helping clients deal with this issue. Integrative behavioral couple therapy continues to be the subject of active research.

Many studies combine Haley's strategic method or the MRI model with structural or other approaches, making determinations about the effectiveness of strategic therapy difficult. In an early study, Watzlawick, Weakland, and Fisch (1974) followed up 97 families about 3 months after treatment. After an average of seven sessions, 40% reported complete symptom relief, 32% considerable relief, and 28% no change. An advantage of the MRI model is its brevity. In a study that divided 40 couples into an immediate-treatment or a waiting-list control group, improvement was found in marital adjustment and decrease in complaints after three sessions of couple counseling (Davidson & Horvath, 1997). A treatment manual was used that, among other techniques, used reframing to help couples see that their conflict could be a way of regulating intimacy. When brief strategic family therapy was compared to a community comparison group, the strategic method was found to have higher engagement and retention in a comparison of 104 families (Coatsworth, Santisteban, McBride, & Szapocznik, 2001). The strategic method was 7 to 12 sessions long and was somewhat similar to Haley's and the MRI method. It emphasized joining with the family and restructuring ineffective family interactions. The community comparison group focused on improving communications and parenting skills. In general, strategic therapists have devoted more attention to presenting case material than to doing research.

Evaluation of the Milan model is difficult because the model has been changing and there are different Milan models. In reviewing Milan systemic family therapy, Carr (1991) found that the Milan approach led to symptomatic change in between 66% and 75% of the cases in 10 studies. A relatively large study (not included in Carr's review) of 118 participants who were randomly assigned to a Milan approach or another approach found that both treatments achieved similar changes in symptoms at the end of a 6-month follow-up (Simpson, 1990). However, the Milan approach was briefer, and families of the identified patients reported more positive changes than did families of patients receiving other therapies. These positive results contrast with the more negative findings of Coleman (1987) and Machal, Feldman, and Sigal (1989), who reported lower success rates and negative reactions to the therapist or team of therapists. These mixed findings are not surprising in light of the fact that Milan therapy has been practiced differently by different people at different times.

Perhaps the best evidence for the effectiveness of Minuchin's structural therapy has come from work with diabetic and anorectic children (Minuchin et al., 1978). Using the level of free fatty acids in the blood as a measure of stress, Minuchin et al. were able to reduce stress levels in diabetic children and their families with structural family therapy. With a group of 43 children suffering from anorexia nervosa, Minuchin et al. reported a 90% improvement rate upon completion of therapy. This positive improvement rate continued on follow-up several years later. The use of enactments is a significant aspect of structural therapy. In a study of 10 family therapy sessions, successful enactments were found to produce changes in the problem by the end of the session (Fellenberg, 2004). Strengthening parental power is another aspect of structural family therapy. When therapists focused on enhancing parental power, family control was measured more positively than when therapists focused less on enhancing parental power (Walsh, 2004). Some family therapists have believed that structural therapy is too aggressive, imposing too much on clients' family interaction style. In a study of 24 videotaped sessions, Hammond and Nichols (2008) report that structural family therapists are empathic with family members as they establish a collaborative therapeutic relationship.

Interest in psychoeducational approaches to families with members who have schizophrenia or other severe mental disorders continues to grow. This interest has been strong due in part to the high cost of inpatient or other intensive care and the disruptiveness of severe mental illness. Fadden (1998) reviewed more than 50 studies that include a diverse set of approaches to psychoeducational interventions. Summarizing these findings, she concluded that psychoeducational interventions significantly decreased the rate of relapse and hospitalizations. These effects were sustainable over time and can be applied to people from many cultures. Effective approaches are educational, focusing on coping skills and dealing with day-to-day problems rather than psychodynamic issues. Education combined with teaching coping skills is more effective in preventing relapse than education alone. Examining the effect of a psychoeducational approach on families of individuals with bipolar disorder, Reinares et al. (2004) found that the family caregivers not only improved their knowledge of bipolar disorder but also were less burdened by taking care of the patient. In a study of Korean Americans, psychoeducational groups helped to reduce the stigma of dealing with family members with severe mental illness and helped give the family members more coping skills, and more power to deal with the patient's crises (Shin, 2004). Using a psychoeducational program with relatives of patients with schizophrenia, Sota et al. (2008) found that relatives, especially mothers, reduced their scores on family expressed emotions and that the identified patient relapsed less frequently. Another study of psychoeducational programs showed that when patients developed a positive alliance to relatives, the relatives became less rejecting and felt less burdened (Smerud & Rosenfarb, 2008). When relatives reported that they had developed a positive alliance, patients were less likely to develop signs of relapse and a need for rehospitalization. However, implementing successful psychoeducational programs for families requires that practitioners have a positive view of such programs, have adequate financial and other resources, and attend to differences between existing and psychoeducational methods. McFarlane, McNary, Dixon, Hornby, and Cimett (2001) reported that agencies in Maine, where most of these conditions were met, implemented family psychoeducational programs in 93% of the agencies; but in Illinois, where many of these conditions were not met, only 10% of the agencies implemented psychoeducational programs. As psychoeducational interventions become more popular, more research is likely to result.

Gender Issues

As shown in Chapter 13, the roles of men and women, in general and in the family, are quite different from each other in the United States, as well as in other cultures. Women are often expected to work and take major responsibility for household chores and child care. Additionally, they are expected to take the major responsibility for relationships with friends and families of origin (Goldenberg & Goldenberg, 2008). On the other hand, men have often taken responsibility for financial support and major family decisions. When children grow and leave the home, women's priorities for themselves may be quite different from those of men, which can lead to marital conflict or divorce (McGoldrick & Hardy, 2008). Women, as they age, may react negatively to having taken responsibility for care of their children and later their aging parents. Until the 1980s, these general differences between men and women and the way they relate in the family were often taken for granted by family therapists and not questioned.

Feminist family therapists have had a significant impact on how family therapists deal with gender issues (Nichols, 2008) by making family therapists aware of their own gender values regarding the roles of men and women and stereotypes about them. This topic has been addressed in depth in *Feminist Family Therapy: Empowerment in Social Context* (Silverstein & Goodrich, 2003). As feminist therapists have observed, the therapist's role is never gender neutral. Family members are likely to bring expectations as to how the therapist will respond based on their own gender-role stereotypes. They are also likely to experience family therapy differently depending on their gender. These expectations in combination with therapists' values about how families operate can limit families' abilities to make positive change.

The traditional view of the family has been that of having a distant but dominant father with a mother who is too involved in her children's behavior. The definition of family is re-examined in *Interventions with Families of Gay, Lesbian, Bisexual, and Transgender People: From the Inside Out* (Bigner & Gottlieb, 2006). Attending to issues of gay and lesbian couples as well as their children is an issue family therapists address (Green, 2008; Nealy, 2008). Feminist therapists have cautioned family therapists against stereotyped views of families that result in blaming the mother for a child's problems (Nichols, 2008). Some feminist therapists have suggested that family therapists need to examine and challenge gender-role beliefs of families (Miller & Bermúdez, 2004), whereas others focus more on equality in relationships (Knudson-Martin & Laughlin, 2005). For many family therapists, child and spousal abuse are substantial issues that they must address (Ball & Hiebert, 2008). Questioning how decisions are made about parenting, work roles, financial decisions, and doing household chores can produce an atmosphere of change and can help a couple relate differently to each other. The questioning of gender-role assumptions has a direct impact on how feminist therapists have viewed family systems theory and resulting therapeutic interventions.

In discussing a variety of approaches, feminist therapists caution against techniques that might bring about change at the expense of reinforcing gender roles. For example, a paradoxical task that might ask a woman to clean and reclean the kitchen several times is reinforcing the role that women belong in the kitchen. Rather, therapists are encouraged to use techniques that help each member of the couple feel more empowered, more likely to share with each other, and more equal in their relationship. By doing so, they can support each other in working with problems related to children. Sharing of responsibility can start at the beginning of therapy. For example, often a wife brings a family to therapy, though the husband may be reluctant to attend. Feminist family therapists encourage the husband to share responsibility for the family, and questions about the family are directed to both husband and wife.

Multicultural Issues

Just as gender issues became important in family therapy in the 1980s, so did the emphasis on the impact of culture on family relationships and values. Books (Greene, Kropf, & Frankel, 2009; Hays, 2008; Ho, Rasheed, & Rasheed 2004; McGoldrick, Giordano, & Garcia-Preto, 2005; McGoldrick & Hardy, 2008) have been written that describe values and characteristics of a variety of ethnic groups. Boyd-Franklin (2008), Boyd-Franklin and Lockwood (2009), and Pinderhughes (2008) explain both issues and approaches to family therapy with African Americans. Akinyela (2008) describes testimony therapy for African American couples. Garcia-Preto (2008) discusses issues when working with Latinas and their families; Smith and Montilla (2009) discuss issue in counseling clients that speak Spanish. Lim and Nakamoto (2008), Sim (2007), and Sim and Wong (2008) describe applications of family therapy in dealing with Asian Americans and South Asians. McGoldrick and Hardy (2008) have discussed the interaction of ethnicity and gender as it affects family therapy in 38 chapters on different cultures and family therapy issues. Increasingly, articles are being written that attend to cultural issues as they affect family therapy. Articles on the interaction between culture and family therapy can provide useful insights for therapists in understanding cultural backgrounds of their clients.

A brief summary of some important issues for families from different cultures is provided by Goldenberg and Goldenberg (2008). They discuss how families, depending on their cultural background, define the family, how family life cycles differ in various cultures, and how child-raising practices can differ across cultures.

> Even the definition of "family" differs in different groups. The dominant white Anglo Saxon Protestant (WASP) focus is on the intact nuclear family, extending back over generations. Blacks expand their definition to include a wide informal network of kin and community. Italians think in terms of tightly knit three- or four-generational families, often including godfathers and old friends; all may be involved in family decision making, may live in close proximity to one another, and may share life-cycle transitions together. The Chinese tend to go even further, including all their ancestors and all their descendants in their definition of family membership (McGoldrick, 1988).

Family life cycle timing is influenced by ethnic considerations. Mexican Americans tend to have longer courtship periods and extended childhoods beyond the dominant American pattern, but shorter adolescent periods and hastened adulthood. Similarly, different groups give different importance to life-cycle transition points. The Irish wake is a ritual that represents a view of death as the most important transition, freeing humans so that they can go on to a happier afterlife. Polish families emphasize weddings, their lengthy celebration reflecting the importance of the family's continuity into the next generation. For Jewish families, the Bar Mitzvah signifies the transition into adulthood, reflecting the high value placed on continued intellectual development (McGoldrick, 1988).

Child rearing practices may also vary greatly. While the dominant American pattern is for the mother to have primary responsibility, blacks often rely on grandparents and extended family members to care for children, especially if the mother is working outside the home. Greeks and Puerto Ricans tend to indulge young infants, but later become strict with children, particularly girls. Adolescent girls from Italian-American families may find themselves in intergenerational conflicts with parents and grandparents as they rebel against traditional female roles of waiting on fathers, brothers, and later, husbands and sons (Goldenberg & Goldenberg, 2008).

Although the information that Goldenberg and Goldenberg (2008) present is a useful example of the type of information available to those who work with families, both they and many other writers warn against the danger of stereotyping clients based on general observations. As Ho, Rasheed, and Rasheed (2004) explain, many issues affect the impact of culture on a family, such as how long families have been established in a new culture, intermarriage, the diversity of neighborhoods, and issues of social class. Family functioning is influenced by cultural traditions, societal expectations such as gender role, and family interactive patterns.

Knowledge of cultural issues can affect the way family therapists work with couples or families. Richeport-Haley (1998) describes Haley's strategic approach, comparing it to culture-focused therapy. Richeport-Haley presents different ways for dealing with an alternative belief system. These include using aspects of the alternative system to accomplish therapeutic goals as well as collaborating with or referring to a local healer. In the example below, she describes both a strategic and culture-focused approach to working with a young South American man.

Problem: A young man in his early 20s was court ordered to therapy for repeated possession and dealing of marijuana. He would be imprisoned if this happened one more time. His mother, who spoke only Spanish, and the eldest son, who translated for her, came to therapy. The goal was to get the boy off marijuana. The intervention was to have the family come up with a strong consequence if the youth relapsed. Once the family realized that they could do something, they had a lengthy discussion of what to do if the youth relapsed. They decided that the consequence would be to ostracize the son from the family for 3 months and to shun him if he took drugs again. The son has not gone back to drugs. The therapist did not need to understand the strong bond of a Latin American family and the difficulty it had in banning a member. The goal of therapy, regardless of ethnic group, was for the family to take charge of its member and make a serious consequence rather than have the community do so.

A Culture-Focused Approach. In contrast to this directive approach, culturally focused therapy would have explored the importance and positive functions of a close-knit family. It would have emphasized the values of forgiveness based on a religious charity ethic. In keeping the communication style of this ethnic group, the therapist might have been authoritarian and told the family exactly what to do rather than letting them decide. (Richeport-Haley, 1998, p. 86)

A number of other case examples in the family therapy literature not only instruct about different values systems within cultures but also alert therapists to the importance of understanding the interaction of their own cultural value system and that of the family.

Family Systems Therapy Applied to the Individual

When working in psychotherapy with an individual, therapists can apply concepts from any of the family systems theories discussed in this chapter. The intergenerational approach of Bowen reminds the therapist of the importance of background across several generations. Intergenerational therapists occasionally do work with one individual and help that individual make appropriate changes in the family (McGoldrick & Carter, 2001). When the structural approach of Minuchin is used in individual therapy, the therapist can listen for ways family members align with each other, are enmeshed in each other's lives, and form coalitions. Hypotheses based on ideas about family subsystems can form interventions that can help the individual deal better with family issues. Using ideas from strategic family systems therapy, therapists can help patients bring about change in their lives, whether related to family issues or not, through the use of straightforward and paradoxical tasks. When experiential family systems therapy is applied to the individual, unconscious reactions to the patient and feelings about the patient can be communicated in much the same way that Whitaker and Satir communicated to the families with whom they worked. As more and more therapists work with both families and individuals, family systems therapy is likely to become better integrated into other therapeutic approaches.

Couples Counseling

The fact that the American Association of Marriage Counselors changed its name to the American Association of Marriage and Family Counselors in 1970 is indicative of the overlap between marriage and family therapy. Because a marriage is a small system, family systems theory can be applied to it. From the point of view of Bowen's intergenerational approach, awareness of the therapist–partner–partner triangular relationship and the ways that each partner is able to differentiate feeling and intellect within himself or herself can be applied directly to marital therapy, as can the concept of the influence of the family of origin. Regarding Minuchin's structural family therapy, attending to the balance in decision making of the partners and to the degree to which they are disengaged or enmeshed with each other can be used in understanding the interactive processes of the couple. Similarly, in Haley's strategic therapy, the therapist can focus on the power distribution within the couple and suggest direct or indirect interventions that will bring about balance and communication between partners. Ways in which Whitaker and Satir, expressive family therapists, attend to and model communication styles and skills apply as well to couples therapy as to family therapy.

Summary

Based in part on early work with families of patients with schizophrenia, family therapy has focused not just on the identified patient but on the entire functioning of the family. Bowen's intergenerational theory deals not only with relationships between two family members and how they involve a third but also on relationships that go back one or more generations. Less concerned with past relationships, Minuchin's structural approach has addressed the flexibility of boundaries within the family and how members can become too close or too distant, thus inhibiting proper family functioning. The strategic therapy of Jay Haley, while incorporating concepts about family boundaries, concentrates on resolving symptoms within the family through direct or indirect means. The experiential approaches of Satir and Whitaker are based in part on intuitive reactions of the therapist to the family and making therapeutic interventions that lead to healthier family functioning. As the field of family therapy has grown, family therapists have tended not only to draw from a variety of family systems therapies but also to incorporate aspects of other theories of psychotherapy in their work. For that reason, I have shown how each of the major theories described in the text can be applied to family therapy.

Although many family therapists see their clients for fewer than 20 or 30 sessions, there has been an emphasis on briefer therapy and innovative approaches to changing family dynamics. A number of feminist therapists and other writers have challenged assumptions about roles within the family based on gender-role and cultural differences. Currently, the development of family therapy is affected by two divergent trends: incorporating a variety of theoretical and other concepts and developing new creative approaches for dealing with families.

Suggested Readings

Bitter, J. (2009). *Theory and practice of family therapy and counseling*. Belmont: CA: Brooks/Cole Cengage. An extensive textbook on family therapy, this book has three chapters on the basic techniques of family therapy and 11 chapters on theories and techniques of family therapy. There are two chapters on the integration of theories of family therapy. The case examples are excellent and frequent.

Goldenberg, I., & Goldenberg, H. (2008). *Family therapy: An overview* (7th ed.). Belmont, CA: Brooks/Cole. Significant theories of family therapy are discussed fully. The background and use of a variety of theoretical approaches are explained in this readable text.

Nichols, M. P. (2008). *Family therapy: Concepts and methods* (8th ed.). Boston: Allyn & Bacon. A more extensive text than that of Goldenberg and Goldenberg, this book goes into detail on many systems of family therapy and their development. Discussion of the history as well as the current trends affecting family therapy is extensive.

Minuchin, S. (1974). *Families and family therapy*. Cambridge, MA: Harvard University Press. This excellent description of Minuchin's theory of structural family therapy is well illustrated with transcripts of therapy sessions. Many techniques are explained, along with their application to different families.

Madanes, C. (1981). *Strategic family therapy*. San Francisco: Jossey-Bass. Describing her approach and that of her former husband, Jay Haley, to strategic family therapy, Madanes explains basic dimensions and elements of their work. Particularly helpful in understanding strategic family therapy is the presentation of 15 case studies that illustrate innovative interventions, including direct and paradoxical suggestions, as well as the use of metaphor.

McGoldrick, M., & Hardy, K. V. (2008). *Re-visioning family therapy: Race, culture, and gender in clinical practice* (2nd ed.). New York: Guilford. An extremely comprehensive book, this text has 38 chapters describing ethnic and gender issues as they relate to families. Most chapters contain helpful case studies.

References

Ackerman, N. W. (1966a). Family psychotherapy—theory and practice. *American Journal of Psychotherapy, 20,* 405–414.

Ackerman, N. W. (1966b). *Treating the troubled family.* New York: Basic Books.

Akinyela, M. M. (2008). Once they come: Testimony therapy and healing questions for African American couples. In M. McGoldrick & K. V. Hardy (Eds.), *Re-visioning family therapy: Race, culture, and gender in clinical practice* (2nd ed., pp. 356–366). New York: Guilford.

Anderson, C. M., Reiss, D., & Hogarty, B. (1986). *Schizophrenia and the family.* New York: Guilford.

Aponte, H., & Van Deusen, J. M. (1981). Structural family therapy. In A. S. Gutman & D. P. Kniskern (Eds.), *Handbook of family therapy* (pp. 310–360). New York: Brunner/Mazel.

Athanasiades, C. (2008). Systemic thinking and circular questioning in therapy with individuals. *Counselling Psychology Review, 23*(3), 5–13.

Ball, D., & Hiebert, W. J. (2008). An ounce of prevention: Stopping violence before it begins. In J. Hamel (Ed.), *Intimate partner and family abuse: A casebook of gender-inclusive therapy* (pp. 29–43). New York: Springer.

Barreto, S. J., Boekamp, J. R., Armstrong, L. M., & Gillen, P. (2004). Community-based interventions for juvenile firestarters: A brief family-centered model. *Psychological Services, 1*(2), 158–168.

Bartle-Haring, S., & Probst, D. (2004). A test of Bowen theory: Emotional reactivity and psychological distress in a clinical sample. *American Journal of Family Therapy, 32*(5), 419–435.

Bateson, G., Jackson, D. D., Haley, J., & Weakland, J. (1956). Towards a theory of schizophrenia. *Behavioral Science, 1,* 251–264.

Baucom, B. R., Atkins, D. C., Simpson, L. E., & Christensen, A. (2009). Prediction of response to treatment in a randomized clinical trial of couple therapy: A 2-year follow-up. *Journal of Consulting and Clinical Psychology, 77*(1), 160–173.

Baucom, D. H., Gordon, K. C., Snyder, D. K., Atkins, D. C., & Christensen, A. (2006). Treating affair couples: Clinical considerations and initial findings. *Journal of Cognitive Psychotherapy, 20*(4), 375–392.

Bertalanffy, C. von. (1968). *General systems theory: Foundation, development, applications.* New York: Braziller.

Bigner, J. J., & Gottlieb, A. R. (Eds.). (2006). *Interventions with families of gay, Lesbian, bisexual, and transgender people: From the inside out.* Binghamton, NY: Haworth.

Bitter, J. (2009). *Theory and practice of family therapy and counseling.* Belmont: CA: Brooks/Cole Cengage.

Boscolo, L., Cecchin, G., Hoffman, L., & Penn, P. (1987). *Milan systemic family therapy: Conversations in theory and practice.* New York: Basic Books.

Bowen, M. (1960). A family concept of schizophrenia. In D. D. Jackson (Ed.), *The etiology of schizophrenia* (pp. 346–372). New York: Basic Books.

Bowen, M. (1966). The use of family theory in clinical practice. *Comprehensive Psychiatry, 7,* 345–374.

Bowen, M. (1975). Family therapy after twenty years. In S. Arieti, D. X. Freedman, & J. E. Dyrud (Eds.), *American handbook of psychiatry V: Treatment* (2nd ed., pp. 367–392). New York: Basic Books.

Bowen, M. (1976). Theory in the practice of psychotherapy. In P. J. Guerin, Jr. (Ed.), *Family therapy: Theory and practice* (pp. 42–90). New York: Gardner.

Bowen, M. (1978). *Family therapy in clinical practice.* New York: Aronson.

Boyd-Franklin, N. (2008). Working with African Americans and trauma: Lessons for clinicians from hurricane Katrina. In M. McGoldrick & K. V. Hardy (Eds.), *Re-visioning family therapy: Race, culture, and gender in clinical practice* (2nd ed., pp. 344–355). New York: Guilford.

Boyd-Franklin, N., & Lockwood, T. W. (2009). Spirituality and religion: Implications for psychotherapy with African American families. In F. Walsh (Ed.), *Spiritual resources in family therapy* (2nd ed., pp. 141–155). New York: Guilford.

Brown, J. H., & Christensen, D. N. (1999). *Family therapy: Theory and practice* (2nd. ed.). Pacific Grove, CA: Brooks/Cole.

Butler, J. F. (2008). The family diagram and genogram: Comparisons and contrasts. *American Journal of Family Therapy, 36*(3), 169–180.

Carr, A. (1991). Milan systemic family therapy: A review of ten empirical investigations. *Journal of Family Therapy, 13,* 237–263.

Cauley, K. C. (2008). Triangles in stepfamilies. In P. Titelman (Ed.), *Triangles: Bowen family systems theory perspectives* (pp. 291–309). New York: Haworth Press.

Christensen, A., Atkins, D. C., Yi, J., Baucom, D. H., & George, W. H. (2006). Couple and individual adjustment for 2 years following a randomized clinical trial comparing traditional versus integrative behavioral couple therapy. *Journal of Consulting and Clinical Psychology, 74*(6), 1180–1191.

Coatsworth, J. D., Santisteban, D. A., McBride, C. K., & Szapocznik, J. (2001). Brief strategic family therapy versus community control: Engagement, retention, and an exploration of the moderating role of adolescent symptom severity. *Family Process, 40*, 313–332.

Coleman, S. (1987). Milan in Bucks County. *Family Therapy Networker, 11*, 42–47.

Connell, G., Mitten, T., & Bumberry, W. (1999). *Reshaping family relationships: The symbolic therapy of Carl Whitaker*. Philadelphia: Brunner/Mazel.

Cooper, S. (1974). Treatment of parents. In S. Arieti & G. Caplan (Eds.), *American handbook of psychiatry II: Child and adolescent psychiatry, sociocultural and community psychiatry* (2nd ed.). New York: Basic Books.

Cromwell, R. E., Olson, D. H., & Fournier, D. G. (1976). Diagnosis and evaluation in marital and family counseling. In D. H. Olson (Ed.), *Treating relationships* (pp. 517–562). Lake Mills, IA: Graphic.

Davidson, G. N. S., & Horvath, A. O. (1997). Three sessions of brief couples therapy: A clinical trial. *Journal of Family Psychology, 11*, 422–435.

Fadden, G. (1998). Research update: Psychoeducational family interventions. *Journal of Family Therapy, 20*, 293–309.

Fellenberg, S. (2004). The contribution of enactments to structural family therapy: A process study. (Doctoral dissertation). *Dissertation Abstracts International: Section B: The Sciences and Engineering, 64* (11–B), 5780.

Friedlander, M. L., & Tuason, M. T. (2000). Processes and outcomes in couples and family therapy. In S. D. Brown & R. W. Lent (Eds.), *Handbook of counseling psychology* (3rd ed., pp. 797–824). New York: Wiley.

Fromm-Reichmann, F. (1948). Notes on the development of treatment of schizophrenics by psychoanalytic psychotherapy. *Psychiatry, 11*, 253–273.

Garcia-Preto, N. (2008). Latinas in the United States: Bridging two worlds. In M. McGoldrick & K. V. Hardy (Eds.), *Re-visioning family therapy: Race, culture, and gender in clinical practice* (2nd ed., pp. 261–274). New York: Guilford.

Goldenberg, I., & Goldenberg, H. (2008). *Family therapy: An overview* (7th ed.). Belmont, CA: Brooks/Cole.

Green, R. (2008). Gay and lesbian couples: Successful coping with minority stress. In M. McGoldrick & K. V. Hardy (Eds.), *Re-visioning family therapy: Race, culture, and gender in clinical practice* (2nd ed., pp. 300–310). New York: Guilford.

Greene, R. R. (2008). General systems theory. In R. R. Greene (Ed.), *Human behavior theory and social work practice* (3rd ed., pp. 165–198). New Brunswick, NJ: Transaction Publishers.

Greene, R. R., Kropf, N., & Frankel, K. (2009). A systems approach: Addressing diverse family forms. In R. R. Greene & N. Kropf (Eds.), *Human behavior theory: A diversity framework* (2nd rev. ed., pp. 167–200). New Brunswick, NJ: AldineTransaction.

Guerin, P. J., Jr., & Guerin, K. B. (1976). Theoretical aspects and clinical relevance of the multi-generational model of family therapy. In P. J. Guerin, Jr. (Ed.), *Family therapy: Theory and practice* (pp. 91–110). New York: Gardner.

Haley, J. (1963). *Strategies of psychotherapy*. New York: Grune & Stratton.

Haley, J. (1971a). Approaches to family therapy. In J. Haley (Ed.), *Changing families: A family therapy reader* (pp. 227–236). New York: Grune & Stratton.

Haley, J. (1971b). Family therapy: A radical change. In J. Haley (Ed.), *Changing families: A family therapy reader* (pp. 272–284). New York: Grune & Stratton.

Haley, J. (1973). *Uncommon therapy: The psychiatric techniques of Milton H. Erickson, M.D.* New York: Norton.

Haley, J. (1976). *Problem-solving therapy*. San Francisco: Jossey-Bass.

Haley, J. (1979). *Leaving home: Therapy with disturbed young people*. New York: McGraw-Hill.

Haley, J. (1984). *Ordeal therapy: Unusual ways to change behavior*. San Francisco: Jossey-Bass.

Haley, J. (1996). *Learning and teaching therapy*. New York: Guilford.

Haley, J., & Richeport-Haley, M. (2007). *Directive family therapy*. New York: Haworth Press.

Hammond, R. T., & Nichols, M. P. (2008). How collaborative is structural family therapy? *Family Journal, 16*(2), 118–124.

Hays, P. A. (2008). *How to help best: Culturally responsive therapy*. Washington, DC: American Psychological Association.

Ho, M. K., Rasheed, J. M., & Rasheed, M. N. (2004). *Family therapy with ethnic minorities* (2nd ed.). Thousand Oaks, CA: Sage.

Keim, J. (2000). Strategic therapy. In F. M. Dattilio & L. J. Bevilacqua (Eds.), *Comparative treatments for relationship dysfunction* (pp. 58–78). New York: Springer.

Kerr, M. (2003). Multigenerational family systems theory of Bowen and its application. In G. P. Sholevar (Ed.), *Textbook of family and couples therapy: Clinical applications* (pp. 103–126). Washington, DC: American Psychiatric Publishing.

Kerr, M. E., & Bowen, M. (1988). *Family evaluation: An approach based on Bowen theory.* New York: W. W. Norton.

Knudson-Martin, C., & Laughlin, M. J. (2005). Gender and sexual orientation in family therapy: Toward a postgender approach. *Family Relations: Interdisciplinary Journal of Applied Family Studies, 54*(1), 101–115.

Laninga, K., Sanders, R. L., & Greenwood, D. E. (2008). The Family Boundaries Game. In C. F. Sori & L. L. Hecker (Eds.), *The therapists' notebook, volume 3: More homework, handouts, and activities for use in psychotherapy* (pp. 159–166). New York: Routledge.

Lebow, J. (1997). The integrative revolution in couple and family therapy. *Family Process, 36,* 1–6.

Lefley, H. P. (2009). *Family psychoeducation for serious mental illness.* New York: Oxford.

Levy, D. (1943). *Maternal overprotection.* New York: Columbia University Press.

Lidz, T., Cornelison, A., Fleck, S., & Terry, D. (1957). The intrafamilial environment of schizophrenic patients: II. Marital schism and marital skew. *American Journal of Psychiatry, 114,* 241–248.

Lim, S., & Nakamoto, T. (2008). Genograms: Use in therapy with Asian families with diverse cultural heritages. *Contemporary Family Therapy: An International Journal, 30*(4), 199–219.

Machal, M., Feldman, R., & Sigal, J. (1989). The unraveling of a treatment program: A follow-up study of the Milan approach to family therapy. *Family Process, 28,* 457–470.

Madanes, C. (1981). *Strategic family therapy.* San Francisco: Jossey-Bass.

Magnuson, S., & Shaw, H. E. (2003). Adaptations of the multifaceted genogram in counseling, training, and supervision. *Family Journal: Counseling and Therapy for Couples and Families, 11*(1), 45–54.

McDaniel S. H., Lusterman, D. D., & Philpot, C. L. (Eds.). (2001). *Casebook for integrating family therapy: An ecosystem approach.* Washington, DC: American Psychological Association.

McFarlane, W. R., McNary, S., Dixon, L., Hornby, H., & Cimett, E. (2001). Predictors of dissemination of family psychoeducation in community mental health centers in Maine and Illinois. *Psychiatric Services, 52,* 935–942.

McGoldrick, M. (1988). Ethnicity and the family life cycle. In B. Carter & M. McGoldrick (Eds.), *The changing family life cycle: A framework for family therapy* (2nd ed., pp. 70–90). New York: Gardner.

McGoldrick, M., & Carter, B. (2001). Advances in coaching: Family therapy with one person. *Journal of Marital and Family Therapy, 27,* 281–300.

McGoldrick, M., Giordano, J., & Garcia-Preto, N. (2005). *Ethnicity and family therapy* (3rd ed.). New York: Guilford.

McGoldrick, M., & Hardy, K. V. (2008). *Re-visioning family therapy: Race, culture, and gender in clinical practice* (2nd ed.). New York: Guilford.

McKnight, A. S. (2003). The impact of cutoff in families raising adolescents. In P. Titelman (Ed.), *Emotional cutoff: Bowen family systems theory perspectives* (pp. 273–287). New York: Haworth.

McLendon, J. A. (2000). The Satir system: Brief therapy strategies. In J. Carlson & L. Sperry (Eds.), *Brief therapy with individuals and couples* (pp. 331–364). Phoenix, AZ: Zeig, Tucker, and Theisen.

Miller, M. M., & Bermúdez, J. M. (2004). Intersecting gender and social exchange theory in family therapy. *Journal of Feminist Family Therapy, 16*(2), 1–24.

Miller, R. B., Anderson, S., & Keala, D. K. (2004). Is Bowen theory valid?: A review of basic research. *Journal of Marital and Family Therapy, 30*(4), 453–466.

Minuchin, P., Colapinto, J., & Minuchin, S. (2007). *Working with families of the poor* (2nd ed.). New York: Guilford.

Minuchin, S. (1974). *Families and family therapy.* Cambridge, MA: Harvard University Press.

Minuchin, S., & Fishman, H. C. (1981). *Family therapy techniques.* Cambridge, MA: Harvard University Press.

Minuchin, S., Rosman, B. L., & Baker, L. (1978). *Psychosomatic families: Anorexia nervosa in context.* Cambridge, MA: Harvard University Press.

Mittelman, B. (1948). The concurrent analysis of married couples. *Psychoanalytic Quarterly, 17,* 182–197.

Murdock, N. L., & Gore, P. A. J. (2004). Stress, coping, and differentiation of self: A test of Bowen theory. *Contemporary Family Therapy: An International Journal, 26*(3), 319–335.

Napier, A. Y., & Whitaker, C. A. (1978). *The family crucible*. New York: Harper & Row.

Nardone, G., & Watzlawick, P. (2005). *Brief strategic therapy: Philosophy, techniques, and research*. Lanham, MD: Jason Aronson.

Nealy, E. C. (2008). Working with LGBT families. In M. McGoldrick & K. V. Hardy (Eds.), *Re-visioning family therapy: Race, culture, and gender in clinical practice* (2nd ed., pp. 289–299). New York: Guilford.

Nichols, M. P. (2008). *Family therapy: Concepts and methods* (8th ed.). Boston: Allyn & Bacon.

Northey, W. F., Jr. (2009). Effectiveness research: A view from the USA. *Journal of Family Therapy, 31*(1), 75–84.

Northey, W. F., Wells, K. C., Silverman, W. K., & Bailey, C. E. (2003). Childhood behavioral and emotional disorders. *Journal of Marital and Family Therapy, 29*(4), 523–545.

Okun, B. E., & Rappaport, L. J. (1980). *Working with families: An introduction to family therapy*. Belmont, CA: Wadsworth.

Papero, D. V. (1983). Family systems theory and therapy. In B. B. Wolman & G. Stricker (Eds.), *Handbook of family and marital therapy* (pp. 137–158). New York: Plenum.

Papero, D. V. (2000). Bowen systems theory. In F. M. Dattilo & L. J. Bevilacqua (Eds.), *Comparative treatments for relationship dysfunction* (pp. 25–44). New York: Springer.

Papp, P. (1980). The Greek chorus and other techniques of paradoxical therapy. *Family Process, 19*, 45–57.

Papp, P. (1984). Setting the terms for therapy. *The Family Therapy Networker, 8*, 42–47.

Pinderhughes, E. (2008). Black genealogy revisited: Restorying an African American family. In M. McGoldrick & K. V. Hardy (Eds.), *Re-visioning family therapy: Race, culture, and gender in clinical practice* (2nd ed., pp. 114–134). New York: Guilford.

Prosky, P. S., & Keith, D. V. (Eds.). (2003). *Family therapy as an alternative to medication: An appraisal of pharmland*. New York: Brunner-Routledge.

Ran, M., Xiang, M., Chan, C. L., Leff, J., Simpson, P., & Huang, M. et al. (2003). Effectiveness of psychoeducational intervention for rural Chinese families experiencing schizophrenia. A randomized controlled trial. *Social Psychiatry and Psychiatric Epidemiology, 38*(2), 69–75.

Reinares, M., Vieta, E., Colom, F., Martínez-Arán, A., Torrent, C., & Comes, M. et al. (2004). Impact of a psychoeducational family intervention on caregivers of stabilized bipolar patients. *Psychotherapy and Psychosomatics, 73*(5), 312–319.

Rhodes, P. (2008). Amplifying deviations in family interactions: Guidelines for trainees in post-Milan family therapy. *Australian and New Zealand Journal of Family Therapy, 29*(1), 34–39.

Richeport-Haley, M. (1998). Ethnicity in family therapy: A comparison of brief strategic therapy and culture-focused therapy. *American Journal of Family Therapy, 26*, 77–90.

Sanderson, J., Kosutic, I., Garcia, M., Melendez, T., Donoghue, J., Perumbilly, S., Franzen, C., & Anderson, S. (2009). The measurement of outcome variables in couple and family therapy research. *American Journal of Family Therapy, 37*(3), 239–257.

Satir, V. M. (1972). *Peoplemaking*. Palo Alto, CA: Science and Behavior Books.

Satir, V. M., & Baldwin, M. (1983). *Satir step by step*. Palo Alto, CA: Science and Behavior Books.

Segal, L. (1982). Brief family therapy. In A. M. Horne & M. M. Ohlsen (Eds.), *Family counseling and therapy* (pp. 279–301). Itasca, IL: F. E. Peacock.

Segal, L. (1987). What is a problem? A brief family therapist's view. *Family Therapy Today, 2*, 1–7.

Selvini-Palazzoli, M., Cirillo, S., Selvini, M., & Sorrentino, A. M. (1989). *Family games: General models of psychotic processes in the family*. New York: Norton.

Shin, S. (2004). Effects of culturally relevant psychoeducation for Korean American families of persons with chronic mental illness. *Research on Social Work Practice, 14*(4), 231–239.

Silverstein, L. B., & Goodrich, T. J. (Eds.). (2003). *Feminist family therapy: Empowerment in social context*. Washington, DC: American Psychological Association.

Sim, T. (2007). Structural family therapy in adolescent drug abuse: A Hong Kong Chinese family. *Clinical Case Studies, 6*(1), 79–99.

Sim, T., & Wong, D. (2008). Working with Chinese families in adolescent drug treatment. *Journal of Social Work Practice, 22*(1), 103–118.

Simpson, L. (1990). The comparative efficacy of Milan family therapy for disturbed children and their families. *Journal of Family Therapy, 13*, 267–284.

Smerud, P. E., & Rosenfarb, I. S. (2008). The therapeutic alliance and family psychoeducation in the treatment of schizophrenia: An exploratory prospective change process study. *Journal of Consulting and Clinical Psychology, 76*(3), 505–510.

Smith, R. L., & Montilla, R. E. (2009). Counseling with Spanish-speaking clients. In C. M. Ellis & J. Carlson (Eds.), *Cross-cultural awareness and social justice in counseling* (pp. 169–184). New York: Routledge.

Sota, S., Shimodera, S., Kii, M., Okamura, K., Suto, K., Suwaki, M., Fujita, H., Fujito, R., & Inoue, S. (2008). Effect of a family psychoeducational program on relatives of schizophrenia patients. *Psychiatry and Clinical Neurosciences, 62*(4), 379–385.

Spiegler, M. D., & Guevremont, D. C. (2010). *Contemporary behavior therapy* (5th ed.). Belmont, CA: Wadsworth.

Sprenkle, D. H., & Piercy, F. P. (2005). *Research methods in family therapy* (2nd ed.). New York: Guilford.

Stratton, P. (2007). Enhancing family therapy's relationships with research. *Australian and New Zealand Journal of Family Therapy, 28*(4), 177–184.

Sullivan, H. S. (1953). *The interpersonal theory of psychiatry*. New York: Norton.

Titelman, P. (Ed.). (2008). *Triangles: Bowen family systems theory perspectives*. New York: Haworth.

Toman, W. (1961). *Family constellation: Its effects on personality and social behavior*. New York: Springer.

Tomm, K. M. (1984). One perspective on the Milan approach: Part 1. Overview of development, theory, and practice. *Journal of Marital and Family Therapy, 10*, 113–125.

Umbarger, C. C. (1983). *Structural family therapy*. New York: Grune & Stratton.

Wahlberg, K. E., & Wynne, L. C. (2001). Possibilities for prevention of schizophrenia: Suggestions from research on genotype-environment interaction. *International Journal of Mental Health, 30*, 91–103.

Walsh, J. E. (2004). Does structural family therapy really change the family structure? An examination of process variables. (Doctoral dissertation). *Dissertation Abstracts International: Section B: The Sciences and Engineering, 64* (12–B), 6317.

Watzlawick, P., Weakland, J. H., & Fisch, R. (1974). *Change: Principles of problem formation and problem resolution*. New York: Norton.

Weakland, J. (1976). Communication theory and clinical change. In P. J. Guerin, Jr. (Ed.), *Family therapy: Theory and practice*. New York: Gardner.

Weeks, G. R., & L'Abate, L. (1982). *Paradoxical psychotherapy: Theory and technique*. New York: Brunner/Mazel.

Weisman, A. (2005). Integrating culturally based approaches with existing interventions for Hispanic/Latino families coping with schizophrenia. *Psychotherapy: Theory, Research, Practice, Training, 42*(2), 178–197.

Whitaker, C. (1976). The hindrance of theory in clinical work. In P. J. Guerin, Jr. (Ed.), *Family therapy: Theory and practice* (pp. 154–164). New York: Gardner.

Whitaker, C. A., & Keith, D. V. (1981). Symbolic-experiential family therapy. In A. S. Gutman & D. P. Kniskern (Eds.), *Handbook of family therapy*. New York: Brunner/Mazel.

Wiener, N. (1948). *Cybernetics, or control and communication in the animal and the machine*. Cambridge, MA: Technology Press.

Wynne, L. C., Ryckoff, I. M., Day, J., & Hirsch, S. I. (1958). Pseudomutuality in the family relationships of schizophrenics. *Psychiatry, 21*, 205–220.

CHAPTER 15

Other Psychotherapies

Outline of Other Psychotherapies

ASIAN PSYCHOTHERAPIES

Asian Theories of Personality

Asian Theories of Psychotherapy
    Mindfulness meditation
    Naikan psychotherapy
    Morita therapy

BODY PSYCHOTHERAPIES

Bioenergetic Analysis

Personality Theory and the Body
    Schizoid character
    Oral character
    Narcissistic character
    Masochistic character
    Rigid character

Psychotherapeutic Approaches
    Body assessment techniques
    Soft techniques
    Hard techniques
    Ethics

INTERPERSONAL PSYCHOTHERAPY

Personality Theory
    Grief
    Interpersonal disputes
    Role transitions
    Interpersonal deficits

Goals

Techniques of Interpersonal Therapy
    Initial phase
    Middle phase
    Starting the session
    Encouragement of affect
    Clarification
    Communication analysis
    Termination

PSYCHODRAMA

Theory of Personality
    Roles and sociometry
    Activity in the present
    Encounter
    Spontaneity and creativity

Theory of Psychotherapy
    Assessment
    Roles in the psychodrama
    The process of psychodrama
    Psychodrama techniques

CREATIVE ARTS THERAPIES

Art Therapy

Dance Movement Therapy

Drama Therapy

Music Therapy

This chapter includes a discussion of five unrelated psychotherapies. They are presented here because they represent innovative approaches to therapy that are different from those in the other chapters. They have not been given a full chapter each because, among other reasons, they are not as widely used as other theories, there is relatively little research, or the problems they treat are limited. Each presents a unique and creative approach to the study of therapy that the other chapters do not. Why are they included in this text? Asian therapy represents a very different cultural view than other theories; body therapy makes use of touch, whereas other therapies do not; Klerman's interpersonal therapy was developed by designing treatment manuals for use with depression; psychodrama uses dramatic acting in large groups; and creative arts therapies have clients use artistic expression.

Asian therapies, body psychotherapies, interpersonal psychotherapy, psychodrama, and creative arts therapies are summarized in this paragraph. A feature of Asian therapies is their emphasis on meditation or quiet reflection and, in some cases, their stress on personal responsibility to others. Both mind and body are important in the body psychotherapies, and assessment is made of movement and physique to make judgments about an individual's personality. Therapeutic techniques include suggestions for movement as well as manipulation of body parts to bring about psychological change. Interpersonal therapy was developed as a treatment for depression. Techniques are based on a review of research and theory and are explained in treatment manuals. Psychodrama is an active system in which clients enact their problems, assisted by the therapist, who directs the psychodrama, and by group or audience members, who may play roles related to the client's concern. Creative arts therapies include art, dance movement, drama therapy, and music. Often seen as an adjunct to psychotherapy, some therapists combine them with traditional verbal therapy to help bring about more awareness of emotions and improved social interactions with others.

Because five very different therapeutic approaches are described in this chapter, the format is quite different than that of the preceding chapters. For all but the creative arts therapies, I describe the background of the theory, a synopsis of the personality theory, and the theory of psychotherapy. Regarding the creative arts therapies, I describe some of their commonalities and then give a brief overview of art, dance movement, drama therapy, and music therapy. Additionally, I give examples of applications for all of the therapeutic approaches. Because each of the five approaches is distinct, references are listed after each of the five sections. I have not included recommended readings but rather suggest any of the references following a section of interest.

Asian Psychotherapies

The teachings of Asian philosophies—Hindu, Buddhist, and Confucian—have had an impact on the psychological development of millions of people in Asia over thousands of years. More so than most Western therapies, Eastern therapies have focused on giving individuals guidance in practicing self-awareness. Meditation is often viewed as a modern therapy, leading to relaxation and stress reduction, even though it has been practiced in the East for millennia. Also, two Japanese therapies, Morita and Naikan, that trace their origins to Buddhist teachings are explained, along with Western adaptations of these therapies.

Background

Ideas about psychology that are embedded in Asian philosophy date back more than 3,000 years. Concepts related to personality theory can be found in the ancient Indian Vedic literature going back to about 750 B.C., which contains some of the teachings of Hinduism. Adding to the abundant literature of Hinduism are the teachings of Gautama Buddha, born in 563 B.C., which have been very influential in Asian philosophy and psychology. Gradually, Buddhist and Hindu teachings spread eastward to China and Japan (Bankart, 2003).

Basic to Indian psychology are four concepts that are important in understanding therapeutic techniques derived from Hindu and Buddhist philosophy: dharma, karma, maya, and atman. *Dharma* refers to rules that describe goodness and appropriate behavior. *Karma* refers to the movement from past incarnations that affect the present and the future. *Maya* refers to distorted perceptions of reality and experience that can be identified as such only with direct attention to our own processes of awareness that come about through internal concentration or meditation. *Atman* refers to a concept of universality in which the self is seen not as individual but as part of the entire cosmos. Thus, the individual is a part of God, a part of universal wisdom, and a part of others, past and future. All of these concepts are teachings that emerge from the abundant literature of India.

Of particular interest in current psychotherapy are the Hindu teachings related to yoga, particularly those related to *hatha yoga*, which deals with the physiological discipline required in separating self from thought processes. Hatha yoga combines meditative and physical exercises; other yoga practices focus mainly on meditative abilities. Research has shown that the practice of yoga can bring about changes in muscle tension, blood pressure, heart rate, and brain waves (Khalsa, 2007). For example, yoga has been shown to reduce symptoms of general anxiety disorder (Dermyer, 2009). Current approaches to meditation that are derived from yoga and other systems are described more fully later.

Concepts developing from Buddhist teachings include the four noble truths and the eightfold path. Embodied in the four noble truths are the ideas that living is subject to suffering, wanting to live causes repeated existence, giving up desire releases one from suffering, and escape from suffering is achieved through adherence to the eightfold path. Following this path means that individuals should have correct beliefs, thoughts, speech, actions, ways of living, effort, mindfulness, and attention to escaping from desire (Olendzki, 2005). These teachings and moral values have influenced thinking in India, China, and Japan for centuries.

About 2,000 years ago, Buddhism was brought to China from India, where its ethical teachings made an impact on the Chinese social system. Practical teachings of Buddhism, along with the teachings of Confucius (551–479 B.C.), helped to structure Chinese values and morality, including presenting oneself so that one's moral views can be judged according to the standards of one's community, submitting to the authority of one's elders (family or community leaders), and observing proper conduct in social situations. Confucius's writings describe the way to achieve perfection. These values are often recognized by psychologists writing about cultural differences between Chinese and Western patients when deciding upon appropriate therapeutic procedures. Around the 6th century, the writings of Confucius and Buddha were brought to Japan. Their influences can be seen later in this section when the relatively recent Morita and Naikan psychotherapies are described.

Asian Theories of Personality

Given the brief amount of space and the vast Hindu, Buddhist, and Confucian literature, as well as other writings, I explain some basic ideas that most Asian

Kathleen Olsen

BUDDHA

philosophies have in common rather than describe an Asian theory of personality. Generally, Asian views of personality emphasize experience rather than logic, focusing on a subjective view. Attention is paid to inner states and watching oneself, as one might watch one's cut finger bleed and feel the pain but not give in to the feeling of pain. Asian philosophies are somewhat similar to those of existential philosophers but dissimilar from many other Western philosophies.

One of the most important concepts is that the self is closely related to the universe. According to Asian philosophies, in understanding the self, one has to understand other aspects of the universe as they relate to the self. Understanding where one's self ends and the rest of the universe begins can give a sense of identity and of knowing oneself. Linked to this concept is the emphasis on social relationships, de-emphasizing the individual and valuing the whole of humanity. If individuals are seen in the context of those around them, then the family, often including the extended family, is important throughout life. The concept of independence, growing and leaving one's family, is a Western concept, as Asian values emphasize responsibility for the family. Given this concept of interdependence, in many Asian cultures many aunts and cousins, as well as parents, may take responsibility for child raising (Bankart, 1997). The emphasis on interdependence applies not only to one's family but also to one's ancestors and to future generations. The concept of reincarnation is consistent with a close relationship to the entire cosmos, past, present, and future.

Buddhist writings have implications for psychopathology and problematic personality development. Whereas many Western psychologists focus on only one state of consciousness, Asian philosophers have described several and believe that fantasies, dreams, and perceptions are often distorted (maya) but can be observed through meditation and other awareness processes that are free of illusions. Ability to achieve other states of consciousness can lead to enlightenment or freedom from psychological pain. Observing one's fantasies and thoughts through the process of meditation can be seen as dehypnosis (Tart, 1986). Whereas hypnosis is the absence of awareness of one's consciousness, meditation provides direct observation of it. However, like hypnosis, higher states of consciousness achieved through meditation can lead to changes in brain waves, breathing rate, and body temperature, a feeling of relaxation, and many other physiological changes (Shapiro & Walsh, 2003).

Psychological health, from an Asian perspective, can be viewed as enlightenment, or a freedom from compulsions, fears, and anxieties. Addictions and aversions are dependencies on things, people, or events. Those with addictions (food, drugs, work, or many other things) believe, "I must have a cigarette, a drink, her love, people's admiration," and so forth. Aversions are the opposite: "I must avoid snakes, food, criticism," and so forth. From an Asian perspective, it is important not to be controlled by fears, dependencies, and feelings. By detaching oneself and reaching other states of consciousness, aversions and addictions no longer have strength. Reynolds (1980) gives an example of two hungry Zen priests walking by a bakery:

> The aroma of baking bread drifted in to the street. "What a lovely smell," the junior priest noted. "It certainly is." A few blocks later the junior monk remarked again, "The odor from that bakery makes me want to eat some bread." "What bakery?" (pp. 93–94)

One can assume that the senior priest, able to move quickly from one state of consciousness to another, could quickly move beyond the tantalizing aroma of the bread. This ability to observe one's own fears, desires, and anxieties is an important principle in the treatment strategies that are discussed next.

Asian Theories of Psychotherapy

In this section, three therapeutic approaches, all dealing with attention to one's own processes, are described. Reynolds (1980) refers to Asian therapies as "quiet" therapies because individuals spend time in isolation dealing with their thoughts and in varied states of awareness. Recently, therapists from a variety of theoretical backgrounds have made use of mindfulness meditation. Mindfulness meditation helps individuals be aware of current experience in a relaxed, alert, and accepting way. Naikan therapy has patients focus on past relationships and their mistakes in dealing with others to bring about better relationships with others and greater contributions to society. Morita therapy was designed as an intensive inpatient therapy to help anxious patients redirect tension away from themselves and has been adapted to outpatient therapy. Each is described here, and its application to different psychological disorders is discussed.

Mindfulness meditation. There are many different varieties of meditation (Kristeller, 2007). They vary in their purposes, for example to develop awareness or concentration. I will describe meditation in general before discussing mindfulness meditation. Although meditation is practiced by relatively few people in the West, it is used by many millions of people in the East (Walsh, 2001). Generally, meditation is applied in the East by people seeking higher psychological or religious levels of self-development, whereas in the West it is often used for stress management, relaxation, and dealing with psychological problems. Implicit in views on meditation is that the usual conscious state is not an optimal state because it is subject to distortions, *maya*, and is not under the control of the individual. Walsh (2001) describes higher states of consciousness as follows:

> Without exclusive identification the me/not me dichotomy is transcended and the individual thus perceives him- or herself as being no thing and every thing. That is, such people experience themselves as both pure awareness (no thing) and the entire universe (every thing). Defenses drop away, because when experiencing oneself as no thing there is nothing to defend; when experiencing oneself as every thing there is nothing to defend against. This experience of unconditioned or pure awareness is apparently very blissful. To those with no experience of these states, such descriptions sound paradoxical if not bizarre. However, there is a remarkable similarity in such descriptions across cultures and centuries by those who have taken these practices to their limits. (p. 370)

Mindfulness meditation is used in dealing with psychological problems. First, I will describe what mindfulness meditation is. Then I will illustrate its use in psychotherapy by using a case example. Next, we will examine several different therapies that integrate it into their therapeutic procedures. Research on meditation is quite extensive and I will review it briefly.

Mindfulness is a way of experiencing ourselves in the present. Mindfulness in our daily lives (everyday mindfulness) is related to agreeableness and being conscientious (Thompson & Waltz, 2007). Everyday mindfulness was found not to be related to mindfulness during meditation (Thompson & Waltz, 2007). In doing mindfulness meditation, one is relaxed, open, and alert (Germer, 2005). The focus in mindfulness meditation is on breathing and focusing awareness on the breathing. By focusing on breathing, following the inhale and exhale, feelings and images are likely to arise (Fulton & Siegel, 2005). Individuals are often tempted to stop thinking about unpleasant events and continue to dwell on pleasant events. With practice, meditators learn to tolerate unpleasant events and not be afraid of them. They tend to accept their thoughts and not be disturbed by regrets or past events.

A summary of a typical brief set of instructions for mindfulness practice will help to illustrate what it is (Germer, 2005). First, one can lie down or sit up. In either case, the spine is kept straight within a comfortable position. Eyes may be closed. Individuals attend to their stomach area. They feel the stomach rise on the inhale and fall on the exhale. Individuals concentrate on the breath, focusing on the full length of the inhale and exhale. As Kabat-Zinn (1990, p. 58) states, it is "as if you were riding the waves of your own breathing." When the mind wanders, individuals notice what it wandered to and then bring it back to focusing on breathing. Always the individual returns to focus on the breathing. This type of exercise is practiced for 15 minutes or more every day. As individuals become practiced at this exercise, they may focus on their breathing at various times during the day. They become aware of their thoughts and feelings without judging them. They also become aware of changes that take place in the way they see and feel about things (Kabat-Zinn, 1990). Retreats are available for individuals to practice meditation in a concentrated and supportive atmosphere. Attending a retreat helps individuals become more practiced and skilled in the use of meditation, including mindfulness meditation. Mindfulness meditation is consistent with the four noble truths and the eightfold path, which are often discussed at retreats (Marlatt et al., 2004). Meditation provides an opportunity to practice values consistent with the four noble truths and the eightfold path.

Fulton and Siegel (2005) describe the case of Richard, which can help to illustrate the benefits of mindfulness meditation as a part of psychotherapy. Richard is a 23-year-old man who was deeply in love with Jessica. She ended the relationship and left Richard to return to her former boyfriend. Richard had many angry thoughts about Jessica and her boyfriend and could not control his continual thinking about them. He was depressed and removed from other areas of his life. He tried mindfulness meditation, which was difficult for him to do at first.

> While meditating, Richard was visited by intense sadness and fear, as well as by violent images, including the dismembering of Jessica and her ex-boyfriend. Sometimes the emotions would be experienced as intense pain in the body—tightness of the throat muscle tension everywhere. The images were also disturbing. Hours would pass, with violent scenes playing like a movie before his eyes. (Fulton & Siegel, 2005, p. 45)

However, with meditation, Richard's thoughts and feelings began to change.

> Because he was practicing intensely, Richard had moments in which his discursive thoughts became quiet. He marveled at small events, such as a flower opening toward the sun and the complex cracks in a stone wall. Along with these experiences came a profound sense of peace—feeling part of this natural world. Personal fears and desires diminished in importance. Interspersed with sadness and violently jealous images, he felt moments of love and compassion toward Jessica. Richard was experiencing moments of "no-self" that produced effects a lot like those we would expect from the "healthy self" his psychotherapy was cultivating. (p. 42)

With therapy and increased use of meditation experiences, Richard experienced improvement in his upset over Jessica's leaving him.

Over time, things began to change. First, through exposure, aversion to these experiences became less prominent. Whereas Richard would ordinarily try to distract himself or take drugs, during the retreat, he practiced staying with whatever arose. Second, the grieving over Jessica's decision seemed to be accelerated by the retreat due to the unflinching exposure to the images and feelings. This seemed to kindle a cathartic experience, even though it occurred in silence. By the end of the 2 weeks, Richard felt more at peace. (p. 45)

The values of mindfulness meditation are important in therapeutic work. Surrey (2005), a relational feminist therapist, describes qualities of the heart that she believes are communicated through attention to Buddhist practices. She describes four principles of *brahma viharas* practices. These include loving kindness or general friendliness, compassion or kindness to another person's sadness, sympathetic joy or being happy for good events in the lives of others, and equanimity, or not having one's successes or failures affect one's view of oneself. Although not a mindfulness practice, these values are very consistent with the psychology underlying mindfulness meditation.

Many theories of therapy now use mindfulness meditation as an important part of their treatment. Acceptance and commitment therapy, described in Chapter 8 (p. 311), has mindfulness as a core concept of its approach. Linehan (Linehan & Dexter-Mazza, 2008) has developed dialectical behavior therapy (also described in Chapter 8, p. 312), which makes great use of mindfulness concepts. Dialectical behavior therapy is an evidence-based therapy designed for the treatment of suicidal patients and those with borderline disorder. Mindfulness-based cognitive therapy, described on page 399 of Chapter 10 shows, how mindfulness meditation can be integrated with cognitive therapy (Teasdale, Segal, & Williams, 2003). Mindfulness values have also been incorporated into behavioral treatment (Wilson & Murrell, 2004) and into cognitive therapy (Ong, Shapiro, & Manber, 2008). Rubin (2004) has shown how principles of Buddhism can be incorporated into psychoanalysis.

There have been many studies that examine the benefits of meditation, showing both physiological and psychological changes (Shapiro & Walsh, 2003). A meta-analysis of 20 studies shows the effectiveness of mindfulness-based meditation to reduce stress in patients and bring about other health benefits (Grossman, Niemann, Schmidt, & Walach, 2004). However, after reviewing 15 controlled studies, Toneatto and Nguyen (2007) conclude that mindfulness-based meditation does not have a consistent effect in reducing depression and anxiety. But some research concludes that mindfulness-based meditation does have a powerful effect on reducing depressive symptoms (Jimenez, 2009). Mindfulness-based meditation has been shown to improve the quality of life in older adults with chronic low back pain (Morone, Lynch, Greco, Tindle, & Weiner, 2008), as well as a sample of adults who attended a 1-week self-development course that include mindfulness meditation (Fernros, Furhoff, & Wändell, 2008). However, Shapiro (1992) warns that meditation practiced by some Westerners can have negative effects such as anxiety, confusion, and feelings of incompleteness and social withdrawal. These effects may be the result of excessive focus on self and isolation from others. Most participants in Shapiro's study reported more positive than negative effects.

Naikan psychotherapy. Developed by Ishin Yoshimoto in the early 1950s, Naikan therapy is based on principles related to Mishirabe, a practice of a subsect of Buddhist priests. It is designed to be applicable to patients with a wide variety of problems, as it views self-centeredness as a problem that many people need to overcome (van Waning, 2009). Individuals should become more accepting of others and more appreciative of the kindness of family members and friends (Tanaka-Matsumi, 2004; Tatsumi, 2003). Showing gratitude to others is a significant aspect of Naikan therapy (Bono, Emmons, & McCullough, 2004). Naikan therapy helps individuals to develop and view their relationships as more healthy and satisfying. Reynolds (1980, 1981, 1993) has described Naikan therapy as it is practiced in its highly structured state in Japan and the adaptations that have been made in the United States.

In Japan, the first week of Naikan therapy is spent in a hospital or similar facility, with individuals being assigned to a small room. From 5 A.M. until about 9 P.M., they are to spend their hours in self-observation, with only brief time spent for meals and bodily functions. About every hour or two the therapist, or teacher, called *sensei*, enters the room to give instructions and to focus self-observations on past relationships, especially with parents. The patient is to be guided by the following three questions:

1. What did I receive from this person?
2. What did I return to this person?
3. What troubles and worries did I cause this person? (Reynolds, 1993, p. 124)

The sensei serves as a confessor, listening to the patient's reports of past relationships. Resentment and anger toward significant people are recognized but overshadowed by the contributions of others to the patient's life, and gradually the patient becomes more sympathetic and accepting of the viewpoints of others.

After this week of intensive self-observation, patients return home to practice, often for a few hours per day, the self-observation they learned in the intensive week of inpatient self-observation. Reynolds (1981) gives an example of an interview that Yoshimoto had with a middle-aged woman, Mrs. O, midway through her intensive inpatient week.

Dr. Yoshimoto: What did you reflect upon for the month of August?

Mrs.O: My husband calls the family together each year in August for a family trip. All the children and grandchildren come. We all go somewhere together. There's nothing so wonderful as that, but I always put on a grumbling face. "Well, since everyone is here, I suppose I'll go too," I'd say and go along with them.

Dr. Yoshimoto: What did you receive from your husband, what did you return to him, and what troubles did you cause him?

Mrs.O: That he took me along on the trip was something I received from him.

Dr. Yoshimoto: And what did you return to him?

Mrs.O: Well, the family asked me to make rice balls for everyone, and though I didn't feel like it, there was no way out of doing it. But I made them too salty.

Dr. Yoshimoto: What troubles did you cause him? (Reynolds, 1981, p. 550)

Although this interviewing style may seem severe, it is consistent with the emphasis on responsible behavior and the need to understand and appreciate the behavior of others. Reynolds (1993) has adapted Naikan therapy to the United States by shortening the lengthy periods of reflection and introducing assignments that lead to recognition of services performed for us by others and of the troubles we cause others. For example, patients may be asked to say "Thank you," while reflecting, to a mental image of a person, in 10 different ways 10 times a day. They may also be asked to write letters of thanks or apology to important people in their lives, to do services for others, and to contribute to the community. Additionally, they are asked to keep a journal or record of past experiences related to the three questions. Reynolds believes that Naikan therapy can help individuals develop a more balanced, less self-centered, and more realistic perspective on life. Other authors have examined how Naikan therapy deals with the mother–child relationship (Ozawa-de Silva, 2007), and how Naikan therapy fits with psychoanalytic values (van Waning, 2009).

Morita therapy. Originated by Morita Masatake around 1915, Morita therapy was designed as an inpatient therapy for patients suffering from *shinkeishitsu* neuroses, which include obsessive-compulsive disorders, panic disorders, and phobic states. Basically, it is a program of isolation in which patients are taught to accept and reinterpret their symptoms (Ishiyama, 2003; Noda, 2009). The patient's attention is shifted from symptoms to address the tasks that life puts before a person. Participation in life without waiting for symptoms to dissipate is encouraged (Chen, 2005).

In traditional Morita therapy as it is practiced in Japan, the patient is hospitalized for 4 to 5 weeks and undergoes four stages of treatment. In the first phase, from 4 to 7 days, individuals are completely inactive except for eating or going to the bathroom. They are told to suffer, worry, and accept their experience. This helps the patient experience his symptoms and the need for changing his lifestyle. Also, the patient learns that isolation is unpleasant and uncomfortable, making social interaction and physical activity more desirable than before. During the next three phases, patients take on increasingly difficult but mundane and tiring tasks and increase their social interactions, while at the same time keeping a diary upon which the therapist writes comments. The therapist's comments and periodic group discussions on the fundamental teachings of Morita therapy are an important aspect of treatment. In this process, the patient learns that thinking needs to be practical and specific, not idealistic and perfectionistic, so that actions can be taken despite symptoms.

Reynolds has adapted Morita therapy for application in the United States. One change has been to make Morita therapy apply to a wider range of disorders than *shinkeishitsu* neuroses. Basically, patients need to have sufficient intellectual development to understand the teachings implicit in Morita therapy. The severe isolated bed rest used by Morita is rarely employed in the United States. Rather, clients may, when appropriate, engage in quiet sitting. Also, the work tasks Reynolds and his colleagues use are not necessarily the repetitive tasks used by Morita but more often simple tasks of living. Additionally, Zen teachings are incorporated to help individuals learn basic principles to redirect their lives.

An example of outpatient Morita therapy with a test-anxious 40-year-old divorced woman illustrates the Morita therapy approach. Ishiyama (in Reynolds, 1989) describes the physiological and psychological symptoms of V, who was worried about her college exams. His approach can be seen by his summary of the first half-hour session and his instructions to the client.

> I explained her anxiety in terms of the desire for living fully: "Where there is a desire, there is anxiety about being unable to fulfill it. The intensity of your anxiety is an indication of the strength of your desire for meaningful academic accomplishment.

Which would you choose, exhausting your energy trying to conquer anxiety or getting your studying done in spite of it?" She agreed that she would prefer to try the latter.

At the end of our thirty-minute session I gave V the following set of instructions:

1. Accept fears and other feelings as they come. Continue studying and abandon any attempts to change the feelings.
2. Acknowledge the anxiety when it appears and continue studying while experiencing it.
3. Notice the fine details of her anxiety. When she cannot get her mind off the anxiety, study it as she would any natural object. (p. 51)

An important part of Morita therapy is the attention to detail, the writing down of the detail in a diary, and the therapist's comments. In a follow-up interview, V found that the active acceptance was helpful in relieving self-blame. Attention shifted from self-evaluation to objective self-observation.

Summary

Mindfulness meditation, Morita, and Naikan therapies all have their roots in Zen Buddhism, which has been influenced by Hindu teachings that originated in India. The Hindu and Buddhist philosophies teach a way of detaching oneself from judgments, events, and blame. Mindfulness meditation helps individuals to experience the present and not dwell on unpleasant thoughts or feelings, thus experiencing less stress. Naikan therapy emphasizes isolation as a way of realizing and developing social responsibility. Morita therapy stresses the development of practical and concrete approaches to reality rather than the search for idealism or perfection. All emphasize self-awareness and social responsibility.

References

Bankart, C. P. (1997). *Talking cures: A history of Western and Eastern psychotherapies.* Pacific Grove, CA: Brooks/Cole.

Bankart, C. P. (2003). Five manifestations of the Buddha in the West: A brief history. In K. H. Dockett, G. R. Dudley-Grant, & Bankart, C. P. (Eds.), *Psychology and Buddhism: From individual to global community* (pp. 45–69). New York, NY: Kluwer Academic/Plenum.

Bono, G., Emmons, R. A., & McCullough, M. E. (2004). Gratitude in practice and the practice of gratitude. In P. A. Linley & S. Joseph (Eds.), *Positive psychology in practice* (pp. 464–481). Hoboken, NJ: Wiley.

Chen, C. P. (2005). Morita therapy: A philosophy of Yin/Yang coexistence. In R. Moodley & W. West (Eds.), *Integrating traditional healing practices into counseling and psychotherapy* (pp. 221–232). Thousand Oaks, CA: Sage.

Dermyer, H. L. (2009). The psychological effects of an integrative Fū-ZEN Dundefined™ yoga-stretch program for the symptom-based treatment of generalized anxiety disorder in randomly assigned adult participants. *Dissertation Abstracts International: Section B: The Sciences and Engineering, 70* (2–B), 1338.

Fernros, L., Furhoff, A., & Wändell, P. E. (2008). Improving quality of life using compound mind-body therapies: Evaluation of a course intervention with body movement and breath therapy, guided imagery, chakra experiencing and mindfulness meditation. *Quality of Life Research: An International Journal of Quality of Life Aspects of Treatment, Care & Rehabilitation, 17*(3), 367–376.

Fulton, P. R., & Siegel, P. R. (2005). Buddhist and Western psychology: Seeking common ground. In C. K. Germer, R. D. Siegel, & P. R. Fulton (Eds.), *Mindfulness and psychotherapy* (pp. 28–51). New York: Guilford.

Germer, K. (2005). Mindfulness: What is it? What does it matter? In C. K. Germer, R. D. Siegel, & P. R. Fulton (Eds.), *Mindfulness and psychotherapy* (pp. 3–27). New York: Guilford.

Grossman, P., Niemann, L., Schmidt, S., & Walach, H. (2004). Mindfulness-based stress reduction and health benefits: A meta-analysis. *Journal of Psychosomatic Research, 57*(1), 35–43.

Ishiyama, F. I. (2003). A bending willow tree: A Japanese (Morita therapy) model of human nature and client change. *Canadian Journal of Counselling, 37*(3), 216–231.

Jimenez, S. (2009). The role of self-acceptance, negative mood regulation, and ruminative brooding on mindfulness and depressive symptoms: A longitudinal, randomized controlled trial of mindfulness meditation vs. relaxation training. *Dissertation Abstracts International: Section B: The Sciences and Engineering, 69* (8–B), 5031.

Kabat-Zinn, J. (1990). *Full catastrophe living: Using the wisdom of your body and mind to face stress, pain, and illness.* New York: Dell.

Khalsa, S. B. S. (2007). Yoga as a therapeutic intervention. In P. M. Lehrer, R. L. Woolfolk, & W. E. Sime (Eds.), *Principles and practice of stress management* (3rd ed., pp. 449–462). New York: Guilford.

Kristeller, J. L. (2007). Mindfulness meditation. In P. M. Lehrer, R. L. Woolfolk, & W. E. Sime (Eds.), *Principles and practice of stress management* (3rd ed., pp. 393–427). New York: Guilford.

Linehan, M. M., & Dexter-Mazza, E. T. (2008). *Dialectical behavior therapy for borderline personality disorder.* New York, NY: Guilford Press.

Marlatt, G. A., Witkiewitz, K., Dillworth, T. M., Bowen, S. W., Parks, G. A., Macpherson, L. M. et al. (2004). Vipassana meditation as a treatment for alcohol and drug use disorders. In S. C. Hayes, V. M. Follette, & M. Linehan (Eds.), *Mindfulness and acceptance: Expanding the cognitive-behavioral tradition* (pp. 261–287). New York: Guilford.

Morone, N. E., Lynch, C. S., Greco, C. M., Tindle, H. A., & Weiner, D. K. (2008). "I felt like a new person." The effects of mindfulness meditation on older adults with chronic pain: Qualitative narrative analysis of diary entries. *Journal of Pain, 9*(9), 841–848.

Noda, F. (2009). Anxiety, acceptance and Japanese healing. In M. Incayawar, R. Wintrob, L. Bouchard, & G. Bartocci (Eds.), *Psychiatrists and traditional healers: Unwitting partners in global mental health* (pp. 167–178). New York: Wiley-Blackwell.

Olendzki, A. (2005). Glossary of terms in Buddhist psychology. In C. K. Germer, R. D. Siegel, & P. R. Fulton (Eds.), *Mindfulness and psychotherapy* (pp. 289–296). New York: Guilford.

Ong, J. C., Shapiro, S. L., & Manber, R. (2008). Combining mindfulness meditation with cognitive-behavior therapy for insomnia: A treatment-development study. *Behavior Therapy, 39*(2), 171–182.

Ozawa-de Silva, C. (2007). Demystifying Japanese therapy: An analysis of Naikan and the Ajase complex through Buddhist thought. *Ethos, 35*(4), 411–446.

Reynolds, D. K. (1980). *The quiet therapies.* Honolulu: University Press of Hawaii.

Reynolds, D. K. (1981). Naikan psychotherapy. In R. J. Corsini (Ed.), *Handbook of innovative psychotherapies* (pp. 544–553). New York: Wiley.

Reynolds, D. K. (1993). *Plunging through the clouds: Constructive living currents.* Albany: State University of New York Press.

Rubin, J. (2004). Psychoanalysis and Buddhism. In U. P. Gielen, J. M. Fish, & J. G. Draguns (Eds.), *Handbook of culture, therapy, and healing* (pp. 253–276). Mahwah, NJ: Erlbaum.

Shapiro, D. H. (1992). Adverse effects of meditation: A preliminary investigation of long-term meditation. *International Journal of Psychosomatics, 39* (Special Issues Nos. 1–4), 62–67.

Shapiro, S. L., & Walsh, R. (2003). An analysis of recent meditation research and suggestions for future directions. *Humanistic Psychologist, 31*(2–3), 86–114.

Surrey, J. L. (2005). Relational psychotherapy, relational mindfulness. In C. K. Germer, R. D. Siegel, & P. R. Fulton (Eds.), *Mindfulness and psychotherapy* (pp. 91–110). New York: Guilford.

Tanaka-Matsumi, J. (2004). Japanese forms of psychotherapy: Naikan therapy and Morita therapy. In U. P. Gielen, J. M. Fish, & J. G. Draguns (Eds.), *Handbook of culture, therapy, and healing* (pp. 277–291). Mahwah, NJ: Erlbaum.

Tart, C. (1986). *Waking up: Overcoming the obstacles to human potential.* Boston: New Science Library/Shambhala.

Tatsumi, N. (2003). Naikan therapy based upon Japanese culture. *International Medical Journal, 10*(3), 195–197.

Teasdale, J. D., Segal, Z. V., & Williams, J. M. G. (2003). Mindfulness training and problem formulation. *Clinical Psychology: Science and Practice, 10*(2), 157–160.

Thompson, B. L., & Waltz, J. (2007). Everyday mindfulness and mindfulness meditation: Overlapping constructs or not? *Personality and Individual Differences, 43*(7), 1875–1885.

Toneatto, T., & Nguyen, L. (2007). Does mindfulness meditation improve anxiety and mood symptoms? A review of the controlled research. *Canadian Journal of Psychiatry / La Revue Canadienne De Psychiatrie, 52*(4), 260–266.

van Waning, A. (2009). Naikan—A Buddhist self-reflective approach: Psychoanalytic and cultural reflections. In S. Akhtar (Ed.), *Freud and the Far East: Psychoanalytic perspectives on the people and culture of China, Japan, and Korea.* (pp. 255–273). Lanham, MD: Jason Aronson.

Walsh, R. (2001). Meditation. In R. J. Corsini (Ed.), *Handbook of innovative psychotherapies* (2nd ed., pp. 368–380). New York: Wiley.

Wilson, K. G., & Murrell, A. R. (2004). Values work in acceptance and commitment therapy: Setting a course for behavioral treatment. In S. C. Hayes, V. M. Follette, & M. Linehan (Eds.), *Mindfulness and acceptance: Expanding the cognitive-behavioral tradition* (pp. 120–151). New York: Guilford.

Body Psychotherapies

Body psychotherapies are characterized by their integration of verbal and bodily processes. By viewing the patient's posture, physique, breathing, musculature, and other physical features, the therapist may make comments about inferred emotional issues or about physical manifestations, or, guided by such observations, may touch the patient to bring about bodily or psychological change. Body therapy began with Wilhelm Reich, a psychoanalyst and a member of the Vienna Psychoanalytic Society from 1921 to 1934. Reich observed his patients carefully, focusing on their breathing and physical changes, especially when they discussed emotional issues. His work was extended by his student, Alexander Lowen, who originated bioenergetic analysis, integrating psychoanalytic concepts with bodily processes. A number of colleagues and students of Lowen, such as John Pierrakos, have developed a variety of strategies for integrating physiological and verbal processes. In this section, Reich and Lowen's views of personality development and psychotherapy are described, along with Smith's integrative approach, which includes concepts from gestalt therapy and those of several body psychotherapists.

Background

Bettmen/Corbis

WILHELM REICH

Wilhelm Reich (1897–1957) was viewed by Freud (Jones, 1957) as an excellent analyst, but he later came to be known for innovative ideas in psychotherapy, some of which were bizarre. His innovative ideas were the integration of body and mind in psychotherapy (Heller, 2007; Young, 2008b). His bizarre ideas dealt with the belief that severe illnesses such as cancer or schizophrenia could be cured by lying in a metal box surrounded by wood (an orgone box) that would pass life-sustaining orgone energy from the universe to the patient. This latter involvement led to Reich's trial and imprisonment for selling orgone accumulators in violation of a federal injunction. This event and some of his ideas in later life have diverted the focus away from his innovative and influential contributions to body psychotherapy (Corrington, 2003; Reich & Higgins, 1999).

One of Reich's (1951, 1972) important contributions is that of muscular armor. Developed in early childhood when the infant's instinctual needs conflict with demands of the parent and others in the environment, the *muscular armor* is a protective mechanism to deal with punishment for acting on instinctual demands, such as urinating in public. The body armor or muscular rigidities that develop are an expression of the neurotic character that reflects the social need to restrain instinctual impulses (Smith, 1985).

To deal with the body armor that had developed, Reich observed and manipulated a patient's body so that emotional energy could be released and life forces could flow freely through the body. This approach, called *vegetotherapy*, reflects Reich's view that all living things possess vital energy that should flow unblocked. Applying this to patients, Reich would have them disrobe and lie down on a bed so that he could observe and feel the blockage or body armor of his patients. By working on muscle knots and exerting pressure in particular areas, Reich (1972) allowed energy to flow in the patients' bodies and dealt with the emotions that would be unlocked along with the muscles. His process was to start at the top of the head and work down to the pelvic area. For example, in working in the neck area, he might find that the patient may express anger toward a brother who was a pain in the neck. Along with working gradually down the body, Reich also helped his patients to breathe more freely. As a result of this therapeutic process, patients would dissolve some of their body armor and become more spontaneous in and out of therapy. Thus, physiological and psychological changes occurred together.

Whereas Freud had viewed libido as an abstract concept representing energy or the driving force of personality, Reich saw energy as a physical force that could be measured, which he first called *bioelectrical energy* and later *orgone* (Corrington, 2003; Reich & Higgins, 1999). When Reich reduced muscular tension, orgone would then flow, and individuals might then experience anxiety, anger, or sexual excitation. Reducing blocks to muscular tension would also reduce neurotic behavior and encourage efficient energy flow. For Reich, full orgiastic potency was not possible in a neurotic personality. Along with full emotional expression, orgiastic potency could be brought about by reducing muscular blockage and allowing energy to flow.

Bioenergetic analysis. A patient and student of Reich's, Alexander Lowen (1910–2008) (Cinotti, 2009), along with John Pierrakos (1921–2001), expanded Reich's work in several ways, including the use of a more varied method of treatment. One of Lowen's (1975, 1997) most important additions was *grounding*, which emphasized that the individual must, literally, be in strong contact with the ground through feet and legs, as well as, figuratively, grounded in the real world. Individuals who are not well grounded may experience a variety of neurotic disorders (to be described later) and may be unable to take a stand on issues, be a pushover for others, and be afraid of falling, literally or figuratively (for example, falling to the back of the class). One implication of Lowen's (1975, 1980) concept of grounding is his work with patients in a variety of positions, such as standing or bending, rather than lying on a bed. Also, Lowen developed a variety of exercises that could be used both in the therapist's office and at home to make patients less dependent on the therapist.

Another important difference between Reich and Lowen is Lowen's (1975) incorporation of psychoanalytic concepts. In bioenergetic analysis, Lowen (1989) used analytic concepts of transference and countertransference, as well as dreams, slips of the tongue, and the working through of Oedipal issues. Also, Lowen saw the pleasure principle as an important value for individuals and viewed it more broadly than did Reich, who focused on sexual fulfillment as an important therapeutic goal. In general, Lowen's approach to working with the body was more flexible than Reich's because he would often work first with concepts related to grounding and then move to other areas of the body, rather than working from the head to the pelvis, as did Reich. Additionally, Lowen has popularized body psychotherapy through his several writings (1958, 1975, 1977, 1980, 1997), his work with therapists in training seminars, and the establishment of the International Institute for Bioenergetic Analysis in New York.

In the following sections, I emphasize Lowen's development of Reich's views of neurotic character types and the physiological characteristics associated with them. Additionally, I summarize Smith's (1985) approach to assessment and therapeutic techniques that include gentle and strong physical interventions to bring about psychological change.

Personality Theory and the Body

As can be seen from Reich and Lowen's approach to therapy and psychological health, viewing the human organism as a unified functioning whole is paramount. A problem that affects one part of the body has an impact on other aspects of physical and psychological functioning. When a person develops skin cancer, it is not just the affected part of the body but the whole individual who is ill. When individuals become depressed, their physiological functioning is affected in many ways. The same would be true with obsessions, anxiety, and all other psychological disorders. Also, if an individual is in a sedentary job and rarely uses the lower body, the lower body does not develop fully, and thus neither does the individual as a whole person (Lowen, 1975).

The focus on unity can be seen in the body's pulsations, such as in the beating of the heart or breathing. In breathing, the whole body participates, not just the lungs. When a person is inhaling, there is a wave beginning in the pelvis and moving upward to the mouth, which is reversed when exhaling (Lowen, 1989). Thus, it follows from the point of view of body psychotherapists that when individuals suffer from a psychological disorder, their breathing changes also. For example, Lowen (1975) noted that he tried to help depressed individuals increase their oxygen intake by getting them to breathe more fully. He observed that when a patient's respiration is more active, her energy level is likely to rise. Changing breathing does not cure the depressive condition; the change is only momentary. However, analyzing other factors related to being depressed physically and psychologically can bring about a more permanent change in depression level, and breathing becomes easier and deeper.

Not only do physiological and psychological disorders affect each other, but they may be affected by past events. Early traumatic experiences may have an impact on how children breathe, stand, walk, or run. Such changes in physiological development may also influence self-image and confidence in physical expression and interaction with others. Trauma, such as child abuse or absence from the mother for prolonged periods, can affect areas of the body such as the throat and mouth, which could be constricted, as in an attempt to reach out to kiss the absent mother. It may also affect breathing patterns that change due to a child hyperventilating for fear of being abandoned.

Using Reich's typology as a beginning, Lowen (1975) described five types of character structures that have developed because of trauma at an early age: schizoid, oral, narcissistic, masochistic, and rigid. It is Lowen's belief that the earlier the trauma occurs to produce the disorder, the more severe it is.

Schizoid character. Traumatized in the uterus or in the first few months after birth, the schizoid personality is characterized by avoiding intimate and affective relationships with others. Thinking tends to be dissociated, and such individuals often are preoccupied with their own fantasy world. Lowen (1975) observed that such individuals may appear to have unexpressive and vacant eyes, a tense body, and arms and legs that are poorly coordinated. When examined, the upper and lower halves of the person's body do not seem to go together. Also, it is not uncommon to notice the head held at an angle to one side and a lack of energy in the face, hands, and feet—the opposite of a vibrant personality.

Oral character. Arising from a deprivation of nurturing within the first 2 years of life, the oral personality is characterized by depression and dependence. Such individuals are apt to feel tired, have low energy, and may feel abandoned or disappointed in self or others. The lower body, particularly the legs and feet, is likely to be thin and underdeveloped, with tension in the shoulders and legs that symbolize that the person has been left alone or abandoned.

Narcissistic character. Developing from incidents related to a feeling of being seduced by the parent (usually before the age of 4) or that the patient is special, the narcissistic character develops a sense of being superior to others and a feeling of grandiosity. This superiority can be seen in the overdevelopment of the upper half of the body in comparison to the weakness in the lower half. In posture, the narcissistic personality tends to show tension in the legs and back when standing (Lowen, 1984).

Masochistic character. Developing as a result of the need to be submissive to an overbearing mother or of strict parenting that makes it difficult for the individual to be free and spontaneous (after the second year of life), the masochistic personality is often characterized by whining, complaining, and suppressed anger. In general, such an individual tends to hold in feelings, and the resulting tension can be seen in tight bodily muscles in the arms and legs. Often the eyes have a look of suffering, and the individual has a whining voice.

Rigid character. Developing around the age of 5, the rigid character is different for males and females and is characterized by Oedipal conflicts in both sexes. The traumatic event is often related to a feeling of rejection from the father for both the boy and the girl. Lowen (1975) described the rigid male as needing to prove himself and having a tendency toward arrogance, competitiveness, and inflexibility. The female rigid character is described as histrionic, shallow, and sentimental and as having eroticized relationships with men. For both male and female, the posture is erect, with rigidity in the back muscles and stiffness in the neck. Lowen attributed this rigidity to being humiliated by the opposite-sex parent during the Oedipal period.

Lowen (1975) pointed out that he treats people, not character types, and that individuals usually exhibit a combination of character types. These character types appear to be able to be identified reliably. Examining pictures of people who represented character types, two bioenergetic experts were in general agreement in their identification of types (Glazer & Friedman, 2009). Furthermore, Lowen developed the psychological and physiological factors of each of these types far more fully than is done here (Lowen, 1975). When working with individuals, Lowen integrated information about the body with information about psychological trauma and proceeded in a gradual manner. He compared this process to putting together the pieces of a jigsaw puzzle (Lowen, 1989). Although Lowen's five character types are often used by therapists who subscribe to bioenergetic principles, other body psychotherapists may use other classification systems.

Psychotherapeutic Approaches

In this section, I describe Smith's (1985, 2001) approach to body psychotherapy, which incorporates many of Lowen's methods used in bioenergetic analysis. The emphasis here is on assessment of the whole person and therapeutic techniques that affect the body in gentle or forceful ways (referred to as soft and hard techniques by Smith). Additionally, I give an example of soft techniques being applied in body psychotherapy and briefly outline important ethical issues.

Body assessment techniques. In using assessment in body psychotherapy, Smith describes two different methods: body reading and body awareness. Body reading makes use of systematic observations by the therapist in attempting to understand energy blockages and tensions within the body. In body awareness methods, the patient is more active and develops awareness of his body.

When reading the body, Smith explains the rationale to the patient, and both agree on what the individual will wear during the reading. Smith (1985, p. 71) then helps individuals to relax and informs them that he will observe the client's body. In some cases, he may next run his fingers along the skin to observe temperature differentials. He then writes down his observations. Body psychotherapists often make use of classification systems such as Lowen's to make hypotheses about the individual's personality. However, body psychotherapists such as Smith also do body reading without a typology. In doing this, Smith looks for tensions and pain within the body that indicate armoring, defensiveness, or areas that are numb or "dead." Additionally, Smith attends to vibrations in the body that indicate an aliveness and energy flow within the body and possible blockages. Hot spots in the body, those that are warm to the therapist's touch, indicate an accumulation of energy that has not been processed. Observations can also be made when the patient is in different body positions, such as standing, lying, or letting the body fall. Although a formal body assessment may be done near the beginning of therapy, the body psychotherapist attends to changes in the body throughout therapy and may make interventions involving the body at any time during therapy.

Soft techniques. Soft or gentle techniques of body psychotherapy do not bring about strong emotional reactions or body awareness as quickly as do abrupt or hard techniques. However, they are less likely than hard techniques to bring out emotional issues that the patient is not yet ready to deal with. One soft technique is to ask the patient to assume a particular posture so that she may be able to experience a blocked feeling. Sometimes Smith might observe the patient holding a body part, such as an arm, in an unusual way. The patient may then be asked to move the arm to a different position and to talk about how it feels in both positions.

Touching is an important technique in soft interventions. A hug or a hand on the back can indicate encouragement and caring. Touching the patient where feelings are inhibited, such as on a hot spot, may draw awareness to a particular feeling.

Another important aspect of soft body work is breathing. Smith agrees with Lowen that every emotional problem affects the patient's breathing. As Smith (1985, p. 120) observes, the average individual breathes 14 to 18 times a minute, or as often as 25,000 times a day. One intervention is to call attention to a patient's nonbreathing, if he holds his breath while discussing an issue in therapy. Another intervention is to teach a patient breathing by having him lie on the floor. Then he, or the therapist, places a hand on his abdomen to teach and encourage full breathing. By teaching breathing, the therapist can later call attention to changes in breathing that occur in the therapy hour, and the patient may be able to develop increased awareness about breathing and emotional issues, as well as ways to change breathing.

A variety of creative approaches can be used to help patients become more aware of their bodies and their related emotional concerns. One technique is to have patients stretch body parts, such as arms and neck, or to rotate their bodies in one direction or another. Tensing a taut body part may lead to awareness of anxiety or other emotions. Using a mirror can help patients deal with their judgments about their bodies and body parts as bad or ugly. All of these techniques—moving, touching, and breathing—are designed to help patients develop awareness of themselves and of repressed emotions.

Sometimes, when clients are cognitively aware but are having difficulty accessing their emotions, soft techniques can be a gentle way of facilitating such access. A well-timed and precisely placed touch can convey the therapist's intimate presence and support, as well as help the client focus on the area of the body where the emotion would be experienced if that experience were allowed. In the following example by Edward Smith (personal communication, April 22, 1998), two soft body techniques, body posturing and touch, are illustrated.

> [Client:] How could she be so cruel? I just don't understand how she could talk to me that way … says she wants to break up … just doesn't know if she really loves me.…
>
> [Therapist:] What are you feeling as you tell me this?
>
> [Client:] I feel she's cruel.
>
> [Therapist:] I know. That's what you're thinking. But, what emotion do you feel?
>
> [Client:] I don't know. Maybe angry … or sad maybe.
>
> [Therapist:] I believe that it may be helpful if you can get in touch with whatever emotions you may have deep down inside.
>
> [Client:] Yeah, it's helped before. It's hard for me to get out of my head.
>
> [Therapist:] I have a suggestion. Would you be willing to lie down on your back and let me sit beside you?
>
> [Client:] I'll give it a try. (He lies down; the therapist sits to his right side.)
>
> [Therapist:] That's good, Joe. Just breathe and see if you can let go. (A minute passes.) Keep breathing. (Another minute passes.) What is happening now?
>
> [Client:] I'm starting to feel a little sad.
>
> [Therapist:] Where in your body do you feel your sadness?
>
> [Client:] Here … and here. (Touching his throat and chest.)
>
> [Therapist:] Joe, would it be all right if I placed my right hand on your chest, along your sternum, like this? (Therapist demonstrates on himself.)
>
> [Client:] Yes.… Go ahead.
>
> [Therapist:] (Placing his right hand gently on Joe's sternum.) Just breathe, feel my touch, and let whatever wants to happen, happen. (Two or three

minutes pass.) (A tear appears in the corner of each of Joe's eyes.) Good, Joe. Let that happen. (Another minute passes.) What are you aware of now?

[Client:] I feel so sad (beginning to sob).

[Therapist:] Good, Joe. Stay with your sadness. I'm right here. (Therapist wiggling his hand gently on Joe's chest.)

[Client:] (Sobbing deeply for two or three minutes. Sobbing subsides.)

[Therapist:] How are you feeling?

[Client:] Whew! Relieved (sighing).

[Therapist:] (Slowly removing his hand.) What would you like now?

Client: I wish I could tell Mary how much she has meant to me and how she's hurt me.

[Therapist:] You can. Let's bring Mary here in fantasy. Sit up as you feel ready and imagine Mary is sitting over here. (Joe sits up.) See Mary as vividly as you can, and when you are ready, speak directly to her.

At this point in the session, having accessed and experienced his hurt and sadness by using body posturing and touch, Joe is ready to clarify his position through a gestalt empty-chair dialogue with Mary (see Chapter 7).

Hard techniques. When using hard techniques, the therapist must use good judgment, as the techniques may be uncomfortable or painful and may bring about intense emotional responses. Uncomfortable postures such as arching the body into a bow, standing on one leg, or lying with legs in the air can bring about vibrating or other bodily responses to which the patient may have an emotional reaction. These postures are related to the concept of grounding, described previously, and may help the individual get in better touch with reality. Smith also discusses deep and heavy massaging of the jaw, neck, and chest that can bring about "energy streaming" and strong emotional reactions. Hard techniques can also be applied to breathing, by pressing hard against different areas of the chest, for instance. Certain techniques are best used in groups. For example, patients can experience the feeling of being safely "contained" by other group members who give them balanced resistance when patients try to strike out with their arms or legs. Thus, the patient can experience rage without any harm or destruction.

Besides direct soft and hard body psychotherapy techniques, Smith uses gestalt expressive techniques. Several of these methods are described in Chapter 7, and a few that particularly emphasize bodily awareness are described here. For example, a patient who is angry at his wife may be pounding the arm of his chair while telling about his wife. The therapist may ask the patient to pound a pillow, imagining that it is his wife, and thus express the emotional energy. It is important to explain that this is a way of understanding the emotional energy and is not a rehearsal or permission for doing this to an individual. Other expressive techniques, discussed in Chapter 7, include exaggerating or repeating an action, such as the pounding of the fist, thus expanding the individual's awareness and enhancing the emotional expression. The gestalt empty-chair technique can be used by substituting a large pillow for the chair (Kepner, 2001) and allowing the patient to kick, pat, hit, or hug the pillow. Expressive, soft, and hard body psychotherapeutic techniques allow the patient to become more aware of bodily and emotional processes and to experience a safe emotional expression.

Body psychotherapy continues to generate interest. In the United States, some therapists with interest in body therapy are members of the United States Association for Body Psychotherapy. In Europe there are a number of body psychotherapy associations (Young, 2008a). Hartley (2009) has collected writings by members of the Chiron Association in *Contemporary Body Psychotherapy: The Chiron Approach*. The Chiron approach to body psychotherapy is an integrative one making use of gestalt techniques (Reynolds, 2009) as well as psychoanalytic concepts, and many others. A concept that is basic to the Chiron approach is that of *self-regulation*, which refers to individuals developing balance, self expression, and improved health in their lives (Carroll, 2009). Body psychotherapy has been evaluated with patients with generalized anxiety disorder who showed more improvement in symptom reduction than a group of patients receiving psychiatric treatment as usual (Levy Berg, Sandell, & Sandahl, 2009). Body psychotherapy has also been used in the treatment of a number of psychological disorders such as depression (Steckler & Young, 2009), schizophrenia (Röhricht, Papadopoulos, Suzuki, & Priebe, 2009), and sexual abuse (Clark, 2009). However, concern about ethical issues prevents a number of therapists from using body psychotherapy.

Ethics. Because body psychotherapies provide intimate contact between patient and therapist, ethical considerations are of primary importance. Smith (1985) emphasizes that the therapist's function is to help the patient grow, not to show how clever or powerful the therapist is. In ethically guided psychotherapy, it is important that the therapist not have sexual intentions or treat the patient in a way that is not in the patient's best interest. Professional codes of ethics forbid therapists' sexual behavior in therapy. The role of touch in body psychotherapy, and therapy in general, is a complex issue that has received recent attention (Asheri, 2009; Kepner, 2001; Smith, Clance, & Imes, 1997). In workshops that body-oriented psychotherapists give, it is important to be aware that many participants may be in therapy with other therapists and to be respectful of that relationship. Another ethical issue concerns the accurate assessment of patients' abilities and pathology so that hard techniques are not used that leave the patient unable to cope with strong emotions. Kepner (2001) states that the therapist must be respectful of the patient and use body-oriented techniques only with the informed consent of the patient.

Summary

Body psychotherapists consider the individual as a whole, believing that bodily and psychological processes are one and the same. One approach to body psychotherapy is that of Lowen's bioenergetics, which is based on the earlier work of Reich. In bioenergetics and other body psychotherapies, assessment is made by attending to posture, musculature, and other aspects of physique. Psychotherapeutic interventions may include work on breathing, posture, blockages in muscles, and bodily manipulation. Observations are integrated with psychotherapeutic procedures, such as psychoanalysis (Lowen) and gestalt therapy (Smith). Interest in body psychotherapies continues in Europe and the United States. Because of the power and intimacy of the techniques, ethical issues are of extreme importance.

References

Asheri, S. (2009). To touch or not to touch: A relational body psychotherapy perspective. In L. Hartley (Ed.), *Contemporary body psychotherapy: The Chiron approach* (pp. 106–120). New York: Routledge.

Carroll, R. (2009). Self-regulation—An evolving concept at the heart of body psychotherapy. In L. Hartley (Ed.), *Contemporary body psychotherapy: The Chiron approach* (pp. 89–105). New York: Routledge.

Cinotti, N. (2009). Obituary: A memory of Alexander Lowen and a reflection on bioenergetic analysis. *International Journal of Psychotherapy*, *13*(2), 68–73.

Clark, J. (2009). Facing the abuser in the abused in body psychotherapy. In L. Hartley (Ed.), *Contemporary body psychotherapy: The Chiron approach*. (pp. 212–225). New York: Routledge.

Corrington, R. S. (2003). *Wilhelm Reich: Psychoanalyst and radical naturalist*. New York: Farrar, Straus and Giroux.

Glazer, R., & Friedman, H. (2009). The construct validity of the bioenergetic–analytic character typology: A multi-method investigation of a humanistic approach to personality. *The Humanistic Psychologist*, *37*(1), 24–48.

Hartley, L. (Ed.). (2009). *Contemporary body psychotherapy: The Chiron approach*. New York: Routledge.

Heller, M. C. (2007). The golden age of body psychotherapy in Oslo II: From vegetotherapy to nonverbal communication. *Body, Movement and Dance in Psychotherapy*, *2*(2), 81–94.

Jones, E. (1957). *The life and works of Sigmund Freud (Vol. 3)*. New York: Basic Books.

Kepner, J. (2001). Touch in gestalt body process psychotherapy: Purpose, practice, and ethics. *Gestalt Review*, *5*, 97–114.

Levy Berg, A., Sandell, R., & Sandahl, C. (2009). Affect-focused body psychotherapy in patients with generalized anxiety disorder: Evaluation of an integrative method. *Journal of Psychotherapy Integration*, *19*(1), 67–85.

Lowen, A. (1958). *The language of the body*. New York: Macmillan.

Lowen, A. (1975). *Bioenergetics*. New York: Penguin.

Lowen, A. (1977). *The way to vibrant health*. New York: Harper & Row.

Lowen, A. (1980). *Fear of life*. New York: Macmillan.

Lowen, A. (1984). *Narcissism: Denial of the true self*. New York: Macmillan.

Lowen, A. (1989). Bioenergetic analysis. In R. J. Corsini & D. Wedding (Eds.), *Current psychotherapies* (4th ed., pp. 573–584). Itasca, IL: Peacock.

Lowen, A. (1997). My evolution as a body-mind therapist: Healing the split in the modern personality. In J. K. Zeig (Ed.), *The evolution of psychotherapy: The third conference* (pp. 135–145). New York: Brunner-Mazel.

Reich, W. (1951). *Selected writings*. New York: Farrar, Straus and Giroux.

Reich, W. (1972). *Character analysis*. New York: Orgone Institute Press.

Reich, W., & Higgins, M. B. (1999). *American odyssey: Letters and journals 1940–1947*. New York: Farrar, Straus, and Giroux.

Reynolds, A. (2009). Gestalt body psychotherapy. In L. Hartley (Ed.), *Contemporary body psychotherapy: The Chiron approach* (pp. 45–59). New York: Routledge/Taylor & Francis Group.

Röhricht, F., Papadopoulos, N., Suzuki, I., & Priebe, S. (2009). Ego-pathology, body experience, and body psychotherapy in chronic schizophrenia. *Psychology and Psychotherapy: Theory, Research and Practice*, *82*(1), 19–30.

Smith, E. W. L. (1985). *The body in psychotherapy*. Jefferson, NC: McFarland.

Smith, E. W. L. (2001). Awe and terror in the living of the resolution of the polarity of insight and expression. *The Psychotherapy Patient*, *11*, 99–121.

Smith, E. W. L., Clance, P. R., & Imes, S. (Eds.). (1997). *Touch in psychotherapy: Theory, research, and practice*. New York: Guilford.

Steckler, L., & Young, C. (2009). Depression and body psychotherapy. *International Journal of Psychotherapy*, *13*(2), 32–41.

Young, C. (2008a). Body-psychotherapy in Europe: EABP & the EAP. *International Journal of Psychotherapy*, *12*(3), 67–74.

Young, C. (2008b). The history and development of body-psychotherapy: The American legacy of Reich. *Body, Movement and Dance in Psychotherapy*, *3*(1), 5–18.

Interpersonal Psychotherapy

Interpersonal psychotherapy was developed by Gerald Klerman (1929–1992) with contributions by his wife, Myrna Weissman, and other colleagues. Interpersonal therapy is different from other theories discussed in this book in several respects. First, it was designed to be a brief system (12 to 16 sessions) to be used in research. A psychiatrist, Klerman believed that all methods of treating psychiatric disorders should be tested before being recommended to the public at large. Thus, if medications such as Prozac should be tested, so should psychotherapy. In order to develop a method that can be researched, Klerman felt it was important to specify a specific disorder and to develop a treatment manual for it. His method was developed to treat depression, and although it has been applied to some other disorders, its application has been done carefully and applied to many fewer disorders than other theories, such as cognitive therapy.

The term *interpersonal therapy* is somewhat confusing, as it has been used for several approaches. Kiesler (1996) has a very different method that focuses on the transactions between individuals, whereas Klerman's (Stuart, 2004; Swartz & Markowitz, 2009; Weissman, Markowitz, & Klerman, 2000, 2007) approach identifies important interpersonal situations and suggests individualistic solutions for clients. Harry Stack Sullivan (1953) also developed a system called interpersonal psychotherapy, which has had some influence on both Kiesler's and Klerman's approaches.

Background

In developing interpersonal psychotherapy, Klerman (Klerman & Weissman, 1993; Klerman, Weissman, Rounsaville, & Chevron, 1984; Markowitz, 2003; Weissman et al., 2000, 2007) was influenced by both early theorists and research on depression. The writings of Adolf Meyer (1957) emphasized the importance of both psychological and biological forces. According to Meyer, psychiatric disorders developed as individuals tried to adapt to their environment. Early experiences with both the family and various social groups influenced individuals' adaptation to their environment. Also, the work of Harry Stack Sullivan (1953) showed the importance of peer relationships in childhood and adolescence as they had an impact on later interpersonal relationships. Another source of theoretical development was John Bowlby's work (1969) in understanding early attachment and bonding with the mother. Although these three theorists were interested in childhood relationships and experiences, they would be considered as outside of the mainstream of psychoanalytic writers.

In developing a brief therapeutic approach to the treatment of depression, Klerman studied psychological research on depression to determine which factors played a role in the onset of depression. Several important conclusions from the research that helped Klerman (Klerman et al., 1984) determine which aspects of depression to treat are described here. Clearly, certain life events created stress that led to depression. The loss of social relationships also contributed to the onset of depression. When women became depressed, they interacted more poorly socially (for example, were nonassertive). Also, social and interpersonal stress, especially stress in marriage, affected the development of depression. Arguments between spouses were related to the onset of depression. Reviewing this research led Klerman to identify four major problem areas that interpersonal therapy should be able to address and treat: grief, interpersonal disputes, role transitions, and interpersonal deficits. Whereas almost all of the theorists described in this book relied on their clinical experience to develop their theoretical approach to therapy, Klerman made significant use of existing psychological data to develop his.

Not only was research important in the development of interpersonal psychotherapy, but so was the continual testing of interpersonal therapy's effectiveness as it was developed. Research, especially on the treatment of depression, continues to be an active area of scientific study. Several meta-analyses have been conducted contrasting interpersonal psychotherapy with cognitive therapy. Weissman (2007) states that cognitive therapy and interpersonal psychotherapy have been the most widely tested psychotherapies for the past 30 years. In a meta-analysis of 13 studies that compared cognitive-behavior therapy to interpersonal therapy, the authors concluded that interpersonal therapy was more effective than cognitive-behavior therapy (de Mello, de Jesus Mari, Bacaltchuk, Verdeli, & Neugebauer, 2005). Combining the results of seven meta-analyses of 53 studies, Cuijpers, van Straten, Andersson, and van Oppen (2008) reported that there were no clear differences in effectiveness between cognitive-behavior therapy and interpersonal therapy, but cognitive therapy had a higher dropout rate than interpersonal psychotherapy. In a meta-analysis of 19 studies that evaluated preventive methods for reducing depression, interpersonal psychotherapy may be seen as more effective in preventing depression than cognitive-behavioral therapy (Cuijpers, van Straten, Smit, Mihalopoulos, & Beekman, 2008).

Research, which is primarily on depression and related disorders, continues to be an important aspect of the development of interpersonal therapy. Interpersonal therapy has been thoroughly studied and is considered to be a research-supported psychological treatment for depression. For example, a specific manual was designed for treating depressed adolescents. When applied to treatment, depressed adolescents after a year or more follow-up had more symptom reduction and better social functioning than those who were deferred for treatment (Mufson, Dorta, Moreau, & Weissman, 2005). After evaluating therapies for adolescent depression and mood disorders, Curry and Becker (2008) and Brunstein-Klomek, Zalsman, and Mufson (2007) conclude that interpersonal psychotherapy is a research-supported psychotherapy for adolescents who suffer from depression and mood disorders.

Interpersonal psychotherapy can be helpful to pregnant women to reduce symptoms of depression and to prepare to be a parent (Spinelli, 2008). In a study of 53 patients who came to an obstetric clinic but were not seeking psychotherapeutic services, those who were offered brief interpersonal psychotherapy were found to have fewer symptoms of depression and to be less likely to have postpartum depression than those who did not have brief interpersonal psychotherapy (Grote et al., 2009). A study of the treatment of women with postpartum depression showed the effectiveness of interpersonal therapy when compared with a waiting-list group (O'Hara, Stuart, Gorman, & Wenzel, 2000). Also, interpersonal psychotherapy was more effective in treating depressed pregnant women than was a parent education program (Spinelli & Endicott, 2003).

Recent attention has been paid to individuals over the age of 65 to 70 who are suffering from depression and received interpersonal psychotherapy (Hinrichsen, 2008a, 2008b). Miller et al. (2007) has developed a model for using interpersonal psychotherapy with older persons with cognitive disabilities and a special version of manualized interpersonal psychotherapy for them (Miller, 2009). After patients have received interpersonal psychotherapy, they may continue to see a therapist once a month. This procedure is called maintenance treatment. In a study of 363 individuals over 70, maintenance medication was found to be superior to a placebo in maintaining improvements, but improvements were not maintained with interpersonal psychotherapy (Dombrovski et al., 2007). However, in another study of 2-year maintenance of interpersonal psychotherapy, the once-a-month sessions of interpersonal psychotherapy worked better with individuals with lower rather than higher cognitive functioning (Carreira et al., 2008). These studies are examples of ongoing research on interpersonal therapy with individuals with depression.

Personality Theory

Klerman (Klerman et al., 1984) was less concerned with the cause of depression than with helping individuals deal with the kinds of issues that affect their lives. As shown previously, Klerman believed that depression was the result of a variety of interpersonal issues. Many of these may have been caused by difficulties in early relationships or problems of attachment within the family. However, to deal with these in a brief treatment approach did not seem to be the most effective way to help individuals deal with their current symptoms of depression. Rather, he believed that there were four interpersonal problem areas that, if they could be alleviated, would help an individual deal with depression: grief, interpersonal disputes, role transitions, and interpersonal deficits.

Grief. Although grief is considered a normal emotion, not a psychiatric disorder, it can provide difficulties for people in mourning, particularly when the reaction is severe and continues over a long period of time. Grief may present a particularly difficult problem when individuals experience the loss of more than one person who is close to them. Furthermore, some individuals are more prone to becoming depressed after losing a close friend or family member than are others. This reaction is often referred to as *complicated bereavement.*

Interpersonal disputes. Often struggles, arguments, or disagreements with others, particularly on a continuing basis, can lead to depression. Sometimes the dispute is with a family member, spouse, child, parent, or other relative. At other times, the dispute may be with someone at work—a boss, a subordinate, or a coworker. Other times disputes are with friends or associates, or people in community organizations, such as in church groups. When individuals are depressed, disputes may be with people in many of these groups.

Role transitions. This is a broad category that includes many different types of life changes. Some are planned for and some are not. Examples of developmental changes are going to college, getting engaged or married, separating or divorcing, dealing with difficult children, or having a child leave the home. Sometimes role transitions have to do with work, such as trying to find a job, dealing with promotion or demotion, or being fired or laid off. Other role transitions may be accidental or not predictable. An individual may develop a serious illness or disease, may be injured in an accident while at work or somewhere else, or have to deal with losing a house to fire or flood. Individuals who are prone to depression may, when faced with one of these situations, see their situation as hopeless or out of control.

Interpersonal deficits. Some individuals may be socially isolated or have few social skills. Individuals who have few friends, "loners," may have difficulty making or sustaining relationships. This can be a default category for patients who do not fit the other categories (Markowitz, 1998). When individuals do not report recent events that may have caused depression, this category is often used. Individuals falling into this category are more likely to have personality disorders than are those in the others. Because this area implies lack of social skills and continuing interpersonal problems, it can be a more difficult area to treat than the other three (Markowitz, 1998).

As the description of these four problem areas shows, the focus of interpersonal therapy is on current problems that deal with relationships. When assessing patient problems, the therapist finds out which ones of the four categories fit the patient's problems. This will have a direct impact on the therapeutic approach the therapist takes. Additionally, the therapist may use such measures as the Hamilton Rating Scale for Depression (Hamilton, 1960) or the Beck Depression Inventory to assess severity of depression. The goals of this brief model are directly related to the assessment.

Goals

The goals of interpersonal therapy are directly related to the specific problem areas that the therapist identifies. Table 15.1 summarizes the goals and treatment for each of the four different problem areas. The four goal areas are described on pages 606 and 607.

Grief. Individuals are helped with the mourning process and to deal with their sadness. They are helped to reestablish interest in relationships and to become involved in both relationships and activities.

Interpersonal disputes. Clients are assisted in understanding disputes or arguments as they relate to depression. They are helped to develop strategies to resolve the dispute or to bring about a change in an impasse. Sometimes they may change their expectations of their problems and relationships with others.

Role transition. When individuals move from one role to the other, they often need to mourn the loss of the old role. Seeing the new role as more positive is one goal. Another is to develop a sense of mastery of the new role or roles and thus increase self-esteem.

Interpersonal deficits. By reducing isolation from others, changes in this problem area can be made. Goals are to develop new relationships or improve ones that may be superficial.

Not only do the problem areas determine the goals for therapy, but the goals determine the specific strategies that are to be used. Table 15.1 lists the specific strategies therapists use to reach each of the goals. The following section describes several techniques used in the three phases of interpersonal therapy.

Techniques of Interpersonal Therapy

The specificity of interpersonal therapy can be seen by the detailed outline in Table 15.1, which fully describes the procedures that Klerman et al. (1984) explain in their treatment manual. Because the approach is detailed so clearly, it can appear to be mechanical (Markowitz, 1998). However, in practice it is quite different. The therapist is an advocate for the patient. Often she may be warm and understanding of the client's difficulty. Clients are encouraged to express their feelings; therapists communicate their understanding of the feelings. In conducting interpersonal therapy, therapists do this in three phases: The initial phase

Table 15.1 Outline of Interpersonal Psychotherapy

I. **The Initial Sessions**
   A. Dealing with depression
      1. Review depressive symptoms.
      2. Give the syndrome a name.
      3. Explain depression as a medical illness and explain the treatment.
      4. Give the patient the "sick role."
      5. Evaluate the need for medication.
   B. Relation of depression to interpersonal context
      1. Review current and past interpersonal relationships as they relate to current depressive symptoms. Determine with the patient the following:
         a. Nature of interaction with significant persons
         b. Expectations of patient and significant persons from one another and whether these were fulfilled
         c. Satisfying and unsatisfying aspects of the relationships
         d. Changes the patient wants in the relationships
   C. Identification of major problem areas
      1. Determine the problem area related to current depression and set the treatment goals.
      2. Determine which relationship or aspect of a relationship is related to the depression and what might change in it.
   D. Explain the IPT concepts and contract
      1. Outline your understanding of the problem.
      2. Agree on treatment goals, determining which problem area will be the focus.
      3. Describe procedures of IPT: "here and now" focus, need for patient to discuss important concerns; review of current interpersonal relations; discussion of practical aspects of treatment—length, frequency, times, fees, policy for missed appointments.

II. **Intermediate Sessions: The Problem Areas**
   A. Grief
      1. Goals
         a. Facilitate the mourning process.
         b. Help the patient reestablish interest and relationships to substitute for what has been lost.
      2. Strategies
         a. Review depressive symptoms.
         b. Relate symptom onset to death of significant other.
         c. Reconstruct the patient's relationship with the deceased.
         d. Describe the sequence and consequences of events just prior to, during, and after the death.
         e. Explore associated feelings (negative as well as positive).
         f. Consider possible ways of becoming involved with others.
   B. Interpersonal disputes
      1. Goals
         a. Identify dispute.
         b. Choose plan of action.
         c. Modify expectations or faulty communication to bring about a satisfactory resolution.

(Continued)

Table 15.1   Outline of Interpersonal Psychotherapy (Continued)

2. Strategies
   a. Review depressive symptoms.
   b. Relate symptom onset to overt or covert dispute with significant other with whom patient is currently involved.
   c. Determine stage of dispute:
      i. Renegotiation (calm down participants to facilitate resolution)
      ii. Impasse (increase disharmony in order to reopen negotiation)
      iii. Dissolution (assist mourning)
   d. Understand how nonreciprocal role expectations relate to dispute:
      i. What are the issues in the dispute?
      ii. What are differences in expectations and values?
      iii. What are the options?
      iv. What is the likelihood of finding alternatives?
      v. What resources are available to bring about change in the relationship?
   e. Are there parallels in other relationships?
      i. What is the patient gaining?
      ii. What unspoken assumptions lie behind the patient's behavior?
   f. How is the dispute perpetuated?
C. Role transitions
   1. Goals
      a. Mourning and acceptance of the loss of the old role.
      b. Help the patient to regard the new role as more positive.
      c. Restore self-esteem by developing a sense of mastery regarding demands of new roles.
   2. Strategies
      a. Review depressive symptoms.
      b. Relate depressive symptoms to difficulty in coping with some recent life change.
      c. Review positive and negative aspects of old and new roles.
      d. Explore feelings about what is lost.
      e. Explore feelings about the change itself.
      f. Explore opportunities in new role.
      g. Realistically evaluate what is lost.
      h. Encourage appropriate release of affect.
      i. Encourage development of social support system and of new skills called for in new role.
D. Interpersonal deficits
   1. Goals
      a. Reduce the patient's social isolation.
      b. Encourage formation of new relationships.
   2. Strategies
      a. Review depressive symptoms.
      b. Relate depressive symptoms to problems of social isolation or unfulfillment.
      c. Review past significant relationships including their negative and positive aspects.
      d. Explore repetitive patterns in relationships.
      e. Discuss patient's positive and negative feelings about therapist and seek parallels in other relationships.

(Continued)

Table 15.1 Outline of Interpersonal Psychotherapy (Continued)

III. Termination
    A. Explicit discussion of termination.
    B. Acknowledgment that termination is a time of grieving.
    C. Move toward recognition of independent competence.

IV. Specific Techniques
    A. Exploratory
    B. Encouragement of affect
    C. Clarification
    D. Communication analysis
    E. Use of therapeutic relationship
    F. Behavior change techniques
    G. Adjunctive techniques

V. Therapist Role
    A. Patient advocate, not neutral
    B. Active, not passive
    C. Therapeutic relationship is not interpreted as transference
    D. Therapeutic relationship is not a friendship

From *Comprehensive Guide to Interpersonal Psychotherapy* by M. M. Weissman, J. C. Markowitz, & G. L. Klerman, pp. 22–25. Copyright © 2000 Basic Books, a Member of Perseus Books Group. Reprinted by permission of Basic Books, a member of Perseus Books, L.L.C.

consists of up to three sessions in which an assessment is made and a framework is set for treatment. The intermediate phase is devoted to work on the four problem areas. The termination phase includes discussion of ending therapy and recognition of competence.

Initial phase. In this phase, a diagnosis, when appropriate, of depression is made and shared with the client. Assessment inventories may be used. Additionally, the therapist assesses the patient's current interpersonal problems in each of the four areas. This helps determine the personal area(s) that the patient and therapist will focus on. Rarely, they will focus on more than two areas (Markowitz, 1998). Then an interpersonal formulation is given to the patient that describes the fact that the person has a medical illness, not a personal weakness. How this is done is shown in the case example on page 610. At this point, the therapist determines if medication, interpersonal therapy, or both should be used. Patients take the sick role in that they are told that being depressed or having an illness is not their fault. By taking the sick role, the patient is encouraged to do something about the illness by coming to therapy to work on it. Since interpersonal therapy follows a medical model, educating the patient about the nature of depression as an illness fits as a part of the initial phase.

An important aspect of the initial phase is to be supportive of the patient and show him that there is hope. The therapist's encouragement and reassurance help build a therapeutic alliance with the patient. The therapist offers initial relief to the patient by telling him that depression is treatable and positive change is likely to occur (but not guaranteed). By coming up with a specific formulation of how the treatment is to proceed, the stage is set for the middle phase of therapy.

Middle phase. Although the interpersonal therapist uses different strategies for each of the four areas (see Table 15.1), some techniques are common to most of these. Many of these techniques are similar to others that are described in this book. However, they are discussed in some detail in Weissman et al. (2000, 2007). All of the techniques deal with interpersonal relationship issues, some more directly than others. Because the role of the therapist is to be supportive and to be on the side of the patient, the therapeutic relationship itself is not typically discussed. However, it may be used as a resource for interpersonal material. The purpose of the therapeutic relationship is to foster relationships outside of therapy. Relationships with others outside of therapy may be long-lasting, but the relationship in a 12- to 16-session model will not be. Common techniques used in interpersonal therapy are described here.

Starting the session. Klerman advocates the use of this question in starting a session: "How have things been since we last met?" (Klerman et al., 1984). The reason for this question is that it asks the patient to bring up recent events, not ones in the distant past. This allows the therapist to discuss events and the moods or feelings that accompany them. By asking for the patient to describe the event in detail, the therapist has significant interpersonal material to work with. Such a question allows the therapist to go into the one or two problem areas that the patient and therapist have decided to work on.

Encouragement of affect. The therapist encourages expression of painful and other emotions. This provides a way of showing understanding of the patient and an opportunity to offer to help with solutions. For example, the therapist may say, "Losing your wife has been so terrible for you," and then may follow it with, "We want to work to help you feel better." This then may lead to, "What might help you feel less depressed?" The therapist wants to find out the patient's desires to explore ways to accomplish the patient's goals.

Clarification. The therapist helps the patient clarify interpersonal relationships that he has just discussed. Sometimes the therapist may point out differences between how patients view their situation and how they actually behave. For example, the therapist may say to the patient, "You say that you are disappointed in your daughter, but I am not clear about how you are disappointed in your daughter in this situation that you just told me about—that time she came home from school late." In this way, the patient can better understand an interpersonal incident that she has just described.

Communication analysis. To analyze an interpersonal situation, the therapist asks the patient to describe exactly what the patient said and what the other person said. Included in this description may be the tone of voice that each used, as well as other details. The more clearly the therapist understands the situation, the more likely the therapist is able to effectively come up with new alternatives to different situations.

Other techniques are used by interpersonal therapists as well as the ones described above. For example, role playing is often used following communication analysis. The therapist can play another person so that the patient can develop new ways for dealing with that person. The therapist may give the patient feedback about the words the patient used, his tone of voice, or his facial expression. Practicing new behaviors to use in interpersonal relationships can be helpful in a variety of situations. In general, the techniques the therapists use will help individuals improve interpersonal interactions in one or more of the four areas.

Termination. Typically termination takes place in the last two or three sessions. There is an explicit discussion that treatment is ending. A positive approach to termination is taken by focusing on graduating from therapy and becoming more independent. However, termination can also be a time of sadness, as the therapist's support will not be available. Acknowledging and discussing this sadness or grief can be very helpful. Because of the emphasis on gains and strengths, termination is a time to credit the patient with accomplishments. However, it is also helpful to discuss the potential that depression may recur. If the therapy has not been particularly successful, the therapist does not want to blame the client but may instead put the blame on interpersonal therapy. At this point, other therapeutic options, such as cognitive therapy or continuation in interpersonal therapy may be discussed.

As can be seen from the above description of the three phases of interpersonal therapy, the therapy is focused throughout on one of the four basic areas (grief, interpersonal disputes, role transitions, or interpersonal deficits). Each of the three phases is clearly related to the others. The treatment (Weissman et al., 2000, 2007) assists the therapist in attending to the goals of the therapy.

An Example of Interpersonal Therapy

The following is a brief example of therapy with a 53-year-old woman with dysthymia, a condition similar to depression. It is a mood disorder in which individuals may have more cognitive concerns such as pessimism and low self-esteem than in typical depression. However, the treatment approach is quite similar. In the following section, Markowitz (1998) describes the beginning of his work with Ms. J. and the interpersonal formulation that he gives to her of her problem. He then goes on to show his approach to dealing with an interpersonal dispute (which he refers to as a role dispute).

> Ms. J., a 53-year-old, married saleswoman in an art gallery, reported lifelong dsythymic disorder. "I'm useless," she said, "Just waiting to die." Raised in an emotionally frigid family, she had married unhappily in her late teens in an attempt to escape her family of origin. Her relationship with her husband was distant, asexual, and angry, but she felt too incapable and incompetent to even consider leaving him. She also felt incompetent socially and at work. She could not recall ever feeling happy or capable. Ms. J had had lengthy treatment with psychodynamic psychotherapy, which had provided some fleeting insights but not relief, and with antidepressant medication, which had produced little response even at high doses. She was dubious about the IPT for dysthymic disorder (IPT-D) definition of her problem as a medical mood disorder but conceded that this was at least a fresh view of things. Her initial Hamilton Depression Rating Scale (Ham-D; Hamilton, 1960) score was 24 on the 24-item version of the scale (significantly depressed). She was passively suicidal but had not made plans or attempts ("I'd only mess it up").
>   The therapist gave a version of the usual IPT-D formulation:
>   I don't think you're useless, you just have a medical illness, dysthymic disorder, that makes you feel that way. You've had it for so long that of course it feels like part of you, but it doesn't have to be that way. I would like to spend the next 16 weeks with you working on a *role transition* in which you move from accepting the depression as part of yourself to distinguishing between depression and your healthy self. If you can do that, you're pretty much bound to feel better and more capable.

Therapy thus focused on the role transition of recognizing her "real" personality in contrast to dysthymic symptoms and on expanding her interpersonal repertoire in her relationship with others. She acknowledged her anger at her husband (a role dispute), felt there was no resolving the chronic role dispute between them, and looked into the possibility of moving out but without much conviction. At the same time, she and the therapist worked on her interactions with coworkers. She had been particularly upset by her interactions with a rude, competitive colleague who interrupted her when she was helping customers.

> *Ms. J:* Rose is rude, interrupts me when I'm dealing with patrons. I don't like her at all.
>
> *[Therapist:]* That sounds understandable. What can you do?
>
> *Ms. J:* I'm not good at doing anything.... I don't feel very effective.... Is there a book I can read on how to be effective?
>
> *[Therapist:]* We'll write it right now. Do you feel that it's appropriate for you to be annoyed? I mean, do you feel Rose is genuinely annoying?
>
> *Ms. J:* I never know if it's me or the other person, but I think some other people have been bothered by her too, even though she often comes across as sweet.
>
> *[Therapist:]* So if it's reasonable to feel angry, what can you say to Rose?
>
> *Ms. J:* "Excuse me, I'll talk to you later?"
>
> *[Therapist:]* Does that get across what you want to say? How do you feel? What do you feel like saying?
>
> *Ms. J:* I feel like telling her to learn some manners!
>
> *[Therapist:]* Okay fine! That sounds right, that makes sense to me; but it's a little blunt. Is there another way to put that? Is there a more direct way to tell her why you want her to learn some manners?
>
> *Ms. J:* I'd like to tell her that it's rude to interrupt, that if she waits I'll get back to her, but that she shouldn't break in.
>
> *[Therapist:]* Fine! Now pretend I'm Rose and say it to me....

Note that this interchange tended to normalize anger as an appropriate response for the patient in noxious interpersonal situations (Markowitz, 1998, pp. 120, 121). Later in therapy, Markowitz addresses an interpersonal dispute dealing with Rose's marriage after making a transition from the situation with Rose. He then summarizes the case from an interpersonal therapy (IPT) point of view.

> Although Ms. J insisted that she was a "slow learner" and unlikely to do anything with her life, in the remaining sessions of the 16-week course of IPT she solidified a shaky sense of social competence at work and began to renegotiate matters with her husband. At the same time, she began looking around for an apartment of her own, with the idea of trying to spend a few months on her own to see whether she could function without her husband. Although she felt "too old to be just starting life at 53," she was taking steps to do so, and her Ham-D score fell to 7, essentially euthymic. In monthly continuation and maintenance sessions she reported that she had neither left her husband nor greatly improved her marriage, but she had a clearer perspective on her role in it, a new appreciation of her husband's failings, and less blame for herself. She put together a resume for new jobs but in the meantime felt new respect from her co-workers and a greater sense of competence in her work.

This case demonstrates how the optimistic, "can-do" approach of IPT can mobilize a doubting patient to action. The therapist supported the patient's feeling of anger, which she had regarded as impotent, and helped her to express it more effectively. For patients whose social skills are shaky, role playing is an important rehearsal of interpersonal skills that can then be used in the world outside the office (Markowitz, 1998, p. 123).

Other Applications of Interpersonal Therapy

As interpersonal therapy has been tested in several research studies, Klerman and his colleagues developed more confidence in this approach, creating treatment manuals and research procedures for applying interpersonal therapy to disorders that are similar to depression. For example, Klerman and Weissman (Weissman et al., 2000, 2007) have developed treatment manuals similar to the original (Klerman et al., 1984) for depressed patients who have marital disputes, for individuals in distress but not considered to be clinically depressed, and for patients who may require more than brief therapy for the reoccurrence of depression. An area of recent attention has been that of depressed adolescents (Brunstein-Klomek et al., 2007; Curry & Becker, 2008; Gunlicks & Mufson, 2009; Young & Mufson, 2008, 2009). Other groups include depressed individuals who have been diagnosed as HIV positive (Ransom et al., 2008) and elderly individuals who are diagnosed with depression (Hinrichsen, 2008a, 2008b; Miller, 2009; Miller et al., 2007). Most applications, such as those discussed, have been to conditions similar to unipolar depression. However, interpersonal therapy has also been applied to individuals with bulimia (Arcelus et al., 2009; Constantino, Arnow, Blasey, & Agras, 2005) as well as those who abuse drugs. When used with drug-abusing patients, interpersonal psychotherapy has not been as successful as it has been for depressed patients (Rounsaville & Carroll, 1993). Interpersonal therapy manuals have been developed for individuals with borderline disorder (Markowitz, Bleiberg, Pessin, & Skodol, 2007), panic symptoms (Cyranowski et al., 2005), and posttraumatic stress disorder (Krupnick et al., 2008; Robertson, Rushton, Batrim, Moore, & Morris, 2007). Interpersonal therapy has also been used in group as well as individual treatment, and it has been shown to be effective in treating depressed adolescents (Mufson, Gallagher, Dorta, & Young, 2004) and depressed individuals in rural Uganda (Bolton et al., 2003; Verdeli et al., 2008). When interpersonal therapy is applied to new disorders, a treatment manual is developed or a previous treatment manual is revised, and then the application is, in most cases, tested in a research study.

Summary

The rationale for interpersonal therapy is rather different from that for other theories of psychotherapy. First, it was developed using a medical model in which a plan was designed to test its effectiveness. Also, interpersonal therapy was created to deal with depression rather than other disorders. A survey of psychological theory and research was made in order to develop a treatment manual that therapists would follow. This brief therapy is designed to be completed in 12 to 16 sessions. The initial sessions assess the patient's problems and educate the patient, when appropriate, about depression. The intermediate sessions focus on bringing about change in the four major problem areas: grief, interpersonal disputes, role transitions, and interpersonal deficits. The treatment manuals specify strategies therapists are to use for each of these problem areas, as well as specific techniques that may be used for all problem areas. The third and final phase is termination, in which therapists discuss the ending of therapy and the recognition of being competent and being on one's own. Interpersonal therapy has been applied to other disorders, but most of these have been similar to depression.

References

Arcelus, J., Whight, D., Langham, C., Baggott, J., McGrain, L., Meadows, L., & Meyer, C. (2009). A case series evaluation of the modified version of interpersonal psychotherapy (IPT) for the treatment of bulimic eating disorders: A pilot study. *European Eating Disorders Review, 17*(4), 260–268.

Bolton, P., Bass, J., Neugebauer, R., Verdeli, H., Clougherty, K. F., & Wickramaratne, P. et al., (2003). Group interpersonal psychotherapy for depression in rural Uganda: A randomized controlled trial. *Journal of the American Medical Association, 289*(23), 3117–3124.

Bowlby, J. (1969). *Attachment and loss* (Vol. 1, Attachment). London: Hogarth.

Brunstein-Klomek, A., Zalsman, G., & Mufson, L. (2007). Interpersonal psychotherapy for depressed adolescents (IPT-A). *Israel Journal of Psychiatry and Related Sciences, 44*(1), 40–46.

Carreira, K., Miller, M. D., Frank, E., Houck, P. R., Morse, J. Q., Dew, M. A., Butters, M. A., & Reynolds, C. F., III. (2008). A controlled evaluation of monthly maintenance interpersonal psychotherapy in late-life depression with varying levels of cognitive function. *International Journal of Geriatric Psychiatry, 23*(11), 1110–1113.

Constantino, M. J., Arnow, B. A., Blasey, C., & Agras, W. S. (2005). The association between patient characteristics and the therapeutic alliance in cognitive-behavioral and interpersonal therapy for bulimia nervosa. *Journal of Consulting and Clinical Psychology, 73*(2), 203–211.

Cuijpers, P., van Straten, A., Andersson, G., & van Oppen, P. (2008). Psychotherapy for depression in adults: A meta-analysis of comparative outcome studies. *Journal of Consulting and Clinical Psychology, 76*(6), 909–922.

Cuijpers, P., van Straten, A., Smit, F., Mihalopoulos, C., & Beekman, A. (2008). Preventing the onset of depressive disorders: A meta-analytic review of psychological interventions. *American Journal of Psychiatry, 165*(10), 1272–1280.

Curry, J. F., & Becker, S. J. (2008). Empirically supported psychotherapies for adolescent depression and mood disorders. In R. G. Steele, T. D. Elkin, & M. C. Roberts (Eds.), *Handbook of evidence-based therapies for children and adolescents: Bridging science and practice* (pp. 161–176). New York: Springer.

Cyranowski, J. M., Frank, E., Shear, M. K., Swartz, H., Fagiolini, A., & Scott, J. et al., (2005). Interpersonal psychotherapy for depression with panic spectrum symptoms: A pilot study. *Depression and Anxiety, 21*(3), 140–142.

De Mello, M. F., De Jesus, M., J., Bacaltchuk, J., Verdeli, H., & Neugebauer, R. (2005). A systematic review of research findings on the efficacy of interpersonal therapy for depressive disorders. *European Archives of Psychiatry and Clinical Neuroscience, 255*(2), 75–82.

Dombrovski, A. Y., Lenze, E. J., Dew, M. A., Mulsant, B. H., Pollock, B. G., Houck, P. R., & Reynolds, C. F., III. (2007). Maintenance treatment for old-age depression preserves health-related quality of life: A randomized, controlled trial of paroxetine and interpersonal psychotherapy. *Journal of the American Geriatrics Society, 55*(9), 1325–1332.

Grote, N. K., Swartz, H. A., Geibel, S. L., Zuckoff, A., Houck, P. R., & Frank, E. (2009). A randomized controlled trial of culturally relevant, brief interpersonal psychotherapy for perinatal depression. *Psychiatric Services, 60*(3), 313–321.

Gunlicks, M. L., & Mufson, L. (2009). Interpersonal psychotherapy for depressed adolescents. In S. Nolen-Hoeksema & L. M. Hilt (Eds.), *Handbook of depression in adolescents* (pp. 511–529). New York: Routledge.

Hamilton, M. (1960). The rating scale for depression. *Journal of Neurological and Neurosurgical Psychiatry, 25*, 56–62.

Hinrichsen, G. A. (2008a). Interpersonal psychotherapy as a treatment for late-life depression. In K. Laidlaw & B. Knight (Eds.), *Handbook of emotional disorders in later life: Assessment and treatment* (pp. 141–164). New York: Oxford University Press.

Hinrichsen, G. A. (2008b). Interpersonal psychotherapy for late life depression: Current status and new applications. *Journal of Rational-Emotive & Cognitive Behavior, 26*(4), 263–275.

Kiesler, B. J. (1996). *Contemporary interpersonal theory and research: Personality, psychopathology, and psychotherapy.* New York: Wiley.

Klerman, G. L., & Weissman, M. M. (Eds.). (1993). *New applications of personal therapy.* Washington, DC: American Psychiatric Press.

Klerman, G. L., Weissman, M. M., Rounsaville, B. J., & Chevron, E. S. (1984). *Interpersonal psychotherapy of depression.* New York: Basic Books.

Krupnick, J. L., Green, B. L., Stockton, P., Miranda, J., Krause, E., & Mete, M. (2008). Group interpersonal psychotherapy for low-income women with post-traumatic stress disorder. *Psychotherapy Research, 18*(5), 497–507.

Markowitz, J. C. (1998). *Interpersonal psychotherapy for dysthymic disorder*. Washington, DC: American Psychiatric Press.

Markowitz, J. C. (2003). Interpersonal psychotherapy. In R. E. Hales & S. C. Yudofsky (Eds.), *The American Psychiatric Publishing textbook of clinical psychiatry* (4th ed., pp. 1207–1223). Washington, DC: American Psychiatric Publishing.

Markowitz, J. C., Bleiberg, K., Pessin, H., & Skodol, A. E. (2007). Adapting interpersonal psychotherapy for borderline personality disorder. *Journal of Mental Health. Special Issue: Developing New Treatments of Personality Disorder, 16*(1), 103–116.

Meyer, A. (1957). *Psychobiology: A science of man*. Springfield, IL: Charles C. Thomas.

Miller, M. D. (2009). *Clinician's guide to interpersonal psychotherapy in late life: Helping cognitively impaired or depressed elders and their caregivers*. New York: Oxford University Press.

Miller, M. D., Richards, V., Zuckoff, A., Martire, L. M., Morse, J., Frank, E., & Reynolds, C. F., III. (2007). A model for modifying interpersonal psychotherapy (IPT) for depressed elders with cognitive impairment. *Clinical Gerontologist, 30*(2), 79–101.

Mufson, L., Dorta, K.P., Moreau, D., & Weissman, M.M. (2005). Efficacy to effectiveness: Adaptations of interpersonal psychotherapy for adolescent depression. In E. D. Hibbs & P. D. Jensen (Eds.), *Psychological treatments for child and adolescent disorders: Empirically based strategies for clinical practice* (2nd ed., pp. 165–186). Washington, DC: American Psychological Association.

Mufson, L., Gallagher, T., Dorta, K. P., & Young, J. F. (2004). A group adaptation of interpersonal psychotherapy for depressed adolescents. *American Journal of Psychotherapy, 58*(2), 220–237.

O'Hara, M. W., Stuart, S., Gorman, L. L., & Wenzel, A. (2000). Efficacy of interpersonal psychotherapy for postpartum depression. *Archives of General Psychiatry, 57*, 1039–1045.

Ransom, D., Heckman, T. G., Anderson, T., Garske, J., Holroyd, K., & Basta, T. (2008). Telephone-delivered, interpersonal psychotherapy for HIV-infected rural persons with depression: A pilot trial. *Psychiatric Services, 59*(8), 871–877.

Robertson, M., Rushton, P., Batrim, D., Moore, E., & Morris, P. (2007). Open trial of interpersonal psychotherapy for chronic post traumatic stress disorder. *Australasian Psychiatry, 15*(5), 375–379.

Rounsaville, B. J., & Carroll, K. (1993). Interpersonal psychotherapy for patients who have used drugs. In G. L. Klerman & M. M. Weissman (Eds.), *New applications of interpersonal psychotherapy* (pp. 319–352). Washington, DC: American Psychiatric Press.

Spinelli, M. (2008). Treating antepartum depression: Interpersonal psychotherapy. In S. D. Stone & A. E. Menken (Eds.), *Perinatal and postpartum mood disorders: Perspectives and treatment guide for the health care practitioner* (pp. 289–307). New York: Springer.

Spinelli, M. G., & Endicott, J. (2003). Controlled clinical trial of interpersonal psychotherapy versus parenting education program for depressed pregnant women. *American Journal of Psychiatry, 160*(3), 555–562.

Stuart, S. (Ed.). (2004). *Brief interpersonal psychotherapy*. Washington, DC: American Psychiatric Press.

Sullivan, H. S. (1953). *The interpersonal theory of psychiatry*. New York: Norton.

Swartz, H. A., & Markowitz, J. C. (2009). Techniques of individual interpersonal psychotherapy. In G. O. Gabbard (Ed.), *Textbook of psychotherapeutic treatments* (pp. 309–338). Arlington, VA: American Psychiatric Publishing.

Verdeli, H., Clougherty, K., Onyango, G., Lewandowski, E., Speelman, L., Betancourt, T. S., Neugebauer, R., Stein, T. R., & Bolton, P. (2008). Group interpersonal psychotherapy for depressed youth in IDP camps in northern Uganda: Adaptation and training. *Child and Adolescent Psychiatric Clinics of North America, 17*(3), 605–624.

Weissman, M. M. (2007). Cognitive therapy and interpersonal psychotherapy: 30 years later. *American Journal of Psychiatry, 164*(5), 693–696.

Weissman, M. M., Markowitz, J. C., & Klerman, G. L. (2000). *Comprehensive guide to interpersonal psychotherapy*. New York: Basic Books.

Weissman, M. M., Markowitz, J. C., & Klerman, G. L. (2007). *Clinician's quick guide to interpersonal psychotherapy*. New York: Oxford University Press.

Young, J. F., & Mufson, L. (2008). *Interpersonal psychotherapy for treatment and prevention of adolescent depression*. New York: Guilford.

Young, J. F., & Mufson, L. (2009). Interpersonal psychotherapy for adolescents. In C. A. Essau (Ed.), *Treatments for adolescent depression: Theory and practice* (pp. 261–282). New York: Oxford University Press.

Psychodrama

Created by Jacob L. Moreno, psychodrama is an approach in which the patient acts out a problem, usually with members of a group or audience who can portray people involved in the problem. The therapist serves as the director of the spontaneous drama, which most frequently takes place before an audience. Attention is paid to the patient's role in relationship with other significant people in her life. A variety of techniques are used to help patients examine their roles from different points of view. By acting out the roles rather than talking about them, patients experience previously unrecognized feelings and attitudes that can lead to changes in behavior.

Background

Born in Bucharest, Romania, Jacob Moreno (1889–1974) was the oldest of six children. At the age of 5, he and his family moved to Vienna (Blatner, 2000). A student of philosophy at the University of Vienna, Moreno became interested in children's play in the Vienna parks when he was about 20 years old. He not only observed their play but also encouraged them to play different roles. Later, Moreno attended medical school at the University of Vienna and became interested in helping disenfranchised social groups, such as prostitutes.

Moreno combined his social interests with his interest in theater and opened the Theatre of Spontaneity in 1921. Because he felt theater was dry and somewhat artificial, he preferred impromptu improvisational dramas. Leaving Vienna for New York in 1925, Moreno applied his ideas to hospitals in the area. He became one of the first group psychotherapists and addressed broader social concerns than could be done in individual therapy. Opening a sanitarium in Beacon, New York, in 1936, he built a theater to be used for psychodrama. In addition to practicing and training therapists in psychodrama, Moreno (1934) carried out group relations research in prisons, schools, and hospitals. In 1940 he worked with Zerka Toeman, whom he later married and who became an active proponent of psychodrama. She worked as a partner with Moreno and continued her work after his death (Blatner, 2000, 2005).

When psychodrama was first developed in the 1930s, it represented a marked change in direction from treating the individual in isolation. It was the precursor for many group therapies, including gestalt and encounter groups. Techniques such as role playing, used in both individual and group therapy, originated from the work of Moreno (1947). In his approach to understanding the personality of individuals, Moreno focused on the variety of roles they played with others and their ability to examine and change these roles (Blatner, 2007).

Theory of Personality

Moreno's view of the roles that individuals enacted with each other represented his major conceptualization of individual personality. Described by his colleagues as an active, creative, energetic, yet unsystematic man, Moreno lectured throughout the world, wrote widely (see Fox, 1987), and could initiate a psychodrama with a large number of people at a moment's notice. These characteristics can be seen in Moreno's views on interpersonal interaction and are reflected in his development of psychodrama.

Roles and sociometry. Role theory examines individuals' relationships with others, such as a woman with her husband, mother, customer, child, or teacher. In particular, Moreno was interested in the changing relationships between individuals and in ways to encourage new changes. In his study of roles, Moreno (Dayton, 2005) developed sociometric testing, which measured the nature of relationships between people in a particular group. By interviewing members of the group, a sociogram can be developed that can determine how each person views the other, for example, as a friend, as someone to be relied on, or as someone skilled in a particular area. In 1937, Moreno founded *Sociometry: A Journal of Inter-Personal Relations,* which later became the *Social Psychology Quarterly,* which published works on psychodrama, small-group behavior, power, class, and gender (Borgatta, 2007; Fields, 2007; Marineau, 2007). Moreno was interested not only in the roles people played in relationship to others but also in role distance. By becoming increasingly objective about an event and able to examine one's own role, role distance is increased. In the case of psychodrama, individuals' role distance can be increased as they play different roles that afford them a new perspective on their relationships with others.

Activity in the present. Although Moreno made use of psychoanalytic concepts in understanding individuals' behavior, he was most interested in current experience. The interaction between psychoanalysis and psychodrama continues to provide insights about early relationships as clients act out their problems (Feasey, 2001). Where psychoanalysis helped individuals understand their past, sociometry provided a way to observe people's relationships to each other in the present. In psychodrama, individuals most often interact with other group members, who play the roles of significant people in their lives. Occasionally, the significant people would be present and act for themselves. For Moreno, psychodrama provided a way to bring past, possible future, or current conflicts or crises into the present. Meaning would be assigned to individuals and events, not as they occurred in the past, but as they were occurring in the present as the individual acted them out in psychodrama.

Encounter. Of interest to Moreno was the interaction that individuals had when they encountered each other in a relationship. Psychodrama provides a way for individuals to experience a number of meaningful encounters in a short period of time. The energy that takes place between individuals in interpersonal exchange is referred to by Moreno as *tele* (Blatner, 2005; Landy, 2008). Moreno also used *tele* to refer to the feeling of caring that developed between individuals in a psychodrama group. As individuals get to know each other and care for each other, tele is increased and group cohesion develops. Tele includes constructs that other theorists would refer to as empathy, transference, or the relationship.

Spontaneity and creativity. Noted for his own spontaneity and creativity, Moreno valued these characteristics in others as signs of living healthily and fully (Schacht, 2007). A spontaneous individual should be able to take initiative and risks when faced with a difficult situation. Using thinking and feeling, individuals should react to an external crisis in a constructive manner, in contrast to acting impulsively, which might lead to negative consequences (Blatner, 2005; Dayton, 2005).

Creativity was highly valued by Moreno, who observed children in the Vienna parks as entering into creative role playing in fantasy situations more readily than did adults. As a part of his work with groups, Moreno often did spontaneity training, in which individuals were encouraged to respond creatively to an unexpected or stressful problem presented by the leader. For example, group members might be presented with situations such as dealing with an angry boss, a tornado, or a stranger with a gun. This emphasis on spontaneous and creative aspects of individual personality, which is found in the writings of humanistic and existential theorists, is clearly apparent in Moreno's writings and in his approach to psychodrama (Schacht, 2007).

Theory of Psychotherapy

Basic to psychodrama is role playing, the process of playing someone else, something else, or oneself in different circumstances. As mentioned previously, individuals play many different roles with different people during the course of their lives. Being aware of how they act toward others in these roles can give individuals the freedom to change their behaviors. By providing many different roles for individuals to play, psychodrama encourages experimentation and learning about new aspects of oneself. Role playing can serve three functions in the course of psychodrama: to assist the leader in assessing how members think and feel, to instruct individuals on new ways to deal with problems, and to train individuals in practicing new skills (Corsini, 1966). Also, the fact that role playing is active helps individuals feel more in control and less passive. Abstract issues, such as frustration about dealing with one's father, become more concrete when they are played out, as the patient must talk to the father, gesture when appropriate, change voice tone and volume, and move physically in relationship to the other players. The specificity and activity of role playing can have several advantages for the participants.

Psychodrama gives individuals an opportunity to test reality, to develop insight into problems, and to express their feelings (catharsis). Reality testing is achieved by playing important situations with real people. Participants may learn that previously held assumptions are no longer valid as they enact various roles and get input from group members. The act of expressing oneself in a role often provides the opportunity to experience strong feelings such as anger, hatred, sadness, joy, or love in ways that thinking or talking about situations does not. By testing reality and experiencing catharsis and insight, individuals are able to learn and try out affective behavior they previously had not considered.

In the following sections, the details of psychodrama are described more fully. Because assessment is quite different in psychodrama than in other therapies, it deserves special consideration. As in a play, individuals have different roles in a psychodrama, and the basic roles are described. Also, *psychodrama* refers not only to playing roles but also to helping individuals enter their roles and learn from them. A number of important techniques have been developed to help individuals learn effectively and cognitively from their psychodrama experience.

Assessment. Unlike other therapies, the psychodrama leader or director must make many assessments about group behavior as the psychodrama unfolds. Although psychodrama is often used in hospital and other institutional settings that have a core of group members, psychodrama is also done in demonstrations or with a group that will not reconvene (Blatner, 2003; Duffy, 2008). The director must assess which problems are appropriate for psychodrama, whether the group member presenting the problem is able to grow from the experience and is not too emotionally vulnerable, and whether other group members are constructively playing their parts. Additionally, leaders must assess when to bring in new members from the group or audience to play parts, when to switch roles, and which roles to initiate. Assessment and the other functions of the director are complicated (Z. T. Moreno, 1987), and individuals need about 2 years of training in psychodrama before they can take the role of director.

Roles in the psychodrama. There are four basic roles in psychodrama: the director, who produces and leads the interactions; the protagonist, the person who presents the problem; the auxiliaries, who portray different people in the protagonist's life; and the audience, who may participate in the enactment as auxiliaries or make comments or ask questions (Landy, 2008). Where possible, the protagonists, auxiliaries, and director act out the psychodrama on a stage large enough to allow freedom of movement. Sometimes, half of a large room may be used for the action and the other half for the audience. Where possible, props are available to be used by the participants.

The director, in addition to assessing the movements and actions of the participants, performs a number of roles (Corey, 2008). The director should establish a tolerant and accepting atmosphere for change in the group while also providing support and direction for the protagonist. During the course of the psychodrama, the director may describe relationships to be explored, scenes to be enacted, or other experiments. If group members attack other members or make inappropriate suggestions, the director intervenes to maintain a helpful and productive atmosphere in the group. Often the director may stop the action to make comments, invite comments from the audience, or make sure that the roles are being properly played out. To be a director takes creativity and the ability to orchestrate the actions of a large group of people (Blatner, 2005).

The protagonist is the person who presents the problem or event that will be explored. Often this person volunteers but may also be selected by the group or director. Although the protagonist initially describes the problem to be explored, the director encourages the protagonist to act it out. To do this, the protagonist selects group members who will play other roles (auxiliaries) and will instruct them how to play the role of a significant other in the protagonist's life, making suggestions if the portrayal is inaccurate. Often the director suggests that the protagonist play a variety of roles or watch the action while others play the role of the protagonist.

Auxiliaries portray significant others in the protagonist's life, such as a sister. Initially their role is to help the protagonist by playing the perceptions of the significant other (Blatner, 2005). The more emotional energy they put into playing this role, the more real it is likely to be for the protagonist. Additionally, when playing such roles, auxiliaries often get insights into their own lives that parallel issues that occur in the psychodrama. Audience members are not passive participants in a psychodrama. At times, they may be called on to be the protagonist or auxiliaries. Also, they may be asked to share experiences or comment on what they are observing. Often they witness enactments that relate to their own lives and develop new insights into their relationships with others. But it is protagonists who are likely to benefit the most from psychodrama (Kim, 2003).

The process of psychodrama. There are three basic phases of a psychodrama: the warm-up phase, the action phase, and the discussion and sharing that take place afterward.

A warm-up phase helps participants get ready for the action phase of psychodrama. The basic aim of the warm-up phase is to develop an atmosphere of trust and safety, along with a willingness to play and try out new behavior (Blatner, 2005). Special warm-up procedures are necessary for individuals who are not a part of an ongoing psychodrama group. Describing the purpose of psychodrama and answering questions about what is to take place is helpful in reassuring new participants. Sometimes it is useful to have pairs, small groups, or the entire group share conflicts they are experiencing that could be material for the psychodrama. As this discussion is going on, the leader assesses appropriate issues to be the focus of the psychodrama and individuals to be protagonists. When a protagonist is selected, the leader listens carefully to his description of the psychodrama scene so that roles can be selected and auxiliaries chosen.

The action phase starts as individuals act out and work through a protagonist's situation. The director may walk around the stage with the protagonist to discuss what could take place (Landy, 2008). Although protagonists should be encouraged to enact situations and events as soon as possible, traumatic events should be saved for later rather than dealt with early on in the session (Corey, 2008). The director takes responsibility for having furniture moved and props made available and for helping the protagonist set the scene for the psychodrama. A creative approach to this is to use miniature objects in a psychodrama (Casson, 2007). As the action progresses, the director may ask members of the audience to play new roles or for the protagonist to change roles with other group members.

When the action phase is concluded, the sharing and discussion phase begins. First, group members, including auxiliaries, share their observations with the protagonist. A part of the director's responsibility is to help the protagonist who has shared a vulnerable part of his life and to ensure that feedback is helpful and not critical or judgmental. For psychodramas that will last only one session, attention must be paid to having effective closure, and the director may facilitate a winding down of the emotional intensity within the group.

Psychodrama techniques. Essential in psychodrama is the acting out of relationships with others. Participants are encouraged to act as if they are in a situation rather than talk about it. Occasionally, they may dialogue with themselves—which is called *monodrama*—by using an empty chair to play two roles, but most often they dialogue with auxiliaries. Some of the more common techniques in the action phase of psychodrama include role reversal, the double technique, the mirror technique, act fulfillment, and future projection (Landy, 2008).

Role reversal is designed to help patients understand the point of view of others and to be more empathic with them. Basically, the protagonist changes roles with an auxiliary to get a different point of view. For example, a man arguing with an auxiliary who is playing his mother may be asked to switch roles, and the auxiliary or another group member then plays the man's role. Moreno (Fox, 1987) gives an example of role reversal when an adolescent boy had told psychiatrists and others that he was worried about turning into or being turned into a girl.

> At a strategic point in his treatment, he was placed in the role of one of the psychiatrists who had heard his disclosure. Acting in the role of the boy, the psychiatrist was to come to the boy—now in the role of the psychiatrist—for advice about his fears. In this way the patient was compelled to act in an advisory capacity toward another person who was exhibiting the same abnormal ideas as those with which he was obsessed. This gave him the opportunity to test for himself the degree of responsibility and stability he had reached in the course of our treatment, and it afforded us a

chance to see what degree of maturity he had attained. He seemed to be acting both himself and the psychiatrist at the same time but, by the technique of reversal, he was forced to objectify his real self and his obsession from what he conceived to be a psychiatrist's point of view. (Fox, 1987, p. 75)

In the *double technique* an auxiliary takes the role of the protagonist and expresses what she perceives to be the protagonist's inner thoughts and feelings. Usually doubles stand close to the protagonist and may speak for her. Additionally, they may enact nonverbal behaviors, such as posture or facial expression. Sometimes multiple doubles are used to express different sides of an individual. Although the role of a double is primarily supportive, it also helps the protagonist develop further insights about her feelings or attitudes. In the following example, Yablonsky (1976) shows how a double, experienced in psychodrama, was able to provide significant insight for a woman who considered herself to be sexually liberated and was critical of the men in her life.

In the center of one interaction, her double, for no special reason, based on what the protagonist said but derived from a feeling as her double, exclaimed, "My problem is that I've never had an orgasm." The protagonist wheeled around to her double, broke into tears, and with amazement said, "How did you know?" The double thus propelled the protagonist into a more honest portraiture and broke past the false image the subject was trying to project. She began to reveal that beneath her sexual braggadocio, she was a frightened little girl who was really afraid of men and sex. Often, a double in a role will have an insight that is not apparent to anyone in the group, including the director, and this will open up the protagonist to his deeper, more honest feelings. (Yablonsky, 1976, pp. 120–121)

In the *mirror technique*, an auxiliary plays the role of the protagonist by mirroring postures, expressions, and words, while the protagonist observes his behavior being reflected by another person. Essentially, mirroring is a feedback process in which the patient sees how someone else perceives him. By looking at ourselves in the "mirror," we can confront ourselves and take a different look at who we are, and thus make changes in our lives (Kellermann, 2007). Mirroring must be done carefully so that the protagonist does not feel ridiculed (Blatner, 2000).

Psychodrama makes use of real and unreal situations to help an individual. The use of fantasy is sometimes called *surplus reality*, such as when a protagonist has a dialogue with an auxiliary who represents a monster in a dream. Another example of surplus reality is that of *act fulfillment*. Here, an individual can have a corrective experience that replaces a hurtful experience from the past. For example, if a young woman remembers being ridiculed by a seventh-grade teacher, she can have an auxiliary play the role of the teacher, confront the teacher, and have a dialogue with him.

Another example of incorporating surplus reality into psychodrama is *future projection*, which is designed to help people clarify concerns about their future. In future projection, a situation is presented, perhaps 4 years from now, where the individual has an interview for graduate school. The protagonist can act out an interview to the best of his ability or can purposefully botch the interview and then experience the feeling of what would happen in that case. In both cases, the audience and/or auxiliaries can give him feedback.

In part because individuals expose themselves and their innermost fears and feelings to others, psychodrama can be a very powerful technique. It is essential that directors are empathic and protective of group members. Although there are many creative techniques other than the ones discussed here, the techniques need to be used by a director who can be creative yet take control of the psychodrama so that emotional destructiveness does not take place. Being able to recognize psychopathology as it emerges in participants is important to prevent damage to others. For example, a manipulative or sociopathic individual who plays the role of an auxiliary may take pleasure in making comments that point out the protagonist's inadequacies in a hurtful way. Although spontaneity and creativity are important products of psychodrama, they must be subservient to the positive goals of insight, growth, and understanding of individuals (Blatner, 2000).

Since the pioneering work of Moreno, psychodrama has continued to grow and develop. In the United States there are more than 400 certified practitioners, and throughout the world more than 15,000 people are trained in psychodrama techniques. Increasingly, practitioners of psychodrama integrate its use with other theories (Adam Blatner, personal communication, January 3, 2010). The American Society for Group Psychotherapy and Psychodrama (ASGPP) provides training and sets standards for the practice of psychodrama and publishes the *Journal of Group Psychotherapy, Psychodrama, and Sociometry*. Some practitioners have extended Moreno's work and have applied it to individual treatment of children in which they are encouraged to act out imaginative ideas. For example, Hoey (1997) describes a 13-year-old girl whose mother died when she was 6 and who had lived in several foster homes but was about to be adopted. To encourage expression Hoey said, "Shall we make up a story about a girl like you? A girl who's lived in lots of places and now has at last found somewhere where she can be happy?" (p. 109). Creativity characterizes those who use psychodrama, and several have combined it with art therapies and drama therapy, while others have used it within a psychodynamic framework (Garfield, 2003).

Summary

Developed by Jacob Moreno in the 1930s, psychodrama makes use of creativity and spontaneity to help individuals test reality, develop insight, and express feelings. In a psychodrama, the therapist takes on the role of the director, choosing the protagonist (the focus of the psychodrama), and uses auxiliaries to play the role of significant others in the protagonist's concerns. Auxiliaries are volunteers from the audience. Using a mixture of playfulness and seriousness and techniques such as role reversal and mirroring, psychodrama offers ways to help individuals grow and see themselves in different ways. The therapist ensures that the psychodrama is a positive experience by seeing that participants are helpful in their roles.

References

Blatner, A. (2000). *Foundations of psychodrama: History, theory, and practice* (4th ed.). New York: Springer.

Blatner, A. (2005). Psychodrama. In R. J. Corsini & D. Wedding (Eds.), *Current psychotherapies* (7th ed., pp. 405–438). Belmont, CA: Brooks/Cole–Thomson.

Blatner, A. (2007). Morenean approaches: Recognizing psychodrama's many facets. *Journal of Group Psychotherapy, Psychodrama & Sociometry*, 59(4), 159–170.

Blatner, A. (Ed.). (2003). "Not mere players": Psychodrama applications in everyday life. In J. Gershoni (Ed.), *Psychodrama in the 21st century: Clinical and educational applications* (pp. 103–115). New York: Springer.

Borgatta, E. F. (2007). Jacob L. *Moreno and sociometry: A mid-century reminiscence. Social Psychology Quarterly*, 70(4), 330–332.

Casson, J. (2007). Psychodrama in miniature. In C. Baim, J. Burmeister, & M. Maciel (Eds.), Psychodrama:

Advances in theory and practice (pp. 201–213). New York: Routledge.

Corey, G. (2008). *Theory and practice of group counseling* (7th ed.) Belmont, CA: Brooks/Cole–Thomson.

Corsini, R. J. (1966). *Role playing in psychotherapy.* Chicago: Aldine-Atherton.

Dayton, T. (2005). *The living stages: A step by step guide to psychodrama, sociometry, and group psychotherapy.* Deerfield Beach, FL: Health Communications.

Duffy, T. K. (2008). Psychodrama. In A. L. Strozier & J. E. Carpenter (Eds.), *Introduction to alternative and complementary therapies* (pp. 129–151). New York: Haworth Press.

Feasey, D. (2001). *Good practice in psychodrama: An analytic perspective.* London, England: Whurr.

Fields, C. D. (2007). Sociometry 1937. *Social Psychology Quarterly, 70*(4), 326–329.

Fox, J. (Ed.). (1987). *The essential Moreno: Writings on psychodrama, group method, and spontaneity.* New York: Springer.

Garfield, S. (Ed.). (2003). Transference in analytic psychodrama. In J. Gershoni (Ed.), *Psychodrama in the 21st century: Clinical and educational applications* (pp. 15–30). New York: Springer.

Hoey, B. (1997). *Who calls the tune? A psychodramatic approach to child therapy.* London: Routledge.

Kellermann, P. F. (2007). Let's face it: Mirroring in psychodrama. In C. Baim, J. Burmeister, & M. Maciel (Eds.), *Psychodrama: Advances in theory and practice* (pp. 83–95). New York: Routledge.

Kim, K. W. (2003). The effects of being the protagonist in psychodrama. *Journal of Group Psychotherapy, Psychodrama & Sociometry, 55*(4), 115–127.

Landy, R. J. (2008). *The couch and the stage: Integrating words and action in psychotherapy.* Lanham, MD: Jason Aronson.

Marineau, R. F. (2007). The birth and development of sociometry: The work and legacy of Jacob Moreno (1889–1974). *Social Psychology Quarterly, 70*(4), 322–325.

Moreno, J. L. (1934). *Who shall survive? A new approach to the problem of human interrelations.* Washington, DC: Nervous and Mental Disease Publishing.

Moreno, J. L. (1947). *Theatre of spontaneity: An introduction to psychodrama.* Beacon, NY: Beacon House.

Moreno, Z. T. (1987). Psychodrama, role theory, and the concept of the social atom. In J. K. Zeig (Ed.), *The evolution of psychotherapy* (pp. 341–366). New York: Brunner/Mazel.

Schacht, M. (2007). Spontaneity-creativity: The psychodramatic concept of change. In C. Baim, J. Burmeister, & M. Maciel (Eds.), *Psychodrama: Advances in theory and practice* (pp. 21–39). New York: Routledge.

Yablonsky, L. (1976). *Psychodrama: Resolving emotional problems through role-playing.* New York: Basic Books.

Creative Arts Therapies

Creative arts therapies include art, drama, dance movement, and music therapies, as they all use creative expression to bring about therapeutic change. Some individuals take advantage of the opportunity to express themselves nonverbally through these media, which leads to increased self-esteem, more productive self-expression, and/or improved social interaction with others.

Creative arts therapies emphasize client use of the artistic medium rather than observation of artistic works. However, music therapists often use recordings in dealing with client affect and moods. The quality of the patient's production is of little importance compared with the meaning that patient and therapist can derive from the work and its ultimate helpfulness to the patient. In this regard, therapists rarely participate in creative expression with clients so as not to inhibit the client, whose work is often artistically inferior to the therapist's.

In most cases, creative arts therapists work as part of a psychotherapeutic team, although increasingly they may work independently, doing psychotherapy as well as creative arts therapy. Traditionally, they have worked in hospitals and institutions for the mentally disabled, particularly with individuals whose verbal communications are limited. Their qualifications are a combination of knowledge and talent in their own area of artistic endeavor, including knowledge of techniques and forms of artistic production, as well as education in working psychotherapeutically with patient problems. Although certain theories of psychotherapy that emphasize enactment, such as gestalt therapy, fit well with creative arts therapy, creative arts therapists have varied backgrounds, and they may combine any one or more of the therapies discussed in this book with their creative specialty. The National Coalition of Creative Art Therapies, which includes six creative arts therapy associations, represents more than 15,000 members. Because psychoanalysis was particularly influential in the 1930s to the 1950s, some creative arts therapists, especially art therapists (Vick, 2003) have been educated to take a psychoanalytic approach to their work.

The development of creative arts therapy has been rapid, taking place within the last 40 or 50 years. Each specialty has at least one association: American Art Therapy Association, Association for Dance and Movement Psychotherapy United Kingdom, National Association for Drama Therapy, and the American Music Therapy Association. Additionally, specialties have one or more journals that publish their contributions: *Art Therapy: Journal of the American Art Therapy Association, The Arts in Psychotherapy: An International Journal, American Journal of Dance Therapy*, and *The Journal of Music Therapy*. Several institutions throughout the world offer master's degree programs in several areas of the creative arts therapies. The variety of approaches available to creative arts therapists is seen not only through their journals but also through textbooks and books of readings on music, art, drama, and dance therapies. Because these therapies are quite specialized and are usually an adjunct to other psychotherapies, only a brief overview can be given in this chapter.

Art Therapy

The broad purpose of art therapy is to help patients deal with emotional conflicts, become more aware of their feelings, and deal with both internal and external problems. To reach these goals, art therapists, when appropriate, provide instruction in the use of a variety of art materials. Typically, materials are selected that fit the needs of the client and the issue being addressed. For example, pastels, crayons, or felt-tip pens might be used when patients are free-associating or using art to express feelings. Other times, clay, paper, canvas, watercolors, or finger paints may be used, depending on the circumstance (Malchiodi, 2003, 2005; Rubin, 2010; Vick, 2003). These materials aid in bringing about the expression of images that are in the human mind before individuals learn to verbally articulate their needs.

Art expression provides the opportunity to depict images that cannot be expressed verbally, to show spatial relationships (such as the patient to his father and mother), and to express oneself without worrying about what one is saying. Unlike verbal expression, art expression is more likely to give a feeling of being creative and to provide the opportunity to increase one's energy level while working physically to develop a tangible product. Furthermore, products of artistic creativity can be referred to in later days or weeks, unlike verbal expression, which fades quickly (Malchiodi, 2005; Rubin, 2010). Suggestions for creative expression may come from the patient, therapist, or both. Therapists may suggest exercises such as having a patient draw an image of herself and then discuss how that image relates to the patient's view of herself. Other exercises might include drawing oneself as one would like to be, drawing one's family, or drawing particular family relationships. In their education and training, art therapists learn the application of a great variety of art media, as well as techniques to help clients express themselves.

As art therapy has developed, so have the variety of means for expression and the populations that therapists work with. With the development of technology has come the use of video recording, easy-to-use photographic equipment, computer graphics, and other methods that aid in creative expression (Rubin, 2010). As art therapy has changed, some art therapists have combined music, movement, and psychodrama in their work. The types of problems and populations that art therapists work with have also expanded to include bereaved children, battered women, incest survivors, group therapy patients, and Alzheimer's patients (Malchiodi, 2005).

A brief example of how art therapy might be used can be seen in Wadeson's (2001) work with Craig, a young man hospitalized with a diagnosis of paranoid schizophrenia. Appearing threatening and dangerous to the staff, Craig was able to make gains by expressing secret desires through his love for drawing and to reduce his sense of isolation through his creative expression and discussion with the art therapist. In describing a drawing, Figure 15.1, that was done on notebook paper with pencil and blue ink, Craig said that the picture represented himself.

> The underneath part is "strong and grasping," the sphere is "selfless" and represents his "mind." He explained that the roots are holding the sphere and that basically the underneath shows "control" of the body over the mind. "In order for the mind to exist, the body controls or comforts it," he said. (Wadeson, 2001, p. 315)

In discussing the relevance of Craig's artwork, (Payne, 2006), Wadeson believed that his art expression provided an opportunity to build a bridge from his fear that people would take his secrets away to interaction with others. Through Wadeson's interest in Craig's imagery, he was able to build trust and to describe his strange inner world to someone he felt understood him. This small example helps show one of many different ways that art therapists may work with patients to help them explore their inner world, to increase communication with others, and to cope more effectively with a variety of problems.

Dance Movement Therapy

The goals of dance movement therapy are to help individuals grow and to interrelate psychological and physiological processes through movement or dance. Individuals can come to understand their own feelings, images, and memories, as well as those of others, by expressing themselves through movement or dance. Although dance movement therapy has its origins in the application of structured dances to individual expression, dance movement therapists rarely teach dances but tend to encourage expression through movement exercises, often making use of music.

Approaches to patients are creative and spontaneous, as dance movement therapists attend to the moods and physical positions of their clients. Implicit in the work of dance therapists is their acknowledgment of the impact that body and mind have on each other as seen in physiological tension, body image, and ordinary movement (Loman, 2005; Payne, 2006). Dance movement therapy allows clients to experience both emotional and physiological feelings

FIGURE 15.1 Craig's drawing.
From "An Eclectic Approach to Art Therapy," by H. Wadeson, in *Approaches to Art Therapy: Theory and Technique*, edited by J. A. Rubin. Copyright © 1987 by Brunner/ Mazel, Inc. Reprinted with permission from the publisher and the author.

simultaneously, which can lead to a better understanding of self. In groups, reaching toward another person, stretching to touch that person, or holding or being held by group members can help interpersonal relationships, as can the awareness of feelings expressed in the bodily movements of others.

Techniques of dance movement therapy are very varied, depending on the nature of the individual or group the therapist is working with. One technique is that of *exaggeration*, in which clients are encouraged to exaggerate a movement, such as a shrug of the shoulder. The client can then be asked to communicate the feeling verbally or to continue moving. Sometimes therapists may find it helpful to copy the actions of a group member to empathically understand what the group member may be experiencing physiologically and affectively. However, this must be done in a way that does not appear to mimic or make fun of the client. Another approach is to translate a client issue into an action. For example, the client wishing to separate from his mother may gradually step backward from the therapist, moving toward the other end of the room, and possibly sharing the experience as he does so. Knowing the clients' cultural background can influence the methods that dance movement therapists use (Hanna, 2004). A vast variety of approaches can be used with clients, ranging from professional dancers to autistic children to those with neurological disabilities. There are many ways that dance movement therapy can be done with groups (Nicholas, 2003). An application of dance movement therapy to seven male adults in a therapeutic community shows how creative approaches to movement can help individuals who are resistant and suffering from severe psychological disorders.

> It seemed like a sign of growing trust when participants started to express more of the anger stored within. They found ways of venting their frustration in punch-like clapping and stomping movements and sometimes even shouting. An evocative image that emerged was Mike Tyson the boxer. When Jeremy complained of obsessive thoughts, which prevented him from stopping talking, I asked him to translate them into movements. His response was a crescendo of fists, shaking violently, and kicking movements. So he found ways of physical outlet for his nervous mental energy and was eventually able to contact some of the depression which was underneath his anger. Then he could even allow the group to hold him in the middle of the circle and rock him soothingly. (Steiner, 1992, pp. 158–159)

And another exercise:

> For what seemed a long time we stayed with small repetitive movements, patting the body, clapping hands, then I introduced my circular band, made of old ties strung together. Everyone held it in one hand and we made some round movements with it. Asked what we were doing, Nigel said "stirring" and Jeremy added "in a cauldron." Encouraged to add ingredients, Nigel put in his sorrow, Jeremy his mother, then me because I had annoyed him by changing "his" music, David added his confrontation, and Billy his anxiety. Thus the group had created a container for the difficult feelings each person experienced. (p. 160)

These brief excerpts suggest how dance movement therapists, using their creativity, can work with individuals to help them integrate psychological and physical processes. Not only do the patients express themselves but they also communicate through bodily energy, rhythm, and touch.

Drama Therapy

The most recently developed of the creative arts therapies, drama therapy can take many forms (Jones, 2007; Landy, 2005, 2008). As defined by Jennings (1992), "Drama therapy is a means of bringing about change in individuals and groups through direct experience of theatre art" (p. 5). For some drama therapists, psychodrama is a form of drama therapy. The range of drama therapeutic approaches runs from Shakespeare to the use of puppets and masks. Jennings (1992) gives an example of how a drama therapist can use lines from Shakespeare's *King Lear*, focusing on King Lear's relationship with his daughters to explore with middle-aged women their relationships with their aging fathers. With seriously ill children, drama therapy allows children to express their emotions by playing roles in fairy tales (Bouzoukis, 2001). Drama therapy has also been used to help children who display problematic sexual behavior by dealing with underlying complex emotional and psychological processes (LeVay, 2005).

Drama therapy has many diverse applications. James (1996) gives an example of a man in his early 20s with limited intellectual functioning who felt "the odds are stacked against me" (pp. 30, 31). Jennings became "the odds" and the young man pushed against him. Later, the young man said that this exercise increased his confidence in his abilities. Although rare, at times it can be helpful to have an audience, such as when a group of patients receiving antipsychotic medications acted out Dickens's *A Christmas Carol* (Andersen-Warren, 1996). Applications of drama therapy reflect knowledge of and expertise in the theater along with a knowledge of theories of psychotherapy (Landy, 2005, 2007, 2008).

In the practice of drama therapy, both drama therapists and their clients can take a dramatic role or the traditional client–therapist roles. In the application of drama therapy, the therapist can direct therapy, observe it, lead a group in imagery exercises, and experience a creative exercise, such as a pretend journey, with a group (Johnson, 1992; Jones, 2007). Drama therapists may improvise a play, use puppets, or use a sand tray (a tray with different toy figures, toy buildings, trees, and so forth). Because they may play many different roles (including that of psychotherapist) with a client and possibly touch the client, transference and countertransference issues can develop more quickly than they might in other forms of therapy (Johnson, 1992). Although this can be true when working with groups, it is accentuated when working individually with clients.

In individual drama therapy, Landy (1992) suggests that drama therapists must attend to the boundaries between client and therapist and to whether clients put too much distance between themselves and the drama therapist or not enough. If the client is underdistanced, the therapist needs to have some distance from the client; if the client is too distant from the therapist, the therapist needs to bridge that gap. Landy gives an example of how the therapist might respond with an overdistant client using an elephant and mouse enactment.

> For example, the client in the role of the mouse makes himself very small. His movements are tiny. His voice is barely audible. He avoids any contact with the therapist in the role of elephant. The therapist fills herself up with the role. As the mouse shrinks, she expands. The smaller he becomes, the larger the therapist becomes. She trumpets, flailing her trunk; she swaggers around the room, knocking things off the table, threatening to crush the mouse under her big, round, wrinkled foot. In her fullness being most threatening, challenging, clumsy, provocative, the therapist/elephant acts at being under-distanced. (Landy, 1992, p. 101)

Aware of her role, the therapist may wish to project the image of a large clumsy authority figure to provoke a response from the client. In this role, the therapist is an actor, ready to suggest that the client change roles with her and play the elephant while she plays the mouse. If the client has difficulty playing the mouse, it is the drama therapist's role to help the client do so. If appropriate, she may play a clever mouse, who can trick the elephant as in a fable, or may encourage the client to play that role. The therapist goes beyond role playing, using acting and directing skills to help the client become more aware of emotions, develop inter-personal skills, and deal with a variety of psychological problems.

Music Therapy

Like other creative arts therapies, music therapy can be applied in several ways. Music therapists make use of music both as a basic stimulus and for its therapeutic applications (Crowe, 2004). Just as retail stores use background music to make the mood of customers more conducive to buying, music therapists may use rhythmic music to stimulate patients or soothing music to calm them down (Frohne-Hagemann, 2007). The therapeutic function of music is seen through many activities such as solo singing, singing accompanied by the music therapist, and drumming. Music therapists may use music to encourage nonviolent behavior, increase verbal behavior, and reduce stress (Crowe, 2004). Although music therapy is used for individuals with diverse problems, such as drug abuse, it is used most frequently for individuals with severe disabilities, such as learning disabilities, schizophrenia, autism, speech and language disorders, visual disabilities, and Alzheimer's disease. For example, (Rio, 2009) shows how music can be used by caregivers for helping older people who suffer from dementia.

The theoretical approaches of music therapists can vary widely, from an emphasis on behavioral evaluation and change (Crowe, 2004) to Odell-Miller's (2003) use of music as a means of enriching psychoanalytic therapy, especially for transference and countertransference issues. One example of the creativity of music therapists is Rogers's (1993) work with sexually abused clients. Different musical instruments, particularly percussion instruments, can be assigned to represent different individuals in a child's life.

> Different instruments may be assigned differing roles for personas. A clear example is a child "B" who repeatedly used a large conga drum to symbolize his father, a small xylophone to represent his mother and a smaller handchime to represent himself. These instruments were then physically positioned to indicate the strength of the relationships between family members. In addition, the way the instruments were played had a clear symbolic meaning; "B" associated the large conga drum with his father and on one level perceived his father as being very dominating; "B" then played the conga very gently. A clear distinction between the visual and auditory perceptions of the conga was apparent (the contrast between size of the instrument and the way it was played). This contrast can be subsequently explored. (Rogers, 1993, p. 211)

This exercise can be seen as a type of musical sculpture, with the physical distance between instruments a part of the sculpture. However, therapists may often improvise and encourage clients to spontaneously express themselves in an active way with a variety of instruments to disclose mood or feeling. Sometimes such exercises may be initiated by the client and other times by the music therapist.

In discussing music therapy, Crowe (2004) describes the physiology and spirituality of music therapy as well as collaboration with other arts therapies, and broad applications to many different populations. Music therapy helped children who have been hospitalized due to trauma as a result of events related to the terrorist attacks of September 11, 2001 (Loewy & Stewart, 2004). As meta-analyses show, music therapy has been helpful in promoting social involvement and increasing emotional and cognitive skills with individuals with dementia (Koger, Chapin, & Brotons, 1999). For such individuals, music that helps people reminisce about earlier times in their lives can be helpful (Ashida, 2000). In a group of adolescents in residential treatment, hip-hop music was helpful because adolescents were able to relate to the rappers' life struggles as played out in the lyrics of the music (Ciardiello, 2003). Music therapists make use of their knowledge of the physiological and psychological processes of individuals, as well as their knowledge of the aesthetic and physical properties of music.

Summary

The creative arts therapies, which include art, dance movement, drama, and music, use innovative therapeutic techniques to encourage the expressive qualities of clients. Although often working with severely disturbed patients, creative arts therapists work with all populations, both individually and in groups. Increasingly there is a trend for creative arts therapists to combine modalities, such as art and drama therapies. Some creative arts therapists work primarily in an adjunctive role with psychotherapists; others may combine psychotherapy with their creative modality.

References

Andersen-Warren, M. (1996). Therapeutic theatre. In S. Mitchell (Ed.), *Dramatherapy: Clinical studies* (pp. 108–135). London: Kingsley.

Ashida, S. (2000). The effect of reminiscence music therapy sessions on changes in depressive symptoms in elderly persons with dementia. *Journal of Music Therapy, 37,* 170–182.

Bouzoukis, C. E. (2001). *Pediatric dramatherapy: They couldn't run so they learned to fly.* London: Kingsley.

Ciardiello, S. (Ed.). (2003). Meet them in the lab: Using hip-hop music therapy groups with adolescents in residential settings. In N. E. Sullivan, E. S. Mesbur, N.C. Lang, D. Goodman, & L. Mitchell (Eds.), *Social work with groups: Social justice through personal, community, and societal change* (pp. 103–117). New York, NY: Haworth Press.

Crowe, B. (2004). *Music and soul making: Toward a new theory of music therapy.* Lanham, MD: Scarecrow Press.

Frohne-Hagemann, I. (Ed.). (2007). *Receptive music therapy: Theory and practice.* Germany: Zeitpunkt Musik.

Hanna, J. L. (2004). Applying anthropological methods in dance/movement therapy research. In R. F. Cruz & C. F. Berrol (Eds.), *Dance/movement therapists in action: A working guide to research options* (pp. 144–165). Springfield, IL: Charles C. Thomas.

James, J. (1996). Dramatherapy with people with learning disabilities. In S. Mitchell (Ed.), *Dramatherapy: Clinical studies* (pp. 15–32). London: Kingsley.

Jennings, S. (1992). "Reason and madness": Therapeutic journeys through *King Lear.* In S. Jennings (Ed.), *Dramatherapy: Theory and practice 2* (pp. 5–18). London: Routledge.

Johnson, D. R. (1992). The dramatherapist's in-role. In S. Jennings (Ed.), *Dramatherapy: Theory and practice 2* (pp. 112–136). London: Routledge.

Jones, P. (2007). *Drama as therapy: Theory, practice and research.* New York: Routledge.

Koger, S. M., Chapin, K., & Brotons, M. (1999). Is music therapy an effective intervention for dementia? A meta-analytic review of literature. *Journal of Music Therapy, 36,* 2–15.

Landy, R. (1992). One on one: The role of the dramatherapist working with individuals. In S. Jennings (Ed.), *Dramatherapy: Theory and practice 2* (pp. 97–111). London: Routledge.

Landy, R. J. (2005). Drama therapy and psychodrama. In C. A. Malchiodi (Ed.), *Expressive therapies* (pp. 90–116). New York: Guilford.

Landy, R. J. (2007). Drama therapy: Past, present, and future. In I. A. Serlin, J. Sonke-Henderson, R. Brandman, & J. Graham-Pole (Eds.), *Whole person healthcare Vol 3: The arts and health* (pp. 143–163). Westport, CT: Praeger.

Landy, R. J. (2008). *The couch and the stage: Integrating words and action in psychotherapy.* Lanham, MD: Jason Aronson.

LeVay, D. (2005). "Little monsters"? Play therapy for children with sexually problematic behavior. In C. Schaefer, J. McCormick, & A. Ohnogi (Eds.), *International handbook of play therapy: Advances in assessment, theory, research, and practice* (pp. 243–262). Lanham, MD: Jason Aronson.

Loewy, J. V., & Stewart, K. (2004). Music therapy to help traumatized children and caregivers. In N. B. Webb (Ed.), *Mass trauma and violence: Helping families and children cope* (pp. 191–215). New York: Guilford.

Loman, S. T. (2005). Dance/movement therapy. In C. A. Malchiodi (Ed.), *Expressive therapies* (pp. 68–89). New York: Guilford.

Malchiodi, C. A. (2003). *Handbook of art therapy*. New York: Guilford.

Malchiodi, C. A. (2005). Art therapy. In C. A. Malchiodi (Ed.), *Expressive therapies* (pp. 16–45). New York: Guilford.

Nicholas, M. (2003). Introduction: Action methods in group therapy. In D. J. Weiner & L. K. Oxford (Eds.), *Action therapy with families and groups: Using creative arts improvisation in clinical practice* (pp. 103–105). Washington, DC: American Psychological Association.

Odell-Miller, H. (Ed.). (2003). Are words enough? Music therapy as an influence in psychoanalytic psychotherapy. In L. King & R. Randall (Eds.), *The future of psychoanalytic psychotherapy* (pp. 153–166). Philadelphia: Whurr.

Payne, H. (Ed.). (2006). *Dance movement therapy: Theory, research and practice* (2nd ed.). New York: Routledge.

Rio, R. (2009). *Connecting through music with people with dementia: A guide for caregivers*. London: Jessica Kingsley.

Rogers, P. (1993). Research in music therapy with sexually abused clients. In H. Payne (Ed.), *Handbook of inquiry in the arts therapies: One river, many currents* (pp. 197–217). London: Kingsley.

Rubin, J. A. (2010). *Introduction to art therapy: Sources & resources* (rev. ed.). New York: Routledge.

Steiner, M. (1992). Alternatives in psychiatry: Dance movement therapy in the community. In H. Payne (Ed.), *Dance movement therapy: Theory and practice* (pp. 141–162). London: Routledge.

Vick, R. M. (2003). A brief history of art therapy. In C. A. Malchiodi (Ed.), *Handbook of art therapy* (pp. 5–15). New York: Guilford.

Wadeson, H. (2001). An eclectic approach to art therapy. In J. A. Rubin (Ed.), *Approaches to art therapy: Theory and technique* (2nd ed., pp. 300–317). New York: Brunner/Mazel.

Summary

Five different therapeutic approaches have been discussed, with each having disparate views on how to produce therapeutic changes. Asian therapies emphasize reflection and contemplation, with some approaches suggesting the importance of responsibility and obligation to others. Body psychotherapies stress attending to posture, movement, and physique to assess psychological problems and then to make interventions that may be physical or psychological. Interpersonal therapy is a research-based approach to treating depression that uses treatment manuals to specify procedures. An established approach, psychodrama is active, done in groups and often in front of an audience. It features the enactment of personal problems. The creative arts therapies use music, artworks, movement, and dramatic expression to help clients express their feelings and become more aware of social interactions. Although each of these approaches is quite different from the others, each provides its unique approach to the application of psychotherapy.

Comparison and Critique

Outline of Comparison and Critique

BASIC CONCEPTS OF PERSONALITY
GOALS OF THERAPY
ASSESSMENT IN THERAPY
THERAPEUTIC TECHNIQUES
DIFFERENTIAL TREATMENT
BRIEF PSYCHOTHERAPY
CURRENT TRENDS
   Common Factors Approach
   Treatment Manuals and Research-Supported
      Psychological Treatment Psychotherapy
   Postmodernism and Constructivism
USING THE THEORY WITH OTHER THEORIES
RESEARCH
   Outcome Research
   Future Directions
GENDER ISSUES
MULTICULTURAL ISSUES
FAMILY THERAPY
GROUP THERAPY

CRITIQUE
   Psychoanalysis
   Jungian Analysis
   Adlerian Therapy
   Existential Therapy
   Person-Centered Therapy
   Gestalt Therapy
   Behavior Therapy
   Rational Emotive Behavior Therapy
   Cognitive Therapy
   Reality Therapy
   Constructivist Theories
      Solution-focused
      Personal construct theory
      Narrative
   Feminist Therapy
   Family Systems Therapy

In this chapter, I compare theories across each of the areas discussed in this book, which provides some background for a critique of the limitations and strengths of each theory. To compare theories, I have summarized the basic concepts of personality, goals, essential approaches to assessment, and the most common techniques applied by each theory. Also, I have selected two disorders—depression and anxiety—to compare the treatment indicated for the major theories discussed in this book. I also summarize and compare how each theory deals with brief psychotherapy, current trends, how theories make use of other theories, research trends, gender and cultural issues as they affect theories differentially, and applications of theories to couples, families, and groups. Because the five separate theories discussed in Chapter 15 (Asian therapies, body

psychotherapies, interpersonal psychotherapy, psychodrama, and creative arts therapies) are described very briefly, they are not included in this review.

Following this comparison, I describe what I consider to be the major limitations and strengths of each theory. These views are subjective and reflect opinions formed from contrasting various aspects of theories with each other. This critique of theories is brief so that you may supplement my views with your own perceptions of the strengths and weaknesses of the theory. Both the comparison of the theories and the critique that I provide should help you as you read about theoretical integration in Chapter 17. Chapter 17 will illustrate three common integrative theories as well as provide information about how you can integrate theories, if you choose to do so.

Basic Concepts of Personality

This section compares the basic concepts of major theories of psychotherapy by grouping theories into three overlapping areas: those that emphasize unconscious processes and/or early development, those dealing with current experience and/or issues related to living, and those dealing with changing actions and/or thoughts. The key concepts associated with each theory are listed for comparison purposes in Table 16.1.

Theories that deal with unconscious forces and/or early development are psychoanalysis, Jungian theory, and Adlerian theory. Concepts of conscious and unconscious forces, as well as the structure of personality (id, ego, and superego), are important to varying degrees to each of the four psychoanalytic views: Drive theory emphasizes psychosexual development, ego psychology focuses on defense mechanisms, and object relations theory uses concepts that concern the infant's relationship with the love object (mother). In self psychology, attention is paid to the importance of the development of narcissism. In relational psychoanalysis, particular attention is paid to the developing relationship between the patient and the psychoanalyst, and the subjective views of the patient are highly valued. Whereas psychoanalytic theory focuses on different views of childhood development, Jungian theory is particularly concerned with the unconscious—more specifically, the collective unconscious. To understand Jungian theory, one must have a grasp of the importance of archetypes, a few of which are listed in Table 16.1. Although Adler believed in the importance of unconscious processes, he was particularly interested in individuals' beliefs, their contributions to society, and their interest in others.

Whereas psychoanalysis, Jungian analysis, and Adlerian therapy focus on past issues and development, existential, person-centered, and gestalt therapy stress present interaction.

Table 16.1   Concepts Basic to Theories of Personality

Psychoanalysis FREUD	Jungian Analysis	Adlerian Therapy
Unconscious	Conscious	Style of life
Conscious	Personal unconscious	Social interest
Structure of personality	Collective unconscious	Inferiority and superiority
Id	Archetypes	Birth order
Ego	Persona	
Superego	Anima, animus	
Defense mechanisms	Shadow	
Drive theory	Self	
Psychosexual stages	Personality attitudes	
Ego psychology	Introversion	
Defense mechanisms	Extraversion	
Adaptive functions	Personality functions	
Adult development	Thinking and feeling	
Object relations	Sensing and intuition	
Childhood relationship with mother	Personality development	
Individuation	Childhood	
Transitional object	Adolescence	
Good-enough mother	Middle age	
True and false self	Old age	
Splitting		
Self psychology		
Narcissism		
Selfobject		
Grandiosity		
Idealized parent		
Relational psychoanalysis		
Interactions with others		
Communication type		
Perception of relationships		
Intersubjectivity		

Existential Therapy	Person-Centered Therapy	Gestalt Therapy
Being-in-the-world	Development of the need for positive regard	Figure and ground
Four ways of being		Contact with self and others
Umwelt	Conditionality	Contact boundaries
Mitwelt	Relationships and self-regard	Disturbances of contact boundaries
Eigenwelt	Fully functioning person	Introjection
Überwelt		Projection
Time and being		Retroflection
Living and dying		Deflection
Freedom, responsibility, and choice		Confluence
Isolation and loving		Awareness
Meaning and meaninglessness		Unfinished business
Self-transcendence		
Striving for authenticity		

Behavior Therapy	Rational Emotive Behavior Therapy	Cognitive Therapy
Classical and operant principles	Responsible hedonism	Automatic thoughts
Positive reinforcement	Humanism	Cognitive schemas
Negative reinforcement	Rationality	Cognitive distortions
Extinction	Unconditional self-acceptance	All-or-nothing thinking

(Continued)

Table 16.1 Concepts Basic to Theories of Personality (Continued)

Behavior Therapy *(continued)*	Rational Emotive Behavior Therapy	Cognitive Therapy
Classical and operant principles	Irrational beliefs about	Selective abstraction
Generalization	Competence and success	Mind reading
Discrimination	Love and approval	Negative prediction
Shaping	Being treated unfairly	Catastrophizing
Observational learning principles	Safety and comfort	Overgeneralization
Self-efficacy	A-B-C theory of personality	Labeling and mislabeling
Attention and retention processes	A. Activating event	Magnification or
Motivational processes	B. Belief	minimization
Motor reproduction processes	C. Consequence	Personalization
	Disturbances about disturbances	

Reality Therapy	Constructivist Therapies	Feminist Therapy	Family Systems Therapy
Responsibility	Solution-focused	Developmental gender	Communication patterns
Choice theory	Listen to complaint	differences	Systems theory
Psychological needs	Motivation to change	Schema theory and	Feedback
Belonging	Attend to expectations for	multiple identities	Homeostasis
Power	solutions	Gilligan's ethic of care	Bowen's intergenerational
Freedom	Narrative therapy	Relational cultural	approach
Fun	Client stories	model	Differentiation of self
Choosing	Setting		Triangulation
Doing	Characterization		Family projection process
Thinking	Plot		Emotional cutoff
Feeling	Theme		Multigenerational
Physiology	Narrative empathy		transmission process
Choosing "crazy"			Minuchin's structural approach
behavior for			Family structure
control			Boundary permeability
			Alignments and coalitions
			Haley's strategic approach
			Power in relationships
			Communication
			Symptom focus

Existential therapy is distinguished by its attention to issues important to being human: living, death, freedom, isolation, loving, meaning, and meaninglessness. Person-centered therapy is concerned with issues that develop or interfere with experiencing self-worth. Awareness of self and contact with self and others, concepts very much related to experiencing the present, are the essence of gestalt therapy.

The behavioral and cognitive therapies are concerned with how people act, learn, and think. In particular, behavior therapists focus on classical and operant principles of behavior, as well as observational learning. In rational emotive behavior therapy (REBT), focus is on the irrational belief systems of individuals that create unhappiness for them. Cognitive therapy attends to thinking and distortions in thought processes that lead to ineffective ways of feeling, behaving, or thinking. Also focusing on doing, thinking, and feeling, reality therapy emphasizes the individual's role in being responsible for or taking control of her own behavior.

Whereas the theories that have just been described attend to psychological factors that affect personality development, feminist therapy examines sociological factors—such as gender and cultural differences—as they relate to the development of individuals and their relationships with others. Also going beyond the individual, family therapists point out the importance of the relationship of members within a family to each other and how these relationships affect individual personality.

In general, each of these theories provides a distinct way of seeing the world that has an impact on its approach to therapy. Constructivist therapies (solution-focused and narrative) emphasize clients' ways of seeing the world or their theory of personality, while integrative theories systematically address the overlap of theories. However, there are several instances of overlap between theories, particularly cognitive, behavior, and REBT therapies, that integrate cognitive and behavioral principles. Sometimes different terms are used for similar concepts in very different theories. For example, Kernberg uses the term *splitting* to describe the tendency of individuals (particularly those with a borderline disorder) to see things as all good or all bad, whereas Beck uses the cognitive term *all-or-nothing thinking* to describe a similar process. For most theories, the concepts that are basic to the theories of personality are quite well developed. In Table 16.1, only the most important are listed.

Goals of Therapy

Following from basic concepts about human personality, goals of therapy for each theory are a reflection of those concepts that the theorists believe are important aims for clients and therapists. Table 16.2 summarizes, in very brief form, aspects of human experience that are seen as the focus of therapeutic change. In general, the emphasis on specificity and clearly defining change is more important for cognitive and behavior therapies than for others. Because therapeutic goals are all stated differently for each theory, comparisons of the goals of therapy are somewhat difficult to make.

Assessment in Therapy

In essence, goals guide therapists as to where they are going; assessment helps them find markers to guide them in bringing about therapeutic change. Although some therapists may make use of personality inventories to learn more about the client, many put the most emphasis on initial interviews, as well as on the therapy sessions, as the assessment process continues throughout therapy. For theories that have cognitive and behavioral goals, the assessment techniques tend to be very specific, with client thoughts and behaviors clearly described. For cognitive therapy, diagnostic classification systems may help guide therapy, along with specific observations and reports. For other therapies, such as Jungian, existential, person-centered, gestalt, family, and constructivist therapies, therapeutic goals are not closely related to the DSM-IV-TR classification system, and assessment methods are unique to each therapy. The brief summary of assessment approaches in Table 16.3 describes concepts, tests, and methods that provide a basis for making therapeutic change.

Table 16.2 Goals of Therapy

Psychoanalysis	Change in personality and character structure; resolve unconscious conflicts within self; reconstruct and reinterpret childhood experiences. *Drive Theory*—increase awareness of sexual and aggressive drives. *Ego Theory*—understand ego defenses and adapt to external world. *Object Relations-Relational Psychoanalysis*—explore and resolve separation and individuation issues. *Self Psychology*—resolve issues dealing with self-absorption or idealized parents.
Jungian Analysis	Individuation; integration of the conscious and unconscious leading to individuation.
Adlerian Therapy	Increase social interest, change self-defeating behaviors, solve problems, modify or change lifestyle.
Existential Therapy	Authenticity; find a meaning for existence and pursue it; fully experience existence.
Person-Centered Therapy	Become more self-directed, increase positive self-regard; the client chooses goals.
Gestalt Therapy	The person's feelings, perceptions, thoughts, and body are in harmony with each other; awareness leads to growth, responsibility, and maturity.
Behavior Therapy	Change specific target behaviors that are clearly and accurately defined. Perform functional analysis, when appropriate, to specify goals.
Rational Emotive Behavior Therapy	Minimize emotional disturbances, decrease self-defeating behaviors, learn a philosophy that will reduce the chances of being disturbed by overwhelming irrational thoughts.
Cognitive Therapy	Remove biases or distortions in thinking to function more effectively and bring about more positive feelings, behavior, and thinking.
Reality Therapy	Help individuals take responsibility for and meet needs for belonging, power, freedom, and fun in satisfying ways.
Constructivist Therapies	*Solution-focused*—make specific goals; solve problems, rate progress. *Narrative therapy*—see lives (stories) in positive ways rather than problem saturated.
Feminist Therapy	Should include changes in societal institutions as well as personal issues; also build self-esteem, improve interpersonal relationships, examine gender roles, and accept one's own body.
Family Systems Therapy	*Bowen*—reduce family stress level and help members become more differentiated. *Minuchin*—alter coalitions and alliances in the family to bring about changes. *Haley*—focus on specific goals; strategies planned to reach goals.

Therapeutic Techniques

Although the various theories have developed techniques growing out of their views of individuals' personalities, some of the techniques or methods overlap, and practitioners borrow from other theories.

Table 16.3   Assessment Approach

Psychoanalysis	Family and social history, structured or unstructured Trial analysis Projective techniques—Rorschach, Thematic Apperception Test
Jungian Analysis	Examine archetypal material in dreams and fantasies Projective techniques Measures of attitude and function—Gray-Wheelwright, Myers-Briggs, Singer-Loomis
Adlerian Therapy	Analyze lifestyle, make observations about family dynamics, birth order, and examine early recollections. Examine basic mistakes (self-defeating behaviors). Assess assets. Questionnaires may be used in addition to interviews.
Existential Therapy	Listen for themes of isolation, meaninglessness, responsibility, and mortality. Also, assess ability to face life honestly. Dreams, objective tests, and projective tests may help.
Person-Centered Therapy	Assessment occurs as therapists empathically understand clients.
Gestalt Therapy	Therapists perceive and construct patterns from patients' words, bodily movements, feelings, and sensations, as they occur. They may do this by focusing on the experiencing cycle, which contains these elements as well as others.
Behavior Therapy	Inquire about antecedents and consequences of behavior; use behavioral reports, ratings, observations, and physiological measurements; use experimental methods to assess progress.
Rational Emotive Behavior Therapy	Assess thoughts and behaviors using interviews and specific questionnaires; use A-B-C theory to identify problems.
Cognitive Therapy	Techniques include interviews with detailed questioning, self-monitoring, thought sampling, and scales and questionnaires about specific problems or attitudes.
Reality Therapy	Use interviews and self-evaluation questionnaires to find what clients "really want" and to assess needs for belonging, power, freedom, and fun. Also assess doing, thinking, feeling, and physiology.
Constructivist Therapies	*Solution-focused*—assess motivation, map sequence of behaviors with mindmaps. *Narrative*—view lives as positive rather than as problem saturated.
Feminist Therapy	Caution against traditional psychological assessment; focus on including sociological factors such as violence, discrimination, and gender role.
Family Systems Therapy	In general, make observations about patterns of family interactions.

For example, most therapists in the course of their work with clients are likely to respond empathically (person-centered therapy) at some point in therapy (particularly during early stages or when clients present emotional issues). The less active techniques of free association and interpretation are usually associated with longer-term therapies such as psychoanalysis and Jungian analysis. More confrontive and direct techniques (confrontations, questions, and directions) are used in brief psychoanalysis and in cognitive, behavioral, REBT, gestalt, and reality therapies. In psychoanalysis and Jungian analysis, techniques emphasize bringing unconscious processes into conscious awareness. In Adlerian, cognitive, and REBT therapy, techniques focus more on cognitive than on behavioral or emotive processes. In behavior and reality therapy, attention is paid first to changing ways of doing but also to beliefs and feelings. In gestalt therapy, primary attention is to awareness of verbal and nonverbal processes, often bringing out emotional feelings, whereas person-centered therapists empathize with their client's experience. Although existential therapists may make use of techniques from any of the previous theories, they attend to issues that are of importance in being human. Feminist therapists may make use of a number of these methods but also examine the social and cultural context and factors outside the client that influence her problems. Family therapists may respond to individuals in a family using some of these approaches but most often are likely to examine the system first and make interventions that may have an impact on two or more members of a family. When solution-focused therapists use techniques, attention is paid to how clients view solutions to their problems and how interventions can be made that fit with the stories of their problems. For convenience, the primary therapeutic techniques that are associated with each theory are listed in Table 16.4 so that further comparison can be made.

Table 16.4   Therapeutic Techniques

Psychoanalysis	Jungian Analysis	Adlerian Therapy
Free association	Bring unconscious into conscious awareness	Immediacy
Neutrality		Encouragement
Empathy	Interpretation of dreams, fantasies	Acting as if
Analyzing resistance	Active imagination	Catching oneself
Interpretation (dreams, free association, etc.)	Creative techniques: poetry, art, sandplay	Creating images
		Spitting in the client's soup
Analysis of transference	Transference	Avoiding the tar baby
Countertransference	Countertransference	Push-button technique
Relational responses		Paradoxical intention
Brief psychoanalysis		Task setting and commitment
Questions		Homework
Restatements		
Confrontations		
Interpretation (limited)		

Existential Therapy	Person-Centered Therapy	Gestalt Therapy
Techniques are not generally used; rather, conditions are present and issues are addressed	Necessary and sufficient conditions for change:	Empathic responding
		Enhancing awareness
	Psychological contact	Awareness statements and questions
Conditions	Psychological vulnerability	Emphasizing and enhancing awareness through
Therapeutic love	Congruence and genuineness	
Resistance	Unconditional positive regard or acceptance	Verbal behavior
Transference		Nonverbal behavior
Issues addressed	Empathy	Feelings
Living and dying	Perception of empathy and acceptance	Dialogue
Freedom, responsibility, and choice		Enactment
Isolation and loving		Dreams
Meaning and meaninglessness		Awareness of self and others

(Continued)

Table 16.4 Therapeutic Techniques (Continued)

Existential Therapy *(continued)*	Person-Centered Therapy	Gestalt Therapy

Frankl's logotherapy techniques
  Attitude modulation
  Dereflection
  Paradoxical intention
  Socratic dialogue
		Awareness of avoidance
		Taking risks
		Creativity

Behavior Therapy	Rational Emotive Behavior Therapy	Cognitive Therapy

Systematic desensitization
Imaginal flooding
In vivo techniques
Virtual reality
Modeling techniques
  Live
  Symbolic
  Role playing
  Participant
  Covert
Cognitive-behavioral techniques
  Self-instructional training
  Stress inoculation
Relaxation techniques
Assertiveness
Exposure and ritual prevention
	Disputing irrational beliefs using
	  A-B-C-D-E model
	Cognitive approaches
	  Coping self-statements
	  Teaching others
	  Problem solving
	Emotive techniques
	  Imagery
	  Role playing
	  Shame attacking
	  Forceful self statements
	    and dialogue
	Behavior methods
	  Activity homework
	  Reinforcement
	  Skill training
	Insight
		Structured sessions
		Guided discovery
		Specifying automatic thoughts
		Homework
		Cognitive interventions
		  Understanding idiosyncratic
		    meaning
		  Challenging absolutes
		  Reattribution
		  Labeling of distortions
		  Decatastrophizing
		  Challenging all-or-nothing thinking
		  Listing advantages and
		    disadvantages
		  Cognitive rehearsal

Reality Therapy	Constructivist Therapies	Feminist Therapy	Family Systems Therapy

Process
  Friendly involvement
  Exploring total behavior
  Evaluating behavior
  Planning to do better
  Commitment to plans
Therapist attitudes
  Don't accept excuses
  No criticism
  Don't give up
Strategies
  Questioning
  Being positive
  Metaphors
  Humor
  Confrontation
  Paradoxical techniques
	Solution-focused
	Pretherapy change
	  Complimenting
	  Miracle question
	  Scaling
	  Assessing motivation
	  Exception-seeking
	  Assessing motivation
	  "The message"
	Narrative therapy
	  Telling the story
	  Externalizing the problem
	  Unique outcomes
	  Alternative narratives
	  Positive narratives
	  Questions about the
	    future
	  Support for client stories
		Gender role analysis and
		  intervention
		Cultural analysis and
		  intervention
		Power analysis and
		  intervention
		Assertiveness training
		Reframing and relabeling
		Demystifying therapy
			Family systems therapy
			Bowen's intergenera-
			  tional approach
			  Genograms
			  Interpretation
			  Coaching
			    Detriangulation
			Minuchin's structural
			  approach
			  Family mapping
			  Accommodating and
			    joining
			  Enactment
			  Changing boundaries
			  Reframing
			Haley's strategic
			  approach
			  Straightforward tasks
			  Paradoxical tasks

Differential Treatment

As has been mentioned previously, theories vary to the degree that they apply different techniques or methods to different disorders. To contrast theoretical approaches, it is more helpful to compare how different theories can be applied to the same disorder than it is to different ones. Table 16.5 gives examples, for most of the theories, as to how a theory can be applied to a particular disorder for a specific client. Because clients differ on so many variables (age, gender, family history, type of problem, temperament, and so forth), it is not possible to say "Use this technique for this disorder." In Table 16.5, a very brief description is given for very complex cases described in this book for the purpose of comparison for depression and anxiety. Returning to the original case in the appropriate chapter can provide much more information about how a particular theoretical orientation might be used to deal with a client.

Because of the particular interests of therapists, certain disorders have come to be associated with different theories.

Table 16.5 Theoretical Approaches Applied to Two Different Disorders

Chapter and Theory	Depression	Anxiety
2. Psychoanalysis	Sam's way of caring and comforting others is related to his eagerness to take care of the analyst.	Mary, 3 years—deals with defense mechanisms and transference.
3. Jungian Analysis	Beth—dream material in a dream series reveals unconscious aspects of depression.	A young woman's dreams reveal her sadness about the death of her brother and the loss of a romantic relationship.
4. Adlerian Therapy	Sheri—early recollections provide insight into distorted perceptions.	Robert builds self-esteem through encouragement, avoids defeat, lessening anxiety.
5. Existential Therapy	Catherine accepts her dispiritedness by bringing detachment to her awareness.	Nathalie must make difficult choices due to her son's behavior toward a friend who later committed suicide.
6. Person-Centered Therapy	A female graduate student assumes more responsibility for self as a result of therapeutic empathic listening.	
7. Gestalt Therapy	A 27-year-old woman deals with feeling worthless by using the two-chair technique.	A young man is continually brought to the present to deal with his issues.
8. Behavior Therapy	Jane, 29—behavior is assessed in detail and she learns self-, time, and child management.	Claire—anxious about husband being away and son's football games. Learns relaxation and worry prevention.
9. Rational Emotive Behavior Therapy	Penny, 14—develops new beliefs and becomes more assertive with brothers.	Ted experiences strong anxiety on a train; therapist disputes irrational beliefs.
10. Cognitive Therapy	Paul, a 38-year-old lawyer with AIDS makes use of the Socratic method, the dysfunctional thought record, and the three-question technique.	Amy—negative thoughts are identified and modified through questions.
11. Reality Therapy	Teresa, 40, little energy—focus is on making choices to do small things and following plans to carry out choices.	Randy, a college student, takes and maintains control over anxious feelings.
13. Feminist Therapy	Ms. B., a graduate student, deals with isolation and guilt by seeking social support and joining relevant groups.	

For example, much of Freud's early work was with female patients who presented symptoms of hysteria. Kohut's work with narcissistic clients has linked this disorder with self psychology. Behavior therapy has been applied to treatment of phobias. Both feminist therapy and gestalt therapy have been used with people who have experienced traumas due to violence (posttraumatic stress disorder).

Some disorders are quite common, and I have tried to give a number of different examples of how theorists approach these problems (alcoholism and drug abuse: existential therapy, gestalt therapy, and cognitive therapy; obsessive-compulsive disorder: existential, cognitive, REBT, behavior, and reality therapy; borderline disorders: object relations, Jungian, Adlerian, existential, person-centered, and feminist; eating disorders: Adlerian therapy, reality therapy, and feminist therapy).

Examining how different theoretical approaches can be applied to a variety of disorders can increase understanding of the theoretical approach. Due to individual differences in clients, in therapists, and in lack of fit between psychological disorders and theories of psychotherapy, prescribing a previously developed treatment plan or method for a specific disorder should be done while considering its appropriateness for the client.

Brief Psychotherapy

In the 1930s and 1940s, much of psychotherapy was psychoanalytically based treatment, which often lasted several years and required three to five sessions per week.

Because of the high cost and time investment from therapist and client, brief methods of psychotherapy have become more and more common. Additionally, many clinics and community services limit the number of sessions per client due to great demands on agency services. Likewise, health maintenance organizations and insurance companies often restrict the number of sessions that they will pay for. Because of these restraints on the length of therapy and because of the large number of practitioners of psychoanalytic therapy, much effort has been directed toward providing a short-term alternative to psychoanalysis that also is consistent with a psychoanalytic view of personality. In Chapter 2, Luborsky's Core Conflictual Relationship Theme method requiring less than 20 sessions is explained. Often brief psychoanalytic therapy tends to limit goals, select patients carefully, focus on specific problems, and be more confrontive and directive than traditional psychoanalytic therapy.

Not all theories have been adapted to a brief or short-term model of psychotherapy. Jungian therapists may work for a year or two with patients and may occasionally stop therapy for a few years and then resume it later. Existential therapy is often used with other theories. When applied with a psychoanalytic perspective, it may be as lengthy as psychoanalytic therapy. However, Frankl's logotherapy is a briefer, more focused method. Both person-centered and gestalt therapies tend to rely on clients to determine the duration of therapy and do not normally use a brief psychotherapeutic method. In contrast, Adlerian therapists often see their clients, on average, for about 20 sessions, with most clients being seen for less than a year. When needed, they do work within a time limit and prefer to do that rather than limit the goals that they address.

Behavior therapy, REBT, cognitive therapy, and reality therapy tend to be short-term treatments; however, a number of factors may determine length of therapy. For behavior therapists, therapy length can depend on the number of target behaviors addressed, the strength of anxiety, or the type of therapy used. For example, a gradual application of behavioral methods takes longer than does flooding. Likewise, imaginal procedures often require more sessions than in vivo exposure. For behavior therapy, REBT, and cognitive therapy, length of treatment is shorter for phobias, and moderate forms of depression than for borderline or obsessive-compulsive disorders. Other factors affecting treatment length are the range and number of problems and the client's willingness to do homework. Many of these comments also apply to reality therapy, in which treatment length varies greatly, with more frequent sessions being needed in the beginning of therapy than toward the end. The problem resolution and symptom relief methods of constructivist therapies (solution-focused and narrative therapies) often require fewer than 10 meetings. For feminist therapy, because it may be combined with any of the theories listed previously, treatment length varies widely.

Considerable attention has been paid to brief therapy in family therapy. Because it may be logistically difficult to get family members together, because some do not wish to attend therapy sessions, and because many family problems present crises, there has been an effort on the part of several family therapy theorists to develop brief methods. The long brief therapy approach of the Milan Associates typically requires about 10 sessions at monthly intervals. Creative approaches such as family systems therapy and constructivist therapies are likely to continue in their popularity as demands for cost-effective solutions with minimal delays are sought by patients, therapists, social agencies, health maintenance organizations, insurance companies, and governmental agencies.

Current Trends

This section will discuss three trends. The first to be discussed is that of common factors. Psychologists have examined a variety of studies to determine the common factors that make up effective psychotherapy. In contrast to this approach, other researchers have focused on specific treatment methods using treatment manuals, called research-supported psychological treatments psychotherapies. Rather than look for factors across many therapies that lead to effective therapy, research-supported psychological treatments examine which theories should be used for which conditions and which disorders. Another influence, which is not related to the common factors or research-supported psychological treatments approach, is that of postmodernism, or social constructionism, which focuses on how clients view their own lives.

Common Factors Approach

Trying to understand the factors that are common to change in psychotherapy and counseling has been an effort that has taken place over a 50-year period. Several writers have shown how attending to and studying common factors can be helpful in the assessment and treatment phases of psychotherapy (Imel & Wampold, 2008; Sparks, Duncan, & Miller, 2008; Weinberger & Rasco, 2007). Also, Castonguay and Beutler (2006) describe in detail in their book, *Principles of Therapeutic Change That Work,* important factors that are considered in understanding components of psychotherapy and counseling. They divide these factors into participant factors and relationship factors. *Participant factors* include characteristics of the client or therapist, such as gender, ethnicity, attachment style, coping style, resistance, and expectations. *Relationship factors* are attributes of the therapeutic interaction and include the therapist's skills that affect the client's improvement. Some of these relationship factors include empathy, positive regard, congruence, the working relationship between therapist and client, consensus about the goals of therapy, self-disclosure, and quality of interpretations. In their book, Castonguay and Beutler (2006) describe how these factors, as well as factors specific to a disorder, affect treatment of depression, anxiety disorders, personality disorders, and substance-abuse disorders. Extensive research on these and other variables helps to describe factors that are common to effective therapy across a wide variety of problems.

Treatment Manuals and Research-Supported Psychological Treatment Psychotherapy

In contrast to the common factors approach, the use of treatment manuals and research-supported psychological treatment is specific for each disorder. Usually designed from one or two theoretical points of view, treatment manuals provide guidelines to therapists as to how to proceed in helping individuals with a specific problem such as fear of blood. Treatment manuals are also effective for training graduate students and others as therapists because they provide guidelines about therapeutic procedures. As health maintenance organizations (HMOs) have desired proof of brief, effective therapy, treatment manuals have been useful in replicating a procedure and showing its effectiveness. Those therapies that provide specific techniques for different problems, such as behavioral and cognitive therapies, are most likely to use manuals.

Much effort has focused on research-supported psychological treatments. As seen in the text, most (but not all) research-supported psychological treatments use behavioral and cognitive approaches. Those research-supported psychological treatments that were mentioned in the text and are considered well established as applications for specific disorders are listed below (Nathan & Gorman, 2007; *Research-Supported Psychological Treatments*, 2009). These treatments are summarized very briefly in Table 16.6 to illustrate some of their most common methods.

In their review of psychotherapy and research, Lambert, Bergin, and Garfield (2004) describe the emphasis on research-supported psychological treatments psychotherapy (empirically supported treatments) and the development of treatment manuals. They believe that their popularity is due to the popularity of cognitive and behavior therapies, the specificity of the DSM-IV-TR, and the requirements by managed care organizations to make treatment more uniform, more effective, and less expensive. There are also efforts by developers of research-supported psychological treatments therapies to make them more usable. For example, Franklin and Foa (2007) have examined how to make exposure and ritual prevention that is used to treat obsessive-compulsive disorder less time intensive in its initial stages. They also examine the issue of training therapists to treat obsessive-compulsive disorder when they may rarely encounter it with their patients. Efforts to make research-supported psychological treatments more available to therapists in general practice continue to be a concern (Nathan & Gorman, 2007). However, as Nathan (2007) notes practitioners have been reluctant to use research-supported psychological treatments.

Postmodernism and Constructivism

Postmodernism, a philosophical movement that has been applied to psychotherapy, has had influences on most theories of therapy, especially solution-focused and narrative therapies.

Table 16.6 Research-Supported Psychological
Treatments Described in the Text

Short-term psychodynamic therapy (Chapter 2)
Depression: These therapies focus on increasing patients' insight into their depression. Some common themes include a focus on how past experiences influence current functioning and the expression of emotions. Other issues are the therapeutic relationship and dealing with uncomfortable topics. Luborsky's Core Conflictual Relationship Themes method described in Chapter 2 is one of the therapies that is used. Therapy is time limited and includes approximately 16 to 20 sessions.

Gestalt Therapy (Chapter 7)
Depression: Some studies suggest that process experiential therapy has been shown to be efficacious in treating depression. Process experiential therapy combines person-centered therapy with gestalt methods, such as use of the empty-chair technique.

Behavior Therapy (Chapter 8)
Depression: Reinforce patient activities and social interactions, rate moods and record events, increase daily activities, and use social skills training.
Obsessive-compulsive disorder: Exposure and ritual prevention are used for an hour or two several times a week. Exposure to the event, such as germs, provokes discomfort. Individuals refrain from rituals.
General anxiety disorder: Techniques include progressive muscle relaxation, self-monitoring, countering automatic thoughts, and worry behavior prevention.
Phobic disorders: In vivo or imaginal exposures, as well as virtual reality therapy, are used for most phobias.
Posttraumatic stress disorder: In eye movement desensitization reprocessing (EMDR), a client history is taken and EMDR is explained. Desensitization takes place when the therapist uses hand movements. The client describes thoughts and images and increases positive thoughts. The therapist focuses on targeted behavior and searches for bodily tensions.
Borderline disorder: Linehan's dialectical behavior therapy (DBT) was designed specifically to deal with borderline disorder. Teaching mindfulness to clients is an important aspect of (DBT). DBT includes individual therapy, group therapy , and instructions on how to manage client crises.

Cognitive Therapy (Chapter 10)
Depression: Assessment of automatic thoughts, cognitive schemas, dysfunctional beliefs. Counters dysfunctional thinking through use of the Socratic method, three-question technique, the Daily Thought Record, and other thought-challenging techniques.
Anxiety: Identify the schema of hypervigilance; assess use of catastrophizing, personalization, magnification, selective abstractions, overgeneralization, and other beliefs. Counter these beliefs with Socratic method and cognitive techniques such as challenging absolutes.
Obsessive-compulsive disorder: There is a focus on dealing with obsessive thoughts that include overestimation of threat, intolerance of uncertainty, too much responsibility, perfectionism, mental control, and overimportance of thoughts. One method of dealing with OCD is the thought-action fusion model that attempts to counter the avoidance that individuals use in trying to deal with obsessional thoughts.
Substance abuse: Focus on being drug free and free of other problems. Deal with cravings and a lack of pleasure from nondrug sources. Focus on dysfunctional beliefs that are anticipatory, relief oriented, and permissive. Change belief system through assessing beliefs, listing addictive beliefs, developing control beliefs, and practicing activating these new beliefs.

Interpersonal Therapy (Chapter 15—Other Psychotherapies)
Depression: Deal with grief, interpersonal disputes, role transitions, or interpersonal deficits. Specific strategies for each are used. The therapy relationship is used to encourage relationships outside of therapy. Common skills used are encouragement of affect, clarification, and communication analysis.

Constructivist ideas remind therapists of the importance of understanding and attending to the clients' ways of seeing their own lives and not imposing a theory in such a way that preconceived ideas about clients interfere with treatment (Neimeyer, 2009). In essence, therapists are recommended to take a step back to see if they are viewing clients' worlds the way their clients do.

The postmodern movement has also given theorists an opportunity to show how their theory is consistent with a constructivist point of view. The postmodern movement, which values the client's view of reality at least as much as the therapist's, is consistent with an approach that values both genders and all cultures equally. The modern, as opposed to postmodern, view is rarely defended by theorists because it can sound like "I know more about my client than he does" or "My view of reality is superior to that of my client." Because of the postmodern influence, almost all theories described in this text can be described as being flexible and consistent with the postmodern position. Most theories show how they can be open to working with the way clients construct reality.

Although these trends do not include all of the concerns that each group of practitioners focuses on, they do represent major issues affecting the practice and theoretical development of various theories.

Using the Theory with Other Theories

As Lambert, Bergin, and Garfield (2004) have noted, there has been a marked trend since the 1950s toward integration of theories. As shown in the next chapter, theories have become increasingly integrative. Some practitioners who subscribe primarily to one theory may find theory A to be helpful, whereas another may find theory B to be useful. For example, one cognitive therapist may find the experiential techniques of gestalt therapy to be helpful, whereas another may find Erickson's adult developmental model (ego psychology) to be helpful.

Although most therapies are becoming increasingly integrative by incorporating techniques from other theories, two discussed in this book are not moving in this direction. Those person-centered therapists who consider Rogers's six conditions to be necessary and sufficient would restrict their approach to empathy, acceptance, and genuineness. Reality therapists make use of a specific model in helping their clients develop control and responsibility in their lives. Although they may use some behavioral techniques, such as positive reinforcement, the structure of reality therapy may make it difficult to more fully integrate ideas from other therapies. In contrast, existential and feminist therapists must make use of other methods because these approaches do not have a sufficient core of techniques to allow complete reliance on the theory. Thus there is considerable divergence in the way many theories are practiced.

Research

The approach of theories of psychotherapy toward research is extremely uneven. Relatively little outcome research has been done with approaches other than cognitive therapy and behavior therapy. In this section, I discuss outcome research related to cognitive therapy and behavior therapy, along with research directions germane to specific theories discussed in this book. I then conclude with a few predictions about the future directions of research in psychotherapy.

Outcome Research

In recent years, research on cognitive and behavioral therapies (including REBT) has been so abundant that meta-analyses have not only been applied to these therapies but also have been done with diagnostic categories, such as depression and general anxiety. In Chapter 8, examples of studies using behavior therapy with obsessive-compulsive disorder, anxiety disorder, and phobia are given. Chapter 10 has examples and summaries of treatment findings for depression, general anxiety, and obsessive-compulsive disorders. Some outcome research has also been done on psychoanalytic treatment. However, this research is more difficult than research on cognitive and behavioral therapies because treatment is lengthy, concepts are difficult to define, and consistency of application of therapeutic techniques is more difficult to ensure. As described in Chapter 2, a few notable studies have been done with relatively small groups of patients (often about 100 or fewer), with research efforts in these studies taking place over a period of 30 years or more. General research findings show that almost all therapeutic treatments showed greater improvements among treatment groups than among control groups that receive no treatment. Comparisons between treatment methods do not show clear patterns and present challenges to the design of studies to show useful differences.

Research procedures and concepts that have been studied for different theories vary widely. Table 16.7 is a synopsis of the areas of research related to theories of psychotherapy.

Future Directions

In summarizing extensive research, Lambert, Bergin, and Garfield (2004) state that about "50% of patients who enter treatment in clinical settings will show *clinically meaningful change* after 13 to 18 sessions of treatment. An additional 25% will meet the same standard after approximately 50 sessions of once-weekly treatment" (p. 11). They raise concerns that limiting treatment may negatively affect patients with relatively severe problems that most need treatment. Lambert, Garfield, and Bergin (2004) believe that psychotherapy research should attend to studying problems in treatment and changing the course of treatment to make it successful. They also see the increase of computer-based interventions that individuals can use in their homes. Viewing mental health as a deep societal problem, they believe that more funding for psychotherapy research should be given and that mental health should be considered a more important part of general overall health systems. Another issue concerns the use of typical patients in psychotherapy research rather than studying patients who are selected for research in evaluating research-supported psychological treatment (Lambert, 2007; Lambert & Vermeersch, 2008).

Gender Issues

For many years, the practice of psychotherapy and particularly psychoanalysis appeared to be influenced by the values of male psychotherapists. Chesler (1972) was an early critic of the practice of psychotherapy, claiming that it devalued aspects of women's roles.

Table 16.7 Research Directions of Theories of
               Psychotherapy

Psychoanalysis	Major areas of research exploration have included defense mechanisms, infant–mother bonding, and the working alliance. Considerably more outcome research has been done using brief psychodynamic therapies than using long-term psychoanalytic therapy or psychoanalysis.
Jungian Analysis	Most research efforts have examined Jung's attitudes and functions of personality. There have been some cross-cultural studies on archetypes.
Adlerian Therapy	Topics of research include birth order, social interest, early recollections, and lifestyles, with a few studies being done on therapeutic interventions.
Existential Therapy	Research on group therapy has been done, as well as research on existential issues such as death, anxiety, spirituality, and responsibility.
Person-Centered Therapy	Carl Rogers's interest in research was partly responsible for a great deal of study on empathy, genuineness, and acceptance in the 1960s and 1970s. Newer research questions the measurement and definitions of these concepts. Some recent therapy research addresses the issue of who will benefit most from different kinds of therapeutic interventions.
Gestalt Therapy	Some areas of controlled research include studies of specific therapeutic techniques such as the empty-chair method and research into contact boundary disturbances.
Behavior Therapy	Researchers have carried out many outcome studies and have developed a variety of measures of therapeutic progress, symptoms, and related issues.
Rational Emotive Behavior Therapy	In addition to outcome research, issues relating to the important concept of irrational beliefs have been examined to provide more information about the definition and description of this topic.
Cognitive Therapy	Cognitive therapy researchers have studied concepts that define depression as well as the treatment of depression itself. Additionally, the effectiveness of therapy with many other disorders has been a topic of investigation.
Reality Therapy	Glasser has deemphasized the importance of research more so than have most other theorists or practitioners of theories. Nevertheless, some research has been done with convicted offenders, high school students, drug abusers, and couples.
Constructivist Therapies	New methodologies have been developed for solution-focused and narrative therapies. There are more outcome studies on solution-focused than narrative therapies.
Feminist Therapy	There have been a few studies comparing feminist therapy to other approaches. Also, some researchers have examined the values and techniques that are important to feminist therapists.
Family Systems Therapy	Although there has been some research on the effectiveness of a variety of family systems approaches, it is relatively limited.

Although a number of theories were concerned with gender issues before Chesler's writings, feminist therapists have had an impact on the attention given to gender and cultural issues as they affect the practice of therapy. Gender issues and how they are dealt with in therapy are summarized here.

Although Freud has been criticized for devaluing women and their role, such comments have not generally been applied to his contemporaries, Jung and Adler. In psychoanalysis, notions of castration anxiety and penis envy have been widely criticized, along with implications made from these concepts that women are lacking in qualities that men possess. Furthermore, object relations theory has been criticized because of its emphasis on the mother–child role and lack of attention to the father's responsibility and parenting. In Jungian analysis, gender is addressed through the study of archetypes. Animus and anima archetypes, which represent the other-sex aspects of an individual, were thoroughly addressed in Jungian therapy. Additionally, female analysts were prominent in the early development of Jungian therapy. For Adler, gender roles were important throughout his theoretical writings. An early advocate of women's rights, Adler saw how neurotic men used stereotypes of masculinity to mask their feelings of inferiority. Adlerians work to help clients deal with gender-role stereotypes.

For existential, person-centered, and gestalt therapists, gender roles are often seen as they relate to important theoretical concepts. For existential therapists, major existential themes of living, responsibility, and meaningfulness affect all individuals, although they may affect males and females differently. When clients hold gender-stereotyped views of themselves or others, a blockage in developing authenticity exists. With regard to genuineness, acceptance, and empathy, Rogers saw these concepts as universally important and believed that therapists should be empathic to gender-related concerns, such as homosexuality. For gestalt therapists, men and women may respond differently to awareness experiments, but empowerment to deal with problems generally results. Miriam Polster (1992) noted that empowerment and awareness need to be directed not only toward individuals but also toward making society more receptive to women's power.

Cognitive and behavior therapists (including REBT and reality therapy) generally use terms that are not related to gender. These therapies tend to emphasize client responsibility. For clients who are unable to make their own choices, such as severely learning-disabled individuals, behavior therapists are particularly careful in not introducing gender bias. Although rational emotive behavior therapists are aware that irrational beliefs differ for men and women, they attend to the irrational beliefs about gender roles in their therapeutic work and have described issues in their writings that affect women in society. Cognitive therapists are aware of the cognitive schemas or beliefs that individuals have about their gender roles, whether toward the place of women in society or toward gay, lesbian, bisexual, or transgendered people (GLBST), and help their clients examine and challenge them. Reality therapists help their clients become more responsible: some men by developing more self-control and some women by not letting others take control of their lives. Each of these therapies approaches gender value issues from its own conceptual perspective.

Naturally, feminist therapy has had the greatest impact on gender issues in therapy. The techniques of gender, cultural, and power analysis and intervention specifically examine and attempt to change roles as experienced by the individual and society as a whole. More so than most therapies, feminist therapy has been concerned about gender roles as they affect GLBST clients.

Roles and relationships of males and females within the family have been an area of concern for family systems therapists. Influenced by feminist therapy, family systems therapists have examined power issues within the family structure and ways in which couples share family duties and responsibilities.

Because of the contribution of feminist therapy and the awareness of therapists about gender issues within each of the theories described in this section, beginning therapists are likely to be exposed to ways in which gender roles affect their own value systems and their practice of psychotherapy or counseling.

Multicultural Issues

To some extent, the infusion of cultural issues into theories of psychotherapy has depended on the interest of the theorists and their adherents. As theories have become more widely known, therapists have applied theoretical principles to their work with a variety of clients from different cultures and have written about this experience, informing their colleagues about the interaction between culture and therapy. Research-supported psychological treatments practices have also been viewed in the context cultural diversity (Sue & Sue, 2008).

For Freud, Jung, and Adler, cultural issues have been prominent, but for very different reasons. Freud's late-19th-century Viennese background influenced his observations about psychological disorders and early childhood development. Erik Erikson's work with Native Americans helped to expand the influence of cultural values on theoretical views of developmental stages. In contrast to Freud, Jung took an active interest in different cultures, traveling widely throughout the world to learn about legends and folklore. Current Jungian analysts are required to have a wide knowledge of myths and folktales in order to understand the collective unconscious of their patients. For Adler, cultural issues are inherent in social interest as it is applied to one's family, neighborhood, and social group. Regarding the practice of psychoanalysis, a continuing issue is the expense of long-term psychotherapy and its availability to individuals who may not have sufficient wealth to afford it, including those from minority groups.

For existential, person-centered, and gestalt therapy, cultural issues emerge in very different ways. Regarding existential therapy, there are similarities between Eastern thought and existential philosophy, which is based primarily on Western European ideas. The themes of living, responsibility, and meaningfulness tend to be universal, cutting across cultures. For Rogers, bringing his therapeutic approach to promote peace and ease conflict between peoples of different nations was an area that he devoted much attention to during the last 20 years of his life. His emphasis on genuineness, acceptance, and empathy as core conditions for change represent cultural values that many found congruent but that others questioned. In a very different way, cultural issues have emerged in gestalt therapy. Because a focus on developing awareness can bring emotional relief that helps individuals deal with cultural injunctions, it can also create an experience that may be difficult to integrate with previously learned cultural values. Although existential, person-centered, and gestalt therapies are related in the sense that existential thought has an impact on their theoretical model, each theory addresses cultural issues differently.

In general, cognitive and behavioral therapies, including REBT and reality therapy, have tended to promote self-sufficiency and responsibility in individuals, which can conflict with cultural beliefs and values. However, recent writings in each of these theories have showed the application of the theory to people from a broad range of cultural groups.

In its emphasis on gender, cultural, and power issues, feminist therapy attends to cultural factors that can affect clients' psychological functioning. Being aware of one's own attitudes and prejudices regarding people from other cultures is a significant aspect of feminist therapy. Techniques of power and cultural analysis and intervention lend themselves to application to people from many different cultures.

For solution-focused and narrative therapies, culture is embedded in the clients' descriptions of their problems. In narrative therapy and personal construct therapy, culture is found as a part of the setting, characters, plot, and theme.

With regard to the practice of family therapy, a knowledge of cultural traditions and values is particularly helpful. Cultures vary as to child-raising practices, relationships with members of extended and immediate families, and traditions such as wakes and weddings. The behavior and attitudes of family members may be appropriate in some societies but inappropriate in other cultural circumstances.

Being aware of one's own values and biases regarding people of different cultures and having a knowledge of cultural values and customs and an understanding of how theoretical and cultural perspectives interact can help therapists practice their theoretical orientations effectively with clients from diverse cultural backgrounds.

Family Therapy

Although theories of psychotherapy differ in terms of how much attention is devoted to family therapy as compared with individual therapy, all apply their theory to individual and family therapy. Relatively few Jungian and existential therapists do family work, preferring individual therapy. Family systems therapy differs from most other family therapy approaches in that the family is viewed as a unit and attention is paid to dysfunctions within the unit rather than to one individual's behavior. Naturally, there are times when family therapists attend to individuals and when nonfamily therapists examine the entire system. This is described fully in Chapter 14.

More and more, therapists are doing all combinations of therapy: individual, couples, and family. As with individual therapy, integration is a growing trend, as therapists combine or make use of aspects of several family systems therapies along with ideas about individual and family therapy from other theories of psychotherapy.

Group Therapy

Just as approaches to individual therapy vary greatly, depending on theoretical orientation, so do approaches toward group therapy. Some therapies (Adlerian, behavior, REBT, cognitive, and reality therapies) tend to be structured, emphasizing the leader's role in educating and directing group members. Others (psychoanalytic, Jungian, existential, gestalt, and feminist therapies) tend to be more open and unstructured. For some theoretical orientations (gestalt, person-centered, and feminist therapies), group approaches are considered as important as individual and are sometimes preferable, whereas for Jungian therapy, group processes are seen as an adjunct to, but not a substitute for, individual therapy. Major features of each theory's contribution to group therapy are described in Table 16.8.

Table 16.8 Group Therapy Approaches

Psychoanalysis	Briefly, psychoanalytic group therapy often focuses on free association, dreams, and other material as it relates to underlying unconscious behavior and early childhood development. Drive and ego therapists are likely to focus on repressed and aggressive drives as they affect group members, as well as the use of ego defenses. For object relations therapists and relational psychoanalysis, issues of separation and individuation as they affect the psychological processes of group members and group interaction are a major focus. For self psychologists, attention is paid to how group members integrate self-concern with concern about others in the group. In general, psychoanalytic group therapists differ as to how much they interpret group processes and deal with transference and countertransference of members to the group leader and other group members.
Jungian Analysis	Used as an adjunct to individual analysis, Jungian groups may make frequent use of dream analysis and also use active imagination.
Adlerian Therapy	A variety of creative approaches to group therapy characterizes Adlerian work. Lifestyle groups help members analyze their lifestyles, which include family relationships, relationships with siblings, and early recollections. Group leaders summarize results of a brief lifestyle analysis, and they and group members make suggestions for change. Other Adlerian groups may combine lectures on social interests, lifestyle, and courage with exercises to promote change.
Existential Therapy	A variety of existential themes are incorporated, and members deal with questions about how meaningful their lives are, how they deal with freedom and responsibility, how they relate to others, and how they behave authentically. Group members relate to each of these issues and discuss how they affect different group members.
Person-Centered Therapy	Rogers believed strongly in the positive power of groups. For him, the leader's role was to facilitate the group, with the notion that the leader could work toward being a participant. In general, the group was unstructured, but the group leader attended to the need to have safety and growth within the group. Rogers devoted a major part of his later life to using groups to develop trust between social or political groups who opposed each other.
Gestalt Therapy	A frequent treatment of choice of gestalt therapists, most gestalt groups use a variety of exercises and experiments to develop awareness among group members. Encouraging open and direct contact between group members, group leaders set limits and work on issues such as family conflicts.

(Continued)

Table 16.8 Group Therapy Approaches (Continued)

Behavior Therapy	Therapists often function as coaches, giving feedback, teaching, demonstrating, and modeling to individuals who share similar target behaviors. Common types of behavior therapy groups are social skills training, in which clients often role play events in their lives, and assertiveness training, in which individuals learn to discriminate among types of behavior and try out assertiveness skills.
Rational Emotive Behavior Therapy	Therapists function educationally, in a direct manner, showing clients how they blame and damn themselves for their behavior. Clients learn to apply REBT principles to their behavior. The therapist may suggest homework and enlist cooperation from members in helping each other with problems.
Cognitive Therapy	Assessing specific behaviors and cognitions is one of the functions of cognitive therapists. They work collaboratively with group members to suggest changes in behavior inside and outside therapy. Specific change strategies focus on cognitive and behavioral interventions. Some groups are targeted toward specific disorders, others toward specific techniques, such as problem-solving groups.
Reality Therapy	Often used as a follow-up to individual reality therapy, group therapy uses the same process of change applied in individual therapy. Principles of choice theory are followed by asking such questions as, What are you doing? What is working for you? What needs to be done to make things better? Therapists take an active approach in encouraging behavior change.
Feminist Therapy	Consciousness-raising groups were the impetus for the development of feminist therapy. A variety of groups focus now on issues such as homelessness, sexual abuse, battered women, and issues related to different ethnic groups. A major focus in feminist therapy groups are gender role issues, which may be dealt with through a variety of therapeutic approaches, including gestalt, solution-focused, and psychoanalytic theories.

Group therapy has several features that individual therapy does not: input from peers, multiple feedback, efficient use of therapists' time, and observational learning. For these reasons, group therapy is likely to continue to be attractive to practitioners of most theories. Organizational problems do present themselves, especially for therapy groups that require a certain type of member, such as incest survivors. Advertising or publicity may be used for such groups.

I have tried to summarize the most important aspects of the theories of personality, therapeutic techniques, and important applications of therapies. Not all significant features have been included. The focus to this point has been on describing differences between theories to show their special features. Next, I describe what I believe are the strengths and weaknesses of each of the theories.

Critique

Basically, when theorists criticize other theories, they find fault with them for not being similar to their own theory. The more dissimilar the two theories, the more numerous and emphatic the criticisms. For example, behavior therapists could criticize psychoanalysis for overemphasizing biology and early childhood development, for not defining concepts clearly, for speculating about unobservable constructs such as the unconscious and ego, for not having testable concepts, for being incredibly inefficient in the frequency and duration of therapy to bring about change, and for having less effective treatment methods than behavior therapy. When criticizing cognitive therapy, behavior therapists have far fewer criticisms. Chiefly, they focus on the emphasis that cognitive therapists may give to unobservable thought processes, but they are less critical of their terms, the testability of procedures, and the effectiveness of therapy. When criticizing cognitive and behavior therapy, psychoanalysts are likely to see the therapies as somewhat similar in that they are superficial and focus on surface issues, pay little attention to past development, tend to ignore unconscious processes such as dreams and fantasies, and do not deal with the importance of parent–child relationships or with the development of individual personality. Any theory can be criticized by using the concepts of personality and psychotherapy of another theory as the basis for criticism.

The more dissimilar a critic's values are from those of the theorist, the greater the chance that the theory will not be respected or treated seriously. For example, values of faculty in academic departments of psychology may favor precise definition, quantitative research, brief therapeutic interventions, and observable behavior, values more compatible with cognitive, behavioral, and REBT therapies than other theories discussed in this book. By contrast, many practicing therapists may have values that stress relationships with clients, understanding many different personality constructs, the influence of the past on the present, and spiritual and unconscious processes, all of which are more compatible with therapies other than behavior, cognitive, and REBT theories. In the discussion that follows, I identify common major limitations and strengths of each theory, devoting one paragraph to limitations and one paragraph to strengths.

Psychoanalysis

Many of the criticisms of psychoanalysis have just been mentioned. Additionally, psychoanalysis can be criticized because it reflects the experiences and values of theorists arising from their own life experiences and observations about patients, which the theorists try to apply to everyone. Just because Freud may have experienced Oedipal feelings and observed Oedipal feelings in his patients does not make it a universal concept. Likewise, Erikson experienced many identity crises in his life and observed them in many others; saying that this is an important construct for most people does not follow logically. Many of the psychoanalytic concepts, such as those just mentioned, are often difficult to define, and psychoanalytic writers may have different definitions in mind when describing a concept such as the ego or transference neurosis. Some critics complain that psychoanalytic writers describe developmental concepts as if everyone has the same cultural experience without looking at the importance of social interactions in later life. A practical criticism of psychoanalysis is that the treatment is extremely time consuming and costly. When psychoanalytic concepts are used in brief therapy, therapists are limited in their goals and in the type of patients they can work with, whereas behavior and cognitive therapists (including Adlerian, REBT, and reality therapists) do not operate with such restrictions.

The strengths of psychodynamic therapies are that they allow individuals to explore, in depth, their early childhood and past as they affect their current functioning, using a drive, ego, object relations, self psychology, or relational model, or a combination. Explanations have been developed to understand resistance, anxiety, and ego defense mechanisms that relate to the individual's psychological functioning. The development of ego, object relations, self psychology, and relational psychoanalysis provides a broad framework for understanding many psychological disorders. Additionally, brief therapies make psychoanalytic approaches more available to those who cannot afford long-term psychotherapy or psychoanalysis.

Jungian Analysis

From an empirical point of view, Jung's theory is the least scientific of all the major theories described in this book. Other than concepts of attitudes and functions (for example, introversion-extraversion), his constructs are the most difficult to define and the least clear and are more like religion than science. Jungian analysis is a long, slow process focusing on bringing unconscious processes into conscious awareness. Little research has been done on concepts such as the collective unconscious and archetypes, and there is no published research on the effectiveness of Jungian analysis. It can be argued that Jungian concepts are not useful or definable and that Jungians are more interested in relating their knowledge about folklore and myth to convoluted archetypes than they are in helping patients with their problems.

A strength of Jungian analysis is its emphasis on the spiritual aspects of humanity, something not measurable by scientific experimentation. Jung's ideas help individuals look inside themselves and understand aspects of their personal and collective unconscious that were previously unavailable to them. Moreover, insight and creativity can develop in the process of Jungian psychotherapy. Furthermore, Jungian analysis provides a means of understanding others' cultures, history, and religion, fostering intellectual development. Individuals wanting greater self-understanding and insight into their self-development rather than removal of specific symptoms are likely to find Jungian analysis instructive and helpful.

Adlerian Therapy

Criticisms of Adlerian therapy are that it does a variety of things but none of them in depth. Because of its emphasis on looking at the past through early recollections and birth order, Adlerian theory is often viewed as simplistic and as fully examining neither conscious nor unconscious processes. Its concepts are difficult to test, and little research supports the effectiveness of its psychotherapeutic approach. Regarding the practice of psychotherapy, too much emphasis may be given to individuals' perceptions of early recollections. Also, many unrelated techniques may be used to bring about change. By focusing on the importance of social interest, the theory tends to ignore important aspects of individual development. Too much emphasis is placed on changing beliefs and not enough on changing behaviors.

The strength of Adlerian psychotherapy is its diversity. It takes into consideration the importance of familial and social factors and their impact on growth and development. It is a practical approach, goal oriented and emphasizing both social and psychological factors. Techniques are geared to change beliefs and behaviors, often within short time periods. More than most therapies, it has an educational emphasis that can be applied to individuals, couples, and families. Perhaps because it is a growth model that acknowledges perceptions of past development and incorporates many therapeutic strategies, it can be applied to a very broad range of client problems.

Existential Therapy

The major criticism of existential psychotherapy is that it is not a system of psychotherapy. Rather, it is a general framework of concepts or issues that some Western European philosophers have seen as important. Although some of the themes may relate to individual anxieties and problems, not all do. Existential therapy offers no guidelines for therapists, and with the exception of a few techniques offered by Frankl, no suggestions for methods for therapists to use. Many of the ideas are intellectual, and clients who are more practical or are not college educated may have difficulty with the philosophical nature of the concepts. Much of the focus in existential psychology is on the negative—death, meaninglessness, and anxiety. Existential psychotherapy offers few specific suggestions for dealing with these issues.

The strength of existential therapy is that it attends to concerns of being human. Other therapies tend to ignore why we are here, why we exist, and our responsibility to ourselves and others. Existential therapy encourages individuals to take a look outside themselves and find meaning in their lives by examining relationships with others as well as confronting major internal life issues. Throughout our lives, people confront many existential crises—marriage, divorce, responsibility for family, death of loved ones, and guilt over past behavior. Existential therapy provides new ways of viewing and understanding such problems.

Person-Centered Therapy

Rogers's view of psychotherapeutic change has been criticized as vague, naive, and limiting. Rogers ignores the unconscious, pays relatively little attention to past development, and follows the client wherever she leads. Empathy is seen as being the cure-all for problems; no consideration of behavioral or cognitive principles is given. Some critics believe that Rogers's view that core conditions are necessary and sufficient for change is simplistic and inaccurate and does not reflect current research. Another criticism is that the therapist is overvalued; there is more to therapeutic change than being empathically understood for an hour or two a week. Many other theorists believe that empathy is not enough for many clients. Therapeutic progress requires structure and direction for specific change. Because clients need direction and suggestions not provided by the person-centered therapist, other therapies should be used to supplement person-centered therapy.

Then again, Rogers has been widely acknowledged for his enormous contribution to psychotherapy by focusing on the client–therapist relationship and on the importance of acceptance, genuineness, and empathy from the therapist. Many therapists find that these concepts are clear and easy to grasp and that they promote client growth and understanding. Although more research is needed, much research has studied the validity of the concepts and shows them to be valuable. Person-centered therapy is particularly suited to couples, family, and group counseling, where the focus is on understanding each other. Many people can profit from the understanding of their experiences, feelings, attitudes, and values that emerges from an empathic relationship with a therapist.

Gestalt Therapy

Criticisms of gestalt therapy have focused on its powerful emotional effect, which can lead an individual to become vulnerable and confused. Also, gestalt therapy, especially Perls's work, has been characterized as developing the individual while sacrificing or ignoring relationships with others. Although dealing with bodily processes, it does not go as far in integrating the mind and body as do body psychotherapies (Chapter 15). The concepts are rather vague and unsystematic. In the hands of therapists who have difficulty separating their own needs (for example, power or sex) from those of the client, gestalt therapy has the potential to damage clients by confusing their awareness of self with awareness of the therapist's needs.

When practiced by a competent therapist, gestalt therapy can help individuals experience feelings and awareness rather than just talk about them. Experimentation in gestalt therapy can develop self-understanding and willingness to apply this learning to relationships outside therapy. As a result, clients often become more creative and assertive in their work and in relationships. Although it should be used with caution with individuals who are suffering from severe disturbances (such as borderline disorders), gestalt therapy can be particularly helpful for those people who are anxious or inhibited.

Behavior Therapy

Sometimes criticized as a piecemeal approach, behavior therapy draws from classical and operant conditioning as well as social learning theory. Attempts to develop an all-encompassing theory of behavior that can be adapted to psychotherapy have failed. Although criticisms that behavior therapy ignores feelings and manipulates its patients no longer apply, behavior therapy can still be criticized for focusing too much on target behaviors and not sufficiently on the whole person or on developmental factors. Changing symptoms may not bring about significant or meaningful change. Furthermore, behavior therapy is seen as focusing too much on changing an individual's behavior; it does not attend sufficiently to a variety of environmental and social conditions. Important existential and social constraints on behavior tend to be ignored.

Behavior therapists have produced a large quantity of research that attests to the effectiveness of their techniques. This research has supported the development of rating and observational techniques, as well as specific therapeutic interventions for many problems. The therapist and client work together, using the therapist's knowledge of techniques to bring about change in a variety of behaviors, including depression, phobia, and sexual disorders. Behavior therapy, often combined with cognitive therapy, is particularly well suited for problems in which a specific target behavior can be identified.

Rational Emotive Behavior Therapy

Criticisms of REBT are both theoretical and practical. Ellis's theory can be seen as a collection of cognitive and behavioral techniques, along with a predilection for convincing clients that their beliefs are wrong. Rather than a coherent theory, REBT tries to convince clients to think more rationally and, if that does not work, tries some other behavioral or cognitive approaches. Unlike cognitive therapies, REBT does not apply different techniques for different disorders. Disputing irrational beliefs, done with all types of problems, can be seen as a way of browbeating clients into changing beliefs, even when they are not convinced to do so. Because REBT focuses so much on cognitive strategies, it tends to ignore behavioral and affective ones.

Ellis pioneered the use of cognitive techniques to bring about therapeutic change in a few sessions or months rather than a few years. His approach is comprehensive and makes use of many different strategies and techniques, but it also helps individuals change irrational beliefs so that future crises and problems can be avoided. The approach is active, featuring homework and role playing as well as record keeping. Ellis's own writings have helped to relieve guilt about sexuality and encouraged individuals to help themselves by no longer blaming themselves. Patients with disorders in which irrational beliefs are an important component, such as anxiety, depression, and phobias, can find REBT helpful.

Cognitive Therapy

Like REBT, Beck's cognitive therapy can be criticized as being simplistic and mere common sense. Rather than straightforward, his concepts of automatic thoughts and cognitive schemas may not be easy for clients to grasp, as they are constructs rather than observable behaviors. Although cognitive therapists say that they do attend to clients' feelings, their emphasis on cognitive distortions can be seen as blaming the client and not being empathic with his distress. There is an overemphasis on the client's responsibility for problems and not enough attention to social forces such as violence that cause problems. Convincing clients that their thinking is distorted, even when added to behavioral and affective approaches, is insufficient to deal with complex client problems.

More than any other theoretical approach, Beck and his colleagues have carefully studied specific cognitive techniques to be used for different psychological disorders. In particular, much work has been done that demonstrates the effectiveness of cognitive approaches to depression and anxiety. Cognitive therapists take a collaborative approach with clients, working with them to bring about changes in thoughts, feelings, and behaviors. By incorporating behavioral, affective, and experiential strategies in a structured manner to bring about specific changes, cognitive therapy represents a broad and effective approach.

Reality Therapy

Glasser's reality therapy has been criticized for being superficial and simplistic. It is a process that clients must accept. Childhood development, transference, dreams, and unconscious processes are ignored. An artificial mechanistic model, using a car as an analogy, oversimplifies very complex human behavior. Existential issues and deep emotions get short shrift in this problem-solving approach. Guidelines are quite simplistic, whereas the actual practice of reality therapy requires many hours of training to deal with clients' resistance to controlling their own behavior.

Unlike many other therapies, reality therapy can be used with people who are resistant to change. It may be particularly effective for hard-to-reach groups such as juvenile offenders, prisoners, and substance abusers. In its emphasis on taking control of one's own behavior and on the positive results that come with acting in accordance with reality principles, reality therapy can be attractive to many clients. Although the approach is not as easy to use as would first appear, with practice it can be used effectively with clients that other therapists might feel are not motivated to change.

Constructivist Theories

Constructivist theories (solution-focused and narrative) provide no real system for understanding individuals. They provide a framework that is too loose to assess the concerns of clients. Solution-focused therapy does not provide an adequate opportunity to assess the full nature of the problem or background factors that have made the problems as difficult as they are. Instead, it rushes in to solve the problem without knowing how it relates to other problems, other individuals, and events in the client's life. Similarly, narrative therapy only offers the opportunity to hear the client's story and then to make judgments about what parts of the story are "problem saturated." Although externalizing the problem by saying "Anger has a voice that speaks to you" is a creative technique, it may be most appropriate for children and of limited application to serious problems. Telling and retelling the story from different points of view may not be enough to help clients make necessary changes in their lives. Constructivist theories do not take the thorough systematic approach that behavioral, cognitive, and other therapies do.

Constructivist therapists understand the problem that clients present from the clients' own point of view without having preconceptions (other theoretical ideas) intervene. Solution-focused therapy is brief and timely. Clients enter therapy because they want help with their problems, not to develop a relationship with the therapist, not to talk about their problems without doing things about them, but to find relief. Solution-focused therapy gets right to the point and through the exception and miracle questions helps individuals deal with a great variety of problems in their lives. Narrative therapy (both personal construct theory and Epston and White's) also helps individuals understand their lives and see ways they have been thinking about their problems that are hurting them. With the therapist's help, clients find solutions that give them a way of viewing themselves, which helps to resolve problems. Unlike other theories, constructivist theories really value the input of clients in resolving their own problems.

Feminist Therapy

Because feminist therapy focuses so much on political and social change, individual responsibility can be ignored. Rather than having any coherent theory, feminist therapy is a conglomeration of diverse ideas about gender development and issues related to treatment of women. Although feminist therapists claim not to be "male bashers," elements of this tendency can be found in their writings. The question arises: Do feminist therapists treat women as more equal than men? Another criticism of feminist therapy is that it is not a therapy but a collection of suggestions about how to infuse feminist ideas into other theories, as feminist therapy does not have sufficient techniques to stand alone.

The strengths of feminist therapy are that it has examined sociological factors, most importantly gender and culture, and pointed out how changes can be made in the practice of psychotherapy to provide more effective therapy for both men and women. Already, feminist therapy has helped make therapists of all theoretical orientations aware of their own attitudes about gender and culture, as well as those of their clients. The political thrust of feminist therapy challenges therapists to work on changing political and social conditions that have contributed to the problems of individuals. Whether a therapist is a feminist therapist or informed by feminist therapy, these practitioners can help their clients by examining both psychological dysfunction and its environmental context.

Family Systems Therapy

The most frequent criticism of family systems therapy is that it tends to ignore individual dysfunction and focuses on interactions between family members. Rather than concentrate on a person's problem (schizophrenia, for example), family systems therapists look at the family's responsibility for the problem. Although Bowen and psychoanalytic approaches do look at the history of the family, structural, strategic, and experiential theories tend to examine present functioning and ignore family development. Many family systems therapies, especially structural and strategic, may manipulate the family without their knowing it by using paradoxical interventions. Such cases provide an authoritative relationship in which clients are unaware of what is being done to them and insight is not valued. Feminist therapy has criticized family systems therapy for not recognizing the wider social context that contributes to role expectations within families. Sometimes family therapists seem more enthralled with new creative approaches to dealing with families than they are with finding a cohesive method of family interventions.

An important contribution of family systems therapy is to recognize that individual problems do not exist in a vacuum and that family members contribute to each other's functioning. By bringing the entire family into treatment, alliances between family members and styles of relating can be observed. The therapist then is able to help family members help each other resolve problems rather than to blame or focus on the "identified patient." Over the last 30 or more years, there has been a trend not only to integrate various family systems therapies but also to integrate individual therapy into family therapy. The importance of treating families can be seen by the fact that not only are there several approaches to family systems theory, but also each theory, except for Jungian analysis, treats family problems.

In characterizing the limitations and strengths of various therapies, a few observations can be made. Evaluations of therapies are subjective, based on the evaluator's values, attitudes, and experience as a therapist, client, or researcher. Clients vary greatly in their cultural background, age, family history, psychological disorder, gender, and many other factors. A therapy that may fit one client may be inappropriate for another. Although most therapies (other than Adlerian, behavioral, cognitive, and psychoanalytic) tend not to have differential treatment for different diagnostic disorders, they recognize psychological dysfunction and bring their perspective on therapy to the problem. By critiquing the limitations and strengths of various therapies, therapists are better able to decide which approaches they want to use in their own approach to therapy.

Summary

Helping people with psychological problems gives therapists an opportunity to increase the satisfaction and happiness and improve the interpersonal relationships of other people. Almost all clients try to deal with their psychological suffering on their own or with the help of friends. Only when that has failed do they seek psychotherapy or counseling. The responsibility to help others ethically and competently is a significant one. Theorists pass on to others their views of how to help individuals in distress. Along with the responsibility of using theory accurately are the satisfaction and excitement that come with helping.

Without the theoretical ideas presented in this book, therapists and counselors would have few guidelines on how to proceed. The thousands of books and articles on ways to help and the research into the effectiveness of helping will continue to increase and to provide guidelines and assistance for the therapist. With continued research and increased therapeutic practice, the theories have become deeper and broader. They have become deeper in that the new aspects or concepts of theories have been developed, critiqued, and modified further. For some theories, research has played an important role in determining aspects of the theory that are particularly effective or need modification. Theories also have become broader, as practitioners of one theory incorporate other techniques and concepts into their work. Additionally, some writers have taken an integrative point of view, essentially developing theories that are broadly based on the concepts and/or techniques of other theories. There are three integrative approaches that will be presented in the next chapter. Also, I will explain how you can use the theories described in the previous chapters to develop your own integrative theory.

For the beginning therapist or counselor, this information can seem exciting at some times and overwhelming at others—overwhelming because there is so much information for beginning therapists, who may feel they need to know their theoretical preference right away. The development of a theoretical style is a gradual one, influenced by readings, by practicum and internship experience, and by supervisors' opinions.

I encourage readers who are choosing to become psychotherapists or counselors to be open to the selection of theoretical points of view. Although the fit between one's own values and personality and those of a theory is important, fit is not the only consideration. Knowledge of the interaction of one's own personality and multicultural values is essential in effective psychotherapy and counseling. The type of client and the work a student anticipates doing often have an impact on the selection of theories. For example, many agencies impose a limit on the number of sessions they can offer their clients, so longer-term therapies (psychoanalysis and Jungian analysis) would be inappropriate in that setting. Some settings may fit well with certain theories: therapists and counselors working with juvenile delinquents may find that behavior or reality therapy approaches fit their needs, whereas those working with individuals in midlife crises may find existential therapy or Jungian analysis to be appropriate.

Some therapists do make small or marked changes in theoretical orientation, depending on changes in their own personal development, the type of clients they work with, and the expectations of a new work setting. Openness to new information and ideas can be seen as a strength rather than as indecisiveness. Choosing the theory that fits best or integrating several theories of psychotherapy or counseling is a long-term process, subject to change due to whom and in what situation you may work.

References

Castonguay, L. G., & Beutler, L. E. (EDS.) (2006). *Principles of psychotherapeutic change that work*. New York: Oxford University Press.

Hesler, P. (1972). *Women and madness*. New York: Doubleday.

Franklin, M. E., & Foa, E. B. (2007). Cognitive treatment of obsessive compulsive personality disorder. In P.E., Nathan & J. M., Gorman (Eds.), *A guide to treatments that work* (3rd ed.). New York: Oxford University Press.

Imel, Z. E., & Wampold, B. E. (2008). The importance of treatment and the science of common factors in psychotherapy. In S. D. Brown & R. W. Lent (Eds.), *Handbook of counseling psychology* (4th ed., pp. 249–266). Hoboken, NJ: Wiley.

Lambert, M. (2007). Presidential address: What we have learned from a decade of research aimed at improving psychotherapy outcome in routine care. *Psychotherapy Research*, 17(1), 1–14

Lambert, M. J. Bergin, A. E., & Garfield, S. L. (2004). Overview and future issues. In Lambert, M. J. (Ed.), *Bergin and Garfield's handbook of psychotherapy and behavior change* (5th ed., pp. 805–821). New York: Wiley.

Lambert, M. J., Garfield, S. L., & Bergin, A. E (2004). Introduction and historical overview. In Lambert, M. J. (Ed.), *Bergin and Garfield's handbook of psychotherapy and behavior change* (5th ed., pp. 3–15). New York: Wiley.

Lambert, M. J., & Vermeersch, D. A. (2008). Measuring and improving psychotherapy outcome in routine practice. In S. D.Brown & R. W.Lent (Eds.), *Handbook of counseling psychology* (4th ed., pp. 233–248). Hoboken, NJ: Wiley.

Nathan, P. E. (2007). Efficacy, effectiveness, and the clinical utility of psychotherapy research. In S. G. Hofmann & J. Weinberger (Eds.), *The art and science of psychotherapy* (pp. 69–83). New York: Routledge.

Nathan, P. E., & Gorman, J. M. (Eds.). (2007). *A guide to treatments that work* (3rd ed.). New York: Oxford University Press.

Neimeyer, R. A. (2009). *Constructivist psychotherapy: Distinctive features*. New York: Routledge.

Polster, M. (1992). *Eve's daughters: The forbidden heroism of women*. San Francisco: Jossey-Bass.

Sparks, J. A., Duncan, B. L., & Miller, S. D. (2008). Common factors in psychotherapy. In J. L. Lebow (Ed.), *Twenty-first-century psychotherapies: Contemporary approaches to theory and practice* (pp. 453–497). Hoboken, NJ: Wiley.

Sue, D., & Sue, D. M. (2008). *Foundations of counseling and psychotherapy: Research-supported psychological treatments practices for a diverse society*. Hoboken, NJ: Wiley.

Weinberger, J., & Rasco, C. (2007). Empirically supported common factors. In S. G. Hofmann & J. Weinberger (Eds.), *The art and science of psychotherapy* (pp. 103–129). New York: Routledge.

CHAPTER 17

Integrative Therapies

Outline of Integrative Therapies

WACHTEL'S CYCLICAL PSYCHODYNAMIC
THEORY
  Psychodynamic treatment
  Behavioral treatments
  Strategies in understanding
  Rationale for using both approaches
  Other approaches used
  Emphasis on therapeutic relationship
  Working toward seamless interventions

Using Wachtel's Cyclical Psychodynamics

Theory as a Model for Your Integrative Theory
  Theoretical integration
  Assimilative model
  Technical eclecticism

PROCHASKA AND COLLEAGUES'
TRANSTHEORETICAL APPROACH

Stages of Change
  Precontemplation
  Contemplation
  Preparation
  Action
  Maintenance

Levels of Psychological Problems
  Symptoms
  Maladaptive thoughts
  Interpersonal conflicts
  Family conflicts
  Intrapersonal conflicts

Processes of Change
  Consciousness raising
  Dramatic relief or catharsis
  Environmental reevaluation
  Self-reevaluation
  Self-liberation
  Social liberation
  Contingency management
  Counterconditioning
  Stimulus control
  Helping relationships

Combining Stages of Change, Levels of
Psychological Problems, and Processes of
Change

Using Prochaska and Colleagues'
Transtheoretical Approach as a Model for Your
Integrative Theory

MULTIMODAL THERAPY

Multimodal Theory of Personality
  Behavior
  Affect
  Sensation
  Imagery
  Cognition
  Interpersonal relationships
  Drugs/biology
  Firing order

Goals of Therapy

Assessment

Treatment Approach
  Tracking
  Bridging
  Using concepts from other theories
  Time tripping
  Deserted island fantasy technique

Using Multimodal Theory as a

Model for Your Integrative Theory

Although there are many integrative approaches to psychotherapy, in this chapter I will describe three integrative theories. Wachtel's cyclical psychodynamics combines the personality theory concepts and psychotherapeutic techniques of several theories, principally psychoanalysis and behavior therapy. Prochaska's transtheoretical approach examines many theories, selecting concepts, techniques, and other factors that effective psychotherapeutic approaches have in common. Both cyclical psychodynamics and the transtheoretical approach use a model called theoretical integration. *Theoretical integration* combines the personality theory concepts and techniques of two or more theories. Similar to this model is the *assimilative* integrative approach, in which the personality theory and the psychotherapeutic techniques of one theory are the major approach and one or more other theories are used to supplement it. In multimodal therapy, a social learning view of personality is the focus (Stricker & Gold, 2005). It influences the use of many treatment techniques, which have been drawn from many theoretical orientations. The model it uses is called technical eclecticism. In *technical eclecticism*, one personality theory is selected and techniques may be used from any theory, but they are used in a way that is consistent with the personality theory that has been selected. Integrative methods provide a means of systematically combining many of the theories that have been described in the previous chapters of this textbook. As I describe each of the three integrative theories (cyclical psychodynamics, transtheoretical, and multimodal), I will explain a method that you can use in making an outline of your own theory that would be similar to each of these.

By combining elements of several theories, therapists can make use of the benefits of many theories. As Prochaska and Norcross (2010) show, there are a wide variety of combinations of integrating theories. For example, psychoanalytic-behavioral integration was popular in the 1970s, and cognitive therapy in combination with behavioral, humanistic, or psychoanalytic therapies was common in the 1980s. Their conclusions, shown in Table 17.1, are based on asking integrative psychotherapists to label their own style (Garfield & Kurtz, 1977; Norcross & Prochaska, 1988). Data from 2003 show the growing popularity of behavioral and cognitive theories (Norcross, Karpiak, & Lister, 2005). However, the data also show a broad range of preferences. This research examined only pairs of integrated therapies; it is likely that some therapists combine three or more therapeutic approaches in their work. As Table 17.1 shows, an integrative approach of long-standing interest is that of behavioral and psychoanalytic theories. Since the 1950s, therapists have used many ways to combine therapies. As different therapeutic approaches developed, practicing therapists tried to integrate and blend different techniques and inform their colleagues about their work. Integrative therapists have described both skills needed to be competent as an integrative therapist and training and supervision methods used in integrative therapy (Boswell, Nelson, Nordberg, McAleavey, & Castonguay, 2010). *The Journal of Psychotherapy Integration* contains articles about issues important to the development of integrative approaches to therapy. As shown in Chapter 1, many therapists practice integrative approaches to therapy.

Wachtel's Cyclical Psychodynamics Theory

Wachtel and his colleagues (Gold & Wachtel, 2006; Wachtel, 2008; Wachtel, Kruk, & McKinney, 2005) have developed an approach that combines behavioral and psychoanalytic ideas and techniques with conceptualizations and methods from some other theories. The integration of behavioral and psychoanalytic therapy would seem, at first, to combine two approaches that are too theoretically distant to be reconciled. However, this pairing has a long history, with Dollard and Miller (1950) developing a unified theory combining the insights of psychoanalysis with the scientific rigor of behavior therapy.

Table 17.1 Most Frequent Combinations of Theoretical Orientations

Combination	1976* %	1976* Rank	1986 %	1986 Rank	2003 %	2003 Rank
Behavioral and cognitive	5	4	12	1	16	1
Cognitive and humanistic			11	2	7	2
Cognitive and psychoanalytic			10	3	7	2
Cognitive and interpersonal			4	12	6	4
Cognitive and systems			<4	14	6	4
Humanistic and interpersonal	3	6	8	4	5	6
Interpersonal and systems			5	7	4	7
Psychoanalytic and systems			4	9	3	8
Interpersonal and psychoanalytic			<4	15	3	8
Behavioral and interpersonal			<4	13	2	10
Behavioral and systems			5	7	2	11
Humanistic and psychoanalytic			<4	12	2	11
Behavioral and humanistic	11	3	8	4	1	13
Behavioral and psychoanalytic	25	1	4	9	<1	14

*Percentages and ranks were not reported for all combinations in the 1976 study (Garfield & Kurtz, 1977). Also data from Norcross and Prochaska (1988) and Norcross, Karpiak, and Lister (2005).

Working in this tradition, Wachtel (Gold & Wachtel, 2006; Wachtel, 1977, 1991, 1993, 1997; Wachtel et al., 2005), with a background in psychoanalysis, has developed a theory that intertwines psychoanalysis and behavior therapy. Others have been attracted to cyclical dynamics because of its emphasis on client strengths as well as relationship and family issues (Ornstein & Ganzer, 2000).

Recognizing that anxiety is common to disorders treated by these methods, Wachtel has developed *cyclical psychodynamics*, a term that comes from his belief that psychological conflicts within oneself create problems in behavior and that problems in behavior create problems within oneself. For example, a person may feel unloved by her parents and be unassertive in her behavior, all the while feeling anger toward her parents. By acting unassertively, she may feel ignored and also feel rage. Thus, the intrapersonal conflict creates behavioral problems, and the behavioral problems create further intrapersonal problems.

In treating patients, Wachtel moves back and forth between helping clients understand their behavior and changing it. Behavioral treatments include relaxation, desensitization, and exposure to anxiety. Psychodynamic treatment includes helping the patient understand past and present unconscious conflicts and how they influence each other. Wachtel deals not only with past issues but also follows how unconscious processes emerge as the end product of anxiety. Thus, unconscious conflicts may cause problems or be the result of problems. Strategies in understanding the client and treating the client come from both behavioral and psychodynamic perspectives. Wachtel inquires into the unconscious problems of the client as well as the behaviors. Also, he may expose the client to anxiety, not just through behavioral procedures but also through interpreting and confronting unconscious processes. However, this exposure is done gradually, and change is brought about in small steps rather than in dramatic interventions.

Wachtel was concerned that a purely psychoanalytic view would mean that individuals' early experiences would appear to not be changed by experiences in their later life. He was attracted to a behavioral point of view that is quite clear in the belief that recent events have an effect on future behaviors of the individual. He was also concerned that insight and knowing about one's issues or problems would not be enough to bring about change. Being familiar with the work of Dollard and Miller (1950), he was able to integrate behavior therapy into psychoanalysis.

Interestingly, Wachtel was not as enthusiastic about integrating cognitive therapy into psychoanalysis. He viewed psychoanalysis as cognitive in its emphasis on thinking about one's concerns and bringing unconscious events into conscious awareness. He wanted to help individuals become more aware of their emotions and be able to change their behaviors. More recently, he has been influenced by a constructivist approach to cognitive therapy (Chapter 12) that focuses on the ways clients think about and address their problems rather than a persuasive approach, such as disputing used in rational emotive behavior therapy (REBT) (Chapter 9), that focuses on persuading individuals to change irrational behaviors.

As the therapy process proceeds, clients are helped to develop insights into clarifying and interpreting thoughts, fantasies, and behaviors. As psychoanalysis and cognitive therapies have been influenced by constructivist approaches, so has Wachtel. This has caused him to take a sharper view of clients' use of language and the way they view the world and the therapeutic relationship. Recognizing that many problems occur within the family, he has also integrated concepts from family therapy (Wachtel et al., 2005).

Wachtel believes that it is not enough to identify and understand one's fears, but that one must be exposed to the fear repeatedly in order to extinguish the behavior. Psychoanalytic interpretation provides one method to expose the fear and extinguish the behavior, as it is a way to help the patient deal with thoughts that have been previously avoided. He suggests that repeating such interpretations is helpful in moving toward extinguishing the fear. Transference can be seen as viewing past experience not only for itself but also as it relates to the client's current life.

Like many current psychoanalysts, Wachtel emphasizes the importance of the client–therapist relationship. The relational psychoanalytic writings of Mitchell (1993) and others have been an important influence on cyclical psychodynamics. Wachtel (Wachtel et al., 2005) sees the therapist as collaborating with the client to make use of interpretations and not feel discouraged by them. In doing this, the therapist attends not just to the client's discussion of past events but also to the reactions and interactions that occur in the present between client and therapist. Change in therapy is seen as being due in part to the effectiveness of the therapeutic relationship.

An Example of Wachtel's Cyclical Psychodynamic Theory: Judy

The following example of Judy, in her mid-40s, who complained of chronic depression and severe somatic symptoms, illustrates how therapists using the cyclical psychodynamic approach conceptualize their clients (Gold & Wachtel, 1993). In the beginning of therapy, Judy and the therapist examined the intrapsychic conflict–behavior–intrapsychic conflict–behavior circle (how psychological issues led to behavioral problems and vice versa) and Judy's anxieties and motivations. Gradually, Judy saw that she was being exploited by others, that she was angry at this exploitation, and that she had developed a sense of helplessness about this problem. Exploration of psychodynamic issues, such as parental attachments, helped Judy make a link between past and present behavior. At this juncture, the therapist combined behavioral and psychoanalytic interventions to break the psychodynamic-behavioral cycle.

> The initial period of such interpretive work became the basis for more active interventions aimed at breaking Judy's vicious circle of compliance, self-deprivation, and anger. The first exercise was a blend of dynamic insight and systematic desensitization. Judy was asked if she could imagine scenes in which she pleasurably spoke her mind in an angry or irritable way with her husband and friends. She gradually moved from timid and tiny expressions and imagery to scenes where her expressions of rage were violent and powerful. As Judy became more comfortable with these ideas and images, she spontaneously gained insight into her anxiety about anger, and about some of the unconscious factors which reinforced her compliant behavior. Judy reported imagining herself frightening other people and taking pleasure in the power which that fear represented. She also learned that her care taking behavior gave her a covert sense of power as well, as it unconsciously provoked fantasies of being better and more capable than the people to whom she acquiesced consciously. (Gold & Wachtel, 1993, pp. 69–70)

An Example of Wachtel's Cyclical Psychodynamic Theory: John N.

The following example shows a more specific integration of behavioral and psychoanalytic theory (Wachtel et al., 2005). It illustrates a "seamless" approach in which behavioral methods are intertwined with psychoanalytic interpretation.

John N. sought therapy because he had failed five times to pass a licensing exam in his professional field (not specified in the case). He had been successful in his field and felt pressure to pass the exam. He had grown up in a prominent Boston family, who were concerned about social status and about being successful. John conveyed his own concern about social status and success in the therapeutic hour. The therapy, unusual for cyclical psychodynamics, lasted only 8 sessions. It was successful in helping John pass the exam. Such a specific goal is not typical of cyclical psychodynamic work. This excerpt from the case illustrates the intertwining of behavioral techniques with psychoanalytic conceptualizations.

> The most interesting developments occurred when John imagined himself visiting the exam room the day before the exam. The aim in this set of imagery exercises was for him to acclimate to the setting in which the exam would take place and thereby to experience a reduction in anxiety. He was asked to look carefully around the room, to touch the various surfaces such as the desk and walls, to experience the lighting, and so forth.
>
> When he began the imaging, however, a fascinating series of associations and new images came forth. At first he spontaneously had the association that the room seemed like a morgue, and then that the rows of desks seemed liked countless graves covering the site of a battlefield. Then he felt overcome with a feeling of impotence. I asked him if he could picture himself as firm and hard, ready to do battle. He did so (I left it ambiguous whether he should take this specifically to mean having an erection or as an image of general body toughness and readiness). He said he felt much better, stronger, and then spontaneously had an image of holding a huge sword and being prepared to take on a dragon. He associated this image to our various discussions of his treating the exam as a worthy opponent, taking it seriously yet being able to master it. He was exhilarated by this image, and I suggested he engage in such imagery at home between sessions, a suggestion he endorsed with great enthusiasm.

counterconditioning, stimulus control, and helping relationships) that cover almost all aspects of possible change and draw on different theories of therapy. They are described in more detail here (Prochaska & Norcross, 2010; Prochaska & DiClemente, 1984, 2005).

Consciousness raising. This refers to interventions that help clients to become more aware of both the causes and consequences of their actions as well as ways to feel better. Typically, such interventions are observations that the therapist makes about the client, interpretations of client statements, and gentle confrontations about issues that they may not have been previously aware of, such as certain defenses that they may have about their concerns. Psychoanalytic, Jungian, Adlerian, existential, gestalt, and feminist therapy help clients raise their consciousness about problems.

Dramatic relief or catharsis. Such experiences are emotional or affective. Expressing the problem to the therapist can lead to relief. Acting out the problem as is done in gestalt therapy with the empty chair would be an example of helping a client to express her feelings about a person or event. A sense of relief is often experienced after expressing emotions. Gestalt therapy does this most directly, but constructivist therapies and psychodrama provide dramatic relief as well.

Environmental reevaluation. By looking at a problem in a wider context, an individual takes a different perspective. In this way an individual can see how the problem affects others or is affected by others. For example, a child who is physically abused can see that the problem is not his fault. Or a man may decide to stop drinking because of the effect that his alcohol consumption is having on his children. Many therapies help with environmental evaluation.

Self-reevaluation. In the process of self-reevaluation, an individual assesses what she needs to do to overcome a significant problem. This involves affective, cognitive, and behavioral changes. The individual examines the advantages and disadvantages of changing. The individual evaluates what she must do or give up in order to change. For example, can one give up the pleasures of drinking in order to deal with problems caused by drinking? Adlerian therapy, cognitive therapy, and REBT are theories that address self-reevaluation.

Self-liberation. Clients choose to address their problems and to make changes. Clients can choose new alternatives in addressing their problems. They can examine their potential for success in changing parts of their lives along with the responsibilities that come with making changes. Sometimes anxiety can result as one examines a need to choose, such as choosing whether or not to have an abortion. Many theories address self-liberation.

Social liberation. Sometimes problems require making small or large social changes. For example, if a woman is being sexually harassed at work by her boss, the therapist may help her develop a strategy or plan for dealing with the problem at work. The plan could also include getting legal or social support along with a plan about how to deal with her boss. Feminist therapy, more than others, addresses this process of change. Family structural therapy and Adlerian therapy also address social liberation.

Contingency management. Reinforcement of behavior, as described in Chapter 8, is an effective example of contingency management. Teaching clients to shape their behavior can be useful in dealing with a variety of problems. Systematic and in vivo desensitization are other ways to manage behaviors. Use of this process often includes conducting a behavioral functional analysis (page 289).

Counterconditioning. By changing the way they respond to problems or stimuli, clients can make positive changes in their lives. Learning new ways of responding can take place by a variety of behavioral modeling techniques or planned practice of how to deal with a situation such as Meichenbaum's self-instructional training (page 299).

Stimulus control. By controlling the environment, individuals can control the way they deal with difficult situations. Meichenbaum's stress inoculation method (pages 299 to 301) is a way of coping with mild stress to deal with more stressful situations. Rehearsing how one can change a difficult situation would be an example of controlling the stimulus.

Helping relationships. A good therapeutic relationship is seen as an important aspect of almost any therapy. In transtheoretical therapy, it is necessary for change to take place. Rogers's person-centered therapy and the existential therapy concept of therapeutic love are examples of using the relationship in psychotherapy to help the client.

Combining Stages of Change, Levels of Psychological Problems, and Processes of Change

Different processes of change (techniques) can be used depending on how ready the client is to make change. In moving from the precontemplation to the contemplation stage, for example, consciousness-raising techniques help clients raise their awareness of the problem. Enacting techniques (dramatic relief) also help in clients' awareness of problems and their desire to make changes. Additionally, reexamining life events (environmental reevaluation) may help clients decide that this is a time to make changes. These techniques start clients on their way to preparing to make changes in their lives.

To move from the contemplation to the preparation stage, clients must self-reevaluate. They do this by deciding on which issues or concerns they wish to change and which they wish to put aside, temporarily or perhaps permanently. Setting goals for therapy is part of the self-reevaluation process. To make changes and move to the action stage, they go through the self-liberation process. Here they examine more closely what it is that they have to do to make changes. They also can examine how likely change is to occur.

When clients move into the action stage, they then are ready to make use of action-oriented processes. The behaviorally based stages of contingency management, counterconditioning, and stimulus control are appropriate here. Depending on the nature of the problem, social liberation strategies may be used as well. These stages continue into the maintenance phase. Follow-up meetings with the therapist may help to check on the action-oriented processes and to provide support.

Throughout the therapy treatment, the helping relationship process is constant. Prochaska and DiClemente (2005) stress the importance of maintaining good therapeutic relationships at all phases of treatment. Without a good relationship between client and therapist, clients will not move through all the stages of change.

Just as certain theories of psychotherapy fit certain types of change processes, certain theories are used most frequently with different levels of problems. Also, some theories are more likely to be used in the contemplation stage, whereas others are more often used in the action and maintenance stages. For example, psychoanalytic therapy is more likely to be used in the precontemplation stage of interpersonal conflicts, and behavior therapy is more likely to be used in the action and maintenance stages of symptom or situational problems. The following is a list of the five levels of psychological problems outlined by Norcross and Prochaska along with the therapeutic approaches presented in this text that most closely fit them:

Symptoms/situational: Behavior therapy, solution-focused therapy
Maladaptive cognitions: Adlerian therapy, REBT, cognitive therapy
Interpersonal conflicts: Family therapy (general), interpersonal therapy, reality therapy, psychodrama
Family systems/conflicts: Bowenian, structural, strategic, experiential, and humanistic family system therapies
Intrapersonal conflicts: Psychoanalytic therapy, Jungian therapy, existential therapy, gestalt therapy, narrative therapy, creative arts therapies

This list is a broad one. There are times that some theories would be used with different levels of problems and at different stages of change. Feminist therapy may fit a variety of levels and stages depending in part on the nature of the problem. Person-centered therapy is likely to be used in each of the different levels.

When using transtheoretical therapy, therapists may employ different strategies. They consider how to help the client (the 10 therapeutic processes), when to use certain processes (the five stages of change), and what it is that needs changing (the five levels of problems). Sometimes they start with the level of problem, working first with symptoms, and then moving to maladaptive cognitions, and so forth. As they move in this direction, the levels become deeper until they reach the intrapersonal conflict level. At other times, such as when working with a phobia of rats, the nature of the problem may require working only at one or two levels. With more difficult and complex problems, therapists may work at all levels. In the case of Mrs. C described below, the therapist works with many change processes and at different levels.

An Example of Prochaska and Colleagues' Transtheoretical Approach: Mrs. C

Because of the many concepts involved in Prochaska and Norcross's transtheoretical approach, presenting an example is difficult. I will briefly summarize Prochaska's work with Mrs. C (Prochaska & Norcross, 2010). Mrs. C presents a broad history of problems, including symptoms of obsessive-compulsive disorder and a recent suicide threat. More than most therapists, Prochaska attends to Mrs. C's motivation for change as she moves from the preparation to action phase. In working with her, he addresses Mrs. C's compulsive handwashing (symptom), her thoughts about dirt (maladaptive thoughts), her relationships with her children (interpersonal), her mother's rules about cleanliness (family), and problems with overcontrolling her feelings (intrapersonal). Having a system of categorization of problems and processes provides a structure that few theories have. This structure also provides a method for determining which therapeutic interventions to make.

Prochaska then chooses from the 10 change processes. When talking about her hospitalization and her obsessive-compulsive disorder, Mrs. C experiences self-liberation and catharsis as Prochaska provides a caring relationship as well as help with family issues as described by Prochaska and Norcross (2010, p. 513).

> A helping relationship was enhanced by meeting twice a week in more person-centered supportive sessions. In these sessions, Mrs. C could share the many thoughts and feelings generated by her hospitalization and treatment. These sessions also helped Mrs. C identify with therapy as she experienced her therapist as caring rather than coercive. The more Mrs. C identified with psychotherapy, the more she relied on self-liberation, as she committed herself more fully to taking action to overcome her chronic compulsions.
>
> The interpersonal level was also addressed through biweekly conjoint sessions for the C family. The family members needed to express the considerable anger and resentment toward Mrs. C that had accumulated over the years. For awhile it looked as though Mrs. C might not return home, because four of the children were adamant about not wanting her back. As the anger dissipated, however, Mr. C and the older children helped the younger children reevaluate their mother, because they shared memories of how Mrs. C was before she became obsessed. Individual sessions with Mr. C also helped him to remember the warm feelings that had been buried under all the frustration and resentment.

Additionally, counterconditioning was used by nurses in the hospital to help Mrs. C cope with her anxiety about compulsive hand washing by being distracted by card playing and watching TV. Prochaska also applied several of the other 10 change processes. This structure assists the therapist in relating assessments of the problems to therapeutic change.

In summary, Prochaska and Norcross (2010) discuss how different processes of change can be applied, depending on the patient's stage of readiness for change and the level of the problem. For example, consciousness raising and dramatic relief may be most appropriate when clients are in the precontemplation or contemplation stage, but counterconditioning and stimulus control may be more appropriate for the action or maintenance stages. By using this multilevel transtheoretical approach, Prochaska and Norcross wish to integrate contributions from many theories and apply them to clients whose problems can be described differentially by their model.

Using Prochaska and Colleagues' Transtheoretical Approach as a Model for Your Integrative Theory

Prochaska and his colleagues have developed a model that can be considered theoretical integration (Prochaska & Norcross, 2010). It draws from most theories that are covered in this textbook. However, the transtheoretical approach applies the theoretical integration model very differently than does Wachtel in his cyclical psychodynamics model. Whereas Wachtel uses theories in their entirety (or almost), Prochaska and his colleagues develop their own unique theory by using the techniques of other theories. Then they group them into their own 10 processes of change. Also, they develop their own five stages of change and five levels of psychological problems. Their theory has many new concepts, whereas Wachtel's does not. Both are valid examples of the theoretical integration model of integrating therapies.

For a student or beginning therapist, it would be very difficult to develop a model that integrates theory in a way similar to that of Prochaska and his colleagues. To develop one's own processes of change from the theories that are discussed in this textbook would be very challenging. However, to attempt to do so might help in understanding the techniques of change that are described in this textbook. It might be easier to take the transtheoretical model and to try and modify it in ways that would reflect your views of theory. For example, would you use different terms than *contingency management, counterconditioning,* and *stimulus control*? These terms are not used in Chapter 8, Behavior Therapy, but are similar to the concepts that are discussed in that chapter. Would you add a category that includes cognitive therapy? Cognitive therapy is only indirectly related to the 10 processes of change as described by Prochaska and his colleagues. Considering these and similar questions might help you if you were to enter the mental health field.

Multimodal Therapy

Courtesy of Arnold Lazarus

ARNOLD LAZARUS

In this section, Lazarus's (1989, 1997, 2001, 2005a, 2005b, 2008) multimodal approach, which is based on a social and cognitive learning theory of personality, is explained, with emphasis on goals of therapy, assessment, and therapeutic techniques.

Arnold Lazarus was born and educated in South Africa. He earned his PhD in 1960 from the University of the Witwatersrand in Johannesburg. During his training, he studied with Joseph Wolpe, a well-known behavior therapist. When Lazarus was a student in South Africa in the 1950s, the predominant theories of psychotherapy were psychoanalysis and person-centered therapy. However, he was also exposed to behavior therapy through lectures by Joseph Wolpe and other behaviorists. Impressed by the scientific basis of behavior therapy and the changes that are produced in patients, Lazarus adopted many of its techniques. However, when examining follow-up studies, Lazarus (1971, 1989) recognized that behavioral methods alone were not usually sufficient to bring about lasting change. He also wanted to know which therapy techniques would be best for which types of people and which types of problems. As he investigated these questions, he was able to use social learning theory as a means for understanding the behavior of his clients.

Multimodal Theory of Personality

The concepts that were important to Lazarus in understanding and treating human behavior are those that are described in the personality theory section of Chapter 8. Included are the principles of classical and operant conditioning and Bandura's work on observational or social learning. Bandura's work was particularly influential on Lazarus's theory and was combined with cognitive beliefs about personality, as described in Chapter 10. His view of human behavior is that individuals learn what to do from observing and experiencing the positive and negative consequences of interactions with others. However, his conceptualization of the social-cognitive model went beyond the specific focus of behavior, cognitive, and rational emotive behavior therapists.

Lazarus's (Lazarus, 2005a, 2005b, 2008) view is that individuals use seven major modalities to experience themselves and their world, which he refers to as BASIC I.D. Each letter and the modality that it stands for is explained here (Lazarus, 1989, 1997, 2005a, 2005b, 2008; Lazarus & Lazarus, 1991).

Behavior: Included in this category are habits, responses, and reactions that can be observed and measured. These include problems with eating, drinking, smoking, crying, and self-control. Also covered are problems with working too little or too much and being too aggressive or not assertive enough.

Affect: A variety of emotions and moods are included, such as being depressed, angry, anxious, happy, helpless, tense, and lonely. Important are feelings that are predominant problems for individuals and those that clients feel they may not be able to control. Feelings of fear and the events that may arouse fear fit in this category.

Sensation: Included are the basic senses of seeing, hearing, touching, tasting, and smelling. Emphasis is given to negative sensations that may include headaches, dizziness, numbness, stomach trouble, hallucinations, or sexual disturbances.

Imagery: Fantasies, mental pictures, images, and dreams fit into this category. Included are images that come through auditory or other sensory mechanisms. Body image and self-image are given special attention.

Cognition: Included are thoughts, ideas, values, and opinions. Of importance are negative thoughts about oneself, such as being stupid, crazy, unattractive, or worthless, as well as positive thoughts, such as being intelligent and honest.

Interpersonal relationships: How one interacts with family, friends, colleagues, teachers, or others fall into this category. Examples include difficulties in relationships with others, including marital and sexual problems.

Drugs/Biology: The entire area of health and medical concerns is covered in this category. Physiological functioning and drugs (prescribed or unprescribed) are considered when understanding the individual's personality. (For clarity, the letter D is used instead of the letter B, because the acronym BASIC I.D. has meaning—basic identification—whereas BASIC I.B. does not). Because this category is broad, it is more accurate to think of it as biology and drugs rather than just drugs. This category is important because all of the other modalities exist in a physiological context.

Lazarus (1997, 2005a, 2005b, 2008) is interested in how individuals use all of these systems and which are most important to the person. He uses the term *firing order* to describe the sequence of modalities that takes place when a person is confronted with an event. An example of the firing order is that of an impulsive person who

> blurts out a stupid remark at a party. A hush descends upon the group, and he understands the air of disapproval. He blushes and begins to perspire and imagines the comments that people will make behind his back. He gets up and walks out of the room. (Lazarus, 1989, p. 16)

The firing order in this situation is behavior-interpersonal-cognition-sensation-imagery-behavior. People react differently to the same situation (with different firing orders), and each individual responds differently to different situations (have different firing orders). In brief, individuals' behaviors, affects, sensations, imageries, cognitions, and interpersonal style of relating are learned through classical and operant conditioning as well as through observational modes. This view of human behavior has a direct impact on the way multimodal therapists conceptualize goals, assessment, and treatment of patient problems.

Goals of Therapy

Client goals for therapy can be seen in a combination of a variety of BASIC I.D. modalities. For example, an individual may seek help to stop smoking (B), seek help to work with fears about being unable to stop (A), be concerned about not having the pleasant sensation of smoking (S), be unable to picture himself as being able to go more than an hour without a cigarette (I), want to change his belief that he is too indecisive to stop smoking (C), be afraid that stopping smoking will make him too irritable with others (I), and be concerned about developing lung cancer through smoking (D). Not all goals are expressed in terms of all modalities, and the strength of each modality varies, depending on the goal. It is important to note that affect can be worked with only through the other modalities, as one cannot directly change emotions, but one can change the behaviors, sensations, imagery, cognition, interpersonal relationships, and biological processes that affect emotions. Thus, a person who is depressed feels better when she is doing productive things, having more positive sensations and images, thinking more rationally, interacting more comfortably with others, and feeling physically better. Lazarus (2005a, 2005b) recognizes the importance of clients' hopes and expectations for improvement early in therapy. It helps clients feel that there is hope for reaching their goals in a relatively brief time (fewer than 40 sessions).

Assessment

Essential to multimodal therapy is a precise and systematic assessment of the BASIC I.D. Assessment is done in three different ways: interviews with the client, having clients fill out their own modality profiles, and assessment instruments such as the Multimodal Life Inventory (Lazarus & Lazarus, 1991). Although assessment predominates in the initial sessions, it continues throughout therapy. The multimodal therapist listens for how problems affect modalities.

> A multimodal elaboration of the statement, "When Mr. Smith has a headache, he worries because he is a hypochondriac," would proceed as follows: When Mr. Smith has a headache, he becomes quiet and withdrawn (behavior), starts feeling anxious (affect), experiences the pain as "an internal hammer with hot spikes driven into the skull" (sensation), and pictures himself dying of a brain tumor (imagery) while convincing himself that the doctors have probably missed something seriously wrong (cognition). During these episodes, he talks monosyllabically while his wife fusses over him (interpersonal) and resorts to aspirins and other painkillers (biological). Multimodal elaboration of any problem not only spells out who or what may be maintaining the ongoing difficulties, but also enables one to pinpoint logical therapeutic approaches by examining the interactive aspects of the identified problems. (Lazarus, 1989, p. 14)

Additionally, the therapist is likely to draw up a chart rating the predominance or importance of each mode on a scale of 0 to 10. This can be done directly, by asking the client how he or she would rate a given modality, or indirectly, based on the therapist's observations.

Often it is helpful for therapists to ask their clients to construct their own modality profiles after the therapist has given the client a description of the BASIC

I.D. Such information gives the therapist insight into clients' views of how their problems fit each modality and familiarizes the client with the seven modalities. The following is an example of a modality profile of a 22-year-old nurse who described his problems as being shy with women, fighting with his mother, and feeling frustrated and depressed (Lazarus, 1989).

B. Stop smoking
    Start exercising
    Start dating
    Shy away from attractive women
A. Depression
    Anger
    Fear
S. Tension
    Blushing
I. I imagine women snickering behind my back.
    Many lonely images
    I often imagine my mother saying: "Who do you think you are?"
C. I am not good enough.
    Attractive women think of me as ugly and dull.
    I'm a loser.
I. My mother thinks I'm ten years old.
    Awkward and shy with attractive women
    Not enough friends
D. Smoke 1 ½–3 packs of cigarettes a day. (Lazarus, 1989, pp. 78–79)

This information is used in addition to that taken from the Multimodal Life History Inventory (Lazarus & Lazarus, 1991). This inventory is more detailed, requesting personal and social history, inquiring about expectations about therapy, requesting descriptions of presenting problems, and having open-ended questions and checklists about each of the seven modalities. Included are a brief medical history and global ratings on each of the seven modalities. With information from the client through the modality profile and the Multimodal Life History Inventory, as well as profiles made by the therapist based on information gathered about each modality, the therapist has an organized and specific method for initiating change with the client.

Sometimes more information is needed from a multimodal assessment, and a "second-order" BASIC I.D. may be necessary, which refers to taking any item on the modality profile and examining it in more detail from each of the seven modalities. For example, in the nurse's modality profile in the previous example, a behavior such as "Start dating," an affect such as "Depression," or a sensation such as "Tension" can each be subject to its own second-order assessment. Thus, one could take the behavior "Start dating" and look at other related behaviors, affects related to it such as fear, sensations such as tingling, images such as being refused a date, cognitions such as "Joan won't want to go out with me," interpersonal relationship issues such as "I don't know what to say on a date," and drug/biology concerns, such as "I sweat profusely before a date." In this way, a second-order assessment could be applied to any of the items on the young man's modality profile or any other modality profile. This detailed assessment approach is used, rather than DSM-IV-TR categories, in multimodal therapy so that the therapist is prepared to implement a variety of therapeutic procedures.

Treatment Approach

By assessing all seven modalities, Lazarus is able to apply a great variety of techniques to bring about therapeutic change. Therapeutic interventions may start in the first session; the multimodal therapist need not wait until a complete assessment is done. Lazarus has applied multimodal therapy to a great variety of outpatients and problems (Lazarus, 1987, 1988, 1997, 2000b, 2005a, 2005b, 2008). In the development of the therapeutic relationship and the application of treatment methodology, Lazarus (1993) describes himself as "an authentic chameleon" who changes his style to fit the client's, both to understand the client and to bring about therapeutic change. Lazarus (2007) values the contribution of Carl Rogers's person-centered therapy, but believes it is not sufficient to produce therapeutic change.

To understand the client and intervene effectively, Lazarus (1989) makes use of tracking and bridging. *Tracking* refers to examining the "firing order" of the modalities of different patients. For example, some patients may react to an adverse event with a sensation (S) of flushing, followed by distorted thoughts, "I must have done something wrong" (C), and images (I) of being yelled at. This might result in unassertive behavior (B). Clients do not display the same firing order consistently, and tracking must be done continuously. Therapeutic treatments may be given that follow the tracking sequence, such as using positive imagery of pleasant scenes if imagery is to be addressed first, or relaxation strategies if behavior is primary. Somewhat similar to tracking, *bridging* refers to attending to the client's current modality before moving into another modality that may be more productive to change. Thus, if an individual uses a cognitive modality to express herself, the therapist stays with that until it seems appropriate to bridge to another modality such as feeling (A). In this way, the therapist tracks the modalities and then moves (or bridges) to another, when appropriate. By doing so, the therapist prevents the client from feeling misunderstood by the therapist, which would occur if the client expressed one modality (such as cognition) and the therapist only reflected feelings (A). In this way, multimodal therapy is very flexible, with the therapist changing modes to make effective therapeutic interventions.

With more than 400 therapies (Corsini & Wedding, 2008) described by various authors and many techniques of therapy available to the therapist, the multimodal therapist has much to choose from. Although other therapists who use Adlerian, REBT, cognitive, or behavioral therapies can draw from a wide variety of affective, behavioral, and cognitive techniques, multimodal therapists draw from an even larger pool, as they also include change methods directed at sensations, imagery, and drug/biology in their repertoire. In *The Practice of Multimodal Therapy*, Lazarus (1989) lists 39 commonly used techniques in multimodal therapy. Of these, about half are behavioral, 25% are cognitive, and the rest come from other theoretical orientations. In taking techniques from other theories, Lazarus uses only the technique, not the conceptualization or reason for the technique. To further understand the range of Lazarus's selective eclecticism, I will describe how he draws from each of the major theories described in this text.

Like psychoanalysts, Lazarus might use free association, not for its value in revealing unconscious processes but rather as it reveals the client's sensations and images. Similarly, multimodal therapists may pay attention to the relationship between themselves and the client (transference), not from the perspective of feelings toward parents being transferred onto the therapist but rather to determine if the therapist is correctly understanding the client's expression of modalities. Some of the techniques of brief psychoanalysis would be shared with multimodal therapy, such as the use of questions, restatements, and confrontations, but brief psychoanalysis aims at understanding childhood dynamics, and multimodal theory uses psychoanalytic techniques to further understand and pursue issues related to the seven modalities as they impede adaptive functioning in the here and now.

Because the conceptual basis of Jungian analysis is so different from that of multimodal therapy, they share few techniques. Where the Jungian approach is to explore dream material as it represents the collective unconscious, the multimodal approach is to find out if there are new associations to a dream or to change the course or ending of the dream. Both Jungian analysis and multimodal theory have an interest in exploring imagery and sensations (although from very different points of view), and multimodal therapists could also use a sand tray with small figures to act out images, as do Jungian therapists.

Adlerian psychotherapy uses many techniques, such as "acting as if," spitting in the client's soup, and catching oneself, which are cognitive approaches that multimodal theorists could use in helping clients change beliefs and behavior. These techniques are action oriented, which is consistent with the multimodal view of change.

The philosophy of existential psychotherapy focuses chiefly on important themes or issues, not techniques. Multimodal therapists work on existential issues, such as dealing with a dying relative, being abandoned by a parent, or leaving college to support oneself, but from the perspective of BASIC I.D. The approaches are so different that existential psychotherapy offers very little to multimodal therapists, who would attend to the seven basic modalities. Possibly, Frankl's concepts of attitude modulation and dereflection could be used to change patient cognitions.

Person-centered therapy emphasizes genuineness, acceptance, and empathy. All of these concepts are important to multimodal therapists and are included in the affect modality. However, Rogers's six conditions for change are neither necessary nor sufficient for multimodal therapists, who use many more methods of intervention (Lazarus, 2007).

Gestalt therapy offers multimodal therapists many creative ideas that deal with the modalities of affect, sensation, and imagery. Use of the empty-chair technique, enacting problems, and awareness exercises tend to develop affect, sensation, and imagery.

Of all the therapies described in this book, behavior therapy has concepts that are most similar to those of multimodal therapy. Therefore, it is not surprising that multimodal therapists would draw heavily on behavior therapy and make use of most of the techniques in Chapter 8.

Both cognitive therapy and REBT offer many strategies that multimodal therapists use to change the cognition and, to a lesser extent, the imagery of the client. Techniques described for REBT and cognitive therapy in Chapters 9 and 10 are consistent with a multimodal approach.

Because reality therapy is tied to a specific process, there is little that multimodal therapy could draw from this theory. Although techniques such as questioning, being positive, using humor, and confronting are shared by both theories, the strong focus on choice and responsibility in reality therapy may not fit well with an emphasis on specific modalities.

Feminist therapy emphasizes culture, gender, power analysis, and intervention. Although multimodal therapists acknowledge the importance of gender and cultural issues, they do not incorporate these directly into the seven modalities. However, both gender-role and power interventions have cognitive and behavioral components that multimodal therapists might use with clients who are dealing with societal and political discrimination.

Multimodal therapists work with both couples and families. Family systems therapy focuses frequently on interpersonal issues, and Minuchin's structural approach does have methods that would be helpful to multimodal therapists in assessing interactions. However, they are more likely to examine how the seven modalities of each member of the couple or family interact with each other than to use a systems theory view.

Lazarus has not made use of a solution-focused approach or narrative therapy. However, a solution-focused approach is consistent with his emphasis on changing behaviors, and his modalities of imagery and cognition are consistent with the emphasis that narrative therapy puts on stories and values.

In addition to drawing from these theories, Lazarus has developed techniques such as time tripping and the deserted island fantasy technique to further develop a client's imagery modality. *Time tripping* refers to having clients picture themselves going backward or forward in time to address particular events or issues. The *deserted island fantasy* technique refers to asking clients what the therapist would learn if he were left alone with the client on a deserted island. This fantasy experience helps the therapist learn more about the cognition, affect, and imagery of the client. Other techniques can be developed by multimodal practitioners, who may make use of ideas from other theories, such as art, drama, dance movement, or music therapies, as well as techniques such as hypnosis. To use multimodal therapy requires empathy for clients, knowledge of social learning theory, ability to assess clients' BASIC I.D., and the application of a variety of strategies to effect changes in the modalities.

An Example of Lazarus's Multimodal Therapy: Mrs. W

An example of a 28-year-old woman who complains of anxiety when going away from home unaccompanied by her husband illustrates a multimodal approach (Lazarus, 1995). The presenting problem is agoraphobia, a disorder that Lazarus would normally treat with in vivo desensitization. He used this method by teaching the client relaxation and deep-breathing techniques and taking walks with the client, gradually increasing the distance between therapist and client. Whereas behavior therapists may stop at this point, Lazarus had information from her Multimodal Life History Inventory showing problems of marital discord, resentment toward parents, and issues related to poor self-esteem. Lazarus's use of switching modalities to meet the client's needs is explained here.

> Initially, a form of role-playing was employed in which Mrs. W attempted to confront her father about certain resentments she had harbored. When she implied that I was not capturing or conveying the essence of her father's tone and demeanor correctly, we switched from role-playing to the two-chair or empty chair technique. Now, while speaking to the empty chair in which she envisioned her father sitting, and then moving to the chair, becoming her father, and talking for him, she achieved a feeling of greater authenticity. This was reflected in considerable emotionality—what she heard herself term "cathartic release." (Lazarus, 1995, p. 30)

Although using gestalt techniques, Lazarus was dealing with affective, sensory, and imagery modalities in a social learning framework. In his further treatment of this client, Lazarus goes on to address other modalities through the use of a great variety of therapeutic techniques. Although this approach has the advantage of being flexible and choosing appropriate techniques to meet a variety of client goals, it has the disadvantage of requiring the ability to identify client BASIC I.D. modalities and requiring a wide knowledge of a variety of techniques.

Using Lazarus's Multimodal Theory as a Model for Your Integrative Theory

Multimodal theory might seem to use a theoretical integration model like Wachtel's cyclical psychodynamic model and Prochaska and colleagues' transtheoretical approach. However, it differs in one important respect from these models. Multimodal theory uses one specific approach to assessing or understanding the client, Bandura's social learning theory, or more broadly behavior personality theory including social learning theory, classical conditioning, and operant conditioning. Lazarus has chosen to use techniques from many theories that are consistent with behavioral personality theory. For this reason his approach is called *technical eclecticism* rather than *theoretical integration*. For example, Lazarus might use the gestalt empty-chair technique to help the client express the modalities of affect, sensation, or imagery, wheras Prochaska and colleagues would use the empty-chair technique in a way that is consistent with gestalt therapy to develop client awareness. Similarly, Lazarus might use the psychoanalytic technique of free association to assist the client in developing the modalities of affect or imagery, but Wachtel would use it in the way Freud intended, to help the client bring unconscious material into consciousness.

For you to use technical eclecticism as an integrative model, you would choose a theory of personality from the second column in Table 17.2 (p. 668). Then, you would look for therapeutic techniques from Table 16.4 on pages 638 and 639. For example if you wanted to develop an experiential integrative theory using the technical eclectic integrative method, you could choose gestalt personality therapy and then identify therapeutic techniques that you might use to help the client experience awareness. These would come from gestalt theory (almost always you would select techniques from the theory that you were using as your guiding personality theory). You might also select behavioral techniques, person-centered techniques, and techniques from narrative therapy. You probably would not want to use more than one theory of personality unless the ones that you chose were consistent with each other like cognitive and behavioral personality theory.

Theorists have developed many integrative models. The most popular and well-known ones have been discussed above. Some therapists or counselors may choose to use just one theory. Others might use an integrative approach such as Wachtel's cyclical psychodynamics, Prochaska and colleagues' transtheoretical approach, or Lazarus's multimodal theory. Yet others may develop their own approach. In this section, I have outlined ways in which therapists and counselors could develop their own integrative therapeutic approach.

Current Trends

Approaches to the integration of theories continue to be popular, including the ones discussed in this chapter—Prochaska's transtheoretical, cyclical psychodynamics, and multimodal. Because the use of several theories allows the therapist to incorporate ways of conceptualizing clients and methods of therapeutic change that complement each other, theoretical combinations are likely to continue to be popular. Furthermore, with health maintenance organizations providing limited payments for psychotherapy, there is a certain amount of pressure on therapists to focus on using whatever methods will work, and work quickly. Additionally, new views of combining theories continue to be a source of discussion. A dilemma facing those who use and do research on integrative therapies is whether to try to agree on which issues and theories to use or to keep developing new approaches (Eubanks-Carter, Burckell, & Goldfried, 2005). Both options seem to be viable at this point. As more theories are developed and tested, there will be more ideas to use to integrate theories into one's own perspective.

Not only are there more well-developed theories, there are more well-developed integrative approaches. Norcross and Goldfried (2005) have compiled a *Handbook of Psychotherapy Integration* that describes more than 15 different approaches to theoretical integration. Only three have been discussed in this chapter. Some approaches are meant to be used widely; others are designed for specific disorders such as depression and anxiety. In some approaches to theoretical integration, the focus is on factors that theories have in common, the *common factors* approach, and drawing the commonalities from existing theories rather than using the theories themselves. This approach is often used as a contrast to the research supported psychological treatments. It has not been widely used as an integrative approach.

Of the three integrative theories that I have described, the transtheoretical approach has drawn the most current interest. The transtheoretical model has been popular for those working with health issues such as smoking, obesity, diabetes, and HIV (Prochaska et al., 2009). Additionally, it has been used with substance abuse and alcohol abuse and other social issues. One reason for its popularity with these issues is the emphasis that the transtheoretical model puts on the processes of change. For example, several studies have examined the processes of change in evaluating smoking cessation (Atak, 2007; Guo, Aveyard, Fielding, & Sutton, 2009; Kleinjan et al., 2008). The transtheoretical model has also been used in weight management with obese patients (Johnson et al., 2008). For individuals with HIV, the transtheoretical model has been used to help compliance with an exercise regimen and to change risky sexual behavior (Basta, Reece, & Wilson, 2008; Gazabon, Morokoff, Harlow, Ward, & Quina, 2007). Dietary interventions are important in managing diabetes, and the transtheoretical model has been used with diabetic patients (Salmela, Poskiparta, Kasila, Vähäsarja, & Vanhala, 2009). Treatment of drug addiction and alcohol abuse is yet another application of the transtheoretical model (Callaghan, Taylor, & Cunningham, 2007; Heather, Hönekopp, Smailes, & UKATT Research Team, 2009; Kennedy & Gregoire, 2009). In addition to health issues, the transtheoretical model has been applied to bullying in school (Evers, Prochaska, Van Marter, Johnson, & Prochaska, 2007) and domestic violence (Brodeur, Rondeau, Brochu, Lindsay, & Phelps, 2009). Many therapists use the transtheoretical model in dealing with psychological disorders; however, there are few recent articles describing this work.

Research

Research on integrative theories has been limited. One problem in doing such research is that it is typical for individuals in comparison groups in a research study to receive very different treatments from each other, while those in a specific treatment group are offered the same techniques. In integrative approaches, many different techniques may be used for individuals within a specific treatment group, causing difficulties in analyzing effectiveness (Schottenbauer, Glass, & Arnkoff, 2005). Also, a number of integrative approaches were developed for specific disorders, making comparisons among integrative approaches difficult. Research on specific integrative approaches varies widely. There is very little research on Wachtel's cyclical psychodynamics model and relatively little on Lazarus's multimodal therapy despite the fact that it is quite well known. In contrast, there has been a significant amount of research on Prochaska's transtheoretical model. Much of this research has been on the stages of change and on the effectiveness of the transtheoretical model in helping individuals with health-related issues.

Recent reviews of research on Prochaska's transtheoretical model have documented studies supporting the theory. Schottenbauer, Glass, and Arnkoff (2005) and Prochaska et al. (2009) review a number of studies that support the use of the stages of change and its effectiveness with health-related issues. Such issues include smoking (a focus of much of the research), other addictive behaviors such as alcohol and drugs, obesity and dietary change, family planning for adolescents, behavior changes in stroke patients, and other issues. A review of 37 studies on the transtheoretical model with seven different health-related issues showed limited evidence for the effectiveness of methods used, based on stages of change (Bridle et al., 2005).

A frequent focus of studies on the transtheoretical model is cigarette smoking (Atak, 2007). Norman, Belicer, Fava, and Prochaska (2000) were able to determine subtypes within the precontemplation and contemplation stages, as well as the preparation stage. Within the contemplation stage, subtypes were identified that include classic contemplators, progressing contemplators, early contemplators, and disengaged contemplators (Anatchkova, Velicer, & Prochaska, 2005). Studying 688 smokers, support was found for the precontemplation and contemplation stages of the transtheoretical model (Schumann et al., 2005). The relationship of stage movement to processes of change has also been studied. Prochaska and colleagues predict that consciousness raising, dramatic relief, environmental reevaluation, and self reevaluation are likely to be associated with the transition from the precontemplation stage to the contemplation stage and that contingency management, helping relationships, counter-conditioning, and stimulus control are likely to be used in the maintenance stage. In a study of 721 adolescents in the Netherlands, the transtheoretical processes of change did not appear to explain adolescent stage transitions with regard to smoking cessation (Kleinjan et al., 2008). In the United Kingdom, forward movement in the processes of change was not clearly associated with stage transition in 1,160 13- and 14-year-olds (Guo et al., 2009). These studies look into predictions made by the transtheoretical model, not the effectiveness of the transtheoretical model as a means of stopping smoking behavior.

In a review of the transtheoretical model, West (2005) is critical of the stages of change model, as he believes that there is little evidence that shows that moving individuals closer to action actually produces sustained change. Wilson and Schlam (2004) criticize the applicability of the transtheoretical model to eating disorders.

Despite this criticism, studies such as one using a culturally diverse sample of inpatient adolescent drug abusers show that individuals in the precontemplation stage had significantly higher treatment dropout rates than did individuals in the contemplation or preparation/action stages (Callaghan et al., 2005). One study showed that individuals moving forward from one process stage to another did not consistently show great improvements in reducing drinking (Callaghan et al., 2007). However, in another study, improvements in limiting drinking were found in clients that moved forward in their process stages (Heather et al., 2009). Examining internal motivation, higher levels of motivation were associated with the contemplation and action stages rather than the precontemplation stage (Kennedy & Gregoire, 2009). The focus on a unique aspect of Prochaska's transtheoretical model, stages of change or readiness, is an interesting one, deserving of more research.

Research on multimodal therapy is quite sparse. Lazarus (2005a) reports on research he has done with his own patients. In tracking patients over a 20-year period, he reports that treatment goals were met with more than 75% of his patients. In a 3-year follow-up study of 20 difficult cases, he reports that 14 were successful in meeting their goals and did not require further therapy. Of the others, two needed medication from time to time, and three did not maintain therapeutic progress. In an earlier study with patients with obsessive-compulsive disorder and those with phobia, Kwee (1984) found that 64% of the individuals with obsessive-compulsive disorder significantly improved, as did 55% with phobias. Of the patients in the study, 70% had suffered with their concerns for more than 4 years and 90% had had previous therapy. In a study comparing nine individuals with treatment-resistant psychosis to a no-treatment group of 12 individuals, those who received multimodal therapy showed a significant reduction in symptoms (Randal, Simpson, & Laidlaw, 2003). There is a need for other researchers to investigate the effectiveness of multimodal therapy.

Gender Issues

When integrative therapies are used, whether transtheoretical, cyclical psychodynamics, or multimodal, they are susceptible to criticisms that are made of the specific theories they borrow from. For example, Prochaska's transtheoretical approach examines symptoms (behavior therapy), maladaptive thoughts (cognitive therapy, family therapy), and intrapersonal conflicts (psychoanalysis, gestalt, and others). Gender issues are different depending on the theory represented in the type of problem the client has. For Wachtel's cyclical psychodynamic theory, gender issues that relate to psychoanalysis, behavior therapy, and family systems therapy (as well as others) apply to a critique of Wachtel's approach. Similarly, in multimodal therapy, which draws heavily on cognitive and behavioral therapies, gender issues that apply to cognitive and behavior therapy apply also to multimodal therapy. Since Lazarus draws on a variety of therapeutic techniques from other theories, concerns about application of those techniques to women may be present.

Multicultural Issues

Prochaska's transtheoretical approach, cyclical psychodynamics, and multimodal therapy make use of theories that vary in their approach to multicultural issues. If integrative theories incorporate part of feminist therapy, they may include a multicultural component to their approach to clients, as it is featured in feminist therapy (Wachtel, 2007). In his book *Race in the Mind of America: Breaking the Vicious Circle between Blacks and Whites*, Wachtel (1999), originator of cyclical psychodynamics, addresses concerns about culture as it affects race relationships. In doing so, he draws upon psychoanalysis and cognitive and behavior therapy, all aspects of cyclical psychodynamics. Two of the change processes of the transtheoretical approach, consciousness raising and self-liberation, address issues that can be important when counseling clients with culturally diverse backgrounds. Prochaska's transtheoretical therapy specifically addresses issues in society that affect the individual. Lazarus's multimodal therapy makes use of seven different therapeutic modalities, some of which can elicit issues that are different depending on cultural background. Culture is likely to affect the images that the therapist uses and that the client perceives, as well as affecting family and friends who influence the client in the interpersonal relationship modality.

Those who study integrative therapy have examined how cultural issues can influence the type of therapy used. Brown (2009), a feminist therapist, describes a model for viewing cultural competence as a means for having an effective approach to psychotherapeutic integration. Wachtel (2008) discusses the importance of attending to cultural values when applying integrative therapy to individuals with different cultural values. Other authors have discussed how integrative psychotherapy can be applied in their own culture: Argentina (Muller, 2008), Chile (Opazo & Bagladi, 2008), Germany and Switzerland (Caspar, 2008), Japan (Iwakabe, 2008), and Portugal (Vasco, 2008). Several other authors have addressed ways of applying integrative therapy with different cultural groups within the United States. In working with an inner-city drug-abusing population, Avants and Margolin (2004) proposed an integrative therapy called spiritual self-schema therapy that makes use of the Buddhist eightfold path (page 584) to help clients use spiritual beliefs in dealing with addiction. Another approach is that of Ubuntu therapy, which makes use of African values that can be incorporated into psychotherapy when counseling African clients (Van Dyk & Nefale, 2005). *Ubuntu* refers to communality, cooperation, and sharing. Thus, there have been many ways of examining how integrative therapies can be applied to individuals with different cultural values.

Summary

This chapter describes three major approaches to integrating theories of psychotherapy. There are more than 15 different integrative theories. All integrative theories combine aspects of one or more theories that are described in this book in order to help their clients. Not only do integrative theories draw from different theories, but they also differ in the ways that they make use of the theories. For each theory, I describe the type of theoretical integration being used: theoretical integration, assimilative, or technical eclectic. Then I explain how each theory can be used as a model for the reader in developing his or her own theory. The three theories described in this chapter are summarized below.

In cyclical psychodynamics, Wachtel starts with psychoanalytic theory and then combines this developmental approach with behavior therapy. The two personality theories are used in assessing problems, and the two methods for client change (techniques) are used to help clients with their problems. Wachtel's cyclical psychodynamics also combines psychoanalysis with constructivist and family systems approaches to therapy as well as with behavior therapy.

Prochaska and his colleagues use a transtheoretical approach. In their model, they assess clients' readiness for change, which ranges from precontemplation (not being willing to change) to action (being committed to change) and then to maintenance (working to continue the change). Problems are then viewed as falling into five levels: symptoms, maladaptive thoughts, interpersonal conflicts, family conflicts, and intrapersonal conflicts. Prochaska and colleagues then draw from 10 techniques to bring about change. Among others, these include consciousness raising, environmental reevaluation, and self-liberation. These techniques give the transtheoretical therapist an opportunity to use many methods in helping clients change.

Multimodal therapy, developed by Arnold Lazarus, is an approach that uses social learning theory to understand the personality and issues of clients. He views client goals from the perspective of BASIC I.D. modalities: Behavior, Affect, Sensation, Imagery, Cognition, Interpersonal Relationships, and Drugs/Biology. Lazarus assesses all seven modalities in his clients and then uses a great variety of techniques to bring about therapeutic change. These techniques are drawn from many different theories.

This chapter, along with Chapter 16, Comparison and Critique, provides a summary of the theories discussed in the other chapters. By providing these summaries, I hope to help you think about which theory or theories you would like to use in counseling or psychotherapy. In this final chapter, I have tried to provide a basis for you to consider which theories you might wish to integrate to use in practice if you choose more than one theory.

At the back of this book is a questionnaire for you to fill out. I would like to hear about your experience with this book, what you like most, and what you like least. Helping others learn about psychotherapy and counseling is important to me, and I would appreciate your feedback.

Suggested Readings

Norcross, J. C., & Goldfried, M. R. (Eds.). (2005). *Handbook of psychotherapy integration* (2nd ed.). New York: Oxford University Press. A very thorough treatment of integrative psychotherapy, this handbook contains chapters written by the developers of more than 15 different approaches to therapeutic integration. Other chapters describe types of integrative approaches, training, outcome research, and future directions in the development of integrative psychotherapy.

Wachtel, P. L. (1997). *Psychoanalysis, behavior therapy and the relational world*. Washington, DC: American Psychological Association. The integration of psychoanalysis and behavior analysis is explained, along with an overview of anxiety, learning, and psychoanalysis. The first chapters are a reprint of Wachtel (1977). The last seven chapters update the theory as it relates to modifications in psychoanalysis, cognitive-behavior theory, and constructivism.

Prochaska, J. O., & Norcross, J. C. (2010). *Systems of psychotherapy: A transtheoretical analysis* (7th ed.). Belmont, CA: Brooks/Cole–Cengage. Chapter 16 provides a good overview of the transtheoretical model as developed by Prochaska, Norcross, and their colleagues.

Lazarus, A. A. (1997). *Brief but comprehensive psychotherapy: The multimodal way*. Baltimore: Johns Hopkins University Press. Lazarus describes multimodal therapy, its techniques and its application. Case material is included, along with explanations about the use of multimodal therapy as it relates to efficient treatment.

References

Anatchkova, M. D., Velicer, W. F., & Prochaska, J. O. (2005). Replication of subtypes for smoking cessation within the contemplation stage of change. *Addictive Behaviors, 30*(5), 915–927.

Atak, N. (2007). A transtheoretical review on smoking cessation. *International Quarterly of Community Health Education, 28*(2), 165–174.

Avants, S. K., & Margolin, A. (2004). Development of spiritual self-schema (3-S) therapy for the treatment of addictive and HIV risk behavior: A convergence of cognitive and Buddhist psychology. *Journal of Psychotherapy Integration, 14*(3), 253–289.

Basta, T. B., Reece, M., & Wilson, M. G. (2008). The transtheoretical model and exercise among individuals living with HIV. *American Journal of Health Behavior, 32*(4), 356–367.

Boswell, J. F., Nelson, D. L., Nordberg, S. S., MCaleavey, A. A., & Castonguay, L.G. (2010). Competency in integrative psychotherapy: Perspectives on training and supervision. *Psychotherapy Theory, Research, Practice, Training 47*(1), 3–11.

Bridle, C., Riemsma, R. P., Pattenden, J., Sowden, A. J., Mather, L., & Watt, I. S. et al. (2005). Systematic review of the effectiveness of health behavior interventions based on the transtheoretical model. *Psychology & Health, 20*(3), 283–301.

Brodeur, N., Rondeau, G., Brochu, S., Lindsay, J., & Phelps, J. (2009). Does the transtheoretical model predict attrition in domestic violence treatment programs? In C. M. Murphy & R. D. Maiuro (Eds.), *Motivational interviewing and stages of change in intimate partner violence* (pp. 159–179). New York: Springer.

Brown, L. S. (2009). Cultural competence: A new way of thinking about integration in therapy. *Journal of Psychotherapy Integration, 19*(4), 340–353.

Callaghan, R. C., Hathaway, A., Cunningham, J. A., Vettese, L. C., Wyatt, S., & Taylor, L. (2005). Does stage-of-change predict dropout in a culturally diverse sample of adolescents admitted to inpatient substance-abuse treatment? A test of the transtheoretical model. *Addictive Behaviors, 30*(9), 1834–1847.

Callaghan, R. C., Taylor, L., & Cunningham, J. A. (2007). Does progressive stage transition mean getting better? A test of the transtheoretical model in alcoholism recovery. *Addiction, 102*(10), 1588–1596.

Caspar, F. (2008). The current status of psychotherapy integration in Germany and Switzerland. *Journal of Psychotherapy Integration, 18*(1), 74–78.

Corsini, R. J., & Wedding, D. (2008). *Current psychotherapies* (8th ed.). Belmont. CA: Brooks/Cole–Cengage.

Dollard, J., & Miller, N. (1950). *Personality and psychotherapy: An analysis in terms of learning, thinking, and culture.* New York: McGraw-Hill.

Eubanks-Carter, C., Burckell, L. A., & Goldfried, M. R. (2005). Future directions in psychotherapy integration. In J. C. Norcross & M. R. Goldfried (Eds.), *Handbook of psychotherapy integration* (2nd ed., pp. 503–521). New York: Oxford University Press .

Evers, K. E., Prochaska, J. O., Van Marter, D. F., Johnson, J. L., & Prochaska, J. M. (2007). Transtheoretical-based bullying prevention effectiveness trials in middle schools and high schools. *Educational Research, 49*(4), 397–414.

Garfield, S. L., & Kurtz, R. (1977). A study of eclectic views. *Journal of Clinical and Consulting Psychology, 45*, 78–83.

Gazabon, S. A., Morokoff, P. J., Harlow, L. L., Ward, R. M., & Quina, K. (2007). Applying the transtheoretical model to ethnically diverse women at risk for HIV. *Health Education & Behavior, 34*(2), 297–314.

Gold, J. R., & Wachtel, P. L. (1993). Cyclical psychodynamics. In G. Stricker & J. R. Gold (Eds.), *Comprehensive handbook of psychotherapy integration* (pp. 59–72). New York: Plenum.

Gold, J., & Wachtel, P. L. (2006). Cyclical psychodynamics. In G. Stricker & J. Gold (Eds.), *A casebook of psychotherapy integration* (pp. 79–87). Washington, DC: American Psychological Association.

Guo, B., Aveyard, P., Fielding, A., & Sutton, S. (2009). Do the transtheoretical model processes of change, decisional balance and temptation predict stage movement? Evidence from smoking cessation in adolescents. *Addiction, 104*(5), 828–838.

Heather, N., Hönekopp, J., Smailes, D., & Ukatt research team. (2009). Progressive stage transition does mean getting better: A further test of the transtheoretical model in recovery from alcohol problems. *Addiction, 104*(6), 949–958.

Iwakabe, S. (2008). Psychotherapy integration in Japan. *Journal of Psychotherapy Integration, 18*(1), 103–125.

Johnson, S. S., Paiva, A. L., Cummins, C. O., Johnson, J. L., Dyment, S. J., Wright, J. A., Prochaska, J. O., Prochaska, J. M., & Sherman, K. (2008). Transtheoretical model-based multiple behavior intervention for weight management: Effectiveness on a population basis. *Preventive Medicine: An International Journal Devoted to Practice and Theory, 46*(3), 238–246.

Kennedy, K., & Gregoire, T. K. (2009). Theories of motivation in addiction treatment: Testing the relationship of the transtheoretical model of change and self-determination theory. *Journal of Social Work Practice in the Addictions*, *9*(2), 163–183.

Kleinjan, M., Brug, J., Van den Eijnden, R. J. J. M., Vermulst, A. A., Van Zundert, R. M. P., & Engels, R. C. M. E. (2008). Associations between the transtheoretical processes of change, nicotine dependence and adolescent smokers' transition through the stages of change. *Addiction*, *103*(2), 331–338.

Kwee, M. G. T. (1984). *Klinische multimodal gedragstherapie*. Lisse, Holland: Swets and Zeitlinger.

Lazarus, A. A. (1971). *Behavior therapy and beyond*. New York: McGraw-Hill.

Lazarus, A. A. (1987). The multimodal approach with adult outpatients. In M. S. Jacobson (Ed.), *Psychotherapists in clinical practice* (pp. 286–326). New York: Guilford.

Lazarus, A. A. (1988). A multimodal perspective on problems of sexual desire. In S. R. Leiblum & R. C. Rosen (Eds.), *Sexual desire disorders* (pp. 145–167). New York: Guilford.

Lazarus, A. A. (1989). *The practice of multimodal therapy*. Baltimore: Johns Hopkins University Press.

Lazarus, A. A. (1993). Tailoring the therapeutic relationship, or being an authentic chameleon. *Psychotherapy*, *30*, 404–407.

Lazarus, A. A. (1995). Different types of eclecticism and integration: Let's be aware of the dangers. *Journal of Psychotherapy Integration*, *5*, 27–39.

Lazarus, A. A. (1997). *Brief but comprehensive therapy: The multimodal way*. New York: Springer.

Lazarus, A. A. (2000). Multimodal strategies with adults. In J. Carlson & L. Sperry (Eds.), *Brief therapy with individuals and couples* (pp. 106–124). Phoenix, AZ: Zeig, Tucker and Theisen.

Lazarus, A. A. (2001). A brief personal account of CT (conditioning therapy), BT behavior therapy, and CBT (cognitive-behavior therapy): Spanning three continents. In W. T. O'Donohue & D. A. Henderson (Eds.), *A history of the behavioral therapies: Founder's personal histories* (pp. 152–162). Reno, NV: Context Press.

Lazarus, A. A. (2005a). Multimodal therapy. In J. C. Norcross & M. R. Goldfried (Eds.), *Handbook of psychotherapy integration* (2nd ed., pp. 105–120). New York: Oxford University Press.

Lazarus, A. A. (2005b). Multimodal therapy. In R. J. Corsini & D. Wedding (Eds.), *Current psychotherapies* (7th ed., pp. 337–371). Belmont, CA: Brooks/Cole–Thomson.

Lazarus, A. A. (2007). On necessity and sufficiency in counseling and psychotherapy (revisited). *Psychotherapy: Theory, Research, Practice, Training*, *44*(3), 253–256.

Lazarus, A. A. (2008). Technical eclecticism and multimodal therapy. In J. L. Lebow (Ed.), *Twenty-first century psychotherapies: Contemporary approaches to theory and practice* (pp. 424–452). Hoboken, NJ: John Wiley.

Lazarus, A. A., & Lazarus, C. N. (1991). *Multimodal life history inventory*. Champaign, IL: Research Press.

Mitchell, S. (1993). *Hope and dread in psychoanalysis*. New York: Basic Books.

Muller, F. J. (2008). Psychotherapy in Argentina: Theoretical orientation and clinical practice. *Journal of Psychotherapy Integration*, *18*(4), 410–420.

Norcross, J. C., & Goldfried, M. R. (Eds.). (2005). *Handbook of psychotherapy integration* (2nd ed.). New York: Oxford University Press.

Norcross, J. C., & Prochaska, J. O. (1988). A study of eclectic (and integrative) views revisited. *Professional Psychology: Research and Practice*, *19*, 170–174.

Norcross, J. C., Karpiak, C. P., & Lister, K. M. (2005). What's an integrationist? A study of self-identified integrative and (occasionally) eclectic psychologists. *Journal of Clinical Psychology*, *61*, 1587–1594.

Norman, G. J., Velicer, W. F., Fava, J. L., & Prochaska, J. O. (2000). Cluster subtypes within stages of change in a representative sample of smokers. *Addictive Behaviors*, *25*, 183–204.

Opazo, R., & Bagladi, V. (2008). Integrative psychotherapy: From Chile with love. *Journal of Psychotherapy Integration*, *18*(1), 126–135.

Ornstein, E. D., & Ganzer, C. (2000). Strengthening the strengths perspective: An integrative relational approach. *Psychoanalytic Social Work*, *7*, 57–78.

Prochaska, J. O., & Diclemente, C. C. (1984). *The transtheoretical approach: Crossing the traditional boundaries of therapy*. Homewood, IL: Dow-Jones-Irwin.

Prochaska, J. O., & Diclemente, C. C. (2005). The transtheoretical approach. In J. C. Norcross & M. R. Goldfried (Eds.), *Handbook of psychotherapy integration* (2nd ed., pp. 147–171). New York: Oxford University Press.

Prochaska, J. O., Johnson, S., & Lee, P. (2009). The transtheoretical model of behavior change. In S. A. Shumaker, J. K. Ockene, & K. A. Riekert (Eds.), *The handbook of health behavior change* (3rd ed., pp. 59–83). New York: Springer.

Prochaska, J. O., & Norcross, J. C. (2010). *Systems of psychotherapy: A transtheoretical analysis* (7th ed.). Belmont, CA: Brooks/Cole–Cengage.

Randal, P., Simpson, A. I. F., & Laidlaw, T. (2003). Can recovery-focused multimodal psychotherapy facilitate symptom and function improvement in people with treatment-resistant psychotic illness? A comparison study. *Australian and New Zealand Journal of Psychiatry, 37*(6), 720–727.

Salmela, S., Poskiparta, M., Kasila, K., Vähäsarja, K., & Vanhala, M. (2009). Transtheoretical model-based dietary interventions in primary care: A review of the evidence in diabetes. *Health Education Research, 24*(2), 237–252.

Schottenbauer, M. A., Glass, C. R., & Arnkoff, D. B. (2005). In J. C. Norcross & M. R. Goldfried (Eds.), *Handbook of psychotherapy integration* (2nd ed., pp. 459–493). New York: Oxford University Press.

Schumann, A., Kohlmann, T., Rumpf, H., Hapke, U., John, U., & Meyer, C. (2005). Longitudinal relationships among transtheoretical model constructs for smokers in the precontemplation and contemplation stages of change. *Annals of Behavioral Medicine, 30*(1), 12–20.

Stricker, G., & Gold, J. (2005). Assimilative psychodynamic psychotherapy. In J. C. Norcross & M. R. Goldfried (Eds.), *Handbook of psychotherapy integration* (2nd ed., pp. 221–240). New York: Oxford University Press.

Van Dyk, G. A. J., & Nefale, M. C. (2005). The split-ego experience of Africans: Ubuntu therapy as a healing alternative. *Journal of Psychotherapy Integration, 15*(1), 48–66.

Vasco, A. B. (2008). Psychotherapy integration in Portugal. *Journal of Psychotherapy Integration, 18*(1), 70–73.

Wachtel, P. L. (1977). *Psychoanalysis and behavior therapy: Toward an integration.* New York: Basic Books.

Wachtel, P. L. (1991). From eclecticism to synthesis: Toward a more seamless psychotherapeutic integration. *Journal of Psychotherapy Integration, 1,* 43–54.

Wachtel, P. L. (1993). *Therapeutic communication: Principles and effective practice.* New York: Guilford.

Wachtel, P. L. (1997). *Psychoanalysis, behavior therapy, and the relational world.* Washington, DC: American Psychological Association.

Wachtel, P. L. (1999). *Race in the mind of America: Breaking the vicious circle between Blacks and Whites.* Florence, KY: Routledge.

Wachtel, P. L. (2007). *Commentary: Making invisibility visible—probing the interface between race and gender.* Washington, DC: American Psychological Association.

Wachtel, P. L. (2008). Psychotherapy from an international perspective. *Journal of Psychotherapy Integration, 18*(1), 66–69.

Wachtel, P. L., Kruk, J. C., & McKinney, M. K. (2005). Cyclical psychodynamics and integrative relational psychotherapy. In J. C. Norcross & M. R. Goldfried (Eds.), *Handbook of psychotherapy integration* (2nd ed., pp. 172–195). New York: Oxford University Press.

West, R. (2005). Time for a change: Putting the transtheoretical (stages of change) model to rest. *Addiction, 100*(8), 1036–1039.

Wilson, G. T., & Schlam, T. R. (2004). The transtheoretical model and motivational interviewing in the treatment of eating and weight disorders. *Clinical Psychology Review, 24*(3), 361–378.

Glossary

Many important terms used in the text are defined here. The theory or theorist that is associated with a definition is in parentheses. Words that are italicized in the definitions are defined in the glossary.

A-B-C model (REBT) The theory that individuals' problems stem not from activating events but from their beliefs about such events. People also experience emotional or behavioral consequences of the activating event.

acceptance (Rogers) Appreciating clients for who they are without valuing or judging them.

acceptance and commitment therapy (behavior) Behavioral techniques are combined with a focus on the client's use of language to eliminate distress. The focus is on accepting a feeling, event, or situation rather than avoiding it. Therapists help clients commit to behavior that fits with client values.

acting as if (Adler) In this technique, patients are asked to "act as if" a behavior will be effective. Patients are encouraged to try on a new role the way they might try on new clothing.

active imagination (Jung) A technique of analysis in which individuals actively focus on experiences or images (in dreams or fantasy), reporting changes in these images or experiences as they concentrate on them.

active schemas (cognitive) Cognitive schemas occurring in everyday events.

affective shift (cognitive) A shift in facial or bodily expressions of emotion or stress that indicates that a cognitive shift has just taken place, often a negative cognitive shift. Often an indication of a hot cognition.

Aha response (Adler) Developing a sudden insight into a solution to a problem as one becomes aware of one's beliefs and behaviors.

alignment (Minuchin) The way in which family members join or oppose each other in dealing with events.

all-or-nothing (cognitive; REBT) Engaging in black-or-white thinking; thinking in extremes, such as all good or all bad, with nothing in the middle.

alpha bias (feminist) The bias that occurs by separating women and men into two specific categories, thus running the risk of treating women as unequal to men. See also beta bias.

alternative narratives (narrative) The process of exploring strengths, special abilities, and aspirations of the family to tell a positive story with good outcomes rather than a problem-saturated story.

altruism (Anna Freud) A defense mechanism in which one learns to become helpful to avoid feeling helpless. Individuals learn that they can satisfy their own egos as well as the demands of society.

amplification (Jung) A process of using knowledge of the history and meaning of symbols to understand unconscious material, such as that arising from patients' dreams.

anal stage (Freud) The second stage of psychosexual development occurring between the ages of about 18 months and 3 years. The anal area becomes the main source of pleasure.

androgyny Possessing both masculine and feminine psychological traits, usually in relatively equal amounts.

anima (Jung) The archetype representing the feminine component of the male personality.

animus (Jung) The archetype that represents the masculine component of the female personality.

anorexia A disorder in which individuals are unable to eat food, may have a severe decrease in appetite, and have an intense fear of becoming obese even when emaciated. Anorexia is diagnosed when individuals lose at least 25% of their normal weight.

anticathexes (Freud) The control or restraint exercised by the ego over the id to keep id impulses out of consciousness.

anxiety An unpleasant feeling of fear and/or apprehension accompanied by physiological changes such as fast pulse, quick breathing, sweating, flushing, muscle aches, and stomach tension.

archetypes (Jung) Universal images or symbols that are pathways from the collective unconscious to the conscious. They take a person's reactions and put them into a pattern, such as a mother (Earth Mother) or animal instincts (shadow).

art therapy A method of helping patients deal with emotional conflicts and awareness of their feelings by using a variety of art media, such as paints, crayons, paper, or sculpting materials.

assertiveness training (behavior; cognitive; feminist; REBT) A technique to teach clients to effectively express positive and negative feelings to others so that they may achieve desired purposes.

assessing motivation (solution-focused) Attention paid to the degree of client motivation to make changes. Scaling questions are often used to assess the motivation for change.

assets (Adler) Assessing the strengths of individuals' lifestyle is an important part of lifestyle assessment, as is assessment of early recollections and basic mistakes.

assimilative approach (integrative) A psychotherapeutic approach in which personality theory and the psychotherapeutic techniques of one theory is the major approach, and one or more other theories are used to supplement it.

atman (Asian) A concept of universality in which the self is not seen as an individual, but as part of the entire universe.

attachment theory (psychoanalysis) The study of infant-mother relationships and patterns of relating to the mother.

attentional processes (behavior) The act of perceiving or watching something and learning from it.

attitude modulation (Frankl) A technique used to change motivations from anxious ones to healthy ones by questioning the client's

rationale and by removing obstacles that interfere with being responsible.

attitudes (Jung) Two ways of interacting with the world see *introversion* and *extraversion*.

audience (psychodrama) People present during the enactment who observe the psychodrama. They may be involved at some point as protagonists or auxiliaries.

authenticity (existential) Being genuine and real, as well as aware of one's being. Authentic individuals deal with moral choices, the meaning of life, and being human.

automatic thoughts (cognitive) Notions or ideas that occur without effort or choice, are usually distorted, and lead to emotional responses. Automatic thoughts can be organized into core beliefs or cognitive schemas.

auxiliaries (psychodrama) Members of a group or audience who play significant roles in the life of the protagonist.

auxiliary function (Jung) The function that takes over when the superior function is not operating. Functions include thinking, feeling, sensing, and intuiting.

avoiding the tar baby (Adler) Although the term *tar baby* has come to have racial and other meanings, Adler used *tar baby* to refer to the therapist being careful when discussing a sticky (tar) issue that is both significant for the patient and causes problems for the patient. This way the therapist does not fall into a trap that the patient sets by using faulty assumptions.

awareness (gestalt) Attending to and observing what is happening in the present. Types of awareness include sensations and actions, feelings, wants, and values or assessments.

BASIC I.D. (multimodal) An acronym that includes the seven fundamental concepts of multimodal therapy behavior, affect, sensation, imagery, cognition, interpersonal relationships, drugs/biology.

basic mistakes (Adler) Self-defeating aspects of individuals' lifestyles that may affect their later behavior. Such mistakes often include avoidance of others, seeking power, a desperate need for security, or faulty values.

being-in-the-world (existential) Derived from the German word *Dasein*, this term refers to examining oneself, others, and one's relationship with the world, thus attaining higher levels of consciousness.

beta bias (feminist) Bias that occurs when treating men and women as identical, thus ignoring important differences between the lives of women and men. See also *alpha bias*.

bibliotherapy A therapeutic technique in which the therapist chooses readings for the client for purposes such as gaining insight into problems, learning new information, and increasing self-esteem.

bioenergetic analysis (body) Developed principally by Alexander Lowen, this is a method of understanding personality in terms of the body and its energy flow. Attention is given to physiology, breathing, and bodily movement.

bipolar self (Kohut) The tension between the grandiose self ("I deserve to get what I want") and an idealized view of the parents forms the two poles of the bipolar self.

birth order (Adler) The idea that place in the family constellation (such as being the youngest child) can have an impact on one's later personality and functioning.

body armor (body) A protective mechanism in the individual to deal with the punishment that comes from acting on instinctual demands, such as defecating in public.

body awareness (body) Patients may move or change positions and develop more awareness of their body.

body psychotherapy (body) A means of integrating psychotherapy and attention to and manipulation of bodily processes.

body reading (body) Systematic observations used to understand energy blockages and tensions within the body.

borderline personality disorder Characteristics include unstable interpersonal relationships and rapid mood changes over a short period of time. Behavior is often erratic, unpredictable, and impulsive in areas such as spending, eating, sex, or gambling. Emotional relationships tend to be intense, with individuals easily becoming angry or disappointed in the relationship.

boundary marking (Minuchin) A technique to change boundaries or interactions among individual family members. An example would be

to change the seating of family members in therapy.

boundary permeability (Minuchin) The degree to which boundaries are flexible among family members and the nature of the contact that family members have with each other. See enmeshed and disengaged families.

boundary situation (existential) An urgent experience that compels an individual to deal with an existential situation.

bridging (multimodal) Being aware of and responding to a client's current modality before introducing another modality to the client.

bulimia Binge eating and inappropriate methods of preventing weight gain, such as vomiting and laxatives, characterize bulimia.

catastrophizing (cognitive; REBT) Exaggerating the potential or real consequences of an event and becoming fearful of the consequences.

catching oneself (Adler) In this technique, patients learn to notice that they are performing behaviors they wish to change. When they catch themselves, they may have an Aha response.

catharsis (psychoanalysis; psychodrama) The expression of feelings that have been previously repressed.

cathect (Freud) Investing psychic energy in a mental representation of a person, behavior, or idea. Infants cathect in objects that gratify their needs.

challenging absolutes (cognitive; REBT) Statements that include words such as *everyone*, *never*, *no one*, and *always* are usually exaggerations, which therapists point out to the client.

characterization (narrative) The people in the story (problem) are the characters. The client is often the protagonist as well as the narrator. People who have conflicts with the client are often the antagonists.

circular questioning (Milan group) An interviewing technique designed to elicit differences in perceptions about events or relationships from different family members.

classical conditioning (behavior) A type of learning in which a neutral stimulus is presented repeatedly with one that reflexively elicits a particular response so the neutral stimulus eventually elicits the response itself (also called *respondent conditioning*).

coalitions (Minuchin) Alliances or affiliations between family members against another family member.

cognitive distortions (cognitive) Systematic errors in reasoning, often stemming from early childhood errors in reasoning; an indication of inaccurate or ineffective information processing.

cognitive rehearsal (cognitive) A means of using imagination to think about having a positive interaction or experience; for example, to imagine a positive interaction with one's future in-laws.

cognitive schemas (cognitive) Ways of thinking that comprise a set of core beliefs and assumptions about how the world operates.

cognitive shift (cognitive) Basically a biased interpretation of life experiences, causing individuals to shift their focus from unbiased to more biased information about themselves or their world.

cognitive spiral (cognitive) The downward spiral of depression in which basic beliefs and schemas can set off a series of negative reactions that may bring about a depressed feeling.

cognitive triad (cognitive) The negative views that individuals have about themselves, their world, and their future.

collective unconscious (Jung) That part of the unconscious that contains memories and images that are universal to the human species, in contrast to the personal unconscious, which is based upon individual experience. Humans have an inherited tendency to form representations of mythological motives, which may vary greatly but maintain basic patterns. Thus individuals may view the universe in similar ways by thinking, feeling, and reacting to common elements such as the moon or water.

common factors (Introduction, Comparison) Factors that are common to changes that take place in psychotherapy and counseling. These include participant and relationship factors.

complementary communication (family systems) A relationship in which there is inequality between two or more members. One is usually submissive to the other.

complex (Jung) A group of associated feelings, thoughts, and memories that have intense emotional content. Complexes may have elements from the personal unconscious and collective unconscious.

complimenting (solution-focused) The client is encouraged as the therapist makes positive statements about client actions. Berg and De Jong discuss three types of complimenting direct, indirect, and self-compliments.

compulsions An irresistible impulse to repeat behaviors continually.

conditional positive regard (Rogers) Receiving praise, attention, or approval from others as a result of behaving in accordance with the expectations of others.

conditionality or conditions of worth (Rogers) The process of evaluating one's own experience based on values or beliefs that others hold.

confluence (gestalt) A contact boundary disturbance in which the separation between oneself and others becomes muted or unclear. Thus, it can be difficult to distinguish one's own perceptions or values from those of another person.

congruence (Rogers) The harmony that takes place when there is no disagreement between individuals' experiences and their views of themselves. For therapists, *congruence* refers to matching one's inner experience with external expressions.

conjoint therapy A type of couples therapy in which one therapist sees both members of the couple at the same time.

conscious or consciousness (Freud) That portion of the mind or mental functioning that individuals are aware of, including sensations and experiences.

consciousness-raising (CR) groups (feminist) A creation of the women's movement in which women met regularly to discuss their lives and issues in them.

constructivism Believing that individuals create their own views or constructs of events or relationships in their own lives.

contact (gestalt) The relationship between "me" and others. Contact involves feeling a connection with others or the world outside oneself while maintaining a separation from it.

contact boundaries (gestalt) The boundaries that distinguish one person (or one aspect of a person) from an object, another person, or another aspect of oneself. Examples include body boundaries, value boundaries, familiarity boundaries, and expressive boundaries.

contingency contract (behavior) A written agreement between the therapist and the client that specifies the consequence that will follow from performing a target behavior.

control theory (reality) A view that individuals try to control the world and themselves as a part of that world in order to satisfy their psychological needs.

conversion reaction A disorder in which a psychological disturbance takes a physical form, such as when the arms or legs are paralyzed, and there is no physiological explanation.

coping question (solution-focused) These questions ask about successful experiences that family members have had in dealing with a problem. They highlight the family members' ability to cope with problems.

countertransference (psychoanalysis) 1. The irrational or neurotic reactions of a therapist toward the patient. 2. The therapist's conscious and unconscious feelings toward the patient. 3. A way of understanding how people in the patient's past may have felt.

covert behavior Behaviors that others cannot directly perceive, such as thinking and feeling.

creating images (Adlerian) The techniques to form a mental picture of doing something, which can have more impact than reminding oneself mentally.

cultural interventions (feminist) Understanding the client's culture and helping him or her make use of interventions that may include the use of lawyers, social agencies, families, or taking action in some way.

cyclical psychodynamics (integrative) An example of the theoretical integration approach to psychotherapy that was developed by Paul Wachtel. Concepts from psychoanalytic theory are combined with those from behavior therapy (and also cognitive and family systems approaches). The cyclical aspect of this view refers to the belief that psychological problems create problems in behavior, and problems in behavior create psychological conflicts or problems.

dance movement therapy A method of helping individuals integrate psychological and physiological processes so that they can better understand their own feelings, thoughts, and memories by expressing themselves through movement or dance.

decatastrophizing (cognitive; REBT) A "what if" technique, in which clients are asked, "What if X happened, what would you do?" It is designed to explore actual rather than feared events.

defense mechanisms (Freud) A means that the ego uses to fight off instinctual outbursts of the id or injunctions by the superego. Ten common ego defense mechanisms are described in Chapter 2.

deflection (gestalt) A contact boundary disturbance in which individuals avoid meaningful contact by being indirect or vague rather than by being direct.

delusions Beliefs that are contrary to reality and that are firmly held despite evidence that they are inaccurate.

denial (Freud) A defense mechanism in which individuals may distort or not acknowledge what they think, feel, or see; for example, not believing that a relative has been killed in an auto accident.

depression An emotional state characterized by deep sadness, feelings of worthlessness, guilt, and withdrawal from others. Other symptoms include difficulty in sleeping, loss of appetite or sexual desire, and loss of interest in normal activities. When not accompanied by manic episodes, it is usually referred to as major depression or unipolar depression.

dereflection (Frankl) A technique in which clients focus away from their problems instead of on them to reduce anxiety.

deserted island fantasy technique (multimodal) A fantasy experience in which clients are asked what the therapist would learn if he or she were alone with the client on a deserted island. It is designed to help the therapist learn more about the client's seven modalities.

detriangulation (Bowen) The process of withdrawing from a family member, usually by a therapist, so as not to be drawn into alliances of one person against another.

dharma (Asian) Rules that describe goodness and appropriate behavior.

dialectical behavior therapy (behavior therapy) An research supported therapy designed for the treatment of suicidal patients and those with borderline disorder. Mindfulness values and meditation techniques have been incorporated into this treatment.

differentiation (Bowen) The process of differentiating one's thinking from one's feeling; the opposite of *fusion*.

director (psychodrama) The person who manages the participants in a psychodrama. The director initiates and organizes a psychodrama and works with the protagonist, auxiliaries, and audience.

discomfort anxiety (REBT) When individuals' comfort level is threatened and they feel they must get what they want (low frustration tolerance). There is a belief that if individuals don't get or do what they want, the results will be awful or catastrophic.

discrimination (behavior) Responding differently to stimuli that are similar based on different cues or antecedent events.

disengaged (Minuchin) A reference to families in which members are isolated or feel unconnected to each other. Boundaries are rigid and nonpermeable.

displacement (Freud) A defense mechanism in which individuals place their feelings not on a dangerous object or person but on one who may be safe. For example, it may be safer to express anger at a friend than at a boss who has been angry with you.

double bind (family systems) A view that when an individual receives an important message with two different meanings and is unable to respond to it, the individual is in an impossible situation. If such messages are repeated over time, some family therapists believe individuals may begin to show signs of schizophrenia.

double technique (psychodrama) A role in which an auxiliary takes the part of the protagonist and expresses his perception of the protagonist's thoughts or feelings.

drama therapy A means of making psychological change by involving individuals in experiences that are related to theater. Sometimes individuals may enact their own spontaneous drama, play the parts of a play that has been written, or observe a play and discuss it. Psychodrama is considered to be one form of drama therapy.

dreams (Jung) Arising from unconscious creativity, "big" dreams represent symbolic material from the collective unconscious; "little" dreams reflect day-to-day activity and may come from the personal unconscious.

drive (Freud) A physiological state of tension, such as hunger, sex, or elimination, that motivates an individual to perform actions to reduce the tension.

drug abuse Using a drug to the extent that individuals have difficulty meeting social and occupational obligations.

early maladaptive schemas (cognitive) Long-standing schemas that individuals assume to be true about themselves and their world. These schemas are resistant to change and cause difficulties in individuals' lives.

early recollections (Adler) Memories of actual incidents that patients recall from their childhood. Adlerians use this information to make inferences about current behavior of children or adults.

eclecticism As applied to psychotherapy, an approach that combines theories or techniques from a wide variety of therapeutic approaches.

ego (Freud) A means of mediating between one's instincts or drives and the external world.

ego (Jung) An expression of personality that includes thoughts, feelings, and behaviors of which we are conscious.

ego ideal (Freud) In the child, a representation of values that are approved of by parents. It is present in the superego as a concern with movement toward perfectionistic goals.

ego anxiety (REBT) Individuals' sense of self-worth is threatened and they feel that they must perform well. There is a belief that if individuals don't get or do what they want, the results will be awful or catastrophic.

Eigenwelt (existential) A way of relating to one's "own world." It refers to being aware of oneself and how we relate to ourselves.

emotional cutoff (Bowen) Given too much stress in a family due to overinvolvement of parents, children may withdraw or cut themselves off emotionally from the family.

empathy (Rogers) To enter the world of another individual without being influenced by one's own views and values is to be empathic with the individual. The therapist, when being empathic, is attuned to the experience, feelings, and sensitivities of the client.

empty chair A technique developed by gestalt therapists and adapted by other theorists in which the patient is asked to play different roles in two chairs. Dialogues between different aspects of the client can then take place.

enactment (family systems) A therapeutic procedure in which families are asked to act out a conflict so that the therapist can work with the actual conflict rather than a report of it.

enactment (gestalt) In enactment, the patient may act out a previous experience or a characteristic. If the patient says he feels like a rat for cheating on his wife, the therapist may ask him to act like a rat.

encounter (psychodrama) The dialogue that takes place between two individuals or two aspects of the same individual upon meeting another individual or another part of themselves.

encounter group (Rogers) A group designed to promote constructive insight, sensitivity to others, and personal growth among its members. The leader facilitates the interactions of the group members.

encouragement (Adler) An important therapeutic technique to build a relationship and to foster client change. Supporting clients in changing beliefs and behaviors is a part of encouragement.

enmeshed (Minuchin) A reference to families in which members are overconcerned and overinvolved in each others' lives. Boundaries are highly permeable.

equifinality (family systems) The ability of a system to arrive at the same destination from different paths or conditions.

eros (Freud) The life instinct, derived from libidinal energy, in opposition to the death instinct (thanatos).

evidence-based psychotherapy or EBP (Introduction, Comparison) Therapies that have been tested to be effective are said to be evidence based. Strict criteria for thorough research procedures are used to determine whether or not therapy is effective. Now replaced by term - *research supported psychological treatments.*

exaggeration (dance movement) Exaggerating a movement so that one can experience feelings

related to the movement, such as anger at the shaking of a fist.

exception-seeking questions (solution focused) Therapists ask about exceptions to the problem. When is the problem not there and what is life like when the problem is not there?

exercises (gestalt) Specific techniques that have been developed to be used in group or individual therapy.

existentialism A philosophical view that emphasizes the importance of existence, including one's responsibility for one's own psychological existence. Related themes include living and dying, freedom, responsibility to self and others, meaningfulness in life, and authenticity.

experiments (gestalt) Creative approaches or techniques used by the therapist to deal with an impasse in therapy brought about by the client's difficulty in achieving awareness.

exposure and ritual prevention (EX/RP) (behavior) A treatment method used primarily with obsessive-compulsive disorders in which patients are exposed to the feared stimulus for an hour or more at a time. They are then asked to refrain from participating in rituals, such as continually checking the door to see if they have closed it.

externalizing the problem (narrative) Making the problem, not the child or family, the opponent. Thus, removing Guilt becomes the focus of therapy rather than the person's guilty feelings.

extinction (behavior) The process of no longer presenting a reinforcement. It is used to decrease or eliminate certain behaviors.

extraversion (Jung) One of the two major attitudes or orientations of personality. Extraversion is associated with valuing objective experience and perceiving and responding to the external world rather than thinking about one's own perceptions or internal world.

eye movement desensitization and reprocessing (EMDR) (behavior) Designed first for post-traumatic stress, EMDR requires that the client visualize an upsetting memory and accompanying physical sensations. The client repeats negative self-statements that he or she associates with the scene. The patient follows the therapist's finger as it moves rapidly back and forth. After completing the eye movements, the client stops thinking about the scene. The procedure is repeated again and again until the client's anxiety is reduced.

factorial designs A research method that can study more than one variable at a time.

false self (Winnicott) When good-enough mothering is not available in infancy, children may act as they believe they are expected to. Basically, they adopt their mother's self rather than develop their own. It is used in contrast with the *true self*.

family constellation (Adler) The number and birth order, as well as the personality characteristics of members of a family; important in determining lifestyle.

family life chronology (Satir) A way of recording significant events in a family's development.

family projection process (Bowen) A means of projecting or transmitting a parental conflict to one or more children.

family sculpting (Satir) A technique in which family members are physically molded or directed to take characteristic poses to represent a view of family relationships.

family structure (Minuchin) The rules that have been developed in the course of family life to determine which members interact with which other members and in what way.

family systems therapy A type of family therapy in which the entire family is seen as a unit or as a system. Focus is often on the interaction of family members.

family therapy Any psychotherapeutic treatment of the family to improve psychological functioning among its members. Most major theories of psychotherapy have applications to family therapy.

feedback (family systems) A communication pattern in which information about the consequences of an event is reintroduced into the system. See *negative feedback* and *positive feedback*.

feeling (Jung) A function of personality in which individuals attend to subjective experiences of pleasure, pain, anger, or other feelings. Its polar opposite is *thinking*.

figure (gestalt) That part of a field that stands out in good contour clearly from the ground.

firing order (multimodal) The sequence of modalities that occurs when an individual perceives an event. For example, interpersonal-sensation-imagery.

first-order change (family systems) A temporary change in the family system to solve a specific problem. Such changes do not alter the basic system of the family. See also *second-order change*.

flooding (behavior) Prolonged in vivo or imagined exposure to stimuli that evoke high levels of anxiety, with no ability to avoid or escape the stimuli. Implosive therapy uses flooding.

free association (psychoanalysis) The patient relates feelings, fantasies, thoughts, memories, and recent events to the analyst spontaneously and without censoring them. These associations give the analyst clues to the unconscious processes of the patient.

friendly involvement (reality) The process of building a relationship with a client that serves as the underpinnings of reality therapy.

fully functioning person (Rogers) A person who meets his or her own need for positive regard rather than relying on the expectations of others. Such individuals are open to new experiences and not defensive.

functional analysis (behavior) Specifying goals and treatment by assessing antecedents and consequences of behavior. Analyze what is maintaining the behavior and propose hypotheses about contributors to the behavior. This information is used to guide the treatment of the behavior and to further specify goals.

functions (Jung) Four ways of perceiving and responding to the world see *thinking*, *feeling*, *sensing*, and *intuiting*.

fusion (family systems) A merging or meshing of thoughts and feelings in a family member; the opposite of *differentiation*. It is most commonly associated with Bowen's theory.

future projection (psychodrama) Playing out a situation that could occur at some time in the future; for example, playing out an interaction with a future mother-in-law.

gender role intervention (feminist) Such interventions deal with reinforcing or helping clients' interventions or helping them deal with gender role obstacles in their lives. Some interventions provide insight into social or political issues that serve as obstacles to clients.

gender-schema (feminist) A set of mental associations in which individuals are seen from the point of view of their gender, as opposed to other characteristics.

generalization (behavior) Transferring the response to one type of stimuli to similar stimuli.

generalized anxiety disorder One of a group of anxiety disorders, it is characterized by a persistent pervasive state of tension. Physical symptoms may include a pounding heart, fast pulse and breathing, sweating, muscle aches, and stomach upset. Individuals may be easily distracted and fearful that something bad is going to happen.

genital stage (Freud) The final stage of psychosexual development, which usually starts about the age of 12 and continues throughout life. The focus of sexual energy is toward members of the other sex rather than toward oneself.

genogram (family systems) A method of charting a family's relationship system. It is essentially a family tree in which ages, sex, marriage dates, and similar information may be diagrammed.

genuineness (Rogers) Similar to congruence, genuineness in the therapist refers to being one's actual self with the client, not phony or affected.

gestalt psychology A psychological approach that studies the organization of experience into patterns or configurations. Gestalt psychologists believe that the whole is greater than the sum of its parts and study, among other issues, the relationship of a figure to its background.

good-enough mother (Winnicott) A mother who adapts to her infant's gestures and needs during early infancy and gradually helps the infant develop independence.

grief (interpersonal therapy) Although a normal process, grief can contribute to depression. When the loss is severe and lengthy or there is more than one loss, this is particularly true.

ground (gestalt) The background that contrasts with the figure in the perceptions of a field.

grounding (body) A concept developed by Alexander Lowen that emphasizes being in contact with the ground literally, through feet and legs, as well as figuratively being grounded in the real world.

guided discovery (cognitive; REBT) A series of questions designed to help the client arrive at logical answers to and conclusions about a certain hypothesis; also called *Socratic dialogue*.

hallucinations Perceiving (seeing, hearing, feeling, tasting, or smelling) things or people that are not there.

hard techniques (body) A method of asking the patient to assume an uncomfortable or painful position or of touching a patient in a somewhat painful way, which may bring about intense emotional responses.

Hatha yoga (Asian) Deals with the physiological discipline required in separating the self from thought processes.

hedonism A philosophical term referring to the concept of seeking pleasure and avoiding pain. In REBT, *responsible hedonism* refers to maintaining pleasure over the long term by avoiding short-term pleasures that may lead to pain, such as alcohol or cocaine.

heterosexism The view that being heterosexual is more normal and better than being homosexual, thus devaluing the lifestyle of gay lesbian, bisexeual, and transgendered individuals.

holding (Winnicott) A feeling of security that develops from the physical holding of the child; also used metaphorically to refer to a caring environment.

homeostasis (family systems) Balance or equilibrium in a system. Such a balance can bring about a stable environment in the system.

homework Specific behaviors or activities that clients are asked to do after therapy sessions.

homophobia The dislike, fear, or hatred of gay lesbian, bisexual, and transgendered people.

hot cognition (cognitive) A strong or highly charged thought or idea that produces powerful emotional reactions.

hot seat (gestalt) A form of group therapy in which individuals work one at a time with the therapist, and the audience observes, occasionally being asked to comment on the therapeutic process.

humanism A philosophy or value system in which human interests and dignity are valued and that takes an individualist, critical, and secular, as opposed to a religious or spiritual, perspective.

hysteria A disorder occurring when psychological disturbances take a physical form and there is no physiological explanation, such as an unexplained paralysis of the arms or legs. This term has been replaced by conversion reaction in common usage.

iatrogenic Refers to a psychological or physical disorder that is induced, aggravated, or made worse by the physician or psychotherapist.

id (Freud) The biological instincts, including sexual and aggressive impulses, that seek pleasure. At birth, the id represents the total personality.

identification (Freud) A defense mechanism in which individuals take on characteristics of another, often a parent, to reduce their own anxieties and internal conflicts. By identifying with the successful parent, an individual can feel successful, even though she has done little that might make her feel productive.

identification with the aggressor (Anna Freud) A defense mechanism in which the individual identifies with an opponent that he or she cannot master, taking on characteristics of that person.

identified patient (family systems) The person whom other members of the family identify as having the problem for which treatment is sought.

immediacy (Adler, gestalt) Communicating the experience of the therapist to the patient about what is happening in the moment.

implosive therapy (behavior) A type of prolonged intense exposure therapy in which the client imagines exaggerated scenes that include hypothesized stimuli.

in vivo (behavior) Latin for "in life," referring to therapeutic procedures that take place in the client's natural environment.

inactive schemas (cognitive) These are cognitive schemas that are triggered by special or unusual events.

incongruence (Rogers) The disharmony that takes place when there is a disagreement between individuals' experience and their view of themselves.

individuation (Jung) The process of integrating opposing elements of personality to become whole. It involves, in part, bringing

unconscious contents into relationship with consciousness.

individuation (object relations) The process of becoming an individual, becoming aware of oneself.

inferior function (Jung) The function (thinking, feeling, sensing, intuiting) that is least well-developed in an individual and may be repressed and unconscious, showing itself in dreams or fantasies.

inferiority (Adler) Feelings of inadequacy and incompetence that develop during infancy and serve as the basis for striving for superiority in order to overcome feelings of inferiority.

inferiority complex (Adler) A strong and pervasive belief that one is not as good as other people. It is usually an exaggerated sense of feelings of inadequacy and insecurity that may result in being defensive or anxious.

instinct (Freud) Basic drives such as hunger, thirst, sex, and aggression that must be fulfilled in order to maintain physical or psychological equilibrium.

intellectualization (Freud) A defense mechanism in which emotional issues are not dealt with directly but rather are handled indirectly by abstract thought.

interpersonal deficits (interpersonal therapy) Social isolation or lack of social skills may cause loneliness and related problems.

interpersonal disputes (interpersonal therapy) Ongoing struggles, disagreements, or arguments with others can contribute to depression. The disputes may occur in the family, at school, at work, or in other situations.

interpretation (Adler) Adlerians express insights to their patients that relate to patients' goals. Interpretations often focus on the family constellation and social interest.

interpretation (psychoanalysis) The process by which the psychoanalyst points out the unconscious meanings of a situation to a patient. Analysts assess their patients' ability to accept interpretations and bring them to conscious awareness.

interrater reliability The degree of agreement between or among raters about their observations of an individual or individuals.

intersection of multiple identities (feminist) Forces that affect the way gender is seen. For example, gender can be seen by examining views of social groups, examining power in relationships, and in understanding individual relationships.

intersubjectivity (psychoanalysis) The view that both analyst and patient influence each other in therapy.

intersubjectivity theory (psychoanalysis) An approach developed by self psychologists and other psychoanalysts that is influenced by constructivism. Emphasis is put on valuing the clients' perceptions and the therapeutic relationship.

intrapsychic processes (psychoanalysis) Impulses, ideas, conflicts, or other psychological phenomena that occur within the mind.

introjection (gestalt) A contact boundary disturbance in which individuals accept information or values from others without evaluating them or without assimilating them into one's personality.

introversion (Jung) One of the two major attitudes or orientations of personality. Introversion represents an orientation toward subjective experiencing and focusing on one's own perception of the external world.

intuiting (Jung) A personality function that stresses having a hunch or guess about something, which may arise from the unconscious. Its polar opposite is *sensing*.

invariant prescription (Milan group) A single directive given to parents, designed to create clear boundaries between parents and children, thus establishing distance between parents and children.

irrational belief (REBT) Unreasonable views or convictions that produce emotional and behavioral problems.

I-sharing (existential) The concept of "I-sharing," a positive term, is one that produces a sense of intimacy In "I-sharing" a sense of connection or fondness develops when people experience a moment in the same way that another does. This creates a sense of existential connectedness that is in contrast to existential isolation.

Jungian analyst A term used for individuals trained at institutions certified by the International Association for Analytic Psychology.

kairos (existential) A Greek word that refers to the critical point at which a disease is expected

to get better or worse. In psychotherapy, it refers to the appropriate timing of a therapeutic intervention.

karma (Asian) Movement from past incarnations that affects the present.

labeling (cognitive) Creating a negative view of oneself based on errors or mistakes that one has made. It is a type of overgeneralizing that affects one's view of oneself.

latency (Freud) Following the phallic stage, there is a relatively calm period before adolescence. When Oedipal issues are resolved, the child enters the latency period.

leagues (narrative) Lists of former clients with similar problems who can give encouragement to battle the problem that the client and others have in common through sharing their stories by letters, email, or a similar means of communicating. Typically, therapists organize and manage leagues.

libido (Freud) The basic driving force of personality, which includes sexual energy but is not limited to it.

life tasks (Adler) There are five basic obligations and opportunities occupation, society, love, self-development, and spiritual development. These are used to help determine therapeutic goals.

lifestyle (Adler) A way of seeking to fulfill particular goals that individuals set in their lives. Individuals use their own patterns of beliefs, cognitive styles, and behaviors as a way of expressing their style of life. Often style of life or lifestyle is a means for overcoming feelings of inferiority.

logotherapy (Frankl) A type of existential therapy that focuses on challenging clients to search for meaning in their lives. It is associated with the techniques of attitude modulation, dereflection, paradoxical intention, and socratic dialogue.

low frustration tolerance (REBT) Inability or difficulty in dealing with events or situations that do not go as planned; for example, getting very angry because someone does not do as you ask.

magnification (cognitive) A cognitive distortion in which an imperfection is exaggerated into something greater than it is.

mandala (Jung) A symbolic representation of the unified wholeness of the Self. Usually, it has four sections representing an effort to achieve wholeness in the four sections (such as the four directions of the winds).

mania or manic episodes   Individuals may demonstrate unfounded elation as indicated by making grandiose plans, being extremely talkative and easily distracted, and engaging in purposeless activity.

marital schism (family systems)   A situation in which one parent tries to undermine the worth of another by competing for sympathy or support from the children.

marital skew (family systems)   A situation in which the psychological disturbance of one parent dominates the family's interactions. An unreal situation for family members is created so that the family can deal with one member's disturbance.

maya (Asian)   A concept derived from Hindu and Buddhist philosophy referring to the distorted perception of reality and experience. Only by directing attention to one's awareness, through concentration or meditation, can reality and experience be perceived more accurately.

meditation (Asian)   Methods for controlling one's mental processes. In concentration meditation, the focus is on a stimulus, such as the act of breathing. In awareness meditation, the purpose is to examine consciousness and the mind.

meta-analysis   A method of statistically summarizing the results of a large number of studies.

methodology   A systematic application of procedures used in research investigations.

mimesis (Minuchin)   A process by which a therapist appears similar to family members by imitating body language, styles, or other features. A way of joining a family system and getting cooperation from a family.

mind reading (cognitive)   The belief that we know the thoughts in another person's mind.

mindfulness (Asian)   A way of experiencing oneself in the present. In doing so, one is relaxed, open, and alert.

mindfulness meditation (Asian)   Focusing awareness on breathing. By focusing on breathing, following the inhale and exhale, feelings and images are likely to arise.

mindmaps (solution-focused)   Diagrams or outlines of the session that are made during or after the session and used for the therapist to focus on organizing the goals and solutions to the problems.

minimization (cognitive)   Making a positive event much less important than it really is.

miracle questions (solution-focused)   What would be different if a miracle happened? Questions like this help to further define the goal.

mirror technique (psychodrama)   A process in which the auxiliary tries to copy the postures, expressions, and words of the protagonist so that the protagonist can view the perceptions of his or her behavior, as held by another person.

mirroring (Kohut)   When the parent shows the child that he or she is happy with the child, the child's grandiose self is supported. The parent reflects or mirrors the child's view of herself.

Mitwelt (existential)   A way in which individuals relate to the world by interacting socially with others. The focus is on human relationships rather than relationships that are biological or physical (*Umwelt*).

modeling (behavior)   A technique in which a client observes the behavior of another person (a model) and then uses the results of that observation.

modernism   Modernists take a rationalist view, believing that there is scientific truth, which can be achieved through advances in technology and science.

monodrama (psychodrama)   A dialogue with oneself in which an individual plays both parts in a scene by alternating between them.

Morita (Asian)   A Japanese therapy designed to help patients redirect tension away from themselves.

motivational processes (behavior)   For observations to be put into action and then continued for some time, reinforcement must be present. Reinforcement brings about motivation.

motor reproduction processes (behavior)   This refers to translating what one has seen into action using motor skills.

multimodal (integrative)   A therapeutic approach developed by Arnold Lazarus that uses personality theory concepts from social learning theory and takes techniques from many other theories, which it applies in a manner that is consistent with social learning theory. The seven major modalities are represented in the acronym BASIC I.D.

multiple identities (feminist) There are many forces that affect the way that gender is seen these include ethnicity, social class, gender orientation, disabilities, and other characteristics.

muscular armor (body) A protective mechanism in the individual to deal with the punishment that comes from acting on instinctual demands, such as defecating in public.

music therapy Patients may listen to or participate in musical experiences through singing or using musical instruments to improve emotional expression, reduce stress, or deal nonverbally with other issues.

musterbation (REBT) Albert Ellis's phrase to characterize the behavior of clients who are inflexible and absolutistic in their thinking, maintaining that they must not fail or that they must have their way.

Naikan (Asian) A Japanese therapy in which patients focus on their mistakes in past relationships to improve relationships with others so that they may contribute to society.

narcissistic personality disorder A pattern of self-importance; need for admiration from others and lack of empathy for others are common characteristics of individuals with this disorder. Boasting or being pretentious and feeling that one is superior to others and deserves recognition are also prominent characteristics.

narradrama (narrative) The combination of drama therapy and narrative therapy in which individuals can act out their stories.

needs (reality) Essential to reality therapy, psychological needs include desires for belonging, power, freedom, and fun.

negative cognitive shift (cognitive) A state in which individuals ignore positive information relevant to themselves and focus on negative information about themselves. See *cognitive shift*.

negative feedback (family systems) Information that flows back to a system to reduce behavior that causes disequilibrium.

negative prediction (cognitive) Believing that something bad is going to happen, even though there is no evidence to support this prediction.

neurosis A large group of disorders characterized by unrealistic anxiety, fears, or obsessions. They are contrasted with more severe *psychotic* disorders.

neurotic anxiety (existential) Anxiety that is out of proportion to a particular event. It is often an indication that an individual is not living authentically and may fail to make choices and assume responsibility.

normal anxiety (existential) Anxiety arising from the nature of being human and dealing with unforeseen forces (the *thrown condition*).

object A term used in psychoanalytic theory to refer, usually, to an important person in a child's life.

object cathexis (Freud) The investment of psychic energy or libido in objects outside the self, such as a person or activity. Such investment is designed to reduce needs.

object relations A study of significant others or love objects in a person's life, focusing on childhood views of the relationship (usually unconsciously).

observational learning (behavior) A type of learning in which people are influenced by observing the behaviors of another.

obsessions Pervasive and uncontrollable recurring thoughts that interfere with day-to-day functioning.

obsessive-compulsive disorder Persistent and uncontrollable thoughts or feelings in which individuals feel compelled to repeat behaviors again and again.

Oedipus complex (Freud) The unconscious sexual desire of the male child for his mother, along with feelings of hostility or fear toward the father. This conflict occurs in the phallic stage.

one-person psychology (psychoanalysis) The view that the patient is influenced by the analyst, but the analyst is not influenced by the patient.

operant conditioning (behavior) A type of learning in which behavior is increased or decreased by systematically changing its consequences.

operational definition An empirical definition that seeks to specify procedures that are used to measure a variable or to distinguish it from others.

oral stage (Freud) The initial stage of psychosexual development, lasting about 18 months. Focus is on gratification through eating and sucking that involves the lips, mouth, and throat.

orgone (body) A physical force that is supposed to power all physiological and psychological functions; developed by Wilhelm Reich.

outcome research A systematic investigation of the effectiveness of a theory of psychotherapy or a technique of psychotherapy or a comparison of techniques or theories of psychotherapy; in contrast to *process research.*

overgeneralization (cognitive) An example of distorted thinking that occurs when individuals make a rule based on a few negative or isolated events and then apply it broadly.

overt behavior Actions that can be directly observed by others.

paradoxical intention A therapeutic strategy in which clients are instructed to engage in and exaggerate behaviors they seek to change. By prescribing the symptom, therapists make patients more aware of their situation and help them achieve distance from the symptoms. For example, a patient who is afraid of mice may be asked to exaggerate his fear of mice, or a patient who hoards paper may be asked to exaggerate that behavior so that living becomes difficult. In this way individuals can become more aware of and more distant from their symptoms.

participant factors (Introduction, Comparison) In a common factors approach, characteristics of the client or therapist, such as gender, ethnicity, attachment style, coping style, resistance, and expectations.

patient-focused research A way of monitoring the progress of clients and then using this information to develop treatment methods.

penis envy (Freud) A woman's desire to be like a man, or, more specifically, a little girl's belief that she has been deprived of a penis and wishes to possess one.

persona (Jung) An archetype representing the roles that people play in response to social demands of others. It is the mask or disguise that individuals assume when superficially interacting with their environment. It may often be at variance with their true identities.

personal unconscious (Jung) Thoughts, feelings, and perceptions that are not accepted by the ego are stored here. Included are distant memories, as well as personal or unresolved moral conflicts that may be emotionally charged.

personality disorders These are characterized by being inflexible, lasting many years or a lifetime, and including traits that make social or occupational functioning difficult.

personality theory A system or way of describing and understanding human behavior.

personalization (cognitive) A cognitive distortion in which an individual takes an event and relates it to himself or herself when there is no relationship. An example would be, "Whenever I want to go skiing, there is no snow." Wanting to go skiing does not cause a lack of snow.

phallic stage (Freud) The third stage of psychosexual development, lasting from about the age of 3 until 5 or 6. The major source of sexual gratification shifts from the anal to the genital region.

phobia Fear of a situation or object out of proportion to the danger of the situation or the threatening qualities of the object. Examples include fears of height, rats, or spiders.

pleasure principle (Freud) The tendency to avoid pain and seek pleasure; the principle by which the *id* operates. It is particularly important in infancy.

plot (narrative) The plot refers to actions that take place in the story (problem). Plots may have several episodes and/or actions. The story may be told more than once. Different plots or views of the plot may develop.

political awareness (feminist) An important goal in feminist therapy; to become aware of biases and discriminations in societal institutions.

positive addiction (reality) Repeating and practicing positive behaviors such as running or meditating so that individuals develop better access to their creativity and the strength to deal with problems in their lives. Discomfort develops when individuals stop these behaviors.

positive feedback (family systems) Information that leads to deviation from the system's norm, bringing about change and a loss of stability.

positive narratives (narrative) Clients' stories about what is going well. Such positive stories can give clients a sense of empowerment.

positive reinforcement (behavior) Process by which the introduction of a stimulus has a consequence of a behavior that increases the likelihood that the behavior will be performed again.

postmodernism A philosophical position that does not assume that there is a fixed truth, but rather that individuals have their own perception of reality or the truth.

posttraumatic stress disorder (PTSD) Extreme reactions to a highly stressful or traumatic event, such as being raped, robbed, or assaulted, define PTSD. Resulting behaviors may include being easily startled, having recurrent dreams or nightmares, or feeling estranged from or afraid of others.

power analysis (feminist) Increasing clients' awareness of the power structure in society and the differences in power between men and women; a five-step set of therapeutic techniques.

power intervention (feminist) Empowering clients can occur in the course of therapeutic discussion. Often encouragement and reinforcement are ways to help clients become more powerful.

preconscious (Freud) Memories of events and experiences that can be retrieved with relatively little effort, such as remembering what one said to a friend yesterday. Information is available to awareness, but not immediately.

pretest-posttest control group design Comparing a group given one treatment with another group given a different treatment or no treatment, by testing individuals before and after therapy.

pretherapy change (solution-focused) Change that takes place before the client arrives at the therapist's office. The therapist asks about and comments on this change.

primary process (Freud) An action of the *id* that satisfies a need, thus reducing drive tension, by producing a mental image of an object.

process research The study of various aspects of psychotherapy. Examples include comparing two or more psychotherapeutic techniques and monitoring a change in personality as a result of the introduction of a technique. It is used in contrast to *outcome research*.

projection (Freud) A defense mechanism in which people attribute their own unacceptable desires to others and do not deal with their own strong sexual or destructive drives.

projection (gestalt) A contact boundary disturbance in which we may ascribe aspects of ourselves to others, such as when we attribute some of our own unacceptable thoughts, feelings, or behaviors to friends.

projective identification (psychoanalysis) Patients take negative aspects of themselves, project them onto someone else, and then identify with or try unconsciously to control that person. In doing so, a part of oneself is "split" off and attributed to another in order to control that other person.

protagonist (psychodrama) The individual who presents a problem that will be the focus of a psychodrama.

pseudomutuality (family systems) Presenting an appearance of open relationships in a family so as to conceal distant or troubled relationships within the family. Members develop roles that they play rather than relating honestly.

pseudoself (Bowen) An expression of values or opinions that other family members may find acceptable rather than one's own values or opinions.

psyche (Jung) Jung's term for personality structure, which includes conscious and unconscious thoughts, feelings, and behaviors.

psychic energy (Jung) Energy of the personality or psyche developing from desiring, motivating, thinking, looking, and so forth.

psychoanalysis Based on the work of Freud and others, psychoanalysis includes free association, dream analysis, and working through transference issues. The patient usually lies on a couch, and sessions are conducted three to five times per week.

psychoanalytic therapy Free association and exploration of unconscious processes may not be emphasized as strongly as in psychoanalysis. Meetings are usually one to three times per week, and the patient sits in a chair.

psychodrama A type of psychotherapy in which patients achieve new insight and alter previously ineffective behaviors by enacting life situations. The therapist serves as director and individuals play out their problems while other group or audience members take the role of important individuals in that person's life (auxiliaries).

psychosis   A broad term for severe mental disorders in which thinking and emotion are so impaired that individuals have lost contact with reality.

puella aeterna (Jung)   A woman who may have difficulty accepting the responsibilities of adulthood and is likely to be still attached to her father.

puer aeternus (Jung)   A man who may have difficulty growing out of adolescence and becoming more responsible.

punctuation (family systems)   The concept that each person in a transaction believes what he or she says is caused by what the other person says. Basically the individual holds the other responsible for his or her reactions.

push-button technique (Adler)   Designed to show patients how they can create whatever feeling they want by thinking about it. The push-button technique asks patients to remember a pleasant incident that they have experienced, become aware of feelings connected to it, and then switch to an unpleasant image and those feelings. Thus patients learn that they have the power to change their own feelings.

questions about the future (narrative)   As change takes place, therapists can assist the client in looking into the future and at potentially positive new stories. For example "If the problem were to continue next week, what meaning would it have for you?"

rationality (REBT)   Thinking, feeling, and acting in ways that will help individuals attain their goals. This is in contrast with irrationality, in which thinking, feeling, and acting are self-defeating and interfere with goal attainment.

rationalization (Freud)   A defense mechanism in which individuals provide a plausible but inaccurate explanation for their failures. An individual who blames her roommate for her own poor performance on an examination may be making excuses for her lack of study and, thus, rationalizing.

reaction formation (Freud)   A defense mechanism in which an acceptable impulse can be avoided by acting in an opposite way. Claiming that you like your occupational choice when you do not can help you avoid dealing with problems that result from not liking your work.

reactivity (behavior)   Occurs when clients change their behaviors because they know that they are being observed.

reality principle (Freud)   A guiding principle of the ego. It allows postponement of gratification so that environmental demands can be met or so that greater pleasure can be obtained at a later time.

reattribution (cognitive)   Helping clients distribute responsibility for an event (such as an argument) so as to place equal responsibility for the event.

reframing (family systems; feminist)   Giving a new or different explanation for an event so that constructive change can occur in the family. In feminist therapy, to help individuals understand how social pressures can affect their problems.

regression (Freud)   A defense mechanism in which an individual retreats to an earlier stage of development that was both more secure and more pleasant. A child hurt by a reprimand of the teacher may suck his thumb and cry, returning to a more secure and less mature time.

relabeling (family systems; feminist)   Attaching a new name to a problem so that therapeutic progress can be made. For example, saying that a client is overwhelmed by an issue rather than "depressed" may allow the client to develop methods to deal with the problem.

relational competence (feminist)   This refers to being able to be empathic toward self and others. It also includes the ability to participate in and build a sense of strength in a community.

relational resilience (feminist)   This refers to growing in a relationship and being able to move forward despite setbacks. Resilience also concerns recognizing when relationships are not mutual and moving on from them.

relational responses (relational psychoanalysis)   Comments on issues that arise during the therapeutic hour that reflect the therapist–patient relationship, rather than transference and countertransference interpretations.

unfinished business (gestalt) Unexpressed feelings from the past that occur in the present and interfere with psychological functioning. They may include feelings, memories, or fantasies from earlier life (often childhood) that can be dealt with in the present.

unique outcomes (narrative) Sometimes called *sparkling moments*, unique outcomes are thoughts, feelings, or actions that occur when the problem starts to dissolve.

virtual reality therapy (behavior) This therapy takes place in a computer-generated environment. Typically, the client can interact with this environment by using a joystick, a headband, a glove with physiological sensors, or a similar device.

word association (Jung) A method developed by Jung and Riklin in which individuals are asked to respond to a word with another word or phrase. Delayed reaction or other physiological response may provide a way of locating complexes that may be disturbing to the individual.

yoga (Asian) Hindu teachings dealing with ethics, lifestyle, body postures, breath control, intellectual study, and meditation.

Name Index

Note: First names of authors are used in the index either when the author's name is found in the index or the author is well known. Also, a dash between page numbers indicates a reference is continued onto the next page, a comma indicates that the reference is contained on that page. If a reference is from a table, the page number is followed by a *t*. If a reference is from a figure, the page number is followed by a *f*.

A

Aaronson, C. J., 403
Abbott, W. J., 439
Abraham, Karl, 32
Abramowitz, J. S., 405
Abrams, L. D., 333
Abrams, M., 333
Ackerman, Nathan, 535, 536, 561
Adams, M. V., 111, 118
Adelman, R., 356, 468, 474
Adler (Epstein), Raissa, 124, 153
Adler, Alexandra, 125
Adler, Alfred, 7, 14, 32, 87, 100, 110, 124, 125–141, 143, 150, 152, 153, 155, 208, 209, 242, 371, 372, 443, 454, 474, 535, 562, 632, 648, 649
Adler, G., 99, 104, 118
Adler, Kurt, 125, 149
Agras, W. S., 612
Ainsworth, Mary, 70
Akinyela, M. M., 477, 573
Albano, A. M., 403
Alberti, R. E., 323
Alexander the Great, 85
Alford, B. A., 373, 377, 389
Ali, S. R., 509, 524
Alicke, M. D., 231
Allan, J. A. B., 113, 118
Alvarez, J., 404, 511
Amendt-Lyon, N., 263, 272
Anatchkova, M. D., 684
Andersen-Warren, M., 627
Anderson, C. M., 567
Andersson, G., 603
Andreasen, N. C., 16, 26
Angel, E., 165
Angus, L. E., 270, 480
Ansbacher, H. L., 126, 153

Ansbacher, R. R., 126, 153
Antoinette, Marie, 419
Antoni, M. H., 195
Antony, M. M., 308
Arcelus, J., 612
Arciniega, M., 153, 154
Arezmendi, T. G., 229
Arlow, Jacob A., 52
Arnau, R. C., 99, 112, 118
Arney, L., 471
Arnkoff, D. B., 684
Arnow, B. A., 612
Arntz, A., 401
Arthur, King, 91
Ashby, J. S., 151
Asheri, S., 600
Ashida, S., 628
Ashton, M. C., 113, 118
Astor, J., 106, 118
Atak, N., 683, 684
Atkins, D. C., 570
Audet, L. R., 247
Austin, C., 471
Austin, S., 113, 118
Avants, S. K., 686
Aveyard, P., 683
Azarian, K., 69
Aziz, R., 118

B

Babacan, H., 501
Bacaltchuk, J., 603
Bachelor, A., 230
Bachofen, Johann, 84
Bagladi, V., 686
Bailey, J. S., 316
Bain, D., 83, 118
Baird, M. K., 488
Baker, L., 549
Baldwin, S. A., 19, 26, 454
Balint, Michael, 41
Ballou, M., 445, 486, 497, 498, 518
Bamks, R., 478
Bandura, Albert, 281, 283, 284, 287, 288, 289, 297, 321, 323, 675, 682
Bankart, C. P., 584, 585
Banks, T., 358
Barber, Jacques, 69, 74
Bard, J., 347
Barenbaum, N. B., 2, 25
Barkham, M., 229

Barlow, D. H., 13, 25, 26, 301, 387
Barnett, L., 171
Barnhofer, T., 399
Barrett, S. E., 489
Barry, H., III, 152
Bartolomucci, C. L., 526
Bassin, A., 425, 428, 447
Basta, T. B., 683
Bastian, Adolf, 84
Bateson, Gregory, 455, 456, 536, 537, 565
Batrim, D., 612
Baucom, B. R., 570
Baum, S. M., 175
Baumgardner, Patricia, 243
Bechtoldt, H., 5, 25
Beck, A. T., 356
Beck, Aaron, 8, 356, 370, 370–374, 374, 376, 377, 379, 382, 384, 389, 390, 392, 393, 396, 397, 399, 400, 401, 402, 403, 404, 405, 409, 410, 635, 657
Beck, Judith S., 370, 380, 381, 383, 386, 387, 402, 406, 410
Becker, S. J., 603, 612
Beebe, J., 94, 103, 111, 118, 121
Beekman, A., 603
Beevers, C. G., 403
Beisser, A. R., 254
Belmont, L., 151
Bem, S. L., 406, 493
Benjamin, G. A. H., 24, 27
Bentilini, J. M., 358
Berg, I. K., 458, 459, 464, 465, 466
Berg, Insoo Kim, 453, 456, 457, 459, 460, 462, 466
Bergin, A. E., 643, 645, 646
Berglund, P., 26
Berliner, P. M., 489
Berman, J. S., 403, 476
Berman, S. L., 170
Bernal, G., 407
Bernard, M. E., 340, 342, 343, 344, 346, 353, 355
Bernauer, F., 317
Bernays, Martha, 30
Bernhardtson, L., 264
Bernheim, Hippolyte, 30
Bertolino, B., 462
Beshai, J. A., 178
Beskow, M., 115, 121
Beuhler, H. A., 121

Beutler, L. E., 10, 17, 25, 26, 229, 642, 643
Beyebach, M., 475
Bhar, S. S., 403
Biaggio, M. K., 195
Bieschke, K. J., 523
Bike, D. H., 5, 25
Binswanger, Ludwig, 164, 165, 166, 167, 168, 200
Bion, Wilfred, 41
Bitter, J. R., 149
Black, D. W., 16, 26
Blackburn, I., 403
Blackledge, J. T., 311
Blanck, Gertrude, 41
Blanck, Rubin, 41
Blane, H. T., 152
Blankstein, K. R., 382
Blanton, P. W., 152
Blasey, C., 612
Blatner, A., 615, 616, 617, 618, 620, 621
Bleiberg, K., 612
Bleuler, Eugen, 84, 87, 109
Bloom, D., 245
Bly, R., 114, 118
Bohart, A. C., 25
Bolton, P., 612
Bono, G., 589
Book, Howard E., 63, 66
Borden, A., 457, 468, 516
Borgatta, E. F., 616
Boring, E. G., 246
Borne, Ludwig, 30
Bornstein, R. F., 194
Boss, Medard, 164, 165, 166, 174, 177, 200
Boswell, J. F., 663
Bouchard, T. J., Jr., 113, 118
Bouzoukis, C. E., 627
Bowen, Murray, 534, 539–544, 547, 548, 564, 569, 570, 575, 576, 659
Bowlby, John, 70, 602
Bowman, C. E., 244
Boy, A. V., 214
Boyd-Franklin, N., 573
Bozarth, J. D., 214, 215, 218, 233
Bozeman, B. N., 475
Brack, C. J., 513
Brack, G., 153
Breshgold, E., 269
Breuer, Josef, 30, 31
Brice-Baker, J., 524
Brickell, J., 419, 431, 432, 433
Bridges, S. K., 466, 468
Bridle, C., 684
Bright, J. A., 390
Brink, D. C., 228
Brink, S. J., 113, 118
Brochu, S., 683
Brockmon, C., 272
Brodeur, N., 683

Brodley, B. T., 209, 214
Brodsky, A. M., 518
Brokke, R., 121
Brooks, G. R., 520, 521
Brotons, M., 628
Brown, C., 474, 509, 510, 519
Brown, C. G., 509
Brown, G., 384, 390, 400
Brown, George, 264
Brown, J. H., 555, 556
Brown, Laura, 196, 477, 486, 487, 489, 490, 497, 499, 503, 506, 510, 514, 518, 520, 522, 523, 525, 527, 686
Brown, T., 423
Brown, T. A., 301, 318
Browne, C. M., 338
Brownell, P., 269
Brucke, Ernst, 30
Brunstein-Klomek, A., 603, 612
Bryant, Herbert, 209
Buber, Martin, 163, 172, 173, 178, 209, 245, 253
Buddha, Gautama, 584
Buehler, H. A., 98, 112
Bugental, Elizabeth, 198
Bugental, James, 165, 166, 174, 178, 179, 180, 184, 185, 186, 189, 190, 191, 192, 201
Bühler, K., 164
Bulmer, L., 474
Bumberry, W., 559
Burch, M. R., 316
Burckell, L. A., 683
Burgess, D., 298
Burness, M. R., 151
Burns, D. D., 403
Burns, M. K., 423, 516
Burstow, B., 505
Burstow, Bonnie, 504, 505, 514, 515
Bussey, K., 321
Butler, A. C., 402, 406
Butler, G., 404

C
Calhoun, G. B., 526
Callaghan, R. C., 683, 685
Callanan, P., 24, 25
Cambray, J., 107, 108, 118
Campbell, J., 110, 118
Campbell, L. F., 5, 25
Camus, Albert, 161, 163, 171, 173
Cann, D. R., 113, 118
Cannon, B., 164, 269
Cantin, S., 519
Capron, E. W., 129
Carr, A., 570
Carreira, K., 604
Carroll, K., 612
Carroll, K. M., 17, 25
Carroll, R., 600
Carter, D. K., 499

Carter, L., 107, 108, 118
Carter, M. M., 407, 497
Carus, Carl Gustav, 84
Caspar, F., 686
Casson, J., 619
Castaldo, D. D., 476
Castellana, F., 104, 118
Castonguay, L. G., 10, 25, 642, 643, 663
Cecchin, G., 566
Cecero, J. J., 5, 27
Chambless, D. L., 18, 25, 319, 404
Chamoun, M., 73
Chan, A., 196
Chapin, K., 628
Charcot, Jean, 30
Charet, F. X., 118
Chasseguet-Smirgel, Janine, 71
Chen, C. P., 590
Cheong, J., 358
Chesler, P., 486, 487, 646
Chessick, Richard D., 66
Chevron, E. S., 602
Childs, E. K., 524
Chima, I. M., 444
Chiu, A. W., 404
Chodorow, Nancy J., 71, 487, 508
Christ, 91
Christensen, A., 570
Christensen, D. N., 555, 556
Ciardiello, S., 629
Cilliers, F., 226, 227
Cimett, E., 572
Cinotti, N., 594
Claessens, M., 193
Clance, P. R., 600
Clark, D. A., 373, 377, 389, 394, 396, 600
Clarke, K. M., 271
Clarkson, P., 241, 248, 250, 254, 276
Clemmens, M. C., 267
Cohen, J. N., 509
Cohn, H. W., 169, 177, 180
Cole, K. L., 519
Coleman, S., 571
Collins, A., 114, 115, 119
Comas-Díaz, L., 196, 489, 523, 524
Combs, G., 474
Comtois, K. A., 316
Conklin, C. A., 406
Connell, G., 559
Connie, E., 466
Connolly, Mary B., 69
Constantino, M. J., 612
Cook, D. A., 485, 493
Cook-Nobles, R., 511
Cooper, M., 166, 168, 176, 177, 184, 401
Cooper, S., 535
Cord-Udy, N., 115
Corey, G., 23, 24, 25, 198, 199, 447, 618, 619
Corey, M., 24, 25
Corrington, R. S., 593, 594

Corry, M. A., 423, 424, 478
Corsini, R. J., 4, 5, 26, 136, 142, 617, 679
Cosman, D., 357, 404
Costa, N. M., 170
Costantino, G., 476, 478
Cottraux, J., 403, 404
Courtney, M., 270, 271
Cowan, E. G., Jr., 172
Crago, M., 229
Craig, M., 174, 176
Crandall, J. E., 152
Crane, C., 399
Crawford, A., 178
Crawford, M., 490, 490–492, 505
Creuzer, George, 84
Criswell, E., 196
Crits-Christoph, P., 25, 66, 68, 69
Croake, J., 148, 151
Crowe, B., 628
Crumbaugh, J. C., 177, 195
Cucherat, M., 403
Cuijpers, P., 603
Cunningham, J. A., 683
Currier, J. M., 476
Curry, J. F., 603, 612
Cyranowski, J. M., 612

D
Dancey, C. P., 358
D'Andrea, M., 485
D'Ardenne, P., 408
Darwin, Charles, 30
Dattilio, F. M., 387, 410
Daugherty, C., 508
David, D., 343, 355, 356, 357, 361, 404
Davidson, K., 390, 392, 401
Davis, D., 406
Davis, D. D., 373
Davis, Elizabeth, 208
Davis, T., 180
Davison, G. C., 358
Dawson, T., 121
Dayton, T., 616
De Jesus Mari, M. J., 603
De Jong, P., 456, 457, 458, 459, 460, 462, 464, 465, 466, 480
De Laszlo, V., 118, 119
De Mello, M. F., 603
De Shazer, S., 453, 456, 457, 458, 459, 460, 462, 475
De Vega, M. H., 475
Dean, J., 153, 521
DeBord, K. A., 523
DeChant, B., 525
Dehon, C., 170
Demler, O., 26
Demorest, Amy, 32
Derlega, V. J., 151
Dermyer, H. L., 584
DeRubeis, R. J., 377, 403, 404

Deutsch, Helene, 71, 242, 487
Dewey, John, 334
Dexter-Mazza, E. T., 588
DeYoung, P. A., 508
Dickens, Charles, 627
Dickerson, V. C., 468
DiClemente, C. C., 669, 671, 672
Diefenbeck, C.A., 376
Dierberger, A. E., 17, 26
DiGiuseppe, R. A., 334, 337, 340, 342, 343, 354, 357, 359
Dinkmeyer, D., Jr., 131, 132, 143, 154
Dinter, L. D., 152
Dixon, L., 572
Dobson, K. S., 390
Dolan, Y., 466
Dollard, J., 285, 316, 663, 665
Dombrovski, A. Y., 604
Donahue, B., 112, 119
Donati, R., 317
Donderi, D. C., 113, 118
Donfrancesco, A., 104, 118
Dorta, K. P., 603, 612
Dostoyevski, Fyodor, 161, 163
Doubrawa, E., 245
Dowd, E. T., 338, 407
Dowd, T., 407
Dozois, D. J. A., 390
Dreikurs, Rudolf, 126, 131, 133, 134, 135, 137, 139, 141, 149, 153
Drob, S., 116, 119
Dryden, W., 333, 334, 335, 336, 337, 338, 340, 341, 344, 346, 347, 348, 349, 350, 356, 358, 361, 362, 363
Du Toit, P.L., 400
Duffy, T. K., 617
Duivenvoorden, H. J., 195
Duncan, B. L., 10, 20, 26
Dunlap, S. J., 406
Dunne, P., 478
Dunn-Johnson, L., 526
Dunwoody, L., 178
Durand, V. M., 13, 25
Durham, Robert C., 69

E
Edmonds, S., 195
Edwards, C. P., 490
Eichenbaum, L., 487, 508
Eitingon, Max, 32
Ekstrom, S., 90, 97, 119
Eliason, G. T., 171
Ellenberger, H. F., 32, 83, 98, 119, 125, 165, 169
Elliot, Helen, 207, 253, 259
Elliot, R., 194, 231, 268, 271
Elliot, R. K., 276
Ellis, A., 443
Ellis, Albert, 8, 228, 317, 332–340, 341, 342, 343, 344, 347, 348, 349, 350, 351, 352, 353, 354, 355, 356, 357,

358, 359, 361, 362, 363, 364, 371, 372, 443, 563, 657
Ellison, J. A., 270
Emery, G., 382, 392
Emmons, M. L., 323
Emmons, R. A., 589
Endicott, J., 603
Enns, C. Z., 486, 487, 488, 496, 497, 499, 505, 508, 509, 510, 517, 518, 523, 525, 527
Enright, J. B., 262
Epictetus, 334, 453
Epp, L. R., 197
Epston, David, 453, 456, 457, 466, 468, 469, 471, 472, 473, 477, 479, 516
Erbaugh, J. K., 384
Erickson, Milton, 443, 453, 454, 455, 456, 553, 565
Eriksen, K., 499, 511
Erikson, Erik, 22, 29, 32, 39, 40, 41, 55, 56, 57, 72, 74, 94, 485, 494, 649, 653
Erikson, Joan, 41
Estes, C. P., 110, 119
Eubanks-Carter, C., 683
Evans, S., 400, 486
Evers, K. E., 683
Eysenck, H. J., 285

F
Fabbro, A., 26
Fabry, J. B., 182, 192
Fadden, G., 571
Fagan, J., 270
Fairbairn, Ronald, 41
Fang-Ru, Y., 475
Farber, B. A., 228
Farmer, E., 408
Farren, C. J., 195
Fava, J. L., 684
Fawcett, J., 2, 26
Feasey, D., 616
Fechner, Gustav, 30
Feder, B., 273, 274
Feder, F., 273, 274
Feder, J., 521
Feeny, N. C., 403
Feldman, R., 571
Fenichel, Otto, 242
Fennell, M., 404
Ferenczi, Sandor, 32, 73
Fernros, L., 588
Feske, U., 319, 322
Few, A. L., 525
Fiedler, F. E., 10, 26
Fielding, A., 683
Fields, C. D., 616
Findling, R. L., 403
Fisch, R., 570
Fizel, L., 151
Fleming, B., 379

Florian, V., 170
Foa, E. B., 643
Fodor, I. E., 269
Fodor, I. G., 359, 402
Fordham, M., 95, 111, 119, 121
Fox, J., 615, 619–620
Frankl, Viktor, 164, 165, 170, 171, 173,
    174, 175, 176, 178, 185, 186, 190,
    192, 193, 195, 197, 200, 201, 228,
    356, 443, 655, 680
Franklin, C., 457, 458, 466, 474
Franklin, M. E., 643
Fransella, F., 454
Franz, R. A., 396
Fredericson, I., 251
Free, M. L., 408, 409
Freeman, A., 343, 373, 376, 379, 380, 382,
    386, 387, 392, 393, 410
Freeman, A. S., 338
Freeman, J., 457, 468, 469, 473, 474
Freeston, M. H., 405
French, S., 195
Fresco, D. M., 400
Fretz, B. R., 26
Fretz, Bruce R., 4, 66
Freud, Anna, 32, 39, 40, 55, 74
Freud, Sigmund, 6, 11, 14, 15, 22, 29–33,
    34, 35, 36, 37, 38, 39, 40, 41, 42, 44,
    47, 51, 55, 56, 65, 67, 69, 70, 71, 72,
    73, 74, 85, 87, 94, 99, 105, 110, 111,
    117, 124, 125, 126, 127, 164, 208,
    242, 243, 370, 371, 487, 494, 534,
    593, 594, 648, 649, 653
Frew, J. E., 259, 272, 273
Friedlander, Sigmund, 243, 244
Friedman, H., 596
Frohne-Hagemann, I., 628
Fromm, Erich, 32
Fromm-Reichmann, F., 535
Frost, R. O., 394
Fry, P. S., 195
Fuhr, R., 254
Fulton, P. R., 587
Furhoff, A., 588

G
Gadol, I., 273
Gaines, J., 262
Gallagher, T., 612
Ganley, A. L., 521
Ganzer, C., 664
Garcia-Preto, N., 573
Garfield, S. L., 621, 643, 645, 646, 663, 664
Gauthier, M., 474
Gay, Peter, 32
Gazabon, S. A., 683
Gelder, M., 404
Geller, S. M., 271
Gelso, C. J., 4, 26, 66
Gelven, M., 163
Gendlin, E. T., 178, 241

Gentile, L., 2, 26
Gergen, M., 517
Germer, R. D., 586, 587
Geronilla, L. S., 423, 434, 436, 437,
    438, 439
Ghaemi, S. N., 169
Gibbard, I., 231
Gilbert, L.A., 497
Gillette, D., 114, 121
Gilligan, Carol, 489, 494, 495, 496, 526
Ginger, S., 269
Ginsburg, G. S., 403
Glass, C. R., 684
Glass, G. V., 317
Glasser, C., 417
Glasser, N., 426, 443
Glasser, W., 8, 417, 418, 419–427, 425,
    428, 429, 430, 431, 432, 433, 434,
    438, 439, 440, 441, 443, 444, 447,
    448, 563, 647*t*, 657
Glauser, A. S., 233
Glazer, R., 596
Gloaguen, V., 403
Goelitz, A., 95, 119
Gold, J. R., 663, 665, 666, 668
Goldenberg, H., 556, 573, 574
Goldenberg, I., 556, 573, 574
Goldfried, M. R., 683, 687
Goldman, R., 258, 264, 270
Goldman, R. N., 270, 276
Goldstein, Kurt, 209, 242, 243, 244
Gonzalez, J. E., 357
Goodheart, C. D., 26
Goodman, Paul, 242, 266
Goodrich, T. J., 518
Goodyear, R. K., 5, 26
Gopalkrishnan, N., 501
Gordon, J., 300, 348
Gordon, K., 570
Gordon, L. B., 270
Gore, K. L., 407
Gorman, J. M., 18, 25, 26, 403
Gorman, L. L., 603
Götestam, K. G., 405
Gottman, J.M., 490
Gould, R. A., 404
Gould, W. B., 164, 171
Graham, E. T., 407
Granger, D. A., 231
Grant, L., 115
Grant, P., 401, 406
Grawe, K., 317
Gray, J. S., 27
Greco, C. M., 588
Greenberg, Jay R., 41, 45
Greenberg, L. G., 271
Greenberg, L. S., 228, 231, 241, 253, 268,
    270, 271, 276
Greenberg, R. L., 392
Greene, B., 72, 508, 524, 525
Greenspan, M., 515, 515–516

Gregoire, T. K., 683, 685
Gremillion, H., 509
Grey, N., 404
Gron, A., 161
Grossman, P., 588
Grote, N.K., 603
Guarnaccia, C. A., 152
Guerin, K. B., 544
Guerin, Philip J., Jr., 544
Guevremont, D. C., 321, 399, 400
Gunlicks, M. L., 612
Guntrip, Harry, 41
Guo, A. H., 98, 121
Guo, B., 683, 684
Guterman, J. T., 356
Guttmann, D., 185, 190
Gyulai, L., 401

H
Haaga, D. A. F., 358
Haaramo, P., 475
Hagedorn, W. B., 477
Hales, R. E., 26
Haley, Jay, 228, 454, 455, 534, 536, 539,
    553, 554, 564, 565, 566, 567, 570,
    574, 575, 576
Hall, C. S., 91, 96, 97, 100, 119
Hall, G. S., 31
Hall, J. A., 119
Hall, R. L., 525
Halstead, K., 523
Hamilton, M., 605
Hammer, A. L., 93, 98, 112, 121
Hammond, R. T., 571
Han, S. S., 231
Handel, M., 511
Handlon, J. H., 251
Hanley, T, 231
Hanna, J. L., 626
Hannah, B., 83, 104, 119
Harding, M. E., 89, 119
Hardy, K. V., 573
Hare-Mustin, R. T., 489, 490, 495
Haris, A.S., 118
Harlow, L. L., 683
Harper, R. A., 333, 336, 347, 363
Harran, S. M., 358
Harrington, G. L., 417, 418, 443
Harrington, N., 337, 338, 340
Harris, A. S., 87, 88, 96, 100, 110, 116,
    118, 119
Harris, E. S., 245, 269
Hart, D. L., 111, 119
Hartley, L., 600
Haucke, C., 111, 119
Hayden, M., 508
Hayes, P. A., 311, 312
Hayes, S. C., 321
Hays, Nicolas, 121
Hays, P. A., 23, 26, 486, 493, 498
Hayward, P., 390

Heather, N., 683, 685
Hedges, Lawrence E., 50
Hefferline, Ralph F., 242, 266
Hegel, G. F. W., 161
Heidegger, Martin, 161, 162, 163, 164
Heimberg, R. G., 387
Heinen, J. R., 2, 26
Heller, M. C., 593
Helms, J. E., 485, 493
Henderson, J. L., 97, 113, 114, 119
Henehan, M. P., 477
Henle, M., 246
Henrion, R., 178, 195
Hertlein, K. M., 311
Hester, R. L., 474
Heymsfield, L., 98, 121
Higginbotham, H. N., 321, 322
Higgins, M. B., 593, 594
Hill, C. E., 21, 26, 98, 121
Hill, M., 486
Hill, M. B., 153
Hillman, J., 89, 111, 119
Hillman, M., 165, 173, 185, 190, 192
Hinrichsen, G. A., 603, 612
Hirschberger, G., 170
Hitler, Adolf, 91, 335
Ho, B., 16, 26
Ho, M. K., 574
Hodge, D. R., 407
Hoey, B., 621
Hoffman, L., 196
Hofmann, S. G., 406
Hogarty, B., 567
Hogenson, G. B., 109, 119
Holdstock, L., 227
Holland, J. M., 476
Hollis, J., 89, 111, 119
Hollon, S. D., 18, 25, 404, 406
Holmbeck, G., 26
Hönekopp, J., 683
Hooker, K., 195
Hooker, K. E., 269
Hoper, J. H., 476
Horn, J. M., 113, 118
Hornby, H., 572
Horney, K., 32, 52, 70, 242, 487, 508
Hoshmand, L. T., 520
Houston, G., 268
Hoyt, M. F., 468
Hubble, M. A., 10, 20, 26
Hudson, g., 407
Hulbeck, Richard, 332
Hull, C. L., 285
Hume, David, 162
Humphrey, K., 245
Huppert, J. D., 26
Hur, Y. M., 113, 118
Hurtado, A., 488
Husserl, Edmund, 162
Hutchinson, G. T., 358
Hutzell, R. R., 185

Hwang, M. G., 444
Hycner, R., 253, 263
Hyde, J. S., 490, 494
Hyland, M. E., 178

I
Iaculo, G., 272
Imes, S., 600
Isebaert, L., 475
Ishak, N. M., 446
Ishiyama, F. I., 590
Ivey, A. E., 485
Iwakabe, S., 686

J
Jack the Ripper, 91
Jacka, B., 113, 119
Jackson, D. D., 536
Jackson, Don, 455, 553, 565
Jackson, Leslie C., 72
Jacobs, L., 251, 252, 253, 254, 268
Jacobson, Edith, 41, 43, 292, 300
Jaffee, S., 494
Jakubowski, 505
James, J., 627
Janet, Pierre, 30, 84
Jasper, K., 161, 162, 163, 477
Javier, Ravael A., 73
Jennings, S., 626, 627
Jimenez, S., 588
Jin, R., 26
Johannsen, B. E., 25
Johnson, A., 520, 524
Johnson, D. R., 627
Johnson, E. P., 152
Johnson, J. L., 683
Johnson, S., 669, 683
Johnson, W. B., 342
Johnson, W. R., 270
Joley, J. M., 26
Jolley, J. M., 21
Jones, Ernest, 32
Jones, J., 343, 407, 593
Jones, Mary Cover, 283, 298
Jones, P., 626, 627
Jones, S. H., 390
Jones, W. H., 151
Jordan, Judith. V., 489, 495–496, 498, 499,
    508, 511, 511–513, 518, 525, 527
Joseph, S., 195
Joseph, S. M., 116, 119
Jourdan, A., 231
Joyce, Marie, 340, 343, 346, 353
Joyce, P., 251, 253, 273
Jung (Rauschenbach), Emma, 84, 89
Jung, Carl, 6, 14, 22, 32, 83–87, 88, 90, 91,
    93, 94, 95, 97, 99, 101, 102, 103, 105,
    109, 110, 111, 112, 114, 115, 116,
    117, 118, 119, 120, 242, 649, 654
Jung, E., 120
Jusoh, A. J., 446

K
Kabat-Zinn, J., 399, 587
Kafka, Frank, 161, 163
Kaklauskas, F. J., 196
Kallivayalil, D., 524
Kalogerakos, F., 270
Kant, Immanuel, 84, 125, 126, 334, 453
Karpiak, C. P., 5, 26, 663
Kaschak, E., 486, 487, 497
Kasila, K., 683
Katzman, G. P., 403
Kaufman, J. A., 140
Kazdin, A. E., 26, 286
Keene-Hagerty, E., 195
Keith, D. V., 559
Kellerman, P. F., 620
Kellogg, S. H., 374, 400
Kelly, F. D., 138
Kelly, George, 371, 372, 453, 454, 456
Kelly, M. S., 457, 458, 466, 474
Kernberg, Otto, 635
Kendall, P. C., 21, 26
Kennedy, K., 683, 685
Kennedy, S. M., 178
Kenny, M. C., 151
Kenward, R., 161
Kepner, E., 274
Kepner, J., 599, 600
Kern, R. M., 148
Kernberg, Otto, 32, 41, 43, 53, 55, 58, 59,
    62, 72, 75
Kessler, R. C., 13, 26
Khalsa, S. B. S., 584
Kierkegaard, Søren, 161, 162, 174
Kiesler, B. J., 602
Kim, J. S., 457, 458, 466, 474, 475
Kim, K. W., 618
Kim, R. I., 444
Kincade, E. A., 486
King, Martin Luther, 127
Kingdon, D. G., 401
Kirby, F. D., 286
Kirsch, J., 120
Kirsch, T. B., 86, 120
Kirschenbaum, H., 231
Kisber, S., 2, 26
Kissane, D. W., 195
Klein, Melanie, 41, 95, 111
Kleinjan, M., 683, 684
Klerman, G. L., 407, 602, 604, 608,
    609, 612
Klerman, Gerald, 602, 603, 604, 605,
    609, 612
Klopfer, Bruno, 98
Klotz, M., 231
Knaus, W. J., 347
Knekt, P., 475
Knoche, L., 490
Knox, J., 111, 120
Kobasa, S. C., 174
Koetting, K., 26

Koffka, Kurt, 245
Koger, S. M., 628
Kohlberg, Lawrence, 494
Kohler, Wolgang, 245
Kohn-Wood, L., 407
Kohut, Heinz, 15, 32, 43, 44, 45, 50, 53, 55, 59, 60, 61, 62, 65, 72, 73, 75, 106, 228, 641
Kondas, D., 272
Koops, M., 474
Koretz, D., 26
Korzybiski, Alfred, 244, 454
Kovacs, M., 384
Kratochvil, C., 403
Kravetz, D., 487, 525
Kress, V. E., 499, 511
Krippner, S., 115, 120
Kristeller, J. L., 586
Krop, H., 298
Krug, O. T., 165, 166
Kruk, J. C., 663
Krupnick, J. L., 612
Kumuru, A., 490
Kupferer, S., 195
Kurtz, R., 663, 664
Kutash, Irwin L, 73
Kuyken, W., 400
Kwee, M. G. T., 685
Kyrios, M., 394

L
Laaksonen, M. A., 475
L'Abate, L., 433, 556
Laidlaw, T., 685
Laing, R. D., 165, 166
Lakhan, R., 361
Lam, D. H., 390, 401
Lambert, M. J., 21, 25, 26, 643, 645, 646
Landau, M. J., 173
Landy, R. J., 616, 618, 619, 626, 627
Lantz, J., 195
Larson, M. W., 390
Lauter, E., 114, 120
Lauver, P. J., 151
Lazarus, A. A., 10, 675, 676, 677, 677–679, 679, 680, 680–682, 681, 682, 685, 686, 687
Leahy, R. L., 387, 401
Lear, King, 627
LeCroy, C. W., 322
Ledley, D. R., 387
Lee, D., 138
Lee, H., 361
Lee, K., 113, 118
Lee, M. Y., 477
Lee, P., 669
Lee, R. G., 244, 246
Lees, M., 508
Lega, L. I., 361
Leibnez, Gottfried, 84
Lerner, G., 488

Leslie, Y. M., 358
Levant, R. F., 17, 25, 26, 521
LeVay, D., 627
Levine, M. d., 406
Levitsky, A., 253, 256
Levy, D., 535
Levy Berg, A., 600
Lewin, Kurt, 243, 244, 269
Lewis, E. L., 407
Lewis, T. F., 127
LichtenBerg, I. K., 475
Lichtenberg, J. W., 26
Lichtenthal, W. G., 195
Lidz, T., 536, 537
Lieberman, M. A., 194
Liese, B. S., 375, 390, 396
Lietaer, G., 195
Lim, S., 573
Lincoln, Abraham, 16
Lindenboim, N., 316
Lindfors, O., 475
Lindgren, Annika, 74
Lindsay, J., 683
Linehan, M. M., 312, 316, 588
Linnenberg, D. M., 445
Lipchik, E., 459
Lister, K. M., 663
Litaer, G., 231
Litwack, L., 444
Lobb, M. S., 242, 263
Lobbestael, J., 401
Lobovits, D, 457, 468
LoCicero, K. A., 151
Lockwood, T. W., 573
Loewy, J. V., 628
Lofgren, T., 475
Loman, S. T., 624
Long, A. E., 173
Longstreth, L. E., 152
Loomis, M., 112, 121
Lowen, A., 593, 594, 595, 596, 597, 600
Lowe-Strong, A., 178
Lowrie, W., 161
Loy, D., 196
Luber, M., 310
Luborsky, Lester, 63, 66, 68, 70
Lukas, E., 190, 192
Lupu, V., 357, 404
Lusterman, D. D., 560
Lynch, C.S., 588
Lynn, S. J., 364
Lyons, L. C., 357

M
Macavei, B., 340
Machal, M., 571
Mackewn, J., 241
Madanes, C., 557
Maddi, S. R., 151, 174
Magnuson, S., 543
Mahalik, J. R., 406, 519

Mahler, Margaret, 41, 43, 44
Mahmud, Z., 446
Mahrer, Alvin, 241
Maidenbaum, A., 115, 120
Maiello, S., 115, 120
Main, R., 109, 120
Maisel, R., 457, 468, 471, 477, 516
Malan, David M., 62
Malchiodi, C. A., 623, 624
Malcolm, W. M., 271
Malgady, R. G., 476, 478
Mallinckrodt, B., 475
Malson, H., 516
Manaster, G., 136, 142, 149
Manber, R., 588
Manchester, K., 443
Maniacci, M. P., 135, 136, 143
Marbley, A. F., 486
Marcel, Gabriel, 163
Marecek, J., 490, 495
Margolin, A., 686
Marin, N. W., 407
Marineau, R. F., 616
Markowitz, J. C., 602, 605, 608, 610, 611, 611–612, 612
Marlatt, G, 300
Marlatt, G. A., 587
Marner, T., 471
Marolla, E. A., 151
Martell, C. R., 406
Martin, S. A., 115, 120
Marx, B. M., 387
Marx, Karl, 125
Masatake, Morita, 590
Maslow, A. H., 209
Matlin, M. W., 487, 490, 491–492, 492, 516
Matthews, G., 395
Mattoon, M. A., 87, 95, 96, 97, 100, 103, 104, 112, 120
Matzko, H., 267
Maxfield, L., 311
May, Rollo, 162, 165, 166, 167, 168, 169, 170, 171, 172, 173, 175, 176, 181, 183, 194, 198, 209
McAleavey, A. A., 663
McAuliffe, G., 499
McBride, O., 178
McCann, J. T., 195
McCarthy, M. L., 357
McCaulley, M. H., 93, 98, 112, 121
McCleery, A., 407
McCullough, M. E., 589
McCully, R., 120
McDaniel, S. H., 560
McDermott, S. P., 406, 485
McFarlane, W. R., 572
McGinn, L. K., 405
McGoldrick, M., 573
McGovern, T. E., 357
McGuire, W., 85, 120

McInerney, J. E., 354
McKinney, M. K., 663
McKnight, A. S., 570
McLean, B. A., 526
McLean, P. D., 405
McLeod, J., 480
McMahon, J., 340, 358
McManus, F., 404
McMichen, P. J., 513
McMullen, E. J., 271
McMullin, R. E., 387, 397
McNary, S., 572
McNeely, R. L., 361
Mcpherson, R., 26
Meara, Naomi M., 49
Mearns, D., 227
Meichenbaum, Donald, 292, 299, 300,
    301, 324, 356, 672
Melnick, J., 254
Mendelson, M., 384
Merikangas, K. R., 26
Metcalf, L., 457, 466
Metcalfe, C., 476
Mettus, C., 98, 121
Meyer, Adolf, 602
Michan, P., 115, 120
Mickel, E., 423, 446
Mihalopoulos, C., 603
Mikulincer, M., 170
Miller, I. W., 403
Miller, J. C., 88, 120
Miller, Jean Baker, 496
Miller, M. D., 603, 612
Miller, M. J., 232
Miller, N. E., 285, 316, 663, 665
Miller, N. J., 357
Miller, S. D., 10, 20, 26, 456, 475
Minkowski, E., 168, 169
Minuchin, Salvador, 534, 539, 545, 546,
    547, 548, 549, 553, 564, 565, 571,
    575, 576, 681
Mirkin, M. P., 518
Mischel, W., 285
Mitchell, K. M., 229
Mitchell, M. L., 21, 26
Mitchell, S., 665
Mitchell, Stephen A., 41, 45, 46, 51, 52,
    54, 55, 61, 66, 75
Mittal, M., 520
Mitten, T., 559
Mjelde-Mossey, L., 477
Mock, J. E., 384
Moeller, Michael L., 53
Mona Lisa, 91
Montilla, R. E., 573
Moore, E., 612
Moore, R., 114, 121
Moreau, D., 603
Moreno, Jacob L., 154, 615, 616, 617,
    619, 621
Moreno, Z. T., 618

Morey, J. R., 111, 121
Morokoff, P. J., 683
Morone, N. E., 588
Morris, M. W., 196
Morris, P., 612
Morrison, A. P., 401
Morrow, S. L., 523
Morton, T., 231
Mosak, H. H., 133, 135, 136, 139, 141,
    143, 150
Mowrer, O. H., 282, 285
Mowrer, W. M., 282
Moyers, B., 118
Mufson, L., 603, 612
Muller, F. J., 686
Muran, E., 359
Murdock, N., 26
Murphy-Shigematsu, L., 477
Murray, Henry, 98, 178
Murrell, A. R., 588
Mwita, M., 127
Myers, J. B., 93, 98, 112, 121

N
Naboulsi, M. A., 178
Nagoshi, C. T., 358
Naimark, H., 359
Najavits, L. M., 17, 26
Nakamoto, T., 573
Nanda, J., 193
Naranjo, C., 265, 266
Nasser, M., 516
Nassif, C., 185
Nathan, P. E., 18, 25, 26, 643
Navabinejad, S., 361
Needleman, L. D. C., 395
Neenan, M., 335, 337, 340, 348
Nefale, M. C., 686
Neimeyer, Greg, 456
Neimeyer, R. A., 19, 26, 403, 453, 454,
    456, 466, 467, 468, 469, 475, 476,
    479, 480
Nelson, D. L., 663
Neugebauer, R., 603
Nevis, E. C., 244
Nevis, S. M., 254
Newlon, B. J., 153, 154
Newman, C. E., 396, 401
Newman, C. F., 406
Nezu, A. M., 18, 21, 25, 26
Nezu, C. M., 18, 21, 25, 26
Ngazimbi, E. E., 477
Nguyen, L., 588
Nicholas, M., 626
Nichols, M. P., 455, 469, 470, 571
Nicoll, W. G., 149
Nielsen, S. L., 361
Niemann, L., 588
Nietzsche, Friedrich, 30, 85, 125, 161,
    162, 334
Nishimura, N., 477

Nnodum, B., 444
Noda, F., 590
Norcross, J. C., 5, 9, 17, 25, 26, 663, 669,
    670, 671, 673, 673–674, 674,
    683, 687
Nordberg, S. S., 663
Nordby, V. J., 91, 119
Nordstrom, F., 475
Norman, G. J., 684
Noronha, D., 521
Novy, C., 474
Nuby, J. F., 113, 121
Nutt, R. L., 520, 521
Nylund, D. A., 477

O
O'Connell, B., 458, 459, 460, 461, 462,
    463, 466, 474, 476, 478, 480
Odell-Miller, H., 628
O'Donnell, D. J., 442
Oedipus, 38
O'Hanlon, B., 462
O'Hara, M., 232
O'Hara, M. W., 603
Okonji, J. M. A., 446
Okun, B. F., 518
O'Leary, E., 228, 249
O'Leary, T. A., 301
Olendzki, A., 584
Ollendick, T. H., 319
O'Neill, B., 269
Ong, J. C., 588
Opazo, R., 686
Orbach, S., 487, 508
Ornstein, E. D., 664
Osokie, J. N., 446
Oswald, R. F., 153
Otto, M. W., 404, 406
Oxford, R. L., 113, 121
Ozawa-de Silva, C., 590

P
Padesky, C. A., 356, 406
Page, R. C., 195
Palmatier, L. L., 443
Palmer, S., 348, 355
Pandora, 114
Papadopoulos, N., 600
Papp, P., 556
Park, S. M., 523
Parker, J.G., 490
Parks, F. M., 477
Parlett, M., 244, 246
Partridge, M. R., 178
Pascual-Leone, A., 271
Passons, W. R., 252, 254, 255, 257, 258,
    276
Patock-Peckham, J. A., 358
Patterson, C. H., 218
Patton, Michael J., 49
Paunonen, S. V., 113, 118

Pavlov, Ivan, 281, 282, 323
Payne, H., 624
Perez, R. M., 523
Perez Foster, R. M., 73
Perls, Fritz, 7, 241, 241–243, 243, 244, 245, 246, 247, 248, 252, 253, 255, 261, 262, 263, 266, 268, 269, 273, 275, 276, 656
Perls, Laura Posner, 242, 243, 245, 271
Perry, C., 121
Perry, J. W., 105, 110, 121
Person, Ethel, 71
Persons, J. B., 390, 392
Pessin, H., 612
Petchkovsky, L., 115, 121
Petersen, S., 443
Peterson, K. A., 405
Petren, S., 26
Peven, D. E., 143, 144, 145
Pfost, K. S., 195
Phelps, J., 683
Philip (father of Alexander the Great), 85
Philippson, P., 268, 269
Philpot, C. L., 561
Piaget, Jean, 371, 372, 453, 454
Piasecki, J., 406
Pierce, P., 519
Pierrakos, John, 593, 594
Pinderhughes, E., 573
Pine, Fred, 47, 53
Pine, G. J., 214
Pinel, E. C., 173
Pokrywa, M. L., 5, 25
Polster, Erving, 246, 247, 248, 249, 250, 251, 258, 263, 275
Polster, Miriam, 246, 247, 248, 249, 250, 251, 255, 258, 261, 272, 275, 648
Popenoe, Paul, 535
Popper, Karl, 334
Portnoy, D., 194
Poskiparta, M., 683
Powers, M. B., 406
Powers, William, 418, 419
Prata, Giuliana, 566
Pretzer, J., 379
Priebe, S., 600
Priest, R., 477
Prince, S. E., 406
Prochaska, J. O., 5, 9, 26, 663, 669, 670, 671, 672, 673–674, 675, 682, 683, 684, 685, 686, 687
Proctor, G., 232
Pulos, S., 446
Purdon, C., 394
Pyszczynski, T., 173

Q
Qalinge, L., 153
Quenk, N. L., 93, 98, 112, 121
Quinn, K., 526, 683

R
Rabin, C. L., 500, 509, 527
Rachman, S., 395
Rahimi, A., 404
Raitasalo, R., 475
Raiz, L., 195
Randal, P., 685
Rank, Otto, 32, 208
Ransom, D., 612
Rapport, Z., 432
Rasheed, J. M., 574
Rasheed, M. N., 574
Raskin, J. D., 466, 468
Rawlings, E. I., 497, 499
Rector, N. A., 401, 406
Reece, M., 683
Reich, W., 242, 243, 244, 593, 594, 595, 600
Reilly-Harrington, N., 401
Reinares, M., 571
Reiss, D., 567
Remer, P., 497, 500, 501, 503, 506, 507, 508, 510, 513, 514, 517, 518, 524, 525, 527
Rendon, Mario, 70
Renna, B., 446
Resnick, R., 264
Reuterlov, H., 475
Reynolds, A. L., 522, 589, 600
Reynolds, D. K., 585, 586, 589, 590
Rhoades, D. R., 196
Rhodes, R., 524
Ricci, R. J., 311
Rice, D. L., 196
Richeport-Haley, M., 574
Riklin, Franz, 84, 97
Rinfret-Raynor, M., 519
Rio, R., 628
Riso, L. P., 400, 401
Rittenhouse, J., 526
Roades, L. A., 513
Roades, R., 499
Roazen, P., 32, 85, 121
Roberts, L. C., 152
Robertson, M., 612
Robichaud, M., 405
Robins, M., 403, 407
Robinson, L. A., 403
Robson, P., 404
Roesler, C., 90, 121
Roffman, E., 518
Rogers, Carl, 7, 207–212, 213, 214, 215, 216, 217, 218, 219, 220, 221, 222, 226, 227, 228, 229, 230, 231, 232, 233, 234, 235, 241, 253, 335, 356, 384, 443, 645, 647t, 648, 649, 651t, 655, 670, 679, 680
Rogers, Donna, 223
Rogers, P., 628
Rogina, J. M., 185
Rohde, P., 403

Röhricht, F., 600
Rondeau, G., 683
Ronen, T., 372
Rorschach, Hermann, 98
Rose, S. D., 322
Rosello, J., 407
Rosen, D. H., 99, 112, 118
Rosenblatt, D., 245
Rosman, B. L., 549
Rothwell, N., 457
Rotter, J. B., 285
Rounsaville, B. J., 17, 25, 602, 612
Rowland, S., 114, 121, 510
Ruberu, M., 407
Rubin, J., 588
Rubin, J. A., 623, 624, 625f
Ruebelt, S. G., 488
Rupprecht, C. S., 114, 120
Rush, A. J., 382
Rushton, P., 612
Russell, Bertrand, 334
Russell, M., 497, 502, 503, 506, 507, 510
Russianoff, P., 359
Ryan, W. J., 519
Rygh, J. L., 374

S
Sachs, Hans, 32
Safren, S. A., 404, 406
Saiger, G. M., 198, 199
Saley, E., 227
Salhany, J., 358
Salkovskis, P. M., 405
Salloway, S., 195
Salmela, S., 683
Salmon, P., 399
Saltzburg, S., 477
Samuels, A., 99, 111, 115, 121
San Roque, C., 115
Sandahl, C., 74, 600
Sandell, R., 600
Sanders, P., 227, 228, 423
Sanderson, W. C., 405
Sandner, D. E., 94, 121
Sanftner, J. L., 519
Santoro, S. O., 5, 26
Sapp, M., 361
Sarlund-Heinrich, P., 519
Sartre, Jean-Paul, 161, 163, 164, 171, 173
Satir, Virginia, 539, 558, 559, 560, 564, 575, 576
Sava, F. A., 404
Savard, M., 269
Sbrocco, T., 407
Schacht, M., 616, 617
Schatz, D. M., 5, 25
Schaverien, J., 89, 104, 121
Schickling, U., 245
Schlam, T. R., 684

Schlosberg, H., 244
Schmidt, S., 588
Schneider, B., 471
Schneider, K. J., 180, 182, 194
Schoenberg, P., 273
Schopenhauer, Arthur, 84, 334
Schor, L., 214
Schottenbauer, M. A., 684
Schramski, T. G., 151
Schulenberg, S. E., 166, 185, 190
Schultz, D. P., 69, 86, 87, 93, 95, 151, 162, 454
Schultz, S. E., 69, 86, 87, 93, 95, 121, 151, 162, 454
Schumann, A., 684
Schwartz-Salant, N., 109, 121
Sciutto, M. J., 358
Sedehi, M., 404
Seem, S. R., 486
Seeman, J., 214
Segal, L., 566
Segal, Z. V., 382, 399, 400, 588
Selvini-Palazzoli, M., 566
Sensky, T., 406
Sequin, C., 178
Serlin, I., 196
Serok, S., 266, 267
Shafiabadi, A., 361
Shafran, R., 404
Shakespeare, William, 627
Shamdasani, S., 83, 85, 89, 90, 121
Shamsaei, F., 404
Shane, P., 245, 246
Shapiro, D., 317
Shapiro, D. A., 229, 317
Shapiro, D. H., 588
Shapiro, Francine, 310, 311
Shapiro, S. L., 585, 588
Shappel, Sandi, 69
Sharf, R. S., 98, 121, 492
Sharifi, H., 361
Sharp, D., 95, 99, 116, 121
Sharp, S. R., 358
Shaw, B. F., 382
Shaw, H. E., 543
Shaw, S. R., 17, 26
Shepherd, I. L., 253, 270
Shields, F., 286
Shillingford, M. A., 477
Shuang-Luo, Z., 475
Shub, N., 247
Shulman, B. H., 133, 143, 144, 145, 154
Shultz, D. P., 121
Si, G., 361
Siegel, P. R., 587
Siev, J., 404
Sigal, J., 571
Sills, C., 251, 253, 273
Silverberg, R. A., 445
Silverman, E. G., 358

Silverman, M. S., 357
Silverstein, L. B., 518
Sim, T., 573
Simek-Morgan, 485
Simi, N. L., 519
Simkin, James, 273
Simon, K. M., 379, 392
Simpson, A. I. F., 685
Singer, J., 112, 114, 121
Singh, J., 232
Skinner, B. F., 281, 282, 283, 323
Sklare, G. B., 458, 461, 462, 474
Skodol, A. E., 612
Slattery, J. M., 486
Slemenson. M., 273
Smailes, D., 683
Smalley, K. B., 521
Smit, F., 603
Smith, E. W. L., 270, 593, 595, 597, 598, 599, 600
Smith, M. L., 317
Smith, R. L., 573
Smuts, Jan, 242
Snyder, D. K., 570
Sodergren, S. C., 178
Sohm, S., 420
Solomon, H. M., 111, 121
Sophocles, 38
Sota, S., 571
Spangler, D. L., 403
Spangler, P., 98, 121
Spence, J. A., 151
Sperry, L. M., 131, 132, 143, 148, 154
Spiegler, M. D., 321, 399, 400
Spinelli, M., 603
Spinoza, Baruch, 30, 334
St. Clair, Michael, 41
Staemmler, F., 273
Stam, H. J., 2, 26
Stampfl, Thomas, 295
Stathopoulou, G., 406
Steckler, L., 600
Steckley, P., 270
Stein, D. J., 373, 400
Stein, M., 86, 121
SteinBerg, I. K., 471
Steiner, M., 626
Steketee, G., 394
Stermac, L., 270
Sternberg, R. J., 26
Stevens, M. J., 195
Stewart, A. E., 453, 475, 485, 628
Stewart, R. B., 175
Stiles, T. C., 405
Stockwell, C., 423
Stolar, N., 401, 406
Stone, Abraham, 535
Stone, Hannah, 535
Streiner, D., 322
Stricker, G., 663, 668
Strümpfel, U., 258, 264, 270, 271

Strunk, D. R., 404
Stuart, S., 602, 603
Sturdivant, S., 497
Sullivan, Harry Stack, 32, 52, 535, 602
Sullwold, E., 116, 121
Surrey, J. L., 588
Sutton, S., 683
Suvak, J., 2, 26
Suyemoto, K. L., 518
Suzuki, I., 600
Swartz, H. A., 602
Sweeney, M., 407, 525
Sweeney, T. J., 131, 133, 154
Swenson, S., 423
Swildens, J. C. A. G., 225, 226
Swinson, R. P., 308
Szadokierski, I., 423
Szentagotai, A., 343, 357, 361, 404
Szymanski, D. M., 488

T
Tafoya, N., 510
Taft, Jessie, 208
Tahir, L., 478
Tanaka-Matsumi, J., 321, 322, 589
Tang, T. Z., 377, 403
Tantillo, M., 519
Target, Mary, 70
Tart, C., 585
Tatsumi, N., 589
Tausch, R., 228
Taylor, L., 683
Taylor, S., 311, 394
Teasdale, J. D., 399, 404, 588
Teresa, Mother, 335
Terjesen, M. D., 358
Ternstrom, A., 475
Teyber, Edward, 61
Thoma, N. C., 5, 27
Thomas, A., 474
Thompson, A., 115, 120
Thompson, B., 99, 112, 118
Thompson, B. L., 586
Thompson, Clara, 72
Thordarson, D. D., 394
Thordarson, D. S, 405
Thorndike, Edward L., 282, 283
Threadgall, R. A., 445
Tillich, Paul, 163, 165, 170, 245
Tindle, H. A., 588
Tobin, S., 269
Todd, G., 401
Toeman, Zerka, 615
Toman, W., 541
Tomer, A., 171
Tomlinson, T. M., 178
Tompkins, M. A., 386, 390, 392
Toneatto, T., 588
Torres, J. B., 361
Trip, S., 358
Truax, C. B., 229

Truscott, D., 2, 3, 27
Tudor, K., 232
Turkington, D., 401
Turner, C. W., 513, 513–514
Twohig, M. P., 405

U
UKATT Research Team, 683
Ulanov, A. B., 88, 105, 106, 121
Unger, R. K., 490–492
U.S. Department of Labor, 492

V
Vähäsarja, K., 683
Vaihinger, Hans, 126, 454
Van der Pompe, G., 195
Van der Velden, I., 474
van Deurzen (van Deurzen-Smith),
    Emmy, 161, 164, 165, 166, 168,
    176, 177, 180, 181, 182, 186, 187,
    189, 193, 194, 197, 198, 201
Van Dyk, G. A. J., 686
Van Marter, D. F., 683
Van Oppen, P., 603
Van Straten, A., 603
Van Vreeswijk, M., 401
Van Waning, A., 589, 590
Vance, D., 423
Vanhala, M., 683
Vasco, A. B., 686
Vasquez, M. J. T., 518
Veldhuis, C. B., 505
Velicer, W. F., 684
Velten, E., 347, 355
Verdeli, H., 603, 612
Verduin, T., 26
Vernon, A., 358
Vick, R. M., 623
Viney, L., 476
Vinogradov, S. C., 194
Virgin Mary, 91
Visser, A., 195
Vogel, P. S., 405
Von Bertalanffy, C., 537
Von Hartman, Eduard, 84
Vontress, C. E., 197

W
Wachtel, Paul, 10, 66, 663, 664, 665,
    667, 669, 674, 675, 682, 685,
    686, 687
Wadeson, H., 624, 625f
Wagner-Moore, L. E., 270
Walach, H., 588
Walen, S., 334, 342, 343, 359
Walker, J., 340, 341
Walker, L. E. A., 506
Walker, L. J. S., 525
Walker, M., 508
Walkup, J., 403
Wallen, R., 246

Wallerstein, Robert S., 67, 70
Walsh, R., 585, 586, 588
Waltz, J., 586
Wampold, B. E., 10, 25, 26
Wändell, P. E., 588
Ward, C. H., 384
Ward, R., 683
Ward, S., 474
Warwar, S. H., 271
Washington, D. O., 404
Watkins, C. E., Jr., 152
Watkins, M., 104, 121
Watson, J., 270, 271
Watson, J. C., 270, 276
Watson, John, 281, 282, 283
Watts, R. E., 127, 128, 150, 208
Watzlawick, P., 244, 570
Weakland, John, 455, 456, 536, 553, 570
Weber, S., 509
Wedding, D., 26, 679
Weeks, G. R., 433, 556
Weems, C. F., 170
WeinBerg, I. K.er, A. D., 374
Weiner, D. K., 588
Weiner, D. N., 332, 333
Weishaar, M., 374, 376
Weiss, B., 231
Weiss, J. F., 195
Weiss, R. D., 17, 26
Weissman, A., 384, 602, 603
Weissman, M. M., 404, 602, 603, 608,
    609, 610, 612
Weisz, J. R., 27, 231
Welfel, E. R., 24, 27
Wells, A., 395, 396, 401, 513
Wen-Feng, L., 475
Wenzel, A., 390, 401, 603
Werth, J. L., Jr., 24, 27
Wertheimer, Max, 245
Wessels, A. B., 195
Wessler, R. L., 334
West, C., 2, 26, 486, 495, 497, 498, 525
West, C. K., 518
West, R., 684
Westbrook, D., 405
Wettersten, K. B., 475
Wheeler, G., 272
Wheelwright, J. B., 98, 112, 121
Wheelwright, J. H., 98, 112, 121
Whipple, V., 445
Whisman, M. A., 380, 384, 390, 392
Whitaker, Carl, 539, 558, 559, 564, 575,
    576
White, J. R., 408
White, M., 480
White, Michael, 453, 456, 457, 466, 468,
    469, 474, 479
Whitmont, E. C., 87, 88, 103, 118, 121
Whittal, M. L., 405
Wieling, E., 520
Wiener, Norbert, 537

Wilde, J., 358
Wilhelm, Richard, 86
Wilkinson, M., 111, 121
Williams, A. C., 72
Williams, J. M. G., 399, 521, 588
Wills, F., 373, 380, 384, 410
Wilson, G. T., 684
Wilson, K. G., 588
Wilson, M. G., 683
Wimer, D. J., 521
Winnicott, Donald, 32, 41, 42, 44, 111
Winstead, B. A., 151
Winter, D., 476
Winter, D. G., 2, 25
Wolf, Alexander, 73
Wolfe, B. E., 194
Wolfe, J. L., 359
Wolman, B., 118
Wolpe, Joseph, 291, 292, 293, 294, 299,
    300, 675
Wolter-Gustafson, C., 232
Wong, D., 573
Wong, P. T. P., 171
Woods, P. J., 357, 358
Woodworth, R., 244
Worell, J., 497, 500, 501, 503, 506, 507,
    508, 510, 513, 514, 517, 518, 520,
    524, 525, 527
Wright, F. D., 396
Wubbolding, Robert E., 419, 420, 423,
    424, 425, 427, 428, 429, 430, 431,
    432, 433, 442, 443, 444, 446,
    447, 448
Wundt, Wilhelm, 30
Wyche, K. F., 509
Wyckoff, L. A., 5, 25
Wynne, Lyman, 537

Y
Yablonsky, L., 620
Yakushko, O., 196
Yalom, Irvin, 165, 166, 169, 170, 171, 172,
    173, 174, 177, 178, 180, 181, 182,
    183, 185, 186, 189, 190, 194, 195,
    198, 199, 200, 201
Yang, M., 196
Yates, B. T., 404
Yates, J., 95, 121
Yeager, R., 354
Yeakle, R., 148
Yeung, F. K. C., 477
Yokoyama, K., 524
Yontef, G. M., 251, 252, 253, 254, 264,
    268, 269
Yoshimoto, Ishin, 588, 589
Young, J. E., 373, 374, 384, 400, 593,
    600, 612
Young, M. J., 196
Young-Bruehl, Elisabeth, 32
Young-Eisendrath, P., 114
Yudofsky, S. C., 26

Z

Zachary, I., 359, 360
Zahm, S., 269
Zalsman, G., 603
Zarabian, M. K., 404

Zare, M., 361
Zeig, J. K., 454, 455
Zeigarnik, B., 244
Zeus, 114
Ziegler, D. J., 335, 358

Zimmerman, J. L., 468, 525
Zimring, F., 217
Zinker, J., 252, 262, 274
Zionts, P., 358
Zunin, L. M., 418, 432

Subject Index

Note: Page numbers in bold indicate an in-depth discussion of the topic. Page numbers followed by an *f* refer to figures. Page numbers followed by a *t* refer to tables.

A

A-B-C theory of personality, 337–339
A-B-C-D-E therapeutic approach, 343–346
Acceptance and commitment therapy (ACT), 311–312
Accommodation, 255, 548
Acting as if, 138–139
Action, 495
Active schemas, 376
Adapting Cognitive Therapy for Depression (Whisman), 390
Addictions, 584
Addressing Cultural Complexities in Practice (Hays), 321
Adlerian therapy, **123–159**
  analysis, 132–133
  anger, 143
  anxiety, 640*t*
  assessment, 132–133
  assets, 136–137
  birth order, 130
  brief therapy, 148–149
  critique, 654–655
  current trends, 149–150
  dreams, 135
  family constellations, 133–134
  family dynamics, 133–134
  family therapy, 562
  gender issues, 152–153
  goals of, 131, 636*t*
  group counseling and therapy, 154
  group therapy approaches, 651*t*
  history of, 124–126
  inferiority complex, 129–130
  influences on, 125–126
  insight, 137–138
  integrative theory of psychotherapy and, 668*t*
  interpretation, 137–138
  life, style of, 127–128
  life and life's demands, misperception of, 136
  mistakes, basic, 136
  multicultural issues, 153–154

overgeneralizations, 136
personality theory, 126–130, 633*t*
psychological disorders, 142–148
recollections, early, 134–135
reorientation, 138
research, 151–152, 647*t*
security, goals of, 136
social interest, 128
superiority complex, 129–130
theories, using with other, 150–151
theories of, 7, 124–131
therapeutic relationship, 131–132
therapeutic techniques, 638*t*
therapy and counseling, theory of, 130–142
values, faulty, 136
worth, minimization or denial of one's, 136
Adolescence, 40, 95, 491
Adulthood, 491–492
Affect, 676
Affective schemas, 377
Alcohol and substance abuse, 354
Alcoholics Anonymous (AA), 355
Alcoholism, 190–191, 354–355
Alignment, 547
All-or-nothing thinking, 635
Alpha bias, 490
Altruism, 39
Amplification, 91
Anal stage, 38, 40
Analysis, bioenergetic, 594–595
Analysis and dreams, 100–103
The Analysis of the Self (Kohut), 43
Analyst, 4
Analytically informed counseling and therapy, 66
Androgyny: The Opposites Within (Singer), 114
Anima, 89
Animus, 89
Animus and Anima (Jung, E.), 84
Anorexia, 15, 434–438, 516–517. *See also* Eating disorders
Anticathexis, 35
Anticipatory beliefs, 397
Anti-suggestion, 141
Anxiety
  case study, 56–57, 186–188, 265–266, 441–442
  disorder, 13–14, 296, 350–353

existential personality theory, 169–170
hierarchies, 292
neurosis, 108–109
rational emotive behavior A-B-C theory of personality, 339
theoretical approaches to, 640*t*
treatments, research supported psychological, 644*t*
types of, 35
Application phase, 300
The Archetypal Imagination (Hollis), 111
Arousal, 289
Art and Science of Love, (Ellis), 333
Art of Solution Focused Therapy (Connie & Metcalf), 466
Art Stimulus Apperceptive Response Test, 214
Asian psychotherapy, **583–591**
  and addictions, 585
  Asian philosophy, impact of, 583–584
  background of, 583
  case study, 587
  Indian psychology, 584
  mindfulness meditation, 586–587
  Morita therapy, 590–591
  Naikan psychotherapy, 588
  personality theory, 584, 669*t*
  theories of, 586
Assertiveness training, 323, 505
Assessment
  Adlerian therapy, 637*t*
  approach, 637*t*
  of behavior, 290
  cognitive therapy, 380–384
  of constructivist therapies, 592
  dreams as, 177–178
  existential psychotherapy, 177–178
  feminist therapy, 499
  in therapy, 635
  initial, 177
  Jungian analysis and therapy, 97
  multimodal therapy, 677–679
  narrative therapy, 468–469
  psychoanalysis, 48
  psychodrama, 617
  reality therapy, 423–424
  of solution focused therapy, 458
  tests, use of objective and projective, 178

Subject Index

Assimilation, 255
Assimilative integrative approach, 663
Association for Behavioral and
    Cognitive Therapies, 284
*Attachment Theory and Research in Clinical
    Work with Adults* (Obegi &
    Berant), 70
Attentional processes, 287–288
Attitude modulation, 185
Attitudes, 91–93, 429
Authentic, 162, 174–175
Automatic thoughts, 374
Auxiliary function, 93
Awareness
    assessment, 250
    avoidance of, 262–263
    dreams and, 260–262
    emphasizing, 256
    enactment and, 260
    example of, 250–251
    feelings, 250, 258
    homework and, 262
    language and, 256–257
    nonverbal behavior and, 257
    questions, 255–256
    self, 250, 257
    self dialogue and, 258–260
    sensations and actions, 250
    statements, 255–256
    values, 250

B
Bad faith, 171
Beck Depression Inventory, 305–306, 605
On Becoming a Person (Rogers), 210
Behavior
    assessment of, 290
    basic principles of, 285
    bed wetting, 282
    multimodal therapy, 676
    positive reinforcement, 285
    target, 289
Behavior: The Control of Perception
    (Powers), 418
Behavior theory of personality, 285–289
Behavior therapy, **281–324**
    acceptance and commitment therapy
        (ACT), 311
    anxiety, 640t
    application phase, 300
    assessment, 637t
    brief, 309
    case study, 281
    classical conditioning, 281–282
    concepts of, 7–8
    conceptual phase, 300
    conditioned response (CR), 281
    conditioned stimulus (CS), 281
    critique, 656
    current status of, 284
    current trends, 309–316

discrimination, 285, 287
extinction, 286
family therapy, 563
feminist, 508–509
generalization, 285–286
goals of, 289, 636t
group therapy, 322, 652t
history of, 281
integrative theory of psychotherapy
    and, 668t
journals of, 284
modeling technique, 297–299
neutral stimulus, 281
observational learning, 287
operant conditioning, 282
personality theory, 633t–634t
reinforcement, negative, 286
reinforcement, positive, 285
research, 647t
shaping, 287
skills acquisition phase, 300
social cognitive theory, 283
summary of, 323–324
theories, using with other, 316–317
theories of, 289–301
therapeutic techniques, 639t
treatments, research supported
    psychological, 644t
unconditioned response (UCR), 281
unconditioned stimulus (UCS), 281
Behavioral assessment, 290
Behavioral interviews, 290
Behavioral observations, 291
Behavioral Practice, 373
Behavioral reports and ratings, 291
Behavioral schemas, 377
Being and Time (Heidegger), 162
Being-for-itself, 166–167
Being-in-the-world, 162, 164, 166
Being-in-the-World (Binswanger), 164
Beliefs, 397
Beta bias, 490
*Better, Deeper, and More Enduring Brief
    Therapy* (Ellis), 346
Betweenness, 163
Bigotry, 524
Bioenergetic analysis, 594–595
Biology, 676
Bipolar depression, 13
Birth order, 130
Bisexual, 522–523
*Biting the Hand That Starves You:
    Inspiring Resistance to Anorexia/
    Bulimia* (Maisel, Epsten &
    Borden), 457, 516
Blacky test, 48
Blamer, 559
Body armor, 243
Body image, 498, 593, 594
Body psychotherapy, **593–600**
    background of, 593

bioenergetic analysis, 594
body assessment techniques, 597
character, 595–596
Chiron approach, 600
concepts of, 9
ethics and, 600
hard techniques, 599
masochistic character, 596
oral character, 596
personality theory, 595
psychotherapeutic approaches to, 597
rigid character, 596
schizoid character, 595–596
self-regulation, 600
soft techniques, 597
summary of, 600
vegetotherapy, 594
Body psychotherapy personality theory,
    669t
Body-boundaries, 248
Borderline disorder, 14, 58–59, 109,
    147–148, 189–190, 225–226,
    511–513, 644t
Borderline personality disorder. *See*
    Borderline disorder
Boundaries, 248–250, 546–547, 549
Bowen's family therapy. *See* Family
    therapy
Bridging, 679
Brief Gestalt Therapy (Houston), 268
Brief psychoanalytic therapy, 62–65
Brief therapy
    Adlerian theory, 148–149
    assessment, 192
    behavior therapy, 309
    cognitive therapy, 398–399
    concern, identifying the, 192
    existential therapy, 191–193
    family systems therapy, 565–567
    feminist therapy, 510–511
    Mental Research Institute, 565–566
    person-centered therapy, 226
    psychotherapy, 641–642
    rational emotive behavior therapy
        (REBT), 355
    resistance, identifying, 192
    searching process, teaching
        the, 192
    termination, 192
British Journal of Gestalt Therapy, 270
British school of Jungian analysis, 111
Buddha/Buddhism, 584–585, 588
Bulimia, 15, 434–438, 516–517. *See also*
    Eating disorders

C
Care, ethics of, 494–495
Carl Rogers on Encounter Groups
    (Rogers), 233
Carl Rogers on Personal Power (Rogers),
    210, 232

Case studies
  alcoholism, 190–191
  anxiety, 56–57, 108–109, 186–188,
    265–266, 350–353, 441–442
  borderline disorder, 58–59, 109,
    147–148, 189–190, 225–226, 511–513
  classical conditioning, 281–282
  covert modeling, 299
  depression, 61–62, 107, 143–145, 189,
    222–223, 264–265, 305–306, 353,
    389–392, 440–441, 513–514
  drug abuse, 438–439
  eating disorders, 146–147, 434–438,
    516–517
  generalized anxiety disorder, 146,
    301–305, 392–393
  grief and loss, 223–225
  guilt and compulsions, 472–473
  hysteria, 55–56
  interpersonal therapy, 610–612
  mindfulness meditation, 587–588
  Mitchell's modes, 46
  narcissistic disorder, 59–61
  narrative therapy, 472–473
  obsessive disorder, 393–394
  obsessive-compulsive disorder, 190,
    306–308, 353–354
  personal construct therapy, 467–468
  phobic disorders, 308–309
  posttraumatic stress disorder (PTSD),
    266–267, 514–516
  Prochaska and colleagues'
    transtheoretical approach,
    673–674
  psychotic disorders, 109–110
  social constructionism, 20
  social learning theory, 283
  social reinforcement, 286
  solution-focused therapy, 463–466
  substance abuse, 267, 396–398
  systemic desensitization, 292–294
  Wachtel's cyclical psychodynamics
    theory, 665–667
Catastrophizing, 377–378
Catching oneself, 139–140, 143
Catharsis, 671
Cathect, 34
Challenging absolutes, 387–388
Changeable schemas, 376
Childhood, 95, 490
Chiron approach, 595
Choice, 171–172, 183–184, 420–421
Choice theory, 419–422
*Choice Theory: A New Psychology of
    Personal Freedom* (Glasser), 418
Circular questioning, 566
Circularity, 538f
Classical conditioning, 281–282
Classical psychoanalysts, 47
Client, 4
Client-centered therapy, 207

*Client-Centered Therapy: Its Current
    Practice, Implications, and Theory*
    (Rogers), 209–210
*Clinical Handbook of Psychological
    Disorder* (Barlow), 387
The Clinical Treatment of the Problem Child
    (Rogers), 208
Clinically meaningful change, 646
Clock time, 168
Closure, 254
*Clues: Investigating Solutions in Brief
    Therapy* (de Shazer), 456
Coalitions, 547
Cognition, 676
*Cognitive Behavioral Workbook for Anxiety:
    A Step-by-Step Program* (Knaus),
    347
Cognitive Behaviour Therapy, 373
Cognitive rehearsal, 389
Cognitive schemas, 377
Cognitive therapy, **369–415**
  anxiety, 640t
  assessment, 380–384, 637t
  concepts of, 8
  critique, 657
  current influences, 373
  depression, 640t
  distortions, 377–378
  family therapy, 563
  feminist, 508–509
  gender issues, 406–407
  goals of, 379–380, 636t
  group therapy, 408–409, 652t
  history of, 370–371
  integrative theory of psychotherapy
    and, 668t
  multicultural issues, 407–408
  OCD, 393–396
  personality theory, 373–378, 633t–634t
  psychological disorders, 389
  research, 402–406, 647t
  session format, 386
  techniques, 387–389
  termination, 386–387
  theoretical influences, 371–373
  theories, using with other, 401–402
  theory of, 379–389
  therapeutic process, 385–387
  therapeutic techniques, 639t
  treatments, research supported
    psychological, 644t
Cognitive Therapy and Research, 373
Cognitive Therapy for Bipolar Disorder
    (Lam, Jones, Hayward, & Bright),
    390
*Cognitive Therapy for Suicidal Patients:
    Scientific and Clinical Applications*
    (Wenzel, et al.), 390
Cognitive Therapy of Substance Abuse (Beck,
    Wright, Newman & Liese), 396
Cognitive triad, 390

Cognitive-behavior, 283–284, 299, 301,
    318, 346
Cognitive-behavioral approach, 271
Cohesiveness, 408
Color blindness, 524
Coming out issues, 522
Commitment, 141
Common factors, 683
Comparison, **631–652**
Compelling schemas, 376
Complementary relationships, 565
Compulsions, 14
Concentration-therapy, 242
The Concept of the Dead
    (Kierkegaard), 161
Conceptional phase, 300
Concepts in theory, 2–3
Conditioned response (CR), 281
Conditioned stimulus (CS), 281
Confluence, 249
Confrontation, 432
Congruent communicator, 559
Coniunctio, 109
Conscience, 35
Conscious, 33
Consciousness, levels of, 87–88
Consciousness-raising (CR), 486, 671
Consciousness-raising (CR) groups, 486
Constellation, 133–134
Constructivism, 19–20
Constructivist approaches, **452–479**. *See
    also* Narrative therapy; Solution-
    focused therapy
  assessment, 637t
  concepts of, 8
  critique, 658
  early family therapy, 454
  early influences, 453–454
  goals of, 636t
  history of, 453
  integrative theory of psychotherapy
    and, 668t
  multicultural issues, 477
  narrative therapy, **466–474**
  personality theory, 634t
  recent, 456–457
  research, 475–476, 647t
  solution focused, **457–466**,
    476–479
  theories of, 474
  therapeutic techniques, 639t
Contact, 247–250, 254
*Contemporary Body Psychotherapy: The
    Chiron Approach* (Hartley), 600
Context, 499
Contingency management, 671–672, 675
*Control Theory: A New Explanation of How
    We Control Our Lives* (Glasser),
    418
Control Theory in the Classroom
    (Glasser), 418

Control Theory in the Practice of Reality Therapy (Glass), 434
Conversion disorder, 14–15
Cooperation Between the Sexes (Ansbacher and Ansbacher), 153
Core Conflictual Relationship Theme Method, 63–66
Core mindfulness skills, 315
Cost-benefit analysis, 347
Counseling. *See also under individual types of counseling*
  Adlerian theory, 130–142
  author's theory of, 24
  couples, 575
  defined, 4
  feminist therapy, 510
  theories of, 5–6
  your theory of, 24
Counseling and Psychotherapy (Rogers), 208–209
Counseling With Choice Theory (Glasser), 418, 434
Counterconditioning, 294, 672, 675
Countertransference, 53–54, 105–106
Couples counseling, 575
Courage, 163
The Courage to Be (Tillich), 165
The Courage to Create (May), 165
Covert modeling, 298–299
CPSS model, 499
Creating images, 140
Creative arts therapies, **621–629**
  art, 623
  dance movement, 624–626
  drama, 626–628
  drawing, Craig's, 625*f*
  integrative theory of psychotherapy and, 669*t*
  music, 628–629
  summary of, 629–630
The Crescent and the Couch: Cross-currents Between Islam and Psychoanalysis (Akhtar), 73
Critique of therapies, **653–661**
The Cry for Myth (May), 165
Cultural. *See also* Multicultural issues
  analysis, 500
  anxiety, 197
  identity, 153
  intervention, 500–501
  relativism, 493
Cultural Competence in Trauma Therapy: Beyond the Flashback (Brown), 514–515
Culture-focused approach, 574
Current trends
  Adlerian theory, 149–150
  behavior therapy, 309–310
  cognitive therapy, 399–401
  common factors, 642–643, 645
  existential therapy, 193

family therapy, 567–569
feminist therapy, 517–519
gestalt, 268–269
integrative therapy, 683
Jungian, 111–112
narrative therapy, 473–474
person-centered therapy, 226–227
psychoanalysis, 65–66
rational emotive behavior therapy (REBT), 355–356
reality therapy, 442–443
societal implications, 226–227
solution focused therapy, 473–474
theoretical purity vs. eclecticism, 227
training, 227
Cyclical psychodynamics, 664

D
Das Man, 162
Dasein, 162, 166
Dasein choosing, 167
Death Anxiety Scale, 178
Death instinct, 33
Decatastrophizing, 388
Decentering, 399
Defense against reality situations, 39
Deflection, 249
Denial, 36
Depression
  Adlerian therapy, 640*t*
  Beck inventory of, 305–306, 605
  behavioral therapy, 640*t*
  bipolar, 13
  case study, 61–62, 107, 143–145, 189, 222–223, 264–265, 305–306, 353, 389–392, 440–441, 513–514
  defined, 13
  Hamilton Rating Scale for Depression, 610
  interpersonal psychotherapy, 603–605, 608
  theoretical approaches to, 640*t*
  treatments, research supported psychological, 644*t*
  unipolar, 13
Depression: Clinical, Experimental, and Theoretical Aspects (Beck), 370
Dereflection, 185
Desensitization, 293
Deserted island fantasy, 681
Desire, 496
Destroying own feelings, 558
Detriangulation, 543–544
Developmental lines, 39
Developmental school of Jungian analysis, 111
Diagnostic and Statistical Manual of Mental Disorders (DSM-IV-TR, American Psychiatric Association, 2000), 12, 16, 97
Diagnostic approach, 253

Dialectical behavior therapy (DBT), 312–316, 588
Dialectical persuasion, 314–315
Differential treatment, 640–641
Differentiation of self, 540
Disconnection, 375
Discrimination, 286–287
Disengaged, 547
Disgust: wisdom, 41
Disorders. *See also under individual types of disorders*
  anxiety, 13–14
  borderline, 14, 109
  conversion, 14–15
  psychological, 12–16, 106–107, 142–148, 186–191
Dispirited condition, 186, 189
Displacement, 36
Distortion, 388, 508
Distress tolerance skills, 315
Diversity, 498
Divorced Without Children: Solution-Focused Therapy With Women at Midlife (Castaldo), 476
Does Psychoanalysis Work? (Galatzer-Levy, Bachrach, Skolnikoff, & Waldron), 67–68
Doing, 421
Double bind, 536
Dramatic relief, 671
Dreams
  Adlerian therapy, 135
  Jungian analysis, compensatory functions of, 103
  Jungian analysis, interpretations of, 51–52, 101–102
  Jungian analysis, material of, 100
  Jungian analysis, structure of, 100–101
Drive theory
  consciousness, levels of, 33–34
  defense mechanisms, 35–37
  drives and instincts, 33
  personality, structure of, 34–35
  psychoanalysis, 33–39, 52–53
  psychosexual stages of development, 37–39
  therapy, goals of, 636*t*
Drives, 33
Drug abuse, 438–439
Drugs, multimodal, 676

E
Early childhood, 40
Eating disorders, 15, 146–147, 434–438, 516–517
Ego, 2, 35
Ego, Hunger and Aggression (Perls), 242
The Ego and the Id (Freud), 31–32
The Ego and the Mechanisms of Defense (Freud, A.), 39

Ego ideal, 35
Ego psychology, 32, 39–41, 53
Ego theory, 636t
Eigenwelt, 167–168, 176, 194
Eight Lessons for a Happier Marriage (Glasser & Glasser), 419
Either/Or (Kierkegaard), 161
EMDR (eye-movement desensitization and reprocessing), 310–311
EMDR and the Art of Psychotherapy with Children (Adler-Tapia & Settle), 310
Emotional allowances, 289
Emotional cutoff, 541
Empathy, 2, 49–50
Empirically supported therapy, 18
Empowerment, 498
Enacting, 255
Enactment, 549
Encouragement, 138–139
Encyclopedia of Sexual Behavior (Ellis), 333
Engagement, 186
Enmeshed, 547
Environmental reevaluation, 671
Epston and White's narrative therapy, **468–473**, 479
Equifinality, 538
Eros, 33
Essential Components of Cognitive-Behavior Therapy for Depression (Persons, Davidson & Tompkins), 390
Ethical issues, 316
Ethics, 23–24
Ethics of care, 494–495
Evaluation, 427
Evaluation interview, 542–543
Every Student Can Succeed (Glasser), 418
Eve's Daughters (Polster), 272
Evidence-based psychotherapy, 18
Exaggeration, 256
Exception seeking questions, 461–462
Existence as real, 176
Existential a priori, 164
Existential and Spiritual Issues in Death Attitudes (Tomer, Eliason, & Wong), 171
Existential Counseling and Psychotherapy in Practice (Van Deurzen), 166
Existential power, 503–504
Existential Psychology: East-West (Hoffman, et. al.), 196
Existential therapy, **161–205**
  anxiety, 169–170, 640t
  assessment, 177–178, 637t
  authenticity, 174–175
  being, four ways of, 167–168
  being-in-the-world, 166–167
  brief therapy, 191–193
  choice, 171–172, 183–184
  and counseling, 176–177
  critique, 655

current trends, 193
defined, 7
depression, 640t
dying, 170–171, 180–181
existential thought, 161–166
family therapy, 562
freedom, 171–172, 182
gender issues, 196
goals of, 176, 636t
group counseling and psychotherapy, 198–199
group therapy approaches, 651t
history of, 161–166
integrative theory of psychotherapy and, 668t
isolation, 172–173, 184–185
living, 170–171, 180–181
loving, 172–173, 184–185
meaning and meaninglessness, 173, 185–186
multicultural issues, 196–198
personality theory, 166–176, 633t
philosophers of, 161–164
philosophy, 163
psychological disorders, 186–191
psychotherapy, 175–186
psychotherapy, originators of existential, 164–165
psychotherapy, recent contributors to existential, 165–166
research, 194–196, 647t
responsibility, 171–172, 182–183
self-transcendence, 173–174
theories, using with other, 194
therapeutic relationship, 178–180
therapeutic techniques, 638t–639t
time and being, 168–169
values, 175
Existential-Integrative Psychotherapy (Schneider), 194
Experience (person-centered)
  change, 220
  exploration, process of, 219
  in therapy, client's, 218–220
  responsibility, 218
  the self, 219–220
  the therapist, 218–219
Experiencing Scale, 178
Experiential therapy, 240–279, 558–559
Explosive level, 248
Expressive-boundaries, 248
Extinction, 286
Extraversion, 91–93
Eye-movement desensitization and reprocessing (EMDR), 310–311

F
Facilitating, 233
False self, 42
Familiarity-boundaries, 248

Families
  Adlerian constellations, 131–134
  Adlerian dynamics, 131–134
  communication patterns in, 536
  conflicts, 673
  counseling, 535
  dynamics, 131–134, 153–154
  law, 568
  life chronology, 559
  nuclear, 540–541
  projection process, 541
  reconstruction, 560
  schizophrenia, communication patterns with members who have, 536
  sculpting, 560
  structure, 546
  subsystem, 546
  systems, 673
Family Based Services: A Solution-Focused Approach (Berg), 456
Family systems therapy, **533–581**. *See also* Families; Family therapy
  assessment, 637t
  Bowen's, techniques of, 542–544
  brief therapy, 565–567
  couples counseling, 575
  critique, 659–660
  current trends, 567–569
  experiential therapy, 558–559
  gender issues, 572–573
  general systems theory, 537–539
  goals of, 542, 636t
  history of, 534–539
  humanistic therapies, 559–560
  individual, applied to the, 575
  individual therapy, theories of, 561–562
  integrative therapy, 560–561
  intergenerational family systems, 539–545
  multicultural issues, 573–575
  personality theory, 634t
  research, 569–572, 647t
  strategic therapy, 553–558
  therapeutic techniques, 639t
Family therapy, **533–581**. *See also* Families; Family systems therapy
  Bowen, Murray, 539–545, 636t
  comparison, 650
  early approaches to, 455
  integrative theory of psychotherapy and, 669t
  psychoanalytic and related influences on, 535–536
  schizophrenia, communication patterns with members who have, 536
  structural, 545–553
Faulty thinking, 508
Feedback, 537–538

Feeling, 92–93, 421
Femaleist, 489
Feminine intuition, 496
Feminist Archetypal Theory (Lauter and Rupprecht), 114
Feminist behavioral and cognitive therapy, 508–509
Feminist Family Therapy: Empowerment in Social Context (Silverstein & Goodrich), 572
Feminist gestalt therapy, 509
Feminist narrative therapy, 509–510
Feminist psychoanalytic theory, 507–508
Feminist therapy. *See also* Gender issues
 anxiety, 640t
 assessment, 499, 637t
 brief therapy, 510–511
 for change not adjustment, 497
 and counseling, 510
 critique, 658–659
 current trends, 517–519
 depression, 640t
 family therapy, 564
 Gay, Lesbian, Bisexual, or Transgender clients (GLBT), 522–523
 gender issues, 485–486, 520–523
 gestalt therapy, 509
 goals of, 497, 636t
 group counseling, 525–526
 group therapy approaches, 652t
 history of, 486–489
 integrative theory of psychotherapy and, 669t
 a multicultural approach, **484–532**
 multicultural issues, 485–486, 523–525
 narrative therapy, 509–510
 personality theory, 489–497, 634t
 psychological disorders, 511–517
 research, 519–520, 647t
 techniques, 500
 terminology, 518, 522
 theories, using with other, 507–510
 theories of, 497–507
 therapeutic relationship, 499–500
 therapeutic techniques, 639t
Fictionalism, 126
Field theory, 244
Firing order, 676
First-order change, 565
Free association, 31, 49
Freedom, 171–172, 182
Freedom and Destiny (May), 165
Function strength, 93
Functional analysis, 289
Functions, 92–93
Fundamental meaning structure, 164
The Future of Psychoanalysis (Chessick), 66

G

Gay, Lesbian, Bisexual, or Transgender clients (GLBT), 522–523, 572
Gender, 485
Gender and Desire: Uncursing Pandora (Young-Eisendrath), 114
Gender issues. *See also* Feminist therapy
 Adlerian theory, 152–153
 behavior therapy, 320–321
 cognitive therapy, 406–407
 comparison, 646, 648–649
 difference and similarities, 489–492
 existential therapy, 196–198
 family systems therapy, 572–573
 feminist therapy, 485–486, 520–523
 gestalt therapy, 271–272
 integrative therapy, 685
 Jungian analysis and therapy, 113–114
 narrative therapy, 477
 person-centered therapy, 232
 psychoanalysis, 70–71
 rational emotive behavior therapy (REBT), 359–360
 reality therapy, 444–445
 solution focused therapy, 476
 theory, 22
Gender-role analysis, 501–502
Gender-role intervention, 502–503
Generalized anxiety disorder, 13–14, 146, 301–305, 318–319, 392–393, 644t
Genital stage, 38–41
Genograms, 543
Geographical location, 154
Gerotranscendence, 41
The Gestalt Approach (Perls), 243
The Gestalt Review, 270
Gestalt therapy, **240–279**
 anxiety, 265–266, 640t
 assessment, 253–254, 637t
 awareness, 250–263
 brief therapy, 268
 contact, 247–248
 creativity, 263–264
 critique, 656
 current trends, 268–269
 defined, 241
 depression, 264–265, 640t
 emotion-focused, 268
 ethics, 264
 family therapy, 562
 feminist, 509
 figure, 246
 gender issues, 271–272
 gestalt psychology, 245–247
 goals of, 252–253, 636t
 ground, 246
 group therapy, 273–274, 651t
 history of, 241–243
 integration, 252, 263–264

integrative theory of psychotherapy and, 668t
 multicultural issues, 272–273
 personality theory, 245–251, 633t
 present, importance of, 251
 psychological disorders, 264–268
 psychotherapy, theory of, 251–264
 research, 269–271, 647t
 risks, 264
 theories, using with other, 269
 therapeutic change, 254–255
 therapeutic techniques, 638t–639t
 treatments, research supported psychological, 644t
Gestalt Therapy: Excitement and Growth in the Human Personality (Perls, Goodman, Hefferline), 242
Gestalt Therapy Verbatim (Perls), 242
Getting Together and Staying Together (Glasser & Glasser), 418–419
Good enough mother, 42
Good faith, 172
Gray-Wheelwright Jungian Type Survey (GW; Wheelwright, Wheelwright, & Buehler), 97–98, 112
Grief and loss, 223–225, 604
Group counseling and psychotherapy
 Adlerian theory, 154
 choice, 198–199
 dying, 198
 existential therapy, 198–199
 feminist therapy, 525–526
 freedom, 198–199
 isolation, 199
 living, 198
 loving, 199
 meaning and meaninglessness, 199
 person-centered therapy, 233–234
 reality therapy, 446–447
 responsibility, 198–199
Group skills training, 315
Group therapy
 Adlerian theory, 154
 approaches, 651t–652t
 assertiveness training in, 322
 behavior therapy, 322
 cognitive therapy, 408–409
 comparison, 650–652
 constructivist approaches, 478
 gestalt therapy, 273–274
 Jungian analysis and therapy, 116
 psychoanalysis, 73–74
 rational emotive behavior therapy (REBT), 361–362
 social skills training in, 322
 theory, 23
A Guide to Treatments that Work (Nathan and Gorman), 18–19
Guided discovery, 385
Guilt and compulsions, 472–473

H

Hamilton Rating Scale for Depression, 605, 610
Handbook of Psychotherapy Integration (Norcross & Goldfried), 683
The Heart and Soul of Change: Delivering What Works in Therapy (Duncan), 10
Hedonism, 334
Heterosexism, 522
Hindu / Hinduism, 584
Holism and Evolution (Smuts), 242
Homeostasis, 538–539
Homework, 142, 386
Homophobia, 522
Homosexuality, 522–523. *See also* Gay, Lesbian, Bisexual, or Transgender clients (GLBT)
How Does Analysis Cure? (Kohut), 43
How to Make Yourself Happy and Remarkably Less Disturbable (Ellis), 333
How to Think and Intervene Like an REBT Therapist (Dryden), 344, 346
Human being, 167
Humanism, 209, 334–335
Humanistic Psychotherapy: The rational Emotive Approach (Ellis), 333
Humanistic therapies, 194, 559–560
Humor, 432
Hypervigilance, 392
Hypochondria, 14
Hysteria, 15, 55–56

I

I, 425–426
I-am, 167
I-boundaries, 248
Id, 34–35
Identification, 37
Identification with the aggressor, 39
Idiosyncratic meaning, 387
I-it, 163
Imagery, 676
Imaginal flooding therapies, 294–295
Imagination, 104
Immediacy, 138
Impaired autonomy, 375
Impaired limits, 375
Impaired performance, 375
Impasse, 248
Implosive level, 248
Implosive therapy, 295
In and Out of the Garbage Pail (Perls), 243
In vivo therapies, 295, 297
Inauthentic, 162, 174–175
Indian psychology, 584
Individual differences, 493
Individual therapy, 313, 561–562
Individuation, 41, 96
Infancy, 40

Inferior function, 93–94
Inferiority complex, 129
Inhibition, 375
Instincts, 33
Institute for Rational Living (Albert Ellis Institute), 332
Instrumental conditioning, 281–283
Integrative therapy, **662–690**
  concepts of, 9–10
  current trends, 683
  family therapy, 560–561
  gender issues, 685
  Lazarus multimodal theory, using as a model for your, 682
  multicultural issues, 685–686
  Prochaska and colleagues' transtheoretical approach, using as a model for your, 674–675
  research, 684–685
  Wachtel's psychodynamics, 663–667
Intellectualization, 37
Intensity, 549
Interrater reliability, 291
Intergenerational family systems, 539–545
Intermittent reinforcement, 286
The International Forum for Logotherapy, 193
The International Gestalt Journal, 270
Interpersonal
  conflicts, 673
  effectiveness skills, 315
  isolation, 172
  power, 503
  relationships, 676
Interpersonal psychotherapy, **602–612**
  applications, 612
  background of, 602
  case study, 610–611
  clarification, 609
  communication analysis and, 609
  deficits, 604–605
  depression, 602–603
  disputes, 604
  and the elderly, 603
  encouragement and, 609
  example of, 610
  goals of, 605
  grief, 604
  initial phase of, 608
  middle phase of, 608–609
  outline of, 606–608
  personality theory, 604
  personality theory, 669t
  pregnancy, 603
  role transition, 604
  session, starting of, 609
  techniques in, 605
  termination of, 610
  treatments, research supported psychological, 644t

Interpretation, 51–53, 137–138, 543
The Interpretations of Dreams (Freud), 31
Intersection of multiple identities, 485
Intersubjectivity, 46
Interventions With Families of Gay, Lesbian, Bisexual, and Transgender People: From the Inside Out (Bigner & Gottlieb), 572
Interviewing for Solutions (De Jong & Berg), 456
Interviews, 142, 380, 382
Intrapersonal conflicts, 673
Intrapersonal isolation, 172
Intrapersonal power, 503
Intraphysic power, 503
Introductory Lectures on Psycho-Analysis (Freud), 31
Introjection, 248–249
Introversion, 91–93
Intuition, 92–93
Invariant prescription, 566
Iron John (Bly), 110
Irrational beliefs, 336–337
Irrationality, 508
I-sharing, 173
Isolation, 184–185, 189
I-thou, 172–173

J

Joining, 548
Jokes and Their Relation to the Unconscious (Freud), 31
Journal of Cognitive Psychotherapy, 373
Journal of Feminist Family Therapy, 564
Journal of Marital and Family Therapy, 568
The Journal of Psychotherapy Integration, 663
Journal of Systemic Therapies, 565
Jung: A Feminist Revision (Rowland), 114
Jungian analysis and therapy, **82–122**
  analysis, 96–97
  anxiety, 640t
  assessment, 97–99, 637t
  brief therapies, 110
  counseling, 96–97
  countertransference, 105–106
  critique, 654
  current trends, 110–111
  depression, 640t
  dreams and analysis, 100–103
  gender issues, 113–114
  goals of, 636t
  group therapy, 116, 651t
  history of, 83–86
  imagination, active, 104
  integrative theory of psychotherapy and, 668t
  multicultural issues, 115–116
  personality theory, 86–96, 633t
  psychological disorders, 106–110
  psychotherapy, 96–97

Jungian analysis and therapy (*continued*)
  research, 112–113, 647*t*
  techniques, other, 104–105
  theories, using with other, 111–112
  therapeutic goals, 96
  therapeutic relationship, 97–99
  therapeutic techniques, 638*t*
  therapy, stages of, 99–100
  transference, 105–106
Jungian analyst, 96

K
Kairos, 168, 182
Keys to Solutions in Brief Therapy (de Shazer), 456
Knowledge, 495

L
Labeling, 378, 388
Language, 153
The Language of Choice Theory (Glasser & Glasser), 418
Latency, 38, 40
Later life, 41
Law, 568
Law of effect, 283
Learning Emotion-Focused Therapy: The Process Experiential Approach to Change (Elliott), 268
Legacy from Fritz (Perls & Baumgardner), 243
Lesbian, 522–523, 572
Libido, 31, 33
Life review, 401
Life tasks, 142
Linearity, 538*f*
Listing advantages and disadvantages, 389
Live modeling, 298
Logotherapy, 185
Logotherapy (Frankl), 165
Long brief therapy, 566–567
Love and Will (May), 165
Love's Executioner, 165
Loving, 184–185
Luborsky's Core Conflictual Relationship Therapy, 474

M
Magnification, 378
Maladaptive cognitions, 673
Maladaptive schemas, 374
Mandala, 91
Man's Search for Himself (May), 165
Man's Search for Meaning (Frankl), 165, 193
Mapping, 548
Maps of Narrative Practice (White), 456
Marital schism, 536–537
Marital skew, 536–537
Masculine protest, 152–153
Mask, 89

Me, 425
Meaning, 173, 185–186, 198–199, 387
The Meaning of Anxiety (May), 165
Meaninglessness, 173, 185–186, 198–199
Medicine, 569
Memories, Dreams, Reflections (Jung), 84–85
Mental control, 394
Mental metabolism, 242
Mental Research Institute (MRI), 565–566
Meta-analysis, 21
Metaphors, 431–432
Middle age, 40, 95
Milan Associates, 566–567
Mimesis, 548
Mind reading, 377
Mindfulness, 193
Mindfulness meditation, 399–400, 586–588, 591
Minimization, 378
Minuchin, 636*t*
Minuchin's symbols for family mapping, 548*f*
Mirroring, 44–45
Mirroring selfobject, 44
Mislabeling, 378
Mitwelt, 167–168, 194
Mobilization, 254
Modeling techniques, 297–299
Models of Meichenbaum, 300, 356
Modernism, 19
Momma and the Meaning of Life (May), 165
Morita therapy, 590–591
Motivational processes, 288
Motivational schemas, 377
Motor reproduction processes, 288
Multicultural Feminist Therapy: Theory in Context (Barrett et al.), 489
Multicultural issues
  Adlerian theory, 153–154
  behavior therapy, 321–322
  cognitive therapy, 407–408
  comparison, 649–650
  constructivist theories, 477
  existential therapy, 196–198
  family systems therapy, 573–575
  feminist therapy, 485–486, 523–525
  gestalt therapy, 272–273
  integrative therapy, 685–686
  Jungian analysis and therapy, 115–116
  person-centered therapy, 232–233
  psychoanalysis, 72–73
  rational emotive behavior therapy (REBT), 361
  reality therapy, 445–446
  theory, 22–23
Multigenerational transmission process, 541
Multimodal theory of personality, 675

Multimodal therapy, 675–682
Multiple identities, 492–493
Murray's TAT, 178
Muscular armor, 593–594
Must, 563
Myers-Briggs Type Indicator (MBTI; Myers, McCaulley, Quenk, & Hammer), 97–98, 111–113

N
Naikan psychotherapy, 588
On Narcissism: An Introduction (Freud), 31
Narcissistic personality disorder, 15, 59–61
Narrative Means to Therapeutic Ends (White & Epstein), 456–457
Narrative therapy, **466–474**
  alternative narratives, 470
  assessment in, 468–469
  case study, 467–468, 472–473
  characterization, 466
  client stories, support of, 471
  constructivist therapy, 636*t*–637*t*
  current trends, 473–474
  Epston and White's, 468
  feminist therapy, 509–510
  future, questions about, 471
  gender issues, 476–477
  goals of, 469
  personal construct, 466
  plot, 466
  positive narratives, 470
  problem, externalizing of, 470
  research, 474, 476
  techniques in, 470–471
  theories, using with other, 474
  unique outcomes of, 470
National Coalition of Creative Art Therapies, 623
Naturalistic observation, 291
Need, 509
Negative feedback, 539
Negative prediction, 377
Negative reinforcement, 286
Neurosis, 13–14
Neurotic anxiety, 168–170
Neutrality, 49–50
A New Guide to Rational Living (Ellis, Harper), 333
The New Handbook of Cognitive Therapy Techniques (McMullin), 387
New Haven Children's Center, 282
A New Psychotherapy for Traditional Men (Brooks), 520
Nondirective therapy, 207
Noölogical, 174
Normal anxiety, 168–169
Notes from Underground (Dostoyevski), 163
Nuclear family emotional systems, 540

O

Object, 29, 44
Object cathexis, 34
Object relations, 41, 636*t*
Object relations psychology, 41–43,
    52–53
Observation, 285
Observational learning, 287
Obsessions, 14
Obsessive disorder, 393–394
Obsessive-compulsive disorder, 14, 190,
    306–308, 318, 353–354, 644*t*
Oedipus complex, 11, 38
Old age, 95
One-person psychology, 65–66
Operant conditioning, 281–283
Operational definitions, 2
Oral incorporation, 37
Oral stage, 37–38, 40
Organismic sensing, 211
Organizations (family therapy), 568
Other directedness, 375
Overgeneralization, 378
Over-vigilance, 375
Own-world, 167–168

P

Paradox and Passion in Psychotherapy
    (Van Deurzen), 166
Paradoxical intention, 141, 185
Paradoxical prescriptions, 433
Paradoxical techniques, 432–433, 556
Participant factors, 642
Participant modeling, 298
Paternalism, 524
Patient, 4
Perfectionism, 394
Performance accomplishments, 289
Permissive beliefs, 397
Persona, 89
Personal construct therapy, 466–467
Personality, basic concepts of, 632–635
Personality and Psychotherapies (Dollard
    and Miller), 316–317
Personality cognitive model, 374
Personality development, 94–95
Personality Theories: Critical Perspectives
    (Ellis, Abrams, & Abrams), 333
Personality theory
    Adlerian therapy, 126–130
    angering/angry, 420
    anxietizing/anxious, 420
    archetype, 89–91
    basic concepts, 633*t*–634*t*
    behavior, 421–422
    and the body, 595
    choice, 420–421
    cognitive therapy, 373–378
    collective unconscious, 88
    conditionality, 212
    conscious level, 87

consciousness, levels of, 87–88
depressed/depressing, 420
development, 212
feminist therapy, 489–497
fully-functioning person, 213
gender differences and similarities,
    489–492
history of, 11
integrative theory of psychotherapy
    and, 668*t*–669*t*
multiple identities, 492–493
needs, 420
personal unconscious, 87–88
personality attitudes and functions,
    91–94
personality development, 94–96
person-centered therapy, 211–213
phobicizing, 420
psychological development, 211
reality, pictures of, 419
reality therapy, 419–422
relational cultural model, 495
relationships, 212–213
schema theory, 492–493
self-regard, 212–213
Personalization, 378
*Person-Centered and Experiential
    Psychotherapy* (Rogers), 211
Person-centered therapy, **207–239**
    acceptance, 215–216, 218
    anxiety, 640*t*
    assessment, 214, 637*t*
    brief therapy, 226
    client change, conditions for, 214–218
    client experience, 218–220
    congruence, 215
    critique, 655–656
    current trends, 226–227
    defined, 7
    depression, 640*t*
    effectiveness of, 230–231
    empathy, 216–218
    family therapy, 562
    gender issues, 232
    genuineness, 215
    goals of, 213–214, 636*t*
    group counseling, 233–234
    group therapy approaches, 651*t*
    history of, 207–211
    incongruence, 215
    integrative theory of psychotherapy
        and, 668*t*
    multicultural issues, 232–233
    perception, 218
    personality theory, 211–213, 633*t*
    presence, 215
    process of, 220–221
    psychological contact, 214–215
    psychological disorders, 221–226
    psychotherapy, theory of, 213–221
    research, 229–231, 647*t*

theories, using with other, 228
therapeutic techniques, 638*t*–639*t*
unconditional positive regard,
    215–216
Phallic stage, 38, 40
Phase, 499
Phenomenology, 244, 275
The Philosophy of "As If" (Vaihinger), 126
Phobias, 14, 296, 319–320
Phobic disorders, 308–309, 644*t*
Phobic layer, 247
Phony layer, 247
Physiological dependency, 15
Physiological measurements, 291
Physiological schemas, 377
Physiology, 421
Placater, 559
*Playful Approaches to Serious Problems:
    Narratives With Children and Their
    Families* (Freeman Epston &
    Lobovits), 457
Positive Addiction (Glasser), 431
Positive feedback, 539
Positive reinforcement, 285, 443
Positive statements, 430–431
Postmodernism, 19
Posttraumatic stress disorder (PTSD),
    15, 266–267, 296–297, 514–516,
    644*t*
Power analysis, 503
Power and Innocence (May), 165
Power intervention, 504–505
The Practice of Multimodal Therapy
    (Lazarus), 679
Preconscious, 33–34
Preschool age, 40
Prescribing the symptom, 141
Pretest-posttest control group design, 21
The Prevention of Anxiety and Depression
    (Dozois, Dobson), 390
Primary process, 34
Principles of behavior, 281–282
Principles of Therapeutic Change That Work
    (Castonguay and Beutler), 10, 642
Prisoners of Hate (Beck), 376
Prochaska and colleagues'
    transtheoretical approach,
    669–674
Professional training and organizations,
    568
Projection, 36, 249
Projection process, 541
Projective identification, 58
Pseudomutuality, 537
Psychoanalysis, **28–81**
    analysis of transference, 52–53
    anxiety, 640*t*
    assessment, 48, 637*t*
    brief psychoanalytic therapy, 62–65
    countertransference, 53–54
    critique, 653–654

Psychoanalysis *(continued)*
current trends, 65–66
depression, 640*t*
dreams, interpretations of, 51–52
drive theory, 33–39
ego psychology, 39–41
empathy, 49–50
family therapy, 561
free association, 49
gender issues, 70–71
group therapy, 73–74, 651*t*
history of, 29–32
integrative theory of psychotherapy and, 668*t*
interpretation, 51–53
interpretation of dreams, 51–52
multicultural issues, 72–73
neutrality, 49–50
object relations psychology, 41–43
personality theory, 633*t*
psychoanalytic counseling, 48–49
psychological disorders, 54–62
psychotherapy, 48–49
relational, 45–47
relational responses, 54
research, 67–70, 647*t*
resistance, 50–51
self psychology, 43–45
theories, using with other, 66–67
therapeutic goals, 47–48
therapeutic techniques, 638*t*
therapy, goals of, 636*t*
treatment, approaches to, 47–54
Psychoanalysis and Daseinsanalysis (Boss), 164
Psychoanalytic counseling, 48–49
Psychoanalytic therapy, 507–508
Psychodrama, **615–621**
activity in the present, 616
assessment, 617
background, 615
creativity, 616–617
encounter, 616
personality theory, 615
process of, 618–619
psychotherapy, theory of, 617
role playing, 617
role therapy, 616
roles in, 618
spontaneity, 616–617
techniques of, 619–621
therapy, 9, 154, 669*t*
The Psychodynamic Approach to Therapeutic Change (Leiper & Maltby), 66
Psychodynamic therapy, 66, 644*t*
Psychoeducational approaches, 567–568
Psychoeducational methods, 347
Psychoeducational modules, 408–409
Psychological dependency, 15
Psychological disorders, **301–321**

Adlerian therapy, 142–148
anxiety, 296–297, 605
assertiveness training, 323
Beck Depression Inventory, 605
case study, 308–309
cognitive therapy, 373–374
defined, 12–16
depression, 305–306, 603, 608, 610
existential therapy, 186–191
feminist therapy, 511–517
gender issues, 320–322
generalized anxiety disorder, 301–305, 318
gestalt therapy, 284–287
group therapy, 322
Hamilton Rating Scale for Depression, 605, 610
Jungian analysis and therapy, 106–110
Morita therapy, 590
multicultural issues, 321
obsessive-compulsive disorder, 306, 318, 353–354
person-centered therapy, 221–226
phobias, 296–297, 308–309, 319–320
posttraumatic stress disorders (PTSD), 296–297
psychoanalysis, 54–62
rational emotive behavior therapy (REBT) and, 350–355
reality therapy, 434–442
social skills training, 322–323
treatment of, 389
Psychological disorders, gestalt therapy, 264–268
On Psychology and Pathology of So-Called Occult Phenomenon (Jung), 83
Psychology of Dementia Praecox (Jung), 85
The Psychopathology of Everyday Life (Freud), 31
Psychosis, 16
Psychotherapy. *See also* Psychoanalysis; Therapy; *under individual psychotherapies*
author's theory of, 24
brief, 16–17, 641–642
defined, 4
evidence-based, 18
feminist therapy, 510
psychoanalysis, 48–49
research directions, 647*t*
research-supported psychological treatments (RSPT), 643, 644*t*, 645
short-term, 16–17
theories of, 5–6, 11–12, 213–221
your theory of, 24
Psychotherapy and the Quest for Happiness (Van Deurzen), 166
Psychotherapy Isn't What You Think (Bugental), 166
Psychotherapy: Research, Practice, and Training, 228

Psychotic Disorders, 109–110
PTSD (posttraumatic stress disorder), 296–297
Puella aeterna, 95
Puer aeternus, 95
Punctuation, 565
Purpose in Life Test, 178, 194
Push-button technique, 141, 143

Q
The Quality School (Glasser), 418
Questioning, 430–431
Questionnaires, 384
Questions, 459–461, 589

R
Race in the Mind of America: Breaking the Vicious Circle between Blacks and Whites (Wachtel), 686
Rational belief: pleasant activating event, 337
Rational belief: unpleasant activating event, 337
Rational beliefs, 337
Rational emotive behavior therapy (REBT), **331–362**
A-B-C theory of personality, 337–339, 350
A-B-C-D-E therapeutic approach, 343–344
activity homework, 349
alcohol and substance abuse, 354–355
anxiety, 640*t*
anxiety disorders, 350
assessment, 340, 637*t*
behavioral methods of, 349
brief therapy, 355
concepts of, 8
core of, 343
cost-benefit analysis, 347
critique, 657
current trends, 355–356
depression, 640*t*
emotive behavior therapy (REBT), 332–333
emotive techniques, 347
family therapy, 563
forceful self-dialogue, 348
forceful self-statements, 348
gender issues, 357–360
goals of, 339–340, 636*t*
group therapy, 361–362, 652*t*
hedonism, 334
history of, 332–333
humanism, 334
imagery, 348
insight, cognitive, 349
integrative theory of psychotherapy and, 668*t*
multicultural issues, 361
penalties, 349

personality theory, 334–339, 633t–634t
philosophical viewpoints, 334
problem solving, 347
psychoeducational methods, 347
psychological disorders, 350
psychotherapy theory, 339–350
reinforcements, 349
research, 357–358, 647t
role playing, 348
self-help form, 341–342
shame attacking exercises, 348
skill training, 349
social factors, 336
summary of, 362–363
teaching others, 347
theories, using with other, 356
therapeutic relationship in, 340
therapeutic techniques, 639t
vulnerability to disturbance, 336
Rational Emotive Behavioral Therapy:
    Distinctive Features (Dryden),
    346
Rational Emotive Therapy: It Works for
    Me-It Can Work for You
    (Ellis), 333
Rational-Emotive Treatment of Alcoholism
    and Substance Abuse (Ellis), 354
Rationalist, 19
Rationality, 335
Rationalization, 36–37
Reaction formation, 36
Reactivity, 291
Reality therapy, **416–451**
    anxiety, 640t
    assessment, 423–424, 637t
    behavior, 426–428
    choice theory, 419–422
    critique, 657–658
    current trends, 442–443
    depression, 640t
    environment, establishing a friendly,
        424
    family therapy, 563–564
    gender issues, 444–445
    goals of, 422–423, 636t
    group counseling, 446–447
    group therapy approaches, 652t
    history of, 417–419
    integrative theory of psychotherapy
        and, 668t
    involvement, friendly, 425–426
    multicultural issues, 445–446
    personality theory, 419–422, 633t–634t
    plans, 428
    process of, 424
    psychological disorders, 434–442
    Reality therapy car, 421f
    research, 443–444, 647t
    resources, 417
    theories, using with other, 443
    theory of, 422–433

therapeutic techniques, 639t
    therapist attitudes, 429
Reality Therapy (Glasser), 417
Reason and Emotion in Psychotherapy, 333
Reattribution, 388
Reauthoring Lives: Interview and Essays
    (White), 456
REBT (rational emotive behavior
    therapy). *See* Rational emotive
    behavior therapy (REBT)
Reflex behavior, 282–283
Reframing, 433, 506, 549
Regression, 37
Rejection, 375
Relabeling, 506
Relational competence, 496
Relational Concepts in Psychoanalysis
    (Greenberg and Mitchell), 45
Relational cultural model, 495
Relational psychoanalysis, 45–47
Relational Psychotherapy: A Primer
    (DeYoung), 508
Relational resilience, 496
Relational responses, 54
Relational Theory and the Practice of
    Psychotherapy (Wachtel), 66
Relational-Cultural Therapy (Jordan), 499
Relationship, helping, 672
Relationship factors, 642
Relaxation, 292, 300
Relief-oriented beliefs, 397
Religious schemas, 376
Renaissance, 211
Repression, 36
Reptest (Role Construct Repertory Test),
    454
Research
    Adlerian therapy, 151–152
    approaches of, 645–646
    behavior therapy, 317
    core conditions, 229–230
    depression, 403–404
    directions, future, 646
    existential therapy, 194–196
    family systems therapy, 569–572
    feminist therapy, 519–520
    general anxiety disorder, 404–405
    integrative therapy, 684–685
    interpersonal therapy and, 603
    Jungian analysis and therapy,
        113–114
    obsessional disorders, 405–406
    outcome, 646
    person-centered therapy, 229–231
    psychoanalysis, 67–70
    rational emotive behavior therapy
        (REBT), 357–358
    reality therapy, 443–444
    solution focused therapy, 475–476
    theories of psychotherapy, directions
        of, 647t

theory, 20–22
Research Methods in Family Therapy
    (Sprenkle & Piercy), 569
Research Supported Psychological
    Treatments (APA), 18–19
Research-Supported Psychological
    Treatments (Nathan & Gorman),
    643
Research-supported psychological
    treatments (RSPT), 18, 643, 644,
    645t
Resistance, 50–51
Resolution, 254
Respondent conditioning, 281–282
Response from the other, 63–64
Response from the self, 63
Responsibility, 171–172, 182–183, 394
Responsible hedonism, 334
The Restoration of the Self
    (Kohut), 43
Retention processes, 288
Retroflection, 249
Role Construct Repertory Test (Reptest),
    454
Rorschach, 48, 178
Rules in theory, 2–3

S
Scales, 384
Scaling, 388–389, 460
Schema-focused cognitive therapy,
    400–401
Schemas
    abandonment/instability, 400
    changing, 379
    cognitive development model, 374–376
    defensiveness/shame, 400
    dialogue, 401
    emotional deprivation, 400
    mistrust/abuse, 400
    modification, 379
    reinterpretation, 379
    social isolation/shame, 400
    theory, 492–493
    therapeutic, 375
    types of, 376–377
Schematic restructuring, 379
Schizophrenia, 16, 536
School age, 40
Schools Without Failure (Glasser), 418
Scientific Foundations of Cognitive Theory
    and Therapy of Depression (Clark,
    Beck & Alford), 390
Secondary process, 35
Second-order change, 565
Selective abstraction, 377
Self, 90
The Self in Psychotic Process (Perry),
    109–110
Self Management and Rational Training
    (SMART), 355

Self psychology, 43–45, 52–53, 636*t*
Self-actualization, 244
Self-efficacy, 288–289
Self-esteem, 497
Self-instructional training, 299
Self-liberation, 671
Self-modeling, 298
Self-monitoring, 382
Self-nurturance, 497
Selfobject, 44–45
Self-reevaluation, 671
Self-regulation, 600
Sensation, 92–93, 254, 676
Sense of worth, 496
Sensuality, 498
Sex Without Guilt (Ellis), 333
Shadow, 89–90
Shaping, 287
Short-term therapies, 16–17
Sibling position, 541–542
Silver Lining Questionnaire, 178
Singer-Loomis Inventory of Personality
    (SLIP; Singer & Loomis), 97–98,
    112
Situational, 673
Skills acquisition phase, 300
Skinner box, 283
Social
    action, 498
    cognitive theory, 281, 283–284
    constructionism, 19–20
    learning theory, 283, 285
    liberation, 671
    reinforcement, 286
    skills training, 322
Social-contextual power, 503
Societal regression, 542
Socratic dialogue, 185–186, 385
Solution focused therapy, **457–466**
    assessing motivation in, 460
    assessment, 458
    bridging statement, 463
    case study, 463
    change, views about, 457
    collaborative relationship and, 459
    compliments, 463
    concepts of, 457
    constructivist therapy, 636*t*–637*t*
    coping questions in, 459
    gender issues, 475–477
    goals of, 458
    group therapy, 478–479
    message of, 462
    mindmaps, 458
    miracle question, 460
    pretherapy change, 459
    questions used in, 460–462
    research, 475–476
    scaling, 460
    techniques in, 458–459
    theories, using with other, 474

*Solution-Focused Brief Therapy in Schools:
    A 360-Degree View of Research and
    Practice* (Kelly, Kim & Franklin),
    466
Solution-Focused Therapy (O'Connell),
    466
Somatic power, 503
Somatoform disorders, 14–15
Specifying automatic thoughts, 386
Spiritual power, 503–504
Spitting on the client's soup, 140
Splitting, 43, 635
Stage, 499
*Standard Edition of the Complete Works of
    Sigmund Freud*, 32
*Staring at the Sun: Overcoming the Terror
    of Death* (Yalom), 171
Stations of the Mind (Glasser),
    418–419
Stimulated observation, 291
Stimulus control, 672, 675
Straightforward tasks, 554–556
Strategic family therapy
    concepts of, 553–554
    example, 557–558
    goals of, 554
    Haley's theory of family
        systems, 553
    techniques of, 554
Strengths, 498
Stress-inoculation training (SIT),
    299–301
Structural family therapy
    concepts of, 546–547
    defined, 545
    example, 550–553
    goals of, 547–548
    techniques, 548
*Studies of Organ Inferiority and Its
    Psychical Compensation* (Adler),
    125
Studies on Hysteria (Freud and Breuer),
    31, 55
Style, 499
Subject, 44
Subjective units of discomfort scale
    (SUDs), 292–295, 310
Sublimation, 36
Substance abuse, 15, 267, 396–398, 644*t*
Substance-dependent, 15
Suicide, 181
Superego, 35
Superior function, 93
Superiority complex, 130
Superreasonable, 559
Symbolic modeling, 298
Symbols, 90–91
Symbols of Transformation (Jung), 85
Symmetrical relationship, 565
Symptom analysis, 97
Symptoms, 673

Synchronicity, 109
Systemic desensitization, 292–294

T
Take Effective Control of Your Life
    (Glasser), 418
*Tales of Solutions: A Collection of Hope-
    Inspiring Stories* (Berg & Dolan),
    466
Tar baby, 140–141
Task setting, 141
Technical eclecticism, 663, 682
Teleoanalytic workshop, 154
Termination, 386–387
Tests, 48, 97, 178
Thanatos, 33
Thematic Apperception
    Test (TAT), 178
Theoretical integration, 663, 667, 682
Theoretical orientations, 664*t*
Theory. *See also under individual theory*
    A-B-C of personality, 337–339
    approaches, 640*t*
    of Asian psychotherapy, 586
    author's, of psychotherapy and
        counseling, 24
    background, 10–11
    of behavior therapy, 290–301
    clarity, 2–3
    comparison, **631–661**
    comprehensiveness, 3
    of constructivist approaches, 474
    counseling, 5–6
    critique, **631–661**
    current trends, 17–20
    defined, 2
    family systems, 539–542
    gender issues, 22
    group therapy, 23
    history, 10–11
    integration, 5
    Jungian analysis, 6–7
    multicultural issues, 22–23
    other theories, using with, 20
    personality, 11, 87–94, 126–130
    precision, 2–3
    primary theoretical orientations of
        psychotherapists in the United
        States, 5*t*
    psychoanalysis, 6
    psychodrama, 617
    of psychotherapy, 5–6, 11–12
    research, 20–22
    testability, 3
    theories, using with other, 645
    therapy, 6–9
    of traits, 285
    treatment manuals, 17–18
    usefulness, 3–4
    your, of psychotherapy and
        counseling, 24

Theory and Measurement of Social Interest (Crandall), 152
Therapeutic relationship, 253, 384–387
Therapy-demystifying strategies, 506–507
Thinking, 92–93, 421
Thinking, all-or-nothing, 377, 388–389
Thou, 163
Thought sampling, 382, 384
Thoughts, overimportance of, 394–396
Threat, overestimation of, 394
Three Essays on Sexuality (Freud), 31
Three question technique, 385
Thrown-world, 167
Time tripping, 681
Time-limited therapy, 16–17
Top dog, 259
Tracking, 679
Traditional pyschoanalysts, 47
Transcend, 163
Transcendent function, 88
The Transcendent Function: Jung's Model of Psychological Growth through Dialogues with the Unconscious (Jung), 88
Transference, analysis of, 52–53
Transference psychosis, 58, 105–106
Transgender, 522–523, 572
Transitional object, 42
Treatment. *See specific therapies*
Treatment manuals, 17–18, 65–66, 401, 643, 645
Triadic reciprocal interaction system, 284
Triangle, 547
Triangulation, 540
The Tribes of the Person-Centered Nation: an Introduction to the Schools of Therapy (Sanders), 227

True self, 42
Two-person psychology, 65–66

U
Überwelt, 167–168, 194
Ultimate rescuer, 181
Umwelt, 167–168, 176, 194
Uncertainty, intolerance of, 394
Unconditioned response (UCR), 281
Unconditioned stimulus (UCS), 281
Unconscious, 34
Underdog, 259
Understanding Gender and Culture in the Helping Process (Rabin), 500
Unfeminine, 493
Unfinished business, 251, 266
Unfinished pleasures, 251
Unipolar depression, 13
United States Association for Body Psychotherapy, 600
Unmanly, 493
Urine alarm, 282

V
Validation and acceptance strategies, 314
Value, 427
Value-boundaries, 248
Vegetotherapy, 594
Verbal persuasion, 289
Vicarious experiences, 289
Viktor Frankl–Recollections: An Autobiography (Frankl), 165
Virtual reality therapy, 296–297

W
Wachtel's cyclical psychodynamics theory, 663–669

Walden Two (Skinner, B.F.), 283
Warning: Psychiatry Can be Hazardous to Your Mental Health (Glasser), 419
A Way of Being (Rogers), 210
WDEP (wants, direction and doing, evaluation and planning), 424
What Are You Doing? (Glasser), 426, 434
When Death Enters the Therapeutic Space: Existential Perspective in Psychotherapy and Counseling (Barnett), 171
Will to power, 162
Willing, 172
Withdrawal, 254
With-world, 167
Wolpe's desensitization method, 291–292
Womanist, 489
Women and Madness (Chesler), 487
Women Who Run with the Wolves (Estes), 110
Words Were Originally Magic (de Shazer), 456
Working Alliance Inventory, 48
Working With the Problem Drinker: A Solution-Focused Approach (Berg), 456
Wounded healer, 99

Y
Young adulthood, 40

Z
Zest, 495

TO THE OWNER OF THIS BOOK:

I hope that you have found *Theories of Psychotherapy and Counseling:Concepts and Cases*, Fifth Edition, useful. So that this book can be improved in a future edition, would you take the time to complete this sheet and return it? Thank you.

School and address:

Department:

Instructor's name:

1. What I like most about this book is:

2. What I like least about this book is:

3. My general reaction to this book is:

4. The name of the course in which I used this book is:

5. Were all of the chapters of the book assigned for you to read?

   If not, which ones weren't?

6. In the space below, or on a separate sheet of paper, please write specific suggestions for improving this book and anything else you'd care to share about your experience in using this book.

BROOKS/COLE
CENGAGE Learning

BUSINESS REPLY MAIL
FIRST-CLASS MAIL   PERMIT NO. 34   BELMONT CA

POSTAGE WILL BE PAID BY ADDRESSEE

Attn: *Seth Dobrin, Acquisitions Editor*

Helping Professions
BrooksCole/Cengage Learning, Inc.
20 Davis Drive
Belmont CA 94002

NO POSTAGE
NECESSARY
IF MAILED
IN THE
UNITED STATES

OPTIONAL:

Your name: _____ Date: _____

May we quote you, either in promotion for *Theories of Psychotherapy and Counseling: Concepts and Cases*, Fifth Edition, or in future publishing ventures?

Yes: _____ No: _____

Sincerely yours,

Richard S. Sharf